neg	negative	отрицательный
neut	neuter	средний род
nn	nouns	имена существительные
nom	nominative (case)	именительный падеж
o.s.	oneself	себя
parl	parliamentary	парламентский термин
part	participle	причастие
partl	particle	частица
pers	person	лицо
pf	perfective	совершенный вид
philos	philosophy	философия
phon	phonetics	фонетика
phot	photography	фотография
phys	physics	физика
pl	plural	множественное число
polit	political	политический термин
poss	possessive	притяжательное
predic	predicate; predicative	сказуемое; предикативный
pref	prefix	префикс
prep	preposition; prepositional (case).	предлог; предложный падеж
pres	present (tense)	настоящее время

sb	substantive	имя существительное
sg	singular	единственное число
sl	slang	сленг
s.o.	someone	кто-нибудь
sth	something	что-нибудь
superl	superlative	превосходная степень
tech	technical	техника
tel	telephony	телефония
theat	theatre	театр, театральный термин
theol	theology	богословие
trans	transitive	переходный глагол
univ	university	университетский жаргон
usu	usually	обычно
v	verb	глагол
v aux	auxiliary verb	вспомогательный глагол
vbl	verbal	отглагольное
vi	intransitive verb	непереходный глагол
voc	vocative (case)	звательный падеж
vt	transitive verb	переходный глагол
vulg	vulgar(ism)	грубое
vv	verbs	глаголы
zool	zoology	зоология

*This dictionary includes some words which are, or are asserted to be, proprietary names or trade marks. These words are labelled (*propr*). The presence or absence of this label should not be regarded as affecting the legal status of any proprietary name or trade mark.

Oxford Russian Minidictionary

Edited by
Della Thompson

OXFORD
UNIVERSITY PRESS

Great Clarendon Street, Oxford OX2 6DP

Oxford University Press is a department of the University of Oxford.
It furthers the University's objective of excellence in research, scholarship, and education by publishing worldwide in

Oxford New York

Auckland Cape Town Dar es Salaam Hong Kong Karachi
Kuala Lumpur Madrid Melbourne Mexico City Nairobi
New Delhi Shanghai Taipei Toronto

With offices in
Argentina Austria Brazil Chile Czech Republic France Greece
Guatemala Hungary Italy Japan Poland Portugal Singapore
South Korea Switzerland Thailand Turkey Ukraine Vietnam

Oxford is a registered trade mark of Oxford University Press in the UK and in certain other countries

Published in the United States
by Oxford University Press Inc., New York

© Oxford University Press 1995, 1997, 2002, 2005, 2006

First published 1995
Reissued with corrections 1997
Revised edition 2002
Reissued with English phonetics 2005
Second edition 2006

All rights reserved. No part of this publication may be reproduced, stored in a retrieval system, or transmitted, in any form or by any means, without the prior permission in writing of Oxford University Press, or as expressly permitted by law, or under terms agreed with the appropriate reprographics rights organization. Enquiries concerning reproduction outside the scope of the above should be sent to the Rights Department, Oxford University Press, at the address above

You must not circulate this book in any other binding or cover and you must impose this same condition on any acquirer

British Library Cataloguing in Publication Data

Data available

Library of Congress Cataloging in Publication Data

Data available

ISBN 978-019-861457-9 (OUP main edition)
ISBN 978-019-920375-8 (Special edition)
ISBN 978-019-920374-1 (Special edition)
ISBN 978-019-920373-4 (Special edition)
ISBN 978-019-953293-3 (Special edition)
ISBN 978-019-955656-4 (Special edition)
ISBN 978-019-955657-1 (Special edition)

10 9 8 7 6 5 4

Typeset in Arial, Argo, and Times by Interactive Sciences Ltd, Gloucester
Printed and bound in Italy by L.E.G.O. S.p.A. Lavis (TN)

Contents

Preface

The *Oxford Russian Minidictionary* is a handy yet extremely comprehensive reference work, designed for students of both Russian and English, as well as for tourists and business people. This new edition has been updated to include the latest familiar terms in areas such as computing and business.

The student of Russian is aided by the provision of inflected forms where these cause difficulty, and the indication of the stressed syllable of every Russian word as well as changes in stress. The student of English is helped by the provision of phonetic transcriptions of English entries and a table of English irregular verbs at the back of the book.

A completely new feature of this edition is the **Phrasefinder**, located in the centre of the dictionary and providing essential words and phrases for everyday use, grouped together according to topic and covering subjects such as travel, food and drink, shopping, using the telephone, and finding overnight accommodation. Thanks are due to Lucy Popova for help in compiling this section.

D.J.T.

Introduction

In order to save space, related words are often grouped together in paragraphs, as are cross-references and compound entries.

The swung dash (~) and the hyphen are also used to save space. The swung dash represents the headword preceding it in bold, or the preceding Russian word, e.g. **Georgian** *n* грузи́н, ~ка. The hyphen is mainly used in giving grammatical forms, to stand for part of the preceding, or (less often) following, Russian word, e.g. **приходи́ть**, (-ожу́, -о́дишь).

Russian headwords are followed by inflexional information where considered necessary. So-called regular inflexions for the purpose of this dictionary are listed in the Appendices.

Where a noun ending is given but not labelled in the singular, it is the genitive ending; other cases are named; in the plural, where cases are identifiable by their endings, they are not labelled, e.g. **сестра́** (*pl* сёстры, сестёр, сёстрам). The gender of Russian nouns can usually be deduced from their endings and it is indicated only in exceptional cases (e.g. for masculine nouns in **-а**, **-я**, and **-ь**, neuter nouns in **-мя**, and all indeclinable nouns).

Verbs are labelled *impf* or *pf* to show their aspect. Where a perfective verb is formed by the addition of a prefix to the imperfective, this is shown at the headword by a light vertical stroke, e.g. **про|лепета́ть**. When a verb requires the use of a case other than the accusative, this is indicated, e.g. **маха́ть** *impf*, **махну́ть** *pf* + *instr* wave, brandish.

Both the comma and the ampersand (&) are used to show alternatives, e.g. **хоте́ть** + *gen*, *acc* means that the Russian verb may govern either the genitive or accusative; **сирота́** *m & f* orphan means that the Russian noun is treated as masculine or feminine according to the sex of the person denoted; **Cossack** *n* каза́к, -а́чка represents the masculine and feminine translations of Cossack; **dilate** *vt & i* расширя́ть(ся) means that the Russian verb forms cover both the transitive and intransitive English verbs.

Stress

The stress of Russian words is shown by an acute accent over the vowel of the stressed syllable. The vowel **ё** has no stress mark since it is almost always stressed. The presence of two stress marks indicates that either of the marked syllables may be stressed.

Changes of stress in inflexion are shown, e.g.

i) **предложи́ть** (-жу́, -жишь)

The absence of a stress mark on the second person singular indicates that the stress is on the preceding syllable and that the rest of the conjugation is stressed in this way.

ii) **нача́ть** (..............; на́чал, -а́, -о)

The final form, на́чало, takes the stress of the first of the two preceding forms when these differ from each other. Forms that are not shown, here на́чали, are stressed like the last form given.

iii) **дождь** (-дя́)

The single form given in brackets is the genitive singular and all other forms have the same stressed syllable.

iv) **душа́** (*acc* -у; *pl* -и)

If only one case-labelled form is given in the singular, it is an exception to the regular paradigm. If only one plural form is given (the nominative), the rest follow this. In other words, in this example, the accusative singular and all the plural forms have initial stress.

v) **скоба́** (*pl* -ы, -а́м)

In the plural, forms that are not shown (here instrumental and prepositional) are stressed like the last form given.

Символы фонтетической транскрипции, используемые в Словаре

Согласные				Гласные			
b	*b*ut	s	*s*it	æ	c*a*t	aɪ	m*y*
d	*d*og	t	*t*op	ɑː	*a*rm	aʊ	h*ow*
f	*f*ew	v	*v*oice	e	b*e*d	eɪ	d*ay*
g	*g*et	w	*w*e	əː	h*er*	əʊ	n*o*
h	*h*e	z	*z*oo	ɪ	s*i*t	eə	h*air*
j	*y*es	ʃ	*sh*e	iː	s*ee*	ɪə	n*ear*
k	*c*at	ʒ	deci*s*ion	ɒ	h*o*t	ɔɪ	b*oy*
l	*l*eg	θ	*th*in	ɔː	s*aw*	ʊə	p*oor*
m	*m*an	ð	*th*is	ʌ	r*u*n	aɪə	f*ire*
n	*n*o	ŋ	ri*ng*	ʊ	p*u*t	aʊə	s*our*
p	*p*en	ʧ	*ch*ip	uː	t*oo*		
r	*r*ed	ʤ	*j*ar	ə	*a*go		

(ə) обозначает безударный беглый гласный, который слышится в таких словах, как gard*e*n, carn*a*l и rhyth*m*.

(r) в конце слова обозначает согласный r, который произносится в случае, если следующее слово начинается с гласного звука, как, например, в *clutter up* и *an acre of land*.

Тильда ˜ обозначает носовой гласный звук, как в некоторых заимствованиях из французского языка, например ɑ̃ в nu*an*ce /'njuːɑ̃s/.

Основное ударение в слове отмечается знаком ' перед ударным слогом.

Вторичное ударение в многосложном слове отмечается знаком ˌ перед соответствующим слогом.

A

а[1] *conj* and, but; **а (не) то́** or else, otherwise.
а[2] *int* oh, ah.
абажу́р lampshade.
абба́тство abbey.
аббревиату́ра abbreviation.
абза́ц indention; paragraph.
абонеме́нт subscription, season ticket. **абоне́нт** subscriber.
абориге́н aborigine.
або́рт abortion; **де́лать** *impf*, **с~** *pf* **~** have an abortion.
абрико́с apricot.
абсолю́тно *adv* absolutely. **абсолю́тный** absolute.
абстра́ктный abstract.
абсу́рд absurdity; the absurd. **абсу́рдный** absurd.
абсце́сс abscess.
аванга́рд advanced guard; vanguard; avant-garde. **аванга́рдный** avant-garde. **аванпо́ст** outpost; forward position.
ава́нс advance (*of money*); *pl* advances, overtures. **ава́нсом** *adv* in advance, on account.
авансце́на proscenium.
авантю́ра (*derog*) adventure; venture; escapade; shady enterprise. **авантюри́ст** (*derog*) adventurer. **авантюри́стка** (*derog*) adventuress. **авантю́рный** adventurous; adventure.
авари́йный breakdown; emergency. **ава́рия** accident, crash; breakdown.
а́вгуст August. **а́вгустовский** August.
а́виа *abbr* (*of* **авиапо́чтой**) by airmail.
авиа- *abbr in comb* (*of* **авиацио́нный**) air-, aero-; aircraft; aviation. **авиакомпа́ния** airline. **~ли́ния** air-route, airway. **~но́сец** (-сца) aircraft carrier. **~по́чта** airmail.
авиацио́нный aviation; flying; aircraft. **авиа́ция** aviation; aircraft; air-force.
авока́до *neut indecl* avocado (pear).
аво́сь *adv* perhaps; **на ~** at random, on the off-chance.
австрали́ец (-и́йца), **австрали́йка** Australian. **австрали́йский** Australian. **Австра́лия** Australia.
австри́ец (-и́йца), **австри́йка** Austrian. **австри́йский** Austrian. **А́встрия** Austria.
авто- *in comb* self-; auto-; automatic; motor-. **автоба́за** motor-transport depot. **~биографи́ческий** autobiographical. **~биогра́фия** autobiography; curriculum vitae. **авто́бус** bus. **~вокза́л** bus-station. **авто́граф** autograph. **~запра́вочная ста́нция** petrol station. **~кра́т** autocrat. **~крати́ческий** autocratic. **~кра́тия** autocracy. **~магистра́ль** motorway. **~маши́на** motor vehicle. **~моби́ль** *m* car. **~но́мия** au-

tonomy. **~но́мный** autonomous; self-contained. **~пило́т** automatic pilot. **~портре́т** self-portrait. **~ру́чка** fountain-pen. **~ста́нция** bus-station. **~стра́да** motorway.

автома́т slot-machine; automatic device, weapon, etc.; sub-machine gun; robot; **(телефо́н-)~** public call-box. **автоматиза́ция** automation. **автоматизи́ровать** *impf* & *pf* automate; make automatic. **автомати́ческий** automatic.

а́втор author; composer; inventor; (*fig*) architect.

авторизо́ванный authorized.

авторите́т authority. **авторите́тный** authoritative.

а́вторск|ий author's; **~ий гонора́р** royalty; **~ое пра́во** copyright. **а́вторство** authorship.

ага́ *int* aha; yes.

аге́нт agent. **аге́нтство** agency. **агенту́ра** (network of) agents.

агита́тор agitator, propagandist; canvasser. **агитацио́нный** propaganda. **агита́ция** propaganda, agitation; campaign. **агити́ровать** *impf* (*pf* **с~**) agitate, campaign; (try to) persuade, win over. **агитпу́нкт** *abbr* agitation centre.

аго́ния agony.

агра́рный agrarian.

агрега́т aggregate; unit.

агресси́вный aggressive. **агре́ссия** aggression. **агре́ссор** aggressor.

агроно́м agronomist. **агроно́мия** agriculture.

ад (*loc* -у́) hell.

ада́птер adapter; (*mus*) pick-up.

адвока́т lawyer. **адвокату́ра** legal profession; lawyers.

администрати́вный administrative. **администра́тор** administrator; manager. **администра́ция** administration; management.

адмира́л admiral.

а́дрес (*pl* -а́) address. **адреса́т** addressee. **а́дресн|ый** address; **~ая кни́га** directory. **адресова́ть** *impf* & *pf* address, send.

а́дский infernal, hellish.

адъюта́нт aide-de-camp; **ста́рший ~** adjutant.

ажу́рн|ый delicate, lacy; **~ая рабо́та** openwork; tracery.

аза́рт heat; excitement; fervour, ardour, passion. **аза́ртн|ый** venturesome; heated; **~ая игра́** game of chance.

а́збука alphabet; ABC.

Азербайджа́н Azerbaijan. **азербайджа́нец** (-нца), **азербайджа́нка** Azerbaijani. **азербайджа́нский** Azerbaijani.

азиа́т, ~ка Asian. **азиа́тский** Asian, Asiatic. **А́зия** Asia.

азо́т nitrogen.

аист stork.

ай *int* oh; oo.

а́йсберг iceberg.

акаде́мик academician. **академи́ческий** academic. **акаде́мия** academy.

аквала́нг aqualung.

акваре́ль water-colour.

аква́риум aquarium.

акведу́к aqueduct.

акклиматизи́ровать *impf* & *pf* acclimatize; **~ся** become acclimatized.

аккомпанеме́нт accompaniment; **под ~**+*gen* to the accompaniment of. **аккомпаниа́тор** accompanist. **аккомпани́ровать** *impf* +*dat* accompany.

акко́рд chord.
аккордео́н accordion.
акко́рдн|ый by agreement; **~ая рабо́та** piece-work.
аккредити́в letter of credit. **аккредитова́ть** *impf* & *pf* accredit.
аккумуля́тор accumulator.
аккура́тный neat, careful; punctual; exact, thorough.
акри́л acrylic. **акри́ловый** acrylic.
акроба́т acrobat.
аксессуа́р accessory; (stage) props.
аксио́ма axiom.
акт act; deed, document; **обвини́тельный ~** indictment.
актёр actor.
акти́в (*comm*) asset(s).
активиза́ция stirring up, making (more) active. **активизи́ровать** *impf* & *pf* make (more) active, stir up. **акти́вный** active.
акти́ровать *impf* & *pf* register, record.
а́ктовый зал assembly hall.
актри́са actress.
актуа́льный topical, urgent.
аку́ла shark.
аку́стика acoustics. **акусти́ческий** acoustic.
акуше́р obstetrician. **акуше́рка** midwife.
акце́нт accent, stress. **акценти́ровать** *impf* & *pf* accent; accentuate.
акционе́р shareholder. **акционе́рный** joint-stock. **а́кция**[1] share; *pl* stock. **а́кция**[2] action.
а́лгебра algebra.
а́либи *neut indecl* alibi.
алиме́нты (*pl*; *gen* -ов) (*law*) maintenance.
алкоголи́зм alcoholism. **алкого́лик** alcoholic. **алкого́ль** *m* alcohol. **алкого́льный** alcoholic.
аллего́рия allegory.
аллерги́я allergy.
алле́я avenue; path, walk.
аллига́тор alligator.
алло́ hello! (*on telephone*).
алма́з diamond.
алта́рь (-я́) *m* altar; chancel, sanctuary.
алфави́т alphabet. **алфави́тный** alphabetical.
а́лчный greedy, grasping.
а́лый scarlet.
альбо́м album; sketch-book.
альмана́х literary miscellany; almanac.
альпи́йский Alpine. **альпини́зм** mountaineering. **альпини́ст**, **альпини́стка** (mountain-)climber.
альт (-а́; *pl* -ы) alto; viola.
альтернати́ва alternative. **альтернати́вный** alternative.
альтруисти́ческий altruistic.
алюми́ний aluminium.
амазо́нка Amazon; horsewoman; riding-habit.
амба́р barn; storehouse, warehouse.
амби́ция pride; arrogance.
амбулато́рия out-patients' department; surgery. **амбулато́рный больно́й** *sb* outpatient.
Аме́рика America. **америка́нец** (-нца), **америка́нка** American. **америка́нский** American; US.
аминокислота́ amino acid.
ами́нь *m* amen.
аммиа́к ammonia.
амни́стия amnesty.
амора́льный amoral; immoral.

амортиза́тор shock-absorber. **амортиза́ция** depreciation; shock-absorption.

ампе́р (*gen pl* **ампе́р**) ampere.

ампута́ция amputation. **ампути́ровать** *impf* & *pf* amputate.

амфетами́н amphetamine.

амфи́бия amphibian.

амфитеа́тр amphitheatre; circle.

ана́лиз analysis; **~ кро́ви** blood test. **анализи́ровать** *impf* & *pf* analyse. **анали́тик** analyst. **аналити́ческий** analytic(al).

ана́лог analogue. **аналоги́чный** analogous. **анало́гия** analogy.

анана́с pineapple.

анархи́ст, ~ка anarchist. **анархи́ческий** anarchic. **ана́рхия** anarchy.

анатоми́ческий anatomical. **анато́мия** anatomy.

анахрони́зм anachronism. **анахрони́ческий** anachronistic.

анга́р hangar.

а́нгел angel. **а́нгельский** angelic.

анги́на sore throat.

англи́йск|ий English; **~ая була́вка** safety-pin. **англича́нин** (*pl* **-ча́не, -ча́н**) Englishman. **англича́нка** Englishwoman. **А́нглия** England, Britain.

анекдо́т anecdote, story; funny thing.

анеми́я anaemia.

анестезио́лог anaesthetist. **анестези́ровать** *impf* & *pf* anaesthetize. **анестези́рующее сре́дство** anaesthetic. **анестези́я** anaesthesia.

анке́та questionnaire, form.

аннекси́ровать *impf* & *pf* annex. **анне́ксия** annexation.

аннули́ровать *impf* & *pf* annul; cancel, abolish.

анома́лия anomaly. **анома́льный** anomalous.

анони́мка anonymous letter. **анони́мный** anonymous.

анонси́ровать *impf* & *pf* announce.

анор́ексия anorexia.

анса́мбль *m* ensemble; company, troupe.

антагони́зм antagonism.

Анта́рктика the Antarctic.

анте́нна antenna; aerial.

антибио́тик antibiotic(s).

антидепресса́нт antidepressant.

антиква́р antiquary; antique-dealer. **антиквариа́т** antique-shop. **антиква́рный** antiquarian; antique.

антило́па antelope.

антипа́тия antipathy.

антисемити́зм anti-Semitism. **антисеми́тский** anti-Semitic.

антисе́птик antiseptic. **антисепти́ческий** antiseptic.

антите́зис (*philos*) antithesis.

антите́ло (*pl* **-а́**) antibody.

антифри́з antifreeze.

анти́чность antiquity. **анти́чный** ancient, classical.

антоло́гия anthology.

антра́кт interval.

антраци́т anthracite.

антреко́т entrecôte, steak.

антрепренёр impresario.

антресо́ли (*pl*; *gen* **-ей**) mezzanine; shelf.

антропо́лог anthropologist. **антропологи́ческий** anthropological. **антрополо́гия** anthropology.

анфила́да suite (of rooms).

анчо́ус anchovy.
аншла́г 'house full' notice.
апартеи́д apartheid.
апати́чный apathetic. **апа́тия** apathy.
апелли́ровать *impf* & *pf* appeal. **апелляцио́нный суд** Court of Appeal. **апелля́ция** appeal.
апельси́н orange; orange-tree. **апельси́нный, апельси́новый** orange.
аплоди́ровать *impf +dat* applaud. **аплодисме́нты** *m pl* applause.
апло́мб aplomb.
Апока́липсис Revelation. **апокалипти́ческий** apocalyptic.
апо́стол apostle.
апостро́ф apostrophe.
аппара́т apparatus; machinery, organs. **аппарату́ра** apparatus, gear; (*comput*) hardware. **аппара́тчик** operator; apparatchik.
аппе́ндикс appendix. **аппендици́т** appendicitis.
аппети́т appetite; **прия́тного ~а!** bon appétit! **аппети́тный** appetizing.
апре́ль *m* April. **апре́льский** April.
апте́ка chemist's. **апте́карь** *m* chemist. **апте́чка** medicine chest; first-aid kit.
ара́б, ара́бка Arab. **ара́бский** Arab, Arabic.
арави́йский Arabian.
аранжи́ровать *impf* & *pf* (*mus*) arrange. **аранжиро́вка** (*mus*) arrangement.
ара́хис peanut.
арби́тр arbitrator. **арбитра́ж** arbitration.
арбу́з water-melon.
аргуме́нт argument. **аргумента́ция** reasoning; arguments. **аргументи́ровать** *impf* & *pf* argue, (try to) prove.
аре́на arena, ring.
аре́нда lease. **аренда́тор** tenant. **аре́ндная пла́та** rent. **арендова́ть** *impf* & *pf* rent.
аре́ст arrest. **арестова́ть** *pf*, **аресто́вывать** *impf* arrest; seize, sequestrate.
аристокра́т, ~ка aristocrat. **аристократи́ческий** aristocratic. **аристокра́тия** aristocracy.
арифме́тика arithmetic. **арифмети́ческий** arithmetical.
а́рия aria.
а́рка arch.
А́рктика the Arctic. **аркти́ческий** arctic.
армату́ра fittings; reinforcement; armature. **армату́рщик** fitter.
арме́йский army.
Арме́ния Armenia.
а́рмия army.
армяни́н (*pl* -я́не, -я́н), **армя́нка** Armenian. **армя́нский** Armenian.
арома́т scent, aroma. **ароматерапи́я** aromatherapy. **арома́тный** aromatic, fragrant.
арсена́л arsenal.
арте́рия artery.
арти́куль *m* (*gram*) article.
артилле́рия artillery.
арти́ст, ~ка artiste, artist; expert. **артисти́ческий** artistic.
артри́т arthritis.
а́рфа harp.
архаи́ческий archaic.
арха́нгел archangel.
архео́лог archaeologist. **археологи́ческий** archaeological. **археоло́гия** archaeology.

архи́в archives. **архиви́ст** archivist. **архи́вный** archive, archival.

архиепи́скоп archbishop. **архиере́й** bishop.

архипела́г archipelago.

архите́ктор architect. **архитекту́ра** architecture. **архитекту́рный** architectural.

арши́н arshin (*71 cm.*).

асбе́ст asbestos.

асимметри́чный asymmetrical. **асимметри́я** asymmetry.

аске́т ascetic. **аскети́зм** asceticism. **аскети́ческий** ascetic.

асоциа́льный antisocial.

аспира́нт, ~ка post-graduate student. **аспиранту́ра** post-graduate course.

аспири́н aspirin.

ассамбле́я assembly.

ассигна́ция banknote.

ассимиля́ция assimilation.

ассисте́нт assistant; junior lecturer, research assistant.

ассортиме́нт assortment.

ассоциа́ция association. **ассоции́ровать** *impf* & *pf* associate.

а́стма asthma. **астмати́ческий** asthmatic.

астро́лог astrologer. **астроло́гия** astrology.

астрона́вт astronaut. **астроно́м** astronomer. **астрономи́ческий** astronomical. **астроно́мия** astronomy.

асфа́льт asphalt.

ата́ка attack. **атакова́ть** *impf* & *pf* attack.

атама́н ataman (*Cossack chieftain*); (gang-)leader.

атеи́зм atheism. **атеи́ст** atheist.

ателье́ *neut indecl* studio; atelier.

а́тлас[1] atlas.

атла́с[2] satin. **атла́сный** satin.

атле́т athlete; strong man. **атле́тика** athletics. **атлети́ческий** athletic.

атмосфе́ра atmosphere. **атмосфе́рный** atmospheric.

а́том atom. **а́томный** atomic.

атташе́ *m indecl* attaché.

аттеста́т testimonial; certificate; pedigree. **аттестова́ть** *impf* & *pf* attest; recommend.

аттракцио́н attraction; sideshow; star turn.

ау́ *int* hi, cooee.

аудито́рия auditorium, lecture-room.

аукцио́н auction.

ауто́псия autopsy.

афе́ра speculation, trickery. **афери́ст** speculator, trickster.

афи́ша placard, poster.

афори́зм aphorism.

А́фрика Africa. **африка́нец** (-нца), **африка́нка** African. **африка́нский** African.

аффе́кт fit of passion; temporary insanity.

ах *int* ah, oh. **а́хать** *impf* (*pf* **а́хнуть**) sigh; exclaim; gasp.

аэро|вокза́л air terminal. **~дина́мика** aerodynamics. **~дро́м** aerodrome, air-field. **~зо́ль** *m* aerosol. **~по́рт** (*loc* -у́) airport.

Б

б *partl*: *see* **бы**

ба́ба (*coll*) (old) woman; **сне́жная ~** snowman.

ба́бочка butterfly.

ба́бушка grandmother; grandma.

бага́ж (-а́) luggage. **бага́жник** carrier; luggage-rack; boot. **ба-**

гáжный вагóн luggage-van.
багóр (-грá) boat-hook.
багрóвый crimson, purple.
бадминтóн badminton.
бáза base; depot; basis; ~ **дáнных** database.
базáр market; din.
бáзис base; basis.
байдáрка canoe.
бáйка flannelette.
бак[1] tank, cistern.
бак[2] forecastle.
бакалáвр (*univ*) bachelor.
бакалéйный grocery. **бакалéя** groceries.
бáкен buoy.
бакенбáрды (*pl*; *gen* -бáрд) side-whiskers.
баклажáн (*gen pl* -ов *or* -жáн) aubergine.
бактéрия bacterium.
бал (*loc* -ý; *pl* -ы́) dance, ball.
балагáн farce.
балалáйка balalaika.
балáнс (*econ*) balance.
баланси́ровать *impf* (*pf* с~) balance; keep one's balance.
балбéс booby.
балдахи́н canopy.
балери́на ballerina. **балéт** ballet.
бáлка[1] beam, girder.
бáлка[2] gully.
балкóн balcony.
балл mark (*in school*); degree; force; **вéтер в пять ~ов** wind force 5.
баллáда ballad.
баллáст ballast.
баллóн container, carboy, cylinder; balloon tyre.
баллоти́ровать *impf* vote; put to the vote; **~ся** stand, be a candidate (**в** *or* **на**+*acc* for).
баловáть *impf* (*pf* **из~**) spoil, pamper; **~ся** play about, get up to tricks; amuse o.s. **баловствó** spoiling; mischief.
Балти́йское мóре Baltic (Sea).
бальзáм balsam; balm.
балюстрáда balustrade.
бамбýк bamboo.
бáмпер bumper.
банáльность banality; platitude. **банáльный** banal.
банáн banana.
бáнда band, gang.
бандáж (-á) truss; belt, band.
бандерóль wrapper; printed matter, book-post.
бáнджо *neut indecl* banjo.
банди́т bandit; gangster.
банк bank.
бáнка jar; tin.
банкéт banquet.
банки́р banker. **банкнóта** banknote. **банкрóт** bankrupt. **банкрóтство** bankruptcy.
банкомáт cash machine.
бант bow.
бáня bath; bath-house.
бар bar; snack-bar.
барабáн drum. **барабáнить** *impf* drum, thump. **барабáнная перепóнка** ear-drum. **барабáнщик** drummer.
барáк wooden barrack, hut.
барáн ram; sheep. **барáнина** mutton; lamb.
барáнка ring-shaped roll; (steering-)wheel.
барахлó old clothes, jumble; odds and ends. **барахóлка** flea market.
барáшек (-шка) young ram; lamb; wing nut; catkin. **барáшковый** lambskin.
бáржá (*gen pl* барж(éй)) barge.
бáрин (*pl* -ре *or* -ры, бар) landowner; sir.

баритóн baritone.
бáрка barge.
бáрмен barman.
барóкко *neut indecl* baroque.
барóметр barometer.
барóн baron. **баронéсса** baroness.
барóчный baroque
баррикáда barricade.
барс snow-leopard.
бáрский lordly; grand.
барсýк (-á) badger.
бархáн dune.
бáрхат (-у) velvet. **бáрхатный** velvet.
бáрыня landowner's wife; madam.
барыш (-á) profit. **бары́шник** dealer; (ticket) speculator.
бáрышня (*gen pl* -шень) young lady; miss.
барьéр barrier; hurdle.
бас (*pl* -ы́) bass.
баскетбóл basket-ball.
баснослóвный mythical, legendary; fabulous. **бáсня** (*gen pl* -сен) fable; fabrication.
басóвый bass.
бассéйн (*geog*) basin; pool; reservoir.
бастовáть *impf* be on strike.
батальóн battalion.
батарéйка, батарéя battery; radiator.
батóн long loaf; stick, bar.
бáтька *m*, **бáтюшка** *m* father; priest. **бáтюшки** *int* good gracious!
бах *int* bang!
бахвáльство bragging.
бахромá fringe.
бац *int* bang! crack!
бацúлла bacillus. **бациллонóситель** *m* carrier.
бачóк (-чкá) cistern.
башкá head.
башлы́к (-á) hood.
башмáк (-á) shoe; **под ~óм у**+*gen* under the thumb of.
бáшня (*gen pl* -шен) tower, turret.
баю́кать *impf* (*pf* **у~**) sing lullabies (to). **бáюшки-баю́** *int* hushabye!
баян accordion.
бдéние vigil. **бдúтельность** vigilance. **бдúтельный** vigilant.
бег (*loc* -ý; *pl* -á) run, running; race. **бéгать** *indet* (*det* **бежáть**) *impf* run.
бегемóт hippopotamus.
беглéц (-á), **беглянка** fugitive.
бéглость speed, fluency, dexterity. **бéглый** rapid, fluent; fleeting, cursory; *sb* fugitive, runaway. **беговóй** running; race. **бегóм** *adv* running, at the double. **беготня́** running about; bustle. **бéгство** flight; escape.
бегýн (-á), **бегýнья** (*gen pl* -ний) runner.
бедá (*pl* -ы) misfortune; disaster; trouble; **~ в том, что** the trouble is (that). **беднéть** *impf* (*pf* **о~**) grow poor. **бéдность** poverty; the poor. **бéдный** (-ден, -днá, -дно) poor. **бедня́га** *m*, **бедня́жка** *m* & *f* poor thing.
бедня́к (-á), **бедня́чка** poor peasant; poor man, poor woman.
бедрó (*pl* бёдра, -дер) thigh; hip.
бéдственный disastrous. **бéдствие** disaster. **бéдствовать** *impf* live in poverty.
бежáть (бегý *det*; *indet* бéгать) *impf* (*pf* **по~**) run; flow; fly; boil over; *impf* & *pf* escape. **бéженец** (-нца), **бéженка** refugee.

без *prep+gen* without; ~ **пяти (минут) три** five (minutes) to three; ~ **четверти** a quarter to.

без-, безъ-, бес- *in comb* in-, un-; non-; -less. **без|алкогóльный** non-alcoholic. **~апелляциóнный** peremptory, categorical. **~бóжие** atheism. **~бóжный** godless; shameless, outrageous. **~болéзненный** painless. **~брáчный** celibate. **~брéжный** boundless. **~вéстный** unknown; obscure. **~вкýсие** lack of taste, bad taste. **~вкýсный** tasteless. **~влáстие** anarchy. **~вóдный** arid. **~возврáтный** irrevocable; irrecoverable. **~возмéздный** free, gratis. **~вóлие** lack of will. **~вóльный** weak-willed. **~врéдный** harmless. **~врéменный** untimely. **~вы́ходный** hopeless, desperate; uninterrupted. **~глáзый** one-eyed; eyeless. **~грáмотный** illiterate. **~грани́чный** boundless, infinite. **~дáрный** untalented. **~дéйственный** inactive. **~дéйствие** inertia, idleness; negligence. **~дéйствовать** *impf* be idle, be inactive; stand idle.

бездéлица trifle. **безделýшка** knick-knack. **бездéльник** idler; ne'er-do-well. **бездéльничать** *impf* idle, loaf.

бéздна abyss, chasm; a huge number, a multitude.

без-. бездоказáтельный unsubstantiated. **~дóмный** homeless. **~дóнный** bottomless; fathomless. **~дорóжье** lack of (good) roads; season when roads are impassable. **~дýмный** unthinking. **~дýшный** heartless; inanimate; lifeless. **~жáлостный** pitiless, ruthless. **~жи́зненный** lifeless. **~забóтный** carefree; careless. **~завéтный** selfless, whole-hearted. **~закóние** lawlessness; unlawful act. **~закóнный** illegal; lawless. **~застéнчивый** shameless, barefaced. **~защи́тный** defenceless. **~звýчный** silent. **~злóбный** good-natured. **~ли́чный** characterless; impersonal. **~лю́дный** uninhabited; sparsely populated; lonely.

безмéн steelyard.

без-. безмéрный immense; excessive. **~мóлвие** silence. **~мóлвный** silent, mute. **~мятéжный** serene, placid. **~надёжный** hopeless. **~надзóрный** neglected. **~накáзанно** *adv* with impunity. **~накáзанный** unpunished. **~нóгий** legless; one-legged. **~нрáвственный** immoral.

безо *prep+gen* = **без** (*used before* **весь** *and* **вся́кий**).

безобрáзие ugliness; disgrace, scandal. **безобрáзничать** *impf* make a nuisance of o.s. **безобрáзный** ugly; disgraceful.

без-. безоговóрочный unconditional. **~опáсность** safety; security. **~опáсный** safe; secure. **~орýжный** unarmed. **~основáтельный** groundless. **~останóвочный** unceasing; non-stop. **~отвéтный** meek, unanswering; dumb. **~отвéтственный** irresponsible. **~откáзно** *adv* without a hitch. **~откáзный** trouble-free, smooth-(running). **~отлагáтельный** urgent. **~относи́тельно** *adv+***к***+dat* irrespective of. **~отчётный** unaccountable. **~оши́бочный** unerring;

correct. **∼рабо́тица** unemployment. **∼рабо́тный** unemployed. **∼разли́чие** indifference. **∼разли́чно** *adv* indifferently; it is all the same. **∼разли́чный** indifferent. **∼рассу́дный** reckless, imprudent. **∼ро́дный** alone in the world; without relatives. **∼ро́потный** uncomplaining; meek. **∼рука́вка** sleeveless pullover. **∼ру́кий** armless; one-armed. **∼уда́рный** unstressed. **∼у́держный** unrestrained; impetuous. **∼укори́зненный** irreproachable.

безу́мец (-мца) madman. **безу́мие** madness. **безу́мный** mad. **безу́мство** madness.

без-. безупре́чный irreproachable, faultless. **∼усло́вно** *adv* unconditionally; of course, undoubtedly. **∼усло́вный** unconditional, absolute; indisputable, **∼успе́шный** unsuccessful. **∼уста́нный** tireless. **∼уте́шный** inconsolable. **∼уча́стие** indifference, apathy. **∼уча́стный** indifferent, apathetic. **∼ымя́нный** nameless, anonymous; **∼ымя́нный па́лец** ring-finger. **∼ыску́сный** artless, ingenuous. **∼ысхо́дный** irreparable; interminable.

бейсбо́л baseball.

бека́р (*mus*) natural.

бека́с snipe.

беко́н bacon.

Белару́сь Belarus.

беле́ть *impf* (*pf* **по∼**) turn white; show white.

белизна́ whiteness. **бели́ла** (*pl*; *gen* -и́л) whitewash; Tippex (*propr*). **бели́ть** (бе́лишь) *impf* (*pf* **вы∼, на∼, по∼**) whitewash; whiten; bleach.

бе́лка squirrel.

беллетри́ст writer of fiction. **беллетри́стика** fiction.

бело- *in comb* white-, leuco-. **белогварде́ец** (-е́йца) White Guard. **∼кро́вие** leukaemia. **∼ку́рый** fair, blonde. **∼ру́с, ∼ру́ска, ∼ру́сский** Belorussian. **∼сне́жный** snow-white.

белови́к (-а́) fair copy. **белово́й** clean, fair.

бело́к (-лка́) white (*of egg, eye*); protein.

белошве́йка seamstress. **белошве́йный** linen.

белу́га white sturgeon. **белу́ха** white whale.

бе́л|ый (бел, -а́, бе́ло́) white; clean, blank; *sb* white person; **∼ая берёза** silver birch; **∼ое кале́ние** white heat; **∼ый медве́дь** polar bear; **∼ые но́чи** white nights, midnight sun.

бельги́ец, -ги́йка Belgian. **бельги́йский** Belgian. **Бе́льгия** Belgium.

бельё linen; bedclothes; underclothes; washing.

бельмо́ (*pl* -а) cataract.

бельэта́ж first floor; dress circle.

бемо́ль *m* (*mus*) flat.

бенефи́с benefit (performance).

бензи́н petrol.

бензо- *in comb* petrol. **бензоба́к** petrol-tank. **∼во́з** petrol tanker. **∼запра́вочная** *sb* filling-station. **∼коло́нка** petrol pump. **∼прово́д** petrol pipe, fuel line.

берёг *etc.*: *see* **бере́чь**

бе́рег (*loc* -у́; *pl* -а́) bank, shore; coast; **на ∼у́ мо́ря** at the seaside. **берегово́й** coast; coastal.

бережёшь *etc.*: *see* **бере́чь. бе-**

режливый thrifty. **бережный** careful.

берёза birch. **Берёзка** hard-currency shop.

беременеть *impf* (*pf* **за~**) be-(come) pregnant. **беременная** pregnant (+*instr* with). **беременность** pregnancy; gestation.

берет beret.

беречь (-регу́, -режёшь; -рёг, -ла́) *impf* take care of; keep; cherish; husband; be sparing of; **~ся** take care; beware (+*gen* of).

берлога den, lair.

беру *etc.*: *see* **брать**

бес devil, demon.

бес-: *see* **без-**

беседа talk, conversation. **беседка** summer-house. **беседовать** *impf* talk, converse.

бесить (бешу́, бе́сишь) *impf* (*pf* **вз~**) enrage; **~ся** go mad; be furious.

бес-. бесконечность infinity; endlessness. **~конечный** endless. **~корыстие** disinterestedness. **~корыстный** disinterested. **~крайний** boundless.

бесовский devilish.

бес-. беспамятство unconsciousness. **~партийный** non-party **~перспективный** without prospects; hopeless. **~печность** carelessness, unconcern. **~платно** *adv* free. **~платный** free. **~плодие** sterility, barrenness. **~плодность** futility. **~плодный** sterile, barren; futile. **~поворотный** irrevocable. **~подобный** incomparable. **~позвоночный** invertebrate.

беспокоить *impf* (*pf* **о~**, **по~**) disturb, bother; trouble; **~ся** worry; trouble. **беспокойный** anxious; troubled; fidgety. **беспокойство** anxiety.

бес-. бесполезный useless. **~помощный** helpless; feeble. **~породный** mongrel, not thoroughbred. **~порядок** (-дка) disorder; untidy state. **~порядочный** disorderly; untidy. **~посадочный** non-stop. **~почвенный** groundless. **~пошлинный** duty-free. **~пощадный** merciless. **~правный** without rights. **~предельный** boundless. **~предметный** aimless; abstract. **~препятственный** unhindered; unimpeded. **~прерывный** continuous. **~престанный** continual.

беспризорник, -ница waif, homeless child. **беспризорный** neglected; homeless; *sb* waif, homeless child.

бес-. беспримерный unparalleled. **~принципный** unscrupulous. **~пристрастие** impartiality. **~пристрастный** impartial. **~просветный** pitch-dark; hopeless; unrelieved. **~путный** dissolute. **~связный** incoherent. **~сердечный** heartless. **~силие** impotence; feebleness. **~сильный** impotent, powerless. **~славный** inglorious. **~следно** *adv* without trace. **~словесный** dumb; silent, meek; (*theat*) walk-on. **~сменный** permanent, continuous. **~смертие** immortality. **~смертный** immortal. **~смысленный** senseless; foolish; meaningless. **~смыслица** nonsense. **~совестный** unscrupulous; shameless. **~сознательный** unconscious; involuntary. **~сонница** insomnia. **~спорный** indisputable. **~срочный** indefinite; without a time limit. **~страстный** impassive. **~стра́шный** fearless. **~сты́дный** shameless. **~та́ктный** tactless.

бестолко́вщина confusion, disorder. **бестолко́вый** muddle-headed, stupid; incoherent.

бес-. бесфо́рменный shapeless. **~хара́ктерный** weak, spineless. **~хи́тростный** artless; unsophisticated. **~хозя́йственный** improvident. **~цве́тный** colourless. **~це́льный** aimless; pointless. **~це́нный** priceless. **~це́нок: за ~це́нок** very cheap, for a song. **~церемо́нный** unceremonious. **~челове́чный** inhuman. **~че́стить** (-е́щу) *impf* (*pf* **о~че́стить**) dishonour. **~че́стный** dishonourable. **~чи́сленный** innumerable, countless.

бесчу́вственный insensible; insensitive. **бесчу́вствие** insensibility; insensitivity.

бес-. бесшу́мный noiseless.

бето́н concrete. **бето́нный** concrete. **бетономеша́лка** concrete-mixer. **бето́нщик** concrete-worker.

бечева́ tow-rope; rope. **бечёвка** cord, string.

бе́шенство rabies; rage. **бе́шеный** rabid; furious.

бешу́ *etc*.: *see* **беси́ть**

библе́йский biblical. **библиографи́ческий** bibliographical. **библиогра́фия** bibliography. **библиоте́ка** library. **библиоте́карь** *m*, **-те́карша** librarian. **би́блия** bible.

бива́к bivouac, camp.

би́вень (-вня) *m* tusk.

бигуди́ *pl indecl* curlers.

бидо́н can; churn.

бие́ние beating; beat.

бижуте́рия costume jewellery.

би́знес business. **бизнесме́н** businessman.

биле́т ticket; card; pass. **биле́тный** ticket.

биллио́н billion.

билья́рд billiards.

бино́кль *m* binoculars.

бинт (-а́) bandage. **бинтова́ть** *impf* (*pf* **за~**) bandage. **бинто́вка** bandaging.

био́граф biographer. **биографи́ческий** biographical. **биогра́фия** biography. **био́лог** biologist. **биологи́ческий** biological. **биоло́гия** biology. **биохи́мия** biochemistry.

би́ржа exchange.

би́рка name-plate; label.

бирюза́ turquoise

бис *int* encore.

би́сер (*no pl*) beads.

бискви́т sponge cake.

бита́ bat.

би́тва battle.

битко́м *adv*: **~ наби́т** packed.

биту́м bitumen.

бить (бью, бьёшь) *impf* (*pf* **за~**, **по~**, **про~**, **уда́рить**) beat; hit; defeat; sound; thump, bang; smash; **~ в цель** hit the target; **~ на**+*acc* strive for; **~ отбо́й** beat a retreat; **~ по**+*dat* damage, wound; **~ся** fight; beat; struggle; break; +*instr* knock, hit, strike; **+над**+*instr* struggle with, rack one's brains over.

бифште́кс beefsteak.

бич (-а́) whip, lash; scourge; homeless person. **бичева́ть** (-чу́ю) *impf* flog; castigate.

бла́го good; blessing.

бла́го- *in comb* well-, good-. **Благове́щение** Annunciation. **~ви́дный** plausible. **~во-**

ле́ние goodwill. **~воспи́танный** well-brought-up.
благодари́ть (-рю́) *impf* (*pf* **по~**) thank. **благода́рность** gratitude; **не сто́ит благода́рности** don't mention it. **благода́рный** grateful. **благодаря́** *prep+dat* thanks to, owing to.
благо-. **благоде́тель** *m* benefactor. **~де́тельница** benefactress. **~де́тельный** beneficial. **~ду́шный** placid; good-humoured. **~жела́тель** *m* well-wisher. **~жела́тельный** well-disposed; benevolent. **~зву́чный** melodious, harmonious. **~надёжный** reliable. **~наме́ренный** well-intentioned. **~полу́чие** well-being; happiness. **~полу́чно** *adv* all right, well; happily; safely. **~полу́чный** happy, successful; safe. **~прия́тный** favourable. **~прия́тствовать** *impf +dat* favour. **~разу́мие** sense; prudence. **~разу́мный** sensible. **~ро́дие**: **ва́ше ~ро́дие** Your Honour. **~ро́дный** noble. **~ро́дство** nobility. **~скло́нность** favour, good graces. **~скло́нный** favourable; gracious. **~слови́ть** *pf*, **благословля́ть** *impf* bless. **~состоя́ние** prosperity. **~твори́тель** *m*, **-ница** philanthropist. **~твори́тельный** charitable, charity. **~тво́рный** salutary; beneficial; wholesome. **~устро́енный** well-equipped, well-planned; with all amenities.
блаже́нный blissful; simple-minded. **блаже́нство** bliss.
бланк form.
блат (*sl*) string-pulling; pull, influence. **блатно́й** criminal.
бледне́ть (-е́ю) *impf* (*pf* **по~**) (grow) pale. **бле́дность** paleness, pallor. **бле́дный** (-ден, -дна́, -о) pale.
блеск brightness, brilliance, lustre; magnificence.
блесну́ть (-ну́, -нёшь) *pf* flash, gleam; shine. **блесте́ть** (-ещу́, -сти́шь *or* бле́щешь) *impf* shine; glitter. **блёстка** sparkle; sequin. **блестя́щий** shining, bright; brilliant.
бле́ять (-е́ет) *impf* bleat.
ближа́йший nearest, closest; next. **бли́же** *comp of* **бли́зкий**, **бли́зко**. **бли́жний** near, close; neighbouring; *sb* neighbour.
близ *prep+gen* near, by. **бли́з|кий** (-зок, -изка́, -о) near; close; imminent; **~кие** *sb pl* one's nearest and dearest, close relatives. **бли́зко** *adv* near (**от**+*gen* to). **близне́ц** (-а́) twin; *pl* Gemini. **близору́кий** short-sighted. **бли́зость** closeness, proximity.
блик patch of light; highlight.
блин (-а́) pancake.
блинда́ж (-а́) dug-out.
блиста́ть *impf* shine; sparkle.
блог (*comput.*) blog, weblog. **бло́ггер** (*comput.*) blogger, weblogger.
блок block, pulley, sheave.
блока́да blockade. **блоки́ровать** *impf* & *pf* blockade; **~ся** form a bloc. **блокно́т** writing-pad, note-book.
блонди́н, **блонди́нка** blond(e).
блоха́ (*pl* -и, -а́м) flea.
блуд lechery. **блудни́ца** whore.
блужда́ть *impf* roam, wander.
блу́за, блу́зка blouse.
блю́дечко saucer; small dish. **блю́до** dish; course. **блю́дце** saucer.
боб (-а́) bean. **бобо́вый** bean.

бобр (-á) beaver.

Бог (*voc* **Бóже**) God; **дай ~** God grant; **~ егó знáет** who knows? **не дай ~** God forbid; **Бóже (мой)!** my God! good God!; **рáди ~а** for God's sake; **слáва ~у** thank God.

богатéть *impf* (*pf* **раз~**) grow rich. **богáтство** wealth. **богáтый** rich, wealthy; *sb* rich man. **богáч** (-á) rich man.

богаты́рь (-я́) *m* hero; strong man.

боги́ня goddess. **Богомáтерь** Mother of God. **богомóлец** (-льца), **богомóлка** devout person; pilgrim. **богомóлье** pilgrimage. **богомóльный** religious, devout. **Богорóдица** the Virgin Mary. **богослóв** theologian. **богослóвие** theology. **богослужéние** divine service. **боготвори́ть** *impf* idolize; deify. **богоху́льство** blasphemy.

бодри́ть *impf.* stimulate, invigorate; **~ся** try to keep up one's spirits. **бóдрость** cheerfulness, courage. **бóдрствовать** be awake; stay awake; keep vigil. **бóдрый** (бодр, -á, -о) cheerful, bright.

боеви́к (-á) smash hit. **боевóй** fighting, battle. **боеголóвка** warhead. **боеприпáсы** (*pl*; *gen* -ов) ammunition. **боеспосóбный** battle-worthy. **боéц** (бойцá) soldier; fighter, warrior.

Бóже: *see* **Бог**. **бóжеский** divine; just. **божéственный** divine. **божествó** deity; divinity. **бóж|ий** God's; **~ья корóвка** ladybird. **божóк** (-жкá) idol.

бой (*loc* -ю́; *pl* -и́, -ёв) battle, action, fight; fighting; slaughtering; striking; breakage(s).

бóйкий (бóек, бойкá, -о) smart, sharp; glib; lively.

бойкóт boycott.

бóйня (*gen pl* бóен) slaughterhouse; butchery.

бок (*loc* -у́; *pl* -á) side; flank; **~ ó ~** side by side; **нá ~** to the side; **на ~у́** on one side; **пóд ~ом** near by; **с ~у** from the side, from the flank; **с ~у нá бок** from side to side.

бокáл glass; goblet.

боковóй side; lateral. **бóком** *adv* sideways.

бокс boxing. **боксёр** boxer.

болвáн blockhead. **болвáнка** pig (*of iron etc.*).

болгáрин (*pl* -гáры), **болгáрка** Bulgarian. **болгáрский** Bulgarian. **Болгáрия** Bulgaria.

бóлее *adv* more; **~ всегó** most of all; **тем ~, что** especially as.

болéзненный sickly; unhealthy; painful. **болéзнь** illness, disease; abnormality.

болéльщик, -щица fan, supporter. **болéть**[1] (-éю) *impf* be ill, suffer. **болéть**[2] (-ли́т) *impf* ache, hurt.

болóтистый marshy. **болóто** marsh, bog.

болтáть[1] *impf* stir; shake; dangle; **~ся** dangle, swing; hang about.

болтáть[2] *impf* chat, natter. **болтли́вый** talkative; indiscreet. **болтовня́** talk; chatter; gossip. **болту́н** (-á), **болту́нья** chatterbox.

боль pain; ache. **больни́ца** hospital. **больни́чный** hospital; **~ листóк** medical certificate. **бóльно**[1] *adv* painfully, badly; *predic+dat* it hurts. **бóльно**[2] *adv* very, terribly. **больнóй** (-лен, -льнá) ill, sick; diseased;

sore; *sb* patient, invalid.

бóльше *comp of* **большóй, мнóго**; bigger, larger; greater; more; **~ не** not any more, no longer; **~ тогó** and what is more; *adv* for the most part. **большевúк** Bolshevik. **бóльш|ий** greater, larger; **~ей чáстью** for the most part. **большинствó** majority. **больш|óй** big, large; great; grown-up; **~áя бýква** capital letter; **~óй пáлец** thumb; big toe; **~úе** *sb pl* grown-ups.

бóмба bomb. **бомбардировáть** *impf* bombard; bomb. **бомбардирóвка** bombardment, bombing. **бомбардирóвщик** bomber. **бомбёжка** bombing. **бомбúть** (-блю́) bomb. **бомбоубéжище** bomb shelter.

бор (*loc* -ý; *pl* -ы́) coniferous forest.

бордóвый wine-red.

бордю́р border.

борéц (-рцá) fighter; wrestler.

бóрзый swift.

бормашúна (dentist's) drill.

бормотáть (-очý, -óчешь) *impf* (*pf* **про~**) mutter, mumble.

бородá (*acc* бóроду; *pl* бóроды, -рóд, -áм) beard. **бородáвка** wart. **бородáтый** bearded.

бороздá (*pl* бóрозды, -óзд, -áм) furrow. **бороздúть** (-зжý) *impf* (*pf* **вз~**) furrow.

боронá (*acc* бóрону; *pl* бóроны, -рóн, -áм) harrow. **боронúть** *impf* (*pf* **вз~**) harrow.

борóться (-рю́сь, бóрешься) *impf* wrestle; struggle, fight.

борт (*loc* -ý; *pl* -á, -óв) side, ship's side; front; **за ~, за ~ом** overboard; **на ~, на ~ý** on board. **бортпроводнúк** (-á) air steward. **бортпроводнúца** air hostess.

борщ (-á) borshch (*beetroot soup*).

борьбá wrestling; struggle, fight.

босикóм *adv* barefoot.

боснúец (-úйца), **боснúйка** Bosnian. **боснúйский** Bosnian. **Бóсния** Bosnia.

босóй (бос, -á, -о) barefooted. **босонóжка** sandal.

бот, бóтик small boat.

ботáник botanist. **ботáника** botany. **ботанúческий** botanical.

ботúнок (-нка; *gen pl* -нок) (*ankle-high*) boot.

бóцман boatswain

бóчка barrel. **бочóнок** (-нка) keg, small barrel.

боязлúвый timid, timorous. **боя́знь** fear, dread.

боя́рин (*pl* -я́ре, -я́р) boyar.

боя́рышник hawthorn.

боя́ться (боюсь) *impf* +*gen* be afraid of, fear; dislike.

брак[1] marriage.

брак[2] defective goods; flaw. **бракoвáть** *impf* (*pf* **за~**) reject.

браконьéр poacher.

бракоразвóдный divorce. **бракосочетáние** wedding.

бранúть *impf* (*pf* **вы́~**) scold; abuse, curse; **~ся** (*pf* **по~**) swear, curse; quarrel. **брáнн|ый** abusive; **~ое слóво** swear-word.

брань bad language; abuse.

браслéт bracelet.

брасс breast stroke.

брат (*pl* -тья, -тьев) brother; comrade; mate; lay brother, monk. **братáться** *impf* (*pf* **по~**) fraternize. **братоубúй-**

ство fratricide. **брáтский** brotherly, fraternal. **брáтство** brotherhood, fraternity.

брать (берý, -рёшь; брал, -á, -o) *impf* (*pf* **взять**) take; obtain; hire; seize; demand, require; surmount, clear; work; +*instr* succeed by means of; **~ся** +**за**+*acc* touch; seize; get down to; +**за**+*acc or inf* undertake; appear, come.

брáчный marriage; mating.

бревéнчатый log. **бревнó** (*pl* брёвна, -вен) log, beam.

бред (*loc* -ý) delirium; raving(s). **брéдить** (-éжу) *impf* be delirious, rave; +*instr* rave about, be infatuated with. **бредóвый** delirious; fantastic, nonsensical.

бредý *etc.*: *see* **брести́**. **брéжу** *etc.*: *see* **брéдить**

брéзгать *impf* (*pf* **по~**) +*inf or instr* be squeamish about. **брезгли́вый** squeamish.

брезéнт tarpaulin.

брéзжить(ся *impf* dawn; gleam faintly, glimmer.

брёл *etc.*: *see* **брéсти**

брелóк charm, pendant.

бремени́ть *impf* (*pf* **о~**) burden. **брéмя** (-мени) *neut* burden; load.

бренчáть (-чý) *impf* strum; jingle.

брести́ (-едý, -едёшь; брёл, -á) *impf* stroll; drag o.s. along.

бретéль, бретéлька shoulder strap.

брешь breach; gap.

брéю *etc.*: *see* **брить**

бригáда brigade; crew, team. **бригади́р** brigadier; team-leader; foreman.

бриллиáнт, брильянт diamond.

британец (-нца), **британка** Briton. **британск|ий** British; **Б~ие островá** the British Isles.

бри́тва razor. **бри́твенный** shaving. **бри́тый** shaved; clean-shaven. **брить** (брéю) *impf* (*pf* **по~**) shave; **~ся** shave (o.s.).

бровь (*pl* -и, -éй) (eye)brow.

брод ford.

броди́ть (-ожý, -óдишь) *impf* wander, roam, stroll; ferment. **бродя́га** *m* & *f* tramp, vagrant. **бродя́жничество** vagrancy. **бродя́чий** vagrant; wandering. **брожéние** ferment, fermentation.

брóкер broker.

броне- *in comb* armoured, armour. **броневи́к** (-á) armoured car. **~вóй** armoured. **~нóсец** (-сца) battleship; armadillo.

брóнза bronze; bronzes. **брóнзовый** bronze; tanned.

брониро́ванный armoured.

брони́ровать *impf* & *pf* (*pf also* **за~**) reserve, book.

бронхи́т bronchitis.

брóня[1] reservation; commandeering.

броня́[2] armour.

бросáть *impf*, **брóсить** (-óшу) *pf* throw (down); leave, desert; give up, leave off; **~ся** throw o.s., rush; +*inf* begin; +*instr* squander; pelt one another with; **~ся в глазá** be striking. **брóский** striking; garish, glaring. **бросóк** (-скá) throw; bound, spurt.

брóшка, брошь brooch.

брошю́ра pamphlet, brochure.

брус (*pl* -сья, -сьев) squared beam, joist; **(параллéльные) ~ья** parallel bars.

брусни́ка red whortleberry; red whortleberries.

брусóк (-скá) bar; ingot.

бру́тто *indecl adj* gross.
бры́згать (-зжу *or* -гаю) *impf*, **бры́знуть** (-ну) *pf* splash; sprinkle. **бры́зги** (брызг) *pl* spray, splashes; fragments.
брыка́ть *impf*, **брыкну́ть** (-ну́, -нёшь) *pf* kick.
брюзга́ *m* & *f* grumbler. **брюзгли́вый** grumbling, peevish. **брюзжа́ть** (-жу́) *impf* grumble.
брю́ква swede.
брю́ки (*pl*; *gen* брюк) trousers.
брюне́т dark-haired man. **брюне́тка** brunette.
брю́хо (*pl* -и) belly; stomach.
брюшно́й abdominal; ~ **тиф** typhoid.
бряца́ть *impf* rattle; clank, clang.
бу́бен (-бна) tambourine. **бубене́ц** (-нца́) small bell.
бу́бны (*pl*; *gen* -бён, *dat* -бна́м) (*cards*) diamonds. **бубно́вый** diamond.
буго́р (-гра́) mound, hillock; bump, lump.
будди́зм Buddhism. **будди́йский** Buddhist. **будди́ст** Buddhist.
бу́дет that will do.
буди́льник alarm-clock. **буди́ть** (бужу́, бу́дишь) *impf* (*pf* **про**~, **раз**~) wake; arouse.
бу́дка box, booth; hut; stall.
бу́дни (*pl*; *gen* **-ней**) *pl* weekdays; working days; humdrum existence. **бу́дний, бу́дничный** weekday; everyday; humdrum.
бу́дто *conj* as if, as though; ~ **(бы), (как)** ~ apparently, ostensibly.
бу́ду *etc.*: *see* **быть. бу́дучи** being. **бу́дущ|ий** future; next; ~**ее** *sb* future. **бу́дущность** future. **бу́дь(те):** *see* **быть**
бужу́: *see* **буди́ть**
бузина́ (*bot*) elder.
буй (*pl* -и́, -ёв) buoy.
бу́йвол buffalo.
бу́йный (бу́ен, буйна́, -о) violent, turbulent; luxuriant, lush. **бу́йство** unruly behaviour. **бу́йствовать** *impf* create an uproar, behave violently.
бук beech.
бука́шка small insect.
бу́ква (*gen pl* букв) letter; ~ **в бу́кву** literally. **буква́льно** *adv* literally. **буква́льный** literal.
буква́рь (-я́) *m* ABC. **буквое́д** pedant.
буке́т bouquet; aroma.
букини́ст second-hand bookseller.
бу́кля curl, ringlet.
бу́ковый beech.
букси́р tug-boat; tow-rope. **букси́ровать** *impf* tow.
буксова́ть *impf* spin, slip.
була́вка pin.
бу́лка roll; white loaf. **бу́лочка** roll, bun. **бу́лочная** *sb* baker's. **бу́лочник** baker.
булы́жник cobble-stone, cobbles.
бульва́р avenue; boulevard.
бульдо́г bulldog.
бульдо́зер bulldozer.
бу́лькать *impf* gurgle.
бульо́н broth.
бум (*sport*) beam.
бума́га cotton; paper; document. **бума́жка** piece of paper; (bank)note. **бума́жник** wallet; paper-maker. **бума́жный** cotton; paper.
бу́нкер bunker.
бунт (*pl* -ы) rebellion; riot; mutiny. **бунта́рь** (-я́) *m* rebel; insurgent. **бунтова́ть(ся** *impf* (*pf*

вз~) rebel; riot. **бунтовщи́к** (-á), **-щи́ца** rebel, insurgent.

бур auger.

бура́в (-á; *pl* -á) auger; gimlet. **бура́вить** (-влю) *impf* (*pf* **про~**) bore, drill.

бура́н snowstorm.

буреве́стник stormy petrel.

буре́ние boring, drilling.

буржуа́ *m indecl* bourgeois. **буржуази́я** bourgeoisie. **буржуа́зный** bourgeois.

бури́льщик borer, driller. **бури́ть** *impf* (*pf* **про~**) bore, drill.

бурли́ть *impf* seethe.

бу́рный (-рен, -рна́, -о) stormy; rapid; energetic.

буров|о́й boring; **~а́я вы́шка** derrick; **~а́я (сква́жина)** borehole; **~о́й стано́к** drilling rig.

бу́рый (бур, -á, -о) brown.

бурья́н tall weeds.

бу́ря storm.

бу́сина bead. **бу́сы** (*pl*; *gen* бус) beads.

бутафо́рия (*theat*) props.

бутербро́д open sandwich.

буто́н bud.

бу́тсы (*pl*; *gen* -ов) *pl* football boots.

буты́лка bottle. **буты́ль** large bottle; carboy.

буфе́т snack bar; sideboard; counter. **буфе́тчик** barman. **буфе́тчица** barmaid.

бух *int* bang, plonk. **бу́хать** *impf* (*pf* **бу́хнуть**) thump, bang; bang down; thunder, thud; blurt out.

буха́нка loaf.

бухга́лтер accountant. **бухгалте́рия** accountancy; accounts department.

бу́хнуть (-ну) *impf* swell.

бу́хта bay.

бушева́ть (-шу́ю) *impf* rage, storm.

буя́н rowdy. **буя́нить** *impf* create an uproar.

бы, б *partl* **I.** *+past tense or inf indicates the conditional or subjunctive.* **II.** **(+ни)** *forms indef prons and conjs.*

быва́лый experienced; former; habitual, familiar. **быва́ть** *impf* be; happen; be inclined to be; **как ни в чём не быва́ло** as if nothing had happened; **быва́ло** *partl* used to, would; **мать быва́ло ча́сто пе́ла э́ту пе́сню** my mother would often sing this song. **бы́вший** former, ex-.

бык (-á) bull, ox; pier.

были́на ancient Russian epic.

бы́ло *partl* nearly, on the point of; (only) just. **был|о́й** past, bygone; **~о́е** *sb* the past. **быль** true story; fact.

быстрота́ speed. **бы́стрый** (быстр, -á, -о) fast, quick.

быт (*loc* -у́) way of life. **бытие́** being, existence; objective reality; **книга́ Бытия́** Genesis. **бытово́й** everyday; social.

быть (*pres 3rd sg* есть, *pl* суть; *fut* бу́ду; *past* был, -á, -о; *imper* бу́дь(те)) *impf* be; be situated; happen. **бытьё** way of life.

бычо́к (-чка́) steer.

бью *etc.*: *see* **бить**

бюдже́т budget.

бюллете́нь *m* bulletin; ballot-paper; doctor's certificate.

бюро́ *neut indecl* bureau; office; writing-desk. **бюрокра́т** bureaucrat. **бюрократи́зм** bureaucracy. **бюрократи́ческий** bureaucratic. **бюрокра́тия** bureaucracy; bureaucrats.

бюст bust. **бюстга́льтер** bra.

В

в, во *prep* **I.** *+acc* into, to; on; at; within; through; **быть в** take after; **в два ра́за бо́льше** twice as big; **в на́ши дни** in our day; **войти́ в дом** go into the house; **в понеде́льник** on Monday; **в тече́ние**+*gen* during; **в четы́ре часа́** at four o'clock **высото́й в три ме́тра** threemetres high; **игра́ть в ша́хматы** play chess; **пое́хать в Москву́** go to Moscow; **сесть в ваго́н** get into the carriage; **смотре́ть в окно́** look out of the window. **II.** *+prep* in; at; **в двадца́том ве́ке** in the twentieth century; **в теа́тре** at the theatre; **в трёх киломе́трах от го́рода** three kilometres from the town; **в э́том году́** this year; **в январе́** in January.

ваго́н carriage, coach; **~-рестора́н** restaurant car. **ваго́нетка** truck, trolley. **вагоновожа́тый** *sb* tram-driver.

ва́жничать *impf* give o.s. airs; *+instr* plume o.s., pride o.s., on. **ва́жность** importance; pomposity. **ва́жный** (-жен, -жна́, -о) important; weighty; pompous.

ва́за vase, bowl.

вазели́н Vaseline (*propr*).

вака́нсия vacancy. **вака́нтный** vacant.

ва́кса (shoe-)polish.

ва́куум vacuum.

вакци́на vaccine.

вал[1] (*loc* -у́; *pl* -ы́) bank; rampart; billow, roller; barrage.

вал[2] (*loc* -у́; *pl* -ы́) shaft.

ва́ленок (-нка; *gen pl* -нок) felt boot.

вале́т knave, Jack.

ва́лик roller, cylinder.

вали́ть[1] *impf* flock, throng.

вали́ть[2] (-лю́, -лишь) *impf* (*pf* **по~, с~**) throw down, bring down; pile up; **~ся** fall, collapse.

валли́ец (-и́йца) Welshman. **валли́йка** Welshwoman.

валово́й gross; wholesale.

валто́рна French horn.

валу́н (-а́) boulder.

вальс waltz. **вальси́ровать** *impf* waltz.

валю́та currency; foreign currency.

валя́ть *impf* (*pf* **на~, с~**) drag; roll; shape; bungle; **~ дурака́** play the fool; **~ся** lie, lie about; roll, wallow.

вам, ва́ми: *see* **вы**

вампи́р vampire.

ванда́л vandal. **вандали́зм** vandalism.

вани́ль vanilla.

ва́нна bath. **ва́нная** *sb* bathroom.

ва́рвар barbarian. **ва́рварский** barbaric. **ва́рварство** barbarity; vandalism.

ва́режка mitten.

варёный boiled. **варе́нье** jam.

вари́ть (-рю́, -ришь) *impf* (*pf* **с~**) boil; cook; **~ся** boil; cook.

вариа́нт version; option; scenario.

вас: *see* **вы**

василёк (-лька́) cornflower.

ва́та cotton wool; wadding.

ватерли́ния water-line. **ватерпа́с** (spirit-)level.

вати́н (sheet) wadding. **ва́тник** quilted jacket. **ва́тный** quilted, wadded.

ватру́шка cheese-cake.

ватт (*gen pl* **ватт**) watt.

ва́учер coupon (*exchangeable*

for government-issued share).
ва́фля (*gen pl* -фель) wafer; waffle.
ва́хта (*naut*) watch. **вахтёр** janitor, porter.
ваш (-его) *m*, **ва́ша** (-ей) *f*, **ва́ше** (-его) *neut*, **ва́ши** (-их) *pl*, *pron* your, yours.
вбега́ть *impf*, **вбежа́ть** (вбегу́) *pf* run in.
вберу́ *etc.*: *see* **вобра́ть**
вбива́ть *impf of* **вбить**
вбира́ть *impf of* **вобра́ть**
вбить (вобью́, -бьёшь) *pf* (*impf* **вбива́ть**) drive in, hammer in.
вблизи́ *adv* (+от+*gen*) close (to), near by.
вбок *adv* sideways, to one side.
вброд *adv*: **переходи́ть ~** ford, wade.
вва́ливать *impf*, **ввали́ть** (-лю́, -лишь) *pf* throw heavily, heave, bundle; **~ся** fall heavily; sink, become sunken; burst in.
введе́ние introduction. **введу́** *etc.*: *see* **ввести́**
ввезти́ (-зу́, -зёшь; ввёз, -ла́) *pf* (*impf* **ввози́ть**) import; bring in.
вве́рить *pf* (*impf* **вверя́ть**) entrust, confide; **~ся** +*dat* trust in, put one's faith in.
вверну́ть (-ну́, -нёшь) *pf*, **ввёртывать** *impf* screw in; insert.
вверх *adv* up, upward(s); **~дном** upside down; **~ (по ле́стнице)** upstairs. **вверху́** *adv* above, overhead.
вверя́ть(ся) *impf of* **вве́рить(ся)**
ввести́ (-еду́, -едёшь; ввёл, -а́) *pf* (*impf* **вводи́ть**) bring in; introduce.
ввиду́ *prep+gen* in view of.
ввинти́ть (-нчу́) *pf*, **вви́нчивать** *impf* screw in.
ввод lead-in. **вводи́ть** (-ожу́, -о́дишь) *impf of* **ввести́**. **вво́дный** introductory; parenthetic.
ввожу́ *see* **вводи́ть, ввози́ть**
ввоз importation; import(s).
ввози́ть (-ожу́, -о́зишь) *impf of* **ввезти́**
вво́лю *adv* to one's heart's content.
ввысь *adv* up, upward(s).
ввяза́ть (-яжу́, -я́жешь) *pf*, **ввя́зывать** *impf* knit in; involve; **~ся** meddle, get or be mixed up (in).
вглубь *adv* & *prep+gen* deep (into), into the depths.
вгляде́ться (-яжу́сь) *pf*, **вгля́дываться** *impf* peer, look closely (**в**+*acc* at).
вгоня́ть *impf of* **вогна́ть**. **вдава́ться** (вдаю́сь, -ёшься) *impf of* **вда́ться**
вдави́ть (-авлю́, -а́вишь) *pf*, **вда́вливать** *impf* press in.
вдалеке́, вдали́ *adv* in the distance, far away. **вдаль** *adv* into the distance.
вда́ться (-а́мся, -а́шься, -а́стся, -адимся; -а́лся, -ла́сь) *pf* (*impf* **вдава́ться**) jut out; penetrate, go in; (*fig*) get immersed.
вдво́е *adv* twice; double; **~ бо́льше** twice as big, as much, as many. **вдвоём** *adv* (the) two together, both. **вдвойне́** *adv* twice, double; doubly.
вдева́ть *impf of* **вдеть**
вде́лать *pf*, **вде́лывать** *impf* set in, fit in.
вдёргивать *impf*, **вдёрнуть** (-ну) *pf* **в**+*acc* thread through.
вдеть (-е́ну) *pf* (*impf* **вдева́ть**) put in, thread.

вдоба́вок *adv* in addition; besides.

вдова́ widow. **вдове́ц** (-вца́) widower.

вдо́воль *adv* enough; in abundance.

вдого́нку *adv* (**за**+*instr*) after, in pursuit (of).

вдоль *adv* lengthwise; **~ и поперёк** far and wide; in detail; *prep*+*gen or* **по**+*dat* along.

вдох breath. **вдохнове́ние** inspiration, **вдохнове́нный** inspired. **вдохнови́ть** (-влю́) *pf*, **вдохновля́ть** *impf* inspire. **вдохну́ть** (-ну́, -нёшь) *pf* (*impf* **вдыха́ть**) breathe in.

вдре́безги *adv* to smithereens.

вдруг *adv* suddenly.

вду́маться *pf*, **вду́мываться** *impf* ponder, meditate; +**в**+*acc* think over. **вду́мчивый** thoughtful.

вдыха́ние inhalation. **вдыха́ть** *impf of* **вдохну́ть**

веб-сайт (*comput*) website. **веб-страни́ца** (*comput*) web page.

вегетариа́нец (-нца), **-нка** vegetarian. **вегетариа́нский** vegetarian.

ве́дать *impf* know; +*instr* manage, handle. **ве́дение**[1] authority, jurisdiction.

веде́ние[2] conducting, conduct; **~ книг** book-keeping.

ве́домость (*gen pl* -е́й) list, register. **ве́домственный** departmental. **ве́домство** department.

ведро́ (*pl* вёдра, -дер) bucket; vedro (*approx 12 litres*).

веду́ *etc.*: *see* **вести́. веду́щий** leading.

ведь *partl* & *conj* you see, you know; isn't it? is it?

ве́дьма witch.

ве́ер (*pl* -а́) fan.

ве́жливость politeness. **ве́жливый** polite.

везде́ *adv* everywhere.

везе́ние luck. **везу́чий** lucky.

везти́ (-зу́, -зёшь; вёз, -ла́) *impf* (*pf* **по~**) convey; bring, take; *impers*+*dat* be lucky; **ему́ не везло́** he had no luck.

век (*loc* -у́; *pl* -а́) century; age; life(time). **век** *adv* for ages.

ве́ко (*pl* -и, век) eyelid.

веково́й ancient, age-old.

ве́ксель (*pl* -я́, -е́й) *m* promissory note, bill (of exchange).

вёл *etc.*: *see* **вести́**

веле́ть (-лю́) *impf* & *pf* order; **не ~** forbid.

велика́н giant. **вели́кий** (вели́к, -а *or* -а́) great; big, large; too big; **~ пост** Lent.

велико- *in comb* great. **Великобрита́ния** Great Britain. **великоду́шие** magnanimity. **~ду́шный** magnanimous. **~ле́пие** splendour. **~ле́пный** splendid.

велича́вый stately, majestic. **велича́йший** greatest, supreme. **вели́чественный** majestic, grand. **вели́чество** Majesty. **вели́чие** greatness, grandeur. **величина́** (*pl* -и́ны, -а́м) size; quantity, magnitude; value; great figure.

велосипе́д bicycle. **велосипеди́ст** cyclist.

вельве́т velveteen; **~ в ру́бчик** corduroy.

вельмо́жа *m* grandee.

ве́на vein.

венге́рец (-рца), **венге́рка** Hungarian. **венге́рский** Hungarian. **венгр** Hungarian. **Ве́нгрия** Hungary.

вendéтта vendetta.

венери́ческий venereal.

вене́ц (-нца́) crown; wreath.
ве́ник besom; birch twigs.
вено́к (-нка́) wreath, garland.
ве́нтиль *m* valve.
вентиля́тор ventilator; extractor (fan). **вентиля́ция** ventilation.
венча́ние wedding; coronation. **венча́ть** *impf* (*pf* **об~, по~, у~**) crown; marry; **~ся** be married, marry. **ве́нчик** halo; corolla; rim; ring, bolt.
ве́ра faith, belief.
вера́нда veranda.
ве́рба willow; willow branch. **ве́рбн|ый; ~ое воскресе́нье** Palm Sunday.
верблю́д camel.
вербова́ть *impf* (*pf* **за~**) recruit; win over. **вербо́вка** recruitment.
верёвка rope; string; cord. **верёвочный** rope.
верени́ца row, file, line, string.
ве́реск heather.
веретено́ (*pl* -тёна) spindle.
вереща́ть (-щу́) *impf* squeal; chirp.
ве́рить *impf* (*pf* **по~**) believe, have faith; *+dat or* **в**+*acc* trust (in), believe in.
вермише́ль vermicelli.
верне́е *adv* rather. **ве́рно** *partl* probably, I suppose. **ве́рность** faithfulness, loyalty.
верну́ть (-ну́, -нёшь) *pf* (*impf* **возвраща́ть**) give back, return; **~ся** return.
ве́рный (-рен, -рна́, -о) faithful, loyal; true; correct; reliable.
ве́рование belief. **ве́ровать** *impf* believe. **вероисповеда́ние** religion; denomination. **вероло́мный** treacherous, perfidious. **вероотсту́пник** apostate. **веротерпи́мость** (religious) toleration. **вероя́тно** *adv* probably. **вероя́тность** probability. **вероя́тный** probable.
ве́рсия version.
верста́ (*pl* вёрсты) verst (*1.06 km.*).
верста́к (-а́) work-bench.
ве́ртел (*pl* -а́) spit, skewer. **верте́ть** (-чу́, -тишь) *impf* turn (round); twirl; **~ся** turn (round), spin. **вертля́вый** fidgety; flighty.
вертика́ль vertical line. **вертика́льный** vertical.
вертолёт helicopter.
верту́шка flirt.
ве́рующий *sb* believer.
верфь shipyard.
верх (*loc* -у́; *pl* -и́) top; summit; height; *pl* upper crust, top brass; high notes. **ве́рхний** upper; top. **верхо́вный** supreme. **верхово́й** riding; *sb* rider. **верхо́вье** (*gen pl* -вьев) upper reaches. **верхола́з** steeple-jack. **верхо́м** *adv* on horseback; astride. **верху́шка** top, summit; apex; top brass.
верчу́ *etc.*: *see* **верте́ть**
верши́на top, summit; peak; apex. **верши́ть** *impf* *+instr* manage, control.
вершо́к vershok (*4.4 cm.*); smattering.
вес (*loc* -у́; *pl* -а́) weight.
весели́ть *impf* (*pf* **раз~**) cheer, gladden; **~ся** enjoy o.s.; amuse o.s. **ве́село** *adv* merrily. **весёлый** (ве́сел, -а́, -о) merry; cheerful. **весе́лье** merriment.
весе́нний spring.
ве́сить (ве́шу) *impf* weigh. **ве́ский** weighty, solid.
весло́ (*pl* вёсла, -сел) oar.

весна́ (*pl* вёсны, -сен) spring. **весно́й** *adv* in (the) spring. **весну́шка** freckle.

вест (*naut*) west; west wind.

вести́ (веду́, -дёшь; вёл, -а́) *impf* (*pf* **по~**) lead, take; conduct; drive; run; keep; **~ себя́** behave, conduct o.s.; **~сь** be the custom.

вестибю́ль *m* (entrance) hall, lobby.

ве́стник herald; bulletin. **весть**[1] (*gen pl* -е́й) news; **без вести** without trace. **весть**[2]: **Бог ~** God knows.

весы́ (*pl*; *gen* -о́в) scales, balance; Libra.

весь (всего́ *m*, **вся**, всей *f*, **всё**, всего́ *neut*, **все**, всех *pl*) *pron* all, the whole of; **всего́ хоро́шего!** all the best!; **всё** everything; **без всего́** without anything; **все** everybody.

весьма́ *adv* very, highly.

ветвь (*gen pl* -е́й) branch; bough.

ве́тер (-тра, *loc* -у́) wind. **ветеро́к** (-рка́) breeze.

ветера́н veteran.

ветерина́р vet.

ве́тка branch; twig.

ве́то *neut indecl* veto.

ве́тошь old clothes, rags.

ве́треный windy; frivolous. **ветров|о́й** wind; **~о́е стекло́** windscreen. **ветря́к** (-а́) wind turbine; windmill.

ве́тхий (ветх, -а́, -о) old; dilapidated; **В~ заве́т** Old Testament.

ветчина́ ham.

ветша́ть *impf* (*pf* **об~**) decay; become dilapidated.

ве́ха landmark.

ве́чер (*pl* -а́) evening; party. **вечери́нка** party. **вече́рний** evening. **вече́рня** (*gen pl* -рен) vespers. **ве́чером** *adv* in the evening.

ве́чно *adv* for ever, eternally. **вечнозелёный** evergreen. **ве́чность** eternity; ages. **ве́чный** eternal.

ве́шалка peg, rack; tab, hanger. **ве́шать** *impf* (*pf* **взве́сить, пове́сить, све́шать**) hang; weigh (out); **~ся** hang o.s.; weigh o.s.

ве́шу *etc.*: *see* **ве́сить**

веща́ние broadcasting. **веща́ть** *impf* broadcast.

вещево́й clothing; **~ мешо́к** hold-all, kit-bag. **веще́ственный** substantial, material, real. **вещество́** substance; matter. **вещь** (*gen pl* -е́й) thing.

ве́ялка winnowing-machine. **ве́яние** winnowing; blowing; trend. **ве́ять** (ве́ю) *impf* (*pf* **про~**) winnow; blow; flutter.

взад *adv* backwards; **~ и вперёд** back and forth.

взаи́мность reciprocity. **взаи́мный** mutual, reciprocal.

взаимо- *in comb* inter-. **взаимоде́йствие** interaction; co-operation. **~де́йствовать** *impf* interact; cooperate. **~отноше́ние** interrelation; *pl* relations. **~по́мощь** mutual aid. **~понима́ние** mutual understanding. **~свя́зь** interdependence, correlation.

взаймы́ *adv*: **взять ~** borrow; **дать ~** lend.

взаме́н *prep+gen* instead of; in return for.

взаперти́ *adv* under lock and key; in seclusion.

взба́лмошный unbalanced, eccentric.

взбега́ть *impf*, **взбежа́ть** (-егу́) *pf* run up.

взберу́сь *etc.*: *see* **взобра́ться.** **вз|беси́ть(ся** (-ешу́(сь, -е́сишь(ся) *pf.* **взбива́ть** *impf of* **взбить.** **взбира́ться** *impf of* **взобра́ться**

взби́тый whipped, beaten. **взбить** (взобью́, -бьёшь) *pf* (*impf* **взбива́ть**) beat (up), whip; shake up.

вз|борозди́ть (-зжу́) *pf.*

вз|бунтова́ться *pf.*

взбуха́ть *impf*, **взбу́хнуть** (-нет; -ух) *pf* swell (out).

взва́ливать *impf*, **взвали́ть** (-лю́, -лишь) *pf* load; **+на**+*acc* saddle with.

взве́сить (-е́шу) *pf* (*impf* **ве́шать, взве́шивать**) weigh.

взвести́ (-еду́, -едёшь; -ёл, -а́) *pf* (*impf* **взводи́ть**) lead up; raise; cock; **+на**+*acc* impute to.

взве́шивать *impf of* **взве́сить**

взвива́ть(ся *impf of* **взви́ть(ся**

взвизг scream; yelp. **взви́згивать** *impf*, **взви́згнуть** (-ну) *pf* scream; yelp.

взвинти́ть (-нчу́) *pf*, **взви́нчивать** *impf* excite, work up; inflate. **взви́нченный** worked up; nervy; inflated.

взвить (взовью́, -ёшь; -ил, -а́, -о) *pf* (*impf* **взвива́ть**) raise; **~ся** rise, be hoisted; soar.

взвод[1] platoon, troop.

взвод[2] notch. **взводи́ть** (-ожу́, -о́дишь) *impf of* **взвести**

взволно́ванный agitated; worried. **вз|волнова́ть(ся** (-ну́ю(сь) *pf.*

взгляд look; glance; opinion. **взгля́дывать** *impf*, **взгляну́ть** (-яну́, -я́нешь) *pf* look, glance.

взго́рье hillock.

вздёргивать *impf*, **вздёрнуть** (-ну) *pf* hitch up; jerk up; turn up.

вздор nonsense. **вздо́рный** cantankerous; foolish.

вздорожа́ние rise in price. **вз|дорожа́ть** *pf.*

вздох sigh. **вздохну́ть** (-ну́, -нёшь) *pf* (*impf* **вздыха́ть**) sigh.

вздра́гивать *impf* (*pf* **вздро́гнуть**) shudder, quiver.

вздремну́ть *pf* have a nap, doze.

вздро́гнуть (-ну) *pf* (*impf* **вздра́гивать**) start; wince.

вздува́ть(ся *impf of* **вздуть**[1]**(ся**

взду́мать *pf* take it into one's head; **не взду́май(те)!** don't you dare!

взду́тие swelling. **взду́тый** swollen. **вздуть**[1] *pf* (*impf* **вздува́ть**) inflate; **~ся** swell.

вздуть[2] *pf* thrash.

вздыха́ть *impf* (*pf* **вздохну́ть**) breathe; sigh.

взима́ть *impf* levy, collect.

взла́мывать *impf of* **взлома́ть.** **вз|леле́ять** *pf.*

взлёт flight; take-off. **взлета́ть** *impf*, **взлете́ть** (-лечу́) *pf* fly (up); take off. **взлётный** take-off; **взлётно-поса́дочная полоса́** runway.

взлом breaking open, breaking in. **взлома́ть** *pf* (*impf* **взла́мывать**) break open; break up. **взло́мщик** burglar.

взлохма́ченный dishevelled.

взмах stroke, wave, flap. **взма́хивать** *impf*, **взмахну́ть** (-ну́, -нёшь) *pf* +*instr* wave, flap.

взмо́рье seaside; coastal waters.

вз|мути́ть (-учу́, -у́ти́шь) *pf.*

взнос payment; fee, dues.

взнузда́ть *pf*, **взну́здывать** *impf* bridle.

взобра́ться (взберу́сь, -ёшься; -а́лся, -ла́сь, -а́ло́сь) *pf* (*impf* **взбира́ться**) climb (up).
взобью́ *etc.*: *see* **взбить**. **взовью́** *etc.*: *see* **взвить**
взойти́ (-йду́, -йдёшь; -ошёл, -шла́) *pf* (*impf* **вос-, всходи́ть**) rise, go up; **на**+*acc* mount.
взор look, glance.
взорва́ть (-ву́, -вёшь; -а́л, -а́, -о) *pf* (*impf* **взрыва́ть**) blow up; exasperate; **~ся** burst, explode.
взро́слый *adj* & *sb* adult.
взрыв explosion; outburst. **взрыва́тель** *m* fuse. **взрыва́ть** *impf*, **взрыть** (-ро́ю) *pf* (*pf also* **взорва́ть**) blow up; **~ся** explode. **взрывно́й** explosive; blasting. **взрывча́тка** explosive. **взры́вчатый** explosive.
взъеро́шенный tousled, dishevelled. **взъеро́шивать** *impf*, **взъеро́шить** (-шу) *pf* tousle, rumple.
взыва́ть *impf of* **воззва́ть**
взыска́ние penalty; exaction. **взыска́тельный** exacting. **взыска́ть** (-ыщу́, -ы́щешь) *pf*, **взы́скивать** *impf* exact, recover; call to account.
взя́тие taking, capture. **взя́тка** bribe. **взя́точничество** bribery.
взя́ть(ся (возьму́(сь, -мёшь(ся; -я́л(ся, -а́(сь, -о(сь) *pf of* **бра́ть(ся**
вибра́ция vibration. **вибри́ровать** *impf* vibrate.
вивисе́кция vivisection.
вид[1] (*loc* -у́) look; appearance; shape, form; condition; view; prospect; sight; aspect; **де́лать вид** pretend; **име́ть в ~у́** intend; mean; bear in mind.
вид[2] kind; species.
вида́ться *impf* (*pf* **по~**) meet.
ви́дение[1] sight, vision. **виде́ние**[2] vision, apparition.
ви́део *neut indecl* video (cassette) recorder; video film; video cassette. **видеоигра́** video game. **видеока́мера** video camera. **видеокассе́та** video cassette. **видеомагнитофо́н** video (cassette) recorder.
ви́деть (ви́жу) *impf* (*pf* **у~**) see; **~ во сне** dream (of); **~ся** see one another; appear. **ви́димо** *adv* evidently. **ви́димость** visibility; appearance. **ви́димый** visible; apparent, evident. **ви́дный** (-ден, -дна́, -о) visible; distinguished.
видоизмене́ние modification. **видоизмени́ть** *pf*, **видоизменя́ть** *impf* modify.
видоиска́тель *m* view-finder.
ви́жу *see* **ви́деть**
ви́за visa.
визг squeal; yelp. **визжа́ть** (-жу́) *impf* squeal, yelp, squeak.
визи́т visit. **визи́тка** business card.
виктори́на quiz.
ви́лка fork; plug. **ви́лы** (*pl*; *gen* вил) pitchfork.
вильну́ть (-ну́, -нёшь) *pf*, **виля́ть** *impf* twist and turn; prevaricate; +*instr* wag.
вина́ (*pl* ви́ны) fault, guilt; blame.
винегре́т Russian salad; medley.
вини́тельный accusative. **вини́ть** *impf* accuse; **~ся** (*pf* **по~**) confess.
ви́нный wine; winy. **вино́** (*pl* -а) wine.
винова́тый guilty. **вино́вник** initiator; culprit. **вино́вный** guilty.
виногра́д vine; grapes. **виногра́дина** grape. **виногра́дник**

vineyard. **виногра́дный** grape; wine. **виноку́ренный заво́д** distillery.
винт (-á) screw. **винти́ть** (-нчу́) *impf* screw up. **винто́вка** rifle. **винтово́й** screw; spiral.
виолонче́ль cello.
вира́ж (-á) turn; bend.
виртуа́льный (*comput*) virtual.
виртуо́з virtuoso. **виртуо́зный** masterly.
ви́рус virus. **ви́русный** virus.
ви́селица gallows. **висе́ть** (вишу́) *impf* hang. **ви́снуть** (-ну; ви́с(нул)) *impf* hang; droop.
ви́ски *neut indecl* whisky.
висо́к (-ска́) (*anat*) temple.
високо́сный год leap-year.
вист whist.
вися́чий hanging; ~ **замо́к** padlock; ~ **мост** suspension bridge.
витами́н vitamin.
витиева́тый flowery, ornate.
вито́й twisted, spiral. **вито́к** (-тка́) turn, coil.
витра́ж (-á) stained-glass window. **витри́на** shop-window; showcase.
вить (вью, вьёшь; вил, -á, -о) *impf* (*pf* с~) twist, wind, weave; ~**ся** wind, twine; curl; twist; whirl.
вихо́р (-хра́) tuft. **вихра́стый** shaggy.
вихрь *m* whirlwind; vortex; **сне́жный** ~ blizzard.
ви́це- *pref* vice-. **вице-адмира́л** vice-admiral. ~**президе́нт** vice-president.
ВИЧ (*abbr of* **ви́рус иммунодефици́та челове́ка**) HIV.
вишнёвый cherry. **ви́шня** (*gen pl* -шен) cherry, cherries; cherry-tree.
вишу́: *see* **висе́ть**
вишь *partl* look, just look!
вка́лывать *impf* (*sl*) work hard; *impf of* **вколо́ть**
вка́пывать *impf of* **вкопа́ть**
вкати́ть (-ачу́, -а́тишь) *pf*, **вка́тывать** *impf* roll in; administer.
вклад deposit; contribution. **вкла́дка, вкладно́й лист** loose leaf, insert. **вкла́дчик** depositor.
вкла́дывать *impf of* **вложи́ть**
вкле́ивать *impf*, **вкле́ить** *pf* stick in.
вкли́ниваться *impf*, **вклини́ться** *pf* edge one's way in.
включа́тель *m* switch. **включа́ть** *impf*, **включи́ть** (-чу́) *pf* include; switch on; plug in; ~**ся в**+*acc* join in, enter into. **включа́я** including. **включе́ние** inclusion, insertion; switching on. **включи́тельно** *adv* inclusive.
вкола́чивать *impf*, **вколоти́ть** (-очу́, -о́тишь) *pf* hammer in, knock in.
вколо́ть (-олю́, -о́лешь) *pf* (*impf* **вка́лывать**) stick (in).
вкопа́ть *pf* (*impf* **вка́пывать**) dig in.
вкось *adv* obliquely.
вкра́дчивый ingratiating. **вкра́дываться** *impf*, **вкра́сться** (-аду́сь, -адёшься) *pf* creep in; insinuate o.s.
вкра́тце *adv* briefly, succinctly.
вкривь *adv* aslant; wrongly, perversely.
вкруг = **вокру́г**
вкруту́ю *adv* hard(-boiled).
вкус taste. **вкуси́ть** (-ушу́, -у́сишь) *pf*, **вкуша́ть** *impf* taste; partake of. **вку́сный** (-сен, -сна́, -о) tasty, nice.

влáга moisture.
влагáлище vagina.
владéлец (-льца), **-лица** owner. **владéние** ownership; possession; property. **владéтель** *m*, **-ница** possessor; sovereign. **владéть** (-éю) *impf* +*instr* own, possess; control.
влады́ка *m* master, sovereign. **влады́чество** dominion, sway.
влáжность humidity; moisture. **влáжный** (-жен, -жнá, -о) damp, moist, humid.
влáмываться *impf of* **вломи́ться**
влáствовать *impf* +(**над**+) *instr* rule, hold sway over. **властели́н** ruler; master. **влáстный** imperious, commanding; empowered, competent. **власть** (*gen pl* -éй) power; authority.
влéво *adv* to the left (**от**+*gen* of).
влезáть *impf*, **влезть** (-зу; влез) *pf* climb in; get in; fit in.
влёк *etc.*: *see* **влечь**
влетáть *impf*, **влетéть** (-ечу́) *pf* fly in; rush in.
влечéние attraction; inclination. **влечь** (-еку́, -ечёшь; влёк, -лá) *impf* draw; attract; ~ **за собóй** involve, entail.
вливáть *impf*, **влить** (волью́, -ёшь; влил, -á, -о) *pf* pour in; instil.
влия́ние influence. **влия́тельный** influential. **влия́ть** *impf* (*pf* **по~**) **на**+*acc* influence, affect.
вложéние enclosure; investment. **вложи́ть** (-ожу́, -óжишь) *pf* (*impf* **вклáдывать**) put in, insert; enclose; invest.
вломи́ться (-млю́сь, -мишься) *pf* (*impf* **влáмываться**) break in.
влюби́ть (-блю́, -бишь) *pf*, **влюбля́ть** *impf* make fall in love (**в**+*acc* with); **~ся** fall in love. **влюблённый** (-лён, -á) in love; *sb* lover.
вмáзать (-áжу) *pf*, **вмáзывать** *impf* cement, putty in.
вмени́ть *pf*, **вменя́ть** *impf* impute; impose. **вменя́емый** (*law*) responsible; sane.
вмéсте *adv* together; ~ **с тем** at the same time, also.
вмести́лище receptacle. **вмести́мость** capacity; tonnage. **вмести́тельный** capacious. **вмести́ть** (-ещу́) *pf* (*impf* **вмещáть**) hold, accommodate; put; **~ся** go in.
вмéсто *prep*+*gen* instead of.
вмешáтельство interference; intervention. **вмешáть** *pf*, **вмéшивать** *impf* mix in; implicate; **~ся** interfere, intervene.
вмещáть(ся *impf of* **вмести́ть(ся**
вмиг *adv* in an instant.
вминáть *impf*, **вмять** (вомну́, -нёшь) *pf* press in, dent. **вмя́тина** dent.
внаём, внаймы́ *adv* to let; for hire.
вначáле *adv* at first.
вне *prep*+*gen* outside; ~ **себя́** beside o.s.
вне- *pref* extra-; outside; -less. **внебрáчный** extra-marital; illegitimate. **~врéменный** timeless. **~клáссный** extracurricular. **~очереднóй** out of turn; extraordinary. **~штáтный** freelance, casual.
внедрéние introduction; inculcation. **внедри́ть** *pf*, **внедря́ть** *impf* inculcate; introduce; **~ся** take root.
внезáпно *adv* suddenly. **вне-**

за́пный sudden.
вне́млю *etc.*: *see* **внима́ть**
внесе́ние bringing in; deposit.
внести́ (-су́, -сёшь; внёс, -ла́) *pf* (*impf* **вноси́ть**) bring in; introduce; deposit; insert.
вне́шне *adv* outwardly. **вне́шний** outer; external; outside; foreign. **вне́шность** exterior; appearance.
вниз *adv* down(wards); ~ **по**+*dat* down. **внизу́** *adv* below; downstairs.
вника́ть *impf*, **вни́кнуть** (-ну; вник) *pf* +**в**+*acc* go carefully into, investigate thoroughly.
внима́ние attention. **внима́тельный** attentive. **внима́ть** *impf* (*pf* **внять**) listen to; heed.
вничью́ *adv*: **око́нчиться** ~ end in a draw; **сыгра́ть** ~ draw.
вновь *adv* anew, again.
вноси́ть (-ошу́, -о́сишь) *impf of* **внести́**
внук grandson; *pl* grandchildren, descendants.
вну́тренний inner; internal. **вну́тренность** interior; *pl* entrails; internal organs. **внутри́** *adv* & *prep*+*gen* inside. **внутрь** *adv* & *prep*+*gen* inside, in; inwards.
внуча́та (*pl*; *gen* -ча́т) grandchildren. **внуча́тый** second, great-; ~ **брат** second cousin; ~ **племя́нник** great-nephew. **вну́чка** grand-daughter.
внуша́ть *impf*, **внуши́ть** (-шу́) *pf* instil; +*dat* inspire with. **внуше́ние** suggestion; reproof. **внуши́тельный** inspiring; imposing.
вня́тный distinct. **внять** (*no fut*; -ял, -а́, -о) *pf of* **внима́ть**
во: *see* **в**
вобра́ть (вберу́, -рёшь; -а́л, -а́, -о) *pf* (*impf* **вбира́ть**) absorb; inhale.
вобью́ *etc.*: *see* **вбить**
вовлека́ть *impf*, **вовле́чь** (-еку́, -ечёшь; -ёк, -екла́) *pf* draw in, involve.
во́время *adv* in time; on time.
во́все *adv* quite; ~ **не** not at all.
во-вторы́х *adv* secondly.
вогна́ть (вгоню́, -о́нишь; -гна́л, -а́, -о) *pf* (*impf* **вгоня́ть**) drive in.
во́гнутый concave. **вогну́ть** (-ну́, -нёшь) *pf* (*impf* **вгиба́ть**) bend or curve inwards.
вода́ (*acc* во́ду, *gen* -ы́; *pl* -ы) water; *pl* the waters; spa.
водвори́ть *pf*, **водворя́ть** *impf* settle, install; establish.
води́тель *m* driver. **води́ть** (вожу́, во́дишь) *impf* lead; conduct; take; drive; ~**ся** be found; associate (with); be the custom.
во́дка vodka. **во́дн|ый** water; ~**ые лы́жи** water-skiing; water-skis.
водо- *in comb* water, water-; hydraulic; hydro-. **водобоя́знь** hydrophobia. ~**воро́т** whirlpool; maelstrom. ~**ём** reservoir. ~**измеще́ние** displacement. ~**ка́чка** water-tower, pumping station. ~**ла́з** diver. ~**ле́й** Aquarius. ~**непроница́емый** waterproof. ~**отво́дный** drainage. ~**па́д** waterfall. ~**по́й** watering-place. ~**прово́д** water-pipe, water-main; water supply. ~**прово́дчик** plumber. ~**разде́л** watershed. ~**ро́д** hydrogen. **во́доросль** water-plant; seaweed. ~**снабже́ние** water supply. ~**сто́к** drain, gutter. ~**храни́лище** reservoir.
водружа́ть *impf*, **водрузи́ть**

(-ужу́) *pf* hoist; erect.

водяни́стый watery. **водяно́й** water.

воева́ть (вою́ю) *impf* wage war.

воево́да *m* voivode; commander.

воеди́но *adv* together.

военко́м military commissar.

военно- *in comb* military; war-. **во́енно-возду́шный** air-, air-force. **во́енно-морско́й** naval. **~пле́нный** *sb* prisoner of war. **во́енно-полево́й суд** court-martial. **~слу́жащий** *sb* serviceman.

вое́нн|ый military; war; *sb* serviceman; **~ое положе́ние** martial law; **~ый суд** court-martial.

вожа́к (-а́) guide; leader. **вожа́тый** *sb* guide; tram-driver.

вожделе́ние desire, lust.

вождь (-я́) *m* leader, chief.

вожжа́ (*pl* -и, -е́й) rein.

вожу́ *etc.*: *see* **води́ть, вози́ть**

воз (*loc* -у́; *pl* -ы́) cart; cart-load.

возбуди́мый excitable. **возбуди́тель** *m* agent; instigator. **возбуди́ть** (-ужу́) *pf*, **возбужда́ть** *impf* excite, arouse; incite. **возбужда́ющ|ий: ~ее сре́дство** stimulant. **возбужде́ние** excitement. **возбуждённый** excited.

возвести́ (-еду́, -дёшь; -вёл, -ла́) *pf* (*impf* **возводи́ть**) elevate; erect; level; **+к+***dat* trace to.

возвести́ть (-ещу́) *pf*, **возвеща́ть** *impf* proclaim.

возводи́ть (-ожу́, -о́дишь) *impf of* **возвести́**

возвра́т return; repayment. **возврати́ть** (-ащу́) *pf*, **возвраща́ть** *impf* (*pf also* **верну́ть**) return, give back; **~ся** return; go back, come back. **возвра́тный** return; reflexive. **возвраще́ние** return.

возвы́сить *pf*, **возвыша́ть** *impf* raise; ennoble; **~ся** rise. **возвыше́ние** rise; raised place. **возвы́шенность** height; loftiness. **возвы́шенный** high; elevated.

возгла́вить (-влю) *pf*, **возглавля́ть** *impf* head.

во́зглас exclamation. **возгласи́ть** (-ашу́) *pf*, **возглаша́ть** *impf* proclaim.

возгора́емый inflammable. **возгора́ться** *impf*, **возгоре́ться** (-рю́сь) *pf* flare up; be seized (with).

воздава́ть (-даю́, -даёшь) *impf*, **возда́ть** (-а́м, -а́шь, -а́ст, -ади́м; -а́л, -а́, -о) *pf* render.

воздвига́ть *impf*, **воздви́гнуть** (-ну; -дви́г) *pf* raise.

возде́йствие influence. **возде́йствовать** *impf* & *pf* **+на+***acc* influence.

возде́лать *pf*, **возде́лывать** *impf* cultivate, till.

воздержа́ние abstinence; abstention. **возде́ржанный** abstemious. **воздержа́ться** (-жу́сь, -жишься) *pf*, **возде́рживаться** *impf* refrain; abstain.

во́здух air. **воздухонепроница́емый** air-tight. **возду́шн|ый** air, aerial; airy; flimsy; **~ый змей** kite; **~ый шар** balloon.

воззва́ние appeal. **воззва́ть** (-зову́, -вёшь) *pf* (*impf* **взыва́ть**) appeal (**о+***prep* for).

воззре́ние opinion, outlook.

вози́ть (вожу́, во́зишь) *impf* convey; carry; bring, take; **~ся** romp, play noisily; busy o.s.; potter about.

возлага́ть *impf of* **возложи́ть**

во́зле *adv* & *prep+gen* by, near; near by; past.
возложи́ть (-жу́, -жишь) *pf* (*impf* **возлага́ть**) lay; place.
возлю́бленный beloved; *sb* sweetheart.
возме́здие retribution.
возмести́ть (-ещу́) *pf*, **возмеща́ть** *impf* compensate for; refund. **возмеще́ние** compensation; refund.
возмо́жно *adv* possibly; *+comp* as ... as possible. **возмо́жность** possibility; opportunity. **возмо́жный** possible.
возмужа́лый mature; grown up. **возмужа́ть** *pf* grow up; gain strength.
возмути́тельный disgraceful. **возмути́ть** (-ущу́) *pf*, **возмуща́ть** *impf* disturb; stir up; rouse to indignation; **~ся** be indignant. **возмуще́ние** indignation. **возмущённый** (-щён, -щена́) indignant.
вознагради́ть (-ажу́) *pf*, **вознагражда́ть** *impf* reward. **вознагражде́ние** reward; fee.
возненави́деть (-и́жу) *pf* conceive a hatred for.
вознесе́ние Ascension. **вознести́** (-несу́, -несёшь; -нёс, -ла́) *pf* (*impf* **возноси́ть**) raise, lift up; **~сь** rise; ascend.
возника́ть *impf*, **возни́кнуть** (-нет; -ни́к) *pf* arise, spring up. **возникнове́ние** rise, beginning, origin.
возни́ца *m* coachman.
возноси́ть(ся (-ошу́(сь, -о́сишь(ся) *impf of* **вознести́(сь. вознoше́ние** raising, elevation.
возня́ row, noise; bother.
возобнови́ть (-влю́) *pf*, **возобновля́ть** *impf* renew; restore; **~ся** begin again. **возобновле́ние** renewal; revival.
возража́ть *impf*, **возрази́ть** (-ажу́) *pf* object. **возраже́ние** objection.
во́зраст age. **возраста́ние** growth, increase. **возраста́ть** *impf*, **возрасти́** (-тёт; -ро́с, -ла́) *pf* grow, increase.
возроди́ть (-ожу́) *pf*, **возрожда́ть** *impf* revive; **~ся** revive. **возрожде́ние** revival; Renaissance.
возро́с *etc.*: *see* **возрасти́. возро́сший** increased.
во́зчик carter, carrier.
возьму́ *etc.*: *see* **взять**
во́ин warrior; soldier. **во́инск|ий** military; **~ая пови́нность** conscription. **во́инственный** warlike. **во́йнствующий** militant.
вой howl(ing); wail(ing).
войду́ *etc.*: *see* **войти́**
во́йлок felt. **во́йлочный** felt.
война́ (*pl* -ы) war.
во́йско (*pl* -а́) army; *pl* troops, forces. **войсково́й** military.
войти́ (-йду́, -йдёшь; вошёл, -шла́) *pf* (*impf* **входи́ть**) go in, come in, enter; get in(to); **~ в систе́му** (*comput*) log on.
вокза́л (railway) station.
во́кмен Walkman (*propr*), personal stereo.
вокру́г *adv* & *prep+gen* round, around.
вол (-а́) ox, bullock.
вола́н flounce; shuttlecock.
волды́рь (-я́) *m* blister; bump.
волево́й strong-willed.
волейбо́л volleyball.
во́лей-нево́лей *adv* willy-nilly.
волк (*pl* -и, -о́в) wolf. **волкода́в** wolf-hound.
волна́ (*pl* -ы, во́лна́м) wave. **вол-**

нение choppiness; agitation; emotion. **волнистый** wavy. **волновать** *impf* (*pf* **вз~**) disturb; agitate; excite; **~ся** be disturbed; worry, be nervous. **волнолом, волнорез** breakwater. **волнующий** disturbing; exciting.

волокита red tape; rigmarole.

волокнистый fibrous, stringy. **волокно** (*pl* -а) fibre.

волоку *etc.*: *see* **волочь**

волос (*pl* -ы, -ос, -ам); *pl* hair. **волосатый** hairy. **волосной** capillary.

волость (*pl* -и, -ей) volost (*administrative division*).

волочить (-очу, -очишь) *impf* drag; **~ся** drag, trail; +**за**+*instr* run after, court. **волочь** (-оку, -очёшь; -ок, -ла) *impf* drag.

волчий wolf's; wolfish. **волчиха, волчица** she-wolf.

волчок (-чка) top; gyroscope.

волчонок (-нка; *pl* -чата, -чат) wolf cub.

волшебник magician; wizard. **волшебница** enchantress. **волшебный** magic, magical; enchanting. **волшебство** magic, enchantment.

вольнонаёмный civilian. **вольность** liberty; license. **вольный** (-лен, -льна, -о, вольны) free; free-style.

вольт[1] (*gen pl* вольт) volt.

вольт[2] (*loc* -у) vault.

вольфрам tungsten.

воля will; liberty.

вомну *etc.*: *see* **вмять**

вон *adv* out; off, away.

вон *partl* there, over there.

вонзать *impf*, **вонзить** (-нжу) *pf* plunge, thrust.

вонь stench. **вонючий** stinking. **вонять** stink.

воображаемый imaginary. **воображать** *impf*, **вообразить** (-ажу) *pf* imagine. **воображение** imagination. **вообразимый** imaginable.

вообще *adv* in general; generally.

воодушевить (-влю) *pf*, **воодушевлять** *impf* inspire. **воодушевление** inspiration; fervour.

вооружать *impf*, **вооружить** (-жу) *pf* arm, equip; **~ся** arm o.s.; take up arms. **вооружение** arming; arms; equipment. **вооружённый** (-жён, -а) armed; equipped.

воочию *adv* with one's own eyes.

во-первых *adv* first, first of all.

вопить (-плю) *impf* yell, howl. **вопиющий** crying; scandalous.

воплотить (-ощу) *pf*, **воплощать** *impf* embody. **воплощение** embodiment.

вопль *m* cry, wail; howling.

вопреки *prep*+*dat* in spite of.

вопрос question; problem. **вопросительный** interrogative; questioning; ~ **знак** question-mark.

вор (*pl* -ы, -ов) thief; criminal.

ворваться (-вусь, -вёшься; -ался, -лась, -алось) *pf* (*impf* **врываться**) burst in.

воркотня grumbling.

воробей sparrow.

вороватый thievish; furtive. **воровать** *impf* (*pf* **с~**) steal. **воровка** woman thief. **воровски** *adv* furtively. **воровской** thieves'. **воровство** stealing; theft.

ворон raven. **ворона** crow.

воронка funnel; crater.

вороно́й black.
во́рот[1] collar; neckband.
во́рот[2] winch; windlass.
воро́та (*pl*; *gen* -ро́т) gate(s); gateway; goal.
вороти́ть (-очу́, -о́тишь) *pf* bring back, get back; turn back; **~ся** return.
воротни́к (-а́) collar.
во́рох (*pl* -а́) heap, pile; heaps.
воро́чать *impf* turn; move; +*instr* have control of; **~ся** move, turn.
ворочу́(сь *etc.*: *see* **вороти́ть(ся**
вороши́ть (-шу́) *impf* stir up; turn (over).
ворс nap, pile.
ворча́ть (-чу́) *impf* grumble; growl. **ворчли́вый** peevish; grumpy.
восвоя́си *adv* home.
восемна́дцатый eighteenth. **восемна́дцать** eighteen. **во́семь** (-сьми́, *instr* -сьмью́ *or* -семью́) eight. **во́семьдесят** (-сьми́десяти, -сьмью́десятью) eighty. **восемьсо́т** (-сьмисо́т, -ста́ми) eight hundred. **во́семью** *adv* eight times.
воск wax, beeswax.
воскли́кнуть (-ну) *pf*, **восклица́ть** *impf* exclaim. **восклица́ние** exclamation. **восклица́тельный** exclamatory; **~ знак** exclamation mark.
восково́й wax; waxy; waxed.
воскреса́ть *impf*, **воскре́снуть** (-ну; -е́с) *pf* rise from the dead; revive. **воскресе́ние** resurrection. **воскресе́нье** Sunday. **воскреси́ть** (-ешу́) *pf*, **воскреша́ть** *impf* resurrect; revive. **воскреше́ние** resurrection; revival.
воспале́ние inflammation. **воспалённый** (-лён, -а́) inflamed. **воспали́ть** *pf*, **воспаля́ть** *impf* inflame; **~ся** become inflamed.
воспита́ние upbringing, education. **воспи́танник, -ница** pupil. **воспи́танный** well-brought-up. **воспита́тель** *m* tutor; educator. **воспита́тельный** educational. **воспита́ть** *pf*, **воспи́тывать** *impf* bring up; foster; educate.
воспламени́ть *pf*, **воспламеня́ть** *impf* ignite; fire; **~ся** ignite; flare up. **воспламеня́емый** inflammable.
вос|по́льзоваться *pf*.
воспомина́ние recollection, memory; *pl* memoirs; reminiscences.
вос|препя́тствовать *pf*.
воспрети́ть (-ещу́) *pf*, **воспреща́ть** *impf* forbid. **воспреще́ние** prohibition. **воспрещённый** (-щён, -а́) prohibited.
восприи́мчивый impressionable; susceptible. **воспринима́ть** *impf*, **восприня́ть** (-иму́, -и́мешь; -и́нял, -а́, -о) *pf* perceive; grasp. **восприя́тие** perception.
воспроизведе́ние reproduction. **воспроизвести́** (-еду́, -едёшь; -вёл, -а́) *pf*, **воспроизводи́ть** (-ожу́, -о́дишь) *impf* reproduce. **воспроизводи́тельный** reproductive.
вос|проти́виться (-влюсь) *pf*.
воссоедине́ние reunification. **воссоедини́ть** *pf*, **воссоединя́ть** *impf* reunite.
восстава́ть (-таю́, -таёшь) *impf of* **восста́ть**.
восста́ние insurrection, uprising.
восстанови́ть (-влю́, -вишь) *pf*

(*impf* **восстанáвливать**) restore; reinstate; recall; ~ **прóтив**+*gen* set against. **восстановлéние** restoration.

восстáть (-áну) *pf* (*impf* **восставáть**) rise (up).

востóк east.

востóрг delight, rapture. **восторгáться**+*instr* be delighted with, go into raptures over. **востóрженный** enthusiastic.

востóчный east, eastern; easterly; oriental.

вострéбование: **до востребования** to be called for, poste restante.

восхвалúть (-лю, -лишь) *pf*, **восхвалять** *impf* praise, extol.

восхитúтельный entrancing; delightful. **восхитúть** (-хищý) *pf*, **восхищáть** *impf* enrapture; ~**ся** +*instr* be enraptured by. **восхищéние** delight; admiration.

восхóд rising. **восходúть** (-ожý, -óдишь) *impf of* **взойти**; ~ **к**+*dat* go back to, date from. **восхождéние** ascent. **восходящий** rising.

восшéствие accession.

восьмáя *sb* eighth; octave. **восьмёрка** eight; figure eight; No. 8; figure of eight.

восьми- *in comb* eight-; octo-. **восьмигрáнник** octahedron. ~**десятый** eightieth. ~**лéтний** eight-year; eight-year-old. ~**сóтый** eight-hundredth. ~**угóльник** octagon. ~**угóльный** octagonal.

восьмóй eighth.

вот *partl* here (is), there (is); this (is); ~ **и всё** and that's all; ~ **как!** no! really? ~ **тáк!** that's right!; ~ **что!** no! not really? **вот-вóт** *adv* just, on the point of; *partl* that's right!

воткнýть (-нý, -нёшь) *pf* (*impf* **втыкáть**) stick in, drive in.

вотрý *etc.*: *see* **втерéть**

воцарúться *pf*, **воцаряться** *impf* come to the throne; set in.

вошёл *etc.*: *see* **войти**

вошь (вши; *gen pl* вшей) louse.

вошью *etc.*: *see* **вшить**

вóю *etc.*: *see* **выть**

воюю *etc.*: *see* **воевáть**

впадáть *impf*, **впасть** (-адý) *pf* flow; lapse; fall in; +**в**+*acc* verge on, approximate to. **впадéние** confluence, (river-)mouth. **впáдина** cavity, hollow; socket. **впáлый** sunken.

впервые *adv* for the first time.

вперёд *adv* forward(s), ahead; in future; in advance; **идти** ~ (*of clock*) be fast. **впередú** *adv* in front, ahead; in (the) future; *prep*+*gen* in front of, before.

впечатлéние impression. **впечатлúтельный** impressionable.

вписáть (-ишý, -ишешь) *pf*, **впúсывать** *impf* enter, insert; ~**ся** be enrolled, join.

впитáть *pf*, **впúтывать** *impf* absorb, take in; ~**ся** soak.

впúхивать *impf*, **впúхнуть** (-нý, -нёшь) *pf* cram in; shove.

вплавь *adv* (by) swimming.

вплестú (-етý, -етёшь; -ёл, -á) *pf*, **вплетáть** *impf* plait in, intertwine; involve.

вплотнýю *adv* close; in earnest.

вплоть *adv*; ~ **до**+*gen* (right) up to.

вполгóлоса *adv* under one's breath.

вполнé *adv* fully, entirely; quite.

впопыхáх *adv* hastily; in one's haste.

впо́ру *adv* at the right time; just right, exactly.
впосле́дствии *adv* subsequently.
впотьма́х *adv* in the dark.
впра́ве *adv*: **быть ~** have a right.
впра́во *adv* to the right (**от**+*gen* of).
впредь *adv* in (the) future; **~ до**+*gen* until.
впро́голодь *adv* half starving.
впро́чем *conj* however, but; though.
впры́скивание injection. **впры́скивать** *impf*, **впры́снуть** (-ну) *pf* inject.
впряга́ть *impf* **впрячь** (-ягу́, -яжёшь; -яг, -ла́) *pf* harness.
впуск admittance. **впуска́ть** *impf*, **впусти́ть** (-ущу́, -у́стишь) *pf* admit, let in.
впусту́ю *adv* to no purpose, in vain.
впущу́ *etc.*: *see* **впусти́ть**
враг (-а́) enemy. **вражда́** enmity. **вражде́бный** hostile. **враждова́ть** be at enmity. **вра́жеский** enemy.
вразбро́д *adv* separately, disunitedly.
вразре́з *adv*: **идти́ ~ с**+*instr* go against.
вразуми́тельный intelligible, clear; persuasive.
врасплóх *adv* unawares.
враста́ть *impf*, **врасти́** (-тёт; врос, -ла́) *pf* grow in; take root.
врата́рь (-я́) *m* goalkeeper.
врать (вру, врёшь; -ал, -а́, -о) *impf* (*pf* **на~, со~**) lie, tell lies; talk nonsense.
врач (-а́) doctor. **враче́бный** medical.
враща́ть *impf* rotate, revolve; **~ся** revolve, rotate. **враще́ние** rotation, revolution.
вред (-а́) harm; damage. **вреди́тель** *m* pest; wrecker; *pl* vermin. **вреди́тельство** wrecking, (act of) sabotage. **вреди́ть** (-ежу́) *impf* (*pf* **по~**) +*dat* harm; damage. **вре́дный** (-ден, -дна́, -о) harmful.
вре́зать (-е́жу) *pf*, **вреза́ть** *impf* cut in; set in; (*sl*) +*dat* hit; **~ся** cut (into); run (into); be engraved; fall in love.
времена́ми *adv* at times. **вре́менно** *adv* temporarily. **временно́й** temporal. **вре́менный** temporary; provisional. **вре́мя** (-мени; *pl* -мена́, -мён, -а́м) *neut* time; tense; **~ го́да** season; **~ от вре́мени** at times, from time to time; **на ~** for a time; **ско́лько вре́мени?** what is the time?; **тем вре́менем** meanwhile.
вро́вень *adv* level, on a level.
вро́де *prep*+*gen* like; *partl* such as, like; apparently.
врождённый (-дён, -а́) innate.
врозь, врозь *adv* separately, apart.
врос *etc.*: *see* **врасти́. вру** *etc.*: *see* **врать**
врун (-а́), **вру́нья** liar.
вруча́ть *impf*, **вручи́ть** (-чу́) *pf* hand, deliver; entrust.
вручну́ю *adv* by hand.
врыва́ть(ся *impf of* **ворва́ться**
вряд (ли) *adv* it's not likely; hardly, scarcely.
всади́ть (-ажу́, -а́дишь) *pf*, **вса́живать** *impf* thrust in; sink in. **вса́дник** rider, horseman. **вса́дница** rider, horsewoman.
вса́сывать *impf of* **всоса́ть**
всё, все *pron*: *see* **весь. всё** *adv* always, all the time; **~ (ещё)** still; *conj* however, nevertheless;

~ же all the same.
все- *in comb* all-, omni-. **все-возмо́жный** of every kind; all possible. **~дозво́ленность** permissiveness. **~ме́рный** of every kind. **~ми́рный** world, world-wide; **Всеми́рная паути́на** the (world-wide) Web; **~могу́щий** omnipotent. **~наро́дно** *adv* publicly. **~наро́дный** national; nation-wide. **~объе́млющий** comprehensive, all-embracing. **~росси́йский** All-Russian. **~си́льный** omnipotent. **~сторо́нний** all-round; comprehensive.
всегда́ always.
всего́ *adv* in all, all told; only.
вселе́нная *sb* universe.
всели́ть *pf*, **вселя́ть** *impf* install, lodge; inspire; **~ся** move in, install o.s.; be implanted.
все́нощная *sb* night service.
всео́бщий general, universal.
всерьёз *adv* seriously, in earnest.
всё-таки *conj & partl* all the same, still. **всеце́ло** *adv* completely.
вска́кивать *impf of* **вскочи́ть**
вскачь *adv* at a gallop.
вскипа́ть *impf*, **вс|кипе́ть** (-плю́) *pf* boil up; flare up.
вс|кипяти́ть(ся (-ячу́(сь) *pf*.
всколыхну́ть (-ну́, -нёшь) *pf* stir; stir up.
вскользь *adv* slightly; in passing.
вско́ре *adv* soon, shortly after.
вскочи́ть (-очу́, -о́чишь) *pf* (*impf* **вска́кивать**) jump up.
вскри́кивать *impf*, **вскри́кнуть** (-ну) *pf* shriek, scream. **вскрича́ть** (-чу́) *pf* exclaim.
вскрыва́ть *impf*, **вскрыть** (-ро́ю) *pf* open; reveal; dissect. **вскры́тие** opening; revelation; post-mortem.
вслед *adv & prep+dat* after; **~ за**+*instr* after, following.
всле́дствие *prep+gen* in consequence of.
вслепу́ю *adv* blindly; blindfold.
вслух *adv* aloud.
вслу́шаться *pf*, **вслу́шиваться** *impf* listen attentively.
всма́триваться *impf*, **всмотре́ться** (-рю́сь, -ри́шься) *pf* look closely.
всмя́тку *adv* soft(-boiled).
всо́вывать *impf of* **всу́нуть**
всоса́ть (-су́, -сёшь) *pf* (*impf* **вса́сывать**) suck in; absorb; imbibe.
вс|паха́ть (-ашу́, -а́шешь) *pf*, **вспа́хивать** *impf* plough up. **вспа́шка** ploughing.
вс|пе́ниться *pf*.
всплеск splash. **всплёскивать** *impf*, **всплесну́ть** (-ну́, -нёшь) *pf* splash; **~ рука́ми** throw up one's hands.
всплыва́ть *impf*, **всплыть** (-ыву́, -ывёшь; -ыл, -а́, -о) *pf* rise to the surface; come to light.
вспомина́ть *impf*, **вспо́мнить** *pf* remember; **~ся** *impers +dat*: **мне вспо́мнилось** I remembered.
вспомога́тельный auxiliary.
вс|поте́ть *pf*.
вспры́гивать *impf*, **вспры́гнуть** (-ну) *pf* jump up.
вспуха́ть *impf*, **вс|пу́хнуть** (-нет; -ух) *pf* swell up.
вспыли́ть *pf* flare up. **вспы́льчивый** hot-tempered.
вспы́хивать *impf*, **вспы́хнуть** (-ну) *pf* blaze up; flare up.

вспышка flash; outburst; outbreak.
вставать (-таю, -таёшь) *impf of* **встать**
вставить (-влю) *pf*, **вставлять** *impf* put in, insert. **вставка** insertion; framing, mounting; inset. **вставн|ой** inserted; set in; **~ые зубы** false teeth.
встать (-ану) *pf* (*impf* **вставать**) get up; stand up.
встревоженный *adj* anxious.
вс|тревожить (-жу) *pf*.
встрепенуться (-нусь, -нёшься) *pf* rouse o.s.; start (up); beat faster.
встретить (-ёчу) *pf*, **встречать** *impf* meet (with); **~ся** meet; be found. **встреча** meeting. **встречный** coming to meet; contrary, head; counter; *sb* person met with; **первый ~** the first person you meet, anybody.
встряска shaking; shock.
встряхивать *impf*, **встряхнуть** (-ну, -нёшь) *pf* shake (up); rouse; **~ся** shake o.s.; rouse o.s.
вступать *impf*, **вступить** (-плю, -пишь) *pf* +**в**+*acc* enter (into); join (in); +**на**+*acc* go up, mount; **~ся** intervene; +**за**+*acc* stand up for. **вступительный** introductory; entrance. **вступление** entry, joining; introduction.
всунуть (-ну) *pf* (*impf* **всовывать**) put in, stick in.
всхлипнуть (-ну) *pf*, **всхлипывать** *impf* sob.
всходить (-ожу, -одишь) *impf of* **взойти**. **всходы** (*pl*; *gen* -ов) (corn-)shoots.
всю: *see* **весь**
всюду *adv* everywhere.
вся: *see* **весь**
всяк|ий any; every, all kinds of; **~ом случае** in any case; **на ~ий случай** just in case; *pron* anyone.
всячески *adv* in every possible way.
втайне *adv* secretly.
вталкивать *impf of* **втолкнуть**.
втаптывать *impf of* **втоптать**.
втаскивать *impf*, **втащить** (-щу, -щишь) *pf* drag in.
втереть (вотру, вотрёшь; втёр) *pf* (*impf* **втирать**) rub in; **~ся** insinuate o.s., worm o.s.
втирать(ся *impf of* **втереть(ся**
втискивать *impf*, **втиснуть** (-ну) *pf* squeeze in; **~ся** squeeze (o.s.) in.
втихомолку *adv* surreptitiously.
втолкнуть (-ну, -нёшь) *pf* (*impf* **вталкивать**) push in.
втоптать (-пчу, -пчешь) *pf* (*impf* **втаптывать**) trample (in).
вторгаться *impf*, **вторгнуться** (-нусь; вторгся, -лась) *pf* invade; intrude. **вторжение** invasion; intrusion.
вторить *impf* play or sing second part; +*dat* repeat, echo. **вторичный** second, secondary. **вторник** Tuesday. **втор|ой** second; **~ое** *sb* second course. **второстепенный** secondary, minor.
второпях *adv* in haste.
в-третьих *adv* thirdly. **втрое** *adv* three times. **втроём** *adv* three (together). **втройне** *adv* three times as much.
втулка plug.
втыкать *impf of* **воткнуть**
втягивать *impf*, **втянуть** (-ну, -нешь) *pf* draw in; **~ся** +**в**+*acc* enter; get used to.
вуаль veil.
вуз *abbr* (*of* **высшее учебное заведение**) higher educational es-

tablishment; college.
вулка́н volcano.
вульга́рный vulgar.
вундерки́нд infant prodigy.
вход entrance; entry. **входи́ть** (-ожу́, -о́дишь) *impf of* **войти́**. **входно́й** entrance.
вхолосту́ю *adv* idle, free.
вцепи́ться (-плю́сь, -пишься) *pf*, **вцепля́ться** *impf* +**в**+*acc* clutch, catch hold of.
вчера́ *adv* yesterday. **вчера́шний** yesterday's.
вчерне́ in rough.
вче́тверо *adv* four times. **вчетверо́м** *adv* four (together).
вши *etc.*: *see* **вошь**
вшива́ть *impf of* **вшить**
вши́вый lousy.
вширь *adv* in breadth; widely.
вшить (вошью́, -ьёшь) *pf* (*impf* **вшива́ть**) sew in.
въе́дливый corrosive; caustic.
въезд entry; entrance. **въезжа́ть** *impf*, **въе́хать** (-е́ду, -е́дешь) *pf* (+**в**+*acc*) ride in(to); drive in(to); crash into.
вы (вас, вам, ва́ми, вас) *pron* you.
выбега́ть *impf*, **вы́бежать** (-егу, -ежишь) *pf* run out.
вы́|белить *pf*.
вы́беру *etc.*: *see* **вы́брать. выбива́ть(ся** *impf of* **вы́бить(ся. выбира́ть(ся** *impf of* **вы́брать(ся**
вы́бить (-бью) *pf* (*impf* **выбива́ть**) knock out; dislodge; **~ся** get out; break loose; come out; **~ся из сил** exhaust o.s.
вы́бор choice; selection; *pl* election(s). **вы́борный** elective; electoral. **вы́борочный** selective.
вы́|бранить *pf*. **выбра́сывать(ся** *impf of* **вы́бросить(ся**
вы́брать (-беру) *pf* (*impf* **выбира́ть**) choose; elect; take out; **~ся** get out.
выбрива́ть *impf*, **вы́брить** (-рею) *pf* shave.
вы́бросить (-ошу) *pf* (*impf* **выбра́сывать**) throw out; throw away; **~ся** throw o.s. out, leap out.
выбыва́ть *impf*, **вы́быть** (-буду) *pf* **из**+*gen* leave, quit.
выва́ливать *impf*, **вы́валить** *pf* throw out; pour out; **~ся** tumble out.
вы́везти (-зу; -ез) *pf* (*impf* **вывози́ть**) take, bring, out; export; rescue.
вы́верить *pf* (*impf* **выверя́ть**) adjust, regulate.
вы́вернуть (-ну) *pf*, **вывёртывать** *impf* turn inside out; unscrew; wrench.
выверя́ть *impf of* **вы́верить**
вы́весить (-ешу) *pf* (*impf* **выве́шивать**) weigh; hang out. **вы́веска** sign; pretext.
вы́вести (-еду; -ел) *pf* (*impf* **выводи́ть**) lead, bring, take, out; drive out; remove; exterminate; deduce; hatch; grow, breed; erect; depict; draw; **~сь** go out of use; become extinct; come out; hatch out.
выве́тривание airing.
выве́шивать *impf of* **вы́весить**
вы́вих dislocation. **выви́хивать** *impf*, **вы́вихнуть** (-ну) *pf* dislocate.
вы́вод conclusion; withdrawal. **выводи́ть(ся** (-ожу́(сь, -о́дишь(ся) *impf of* **вы́вести(сь. вы́водок** (-дка) brood; litter.
вывожу́ *see* **выводи́ть, вывози́ть**

вы́воз export; removal. **вывози́ть** (-ожу́, -о́зишь) *impf of* **вы́везти. вывозно́й** export.

вы́гадать *pf*, **выга́дывать** *impf* gain, save.

вы́гиб curve. **выгиба́ть** *impf of* **вы́гнуть**

вы́|гладить (-ажу) *pf*.

вы́глядеть (-яжу) *impf* look, look like. **выгля́дывать** *impf*, **вы́глянуть** (-ну) *pf* look out; peep out.

вы́гнать (-гоню) *pf* (*impf* **выгоня́ть**) drive out; distil.

вы́гнутый curved, convex. **вы́гнуть** (-ну) *pf* (*impf* **выгиба́ть**) bend, arch.

выгова́ривать *impf*, **вы́говорить** *pf* pronounce, speak; +*dat* reprimand; **~ся** speak out. **вы́говор** pronunciation; reprimand.

вы́года advantage; gain. **вы́годный** advantageous; profitable.

вы́гон pasture; common. **выгоня́ть** *impf of* **вы́гнать**

выгора́ть *impf*, **вы́гореть** (-рит) *pf* burn down; fade.

вы́|гравировать *pf*.

выгружа́ть *impf*, **вы́грузить** (-ужу) *pf* unload; disembark. **вы́грузка** unloading; disembarkation.

выдава́ть (-даю, -даёшь) *impf*, **вы́дать** (-ам, -ашь, -аст, -адим) *pf* give (out), issue; betray; extradite; +**за**+*acc* pass off as; **~ся** protrude; stand out; present itself. **вы́дача** issue; payment; extradition. **выдаю́щийся** prominent.

выдвига́ть *impf*, **вы́двинуть** (-ну) *pf* move out; pull out; put forward, nominate; **~ся** move forward, move out; come out; get on (in the world). **выдвиже́ние** nomination; promotion.

выделе́ние secretion; excretion; isolation; apportionment.

вы́делить *pf*, **выделя́ть** *impf* pick out; detach; allot; secrete; excrete; isolate; **~ курси́вом** italicize; **~ся** stand out, be noted (+*instr* for).

выдёргивать *impf of* **вы́дернуть**

вы́держанный consistent; self-possessed; firm; matured, seasoned. **вы́держать** (-жу) *pf*, **выде́рживать** *impf* bear; endure; contain o.s.; pass (*exam*); sustain. **вы́держка**[1] endurance; self-possession; exposure.

вы́держка[2] excerpt.

вы́дернуть *pf* (*impf* **выдёргивать**) pull out.

вы́дохнуть (-ну) *pf* (*impf* **выдыха́ть**) breathe out; **~ся** have lost fragrance or smell; be past one's best.

вы́дра otter.

вы́|драть (-деру) *pf*. **вы́|дрессировать** *pf*.

выдува́ть *impf of* **вы́дуть**

вы́думанный made-up, fabricated. **вы́думать** *pf*, **выду́мывать** *impf* invent; fabricate. **вы́думка** invention; device; inventiveness.

вы́дуть *pf* (*impf* **выдува́ть**) blow; blow out.

выдыха́ние exhalation. **выдыха́ть(ся** *impf of* **вы́дохнуть(ся**

вы́езд departure; exit. **выездн|о́й** exit; **~ая се́ссия суда́** assizes. **выезжа́ть** *impf of* **вы́ехать**

вы́емка taking out; excavation; hollow.

вы́ехать (-еду) *pf* (*impf* **выез-**

жа́ть) go out, depart; drive out, ride out; move (house).

вы́жать (-жму, -жмешь) *pf* (*impf* **выжима́ть**) squeeze out; wring out.

вы́жечь (-жгу) *pf* (*impf* **выжига́ть**) burn out; cauterize.

выжива́ние survival. **выжива́ть** *impf of* **вы́жить**

выжига́ть *impf of* **вы́жечь**

выжида́тельный waiting; temporizing.

выжима́ть *impf of* **вы́жать**

вы́жить (-иву) *pf* (*impf* **выжива́ть**) survive; hound out; ~ **из ума́** become senile.

вы́звать (-зову) *pf* (*impf* **вызыва́ть**) call (out); send for; challenge; provoke; ~**ся** volunteer.

выздора́вливать *impf*, **вы́здороветь** (-ею) *pf* recover. **выздоровле́ние** recovery; convalescence.

вы́зов call; summons; challenge.

вы́золоченный gilt.

вызу́бривать *impf*, **вы́|зубрить** *pf* learn by heart.

вызыва́ть(ся *impf of* **вы́звать(ся**. **вызыва́ющий** defiant; provocative.

вы́играть *pf*, **выи́грывать** *impf* win; gain. **вы́игрыш** win; gain; prize. **вы́игрышный** winning; advantageous.

вы́йти (-йду; -шел, -шла) *pf* (*impf* **выходи́ть**) go out; come out; get out; appear; turn out; be used up; have expired; ~ **в свет** appear; ~ **за́муж** (**за**+*acc*) marry; ~ **из себя́** lose one's temper; ~ **из систе́му** (*comput*) log off.

выка́лывать *impf of* **вы́колоть**. **выка́пывать** *impf of* **вы́копать**

выка́рмливать *impf of* **вы́кормить**

вы́качать *pf*, **выка́чивать** *impf* pump out.

выки́дывать *impf*, **вы́кинуть** *pf* throw out, reject; put out; miscarry, abort; ~ **флаг** hoist a flag. **вы́кидыш** miscarriage, abortion.

вы́кладка laying out; lay-out; facing; kit; computation, calculation. **выкла́дывать** *impf of* **вы́ложить**

выключа́тель *m* switch. **выключа́ть** *impf*, **вы́ключить** (-чу) *pf* turn off, switch off; remove, exclude.

выкола́чивать *impf*, **вы́колотить** (-лочу) *pf* knock out, beat out; beat; extort, wring out.

вы́колоть (-лю) *pf* (*impf* **выка́лывать**) put out; gouge out; tattoo.

вы́|копать *pf* (*impf also* **выка́пывать**) dig; dig up, dig out; exhume; unearth.

вы́кормить (-млю) *pf* (*impf* **выка́рмливать**) rear, bring up.

вы́корчевать (-чую) *pf*, **выкорчёвывать** *impf* uproot, root out; eradicate.

выкра́ивать *impf of* **вы́кроить**

вы́|красить (-ашу) *pf*, **выкра́шивать** *impf* paint; dye.

выкри́кивать *impf*, **вы́крикнуть** (-ну) *pf* cry out; yell.

вы́кроить *pf* (*impf* **выкра́ивать**) cut out; find (*time etc.*). **вы́кройка** pattern.

вы́крутить (-учу) *pf*, **выкру́чивать** *impf* unscrew; twist; ~**ся** extricate o.s.

вы́куп ransom; redemption.

вы́|купать[1]**(ся** *pf*.

выкупа́ть[2] *impf*, **вы́купить**

(-плю) *pf* ransom, redeem.
вы́лазка sally, sortie; excursion.
выла́мывать *impf of* **вы́ломать**
вылеза́ть *impf*, **вы́лезти** (-зу; -лез) *pf* climb out; come out.
вы́|лепить (-плю) *pf*.
вы́лет flight; take-off. **вылета́ть** *impf*, **вы́лететь** (-ечу) *pf* fly out; take off.
вылечивать *impf*, **вы́лечить** (-чу) *pf* cure; **~ся** recover, be cured.
вылива́ть(ся *pf of* **вы́лить(ся**
вы́|линять *pf*.
вы́лить (-лью) *pf* (*impf* **вылива́ть**) pour out; cast, found; **~ся** flow (out); be expressed.
вы́ложить (-жу) *pf* (*impf* **выкла́дывать**) lay out.
вы́ломать *pf*, **вы́ломить** (-млю) *pf* (*impf* **выла́мывать**) break open.
вы́лупиться (-плюсь) *pf*, **вылупля́ться** *impf* hatch (out).
вы́лью *etc.*: *see* **вы́лить**
вы́|мазать (-мажу) *pf*, **выма́зывать** *impf* smear, dirty.
выма́нивать *impf*, **вы́манить** *pf* entice, lure.
вы́мереть (-мрет; -мер) *pf* (*impf* **вымира́ть**) die out; become extinct. **вы́мерший** extinct.
вы́мести (-ету) *pf*, **вы́метать** *impf* sweep (out).
вымога́тельство blackmail, extortion. **вымога́ть** *impf* extort.
вымока́ть *impf*, **вы́мокнуть** (-ну; -ок) *pf* be drenched; soak; rot.
вы́молвить (-влю) *pf* say, utter.
вы́|мостить (-ощу) *pf*. **вы́мою** *etc.*: *see* **вы́мыть**
вы́мпел pennant.
вы́мрет *see* **вы́мереть. вымыва́ть(ся** *impf of* **вы́мыть(ся**
вы́мысел (-сла) invention, fabrication; fantasy.
вы́|мыть (-мою) *pf* (*impf also* **вымыва́ть**) wash; wash out, off; wash away; **~ся** wash o.s.
вы́мышленный fictitious.
вы́мя (-мени) *neut* udder.
вына́шивать *impf of* **вы́носить²**
вы́нести (-су; -нес) *pf* (*impf* **выноси́ть¹**) carry out, take out; carry away; endure.
вынима́ть *impf of* **вы́нуть**
вы́нос carrying out. **выноси́ть¹** (-ошу́, -о́сишь) *impf of* **вы́нести. вы́носить²** *pf* (*impf* **вына́шивать**) bear; nurture. **вы́носка** carrying out; removal; footnote. **выно́сливость** endurance; hardiness.
вы́нудить (-ужу) *pf*, **вынужда́ть** *impf* force, compel. **вы́нужденный** forced.
вы́нуть (-ну) *pf* (*impf* **вынима́ть**) take out.
вы́пад attack; lunge. **выпада́ть** *impf of* **вы́пасть**
выпа́лывать *impf of* **вы́полоть**
выпа́ривать *impf*, **вы́парить** evaporate; steam.
выпа́рывать *impf of* **вы́пороть²**
вы́пасть (-аду; -ал) *pf* (*impf* **выпада́ть**) fall out; fall; occur, turn out; lunge.
выпека́ть *impf*, **вы́печь** (-еку; -ек) *pf* bake.
выпива́ть *impf of* **вы́пить**; enjoy a drink. **вы́пивка** drinking bout; drinks.

выпи́ливать *impf*, **вы́пилить** *pf* saw, cut out.
вы́писать (-ишу) *pf*, **выпи́сывать** *impf* copy out; write out; order; subscribe to; send for; discharge, release; **~ся** be discharged; check out. **вы́писка** writing out; extract; ordering, subscription; discharge.
вы́|пить (-пью) *pf* (*impf also* **выпива́ть**) drink; drink up.
вы́плавить (-влю) *pf*, **выплавля́ть** *impf* smelt. **вы́плавка** smelting; smelted metal.
вы́плата payment. **вы́платить** (-ачу) *pf*, **выпла́чивать** *impf* pay (out); pay off.
выплёвывать *impf of* **вы́плюнуть**
выплыва́ть *impf*, **вы́плыть** (-ыву) *pf* swim out, sail out; emerge; crop up.
вы́плюнуть (-ну) *pf* (*impf* **выплёвывать**) spit out.
выполза́ть *impf*, **вы́ползти** (-зу; -олз) *pf* crawl out.
выполне́ние execution, carrying out; fulfilment. **вы́полнить** *pf*, **выполня́ть** *impf* execute, carry out; fulfil.
вы́|полоскать (-ощу) *pf*.
вы́|полоть (-лю) *pf* (*impf also* **выпа́лывать**) weed out; weed.
вы́|пороть[1] (-рю) *pf*.
вы́пороть[2] (-рю) *pf* (*impf* **выпа́рывать**) rip out, rip up.
вы́|потрошить (-шу) *pf*.
вы́правка bearing; correction.
выпра́шивать *impf of* **вы́просить**; solicit.
выprова́живать *impf*, **вы́проводить** (-ожу) *pf* send packing.
вы́просить (-ошу) *pf* (*impf* **выпра́шивать**) (ask for and) get.
выпряга́ть *impf of* **вы́прячь**
вы́прямить (-млю) *pf*, **выпрямля́ть** *impf* straighten (out); rectify; **~ся** become straight; draw o.s. up.
вы́прячь (-ягу; -яг) *pf* (*impf* **выпряга́ть**) unharness.
вы́пуклый protuberant; bulging; convex.
вы́пуск output; issue; discharge; part, instalment; final-year students; omission. **выпуска́ть** *impf*, **вы́пустить** (-ущу) *pf* let out; issue; produce; omit. **выпускни́к** (-а́), **-и́ца** final-year student. **выпускн|о́й** discharge; exhaust; **~о́й экза́мен** finals, final examination.
вы́путать *pf*, **выпу́тывать** *impf* disentangle; **~ся** extricate o.s.
вы́пью *etc.*: *see* **вы́пить**
выраба́тывать *impf*, **вы́работать** *pf* work out; work up; draw up; produce, make; earn. **вы́работка** manufacture; production; working out; drawing up; output; make.
выра́внивать(ся *impf of* **вы́ровнять(ся**
выража́ть *impf*, **вы́разить** (-ажу) *pf* express; **~ся** express o.s. **выраже́ние** expression. **вырази́тельный** expressive.
выраста́ть *impf*, **вы́расти** (-ту; -рос) *pf* grow, grow up. **вы́растить** (-ащу) *pf*, **выра́щивать** *impf* bring up; breed; cultivate.
вы́рвать[1] (-ву) *pf* (*impf* **вырыва́ть**[2]) pull out, tear out; extort; **~ся** break loose, break free; escape; shoot.
вы́|рвать[2] (-ву) *pf*.
вы́рез cut; décolletage. **вы́резать** (-ежу) *pf*, **выреза́ть** *impf*, **выре́зывать** *impf* cut (out); engrave. **вы́резка** cutting out, ex-

cision; cutting; fillet.
вы́ровнять *pf* (*impf* **выра́внивать**) level; straighten (out); draw up; **~ся** become level; equalize; catch up.
вы́родиться *pf*, **вырожда́ться** *impf* degenerate. **вы́родок** (-дка) degenerate; black sheep. **вырожде́ние** degeneration.
вы́ронить *pf* drop.
вы́рос *etc.*: *see* **вы́расти**
вы́рою *etc.*: *see* **вы́рыть**
выруба́ть *impf*, **вы́рубить** (-блю) *pf* cut down; cut (out); carve (out). **вы́рубка** cutting down; hewing out.
вы́|ругать(ся *pf*.
выру́ливать *impf*, **вы́|рулить** *pf* taxi.
выруча́ть *impf*, **вы́ручить** (-чу) *pf* rescue; help out; gain; make. **вы́ручка** rescue; gain; proceeds; earnings.
вырыва́ть[1] *impf*, **вы́|рыть** (-рою) *pf* dig up, unearth.
вырыва́ть[2]**(ся** *impf of* **вы́рвать(ся**
вы́садить (-ажу) *pf*, **выса́живать** *impf* set down; put ashore; transplant; smash; **~ся** alight; disembark. **вы́садка** disembarkation; landing; transplanting.
выса́сывать *impf of* **вы́сосать**
вы́свободить (-божу) *pf*, **высвобожда́ть** *impf* free; release.
высека́ть *impf of* **вы́сечь**[2]
выселе́ние eviction. **вы́селить** *pf*, **выселя́ть** *impf* evict; evacuate, move; **~ся** move, remove.
вы́|сечь[1] (-еку; -сек) *pf*. **вы́сечь**[2] (-еку; -сек) (*impf* **высека́ть**) cut (out); carve.
вы́сидеть (-ижу) *pf*, **выси́живать** *impf* sit out; stay; hatch.
вы́ситься *impf* rise, tower.
выска́бливать *impf of* **вы́скоблить**
вы́сказать (-кажу) *pf*, **выска́зывать** *impf* express; state; **~ся** speak out. **выска́зывание** utterance; pronouncement.
выска́кивать *impf of* **вы́скочить**
вы́скоблить *pf* (*impf* **выска́бливать**) scrape out; erase; remove.
вы́скочить (-чу) *pf* (*impf* **выска́кивать**) jump out; spring out; **~ с**+*instr* come out with. **вы́скочка** upstart.
вы́слать (вы́шлю) *pf* (*impf* **высыла́ть**) send (out); exile; deport.
вы́следить (-ежу) *pf*, **высле́живать** *impf* trace; shadow.
выслу́живать *impf*, **вы́служить** (-жу) *pf* qualify for; serve (out); **~ся** gain promotion; curry favour.
вы́слушать *pf*, **выслу́шивать** *impf* hear out; sound; listen to.
высме́ивать *impf*, **вы́смеять** (-ею) *pf* ridicule.
вы́|сморкать(ся *pf*. **высо́вывать(ся** *impf of* **вы́сунуть(ся**
высо́кий (-о́к, -а́, -о́ко́) high; tall; lofty; elevated.
высоко- *in comb* high-, highly. **высокоблагоро́дие** (your) Honour, Worship. **~во́льтный** high-tension. **~го́рный** mountain. **~ка́чественный** high-quality. **~квалифици́рованный** highly qualified. **~ме́рие** haughtiness. **~ме́рный** haughty. **~па́рный** high-flown; bombastic. **~часто́тный** high-frequency.
вы́сосать (-осу) *pf* (*impf* **выса́сывать**) suck out.

высота́ (*pl* -ы) height, altitude. **высо́тный** high-altitude; high-rise.

вы́|сохнуть (-ну; -ох) *pf* (*impf also* **высыха́ть**) dry (out); dry up; wither (away).

вы́спаться (-плюсь, -пишься) *pf* (*impf* **высыпа́ться**[2]) have a good sleep.

вы́ставить (-влю) *pf*, **выставля́ть** *impf* display, exhibit; post; put forward; set down; take out; +*instr* represent as; **~ся** show off. **вы́ставка** exhibition.

выста́ивать *impf of* **вы́стоять**

вы́|стегать *pf*. **вы́|стирать** *pf*.

вы́стоять (-ою) *pf* (*impf* **выста́ивать**) stand; stand one's ground.

вы́страдать *pf* suffer; gain through suffering.

выстра́ивать(ся *impf of* **вы́строить(ся**

вы́стрел shot; report. **вы́стрелить** *pf* shoot, fire.

вы́|строгать *pf*.

вы́строить *pf* (*impf* **выстра́ивать**) build; draw up, order, arrange; form up. **~ся** form up.

вы́ступ protuberance, projection. **выступа́ть** *impf*, **вы́ступить** (-плю) *pf* come forward; come out; perform; speak; +**из**+*gen* go beyond. **выступле́ние** appearance, performance; speech; setting out.

вы́сунуть (-ну) *pf* (*impf* **высо́вывать**) put out, thrust out; **~ся** show o.s., thrust o.s. forward.

вы́|сушить(ся (-шу(сь) *pf*.

вы́сший highest; high; higher.

высыла́ть *impf of* **вы́слать**. **вы́сылка** sending, dispatch; expulsion, exile.

вы́сыпать (-плю) *pf*, **высыпа́ть** *impf* pour out; spill; **~ся**[1] pour out; spill.

высыпа́ться[2] *impf of* **вы́спаться**

высыха́ть *impf of* **вы́сохнуть**

высь height; summit.

выта́лкивать *impf of* **вы́толкать**, **вы́толкнуть**. **выта́скивать** *impf of* **вы́тащить**. **вытача́ивать** *impf of* **вы́точить**

вы́|тащить (-щу) *pf* (*impf also* **выта́скивать**) drag out; pull out.

вы́|твердить (-ржу) *pf*.

вытека́ть *impf* (*pf* **вы́течь**); **~ из**+*gen* flow from, out of; result from.

вы́тереть (-тру; -тер) *pf* (*impf* **вытира́ть**) wipe (up); dry; wear out.

вы́терпеть (-плю) *pf* endure.

вы́тертый threadbare.

вы́теснить *pf*, **вытесня́ть** *impf* force out; oust; displace.

вы́течь (-чет; -ек) *pf* (*impf* **вытека́ть**) flow out, run out.

вытира́ть *impf of* **вы́тереть**

вы́толкать *pf*, **вы́толкнуть** (-ну) *pf* (*impf* **выта́лкивать**) throw out; push out.

вы́точенный turned. **вы́|точить** (-чу) *pf* (*impf also* **вытача́ивать**) turn; sharpen; gnaw through.

вы́|травить (-влю) *pf*, **вытра́вливать** *impf*, **вытравля́ть** *impf* exterminate, destroy; remove; etch; trample down, damage.

вытрезви́тель *m* detoxification centre. **вы́трезвить(ся** (-влю(сь) *pf*, **вытрезвля́ть(ся** *impf* sober up.

вы́тру *etc.*: *see* **вы́тереть**

вы́|трясти (-су; -яс) *pf* shake out.

вытря́хивать *impf*, **вы́трях-нуть** (-ну) *pf* shake out.

выть (во́ю) *impf* howl; wail.

вытя́гивать *impf*, **вы́тянуть** (-ну) *pf* stretch (out); extend; extract; endure; **~ся** stretch, stretch out, stretch o.s.; shoot up; draw o.s. up. **вы́тяжка** drawing out, extraction; extract.

вы́|утюжить (-жу) *pf*.

выу́чивать *impf*, **вы́|учить** (-чу) *pf* learn; teach; **~ся** +*dat or inf* learn.

выха́живать *impf of* **вы́ходить²**

вы́хватить (-ачу) *pf*, **выхва́тывать** *impf* snatch out, up, away; pull out.

вы́хлоп exhaust. **выхлопно́й** exhaust, discharge.

вы́ход going out; departure; way out, exit; vent; appearance; yield; **~ за́муж** marriage. **вы́ходец** (-дца) emigrant; immigrant.

выходи́ть¹ (-ожу́, -о́дишь) *impf of* **вы́йти**; +**на**+*acc* look out on.

вы́ходить² (-ожу) *pf* (*impf* **выха́живать**) nurse; rear, bring up.

вы́ходка trick; prank.

выходн|о́й exit; going-out, outgoing; discharge; **~о́й день** day off; **~о́й** *sb* person off duty; day off. **выхожу́** *etc.*: *see* **выходи́ть¹**. **вы́хожу** *etc.*: *see* **вы́ходить²**

вы́цвести (-ветет) *pf*, **выцвета́ть** *impf* fade. **вы́цветший** faded.

вычёркивать *impf*, **вы́черкнуть** (-ну) *pf* cross out.

вы́черпать *pf*, **выче́рпывать** *impf* bale out.

вы́честь (-чту; -чел, -чла) *pf* (*impf* **вычита́ть**) subtract. **вы́чет** deduction.

вычисле́ние calculation. **вычисли́тель** *m* calculator. **вычисли́тельн|ый** calculating, computing; **~ая маши́на** computer; **~ая те́хника** computers; **вы́числить** *pf*, **вычисля́ть** *impf* calculate, compute.

вы́|чистить (-ищу) *pf* (*impf also* **вычища́ть**) clean, clean up.

вычита́ние subtraction. **вычита́ть** *impf of* **вы́честь**

вычища́ть *impf of* **вы́чистить**.

вы́чту *etc.*: *see* **вы́честь**

вы́швырнуть (-ну) *pf*, **вышвы́ривать** *impf* chuck out.

вы́ше higher, taller; *prep*+*gen* beyond; over; *adv* above.

выше- *in comb* above-, afore-. **вышеизло́женный** foregoing. **~на́званный** afore-named. **~ска́занный**, **~ука́занный** aforesaid. **~упомя́нутый** afore-mentioned.

вы́шел *etc.*: *see* **вы́йти**

вышиба́ла *m* chucker-out. **вышиба́ть** *impf*, **вы́шибить** (-бу; -иб) *pf* knock out; chuck out.

вышива́ние embroidery, needlework. **вышива́ть** *impf of* **вы́шить**. **вы́шивка** embroidery.

вышина́ height.

вы́шить (-шью) *pf* (*impf* **вышива́ть**) embroider. **вы́шитый** embroidered.

вы́шка tower; **(бурова́я) ~** derrick.

вы́шлю *etc.*: *see* **вы́слать**. **вы́шью** *etc.*: *see* **вы́шить**

вы́явить (-влю) *pf*, **выявля́ть** *impf* reveal; make known; expose; **~ся** come to light, be revealed.

выясне́ние elucidation; explanation. **вы́яснить** *pf*, **выясня́ть** *impf* elucidate; explain; **~ся** become clear; turn out.

Вьетна́м Vietnam. **вьетна́мец, -мка** Vietnamese. **вьетна́мский** Vietnamese.

вью *etc.*: *see* **вить**

вью́га snow-storm, blizzard.

вьюно́к (-нка́) bindweed.

вью́чн|ый pack; **~ое живо́тное** beast of burden.

вью́щийся climbing; curly.

вяжу́ *etc.*: **вяза́ть. вя́жущий** binding; astringent.

вяз elm.

вяза́ние knitting, crocheting; binding, tying. **вя́занка**[1] knitted garment. **вяза́нка**[2] bundle. **вя́заный** knitted, crocheted. **вяза́нье** knitting; crochet(-work). **вяза́ть** (вяжу́, вя́жешь) *impf* (*pf* **с~**) tie, bind; knit, crochet; be astringent; **~ся** accord; tally. **вя́зка** tying; knitting, crocheting; bunch.

вя́зкий (-зок, -зка́, -о) viscous; sticky; boggy. **вя́знуть** (-ну; вяз(нул), -зла) *impf* (*pf* **за~, у~**) stick, get stuck.

вя́зовый elm.

вязь ligature; arabesque.

вя́леный dried; sun-cured.

вя́лый limp; sluggish; slack. **вя́нуть** (-ну; вял) *impf* (*pf* **за~, у~**) fade, wither; flag.

Г

г. *abbr* (*of* **год**) year; (*of* **го́род**) city; (*of* **господи́н**) Mr.

г *abbr* (*of* **грамм**) gram.

га *abbr* (*of* **гекта́р**) hectare.

га́вань harbour.

гага́чий пух eiderdown.

гад reptile; repulsive person; *pl.* vermin.

гада́лка fortune-teller. **гада́ние** fortune-telling; guess-work. **гада́ть** *impf* (*pf* **по~**) tell fortunes; guess.

га́дина reptile; repulsive person; *pl* vermin. **га́дить** (га́жу) *impf* (*pf* **на~**) +**в**+*prep*, **на**+*acc*, *prep* foul, dirty, defile. **га́дкий** (-док, -дка́, -о) nasty, vile repulsive. **га́дость** filth, muck; dirty trick; *pl* filthy expressions. **гадю́ка** adder, viper; repulsive person.

га́ечный ключ spanner, wrench.

газ[1] gauze.

газ[2] gas; wind; **дать ~** step on the gas; **сба́вить ~** reduce speed.

газе́та newspaper. **газе́тчик** journalist; newspaper-seller.

газиро́ванный aerated. **га́зовый** gas.

газо́н lawn. **газонокоси́лка** lawn-mower.

газопрово́д gas pipeline; gas-main.

га́йка nut; female screw.

гала́ктика galaxy.

галантере́йный магази́н haberdasher's. **галантере́я** haberdashery.

гала́нтный gallant.

галере́я gallery. **галёрка** gallery, gods.

галифе́ *indecl pl* riding-breeches.

га́лка jackdaw.

галлюцина́ция hallucination.

гало́п gallop.

га́лочка tick.

га́лстук tie; neckerchief.

галу́шка dumpling.

га́лька pebble; pebbles, shingle.

гам din, uproar.
гама́к (-а́) hammock.
га́мма scale; gamut; range.
гангре́на gangrene.
га́нгстер gangster.
ганте́ль dumb-bell.
гара́ж (-а́) garage.
гаранти́ровать *impf* & *pf* guarantee. **гара́нтия** guarantee.
гардеро́б wardrobe; cloakroom. **гардеро́бщик, -щица** cloakroom attendant.
гарди́на curtain.
гармонизи́ровать *impf* & *pf* harmonize.
гармо́ника accordion, concertina. **гармони́ческий, гармони́чный** harmonious. **гармо́ния** harmony; concord. **гармо́нь** accordion, concertina.
гарнизо́н garrison.
гарни́р garnish; vegetables.
гарниту́р set; suite.
гарь burning; cinders.
гаси́тель *m* extinguisher; suppressor. **гаси́ть** (гашу́, га́сишь) *impf* (*pf* **за~, по~**) extinguish; suppress. **га́снуть** (-ну; гас) *impf* (*pf* **за~, по~, у~**) be extinguished, go out; grow feeble.
гастро́ли *f pl* tour; guest-appearance, performance. **гастроли́ровать** *impf* (be on) tour.
гастроно́м gourmet; provision shop. **гастрономи́ческий** gastronomic; provision. **гастроно́мия** gastronomy; provisions; delicatessen.
гауптва́хта guardroom.
гаши́ш hashish.
гварде́ец (-е́йца) guardsman. **гварде́йский** guards'. **гва́рдия** Guards.
гво́здик tack. **гвозди́ка** pink(s), carnation(s); cloves. **гво́здики** (-ов) *pl* stilettos.
гвоздь (-я́; *pl* -и, -е́й) *m* nail; tack; crux; highlight, hit.
гг. *abbr* (*of* **го́ды**) years.
где *adv* where; **~ бы ни** wherever. **где́-либо** *adv* anywhere. **где́-нибудь** *adv* somewhere; anywhere. **где́-то** *adv* somewhere.
гекта́р hectare.
ге́лий helium.
гемоглоби́н haemoglobin.
геморро́й haemorrhoids. **гемофили́я** haemophilia.
ген gene.
ге́незис origin, genesis.
генера́л general. **генера́льн|ый** general; **~ая репети́ция** dress rehearsal.
генера́тор generator.
гене́тик geneticist. **гене́тика** genetics. **генети́ческий** genetic.
гениа́льный brilliant. **ге́ний** genius.
ге́ном genome.
гео- *in comb* geo-. **гео́граф** geographer. **~графи́ческий** geographical. **~гра́фия** geography. **гео́лог** geologist. **~логи́ческий** geological. **~ло́гия** geology. **~метри́ческий** geometric. **~ме́трия** geometry.
георги́н dahlia.
геофи́зика geophysics.
гепа́рд cheetah.
гепати́т hepatitis.
гера́нь geranium.
герб arms, coat of arms. **ге́рбов|ый** heraldic; **~ая печа́ть** official stamp.
геркуле́с Hercules; rolled oats.
герма́нец (-нца) ancient German. **Герма́ния** Germany. **гер-**

ма́нский Germanic.
гермафроди́т hermaphrodite.
гермети́чный hermetic; hermetically sealed; air-tight.
герои́зм heroism. **герои́ня** heroine. **герои́ческий** heroic. **геро́й** hero. **геро́йский** heroic.
герц (*gen pl* **герц**) hertz.
ге́рцог duke. **герцоги́ня** duchess.
г-жа *abbr* (*of* **госпожа́**) Mrs.; Miss.
гиаци́нт hyacinth.
ги́бель death; destruction, ruin; loss; wreck; downfall. **ги́бельный** disastrous, fatal.
ги́бкий (-бок, -бка́, -бко) flexible, adaptable, versatile; supple. **ги́бкость** flexibility; suppleness.
ги́бнуть (-ну; ги́б(нул)) *impf* (*pf* **по~**) perish.
гибри́д hybrid.
гига́нт giant. **гига́нтский** gigantic.
гигие́на hygiene. **гигиени́ческий, -и́чный** hygienic, sanitary.
гид guide.
гидравли́ческий hydraulic.
гидро- *pref* hydro-. **~электроста́нция** hydro-electric power-station.
гие́на hyena.
ги́льза cartridge-case; sleeve; (cigarette-)wrapper.
гимн hymn.
гимна́зия grammar school, high school.
гимна́ст gymnast. **гимна́стика** gymnastics. **гимнасти́ческий** gymnastic.
гинеко́лог gynaecologist. **гинеколо́гия** gynaecology.
гипе́рбола hyperbole.
гипно́з hypnosis. **гипнотизёр** hypnotist. **гипнотизи́ровать** *impf* (*pf* **за~**) hypnotize. **гипноти́ческий** hypnotic.
гипо́теза hypothesis. **гипотети́ческий** hypothetical.
гиппопота́м hippopotamus.
гипс gypsum, plaster (of Paris); plaster cast. **ги́псовый** plaster.
гирля́нда garland.
ги́ря weight.
гистерэктоми́я hysterectomy.
гита́ра guitar.
гл. *abbr* (*of* **глава́**) chapter.
глав- *abbr in comb* head, chief, main.
глава́ (*pl* -ы) head; chief; chapter; cupola. **глава́рь** (-я́) *m* leader, ring-leader. **главк** central directorate. **главнокома́ндующий** *sb* commander-in-chief. **гла́вн|ый** chief, main; **~ым о́бразом** chiefly, mainly, for the most part; **~ое** *sb* the main thing; the essentials.
глаго́л verb.
гла́дить (-а́жу) *impf* (*pf* **вы́~, по~**) stroke; iron. **гла́дкий** smooth; plain. **гла́дко** *adv* smoothly. **гладь** smooth surface.
глаз (*loc* -у́; *pl* -а́, глаз) eye; **в ~а́** to one's face; **за ~а́+*gen*** behind the back of; **смотре́ть во все ~а́** be all eyes.
глазиро́ванный glazed; glossy; iced; glacé.
глазни́ца eye-socket. **глазно́й** eye; optic; **~ врач** oculist. **глазо́к** (-зка́) peephole.
глазу́нья fried eggs.
глазу́рь glaze; syrup; icing.
гла́нды (гланд) *pl* tonsils.
гла́сность publicity; glasnost, openness. **гла́сный** public; vowel; *sb* vowel.
гли́на clay. **гли́нистый** clayey.

гли́няный clay; clayey.
гли́ссер speed-boat.
глист (*intestinal*) worm.
глицери́н glycerine.
глоба́льный global; extensive.
гло́бус globe.
глота́ть *impf* swallow. **гло́тка** gullet; throat. **глото́к** (-тка́) gulp; mouthful.
гло́хнуть (-ну; глох) *impf* (*pf* **за~, о~**) become deaf; die away, subside; grow wild.
глубина́ (*pl* -ы) depth; heart, interior. **глубо́кий** (-о́к, -а́, -о́ко́) deep; profound; late, advanced, extreme. **глубокомы́слие** profundity. **глубокоуважа́емый** (*in formal letters*) dear.
глуми́ться (-млю́сь) *impf* mock, jeer (**над**+*instr* at). **глумле́ние** mockery.
глупе́ть (-е́ю) *impf* (*pf* **по~**) grow stupid. **глупе́ц** (-пца́) fool. **глу́пость** stupidity. **глу́пый** (глуп, -а́, -о) stupid.
глуха́рь (-я́) *m* capercaillie. **глух|о́й** (глух, -а́, -о) deaf; muffled; obscure, vague; dense; wild; remote; deserted; sealed; blank; **~о́й, ~а́я** *sb* deaf man, woman. **глухонемо́й** deaf and dumb; *sb* deaf mute. **глухота́** deafness. **глуши́тель** *m* silencer. **глуши́ть** (-шу́) *impf* (*pf* **за~, о~**) stun; muffle; dull; jam; extinguish; stifle; suppress. **глушь** backwoods.
глы́ба clod; lump, block.
глюко́за glucose.
гляде́ть (-яжу́) *impf* (*pf* **по~, гля́нуть**) look, gaze, peer; **~ в о́ба** be on one's guard; **(того́ и) гляди́** it looks as if; I'm afraid; **гля́дя по**+*dat* depending on.
гля́нец (-нца) gloss, lustre; polish.
гля́нуть (-ну) *pf* (*impf* **гляде́ть**) glance.
гм *int* hm!
г-н *abbr* (*of* **господи́н**) Mr.
гнать (гоню́, го́нишь; гнал, -а́, -о) *impf* drive; urge (on); hunt, chase; persecute; distil; **~ся за**+*instr* pursue.
гнев anger, rage. **гне́ваться** *impf* (*pf* **раз~**) be angry. **гне́вный** angry.
гнедо́й bay.
гнездо́ (*pl* гнёзда) nest.
гнёт weight; oppression. **гнету́щий** oppressive.
гни́да nit.
гние́ние decay, putrefaction, rot. **гнило́й** (-ил, -а́, -о) rotten; muggy. **гнить** (-ию́, -иёшь; -ил, -а́, -о) *impf* (*pf* **с~**) rot. **гное́ние** suppuration. **гнои́ться** *impf* (*pf* **с~**) suppurate, discharge matter. **гной** pus. **гнойни́к** abscess; ulcer. **гно́йный** purulent.
гну́сный (-сен, -сна́, -о) vile.
гнуть (гну, гнёшь) *impf* (*pf* **со~**) bend; aim at; **~ся** bend; stoop.
гнуша́ться *impf* (*pf* **по~**) disdain; +*gen or instr* shun; abhor.
гобеле́н tapestry.
гобо́й oboe.
гове́ть (-е́ю) *impf* fast.
говно́ (*vulg*) shit.
говори́ть *impf* (*pf* **по~, сказа́ть**) speak, talk; say; tell; **~ся: как говори́тся** as they say.
говя́дина beef. **говя́жий** beef.
го́гот cackle; loud laughter. **гогота́ть** (-очу́, -о́чешь) *impf* cackle; roar with laughter.
год (*loc* -у́; *pl* -ы *or* -а́, *gen* -о́в *or* лет) year. **года́ми** *adv* for years (on end).
годи́ться, (-жу́сь) *impf* be fit, suitable; serve.

годи́чный a year's; annual.

го́дный (-ден, -дна́, -о, -ы *or* -ы́) fit, suitable; valid.

годова́лый one-year-old. **годово́й** annual. **годовщи́на** anniversary.

гожу́сь *etc.*: *see* **годи́ться**

гол goal.

голени́ще (boot-)top. **го́лень** shin.

голла́ндец (-дца) Dutchman. **Голла́ндия** Holland. **голла́ндка** Dutchwoman; tiled stove. **голла́ндский** Dutch.

голова́ (*acc* го́лову; *pl* го́ловы, -о́в, -а́м) head. **голова́стик** tadpole. **голо́вка** head; cap, nose, tip. **головн|о́й** head; leading; **~а́я боль** headache; **~о́й мозг** brain, cerebrum; **~о́й убо́р** headgear, headdress. **головокруже́ние** dizziness. **головоло́мка** puzzle. **головоре́з** cutthroat; rascal.

го́лод hunger; famine; acute shortage. **голода́ние** starvation; fasting. **голода́ть** *impf* go hungry, starve; fast. **голо́дный** (го́лоден, -дна́, -о, -ы *or* -ы́) hungry. **голодо́вка** hunger-strike.

гололёд, гололе́дица (period of) black ice.

го́лос (*pl* -а́) voice; part; vote. **голоси́ть** (-ошу́) *impf* sing loudly; cry; wail.

голосло́вный unsubstantiated, unfounded.

голосова́ние voting; poll. **голосова́ть** *impf* (*pf* **про~**) vote; vote on.

голосов|о́й vocal; **~а́я по́чта** voice mail.

голу́бка pigeon; (my) dear, darling. **голубо́й** light blue. **голу́бчик** my dear (fellow); darling.

го́лубь *m* pigeon, dove. **голубя́тня** (*gen pl* -тен) dovecot, pigeon-loft.

го́лый (гол, -ла́, -ло) naked, bare.

гольф golf.

го́мон hubbub.

гомосексуали́ст homosexual. **гомосексуа́льный** homosexual.

гондо́ла gondola.

гоне́ние persecution. **го́нка** race; dashing; haste.

гонора́р fee.

го́ночный racing.

гонча́р (-а́) potter.

го́нщик racing driver *or* cyclist.

гоню́ *etc.*: *see* **гнать**. **гоня́ть** *impf* drive; send on errands; **~ся** +**за**+*instr* chase, hunt.

гора́ (*acc* го́ру; *pl* го́ры, -а́м) mountain; hill; **в го́ру** uphill; **по́д гору** downhill.

гора́здо *adv* much, far, by far.

горб (-а́, *loc* -у́) hump; bulge. **горба́тый** hunchbacked. **го́рбить** (-блю) *impf* (*pf* **с~**) arch, hunch; **~ся** stoop. **горбу́н** (-а́) *m*, **горбу́нья** (*gen pl* -ний) hunchback. **горбу́шка** (*gen pl* -шек) crust (*of loaf*).

горди́ться (-ржу́сь) *impf* put on airs; +*instr* be proud of. **го́рдость** pride. **го́рдый** (горд, -а́, -о, го́рды́) proud. **горды́ня** arrogance.

го́ре grief, sorrow; trouble. **горева́ть** (-рю́ю) *impf* grieve.

горе́лка burner. **горе́лый** burnt. **горе́ние** burning, combustion; enthusiasm.

го́рестный sad; mournful. **го́ресть** sorrow; *pl* misfortunes.

горе́ть (-рю́) *impf* burn; be on fire.

го́рец (-рца) mountain-dweller.

го́речь bitterness; bitter taste.
горизо́нт horizon. **горизонта́ль** horizontal. **горизонта́льный** horizontal.
гори́стый mountainous, hilly. **го́рка** hill; hillock; steep climb.
го́рло throat; neck. **горлово́й** throat; guttural; raucous. **го́рлышко** neck.
гормо́н hormone.
горн[1] furnace, forge.
горн[2] bugle.
го́рничная *sb* maid, chambermaid.
горнорабо́чий *sb* miner.
горноста́й ermine.
го́рный mountain; mountainous; mineral; mining. **горня́к** (-а́) miner.
го́род (*pl* -а́) town; city. **городо́к** (-дка́) small town. **городско́й** urban; city; municipal. **горожа́нин** (*pl* -а́не, -а́н) *m*, **-жа́нка** town-dweller.
гороско́п horoscope.
горо́х pea, peas. **горо́шек** (-шка) spots, spotted pattern; **души́стый ~** sweet peas; **зелёный ~** green peas. **горо́шина** pea.
горсове́т *abbr* (*of* **городско́й сове́т**) city soviet, town soviet.
горсть (*gen pl* -е́й) handful.
горта́нный guttural. **горта́нь** larynx.
горчи́ца mustard. **горчи́чник** mustard plaster.
горшо́к (-шка́) flowerpot; pot; potty; chamber-pot.
го́рький (-рек, -рька́, -о) bitter.
горю́ч|ий combustible; **~ее** *sb* fuel. **горя́чий** (-ря́ч, -а́) hot; passionate; ardent.
горячи́ться (-чу́сь) *impf* (*pf* **раз~**) get excited. **горя́чка** fever; feverish haste. **горя́чность** zeal.
гос- *abbr in comb* (*of* **госуда́рственный**) state.
го́спиталь *m* (military) hospital.
го́споди *int* good heavens! **господи́н** (*pl* -ода́, -о́д, -а́м) master; gentleman; Mr; *pl* ladies and gentlemen. **господство** supremacy. **госпо́дствовать** *impf* hold sway; prevail. **Госпо́дь** (Го́спода, *voc* Го́споди) *m* God, the Lord. **госпожа́** lady; Mrs.
гостеприи́мный hospitable. **гостеприи́мство** hospitality.
гости́ная *sb* sitting-room, living-room, drawing-room. **гости́ница** hotel. **гости́ть** (гощу́) *impf* stay, be on a visit. **гость** (*gen pl* -е́й) *m*, **го́стья** (*gen pl* -ий) guest, visitor.
госуда́рственный State, public. **госуда́рство** State. **госуда́рыня, госуда́рь** *m* sovereign; Your Majesty.
готи́ческий Gothic.
гото́вить (-влю) *impf* (*pf* **с~**) prepare; **~ся** prepare (o.s.); be at hand. **гото́вность** readiness. **гото́вый** ready.
гофриро́ванный corrugated; waved; pleated.
грабёж robbery; pillage. **граби́тель** *m* robber. **граби́тельский** predatory; exorbitant. **гра́бить** (-блю) *impf* (*pf* **о~**) rob, pillage.
гра́бли (-бель *or* -блей) *pl* rake.
гравёр, гравиро́вщик engraver.
гра́вий gravel. **гравирова́ть** *impf* (*pf* **вы́~**) engrave; etch. **гравиро́вка** engraving.
гравитацио́нный gravitational.
гравю́ра engraving, print; etching.
град[1] city, town.

град² hail; volley. **гра́дина** hailstone.

гра́дус degree. **гра́дусник** thermometer.

граждани́н (*pl* гра́ждане, -дан), **гражда́нка** citizen. **гражда́нский** civil; civic; civilian. **гражда́нство** citizenship.

грамза́пись (gramophone) recording.

грамм gram.

грамма́тика grammar. **граммати́ческий** grammatical.

гра́мота reading and writing; official document; deed. **гра́мотность** literacy. **гра́мотный** literate; competent.

грампласти́нка (gramophone) record.

грана́т pomegranate; garnet. **грана́та** shell, grenade.

грандио́зный grandiose.

гранёный cut, faceted; cut-glass.

грани́т granite.

грани́ца border; boundary, limit; **за грани́цей, за грани́цу** abroad. **грани́чить** *impf* border.

грант grant.

грань border, verge; side, facet.

граф count; earl.

графа́ column. **гра́фик** graph; chart; schedule; graphic artist. **гра́фика** drawing; graphics; script.

графи́н carafe; decanter.

графи́ня countess.

графи́т graphite.

графи́ческий graphic.

графлёный ruled.

гра́фство county.

грацио́зный graceful. **гра́ция** grace.

грач (-а́) rook.

гребёнка comb. **гре́бень** (-бня) *m* comb; crest. **гребе́ц** (-бца́) rower, oarsman. **гребно́й** rowing. **гребу́** *etc.*: *see* **грести́**

грёза day-dream, dream. **гре́зить** (-е́жу) *impf* dream.

грек Greek.

гре́лка hot-water bottle.

греме́ть *impf* (*pf* **про~**) thunder, roar; rattle; resound. **гре-му́чая змея́** rattlesnake.

грести́ (-ебу́, -ебёшь; грёб, -бла́) *impf* row; rake.

греть (-е́ю) *impf* warm, heat; **~ся** warm o.s., bask.

грех (-а́) sin. **грехо́вный** sinful. **грехопаде́ние** the Fall; fall.

Гре́ция Greece. **гре́цкий оре́х** walnut. **греча́нка** Greek. **гре́ческий** Greek, Grecian.

гречи́ха buckwheat. **гре́чневый** buckwheat.

греши́ть (-шу́) *impf* (*pf* **по~, со~**) sin. **гре́шник, -ница** sinner. **гре́шный** (-шен, -шна́, -о) sinful.

гриб (-а́) mushroom. **грибно́й** mushroom.

гри́ва mane.

гри́венник ten-copeck piece.

грим make-up; grease-paint.

гримирова́ть *impf* (*pf* **за~**) make up; +*instr* make up as.

грипп flu.

гриф neck (*of violin etc.*).

гри́фель *m* pencil lead.

гроб (*loc* -у́; *pl* -ы́ *or* -а́) coffin; grave. **гробни́ца** tomb. **гробово́й** coffin; deathly. **гробовщи́к** (-а́) coffin-maker; undertaker.

гроза́ (*pl* -ы) (thunder-)storm.

гроздь (*pl* -ди *or* -дья, -де́й *or* -дьев) cluster, bunch.

грози́ть(ся (-ожу́(сь) *impf* (*pf* **по~, при~**) threaten. **гро́зный** (-зен, -зна́, -о) menacing; terrible; severe.

гром (*pl* -ы, -о́в) thunder.
грома́да mass; bulk, pile. **грома́дный** huge, colossal.
громи́ть (-млю́) *impf* destroy; smash, rout.
гро́мкий (-мок, -мка́, -о) loud; famous; notorious; fine-sounding. **гро́мко** *adv* loud(ly); aloud. **громкоговори́тель** *m* loud-speaker. **громово́й** thunder; thunderous; crushing. **громогла́сный** loud; public.
громозди́ть (-зжу́) *impf* (*pf* **на~**) pile up; **~ся** tower; clamber up. **громо́здкий** cumbersome.
гро́мче *comp of* **гро́мкий, гро́мко**
гроссме́йстер grand master.
гроте́скный grotesque.
гро́хот crash, din.
грохота́ть (-очу́, -о́чешь) *impf* (*pf* **про~**) crash; rumble; roar.
грош (-а́) half-copeck piece; farthing. **грошо́вый** cheap; trifling.
грубе́ть (-е́ю) *impf* (*pf* **за~, о~, по~**) grow coarse. **груби́ть** (-блю́) *impf* (*pf* **на~**) be rude. **грубия́н** boor. **гру́бость** rudeness; coarseness; rude remark. **гру́бый** (груб, -а́, -о) coarse; rude.
гру́да heap, pile.
груди́на breastbone. **груди́нка** brisket; breast. **грудно́й** breast, chest; pectoral. **грудь** (-и́ *or* -и, *instr* -ю, *loc* -и́; *pl* -и, -е́й) breast; chest.
груз load; burden.
грузи́н (*gen pl* -и́н), **грузи́нка** Georgian. **грузи́нский** Georgian.
грузи́ть (-ужу́, -у́зишь) *impf* (*pf* **за~, на~, по~**) load; **~ся** load, take on cargo.
Гру́зия Georgia.
гру́зный (-зен, -зна́, -о) weighty; bulky. **грузови́к** (*gen* -а́) lorry, truck. **грузово́й** goods, cargo. **гру́зчик** stevedore; loader.
грунт ground, soil; priming. **грунтова́ть** *impf* (*pf* **за~**) prime. **грунтово́й** soil, earth; priming.
гру́ппа group. **группирова́ть** *impf* (*pf* **с~**) group; **~ся** group, form groups. **группиро́вка** grouping. **группово́й** group; team.
грусти́ть (-ущу́) *impf* grieve, mourn; **+по**+*dat* pine for. **гру́стный** (-тен, -тна́, -о) sad. **грусть** sadness.
гру́ша pear.
гры́жа hernia, rupture.
грызть (-зу́, -зёшь; грыз) *impf* (*pf* **раз~**) gnaw; nag; **~ся** fight; squabble. **грызу́н** (-а́) rodent.
гряда́ (*pl* -ы, -а́м) ridge; bed; row, series; bank. **гря́дка** (flower-)bed.
грядý́щий approaching; future.
гря́зный (-зен, -зна́, -о) muddy; dirty. **грязь** (*loc* -и́) mud; dirt, filth; *pl* mud-cure.
гря́нуть (-ну) *pf* ring out, crash out; strike up.
губа́ (*pl* -ы, -а́м) lip; *pl* pincers.
губерна́тор governor. **губе́рния** province. **губе́рнский** provincial.
губи́тельный ruinous; pernicious. **губи́ть** (-блю́, -бишь) *impf* (*pf* **по~**) ruin; spoil.
гу́бка sponge.
губна́я пома́да lipstick.
гу́бчатый porous, spongy.
гуверна́нтка governess. **гувернёр** tutor.
гуде́ть (гужу́) *impf* (*pf* **про~**) hum; drone; buzz; hoot. **гудо́к**

(-дка́) hooter, siren, horn, whistle; hoot.
гудро́н tar. **гудро́нный** tar, tarred.
гул rumble. **гу́лкий** (-лок, -лка́, -о) resonant; booming.
гуля́нье (*gen pl* -ний) walk; fête; outdoor party. **гуля́ть** *impf* (*pf* **по~**) stroll; go for a walk; have a good time.
гуманита́рный of the humanities; humane. **гума́нный** humane.
гумно́ (*pl* -а, -мен *or* -мён, -ам) threshing-floor; barn.
гурт (-а́) herd; flock. **гуртовщи́к** (-а́) herdsman. **гурто́м** *adv* wholesale; en masse.
гуса́к (-а́) gander.
гу́сеница caterpillar; (caterpillar) track. **гу́сеничный** caterpillar.
гусёнок (-нка; *pl* -ся́та, -ся́т) gosling. **гуси́н|ый** goose; **~ая ко́жа** goose-flesh.
густе́ть (-е́ет) *impf* (*pf* **за~**) thicken. **густо́й** (густ, -а́, -о) thick, dense; rich. **густота́** thickness, density; richness.
гусы́ня goose. **гусь** (*pl* -и, -е́й) *m* goose. **гусько́м** *adv* in single file.
гутали́н shoe-polish.
гу́ща grounds, sediment; thicket; thick. **гу́ще** *comp of* **густо́й**.
ГЭС *abbr* (*of* **гидроэлектроста́нция**) hydro-electric power station.

Д

д. *abbr* (*of* **дере́вня**) village; (*of* **дом**) house.
да *conj* and; but.
да *partl* yes; really? well; *+3rd pers of v*, may, let; **да здра́вствует...!** long live ...!
дава́ть (даю́, -ёшь) *impf of* **дать; дава́й(те)** let us, let's; come on; **~ся** yield; come easy.
дави́ть (-влю́, -вишь) *impf* (*pf* **за~, по~, раз~, у~**) press; squeeze; crush; oppress; **~ся** choke; hang o.s. **да́вка** crushing; crush. **давле́ние** pressure.
да́вний ancient; of long standing. **давно́** *adv* long ago; for a long time. **да́вность** antiquity; remoteness; long standing. **давны́м-давно́** *adv* long long ago.
дади́м *etc.*: *see* **дать. даю́** *etc.*: *see* **дава́ть**
да́же *adv* even.
да́лее *adv* further; **и так ~** and so on, etc. **далёкий** (-ёк, -а́, -ёко́) distant, remote; far (-away). **далеко́** *adv* far; far off; by a long way; **~ за** long after; **~ не** far from. **даль** (*loc* -и́) distance. **дальне́йший** further. **да́льний** distant, remote; long; **~ Восто́к** the Far East. **дальнозо́ркий** long-sighted. **да́льность** distance; range. **да́льше** *adv* further; then, next; longer.
дам *etc.*: *see* **дать**
да́ма lady; partner; queen.
да́мба dike; dam.
да́мский ladies'.
Да́ния Denmark.
да́нные *sb pl* data; facts. **да́нный** given, present. **дань** tribute; debt.
данти́ст dentist.
дар (*pl* -ы́) gift. **дари́ть** (-рю́, -ришь) *impf* (*pf* **по~**) *+dat* give, make a present.
дарова́ние talent. **дарова́ть** *impf* & *pf* grant, confer. **даро-**

ви́тый gifted. **дарово́й** free (of charge). **да́ром** *adv* free, gratis; in vain.

да́та date.

да́тельный dative.

дати́ровать *impf* & *pf* date.

да́тский Danish. **датча́нин** (*pl* -а́не, -а́н), **датча́нка** Dane.

дать (дам, дашь, даст, дади́м; дал, -а́, да́ло́) *pf* (*impf* **дава́ть**) give; grant; let; ~ **взаймы́** lend; **~ся** *pf of* **дава́ться**

да́ча dacha; **на да́че** in the country. **да́чник** (holiday) visitor.

два *m* & *neut*, **две** *f* (двух, -ум, -умя́, -ух) two. **двадцатиле́тний** twenty-year; twenty-year-old. **двадца́т|ый** twentieth; **~ые го́ды** the twenties. **два́дцать** (-и́, *instr* -ью́) twenty. **два́жды** *adv* twice; double. **двена́дцатый** twelfth. **двена́дцать** twelve.

дверь (*loc* -и́; *pl* -и, -е́й, *instr* -я́ми *or* -ьми́) door.

две́сти (двухсо́т, -умста́м, -умяста́ми, -ухста́х) two hundred.

дви́гатель *m* engine, motor; motive force. **дви́гать** (-аю *or* -и́жу) *impf*, **дви́нуть** (-ну) *pf* move; set in motion; advance; **~ся** move; advance; get started. **движе́ние** movement; motion; exercise; traffic. **дви́жимость** chattels; personal property. **дви́жимый** movable; moved. **дви́жущий** motive.

двое́ (-и́х) two; two pairs.

двое- *in comb* two-; double(-). **двоебо́рье** biathlon. **~же́нец** (-нца) bigamist. **~жёнство** bigamy. **~то́чие** colon.

двои́ться *impf* divide in two; appear double; **у него́ двои́лось в глаза́х** he saw double. **двои́чный** binary. **дво́йка** two; figure 2; No. 2. **двойни́к** (-а́) double. **двойно́й** double, twofold; binary. **дво́йня** (*gen pl* -оен) twins. **дво́йственный** two-faced; dual.

двор (-а́) yard; courtyard; homestead; court. **дворе́ц** (-рца́) palace. **дво́рник** yard caretaker; windscreen-wiper. **дво́рня** servants. **дворо́вый** yard, courtyard; *sb* house-serf. **дворяни́н** (*pl* -я́не, -я́н), **дворя́нка** member of the nobility or gentry. **дворя́нство** nobility, gentry.

двою́родн|ый; **~ый брат**, **~ая сестра́** (first) cousin; **~ый дя́дя**, **~ая тётка** first cousin once removed. **двоя́кий** double; twofold.

дву-, **двух-** *in comb* two-; bi-; double. **двубо́ртный** double-breasted. **~ли́чный** two-faced. **~но́гий** two-legged. **~ру́чный** two-handed; two-handled. **~ру́шник** double-dealer. **~смы́сленный** ambiguous. **~(х)спа́льный** double. **~сторо́нний** double-sided; two-way; bilateral. **~хгоди́чный** two-year. **~хле́тний** two-year; two-year-old; biennial. **~хме́стный** two-seater; two-berth. **~хмото́рный** twin-engined. **~хсотле́тие** bicentenary. **~хсо́тый** two-hundredth. **~хта́ктный** two-stroke. **~хэта́жный** two-storey. **~язы́чный** bilingual.

деба́ты (-ов) *pl* debate.

де́бет debit. **дебетова́ть** *impf* & *pf* debit.

деби́т yield, output.

де́бри (-ей) *pl* jungle; thickets; the wilds.

дебю́т début.

дéва maid, maiden; Virgo.
девальвáция devaluation.
девáться *impf of* **дéться**
девúз motto; device.
девúца spinster; girl. **дéвич|ий** girlish, maidenly; **~ья фамúлия** maiden name. **дéвка** wench, lass; tart. **дéвочка** (little) girl. **дéвственник, -ица** virgin. **дéвственный** virgin; innocent. **дéвушка** girl. **девчóнка** girl.
девянóсто ninety. **девянóстый** ninetieth. **девя́тка** nine; figure 9; No. 9. **девятнáдцатый** nineteenth. **девятнáдцать** nineteen. **девя́тый** ninth. **дéвять** (-ú, *instr* -ью́) nine. **девятьсóт** (-тисóт, -тистáм, -тьюстáми, -тистáх) nine hundred.
дегенерúровать *impf & pf* degenerate.
дёготь (-гтя) tar.
дегустáция tasting.
дед grandfather; grandad. **дéдушка** grandfather; grandad.
деепричáстие adverbial participle.
дежу́рить *impf* be on duty. **дежу́рный** duty; on duty; *sb* person on duty. **дежу́рство** (being on) duty.
дезертúр deserter. **дезертúровать** *impf & pf* desert.
дезинфéкция disinfection. **дезинфицúровать** *impf & pf* disinfect.
дезодорáнт deodorant; air-freshener.
дезориентáция disorientation. **дезориентúровать** *impf & pf* disorient; **~ся** lose one's bearings.
дéйственный efficacious; effective. **дéйствие** action; operation; effect; act. **действúтельно** *adv* really; indeed. **действúтельность** reality; validity; efficacy. **действúтельный** actual; valid; efficacious; active. **дéйствовать** *impf* (*pf* **по~**) affect, have an effect; act; work. **дéйствующ|ий** active; in force; working; **~ее лицó** character; **~ие лúца** cast.
декабрúст Decembrist. **декáбрь** (-я́) *m* December. **декáбрьский** December.
декáда ten-day period *or* festival.
декáн dean. **деканáт** office of dean.
декламáция recitation, declamation. **декламúровать** *impf* (*pf* **про~**) recite, declaim.
декларáция declaration.
декоратúвный decorative. **декорáтор** scene-painter. **декорáция** scenery.
декрéт decree; maternity leave. **декрéтный óтпуск** maternity leave.
дéланный artificial, affected. **дéлать** *impf* (*pf* **с~**) make; do; **~ вид** pretend; **~ся** become; happen.
делегáт delegate. **делегáция** delegation; group.
делёж (-á), **делёжка** sharing; partition. **делéние** division; point (*on a scale*).
делéц (-льцá) smart operator.
деликáтный delicate.
делúмое *sb* dividend. **делúмость** divisibility. **делúтель** *m* divisor. **делúть** (-лю́, -лишь) *impf* (*pf* **по~, раз~**) divide; share; **~ шесть нá три** divide six by three; **~ся** divide; be divisible; +*instr* share.
дéло (*pl* -á) business; affair; matter; deed; thing; case;

в са́мом де́ле really, indeed; **~ в том** the point is; **как (ва́ши) дела́?** how are things?; **на са́мом де́ле** in actual fact; **по де́лу, по дела́м** on business. **делови́тый** business-like, efficient. **делово́й** business; business-like. **де́льный** efficient; sensible.
де́льта delta.
дельфи́н dolphin.
демаго́г demagogue.
демобилиза́ция demobilization. **демобилизова́ть** *impf & pf* demobilize.
демокра́т democrat. **демократиза́ция** democratization. **демократизи́ровать** *impf & pf* democratize. **демократи́ческий** democratic. **демокра́тия** democracy.
де́мон demon.
демонстра́ция demonstration. **демонстри́ровать** *impf & pf* demonstrate.
де́нежный monetary; money; **~ перево́д** money order.
де́нусь *etc.*: *see* **де́ться**
день (**дня**) *m* day; afternoon; **днём** in the afternoon; **на днях** the other day; one of these days; **че́рез ~** every other day.
де́ньги (**-нег, -ьга́м**) *pl* money.
департа́мент department.
депо́ *neut indecl* depot.
депорта́ция deportation. **депорти́ровать** *impf & pf* deport.
депута́т (*parl*) deputy; delegate.
дёргать *impf* (*pf* **дёрнуть**) pull, tug; pester; **~ся** twitch; jerk.
дереве́нский village; rural. **дере́вня** (*pl* **-и, -ве́нь, -вня́м**) village; the country. **де́рево** (*pl* **-е́вья, -ьев**) tree; wood. **деревя́нный** wood; wooden.
держа́ва power. **держа́ть** (**-жу́, -жишь**) *impf* hold; support; keep; **~ пари́** bet; **~ себя́** behave; **~ся** **+за+***acc* hold on to; be held up; hold o.s.; hold out; *+gen* keep to.
дерза́ние daring. **дерза́ть** *impf*, **дерзну́ть** (**-ну́, -нёшь**) *pf* dare. **де́рзкий** impudent; daring. **де́рзость** impertinence; daring.
дёрн turf.
дёрнуть(ся (**-ну(сь)** *pf of* **дёргать(ся**
деру́ *etc.*: *see* **драть**
деса́нт landing; landing force.
десе́рт dessert.
де́скать *partl indicating reported speech.*
десна́ (*pl* **дёсны, -сен**) gum.
де́спот despot.
десятиле́тие decade; tenth anniversary. **десятиле́тка** ten-year (*secondary*) school. **десятиле́тний** ten-year; ten-year-old. **десяти́чный** decimal. **деся́тка** ten; figure 10; No. 10; tenner (*10-rouble note*). **деся́ток** (**-тка**) ten; decade. **деся́тый** tenth. **де́сять** (**-и́,** *instr* **-ью́**) ten.
дета́ль detail; part, component. **дета́льный** detailed; minute.
детдо́м (*pl* **-а́**) children's home.
детекти́в detective story.
детёныш young animal; *pl* young. **де́ти** (**-те́й, -тям, -тьми́, -тях**) *pl* children. **детса́д** (*pl* **-ы́**) kindergarten.
де́тская *sb* nursery. **де́тский** children's; childish. **де́тство** childhood.
де́ться (**де́нусь**) *pf* (*impf* **дева́ться**) get to, disappear to.
дефе́кт defect.
дефи́с hyphen.

дефици́т deficit; shortage. **дефици́тный** scarce.
дешеве́ть (-е́ет) *impf* (*pf* **по~**) fall in price. **деше́вле** *comp of* **дёшево, дешёвый. дёшево** *adv* cheap, cheaply. **дешёвый** (дёшев, -а́, -о) cheap.
де́ятель *m*: **госуда́рственный ~** statesman; **обще́ственный ~** public figure. **де́ятельность** activity; work. **де́ятельный** active, energetic.
джаз jazz.
дже́мпер pullover.
джентльме́н gentleman.
джинсо́вый denim. **джи́нсы** (-ов) *pl* jeans.
джо́йстик joystick.
джу́нгли (-ей) *pl* jungle.
диабе́т diabetes. **диабе́тик** diabetic.
диа́гноз diagnosis.
диагона́ль diagonal
диагра́мма diagram.
диале́кт dialect. **диале́ктика** dialectics.
диало́г dialogue.
диа́метр diameter.
диапазо́н range; band.
диапозити́в slide.
диафра́гма diaphragm.
дива́н sofa; divan.
диверса́нт saboteur. **диве́рсия** sabotage.
диви́зия division.
ди́вный marvellous. **ди́во** wonder, marvel.
дида́ктика didactics.
дие́з (*mus*) sharp.
дие́та diet. **диети́ческий** dietetic.
диза́йн design. **диза́йнер** designer.
ди́зель *m* diesel; diesel engine. **ди́зельный** diesel.
дизентери́я dysentery.
дика́рь (-я́) *m*, **дика́рка** savage. **ди́кий** wild; savage; queer; preposterous. **дикобра́з** porcupine. **дикорасту́щий** wild. **ди́кость** wildness, savagery; absurdity.
дикта́нт dictation. **дикта́тор** dictator. **диктату́ра** dictatorship.
диктова́ть *impf* (*pf* **про~**) dictate. **ди́ктор** announcer. **ди́кция** diction.
диле́мма dilemma.
дилета́нт dilettante.
дина́мика dynamics.
динами́т dynamite.
динами́ческий dynamic.
дина́стия dynasty.
диноза́вр dinosaur.
дипло́м diploma; degree; degree work. **диплома́т** diplomat. **дипломати́ческий** diplomatic.
директи́ва instructions; directives. **дире́ктор** (*pl* **~а́**) director; principal. **дире́кция** management.
дирижа́бль *m* airship, dirigible.
дирижёр conductor. **дирижи́ровать** *impf* +*instr* conduct.
диск disc, disk; dial; discus.
ди́скант treble.
дисково́д disk drive.
дискоте́ка discotheque.
дискре́тный discrete.
дискримина́ция discrimination.
диску́ссия discussion, debate.
диспансе́р clinic.
диспе́тчер controller.
ди́спут public debate.
диссерта́ция dissertation, thesis.
дистанцио́нный distance, dis-

tant, remote; remote-control. **дистáнция** distance; range; region.

дисциплина discipline.

дитя́ (дитя́ти; *pl* дéти, -éй) *neut* child; baby.

дифтерия diphtheria.

дифтóнг diphthong.

диффамáция libel.

дичь game.

длинá length. **длинный** (-нен, -ннá, -о) long. **длительность** duration. **длительный** long, protracted. **длиться** *impf* (*pf* **про~**) last.

для *prep+gen* for; for the sake of; **~ тогó, чтóбы...** in order to.

дневáльный *sb* (*mil*) orderly. **дневник** (-á) diary, journal. **дневнóй** day; daily. **днём** *adv* in the day time; in the afternoon. **дни** *etc.*: *see* **день**

днище bottom.

ДНК *abbr* (*of* **дезоксирибонуклеиновая кислотá**) DNA.

дно (дна; *pl* дóнья, -ьев) bottom.

до *prep+gen* (up) to; as far as; until; before; to the point of; **до нáшей э́ры** BC; **до сих пор** till now; **до тех пор** till then, before; **до тогó, как** before; **до тогó, что** to such an extent that, until; **мне не до** I'm not in the mood for.

добáвить (-влю) *pf*, **добавля́ть** *impf* (+*acc or gen*) add. **добáвка** addition; second helping. **добавлéние** addition; supplement; extra. **добáвочный** additional.

добегáть *impf*, **добежáть** (-егý) *pf* **+до+***gen* run to, as far as; reach.

добивáть *impf*, **добить** (-бью, -бьёшь) *pf* finish (off); **~ся** +*gen* get, obtain; **~ся своегó** get one's way.

добирáться *impf of* **добрáться**

дóблесть valour.

добрáться (-берýсь, -ёшься; -áлся, -лáсь, -áлóсь) *pf* (*impf* **добирáться**) **+до+***gen* get to, reach.

добрó good; **~ пожáловать!** welcome!; **э́то не к добрý** it is a bad sign.

добро- *in comb* good-, well-. **доброво́лец** (-льца) volunteer. **~вóльно** *adv* voluntarily. **~вóльный** voluntary. **~дéтель** virtue. **~дéтельный** virtuous. **~дýшие** good nature. **~дýшный** good-natured. **~желáтельный** benevolent. **~кáчественный** of good quality; benign. **~сóвестный** conscientious.

добротá goodness, kindness.

добрóтный of good quality.

дóбрый (добр, -á, -о, дóбры́) good; kind; **бýдьте добры́** +*imper* please; would you be kind enough to.

добывáть *impf*, **добыть** (-бýду; дóбыл, -á, -о) *pf* get, obtain, procure; mine. **добы́ча** output; mining; booty.

добью́ *etc.*: *see* **добить. доведý** *etc.*: *see* **довести**

довезти (-езý, -езёшь; -вёз, -лá) *pf* (*impf* **довозить**) take (to), carry (to), drive (to).

довéренность warrant; power of attorney. **довéренный** trusted; *sb* agent, proxy. **довéрие** trust, confidence. **довéрить** *pf* (*impf* **доверя́ть**) entrust; **~ся** +*dat* trust in; confide in.

дóверху *adv* to the top.

довéрчивый trustful, credu-

lous. **доверя́ть** *impf of* **довéрить**; (+*dat*) to trust.
довéсок (-ска) makeweight.
довести́ (-едý, -едёшь; -вёл, -á) *pf*, **доводи́ть** (-ожý, -óдишь) *impf* lead, take (to); bring, drive (to). **дóвод** argument, reason.
довоéнный pre-war.
довози́ть (-ожý, -óзишь) *impf of* **довезти́**
довóльно *adv* enough; quite, fairly. **довóльный** satisfied; pleased. **довóльство** contentment. **довóльствоваться** *impf* (*pf* **у~**) be content.
догада́ться *pf*, **догáдываться** *impf* guess; suspect. **догáдка** surmise, conjecture. **догáдливый** quick-witted.
дóгма dogma.
догна́ть (-гоню́, -гóнишь; -гнáл, -á, -о) *pf* (*impf* **догоня́ть**) catch up (with).
договáриваться *impf*, **договори́ться** *pf* come to an agreement; arrange. **дóговóр** (*pl* -ы *or* -á, -óв) agreement; contract; treaty. **договóрный** contractual; agreed.
догоня́ть *impf of* **догна́ть**
догорáть *impf*, **догорéть** (-ри́т) *pf* burn out, burn down.
доéду *etc.*: *see* **доéхать. доезжáть** *impf of* **доéхать**
доéхать (-éду) *pf* (*impf* **доезжáть**) +**до**+*gen* reach, arrive at.
дождáться (-дýсь, -дёшься; -áлся, -лáсь, -áлóсь) *pf* +*gen* wait for, wait until.
дождеви́к (-á) raincoat. **дождевóй** rain(y). **дождли́вый** rainy. **дождь** (-я́) *m* rain; **~ идёт** it is raining.
доживáть *impf*, **дожи́ть** (-ивý, -ивёшь; дóжил, -á, -о) *pf* live out; spend.
дожидáться *impf* +*gen* wait for.
дóза dose.
дозвóлить *pf*, **дозволя́ть** *impf* permit.
дозвони́ться *pf* get through, reach by telephone.
дозóр patrol.
дозревáть *impf*, **дозрéть** (-éет) *pf* ripen.
доистори́ческий prehistoric.
дои́ть *impf* (*pf* **по~**) milk.
дойти́ (дойдý, -дёшь; дошёл, -шлá) *pf* (*impf* **доходи́ть**) +**до**+*gen* reach; get through to.
док dock.
доказáтельный conclusive. **доказáтельство** proof, evidence. **доказáть** (-ажý, -áжешь) *pf*, **докáзывать** *impf* demonstrate, prove.
докати́ться (-ачýсь, -áтишься) *pf*, **докáтываться** *impf* roll; boom; +**до**+*gen* sink into.
доклáд report; lecture. **доклáдная (запи́ска)** report; memo. **доклáдчик** speaker, lecturer. **доклáдывать** *impf of* **доложи́ть**
дóкрасна́ *adv* to red heat; to redness.
дóктор (*pl* -á) doctor. **дóкторский** doctoral. **дóкторша** woman doctor; doctor's wife.
доктри́на doctrine.
докумéнт document; deed. **документáльный** documentary. **документáция** documentation; documents.
долби́ть (-блю́) *impf* hollow; chisel; repeat; swot up.
долг (*loc* -ý; *pl* -и́) duty; debt; **взять в ~** borrow; **дать в ~** lend.
дóлгий (дóлог, -лгá, -о) long.

до́лго *adv* long, (for) a long time. **долгове́чный** lasting; durable. **долгожда́нный** long-awaited. **долгоигра́ющая пласти́нка** LP.

долголе́тие longevity. **долголе́тний** of many years; long-standing. **долгосро́чный** long-term.

долгота́ (*pl* -ы) length; longitude.

долево́й lengthwise. **до́лее** *adv* longer.

должа́ть *impf* (*pf* **за~**) borrow.

до́лжен (-жна́) *predic*+*dat* in debt to; +*inf* obliged, bound; likely; must, have to, ought to; **должно́ быть** probably. **должни́к** (-а́), **-ни́ца** debtor. **до́лжное** *sb* due. **должностно́й** official. **до́лжность** (*gen pl* -е́й) post, office; duties. **до́лжный** due, fitting.

доли́на valley.

до́ллар dollar.

доложи́ть[1] (-ожу́, -о́жишь) *pf* (*impf* **докла́дывать**) add.

доложи́ть[2] (-ожу́, -о́жишь) *pf* (*impf* **докла́дывать**) +*acc* or **о**+*prep* report; announce.

доло́й *adv* away, off; +*acc* down with!

долото́ (*pl* -а) chisel.

до́лька segment; clove.

до́льше *adv* longer.

до́ля (*gen pl* -е́й) portion; share; lot, fate.

дом (*pl* -а́) house; home. **до́ма** *adv* at home. **дома́шн|ий** house; home; domestic; home-made; **~яя хозя́йка** housewife.

до́менн|ый blast-furnace; **~ая печь** blast-furnace.

домини́ровать *impf* dominate, predominate.

домкра́т jack.

до́мна blast-furnace.

домовладе́лец (-льца), **-лица** house-owner; landlord. **домово́дство** housekeeping; domestic science. **домо́вый** house; household; housing.

домога́тельство solicitation; bid. **домога́ться** *impf* +*gen* solicit, bid for.

домо́й *adv* home, homewards.

домохозя́йка housewife. **домрабо́тница** domestic servant, maid.

домофо́н entryphone (*propr*).

доне́льзя *adv* in the extreme.

донесе́ние dispatch, report. **донести́** (-су́, -сёшь; -нёс, -сла́) *pf* (*impf* **доноси́ть**) report, announce; +*dat* inform; +**на**+*acc* inform against; **~сь** be heard; +**до**+*gen* reach.

до́низу *adv* to the bottom; **све́рху ~** from top to bottom.

до́нор donor.

доно́с denunciation, information. **доноси́ть(ся** (-ношу́(сь, -но́сишь(ся) *impf of* **донести́(сь**

доно́счик informer.

донско́й Don.

доны́не *adv* hitherto.

до́нья *etc.*: *see* **дно**

до н.э. *abbr* (*of* **до на́шей э́ры**) BC.

допла́та additional payment, excess fare. **доплати́ть** (-ачу́, -а́тишь) *pf*, **допла́чивать** *impf* pay in addition; pay the rest.

допо́длинно *adv* for certain. **допо́длинный** authentic, genuine.

дополне́ние supplement, addition; (*gram*) object. **дополни́тельно** *adv* in addition. **дополни́тельный** supplementary, additional. **допо́лнить** *pf*, **дополня́ть** *impf* supplement.

допрашивать *impf*, **допросить** (-ошу́, -о́сишь) *pf* interrogate. **допро́с** interrogation.
до́пуск right of entry, admittance. **допуска́ть** *impf*, **допусти́ть** (-ущу́, -у́стишь) *pf* admit; permit; tolerate; suppose. **допусти́мый** permissible, acceptable. **допуще́ние** assumption.
дореволюцио́нный pre-revolutionary.
доро́га road; way; journey; route; **по доро́ге** on the way.
до́рого *adv* dear, dearly. **дорогови́зна** high prices. **дорого́й** (до́рог, -а́, -о) dear.
доро́дный portly.
дорожа́ть *impf* (*pf* **вз~, по~**) rise in price, go up. **доро́же** *comp of* **до́рого, дорого́й. дорожи́ть** (-жу́) *impf* +*instr* value.
доро́жка path; track; lane; runway; strip, runner, stair-carpet. **доро́жный** road; highway; travelling.
доса́да annoyance. **досади́ть** (-ажу́) *pf*, **досажда́ть** *impf* +*dat* annoy. **доса́дный** annoying. **доса́довать** be annoyed (**на**+*acc* with).
доска́ (*acc* до́ску; *pl* -и, -со́к, -ска́м) board; slab; plaque.
досло́вный literal; word-for-word.
досмо́тр inspection.
доспе́хи *pl* armour.
досро́чный ahead of time, early.
достава́ть(ся (-таю́(сь, -ёшь(ся) *impf of* **доста́ть(ся**
доста́вить (-влю) *pf*, **доставля́ть** *impf* deliver; supply; cause, give. **доста́вка** delivery.
доста́ну *etc.*: *see* **доста́ть**
доста́ток (-тка) sufficiency; prosperity. **доста́точно** *adv* enough, sufficiently. **доста́точный** sufficient; adequate.
доста́ть (-а́ну) *pf* (*impf* **достава́ть**) take (out); get, obtain; +*gen or* **до**+*gen* touch; reach; *impers* suffice; **~ся** +*dat* be inherited by; fall to the lot of; **ему́ доста́нется** he'll catch it.
достига́ть *impf*, **дости́гнуть, дости́чь** (-и́гну; -сти́г) *pf* +*gen* reach, achieve; +*gen or* **до**+*gen* reach. **достиже́ние** achievement.
достове́рный reliable, trustworthy; authentic.
досто́инство dignity; merit; value. **досто́йный** deserved; suitable; worthy; +*gen* worthy of.
достопримеча́тельность sight, notable place.
достоя́ние property.
до́ступ access. **досту́пный** accessible; approachable; reasonable; available.
досу́г leisure, (spare) time. **досу́жий** leisure; idle.
до́сыта *adv* to satiety.
досье́ *neut indecl* dossier.
досяга́емый attainable.
дота́ция grant, subsidy.
дотла́ utterly; to the ground.
дотра́гиваться *impf*, **дотро́нуться** (-нусь) *pf* +**до**+*gen* touch.
дотя́гивать *impf*, **дотяну́ть** (-яну́, -я́нешь) *pf* draw, drag, stretch out; hold out; live; put off; **~ся** stretch, reach; drag on.
до́хлый dead; sickly. **до́хнуть**[1] (-нет; дох) (*pf* **из~, по~, с~**) die; kick the bucket.
дохну́ть[2] (-ну́, -нёшь) *pf* draw a breath.
дохо́д income; revenue. **дохо-**

ди́ть (-ожу́, -о́дишь) *impf of* **дойти́**. **дохо́дный** profitable. **дохо́дчивый** intelligible.
доце́нт reader, senior lecturer.
до́чиста *adv* clean; completely.
до́чка daughter. **дочь** (-чери, *instr* -черью; *pl* -чери, -черéй, *instr* -черьми́) daughter.
дошёл *etc.*: *see* **дойти́**
дошко́льник, -ница child under school age. **дошко́льный** pre-school.
доща́тый plank, board. **доще́чка** small plank, board; plaque.
доя́рка milkmaid.
драгоце́нность jewel; treasure; *pl* jewellery; valuables. **драгоце́нный** precious.
дразни́ть (-ню́, -нишь) *impf* tease.
дра́ка fight.
драко́н dragon.
дра́ма drama. **драмати́ческий** dramatic. **драмату́рг** playwright. **драматурги́я** dramatic art; plays.
драп thick woollen cloth.
драпиро́вка draping; curtain; hangings. **драпиро́вщик** upholsterer.
драть (деру́, -рёшь; драл, -á, -о) *impf* (*pf* **вы́~**, **за~**, **со~**) tear (up); irritate; make off; flog; **~ся** fight.
дре́безги *pl*; **в ~** to smithereens. **дребезжа́ть** (-жи́т) *impf* jingle, tinkle.
древеси́на wood; timber. **древе́сный** wood; **~ у́голь** charcoal.
дре́вко (*pl* -и, -ов) pole, staff; shaft.
древнегре́ческий ancient Greek. **древнеевре́йский** Hebrew. **древнеру́сский** Old Russian. **дре́вний** ancient; aged. **дре́вность** antiquity.
дрейф drift; leeway. **дрейфова́ть** *impf* drift.
дрема́ть (-млю́, -млешь) *impf* doze; slumber. **дремо́та** drowsiness.
дрему́чий dense.
дрессиро́ванный trained; performing. **дрессирова́ть** *impf* (*pf* **вы́~**) train; school. **дрессиро́вка** training. **дрессиро́вщик** trainer.
дроби́ть (-блю́) *impf* (*pf* **раз~**) break up, smash; crush; **~ся** break to pieces, smash. **дробови́к** (-á) shot-gun. **дробь** (small) shot; drumming; fraction. **дро́бный** fractional.
дрова́ (дров) *pl* firewood.
дро́гнуть (-ну) *pf*, **дрожа́ть** (-жу́) *impf* tremble; shiver; quiver.
дро́жжи (-е́й) *pl* yeast.
дрожь shivering, trembling.
дрозд (-á) thrush; **чёрный ~** blackbird.
дро́ссель *m* throttle, choke.
дро́тик javelin, dart.
друг[1] (*pl* -узья́, -зе́й) friend; boyfriend. **друг**[2]: **~ дру́га (дру́гу)** each other, one another. **друго́й** other, another; different; **на ~ день** (the) next day. **дру́жба** friendship. **дружелю́бный, дру́жеский, дру́жественный** friendly. **дружи́ть** (-жу́, -у́жишь) *impf* be friends. **дру́жный** (-жен, -жнá, -о) friendly; harmonious; simultaneous, general; concerted.
дря́блый (дрябл, -á, -о) flabby.
дря́зги (-зг) *pl* squabbles.
дрянно́й worthless; good-for-nothing. **дрянь** rubbish.

дряхле́ть (-е́ю) *impf* (*pf* **о~**) become decrepit. **дря́хлый** (-хл, -ла́, -о) decrepit, senile.

дуб (*pl* -ы́) oak; blockhead. **дуби́на** club, cudgel; blockhead. **дуби́нка** truncheon, baton.

дублёнка sheepskin coat.

дублёр understudy. **дублика́т** duplicate. **дубли́ровать** duplicate; understudy; dub.

дубо́вый oak; coarse; clumsy.

дуга́ (*pl* -и) arc; arch.

ду́дка pipe, fife.

ду́ло muzzle; barrel.

ду́ма thought; Duma (*lower house of Russian parliament*). **ду́мать** *impf* (*pf* **по~**) think; +*inf* think of, intend. **ду́маться** *impf* (*impers* +*dat*) seem.

дунове́ние puff, breath.

дупло́ (*pl* -а, -пел) hollow; hole; cavity.

ду́ра, дура́к (-а́) fool. **дура́чить** (-чу) *impf* (*pf* **о~**) fool, dupe; **~ся** play the fool.

дуре́ть (-е́ю) *impf* (*pf* **о~**) grow stupid.

дурма́н narcotic; intoxicant. **дурма́нить** *impf* (*pf* **о~**) stupefy.

дурно́й (-рен, -рна́, -о) bad, evil; ugly; **мне ду́рно** I feel faint, sick. **дурнота́** faintness; nausea.

ду́тый hollow; inflated. **дуть** (ду́ю) *impf* (*pf* **по~**) blow; **ду́ет** there is a draught. **ду́ться** (ду́юсь) *impf* pout; sulk.

дух spirit; spirits; heart; mind; breath; ghost; smell; **в ~е** in a good mood; **не в моём ~е** not to my taste; **ни слу́ху ни ~у** no news, not a word. **духи́** (-о́в) *pl* scent, perfume. **Ду́хов день** Whit Monday. **духове́нство** clergy. **духови́дец** (-дца) clairvoyant; medium. **духо́вка** oven.

духо́вный spiritual; ecclesiastical. **духово́й** wind. **духота́** stuffiness, closeness.

душ shower(-bath).

душа́ (*acc* -у; *pl* -и) soul; heart; feeling; spirit; inspiration; **в душе́** inwardly; at heart; **от всей души́** with all one's heart.

душева́я *sb* shower-room.

душевнобольно́й mentally ill, insane; *sb* mental patient; lunatic. **душе́вный** mental; sincere, cordial.

души́стый fragrant; **~ горо́шек** sweet pea(s).

души́ть (-шу́, -шишь) *impf* (*pf* **за~**) strangle; stifle, smother.

души́ться (-шу́сь, -шишься) *impf* (*pf* **на~**) use, put on, perfume.

ду́шный (-шен, -шна́, -о) stuffy, close.

дуэ́ль duel.

дуэ́т duet.

ды́бом *adv* on end; **у меня́ во́лосы вста́ли ~** my hair stood on end. **дыбы́: станови́ться на ~** rear; resist.

дым (*loc* -у́; *pl* -ы́) smoke. **дыми́ть** (-млю́) *impf* (*pf* **на~**) smoke; **~ся** smoke; billow. **ды́мка** haze. **ды́мный** smoky. **дымов|о́й: ~а́я труба́** flue, chimney. **дымо́к** (-мка́) puff of smoke. **дымохо́д** flue.

ды́ня melon.

дыра́ (*pl* -ы), **ды́рка** (*gen pl* -рок) hole; gap.

дыха́ние breathing; breath. **дыха́тельн|ый** respiratory; breathing; **~ое го́рло** windpipe. **дыша́ть** (-шу́, -шишь) *impf* breathe.

дья́вол devil. **дья́вольский** devilish, diabolical.

дья́кон (*pl* -а́) deacon.

дюжина dozen.
дюйм inch.
дюна dune.
дядя (*gen pl* -ей) *m* uncle.
дятел (-тла) woodpecker.

Е

евангелие gospel; the Gospels. **евангелический** evangelical.
еврей, еврейка Jew; Hebrew. **еврейский** Jewish.
евро *neut indecl* euro
Европа Europe. **европеец** (-ейца) European. **европейский** European.
Египет Egypt. **египетский** Egyptian. **египтянин** (*pl* -яне, -ян), **египтянка** Egyptian.
его *see* **он, оно**; *pron* his; its.
еда food; meal.
едва *adv* & *conj* hardly; just; scarcely; ~ **ли** hardly; ~ **(ли) не** almost, all but.
едим *etc.*: *see* **есть**[1]
единение unity. **единица** (figure) one; unity; unit; individual. **единичный** single; individual.
едино- *in comb* mono-, uni-; one; co-. **единобрачие** monogamy. **~властие** autocracy. **~временно** *adv* only once; simultaneously. **~гласие, ~душие** unanimity. **~гласный, ~душный** unanimous. **~кровный брат** half-brother. **~мыслие** like-mindedness; agreement. **~мышленник** like-minded person. **~утробный брат** half-brother.
единственно *adv* only, solely. **единственный** only, sole. **единство** unity. **единый** one; single; united.
едкий (едок, едка, -о) caustic; pungent.
едок (-а) mouth, head; eater.
еду *etc.*: *see* **ехать**
её *see* **она**; *pron* her, hers; its.
ёж (ежа) hedgehog.
еже- *in comb* every; -ly. **ежегодник** annual, year-book. **~годный** annual. **~дневный** daily. **~месячник, ~месячный** monthly. **~недельник, ~недельный** weekly.
ежевика (*no pl*; *usu collect*) blackberry; blackberries; blackberry bush.
ежели *conj* if.
ёжиться (ёжусь) *impf* (*pf* **съ~**) huddle up; shrink away.
езда ride, riding; drive, driving; journey. **ездить** (езжу) *impf* go; ride, drive; ~ **верхом** ride. **ездок** (-а) rider.
ей *see* **она**
ей-богу *int* really! truly!
ел *etc.*: *see* **есть**[1]
еле *adv* scarcely; only just. **еле-еле** *emphatic variant of* **еле**
ёлка fir-tree, spruce; Christmas tree. **ёлочка** herring-bone pattern. **ёлочный** Christmas-tree. **ель** fir-tree; spruce.
ем *etc.*: *see* **есть**[1]
ёмкий capacious. **ёмкость** capacity.
ему *see* **он, оно**
епископ bishop.
ересь heresy. **еретик** (-а) heretic. **еретический** heretical.
ёрзать *impf* fidget.
ерошить (-шу) *impf* (*pf* **взъ~**) ruffle, rumple.
ерунда nonsense.
если *conj* if; ~ **бы** if only; ~ **бы не** but for, if it were not for; ~ **не** unless.

ест *see* **есть**[1]

естéственно *adv* naturally. **естéственный** natural. **естествó** nature; essence. **естествознáние** (natural) science.

есть[1] (ем, ешь, ест, едим; ел) *impf* (*pf* **съ~**) eat; corrode, eat away.

есть[2] *see* **быть**; is, are; there is, there are; **у меня ~** I have.

ефрéйтор lance-corporal.

éхать (éду) *impf* (*pf* **по~**) go; ride, drive; travel; **~ верхóм** ride.

ехи́дный malicious, spiteful.

ешь *see* **есть**[1]

ещё *adv* still; yet; (some) more; any more; yet, further; again; +*comp* still, even; **всё ~** still; **~ бы!** of course! and how!; **~ не, нет ~** not yet; **~ раз** once more; **кто ~?** who else? **покá ~** for the time being. **что ~?** what else?

éю *see* **онá**

Ж

ж *conj*: *see* **же**

жáба toad.

жáбра (*gen pl* -бр) gill.

жáворонок (-нка) lark.

жáдничать *impf* be greedy; be mean. **жáдность** greed; meanness. **жáдный** (-ден, -днá, -о) greedy; avid; mean.

жáжда thirst; +*gen* thirst, craving for. **жáждать** (-ду) *impf* thirst, yearn.

жакéт, жакéтка jacket.

жалéть (-éю) *impf* (*pf* **по~**) pity, feel sorry for; regret; +*acc or gen* grudge.

жáлить *impf* (*pf* **у~**) sting, bite.

жáлкий (-лок, -лкá, -о) pitiful.

жáлко *predic*: *see* **жаль**

жáло sting.

жáлоба complaint. **жáлобный** plaintive.

жáлованье salary. **жáловать** *impf* (*pf* **по~**) +*acc or dat of person, instr or acc of thing* grant, bestow on; **~ся** complain (**на**+*acc* of, about).

жáлостливый compassionate. **жáлостный** piteous; compassionate. **жáлость** pity. **жаль, жáлко** *predic, impers* (it is) a pity; +*dat* it grieves; +*gen* grudge; **как ~** what a pity; **мне ~ егó** I'm sorry for him.

жалюзи́ *neut indecl* Venetian blind.

жанр genre.

жар (*loc* -ý) heat; heat of the day; fever; (high) temperature; ardour. **жарá** heat; hot weather.

жаргóн slang.

жáреный roast; grilled; fried. **жáрить** *impf* (*pf* **за~, из~**) roast; grill; fry; scorch, burn; **~ся** roast, fry. **жáрк|ий** (-рок, -ркá, -о) hot; passionate; **-óе** *sb* roast (meat). **жарóвня** (*gen pl* -вен) brazier. **жар-пти́ца** Firebird. **жáрче** *comp of* **жáркий**

жáтва harvest. **жать**[1] (жну, жнёшь) *impf* (*pf* **с~**) reap, cut.

жать[2] (жму, жмёшь) *impf* press, squeeze; pinch; oppress.

жвáчка chewing, rumination; cud; chewing-gum. **жвáчн|ый** ruminant; **~ое** *sb* ruminant.

жгу *etc.*: *see* **жечь**

жгут (-á) plait; tourniquet.

жгýчий burning. **жёг** *etc.*: *see* **жечь**

ждать (жду, ждёшь; -ал, -á, -о) *impf* +*gen* wait (for); expect.

же, ж *conj* but; and; however; also; *partl* giving emphasis or expressing identity; **мне же кáжется** it seems to me, however; **сегóдня же** this very day; **что же ты дéлаешь?** what on earth are you doing?

жевáтельная резúнка chewing-gum. **жевáть** (жую, жуёшь) *impf* chew; ruminate.

жезл (-á) rod; staff.

желáние wish, desire. **желáнный** longed-for; beloved. **желáтельный** desirable; advisable. **желáть** *impf* (*pf* **по~**) +*gen* wish for, desire; want.

желé *neut indecl* jelly.

железá (*pl* жéлезы, -лёз, -зáм) gland; *pl* tonsils.

железнодорóжник railwayman. **железнодорóжный** railway. **желéзн|ый** iron; **~ая дорóга** railway. **желéзо** iron.

железобетóн reinforced concrete.

жёлоб (*pl* -á) gutter. **желобóк** (-бкá) groove, channel, flute.

желтéть (-éю) *impf* (*pf* **по~**) turn yellow; be yellow. **желтóк** (-ткá) yolk. **желтýха** jaundice. **жёлтый** (жёлт, -á, жёлтó) yellow.

желýдок (-дка) stomach. **желýдочный** stomach; gastric.

жёлудь (*gen pl* -éй) *m* acorn.

жёлчный bilious; gall; irritable. **жёлчь** bile, gall.

жемáниться *impf* mince, put on airs. **жемáнный** mincing, affected. **жемáнство** affectedness.

жéмчуг (*pl* -á) pearl(s). **жемчýжина** pearl. **жемчýжный** pear(ly).

женá (*pl* жёны) wife. **женáтый** married.

женúть (-ню́, -нишь) *impf* & *pf* (*pf also* **по~**) marry. **женúтьба** marriage. **женúться** (-нюсь, -нишься) *impf* & *pf* (+**на**+*prep*) marry, get married (to). **женúх** (-á) fiancé; bridegroom. **жéнский** woman's; feminine; female. **жéнственный** womanly, feminine. **жéнщина** woman.

жердь (*gen pl* -éй) pole; stake.

жеребёнок (-нка; *pl* -бя́та, -бя́т) foal. **жеребéц** (-бцá) stallion.

жеребьёвка casting of lots.

жерлó (*pl* -а) muzzle; crater.

жёрнов (*pl* -á, -óв) millstone.

жéртва sacrifice; victim. **жéртвенный** sacrificial. **жéртвовать** *impf* (*pf* **по~**) present, make a donation (of); +*instr* sacrifice.

жест gesture. **жестикулúровать** *impf* gesticulate.

жёсткий (-ток, -ткá, -о) hard, tough; rigid, strict; **~ диск** (*comput*) hard disk.

жестóкий (-тóк, -á, -о) cruel; severe. **жестóкость** cruelty.

жесть tin(-plate). **жестянóй** tin.

жетóн medal; counter; token.

жечь (жгу, жжёшь; жёг, жгла) *impf* (*pf* **с~**) burn; **~ся** burn, sting; burn o.s.

живúтельный invigorating.

жúвность poultry, fowl.

жив|óй (жив, -á, -о) living, alive; lively; vivid; brisk; animated; bright; **на ~ýю нúтку** hastily, anyhow; **шить на ~ýю нúтку** tack. **живопúсец** (-сца) painter. **живопúсный** picturesque. **жúвопись** painting. **жúвость** liveliness.

живóт (-á) abdomen; stomach. **животновóдство** animal husbandry. **живóтное** *sb* animal. **живóтный** animal.

живý *etc.*: *see* **жить**. **живýчий**

hardy. **живьём** *adv* alive.
жи́дк|ий (-док, -дка́, -о) liquid; watery; weak; sparse; **~ий криста́лл** liquid crystal. **жи́дкость** liquid, fluid; wateriness, weakness. **жи́жа** sludge; slush; liquid. **жи́же** *comp of* **жи́дкий**
жи́зненный life, of life; vital; living; **~ у́ровень** standard of living. **жизнеописа́ние** biography. **жизнера́достный** cheerful. **жизнеспосо́бный** capable of living; viable. **жизнь** life.
жи́ла vein; tendon, sinew.
жиле́т, жиле́тка waistcoat.
жиле́ц (-льца́), **жили́ца** lodger; tenant; inhabitant.
жили́ще dwelling, abode. **жили́щный** housing; living.
жи́лка vein; fibre; streak.
жил|о́й dwelling; habitable; **~о́й дом** dwelling house; block of flats; **~а́я пло́щадь, жилпло́щадь** floor-space; housing, accommodation. **жильё** habitation; dwelling.
жир (*loc* -у́; *pl* -ы) fat; grease. **жире́ть** (-ре́ю) *impf* (*pf* **о~, раз~**) grow fat. **жи́рный** (-рен, -рна́, -о) fatty; greasy; rich. **жирово́й** fatty; fat.
жира́ф giraffe.
жите́йский worldly; everyday. **жи́тель** *m* inhabitant; dweller. **жи́тельство** residence. **жи́тница** granary. **жи́то** corn, cereal. **жить** (живу́, -вёшь; жил, -а́, -о) *impf* live. **житьё** life; existence; habitation.
жму *etc.*: *see* **жать**[2]
жму́риться *impf* (*pf* **за~**) screw up one's eyes, frown.
жнивьё (*pl* -нья, -ньев) stubble (-field). **жну** *etc.*: *see* **жать**[1]
жоке́й jockey.
жонглёр juggler.
жрать (жру, жрёшь; -ал, -а́, -о) guzzle.
жре́бий lot; fate, destiny; **~ бро́шен** the die is cast.
жрец priest. **жри́ца** priestess.
жужжа́ть (-жжу́) hum, buzz, drone; whiz(z).
жук (-а́) beetle.
жу́лик petty thief; cheat. **жу́льничать** *impf* (*pf* **с~**) cheat.
жура́вль (-я́) *m* crane.
жури́ть *impf* reprove.
журна́л magazine, periodical. **журнали́ст** journalist. **журнали́стика** journalism.
журча́ние babble; murmur. **журча́ть** (-чи́т) *impf* babble, murmur.
жу́ткий (-ток, -тка́, -о) uncanny; terrible, terrifying. **жу́тко** *adv* terrifyingly; terribly, awfully.
жую́ *etc.*: *see* **жева́ть**
жюри́ *neut indecl* judges.

З

за *prep* **I.** +*acc* (*indicating motion or action*) *or instr* (*indicating rest or state*) behind; beyond; across, the other side of; at; to; **за́ го́род, за́ го́родом** out of town; **за рубежо́м** abroad; **сесть за роя́ль** sit down at the piano; **сиде́ть за роя́лем** be at the piano; **за́ угол, за угло́м** round the corner. **II.** +*acc* after; over; during, in the space of; by; for; to; **за ва́ше здоро́вье!** your health!; **вести́ за́ руку** lead by the hand; **далеко́ за́ по́лночь** long after midnight; **за два дня до**+*gen* two days before; **за́ три киломе́тра от дере́вни** three kilometres from the village; **пла-**

тúть за билéт pay for a ticket; **за послéднее врéмя** lately. III. +*instr* after; for; because of; at, during; **год за гóдом** year after year; **идтú за молокóм** go for milk; **за обéдом** at dinner.

забáва amusement; game; fun. **забавля́ть** *impf* amuse; **~ся** amuse o.s. **забáвный** amusing, funny.

забастовáть *pf* strike; go on strike. **забастóвка** strike. **забастóвщик** striker.

забвéние oblivion.

забéг heat, race. **забегáть** *impf*, **забежáть** (-егý) *pf* run up; +к+*dat* drop in on; **~ вперёд** run ahead; anticipate.

за|берéменеть (-ею) *pf* become pregnant.

заберý *etc.*: *see* **забрáть**

забивáние jamming. **забивáть(ся** *impf of* **забúть(ся**[1]

забинтовáть *pf*, **забинтóвывать** *impf* bandage.

забирáть(ся *impf of* **забрáть(ся**

забúтый downtrodden. **забúть**[1] (-бью, -бьёшь) *pf* (*impf* **забивáть**) drive in, hammer in; score; seal, block up; obstruct; choke; jam; cram; beat up; beat; **~ся** hide, take refuge; become cluttered *or* clogged; +в+*acc* get into, penetrate. **за|бúть(ся**[2] *pf* begin to beat. **забия́ка** *m* & *f* squabbler; bully.

заблаговрéменно *adv* in good time; well in advance. **заблаговрéменный** timely.

заблестéть (-ещý, -естúшь *or* -éщешь) *pf* begin to shine, glitter, glow.

заблудúться (-ужýсь, -ýдишься) *pf* get lost. **заблýдший** lost, stray. **заблуждáться** *impf* be mistaken. **заблуждéние** error; delusion.

забóй (pit-)face.

заболевáемость sickness rate. **заболевáние** sickness, illness; falling ill. **заболевáть**[1] *impf*, **заболéть**[1](-éю) *pf* fall ill; +*instr* go down with. **заболевáть**[2] *impf*, **заболéть**[2] (-лúт) *pf* (begin to) ache, hurt.

забóр[1] fence.

забóр[2] taking away; obtaining on credit.

забóта concern; care; trouble(s). **забóтить** (-óчу) *impf* (*pf* **о~**) trouble, worry; **~ся** *impf* (*pf* **по~**) worry; take care (**о**+*prep* of); take trouble; care. **забóтливый** solicitous, thoughtful.

за|браковáть *pf*.

забрáсывать *impf of* **забросáть, забрóсить**

забрáть (-берý, -берёшь; -áл, -á, -о) *pf* (*impf* **забирáть**) take; take away; seize; appropriate; **~ся** climb; get to, into.

забредáть *impf*, **забрестú** (-едý, -едёшь; -ёл, -á) *pf* stray, wander; drop in.

за|бронúровать *pf*.

забросáть *pf* (*impf* **забрáсывать**) fill up; bespatter, deluge. **забрóсить** (-óшу) *pf* (*impf* **забрáсывать**) throw; abandon; neglect. **забрóшенный** neglected; deserted.

забры́згать *pf*, **забры́згивать** *impf* splash, bespatter.

забывáть *impf*, **забы́ть** (-бýду) *pf* forget; **~ся** doze off; lose consciousness; forget o.s. **забы́вчивый** forgetful. **забытьё** oblivion; drowsiness.

забью́ *etc.*: *see* **забúть**

завáливать *impf*, **завалúть**

(-лю́, -лишь) *pf* block up; pile; cram; overload; knock down; make a mess of; **~ся** fall; collapse; tip up.
зава́ривать *impf*, **завари́ть** (-арю́, -а́ришь) *pf* make; brew; weld. **зава́рка** brewing; brew; welding.
заведе́ние establishment. **заве́довать** *impf* +*instr* manage.
заве́домо *adv* wittingly. **заве́домый** notorious, undoubted.
заведу́ *etc.*: *see* **завести́**
заве́дующий *sb* (+*instr*) manager; head.
завезти́ (-зу́, -зёшь; -ёз, -ла́) *pf* (*impf* **завози́ть**) convey, deliver.
за|вербова́ть *pf*.
завери́тель *m* witness. **заве́рить** *pf* (*impf* **заверя́ть**) assure; certify; witness.
заверну́ть (-ну́, -нёшь) *pf* (*impf* **завёртывать, завора́чивать**) wrap, wrap up; roll up; screw tight, screw up; turn (off); drop in, call in.
заверте́ться (-рчу́сь, -ртишься) *pf* begin to turn *or* spin; lose one's head.
завёртывать *impf of* **заверну́ть**
заверша́ть *impf*, **заверши́ть** (-шу́) *pf* complete, conclude. **заверше́ние** completion; end.
заверя́ть *impf of* **заве́рить**
заве́са veil, screen. **заве́сить** (-е́шу) *pf* (*impf* **заве́шивать**) curtain (off).
завести́ (-еду́, -ёшь; -вёл, -а́) *pf* (*impf* **заводи́ть**) take, bring; drop off; start up; acquire; introduce; wind (up), crank; **~сь** be; appear; be established; start.
заве́т behest, bidding, ordinance; Testament. **заве́тный** cherished; secret.
заве́шивать *impf of* **заве́сить**
завеща́ние will, testament. **завеща́ть** bequeath.
завзя́тый inveterate.
завива́ть(ся *impf of* **зави́ть(ся.** **зави́вка** waving; wave.
зави́дно *impers*+*dat*: **мне ~** I feel envious. **зави́дный** enviable. **зави́довать** *impf* (*pf* **по~**) +*dat* envy.
завинти́ть (-нчу́) *pf*, **зави́нчивать** *impf* screw up.
зависа́ть *impf*, **зави́снуть** (-нет, -ви́с(нул)) *pf* (*comput*) crash.
зави́сеть (-и́шу) *impf* **+от**+*gen* depend on. **зави́симость** dependence; **в зави́симости от** depending on, subject to. **зави́симый** dependent.
зави́стливый envious. **за́висть** envy.
завито́й (за́вит, -а́, -о) curled, waved. **завито́к** (-тка́) curl, lock; flourish. **зави́ть** (-вью́, -вьёшь; -и́л, -а́, -о) *pf* (*impf* **завива́ть**) curl, wave; **~ся** curl, wave, twine; have one's hair curled.
завладева́ть *impf*, **завладе́ть** (-е́ю) *pf* +*instr* take possession of; seize.
завлека́тельный alluring; fascinating. **завлека́ть** *impf*, **завле́чь** (-еку́, -ечёшь; -лёк, -ла́) *pf* lure; fascinate.
заво́д[1] factory; works; studfarm.
заво́д[2] winding mechanism. **заводи́ть(ся** (-ожу́(сь, -о́дишь(ся) *impf of* **завести́(сь.** **заводно́й** clockwork; winding, cranking.
заводско́й factory; *sb* factory worker. **заво́дчик** factory owner.
за́водь backwater.

завоева́ние winning; conquest; achievement. **завоева́тель** *m* conqueror. **завоева́ть** (-ою́ю) *pf*, **завоёвывать** *impf* conquer; win, gain; try to get.

завожу́ *etc.*: *see* **заводи́ть, завози́ть**

заво́з delivery; carriage. **завози́ть** (-ожу́, -о́зишь) *impf of* **завезти́**

завора́чивать *impf of* **заверну́ть. заворо́т** turn, turning; sharp bend.

заво́ю *etc.*: *see* **завы́ть**

завсегда́ *adv* always. **завсегда́тай** habitué, frequenter.

за́втра tomorrow. **за́втрак** breakfast; lunch. **за́втракать** *impf* (*pf* **по~**) have breakfast; have lunch. **за́втрашний** tomorrow's; **~ день** tomorrow.

завыва́ть *impf*, **завы́ть** (-во́ю) *pf* (begin to) howl.

завяза́ть (-яжу́, -я́жешь) *pf* (*impf* **завя́зывать**) tie, tie up; start; **~ся** start; arise; (*of fruit*) set. **завя́зка** string, lace; start; opening.

за|вя́знуть (-ну; -я́з) *pf*. **завя́зывать(ся** *impf of* **завяза́ть(ся**

за|вя́нуть (-ну; -я́л) *pf*.

загада́ть *pf*, **зага́дывать** *impf* think of; plan ahead; guess at the future; **~ зага́дку** ask a riddle. **зага́дка** riddle; enigma. **зага́дочный** enigmatic, mysterious.

зага́р sunburn, tan.

за|гаси́ть (-ашу́, -а́сишь) *pf*.

за|га́снуть (-ну) *pf*.

загво́здка snag; difficulty.

заги́б fold; exaggeration. **загиба́ть** *impf of* **загну́ть**

за|гипнотизи́ровать *pf*.

загла́вие title; heading. **загла́вн|ый** title; **~ая бу́ква** capital letter.

загла́дить (-а́жу) *pf*, **загла́живать** *impf* iron, iron out; make up for; expiate; **~ся** iron out, become smooth; fade.

за|гло́хнуть (-ну; -гло́х) *pf*.

заглуша́ть *impf*, **за|глуши́ть** (-шу́) *pf* drown, muffle; jam; suppress, stifle; alleviate.

загляде́нье lovely sight. **загляде́ться** (-яжу́сь) *pf*, **загля́дываться** *impf* **на**+*acc* stare at; be lost in admiration of. **загля́дывать** *impf*, **загляну́ть** (-ну́, -нешь) *pf* peep; drop in.

загна́ть (-гоню́, -го́нишь; -а́л, -а́, -о) *pf* (*impf* **загоня́ть**) drive in, drive home; drive; exhaust.

загнива́ние decay; suppuration. **загнива́ть** *impf*, **загни́ть** (-ию́, -иёшь; -и́л, -а́, -о) *pf* rot; decay; fester.

загну́ть (-ну́, -нёшь) *pf* (*impf* **загиба́ть**) turn up, turn down; bend.

загова́ривать *impf*, **заговори́ть** *pf* begin to speak; tire out with talk; cast a spell over; protect with a charm (**от**+*gen* against). **за́говор** plot; spell. **загово́рщик** conspirator.

заголо́вок (-вка) title; heading; headline.

заго́н enclosure, pen; driving in. **загоня́ть**[1] *impf of* **загна́ть. загоня́ть**[2] *pf* tire out; work to death.

загора́живать *impf of* **загороди́ть**

загора́ть *impf*, **загоре́ть** (-рю́) *pf* become sunburnt; **~ся** catch fire; blaze; *impers*+*dat* want very much. **загоре́лый** sunburnt.

загороди́ть (-рожу́, -ро́дишь) *pf*

(*impf* **загора́живать**) enclose, fence in; obstruct. **загоро́дка** fence, enclosure.

за́городный suburban; country.

загота́вливать *impf*, **заготовля́ть** *impf*, **загото́вить** (-влю) *pf* lay in (a stock of); store; prepare. **загото́вка** (State) procurement.

загради́ть (-ажу́) *pf*, **загражда́ть** *impf* block, obstruct; bar. **загражде́ние** obstruction; barrier.

грани́ца abroad, foreign parts. **заграни́чный** foreign.

загреба́ть *impf*, **загрести́** (-ебу́, -ебёшь; -ёб, -ла́) *pf* rake up, gather; rake in.

загри́вок (-вка) withers; nape (of the neck).

за|гримирова́ть *pf*.

загроможда́ть *impf*, **загромозди́ть** (-зжу́) *pf* block up, encumber; cram.

загружа́ть *impf*, **за|грузи́ть** (-ужу́, -у́зишь) *pf* load; feed; (*comput*) boot; load; download; **~ся** +*instr* load up with, take on. **загру́зка** loading, feeding; charge, load, capacity.

за|грунтова́ть *pf*.

загрусти́ть (-ущу́) *pf* grow sad.

загрязне́ние pollution. **за|грязни́ть** *pf*, **загрязня́ть** *impf* soil; pollute; **~ся** become dirty.

загс *abbr* (*of* **(отде́л) за́писи а́ктов гражда́нского состоя́ния**) registry office.

загуби́ть (-блю́, -бишь) *pf* ruin; squander, waste.

загуля́ть *pf*, **загу́ливать** *impf* take to drink.

за|густе́ть *pf*.

зад (*loc* -у́; *pl* -ы́) back; hindquarters; buttocks; **~ом наперёд** back to front.

задава́ть(ся) (-даю́(сь) *impf of* **зада́ть(ся**

задави́ть (-влю́, -вишь) *pf* crush; run over.

задади́м *etc.*, **зада́м** *etc.*: *see* **зада́ть**

зада́ние task, job.

зада́тки (-тков) *pl* abilities, promise.

зада́ток (-тка) deposit, advance.

зада́ть (-а́м, -а́шь, -а́ст, -ади́м; за́дал, -а́, -о) *pf* (*impf* **задава́ть**) set; give; **~ вопро́с** ask a question; **~ся** turn out well; succeed; **~ся мы́слью, це́лью** make up one's mind. **зада́ча** problem; task.

задвига́ть *impf*, **задви́нуть** (-ну) *pf* bolt; bar; push; **~ся** shut; slide. **задви́жка** bolt; catch.

задво́рки (-рок) *pl* back yard; backwoods.

задева́ть *impf of* **заде́ть**

заде́лать *pf*, **заде́лывать** *impf* do up; block up, close up.

заде́ну *etc.*: *see* **заде́ть**. **задёргивать** *impf of* **задёрнуть**

задержа́ние detention. **задержа́ть** (-жу́, -жишь) *pf*, **заде́рживать** *impf* delay; withhold; arrest; **~ся** stay too long; be delayed. **заде́ржка** delay.

задёрнуть (-ну) *pf* (*impf* **задёргивать**) pull; draw.

задеру́ *etc.*: *see* **задра́ть**

заде́ть (-е́ну) *pf* (*impf* **задева́ть**) brush (against), graze; offend; catch (against).

задира *m* & *f* bully; trouble-maker. **задира́ть** *impf of* **задра́ть**

за́дн|ий back, rear; **дать ~ий ход** reverse; **~яя мысль** ulteri-

motive; **~ий план** background; **~ий прохо́д** anus. **за́дник** back; backdrop.
задо́лго *adv* **+до+***gen* long before.
за|должа́ть *pf*. **задо́лженность** debts.
задо́р fervour. **задо́рный** provocative; fervent.
задохну́ться (-ну́сь, -нёшься; -о́хся *or* -у́лся) *pf* (*impf* **задыха́ться**) suffocate; choke; pant.
за|дра́ть (-деру́, -дерёшь; -а́л, -а́, -о) *pf* (*impf also* **задира́ть**) tear to pieces, kill; lift up; break; provoke, insult.
задрема́ть (-млю́, -млешь) *pf* doze off.
задрожа́ть (-жу́) *pf* begin to tremble.
задува́ть *impf of* **заду́ть**
заду́мать *pf*, **заду́мывать** *impf* plan; intend; think of; **~ся** become thoughtful; meditate. **заду́мчивость** reverie. **заду́мчивый** pensive.
заду́ть (-у́ю) *pf* (*impf* **задува́ть**) blow out; begin to blow.
задуше́вный sincere; intimate.
за|души́ть (-ушу́, -у́шишь) *pf*.
задыха́ться *impf of* **задохну́ться**
заеда́ть *impf of* **зае́сть**
зае́зд calling in; lap, heat. **зае́здить** (-зжу) *pf* override; wear out. **заезжа́ть** *impf of* **зае́хать**. **зае́зженный** hackneyed; worn out. **зае́зжий** visiting.
заём (за́йма) loan.
зае́сть (-е́м, -е́шь, -е́ст, -еди́м) *pf* (*impf* **заеда́ть**) torment; jam; entangle.
зае́хать (-е́ду) *pf* (*impf* **заезжа́ть**) call in; enter, ride in, drive in; reach; **+за+***acc* go past; **+за+***instr* call for, fetch.
за|жа́рить(ся *pf*.
зажа́ть (-жму́, -жмёшь) *pf* (*impf* **зажима́ть**) squeeze; grip; suppress.
заже́чь (-жгу́, -жжёшь; -жёг, -жгла́) *pf* (*impf* **зажига́ть**) set fire to; kindle; light; **~ся** catch fire.
зажива́ть *impf of* **зажи́ть**. **заживи́ть** (-влю́) *pf*, **заживля́ть** *impf* heal. **за́живо** *adv* alive.
зажига́лка lighter. **зажига́ние** ignition. **зажига́тельный** inflammatory; incendiary. **зажига́ть(ся** *impf of* **заже́чь(ся**
зажи́м clamp; terminal; suppression. **зажима́ть** *impf of* **зажа́ть**. **зажимно́й** tight-fisted.
зажи́точный prosperous. **зажи́ть** (-иву́, -ивёшь; -ил, -а́, -о) *pf* (*impf* **зажива́ть**) heal; begin to live.
зажму́ *etc*.: *see* **зажа́ть**. **за|жму́риться** *pf*.
зазвене́ть (-и́т) *pf* begin to ring.
зазелене́ть (-е́ет) *pf* turn green.
заземле́ние earthing; earth. **заземли́ть** *pf*, **заземля́ть** *impf* earth.
зазнава́ться (-наю́сь, -наёшься) *impf*, **зазна́ться** *pf* give o.s. airs.
зазу́брина notch.
за|зубри́ть (-рю́, -у́бри́шь) *pf*.
заи́грывать *impf* flirt.
за́ика *m* & *f* stammerer. **заика́ние** stammer. **заика́ться** *impf*, **заикну́ться** (-ну́сь, -нёшься) *pf* stammer, stutter; **+о+***prep* mention.
заи́мствование borrowing. **заи́мствовать** *impf* & *pf* (*pf also* **по~**) borrow.
заинтересо́ванный interested. **заинтересова́ть** *pf*, **за-**

интересо́вывать *impf* interest; **~ся** +*instr* become interested in.

заи́скивать *impf* ingratiate o.s.

зайду́ *etc.*: *see* **зайти́. займу́** *etc.*: *see* **заня́ть**

зайти́ (-йду́, -йдёшь; зашёл, -шла́) *pf* (*impf* **заходи́ть**) call; drop in; set; **+в**+*acc* reach; **+за**+*acc* go behind, turn; **+за** +*instr* call for, fetch.

за́йчик little hare (*esp. as endearment*); reflection of sunlight. **зайчи́ха** doe hare.

закабали́ть *pf*, **закабаля́ть** *impf* enslave.

закады́чный intimate, bosom.

зака́з order; **на ~** to order. **заказа́ть** (-ажу́, -а́жешь) *pf*, **зака́зывать** *impf* order; book. **заказн|о́й** made to order; **~о́е (письмо́)** registered letter. **зака́зчик** customer, client.

зака́л temper; cast. **зака́ливать** *impf*, **закали́ть** (-лю́) *pf* (*impf also* **закаля́ть**) temper; harden. **зака́лка** tempering, hardening.

зака́лывать *impf of* **заколо́ть. закаля́ть** *impf of* **закали́ть. зака́нчивать(ся** *impf of* **зако́нчить(ся**

зака́пать *pf*, **зака́пывать**[1] *impf* begin to drip; rain; spot.

зака́пывать[2] *impf of* **закопа́ть**

зака́т sunset. **заката́ть** *pf*, **зака́тывать**[1] *impf* begin to roll; roll up; roll out. **закати́ть** (-ачу́, -а́тишь) *pf*, **зака́тывать**[2] *impf* roll; **~ся** roll; set.

заква́ска ferment; leaven.

закида́ть *pf*, **заки́дывать**[1] *impf* shower; bespatter.

заки́дывать[2] *impf*, **заки́нуть** (-ну) *pf* throw (out, away).

закипа́ть *impf*, **закипе́ть** (-пи́т) *pf* begin to boil.

закиса́ть *impf*, **заки́снуть** (-ну; -и́с, -ла) *pf* turn sour; become apathetic. **за́кись** oxide.

закла́д pawn; pledge; bet; **би́ться об ~** bet; **в ~е** in pawn. **закла́дка** laying; bookmark. **закладно́й** pawn. **закла́дывать** *impf of* **заложи́ть**

закле́ивать *impf*, **закле́ить** *pf* glue up.

за|клейми́ть (-млю́) *pf*.

заклепа́ть *pf*, **заклёпывать** *impf* rivet. **заклёпка** rivet; riveting.

заклина́ние incantation; spell. **заклина́ть** *impf* invoke; entreat.

заключа́ть *impf*, **заключи́ть** (-чу́) *pf* conclude; enter into; contain; confine. **заключа́ться** consist; lie, be. **заключе́ние** conclusion; decision; confinement. **заключённый** *sb* prisoner. **заключи́тельный** final, concluding.

закля́тие pledge. **закля́тый** sworn.

закова́ть (-кую́, -куёшь) *pf*, **зако́вывать** *impf* chain; shackle.

закола́чивать *impf of* **заколоти́ть**

заколдо́ванный bewitched; **~ круг** vicious circle. **заколдова́ть** *pf* bewitch; lay a spell on.

зако́лка hair-grip; hair-slide.

заколоти́ть (-лочу́, -ло́тишь) *pf* (*impf* **закола́чивать**) board up; knock in; knock insensible.

за|коло́ть (-олю́, -о́лешь) *pf* (*impf also* **зака́лывать**) stab; pin up; (*impers*) **у меня́ заколо́ло в боку́** I have a stitch.

зако́н law. **законнорождённый** legitimate. **зако́нность** legality. **зако́нный** legal; legitimate.

законо- *in comb* law, legal. **зако-**

нове́дение law, jurisprudence. **~да́тельный** legislative. **~да́тельство** legislation. **~ме́рность** regularity, normality. **~ме́рный** regular, natural. **~прое́кт** bill.

за|консерви́ровать *pf.* **за|конспекти́ровать** *pf.*

зако́нченность completeness. **зако́нченный** finished; accomplished. **зако́нчить** (-чу) *pf* (*impf* **зака́нчивать**) end, finish; **~ся** end, finish.

закопа́ть *pf* (*impf* **зака́пывать²**) begin to dig; bury.

закопте́лый sooty, smutty. **за|копте́ть** (-ти́т) *pf.* **за|копти́ть** (-пчу́) *pf.*

закорене́лый deep-rooted; inveterate.

закосне́лый incorrigible.

закоу́лок (-лка) alley; nook.

закочене́лый numb with cold. **за|кочене́ть** (-е́ю) *pf.*

закра́дываться *impf of* **закра́сться**

закра́сить (-а́шу) *pf* (*impf* **закра́шивать**) paint over.

закра́сться (-аду́сь, -адёшься) *pf* (*impf* **закра́дываться**) steal in, creep in.

закра́шивать *impf of* **закра́сить**

закрепи́тель *m* fixative. **закрепи́ть** (-плю́) *pf*, **закрепля́ть** *impf* fasten; fix; consolidate; +за+*instr* assign to; **~ за собо́й** secure.

закрепости́ть (-ощу́) *pf*, **закрепоща́ть** *impf* enslave. **закрепоще́ние** enslavement; slavery, serfdom.

закрича́ть (-чу́) *pf* cry out; begin to shout.

закро́йщик cutter.

закро́ю *etc.*: *see* **закры́ть**

закругле́ние rounding; curve. **закругли́ть** (-лю́) *pf*, **закругля́ть** *impf* make round; round off; **~ся** become round; round off.

закружи́ться (-ужу́сь, -у́жишься) *pf* begin to whirl *or* go round.

за|крути́ть (-учу́, -у́тишь) *pf*, **закру́чивать** *impf* twist, twirl; wind round; turn; screw in; turn the head of; **~ся** twist, twirl, whirl; wind round.

закрыва́ть *impf*, **закры́ть** (-ро́ю) *pf* close, shut; turn off; close down; cover; **~ся** close, shut; end; close down; cover o.s.; shelter. **закры́тие** closing; shutting; closing down; shelter. **закры́тый** closed, shut; private.

закули́сный behind the scenes; backstage.

закупа́ть *impf*, **закупи́ть** (-плю́, -пишь) *pf* buy up; stock up with. **заку́пка** purchase.

заку́поривать *impf*, **заку́порить** *pf* cork; stop up; coop up. **заку́порка** corking; thrombosis.

заку́почный purchase. **заку́пщик** buyer.

заку́ривать *impf*, **закури́ть** (-рю́, -ришь) *pf* light up; begin to smoke.

закуси́ть (-ушу́, -у́сишь) *pf*, **заку́сывать** *impf* have a snack; bite. **заку́ска** hors-d'oeuvre; snack. **заку́сочная** *sb* snack-bar.

за|ку́тать *pf*, **заку́тывать** *impf* wrap up; **~ся** wrap o.s. up.

зал hall; **~ ожида́ния** waiting-room.

залега́ть *impf of* **зале́чь**

за|ледене́ть (-е́ю) *pf.*

залежа́лый stale, long unused. **залежа́ться** (-жу́сь) *pf*, **залёжи-**

ваться *impf* lie too long; find no market; become stale. **за́лежь** deposit, seam; stale goods.

залеза́ть *impf*, **зале́зть** (-зу; -éз) *pf* climb, climb up; get in; creep in.

за|лепи́ть (-плю́, -пишь) *pf*, **залепля́ть** *impf* paste over; glue up.

залета́ть *impf*, **залете́ть** (-ечу́) *pf* fly; +**в**+*acc* fly into.

зале́чивать *impf*, **залечи́ть** (-чу́, -чишь) *pf* heal, cure; **~ся** heal (up).

зале́чь (-ля́гу, -ля́жешь; залёг, -ла́) *pf* (*impf* **залега́ть**) lie down; lie low; lie, be deposited.

зали́в bay; gulf. **залива́ть** *impf*, **зали́ть** (-лью́, -льёшь; за́лил, -а́, -о) *pf* flood, inundate; spill on; extinguish; spread; **~ся** be flooded; pour, spill; +*instr* break into.

зало́г deposit; pledge; security, mortgage; token; voice. **заложи́ть** (-жу́, -жишь) *pf* (*impf* **закла́дывать**) lay; put; mislay; pile up; pawn, mortgage; harness; lay in. **зало́жник** hostage.

залп volley, salvo; **~ом** without pausing for breath.

залью́ *etc.*: *see* **зали́ть. заля́гу** *etc.*: *see* **зале́чь**

зам *abbr* (*of* **замести́тель**) assistant, deputy. **зам-** *abbr in comb* (*of* **замести́тель**) assistant, deputy, vice-.

за|ма́зать (-а́жу) *pf*, **зама́зывать** *impf* paint over; putty; smear; soil; **~ся** get dirty. **зама́зка** putty; puttying.

зама́лчивать *impf of* **замолча́ть**

зама́нивать *impf*, **замани́ть** (-ню́, -нишь) *pf* entice; decoy. **зама́нчивый** tempting.

за|марино́вать *pf*.

за|маскирова́ть *pf*, **замаскиро́вывать** *impf* mask; disguise; **~ся** disguise o.s.

зама́хиваться *impf*, **замахну́ться** (-ну́сь, -нёшься) *pf* +*instr* raise threateningly.

зама́чивать *impf of* **замочи́ть**

замедле́ние slowing down, deceleration; delay. **заме́длить** *pf*, **замедля́ть** *impf* slow down; slacken; delay; **~ся** slow down.

замёл *etc.*: *see* **замести́**

заме́на substitution; substitute. **замени́мый** replaceable. **замени́тель** *m* (+*gen*) substitute (for). **замени́ть** (-ню́, -нишь) *pf*, **заменя́ть** *impf* replace; be a substitute for.

замере́ть (-мру́, -мрёшь; за́мер, -ла́, -о) *pf* (*impf* **замира́ть**) stand still; freeze; die away.

замерза́ние freezing. **замерза́ть** *impf*, **за|мёрзнуть** (-ну; замёрз) *pf* freeze (up); freeze to death.

заме́рить *pf* (*impf* **замеря́ть**) measure, gauge.

замеси́ть (-ешу́, -е́сишь) *pf* (*impf* **заме́шивать**²) knead.

замести́ (-ету́, -етёшь; -мёл, -а́) *pf* (*impf* **замета́ть**) sweep up; cover.

замести́тель *m* substitute; assistant, deputy, vice-. **замести́ть** (-ещу́) *pf* (*impf* **замеща́ть**) replace; deputize for.

замета́ть *impf of* **замести́**

заме́тить (-е́чу) *pf* (*impf* **замеча́ть**) notice; note; remark. **заме́тка** mark; note. **заме́тный** noticeable; outstanding.

замеча́ние remark; reprimand. **замеча́тельный** remarkable;

splendid. **замеча́ть** *impf of* **заме́тить**

замеша́тельство confusion; embarrassment. **замеша́ть** *pf*, **заме́шивать**[1] *impf* mix up, entangle. **заме́шивать**[2] *impf of* **замеси́ть**

замеща́ть *impf of* **замести́ть**. **замеще́ние** substitution; filling.

зами́нка hitch; hesitation.

замира́ть *impf of* **замере́ть**

за́мкнутый reserved; closed, exclusive. **замкну́ть** (-ну́, -нёшь) *pf* (*impf* **замыка́ть**) lock; close; **~ся** close; shut o.s. up; become reserved.

за́мок[1] (-мка) castle.

замо́к[2] (-мка́) lock; padlock; clasp.

замолка́ть *impf*, **замо́лкнуть** (-ну; -мо́лк) *pf* fall silent; stop.

замолча́ть (-чу́) *pf* (*impf* **замалчивать**) fall silent; cease corresponding; hush up.

замора́живать *impf*, **заморо́зить** (-ро́жу) *pf* freeze. **заморо́женный** frozen; iced. **за́морозки** (-ов) *pl* (slight) frosts.

замо́рский overseas.

за|мочи́ть (-чу́, -чишь) *pf* (*impf also* **зама́чивать**) wet; soak; ret.

замо́чная сква́жина keyhole.

замру́ *etc.*: *see* **замере́ть**

за́муж *adv*: **вы́йти ~** (**за**+*acc*) marry. **за́мужем** *adv* married (**за**+*instr* to).

за|му́чить (-чу) *pf* torment; wear out; bore to tears. **за|му́читься** (-чусь) *pf*.

за́мша suede.

замыка́ние locking; short circuit. **замыка́ть(ся** *impf of* **замкну́ть(ся**

за́мысел (-сла) project, plan.

замы́слить *pf*, **замышля́ть** *impf* plan; contemplate.

за́навес, занаве́ска curtain.

занести́ (-су́, -сёшь; -ёс, -ла́) *pf* (*impf* **заноси́ть**) bring; note down; (*impers*) cover with snow etc.; (*impers*) skid.

занима́ть *impf* (*pf* **заня́ть**) occupy; interest; engage; borrow; **~ся** +*instr* be occupied with; work at; study.

зано́за splinter. **занози́ть** (-ожу́) *pf* get a splinter in.

зано́с snow-drift; skid. **заноси́ть** (-ошу́, -о́сишь) *impf of* **занести́**. **зано́счивый** arrogant.

заня́тие occupation; *pl* studies. **занято́й** busy. **за́нятый** (-нят, -а́, -о) occupied; taken; engaged. **заня́ть(ся** (займу́(сь, -мёшь(ся; за́нял(ся, -а́(сь, -о(сь) *pf of* **занима́ть(ся**

заодно́ *adv* in concert; at one; at the same time.

заостри́ть *pf*, **заостря́ть** *impf* sharpen; emphasize.

зао́чник, -ница student taking correspondence course; external student. **зао́чно** *adv* in one's absence; by correspondence course. **зао́чный курс** correspondence course.

за́пад west. **за́падный** west, western; westerly.

западня́ (*gen pl* -не́й) trap; pitfall, snare.

за|пакова́ть *pf*, **запако́вывать** *impf* pack; wrap up.

запа́л ignition; fuse. **запа́льная свеча́** (spark-)plug.

запа́с reserve; supply; hem. **запаса́ть** *impf*, **запасти́** (-су́, -сёшь; -а́с, -ла́) *pf* lay in a stock of; **~ся** +*instr* stock up with. **запасно́й, запа́сный** spare; reserve; **~ вы́ход** emergency exit.

за́пах smell.
запа́хивать *impf*, **запахну́ть²** (-ну́, -нёшь) *pf* wrap up.
запа́хнуть¹ (-ну; -а́х) *pf* begin to smell.
за|па́чкать *pf*.
запева́ть *impf of* **запе́ть**; lead the singing.
запека́ть(ся *impf of* **запе́чь(ся**. **запеку́** *etc.*: *see* **запе́чь**
за|пелена́ть *pf*.
запере́ть (-пру́, -прёшь; за́пер, -ла́, -ло) *pf* (*impf* **запира́ть**) lock; lock in; bar; **~ся** lock o.s. in.
запе́ть (-пою́, -поёшь) *pf* (*impf* **запева́ть**) begin to sing.
запеча́тать *pf*, **запеча́тывать** *impf* seal. **запечатлева́ть** *impf*, **запечатле́ть** (-е́ю) *pf* imprint, engrave.
запе́чь (-еку́, -ечёшь; -пёк, -ла́) *pf* (*impf* **запека́ть**) bake; **~ся** bake; become parched; clot, coagulate.
запива́ть *impf of* **запи́ть**
запина́ться *impf of* **запну́ться**. **запи́нка** hesitation.
запира́ть(ся *impf of* **запере́ть(ся**
записа́ть (-ишу́, -и́шешь) *pf*, **запи́сывать** *impf* note; take down; record; enter; enrol; **~ся** register, enrol (**в**+*acc* at, in). **запи́ска** note. **записн|о́й** note; inveterate; **~а́я кни́жка** notebook. **за́пись** recording; registration; record.
запи́ть (-пью́, -пьёшь; за́пи́л, -а́, -о) *pf* (*impf* **запива́ть**) begin drinking; wash down (with).
запиха́ть *pf*, **запи́хивать** *impf*, **запихну́ть** (-ну́, -нёшь) *pf* push in, cram in.
запишу́ *etc.*: *see* **записа́ть**
запла́кать (-а́чу) *pf* begin to cry.
за|плани́ровать *pf*.
запла́та patch.
за|плати́ть (-ачу́, -а́тишь) *pf* pay (**за**+*acc* for).
запла́чу *etc.*: *see* **запла́кать**. **заплачу́** *see* **заплати́ть**
заплести́ (-ету́, -етёшь; -ёл, -а́) *pf*, **заплета́ть** *impf* plait.
за|пломбирова́ть *pf*.
заплы́в heat, round. **заплыва́ть** *impf*, **заплы́ть** (-ыву́, -ывёшь; -ы́л, -а́, -о) *pf* swim in, sail in; swim out, sail out; be bloated.
запну́ться (-ну́сь, -нёшься) *pf* (*impf* **запина́ться**) hesitate; stumble.
запове́дник reserve; preserve; **госуда́рственный ~** national park. **запове́дный** prohibited. **за́поведь** precept; commandment.
заподо́зривать *impf*, **заподо́зрить** *pf* suspect (**в**+*prep* of).
запозда́лый belated; delayed. **запозда́ть** *pf* (*impf* **запа́здывать**) be late.
запо́й hard drinking.
заполза́ть *impf*, **заползти́** *pf* (-зу́, -зёшь; -о́лз, -зла́) creep, crawl.
запо́лнить *pf*, **заполня́ть** *impf* fill (in, up).
запомина́ть *impf*, **запо́мнить** *pf* remember; memorize; **~ся** stay in one's mind.
за́понка cuff-link; stud.
запо́р bolt; lock; constipation.
за|поте́ть (-е́ет) *pf* mist over.
запою́ *etc.*: *see* **запе́ть**
запра́вить (-влю) *pf*, **заправля́ть** *impf* tuck in; prepare; refuel; season, dress; mix in; **~ся** refuel. **запра́вка** refuelling; seasoning, dressing.

запра́шивать *impf of* **запроси́ть**

запре́т prohibition, ban. **запрети́ть** (-ещу́) *pf*, **запреща́ть** *impf* prohibit, ban. **запре́тный** forbidden. **запреще́ние** prohibition.

за|программи́ровать *pf.*

запро́с inquiry; overcharging; *pl* needs. **запроси́ть** (-ошу́, -о́сишь) *pf* (*impf* **запра́шивать**) inquire.

за́просто *adv* without ceremony.

запрошу́ *etc.*: *see* **запроси́ть**.

запру́ *etc.*: *see* **запере́ть**

запру́да dam, weir; mill-pond.

запряга́ть *impf*, **запря́чь** (-ягу́, -яжёшь; -я́г, -ла́) *pf* harness; yoke.

запуга́ть *pf*, **запу́гивать** *impf* cow, intimidate.

за́пуск launching. **запуска́ть** *impf*, **запусти́ть** (-ущу́, -у́стишь) *pf* thrust (in); start; launch; (+*acc or instr*) fling; neglect. **запусте́лый** neglected; desolate. **запусте́ние** neglect; desolation.

за|пу́тать *pf*, **запу́тывать** *impf* tangle; confuse; **~ся** get tangled; get involved.

запущу́ *etc.*: *see* **запусти́ть**

запча́сть (*gen pl* -е́й) *abbr* (*of* **запасна́я часть**) spare part.

запыха́ться *pf* be out of breath.

запью́ *etc.*: *see* **запи́ть**

запя́стье wrist.

запята́я *sb* comma.

за|пятна́ть *pf.*

зараба́тывать *impf*, **зарабо́тать** *pf* earn; start (up). **за́работн|ый: ~ая пла́та** wages; pay. **за́работок** (-тка) earnings.

заража́ть *impf*, **зарази́ть** (-ажу́) *pf* infect; **~ся** +*instr* be infected with, catch. **зара́за** infection. **зарази́тельный** infectious. **зара́зный** infectious.

зара́нее *adv* in good time; in advance.

зараста́ть *impf*, **зарасти́** (-ту́, -тёшь; -ро́с, -ла́) *pf* be overgrown; heal.

за́рево glow.

за|регистри́ровать(ся *pf.*

за|ре́зать (-е́жу) *pf* kill, knife; slaughter.

зарека́ться *impf of* **заре́чься**

зарекомендова́ть *pf*: **~ себя́** +*instr* show o.s. to be.

заре́чься (-еку́сь, -ечёшься; -ёкся, -екла́сь) *pf* (*impf* **зарека́ться**) +*inf* renounce.

за|ржаве́ть (-е́ет) *pf.*

зарисо́вка sketching; sketch.

зароди́ть (-ожу́) *pf*, **зарожда́ть** *impf* generate; **~ся** be born; arise. **заро́дыш** foetus; embryo. **зарожде́ние** conception; origin.

заро́к vow, pledge.

заро́с *etc.*: *see* **зарасти́**

заро́ю *etc.*: *see* **зары́ть**

зарпла́та *abbr* (*of* **за́работная пла́та**) wages; pay.

заруба́ть *impf of* **заруби́ть**

зарубе́жный foreign.

зарубе́жье foreign countries.

заруби́ть (-блю́, -бишь) *pf* (*impf* **заруба́ть**) kill, cut down; notch.

зару́бка notch.

заруча́ться *impf*, **заручи́ться** (-учу́сь) *pf* +*instr* secure.

зарыва́ть *impf*, **зары́ть** (-ро́ю) *pf* bury.

заря́ (*pl* **зо́ри, зорь**) dawn.

заря́д charge; supply. **заряди́ть** (-яжу́, -я́дишь) *pf*, **заряжа́ть** *impf* load; charge; stoke; **~ся** be loaded; be charged. **зарядка** loading; charging; exercises.

засáда ambush. **засади́ть** (-ажу́, -áдишь) *pf*, **засáживать** *impf* plant; drive; set (**за**+*acc* to); ~ **(в тюрьму́)** put in prison. **засáживаться** *impf of* **засéсть**

засáливать *impf of* **засоли́ть**

засвети́ть (-ечу́, -éтишь) *pf* light; ~**ся** light up.

за|свидéтельствовать *pf.*

засéв sowing; seed; sown area. **засевáть** *impf of* **засéять**

заседáние meeting; session. **заседáть** *impf* sit, be in session.

засéивать *impf of* **засéять.** **засéк** *etc.*: *see* **засéчь.** **засекáть** *impf of* **засéчь**

засекрéтить (-рéчу) *pf*, **засекрéчивать** *impf* classify as secret; clear, give access to secret material.

засеку́ *etc.*: *see* **засéчь.** **засéл** *etc.*: *see* **засéсть**

заселéние settlement. **засели́ть** *pf*, **заселя́ть** *impf* settle; colonize; populate.

засéсть (-ся́ду; -сéл) *pf* (*impf* **засáживаться**) sit down; sit tight; settle; lodge in.

засéчь (-еку́, -ечёшь; -ёк, -лá) *pf* (*impf* **засекáть**) flog to death; notch.

засéять (-éю) *pf* (*impf* **засевáть, засéивать**) sow.

заси́лье dominance, sway.

заслони́ть *pf*, **заслоня́ть** *impf* cover, screen; push into the background. **заслóнка** (*furnace, oven*) door.

заслу́га merit, desert; service. **заслу́женный** deserved, merited; Honoured; time-honoured. **заслу́живать** *impf*, **заслужи́ть** (-ужу́, -у́жишь) *pf* deserve; earn; +*gen* be worthy of.

засмея́ться (-еюсь, -еёшься) begin to laugh.

заснимáть *impf of* **засня́ть**

засну́ть (-ну́, -нёшь) *pf* (*impf* **засыпáть**) fall asleep.

засня́ть (-ниму́, -и́мешь; -я́л, -á, -о) *pf* (*impf* **заснимáть**) photograph.

засóв bolt, bar.

засóвывать *impf of* **засу́нуть**

засóл salting, pickling. **засоли́ть** (-олю́, -óли́шь) *pf* (*impf* **засáливать**) salt, pickle.

засорéние littering; contamination; obstruction. **засори́ть** *pf*, **засоря́ть** *impf* litter; get dirt into; clog.

за|сóхнуть (-ну; -сóх) *pf* (*impf also* **засыхáть**) dry (up); wither.

застáва gate; outpost.

заставáть (-таю́, -таёшь) *impf of* **застáть**

застáвить (-влю) *pf*, **заставля́ть** *impf* make; compel.

застáиваться *impf of* **застоя́ться.** **застáну** *etc.*: *see* **застáть**

застáть (-áну) *pf* (*impf* **заставáть**) find; catch.

застёгивать *impf*, **застегну́ть** (-ну́, -нёшь) *pf* fasten, do up. **застёжка** fastening; clasp, buckle; ~**-мóлния** zip.

застекли́ть *pf*, **застекля́ть** *impf* glaze.

застéнок (-нка) torture chamber.

застéнчивый shy.

застигáть *impf*, **засти́гнуть, засти́чь** (-и́гну; -сти́г) *pf* catch; take unawares.

засти́чь *see* **засти́гнуть**

застóй stagnation. **застóйный** stagnant.

за|стóпориться *pf.*

застоя́ться (-и́тся) *pf* (*impf* **заста́иваться**) stagnate; stand too long.
застра́ивать *impf of* **застро́ить**
застрахо́ванный insured. **за|страхова́ть** *pf*, **застрахо́вывать** *impf* insure.
застрева́ть *impf of* **застря́ть**
застрели́ть (-елю́, -е́лишь) *pf* shoot (dead); **~ся** shoot o.s.
застро́ить (-о́ю) *pf* (*impf* **застра́ивать**) build over, on, up. **застро́йка** building.
застря́ть (-я́ну) *pf* (*impf* **застрева́ть**) stick; get stuck.
за́ступ spade.
заступа́ться *impf*, **заступи́ться** (-плю́сь, -пишься) *pf* +**за**+*acc* stand up for. **засту́пник** defender. **засту́пничество** protection; intercession.
застыва́ть *impf*, **засты́ть** (-ы́ну) *pf* harden, set; become stiff; freeze; be petrified.
засу́нуть (-ну) *pf* (*impf* **засо́вывать**) thrust in, push in.
за́суха drought.
засы́пать[1] (-плю) *pf*, **засыпа́ть** *impf* fill up; strew.
засыпа́ть[2] *impf of* **засну́ть**
засыха́ть *impf of* **засо́хнуть**. **загя́ду** *etc.*: *see* **засе́сть**
затаённый (-ён, -ена́) secret; repressed. **зата́ивать** *impf*, **затаи́ть** *pf* suppress; conceal; harbour; **~ дыха́ние** hold one's breath.
зата́пливать *impf of* **затопи́ть**. **зата́птывать** *impf of* **затопта́ть**
зата́скивать *impf*, **затащи́ть** (-щу́, -щишь) *pf* drag in; drag off; drag away.
затвердева́ть *impf*, **за|тверде́ть** (-е́ет) *pf* become hard; set.
затверде́ние hardening; callus.
затво́р bolt; lock; shutter; flood-gate. **затвори́ть** (-рю́, -ришь) *pf*, **затворя́ть** *impf* shut, close; **~ся** shut o.s. up, lock o.s. in. **затво́рник** hermit, recluse.
затева́ть *impf of* **зате́ять**
затёк *etc.*: *see* **затёчь**. **затека́ть** *impf of* **затёчь**
зате́м *adv* then, next; **~ что** because.
затемне́ние darkening, obscuring; blacking out; black-out. **затемни́ть** *pf*, **затемня́ть** *impf* darken, obscure; black out.
зате́ривать *impf*, **затеря́ть** *pf* lose, mislay; **~ся** be lost; be mislaid; be forgotten.
затёчь (-ечёт, -еку́т; -тёк, -кла́) *pf* (*impf* **затека́ть**) pour, flow; swell up; become numb.
зате́я undertaking, venture; escapade; joke. **зате́ять** *pf* (*impf* **затева́ть**) undertake, venture.
затиха́ть *impf*, **зати́хнуть** (-ну; -ти́х) *pf* die down, abate; fade. **зати́шье** calm; lull.
заткну́ть (-ну́, -нёшь) *pf* (*impf* **затыка́ть**) stop up; stick, thrust.
затмева́ть *impf*, **затми́ть** (-ми́шь) *pf* darken; eclipse; overshadow. **затме́ние** eclipse.
зато́ *conj* but then, but on the other hand.
затону́ть (-о́нет) *pf* sink, be submerged.
затопи́ть[1] (-плю́, -пишь) *pf* (*impf* **зата́пливать**) light; turn on the heating.
затопи́ть[2] (-плю́, -пишь) *pf*, **затопля́ть** *impf* flood, submerge; sink.
затопта́ть (-пчу́, -пчешь) *pf* (*impf* **зата́птывать**) trample (down).

зато́р obstruction, jam; congestion.

за|тормози́ть (-ожу́) *pf.*

затача́ть *impf*, **заточи́ть** (-чу́) *pf* incarcerate. **заточе́ние** incarceration.

затра́гивать *impf of* **затро́нуть**

затра́та expense; outlay. **затра́тить** (-а́чу) *pf*, **затра́чивать** *impf* spend.

затре́бовать *pf* request, require; ask for.

затро́нуть (-ну) *pf* (*impf* **затра́гивать**) affect; touch (on).

затрудне́ние difficulty. **затрудни́тельный** difficult. **затрудни́ть** *pf*, **затрудня́ть** *impf* trouble; make difficult; hamper; **~ся** +*inf or instr* find difficulty in.

за|тупи́ться (-пится) *pf.*

за|туши́ть (-шу́, -шишь) *pf* extinguish; suppress.

за́тхлый musty, mouldy; stuffy.

затыка́ть *impf of* **заткну́ть**

заты́лок (-лка) back of the head; scrag-end.

затя́гивать *impf*, **затяну́ть** (-ну́, -нешь) *pf* tighten; cover; close, heal; spin out; **~ся** be covered; close; be delayed; drag on; inhale. **затя́жка** inhaling; prolongation; delaying, putting off; lagging. **затяжно́й** long-drawn-out.

зауря́дный ordinary; mediocre.

зау́треня morning service.

зау́чивать *impf*, **заучи́ть** (-чу́, -чишь) *pf* learn by heart.

за|фаршировать *pf.* **за|фиксировать** *pf.* **за|фрахтова́ть** *pf.*

захва́т seizure, capture. **захвати́ть** (-ачу́, -а́тишь) *pf*, **захва́тывать** *impf* take; seize; thrill. **захва́тнический** aggressive. **захва́тчик** aggressor. **захва́тывающий** gripping.

захлебну́ться (-ну́сь, -нёшься) *pf*, **захлёбываться** *impf* choke (от+*gen* with).

захлестну́ть (-ну́, -нёшь) *pf*, **захлёстывать** *impf* flow over, swamp, overwhelm.

захло́пнуть (-ну) *pf*, **захло́пывать** *impf* slam, bang; **~ся** slam (to).

захо́д sunset; calling in. **заходи́ть** (-ожу́, -о́дишь) *impf of* **зайти́**

захолу́стный remote, provincial. **захолу́стье** backwoods.

за|хорони́ть (-ню́, -нишь) *pf.*

за|хоте́ть(ся (-очу́(сь, -о́чешь(ся, -оти́м(ся) *pf.*

зацвести́ (-етёт; -вёл, -а́) *pf*, **зацвета́ть** *impf* come into bloom.

зацепи́ть (-плю́, -пишь) *pf*, **зацепля́ть** *impf* hook; engage; sting; catch (за+*acc* on); **~ся** за+*acc* catch on; catch hold of.

зачасту́ю *adv* often.

зача́тие conception. **зача́ток** (-тка) embryo; rudiment; germ. **зача́точный** rudimentary. **зача́ть** (-чну́, -чнёшь; -ча́л, -а́, -о) *pf* (*impf* **зачина́ть**) conceive.

зачёл *etc.*: *see* **заче́сть**

заче́м *adv* why; what for. **заче́м-то** *adv* for some reason.

зачёркивать *impf*, **зачеркну́ть** (-ну́, -нёшь) *pf* cross out.

зачерпну́ть (-ну́, -нёшь) *pf*, **заче́рпывать** *impf* scoop up; draw up.

за|черстве́ть (-е́ет) *pf.*

заче́сть (-чту́, -чтёшь; -чёл, -чла́) *pf* (*impf* **зачи́тывать**) take into account, reckon as credit. **зачёт**

test; **получи́ть, сдать ~ по**+*dat* pass a test in; **поста́вить ~ по**+*dat* pass in. **зачётная кни́жка** (student's) record book.

зачина́ть *impf of* **зача́ть. зачи́нщик** instigator.

зачи́слить *pf*, **зачисля́ть** *impf* include; enter; enlist; **~ся** join, enter.

зачи́тывать *impf of* **заче́сть. зачту́** *etc.*: *see* **заче́сть. зашёл** *etc.*: *see* **зайти́**

зашива́ть *impf*, **заши́ть** (-шью́, -шьёшь) *pf* sew up.

за|шифрова́ть *pf*, **зашифро́вывать** *impf* encipher, encode.

за|шнурова́ть *pf*, **зашнуро́вывать** *impf* lace up.

за|шпаклева́ть (-лю́ю) *pf*. **за|што́пать** *pf*. **за|штрихова́ть** *pf*. **зашью́** *etc.*: *see* **заши́ть**

защи́та defence; protection. **защити́ть** (-ищу́) *pf*, **защища́ть** *impf* defend, protect. **защи́тник** defender. **защи́тный** protective.

заяви́ть (-влю́, -вишь) *pf*, **заявля́ть** *impf* announce, declare; **~ся** turn up. **зая́вка** claim; demand. **заявле́ние** statement; application.

за́яц (за́йца) hare; stowaway; **е́хать за́йцем** travel without a ticket.

зва́ние rank; title. **зва́ный** invited; **~ обе́д** banquet, dinner. **зва́тельный** vocative. **звать** (зову́, -вёшь; звал, -а́, -о) *impf* (*pf* **по~**) call; ask, invite; **как вас зову́т?** what is your name?; **~ся** be called.

звезда́ (*pl* звёзды) star. **звёздный** star; starry; starlit; stellar. **звёздочка** little star; asterisk.

звене́ть (-ню́) *impf* ring; +*instr* jingle, clink.

звено́ (*pl* зве́нья, -ьев) link; team, section; unit; component. **звеньево́й** *sb* section leader.

звери́нец (-нца) menagerie. **зверово́дство** fur farming. **зве́рский** brutal; terrific. **зве́рство** atrocity. **зве́рствовать** *impf* commit atrocities. **зверь** (*pl* -и, -е́й) *m* wild animal.

звон ringing (sound); peal, chink, clink. **звони́ть** *impf* (*pf* **по~**) ring; ring up; **~ кому́-нибу́дь (по телефо́ну)** ring s.o. up. **зво́нкий** (-нок, -нка́, -о) ringing, clear. **звоно́к** (-нка́) bell; (*telephone*) call.

звук sound.

звуко- *in comb* sound. **звукоза́пись** (sound) recording. **~изоля́ция** sound-proofing. **~непроница́емый** sound-proof. **~снима́тель** *m* pick-up.

звуково́й sound; audio; acoustic. **звуча́ние** sound(ing); vibration. **звуча́ть** (-чи́т) *impf* (*pf* **про~**) be heard; sound. **зву́чный** (-чен, -чна́, -о) sonorous.

зда́ние building.

здесь *adv* here. **зде́шний** local; **не ~** a stranger here.

здоро́ваться *impf* (*pf* **по~**) exchange greetings. **здо́рово** *adv* splendidly; very (much); well done!; great! **здоро́вый** healthy, strong; well; wholesome, sound. **здоро́вье** health; **за ва́ше ~!** your health! **как ва́ше ~?** how are you? **здра́вница** sanatorium.

здравомы́слящий sensible, judicious. **здравоохране́ние** public health.

здра́вствовать *impf* be healthy; prosper. **здра́в-**

ствуй(те) how do you do?; hello! **да здра́вствует!** long live! **здра́вый** sensible; **~ смысл** common sense.

зе́бра zebra.

зева́ть *impf*, **зевну́ть** (-ну́, -нёшь) *pf* yawn; gape; (*pf also* **про~**) miss, let slip, lose. **зево́к** (-вка́), **зево́та** yawn.

зелене́ть (-е́ет) *impf* (*pf* **по~**) turn green; show green. **зелёный** (зе́лен, -а́, -о) green; **~ лук** spring onions. **зе́лень** green; greenery; greens.

земе́льный land.

земле- *in comb* land; earth. **землевладе́лец** (-льца) landowner. **~де́лец** (-льца) farmer. **~де́лие** farming, agriculture. **~де́льческий** agricultural. **~ко́п** navvy. **~ро́йный** excavating. **~трясе́ние** earthquake.

земля́ (*acc* -ю; *pl* -и, земе́ль, -ям) earth; ground; land; soil. **земля́к** (-а́) fellow-countryman. **земляни́ка** (*no pl*; *usu collect*) wild strawberry; wild strawberries. **земля́нка** dug-out; mud hut. **земляно́й** earthen; earth. **земля́чка** countrywoman. **земно́й** earthly; terrestrial; ground; mundane; **~ шар** the globe.

зени́т zenith. **зени́тный** zenith; anti-aircraft.

зе́ркало (*pl* -а́) mirror. **зерка́льный** mirror; smooth; plate-glass.

зерни́стый grainy. **зерно́** (*pl* зёрна, зёрен) grain; seed; kernel, core; **ко́фе в зёрнах** coffee beans. **зерново́й** grain. **зерновы́е** *sb pl* cereals. **зернохрани́лище** granary.

зигза́г zigzag.

зима́ (*acc* -у; *pl* -ы) winter. **зи́мний** winter, wintry. **зимова́ть** *impf* (*pf* **пере~, про~**) spend the winter; hibernate. **зимо́вка** wintering; hibernation. **зимо́вье** winter quarters. **зимо́й** *adv* in winter.

зия́ть *impf* gape, yawn.

злак grass; cereal.

злить (злю) *impf* (*pf* **обо~, о~, разо~**) anger; irritate; **~ся** be angry, be in a bad temper; rage. **зло** (*gen pl* зол) evil; harm; misfortune; malice.

зло- *in comb* evil, harm, malice. **злове́щий** ominous. **~во́ние** stink. **~во́нный** stinking. **~ка́чественный** malignant; pernicious. **~па́мятный** rancorous, unforgiving. **~ра́дный** malevolent, gloating. **~сло́вие** malicious gossip. **~умы́шленник** malefactor; plotter. **~язы́чный** slanderous.

зло́ба spite; anger; **~ дня** topic of the day, latest news. **зло́бный** malicious. **злободне́вный** topical. **злоде́й** villain. **злоде́йский** villainous. **злоде́йство** villainy; crime, evil deed. **злодея́ние** crime, evil deed. **злой** (зол, зла) evil; wicked; malicious; vicious; bad-tempered; severe. **зло́стный** malicious; intentional. **злость** malice; fury.

злоупотреби́ть (-блю́) *pf*, **злоупотребля́ть** *impf* +*instr* abuse. **злоупотребле́ние** +*instr* abuse of.

зме́йный snake; cunning. **змей** snake; dragon; kite. **змея́** (*pl* -и) snake.

знак sign; mark; symbol.

знако́мить (-млю) *impf* (*pf* **о~, по~**) acquaint; introduce; **~ся** become acquainted; get to know; **+с+***instr* meet, make the acquaintance of. **знако́мство** acquaintance; (circle of) acquaintances. **знако́м|ый** familiar; **быть ~ым с**+*instr* be acquainted with, know; **~ый, ~ая** *sb* acquaintance.

знамена́тель *m* denominator.

знамена́тельный significant.

зна́мение sign. **знамени́тость** celebrity. **знамени́тый** celebrated, famous. **зна́мя** (-мени; *pl* -мёна) *neut* banner; flag.

зна́ние knowledge.

зна́тный (-тен, -тна́, -о) distinguished; aristocratic; splendid.

знато́к (-а́) expert; connoisseur.

знать *impf* know; **дать ~** inform, let know.

значе́ние meaning; significance; importance. **зна́чит** so then; that means. **значи́тельный** considerable; important; significant. **зна́чить** (-чу) *impf* mean; signify; be of importance; **~ся** be; be mentioned, appear. **значо́к** (-чка́) badge; mark.

зна́ющий expert; learned.

знobи́ть *impf, impers+acc*: **меня́**, *etc.*, **знобит** I feel shivery.

зной intense heat. **зно́йный** hot; burning.

зов call, summons. **зову́** *etc.*: *see* **звать**

зо́дчество architecture. **зо́дчий** *sb* architect.

зол *see* **зло, злой**

зола́ ashes, cinders.

золо́вка sister-in-law (*husband's sister*).

золоти́стый golden. **зо́лото** gold. **золото́й** gold; golden.

золочёный gilt, gilded.

зо́на zone; region.

зонд probe. **зонди́ровать** *impf* sound, probe.

зонт (-а́), **зо́нтик** umbrella.

зоо́лог zoologist. **зоологи́ческий** zoological. **зооло́гия** zoology. **зоопа́рк** zoo. **зооте́хник** livestock specialist.

зо́ри *etc.*: *see* **заря́**

зо́ркий (-рок, -рка́, -о) sharp-sighted; perspicacious.

зрачо́к (-чка́) pupil (*of the eye*).

зре́лище sight; spectacle.

зре́лость ripeness; maturity; **аттеста́т зре́лости** school-leaving certificate. **зре́лый** (зрел, -а́, -о) ripe, mature.

зре́ние (eye)sight, vision; **то́чка зре́ния** point of view.

зреть (-е́ю) *impf* (*pf* **со~**) ripen; mature.

зри́мый visible.

зри́тель *m* spectator, observer; *pl* audience. **зри́тельный** visual; optic; **~ зал** hall, auditorium.

зря *adv* in vain.

зуб (*pl* -ы *or* -бья, -о́в *or* -бьев) tooth; cog. **зуби́ло** chisel. **зубно́й** dental; tooth; **~ врач** dentist. **зубоврачéбный** dentists', dental; **~ кабине́т** dental surgery. **зубочи́стка** toothpick.

зубр (European) bison; die-hard.

зубри́ть (-рю́, зу́бри́шь) *impf* (*pf* **вы́~, за~**) cram.

зубча́тый toothed; serrated.

зуд itch. **зуде́ть** (-и́т) itch.

зы́бкий (-бок, -бка́, -о) unsteady, shaky; vacillating. **зыбь** (*gen pl* -е́й) ripple, rippling.

зюйд (*naut*) south; south wind.

зя́блик chaffinch.

зя́бнуть (-ну; зяб) *impf* suffer from cold, feel the cold.

зябь land ploughed in autumn for spring sowing.

зять (*pl* -тья́, -тьёв) son-in-law; brother-in-law (*sister's husband or husband's sister's husband*).

И, Й

и *conj* and; even; too; (*with neg*) either; **и... и** both ... and.
и́бо *conj* for.
и́ва willow.
игла́ (*pl* -ы) needle; thorn; spine; quill. **иглоука́лывание** acupuncture.
игнори́ровать *impf* & *pf* ignore.
и́го yoke.
иго́лка needle.
иго́рный gaming, gambling. **игра́** (*pl* -ы) play, playing; game; hand; turn; ~ **слов** pun. **игра́льн|ый** playing; **~ые ко́сти** dice. **игра́ть** *impf* (*pf* **сыгра́ть**) play; act; ~ **в**+*acc* play (*game*); ~ **на**+*prep* play (*an instrument*). **игри́вый** playful. **игро́к** (-а́) player; gambler. **игру́шка** toy.
идеа́л ideal. **идеали́зм** idealism. **идеа́льный** ideal.
иде́йный high-principled; acting on principle; ideological.
идеологи́ческий ideological. **идеоло́гия** ideology.
идёт *etc.*: *see* **идти́**
иде́я idea; concept.
иди́ллия idyll.
идио́т idiot.
и́дол idol.
идти́ (иду́, идёшь; шёл, шла) *impf* (*pf* **пойти́**) go; come; run, work; pass; go on, be in progress; be on; fall; +(к+)*dat* suit.
иере́й priest.
иждиве́нец (-нца), **-ве́нка** dependant. **иждиве́ние** maintenance; **на иждиве́нии** at the expense of.
из, изо *prep*+*gen* from, out of, of.
изба́ (*pl* -ы) izba (*hut*).
изба́вить (-влю) *pf*, **избавля́ть** *impf* save, deliver; **~ся** be saved, escape; **~ся от** get rid of; get out of.
избало́ванный spoilt. **из|балова́ть**
избега́ть *impf*, **избе́гнуть** (-ну; -бе́г(нул)) *pf*, **избежа́ть** (-егу́) *pf* +*gen or inf* avoid; escape.
изберу́ *etc.*: *see* **избра́ть**
избива́ть *impf of* **изби́ть**. **избие́ние** slaughter, massacre; beating, beating-up.
избира́тель *m*, **~ница** elector, voter. **избира́тельный** electoral; election. **избира́ть** *impf of* **избра́ть**
изби́тый trite, hackneyed. **изби́ть** (изобью́, -бьёшь) *pf* (*impf* **избива́ть**) beat unmercifully, beat up; massacre.
и́збранн|ый selected; select; **~ые** *sb pl* the élite. **избра́ть** (-беру́, -берёшь; -а́л, -а́, -о) *pf* (*impf* **избира́ть**) elect; choose.
избы́ток (-тка) surplus; abundance. **избы́точный** surplus; abundant.
и́зверг monster. **изверже́ние** eruption; expulsion; excretion.
изверну́ться (-ну́сь, -нёшься) *pf* (*impf* **извора́чиваться**) dodge, be evasive.
изве́стие news; information; *pl* proceedings. **извести́ть** (-ещу́) *pf* (*impf* **извеща́ть**) inform, notify.
извёстка lime.
изве́стно it is (well) known; of course, certainly. **изве́стность** fame, reputation. **изве́стный**

known; well-known, famous; notorious; certain.

известня́к (-á) limestone. **и́звесть** lime.

извеща́ть *impf of* **извести́ть.** **извеще́ние** notification; advice.

извива́ться *impf* coil; writhe; twist, wind; meander. **изви́лина** bend, twist. **изви́листый** winding; meandering.

извине́ние excuse; apology. **извини́ть** *pf*, **извиня́ть** *impf* excuse; **извини́те (меня́)** excuse me, (I'm) sorry; **~ся** apologize; excuse o.s.

изви́ться (изовью́сь, -вьёшься; -и́лся, -áсь, -ось) *pf* coil; writhe.

извлека́ть *impf*, **извле́чь** (-еку́, -ечёшь; -ёк, -лá) *pf* extract; derive, elicit.

извне́ *adv* from outside.

изво́зчик cabman; carrier.

извора́чиваться *impf of* **изверну́ться.** **изворо́т** bend, twist; *pl* tricks, wiles. **изворо́тливый** resourceful; shrewd.

изврати́ть (-ащу́) *pf*, **извраща́ть** *impf* distort; pervert. **извраще́ние** perversion; distortion. **извращённый** perverted, unnatural.

изги́б bend, twist. **изгиба́ть(ся** *impf of* **изогну́ть(ся**

изгна́ние banishment; exile. **изгна́нник** exile. **изгна́ть** (-гоню́, -го́нишь; -áл, -á, -о) *pf* (*impf* **изгоня́ть**) banish; exile.

изголо́вье bed-head.

изголода́ться be famished, starve; **+по**+*dat* yearn for.

изгоню́ *etc.*: *see* **изгна́ть.** **изгоня́ть** *impf of* **изгна́ть**

и́згородь fence, hedge.

изгота́вливать *impf*, **изгото́вить** (-влю) *pf*, **изготовля́ть** *impf* make, manufacture; **~ся** get ready. **изготовле́ние** making, manufacture.

издава́ть (-даю́, -даёшь) *impf of* **изда́ть**

и́здавна *adv* from time immemorial; for a very long time.

издади́м *etc.*: *see* **изда́ть**

издалека́, и́здали *advs* from afar.

изда́ние publication; edition; promulgation. **изда́тель** *m* publisher. **изда́тельство** publishing house. **изда́ть** (-áм, -áшь, -áст, -ади́м; -áл, -á, -о) *pf* (*impf* **издава́ть**) publish; promulgate; produce; emit; **~ся** be published.

издева́тельство mockery; taunt. **издева́ться** *impf* (**+над** +*instr*) mock (at).

изде́лие work; make; article; *pl* wares.

изде́ржки (-жек) *pl* expenses; costs; cost.

из|до́хнуть *pf.*

из|жа́рить(ся *pf.*

изжо́га heartburn.

из-за *prep+gen* from behind; because of.

излага́ть *impf of* **изложи́ть**

излече́ние treatment; recovery; cure. **излечи́ть** (-чу́, -чишь) cure; **~ся** be cured; **+от**+*gen* rid o.s. of.

изли́шек (-шка) surplus; excess. **изли́шество** excess; over-indulgence. **изли́шний** (-шен, -шня) superfluous.

изложе́ние exposition; account. **изложи́ть** (-жу́, -жишь) *pf* (*impf* **излага́ть**) expound; set forth; word.

изло́м break, fracture; sharp bend. **излома́ть** *pf* break; smash; wear out; warp.

излуча́ть *impf* radiate, emit. **излуче́ние** radiation; emanation.

из|ма́зать (-а́жу) *pf* dirty, smear all over; use up; **~ся** get dirty, smear o.s. all over.

изме́на betrayal; treason; infidelity.

измене́ние change, alteration; inflection. **измени́ть**[1] (-ню́, -нишь) *pf* (*impf* **изменя́ть**[1]) change, alter; **~ся** change.

измени́ть[2] (-ню́, -нишь) *pf* (*impf* **изменя́ть**[2]) *+dat* betray; be unfaithful to. **изме́нник, -ица** traitor.

изменя́емый variable. **изменя́ть**[1,2](**ся** *impf of* **измени́ть**[1,2](**ся**

измере́ние measurement, measuring. **изме́рить** *pf*, **измеря́ть** *impf* measure, gauge.

изможденный (-ён, -а́) worn out.

из|му́чить (-чу) *pf* torment; tire out, exhaust; **~ся** be exhausted. **измученный** worn out.

измышле́ние fabrication, invention.

измя́тый crumpled, creased; haggard, jaded. **из|мя́ть(ся** (изомну́(сь, -нёшь(ся) *pf*.

изна́нка wrong side; seamy side.

из|наси́ловать *pf* rape, assault.

изна́шивание wear (and tear). **изна́шивать(ся** *impf of* **износи́ть(ся**

изне́женный pampered; delicate; effeminate.

изнемога́ть *impf*, **изнемо́чь** (-огу́, -о́жешь; -о́г, -ла́) *pf* be exhausted. **изнеможе́ние** exhaustion.

изно́с wear; wear and tear; deterioration. **износи́ть** (-ошу́, -о́сишь) *pf* (*impf* **изна́шивать**) wear out; **~ся** wear out; be used up. **изно́шенный** worn out; threadbare.

изнуре́ние exhaustion. **изнурённый** (-ён, -ена́) exhausted, worn out; jaded. **изнури́тельный** exhausting.

изнутри́ *adv* from inside, from within.

изо *see* **из**

изоби́лие abundance, plenty. **изоби́ловать** *impf* *+instr* abound in, be rich in. **изоби́льный** abundant.

изоблича́ть *impf*, **изобличи́ть** (-чу́) *pf* expose; show. **изобличе́ние** exposure; conviction.

изобража́ть *impf*, **изобрази́ть** (-ажу́) *pf* represent, depict, portray (*+instr* as); **~ из себя́***+acc* make o.s. out to be. **изображе́ние** image; representation; portrayal. **изобрази́тельн|ый** graphic; decorative; **~ые иску́сства** fine arts.

изобрести́ (-ету́, -етёшь; -ёл, -а́) *pf*, **изобрета́ть** *impf* invent; devise. **изобрета́тель** *m* inventor. **изобрета́тельный** inventive. **изобрете́ние** invention.

изобью *etc.*: *see* **изби́ть. изовью́сь** *etc.*: *see* **изви́ться**

изо́гнутый bent, curved; winding. **изогну́ть(ся** (-ну́(сь, -нёшь(ся) *pf* (*impf* **изгиба́ть(ся**) bend, curve.

изоли́ровать *impf* & *pf* isolate; insulate. **изоля́тор** insulator; isolation ward; solitary confinement cell. **изоля́ция** isolation; quarantine; insulation.

изомну́(сь *etc.*: *see* **измя́ть**

изо́рванный tattered, torn. **изорва́ть** (-ву́, -вёшь; -а́л, -а́, -о)

pf tear, tear to pieces; **~ся** be in tatters.
изощрённый (-рён, -á) refined; keen. **изощри́ться** *pf*, **изощря́ться** *impf* acquire refinement; excel.
из-под *prep+gen* from under.
Изра́иль *m* Israel. **изра́ильский** Israeli.
из|расхо́довать(ся *pf*.
и́зредка *adv* now and then.
изре́зать (-е́жу) *pf* cut up.
изрече́ние dictum, saying.
изры́ть (-ро́ю) *pf* dig up, plough up. **изры́тый** pitted.
изря́дно *adv* fairly, pretty. **изря́дный** fair, handsome; fairly large.
изуве́чить (-чу) *pf* maim, mutilate.
изуми́тельный amazing. **изуми́ть** (-млю́) *pf*, **изумля́ть** *impf* amaze; **~ся** be amazed. **изумле́ние** amazement.
изумру́д emerald.
изуро́дованный maimed; disfigured. **из|уро́довать** *pf*.
изуча́ть *impf*, **изучи́ть** (-чу́, -чишь) *pf* learn, study. **изуче́ние** study.
изъе́здить (-зжу) *pf* travel all over; wear out.
изъяви́ть (-влю́, -вишь) *pf*, **изъявля́ть** *impf* express.
изъя́н defect, flaw.
изъя́тие withdrawal; removal; exception. **изъя́ть** (изыму́, -мешь) *pf*. **изыма́ть** *impf* withdraw.
изыска́ние investigation, research; prospecting; survey. **изы́сканный** refined. **изыска́ть** (-ыщу́, -ы́щешь) *pf*, **изы́скивать** *impf* search out; (try to) find.
изю́м raisins.
изя́щество elegance, grace. **изя́щный** elegant, graceful.
ика́ть *impf*, **икну́ть** (-ну́, -нёшь) *pf* hiccup.
ико́на icon.
ико́та hiccup, hiccups.
икра́[1] (hard) roe; caviare.
икра́[2] (*pl* -ы) calf (*of leg*).
ил silt; sludge.
и́ли *conj* or; **~... ~** either ... or.
и́листый muddy, silty.
иллюзиони́ст conjurer. **иллю́зия** illusion.
иллюмина́тор porthole. **иллюмина́ция** illumination.
иллюстра́ция illustration. **иллюстри́ровать** *impf* & *pf* illustrate.
им *see* **он, оно́, оно́**
им. *abbr* (*of* **и́мени**) named after.
и́мени *etc.*: *see* **и́мя**
име́ние estate.
имени́ны (-и́н) *pl* name-day (party). **имени́тельный** nominative. **и́менно** *adv* namely; exactly, precisely; **вот ~!** exactly!
име́ть (-е́ю) *impf* have; **~ де́ло с**+*instr* have dealings with; **~ ме́сто** take place; **~ся** be; be available.
и́ми *see* **они́**
имита́ция imitation. **имити́ровать** *impf* imitate.
иммигра́нт, ~ка immigrant.
иммигра́ция immigration.
императо́р emperor. **императо́рский** imperial. **императри́ца** empress. **империали́зм** imperialism. **империали́ст** imperialist. **империалисти́ческий** imperialist(ic). **импе́рия** empire.
и́мпорт import. **импорти́ро-**

вать *impf* & *pf* import. **и́мпортный** import(ed).

импровиза́ция improvisation. **импровизи́ровать** *impf* & *pf* improvise.

и́мпульс impulse.

иму́щество property.

и́мя (и́мени; *pl* имена́, -ён) *neut* name; first name; noun; **~ прилага́тельное** adjective; **~ существи́тельное** noun; **~ числи́тельное** numeral.

и́на́че *adv* differently, otherwise; **так или ~** in any event; *conj* otherwise, or else.

инвали́д disabled person; invalid. **инвали́дность** disablement, disability.

инвента́рь (-я́) *m* stock; equipment; inventory.

инде́ец (-е́йца) (American) Indian. **инде́йка** (*gen pl* -е́ек) turkey(-hen). **инде́йский** (American) Indian.

и́ндекс index; code.

индиа́нка Indian; American Indian. **инди́ец** (-и́йца) Indian.

индивидуали́зм individualism. **индивидуа́льность** individuality. **индивидуа́льный** individual. **индиви́дуум** individual.

инди́йский Indian. **И́ндия** India. **инду́с, инду́ска** Hindu.

индустриализа́ция industrialization. **индустриализи́ровать** *impf* & *pf* industrialize. **индустриа́льный** industrial. **инду́стрия** industry.

индю́к, индю́шка turkey.

и́ней hoar-frost.

ине́ртность inertia; sluggishness. **ине́рция** inertia.

инжене́р engineer; **~-меха́ник** mechanical engineer; **~-строи́тель** *m* civil engineer.

инжи́р fig.

инициа́л initial.

инициати́ва initiative. **инициа́тор** initiator.

инквизи́ция inquisition.

инкруста́ция inlaid work, inlay.

инкуба́тор incubator.

ино- *in comb* other, different; hetero-. **иногоро́дний** of, from, another town. **~ро́дный** foreign. **~сказа́тельный** allegorical. **~стра́нец** (-нца), **~стра́нка** (*gen pl* -нок) foreigner. **~стра́нный** foreign. **~язы́чный** foreign.

иногда́ *adv* sometimes.

ино́й different; other; some; **~ раз** sometimes.

и́нок monk. **и́нокиня** nun.

инотде́л foreign department.

инсектици́д insecticide.

инспе́ктор inspector. **инспе́кция** inspection; inspectorate.

инста́нция instance.

инсти́нкт instinct. **инстинкти́вный** instinctive.

институ́т institute.

инстру́ктор instructor. **инстру́кция** instructions.

инструме́нт instrument; tool.

инсули́н insulin.

инсцениро́вка dramatization, adaptation; pretence.

интегра́ция integration.

интелле́кт intellect. **интеллектуа́льный** intellectual.

интеллиге́нт intellectual. **интеллиге́нтный** cultured, educated. **интеллиге́нция** intelligentsia.

интенси́вность intensity. **интенси́вный** intensive.

интеракти́вный interactive.

интерва́л interval.

интерве́нция intervention.
интервью́ *neut indecl* interview.
интере́с interest. **интере́сный** interesting. **интересова́ть** *impf* interest; **~ся** be interested (+*instr* in).
интерна́т boarding-school.
интернациона́льный international.
Интерне́т the Internet; **в ~е** on the Internet.
интерни́ровать *impf & pf* intern.
интерпрета́ция interpretation. **интерпрети́ровать** *impf & pf* interpret.
интерье́р interior.
инти́мный intimate.
интона́ция intonation.
интри́га intrigue; plot. **интригова́ть** *impf*, (*pf* **за~**) intrigue.
интуи́ция intuition.
инфа́ркт infarct; coronary (thrombosis), heart attack.
инфекцио́нный infectious. **инфе́кция** infection.
инфля́ция inflation.
информа́тика IT.
информа́ция information.
инфракра́сный infra-red.
ио́д *etc.*: *see* **йод**
ио́н ion.
ипохо́ндрик hypochondriac. **ипохо́ндрия** hypochondria.
ипподро́м racecourse.
Ира́к Iraq. **ира́кец** (-кца) Iraqi. **ира́кский** Iraqi.
Ира́н Iran. **ира́нец** (-нца), **ира́нка** Iranian. **ира́нский** Iranian.
ирла́ндец (-дца) Irishman. **Ирла́ндия** Ireland. **ирла́ндка** Irishwoman. **ирла́ндский** Irish.
ирони́ческий ironic. **иро́ния** irony.
ирригáция irrigation.
иск suit, action.
искажа́ть *impf*, **искази́ть** (-ажу́) *pf* distort, pervert; misrepresent. **искаже́ние** distortion, perversion.
искале́ченный crippled, maimed. **искале́чить** (-чу́) *pf* cripple, maim; break.
иска́ть (ищу́, и́щешь) *impf* (+*acc or gen*) seek, look for.
исключа́ть *impf*, **исключи́ть** (-чу́) *pf* exclude; eliminate; expel. **исключа́я** *prep+gen* except. **исключе́ние** exception; exclusion; expulsion; elimination; **за исключе́нием** +*gen* with the exception of. **исключи́тельно** *adv* exceptionally; exclusively. **исключи́тельный** exceptional; exclusive.
иско́нный primordial.
ископа́емое *sb* mineral; fossil. **ископа́емый** fossilized, fossil.
искорени́ть *pf*, **искореня́ть** *impf* eradicate.
и́скоса *adv* askance; sidelong.
и́скра spark.
и́скренний sincere. **и́скренность** sincerity.
искривле́ние bend; distortion, warping.
ис|купа́ть[1]**(ся** *pf*.
искупа́ть[2] *impf*, **искупи́ть** (-плю́, -пишь) *pf* atone for; make up for. **искупле́ние** redemption, atonement.
искуси́ть (-ушу́) *pf of* **искуша́ть**
иску́сный skilful; expert. **иску́сственный** artificial; feigned. **иску́сство** art; skill. **искусствове́д** art historian.
искуша́ть *impf* (*pf* **искуси́ть**) tempt; seduce. **искуше́ние** temptation, seduction.

испа́нец (-нца) Spaniard. **Испа́ния** Spain. **испа́нка** Spanish woman. **испа́нский** Spanish.

испаре́ние evaporation; *pl* fumes. **испари́ться** *pf*, **испаря́ться** *impf* evaporate.

ис|па́чкать *pf*. **ис|пе́чь** (-еку́, -ечёшь) *pf*.

испове́довать *impf* & *pf* confess; profess; **~ся** confess; make one's confession; **+в**+*prep* unburden o.s. of. **и́споведь** confession.

исподтишка́ *adv* in an underhand way; on the quiet.

исполи́н giant. **исполи́нский** gigantic.

исполко́м *abbr* (*of* **исполни́тельный комите́т**) executive committee.

исполне́ние fulfilment, execution. **исполни́тель** *m*, **~ница** executor; performer. **исполни́тельный** executive. **испо́лнить** *pf*, **исполня́ть** *impf* carry out, execute; fulfil; perform; **~ся** be fulfilled.

испо́льзование utilization. **испо́льзовать** *impf* & *pf* make (good) use of, utilize.

ис|по́ртить(ся (-рчу(сь) *pf*. **испо́рченный** depraved; spoiled; rotten.

исправи́тельный correctional; corrective. **испра́вить** (-влю) *pf*, **исправля́ть** *impf* rectify, correct; mend; reform; **~ся** improve, reform. **исправле́ние** repairing; improvement; correction. **испра́вленный** improved, corrected; revised; reformed. **испра́вный** in good order; punctual; meticulous.

ис|про́бовать *pf*.

испу́г fright. **ис|пуга́ть(ся** *pf*.

испуска́ть *impf*, **испусти́ть** (-ущу́, -у́стишь) *pf* emit, let out.

испыта́ние test, trial; ordeal. **испыта́ть** *pf*, **испы́тывать** *impf* test; try; experience.

иссле́дование investigation; research. **иссле́дователь** *m* researcher; investigator. **иссле́довательский** research. **иссле́довать** *impf* & *pf* investigate, examine; research into.

истаска́ться *pf*, **иста́скиваться** *impf* wear out; be worn out.

истека́ть *impf of* **исте́чь**. **исте́кший** past.

исте́рика hysterics. **истери́ческий** hysterical. **истери́я** hysteria.

истече́ние outflow; expiry. **исте́чь** (-ечёт; -тёк, -ла́) *pf* (*impf* **истека́ть**) elapse; expire.

и́стина truth. **и́стинный** true.

истлева́ть *impf*, **истле́ть** (-е́ю) *pf* rot, decay; be reduced to ashes.

исто́к source.

истолкова́ть *pf*, **истолко́вывать** *impf* interpret; comment on.

ис|толо́чь (-лку́, -лчёшь; -ло́к, -лкла́) *pf*.

исто́ма languor.

исторга́ть *impf*, **исто́ргнуть** (-ну; -о́рг) *pf* throw out.

исто́рик historian. **истори́ческий** historical; historic. **исто́рия** history; story; incident.

исто́чник spring; source.

истоща́ть *impf*, **истощи́ть** (-щу́) *pf* exhaust; emaciate. **истоще́ние** emaciation; exhaustion.

ис|тра́тить (-а́чу) *pf*.

истреби́тель *m* destroyer; fighter. **истреби́ть** (-блю́) *pf*,

истребля́ть *impf* destroy; exterminate.
ис|тупи́ться (-пится) *pf.*
истяза́ние torture. **истяза́ть** *impf* torture.
исхо́д outcome; end; Exodus. **исходи́ть** (-ожу́, -о́дишь) *impf* (+**из** *or* **от**+*gen*) issue (from), come (from); proceed (from). **исхо́дный** initial; departure.
исхуда́лый undernourished, emaciated.
исцеле́ние healing; recovery. **исцели́ть** *pf*, **исцеля́ть** *impf* heal, cure.
исчеза́ть *impf*, **исче́знуть** (-ну; -ез) *pf* disappear, vanish. **исчезнове́ние** disappearance.
исче́рпать *pf*, **исче́рпывать** *impf* exhaust; conclude. **исче́рпывающий** exhaustive.
исчисле́ние calculation; calculus.
ита́к *conj* thus; so then.
Ита́лия Italy. **италья́нец** (-нца), **италья́нка** Italian. **италья́нский** Italian.
ИТАР-ТА́СС *abbr* (*of* **Информацио́нное телегра́фное аге́нтство Росси́и**; *see* **ТАСС**) ITAR-Tass.
и т.д. *abbr* (*of* **и так да́лее**) etc., and so on.
ито́г sum; total; result. **итого́** *adv* in all, altogether.
и т.п. *abbr* (*of* **и тому́ подо́бное**) etc., and so on.
иуде́й, иуде́йка Jew. **иуде́йский** Judaic.
их their, theirs; *see* **они́**.
иша́к (-а́) donkey.
ище́йка bloodhound; police dog.
ищу́ *etc.*: *see* **иска́ть**
ию́ль *m* July. **ию́льский** July.
ию́нь *m* June. **ию́ньский** June.
йо́га yoga.
йод iodine.
йо́та iota.

К

к, ко *prep*+*dat* to, towards; by; for; on; on the occasion of; **к пе́рвому января́** by the first of January; **к тому́ вре́мени** by then; **к тому́ же** besides, moreover; **к чему́?** what for?
-ка *partl modifying force of imper or expressing decision or intention*; **да́йте-ка пройти́** let me pass, please; **скажи́-ка мне** do tell me.
каба́к (-а́) tavern.
кабала́ servitude.
каба́н (-а́) wild boar.
кабаре́ *neut indecl* cabaret.
кабачо́к (-чка́) marrow.
ка́бель *m* cable. **ка́бельтов** cable, hawser.
каби́на cabin; booth; cockpit; cubicle; cab. **кабине́т** study; surgery; room; office; Cabinet.
каблу́к (-а́) heel.
кабота́ж coastal shipping. **кабота́жный** coastal.
кабы if.
кавале́р knight; partner, gentleman. **кавалери́йский** cavalry. **кавалери́ст** cavalryman. **кавале́рия** cavalry.
ка́верзный tricky.
Кавка́з the Caucasus. **кавка́зец** (-зца́), **кавка́зка** Caucasian. **кавка́зский** Caucasian.
кавы́чки (-чек) *pl* inverted commas, quotation marks.
каде́т cadet. **каде́тский ко́рпус** military school.
ка́дка tub, vat.

кадр frame, still; close-up; cadre; *pl* establishment; staff; personnel; specialists. **кáдровый** (*mil*) regular; skilled, trained.

кадык (-á) Adam's apple.

каждодневный daily, everyday. **кáждый** each, every; *sb* everybody.

кáжется *etc.*: *see* **казáться**

казáк (-á; *pl* -áки, -áков), **казáчка** Cossack.

казáрма barracks.

казáться (кажýсь, кáжешься) *impf* (*pf* **по~**) seem, appear; *impers* **кáжется, казáлось** apparently; **казáлось бы** it would seem; *+dat*: **мне кáжется** it seems to me; I think.

Казахстáн Kazakhstan. **казáчий** Cossack.

каземáт casemate.

казённый State; government; fiscal; public; formal; banal, conventional. **казнá** Exchequer, Treasury; public purse; the State. **казначéй** treasurer, bursar; paymaster.

казинó *neut indecl* casino.

казнить *impf* & *pf* execute; punish; castigate. **казнь** execution.

каймá (*gen pl* каём) border, edging.

как *adv* how; what; **вот ~!** you don't say!; **~ вы дýмаете?** what do you think?; **~ его зовýт?** what is his name?; **~ же** naturally, of course; **~ же так?** how is that?; **~ ни** however. **как** *conj* as; like; when; since; *+neg* but, except, than; **в то врéмя ~** while, whereas; **~ мóжно, ~ нельзя́**+*comp* as ... as possible; **~ мóжно скорée** as soon as possible; **~ нельзя́ лýчше** as well as possible; **~ тóлько** as soon as, when; **мéжду тем, ~** while, whereas. **как бýдто** *conj* as if; *partl* apparently. **как бы** how; as if; **как бы... не** what if, supposing; **как бы... ни** however. **кáк-либо** *adv* somehow. **кáк-нибудь** *adv* somehow; anyhow. **как раз** *adv* just, exactly. **как-то** *adv* somehow; once.

какáо *neut indecl* cocoa.

какóв (-á, -ó, -ы) *pron* what, what sort (of); **~ он?** what is he like?; **~ он собóй?** what does he look like?; **погóда-то каковá!** what weather! **каковó** *adv* how. **какóй** *pron* what; (such) as; which; **~... ни** whatever, whichever. **какóй-либо, какóй-нибудь** *prons* some; any; only. **какóй-то** *pron* some; a; a kind of.

как раз, кáк-то *see* **как**

кáктус cactus.

кал faeces, excrement.

каламбýр pun.

калéка *m* & *f* cripple.

календáрь (-я́) *m* calendar.

калéние incandescence.

калéчить (-чу) *impf* (*pf* **ис~, по~**) cripple, maim; **~ся** become a cripple.

калибр calibre; bore; gauge.

кáлий potassium.

калитка (wicket-)gate.

каллигрáфия calligraphy.

калóрия calorie.

калóша galosh.

кáлька tracing-paper; tracing.

калькуля́ция calculation.

кальсóны (-н) *pl* long johns.

кáльций calcium.

кáмбала flat-fish; plaice; flounder.

каменистый stony, rocky. **каменноугóльный** coal; **~ бас-**

се́йн coal-field. **ка́менный** stone; rock; stony; hard, immovable; ~ **век** Stone Age; ~ **у́голь** coal. **каменоло́мня** (*gen pl* -мен) quarry. **ка́менщик** (stone)mason; bricklayer. **ка́мень** (-мня; *pl* -мни, -мне́й) *m* stone.

ка́мера chamber; cell; camera; inner tube, (football) bladder; ~ **хране́ния** cloak-room, left-luggage office. **ка́мерный** chamber. **камерто́н** tuning-fork.

ками́н fireplace; fire.

камко́рдер camcorder.

камо́рка closet, very small room.

кампа́ния campaign; cruise.

камы́ш (-а́) reed, rush; cane.

кана́ва ditch; gutter.

Кана́да Canada. **кана́дец** (-дца), **кана́дка** Canadian. **кана́дский** Canadian.

кана́л canal; channel. **канализа́ция** sewerage (system).

канаре́йка canary.

кана́т rope; cable.

канва́ canvas; groundwork; outline, design.

кандалы́ (-о́в) *pl* shackles.

кандида́т candidate; ~ **нау́к** person with higher degree. **кандидату́ра** candidature.

кани́кулы (-ул) *pl* vacation; holidays.

кани́стра can, canister.

канони́ческий canon(ical).

кано́э *neut indecl* canoe.

кант edging; mount. **кантова́ть** *impf*; **«не ~»** 'this way up'.

кану́н eve.

ка́нуть (-ну) *pf* drop, sink; **как в во́ду** ~ vanish into thin air.

канцеля́рия office. **канцеля́рский** office; clerical. **канцеля́рщина** red-tape.

ка́нцлер chancellor.

ка́пать (-аю *or* -плю) *impf* (*pf* **ка́пнуть, на~**) drip, drop; trickle; +*instr* spill.

капе́лла choir; chapel.

ка́пелька small drop; a little; ~ **росы́** dew-drop.

капельме́йстер conductor; bandmaster.

капилля́р capillary.

капита́л capital. **капитали́зм** capitalism. **капитали́ст** capitalist. **капиталисти́ческий** capitalist. **капита́льный** capital; main, fundamental; major.

капита́н captain; skipper.

капитули́ровать *impf* & *pf* capitulate. **капитуля́ция** capitulation.

капка́н trap.

ка́пля (*gen pl* -пель) drop; bit, scrap. **ка́пнуть** (-ну) *pf of* **ка́пать**

капо́т hood, cowl, cowling; bonnet; house-coat.

капри́з caprice. **капри́зничать** *impf* play up. **капри́зный** capricious.

капу́ста cabbage.

капюшо́н hood.

ка́ра punishment.

кара́бкаться *impf* (*pf* **вс~**) clamber.

карава́н caravan; convoy.

кара́кули *f pl* scribble.

караме́ль caramel; caramels.

каранда́ш (-а́) pencil.

каранти́н quarantine.

кара́т carat.

кара́тельный punitive. **кара́ть** *impf* (*pf* **по~**) punish.

карау́л guard; watch; ~! help! **карау́лить** *impf* guard; lie in wait for. **карау́льный** guard; *sb* sentry, sentinel, guard.

карбюра́тор carburettor.

каре́та carriage, coach.

ка́рий brown; hazel.

карикату́ра caricature; cartoon.

карка́с frame; framework.

ка́ркать *impf*, **ка́ркнуть** (-ну) *pf* caw, croak.

ка́рлик, ка́рлица dwarf; pygmy. **ка́рликовый** dwarf; pygmy.

карма́н pocket. **карма́нник** pickpocket. **карма́нный** *adj* pocket.

карни́з cornice; ledge.

карп carp.

ка́рта map; (playing-)card.

карта́вить (-влю) *impf* burr.

картёжник gambler.

карте́чь case-shot, grape-shot.

карти́на picture; scene. **карти́нка** picture; illustration. **карти́нный** picturesque; picture.

карто́н cardboard. **карто́нка** cardboard box.

картоте́ка card-index.

карто́фель *m* potatoes; potato(-plant). **карто́фельн|ый** potato; **~ое пюре́** mashed potatoes.

ка́рточка card; season ticket; photo. **ка́рточный** card.

карто́шка potatoes; potato.

ка́ртридж cartridge.

карусе́ль merry-go-round.

ка́рцер cell, lock-up.

карье́р[1] full gallop.

карье́р[2] quarry; sand-pit.

карье́ра career. **карьери́ст** careerist.

каса́ние contact. **каса́тельная** *sb* tangent. **каса́ться** *impf* (*pf* **косну́ться**) +*gen* or **до**+*gen* touch; touch on; concern; **что каса́ется** as regards.

ка́ска helmet.

каска́д cascade.

каспи́йский Caspian.

ка́сса till; cash-box; booking-office; box-office; cash-desk; cash.

кассе́та cassette. **кассе́тный магнитофо́н** cassette recorder.

касси́р, касси́рша cashier.

кастра́т eunuch. **кастра́ция** castration. **кастри́ровать** *impf* & *pf* castrate, geld.

кастрю́ля saucepan.

катало́г catalogue.

ката́ние rolling; driving; **~ верхо́м** riding; **~ на конька́х** skating.

катапу́льта catapult. **катапульти́ровать(ся** *impf* & *pf* catapult.

ката́р catarrh.

катара́кта cataract.

катастро́фа catastrophe. **катастрофи́ческий** catastrophic.

ката́ть *impf* roll; (take for a) drive; **~ся** (*pf* **по~**) roll, roll about; go for a drive; **~ся верхо́м** ride, go riding; **~ся на конька́х** skate, go skating.

категори́ческий categorical. **катего́рия** category.

ка́тер (*pl* -á) cutter; launch.

кати́ть (-ачу́, -а́тишь) *impf* bowl along, rip, tear; **~ся** rush, tear; flow, stream, roll; **кати́сь, кати́тесь** get out! clear off! **като́к** (-тка́) skating-rink; roller.

като́лик, католи́чка Catholic. **католи́ческий** Catholic.

ка́торга penal servitude, hard labour. **ка́торжник** convict. **ка́торжн|ый** penal; **~ые рабо́ты** hard labour; drudgery.

кату́шка reel, bobbin; spool; coil.
каучу́к rubber.
кафе́ *neut indecl* café.
ка́федра pulpit; rostrum; chair; department.
ка́фель *m* Dutch tile.
кача́лка rocking-chair. **кача́ние** rocking, swinging; pumping. **кача́ть** *impf* (*pf* **качну́ть**) +*acc or instr* rock, swing; shake; **~ся** rock, swing; roll; reel. **каче́ли** (-ей) *pl* swing.
ка́чественный qualitative; high-quality. **ка́чество** quality; **в ка́честве**+*gen* as, in the capacity of.
ка́чка rocking; tossing.
качну́ть(ся (-ну́(сь, -нёшь(ся) *pf of* **кача́ть(ся**. **качу́** *etc.*: *see* **кати́ть**
ка́ша gruel, porridge; **завари́ть ка́шу** stir up trouble.
ка́шель (-шля) cough. **ка́шлянуть** (-ну) *pf*, **ка́шлять** *impf* (have a) cough.
кашта́н chestnut. **кашта́новый** chestnut.
каю́та cabin, stateroom.
ка́ющийся penitent. **ка́яться** (ка́юсь) *impf* (*pf* **по~**, **рас~**) repent; confess; **ка́юсь** I (must) confess.
кв. *abbr* (*of* **квадра́тный**) square; (*of* **кварти́ра**) flat.
квадра́т square; quad; **в квадра́те** squared; **возвести́ в ~** square. **квадра́тный** square; quadratic.
ква́кать *impf*, **ква́кнуть** (-ну) *pf* croak.
квалифика́ция qualification. **квалифици́рованный** qualified, skilled.
квант, ква́нта quantum. **ква́нтовый** quantum.
кварта́л block; quarter. **кварта́льный** quarterly.
кварте́т quartet.
кварти́ра flat; apartment(s); quarters. **квартира́нт, -ра́нтка** lodger; tenant. **кварти́рная пла́та, квартпла́та** rent.
кварц quartz.
квас (*pl* **~ы́**) kvass. **ква́сить** (-а́шу) *impf* sour; pickle. **ква́шеная капу́ста** sauerkraut.
кве́рху *adv* up, upwards.
квит, кви́ты quits.
квита́нция receipt. **квито́к** (-тка́) ticket, check.
КГБ *abbr* (*of* **Комите́т госуда́рственной безопа́сности**) KGB.
ке́гля skittle.
кедр cedar.
ке́ды (-ов) *pl* trainers.
кекс (fruit-)cake.
ке́лья (*gen pl* -лий) cell.
кем *see* **кто**
ке́мпинг campsite.
кенгуру́ *m indecl* kangaroo.
ке́пка cloth cap.
кера́мика ceramics.
keroга́з stove. **кероси́н** paraffin. **кероси́нка** paraffin stove.
ке́та Siberian salmon. **ке́тов|ый**: **~ая икра́** red caviare.
кефи́р kefir, yoghurt.
киберне́тика cybernetics.
кива́ть *impf*, **кивну́ть** (-ну́, -нёшь) *pf* (**голово́й**) nod (one's head); (+**на**+*acc*) motion (to). **киво́к** (-вка́) nod.
кида́ть *impf* (*pf* **ки́нуть**) throw, fling; **~ся** fling o.s.; rush; +*instr* throw.
кий (-я́; *pl* -и́, -ёв) (*billiard*) cue.
килев|о́й keel; **~а́я ка́чка** pitching.
кило́ *neut indecl* kilo. **килова́тт**

kilowatt. **килогра́мм** kilogram. **киломе́тр** kilometre.

киль *m* keel; fin. **кильва́тер** wake.

ки́лька sprat.

кинжа́л dagger.

кино́ *neut indecl* cinema.

кино- *in comb* film-, cine-. **киноаппара́т** cinecamera. **~арти́ст, ~арти́стка** film actor, actress. **~журна́л** news-reel. **~за́л** cinema; auditorium. **~звезда́** film-star. **~зри́тель** *m* film-goer. **~карти́на** film. **~опера́тор** camera-man. **~плёнка** film. **~режиссёр** film director. **~теа́тр** cinema. **~хро́ника** news-reel.

ки́нуть(ся (-ну(сь) *pf of* **кида́ть(ся**

кио́ск kiosk, stall.

ки́па pile, stack; bale.

кипари́с cypress.

кипе́ние boiling. **кипе́ть** (-плю́) *impf* (*pf* **вс~**) boil, seethe.

кипу́чий boiling, seething; ebullient. **кипяти́льник** kettle, boiler. **кипяти́ть** (-ячу́) *impf* (*pf* **вс~**) boil; **~ся** boil; get excited. **кипято́к** (-тка́) boiling water. **кипячёный** boiled.

Кирги́зия Kirghizia.

кирка́ pick(axe).

кирпи́ч (-а́) brick; bricks. **кирпи́чный** brick; brick-red.

кисе́ль *m* kissel, blancmange.

кисе́т tobacco-pouch.

кисея́ muslin.

кислоро́д oxygen. **кислота́** (*pl* -ы) acid; acidity. **кисло́тный** acid. **ки́слый** sour; acid. **ки́снуть** (-ну; кис) *impf* (*pf* **про~**) turn sour.

ки́сточка brush; tassel. **кисть** (*gen pl* -е́й) cluster, bunch; brush; tassel; hand.

кит (-а́) whale.

кита́ец (-а́йца; *pl* -цы, -цев) Chinese. **Кита́й** China. **кита́йский** Chinese. **китая́нка** Chinese (woman).

китобо́й whaler. **кито́вый** whale.

кичи́ться (-чу́сь) *impf* plume o.s.; strut. **кичли́вость** conceit. **кичли́вый** conceited.

кише́ть (-ши́т) *impf* swarm, teem.

кише́чник bowels, intestines. **кише́чный** intestinal. **кишка́** gut, intestine; hose.

клавеси́н harpsichord. **клавиату́ра** keyboard. **кла́виша** key. **кла́вишный: ~ инструме́нт** keyboard instrument.

клад treasure.

кла́дбище cemetery, graveyard.

кла́дка laying; masonry. **кладова́я** *sb* pantry; store-room. **кладовщи́к** (-а́) storeman. **кладу́** *etc.*: *see* **класть**

кла́няться *impf* (*pf* **поклони́ться**) +*dat* bow to; greet.

кла́пан valve; vent.

кларне́т clarinet.

класс class; class-room. **кла́ссик** classic. **кла́ссика** the classics. **классифици́ровать** *impf* & *pf* classify. **класси́ческий** classical. **кла́ссный** class; first-class. **кла́ссовый** class.

класть (-аду́, -адёшь; -ал) *impf* (*pf* **положи́ть, сложи́ть**) lay; put.

клева́ть (клюю́, клюёшь) *impf* (*pf* **клю́нуть**) peck; bite.

кле́вер (*pl* -а́) clover.

клевета́ slander; libel. **клевета́ть** (-ещу́, -е́щешь) *impf* (*pf* **на~**) +**на**+*acc* slander; libel. **клеветни́к** (-а́), **-ни́ца** slanderer. **клеветни́ческий** slanderous; libellous.

клеёнка oilcloth. **кле́ить** *impf* (*pf* **с~**) glue; stick; **~ся** stick; become sticky. **клей** (*loc* -ю́; *pl* -и́) glue, adhesive. **кле́йкий** sticky.

клейми́ть (-млю́) *impf* (*pf* **за~**) brand; stamp; stigmatize. **клеймо́** (*pl* -а) brand; stamp; mark.

кле́йстер paste.

клён maple.

клепа́ть *impf* rivet.

кле́тка cage; check; cell. **кле́точка** cellule. **кле́точный** cellular. **клетча́тка** cellulose. **кле́тчатый** checked.

клёш flare.

клешня́ (*gen pl* -е́й) claw.

кле́щи (-е́й) *pl* pincers, tongs.

клие́нт client. **клиенту́ра** clientèle.

кли́зма enema.

клик cry, call. **кли́кать** (-и́чу) *impf*, **кли́кнуть** (-ну) *pf* call.

кли́макс menopause.

кли́мат climate. **климати́ческий** climatic.

клин (*pl* -нья, -ньев) wedge. **кли́нок** (-нка́) blade.

кли́ника clinic. **клини́ческий** clinical.

клипс clip-on ear-ring.

клич call. **кли́чка** name; nickname. **кли́чу** *etc.*: *see* **кли́кать**

клок (-а́; *pl* -о́чья, -ьев *or* -и́, -о́в) rag, shred; tuft.

клёкот bubbling; gurgling. **клокота́ть** (-о́чет) *impf* bubble; gurgle; boil up.

клони́ть (-ню́, -нишь) *impf* bend; incline; +к+*dat* drive at; **~ся** bow, bend; +к+*dat* near, approach.

клон clone.

клоп (-а́) bug.

кло́ун clown.

клочо́к (-чка́) scrap, shred. **кло́чья** *etc.*: *see* **клок**

клуб[1] club.

клуб[2] (*pl* -ы́) puff; cloud.

клу́бень (-бня) *m* tuber.

клуби́ться *impf* swirl; curl.

клубни́ка (*no pl*; *usu collect*) strawberry; strawberries.

клубо́к (-бка́) ball; tangle.

клу́мба (flower-)bed.

клык (-а́) fang; tusk; canine (*tooth*).

клюв beak.

клю́ква cranberry; cranberries.

клю́нуть (-ну) *pf of* **клева́ть**

ключ[1] (-а́) key; clue; keystone; clef; wrench, spanner.

ключ[2] (-а́) spring; source.

ключево́й key. **ключи́ца** collarbone.

клю́шка (hockey) stick; (golf-) club.

клюю́ *etc.*: *see* **клева́ть**

кля́кса blot, smudge.

кляну́ *etc.*: *see* **клясть**

кля́нчить (-чу́) *impf* (*pf* **вы~**) beg.

кляп gag.

клясть (-яну́, -янёшь; -ял, -а́, -о) *impf* curse; **~ся** (*pf* **по~ся**) swear, vow. **кля́тва** oath, vow. **кля́твенный** on oath.

кни́га book.

книго- *in comb* book, biblio-. **книгове́дение**[1] bibliography. **~веде́ние**[2] book-keeping. **~изда́тель** *m* publisher. **~лю́б** bibliophile. **~храни́лище** library; book-stack.

кни́жечка booklet. **кни́жка** book; note-book; bank-book. **кни́жный** book; bookish.

кни́зу *adv* downwards. **кно́пка** drawing-pin; press-stud; (push-)button, knob. **кнут** (-а́) whip. **княги́ня** princess. **кня́жество** principality. **княжна́** (*gen pl* -жо́н) princess. **князь** (*pl* -зья́, -зе́й) *m* prince. **ко** *see* к *prep*. **коали́ция** coalition. **кобура́** holster. **кобы́ла** mare; (vaulting-)horse. **ко́ваный** forged; wrought; terse. **кова́рный** insidious, crafty; perfidious. **кова́рство** insidiousness, craftiness; perfidy. **кова́ть** (кую́, -ёшь) *impf* (*pf* **под∼**) forge; hammer; shoe. **ковёр** (-вра́) carpet; rug; mat. **кове́ркать** *impf* (*pf* **ис∼**) distort, mangle, ruin. **ко́вка** forging; shoeing. **коври́жка** honeycake, gingerbread. **ко́врик** rug; mat. **ковче́г** ark. **ковш** (-а́) scoop, ladle. **ковы́ль** *m* feather-grass. **ковыля́ть** *impf* hobble. **ковырну́ть** (-ну́, -нёшь) *pf*, **ковыря́ть** *impf* dig into; tinker; **+в+***prep* pick (at); **∼ся** rummage; tinker. **когда́** *adv* when; **∼ (бы) ни** whenever; *conj* when; while, as; if. **когда́-либо, когда́-нибудь** *advs* some time; ever. **когда́-то** *adv* once; formerly; some time. **кого́** *see* **кто** **ко́готь** (-гтя; *pl* -гти, -гте́й) *m* claw; talon. **код** code. **кодеи́н** codeine. **ко́декс** code. **ко́е-где́** *adv* here and there. **ко́е-ка́к** *adv* anyhow; somehow (or other). **ко́е-како́й** *pron* some. **ко́е-кто́** *pron* somebody; some people. **ко́е-что́** (-чего́) *pron* something; a little. **ко́жа** skin; leather; peel. **ко́жанка** leather jacket. **ко́жаный** leather. **коже́венный** leather; tanning. **ко́жный** skin. **кожура́** rind, peel, skin. **коза́** (*pl* -ы) goat, nanny-goat. **козёл** (-зла́) billy-goat. **козеро́г** ibex; Capricorn. **ко́зий** goat; **∼ пух** angora. **козлёнок** (-нка; *pl* -ля́та, -ля́т) kid. **ко́злы** (-зел) *pl* coach driver's seat; trestle(s); saw-horse. **ко́зни** (-ей) *pl* machinations. **козырёк** (-рька́) peak. **козырно́й** trump. **козырну́ть** (-ну́, -нёшь) *pf*, **козыря́ть** *impf* lead trumps; trump; play one's trump card; salute. **ко́зырь** (*pl* -и, -е́й) *m* trump. **ко́йка** (*gen pl* ко́ек) berth, bunk; bed. **кокаи́н** cocaine. **ко́ка-ко́ла** Coca-Cola (*propr*). **коке́тка** coquette. **коке́тство** coquetry. **коклю́ш** whooping-cough. **ко́кон** cocoon. **коко́с** coconut. **кокс** coke. **кокте́йль** *m* cocktail. **кол** (-а́; *pl* -лья, -ьев) stake, picket. **ко́лба** retort. **колбаса́** (*pl* -ы) sausage. **колго́тки** (-ток) *pl* tights. **колдова́ть** *impf* practise witchcraft. **колдовство́** sorcery. **колду́н** (-а́) sorcerer, wizard. **колду́нья** (*gen pl* -ний) witch, sorceress.

колеба́ние oscillation; variation; hesitation. **колеба́ть** (-éблю) *impf* (*pf* **по~**) shake; **~ся** oscillate; fluctuate; hesitate.

коле́но (*pl* -и, -ей, -ям) knee; (*in pl*) lap. **коле́нчатый** crank, cranked; bent; **~ вал** crankshaft.

колесни́ца chariot. **колесо́** (*pl* -ёса) wheel.

колея́ rut; track, gauge.

ко́лика (*usu pl*) colic; stitch.

коли́чественн|ый quantitative; **~ое числи́тельное** cardinal number. **коли́чество** quantity; number.

колле́га *m* & *f* colleague. **колле́гия** board; college.

коллекти́в collective. **коллективиза́ция** collectivization. **коллекти́вный** collective. **коллекционе́р** collector. **колле́кция** collection.

колли́зия clash, conflict.

коло́да block; pack (*of cards*).

коло́дец (-дца) well.

ко́локол (*pl* -á, -óв) bell. **колоко́льный** bell. **колоко́льня** bell-tower. **колоко́льчик** small bell; bluebell.

колониали́зм colonialism. **колониа́льный** colonial. **колониза́тор** colonizer. **колониза́ция** colonization. **колонизова́ть** *impf* & *pf* colonize. **коло́ния** colony.

коло́нка geyser; (*street*) water fountain; stand-pipe; column; **бензи́новая ~** petrol pump. **коло́нна** column.

колори́т colouring, colour. **колори́тный** colourful, graphic.

ко́лос (-óсья, -ьев) ear. **колоси́ться** *impf* form ears.

колосса́льный huge; terrific.

колоти́ть (-очу́, -о́тишь) *impf* (*pf* **по~**) beat; pound; thrash; smash; **~ся** pound, thump; shake.

коло́ть[1] (-лю́, -лешь) *impf* (*pf* **рас~**) break, chop.

коло́ть[2] (-лю́, -лешь) *impf* (*pf* **за~**, **кольну́ть**) prick; stab; sting; slaughter; **~ся** prick.

колпа́к (-á) cap; hood, cowl.

колхо́з *abbr* (*of* **коллекти́вное хозя́йство**) kolkhoz, collective farm. **колхо́зник, ~ица** kolkhoz member. **колхо́зный** kolkhoz.

колыбе́ль cradle.

колыха́ть (-ы́шу) *impf*, **колыхну́ть** (-ну́, -нёшь) *pf* sway, rock; **~ся** sway; flutter.

кольну́ть (-ну́, -нёшь) *pf of* **коло́ть**

кольцо́ (*pl* -а, -лéц, -льцам) ring.

колю́ч|ий prickly; sharp; **~ая про́волока** barbed wire. **колю́чка** prickle; thorn.

коля́ска carriage; pram; sidecar.

ком (*pl* -мья, -мьев) lump; ball.

ком *see* **кто**

кома́нда command; order; detachment; crew; team. **команди́р** commander. **командирова́ть** *impf* & *pf* post, send on a mission. **командиро́вка** posting; mission, business trip. **командиро́вочные** *sb pl* travelling expenses. **кома́ндование** command. **кома́ндовать** *impf* (*pf* **с~**) give orders; be in command; *+instr* command. **кома́ндующий** *sb* commander.

кома́р (-á) mosquito.

комба́йн combine harvester.

комбина́т industrial complex. **комбина́ция** combination;

manoeuvre; slip. **комбинезóн** overalls, boiler suit; dungarees. **комбини́ровать** *impf* (*pf* **с~**) combine.

комéдия comedy.

комендáнт commandant; manager; warden. **комендатýра** commandant's office.

комéта comet.

кóмик comic actor; comedian. **кóмикс** comic, comic strip.

комиссáр commissar.

комиссионéр (commission-) agent, broker. **комиссиóнн|ый** commission; **~ый магази́н** second-hand shop; **~ые** *sb pl* commission. **коми́ссия** commission; committee.

комитéт committee.

коми́ческий comic; comical. **коми́чный** comical, funny.

кóмкать *impf* (*pf* **с~**) crumple.

комментáрий commentary; *pl* comment. **комментáтор** commentator. **комменти́ровать** *impf* & *pf* comment (on).

коммерсáнт merchant; businessman **коммéрция** commerce. **коммéрческий** commercial.

коммивояжёр commercial traveller.

коммýна commune. **коммунáльный** communal; municipal. **коммуни́зм** communism.

коммуникáция communication.

коммуни́ст, ~ка communist. **коммунисти́ческий** communist.

коммутáтор switchboard.

коммюникé *neut indecl* communiqué.

кóмната room. **кóмнатный** room; indoor.

комóд chest of drawers.

комóк (-мкá) lump.

компáкт-ди́ск compact disc. **компáктный** compact.

компáния company. **компаньóн, ~ка** companion; partner.

компáртия Communist Party.

кóмпас compass.

компенсáция compensation. **компенси́ровать** *impf* & *pf* compensate.

кóмплекс complex. **кóмплексный** complex, compound, composite; combined. **комплéкт** (complete) set; complement; kit. **комплектовáть** *impf* (*pf* **с~, у~**) complete; bring up to strength. **комплéкция** build; constitution.

комплимéнт compliment.

компози́тор composer. **компози́ция** composition.

компонéнт component.

компóст compost.

компóстер punch. **компости́ровать** *impf* (*pf* **про~**) punch.

компóт stewed fruit.

компрéссор compressor.

компромети́ровать *impf* (*pf* **с~**) compromise. **компроми́сс** compromise.

компьютер computer.

комсомóл Komsomol. **комсомóлец** (-льца), **-лка** Komsomol member. **комсомóльский** Komsomol.

комý *see* **кто**

комфóрт comfort.

конвéйер conveyor.

конвéрт envelope; sleeve.

конвои́р escort. **конвои́ровать** *impf* escort. **конвóй** escort, convoy.

конгрéсс congress.

конденсáтор condenser.

конди́терская *sb* confectioner's, cake shop.
кондиционе́р air-conditioner. **кондицио́нный** air-conditioning.
конду́ктор (*pl* -á), **-торша** conductor; guard.
конево́дство horse-breeding.
конёк (-нька́) *dim of* **конь**; hobby(-horse).
коне́ц (-нца́) end; **в конце́ концо́в** in the end, after all. **коне́чно** *adv* of course. **коне́чность** extremity. **коне́чный** final, last; ultimate; finite.
кони́ческий conic, conical.
конкре́тный concrete.
конкуре́нт competitor. **конкуре́нция** competition. **конкури́ровать** *impf* compete. **ко́нкурс** competition; contest.
ко́нница cavalry. **ко́нный** horse; mounted; equestrian; **~ заво́д** stud.
конопля́ hemp.
консервати́вный conservative. **консерва́тор** Conservative.
консервато́рия conservatoire.
консерви́ровать *impf* & *pf* (*pf also* **за~**) preserve; can, bottle. **консе́рвн|ый** preserving; **~ая ба́нка** tin; **~ый нож** tin-opener. **консе́рвооткрыва́тель** *m* tin-opener. **консе́рвы** (-ов) *pl* tinned goods.
конси́лиум consultation.
конспе́кт synopsis, summary. **конспекти́ровать** *impf* (*pf* **за~**, **про~**) make an abstract of.
конспирати́вный secret, clandestine. **конспира́ция** security.
констата́ция ascertaining; establishment. **констати́ровать** *impf* & *pf* ascertain; establish.
конституцио́нный constitutional. **конститу́ция** constitution.
конструи́ровать *impf* & *pf* (*pf also* **с~**) construct; design. **конструкти́вный** structural; constructional; constructive. **констру́ктор** designer, constructor. **констру́кция** construction; design.
ко́нсул consul. **ко́нсульство** consulate.
консульта́ция consultation; advice; clinic; tutorial. **консульти́ровать** *impf* (*pf* **про~**) advise; **+с+*instr*** consult; **~ся** obtain advice; **+с+*instr*** consult.
конта́кт contact. **конта́ктные ли́нзы** *f pl* contact lenses.
конте́йнер container.
конте́кст context.
контине́нт continent.
конто́ра office. **конто́рский** office.
контраба́нда contraband. **контрабанди́ст** smuggler.
контраба́с double-bass.
контра́кт contract.
контра́льто *neut*/*fem indecl* contralto (*voice*/*person*).
контрама́рка complimentary ticket.
контрапу́нкт counterpoint.
контра́ст contrast.
контрибу́ция indemnity.
контрнаступле́ние counter-offensive.
контролёр inspector; ticket-collector. **контроли́ровать** *impf* (*pf* **про~**) check; inspect. **контро́ль** *m* control; check; inspection. **контро́льн|ый** control; **~ая рабо́та** test.
контрразве́дка counter-

intelligence; security service. **контрреволю́ция** counter-revolution.

контýзия bruising; shell-shock.

ко́нтур contour, outline; circuit.

конура́ kennel.

ко́нус cone.

конфедера́ция confederation.

конфере́нция conference.

конфе́та sweet.

конфискова́ть *impf* & *pf* confiscate.

конфли́кт conflict.

конфо́рка ring (*on stove*).

конфýз discomforture, embarrassment. **конфýзить** (-ýжу) *impf* (*pf* **с~**) confuse, embarrass; **~ся** feel embarrassed.

концентра́т concentrate. **концентрацио́нный** concentration. **концентра́ция** concentration. **концентри́ровать(ся** *impf* (*pf* **с~**) concentrate.

конце́пция conception.

конце́рт concert; concerto. **концертме́йстер** leader. **конце́ртный** concert.

концла́герь *abbr* (*of* **концентрацио́нный ла́герь**) concentration camp.

конча́ть *impf*, **ко́нчить** *pf* finish; end; +*inf* stop; **~ся** end, finish; expire. **ко́нчик** tip. **кончи́на** decease.

конь (-я́; *pl* -и, -е́й) *m* horse; knight. **коньки́** (-о́в) *pl* skates; **~ на ро́ликах** roller skates. **конькобе́жец** (-жца) skater.

конья́к (-а́) cognac.

ко́нюх groom, stable-boy. **коню́шня** (*gen pl* -шен) stable.

кооперати́в cooperative. **кооперати́вный** cooperative. **коопера́ция** cooperation.

координа́та coordinate. **координа́ция** coordination.

копа́ть *impf* (*pf* **копнýть, вы́~**) dig; dig up, dig out; **~ся** rummage.

копе́йка copeck.

ко́пи (-ей) *pl* mines.

копи́лка money-box.

копи́рка carbon paper. **копирова́льный** copying. **копи́ровать** *impf* (*pf* **с~**) copy; imitate.

копи́ть (-плю́, -пишь) *impf* (*pf* **на~**) save (up); accumulate; **~ся** accumulate.

ко́пия copy.

копна́ (*pl* -ы, -пён) shock, stook.

копнýть (-нý, -нёшь) *pf of* **копа́ть**

ко́поть soot.

копте́ть (-пчý) *impf* swot; vegetate. **копти́ть** (-пчý) *impf* (*pf* **за~, на~**) smoke, cure; blacken with smoke. **копче́ние** smoking; smoked foods. **копчёный** smoked.

копы́то hoof.

копьё (*pl* -я, -пий) spear, lance.

кора́ bark; cortex; crust.

корабе́льный ship; naval. **кораблевожде́ние** navigation. **кораблекруше́ние** shipwreck. **кораблестрое́ние** shipbuilding. **кора́бль** (-я́) *m* ship, vessel; nave.

кора́лл coral.

коре́йский Korean. **Коре́я** Korea.

корена́стый thickset. **корени́ться** *impf* be rooted. **коренно́й** radical, fundamental; native. **ко́рень** (-рня; *pl* -и, -е́й) *m* root. **корешо́к** (-шка́) root(let); spine; counterfoil.

корзи́на, корзи́нка basket.

коридо́р corridor.
кори́ца cinnamon.
кори́чневый brown.
ко́рка crust; rind, peel.
корм (*loc* -у́; *pl* -а́) fodder.
корма́ stern.
корми́лец (-льца) bread-winner. **корми́ть** (-млю́, -мишь) *impf* (*pf* **на~**, **по~**, **про~**) feed; **~ся** feed; +*instr* live on, make a living by. **кормле́ние** feeding. **кормово́й**[1] fodder.
кормово́й[2] stern.
корнево́й root; radical. **корнепло́ды** (-ов) root-crops.
коро́бить (-блю) *impf* (*pf* **по~**) warp; jar upon; **~ся** (*pf also* **с~ся**) warp.
коро́бка box.
коро́ва cow.
короле́ва queen. **короле́вский** royal. **короле́вство** kingdom. **коро́ль** (-я́) *m* king.
коромы́сло yoke; beam; rocking shaft.
коро́на crown.
коронаротромбо́з coronary (thrombosis).
коро́нка crown. **коронова́ть** *impf* & *pf* crown.
коро́ткий (ко́ро́ток, -тка́, ко́ро́тко́, ко́ро́тки́) short; intimate. **ко́ротко** *adv* briefly; intimately. **коротково́лновый** short-wave. **коро́че** *comp of* **коро́ткий, ко́ротко**
корпора́ция corporation.
ко́рпус (*pl* -ы, -ов *or* -а́, -о́в) corps; services; building; hull; housing, case; body.
корректи́ровать *impf* (*pf* **про~**, **с~**) correct, edit. **корре́ктный** correct, proper. **корре́ктор** (*pl* -а́) proof-reader. **корректу́ра** proof-reading; proof.
корреспонде́нт correspondent. **корреспонде́нция** correspondence.
корро́зия corrosion.
корру́пция corruption.
корт (tennis-)court.
корте́ж cortège; motorcade.
ко́ртик dirk.
ко́рточки (-чек) *pl*; **сиде́ть на ко́рточках** squat.
корчева́ть (-чу́ю) *impf* root out.
ко́рчить (-чу) *impf* (*pf* **с~**) contort; *impers* convulse; **~ из себя́** pose as; **~ся** writhe.
ко́ршун kite.
коры́стный mercenary. **коры́сть** avarice; profit.
коры́то trough; wash-tub.
корь measles.
коса́[1] (*acc* -у; *pl* -ы) plait, tress.
коса́[2] (*acc* ко́су́; *pl* -ы) spit.
коса́[3] (*acc* ко́су́; *pl* -ы) scythe.
ко́свенный indirect.
коси́лка mowing-machine, mower. **коси́ть**[1] (кошу́, ко́сишь) *impf* (*pf* **с~**) cut; mow (down).
коси́ть[2] (кошу́) *impf* (*pf* **по~**, **с~**) squint; be crooked; **~ся** slant; look sideways; look askance.
косме́тика cosmetics, make-up.
косми́ческий cosmic; space. **космодро́м** spacecraft launching-site. **космона́вт, -на́втка** cosmonaut, astronaut.
ко́смос cosmos; (outer) space.
косноязы́чный tongue-tied.
косну́ться (-ну́сь, -нёшься) *pf of* **каса́ться**
косогла́зие squint. **косо́й** (кос, -а́, -о) slanting; oblique; sidelong; squinting, cross-eyed.
костёр (-тра́) bonfire; camp-fire.
костля́вый bony. **ко́стный**

bone. **ко́сточка** (small) bone; stone.

косты́ль (-я́) *m* crutch.

кость (*loc* и́; *pl* -и, -е́й) bone; die.

костю́м clothes; suit. **костюмиро́ванный** fancy-dress.

костяно́й bone; ivory.

косы́нка (*triangular*) headscarf, shawl.

кот (-а́) tom-cat.

котёл (-тла́) boiler; copper, cauldron. **котело́к** (-лка́) pot; mess-tin; bowler (hat). **коте́льная** *sb* boiler-room, -house.

котёнок (-нка; *pl* -тя́та, -тя́т) kitten. **ко́тик** fur-seal; sealskin.

котле́та rissole; burger; **отбивна́я** ~ chop.

котлова́н foundation pit, trench.

кото́мка knapsack.

кото́рый *pron* which, what; who; that; ~ **час?** what time is it?

котя́та *etc.*: *see* **котёнок**

ко́фе *m indecl* coffee. **кофева́рка** percolator. **кофеи́н** caffeine.

ко́фта, ко́фточка blouse, top.

коча́н (-а́ *or* -чна́) (cabbage-) head.

кочева́ть (-чу́ю) *impf* be a nomad; wander; migrate. **коче́вник** nomad. **кочево́й** nomadic.

кочега́р stoker, fireman. **кочега́рка** stokehold, stokehole.

кочене́ть *impf* (*pf* **за~, о~**) grow numb.

кочерга́ (*gen pl* -рёг) poker.

ко́чка hummock.

кошелёк (-лька́) purse.

ко́шка cat.

кошма́р nightmare. **кошма́рный** nightmarish.

кошу́ *etc.*: *see* **коси́ть**

кощу́нство blasphemy.

коэффицие́нт coefficient.

КП *abbr* (*of* **Коммунисти́ческая па́ртия**) Communist Party.

КПСС *abbr* (*of* **Коммунисти́ческая па́ртия Сове́тского Сою́за**) Communist Party of the Soviet Union, CPSU.

краб crab.

кра́деный stolen. **краду́** *etc.*: *see* **красть**

кра́жа theft; ~ **со взло́мом** burglary.

край (*loc* -ю́; *pl* -я́, -ёв) edge; brink; land; region. **кра́йне** *adv* extremely. **кра́йний** extreme; last; outside, wing; **по кра́йней ме́ре** at least. **кра́йность** extreme; extremity.

крал *etc.*: *see* **красть**

кран tap; crane.

крапи́ва nettle.

краса́вец (-вца) handsome man. **краса́вица** beauty. **краси́вый** beautiful; handsome.

краси́тель *m* dye. **кра́сить** (-а́шу) *impf* (*pf* **вы~, о~, по~**) paint; colour; dye; stain; **~ся** (*pf* **на~**) make-up. **кра́ска** paint, dye; colour.

красне́ть (-е́ю) *impf* (*pf* **по~**) blush; redden; show red.

красноарме́ец (-е́йца) Red Army man. **красноарме́йский** Red Army. **красноречи́вый** eloquent.

краснота́ redness. **красну́ха** German measles. **кра́сн|ый** (-сен, -сна́, -о) red; beautiful; fine; **~ое де́рево** mahogany; **~ая сморо́дина** (*no pl*; *usu collect*) redcurrant; redcurrants; **~ая строка́** (first line of) new paragraph.

красовáться *impf* impress by one's beauty; show off. **красотá** (*pl* -ы) beauty. **крáсочный** paint; ink; colourful.

красть (-адý, -адёшь; крал) *impf* (*pf* **у~**) steal; **~ся** creep.

крáтер crater.

крáткий (-ток, -ткá, -о) short; brief. **кратковрéменный** brief; transitory. **краткосрóчный** short-term.

крáтное *sb* multiple.

кратчáйший *superl of* **крáткий**. **крáтче** *comp of* **крáткий, крáтко**

крах crash; failure.

крахмáл starch. **крахмáлить** *impf* (*pf* **на~**) starch.

крáше *comp of* **красúвый, красúво**

крáшеный painted; coloured; dyed; made up. **крáшу** *etc.*: *see* **крáсить**

кревéтка shrimp; prawn.

кредúт credit. **кредúтный** credit. **кредитóр** creditor. **кредитоспосóбный** solvent.

крéйсер (*pl* -á, -óв) cruiser.

крем cream.

крематóрий crematorium.

кремéнь (-мня́) *m* flint.

кремль (-я́) *m* citadel; Kremlin.

крéмний silicon.

крéмовый cream.

крен list, heel; bank. **кренúться** *impf* (*pf* **на~**) heel over, list; bank.

крепúть (-плю́) *impf* strengthen; support; make fast; constipate; **~ся** hold out. **крéпк|ий** (-пок, -пкá, -о) strong; firm; **~ие напúтки** spirits. **креплéние** strengthening; fastening.

крéпнуть (-ну; -еп) *impf* (*pf* **о~**) get stronger.

крепостнúчество serfdom. **крепостн|óй** serf; **~óе прáво** serfdom; **~óй** *sb* serf.

крéпость fortress; strength.

крéпче *comp of* **крéпкий, крéпко**

крéсло (*gen pl* -сел) arm-chair; stall.

крест (-á) cross. **крестúны** (-úн) *pl* christening. **крестúть** (крещý, -éстишь) *impf & pf* (*pf also* **о~, пере~**) christen; make sign of the cross over; **~ся** cross o.s.; be christened. **крест-нáкрест** *adv* crosswise. **крéстник, крéстница** god-child. **крёстн|ый**; **~ая (мать)** godmother; **~ый отéц** godfather. **крестóвый похóд** crusade. **крестонóсец** (-сца) crusader.

крестья́нин (*pl* -я́не, -я́н), **крестья́нка** peasant. **крестья́нский** peasant. **крестья́нство** peasantry.

крещéние christening; Epiphany. **крещён|ый** (-ён, -енá) baptized; *sb* Christian. **крещý** *etc.*: *see* **крестúть**

кривáя *sb* curve. **кривизнá** crookedness; curvature. **кривúть** (-влю́) *impf* (*pf* **по~, с~**) bend, distort; **~ душóй** go against one's conscience; **~ся** become crooked or bent; make a wry face. **кривля́ться** *impf* give o.s. airs.

кривóй (крив, -á, -о) crooked; curved; one-eyed.

крúзис crisis.

крик cry, shout.

крúкет cricket.

крúкнуть (-ну) *pf of* **кричáть**

криминáльный criminal.

кристáлл crystal. **кристаллúческий** crystal.

critéрий criterion.

крúтик critic. **крúтика** criticism;

critique. **критиковáть** *impf* criticize. **критúческий** critical.

кричáть (-чý) *impf* (*pf* **крúкнуть**) cry, shout.

кров roof; shelter.

кровáвый bloody.

кровáтка, кровáть bed.

кровенóсный blood-; circulatory.

крóвля (*gen pl* -вель) roof.

крóвный blood; thoroughbred; vital, intimate.

крово- *in comb* blood. **кровожáдный** bloodthirsty. **~излия́ние** haemorrhage. **~обращéние** circulation. **~пролúтие** bloodshed. **~пролúтный** bloody. **~смешéние** incest. **~течéние** bleeding; haemorrhage. **~точúть** (-чúт) *impf* bleed.

кровь (*loc* -ú) blood. **кровянóй** blood.

кроúть (кроя́) *impf* (*pf* **с~**) cut (out). **крóйка** cutting out.

крокодúл crocodile.

крóлик rabbit.

кроль *m* crawl(-stroke).

крольчúха she-rabbit, doe.

крóме *prep+gen* except; besides; **~ тогó** besides, moreover.

крóмка edge.

крóна crown; top.

кронштéйн bracket; corbel.

кропотлúвый painstaking; laborious.

кросс cross-country race.

кроссвóрд crossword (puzzle).

крот (-á) mole.

крóткий (-ток, -ткá, -тко) meek, gentle. **крóтость** gentleness; mildness.

крóхотный, крóшечный tiny. **крóшка** crumb; a bit.

круг (*loc* -ý; *pl* -ú) circle; circuit; sphere. **круглосýточный** round-the-clock. **крýглый** (кругл, -á, -о) round; complete; **~ год** all the year round. **круговóй** circular; all-round. **кругозóр** prospect; outlook. **кругóм** *adv* around; *prep+gen* round. **кругосвéтный** round-the-world.

кружевнóй lace; lacy. **крýжево** (*pl* -á, -ев, -áм) lace.

кружúть (-ужý, -ýжишь) *impf* whirl, spin round; **~ся** whirl, spin round.

крýжка mug.

кружóк (-жкá) circle, group.

круúз cruise.

крупá (*pl* -ы) groats; sleet. **крупúца** grain.

крýпный large, big; great; coarse; **~ый план** close-up.

крутизнá steepness.

крутúть (-учý, -ýтишь) *impf* (*pf* **за~, с~**) twist, twirl; roll; turn, wind; **~ся** turn, spin; whirl.

крутóй (крут, -á, -о) steep; sudden; sharp; severe; drastic. **крýча** steep slope. **крýче** *comp of* **крутóй, крýто**

кручý *etc.*: *see* **крутúть**

крушéние crash; ruin; collapse.

крыжóвник gooseberries; gooseberry bush.

крылáтый winged. **крылó** (*pl* -лья, -льев) wing; vane; mudguard.

крыльцó (*pl* -а, -лéц, -цáм) porch; (front, back) steps.

Крым the Crimea. **кры́мский** Crimean.

кры́са rat.

крыть (крóю) *impf* cover; roof; trump; **~ся** be, lie; be concealed. **кры́ша** roof. **кры́шка** lid.

крюк (-á; *pl* -ки́, -ко́в *or* -ю́чья, -чьев) hook; detour. **крючо́к** (-чка́) hook.

кря́ду *adv* in succession.

кряж ridge.

кря́кать *impf*, **кря́кнуть** (-ну) *pf* quack.

кряхте́ть (-хчу́) *impf* groan.

кста́ти *adv* to the point; opportunely; at the same time; by the way.

кто (кого́, кому́, кем, ком) *pron* who; anyone; ~ **(бы) ни** whoever. **кто́-либо, кто́-нибудь** *prons* anyone; someone. **кто́-то** *pron* someone.

куб (*pl* -ы́) cube; boiler; **в** ~**е** cubed.

ку́бик brick, block.

куби́нский Cuban.

куби́ческий cubic; cube.

ку́бок (-бка) goblet; cup.

кубоме́тр cubic metre.

кувши́н jug; pitcher. **кувши́нка** water-lily.

кувырка́ться *impf*, **кувыркну́ться** (-ну́сь) *pf* turn somersaults. **кувырко́м** *adv* head over heels; topsy-turvy.

куда́ *adv* where (to); what for; +*comp* much, far; ~ **(бы) ни** wherever. **куда́-либо, куда́-нибудь** *adv* anywhere, somewhere. **куда́-то** *adv* somewhere.

ку́дри (-е́й) *pl* curls. **кудря́вый** curly; florid.

кузне́ц (-á) blacksmith. **кузне́чик** grasshopper. **ку́зница** forge, smithy.

ку́зов (*pl* -á) basket; body.

ку́кла doll; puppet. **ку́колка** dolly; chrysalis. **ку́кольный** doll's; puppet.

кукуру́за maize.

куку́шка cuckoo.

кула́к (-á) fist; kulak. **кула́цкий** kulak. **кула́чный** fist.

кулёк (-лька́) bag.

кули́к (-á) sandpiper.

кулина́рия cookery. **кулина́рный** culinary.

кули́сы (-и́с) wings; **за кули́сами** behind the scenes.

кули́ч (-á) Easter cake.

кулуа́ры (-ов) *pl* lobby.

кульмина́ция culmination.

культ cult. **культиви́ровать** *impf* cultivate.

культу́ра culture; standard; cultivation. **культури́зм** bodybuilding. **культу́рно** *adv* in a civilized manner. **культу́рный** cultured; cultivated; cultural.

куми́р idol.

кумы́с koumiss (*fermented mare's milk*).

куни́ца marten.

купа́льный bathing. **купа́льня** bathing-place. **купа́ть** *impf* (*pf* **вы́**~, **ис**~) bathe; bath; ~**ся** bathe; take a bath.

купе́ *neut indecl* compartment.

купе́ц (-пца́) merchant. **купе́ческий** merchant. **купи́ть** (-плю́, -пишь) *pf* (*impf* **покупа́ть**) buy.

ку́пол (*pl* -á) cupola, dome.

купо́н coupon.

купчи́ха merchant's wife; female merchant.

кура́нты (-ов) *pl* chiming clock; chimes.

курга́н barrow; tumulus.

куре́ние smoking. **кури́льщик, -щица** smoker.

кури́ный hen's; chicken's.

кури́ть (-рю́, -ришь) *impf* (*pf* **по**~) smoke; ~**ся** burn; smoke.

ку́рица (*pl* ку́ры, кур) hen, chicken.

куро́к (-рка́) cocking-piece; **взве-**

сти́ ~ cock a gun; **спусти́ть** ~ pull the trigger.
куропа́тка partridge.
куро́рт health-resort; spa.
курс course; policy; year; exchange rate. **курса́нт** student.
курси́в italics.
курси́ровать *impf* ply.
курсо́р (*comput*) cursor.
ку́ртка jacket.
курча́вый curly(-headed).
ку́ры *etc.*: *see* **ку́рица**
курьёз a funny thing. **курьёзный** curious.
курье́р messenger; courier. **курье́рский** express.
куря́тник hen-house.
куря́щий *sb* smoker.
куса́ть *impf* bite; sting; **~ся** bite.
кусо́к (-ска́) piece; lump. **кусо́чек** (-чка) piece.
куст (-а́) bush, shrub. **куста́рник** bush(es), shrub(s).
куста́рн|ый hand-made; handicrafts; primitive; **~ая промы́шленность** cottage industry. **куста́рь** (-я́) *m* craftsman.
ку́тать *impf* (*pf* **за~**) wrap up; **~ся** muffle o.s. up.
кути́ть (кучу́, ку́тишь) *impf*, **кутну́ть** (-ну́, -нёшь) *pf* carouse; go on a binge.
куха́рка cook. **ку́хня** (*gen pl* -хонь) kitchen; cuisine. **ку́хонный** kitchen.
ку́ча heap; heaps.
ку́чер (*pl* -а́) coachman.
ку́чка small heap *or* group.
кучу́ *see* **кути́ть**
куша́к (-а́) sash; girdle.
ку́шанье food; dish. **ку́шать** *impf* (*pf* **по~, с~**) eat.
куше́тка couch.
кую́ *etc.*: *see* **кова́ть**

Л

лабора́нт, -а́нтка laboratory assistant. **лаборато́рия** laboratory.
ла́ва lava.
лави́на avalanche.
ла́вка bench; shop. **ла́вочка** small shop.
лавр bay tree, laurel.
ла́герный camp. **ла́герь** (*pl* -я́ *or* -и, -е́й *or* -ей) *m* camp; campsite.
лад (*loc* -у́; *pl* -ы́, -о́в) harmony; manner, way; stop, fret.
ла́дан incense.
ла́дить (ла́жу) *impf* get on, be on good terms. **ла́дно** *adv* all right; very well! **ла́дный** fine, excellent; harmonious.
ладо́нь palm.
ладья́ rook, castle; boat.
ла́жу *etc.*: *see* **ла́дить, ла́зить**
лазаре́т field hospital; sick-bay.
ла́зать *see* **ла́зить. лазе́йка** hole; loop-hole.
ла́зер laser.
ла́зить (ла́жу), **ла́зать** *impf* climb, clamber.
лазу́рный sky-blue, azure. **лазу́рь** azure.
лазу́тчик scout; spy.
лай bark, barking. **ла́йка**[1] (Siberian) husky, laika.
ла́йка[2] kid. **ла́йковый** kid; kidskin.
ла́йнер liner; airliner.
лак varnish, lacquer.
лака́ть *impf* (*pf* **вы~**) lap.
лаке́й footman, man-servant; lackey.
лакирова́ть *impf* (*pf* **от~**) varnish; lacquer.
ла́кмус litmus.

ла́ковый varnished, lacquered. **ла́комиться** (-млюсь) *impf* (*pf* **по~**) +*instr* treat o.s. to. **ла́комка** *m* & *f* gourmand. **ла́комство** delicacy. **ла́комый** dainty, tasty; +**до** fond of.
лакони́чный laconic.
ла́мпа lamp; valve, tube. **лампа́да** icon-lamp. **ла́мпочка** lamp; bulb.
ландша́фт landscape.
ла́ндыш lily of the valley.
лань fallow deer; doe.
ла́па paw; tenon.
ла́поть (-птя; *pl* -и, -е́й) *m* bast shoe.
ла́почка pet, sweetie.
лапша́ noodles; noodle soup.
ларёк (-рька́) stall. **ларь** (-я́) *m* chest; bin.
ла́ска[1] caress.
ла́ска[2] weasel.
ласка́ть *impf* caress, fondle; **~ся** +**к**+*dat* make up to; fawn upon. **ла́сковый** affectionate, tender.
ла́сточка swallow.
латви́ец (-йица), **-и́йка** Latvian. **латви́йский** Latvian. **Ла́твия** Latvia.
лати́нский Latin.
лату́нь brass.
ла́ты (лат) *pl* armour.
латы́нь Latin.
латы́ш, латы́шка Latvian, Lett. **латы́шский** Latvian, Lettish.
лауреа́т prize-winner.
ла́цкан lapel.
лачу́га hovel, shack.
ла́ять (ла́ю) *impf* bark.
лба *etc.*: *see* **лоб**
лгать (лгу, лжёшь; лгал, -а́, -о) *impf* (*pf* **на~, со~**) lie; tell lies; +**на**+*acc* slander. **лгун** (-а́), **лгу́нья** liar.
лебеди́ный swan. **лебёдка** swan, pen; winch. **ле́бедь** (*pl* -и, -е́й) *m* swan, cob.
лев (льва) lion.
левобере́жный left-bank.
левша́ (*gen pl* -е́й) *m* & *f* left-hander. **ле́вый** *adj* left; left-hand; left-wing.
лёг *etc.*: *see* **лечь**
лега́льный legal.
леге́нда legend. **легенда́рный** legendary.
лёгк|ий (-гок, -гка́, лёгки) light; easy; slight, mild; **~ая атле́тика** field and track events. **легко́** *adv* easily, lightly, slightly.
легко- *in comb* light; easy, easily. **легкове́рный** credulous. **~ве́с** light-weight. **~мы́сленный** thoughtless; flippant, frivolous, superficial. **~мы́слие** flippancy, frivolity.
легков|о́й: ~а́я маши́на (private) car. **лёгкое** *sb* lung. **лёгкость** lightness; easiness. **ле́гче** *comp of* **лёгкий, легко́**
лёд (льда, *loc* -у) ice. **ледене́ть** (-е́ю) *impf* (*pf* **за~, о~**) freeze; grow numb with cold. **ледене́ц** (-нца́) fruit-drop. **леденя́щий** chilling, icy.
ле́ди *f indecl* lady.
ле́дник[1] ice-box; refrigerator van. **ледни́к**[2] (-а́) glacier. **леднико́вый** glacial; **~ пери́од** Ice Age. **ледо́вый** ice. **ледоко́л** ice-breaker. **ледяно́й** ice; icy.
лежа́ть (-жу́) *impf* lie; be, be situated. **лежа́чий** lying (down).
ле́звие (cutting) edge; razor-blade.
лезть (-зу; лез) *impf* (*pf* **по~**) climb; clamber, crawl; get, go; fall out.
лейбори́ст Labourite.
ле́йка watering-can.

лейтена́нт lieutenant.
лека́рство medicine.
ле́ксика vocabulary. **лексико́н** lexicon; vocabulary.
ле́ктор lecturer. **ле́кция** lecture.
леле́ять (-е́ю) *impf* (*pf* **вз~**) cherish, foster.
лён (льна) flax.
лени́вый lazy.
ленингра́дский (of) Leningrad. **ле́нинский** (of) Lenin; Leninist.
лени́ться (-ню́сь, -нишься) *impf* (*pf* **по~**) be lazy; *+inf* be too lazy to.
ле́нта ribbon; band; tape.
лентя́й, -я́йка lazy-bones. **лень** laziness.
лепесто́к (-тка́) petal.
ле́пет babble; prattle. **лепета́ть** (-ечу́, -е́чешь) *impf* (*pf* **про~**) babble, prattle.
лепёшка scone; tablet, pastille.
лепи́ть (-плю́, -пишь) *impf* (*pf* **вы́~, за~, с~**) model, fashion; mould; **~ся** cling; crawl. **ле́пка** modelling. **лепно́й** modelled, moulded.
лес (*loc* -у́; *pl* -а́) forest, wood; *pl* scaffolding.
ле́са́ (*pl* ле́сы) fishing-line.
лесни́к (-а́) forester. **лесни́чий** *sb* forestry officer; forest warden. **десно́й** forest.
лесо- *in comb* forest, forestry; timber wood. **лесово́дство** forestry. **~загото́вка** logging. **~пи́лка, ~пи́льня** (*gen pl* -лен) sawmill. **~ру́б** woodcutter.
ле́стница stairs, staircase; ladder.
ле́стный flattering. **лесть** flattery.
лёт (*loc* -у́) flight, flying.
лета́ (лет) *pl* years; age; **ско́лько вам лет?** how old are you?
лета́тельный flying. **лета́ть** *impf*, **лете́ть** (лечу́) *impf* (*pf* **полете́ть**) fly; rush; fall.
ле́тний summer.
лётный flying, flight.
ле́то (*pl* -а́) summer; *pl* years. **ле́том** *adv* in summer.
ле́топись chronicle.
летосчисле́ние chronology.
лету́ч|ий flying; passing; brief; volatile; **~ая мышь** bat. **лётчик, -чица** pilot.
лече́бница clinic. **лече́бный** medical; medicinal. **лече́ние** (medical) treatment. **лечи́ть** (-чу́, -чишь) *impf* treat (**от** for); **~ся** be given, have treatment (**от** for).
лечу́ *etc.*: *see* **лете́ть, лечи́ть**
лечь (ля́гу, ля́жешь; лёг, -ла́) *pf* (*impf* **ложи́ться**) lie, lie down; go to bed.
лещ (-а́) bream.
лжесвиде́тельство false witness.
лжец (-а́) liar. **лжи́вый** lying; deceitful.
ли, ль *interrog partl* & *conj* whether, if; **ли,... ли** whether ... or; **ра́но ли, по́здно ли** sooner or later.
либера́л liberal. **либера́льный** liberal.
ли́бо *conj* or; **~... ~** either ... or.
ли́вень (-вня) *m* heavy shower, downpour.
ливре́я livery.
ли́га league.
ли́дер leader. **лиди́ровать** *impf* & *pf* be in the lead.
лиза́ть (лижу́, -ешь) *impf*, **лизну́ть** (-ну́, -нёшь) *pf* lick.
ликвида́ция liquidation; aboli-

tion. **ликвидировать** *impf & pf* liquidate; abolish.

ликёр liqueur.

ликование rejoicing. **ликовать** *impf* rejoice.

лилия lily.

лиловый lilac, violet.

лиман estuary.

лимит limit.

лимон lemon. **лимонад** lemonade; squash. **лимонный** lemon.

лимфа lymph.

лингвист linguist. **лингвистика** linguistics. **лингвистический** linguistic.

линейка ruler; line. **линейный** linear; ~ **корабль** battleship.

линза lens.

линия line.

линолеум lino(leum).

линять *impf* (*pf* **вы~, по~, с~**) fade; moult.

липа lime tree.

липкий (-пок, -пка, -о) sticky. **липнуть** (-ну; лип) *impf* stick.

липовый lime.

лира lyre. **лирик** lyric poet. **лирика** lyric poetry. **лирический** lyric; lyrical.

лиса (*pl* -ы), **-сица** fox.

лист (-а; *pl* -ы *or* -ья, -ов *or* -ьев) leaf; sheet; page; form; **играть с ~а** play at sight. **листать** *impf* leaf through. **листва** foliage. **лиственница** larch **лиственный** deciduous. **листовка** leaflet. **листовой** sheet, plate; leaf. **листок** (-тка) *dim of* **лист**; leaflet; form, pro-forma.

Литва Lithuania.

литейный founding, casting.

литератор man of letters. **литература** literature. **литературный** literary.

литовец (-вца), **литовка** Lithuanian. **литовский** Lithuanian.

литой cast.

литр litre.

лить (лью, льёшь; лил, -а, -о) *impf* (*pf* **с~**) pour; shed; cast, mould. **литьё** founding, casting, moulding; castings, mouldings. **литься** (льётся; лился, -ась, лилось) *impf* flow; pour.

лиф bodice. **лифчик** bra.

лифт lift.

лихой[1] (лих, -а, -о) dashing, spirited.

лихой[2] (лих, -а, -о, лихи) evil.

лихорадка fever. **лихорадочный** feverish.

лицевой facial; exterior; front.

лицемер hypocrite. **лицемерие** hypocrisy. **лицемерный** hypocritical.

лицо (*pl* -а) face; exterior; right side; person; **быть к лицу** +*dat* suit, befit. **личинка** larva, grub; maggot. **лично** *adv* personally, in person. **личность** personality; person. **личный** personal; private; ~ **состав** staff, personnel.

лишай lichen; herpes; shingles. **лишайник** lichen.

лишать(ся *impf of* **лишить(ся**

лишение deprivation; privation. **лишённый** (-ён, -ена) +*gen* lacking in, devoid of. **лишить** (-шу) *pf* (*impf* **лишать**) +*gen* deprive of; **~ся** +*gen* lose, be deprived of. **лишн|ий** superfluous; unnecessary; spare; ~ **раз** once more; **с ~им** odd, and more.

лишь *adv* only; *conj* as soon as; ~ **бы** if only, provided that.

лоб (лба, *loc* лбу) forehead.

лобзик fret-saw.

ловить (-влю, -вишь) *impf* (*pf*

поймать) catch, try to catch.
ло́вкий (-вок, -вка́, -о) adroit; cunning. **ло́вкость** adroitness; cunning.
ло́вля (*gen pl* -вель) catching, hunting; fishing-ground. **лову́шка** trap.
ло́вче *comp of* **ло́вкий**
логари́фм logarithm.
ло́гика logic. **логи́ческий, логи́чный** logical.
ло́говище, ло́гово den, lair.
ло́дка boat.
ло́дырничать *impf* loaf, idle about. **ло́дырь** *m* loafer, idler.
ло́жа box; (masonic) lodge.
ложби́на hollow.
ло́же couch; bed.
ложи́ться (-жу́сь) *impf of* **лечь**
ло́жка spoon.
ло́жный false. **ложь** (лжи) lie, falsehood.
лоза́ (*pl* -ы) vine.
ло́зунг slogan, catchword.
лока́тор radar *or* sonar apparatus.
локомоти́в locomotive.
ло́кон lock, curl.
ло́коть (-ктя; *pl* -и, -е́й) *m* elbow.
лом (*pl* -ы, -о́в) crowbar; scrap, waste. **ло́маный** broken. **лома́ть** *impf* (*pf* **по~, с~**) break; cause to ache; **~ся** break; crack; put on airs; be obstinate.
ломба́рд pawnshop.
ло́мберный стол card-table.
ломи́ть (ло́мит) *impf* break; break through, rush; *impers* cause to ache; **~ся** be (near to) breaking. **ло́мка** breaking; *pl* quarry. **ло́мкий** (-мок, -мка́, -о) fragile, brittle.
ломо́ть (-мтя́; *pl* -мти́) *m* large slice; hunk; chunk. **ло́мтик** slice.
ло́но bosom, lap.
ло́пасть (*pl* -и, -е́й) blade; fan, vane; paddle.
лопа́та spade; shovel. **лопа́тка** shoulder-blade; shovel; trowel.
ло́паться *impf*, **ло́пнуть** (-ну) *pf* burst; split; break; fail; crash.
лопу́х (-а́) burdock.
лорд lord.
лоси́на elk-skin, chamois leather; elk-meat.
лоск lustre, shine.
лоску́т (-а́; *pl* -ы́ *or* -ья, -о́в *or* -ьев) rag, shred, scrap.
лосни́ться *impf* be glossy, shine.
ло́со́сь *m* salmon.
лось (*pl* -и, -е́й) *m* elk.
лосьо́н lotion; aftershave; cream.
лот lead, plummet.
лотере́я lottery, raffle.
лото́к (-тка́) hawker's stand *or* tray; chute; gutter; trough.
лохма́тый shaggy; dishevelled.
лохмо́тья (-ьев) *pl* rags.
ло́цман pilot.
лошади́ный horse; equine. **ло́шадь** (*pl* -и, -е́й, *instr* -дьми́ *or* -дя́ми) horse.
лощёный glossy, polished.
лощи́на hollow, depression.
лоя́льный fair, honest; loyal.
лубо́к (-бка́) splint; popular print.
луг (*loc* -у́; *pl* -а́) meadow.
лу́жа puddle.
лужа́йка lawn, glade.
лужёный tin-plated.
лук[1] onions.
лук[2] bow.
лука́вить (-влю) *impf* (*pf* **с~**) be cunning. **лука́вство** craftiness.
лука́вый crafty, cunning.
лу́ковица onion; bulb

луна́ (*pl* -ы) moon. **луна́тик** sleep-walker.
лу́нка hole; socket.
лу́нный moon; lunar.
лу́па magnifying-glass.
лупи́ть (-плю́, -пишь) *impf* (*pf* **от~**) flog.
луч (-а́) ray; beam. **лучево́й** ray, beam; radial; radiation. **лучеза́рный** radiant.
лучи́на splinter.
лу́чше better; **~ всего́, ~ всех** best of all. **лу́чш|ий** better; best; **в ~ем слу́чае** at best; **всё́го ~его!** all the best!
лы́жа ski. **лы́жник** skier. **лы́жный спорт** skiing. **лыжня́** ski-track.
лы́ко bast.
лысе́ть (-е́ю) *impf* (*pf* **об~, по~**) grow bald. **лы́сина** bald spot; blaze. **лы́сый** (лыс, -а́, -о) bald.
ль *see* **ли**
льва *etc*.: *see* **лев. льви́ный** lion, lion's. **льви́ца** lioness.
льго́та privilege; advantage. **льго́тный** privileged; favourable.
льда *etc*.: *see* **лёд. льди́на** block of ice; ice-floe.
льна *etc*.: *see* **лён. льново́дство** flax-growing.
льнуть (-ну, -нёшь) *impf* (*pf* **при~**) +к+*dat* cling to; have a weakness for; make up to.
льняно́й flax, flaxen; linen; linseed.
льсте́ц (-а́) flatterer. **льсти́вый** flattering; smooth-tongued. **льстить** (льщу) *impf* (*pf* **по~**) +*dat* flatter.
лью *etc*.: *see* **лить**
любе́зность courtesy; kindness; compliment. **любе́зн|ый** courteous; obliging; kind; **бу́дьте ~ы** be so kind (as to).
люби́мец (-мца), **-мица** pet, favourite. **люби́мый** beloved; favourite. **люби́тель** *m*, **-ница** lover; amateur. **люби́тельский** amateur. **люби́ть** (-блю́, -бишь) *impf* love; like.
любова́ться *impf* (*pf* **по~**) +*instr or* **на**+*acc* admire.
любо́вник lover. **любо́вница** mistress. **любо́вный** love-; loving. **любо́вь** (-бви́, *instr* -бо́вью) love.
любозна́тельный inquisitive.
любо́й any; either; *sb* anyone.
любопы́тный curious; inquisitive. **любопы́тство** curiosity.
лю́бящий loving.
лю́ди (-е́й, -ям, -дьми́, -ях) *pl* people. **лю́дный** populous; crowded. **людое́д** cannibal; ogre. **людско́й** human.
люк hatch(way); trap; manhole.
лю́лька cradle.
люминесце́нтный luminescent. **люминесце́нция** luminescence.
лю́стра chandelier.
лю́тня (*gen pl* -тен) lute.
лю́тый (лют, -а́, -о) ferocious.
ляга́ть *impf*, **лягну́ть** (-ну́, -нёшь) *pf* kick; **~ся** kick.
ля́гу *etc*.: *see* **лечь**
лягу́шка frog.
ля́жка thigh, haunch.
ля́згать *impf* clank; +*instr* rattle.
ля́мка strap; **тяну́ть ля́мку** toil.

М

мавзоле́й mausoleum.
мавр, маврита́нка Moor. **маврита́нский** Moorish.

магази́н shop.

маги́стр (holder of) master's degree.

магистра́ль main; main line, main road.

маги́ческий magic(al). **ма́гия** magic.

магнети́зм magnetism.

ма́гний magnesium.

магни́т magnet. **магни́тный** magnetic. **магнитофо́н** tape-recorder.

мада́м *f indecl* madam, madame.

мажо́р major (key); cheerful mood. **мажо́рный** major; cheerful.

ма́зать (ма́жу) *impf* (*pf* **вы**~, **за**~, **из**~, **на**~, **по**~, **про**~) oil, grease; smear, spread; soil; ~**ся** get dirty; make up. **мазо́к** (-зка́) touch, dab; smear. **мазу́т** fuel oil. **мазь** ointment; grease.

маи́с maize.

май May. **ма́йский** May.

ма́йка T-shirt.

майо́р major.

мак poppy, poppy-seeds.

макаро́ны (-н) *pl* macaroni.

мака́ть *impf* (*pf* **макну́ть**) dip.

маке́т model; dummy.

макну́ть (-ну́, -нёшь) *pf of* **мака́ть**

макре́ль mackerel.

максима́льный maximum. **ма́ксимум** maximum; at most.

макулату́ра waste paper; pulp literature.

маку́шка top; crown.

мал *etc.*: *see* **ма́лый**

малахи́т malachite.

мале́йший least, slightest. **ма́ленький** little; small.

мали́на (*no pl*; *usu collect*) raspberry; raspberries; raspberry-bush. **мали́новый** raspberry.

ма́ло *adv* little, few; not enough; ~ **того́** moreover; ~ **того́ что...** not only ....

мало- *in comb* (too) little. **малова́жный** of little importance. ~**вероя́тный** unlikely. ~**гра́мотный** semi-literate; crude. ~**ду́шный** faint-hearted. ~**иму́щий** needy. ~**кро́вие** anaemia. ~**ле́тний** young; juvenile; minor. ~**о́пытный** inexperienced. ~**чи́сленный** small (in number), few.

мало-ма́льски *adv* in the slightest degree; at all. **малопома́лу** *adv* little by little.

ма́л|ый (мал, -а́) little, (too) small; **са́мое** ~**ое** at the least; *sb* fellow; lad. **малы́ш** (-а́) kiddy; little boy. **ма́льчик** boy. **мальчи́шка** *m* urchin, boy. **мальчуга́н** little boy. **малю́тка** *m* & *f* baby.

маля́р (-а́) painter, decorator.

маляри́я malaria.

ма́ма mother, mummy. **мама́ша** mummy. **ма́мин** mother's.

ма́монт mammoth.

мандари́н mandarin, tangerine.

манда́т warrant; mandate.

манёвр manoeuvre; shunting. **маневри́ровать** *impf* (*pf* **с**~) manoeuvre; shunt; +*instr* make good use of.

мане́ж riding-school.

манеке́н dummy; mannequin. **манеке́нщик, -щица** model.

мане́ра manner; style. **мане́рный** affected.

манже́та cuff.

маникю́р manicure.

манипули́ровать *impf* manipulate. **манипуля́ция** manipulation; machination.

мани́ть (-ню́, -нишь) *impf* (*pf* **по~**) beckon; attract; lure.
манифе́ст manifesto. **манифеста́ция** demonstration.
мани́шка (false) shirt-front.
ма́ния mania; **~ вели́чия** megalomania.
ма́нная ка́ша semolina.
мано́метр pressure-gauge.
ма́нтия cloak; robe, gown.
мануфакту́ра manufacture; textiles.
манья́к maniac.
марафо́нский бег marathon.
ма́рганец (-нца) manganese.
маргари́н margarine.
маргари́тка daisy.
марино́ванный pickled. **маринова́ть** *impf* (*pf* **за~**) pickle; put off.
марионе́тка puppet.
ма́рка stamp; counter; brand; trade-mark; grade; reputation.
ма́ркетинг marketing.
ма́ркий easily soiled.
маркси́зм Marxism. **маркси́ст** Marxist. **маркси́стский** Marxist.
ма́рлевый gauze. **ма́рля** gauze; cheesecloth.
мармела́д fruit jellies.
ма́рочный high-quality.
Марс Mars.
март March. **ма́ртовский** March.
марты́шка marmoset; monkey.
марш march.
ма́ршал marshal.
маршірова́ть *impf* march.
маршру́т route, itinerary.
ма́ска mask. **маскара́д** masked ball; masquerade. **маскирова́ть** *impf* (*pf* **за~**) disguise; camouflage. **маскиро́вка** disguise; camouflage.
Ма́сленица Shrovetide.
маслёнка butter-dish; oil-can.
масли́на olive. **ма́сло** (*pl* -а́, ма́сел, -сла́м) butter; oil; oil paints. **маслобо́йка** churn. **маслобо́йня** (*gen pl* -óен), **маслозаво́д** dairy. **масляни́стый** oily. **ма́сляный** oil.
ма́сса mass; a lot, lots.
масса́ж massage. **масси́ровать** *impf* & *pf* massage.
масси́в massif; expanse, tract. **масси́вный** massive.
ма́ссовый mass.
ма́стер (*pl* -а́), **мастери́ца** foreman, forewoman; (master) craftsman; expert. **мастери́ть** *impf* (*pf* **с~**) make, build. **мастерска́я** *sb* workshop. **мастерско́й** masterly. **мастерство́** craft; skill.
масти́ка mastic; putty; floor-polish.
масти́тый venerable.
масть (*pl* -и, -е́й) colour; suit.
масшта́б scale.
мат[1] checkmate.
мат[2] mat.
мат[3] foul language.
матема́тик mathematician. **матема́тика** mathematics. **математи́ческий** mathematical.
материа́л material. **материали́зм** materialism. **материалисти́ческий** materialist. **материа́льный** material.
матери́к (-а́) continent; mainland. **материко́вый** continental.
матери́нский maternal, motherly. **матери́нство** maternity.
мате́рия material; pus; topic.
ма́тка womb; female.
ма́товый matt; frosted.

матра́с, матра́ц mattress.
матрёшка Russian doll.
ма́трица matrix; die, mould.
матро́с sailor, seaman.
матч match.
мать (ма́тери, *instr* -рью; *pl* -тери, -ре́й) mother.
ма́фия Mafia.
мах swing, stroke. **маха́ть** (машу́, ма́шешь) *impf*, **махну́ть** (-ну́, -нёшь) *pf* +*instr* wave; brandish; wag; flap; go; rush.
махина́ция machinations.
махови́к (-а́) fly-wheel.
махро́вый dyed-in-the-wool; terry.
ма́чеха stepmother.
ма́чта mast.
маши́на machine; car. **машина́льный** mechanical. **машини́ст** operator; engine-driver; scene-shifter. **машини́стка** typist; **~-стенографи́стка** shorthand-typist. **маши́нка** machine; typewriter; sewing-machine. **машинопи́сный** typewritten. **маши́нопись** typing; typescript. **машинострое́ние** mechanical engineering.
мая́к (-а́) lighthouse; beacon.
ма́ятник pendulum. **ма́яться** *impf* toil; suffer; languish.
мгла haze; gloom.
мгнове́ние instant, moment. **мгнове́нный** instantaneous, momentary.
ме́бель furniture. **меблиро́ванный** furnished. **меблиро́вка** furnishing; furniture.
мегава́тт (*gen pl* -а́тт) megawatt. **мего́м** megohm. **мегато́нна** megaton.
мёд (*loc* -у́; *pl* -ы́) honey.
меда́ль medal. **медальо́н** medallion.
медве́дица she-bear. **медве́дь** *m* bear. **медве́жий** bear('s). **медвежо́нок** (-нка; *pl* -жа́та, -жа́т) bear cub.
ме́дик medical student; doctor. **медикаме́нты** (-ов) *pl* medicines.
медици́на medicine. **медици́нский** medical.
ме́дленный slow. **медли́тельный** sluggish; slow. **ме́длить** *impf* linger; be slow.
ме́дный copper; brass.
медо́вый honey; **~ ме́сяц** honeymoon.
медосмо́тр medical examination, check-up. **медпу́нкт** first aid post. **медсестра́** (*pl* -сёстры, -сестёр, -сёстрам) nurse.
меду́за jellyfish.
медь copper.
меж *prep*+*instr* between.
меж- *in comb* inter-.
межа́ (*pl* -и, меж, -а́м) boundary.
междоме́тие interjection.
ме́жду *prep*+*instr* between; among; **~ про́чим** incidentally, by the way; **~ тем** meanwhile; **~ тем, как** while.
между- *in comb* inter-. **междугоро́дный** inter-city. **~наро́дный** international.
межконтинента́льный intercontinental. **межплане́тный** interplanetary.
мезони́н attic (storey); mezzanine (floor).
Ме́ксика Mexico.
мел (*loc* -у́) chalk.
мёл *etc.*: *see* **мести́**
меланхо́лия melancholy.
меле́ть (-е́ет) *impf* (*pf* **об~**) grow shallow.
мелиора́ция land improvement.

ме́лкий (-лок, -лка́, -о) small; shallow; fine; petty. **ме́лко** *adv* fine, small. **мелкобуржуа́зный** petty bourgeois. **мелково́дный** shallow.

мелоди́чный melodious, melodic. **мело́дия** melody.

ме́лочный petty. **ме́лочь** (*pl* -и, -е́й) small items; (small) change; *pl* trifles, trivialities.

мель (*loc* -и́) shoal; bank; **на мели́** aground.

мелька́ть *impf*, **мелькну́ть** (-ну́, -нёшь) *pf* be glimpsed fleetingly. **ме́льком** *adv* in passing; fleetingly.

ме́льник miller. **ме́льница** mill.

мельча́йший *superl of* **ме́лкий. ме́льче** *comp of* **ме́лкий, ме́лко.**

мелюзга́ small fry.

мелю́ *etc.*: *see* **моло́ть**

мембра́на membrane; diaphragm.

мемора́ндум memorandum.

мемуа́ры (-ов) *pl* memoirs.

ме́на exchange, barter.

ме́неджер manager.

ме́нее *adv* less; **тем не ~** none the less.

мензу́рка measuring-glass.

менов́ой exchange; barter.

менуэ́т minuet.

ме́ньше smaller; less. **меньшеви́к** (-а́) Menshevik. **ме́ньший** lesser, smaller; younger. **меньшинство́** minority.

меню́ *neut indecl* menu.

меня́ *see* **я** *pron*

меня́ть *impf* (*pf* **об~, по~**) change; exchange; **~ся** change; +*instr* exchange.

ме́ра measure.

мере́щиться (-щусь) *impf* (*pf* **по~**) seem, appear.

мерза́вец (-вца) swine, bastard. **ме́рзкий** (-зок, -зка́, -о) disgusting.

мерзлота́: **ве́чная ~** permafrost. **мёрзнуть** (-ну; мёрз) *impf* (*pf* **за~**) freeze.

ме́рзость vileness; abomination.

меридиа́н meridian.

мери́ло standard, criterion.

ме́рин gelding.

ме́рить *impf* (*pf* **по~, с~**) measure; try on. **ме́рка** measure.

ме́рный measured; rhythmical.

мероприя́тие measure.

мертве́ть (-е́ю) *impf* (*pf* **о~, по~**) grow numb; be benumbed. **мертве́ц** (-а́) corpse, dead man. **мёртвый** (мёртв, -а́, мёртво́) dead.

мерца́ть *impf* twinkle; flicker.

меси́ть (мешу́, ме́сишь) *impf* (*pf* **с~**) knead.

ме́сса Mass.

места́ми *adv* here and there, in places. **месте́чко** (*pl* -и, -чек) small town.

мести́ (мету́, -тёшь; мёл, -а́) *impf* sweep; whirl.

ме́стность terrain; locality; area. **ме́стный** local; locative. **-ме́стный** *in comb* -berth, -seater. **ме́сто** (*pl* -а́) place; site; seat; room; job. **местожи́тельство** (place of) residence. **местоиме́ние** pronoun. **местонахожде́ние** location, whereabouts. **месторожде́ние** deposit; layer.

месть vengeance, revenge.

ме́сяц month; moon. **ме́сячный** monthly; *sb pl* period.

мета́лл metal. **металли́ческий** metal, metallic. **металлу́ргия** metallurgy.

мета́н methane.

мета́ние throwing, flinging. **мета́ть**[1] (мечу́, ме́чешь) *impf* (*pf* **метну́ть**) throw, fling; **~ся** rush about; toss (and turn).

мета́ть[2] *impf* (*pf* **на~, с~**) tack.

метафи́зика metaphysics.

мета́фора metaphor.

метёлка panicle.

мете́ль snow-storm.

метео́р meteor. **метеори́т** meteorite. **метеоро́лог** meteorologist. **метеорологи́ческий** meteorological. **метеороло́гия** meteorology.

метеосво́дка weather report. **метеоста́нция** weather-station.

ме́тить[1] (ме́чу) *impf* (*pf* **на~, по~**) mark.

ме́тить[2] (ме́чу) *impf* (*pf* **на~**) aim; mean.

ме́тка marking, mark.

ме́ткий (-ток, -тка́, -о) well-aimed, accurate.

метла́ (*pl* мётлы, -тел) broom.

метну́ть (-ну́, -нёшь) *pf of* **мета́ть**[1]

ме́тод method. **мето́дика** method(s); methodology. **методи́чный** methodical. **методоло́гия** methodology.

метр metre.

ме́трика birth certificate. **метри́ческ|ий**[1]: **~ое свиде́тельство** birth certificate.

метри́ческий[2] metric; metrical.

метро́ *neut indecl*, **метрополите́н** Metro; underground.

мету́ *etc.*: *see* **мести́**

мех[1] (*loc* -у́; *pl* -а́) fur.

мех[2] (*pl* -и́) wine-skin, water-skin; *pl* bellows.

механиза́ция mechanization. **механи́зм** mechanism; gear(ing). **меха́ник** mechanic. **меха́ника** mechanics; trick; knack. **механи́ческий** mechanical; mechanistic.

мехово́й fur.

меч (-а́) sword.

ме́ченый marked.

мече́ть mosque.

мечта́ (day-)dream. **мечта́тельный** dreamy. **мечта́ть** *impf* dream.

ме́чу *etc.*: *see* **ме́тить. мечу́** *etc.*: *see* **мета́ть**

меша́лка mixer.

меша́ть[1] *impf* (*pf* **по~**) +*dat* hinder; prevent; disturb.

меша́ть[2] *impf* (*pf* **по~, с~**) stir; mix; mix up; **~ся** (**в**+*acc*) interfere (in), meddle (with).

мешо́к (-шка́) bag; sack. **мешкови́на** sacking, hessian.

мещани́н (*pl* -а́не, -а́н) petty bourgeois; Philistine. **меща́нский** bourgeois, narrow-minded; Philistine. **меща́нство** petty bourgeoisie; philistinism, narrow-mindedness.

миг moment, instant.

мига́ть *impf*, **мигну́ть** (-ну́, -нёшь) *pf* blink; wink, twinkle.

ми́гом *adv* in a flash.

мигра́ция migration.

мигре́нь migraine.

мизантро́п misanthrope.

мизи́нец (-нца) little finger; little toe.

микро́б microbe.

микроволно́вая печь microwave oven.

микро́н micron.

микрооргани́зм micro-organism.

микроско́п microscope. **ми-**

кроскопи́ческий microscopic.
микросхéма microchip.
микрофóн (*gen pl* -н) microphone.
ми́ксер (*cul*) mixer, blender.
микстýра medicine, mixture.
ми́ленький pretty; sweet; dear.
милитари́зм militarism.
милиционéр militiaman, policeman. **мили́ция** militia, police force.
миллиáрд billion, a thousand million. **миллимéтр** millimetre. **миллиóн** million. **миллионéр** millionaire.
милосéрдие mercy, charity. **милосéрдный** merciful, charitable.
ми́лостивый gracious, kind. **ми́лостыня** alms. **ми́лость** favour, grace. **ми́лый** (мил, -á, -о) nice; kind; sweet; dear.
ми́ля mile.
ми́мика (facial) expression; mimicry.
ми́мо *adv* & *prep +gen* by, past. **мимолётный** fleeting. **мимохóдом** *adv* in passing.
ми́на[1] mine; bomb.
ми́на[2] expression, mien.
миндáль (-я́) *m* almond(-tree); almonds.
минерáл mineral. **минералóгия** mineralogy. **минерáльный** mineral.
миниатю́ра miniature. **миниатю́рный** miniature; tiny.
минимáльный minimum. **ми́нимум** minimum.
министéрство ministry. **мини́стр** minister.
миновáть *impf* & *pf* pass; *impers+dat* escape.
миномёт mortar. **минонóсец** (-сца) torpedo-boat.
минóр minor (key); melancholy.
минýвш|ий past; **~ее** *sb* the past.
ми́нус minus.
минýта minute. **минýтный** minute; momentary.
минýть (-нешь; ми́нул) *pf* pass.
мир[1] (*pl* -ы́) world.
мир[2] peace.
мирáж mirage.
мири́ть *impf* (*pf* **по~, при~**) reconcile; **~ся** be reconciled. **ми́рный** peace; peaceful.
мировоззрéние (world-)outlook; philosophy. **мировóй** world. **мироздáние** universe.
миролюби́вый peace-loving.
ми́ска basin, bowl.
мисс *f indecl* Miss.
миссионéр missionary.
ми́ссис *f indecl* Mrs.
ми́ссия mission.
ми́стер Mr.
ми́стика mysticism.
мистификáция hoax.
ми́тинг mass meeting; rally.
митрополи́т metropolitan.
миф myth. **мифи́ческий** mythical. **мифологи́ческий** mythological. **мифолóгия** mythology.
ми́чман warrant officer.
мишéнь target.
ми́шка (Teddy) bear.
младéнец (-нца) baby; infant. **млáдший** younger; youngest; junior.
млекопитáющие *sb pl* mammals. **Млéчный Путь** Milky Way.
мне *see* **я** *pron*
мнéние opinion.
мни́мый imaginary; sham. **мни́тельный** hypochondriac;

mistrustful. **мнить** (мню) *impf* think.

мно́гие *sb pl* many (people); **~ое** *sb* much, a great deal. **мно́го** *adv+gen* much; many; **на ~** by far.

много- *in comb* many-, poly-, multi-, multiple-. **многобо́рье** combined event. **~гра́нный** polyhedral; many-sided. **~де́тный** having many children. **~жёнство** polygamy. **~значи́тельный** significant. **~кра́тный** repeated; frequentative. **~ле́тний** lasting, living, many years; of many years' standing; perennial. **~лю́дный** crowded. **~национа́льный** multinational. **~обеща́ющий** promising. **~обра́зие** diversity. **~сло́вный** verbose. **~сторо́нний** multi-lateral; many-sided, versatile. **~то́чие** dots, omission points. **~уважа́емый** respected; Dear. **~уго́льный** polygonal. **~цве́тный** multicoloured; multiflorous. **~чи́сленный** numerous. **~эта́жный** many-storeyed. **~язы́чный** polyglot.

мно́жественный plural. **мно́жество** great number. **мно́жить** (-жу) *impf* (*pf* **у~**) multiply; increase.

мной *etc.*: *see* **я** *pron.* **мну** *etc.*: *see* **мять**

мобилиза́ция mobilization. **мобилизова́ть** *impf* & *pf* mobilize.

мог *etc.*: *see* **мочь**

моги́ла grave. **моги́льный** (of the) grave; sepulchral.

могу́ *etc.*: *see* **мочь. могу́чий** mighty. **могу́щественный** powerful. **могу́щество** power, might.

мо́да fashion.

модели́ровать *impf* & *pf* design. **моде́ль** model; pattern. **моделье́р** fashion designer. **моде́льный** model; fashionable.

модернизи́ровать *impf* & *pf* modernize.

моде́м (*comput*) modem.

моди́стка milliner.

модифика́ция modification. **модифици́ровать** *impf* & *pf* modify.

мо́дный (-ден, -дна́, -о) fashionable; fashion.

мо́жет *see* **мочь**

можжеве́льник juniper.

мо́жно one may, one can; it is permissible; it is possible; **как ~**+*comp* as … as possible; **как ~ скоре́е** as soon as possible.

моза́ика mosaic; jigsaw.

мозг (*loc* -у́; *pl* -и́) brain; marrow. **мозгово́й** cerebral.

мозо́ль corn; callus.

мой (моего́) *m*, **моя́** (мое́й) *f*, **моё** (моего́) *neut*, **мои́** (-и́х) *pl pron* my; mine; **по-мо́ему** in my opinion; in my way.

мо́йка washing.

мо́кнуть (-ну; мок) *impf* get wet; soak. **мокро́та** phlegm. **мо́крый** wet, damp.

мол (*loc* -у́) mole, pier.

молва́ rumour, talk.

моле́бен (-бна) church service.

моле́кула molecule. **молекуля́рный** molecular.

моли́тва prayer. **моли́ть** (-лю́, -лишь) *impf* pray; beg; **~ся** (*pf* **по~ся**) pray.

моллю́ск mollusc.

молниено́сный lightning. **мо́лния** lightning; zip(-fastener).

молодёжь youth, young people. **молоде́ть** (-е́ю) *impf* (*pf* **по~**) get younger, look younger. **молоде́ц** (-дца́) fine fellow *or* girl; **~!** well done! **молодожёны** (-ов) *pl* newly-weds. **молодо́й** (мо́лод, -а́, -о) young. **мо́лодость** youth. **моло́же** *comp of* **молодо́й**

молоко́ milk.

мо́лот hammer. **молоти́ть** (-очу́, -о́тишь) *impf* (*pf* **с~**) thresh; hammer. **молото́к** (-тка́) hammer. **мо́лотый** ground. **моло́ть** (мелю́, ме́лешь) *impf* (*pf* **с~**) grind, mill.

моло́чная *sb* dairy. **моло́чный** milk; dairy; milky.

мо́лча *adv* silently, in silence. **молчали́вый** silent, taciturn; tacit. **молча́ние** silence. **молча́ть** (-чу́) *impf* be *or* keep silent.

моль moth.

мольба́ entreaty.

мольбе́рт easel.

моме́нт moment; feature. **момента́льно** *adv* instantly. **момента́льный** instantaneous.

мона́рх monarch. **монархи́ст** monarchist.

монасты́рь (-я́) *m* monastery; convent. **мона́х** monk. **мона́хиня** nun.

монго́л, ~ка Mongol.

моне́та coin.

моногра́фия monograph.

моноли́тный monolithic.

моноло́г monologue.

монопо́лия monopoly.

моното́нный monotonous.

монта́ж (-а́) assembling, mounting; editing. **монта́жник** rigger, fitter. **монтёр** fitter, mechanic. **монти́ровать** *impf* (*pf* **с~**) mount; install, fit; edit.

монуме́нт monument. **монумента́льный** monumental.

мора́ль moral; morals, ethics. **мора́льный** moral; ethical.

морг morgue.

морга́ть *impf*, **моргну́ть** (-ну́, -нёшь) *pf* blink; wink.

мо́рда snout, muzzle; (ugly) mug.

мо́ре (*pl* -я́, -е́й) sea.

морепла́вание navigation. **морепла́ватель** *m* seafarer. **морехо́дный** nautical.

морж (-а́), **моржи́ха** walrus.

Мо́рзе *indecl* Morse; **а́збука ~** Morse code.

мори́ть *impf* (*pf* **у~**) exhaust; **~ го́лодом** starve.

морко́вка carrot. **морко́вь** carrots.

моро́женое *sb* ice-cream. **моро́женый** frozen, chilled. **моро́з** frost; *pl* intensely cold weather. **морози́лка** freezer compartment; freezer. **морози́льник** deep-freeze. **моро́зить** (-о́жу) freeze. **моро́зный** frosty.

мороси́ть *impf* drizzle.

морск|о́й sea; maritime; marine, nautical; **~а́я сви́нка** guinea-pig; **~о́й флот** navy, fleet.

мо́рфий morphine.

морщи́на wrinkle; crease. **мо́рщить** (-щу) *impf* (*pf* **на~, по~, с~**) wrinkle; pucker; **~ся** knit one's brow; wince; crease, wrinkle.

моря́к (-а́) sailor, seaman.

москви́ч (-а́), **~ка** Muscovite. **моско́вский** (of) Moscow.

мост (мо́ста́, *loc* -у́; *pl* -ы́) bridge. **мо́стик** bridge. **мости́ть** (-ощу́) *impf* (*pf* **вы~**) pave. **мостки́** (-о́в) *pl* planked footway. **мо-**

стова́я *sb* roadway; pavement. **мостово́й** bridge.

мота́ть[1] *impf* (*pf* **мотну́ть, на~**) wind, reel.

мота́ть[2] *impf* (*pf* **про~**) squander.

мота́ться *impf* dangle; wander; rush about.

моти́в motive; reason; tune; motif. **мотиви́ровать** *impf & pf* give reasons for, justify. **мотиви́ровка** reason(s); justification.

мотну́ть (-ну́, -нёшь) *pf of* **мота́ть**

мото- *in comb* motor-, engine-. **мотого́нки** (-нок) *pl* motor-cycle races. **~пе́д** moped. **~пехо́та** motorized infantry. **~ро́ллер** (motor-)scooter. **~цикл** motor cycle.

мото́к (-тка́) skein, hank.

мото́р motor, engine. **мотори́ст** motor-mechanic. **мото́рный** motor; engine.

моты́га hoe, mattock.

мотылёк (-лька́) butterfly, moth.

мох (мха *or* мо́ха, *loc* мху; *pl* мхи, мхов) moss. **мохна́тый** hairy, shaggy.

моча́ urine.

моча́лка loofah.

мочево́й пузы́рь bladder. **мочи́ть** (-чу́, -чишь) *impf* (*pf* **за~, на~**) wet, moisten; soak; **~ся** (*pf* **по~ся**) urinate.

мо́чка ear lobe.

мочь (могу́, мо́жешь; мог, -ла́) *impf* (*pf* **с~**) be able; **мо́жет (быть)** perhaps.

моше́нник rogue. **моше́нничать** *impf* (*pf* **с~**) cheat, swindle. **моше́ннический** rascally.

мо́шка midge. **мошкара́** (swarm of) midges.

мо́щность power; capacity. **мо́щный** (-щен, -щна́, -о) powerful.

мощу́ *etc.*: *see* **мости́ть**

мощь power.

мо́ю *etc.*: *see* **мыть. мо́ющий** washing; detergent.

мрак darkness, gloom. **мракобе́с** obscurantist.

мра́мор marble. **мра́морный** marble.

мра́чный dark; gloomy.

мсти́тельный vindictive. **мстить** (мщу) *impf* (*pf* **ото~**) take vengeance on; **+за+***acc* avenge.

мудре́ц (-а́) sage, wise man. **му́дрость** wisdom. **му́дрый** (-др, -а́, -о) wise, sage.

муж (*pl* -жья́ *or* -и́) husband. **мужа́ть** *impf* grow up; mature; **~ся** take courage. **мужепо́добный** mannish; masculine. **му́жественный** manly, steadfast. **му́жество** courage.

мужи́к (-а́) peasant; fellow.

мужско́й masculine; male. **мужчи́на** *m* man.

му́за muse.

музе́й museum.

му́зыка music. **музыка́льный** musical. **музыка́нт** musician.

му́ка[1] torment.

мука́[2] flour.

мультиплика́ция, мультфи́льм cartoon film.

му́мия mummy.

мунди́р (full-dress) uniform.

мундшту́к (-а́) mouthpiece; cigarette-holder.

муниципа́льный municipal.

мураве́й (-вья́) ant. **мураве́йник** ant-hill.

мурлы́кать (-ы́чу *or* -каю) *impf* purr.

мускáт nutmeg.

мýскул muscle. **мýскульный** muscular.

мýсор refuse; rubbish. **мýсорный я́щик** dustbin.

мусульмáнин (*pl* -мáне, -мáн), **-áнка** Muslim.

мути́ть (мучý, мýти́шь) *impf* (*pf* **вз~**) make muddy; stir up, upset. **мýтный** (-тен, -тнá, -о) turbid, troubled; dull. **муть** sediment; murk.

мýха fly.

мучéние torment, torture. **мýченик, мýченица** martyr. **мучи́тельный** agonizing. **мýчить** (-чу) *impf* (*pf* **за~, из~**) torment; harass; **~ся** torment o.s.; suffer agonies.

мучнóй flour, meal; starchy.

мха *etc.*: *see* **мох**

мчать (мчу) *impf* rush along, whirl along; **~ся** rush.

мщу *etc.*: *see* **мсти́ть**

мы (нас, нам, нáми, нас) *pron* we; **мы с вáми** you and I.

мы́лить *impf* (*pf* **на~**) soap; **~ся** wash o.s. **мы́ло** (*pl* -á) soap. **мы́льница** soap-dish. **мы́льный** soap, soapy.

мыс cape, promontory.

мы́сленный mental. **мы́слимый** conceivable. **мысли́тель** *m* thinker. **мы́слить** *impf* think; conceive. **мысль** thought; idea. **мы́слящий** thinking.

мыть (мóю) *impf* (*pf* **вы́~, по~**) wash; **~ся** wash (o.s.).

мычáть (-чý) *impf* (*pf* **про~**) low, moo; bellow; mumble.

мышелóвка mousetrap.

мы́шечный muscular.

мышлéние thinking, thought.

мы́шца muscle.

мышь (*gen pl* -éй) mouse.

мэр mayor. **мэ́рия** town hall.

мя́гкий (-гок, -гкá, -о) soft; mild; **~ знак** soft sign, the letter **ь**.

мя́гче *comp of* **мя́гкий, мя́гко.**

мя́коть fleshy part, flesh; pulp.

мяси́стый fleshy; meaty. **мясни́к** (-á) butcher. **мяснóй** meat. **мя́со** meat; flesh. **мясорýбка** mincer.

мя́та mint; peppermint.

мятéж (-á) mutiny, revolt. **мятéжник** mutineer, rebel. **мятéжный** rebellious; restless.

мя́тный mint, peppermint.

мять (мну, мнёшь) *impf* (*pf* **из~, раз~, с~**) work up; knead; crumple; **~ся** become crumpled; crush (easily).

мяýкать *impf* miaow.

мяч (-á), **мя́чик** ball.

Н

на[1] *prep* **I.** +*acc* on; on to, to, into; at; till, until; for; by. **II.** +*prep* on, upon; in; at.

на[2] *partl* here; here you are.

набáвить (-влю) *pf*, **набавля́ть** *impf* add (to), increase.

набáт alarm-bell.

набéг raid, foray.

набекрéнь *adv* aslant.

на|бели́ть (-éли́шь) *pf*. **нáбело** *adv* without corrections.

нáбережная *sb* embankment, quay.

наберý *etc.*: *see* **набрáть**

набивáть(ся *impf of* **наби́ть(ся. наби́вка** stuffing, padding; (textile) printing.

набирáть(ся *impf of* **набрáть(ся**

наби́тый packed, stuffed; crowded. **наби́ть** (-бью, -бьёшь) *pf* (*impf* **набива́ть**) stuff, pack, fill; smash; print; hammer, drive; **~ся** crowd in.

наблюда́тель *m* observer. **наблюда́тельный** observant; observation. **наблюда́ть** *impf* observe,watch; +**за**+*instr* look after; supervise. **наблюде́ние** observation; supervision.

на́божный devout, pious.

на́бок *adv* on one side, crooked.

наболе́вший sore, painful.

набо́р recruiting; collection, set; type-setting.

набра́сывать(ся *impf of* **наброса́ть, набро́сить(ся**

набра́ть (-беру́, -берёшь; -а́л, -а́, -о) *pf* (*impf* **набира́ть**) gather; enlist; compose, set up; **~ но́мер** dial a number; **~ся** assemble, collect; +*gen* find, acquire, pick up; **~ся сме́лости** pluck up courage.

набрести́ (-еду́, -дёшь; -ёл, -ела́) *pf* +**на**+*acc* come across.

наброса́ть *pf* (*impf* **набра́сывать**) throw (down); sketch; jot down. **набро́сить** (-о́шу) *pf* (*impf* **набра́сывать**) throw; **~ся** throw o.s.; **~ся на** attack. **набро́сок** (-ска) sketch, draft.

набуха́ть *impf*, **набу́хнуть** (-нет; -у́х) *pf* swell.

набью́ *etc.*: *see* **наби́ть**

наважде́ние delusion.

нава́ливать *impf*, **навали́ть** (-лю́, -лишь) *pf* heap, pile up; load; **~ся** lean; +**на**+*acc* fall (up)on.

наведе́ние laying (on); placing.

наведу́ *etc.*: *see* **навести́**

наве́к, наве́ки *adv* for ever.

навёл *etc.*: *see* **навести́**

наве́рно, наве́рное *adv* probably. **наверняка́** *adv* certainly, for sure.

наверста́ть *pf*, **навёрстывать** *impf* make up for.

наве́рх *adv* up(wards); upstairs. **наверху́** *adv* above; upstairs.

наве́с awning.

наве́сить (-е́шу) *pf* (*impf* **наве́шивать**) hang (up). **навесно́й** hanging.

навести́ (-еду́, -едёшь; -вёл, -а́) *pf* (*impf* **наводи́ть**) direct; aim; cover (with), spread; introduce, bring; make.

навести́ть (-ещу́) *pf* (*impf* **навеща́ть**) visit.

наве́шать *pf*, **наве́шивать**[1] *impf* hang (out); weigh out.

наве́шивать[2] *impf of* **наве́сить. навеща́ть** *impf of* **навести́ть**

на́взничь *adv* backwards, on one's back.

навзры́д *adv*: **пла́кать ~** sob.

навига́ция navigation.

нависа́ть *impf*, **нави́снуть** (-нет; -ви́с) *pf* overhang, hang (over); threaten. **нави́сший** beetling.

навлека́ть *impf*, **навле́чь** (-еку́, -ечёшь; -ёк, -ла́) *pf* bring, draw; incur.

наводи́ть (-ожу́, -о́дишь) *impf of* **навести́; наводя́щий вопро́с** leading question. **наво́дка** aiming; applying.

наводне́ние flood. **наводни́ть** *pf*, **наводня́ть** *impf* flood; inundate.

наво́з dung, manure.

на́волочка pillowcase.

на|вра́ть (-ру́, -рёшь; -а́л, -а́, -о) *pf* tell lies, romance; talk nonsense; +**в**+*prep* make mistake(s) in.

навреди́ть (-ежу́) *pf* +*dat* harm.
навсегда́ *adv* for ever.
навстре́чу *adv* to meet; **идти́ ~** go to meet; meet halfway.
навы́ворот *adv* inside out; back to front.
на́вык experience, skill.
навы́нос *adv* to take away.
навы́пуск *adv* worn outside.
навью́чивать *impf*, **на|вью́чить** (-чу) *pf* load.
навяза́ть (-яжу́, -я́жешь) *pf*, **навя́зывать** *impf* tie, fasten; thrust, foist; **~ся** thrust o.s. **навя́зчивый** importunate; obsessive.
на|га́дить (-а́жу) *pf*.
нага́н revolver.
нагиба́ть(ся *impf of* **нагну́ть(ся**
нагишо́м *adv* stark naked.
нагле́ц (-а́) impudent fellow. **на́глость** impudence. **на́глый** (нагл, -а́, -о) impudent.
нагля́дный clear, graphic; visual.
нагна́ть (-гоню́, -го́нишь; -а́л, -а́, -о) *pf* (*impf* **нагоня́ть**) overtake, catch up (with); inspire, arouse.
нагнести́ (-ету́, -етёшь) *pf*, **нагнета́ть** *impf* compress; supercharge.
нагное́ние suppuration. **нагнои́ться** *pf* suppurate.
нагну́ть (-ну́, -нёшь) *pf* (*impf* **нагиба́ть**) bend; **~ся** bend, stoop.
нагова́ривать *impf*, **наговори́ть** *pf* slander; talk a lot (of); record.
наго́й (наг, -а́, -о) naked, bare.
на́голо́ *adv* naked, bare.
нагоня́ть *impf of* **нагна́ть**
нагора́ть *impf*, **нагоре́ть** (-ри́т) *pf* be consumed; *impers*+*dat* be scolded.
наго́рный upland, mountain; mountainous.
нагота́ nakedness, nudity.
награ́бить (-блю) *pf* amass by dishonest means.
награ́да reward; decoration; prize. **награди́ть** (-ажу́) *pf*, **награжда́ть** *impf* reward; decorate; award prize to.
нагрева́тельный heating. **нагрева́ть** *impf*, **нагре́ть** (-е́ю) *pf* warm, heat; **~ся** get hot, warm up.
нагроможда́ть *impf*, **на|громозди́ть** (-зжу́) *pf* heap up, pile up. **нагроможде́ние** heaping up; conglomeration.
на|груби́ть (-блю́) *pf*.
нагружа́ть *impf*, **на|грузи́ть** (-ужу́, -у́зишь) *pf* load; **~ся** load o.s. **нагру́зка** loading; load; work; commitments.
нагря́нуть (-ну) *pf* appear unexpectedly.
над, надо *prep*+*instr* over, above; on, at.
надави́ть (-влю́, -вишь) *pf*, **нада́вливать** *impf* press; squeeze out; crush.
надба́вка addition, increase.
надвига́ть *impf*, **надви́нуть** (-ну) *pf* move, pull, push; **~ся** approach.
на́двое *adv* in two.
надгро́бие epitaph. **надгро́бный** (*on or over a*) grave.
надева́ть *impf of* **наде́ть**
наде́жда hope. **надёжность** reliability. **надёжный** reliable.
наде́л allotment.
наде́лать *pf* make; cause; do.
надели́ть (-лю́, -лишь) *pf*, **наделя́ть** *impf* endow, provide.
наде́ть (-е́ну) *pf* (*impf* **надева́ть**) put on.

надéяться (-éюсь) *impf* (*pf* **по~**) hope; rely.

надзирáтель *m* overseer, supervisor. **надзирáть** *impf* **+за+***instr* supervise, oversee. **надзóр** supervision; surveillance.

надлáмывать(ся *impf of* **надломи́ть(ся**

надлежáщий fitting, proper, appropriate. **надлежи́т** (-жáло) *impers* (*+dat*) it is necessary, required.

надлóм break; crack; breakdown. **надломи́ть** (-млю́, -мишь) *pf* (*impf* **надлáмывать**) break; crack; breakdown; **~ся** break, crack, breakdown. **надлóмленный** broken.

надмéнный haughty, arrogant.

нáдо[1] (*+dat*) it is necessary; I (*etc.*) must, ought to; I (*etc.*) need. **нáдобность** necessity, need.

надо[2]: *see* **над.**

надоедáть *impf*, **надоéсть** (-éм, -éшь, -éст, -еди́м) *pf* *+dat* bore, pester. **надоéдливый** boring, tiresome.

надóлго *adv* for a long time.

надорвáть (-вý, -вёшь; -áл, -á, -о) *pf* (*impf* **надрывáть**) tear; strain; **~ся** tear; overstrain o.s.

нáдпись inscription.

надрéз cut, incision. **надрéзать** (-éжу) *pf*, **надрезáть** *impf*, **надрéзывать** *impf* make an incision in.

надругáтельство outrage. **надругáться** *pf* **+над+***instr* outrage, insult.

надры́в tear; strain; breakdown; outburst. **надрывáть(ся** *impf of* **надорвáть(ся. надры́вный** hysterical; heartrending.

надстáвить (-влю) *pf*, **надставля́ть** *impf* lengthen.

надстрáивать *impf*, **надстрóить** (-óю) *pf* build on top; extend upwards. **надстрóйка** building upwards; superstructure.

надувáтельство swindle. **надувáть(ся** *impf. of* **надýть(ся. надувнóй** pneumatic, inflatable.

надýманный far-fetched.

надýтый swollen; haughty; sulky. **надýть** (-ýю) *pf* (*impf* **надувáть**) inflate; swindle; **~ся** swell out; sulk.

на|души́ть(ся (-шý(сь, -шишь(ся) *pf.*

наедáться *impf of* **наéсться**

наединé *adv* privately, alone.

наéзд flying visit; raid. **наéздник, -ица** rider. **наезжáть** *impf of* **наéздить, наéхать**; pay occasional visits.

наём (нáйма) hire; renting; **взять в ~** rent; **сдать в ~** let. **наёмник** hireling; mercenary. **наёмный** hired, rented.

наéсться (-éмся, -éшься, -éстся, -еди́мся) *pf* (*impf* **наедáться**) eat one's fill; stuff o.s.

наéхать (-éду) *pf* (*impf* **наезжáть**) arrive unexpectedly; **+на+***acc* run into, collide with.

нажáть (-жмý, -жмёшь) *pf* (*impf* **нажимáть**) press; put pressure (on).

наждáк (-á) emery. **наждáчная бумáга** emery paper.

нажи́ва profit, gain.

наживáть(ся *impf of* **нажи́ть(ся**

нажи́м pressure; clamp. **нажимáть** *impf of* **нажáть.**

нажи́ть (-ивý, -ивёшь; нáжил, -á, -о) *pf* (*impf* **наживáть**) acquire;

contract, incur; **~ся** (-жи́лся, -áсь) get rich.

нажму́ *etc.*: *see* **нажа́ть**

наза́втра *adv* (the) next day.

наза́д *adv* back(wards); **(тому́)** ~ ago.

назва́ние name; title. **назва́ть** (-зову́, -зовёшь; -áл, -á, -o) *pf* (*impf* **называ́ть**) call, name; **~ся** be called.

назе́мный ground, surface.

на́зло́ *adv* out of spite; to spite.

назнача́ть *impf*, **назна́чить** (-чу) *pf* appoint; fix, set; prescribe. **назначе́ние** appointment; fixing, setting; prescription.

назову́ *etc.*: *see* **назва́ть**

назо́йливый importunate.

назрева́ть *impf*, **назре́ть** (-е́ет) *pf* ripen, mature; become imminent.

называ́емый: так ~ so-called.

называ́ть(ся *impf of* **назва́ть(ся.**

наибо́лее *adv* (the) most. **наибо́льший** greatest, biggest.

наи́вный naive.

наивы́сший highest.

наигра́ть *pf*, **наи́грывать** *impf* win; play, pick out.

наизна́нку *adv* inside out.

наизу́сть *adv* by heart.

наилу́чший best.

наименова́ние name; title.

на́искось *adv* obliquely.

найму́ *etc.*: *see* **наня́ть**

найти́ (-йду́, -йдёшь; нашёл, -шла́, -шло́) *pf* (*impf* **находи́ть**) find; **~сь** be found; be, be situated.

наказа́ние punishment. **наказа́ть** (-ажу́, -а́жешь) *pf*, **нака́зывать** *impf* punish.

нака́л incandescence. **нака́ливать** *impf*, **накали́ть** *pf*, **накаля́ть** *impf* heat; make red-hot; strain, make tense; **~ся** glow, become incandescent; become strained.

нака́лывать(ся *impf of* **наколо́ть(ся**

накану́не *adv* the day before.

нака́пливать(ся *impf of* **накопи́ть(ся**

накача́ть *pf*, **нака́чивать** *impf* pump (up).

наки́дка cloak, cape; extra charge. **наки́нуть** (-ну) *pf*, **наки́дывать** *impf* throw; throw on; **~ся** throw o.s.; **~ся на** attack.

на́кипь scum; scale.

накладна́я *sb* invoice. **наклад|но́й** laid on; false; **~ы́е расхо́ды** overheads. **накла́дывать** *impf of* **наложи́ть**

на|клевета́ть (-ещу́, -е́щешь) *pf.*

накле́ивать *impf*, **накле́ить** *pf* stick on. **накле́йка** sticking (on, up); label.

накло́н slope, incline. **наклоне́ние** inclination; mood. **наклони́ть** (-ню́, -нишь) *pf*, **наклоня́ть** *impf* incline, bend; **~ся** stoop, bend. **накло́нный** inclined, sloping.

нако́лка pinning; (*pinned-on*) ornament for hair; tattoo. **наколо́ть**[1] (-лю́, -лешь) *pf* (*impf* **нака́лывать**) prick; pin; **~ся** prick o.s.

наколо́ть[2] (-лю́, -лешь) *pf* (*impf* **нака́лывать**) chop.

наконе́ц *adv* at last. **наконе́чник** tip, point.

на|копи́ть (-плю́, -пишь) *pf*, **накопля́ть** *impf* (*impf also* **нака́пливать**) accumulate; **~ся** accumulate. **накопле́ние** accumulation.

на|копти́ть (-пчу́) *pf.* **на|кор-**

ми́ть (-млю́, -ми́шь) *pf.*

накра́сить (-а́шу) *pf* paint; make up. **на|кра́ситься** (-а́шусь) *pf.*

на|крахма́лить *pf.*

на|крени́ть *pf.* **накрени́ться** (-ни́тся) *pf*, **накреня́ться** *impf* tilt; list.

накрича́ть (-чу́) *pf* (+**на**+*acc*) shout (at).

накро́ю *etc.*: *see* **накры́ть**

накрыва́ть *impf*, **накры́ть** (-ро́ю) *pf* cover; catch; **~ (на) стол** lay the table; **~ся** cover o.s.

накури́ть (-рю́, -ри́шь) *pf* fill with smoke.

налага́ть *impf of* **наложи́ть**

нала́дить (-а́жу) *pf*, **нала́живать** *impf* regulate, adjust; repair; organize; **~ся** come right; get going.

на|лга́ть (-лгу́, -лжёшь; -а́л, -а́, -о) *pf.*

нале́во *adv* to the left.

налёг *etc.*: *see* **нале́чь. налега́ть** *impf of* **нале́чь**

налегке́ *adv* lightly dressed; without luggage.

налёт raid; flight; thin coating. **налета́ть**[1] *pf* have flown. **налета́ть**[2] *impf*, **налете́ть** (-лечу́) *pf* swoop down; come flying; spring up.

нале́чь (-ля́гу, -ля́жешь; -лёг, -ла́) *pf* (*impf* **налега́ть**) lean, apply one's weight, lie; apply o.s.

налжёшь *etc.*: *see* **налга́ть**

налива́ть(ся *impf of* **нали́ть(ся. нали́вка** fruit liqueur.

нали́ть (-лью́, -льёшь; на́лил, -а́, -о) *pf* (*impf* **налива́ть**) pour (out), fill; **~ся** (-и́лся, -а́сь, -и́ло́сь) pour in; ripen.

налицо́ *adv* present; available.

нали́чие presence. **нали́чн|ый** on hand; cash; **~ые (де́ньги)** ready money.

нало́г tax. **налогоплате́льщик** taxpayer. **нало́женн|ый: ~ым платежо́м** C.O.D. **наложи́ть** (-жу́, -жишь) *pf* (*impf* **накла́дывать, налага́ть**) lay (in, on), put (in, on); apply; impose.

налью́ *etc.*: *see* **нали́ть**

наля́гу *etc.*: *see* **нале́чь**

нам *etc.*: *see* **мы**

на|ма́зать (-а́жу) *pf*, **нама́зывать** *impf* oil, grease; smear, spread.

нама́тывать *impf of* **намота́ть.**

нама́чивать *impf of* **намочи́ть**

намёк hint. **намека́ть** *impf*, **намекну́ть** (-ну́, -нёшь) *pf* hint.

намерева́ться *impf* +*inf* intend to. **наме́рен** *predic*: **я ~(а)**+*inf* I intend to. **наме́рение** intention. **наме́ренный** intentional.

на|мета́ть *pf.* **на|ме́тить**[1] (-е́чу) *pf.*

наме́тить[2] (-е́чу) *pf* (*impf* **намеча́ть**) plan; outline; nominate; **~ся** be outlined, take shape.

намно́го *adv* much, far.

намока́ть *impf*, **намо́кнуть** (-ну) *pf* get wet.

намо́рдник muzzle.

на|мо́рщить(ся (-щу(сь) *pf.*

на|мота́ть *pf* (*impf also* **нама́тывать**) wind, reel.

на|мочи́ть (-очу́, -о́чишь) *pf* (*impf also* **нама́чивать**) wet; soak; splash, spill.

намы́ливать *impf*, **на|мы́лить** *pf* soap.

нанести́ (-су́, -сёшь; -ёс, -ла́) *pf* (*impf* **наноси́ть**) carry, bring; draw, plot; inflict.

на|низа́ть (-ижу́, -и́жешь) *pf*, **на-**

ни́зывать *impf* string, thread.
нанима́тель *m* tenant; employer. **нанима́ть(ся** *impf of* **наня́ть(ся**
наноси́ть (-ошу́, -о́сишь) *impf of* **нанести́**
наня́ть (найму́, -мёшь; на́нял, -а́, -о) *pf* (*impf* **нанима́ть**) hire; rent; **~ся** get a job.
наоборо́т *adv* on the contrary; back to front; the other, the wrong, way (round); vice versa.
нао́тмашь *adv* violently.
наотре́з *adv* flatly, point-blank.
напада́ть *impf of* **напа́сть. напада́ющий** *sb* forward. **нападе́ние** attack; forwards.
напа́рник co-driver, (work-)mate.
напа́сть (-аду́, -адёшь; -а́л) *pf* (*impf* **напада́ть**) **на**+*acc* attack; descend on; seize; come upon. **напа́сть** misfortune.
напе́в tune. **напева́ть** *impf of* **напе́ть**
наперебо́й *adv* interrupting, vying with, one another.
напере́д *adv* in advance.
напереко́р *adv*+*dat* in defiance of, counter to.
напёрсток (-тка) thimble.
напе́ть (-пою́, -поёшь) *pf* (*impf* **напева́ть**) sing; hum, croon.
на|печа́тать(ся *pf*. **напива́ться** *impf of* **напи́ться**
напи́льник file.
на|писа́ть (-ишу́, -и́шешь) *pf*.
напи́ток (-тка) drink. **напи́ться** (-пью́сь, -пьёшься; -и́лся, -а́сь, -и́ло́сь) *pf* (*impf* **напива́ться**) quench one's thirst, drink; get drunk.
напиха́ть *pf*, **напи́хивать** *impf* cram, stuff.
на|плева́ть (-люю́, -люёшь) *pf*; **~!** to hell with it! who cares?
наплы́в influx; accumulation; canker.
наплюю́ *etc.*: *see* **наплева́ть**
напова́л outright.
наподо́бие *prep*+*gen* like, not unlike.
на|пои́ть (-ою́, -о́ишь) *pf*.
напока́з *adv* for show.
наполни́тель *m* filler. **напо́лнить(ся** *pf*, **наполня́ть(ся** *impf* fill.
наполови́ну *adv* half.
напомина́ние reminder. **напомина́ть** *impf*, **напо́мнить** *pf* (+*dat*) remind.
напо́р pressure. **напо́ристый** energetic, pushing.
напосле́док *adv* in the end; after all.
напою́ *etc.*: *see* **напе́ть, напои́ть**
напр. *abbr* (*of* **наприме́р**) e.g., for example.
напра́вить (-влю) *pf*, **направля́ть** *impf* direct; send; sharpen; **~ся** make (for), go (towards). **направле́ние** direction; trend; warrant; order. **напра́вленный** purposeful.
напра́во *adv* to the right.
напра́сно *adv* in vain, for nothing; unjustly, mistakenly.
напра́шиваться *impf of* **напроси́ться**
наприме́р for example.
на|прока́зничать *pf*.
напрока́т *adv* for, on, hire.
напролёт *adv* through, without a break.
напроло́м *adv* straight, regardless of obstacles.
напроси́ться (-ошу́сь, -о́сишься) *pf* (*impf* **напра́шиваться**) thrust o.s.; suggest itself; **~ на** ask for, invite.

напро́тив *adv* opposite; on the contrary. **напро́тив** *prep+gen* opposite.

напряга́ть(ся *impf of* **напря́чь(ся. напряже́ние** tension; exertion; voltage. **напряжённый** tense; intense; intensive.

напрями́к *adv* straight (out).

напря́чь (-ягу́, -яжёшь; -я́г, -гла́) *pf* (*impf* **напряга́ть**) strain; **~ся** strain o.s.

на|пуга́ть(ся *pf.* **на|пу́дриться** *pf.*

напуска́ть *impf*, **напусти́ть** (-ущу́, -у́стишь) *pf* let in; let loose; **~ся +на**+*acc* fly at, go for.

напу́тать *pf* **+в**+*prep* make a mess of.

на|пыли́ть *pf.*

напью́сь *etc.*: *see* **напи́ться**

наравне́ *adv* level; equally.

нараспа́шку *adv* unbuttoned.

нараста́ние growth, accumulation. **нараста́ть** *impf*, **нарасти́** (-тёт; -ро́с, -ла́) *pf* grow; increase.

нарасхва́т *adv* very quickly, like hot cakes.

нарва́ть[1] (-рву́, -рвёшь; -а́л, -а́, -о) *pf* (*impf* **нарыва́ть**) pick; tear up.

нарва́ть[2] (-вёт; -а́л, -а́, -о) *pf* (*impf* **нарыва́ть**) gather.

нарва́ться (-ву́сь, -вёшься; -а́лся, -ала́сь, -а́ло́сь) *pf* (*impf* **нарыва́ться**) **+на**+*acc* run into, run up against.

наре́зать (-е́жу) *pf*, **нареза́ть** *impf* cut (up), slice, carve; thread, rifle.

наре́чие[1] dialect.

наре́чие[2] adverb.

на|рисова́ть *pf.*

нарко́з narcosis. **наркома́н, -ма́нка** drug addict. **наркома́ния** drug addiction. **нарко́тик** narcotic.

наро́д people. **наро́дность** nationality; national character. **наро́дный** national; folk; popular; people's.

наро́с *etc.*: *see* **нарасти́**

наро́чно *adv* on purpose, deliberately. **на́рочный** *sb* courier.

нару́жность exterior. **нару́жный** external, outward. **нару́жу** *adv* outside.

нару́чник handcuff. **нару́чный** wrist.

наруше́ние breach; infringement. **наруши́тель** *m* transgressor. **нару́шить** (-шу) *pf*, **наруша́ть** *impf* break; disturb, infringe, violate.

нарци́сс narcissus; daffodil.

на́ры (нар) *pl* plank-bed.

нары́в abscess, boil. **нарыва́ть(ся** *impf of* **нарва́ть(ся**

наря́д[1] order, warrant.

наря́д[2] attire; dress. **наряди́ть** (-яжу́) *pf* (*impf* **наряжа́ть**) dress (up); **~ся** dress up. **наря́дный** well-dressed.

наряду́ *adv* alike, equally; side by side.

наряжа́ть(ся *impf of* **наряди́ть(ся. нас** *see* **мы**

насади́ть (-ажу́, -а́дишь) *pf*, **насажда́ть** *impf* (*impf also* **наса́живать**) plant; propagate; implant. **наса́дка** setting, fixing. **насажде́ние** planting; plantation; propagation. **наса́живать** *impf of* **насади́ть**

насеко́мое *sb* insect.

населе́ние population. **населённость** density of population. **населённый** populated; **~ пункт** settlement; built-up area. **населить** *pf*, **населять** *impf* settle, people.

насилие violence, force. **насиловать** *impf* (*pf* **из~**) coerce; rape. **насилу** *adv* with difficulty. **насильник** aggressor; rapist; violator. **насильно** *adv* by force. **насильственный** violent, forcible.

наскакивать *impf of* **наскочить**

насквозь *adv* through, throughout.

насколько *adv* how much?, how far?; as far as.

наскоро *adv* hastily.

наскочить (-очу, -очишь) *pf* (*impf* **наскакивать**) +**на**+*acc* run into, collide with; fly at.

наскучить (-чу) *pf* bore.

насладиться (-ажусь) *pf*, **наслаждаться** *impf* (+*instr*) enjoy, take pleasure. **наслаждение** pleasure, enjoyment.

наследие legacy; heritage. **на|следить** (-ежу) *pf*. **наследник** heir; successor. **наследница** heiress. **наследный** next in succession. **наследовать** *impf* & *pf* (*pf also* **у~**) inherit, succeed to. **наследственность** heredity. **наследственный** hereditary, inherited. **наследство** inheritance; heritage.

насмерть *adv* to (the) death.

на|смешить (-шу) *pf* **насмешка** mockery; gibe. **насмешливый** mocking.

насморк runny nose; cold.

на|сорить *pf*.

насос pump.

наспех *adv* hastily.

на|сплетничать *pf*. **наставать** (-таёт) *impf of* **настать**

наставление exhortation; directions, manual.

наставник tutor, mentor.

настаивать[1] *impf of* **настоять**[1].

настаивать[2]**(ся** *impf of* **настоять**[2]**(ся**

настать (-анет) *pf* (*impf* **наставать**) come, begin, set in.

настежь *adv* wide (open).

настелю *etc.*: *see* **настлать**

настигать *impf*, **настигнуть**, **настичь** (-игну; -иг) *pf* catch up with, overtake.

настил flooring, planking. **настилать** *impf of* **настлать**

настичь *see* **настигать**

настлать (-телю, -телешь) *pf* (*impf* **настилать**) lay, spread.

настойка liqueur, cordial.

настойчивый persistent; urgent.

настолько *adv* so, so much.

настольный table, desk; reference.

настораживать *impf*, **насторожить** (-жу) *pf* set; prick up; **~ся** prick up one's ears. **настороженный** (-ен, -енна) guarded; alert.

настоятельный insistent; urgent. **настоять**[1] (-ою) *pf* (*impf* **настаивать**[1]) insist.

настоять[2] (-ою) *pf* (*impf* **настаивать**[2]) brew; **~ся** draw, stand.

настоящее *sb* the present. **настоящий** (the) present, this; real, genuine.

настраивать(ся *impf of* **настроить(ся**

настричь (-игу, -ижёшь; -иг) *pf* shear, clip.

настроение mood. **настроить** (-ою) *pf* (*impf* **настраивать**) tune (in); dispose; **~ся** dispose o.s. **настройка** tuning. **настройщик** tuner.

на|строчи́ть (-чу́) *pf.*

наступа́тельный offensive.

наступа́ть[1] *impf of* **наступи́ть**[1]

наступа́ть[2] *impf of* **наступи́ть**[2]. **наступа́ющий**[1] coming.

наступа́ющий[2] *sb* attacker.

наступи́ть[1] (-плю́, -пишь) *pf* (*impf* **наступа́ть**[1]) tread; attack; advance.

наступи́ть[2] (-у́пит) *pf* (*impf* **наступа́ть**[2]) come, set in. **наступле́ние**[1] coming.

наступле́ние[2] offensive, attack.

насу́питься (-плюсь) *pf*, **насу́пливаться** *impf* frown.

на́сухо *adv* dry. **насуши́ть** (-шу́, -шишь) *pf* dry.

насу́щный urgent, vital; **хлеб ~** daily bread.

насчёт *prep+gen* about, concerning; as regards. **насчита́ть** *pf*, **насчи́тывать** *impf* count; hold; **~ся** +*gen* number.

насы́пать (-плю) *pf*, **насыпа́ть** *impf* pour in, on; fill; spread; heap up. **на́сыпь** embankment.

насы́тить (-ы́щу) *pf*, **насыща́ть** *impf* satiate; saturate; **~ся** be full; be saturated.

ната́лкивать(ся *impf of* **натолкну́ть(ся**. **ната́пливать** *impf of* **натопи́ть**

натаска́ть *pf*, **ната́скивать** *impf* train; coach, cram; bring in, lay in.

натвори́ть *pf* do, get up to.

натере́ть (-тру́, -трёшь; -тёр) *pf* (*impf* **натира́ть**) rub on, in; polish; chafe; grate; **~ся** rub o.s.

на́тиск onslaught.

наткну́ться (-ну́сь, -нёшься) *pf* (*impf* **натыка́ться**) +**на**+*acc* run into; strike, stumble on.

натолкну́ть (-ну́, -нёшь) *pf* (*impf* **ната́лкивать**) push; lead; **~ся** run against, across.

натопи́ть (-плю́, -пишь) *pf* (*impf* **ната́пливать**) heat (up); stoke up; melt.

на|точи́ть (-чу́, -чишь) *pf.*

натоща́к *adv* on an empty stomach.

натрави́ть (-влю́, -вишь) *pf*, **натра́вливать** *impf*, **натравля́ть** *impf* set (on); stir up.

на|тренирова́ть(ся *pf.*

на́трий sodium.

нату́ра nature. **натура́льный** natural; genuine. **нату́рщик, -щица** artist's model.

натыка́ть(ся *impf of* **наткну́ть(ся**

натюрмо́рт still life.

натя́гивать *impf*, **натяну́ть** (-ну́, -нешь) *pf* stretch; draw; pull (on); **~ся** stretch. **натя́нутость** tension. **натя́нутый** tight; strained.

науга́д *adv* at random.

нау́ка science; learning.

нау́тро *adv* (the) next morning.

на|учи́ть(ся (-чу́(сь, -чишь(ся) *pf.*

нау́чн|ый scientific; **~ая фанта́стика** science fiction.

нау́шник ear-flap; ear-phone.

нафтали́н naphthalene.

наха́л, -ха́лка impudent creature. **наха́льный** impudent. **наха́льство** impudence.

нахвата́ть *pf*, **нахва́тывать** *impf* pick up, get hold of; **~ся** +*gen* pick up.

нахле́бник hanger-on.

нахлы́нуть (-нет) *pf* well up; surge; gush.

на|хму́рить(ся *pf.*

находи́ть(ся (-ожу́(сь, -о́дишь(ся) *impf of* **найти́(сь**. **на-**

хóдка find. **нахóдчивый** resourceful, quick-witted.

нацéливать *impf*, **на|цéлить** *pf* aim; **~ся** (take) aim.

нацéнка surcharge, mark-up.

нацúзм Nazism. **национализáция** nationalization. **национализúровать** *impf* & *pf* nationalize. **националúзм** nationalism. **националистúческий** nationalist(ic). **национáльность** nationality; ethnic group. **национáльный** national. **нацúст, -úстка** Nazi. **нацúстский** Nazi. **нáция** nation. **нацмéн, -мéнка** *abbr* member of national minority.

начáло beginning; origin; principle, basis. **начáльник** head, chief; boss. **начáльный** initial; primary. **начáльство** the authorities; command. **начáть** (-чнý, -чнёшь; нáчал, -á, -о) *pf* (*impf* **начинáть**) begin; **~ся** begin.

начертáть *pf* trace, inscribe.

на|чертúть (-рчý, -ртишь) *pf*.

начинáние undertaking. **начинáть(ся** *impf of* **начáть(ся**. **начинáющий** *sb* beginner.

начинúть *pf*, **начинять** *impf* stuff, fill. **начúнка** stuffing, filling.

начúстить (-úщу) *pf* (*impf* **начищáть**) clean. **нáчисто** *adv* clean; flatly, decidedly; openly, frankly. **начистотý** *adv* openly, frankly.

начúтанность learning; wide reading. **начúтанный** well-read.

начищáть *impf of* **начúстить**

наш (-его) *m*, **нáша** (-ей) *f*, **нáше** (-его) *neut*, **нáши** (-их) *pl*, *pron* our, ours.

нашатúрный спирт ammonia. **нашатúрь** (-я́) *m* sal-ammoniac; ammonia.

нашёл *etc.*: *see* **найтú**

нашéствие invasion.

нашивáть *impf*, **нашúть** (-шью́, -шьёшь) *pf* sew on. **нашúвка** stripe, chevron; tab.

нашлёпать *impf* slap.

нашумéть (-млю́) *pf* make a din; cause a sensation.

нашью́ *etc.*: *see* **нашúть**

нащýпать *pf*, **нащýпывать** *impf* grope for.

на|электризовáть *pf*.

наявý *adv* awake; in reality.

не *partl* not.

не- *pref* un-, in-, non-, mis-, dis-; -less; not. **неаккурáтный** careless; untidy; unpunctual. **небезразлúчный** not indifferent. **небезызвéстный** not unknown; notorious; well-known.

небесá *etc.*: *see* **нéбо²**. **небéсный** heavenly; celestial.

не-. неблагодáрный ungrateful; thankless. **неблагонадёжный** unreliable. **неблагополýчный** unsuccessful, bad, unfavourable. **неблагоприя́тный** unfavourable. **неблагоразýмный** imprudent. **неблагорóдный** ignoble, base.

нёбо¹ palate.

нéбо² (*pl* -бесá, -бéс) sky; heaven.

не-. небогáтый of modest means, modest. **небольшóй** small, not great; **с небольшúм** a little over.

небосвóд firmament. **небосклóн** horizon. **небоскрёб** skyscraper.

небóсь *adv* I dare say; probably.

не-. небрéжный careless. **небывáлый** unprecedented; fantastic. **небыли́ца** fable, cock-and-bull story. **небытие́** non-existence. **небьющийся** unbreakable. **нева́жно** *adv* not too well, indifferently. **нева́жный** unimportant; indifferent. **невдалеке́** *adv* not far away. **неве́дение** ignorance. **неве́домый** unknown; mysterious. **неве́жа** *m* & *f* boor, lout. **неве́жда** *m* & *f* ignoramus. **неве́жественный** ignorant. **неве́жество** ignorance. **неве́жливый** rude. **невели́кий** (-и́к, -а́, -и́ко́) small. **неве́рие** unbelief, atheism; scepticism. **неве́рный** (-рен, -рна́, -о) incorrect, wrong; inaccurate, unsteady; unfaithful. **невероя́тный** improbable; incredible. **неве́рующий** unbelieving; *sb* atheist. **невесёлый** joyless, sad. **невесо́мый** weightless; imponderable.

неве́ста fiancée; bride. **неве́стка** daughter-in-law; brother's wife, sister-in-law.

не-. невзго́да adversity. **невзира́я на** *prep+acc* regardless of. **невзнача́й** *adv* by chance. **невзра́чный** unattractive, plain. **неви́данный** unprecedented, unheard-of. **неви́димый** invisible. **неви́нность** innocence. **неви́нный, невино́вный** innocent. **невменя́емый** irresponsible. **невмеша́тельство** non-intervention; non-interference. **невмоготу́, невмо́чь** *advs* unbearable, too much (for). **невнима́тельный** inattentive, thoughtless.

не́вод seine(-net).

не-. невозврати́мый, невозвра́тный irrevocable, irrecoverable. **невозмо́жный** impossible. **невозмути́мый** imperturbable.

нево́льник, -ница slave. **нево́льный** involuntary; unintentional; forced. **нево́ля** captivity; necessity.

не-. невообрази́мый unimaginable, inconceivable. **невооружённ|ый** unarmed; **~ным гла́зом** with the naked eye. **невоспи́танный** ill-bred, bad-mannered. **невоспламеня́ющийся** non-flammable. **невосприи́мчивый** unreceptive; immune.

невралги́я neuralgia.

невреди́мый safe, unharmed.

невро́з neurosis. **неврологи́ческий** neurological. **невроти́ческий** neurotic.

не-. невы́годный disadvantageous; unprofitable. **невы́держанный** lacking self-control; unmatured. **невыноси́мый** unbearable. **невыполни́мый** impracticable. **невысо́кий** (-со́к, -а́, -о́ко́) low; short.

не́га luxury; bliss.

негати́вный negative.

не́где *adv* (there is) nowhere.

не-. неги́бкий (-бок, -бка́, -о) inflexible, stiff. **негла́сный** secret. **неглубо́кий** (-о́к, -а́, -о) shallow. **неглу́пый** (-у́п, -а́, -о) sensible, quite intelligent. **него́дный** (-ден, -дна́, -о) unfit, unsuitable; worthless. **негодова́ние** indignation. **негодова́ть** *impf* be indignant. **негодя́й** scoundrel. **негостеприи́мный** inhospitable.

негр Negro, black man.

негра́мотность illiteracy. **негра́мотный** illiterate.

негритя́нка Negress, black woman. **негритя́нский** Negro.

не-. негро́мкий (-мок, -мка́, -о) quiet. **неда́вний** recent. **не-**

дáвно *adv* recently. **недалёкий** (-ёк, -á, -ёкó) near; short; not bright, dull-witted. **недалёкó** *adv* not far, near. **недáром** *adv* not for nothing, not without reason. **недви́жимость** real estate. **недви́жимый** immovable. **недвусмы́сленный** unequivocal. **недействи́тельный** ineffective; invalid. **недели́мый** indivisible.

недéльный of a week, week's. **недéля** week.

не-. недёшево *adv* dear(ly). **недоброжелáтель** *m* ill-wisher. **недоброжелáтельность** hostility. **недоброкáчественный** of poor quality. **недобросóвестный** unscrupulous; careless. **недóбрый** (-óбр, -брá, -о) unkind; bad. **недовéрие** distrust. **недовéрчивый** distrustful **недовóльный** dissatisfied. **недовóльство** dissatisfaction. **недоедáние** malnutrition. **недоедáть** *impf* be undernourished.

не-. недóлгий (-лог, -лгá, -о) short, brief. **недóлго** *adv* not long. **недолговéчный** short-lived. **недомогáние** indisposition. **недомогáть** *impf* be unwell. **недомы́слие** thoughtlessness. **недонóшенный** premature. **недооцéнивать** *impf*, **недооцени́ть** (-ню́, -нишь) *pf* underestimate; underrate. **недооцéнка** underestimation. **недопусти́мый** inadmissible, intolerable. **недоразумéние** misunderstanding. **недорогóй** (-дóрог, -á, -о) inexpensive. **недосмотрéть** (-рю́,-ришь) *pf* overlook. **недоспáть** (-плю́; -áл, -á, -о) *pf* (*impf* **недосыпáть**) not have enough sleep.

недоставáть (-таёт) *impf*, **недостáть** (-áнет) *pf impers* be missing, be lacking. **недостáток** (-тка) shortage, deficiency. **недостáточный** insufficient, inadequate. **недостáча** lack, shortage.

не-. недостижи́мый unattainable. **недостóйный** unworthy, **недостýпный** inaccessible. **недосчитáться** *pf*, **недосчи́тываться** *impf* miss, find missing, be short (of). **недосыпáть** *impf of* **недоспáть**. **недосягáемый** unattainable.

недоумевáть *impf* be at a loss, be bewildered. **недоумéние** bewilderment.

не-. недоýчка *m* & *f* half-educated person. **недочёт** deficit; defect.

нéдра (недр) *pl* depths, heart, bowels.

не-. нéдруг enemy. **недружелю́бный** unfriendly.

недýг illness, disease.

недурнóй not bad; not bad-looking.

не-. неестéственный unnatural. **неждáнный** unexpected. **нежелáние** unwillingness. **нежелáтельный** undesirable.

нéжели than.

неженáтый unmarried.

нéженка *m* & *f* mollycoddle.

нежилóй uninhabited; uninhabitable.

нéжиться (-жусь) *impf* luxuriate, bask. **нéжность** tenderness; *pl* endearments. **нéжный** tender; affectionate.

не-. незабвéнный unforgettable. **незабýдка** forget-me-not. **незабывáемый** unforgettable. **незави́симость** independence. **незави́симый** independent.

незадо́лго *adv* not long. **незаконнорождённый** illegitimate. **незако́нный** illegal, illicit; illegitimate. **незако́нченный** unfinished. **незамени́мый** irreplaceable. **незамерза́ющий** ice-free; anti-freeze. **незаме́тный** imperceptible. **незаму́жняя** unmarried. **незапа́мятный** immemorial. **незаслу́женный** unmerited. **незауря́дный** uncommon, outstanding.

не́зачем *adv* there is no need.

не-. **незащищённый** unprotected. **незва́ный** uninvited. **нездоро́виться** *impf*, *impers* +*dat*: **мне нездоро́вится** I don't feel well. **нездоро́вый** unhealthy. **нездоро́вье** ill health. **незнако́мец** (-мца), **незнако́мка** stranger. **незнако́мый** unknown, unfamiliar. **незна́ние** ignorance. **незначи́тельный** insignificant. **незре́лый** unripe, immature. **незри́мый** invisible. **незы́блемый** unshakable, firm. **неизбе́жность** inevitability. **неизбе́жный** inevitable. **неизве́данный** unknown.

неизве́стность uncertainty; ignorance; obscurity. **неизве́стный** unknown; *sb* stranger.

не-. **неизлечи́мый** incurable. **неизме́нный** unchanged, unchanging; devoted. **неизменя́емый** unalterable. **неизмери́мый** immeasurable, immense. **неизу́ченный** unstudied; unexplored. **неиму́щий** poor. **неинтере́сный** uninteresting. **неи́скренний** insincere. **неискушённый** inexperienced, unsophisticated. **неисполни́мый** impracticable. **неисправи́мый** incorrigible; irreparable. **неиспра́вный** out of order, defective; careless. **неиссле́дованный** unexplored. **неиссяка́емый** inexhaustible. **неи́стовство** fury, frenzy; atrocity. **неи́стовый** furious, frenzied, uncontrolled. **неистощи́мый, неисчерпа́емый** inexhaustible. **неисчисли́мый** innumerable.

нейло́н, нейло́новый nylon.

нейро́н neuron.

нейтрализа́ция neutralization. **нейтрализова́ть** *impf* & *pf* neutralize. **нейтралите́т** neutrality. **нейтра́льный** neutral. **нейтро́н** neutron.

неквалифици́рованный unskilled.

не́кий *pron* a certain, some.

не́когда[1] *adv* once, formerly.

не́когда[2] *adv* there is no time; **мне ~** I have no time.

не́кого (не́кому, не́кем, не́ о ком) *pron* there is nobody.

некомпете́нтный not competent, unqualified.

не́котор|ый *pron* some; **~ые** *sb pl* some (people).

некраси́вый plain, ugly; not nice.

некроло́г obituary.

некста́ти *adv* at the wrong time, out of place.

не́кто *pron* somebody; a certain.

не́куда *adv* there is nowhere.

не-. **некульту́рный** uncivilized, uncultured. **некуря́щий** *sb* non-smoker. **нела́дный** wrong. **нелега́льный** illegal. **нелёгкий** not easy; heavy. **нele̍пость** absurdity, nonsense. **нele̍пый** absurd. **нело́вкий** awkward. **нело́вкость** awkwardness.

нельзя́ *adv* it is impossible; it is not allowed.

не-. нелюби́мый unloved. **нелюди́мый** unsociable. **нема́ло** *adv* quite a lot (of). **нема́лый** considerable. **неме́дленно** *adv* immediately. **неме́дленный** immediate.

неме́ть (-е́ю) *impf* (*pf* **о~**) become dumb. **не́мец** (-мца) German. **неме́цкий** German.

немину́емый inevitable.

не́мка German woman.

немно́гие *sb pl* (a) few. **немно́го** *adv* a little; some; a few. **немно́жко** *adv* a little.

немо́й (нем, -á, -о) dumb, mute, silent. **немота́** dumbness.

не́мощный feeble.

немы́слимый unthinkable.

ненави́деть (-и́жу) *impf* hate. **ненави́стный** hated; hateful. **не́нависть** hatred.

не-. ненагля́дный beloved. **ненадёжный** unreliable. **ненадо́лго** *adv* for a short time. **нена́стье** bad weather. **ненасы́тный** insatiable. **ненорма́льный** abnormal. **нену́жный** unnecessary, unneeded. **необду́манный** thoughtless, hasty. **необеспе́ченный** without means, unprovided for. **необита́емый** uninhabited. **необозри́мый** boundless, immense. **необосно́ванный** unfounded, groundless. **необрабо́танный** uncultivated; crude; unpolished. **необразо́ванный** uneducated.

необходи́мость necessity. **необходи́мый** necessary.

не-. необъясни́мый inexplicable. **необъя́тный** immense. **необыкнове́нный** unusual. **необыча́йный** extraordinary. **необы́чный** unusual. **необяза́тельный** optional. **неограни́ченный** unlimited. **неоднокра́тный** repeated. **неодобри́тельный** disapproving. **неодушевлённый** inanimate.

неожи́данность unexpectedness. **неожи́данный** unexpected, sudden.

неоклассици́зм neoclassicism.

не-. неоко́нченный unfinished. **неопла́ченный** unpaid. **неопра́вданный** unjustified. **неопределённый** indefinite; infinitive; vague. **неопровержи́мый** irrefutable. **неопублико́ванный** unpublished. **нео́пытный** inexperienced. **неоргани́ческий** inorganic. **неоспори́мый** incontestable. **неосторо́жный** careless. **неосуществи́мый** impracticable. **неотврати́мый** inevitable.

не́откуда *adv* there is nowhere.

не-. неотло́жный urgent. **неотрази́мый** irresistible. **неотсту́пный** persistent. **неотъе́млемый** inalienable. **неофициа́льный** unofficial. **неохо́та** reluctance. **неохо́тно** *adv* reluctantly. **неоцени́мый** inestimable, invaluable. **непарти́йный** non-party; unbefitting a member of the (Communist) Party. **непереводи́мый** untranslatable. **неперехо́дный** intransitive. **неплатёжеспосо́бный** insolvent.

не-. непло́хо *adv* not badly, quite well. **неплохо́й** not bad, quite good. **непобеди́мый** invincible. **неповинове́ние** insubordination. **неповоро́тливый** clumsy. **неповтори́мый** inimitable, unique. **непого́да** bad weather. **непогреши́мый**

infallible. **неподалёку** *adv* not far (away). **неподви́жный** motionless, immovable; fixed. **неподде́льный** genuine; sincere. **неподку́пный** incorruptible. **неподража́емый** inimitable. **неподходя́щий** unsuitable, inappropriate. **непоколеби́мый** unshakable, steadfast. **непоко́рный** recalcitrant, unruly.

не-. непола́дки (-док) *pl* defects. **неполноце́нность; ко́мплекс неполноце́нности** inferiority complex. **неполноце́нный** defective; inadequate. **непо́лный** incomplete; not (a) full. **непоме́рный** excessive. **непонима́ние** incomprehension, lack of understanding. **непоня́тный** incomprehensible. **непоправи́мый** irreparable. **непоря́док** (-дка) disorder. **непоря́дочный** dishonourable. **непосе́да** *m* & *f* fidget. **непоси́льный** beyond one's strength. **непосле́довательный** inconsistent. **непослуша́ние** disobedience. **непослу́шный** disobedient. **непосре́дственный** immediate; spontaneous. **непостижи́мый** incomprehensible. **непостоя́нный** inconstant, changeable. **непохо́жий** unlike; different.

не-. непра́вда untruth. **неправдоподо́бный** improbable. **непра́вильно** *adv* wrong. **непра́вильный** irregular; wrong. **непра́вый** wrong. **непракти́чный** unpractical. **непревзойдённый** unsurpassed. **непредви́денный** unforeseen. **непредубеждённый** unprejudiced. **непредусмо́тренный** unforeseen. **непредусмотри́тельный** short-sighted. **непрекло́нный** inflexible; adamant. **непрело́жный** immutable.

не-. непреме́нно *adv* without fail. **непреме́нный** indispensable. **непреодоли́мый** insuperable. **непререка́емый** unquestionable. **непреры́вно** *adv* continuously. **непреры́вный** continuous. **непреста́нный** incessant. **неприве́тливый** unfriendly; bleak. **непривлека́тельный** unattractive. **непривы́чный** unaccustomed. **неприглядный** unattractive. **непригодный** unfit, useless. **неприе́млемый** unacceptable. **неприкоснове́нность** inviolability, immunity. **неприкоснове́нный** inviolable; reserve. **неприли́чный** indecent. **непримири́мый** irreconcilable. **непринуждённый** unconstrained; relaxed. **неприспосо́бленный** unadapted; maladjusted. **непристо́йный** obscene. **непристу́пный** inaccessible. **непритяза́тельный, неприхотли́вый** unpretentious, simple. **неприя́зненный** hostile, inimical. **неприя́знь** hostility. **неприя́тель** *m* enemy. **неприя́тельский** enemy. **неприя́тность** unpleasantness; trouble. **неприя́тный** unpleasant.

не-. непрове́ренный unverified. **непрогля́дный** pitch-dark. **непрое́зжий** impassable. **непрозра́чный** opaque. **непроизводи́тельный** unproductive. **непроизво́льный** involuntary. **непромока́емый** waterproof. **непроница́емый** impenetrable. **непрости́тельный** unforgivable. **непроходи́мый** impassable. **непро́чный** (-чен, -чна́, -о) fragile, flimsy.

не прочь *predic* not averse.

не-. непро́шеный uninvited, unsolicited. **неработоспосо́бный** disabled. **нерабо́чий:** ~ **день** day off. **нера́венство** inequality. **неравноме́рный** uneven. **нера́вный** unequal. **неради́вый** lackadaisical. **неразбери́ха** muddle. **неразбо́рчивый** not fastidious; illegible. **неразвито́й** (-ра́звит, -á, -о) undeveloped; backward. **неразгово́рчивый** taciturn. **неразделённый:** ~**ая любо́вь** unrequited love. **неразличи́мый** indistinguishable. **неразлу́чный** inseparable. **неразрешённый** unsolved; forbidden. **неразреши́мый** insoluble. **неразры́вный** indissoluble. **неразу́мный** unwise; unreasonable. **нераствори́мый** insoluble.

нерв nerve. **не́рвничать** *impf* fret, be nervous. **нервнобольно́й** *sb* neurotic. **не́рвный** (-вен, -вна́, -о) nervous; nerve; irritable. **нерво́зный** nervy, irritable.

не-. нереа́льный unreal; unrealistic. **нере́дкий** (-док, -дка́, -о) not infrequent, not uncommon. **нереши́тельность** indecision. **нереши́тельный** indecisive, irresolute. **нержаве́ющая сталь** stainless steel. **неро́вный** (-вен, -вна́, -о) uneven, rough; irregular. **неруши́мый** inviolable.

неря́ха *m* & *f* sloven. **неря́шливый** slovenly.

не-. несбы́точный unrealizable. **несваре́ние желу́дка** indigestion. **несве́жий** (-е́ж, -á) not fresh; tainted; weary. **несвоевре́менный** ill-timed; overdue. **несво́йственный** not characteristic. **несгора́емый** fireproof. **несерьёзный** not serious.

несессе́р case.

несимметри́чный asymmetrical.

нескла́дный incoherent; awkward.

несклоня́емый indeclinable.

не́сколько (-их) *pron* some, several; *adv* somewhat.

не-. нескونча́емый interminable. **нескро́мный** (-мен, -мна́, -о) immodest; indiscreet. **несло́жный** simple. **несль́ıханный** unprecedented. **несль́ıшный** inaudible. **несме́тный** countless, incalculable. **несмолка́емый** ceaseless.

несмотря́ на *prep+acc* in spite of.

не-. несно́сный intolerable. **несоблюде́ние** non-observance. **несовершенноле́тний** under-age; *sb* minor. **несоверше́нный** imperfect, incomplete; imperfective. **несоверше́нство** imperfection. **несовмести́мый** incompatible. **несогла́сие** disagreement. **несогласо́ванный** uncoordinated. **несозна́тельный** irresponsible. **несоизмери́мый** incommensurable. **несокруши́мый** indestructible. **несомне́нный** undoubted, unquestionable. **несообра́зный** incongruous. **несоотве́тствие** disparity. **несостоя́тельный** insolvent; of modest means; untenable. **неспе́лый** unripe. **неспоко́йный** restless; uneasy. **неспосо́бный** not bright; incapable. **несправедли́вость** injustice. **несправедли́вый** unjust, unfair; incorrect. **не-**

сравне́нный (-е́нен, -е́нна) incomparable. **несравни́мый** incomparable. **нестерпи́мый** unbearable.

нести́ (-су́, -сёшь; нёс, -ла́) *impf* (*pf* **по~, с~**) carry; bear; bring, take; suffer; incur; lay; **~сь** rush, fly; float, be carried.

не-. несто́йкий unstable. **несуще́ственный** immaterial, inessential.

несу́ *etc.*: *see* **нести́**

несхо́дный unlike, dissimilar.

несчастли́вый unfortunate, unlucky; unhappy. **несча́стный** unhappy, unfortunate; **~ слу́чай** accident. **несча́стье** misfortune; **к несча́стью** unfortunately.

несчётный innumerable.

нет *partl* no, not; nothing. **нет, не́ту** there is not, there are not.

не-. нетакти́чный tactless. **нетвёрдый** (-ёрд, -а́, -о) unsteady, shaky. **нетерпели́вый** impatient. **нетерпе́ние** impatience. **нетерпи́мый** intolerable, intolerant. **нетороплúвый** leisurely. **нето́чный** (-чен, -чна́, -о) inaccurate, inexact. **нетре́звый** drunk. **нетро́нутый** untouched; chaste, virginal. **нетрудово́й дохо́д** unearned income. **нетрудоспосо́бность** disability.

не́тто *indecl adj & adv* net(t).

не́ту *see* **нет**

не-. неубеди́тельный unconvincing. **неуваже́ние** disrespect. **неуве́ренность** uncertainty. **неуве́ренный** uncertain. **неувяда́емый, неувяда́ющий** unfading. **неугомо́нный** indefatigable. **неуда́ча** failure. **неуда́чливый** unlucky. **неуда́чник, -ница** unlucky person, failure. **неуда́чный** unsuccessful, unfortunate. **неудержи́мый** irrepressible. **неудо́бный** uncomfortable; inconvenient; embarrassing. **неудо́бство** discomfort; inconvenience; embarrassment. **неудовлетворе́ние** dissatisfaction. **неудовлетворённый** dissatisfied. **неудовлетвори́тельный** unsatisfactory. **неудово́льствие** displeasure.

неуже́ли? *partl* really?

не-. неузнава́емый unrecognizable. **неукло́нный** steady; undeviating. **неуклю́жий** clumsy. **неулови́мый** elusive; subtle. **неуме́лый** inept; clumsy. **неуме́ренный** immoderate. **неуме́стный** inappropriate; irrelevant. **неумоли́мый** implacable, inexorable. **неумы́шленный** unintentional.

не-. неупла́та non-payment. **неуравнове́шенный** unbalanced. **неурожа́й** bad harvest. **неуро́чный** untimely, inopportune. **неуря́дица** disorder, mess. **неуспева́емость** poor progress. **неусто́йка** forfeit. **неусто́йчивый** unstable; unsteady. **неусту́пчивый** unyielding. **неуте́шный** inconsolable. **неутоли́мый** unquenchable. **неутоми́мый** tireless. **не́уч** ignoramus. **неучти́вый** discourteous. **неуязви́мый** invulnerable.

нефри́т jade.

нефте- *in comb* oil, petroleum. **нефтено́сный** oil-bearing. **~перего́нный заво́д** oil refinery. **~прово́д** (oil) pipeline. **~проду́кты** (-ов) *pl* petroleum products.

нефть oil, petroleum. **нефтяно́й** oil, petroleum.

не-. нехва́тка shortage. **нехорошо́** *adv* badly. **нехоро́ш|ий** (-о́ш, -а́) bad; **~о́** it is bad, it is wrong. **не́хотя** *adv* unwillingly; unintentionally. **нецелесообра́зный** inexpedient; pointless. **нецензу́рный** unprintable. **нечаянный** unexpected; accidental.

не́чего (не́чему, -чем, не́ о чем) *pron* (*with separable pref*) (there is) nothing.

нечелове́ческий inhuman, superhuman.

нече́стный dishonest, unfair.

нечётный odd.

нечистопло́тный dirty; slovenly; unscrupulous. **нечистота́** (*pl* -о́ты, -о́т) dirtiness, filth; *pl* sewage. **нечи́стый** (-и́ст, -а́, -о) dirty, unclean; impure; unclear. **не́чисть** evil spirits; scum.

нечленоразде́льный inarticulate.

не́что *pron* something.

не-. неэконо́мный uneconomical. **неэффекти́вный** ineffective; inefficient. **нея́вка** failure to appear. **нея́ркий** dim, faint; dull, subdued. **нея́сный** (-сен, -сна́, -о) not clear; vague.

ни *partl* not a; **ни оди́н (одна́, одно́)** not a single; (*with prons and pronominal advs*) -ever; **кто... ни** whoever. **ни** *conj*: **ни... ни** neither … nor; **ни то ни сё** neither one thing nor the other.

ни́ва cornfield, field.

ниве́ли́р level.

нигде́ *adv* nowhere.

нидерла́ндец (-дца; *gen pl* -дцев) Dutchman. **нидерла́ндка** Dutchwoman. **нидерла́ндский** Dutch. **Нидерла́нды** (-ов) *pl* the Netherlands.

ни́же *adj* lower, humbler; *adv* below; *prep+gen* below, beneath. **нижесле́дующий** following. **ни́жн|ий** lower, under-; **~ее бельё** underclothes; **~ий эта́ж** ground floor. **низ** (*loc* -у́; *pl* -ы́) bottom; *pl* lower classes; low notes.

низа́ть (нижу́, ни́жешь) *impf* (*pf* **на~**) string, thread.

низверга́ть *impf*, **низве́ргнуть** (-ну; -е́рг) *pf* throw down, overthrow; **~ся** crash down; be overthrown. **низверже́ние** overthrow.

низи́на low-lying place. **ни́зкий** (-зок, -зка́, -о) low; base. **низкопокло́нство** servility. **низкопро́бный** low-grade. **низкоро́слый** undersized. **низкосо́ртный** low-grade.

ни́зменность lowland; baseness. **ни́зменный** low-lying; base.

низо́вье (*gen pl* -ьев) the lower reaches. **ни́зость** baseness, meanness. **ни́зш|ий** lower, lowest; **~ее образова́ние** primary education.

ника́к *adv* in no way. **никако́й** *pron* no; no … whatever

ни́кель *m* nickel.

нике́м *see* **никто́**. **никогда́** *adv* never. **никто́** (-кого́, -кому́, -ке́м, ни о ко́м) *pron* (*with separable pref*) nobody, no one. **никуда́** nowhere. **никчёмный** useless.

нима́ло *adv* not in the least.

нимб halo, nimbus.

ни́мфа nymph; pupa.

ниотку́да *adv* from nowhere.

нипочём *adv* it is nothing; dirt cheap; in no circumstances.

ниско́лько *adv* not at all.

ниспровергáть *impf*, **ниспровéргнуть** (-ну; -éрг) *pf* overthrow. **ниспровержéние** overthrow.

нисходя́щий descending.

ни́тка thread; string; **до ни́тки** to the skin; **на живу́ю ни́тку** hastily, anyhow. **ни́точка** thread. **нить** thread; filament.

ничегó *etc.*: *see* **ничтó**. **ничегó** *adv* all right; it doesn't matter, never mind; *as indecl adj* not bad, pretty good. **ничéй** (-чья́, -чьё) *pron* nobody's; **ничья́ земля́** no man's land. **ничья́** *sb* draw; tie.

ничкóм *adv* face down, prone.

ничтó (-чегó, -чему́, -чéм, ни о чём) *pron* (*with separable pref*) nothing. **ничтóжество** nonentity, nobody. **ничтóжный** insignificant; worthless.

ничу́ть *adv* not a bit.

ничьё, ничья́: *see* **ничéй**

ни́ша niche, recess.

ни́щенка beggar-woman. **ни́щенский** beggarly. **нищетá** poverty. **ни́щий** (нищ, -á, -е) destitute, poor; *sb* beggar.

но *conj* but; still.

новáтор innovator. **новáторский** innovative. **новáторство** innovation.

Нóвая Зелáндия New Zealand.

новéйший newest, latest.

новéлла short story.

нóвенький brand-new.

новизнá novelty; newness. **нови́нка** novelty. **новичóк** (-чкá) novice.

ново- *in comb* new(ly). **новобрáнец** (-нца) new recruit. **~брáчный** *sb* newly-wed. **~введéние** innovation. **~гóдний** new year's. **~зелáндец** (-дца; *gen pl* -дцев), **~зелáндка** New-Zealander. **~зелáндский** New Zealand. **~лу́ние** new moon. **~прибы́вший** newly-arrived; *sb* newcomer. **~рождённый** newborn. **~сёл** new settler. **~сéлье** new home; house-warming. **новострóйка** new building.

нóвость (*gen pl* -éй) news; novelty. **нóвшество** innovation, novelty. **нóвый** (нов, -á, -о) new; modern; **~ год** New Year.

ногá (*acc* нóгу; *pl* нóги, ног, ногáм) foot, leg.

нóготь (-гтя; *gen pl* -тéй) *m* finger-nail, toe-nail.

нож (-á) knife.

нóжка small foot or leg; leg; stem, stalk.

нóжницы (-иц) *pl* scissors, shears.

нóжны (-жен) *pl* sheath, scabbard.

ножóвка saw, hacksaw.

ноздря́ (*pl* -и, -éй) nostril.

нокáут knock-out. **нокаути́ровать** *impf* & *pf* knock out.

нолевóй, нулевóй zero. **ноль** (-я́), **нуль** (-я́) *m* nought, zero, nil.

номенклату́ра nomenclature; top positions in government.

нóмер (*pl* -á) number; size; (hotel-)room; item; trick. **номерóк** (-ркá) tag; label, ticket.

номинáл face value. **номинáльный** nominal.

норá (*pl* -ы) burrow, hole.

Норвéгия Norway. **норвéжец** (-жца), **норвéжка** Norwegian. **норвéжский** Norwegian.

норд (*naut*) north; north wind.

нóрка mink.

нóрма standard, norm; rate.

нормализа́ция standardization. **норма́льно** all right, OK. **норма́льный** normal; standard. **нормирова́ние, нормиро́вка** regulation; rate-fixing; rationing. **нормирова́ть** *impf* & *pf* regulate, standardize; ration.

нос (*loc* -ý; *pl* -ы́) nose; beak; bow, prow. **но́сик** (*small*) nose; spout.

носи́лки (-лок) *pl* stretcher; litter. **носи́льщик** porter. **носи́тель** *m*, **~ница** (*fig*) bearer; (*med*) carrier. **носи́ть** (-ошу́, -о́сишь) *impf* carry, bear; wear; **~ся** rush, tear along, fly; float, be carried; wear. **но́ска** carrying, wearing. **но́ский** hard-wearing.

носово́й nose; nasal; **~ плато́к** (pocket) handkerchief. **носо́к** (-ска́) little nose; toe; sock. **носоро́г** rhinoceros.

но́та note; *pl* music. **нота́ция** notation; lecture, reprimand.

нота́риус notary.

ночева́ть (-чу́ю) *impf* (*pf* **пере~**) spend the night. **ночёвка** spending the night. **ночле́г** place to spend the night; passing the night. **ночле́жка** doss-house. **ночни́к** (-а́) night-light. **ночн|о́й** night, nocturnal; **~а́я руба́шка** nightdress; **~о́й горшо́к** potty; chamber-pot. **ночь** (*loc* -и́; *gen pl* -е́й) night. **но́чью** *adv* at night.

но́ша burden. **но́шеный** worn; second-hand.

но́ю *etc.*: *see* **ныть**

ноя́брь (-я́) *m* November. **ноя́брьский** November.

нрав disposition, temper; *pl* customs, ways. **нра́виться** (-влюсь) *impf* (*pf* **по~**) +*dat* please; **мне нра́вится** I like. **нра́вственность** morality, morals. **нра́вственный** moral.

ну *int* & *partl* well, well then.

ну́дный tedious.

нужда́ (*pl* -ы) need. **нужда́ться** *impf* be in need; +**в**+*prep* need, require. **ну́жн|ый** (-жен, -жна́, -о, ну́жны́) necessary; **~о** it is necessary; +*dat* I, *etc.*, must, ought to, need.

нулево́й, нуль *see* **нолево́й, ноль**

нумера́ция numeration; numbering. **нумерова́ть** *impf* (*pf* **про~**) number.

нутро́ inside, interior; instinct(s).

ны́не *adv* now; today. **ны́нешний** present; today's. **ны́нче** *adv* today; now.

нырну́ть (-ну́, -нёшь) *pf*, **ныря́ть** *impf* dive.

ныть (но́ю) *impf* ache; whine. **нытьё** whining.

н.э. *abbr* (*of* **на́шей э́ры**) AD.

нюх scent; flair. **ню́хать** *impf* (*pf* **по~**) smell, sniff.

ня́нчить (-чу) *impf* nurse, look after; **~ся с**+*instr* nurse; fuss over. **ня́нька** nanny. **ня́ня** (*children's*) nurse, nanny.

О

о, об, обо *prep* **I.** +*prep* of, about, concerning. **II.** +*acc* against; on, upon.

о *int* oh!

оа́зис oasis.

об *see* **о** *prep*.

о́ба (обо́их) *m* & *neut*, **о́бе** (обе́их) *f* both.

обалдева́ть *impf*, **обалде́ть**

(-éю) *pf* go crazy; become dulled; be stunned.
обанкрóтиться (-óчусь) *pf* go bankrupt.
обаяние fascination, charm. **обаятельный** fascinating, charming.
обвáл fall(ing); crumbling; collapse; caving-in; landslide; **(снéжный)** ~ avalanche. **обвалить** (-лю́, -лишь) *pf* (*impf* **обвáливать**) cause to fall *or* collapse; crumble; heap round; **~ся** collapse, cave in; crumble.
обвалять *pf* (*impf* **обвáливать**) roll.
обвáривать *impf*, **обварить** (-рю́, -ришь) *pf* pour boiling water over; scald; **~ся** scald o.s.
обведу́ *etc.*: *see* **обвести́. обвёл** *etc.*: *see* **обвести́. об|венчáть(ся** *pf.*
обернýть (-нý, -нёшь) *pf*, **обвёртывать** *impf* wrap, wrap up.
обвéс short weight. **обвéсить** (-éшу) *pf* (*impf* **обвéшивать**) cheat in weighing.
обвести́ (-едý, -едёшь; -ёл, -елá) *pf* (*impf* **обводи́ть**) lead round, take round; encircle; surround; outline; dodge.
обвéтренный weather-beaten.
обветшáлый decrepit. **об|ветшáть** *pf.*
обвéшивать *impf of* **обвéсить. обвивáть(ся** *impf of* **обви́ть(ся**
обвинéние charge, accusation; prosecution. **обвини́тель** *m* accuser; prosecutor. **обвини́тельный** accusatory; ~ **акт** indictment; ~ **приговóр** verdict of guilty. **обвини́ть** *pf*, **обвинять** *impf* prosecute, indict; **+в+***prep* accuse of, charge with. **обвиняемый** *sb* the accused; defendant.
обви́ть (обовью́, обовьёшь; обви́л, -á, -о) *pf* (*impf* **обвивáть**) wind round; **~ся** wind round.
обводи́ть (-ожý, -óдишь) *impf of* **обвести́**
обворáживать *impf*, **обворожи́ть** (-жý) *pf* charm, enchant. **обворожи́тельный** charming, enchanting.
обвязáть (-яжý, -яжешь) *pf*, **обвязывать** *impf* tie round; **~ся** *+instr* tie round o.s.
обгóн passing. **обгонять** *impf of* **обогнáть**
обгорáть *impf*, **обгорéть** (-рю́) *pf* be burnt, be scorched. **обгорéлый** burnt, charred, scorched.
обдéлать *pf* (*impf* **обдéлывать**) finish; polish, set; manage, arrange.
обдели́ть (-лю́, -лишь) *pf* (*impf* **обделять**) *+instr* do out of one's (fair) share of.
обдéлывать *impf of* **обдéлать. обделять** *impf of* **обдели́ть**
обдерý *etc.*: *see* **ободрáть. обдирáть** *impf of* **ободрáть**
обдýманный deliberate, well-considered. **обдýмать** *pf*, **обдýмывать** *impf* consider, think over.
óбе: *see* **óба. обегáть** *impf of* **обежáть. обегý** *etc.*: *see* **обежáть**
обéд dinner, lunch. **обéдать** *impf* (*pf* **по~**) have dinner, have lunch, dine. **обéденный** dinner.
обеднéвший impoverished. **обеднéние** impoverishment. **о|беднéть** (-éю) *pf.*
обéдня (*gen pl* -ден) Mass.

обежа́ть (-егу́) *pf* (*impf* **обега́ть**) run round; run past.

обезбо́ливание anaesthetization. **обезбо́ливать** *impf*, **обезбо́лить** *pf* anaesthetize.

обезвре́дить (-е́жу) *pf*, **обезвре́живать** *impf* render harmless.

обездо́ленный unfortunate, hapless.

обеззара́живающий disinfectant.

обезли́ченный depersonalized; robbed of individuality.

обезобра́живать *impf*, **о|безобра́зить** (-а́жу) *pf* disfigure.

обезопа́сить (-а́шу) *pf* secure.

обезору́живать *impf*, **обезору́жить** (-жу) *pf* disarm.

обезу́меть (-ею) *pf* lose one's senses, lose one's head.

обезья́на monkey; ape.

обели́ть *pf*, **обеля́ть** *impf* vindicate; clear of blame.

оберега́ть *impf*, **обере́чь** (-егу́, -ежёшь; -рёг, -ла́) *pf* guard; protect.

оберну́ть (-ну́, -нёшь) *pf*, **обёртывать** *impf* (*impf also* **обора́чивать**) twist; wrap up; turn; **~ся** turn (round); turn out; +*instr or* **в**+*acc* turn into. **обёртка** wrapper; (dust-) jacket, cover. **обёрточный** wrapping.

оберу́ *etc.*: *see* **обобра́ть**

обескура́живать *impf*, **обескура́жить** (-жу) *pf* discourage; dishearten.

обескро́вить (-влю) *pf*, **обескро́вливать** *impf* drain of blood, bleed white; render lifeless.

обеспе́чение securing, guaranteeing; ensuring; provision; guarantee; security. **обеспе́ченность** security; +*instr* provision of. **обеспе́ченный** well-to-do; well provided for. **обеспе́чивать** *impf*, **обеспе́чить** (-чу) *pf* provide for; secure; ensure; protect; +*instr* provide with.

о|беспоко́ить(ся *pf*.

обесси́леть (-ею) *pf* grow weak, lose one's strength. **обесси́ливать** *impf*, **обесси́лить** *pf* weaken.

о|бесла́вить (-влю) *pf*.

обессме́ртить (-рчу) *pf* immortalize.

обесцене́ние depreciation. **обесце́нивать** *impf*, **обесце́нить** *pf* depreciate; cheapen; **~ся** depreciate.

о|бесче́стить (-е́щу) *pf*.

обе́т vow, promise. **обетова́нный** promised. **обеща́ние** promise. **обеща́ть** *impf* & *pf* (*pf also* **по~**) promise.

обжа́лование appeal. **обжа́ловать** *pf* appeal against.

обже́чь (обожгу́, обожжёшь; обжёг, обожгла́) *pf*, **обжига́ть** *impf* burn; scorch; bake; **~ся** burn o.s.; burn one's fingers.

обжо́ра *m* & *f* glutton. **обжо́рство** gluttony.

обзавести́сь (-еду́сь, -едёшься; -вёлся, -ла́сь) *pf*, **обзаводи́ться** (-ожу́сь, -о́дишься) *impf* +*instr* provide o.s. with; acquire.

обзову́ *etc.*: *see* **обозва́ть**

обзо́р survey, review.

обзыва́ть *impf of* **обозва́ть**

обива́ть *impf of* **оби́ть**. **оби́вка** upholstering; upholstery.

оби́да offence, insult; nuisance. **оби́деть** (-и́жу) *pf*, **обижа́ть** *impf* offend; hurt, wound; **~ся** take offence; feel hurt. **оби́дный** offensive; annoying. **оби́д-**

чивый touchy. **обиженный** offended.

обилие abundance. **обильный** abundant.

обирать *impf of* **обобрать**

обитаемый inhabited. **обитатель** *m* inhabitant. **обитать** *impf* live.

обить (обобью, -ьёшь) *pf* (*impf* **обивать**) upholster; knock off.

обиход custom, (general) use, practice. **обиходный** everyday.

обкладывать(ся *impf of* **обложить(ся**

обкрадывать *impf of* **обокрасть**

облава raid; cordon, cordoning off.

облагаемый taxable. **облагать(ся** *impf of* **обложить(ся: ~ся налогом** be liable to tax.

обладание possession. **обладатель** *m* possessor. **обладать** *impf* +*instr* possess.

облако (*pl* -á, -óв) cloud.

обламывать(ся *impf of* **обломать(ся, обломиться**

областной regional. **область** (*gen pl* -éй) region; field, sphere.

облачность cloudiness. **облачный** cloudy.

облёг *etc.*: *see* **облечь. облегать** *impf of* **облечь**

облегчать *impf*, **облегчить** (-чý) *pf* lighten; relieve; alleviate; facilitate. **облегчение** relief.

обледенелый ice-covered. **обледенение** icing over. **обледенеть** (-éет) *pf* become covered with ice.

облезлый shabby; mangy.

облекать(ся *impf of* **облечь²(ся. облеку** *etc.*: *see* **облечь²**

облепить (-плю, -пишь) *pf*, **облеплять** *impf* stick to, cling to; throng round; plaster.

облетать *impf*, **облететь** (-лечý) fly (round); spread (all over); fall.

облечь¹ (-ля́жет; -лёг, -лá) *pf* (*impf* **облегать**) cover, envelop; fit tightly.

облечь² (-екý, -ечёшь; -ёк, -клá) *pf* (*impf* **облекать**) clothe, invest; **~ся** clothe o.s.; +*gen* take the form of.

обливать(ся *impf of* **облить(ся**

облигация bond.

облизать (-ижý, -йжешь) *pf*, **облизывать** *impf* lick (all over); **~ся** smack one's lips.

облик look, appearance.

облитый (óблит, -á, -о) covered, enveloped. **облить** (оболью, -льёшь; óблил, -илá, -о) *pf* (*impf* **обливать**) pour, sluice, spill; **~ся** sponge down, take a shower; pour over o.s.

облицевать (-цýю) *pf*, **облицовывать** *impf* face. **облицовка** facing; lining.

обличать *impf*, **обличить** (-чý) *pf* expose; reveal; point to. **обличение** exposure, denunciation. **обличительный** denunciatory.

обложение taxation; assessment. **обложить** (-жý, -жишь) *pf* (*impf* **обкладывать, облагать**) edge; face; cover; surround; assess; **кругом обложило (небо)** the sky is completely overcast; **~ налогом** tax; **~ся** +*instr* surround o.s. with. **обложка** (dust-)cover; folder.

облокачиваться *impf*, **облокотиться** (-очýсь, -óтишься) *pf* **на**+*acc* lean one's elbows on.

облома́ть *pf* (*impf* **обла́мывать**) break off; **~ся** break off. **обломи́ться** (-ло́мится) *pf* (*impf* **обла́мываться**) break off. **обло́мок** (-мка) fragment.

облу́пленный chipped.

облучи́ть (-чу́) *pf*, **облуча́ть** *impf* irradiate. **облуче́ние** irradiation.

об|лысе́ть (-е́ю) *pf.*

обля́жет *etc.*: *see* **обле́чь¹**

обма́зать (-а́жу) *pf*, **обма́зывать** *impf* coat; putty; besmear; **~ся** +*instr* get covered with.

обма́кивать *impf*, **обмакну́ть** (-ну́, -нёшь) *pf* dip.

обма́н deceit; illusion; **~ зре́ния** optical illusion. **обма́нный** deceitful. **обману́ть** (-ну́, -нешь) *pf*, **обма́нывать** *impf* deceive; cheat; **~ся** be deceived. **обма́нчивый** deceptive. **обма́нщик** deceiver; fraud.

обма́тывать(ся *impf of* **обмота́ть(ся**

обма́хивать *impf*, **обмахну́ть** (-ну́, -нёшь) *pf* brush off; fan; **~ся** fan o.s.

обмёл *etc.*: *see* **обмести́**

обмеле́ние shallowing. **об|меле́ть** (-е́ет) *pf* become shallow.

обме́н exchange; barter; **в ~ за**+*acc* in exchange for; **~ веще́ств** metabolism. **обме́нивать** *impf*, **обмени́ть** (-ню́, -нишь) *pf*, **об|меня́ть** *pf* exchange; **~ся** +*instr* exchange. **обме́нный** exchange.

обме́р measurement; false measure.

обмере́ть (обомру́, -рёшь; о́бмер, -ла́, -ло) *pf* (*impf* **обмира́ть**) faint; **~ от у́жаса** be horror-struck.

обме́ривать *impf*, **обме́рить** *pf* measure; cheat in measuring.

обмести́ (-ету́, -етёшь; -мёл, -а́) *pf*, **обмета́ть¹** *impf* sweep off, dust.

обмета́ть² (-ечу́ *or* -а́ю, -е́чешь *or* -а́ешь) *pf* (*impf* **обмётывать**) oversew.

обмету́ *etc.*: *see* **обмести́.**

обмётывать *impf of* **обмета́ть.**

обмира́ть *impf of* **обмере́ть**

обмо́лвиться (-влюсь) *pf* make a slip of the tongue; +*instr* say, utter. **обмо́лвка** slip of the tongue.

обморо́женный frost-bitten.

о́бморок fainting-fit, swoon.

обмота́ть *pf* (*impf* **обма́тывать**) wind round; **~ся** +*instr* wrap o.s. in. **обмо́тка** winding; *pl* puttees.

обмо́ю *etc.*: *see* **обмы́ть**

обмундирова́ние fitting out (with uniform); uniform. **обмундирова́ть** *pf*, **обмундиро́вывать** *impf* fit out (with uniform).

обмыва́ть *impf*, **обмы́ть** (-мо́ю) *pf* bathe, wash; **~ся** wash, bathe.

обмяка́ть *impf*, **обмя́кнуть** (-ну; -мя́к) *pf* become soft *or* flabby.

обнадёживать *impf*, **обнадёжить** (-жу) *pf* reassure.

обнажа́ть *impf*, **обнажи́ть** (-жу́) *pf* bare, uncover; reveal. **обнажённый** (-ён, -ена́) naked, bare; nude.

обнаро́довать *impf* & *pf* promulgate.

обнару́же́ние revealing; discovery; detection. **обнару́живать** *impf*, **обнару́жить** (-жу) *pf* display; reveal; discover; **~ся** come to light.

обнести́ (-су́, -сёшь; -нёс, -ла́) *pf* (*impf* **обноси́ть**) enclose; +*instr* serve round; pass over, leave out.

обнима́ть(ся *impf* *of* **обня́ть(ся. обниму́** *etc.*: *see* **обня́ть**

обнища́ние impoverishment.

обнови́ть (-влю́) *pf*, **обновля́ть** *impf* renovate; renew. **обно́вка** new acquisition; new garment. **обновле́ние** renovation, renewal.

обноси́ть (-ошу́, -о́сишь) *impf of* **обнести́**; **~ся** *pf* have worn out one's clothes.

обня́ть (-ниму́, -ни́мешь; о́бнял, -а́, -о) *pf* (*impf* **обнима́ть**) embrace; clasp; **~ся** embrace; hug one another.

обо *see* **о** *prep.*

обобра́ть (оберу́, -рёшь; обобра́л, -а́, -о) *pf* (*impf* **обира́ть**) rob; pick.

обобща́ть *impf*, **обобщи́ть** (-щу́) *pf* generalize. **обобще́ние** generalization. **обобществи́ть** (-влю́) *pf*, **обобществля́ть** *impf* socialize; collectivize. **обобществле́ние** socialization; collectivization.

обобью́ *etc.*: *see* **оби́ть. обовью́** *etc.*: *see* **обви́ть**

обогати́ть (-ащу́) *pf*, **обогаща́ть** *impf* enrich; **~ся** become rich; enrich o.s. **обогаще́ние** enrichment.

обогна́ть (обгоню́, -о́нишь; обогна́л, -а́, -о) *pf* (*impf* **обгоня́ть**) pass; outstrip.

обогну́ть (-ну́, -нёшь) *pf* (*impf* **огиба́ть**) round, skirt; bend round.

обогрева́тель *m* heater. **обогрева́ть** *impf*, **обогре́ть** (-е́ю) *pf* heat, warm; **~ся** warm up.

о́бод (*pl* -о́дья, -ьев) rim. **ободо́к** (-дка́) thin rim, narrow border.

обо́дранный ragged. **ободра́ть** (обдеру́, -рёшь; -а́л, -а́, -о) *pf* (*impf* **обдира́ть**) skin, flay; peel; fleece.

ободре́ние encouragement, reassurance. **ободри́тельный** encouraging, reassuring. **ободри́ть** *pf*, **ободря́ть** *impf* encourage, reassure; **~ся** cheer up, take heart.

обожа́ть *impf* adore.

обожгу́ *etc.*: *see* **обже́чь**

обожестви́ть (-влю́) *pf*, **обожествля́ть** *impf* deify.

обожжённый (-ён, -ена́) burnt, scorched.

обо́з string of vehicles; transport.

обозва́ть (обзову́, -вёшь; -а́л, -а́, -о) *pf* (*impf* **обзыва́ть**) call; call names.

обозлённый (-ён, -а́) angered; embittered. **обо|зли́ть** *pf*, **о|зли́ть** *pf* anger; embitter; **~ся** get angry.

обozна́ться *pf* mistake s.o. for s.o. else.

обознача́ть *impf*, **обозна́чить** (-чу) *pf* mean; mark; **~ся** appear, reveal o.s. **обозначе́ние** sign, symbol.

обозрева́тель *m* reviewer; columnist. **обозрева́ть** *impf*, **обозре́ть** (-рю́) *pf* survey. **обозре́ние** survey; review; revue. **обозри́мый** visible.

обо́и (-ев) *pl* wallpaper.

обо́йма (*gen pl* **-о́йм**) cartridge clip.

обойти́ (-йду́, -йдёшь; -ошёл, -ошла́) *pf* (*impf* **обходи́ть**) go round; pass; avoid; pass over;

~сь manage, make do; +с+*instr* treat.
обокра́сть (обкраду́, -дёшь) *pf* (*impf* **обкра́дывать**) rob.
оболо́чка casing; membrane; cover, envelope, jacket; shell.
обольсти́тель *m* seducer. **обольсти́тельный** seductive. **обольсти́ть** (-льщу́) *pf*, **обольща́ть** *impf* seduce. **обольще́ние** seduction; delusion.
оболью́ *etc.*: *see* **обли́ть**
обомру́ *etc.*: *see* **обмере́ть**
обоня́ние (sense of) smell. **обоня́тельный** olfactory.
обопру́ *etc.*: *see* **опере́ть**
обора́чивать(ся *impf of* **оберну́ть(ся, обороти́ть(ся**
обо́рванный torn, ragged. **оборва́ть** (-ву́, -вёшь; -а́л, -а́, -о) *pf* (*impf* **обрыва́ть**) tear off; break; snap; cut short; **~ся** break; snap; fall; stop suddenly.
обо́рка frill, flounce.
оборо́на defence. **оборони́тельный** defensive. **оборони́ть** *pf*, **обороня́ть** *impf* defend; **~ся** defend o.s. **оборо́нный** defence, defensive.
оборо́т turn; revolution; circulation; turnover; back; **~ ре́чи** (turn of) phrase; **смотри́ на ~е** P.T.O. **обороти́ть** (-рочу́, -ро́тишь) *pf* (*impf* **обора́чивать**) turn; **~ся** turn (round); +*instr or* **в**+*acc* turn into. **оборо́тный** circulating; reverse; **~ капита́л** working capital.
обору́дование equipping; equipment. **обору́довать** *impf* & *pf* equip.
обоснова́ние basing; basis, ground. **обосно́ванный** well-founded. **обоснова́ть** *pf*, **обосно́вывать** *impf* ground, base; substantiate; **~ся** settle down.
обосо́бленный isolated, solitary.
обостре́ние aggravation. **обострённый** keen; strained; sharp, pointed. **обостри́ть** *pf*, **обостря́ть** *impf* sharpen; strain; aggravate; **~ся** become strained; be aggravated; become acute.
оботру́ *etc.*: *see* **обтере́ть**
обо́чина verge; shoulder, edge.
обошёл *etc.*: *see* **обойти́. обошью́** *etc.*: *see* **обши́ть**
обою́дный mutual, reciprocal.
обраба́тывать *impf*, **обрабо́тать** *pf* till, cultivate; work, work up; treat, process. **обрабо́тка** working (up); processing; cultivation.
об|ра́довать(ся *pf*.
о́браз shape, form; image; manner; way; icon; **гла́вным ~ом** mainly; **таки́м ~ом** thus. **образе́ц** (-зца́) model; pattern; sample. **о́бразный** graphic; figurative. **образова́ние** formation; education. **образо́ванный** educated. **образова́тельный** educational. **образова́ть** *impf* & *pf*, **образо́вывать** *impf* form; **~ся** form; arise; turn out well.
образу́мить (-млю) *pf* bring to reason; **~ся** see reason.
образцо́вый model. **обра́зчик** specimen, sample.
обра́мить (-млю) *pf*, **обрамля́ть** *impf* frame.
обраста́ть *impf*, **обрасти́** (-ту́, -тёшь; -ро́с, -ла́) *pf* be overgrown.
обрати́мый reversible, convertible. **обрати́ть** (-ащу́) *pf*, **обраща́ть** *impf* turn; convert; **~ внима́ние на**+*acc* pay *or* draw attention to; **~ся** turn; appeal;

apply; address; **+в**+*acc* turn into; **+с**+*instr* treat; handle. **обра́тно** *adv* back; backwards; conversely; **~ пропорциона́льный** inversely proportional. **обра́тный** reverse; return; opposite; inverse. **обраще́ние** appeal, address; conversion; (**+с**+*instr*) treatment (of); handling (of); use (of).

обре́з edge; sawn-off gun; **в ~**+*gen* only just enough. **обре́зать** (-е́жу) *pf*, **обреза́ть** *impf* cut (off); clip, trim; pare; prune; circumcise; **~ся** cut o.s. **обре́зок** (-зка) scrap; *pl* ends; clippings.

обрека́ть *impf of* **обре́чь. обреку́** *etc.*: *see* **обре́чь. обрёл** *etc.*: *see* **обрести́**

обремени́тельный onerous. **о|бремени́ть** *pf*, **обременя́ть** *impf* burden.

обрести́ (-ету́, -етёшь; -рёл, -а́) *pf*, **обрета́ть** *impf* find.

обрече́ние doom. **обречённый** doomed. **обре́чь** (-еку́, -ечёшь; -ёк, -ла́) *pf* (*impf* **обрека́ть**) doom.

обрисова́ть *pf*, **обрисо́вывать** *impf* outline, depict; **~ся** appear (in outline).

оброни́ть (-ню́, -нишь) *pf* drop; let drop.

обро́с *etc.*: *see* **обрасти́.**

обруба́ть *impf*, **обруби́ть** (-блю́, -бишь) *pf* chop off; cut off. **обру́бок** (-бка) stump.

об|руга́ть *pf.*

о́бруч (*pl* -и, -е́й) hoop. **обруча́льн|ый** engagement; **~ое кольцо́** betrothal ring, wedding ring. **обруча́ть** *impf*, **обручи́ть** (-чу́) betroth; **~ся +с**+*instr* become engaged to. **обруче́ние** engagement.

обру́шивать *impf*, **об|ру́шить** (-шу) *pf* bring down; **~ся** come down, collapse.

обры́в precipice. **обрыва́ть(ся** *impf of* **оборва́ть(ся. обры́вок** (-вка) scrap; snatch.

обры́згать *pf*, **обры́згивать** *impf* splash; sprinkle.

обрю́зглый flabby.

обря́д rite, ceremony.

обсервато́рия observatory.

обслу́живание service; maintenance. **обслу́живать** *impf*, **обслужи́ть** (-жу́, -жишь) *pf* serve; operate.

обсле́дование inspection. **обсле́дователь** *m* inspector. **обсле́довать** *impf* & *pf* inspect.

обсо́хнуть (-ну; -о́х) *pf* (*impf* **обсыха́ть**) dry (off).

обста́вить (-влю) *pf*, **обставля́ть** *impf* surround; furnish; arrange. **обстано́вка** furniture; situation, conditions; set.

обстоя́тельный thorough, reliable; detailed. **обстоя́тельство** circumstance. **обстоя́ть** (-ои́т) *impf* be; go; **как обстои́т де́ло?** how is it going?

обстре́л firing, fire; **под ~ом** under fire. **обстре́ливать** *impf*, **обстреля́ть** *pf* fire at; bombard.

обступа́ть *impf*, **обступи́ть** (-у́пит) *pf* surround.

обсуди́ть (-ужу́, -у́дишь) *pf*, **обсужда́ть** *impf* discuss. **обсужде́ние** discussion.

обсчита́ть *pf*, **обсчи́тывать** *impf* shortchange; **~ся** miscount, miscalculate.

обсы́пать (-плю) *pf*, **обсыпа́ть** *impf* strew; sprinkle.

обсыха́ть *impf of* **обсо́хнуть. обта́чивать** *impf of* **обточи́ть**

обтека́емый streamlined.

обтере́ть (оботру́, -трёшь; обтёр) *pf* (*impf* **обтира́ть**) wipe; rub; **~ся** dry o.s.; sponge down.

о(б)теса́ть (-ешу́, -е́шешь) *pf*, **о(б)тёсывать** *impf* rough-hew; teach good manners to; trim.

обтира́ние sponge-down. **обтира́ть(ся** *pf of* **обтере́ть(ся**

обточи́ть (-чу́, -чишь) *pf* (*impf* **обта́чивать**) grind; machine.

обтрёпанный frayed; shabby.

обтя́гивать *impf*, **обтяну́ть** (-ну́, -нешь) *pf* cover; fit close. **обтя́жка** cover; skin; **в обтя́жку** close-fitting.

обува́ть(ся *impf of* **обу́ть(ся.**

о́бувь footwear; boots, shoes.

обу́гливать *impf*, **обу́глить** *pf* char; carbonize; **~ся** char, become charred.

обу́за burden.

обузда́ть *pf*, **обу́здывать** *impf* bridle, curb.

обурева́ть *impf* grip; possess.

обусло́вить (-влю) *pf*, **обусло́вливать** *impf* cause; +*instr* make conditional on; **~ся** +*instr* be conditional on; depend on.

обу́тый shod. **обу́ть** (-у́ю) *pf* (*impf* **обува́ть**) put shoes on; **~ся** put on one's shoes.

о́бу́х butt, back.

обуча́ть *impf*, **об|учи́ть** (-чу́, -чишь) *pf* teach; train; **~ся** +*dat or inf* learn. **обуче́ние** teaching; training.

обхва́т girth; **в ~е** in circumference. **обхвати́ть** (-ачу́, -а́тишь) *pf*, **обхва́тывать** *impf* embrace; clasp.

обхо́д round(s); roundabout way; bypass. **обходи́тельный** courteous; pleasant. **обходи́ть(ся** (-ожу́(сь, -о́дишь(ся) *impf of* **обойти́(сь. обхо́дный** roundabout.

обша́ривать *impf*, **обша́рить** *pf* rummage through, ransack.

обшива́ть *impf of* **обши́ть. обши́вка** edging; trimming; boarding, panelling; plating.

обши́рный extensive; vast.

обши́ть (обошью́, -шьёшь) *pf* (*impf* **обшива́ть**) edge; trim; make outfit(s) for; plank.

обшла́г (-а́; *pl* -а́, -о́в) cuff.

обща́ться *impf* associate.

обще- *in comb* common(ly), general(ly). **общедосту́пный** moderate in price; popular. **~жи́тие** hostel. **~изве́стный** generally known. **~наро́дный** national, public. **~образова́тельный** of general education. **~при́нятый** generally accepted. **~сою́зный** *hist* All-Union. **~челове́ческий** common to all mankind; universal.

обще́ние contact; social intercourse. **обще́ственность** (the) public; public opinion; community. **обще́ственный** social, public; voluntary. **о́бщество** society; company.

о́бщ|ий general; common; **в ~ем** on the whole, in general. **общи́на** community; commune.

об|щипа́ть (-плю́, -плешь) *pf.*

общи́тельный sociable. **о́бщность** community.

объеда́ть(ся *impf of* **объе́сть(ся**

объедине́ние unification; merger; union, association. **объединённый** (-ён, -а́) united. **объедини́тельный** unifying. **объедини́ть** *pf*, **объединя́ть** *impf* unite; join; combine; **~ся** unite.

объе́дки (-ов) *pl* leftovers, scraps.

объе́зд riding round; detour.

объе́здить (-зжу, -здишь) *pf* (*impf* **объезжа́ть**) travel over; break in.

объезжа́ть *impf of* **объе́здить, объе́хать**

объе́кт object; objective; establishment, works. **объекти́в** lens. **объекти́вность** objectivity. **объекти́вный** objective.

объём volume; scope. **объёмный** by volume, volumetric.

объе́сть (-е́м, -е́шь, -е́ст, -еди́м) *pf* (*impf* **объеда́ть**) gnaw (round), nibble; **~ся** overeat.

объе́хать (-е́ду) *pf* (*impf* **объезжа́ть**) drive *or* go round; go past; travel over.

объяви́ть (-влю́, -вишь) *pf*, **объявля́ть** *impf* declare, announce; **~ся** turn up; *+instr* declare o.s. **объявле́ние** declaration, announcement; advertisement.

объясне́ние explanation. **объясни́мый** explainable. **объясни́ть** *pf*, **объясня́ть** *impf* explain; **~ся** be explained; make o.s. understood; **+с+***instr* have it out with.

объя́тие embrace.

обыва́тель *m* Philistine. **обыва́тельский** narrow-minded.

обыгра́ть *pf*, **обы́грывать** *impf* beat (*in a game*).

обы́денный ordinary; everyday.

обыкнове́ние habit. **обыкнове́нно** *adv* usually. **обыкнове́нный** usual; ordinary.

о́быск search. **обыска́ть** (-ыщу́, -ы́щешь) *pf*, **обы́скивать** *impf* search.

обы́чай custom; usage. **обы́чно** *adv* usually. **обы́чный** usual.

обя́занность duty; responsibility. **обя́занный** (*+inf*) obliged; *+dat* indebted to (*+instr* for). **обяза́тельно** *adv* without fail. **обяза́тельный** obligatory. **обяза́тельство** obligation; commitment. **обяза́ть** (-яжу́, -я́жешь) *pf*, **обя́зывать** *impf* bind; commit; oblige; **~ся** pledge o.s., undertake.

ова́л oval. **ова́льный** oval.

ова́ция ovation.

овдове́ть (-е́ю) *pf* become a widow, widower.

овёс (овса́) oats.

ове́чка *dim of* **овца́**; harmless person.

овладева́ть *impf*, **овладе́ть** (-е́ю) *pf +instr* seize; capture; master.

о́вод (*pl* -ы *or* -а́) gadfly.

о́вощ (*pl* -и, -е́й) vegetable. **овощно́й** vegetable.

овра́г ravine, gully.

овся́нка oatmeal; porridge. **овся́ный** oat, oatmeal.

овца́ (*pl* -ы, ове́ц, о́вцам) sheep; ewe. **овча́рка** sheep-dog. **овчи́на** sheepskin.

ога́рок (-рка) candle-end.

огиба́ть *impf of* **обогну́ть**

оглавле́ние table of contents.

огласи́ть (-ашу́) *pf*, **оглаша́ть** *impf* announce; fill (with sound); **~ся** resound. **огла́ска** publicity. **оглаше́ние** publication.

огло́бля (*gen pl* -бель) shaft.

о|гло́хнуть (-ну; -о́х) *pf*.

оглуша́ть *impf*, **о|глуши́ть** (-шу́) *pf* deafen; stun. **оглуши́тельный** deafening.

огляде́ть (-яжу́) *pf*, **огля́ды-**

вать *impf*, **огляну́ть** (-ну́, -нешь) *pf* look round; look over; **~ся** look round; look back. **огля́дка** looking back.

огнево́й fire; fiery. **о́гненный** fiery. **огнеопа́сный** inflammable. **огнеприпа́сы** (-ов) *pl* ammunition. **огнесто́йкий** fireproof. **огнестре́льн|ый: ~ое ору́жие** firearm(s). **огнетуши́тель** *m* fire-extinguisher. **огнеупо́рный** fire-resistant.

ого́ *int* oho!

огова́ривать *impf*, **оговори́ть** *pf* slander; stipulate (for); **~ся** make a proviso; make a slip (of the tongue). **огово́р** slander. **огово́рка** reservation, proviso; slip of the tongue.

оголённый bare, nude. **оголи́ть** *pf* (*impf* **оголя́ть**) bare; strip; **~ся** strip o.s.; become exposed.

оголя́ть(ся *impf of* **оголи́ть(ся**

огонёк (-нька́) (*small*) light; zest. **ого́нь** (огня́) *m* fire; light.

огора́живать *impf*, **огороди́ть** (-рожу́, -ро́дишь) *pf* fence in, enclose; **~ся** fence o.s. in. **огоро́д** kitchen-garden. **огоро́дный** kitchen-garden.

огорча́ть *impf*, **огорчи́ть** (-чу́) *pf* grieve, pain; **~ся** grieve, be distressed. **огорче́ние** grief; chagrin.

о|гра́бить (-блю) *pf*. **ограбле́ние** robbery; burglary.

огра́да fence. **огради́ть** (-ажу́) *pf*, **огражда́ть** *impf* guard, protect.

ограниче́ние limitation, restriction. **ограни́ченный** limited. **ограни́чивать** *impf*, **ограни́чить** (-чу) *pf* limit, restrict; **~ся** *+instr* limit *or* confine o.s. to; be limited to.

огро́мный huge; enormous.

о|грубе́ть (-е́ю) *pf*.

огры́зок (-зка) bit, end; stub.

огуре́ц (-рца́) cucumber.

ода́лживать *impf of* **одолжи́ть**

одарённый gifted. **ода́ривать** *impf*, **одари́ть** *pf*, **одаря́ть** *impf* give presents (to); *+instr* endow with.

одева́ть(ся *impf of* **оде́ть(ся**

оде́жда clothes; clothing.

одеколо́н eau-de-Cologne.

одели́ть *pf*, **оделя́ть** *impf* (*+instr*) present (with); endow (with).

оде́ну *etc.*: *see* **оде́ть**. **одёргивать** *impf of* **одёрнуть**

о|деревене́ть (-е́ю) *pf*.

одержа́ть (-жу́, -жишь) *pf*, **одерживать** *impf* gain. **одержи́мый** possessed.

одёрнуть (-ну) *pf* (*impf* **одёргивать**) pull down, straighten.

оде́тый dressed; clothed. **оде́ть** (-е́ну) *pf* (*impf* **одева́ть**) dress; clothe; **~ся** dress (o.s.). **одея́ло** blanket. **одея́ние** garb, attire.

оди́н (одного́), **одна́** (одно́й), **одно́** (одного́); *pl* **одни́** (одни́х) one; a, an; a certain; alone; only; nothing but; same; **одно́ и то же** the same thing; **оди́н на оди́н** in private; **оди́н раз** once; **одни́м сло́вом** in a word; **по одному́** one by one.

одина́ковый identical, the same, equal.

оди́ннадцатый eleventh. **оди́ннадцать** eleven.

одино́кий solitary; lonely; single. **одино́чество** solitude; loneliness. **одино́чка** *m* & *f* (one) person alone. **одино́чн|ый** individual; one-man; single; **~ое заключе́ние** solitary confinement.

одичáлый wild.
однáжды *adv* once; one day; once upon a time.
однáко *conj* however.
одно- *in comb* single, one; uni-, mono-, homo-. **однобóкий** one-sided. **~врéмéнно** *adv* simultaneously, at the same time. **~врéмéнный** simultaneous. **~зву́чный** monotonous. **~знáчащий** synonymous. **~знáчный** synonymous; one-digit. **~имённый** of the same name. **~клáссник** classmate. **~клéточный** unicellular. **~крáтный** single. **~лéтний** one-year; annual. **~мéстный** single-seater. **~обрáзие, ~образность** monotony. **~обрáзный** monotonous. **~рóдность** homogeneity, uniformity. **~рóдный** homogeneous; similar. **~сторóнний** one-sided; unilateral; one-way. **~фами́лец** (-льца) person of the same surname. **~цвéтный** one-colour; monochrome. **~этáжный** one-storeyed.
одобрéние approval. **одобри́тельный** approving. **одóбрить** *pf*, **одобря́ть** *impf* approve (of).
одолевáть *impf*, **одолéть** (-éю) *pf* overcome.
одолжáть *impf*, **одолжи́ть** (-жу́) *pf* lend; **+у**+*gen* borrow from. **одолжéние** favour.
о|дряхлéть (-éю) *pf*.
одувáнчик dandelion.
оду́маться *pf*, **оду́мываться** *impf* change one's mind.
одурéлый stupid. **о|дурéть** (-éю) *pf*.
одурмáнивать *impf*, **о|дурмáнить** *pf* stupefy. **одуря́ть** *impf* stupefy.
одухотворённый inspired; spiritual. **одухотвори́ть** *pf*, **одухотворя́ть** *impf* inspire.
одушеви́ть (-влю́) *pf*, **одушевля́ть** *impf* animate. **одушевлéние** animation.
оды́шка shortness of breath.
ожерéлье necklace.
ожесточáть *impf*, **ожесточи́ть** (-чу́) *pf* embitter, harden. **ожесточéние** bitterness. **ожесточённый** bitter; hard.
оживáть *impf of* **ожи́ть**
оживи́ть (-влю́) *pf*, **оживля́ть** *impf* revive; enliven; **~ся** become animated. **оживлéние** animation; reviving; enlivening. **оживлённый** animated, lively.
ожидáние expectation; waiting. **ожидáть** *impf +gen or acc* wait for; expect.
ожирéние obesity. **о|жирéть** (-éю) *pf*.
ожи́ть (-иву́, -ивёшь; óжил, -á, -о) *pf* (*impf* **оживáть**) come to life, revive.
ожóг burn, scald.
озабóченность preoccupation; anxiety. **озабóченный** preoccupied; anxious.
озаглáвить (-лю) *pf*, **озаглáвливать** *impf* entitle; head.
озадáчивать *impf*, **озадáчить** (-чу) *pf* perplex, puzzle.
озари́ть *pf*, **озаря́ть** *impf* light up, illuminate; **~ся** light up.
оздорови́тельный бег jogging. **оздоровлéние** sanitation.
озелени́ть *pf*, **озеленя́ть** *impf* plant (*with trees etc.*).
óзеро (*pl* озёра) lake.
ози́мые *sb* winter crops. **ози́мый** winter. **óзимь** winter crop.

озира́ться *impf* look round; look back.

о|зли́ть(ся: *see* **обозли́ть(ся**

озло́бить (-блю) *pf*, **озлобля́ть** *impf* embitter; **~ся** grow bitter. **озлобле́ние** bitterness, animosity. **озло́бленный** embittered.

о|знако́мить (-млю) *pf*, **ознакомля́ть** *impf* **с+***instr* acquaint with; **~ся с+***instr* familiarize o.s. with.

ознаменова́ть *pf*, **ознамено́вывать** *impf* mark; celebrate.

означа́ть *impf* mean, signify.

озно́б shivering, chill.

озо́н ozone.

озорни́к (-á) mischief-maker. **озорно́й** naughty, mischievous. **озорство́** mischief.

озя́бнуть (-ну; озя́б) *pf* be cold, be freezing.

ой *int* oh.

оказа́ть (-ажу́, -а́жешь) *pf* (*impf* **ока́зывать**) render, provide, show; **~ся** turn out, prove; find o.s., be found.

ока́зия unexpected event, funny thing.

ока́зывать(ся *impf of* **оказа́ть(ся**

окамене́лость fossil. **окамене́лый** fossilized; petrified. **о|камене́ть** (-е́ю) *pf*.

оканто́вка mount.

ока́нчивать(ся *impf of* **око́нчить(ся. ока́пывать(ся** *impf of* **окопа́ть(ся**

окая́нный damned, cursed.

океа́н ocean. **океа́нский** ocean; oceanic.

оки́дывать *impf*, **оки́нуть** (-ну) *pf*; **~ взгля́дом** take in at a glance, glance over.

о́кисел (-сла) oxide. **окисле́ние** oxidation. **о́кись** oxide.

оккупа́нт invader. **оккупа́ция** occupation. **оккупи́ровать** *impf* & *pf* occupy.

окла́д salary scale; (basic) pay.

оклевета́ть (-ещу́, -е́щешь) *pf* slander.

окле́ивать *impf*, **окле́ить** *pf* cover; paste over; **~ обо́ями** paper.

окно́ (*pl* о́кна) window.

о́ко (*pl* о́чи, оче́й) eye.

око́вы (око́в) *pl* fetters.

околдова́ть *pf*, **околдо́вывать** *impf* bewitch.

о́коло *adv* & *prep+gen* by; close (to), near; around; about.

око́льный roundabout.

око́нный window.

оконча́ние end; conclusion, termination; ending. **оконча́тельный** final. **око́нчить** (-чу) *pf* (*impf* **ока́нчивать**) finish, end; **~ся** finish, end.

око́п trench. **окопа́ть** *pf* (*impf* **ока́пывать**) dig round; **~ся** entrench o.s., dig in. **око́пный** trench.

о́корок (*pl* -á, -о́в) ham, gammon.

окочене́лый stiff with cold. **о|кочене́ть** (-е́ю) *pf*.

око́шечко, око́шко (*small*) window.

окра́ина outskirts, outlying districts.

о|кра́сить (-а́шу) *pf*, **окра́шивать** *impf* paint, colour; dye. **окра́ска** painting; colouring; dyeing; colouration.

о|кре́пнуть (-ну) *pf*. **о|крести́ть(ся** (-ещу́(сь, -е́стишь(ся) *pf*.

окре́стность environs. **окре́стный** neighbouring.

о́крик hail; shout. **окри́кивать** *impf*, **окри́кнуть** (-ну) *pf* hail, call, shout to.

окрова́вленный blood-stained.

о́круг (*pl* ~а́) district. **окру́га** neighbourhood. **округли́ть** *pf*, **округля́ть** *impf* round; round off. **окру́глый** rounded. **окружа́ть** *impf*, **окружи́ть** (-жу́) *pf* surround; encircle. **окружа́ющ|ий** surrounding; ~**ее** *sb* environment; ~**ие** *sb pl* associates. **окруже́ние** encirclement; environment. **окружно́й** district. **окру́жность** circumference.

окрыли́ть *pf*, **окрыля́ть** *impf* inspire, encourage.

окта́ва octave.

окта́н octane.

октя́брь (-я́) *m* October. **октя́брьский** October.

окули́ст oculist.

окуна́ть *impf*, **окуну́ть** (-ну́, -нёшь) *pf* dip; ~**ся** dip; plunge; become absorbed.

о́кунь (*pl* -и, -е́й) *m* perch.

окупа́ть *impf*, **окупи́ть** (-плю́, -пишь) *pf* compensate, repay; ~**ся** be repaid, pay for itself.

оку́рок (-рка) cigarette-end.

оку́тать *pf*, **оку́тывать** *impf* wrap up; shroud, cloak.

оку́чивать *impf*, **оку́чить** (-чу) *pf* earth up.

ола́дья (*gen pl* -ий) fritter; drop-scone.

оледене́лый frozen. **о|ледене́ть** (-е́ю) *pf*.

оле́ний deer, deer's; reindeer. **оле́нина** venison. **оле́нь** *m* deer; reindeer.

оли́ва olive. **оли́вковый** olive; olive-coloured.

олига́рхия oligarchy.

олимпиа́да olympiad; Olympics. **олимпи́йск|ий** Olympic; Olympian; ~**ие игры** Olympic games.

оли́фа drying oil (*e.g. linseed oil*).

олицетворе́ние personification; embodiment. **олицетвори́ть** *pf*, **олицетворя́ть** *impf* personify, embody.

о́лово tin. **оловя́нный** tin.

ом ohm.

ома́р lobster.

омерзе́ние loathing. **омерзи́тельный** loathsome.

омертве́лый stiff, numb; necrotic. **о|мертве́ть** (-е́ю) *pf*.

омле́т omelette.

омоложе́ние rejuvenation.

омо́ним homonym.

омо́ю *etc.*: *see* **омы́ть**

омрача́ть *impf*, **омрачи́ть** (-чу́) *pf* darken, cloud.

о́мут whirlpool; maelstrom.

омыва́ть *impf*, **омы́ть** (омо́ю) *pf* wash; ~**ся** be washed.

он (его́, ему́, им, о нём) *pron* he. **она́** (её, ей, ей (е́ю), о ней) *pron* she.

онда́тра musk-rat.

онеме́лый numb. **о|неме́ть** (-е́ю) *pf*.

они́ (их, им, и́ми, о них) *pron* they. **оно́** (его́, ему́, им, о нём) *pron* it; this, that.

опада́ть *impf of* **опа́сть**.

опа́здывать *impf of* **опозда́ть**

опа́ла disgrace.

о|пали́ть *pf*.

опа́ловый opal.

опа́лубка casing.

опаса́ться *impf* +*gen* fear; avoid, keep off. **опасе́ние** fear; apprehension.

опа́сность danger; peril. **опа́сный** dangerous.

опа́сть (-адёт) *pf* (*impf* **опада́ть**) fall, fall off; subside.

опе́ка guardianship; trusteeship. **опека́емый** *sb* ward. **опека́ть** *impf* be guardian of; take care of. **опеку́н** (-а́), **-у́нша** guardian; tutor; trustee.

о́пера opera.

операти́вный efficient; operative, surgical; operation(s), operational. **опера́тор** operator; cameraman. **операцио́нн|ый** operating; **~ая** *sb* operating theatre. **опера́ция** operation.

опереди́ть (-режу́) *pf*, **опережа́ть** *impf* outstrip, leave behind.

опере́ние plumage.

опере́тта, -е́тка operetta.

опере́ть (обопру́, -прёшь; опёр, -ла́) *pf* (*impf* **опира́ть**) +**о**+*acc* lean against; **~ся на** *or* **о**+*acc* lean on, lean against.

опери́ровать *impf* & *pf* operate on; operate, act; +*instr* use.

о́перный opera; operatic.

о|печа́лить(ся *pf*.

опеча́тать *pf* (*impf* **опеча́тывать**) seal up.

опеча́тка misprint.

опеча́тывать *impf of* **опеча́тать**

опе́шить (-шу) *pf* be taken aback.

опи́лки (-лок) *pl* sawdust; filings.

опира́ть(ся *impf of* **опере́ть(ся**

описа́ние description. **описа́тельный** descriptive. **описа́ть** (-ишу́, -и́шешь) *pf*, **опи́сывать** *impf* describe; **~ся** make a slip of the pen. **опи́ска** slip of the pen. **о́пись** inventory.

о́пиум opium.

опла́кать (-а́чу) *pf*, **опла́кивать** *impf* mourn for; bewail.

опла́та payment. **оплати́ть** (-ачу́, -а́тишь) *pf*, **опла́чивать** *impf* pay (for).

опла́чу *etc.*: *see* **опла́кать.**

оплачу́ *etc.*: *see* **оплати́ть**

оплеу́ха slap in the face.

оплодотвори́ть *pf*, **оплодотворя́ть** *impf* impregnate; fertilize.

о|пломбирова́ть *pf*.

опло́т stronghold, bulwark.

опло́шность blunder, mistake.

оповести́ть (-ещу́) *pf*, **оповеща́ть** *impf* notify. **оповеще́ние** notification.

опозда́вший *sb* late-comer. **опозда́ние** lateness; delay. **опозда́ть** *pf* (*impf* **опа́здывать**) be late; +**на**+*acc* miss.

опознава́тельный distinguishing; **~ знак** landmark. **опознава́ть** (-наю́, -наёшь) *impf*, **опозна́ть** *pf* identify. **опозна́ние** identification.

о|позо́рить(ся *pf*.

ополза́ть *impf*, **оползти́** (-зёт; -о́лз, -ла́) *pf* slip, slide. **о́ползень** (-зня) *m* landslide.

ополче́ние militia.

опо́мниться *pf* come to one's senses.

опо́р: **во весь ~** at full speed.

опо́ра support; pier; **то́чка опо́ры** fulcrum, foothold.

опора́жнивать *impf of* **опорожни́ть**

опо́рный support, supporting, supported; bearing.

опоро́жни́ть *pf*, **опорожня́ть** *impf* (*impf also* **опора́жнивать**) empty.

о|поро́чить (-чу) *pf*.

опохмели́ться *pf*, **опохмеля́ться** *impf* take a hair of the

dog that bit you.
опóшлить *pf*, **опошля́ть** *impf* vulgarize, debase.
опоя́сать (-я́шу) *pf*, **опоя́сывать** *impf* gird; girdle.
оппозицио́нный opposition. **оппози́ция** opposition.
оппортуни́зм opportunism.
опрáва setting, mounting; spectacle frames.
оправдáние justification; excuse; acquittal. **оправдáтельный приговóр** verdict of not guilty. **оправдáть** *pf*, **оправдывать** *impf* justify; excuse; acquit; ~**ся** justify o.s.; be justified.
опрáвить (-влю) *pf*, **оправля́ть** *impf* set right, adjust; mount; ~**ся** put one's dress in order; recover; +**от**+*gen* get over.
опрáшивать *impf of* **опроси́ть**
определéние definition; determination; decision. **определённый** definite; certain. **определи́мый** definable. **определи́ть** *pf*, **определя́ть** *impf* define; determine; appoint; ~**ся** be formed; be determined; find one's position.
опровергáть *impf*, **опровéргнуть** (-ну; -вéрг) *pf* refute, disprove. **опровержéние** refutation; denial.
опроки́дывать *impf*, **опроки́нуть** (-ну) *pf* overturn; topple; ~**ся** overturn; capsize.
опромéтчивый rash, hasty.
опрóс (cross-)examination; (opinion) poll. **опроси́ть** (-ошу́, -óсишь) *pf* (*impf* **опрáшивать**) question; (cross-)examine. **опрóсный лист** questionnaire.
опры́скать *pf*, **опры́скивать** *impf* sprinkle; spray.
опря́тный neat, tidy.
óптик optician. **óптика** optics. **опти́ческий** optic, optical.
оптимáльный optimal. **оптими́зм** optimism. **оптими́ст** optimist. **оптимисти́ческий** optimistic.
оптóвый wholesale. **óптом** *adv* wholesale.
опубликовáние publication; promulgation. **о|публиковáть** *pf*, **опубликóвывать** *impf* publish; promulgate.
опускáть(ся *impf of* **опусти́ть(ся**
опустéлый deserted. **о|пустéть** (-éет) *pf*.
опусти́ть (-ущу́, -ýстишь) *pf* (*impf* **опускáть**) lower; let down; turn down; omit; post; ~**ся** lower o.s.; sink; fall; go down; go to pieces.
опустошáть *impf*, **опустоши́ть** (-шу́) *pf* devastate. **опустошéние** devastation. **опустоши́тельный** devastating.
опýтать *pf*, **опýтывать** *impf* entangle; ensnare.
опухáть *impf*, **о|пýхнуть** (-ну; опýх) *pf* swell, swell up. **óпухоль** swelling; tumour.
опýшка edge of a forest; trimming.
опущу́ *etc.*: *see* **опусти́ть**
опылéние pollination. **опыли́ть** *pf*, **опыля́ть** *impf* pollinate.
óпыт experience; experiment. **óпытный** experienced; experimental.
опьянéние intoxication. **о|пьянéть** (-éю) *pf*, **о|пьяни́ть** *pf*, **опьяня́ть** *impf* intoxicate, make drunk.
опя́ть *adv* again.
орáва crowd, horde.
орáкул oracle.

орангута́нг orangutan.
ора́нжевый orange. **оранжере́я** greenhouse, conservatory.
ора́тор orator. **орато́рия** oratorio.
ора́ть (ору́, орёшь) *impf* yell.
орби́та orbit; (eye-)socket.
о́рган[1] organ; body. **орга́н**[2] (*mus*) organ. **организа́тор** organizer. **организацио́нный** organization(al). **организа́ция** organization. **органи́зм** organism. **организо́ванный** organized. **организова́ть** *impf* & *pf* (*pf also* с~) organize; ~ся be organized; organize. **органи́ческий** organic.
о́ргия orgy.
орда́ (*pl* -ы) horde.
о́рден (*pl* -а́) order.
о́рдер (*pl* -а́) order; warrant; writ.
ордина́та ordinate.
ордина́тор house-surgeon.
орёл (орла́) eagle; ~ **или ре́шка?** heads or tails?
орео́л halo.
оре́х nut, nuts; walnut. **оре́ховый** nut; walnut. **оре́шник** hazel; hazel-thicket.
оригина́л original; eccentric. **оригина́льный** original.
ориента́ция orientation. **ориенти́р** landmark; reference point. **ориенти́роваться** *impf* & *pf* orient o.s.; +на+*acc* head for; aim at. **ориентиро́вка** orientation. **ориентиро́вочный** reference; tentative; approximate.
орке́стр orchestra.
орли́ный eagle; aquiline.
орна́мент ornament; ornamental design.
о|робе́ть (-е́ю) *pf.*
ороси́тельный irrigation. **ороси́ть** (-ошу́) *pf*, **ороша́ть** *impf* irrigate. **ороше́ние** irrigation; **поля́ ороше́ния** sewage farm.
ору́ *etc.*: *see* **ора́ть**
ору́дие instrument; tool; gun. **оруди́йный** gun. **ору́довать** *impf* +*instr* handle; run. **оруже́йный** arms; gun. **ору́жие** arm, arms; weapons.
орфографи́ческий orthographic(al). **орфогра́фия** orthography, spelling.
оса́ (*pl* -ы) wasp.
оса́да siege. **осади́ть**[1] (-ажу́) *pf* (*impf* **осажда́ть**) besiege.
осади́ть[2] (-ажу́, -а́дишь) *pf* (*impf* **оса́живать**) check; force back; rein in; take down a peg.
оса́дный siege.
оса́док (-дка) sediment; fall-out; after-taste; *pl* precipitation, fall-out. **оса́дочный** sedimentary.
осажда́ть *impf of* **осади́ть**[1]
оса́живать *impf of* **осади́ть**[2]. **осажу́** *see* **осади́ть**[1,2]
оса́нка carriage, bearing.
осва́ивать(ся *impf of* **осво́ить(ся**
осведоми́тельный informative; information. **осве́домить** (-млю) *pf*, **осведомля́ть** *impf* inform; ~ся о+*prep* inquire about, ask after. **осведомле́ние** notification. **осведомлённый** well-informed, knowledgeable.
освежа́ть *impf*, **освежи́ть** (-жу́) *pf* refresh; air. **освежи́тельный** refreshing.
освети́тельный illuminating. **освети́ть** (-ещу́) *pf*, **освеща́ть** *pf* light up; illuminate; throw light on; ~ся light up. **освеще́-**

ние lighting, illumination. **освещённый** (-ён, -á) lit.

о|свидетельствовать *pf.*

освистáть (-ищý, -йщешь) *pf*, **освистывать** *impf* hiss (off); boo.

освободитель *m* liberator. **освободительный** liberation, emancipation. **освободить** (-ожý) *pf*, **освобождáть** *impf* liberate; emancipate; dismiss; vacate; empty; **~ся** free o.s.; become free. **освобождéние** liberation; release; emancipation; vacation. **освобождённый** (-ён, -á) freed, free; exempt.

освоéние mastery; opening up. **освóить** *pf* (*impf* **осваивать**) master; become familiar with; **~ся** familiarize o.s.

освящённый (-ён, -енá) consecrated; sanctified; **~ векáми** time-honoured.

оседáть *impf of* **осéсть**

о|седлáть *pf*, **осёдлывать** *impf* saddle.

осéдлый settled.

осекáться *impf of* **осéчься**

осёл (-слá) donkey; ass.

оселóк (-лкá) touchstone; whetstone.

осенить *pf* (*impf* **осенять**) overshadow; dawn upon.

осéнний autumn(al). **óсень** autumn. **óсенью** *adv* in autumn.

осенять *impf of* **осенить**

осéсть (осяду; осéл) *pf* (*impf* **оседáть**) settle; subside.

осётр (-á) sturgeon. **осетрина** sturgeon.

осéчка misfire. **осéчься** (-екýсь, -ечёшься; -ёкся, -еклáсь) *pf* (*impf* **осекáться**) stop short.

осиливать *impf*, **осилить** *pf* overpower; master.

осина aspen.

о|сипнуть (-ну; осип) get hoarse.

осиротéлый orphaned. **осиротéть** (-éю) *pf* be orphaned.

оскáливать *impf*, **о|скáлить** *pf*; **~ зýбы, ~ся** bare one's teeth.

о|скандáлить(ся *pf.*

осквернить *pf*, **осквернять** *impf* profane; defile.

оскóлок (-лка) splinter; fragment.

оскóмина bitter taste (in the mouth); **набить оскóмину** set the teeth on edge.

оскорбительный insulting, abusive. **оскорбить** (-блю) *pf*, **оскорблять** *impf* insult; offend; **~ся** take offence. **оскорблéние** insult. **оскорблённый** (-ён, -á) insulted.

ослабевáть *impf*, **о|слабéть** (-éю) *pf* weaken; slacken. **ослáбить** (-блю) *pf*, **ослаблять** *impf* weaken; slacken. **ослаблéние** weakening; slackening, relaxation.

ослепительный blinding, dazzling. **ослепить** (-плю) *pf*, **ослеплять** *impf* blind, dazzle. **ослеплéние** blinding, dazzling; blindness. **о|слéпнуть** (-ну; -éп) *pf.*

ослиный donkey; asinine. **ослица** she-ass.

осложнéние complication. **осложнить** *pf*, **осложнять** *impf* complicate; **~ся** become complicated.

ослышаться (-шусь) *pf* mishear.

осмáтривать(ся *impf of* **осмотрéть(ся**. **осмéивать** *impf of* **осмеять**

о|смелéть (-éю) *pf*. **осмéли-**

ваться *impf*, **осмелиться** *pf* dare; venture.
осмеять (-ею, -еёшь) *pf* (*impf* **осмеивать**) ridicule.
осмотр examination, inspection. **осмотреть** (-рю, -ришь) *pf* (*impf* **осматривать**) examine, inspect; look round; **~ся** look round. **осмотрительный** circumspect.
осмысленный sensible, intelligent. **осмысливать** *impf*, **осмыслить** *pf*, **осмыслять** *impf* interpret; comprehend.
оснастить (-ащу) *pf*, **оснащать** *impf* fit out, equip. **оснастка** rigging. **оснащение** fitting out; equipment.
основа base, basis, foundation; *pl* fundamentals; stem (*of a word*). **основание** founding, foundation; base; basis; reason; **на каком основании?** on what grounds? **основатель** *m* founder. **основательный** well-founded; solid; thorough. **основать** (-ную, -нуёшь) *pf*, **основывать** *impf* found; base; **~ся** settle; be founded, be based. **основной** fundamental, basic; main; **в основном** in the main, on the whole. **основоположник** founder.
особа person. **особенно** *adv* especially. **особенность** peculiarity; **в особенности** in particular. **особенный** special, particular, peculiar. **особняк** (-а) private residence; detached house. **особняком** *adv* by o.s. **особо** *adv* apart; especially. **особый** special; particular.
осознавать (-наю, -наёшь) *impf*, **осознать** *pf* realize.
осока sedge.
оспа smallpox; pock-marks.
оспаривать *impf*, **оспорить** *pf* dispute; contest.
о|срамить(ся (-млю(сь) *pf*. **оставаться** (-таюсь, -таёшься) *impf of* **остаться**
ост (*naut*) east; east wind.
оставить (-влю) *pf*, **оставлять** *impf* leave; abandon; reserve.
остальн|ой the rest of; **~ое** *sb* the rest; **~ые** *sb pl* the others.
останавливать(ся *impf of* **остановить(ся**
останки (-ов) *pl* remains.
остановить (-влю, -вишь) *pf* (*impf* **останавливать**) stop; restrain; **~ся** stop, halt; stay; **+на**+*prep* dwell on; settle on. **остановка** stop.
остаток (-тка) remainder; rest; residue; *pl* remains; leftovers. **остаться** (-анусь) *pf* (*impf* **оставаться**) remain; stay; *impers* it remains, it is necessary; **нам не остаётся ничего другого, как** we have no choice but.
остеклить *pf*, **остеклять** *impf* glaze.
остервенеть *pf* become enraged.
остерегать *impf*, **остеречь** (-регу, -режёшь; -рёг, -ла) *pf* warn; **~ся** (+*gen*) beware (of).
остов frame, framework; skeleton.
о|столбенеть (-ею) *pf*.
осторожно *adv* carefully; **~!** look out! **осторожность** care, caution. **осторожный** careful, cautious.
остригать(ся *impf of* **остричь(ся**
остриё point; spike; (cutting) edge. **острить**[1] *impf* sharpen. **острить**[2] *impf* (*pf* **с~**) be witty.
о|стричь (-игу, -ижёшь; -иг) *pf*

(*impf also* **остригáть**) cut, clip; **~ся** have one's hair cut.

óстров (*pl* -á) island. **островóк** (-вкá) islet; **~ безопáсности** (traffic) island.

острóта[1] witticism, joke. **остротá**[2] sharpness; keenness; pungency.

остроу́мие wit. **остроу́мный** witty.

óстрый (остр, -á, -о) sharp; pointed; acute; keen. **остря́к** (-á) wit.

о|студи́ть (-ужу́, -у́дишь) *pf*, **остужáть** *impf* cool.

оступáться *impf*, **оступи́ться** (-плю́сь, -пишься) *pf* stumble.

остывáть *impf*, **осты́ть** (-ы́ну) *pf* get cold; cool down.

осуди́ть (-ужу́, -у́дишь) *pf*, **осуждáть** *impf* condemn; convict. **осуждéние** condemnation; conviction. **осуждённый** (-ён, -á) condemned, convicted; *sb* convict.

осу́нуться (-нусь) *pf* grow thin, become drawn.

осушáть *impf*, **осуши́ть** (-шу́, -шишь) *pf* drain; dry. **осушéние** drainage.

осуществи́мый feasible. **осуществи́ть** (-влю́) *pf*, **осуществля́ть** *impf* realize, bring about; accomplish; **~ся** be fulfilled, come true. **осуществлéние** realization; accomplishment.

осчастли́вить (-влю) *pf*, **осчастли́вливать** *impf* make happy.

осы́пать (-плю) *pf*, **осыпáть** *impf* strew; shower; **~ся** crumble; fall. **óсыпь** scree.

ось (*gen pl* -éй) axis; axle.

осьминóг octopus.

ося́ду *etc.*: *see* **осéсть**

осязáемый tangible. **осязáние** touch. **осязáтельный** tactile; tangible. **осязáть** *impf* feel.

от, ото *prep+gen* from; of; against.

отáпливать *impf of* **отопи́ть**

отáра flock (*of sheep*).

отбáвить (-влю) *pf*, **отбавля́ть** *impf* pour off; **хоть отбавля́й** more than enough.

отбегáть *impf*, **отбежáть** (-егу́) *pf* run off.

отберу́ *etc.*: *see* **отобрáть**

отбивáть(ся *impf of* **отби́ть(ся**

отбивнáя котлéта cutlet, chop.

отбирáть *impf of* **отобрáть**

отби́ть (отобью́, -ёшь) *pf* (*impf* **отбивáть**) beat (off), repel; win over; break off; **~ся** break off; drop behind; **+от+***gen* defend o.s. against.

óтблеск reflection.

отбóй repelling; retreat; ringing off; **бить ~** beat a retreat; **дать ~** ring off.

отбóйный молотóк (-ткá) pneumatic drill.

отбóр selection. **отбóрный** choice, select(ed).

отбрáсывать *impf*, **отбрóсить** (-óшу) *pf* throw off *or* away; hurl back; reject; **~ тень** cast a shadow. **отбрóсы** (-ов) *pl* garbage.

отбывáть *impf*, **отбы́ть** (-бу́ду; óтбыл, -á, -о) *pf* depart; serve (*a sentence*).

отвáга courage, bravery.

отвáживаться *impf*, **отвáжиться** (-жусь) *pf* dare. **отвáжный** courageous.

отвáл dump, slag-heap; casting off; **до ~а** to satiety. **отвáливать** *impf*, **отвали́ть** (-лю́,

-лишь) *pf* push aside; cast off; fork out.
отва́р broth; decoction. **отва́ривать** *impf*, **отвари́ть** (-рю́, -ришь) *pf* boil. **отварно́й** boiled.
отве́дать *pf* (*impf* **отве́дывать**) taste, try.
отведу́ *etc.*: *see* **отвести́**
отве́дывать *impf of* **отве́дать**
отвезти́ (-зу́, -зёшь; -вёз, -ла́) *pf* (*impf* **отвози́ть**) take *or* cart away.
отвёл *etc.*: *see* **отвести́**
отверга́ть *impf*, **отве́ргнуть** (-ну; -ве́рг) *pf* reject; repudiate.
отве́рженный outcast.
отверну́ть (-ну́, -нёшь) *pf* (*impf* **отвёртывать**, **отвора́чивать**) turn aside; turn down; turn on; unscrew; screw off; **~ся** turn away; come unscrewed.
отве́рстие opening; hole.
отверте́ть (-рчу́, -ртишь) *pf* (*impf* **отвёртывать**) unscrew; twist off; **~ся** come unscrewed; get off. **отвёртка** screwdriver.
отвёртывать(ся *impf of* **отверну́ть(ся**, **отверте́ть(ся**
отве́с plumb; vertical slope. **отве́сить** (-е́шу) *pf* (*impf* **отве́шивать**) weigh out. **отве́сный** perpendicular, sheer.
отвести́ (-еду́, -едёшь; -вёл, -а́) *pf* (*impf* **отводи́ть**) lead, take; draw *or* take aside; deflect; draw off; reject; allot.
отве́т answer.
ответви́ться *pf*, **ответвля́ться** *impf* branch off. **ответвле́ние** branch, offshoot.
отве́тить (-е́чу) *pf*, **отвеча́ть** *impf* answer; +**на**+*acc* reply to; +**за**+*acc* answer for. **отве́тный** in reply, return. **отве́тственность** responsibility. **отве́тственный** responsible. **отве́тчик** defendant.
отве́шивать *impf of* **отве́сить**.
отве́шу *etc.*: *see* **отве́сить**
отвинти́ть (-нчу́) *pf*, **отви́нчивать** *impf* unscrew.
отвиса́ть *impf*, **отви́снуть** (-нет; -и́с) *pf* hang down, sag. **отви́слый** hanging, baggy.
отвлека́ть *impf*, **отвле́чь** (-еку́, -ечёшь; -влёк, -ла́) *pf* distract, divert; **~ся** be distracted. **отвлечённый** abstract.
отво́д taking aside; diversion; leading, taking; rejection; allotment. **отводи́ть** (-ожу́, -о́дишь) *impf of* **отвести́**.
отвоева́ть (-ою́ю) *pf*, **отвоёвывать** *impf* win back; spend in fighting.
отвози́ть (-ожу́, -о́зишь) *impf of* **отвезти́**. **отвора́чивать(ся** *impf of* **отверну́ть(ся**
отвори́ть (-рю́, -ришь) *pf* (*impf* **отворя́ть**) open; **~ся** open.
отворя́ть(ся *impf of* **отвори́ть(ся**. **отвою́ю** *etc.*: *see* **отвоева́ть**
отврати́тельный disgusting. **отвраще́ние** disgust, repugnance.
отвыка́ть *impf*, **отвы́кнуть** (-ну; -вы́к) *pf* +**от** *or inf* lose the habit of; grow out of.
отвяза́ть (-яжу́, -я́жешь) *pf*, **отвя́зывать** *impf* untie, unfasten; **~ся** come untied, come loose; +**от**+*gen* get rid of; leave alone.
отгада́ть *pf*, **отга́дывать** *impf* guess. **отга́дка** answer.
отгиба́ть(ся *impf of* **отогну́ть(ся**
отгла́дить (-а́жу) *pf*, **отгла́живать** *impf* iron (out).
отгова́ривать *impf*, **отговори́ть** *pf* dissuade; **~ся** +*instr*

plead. **отгово́рка** excuse, pretext.
отголо́сок (-ска) echo.
отгоня́ть *impf of* **отогна́ть**
отгора́живать *impf*, **отгороди́ть** (-ожу́, -о́дишь) *pf* fence off; partition off; **~ся** shut o.s. off.
отдава́ть[1]**(ся** (-даю́(сь) *impf of* **отда́ть(ся**. **отдава́ть**[2] (-аёт) *impf impers+instr* taste of; smell of; smack of; **от него́ отдаёт во́дкой** he reeks of vodka.
отдале́ние removal; distance. **отдалённый** remote. **отдали́ть** *pf*, **отдаля́ть** *impf* remove; estrange; postpone; **~ся** move away; digress.
отда́ть (-а́м, -а́шь, -а́ст, -ади́м; о́тдал, -а́, -о) *pf* (*impf* **отдава́ть**[1]) give back, return; give; give up; give away; recoil; cast off; **~ся** give o.s. (up); resound. **отда́ча** return; payment; casting off; efficiency; output; recoil.
отде́л department; section.
отде́лать *pf* (*impf* **отде́лывать**) finish, put the finishing touches to; trim; **~ся +от**+*gen* get rid of; +*instr* get off with.
отделе́ние separation; department; compartment; section. **отдели́ть** (-елю́, -е́лишь) *pf* (*impf* **отделя́ть**) separate; detach; **~ся** separate; detach o.s.; get detached.
отде́лка finishing; finish, decoration. **отде́лывать(ся** *impf of* **отде́лать(ся**
отде́льно separately; apart. **отде́льный** separate. **отделя́ть(ся** *impf of* **отдели́ть(ся**
отдёргивать *impf*, **отдёрнуть** (-ну) *pf* draw *or* pull aside *or* back.
отдеру́ *etc.*: *see* **отодра́ть. отдира́ть** *impf of* **отодра́ть**
отдохну́ть (-ну́, -нёшь) *pf* (*impf* **отдыха́ть**) rest.
отду́шина air-hole, vent.
о́тдых rest. **отдыха́ть** *impf* (*pf* **отдохну́ть**) rest; be on holiday.
отдыша́ться (-шу́сь, -шишься) *pf* recover one's breath.
отека́ть *impf of* **оте́чь.**
о|тели́ться (-е́лится) *pf.*
оте́ль *m* hotel.
отеса́ть *etc.*: *see* **обтеса́ть**
оте́ц (отца́) father. **оте́ческий** fatherly, paternal. **оте́чественный** home, native. **оте́чество** native land, fatherland.
оте́чь (-еку́, -ечёшь; отёк, -ла́) *pf* (*impf* **отека́ть**) swell (up).
отжива́ть *impf*, **отжи́ть** (-иву́, -ивёшь; о́тжил, -а́, -о) *pf* become obsolete *or* outmoded. **отжи́вший** obsolete; outmoded.
о́тзвук echo.
о́тзыв[1] opinion; reference; review; response. **отзы́в**[2] recall. **отзыва́ть(ся** *impf of* **отозва́ть(ся. отзы́вчивый** responsive.
отка́з refusal; repudiation; failure; natural. **отказа́ть** (-ажу́, -а́жешь) *pf*, **отка́зывать** *impf* break down; (+*dat* **в**+*prep*) refuse, deny (*s.o. sth*); **~ся** (**+от**+*gen or* +*inf*) refuse; turn down; renounce, give up.
отка́лывать(ся *impf of* **отколо́ть(ся. отка́пывать** *impf of* **откопа́ть. отка́рмливать** *impf of* **откорми́ть**
откати́ть (-ачу́, -а́тишь) *pf*, **отка́тывать** *impf* roll away; **~ся** roll away *or* back; be forced back.
откача́ть *pf*, **отка́чивать** *impf* pump out; give artificial respiration to.
отка́шливаться *impf*, **отка́шляться** *pf* clear one's throat.

откидно́й folding, collapsible. **отки́дывать** *impf*, **отки́нуть** (-ну) *pf* fold back; throw aside.

откла́дывать *impf of* **отложи́ть**

откле́ивать *impf*, **откле́ить** (-е́ю) *pf* unstick; **~ся** come unstuck.

о́тклик response; comment; echo. **отклика́ться** *impf*, **откли́кнуться** (-нусь) *pf* answer, respond.

отклоне́ние deviation; declining, refusal; deflection. **отклони́ть** (-ню́, -нишь) *pf*, **отклоня́ть** *impf* deflect; decline; **~ся** deviate; diverge.

отключа́ть *impf*, **отключи́ть** (-чу́) *pf* cut off, disconnect.

отколоти́ть (-очу́, -о́тишь) *pf* knock off; beat up.

отколо́ть (-лю́, -лешь) *pf* (*impf* **отка́лывать**) break off; chop off; unpin; **~ся** break off; come unpinned; break away.

откопа́ть *pf* (*impf* **отка́пывать**) dig up; exhume.

откорми́ть (-млю́, -мишь) *pf* (*impf* **отка́рмливать**) fatten.

отко́с slope.

открепи́ть (-плю́) *pf*, **открепля́ть** *impf* unfasten; **~ся** become unfastened.

открове́ние revelation. **открове́нный** frank; outspoken; unconcealed. **откро́ю** *etc.*: *see* **откры́ть**

открути́ть (-учу́, -у́тишь) *pf*, **откру́чивать** *impf* untwist, unscrew.

открыва́ть *impf*, **откры́ть** (-ро́ю) *pf* open; reveal; discover; turn on; **~ся** open; come to light, be revealed. **откры́тие** discovery; revelation; opening. **откры́тка** postcard, card. **откры́то** openly. **откры́тый** open.

отку́да *adv* from where; from which; how; **~ ни возьми́сь** from out of nowhere. **отку́да-либо, -нибудь** from somewhere or other. **отку́да-то** from somewhere.

отку́поривать *impf*, **отку́порить** *pf* uncork.

откуси́ть (-ушу́, -у́сишь) *pf*, **отку́сывать** *impf* bite off.

отлага́тельство delay. **отлага́ть** *impf of* **отложи́ть**

от|лакирова́ть *pf*. **отла́мывать** *impf of* **отлома́ть, отломи́ть**

отлепи́ть (-плю́, -пишь) *pf* unstick, take off; **~ся** come unstuck, come off.

отлёт flying away; departure. **отлета́ть** *impf*, **отлете́ть** (-лечу́) *pf*, fly, fly away, fly off; rebound.

отли́в ebb, ebb-tide; tint; play of colours. **отлива́ть** *impf*, **отли́ть** (отолью́; о́тли́л, -а́, -о) *pf* pour off; pump out; cast, found; (*no pf*) *+instr* be shot with. **отли́вка** casting; moulding.

отлича́ть *impf*, **отличи́ть** (-чу́) *pf* distinguish; **~ся** distinguish o.s.; differ; *+instr* be notable for. **отли́чие** difference; distinction; **знак отли́чия** order, decoration; **с отли́чием** with honours. **отли́чник** outstanding student, worker, etc. **отличи́тельный** distinctive; distinguishing. **отли́чный** different; excellent.

отло́гий sloping.

отложе́ние sediment; deposit. **отложи́ть** (-ожу́, -о́жишь) *pf* (*impf* **откла́дывать, отлага́ть**) put aside; postpone; deposit.

отлома́ть, отломи́ть (-млю́,

-мишь) *pf* (*impf* **отла́мывать**) break off.

от|лупи́ть *pf.*

отлуча́ть *impf*, **отлучи́ть** (-чу́) *pf* **(от це́ркви)** excommunicate; **~ся** absent o.s. **отлу́чка** absence.

отлы́нивать *impf* **+от**+*gen* shirk.

отма́хиваться *impf*, **отмахну́ться** (-ну́сь, -нёшься) *pf* **от**+*gen* brush off; brush aside.

отмежева́ться (-жу́юсь) *pf*, **отмежёвываться** *impf* **от**+*gen* dissociate o.s. from.

о́тмель (sand-)bank.

отме́на abolition; cancellation. **отмени́ть** (-ню́, -нишь) *pf*, **отменя́ть** *impf* repeal; abolish; cancel.

отмере́ть (отомрёт; о́тмер, -ла́, -ло) *pf* (*impf* **отмира́ть**) die off; die out.

отме́ривать *impf*, **отме́рить** *pf*, **отмеря́ть** *impf* measure off.

отмести́ (-ету́, -етёшь; -ёл, -á) *pf* (*impf* **отмета́ть**) sweep aside.

отмета́ть *impf of* **отмести́**

отме́тить (-е́чу) *pf*, **отмеча́ть** *impf* mark, note; celebrate; **~ся** sign one's name; sign out. **отме́тка** note; mark.

отмира́ть *impf of* **отмере́ть**

отмора́живать *impf*, **отморо́зить** (-о́жу) *pf* injure by frost-bite. **отморо́жение** frost-bite. **отморо́женный** frost-bitten.

отмо́ю *etc.*: *see* **отмы́ть**

отмыва́ть *impf*, **отмы́ть** (-мо́ю) *pf* wash clean; wash off; **~ся** wash o.s. clean; come out.

отмыка́ть *impf of* **отомкну́ть**

отмы́чка master key.

отнести́ (-су́, -сёшь; -нёс, -ла́) *pf* (*impf* **относи́ть**) take; carry away; ascribe, attribute; **~сь к**+*dat* treat; regard; apply to; concern, have to do with.

отнима́ть(ся *impf of* **отня́ть(ся**

относи́тельно *adv* relatively; *prep*+*gen* concerning. **относи́тельность** relativity. **относи́тельный** relative. **относи́ть(ся** (-ошу́(сь, -о́сишь(ся) *impf of* **отнести́(сь. отноше́ние** attitude; relation; respect; ratio; **в отноше́нии**+*gen*, **по отноше́нию к**+*dat* with regard to; **в прямо́м (обра́тном) отноше́нии** in direct (inverse) ratio.

отны́не *adv* henceforth.

отню́дь not at all.

отня́тие taking away; amputation. **отня́ть** (-ниму́, -ни́мешь; о́тнял, -á, -о) *pf* (*impf* **отнима́ть**) take (away); amputate; **~ от груди́** wean; **~ся** be paralysed.

ото: *see* **от**

отобража́ть *impf*, **отобрази́ть** (-ажу́) *pf* reflect; represent. **отображе́ние** reflection; representation.

отобра́ть (отберу́, -рёшь; отобра́л, -á, -о) *pf* (*impf* **отбира́ть**) take (away); select.

отобью́ *etc.*: *see* **отби́ть**

отовсю́ду *adv* from everywhere.

отогна́ть (отгоню́, -о́нишь; отогна́л, -á, -о) *pf* (*impf* **отгоня́ть**) drive away, off.

отогну́ть (-ну́, -нёшь) *pf* (*impf* **отгиба́ть**) bend back; **~ся** bend.

отогрева́ть *impf*, **отогре́ть** (-е́ю) *pf* warm.

отодвига́ть *impf*, **отодви́нуть** (-ну) *pf* move aside; put off.

отодра́ть (отдеру́, -рёшь; отодра́л, -á, -о) *pf* (*impf* **отдира́ть**) tear off, rip off.

отож(д)ествить (-влю) *pf*, **отож(д)ествлять** *impf* identify.
отозвать (отзову, -вёшь; отозвал, -а, -о)*pf* (*impf* **отзывать**) take aside; recall; **~ся на**+*acc* answer; **на**+*acc or prep* tell on; have an affect on.
отойти (-йду, -йдёшь; отошёл, -шла) *pf* (*impf* **отходить**) move away; depart; withdraw; digress; come out; recover.
отолью *etc.*: *see* **отлить. отомрёт** *etc.*: *see* **отмереть.**
ото|мстить (-мщу) *pf.*
отомкнуть (-ну, -нёшь) *pf* (*impf* **отмыкать**) unlock, unbolt.
отопительный heating. **отопить** (-плю, -пишь) *pf* (*impf* **отапливать**) heat. **отопление** heating.
отопру *etc.*: *see* **отпереть. отопью** *etc.*: *see* **отпить**
оторванный cut off, isolated. **оторвать** (-ву, -вёшь) *pf* (*impf* **отрывать**) tear off; tear away; **~ся** come off, be torn off; be cut off, lose touch; break away; tear o.s. away; **~ся от земли** take off.
оторопеть (-ею) *pf* be struck dumb.
отослать (-ошлю, -ошлёшь) *pf* (*impf* **отсылать**) send (off); send back; +**к**+*dat* refer to.
отоспаться (-сплюсь; -ался, -алась, -ось) *pf* (*impf* **отсыпаться**) catch up on one's sleep.
отошёл *etc.*: *see* **отойти. отошлю** *etc.*: *see* **отослать**
отпадать *impf of* **отпасть.**
от|парировать *pf.* **отпарывать** *impf of* **отпороть**
отпасть (-адёт) *pf* (*impf* **отпадать**) fall off; fall away; pass.
отпевание funeral service.
отпереть (отопру, -прёшь; отпер, -ла, -ло) *pf* (*impf* **отпирать**) unlock; **~ся** open; **+от**+*gen* deny; disown.
от|печатать *pf*, **отпечатывать** *impf* print (off); type (out); imprint. **отпечаток** (-тка) imprint, print.
отпивать *impf of* **отпить**
отпиливать *impf*, **отпилить** (-лю, -лишь) *pf* saw off.
от|пирательство denial. **отпирать(ся** *impf of* **отпереть(ся**
отпить (отопью, -пьёшь; отпил, -а, -о) *pf* (*impf* **отпивать**) take a sip of.
отпихивать *impf*, **отпихнуть** (-ну, -нёшь) *pf* push off; shove aside.
отплатить (-ачу, -атишь) *pf*, **отплачивать** *impf* +*dat* pay back.
отплывать *impf*, **отплыть** (-ыву, -ывёшь; -ыл, -а, -о) *pf* (set) sail; swim off. **отплытие** sailing, departure.
отповедь rebuke.
отползать *impf*, **отползти** (-зу, -зёшь; -олз, -ла) *pf* crawl away.
от|полировать *pf.* **от|полоскать** (-ощу) *pf.*
отпор repulse; rebuff.
отпороть (-рю, -решь) *pf* (*impf* **отпарывать**) rip off.
отправитель *m* sender. **отправить** (-влю) *pf*, **отправлять** *impf* send, dispatch; **~ся** set off, start. **отправка** dispatch. **отправление** sending; departure; performance. **отправн|ой: ~ой пункт, ~ая точка** starting-point.
от|праздновать *pf.*
отпрашиваться *impf*, **отпроситься** (-ошусь, -осишься) *pf* ask for leave, get leave.
отпрыгивать *impf*, **отпрыг-**

нуть (-ну) *pf* jump *or* spring back *or* aside.

о́тпрыск offshoot, scion.

отпряга́ть *impf of* **отпря́чь**

отпря́нуть (-ну) *pf* recoil, start back.

отпря́чь (-ягу́, -яжёшь; -я́г, -ла́) *pf* (*impf* **отпряга́ть**) unharness.

отпу́гивать *impf*, **отпугну́ть** (-ну́, -нёшь) *pf* frighten off.

о́тпуск (*pl* -а́) leave, holiday(s). **отпуска́ть** *impf*, **отпусти́ть** (-ущу́, -у́стишь) *pf* let go, let off; set free; release; slacken; (let) grow; allot; remit. **отпускни́к** (-а́) person on leave. **отпускно́й** holiday; leave. **отпуще́ние** remission; **козёл отпуще́ния** scapegoat.

отраба́тывать *impf*, **отрабо́тать** *pf* work off; master. **отрабо́танный** worked out; waste, spent, exhaust.

отра́ва poison. **отрави́ть** (-влю́, -вишь) *pf*, **отравля́ть** *impf* poison.

отра́да joy, delight. **отра́дный** gratifying, pleasing.

отража́тель *m* reflector; scanner. **отража́ть** *impf*, **отрази́ть** (-ажу́) *pf* reflect; repulse; **~ся** be reflected; **+на**+*prep* affect. **отраже́ние** reflection; repulse.

о́трасль branch.

отраста́ть *impf*, **отрасти́** (-тёт; отро́с, -ла́) *pf* grow. **отрасти́ть** (-ащу́) *pf*, **отра́щивать** *impf* (let) grow.

от|реаги́ровать *pf*. **от|регули́ровать** *pf*. **от|редакти́ровать** *pf*.

отре́з cut; length. **отре́зать** (-е́жу) *pf*, **отреза́ть** *impf* cut off; snap.

о|трезве́ть (-е́ю) *pf*. **отрезви́ть** (-влю́, -ви́шь) *pf*, **отрезвля́ть** *impf* sober; **~ся** sober up.

отре́зок (-зка) piece; section; segment.

отрека́ться *impf of* **отре́чься**

от|рекомендова́ть(ся *pf*.

отрёкся *etc.*: *see* **отре́чься**.

от|ремонти́ровать *pf*. **от|репети́ровать** *pf*.

отре́пье, отре́пья (-ьев) *pl* rags.

от|реставри́ровать *pf*.

отрече́ние renunciation; **~ от престо́ла** abdication. **отре́чься** (-еку́сь, -ечёшься) *pf* (*impf* **отрека́ться**) renounce.

отреша́ться *impf*, **отреши́ться** (-шу́сь) *pf* renounce; get rid of.

отрица́ние denial; negation. **отрица́тельный** negative. **отрица́ть** *impf* deny.

отро́с *etc.*: *see* **отрасти́**. **отро́сток** (-тка) shoot, sprout; appendix.

о́трочество adolescence.

отруба́ть *impf of* **отруби́ть**

о́труби (-ей) *pl* bran.

отруби́ть (-блю́, -бишь) *pf* (*impf* **отруба́ть**) chop off; snap back.

от|руга́ть *pf*.

отры́в tearing off; alienation, isolation; **в ~е от**+*gen* out of touch with; **~ (от земли́)** takeoff. **отрыва́ть(ся** *impf of* **оторва́ть(ся**. **отры́вистый** staccato; disjointed. **отрывно́й** tear-off. **отры́вок** (-вка) fragment, excerpt. **отры́вочный** fragmentary, scrappy.

отры́жка belch; throw-back.

от|ры́ть (-ро́ю) *pf*.

отря́д detachment; order.

отря́хивать *impf*, **отряхну́ть** (-ну́, -нёшь) *pf* shake down *or* off.

от|салютова́ть *pf*.

отса́сывание suction. **отса́-**

сывать *impf of* **отсосáть**

отсвéчивать *impf* be reflected; *+instr* shine with.

отсéв sifting, selection; dropping out. **отсевáть(ся, отсéивать(ся** *impf of* **отсéять(ся**

отсéк compartment. **отсекáть** *impf*, **отсéчь** (-екý, -ечёшь; -сёк, -лá) *pf* chop off.

отсéять (-éю) *pf* (*impf* **отсевáть, отсéивать**) sift, screen; eliminate; **~ся** drop out.

отсидéть (-ижý) *pf*, **отси́живать** *impf* make numb by sitting; sit through; serve out.

отскáкивать *impf*, **отскочи́ть** (-чý, -чишь) *pf* jump aside *or* away; rebound; come off.

отслýживать *impf*, **отслужи́ть** (-жý, -жишь) *pf* serve one's time; be worn out.

отсосáть (-осý, -осёшь) *pf* (*impf* **отсáсывать**) suck off, draw off.

отсóхнуть (-нý) *pf* (*impf* **отсыхáть**) wither.

отсрóчивать *impf*, **отсрóчить** *pf* postpone, defer. **отсрóчка** postponement, deferment.

отставáние lag; lagging behind. **отставáть** (-тaю, -аёшь) *impf of* **отстáть**

отстáвить (-влю) *pf*, **отставля́ть** *impf* set *or* put aside. **отстáвка** resignation; retirement; **в отстáвке** retired; **вы́йти в отстáвку** resign, retire. **отставнóй** retired.

отстáивать(ся *impf of* **отстоя́ть(ся**

отстáлость backwardness. **отстáлый** backward. **отстáть** (-áну) *pf* (*impf* **отставáть**) fall behind; lag behind; become detached; lose touch; break (off); be slow. **отстаю́щий** *sb* backward pupil.

от|стегáть *pf.*

отстёгивать *impf*, **отстегнýть** (-нý, -нёшь) *pf* unfasten, undo; **~ся** come unfastened *or* undone.

отстоя́ть[1] (-ою́) *pf* (*impf* **отстáивать**) defend; stand up for. **отстоя́ть**[2] (-ои́т) *impf* **на**+*acc* be ... distant (**от**+*gen* from). **отстоя́ться** *pf* (*impf* **отстáиваться**) settle; become stabilized.

отстрáивать(ся *impf of* **отстрóить(ся**

отстранéние pushing aside; dismissal. **отстрани́ть** *pf*, **отстраня́ть** *impf* push aside; remove; suspend; **~ся** move away; keep aloof; **~ся от** dodge.

отстрéливаться *impf*, **отстреля́ться** *pf* fire back.

отстригáть *impf*, **отстри́чь** (-игý, -ижёшь; -ри́г) *pf* cut off.

отстрóить *pf* (*impf* **отстрáивать**) finish building; build up.

отступáть *impf*, **отступи́ть** (-плю́, -пишь) *pf* step back; recede; retreat; back down; **~ от**+*gen* give up; deviate from; **~ся от**+*gen* give up; go back on. **отступлéние** retreat; deviation; digression. **отступн|óй: ~ы́е дéньги, ~óе** *sb* indemnity, compensation. **отступя́** *adv* (farther) off, away (**от**+*gen* from).

отсýтствие absence; lack. **отсýтствовать** *impf* be absent. **отсýтствующий** absent; *sb* absentee.

отсчитáть *pf*, **отсчи́тывать** *impf* count off.

отсылáть *impf of* **отослáть**

отсы́пать (-плю) *pf*, **отсыпáть** *impf* pour out; measure off.

отсыпáться *impf of* **отоспáться**
отсырéлый damp. **от|сырéть** (-éет) *pf.*
отсыхáть *impf of* **отсóхнуть**
отсю́да *adv* from here; hence.
оттáивать *impf of* **оттáять**
оттáлкивать *impf of* **оттолкнýть. оттáлкивающий** repulsive, repellent.
оттáчивать *impf of* **отточи́ть**
оттáять (-áю) *pf* (*impf* **оттáивать**) thaw out.
оттéнок (-нка) shade, nuance; tint.
óттепель thaw.
оттесни́ть *pf*, **оттесня́ть** *impf* drive back; push aside.
óттиск impression; off-print, reprint.
оттогó *adv* that is why; ~, **что** because.
оттолкнýть (-нý, -нёшь) *pf* (*impf* **оттáлкивать**) push away; antagonize; **~ся** push off.
оттопы́ренный protruding. **оттопы́ривать** *impf*, **оттопы́рить** *pf* stick out; **~ся** protrude; bulge.
отточи́ть (-чý, -чишь) *pf* (*impf* **оттáчивать**) sharpen.
оттýда *adv* from there.
оття́гивать *impf*, **оттянýть** (-нý, -нешь) *pf* draw out; draw off; delay. **оття́жка** delay.
отупéние stupefaction. **о|т-упéть** (-éю) *pf* sink into torpor.
от|утю́жить (-жу) *pf.*
отучáть *impf*, **отучи́ть** (-чý, -чишь) *pf* break (of); **~ся** break o.s. (of).
отхáркать *pf*, **отхáркивать** *impf* expectorate.
отхвати́ть (-чý, -тишь) *pf*, **отхвáтывать** *impf* snip *or* chop off.
отхлебнýть (-нý, -нёшь) *pf*, **отхлёбывать** *impf* sip, take a sip of.
отхлы́нуть (-нет) *pf* flood *or* rush back.
отхóд departure; withdrawal. **отходи́ть** (-ожý, -óдишь) *impf of* **отойти́. отхóды** (-ов) *pl* waste.
отцвести́ (-етý, -етёшь; -ёл, -á) *pf*, **отцветáть** *impf* finish blossoming, fade.
отцепи́ть (-плю́, -пишь) *pf*, **отцепля́ть** *impf* unhook; uncouple.
отцóвский father's; paternal.
отчáиваться *impf of* **отчáяться**
отчáливать *impf*, **отчáлить** *pf* cast off.
отчáсти *adv* partly.
отчáяние despair. **отчáянный** desperate. **отчáяться** (-áюсь) *pf* (*impf* **отчáиваться**) despair.
отчегó *adv* why. **отчегó-либо, -нибудь** *adv* for some reason or other. **отчегó-то** *adv* for some reason.
от|чекáнить *pf.*
óтчество patronymic.
отчёт account; **отдáть себé ~ в**+*prep* be aware of, realize. **отчётливый** distinct; clear. **отчётность** book-keeping; accounts. **отчётный** *adj*: **~ год** financial year, current year; **~ доклáд** report.
отчи́зна native land. **óтчий** paternal. **óтчим** step-father.
отчислéние deduction; dismissal. **отчи́слить** *pf*, **отчисля́ть** *impf* deduct; dismiss.
отчитáть *pf*, **отчи́тывать** *impf* tell off; **~ся** report back.
отчуждéние alienation; estrangement.
отшатнýться (-нýсь, -нёшься) *pf*, **отшáтываться** *impf* start

back, recoil; **+от+***gen* give up, forsake.
отшвы́ривать *impf*, **отшвырну́ть** (-ну́, -нёшь) *pf* fling away; throw off.
отше́льник hermit; recluse.
отшлёпать *pf* spank.
от|шлифова́ть *pf*. **от|штукату́рить** *pf*.
отщепе́нец (-нца) renegade.
отъе́зд departure. **отъезжа́ть** *impf*, **отъе́хать** (-е́ду) *pf* drive off, go off.
отъя́вленный inveterate.
отыгра́ть *pf*, **оты́грывать** *impf* win back; **~ся** win back what one has lost.
отыска́ть (-ыщу́, -ы́щешь) *pf*, **оты́скивать** *impf* find; look for; **~ся** turn up, appear.
отяготи́ть (-ощу́) *pf*, **отягоща́ть** *impf* burden.
офице́р officer. **офице́рский** officer's, officers'.
официа́льный official.
официа́нт waiter. **официа́нтка** waitress.
официо́з semi-official organ. **официо́зный** semi-official.
оформи́тель *m* designer; stage-painter. **офо́рмить** (-млю) *pf*, **оформля́ть** *impf* design; put into shape; make official; process; **~ся** take shape; go through the formalities. **оформле́ние** design; mounting, staging; processing.
ох *int* oh! ah!
оха́пка armful.
о|характеризова́ть *pf*.
о́хать *impf* (*pf* **о́хнуть**) moan; sigh.
охва́т scope; inclusion; outflanking. **охвати́ть** (-ачу́, -а́тишь) *pf*, **охва́тывать** *impf* envelop; seize; comprehend.
охладева́ть *impf*, **охладе́ть** (-е́ю) *pf* grow cold. **охлади́ть** (-ажу́) *pf*, **охлажда́ть** *impf* cool; **~ся** become cool, cool down. **охлажде́ние** cooling; coolness.
о|хмеле́ть (-е́ю) *pf*. **о́хнуть** (-ну) *pf of* **о́хать**
охо́та[1] hunt, hunting; chase.
охо́та[2] wish, desire.
охо́титься (-о́чусь) *impf* hunt.
охо́тник[1] hunter.
охо́тник[2] volunteer; enthusiast.
охо́тничий hunting.
охо́тно *adv* willingly, gladly.
о́хра ochre.
охра́на guarding; protection; guard. **охрани́ть** *pf*, **охраня́ть** *impf* guard, protect.
охри́плый, охри́пший hoarse.
о|хри́пнуть (-ну; охри́п) *pf* become hoarse.
о|цара́пать(ся *pf*.
оце́нивать *impf*, **оцени́ть** (-ню́, -нишь) *pf* estimate; appraise. **оце́нка** estimation; appraisal; estimate. **оце́нщик** valuer.
о|цепене́ть (-е́ю) *pf*.
оцепи́ть (-плю́, -пишь) *pf*, **оцепля́ть** *impf* surround; cordon off.
оча́г (-а́) hearth; centre; breeding ground; hotbed.
очарова́ние charm, fascination. **очарова́тельный** charming. **очарова́ть** *pf*, **очаро́вывать** *impf* charm, fascinate.
очеви́дец (-дца) eye-witness.
очеви́дно *adv* obviously, evidently. **очеви́дный** obvious.
о́чень *adv* very; very much.
очередно́й next in turn; usual, regular; routine. **о́чередь** (*gen pl* -е́й) turn; queue.

о́черк essay, sketch.
о|черни́ть *pf.*
о|черстве́ть (-е́ю) *pf.*
очерта́ние outline(s), contour(s). **очерти́ть** (-рчу́, -ртишь) *pf*, **очё́рчивать** *impf* outline.
о́чи *etc.*: *see* **о́ко**
очисти́тельный cleansing. **о|чи́стить** (-и́щу) *pf*, **очища́ть** *impf* clean; refine; clear; peel; **~ся** clear o.s.; become clear (**от**+*gen* of). **очи́стка** cleaning; purification; clearance. **очи́стки** (-ов) *pl* peelings. **очище́ние** cleansing; purification.
очки́ (-о́в) *pl* spectacles. **очко́** (*gen pl* -о́в) pip; point. **очко́вая змея́** cobra.
очну́ться (-ну́сь, -нёшься) *pf* wake up; regain consciousness.
о́чн|ый: ~ое обуче́ние classroom instruction; **~ая ста́вка** confrontation.
очути́ться (-у́тишься) *pf* find o.s.
оше́йник collar.
ошеломи́тельный stunning. **ошеломи́ть** (-млю́) *pf*, **ошеломля́ть** *impf* stun.
ошиба́ться *impf*, **ошиби́ться** (-бу́сь, -бёшься; -и́бся) *pf* be mistaken, make a mistake; be wrong. **оши́бка** mistake; error. **оши́бочный** erroneous.
ошпа́ривать *impf*, **о|шпа́рить** *pf* scald.
о|штрафова́ть *pf.* **о|штукату́рить** *pf.*
ощети́ниваться *impf*, **о|щети́ниться** *pf* bristle (up).
о|щипа́ть (-плю́, -плешь) *pf*, **ощи́пывать** *impf* pluck.
ощу́пать *pf*, **ощу́пывать** *impf* feel; grope about. **о́щупь: на ~** to the touch; by touch. **о́щупью** *adv* gropingly; by touch.
ощути́мый, ощути́тельный perceptible; appreciable. **ощути́ть** (-ущу́) *pf*, **ощуща́ть** *impf* feel, sense. **ощуще́ние** sensation; feeling.

П

па *neut indecl* dance step.
павильо́н pavilion; film studio.
павли́н peacock.
па́водок (-дка) (sudden) flood.
па́вший fallen.
па́губный pernicious, ruinous.
па́даль carrion.
па́дать *impf* (*pf* **пасть, упа́сть**) fall; **~ ду́хом** lose heart. **паде́ж** (-а́) case. **паде́ние** fall; degradation; incidence. **па́дкий на**+*acc or* **до**+*gen* having a weakness for.
па́дчерица step-daughter.
паёк (пайка́) ration.
па́зуха bosom; sinus; axil.
пай (*pl* -и́, -ёв) share. **па́йщик** shareholder.
паке́т package; packet; paper bag.
Пакиста́н Pakistan. **пакиста́нец** (-нца), **-а́нка** Pakistani. **пакиста́нский** Pakistani.
па́кля tow; oakum.
упакова́ть *impf* (*pf* **за~, у~**) pack.
па́костный dirty, mean. **па́кость** dirty trick; obscenity.
пакт pact.
пала́та chamber, house. **пала́тка** tent; stall, booth.
пала́ч (-а́) executioner.
па́лец (-льца) finger; toe.
палиса́дник (*small*) front garden.
палиса́ндр rosewood.

пали́тра palette.
пали́ть[1] *impf* (*pf* **о~, с~**) burn; scorch.
пали́ть[2] *impf* (*pf* **вы́~, пальну́ть**) fire, shoot.
па́лка stick; walking-stick.
пало́мник pilgrim. **пало́мничество** pilgrimage.
па́лочка stick; bacillus; wand; baton.
па́луба deck.
пальба́ fire.
па́льма palm(-tree). **па́льмовый** palm.
пальну́ть (-ну́, -нёшь) *pf of* **пали́ть**
пальто́ *neut indecl* (over)coat.
паля́щий burning, scorching.
па́мятник monument; memorial. **па́мятный** memorable; memorial. **па́мять** memory; consciousness; **на ~** as a keepsake.
панаце́я panacea.
пане́ль footpath; panel(ling), wainscot(ing). **пане́льный** panelling.
па́ника panic. **паникёр** alarmist.
панихи́да requiem.
пани́ческий panic; panicky.
панно́ *neut indecl* panel.
панора́ма panorama.
пансио́н boarding-house; board and lodging. **пансиона́т** holiday hotel. **пансионе́р** boarder; guest.
пантало́ны (-о́н) *pl* knickers.
панте́ра panther.
пантоми́ма mime.
па́нцирь *m* armour, coat of mail.
па́па[1] *m* pope.
па́па[2] *m*, **папа́ша** *m* daddy.
папа́ха tall fur cap.
папиро́са (*Russian*) cigarette.
па́пка file; folder.
па́поротник fern.
пар[1] (*loc* -у́; *pl* -ы́) steam.
пар[2] (*loc* -у́; *pl* -ы́) fallow.
па́ра pair; couple; (two-piece) suit.
пара́граф paragraph.
пара́д parade; review. **пара́дн|ый** parade; gala; main, front; **~ая фо́рма** full dress (uniform).
парадо́кс paradox. **парадокса́льный** paradoxical.
парази́т parasite.
парализова́ть *impf & pf* paralyse. **парали́ч** (-а́) paralysis.
паралле́ль parallel. **паралле́льный** parallel.
пара́метр parameter.
парано́йя paranoia.
парашю́т parachute.
паре́ние soaring.
па́рень (-рня; *gen pl* -рне́й) *m* lad; fellow.
пари́ *neut indecl* bet; **держа́ть ~** bet, lay a bet.
пари́к (-а́) wig. **парикма́хер** hairdresser. **парикма́херская** *sb* hairdresser's.
пари́ровать *impf & pf* (*pf also* **от~**) parry, counter.
парите́т parity.
пари́ть[1] *impf* soar, hover.
па́рить[2] *impf* steam; stew; *impers* **па́рит** it is sultry; **~ся** (*pf* **по~ся**) steam, sweat; stew.
парк park; depot; stock.
парке́т parquet.
парла́мент parliament. **парламента́рный** parliamentarian.
парламентёр envoy; bearer of flag of truce. **парла́ментский** parliamentary; **~ зако́н** Act of Parliament.
парни́к (-а́) hotbed; seed-bed.

парнико́в|ый *adj*: **~ые расте́ния** hothouse plants.
парни́шка *m* boy, lad.
парно́й fresh; steamy.
па́рный (forming a) pair; twin.
паро- *in comb* steam-. **парово́з** (steam-)engine, locomotive. **~обра́зный** vaporous. **~хо́д** steamer; steamship. **~хо́дство** steamship-line.
парово́й steam; steamed.
паро́дия parody.
паро́ль *m* password.
паро́м ferry(-boat).
парт- *abbr in comb* Party. **партбиле́т** Party (membership) card. **~ко́м** Party committee. **~организа́ция** Party organization.
па́рта (*school*) desk.
парте́р stalls; pit.
партиза́н (*gen pl* -а́н) partisan; guerilla. **партиза́нский** partisan, guerilla; unplanned.
парти́йный party; Party; *sb* Party member.
партиту́ра (*mus*) score.
па́ртия party; group; batch; game, set; part.
партнёр partner.
па́рус (*pl* -а́, -о́в) sail. **паруси́на** canvas. **па́русник** sailing vessel. **па́русный** sail; **~ спорт** sailing.
парфюме́рия perfumes.
парча́ (*gen pl* -е́й) brocade.
па́сека apiary, beehive.
пасётся *see* **пасти́сь**
па́сквиль *m* lampoon; libel.
па́смурный overcast; gloomy.
па́спорт (*pl* -а́) passport.
пасса́ж passage; arcade.
пассажи́р passenger.
пасси́вный passive.
па́ста paste.
па́стбище pasture.
па́ства flock.
пасте́ль pastel.
пастерна́к parsnip.
пасти́ (-су́, -сёшь; пас, -ла́) *impf* graze; tend.
пасти́сь (-сётся; па́сся, -ла́сь) *impf* graze. **пасту́х** (-а́) shepherd. **па́стырь** *m* pastor.
пасть[1] mouth; jaws.
пасть[2] (паду́, -дёшь; пал) *pf of* **па́дать**
Па́сха Easter; Passover.
па́сынок (-нка) stepson, stepchild.
пат stalemate.
пате́нт patent.
патети́ческий passionate.
па́тока treacle; syrup.
патоло́гия pathology.
патриа́рх patriarch.
патрио́т, ~ка patriot. **патриоти́зм** patriotism. **патриоти́ческий** patriotic.
патро́н cartridge; chuck; lamp-socket.
патру́ль (-я́) *m* patrol.
па́уза pause; (*also mus*) rest.
пау́к (-а́) spider. **паути́на** cobweb; gossamer; web.
па́фос zeal, enthusiasm.
пах (*loc* -у́) groin.
па́харь *m* ploughman. **паха́ть** (пашу́, па́шешь) *impf* (*pf* **вс~**) plough.
па́хнуть[1] (-ну; пах) *impf* smell (+*instr* of).
пахну́ть[2] (-нёт) *pf* puff, blow.
па́хота ploughing. **па́хотный** arable.
паху́чий odorous, strong-smelling.
пацие́нт, ~ка patient.
пацифи́зм pacificism. **пацифи́ст** pacifist.

па́чка bundle; packet, pack; tutu.

па́чкать *impf* (*pf* **за~, ис~**) dirty, soil, stain.

пашу́ *etc.*: *see* **паха́ть. па́шня** (*gen pl* -шен) ploughed field.

паште́т pâté.

пая́льная ла́мпа blow-lamp. **пая́льник** soldering iron. **пая́ть** (-я́ю) *impf* solder.

пая́ц clown, buffoon.

певе́ц (-вца́), **певи́ца** singer. **певу́чий** melodious. **пе́вчий** singing; *sb* chorister.

пе́гий piebald.

педаго́г teacher; pedagogue. **педаго́гика** pedagogy. **педагоги́ческий** pedagogical; educational; ~ **институ́т** (teachers') training college.

педа́ль pedal.

педиа́тр paediatrician. **педиатри́ческий** paediatric.

педикю́р chiropody.

пейза́ж landscape; scenery.

пёк *see* **печь. пека́рный** baking. **пека́рня** (*gen pl* -рен) bakery. **пе́карь** (*pl* -я́, -е́й) *m* baker. **пе́кло** scorching heat; hell-fire. **пеку́** *etc.*: *see* **печь**

пелена́ (*gen pl* -лён) shroud. **пелена́ть** *impf* (*pf* **за~**) swaddle; put a nappy on.

пе́ленг bearing. **пеленгова́ть** *impf* & *pf* take the bearings of.

пелёнка nappy.

пельме́нь *m* meat dumpling.

пе́на foam; scum; froth.

пена́л pencil-case.

пе́ние singing.

пе́нистый foamy; frothy. **пе́ниться** *impf* (*pf* **вс~**) foam.

пе́нка skin. **пенопла́ст** plastic foam.

пеницилли́н penicillin.

пенсионе́р, пенсионе́рка pensioner. **пенсио́нный** pensionable. **пе́нсия** pension.

пень (пня) *m* stump, stub.

пенька́ hemp.

пе́пел (-пла) ash, ashes. **пе́пельница** ashtray.

перве́йший the first; first-class. **пе́рвенец** (-нца) first-born. **пе́рвенство** first place; championship. **пе́рвенствовать** *impf* take first place; take priority. **перви́чный** primary.

перво- *in comb* first; prime. **первобы́тный** primitive; primeval. **~исто́чник** source; origin. **~кла́ссный** first-class. **~ку́рсник** first-year student. **~нача́льный** original; primary. **~со́ртный** best-quality; first-class. **~степе́нный** paramount.

пе́рвое *sb* first course. **пе́рвый** first; former.

перга́мент parchment.

перебега́ть *impf*, **перебежа́ть** (-бегу́) *pf* cross, run across; desert. **перебе́жчик** deserter; turncoat.

переберу́ *etc.*: *see* **перебра́ть**

перебива́ть(ся *impf of* **переби́ть(ся**

перебира́ть(ся *impf of* **перебра́ть(ся**

переби́ть (-бью́, -бьёшь) *pf* (*impf* **перебива́ть**) interrupt; slaughter; beat; break; re-upholster; **~ся** break; make ends meet. **перебо́й** interruption; stoppage; irregularity.

перебо́рка sorting out; partition; bulkhead.

переборо́ть (-рю́, -решь) *pf* overcome.

переборщи́ть (-щу́) *pf* go too far; overdo it.

перебра́сывать(ся *impf of* **перебро́сить(ся**

перебра́ть (-беру́, -берёшь; -а́л, -а́, -о) *pf* (*impf* **перебира́ть**) sort out; look through; turn over in one's mind; finger; **~ся** get over, cross; move.

перебро́сить (-о́шу) *pf* (*impf* **перебра́сывать**) throw over; transfer; **~ся** fling o.s.; spread. **перебро́ска** transfer.

перебью́ *etc.*: *see* **переби́ть**

перева́л crossing; pass. **перева́ливать** *impf*, **перевали́ть** (-лю́, -лишь) *pf* transfer, shift; cross, pass.

перева́ривать *impf*, **перевари́ть** (-рю́, -ришь) *pf* reheat; overcook; digest; tolerate.

переведу́ *etc.*: *see* **перевести́**

перевезти́ (-зу́, -зёшь; -вёз, -ла́) *pf* (*impf* **перевози́ть**) take across; transport; (re)move.

переверну́ть (-ну́, -нёшь) *pf*, **перевёртывать** *impf* (*impf also* **перевора́чивать**) turn (over); upset; turn inside out; **~ся** turn (over).

переве́с preponderance; advantage. **переве́сить** (-е́шу) *pf* (*impf* **переве́шивать**) re-weigh; outweigh; tip the scales; hang elsewhere.

перевести́ (-веду́, -ведёшь; -вёл, -а́) *pf* (*impf* **переводи́ть**) take across; transfer, move, shift; translate; convert; **~сь** be transferred; run out; become extinct.

переве́шивать *impf of* **переве́сить. перевира́ть** *impf of* **перевра́ть**

перево́д transfer, move, shift; translation; conversion; waste. **переводи́ть(ся** (-ожу́(сь, -о́дишь(ся) *impf of* **перевести́(сь. переводн|о́й**: **~а́я бума́га** carbon paper; **~а́я карти́нка** transfer. **перево́дный** transfer; translated. **перево́дчик, ~ица** translator; interpreter.

перево́з transporting; ferry. **перевози́ть** (-ожу́, -о́зишь) *impf of* **перевезти́. перево́зка** conveyance. **перево́зчик** ferryman; removal man.

перевооружа́ть *impf*, **перевооружи́ть** (-жу́) *pf* rearm; **~ся** rearm. **перевооруже́ние** rearmament.

перевоплоти́ть (-лощу́) *pf*, **перевоплоща́ть** *impf* reincarnate; **~ся** be reincarnated. **перевоплоще́ние** reincarnation.

перевора́чивать(ся *impf of* **переверну́ть(ся. переворо́т** revolution; overturn; cataclysm; **госуда́рственный ~** coup d'état.

перевоспита́ние re-education. **перевоспита́ть** *pf*, **перевоспи́тывать** *impf* re-educate.

перевра́ть (-ру́, -рёшь; -а́л, -а́, -о) *pf* (*impf* **перевира́ть**) garble; misquote.

перевыполне́ние overfulfilment. **перевы́полнить** *pf*, **перевыполня́ть** *impf* overfulfil.

перевяза́ть (-яжу́, -я́жешь) *pf*, **перевя́зывать** *impf* bandage; tie up; re-tie. **перевя́зка** dressing, bandage.

переги́б bend; excess, extreme. **перегиба́ть(ся** *impf of* **перегну́ть(ся**

перегля́дываться *impf*, **перегляну́ться** (-ну́сь, -нешься) *pf* exchange glances.

перегна́ть (-гоню́, -го́нишь; -а́л,

-а́, -о) *pf* (*impf* **перегоня́ть**) outdistance; surpass; drive; distil.
перегно́й humus.
перегну́ть (-ну́, -нёшь) *pf* (*impf* **перегиба́ть**) bend; ~ **па́лку** go too far; ~**ся** bend; lean over.
перегова́ривать *impf*, **переговори́ть** *pf* talk; out-talk; ~**ся** (**с**+*instr*) exchange remarks (with). **перегово́ры** (-ов) *pl* negotiations, parley. **перегово́рный** *adj*: ~ **пункт** public call-boxes; trunk-call office.
перего́н driving; stage. **перего́нка** distillation. **перего́нный** distilling, distillation. **перегоню́** *etc.*: *see* **перегна́ть. перегоня́ть** *impf of* **перегна́ть**
перегора́живать *impf of* **перегороди́ть**
перегора́ть *impf*, **перегоре́ть** (-ри́т) *pf* burn out, fuse.
перегороди́ть (-рожу́, -ро́ди́шь) *pf* (*impf* **перегора́живать**) partition off; block. **перегоро́дка** partition.
перегре́в overheating. **перегрева́ть** *impf*, **перегре́ть** (-е́ю) *pf* overheat; ~**ся** overheat.
перегружа́ть *impf*, **перегрузи́ть** (-ужу́, -у́зишь) *pf* overload; transfer. **перегру́зка** overload; transfer.
перегрыза́ть *impf*, **перегры́зть** (-зу́, -зёшь; -гры́з) *pf* gnaw through.
пе́ред, пе́редо, пред, пре́до *prep*+*instr* before; in front of; compared to. **перёд** (пе́реда; *pl* -а́) front, forepart.
передава́ть (-даю́, -даёшь) *impf*, **переда́ть** (-а́м, -а́шь, -а́ст, -ади́м; пе́редал, -а́, -о) *pf* pass, hand, hand over; transfer; hand down; make over; tell; communicate; convey; give too much; ~**ся** pass; be transmitted; be communicated; be inherited. **переда́тчик** transmitter. **переда́ча** passing; transmission; communication; transfer; broadcast; drive; gear, gearing.
передвига́ть *impf*, **передви́нуть** (-ну) *pf* move, shift; ~**ся** move, shift. **передвиже́ние** movement; transportation. **передви́жка** movement; *in comb* travelling; itinerant. **передвижно́й** movable, mobile.
переде́лать *pf*, **переде́лывать** *impf* alter; refashion. **переде́лка** alteration.
передёргивать(ся *impf of* **передёрнуть(ся**
передержа́ть (-жу́, -жишь) *pf*, **переде́рживать** *impf* overdo; overcook; overexpose.
передёрнуть (-ну) *pf* (*impf* **передёргивать**) pull aside *or* across; cheat; distort; ~**ся** wince.
пере́дний front; ~ **план** foreground. **пере́дник** apron. **пере́дняя** *sb* (entrance) hall, lobby. **пе́редо:** *see* **пе́ред. передови́к** (-а́) exemplary worker. **передови́ца** leading article. **передово́й** advanced; foremost; leading.
передохну́ть (-ну́, -нёшь) *pf* pause for breath.
передра́знивать *impf*, **передразни́ть** (-ню́, -нишь) *pf* mimic.
переду́мать *pf*, **переду́мывать** *impf* change one's mind.
переды́шка respite.
перее́зд crossing; move. **переезжа́ть** *impf*, **перее́хать** (-е́ду) *pf* cross; run over, knock down; move (house).
пережа́ривать *impf*, **пережа-**

рить *pf* overdo, overcook.

переждáть (-жду́, -ждёшь; -áл, -á, -o) *pf* (*impf* **пережидáть**) wait for the end of.

пережёвывать *impf* chew; repeat over and over again.

переживáние experience. **переживáть** *impf of* **пережúть**

пережидáть *impf of* **переждáть**

пережитóе *sb* the past. **пережúток** (-тка) survival; vestige. **пережúть** (-иву́, -ивёшь; пéрежил, -á, -o) *pf* (*impf* **переживáть**) experience; go through; endure; outlive.

перезарядúть (-яжу́, -я́дишь) *pf*, **перезаряжáть** *impf* recharge, reload.

перезвáнивать *impf*, **перезвонúть** *pf* +*dat* ring back.

пере|зимовáть *pf.*

перезрéлый overripe.

переигрáть *pf*, **переúгрывать** *impf* play again; overact.

переизбирáть *impf*, **переизбрáть** (-беру́, -берёшь; -брáл, -á, -o) *pf* re-elect. **переизбрáние** re-election.

переиздавáть (-даю́, -даёшь) *impf*, **переиздáть** (-áм, -áшь, -áст, -адúм; -áл, -á, -o) *pf* republish, reprint. **переиздáние** republication; new edition.

переименовáть *pf*, **переименóвывать** *impf* rename.

перейму́ *etc.*: *see* **перенять**

перейтú (-йду́, -йдёшь; перешёл, -шлá) *pf* (*impf* **переходúть**) cross; go, walk, pass; move, change, switch; turn (**в**+*acc* to, into).

перекáпывать *impf of* **перекопáть**

перекатúть (-чу́, -тишь) *pf*, **перекáтывать** *impf* roll; **~ся** roll.

перекачáть *pf*, **перекáчивать** *impf* pump (across).

переквалифицúроваться *impf* & *pf* retrain.

перекúдывать *impf*, **перекúнуть** (-ну) *pf* throw over; **~ся** leap.

пéрекись peroxide.

переклáдина cross-beam; joist; horizontal bar.

переклáдывать *impf of* **переложúть**

переклúчка roll-call.

переключáтель *m* switch. **переключáть** *impf*, **переключúть** (-чу́) *pf* switch (over); **~ся** switch (over) (**на**+*acc* to).

перековáть (-ку́ю, -куёшь) *pf*, **перекóвывать** *impf* re-shoe; re-forge.

перекопáть *pf* (*impf* **перекáпывать**) dig (all of); dig again.

перекосúть (-ошу́, -óсишь) *pf* warp; distort; **~ся** warp; become distorted.

перекочевáть (-чу́ю) *pf*, **перекочёвывать** *impf* migrate.

перекóшенный distorted, twisted.

перекрáивать *impf of* **перекроúть**

перекрáсить (-áшу) *pf*, **перекрáшивать** *impf* (re-)paint; (re-)dye; **~ся** change colour; turn one's coat.

пере|крестúть (-ещу́, -éстишь) *pf*, **перекрéщивать** *impf* cross; **~ся** cross, intersect; cross o.s. **перекрёстн|ый** cross; **~ый допрóс** cross-examination; **~ый огóнь** cross-fire; **~ая ссы́лка** cross-reference. **перекрёсток** (-тка) cross-roads, crossing.

перекрúкивать *impf*, **пере-**

крича́ть (-чу́) *pf* shout down.

перекройть (-ою́) *pf* (*impf* **перекра́ивать**) cut out again; reshape.

перекрыва́ть *impf*, **перекры́ть** (-ро́ю) *pf* re-cover; exceed. **перекры́тие** ceiling.

перекую́ *etc.*: *see* **перекова́ть**

перекупа́ть *impf*, **перекупи́ть** (-плю́, -пишь) *pf* buy up; buy by outbidding s.o. **переку́пщик** second-hand dealer.

перекуси́ть (-ушу́, -у́сишь) *pf*, **перееку́сывать** *impf* bite through; have a snack.

перелага́ть *impf of* **переложи́ть**

перела́мывать *impf of* **переломи́ть**

перелеза́ть *impf*, **переле́зть** (-зу; -ез) *pf* climb over.

переле́сок (-ска) copse.

перелёт migration; flight. **перелета́ть** *impf*, **перелете́ть** (-лечу́) *pf* fly over. **перелётный** migratory.

перелива́ние decanting; transfusion. **перелива́ть** *impf of* **перели́ть**. **перелива́ться** *impf of* **перели́ться**; gleam; modulate.

перелиста́ть *pf*, **перели́стывать** *impf* leaf through.

перели́ть (-лью́, -льёшь; -ил, -а́, -о) *pf* (*impf* **перелива́ть**) pour; decant; let overflow; transfuse. **перели́ться** (-льётся; -ли́лся, -лила́сь, -ли́ло́сь) *pf* (*impf* **перелива́ться**) flow; overflow.

перелицева́ть (-цу́ю) *pf*, **перелицо́вывать** *impf* turn; have turned.

переложе́ние arrangement. **переложи́ть** (-жу́, -жишь) *pf* (*impf* **перекла́дывать**, **перелага́ть**) put elsewhere; shift; transfer; interlay; put in too much; set; arrange; transpose.

перело́м breaking; fracture; turning-point, crisis; sudden change. **перелома́ть** *pf* break; **~ся** break, be broken. **переломи́ть** (-млю́, -мишь) *pf* (*impf* **перела́мывать**) break in two; master. **перело́мный** critical.

перелью́ *etc.*: *see* **перели́ть**

перема́нивать *impf*, **перемани́ть** (-ню́, -нишь) *pf* win over; entice.

перемежа́ться *impf* alternate.

переме́на change; break. **перемени́ть** (-ню́, -нишь) *pf*, **переменя́ть** *impf* change; **~ся** change. **переме́нный** variable; **~ ток** alternating current. **переме́нчивый** changeable.

перемести́ть (-мещу́) *pf* (*impf* **перемеща́ть**) move; transfer; **~ся** move.

перемеша́ть *pf*, **переме́шивать** *impf* mix; mix up; shuffle; **~ся** get mixed (up).

перемеща́ть(ся *impf of* **перемести́ть(ся**. **перемеще́ние** transference; displacement. **перемещённ|ый** displaced; **~ые ли́ца** displaced persons.

переми́рие armistice, truce.

перемыва́ть *impf*, **перемы́ть** (-мо́ю) *pf* wash (up) again.

перенапряга́ть *impf*, **перенапря́чь** (-ягу́, -яжёшь: -я́г, -ла́) *pf* overstrain.

перенаселе́ние overpopulation. **перенаселённый** (-лён, -а́) overpopulated; overcrowded.

перенести́ (-су́, -сёшь; -нёс, -ла́) *pf* (*impf* **переноси́ть**) carry, move, take; transfer; take over; postpone; endure, bear; **~сь** be carried; be carried away.

перенима́ть *impf of* **переня́ть**

перено́с transfer; word division; **знак ~а** end-of-line hyphen. **переноси́мый** endurable. **переноси́ть(ся** (-ошу́(сь, -о́сишь(ся) *impf of* **перенести́(сь**

перено́сица bridge (*of the nose*).

перено́ска carrying over; transporting; carriage. **перено́сный** portable; figurative. **перено́счик** carrier.

пере|ночева́ть (-чу́ю) *pf.* **переношу́** *etc.*: *see* **переноси́ть**

переня́ть (-ейму́, -еймёшь; пе́реня́л, -а́, -о) *pf* (*impf* **перенима́ть**) imitate; adopt.

переобору́довать *impf* & *pf* re-equip.

переобува́ться *impf*, **переобу́ться** (-у́юсь, -у́ешься) *pf* change one's shoes.

переодева́ться *impf*, **переоде́ться** (-е́нусь) *pf* change (one's clothes).

переосвиде́тельствовать *impf* & *pf* re-examine.

переоце́нивать *impf*, **переоцени́ть** (-ню́, -нишь) *pf* overestimate; revalue. **переоце́нка** overestimation; revaluation.

перепа́чкать *pf* make dirty; **~ся** get dirty.

пе́репел (*pl* -а́) quail.

перепелена́ть *pf* change (*a baby*).

перепеча́тать *pf*, **перепеча́тывать** *impf* reprint. **перепеча́тка** reprint.

перепи́ливать *impf*, **перепили́ть** (-лю́, -лишь) *pf* saw in two.

переписа́ть (-ишу́, -и́шешь) *pf*, **перепи́сывать** *impf* copy; re-write; make a list of. **перепи́ска** copying; correspondence. **перепи́сываться** *impf* correspond. **пе́репись** census.

перепла́вить (-влю) *pf*, **переплавля́ть** *impf* smelt.

переплати́ть (-ачу́, -а́тишь) *pf*, **перепла́чивать** *impf* overpay.

переплести́ (-лету́, -летёшь; -лёл, -а́) *pf*, **переплета́ть** *impf* bind; interlace, intertwine; re-plait; **~ся** interlace, interweave; get mixed up. **переплёт** binding. **переплётчик** bookbinder.

переплыва́ть *impf*, **переплы́ть** (-ыву́, -ывёшь; -ы́л, -а́, -о) *pf* swim *or* sail across.

переподгото́вка further training; refresher course.

переполза́ть *impf*, **переползти́** (-зу́, -зёшь; -о́лз, -ла́) *pf* crawl *or* creep across.

переполне́ние overfilling; overcrowding. **перепо́лненный** overcrowded; too full. **перепо́лнить** *pf*, **переполня́ть** *impf* overfill; overcrowd.

переполо́х commotion.

перепо́нка membrane; web.

перепра́ва crossing; ford.

перепра́вить (-влю) *pf*, **переправля́ть** *impf* convey; take across; forward; **~ся** cross, get across.

перепродава́ть (-даю́, -даёшь) *impf*, **перепрода́ть** (-а́м, -а́шь, -а́ст, -ади́м; -про́да́л, -а́, -о) *pf* re-sell. **перепрода́жа** re-sale.

перепроизво́дство overproduction.

перепры́гивать *impf*, **перепры́гнуть** (-ну) *pf* jump (over).

перепуга́ть *pf* frighten, scare; **~ся** get a fright.

пере|пу́тать *pf*, **перепу́тывать** *impf* tangle; confuse, mix up.

перепу́тье cross-roads.

перераба́тывать *impf*, **перерабо́тать** *pf* convert; treat;

re-make; re-cast; process; work overtime; overwork; **~ся** overwork. **перерабо́тка** processing; reworking; overtime work.

перераспределе́ние redistribution. **перераспредели́ть** *pf*, **перераспределя́ть** *impf* redistribute.

перераста́ние outgrowing; escalation; development (into). **перераста́ть** *impf*, **перерасти́** (-ту́, -тёшь; -ро́с, -ла́) *pf* outgrow; develop.

перерасхо́д over-expenditure; overdraft. **перерасхо́довать** *impf* & *pf* expend too much of.

перерасчёт recalculation.

перерва́ть (-ву́, -вёшь; -а́л, -а́, -о) *pf* (*impf* **перерыва́ть**) break, tear asunder; **~ся** break, come apart.

перере́зать (-е́жу) *pf*, **перереза́ть** *impf*, **перере́зывать** *impf* cut; cut off; kill.

перероди́ть (-ожу́) *pf*, **перерожда́ть** *impf* regenerate; **~ся** be reborn; be regenerated; degenerate. **перерожде́ние** regeneration; degeneration.

переро́с *etc.*: *see* **перерасти́**.

переро́ю *etc.*: *see* **переры́ть**

переруба́ть *impf*, **переруби́ть** (-блю́, -бишь) *pf* chop in two.

переры́в break; interruption; interval.

перерыва́ть[1]**(ся** *impf of* **перерва́ть(ся**

перерыва́ть[2] *impf*, **переры́ть** (-ро́ю) *pf* dig up; rummage through.

пересади́ть (-ажу́, -а́дишь) *pf*, **переса́живать** *impf* transplant; graft; seat somewhere else. **переса́дка** transplantation; grafting; change.

переса́живаться *impf of* **пересе́сть**. **переса́ливать** *impf of* **пересоли́ть**

пересдава́ть (-даю́сь) *impf*, **пересда́ть** (-а́м, -а́шь, -а́ст, -адим; -да́л, -а́, -о) *pf* sublet; re-sit.

пересека́ть(ся *impf of* **пересе́чь(ся**

пересе́ленец (-нца) settler; immigrant. **пересе́ле́ние** migration; immigration, resettlement; moving. **пересели́ть** *pf*, **переселя́ть** *impf* move; **~ся** move; migrate.

пересе́сть (-ся́ду) *pf* (*impf* **переса́живаться**) change one's seat; change (*trains etc.*).

пересече́ние crossing, intersection. **пересе́чь** (-секу́, -сечёшь; -сёк, -ла́) *pf* (*impf* **пересека́ть**) cross; intersect; **~ся** cross, intersect.

переси́ливать *impf*, **переси́лить** *pf* overpower.

переска́з (re)telling; exposition. **пересказа́ть** (-ажу́, -а́жешь) *pf*, **переска́зывать** *impf* retell.

переска́кивать *impf*, **перескочи́ть** (-чу́, -чишь) *pf* jump *or* skip (over).

пересла́ть (-ешлю́, -шлёшь) *pf* (*impf* **пересыла́ть**) send; forward.

пересма́тривать *impf*, **пересмотре́ть** (-трю́, -тришь) *pf* look over; reconsider. **пересмо́тр** revision; reconsideration; review.

пересоли́ть (-олю́, -о́ли́шь) *pf* (*impf* **переса́ливать**) over-salt; overdo it.

пересо́хнуть (-нет; -о́х) *pf* (*impf* **пересыха́ть**) dry up, become parched.

переспа́ть (-плю́; -а́л, -а́, -о) *pf* oversleep; spend the night.

переспе́лый overripe.

переспра́шивать *impf*, **пере-**

спроси́ть (-ошу́, -о́сишь) *pf* ask again.

перестава́ть (-таю́, -таёшь) *impf of* **переста́ть**

переста́вить (-влю) *pf*, **переставля́ть** *impf* move; re-arrange; transpose. **перестано́вка** rearrangement; transposition.

переста́ть (-а́ну) *pf* (*impf* **перестава́ть**) stop, cease.

перестрада́ть *pf* have suffered.

перестра́ивать(ся *impf of* **перестро́ить(ся**

перестрахо́вка re-insurance; overcautiousness.

перестре́лка exchange of fire. **перестреля́ть** *pf* shoot (down).

перестро́ить *pf* (*impf* **перестра́ивать**) rebuild; reorganize; retune; **~ся** re-form; reorganize o.s.; switch over (**на**+*acc* to). **перестро́йка** reconstruction; reorganization; retuning; perestroika.

переступа́ть *impf*, **переступи́ть** (-плю́, -пишь) *pf* step over; cross; overstep.

пересчита́ть *pf*, **пересчи́тывать** *impf* (*pf also* **перече́сть**) re-count; count.

пересыла́ть *impf of* **пересла́ть. пересы́лка** sending, forwarding.

пересыпа́ть *impf*, **пересы́пать** (-плю, -плешь) *pf* pour; sprinkle; pour too much.

пересыха́ть *impf of* **пересо́хнуть. пересяду** *etc.*: *see* **пересе́сть. перета́пливать** *impf of* **перетопи́ть**

перета́скивать *impf*, **перетащи́ть** (-щу́, -щишь) *pf* drag (over, through); move.

перетере́ть (-тру́, -трёшь; -тёр) *pf*, **перетира́ть** *impf* wear out, wear down; grind; wipe; **~ся** wear out *or* through.

перетопи́ть (-плю́, -пишь) *pf* (*impf* **перета́пливать**) melt.

перетру́ *etc.*: *see* **перетере́ть**

пере́ть (пру, прёшь; пёр, -ла) *impf* go; make *or* force one's way; haul; come out.

перетя́гивать *impf*, **перетяну́ть** (-ну́, -нешь) *pf* pull, draw; win over; outweigh.

переубеди́ть *pf*, **переубежда́ть** *impf* make change one's mind.

переу́лок (-лка) side street, alley, lane.

переустро́йство reconstruction, reorganization.

переутоми́ть (-млю́) *pf*, **переутомля́ть** *impf* overtire; **~ся** overtire o.s. **переутомле́ние** overwork.

переучёт stock-taking.

переу́чивать *impf*, **переучи́ть** (-чу́, -чишь) *pf* teach again.

перефрази́ровать *impf* & *pf* paraphrase.

перехвати́ть (-ачу́, -а́тишь) *pf*, **перехва́тывать** *impf* intercept; snatch a bite (of); borrow.

перехитри́ть *pf* outwit.

перехо́д transition; crossing; conversion. **переходи́ть** (-ожу́, -о́дишь) *impf of* **перейти́. перехо́дный** transitional; transitive. **переходя́щий** transient; intermittent; brought forward.

пе́рец (-рца) pepper.

перечёл *etc.*: *see* **перече́сть**

пе́речень (-чня) *m* list, enumeration.

перечёркивать *impf*, **перечеркну́ть** (-ну́, -нёшь) *pf* cross out, cancel.

перечéсть (-чтý, -чтёшь; -чёл, -члá) *pf*: *see* **пересчитáть, перечитáть**

перечислéние enumeration; transfer. **перечúслить** *pf*, **перечисля́ть** *impf* enumerate; transfer.

перечитáть *pf*, **перечúтывать** *impf* (*pf also* **перечéсть**) re-read.

перéчить (-чу) *impf* contradict; cross, go against.

пéречница pepper-pot.

перечтý *etc.*: *see* **перечéсть**. **перéчу** *etc.*: *see* **перéчить**

перешáгивать *impf*, **перешагнýть** (-нý, -нёшь) *pf* step over.

перешéек (-éйка) isthmus, neck.

перешёл *etc.*: *see* **перейтú**

перешивáть *impf*, **перешúть** (-шью́, -шьёшь) *pf* alter; have altered.

перешлю́ *etc.*: *see* **переслáть**

переэкзаменовáть *pf.*, **переэкзаменóвывать** *impf* re-examine; **~ся** retake an exam.

перúла (-úл) *pl* railing(s); banisters.

перúна feather-bed.

перúод period. **периóдика** periodicals. **периодúческий** periodical; recurring.

пéристый feathery; cirrus.

перифери́я periphery.

перламýтр mother-of-pearl. **перламýтровый** mother-of-pearl. **перлóв|ый**: **~ая крупá** pearl barley.

перманéнт perm. **перманéнтный** permanent.

пернáтый feathered. **пернáтые** *sb pl* birds. **перó** (*pl* пéрья, -ьев) feather; nib. **перочúнный нож, нóжик** penknife.

перпендикуля́рный perpendicular.

перрóн platform.

перс Persian. **персúдский** Persian.

пéрсик peach.

персия́нка Persian woman.

персóна person; **сóбственной персóной** in person. **персонáж** character; personage. **персонáл** personnel, staff. **персонáльный** personal.

перспектúва perspective; vista; prospect. **перспектúвный** perspective; long-term; promising.

пéрстень (-тня) *m* ring.

перфокáрта punched card.

пéрхоть dandruff.

перчáтка glove.

пéрчить (-чу) *impf* (*pf* **по~**) pepper.

пёс (пса) dog.

пéсенник song-book; (choral) singer; song-writer. **пéсенный** song; of songs.

песéц (-цá) (polar) fox.

песнь (*gen pl* -ей) song; canto.

пéсня (*gen pl* -сен) song.

песóк (-скá) sand. **песóчный** sand; sandy.

пессимúзм pessimism. **пессимúст** pessimist. **пессимистúческий** pessimistic.

пестротá diversity of colours; diversity. **пёстрый** variegated; diverse; colourful.

песчáник sandstone. **песчáный** sandy. **песчúнка** grain of sand.

петербýргский (of) St Petersburg.

петúция petition.

петлúца buttonhole; tab. **пéтля** (*gen pl* -тель) loop; noose; but-

tonhole; stitch; hinge.
петру́шка[1] parsley.
петру́шка[2] *m* Punch; *f* Punch-and-Judy show.
пету́х (-á) cock. **петушóк** (-шкá) cockerel.
петь (пою́, поёшь) *impf* (*pf* **про~, с~**) sing.
пехóта infantry, foot. **пехоти́нец** (-нца) infantryman. **пехóтный** infantry.
печа́лить *impf* (*pf* **о~**) sadden; **~ся** grieve, be sad. **печа́ль** sorrow. **печа́льный** sad.
печа́тать *impf* (*pf* **на~, от~**) print; **~ся** write, be published; be at the printer's. **печа́тн|ый** printing; printer's; printed; **~ые бу́квы** block capitals; **~ый станóк** printing-press. **печа́ть** seal, stamp; print; printing; press.
печéние baking.
печёнка liver.
печёный baked.
пéчень liver.
печéнье pastry; biscuit. **пéчка** stove. **печнóй** stove; oven; kiln.
печь (*loc* -и́; *gen pl* -éй) stove; oven; kiln. **печь** (пеку́, -чёшь; пёк, -лá) *impf* (*pf* **ис~**) bake; **~ся** bake.
пешехóд pedestrian. **пешехóдный** pedestrian; foot-. **пéший** pedestrian; foot. **пéшка** pawn.
пешкóм *adv* on foot.
пещéра cave. **пещéрный** cave; **~ человéк** cave-dweller.
пиани́но *neut indecl* (upright) piano. **пиани́ст, ~ка** pianist.
пивна́я *sb* pub. **пивнóй** beer.
пи́во beer. **пивова́р** brewer.
пигмéй pygmy.
пиджа́к (-á) jacket.
пижа́ма pyjamas.
пижóн dandy.
пик peak; **часы́ пик** rush-hour.
пи́ка lance.
пика́нтный piquant; spicy.
пика́п pick-up (van).
пикé *neut indecl* dive.
пикéт picket. **пикéтчик** picket.
пи́ки (пик) *pl* (*cards*) spades.
пики́ровать *impf* & *pf* (*pf also* **с~**) dive.
пикирóвщик, пики́рующий бомбардирóвщик dive-bomber.
пикни́к (-á) picnic.
пи́кнуть (-ну) *pf* squeak; make a sound.
пи́ковый of spades.
пила́ (*pl* -ы) saw; nagger. **пилёный** sawed, sawn. **пили́ть** (-лю́, -лишь) *impf* saw; nag (at). **пи́лка** sawing; fret-saw; nail-file.
пилóт pilot.
пилóтка forage-cap.
пилоти́ровать *impf* pilot.
пилю́ля pill.
пина́ть *impf* (*pf* пнуть) kick.
пинóк (-нкá) kick.
пингви́н penguin.
пинцéт tweezers.
пиóн peony.
пионéр pioneer. **пионéрский** pioneer.
пипéтка pipette.
пир (*loc* -у́; *pl* -ы́) feast, banquet. **пирова́ть** *impf* feast.
пирами́да pyramid.
пира́т pirate.
пирóг (-á) pie. **пирóжное** *sb* cake, pastry. **пирожóк** (-жкá) pasty.
пирс pier.
пиру́эт pirouette.
пи́ршество feast; celebration.
пи́саный handwritten. **пи́сарь** (*pl* -я́) *m* clerk. **писа́тель** *m*, **пи-**

са́тельница writer, author. **писа́ть** (пишу́, пи́шешь) *impf* (*pf* **на~**) write; paint; **~ ма́слом** paint in oils; **~ся** be spelt.

писк squeak, chirp. **пискли́вый** squeaky. **пи́скнуть** (-ну) *pf of* **пища́ть**

пистоле́т pistol; gun; **~-пулемёт** sub-machine gun.

писто́н (percussion-)cap; piston.

писчебума́жный stationery.

пи́счая бума́га writing paper.

пи́сьменно *adv* in writing.

пи́сьменность literature.

пи́сьменный writing, written.

письмо́ (*pl* -а, -сем) letter.

пита́ние nourishment; feeding. **пита́тельный** nutritious; alimentary; feed. **пита́ть** *impf* feed; nourish; supply; **~ся** feed; eat; live; +*instr* feed on.

пито́мец (-мца) charge; pupil; alumnus. **пито́мник** nursery.

пить (пью, пьёшь; пил, -а́, -о) *impf* (*pf* **вы́~**) drink. **питьево́й** drinkable; drinking.

пиха́ть *impf*, **пихну́ть** (-ну́, -нёшь) *pf* push, shove.

пи́хта (silver) fir.

пи́чкать *impf* (*pf* **на~**) stuff.

пи́шущ|ий writing; **~ая маши́нка** typewriter.

пи́ща food.

пища́ть (-щу́) *impf* (*pf* **пи́скнуть**) squeak; cheep.

пищеваре́ние digestion. **пищево́д** oesophagus, gullet. **пищево́й** food.

пия́вка leech.

ПК *abbr* (*of* **персона́льный компью́тер**) PC (*personal computer*).

пла́вание swimming; sailing; voyage. **пла́вательный** swimming; **~ бассе́йн** swimming-pool. **пла́вать** *impf* swim; float; sail. **плавба́за** depot ship, factory ship.

плави́льный melting, smelting. **плави́льня** foundry. **пла́вить** (-влю) *impf* (*pf* **рас~**) melt, smelt; **~ся** melt. **пла́вка** fusing; melting.

пла́вки (-вок) *pl* bathing trunks.

пла́вкий fusible; fuse. **плавле́ние** melting.

плавни́к (-а́) fin; flipper. **пла́вный** smooth, flowing; liquid.

плаву́чий floating.

плагиа́т plagiarism. **плагиа́тор** plagiarist.

пла́зма plasma.

плака́т poster; placard.

пла́кать (-а́чу) *impf* cry, weep; **~ся** complain, lament; +**на**+*acc* complain of; bemoan.

пла́кса cry-baby. **плакси́вый** whining. **плаку́чий** weeping.

пла́менный flaming; ardent.

пла́мя (-мени) *neut* flame; blaze.

план plan

планёр glider. **планери́зм** gliding. **планери́ст** glider-pilot.

плане́та planet. **плане́тный** planetary.

плани́рование[1] planning.

плани́рование[2] gliding; glide.

плани́ровать[1] *impf* (*pf* **за~**) plan.

плани́ровать[2] *impf* (*pf* **с~**) glide (down).

пла́нка lath, slat.

пла́новый planned, systematic; planning. **планоме́рный** systematic, planned.

планта́ция plantation.

пласт (-а́) layer; stratum. **пласти́на** plate. **пласти́нка** plate; (*gramophone*) record.

пласти́ческий, пласти́чный plastic. **пластма́сса** plastic. **пластма́ссовый** plastic.

пла́стырь *m* plaster.

пла́та pay; charge; fee. **платёж** (-á) payment. **платёжеспосо́бный** solvent. **платёжный** pay.

пла́тина platinum.

плати́ть (-ачу́, -а́тишь) *impf* (*pf* **за~, у~**) pay; **~ся** (*pf* **по~ся**) **за**+*acc* pay for. **пла́тный** paid; requiring payment.

плато́к (-тка́) shawl; head-scarf; handkerchief.

платони́ческий platonic.

платфо́рма platform; truck.

пла́тье (*gen pl* -ьев) clothes, clothing; dress; gown. **платяно́й** clothes.

плафо́н ceiling; lamp shade.

плацда́рм bridgehead, beachhead; base; springboard.

плацка́рта reserved-seat ticket.

плач weeping. **плаче́вный** lamentable. **пла́чу** *etc.*: *see* **пла́кать**

плачу́ *etc.*: *see* **плати́ть**

плашмя́ *adv* flat, prone.

плащ (-á) cloak; raincoat.

плебе́й plebeian.

плева́тельница spittoon. **плева́ть** (плюю́, плюёшь) *impf* (*pf* **на~, плю́нуть**) spit; *inf*+*dat*: **мне ~** I don't give a damn (**на**+*acc* about); **~ся** spit. **плево́к** (-вка́) spit, spittle.

плеври́т pleurisy.

плед rug; plaid.

плёл *etc.*: *see* **плести́**

племенно́й tribal; pedigree. **пле́мя** (-мени; *pl* -мена́, -мён) *neut* tribe. **племя́нник** nephew. **племя́нница** niece.

плен (*loc* -ý) captivity.

плена́рный plenary.

плени́тельный captivating. **плени́ть** *pf* (*impf* **пленя́ть**) captivate; **~ся** be captivated.

плёнка film; tape; pellicle.

пле́нник prisoner. **пле́нный** captive.

пле́нум plenary session.

пленя́ть(ся *impf of* **плени́ть(ся**

пле́сень mould.

плеск splash, lapping. **плеска́ть** (-ещу́, -е́щешь) *impf* (*pf* **плесну́ть**) splash; lap; **~ся** splash; lap.

пле́сневеть (-еет) *impf* (*pf* **за~**) go mouldy, grow musty.

плесну́ть (-ну́, -нёшь) *pf of* **плеска́ть**

плести́ (-ету́, -етёшь; плёл, -á) *impf* (*pf* **с~**) plait; weave; **~сь** trudge along. **плете́ние** plaiting; wickerwork. **плетёный** wattled; wicker. **плете́нь** (-тня́) *m* wattle fencing. **плётка, плеть** (*gen pl* -е́й) lash.

пле́чико (*pl* -и, -ов) shoulder-strap; *pl* coat-hanger. **плечи́стый** broad-shouldered. **плечо́** (*pl* -и, -áм) shoulder.

плеши́вый bald. **плеши́на, плешь** bald patch.

плещу́ *etc.*: *see* **плеска́ть**

пли́нтус plinth; skirting-board.

плис velveteen.

плиссирова́ть *impf* pleat.

плита́ (*pl* -ы) slab; flag-(stone); stove, cooker; **моги́льная ~** gravestone. **пли́тка** tile; (thin) slab; stove, cooker; **~ шокола́да** bar of chocolate. **пли́точный** tiled.

пловéц (-вцá), **пловчи́ха** swimmer. **плову́чий** floating; buoyant.

плод (-á) fruit. **плоди́ть** (-ожу́) *impf* (*pf* **рас~**) produce, procreate; **~ся** propagate.

плодо- *in comb* fruit-. **плодо-**

ви́тый fruitful, prolific; fertile. **~во́дство** fruit-growing. **~но́сный** fruit-bearing, fruitful. **~овощно́й** fruit and vegetable. **~ро́дный** fertile. **~тво́рный** fruitful.

пло́мба seal; filling. **пломбирова́ть** *impf* (*pf* **за~, о~**) fill; seal.

пло́ский (-сок, -ска́, -о) flat; trivial.

плоско- *in comb* flat. **плоского́рье** plateau. **~гу́бцы** (-ев) *pl* pliers. **~до́нный** flat-bottomed.

пло́скость (*gen pl* -е́й) flatness; plane; platitude.

плот (-а́) raft.

плоти́на dam; weir; dyke.

пло́тник carpenter.

пло́тность solidity; density. **пло́тный** (-тен, -тна́, -о) thick; compact; dense; solid, strong; hearty.

плотоя́дный carnivorous.

плоть flesh.

плохо́й bad; poor.

площа́дка area, (sports) ground, court, playground; site; landing; platform. **пло́щадь** (*gen pl* -е́й) area; space; square.

плуг (*pl* -и́) plough.

плут (-а́) cheat, swindler; rogue. **плутова́тый** cunning. **плутовско́й** roguish; picaresque.

плуто́ний plutonium.

плыть (-ыву́, -ывёшь; плыл, -а́, -о) *impf* swim; float; sail.

плю́нуть (-ну) *pf of* **плева́ть**

плюс plus; advantage.

плюш plush.

плющ (-а́) ivy.

плюю́ *etc.*: *see* **плева́ть**

пляж beach.

пляса́ть (-яшу́, -я́шешь) *impf* (*pf* **с~**) dance. **пля́ска** dance; dancing.

пневмати́ческий pneumatic.

пневмони́я pneumonia.

пнуть (пну, пнёшь) *pf of* **пина́ть**

пня *etc.*: *see* **пень**

по *prep* **I.** +*dat* on; along; round, about; by; over; according to; in accordance with; for; in; at; by (reason of); on account of; from; **по понеде́льникам** on Mondays; **по профе́ссии** by profession; **по ра́дио** over the radio. **II.** +*dat or acc of cardinal number, forms distributive number*: **по́ два, по́ двое** in twos, two by two; **по пять рубле́й шту́ка** at five roubles each. **III.** +*acc* to, up to; for, to get; **идти́ по во́ду** go to get water; **по пе́рвое сентября́** up to (and including) 1st September. **IV.** +*prep* on, (immediately) after; **по прибы́тии** on arrival.

по- *pref* **I.** *in comb +dat of adjs, or with advs in* **-и**, *indicates manner, use of a named language, or accordance with the opinion or wish of*: **говори́ть по-ру́сски** speak Russian; **жить по-ста́рому** live in the old style; **по-мо́ему** in my opinion. **II.** *in comb with adjs and nn, indicates situation along or near a thing*: **помо́рье** seaboard, coastal region. **III.** *in comb with comp of adjs indicates a smaller degree of comparison*: **поме́ньше** a little less.

поба́иваться *impf* be rather afraid.

побе́г[1] flight; escape.

побе́г[2] shoot; sucker.

побегу́шки: **быть на побегу́шках** run errands.

побе́да victory. **победи́тель** *m* victor; winner. **победи́ть** *pf*

(*impf* **побежда́ть**) conquer; win. **побе́дный, победоно́сный** victorious, triumphant.
по|бежа́ть *pf.*
побежда́ть *impf of* **победи́ть**
по|беле́ть (-е́ю) *pf.* **по|бели́ть** *pf.* **побе́лка** whitewashing.
побере́жный coastal. **побере́жье** (sea-)coast.
по|беспоко́ить(ся *pf.*
побира́ться *impf* beg; live by begging.
по|би́ть(ся (-бью́(сь, -бьёшь(ся) *pf.* **по|благодари́ть** *pf.*
побла́жка indulgence.
по|бледне́ть (-е́ю) *pf.*
поблёскивать *impf* gleam.
побли́зости *adv* nearby.
побо́и (-ев) *pl* beating. **побо́ище** slaughter; bloody battle.
побо́рник champion, advocate.
поборо́ть (-рю́, -решь) *pf* overcome.
побо́чный secondary; done on the side; ~ **проду́кт** by-product.
по|брани́ться *pf.*
по|брата́ться *pf.* **побрати́м** twin town.
по|бре́згать *pf.* **по|бри́ть(ся** (-бре́ю(сь) *pf.*
побуди́тельный stimulating.
побуди́ть (-ужу́) *pf*, **побужда́ть** *impf* induce, prompt. **побужде́ние** motive; inducement.
побыва́ть *pf* have been, have visited; look in, visit. **побы́вка** leave. **побы́ть** (-бу́ду, -дешь; по́был, -а́, -о) *pf* stay (for a short time).
побью́(сь *etc.*: *see* **поби́ть(ся**
пова́диться (-а́жусь) get into the habit (of). **пова́дка** habit.
по|вали́ть(ся (-лю́(сь, -лишь(ся) *pf.*
пова́льно *adv* without exception. **пова́льный** general, mass.
по́вар (*pl* -а́) cook, chef. **пова́ренный** culinary; cookery, cooking.
по-ва́шему *adv* in your opinion.
пове́дать *pf* disclose; relate.
поведе́ние behaviour.
поведу́ *etc.*: *see* **повести́.**
по|везти́ (-зу́, -зёшь; -вёз, -ла́) *pf.* **повёл** *etc.*: *see* **повести́**
повелева́ть *impf* +*instr* rule (over); +*dat* command. **повеле́ние** command. **повели́тельный** imperious; imperative.
по|венча́ть(ся *pf.*
поверга́ть *impf*, **пове́ргнуть** (-ну; -ве́рг) *pf* throw down; plunge.
пове́ренная *sb* confidante. **пове́ренный** *sb* attorney; confidant; ~ **в дела́х** chargé d'affaires. **по|ве́рить**[1]. **пове́рить**[2] *pf* (*impf* **поверя́ть**) check; confide. **пове́рка** check; roll-call.
поверну́ть (-ну́, -нёшь) *pf*, **повёртывать** *impf* (*impf also* **повора́чивать**) turn; ~**ся** turn.
пове́рх *prep*+*gen* over. **пове́рхностный** surface, superficial. **пове́рхность** surface.
пове́рье (*gen pl* -ий) popular belief, superstition. **поверя́ть** *impf of* **пове́рить**[2]
пове́са playboy.
по|весели́ть (-е́ю) *pf.*
повесели́ть *pf* cheer (up), amuse; ~**ся** have fun.
пове́сить(ся (-ве́шу(сь) *pf of* **ве́шать(ся**
повествова́ние narrative, narration. **повествова́тельный** narrative. **повествова́ть** *impf*

+**о**+*prep* narrate, relate.
по|вести́ (-еду́, -едёшь; -вёл, -а́) *pf* (*impf* **поводи́ть**) +*instr* move.
пове́стка notice; summons; ~ (**дня**) agenda.
по́весть (*gen pl* -е́й) story, tale.
пове́трие epidemic; craze.
пове́шу *etc.*: *see* **пове́сить**.
по|вздо́рить *pf.*
повзросле́ть (-е́ю) *pf* grow up.
по|вида́ть(ся *pf.*
по-ви́димому apparently.
пови́дло jam.
по|вини́ться *pf.*
пови́нность duty, obligation; **во́инская** ~ conscription. **пови́нный** guilty.
повинова́ться *impf* & *pf* obey. **повинове́ние** obedience.
повиса́ть *impf*, **по|ви́снуть** (-ну; -ви́с) *pf* hang (on); hang down, droop.
повле́чь (-еку́, -ечёшь; -ёк, -ла́) *pf* (**за собо́й**) entail, bring in its train.
по|влия́ть *pf.*
по́вод[1] occasion, cause; **по** ~**у**+*gen* as regards, concerning.
по́вод[2] (*loc* -у́; *pl* -о́дья, -ьев) rein; **быть на** ~**у́ у**+*gen* be under the thumb of. **поводи́ть** (-ожу́, -о́дишь) *impf of* **повести́**. **поводо́к** (-дка́) leash. **поводы́рь** (-я́) *m* guide.
пово́зка cart; vehicle.
повора́чивать(ся *impf of* **поверну́ть(ся, повороти́ть(ся**; **повора́чивайся, -айтесь!** get a move on!
поворо́т turn, turning; bend; turning-point. **повороти́ть(ся** (-рочу́(сь, -ро́тишь(ся) *pf* (*impf* **повора́чивать(ся**) turn. **поворо́тливый** agile, nimble; manoeuvrable. **поворо́тный** turning; rotary; revolving.
по|вреди́ть (-ежу́) *pf*, **поврежда́ть** *impf* damage; injure; ~**ся** be damaged; be injured. **поврежде́ние** damage, injury.
повремени́ть *pf* wait a little; +**с**+*instr* delay over.
повседне́вный daily; everyday.
повсеме́стно *adv* everywhere. **повсеме́стный** universal, general.
повста́нец (-нца) rebel, insurgent. **повста́нческий** rebel; insurgent.
повсю́ду *adv* everywhere.
повторе́ние repetition. **повтори́ть** *pf*, **повторя́ть** *impf* repeat; ~**ся** repeat o.s.; be repeated; recur. **повто́рный** repeated.
повы́сить (-ы́шу) *pf*, **повыша́ть** *impf* raise, heighten; ~**ся** rise. **повыше́ние** rise; promotion. **повы́шенный** heightened, high.
повяза́ть (-яжу́, -я́жешь) *pf*, **повя́зывать** *impf* tie. **повя́зка** band; bandage.
по|гада́ть *pf.*
пога́нка toadstool. **пога́ный** foul; unclean.
погаса́ть *impf*, **по|га́снуть** (-ну) *pf* go out, be extinguished. **по|гаси́ть** (-ашу́, -а́сишь) *pf.* **погаша́ть** *impf* liquidate, cancel. **пога́шенный** used, cancelled, cashed.
погиба́ть *impf*, **по|ги́бнуть** (-ну; -ги́б) *pf* perish; be lost. **поги́бель** ruin. **поги́бший** lost; ruined; killed.
по|гла́дить (-а́жу) *pf.*
поглоти́ть (-ощу́, -о́тишь) *pf*, **поглоща́ть** *impf* swallow up; ab-

sorb. **поглоще́ние** absorption.

по|глупе́ть (-е́ю) *pf.*

по|гляде́ть (-яжу́) *pf.* **погля́дывать** *impf* glance (from time to time); +**за**+*instr* keep an eye on.

погна́ть (-гоню́, -го́нишь; -гна́л, -а́, -о) *pf* drive; **~ся за**+*instr* run after; start in pursuit of.

по|гну́ть(ся (-ну́(сь, -нёшь(ся) *pf.*

по|гнуша́ться *pf.*

поговори́ть *pf* have a talk.

погово́рка saying, proverb.

пого́да weather.

погоди́ть (-ожу́) *pf* wait a little; **немно́го погодя́** a little later.

поголо́вно *adv* one and all. **поголо́вный** general; capitation. **поголо́вье** number.

пого́н (*gen pl* -о́н) shoulder-strap.

пого́нщик driver. **погоню́** *etc.*: *see* **погна́ть. пого́ня** pursuit, chase. **погоня́ть** *impf* urge on, drive.

погорячи́ться (-чу́сь) *pf* get worked up.

пого́ст graveyard.

пограни́чник frontier guard. **пограни́чный** frontier.

по́греб (*pl* -а́) cellar. **погреба́льный** funeral. **погреба́ть** *impf of* **погрести́. погребе́ние** burial.

погрему́шка rattle.

погрести́[1] (-ебу́, -ебёшь; -рёб, -ла́) *pf* (*impf* **погреба́ть**) bury.

погрести́[2] (-ебу́, -ебёшь; -рёб, -ла́) *pf* row for a while.

погре́ть (-е́ю) *pf* warm; **~ся** warm o.s.

по|греши́ть (-шу́) *pf* sin; err. **погре́шность** error, mistake.

по|грози́ть(ся (-ожу́(сь) *pf.*

по|грубе́ть (-е́ю) *pf.*

погружа́ть *impf*, **по|грузи́ть** (-ужу́, -у́зишь) *pf* load; ship; dip, plunge, immerse; **~ся** sink, plunge; dive; be plunged, absorbed. **погруже́ние** submergence; immersion; dive. **погру́зка** loading; shipment.

погряза́ть *impf*, **по|гря́знуть** (-ну; -я́з) *pf* be bogged down; wallow.

по|губи́ть (-блю́, -бишь) *pf.*

по|гуля́ть *pf.*

под, подо *prep* **I.** +*acc or instr* under; near, close to; **взять по́д руку**+*acc* take the arm of; **~ ви́дом**+*gen* under the guise of; **по́д гору** downhill; **~ Москво́й** in the environs of Moscow. **II.** +*instr* occupied by, used as; (meant, implied) by; in, with; **говя́дина ~ хре́ном** beef with horse-radish. **III.** +*acc* towards; to (the accompaniment of); in imitation of; on; for, to serve as; **ему́ ~ пятьдеся́т (лет)** he is getting on for fifty.

подава́ть(ся (-даю́(сь, -даёшь(ся) *impf of* **пода́ть(ся**

подави́ть (-влю́, -вишь) *pf*, **подавля́ть** *impf* suppress; depress; overwhelm. **по|дави́ться** (-влю́сь, -вишься) *pf.* **подавле́ние** suppression; repression. **пода́вленность** depression. **пода́вленный** suppressed; depressed. **подавля́ющий** overwhelming.

пода́вно *adv* all the more.

пода́гра gout.

пода́льше *adv* a little further.

по|дари́ть (-рю́, -ришь) *pf.* **пода́рок** (-рка) present.

пода́тливый pliant, pliable.

по́дать (*gen pl* -е́й) tax. **пода́ть** (-а́м, -а́шь, -а́ст, -ади́м; по́дал, -а́, -о) *pf* (*impf* **подава́ть**) serve;

give; put, move, turn; put forward, present, hand in; **~ся** move; give way; yield; **+на**+*acc* set out for. **пода́ча** giving, presenting; serve; feed, supply. **пода́чка** handout, crumb. **подаю** *etc.*: *see* **подава́ть. подая́ние** alms.

подбега́ть *impf*, **подбежа́ть** (-егу́) *pf* come running (up).

подбива́ть *impf of* **подби́ть**

подберу́ *etc.*: *see* **подобра́ть.**

подбира́ть(ся *impf of* **подобра́ть(ся**

подби́ть (-добью́, -добьёшь) *pf* (*impf* **подбива́ть**) line; re-sole; bruise; put out of action; incite.

подбодри́ть *pf*, **подбодря́ть** *impf* cheer up, encourage; **~ся** cheer up, take heart.

подбо́р selection, assortment.

подборо́док (-дка) chin.

подбоче́нившись *adv* with hands on hips.

подбра́сывать *impf*, **подбро́сить** (-ро́шу) *pf* throw up.

подва́л cellar; basement. **подва́льный** basement, cellar.

подведу́ *etc.*: *see* **подвести́**

подвезти́ (-зу́, -зёшь; -вёз, -ла́) *pf* (*impf* **подвози́ть**) bring, take; give a lift.

подвене́чный wedding.

подверга́ть *impf*, **подве́ргнуть** (-ну; -ве́рг) *pf* subject; expose; **~ся** *+dat* undergo. **подве́рженный** subject, liable.

подверну́ть (-ну́, -нёшь) *pf*, **подвёртывать** *impf* turn up; tuck under; sprain; tighten; **~ся** be sprained; be turned up; be tucked under.

подве́сить (-е́шу) *pf* (*impf* **подве́шивать**) hang up, suspend.

подвесно́й hanging, suspended.

подвести́ (-еду́, -едёшь; -вёл, -а́) *pf* (*impf* **подводи́ть**) lead up, bring up; place (under); bring under, subsume; let down; **~ ито́ги** reckon up; sum up.

подве́шивать *impf of* **подве́сить**

по́двиг exploit, feat.

подвига́ть(ся *impf of* **подви́нуть(ся**

подви́жник religious ascetic; champion.

подвижно́й mobile; **~ соста́в** rolling-stock. **подви́жность** mobility. **подви́жный** mobile; lively; agile.

подвиза́ться *impf* (**в** *or* **на** *+prep*) work (in).

подви́нуть (-ну) *pf* (*impf* **подвига́ть**) move; push; advance; **~ся** move; advance.

подвла́стный *+dat* subject to; under the control of.

подво́да cart. **подводи́ть** (-ожу́, -о́дишь) *impf of* **подвести́**

подво́дн|ый submarine; underwater; **~ая скала́** reef.

подво́з transport; supply. **подвози́ть** (-ожу́, -о́зишь) *impf of* **подвезти́**

подворо́тня (*gen pl* -тен) gateway.

подво́х trick.

подвы́пивший tipsy.

подвяза́ть (-яжу́, -я́жешь) *pf*, **подвя́зывать** *impf* tie up. **подвя́зка** garter; suspender.

подгиба́ть *impf of* **подогну́ть**

подгляде́ть (-яжу́) *pf*, **подгля́дывать** *impf* peep; spy.

подгова́ривать *impf*, **подговори́ть** *pf* incite.

подгоню́ *etc.*: *see* **подогна́ть.**

подгоня́ть *impf of* **подогна́ть**
подгора́ть *impf*, **подгоре́ть** (-ри́т) *pf* get a bit burnt. **подгоре́лый** slightly burnt.
подготови́тельный preparatory. **подгото́вить** (-влю) *pf*, **подгота́вливать** *impf* prepare; **~ся** prepare, get ready. **подгото́вка** preparation, training.
поддава́ться (-даю́сь, -даёшься) *impf of* **подда́ться**
подда́кивать *impf* agree, assent.
по́дданный *sb* subject; citizen. **по́дданство** citizenship. **подда́ться** (-а́мся, -а́шься, -а́стся, -ади́мся; -а́лся, -ла́сь) *pf* (*impf* **поддава́ться**) yield, give way.
подде́лать *pf*, **подде́лывать** *impf* counterfeit; forge. **подде́лка** falsification; forgery; imitation. **подде́льный** false, counterfeit.
поддержа́ть (-жу́, -жишь) *pf*, **подде́рживать** *impf* support; maintain. **подде́ржка** support.
по|де́йствовать *pf*.
поде́лать *pf* do; **ничего́ не поде́лаешь** it can't be helped.
по|дели́ть(ся (-лю́(сь, -лишь(ся) *pf*.
поде́лка *pl* small (hand-made) articles.
подело́м *adv*: **~ ему́** (*etc.*) it serves him (*etc.*) right.
подённый by the day. **подёнщик, -ица** day-labourer.
подёргиваться *impf* twitch.
поде́ржанный second-hand.
подёрнуть (-нет) *pf* cover.
подеру́ *etc.*: *see* **подра́ть. по|дешеве́ть** (-е́ет) *pf*.
поджа́ривать(ся *impf*, **поджа́рить(ся** *pf* fry, roast, grill; toast. **поджа́ристый** brown(ed).
поджа́рый lean, wiry.
поджа́ть (-дожму́, -дожмёшь) *pf* (*impf* **поджима́ть**) draw in, draw under; **~ гу́бы** purse one's lips.
подже́чь (-дожгу́, -ожжёшь; -жёг, -дожгла́) *pf*, **поджига́ть** *impf* set fire to; burn. **поджига́тель** *m* arsonist; instigator.
поджида́ть *impf* (+*gen*) wait (for).
поджима́ть *impf of* **поджа́ть**
поджо́г arson.
подзаголо́вок (-вка) subtitle, sub-heading.
подзащи́тный *sb* client.
подземе́лье (*gen pl* -лий) cave; dungeon. **подзе́мный** underground.
подзову́ *etc.*: *see* **подозва́ть**
подзо́рная труба́ telescope.
подзыва́ть *impf of* **подозва́ть**
по|диви́ться (-влю́сь) *pf*.
подка́пывать(ся *impf of* **подкопа́ть(ся**
подкарау́ливать *impf*, **подкарау́лить** *pf* be on the watch (for).
подкати́ть (-ачу́, -а́тишь) *pf*, **подка́тывать** *impf* roll up, drive up; roll.
подка́шивать(ся *impf of* **подкоси́ть(ся**
подки́дывать *impf*, **подки́нуть** (-ну) *pf* throw up. **подки́дыш** foundling.
подкла́дка lining. **подкла́дывать** *impf of* **подложи́ть**
подкле́ивать *impf*, **подкле́ить** *pf* glue (up); mend.
подко́ва (horse-)shoe. **под|кова́ть** (-кую́, -ёшь) *pf*, **подко́вывать** *impf* shoe.
подко́жный hypodermic.
подкоми́ссия, подкомите́т sub-committee.

подко́п undermining; underground passage. **подкопа́ть** *pf* (*impf* **подка́пывать**) undermine; **~ся под**+*acc* undermine; burrow under.

подкоси́ть (-ошу́, -о́сишь) *pf* (*impf* **подка́шивать**) cut down; **~ся** give way.

подкра́дываться *impf of* **подкра́сться**

подкра́сить (-а́шу) *pf* (*impf* **подкра́шивать**) touch up; **~ся** make up lightly.

подкра́сться (-аду́сь, -адёшься) *pf* (*impf* **подкра́дываться**) sneak up.

подкра́шивать(ся *impf of* **подкра́сить(ся. подкра́шу** *etc.*: *see* **подкра́сить**

подкрепи́ть (-плю́) *pf*, **подкрепля́ть** *impf* reinforce; support; corroborate; fortify; **~ся** fortify o.s. **подкрепле́ние** confirmation; sustenance; reinforcement.

подкрути́ть (-учу́, -у́тишь) *pf* (*impf* **подкру́чивать**) tighten up.

по́дкуп bribery. **подкупа́ть** *impf*, **подкупи́ть** (-плю́, -пишь) *pf* bribe; win over.

подла́диться (-а́жусь) *pf*, **подла́живаться** *impf* +**к**+*dat* adapt o.s. to; make up to.

подла́мываться *impf of* **подломи́ться**

по́дле *prep*+*gen* by the side of, beside.

подлежа́ть (-жу́) *impf* +*dat* be subject to; **не подлежи́т сомне́нию** it is beyond doubt. **подлежа́щее** *sb* subject. **подлежа́щий**+*dat* subject to.

подлеза́ть *impf*, **подле́зть** (-зу; -е́з) *pf* crawl (under).

подле́сок (-ска) undergrowth.

подле́ц (-а́) scoundrel.

подлива́ть *impf of* **подли́ть. подли́вка** sauce, dressing; gravy.

подли́за *m* & *f* toady. **подлиза́ться** (-ижу́сь, -и́жешься) *pf*, **подли́зываться** *impf* +**к**+*dat* suck up to.

по́длинник original. **по́длинно** *adv* really. **по́длинный** genuine; authentic; original; real.

подли́ть (-долью́, -дольёшь; по́дли́л, -а́, -о) *pf* (*impf* **подлива́ть**) pour; add.

подло́г forgery.

подло́дка submarine.

подложи́ть (-жу́, -жишь) *pf* (*impf* **подкла́дывать**) add; **+под**+*acc* lay under; line.

подло́жный false, spurious; counterfeit, forged.

подлоко́тник arm (*of chair*).

подломи́ться (-о́мится) *pf* (*impf* **подла́мываться**) break; give way.

по́длость meanness, baseness; mean trick. **по́длый** (подл, -а́, -о) mean, base.

подма́зать (-а́жу) *pf*, **подма́зывать** *impf* grease; bribe.

подмасте́рье (*gen pl* -ьев) *m* apprentice.

подме́н, подме́на replacement. **подме́нивать** *impf*, **подмени́ть** (-ню́, -нишь) *pf*, **подменя́ть** *impf* replace.

подмести́ (-ету́, -етёшь; -мёл, -а́) *pf*, **подмета́ть**[1] *impf* sweep.

подмета́ть[2] *pf* (*impf* **подмётывать**) tack.

подме́тить (-е́чу) *pf* (*impf* **подмеча́ть**) notice.

подмётка sole.

подмётывать *impf of* **подме-**

тáть[2]. **подмечáть** *impf of* **подмéтить**

подмешáть *pf*, **подмéшивать** *impf* mix in, stir in.

подмúгивать *impf*, **подмигнýть** (-нý, -нёшь) *pf* +*dat* wink at.

подмóга help.

подмокáть *impf*, **подмóкнуть** (-нет; -мóк) *pf* get damp, get wet.

подморáживать *impf*, **подморóзить** *pf* freeze.

подмоскóвный (situated) near Moscow.

подмóстки (-ов) *pl* scaffolding; stage.

подмóченный damp; tarnished.

подмывáть *impf*, **подмы́ть** (-óю) *pf* wash; wash away; **егó так и подмывáет** he feels an urge (to).

подмы́шка armpit.

подневóльный dependent; forced.

поднестú (-сý, -сёшь; -ёс, -лá) *pf* (*impf* **подносúть**) present; take, bring.

поднимáть(ся *impf of* **поднять(ся**

подновúть (-влю) *pf*, **подновля́ть** *impf* renew, renovate.

подногóтная *sb* ins and outs.

поднóжие foot; pedestal. **поднóжка** running-board. **поднóжный корм** pasture.

поднóс tray. **подносúть** (-ошý, -óсишь) *impf of* **поднестú**. **подношéние** giving; present.

подня́тие raising. **подня́ть** (-нимý, -ни́мешь; пóднял, -á, -о) *pf* (*impf* **поднимáть, подымáть**) raise; lift (up); rouse; **~ся** rise; go up.

подо *see* **под**

подобáть *impf* befit, become. **подобáющий** proper.

подóбие likeness; similarity. **подóб|ный** like, similar; **и томý ~ое** and so on, and such like; **ничегó ~ого!** nothing of the sort!

подобострáстие servility. **подобострáстный** servile.

подобрáть (-дберý, -дберёшь; -брáл, -á, -о) *pf* (*impf* **подбирáть**) pick up; tuck up, put up; pick; **~ся** steal up.

подобью *etc.*: *see* **подбúть**

подогнáть (-дгоню, -дгóнишь; -áл, -á, -о) *pf* (*impf* **подгоня́ть**) drive; urge on; adjust.

подогнýть (-нý, -нёшь) *pf* (*impf* **подгибáть**) tuck in; bend under.

подогревáть *impf*, **подогрéть** (-éю) *pf* warm up.

пододвигáть *impf*, **пододвúнуть** (-ну) *pf* move up.

пододея́льник blanket cover; top sheet.

подожгý *etc.*: *see* **поджéчь**

подождáть (-дý, -дёшь; -áл, -á, -о) *pf* wait (+*gen or acc* for).

подожмý *etc.*: *see* **поджáть**

подозвáть (-дзовý, -дзовёшь; -áл, -á, -о) *pf* (*impf* **подзывáть**) call to; beckon.

подозревáемый suspected; suspect. **подозревáть** *impf* suspect. **подозрéние** suspicion. **подозрúтельный** suspicious.

по|доúть (-ою, -óишь) *pf*.

подойтú (-йдý, -йдёшь; -ошёл, -шлá) *pf* (*impf* **подходúть**) approach; come up; +*dat* suit, fit.

подокóнник window-sill.

подóл hem.

подóлгу *adv* for ages; for hours (*etc.*) on end.

подолью́ *etc.*: *see* **подли́ть**
подо́нки (-ов) *pl* dregs; scum.
подоплёка underlying cause.
подопру́ *etc.*: *see* **подпере́ть**
подо́пытный experimental.
подорва́ть (-рву́, -рвёшь; -а́л, -а́, -о) *pf* (*impf* **подрыва́ть**) undermine; blow up.
по|дорожа́ть *pf*.
подоро́жник plantain. **подоро́жный** roadside.
подосла́ть (-ошлю́, -ошлёшь) *pf* (*impf* **подсыла́ть**) send (secretly).
подоспева́ть *impf*, **подоспе́ть** (-е́ю) *pf* arrive, appear (in time).
подостла́ть (-дстелю́, -дсте́лешь) *pf* (*impf* **подстила́ть**) lay under.
подотде́л section, subdivision.
подотру́ *etc.*: *see* **подтере́ть**
подотчётный accountable.
по|до́хнуть (-ну) *pf* (*impf also* **подыха́ть**).
подохо́дный нало́г income-tax.
подо́шва sole; foot.
подошёл *etc.*: *see* **подойти́. подошлю́** *etc.*: *see* **подосла́ть подошью́** *etc.*: *see* **подши́ть.**
подпада́ть *impf*, **подпа́сть** (-аду́, -адёшь; -а́л) *pf* **под**+*acc* fall under.
подпева́ть *impf* (+*dat*) sing along (with).
подпере́ть (-допру́; -пёр) *pf* (*impf* **подпира́ть**) prop up.
подпи́ливать *impf*, **подпили́ть** (-лю́, -лишь) *pf* saw; saw a little off.
подпира́ть *impf of* **подпере́ть**
подписа́ние signing. **подписа́ть** (-ишу́, -и́шешь) *pf*, **подпи́сывать** *impf* sign; **~ся** sign; subscribe. **подпи́ска** subscription. **подписно́й** subscription. **подпи́счик** subscriber. **по́дпись** signature.
подплыва́ть *impf*, **подплы́ть** (-ыву́, -ывёшь; -плы́л, -а́, -о) *pf* **к**+*dat* swim *or* sail up to.
подполза́ть *impf*, **подползти́** (-зу́, -зёшь; -по́лз, -ла́) *pf* creep up (**к**+*dat* to); **+под**+*acc* crawl under.
подполко́вник lieutenant-colonel.
подпо́лье cellar; underground. **подпо́льный** underfloor; underground.
подпо́ра, подпо́рка prop, support.
подпо́чва subsoil.
подпра́вить (-влю) *pf*, **подправля́ть** *impf* touch up, adjust.
подпры́гивать *impf*, **подпры́гнуть** (-ну) *pf* jump up (and down).
подпуска́ть *impf*, **подпусти́ть** (-ущу́, -у́стишь) *pf* allow to approach.
подраба́тывать *impf*, **подрабо́тать** *pf* earn on the side; work up.
подра́внивать *impf of* **подровня́ть**
подража́ние imitation. **подража́ть** *impf* imitate.
подразделе́ние subdivision. **подраздели́ть** *pf*, **подразделя́ть** *impf* subdivide.
подразумева́ть *impf* imply, mean; **~ся** be meant, be understood.
подраста́ть *impf*, **подрасти́** (-ту́, -тёшь; -ро́с, -ла́) *pf* grow.
по|дра́ть(ся (-деру́(сь, -дерёшь(ся, -а́л(ся, -ла́(сь, -о́(сь *or* -о(сь) *pf*.
подре́зать (-е́жу) *pf*, **подреза́ть** *impf* cut; clip, trim.

подро́бно *adv* in detail. **подро́бность** detail. **подро́бный** detailed.

подровня́ть *pf* (*impf* **подра́внивать**) level, even; trim.

подро́с *etc.*: *see* **подрасти́**. **подро́сток** (-тка) adolescent; youth.

подро́ю *etc.*: *see* **подры́ть**

подруба́ть[1] *impf*, **подруби́ть** (-блю́, -бишь) *pf* chop down; cut short(er).

подруба́ть[2] *impf*, **подруби́ть** (-блю́, -бишь) *pf* hem.

подру́га friend; girlfriend. **по-дру́жески** *adv* in a friendly way. **подружи́ться** (-жу́сь) *pf* make friends.

по-друго́му *adv* differently.

подру́чный at hand; improvised; *sb* assistant.

подры́в undermining; injury.

подрыва́ть[1] *impf of* **подорва́ть**

подрыва́ть[2] *impf*, **подры́ть** (-ро́ю) *pf* undermine, sap. **подрывно́й** blasting, demolition; subversive.

подря́д[1] *adv* in succession.

подря́д[2] contract. **подря́дчик** contractor.

подса́живаться *impf of* **подсе́сть**

подса́ливать *impf of* **подсоли́ть**

подсве́чник candlestick.

подсе́сть (-ся́ду; -се́л) *pf* (*impf* **подса́живаться**) sit down (к+*dat* near).

подсказа́ть (-ажу́, -а́жешь) *pf*, **подска́зывать** *impf* prompt; suggest. **подска́зка** prompting.

подска́кивать *impf*, **подскочи́ть** (-чу́, -чишь) *pf* jump (up); soar; come running.

подсласти́ть (-ащу́) *pf*, **подсла́щивать** *impf* sweeten.

подсле́дственный under investigation.

подслу́шать *pf*, **подслу́шивать** *impf* overhear; eavesdrop, listen.

подсма́тривать *impf*, **подсмотре́ть** (-рю́, -ришь) *pf* spy (on).

подсне́жник snowdrop.

подсо́бный subsidiary; auxiliary.

подсо́вывать *impf of* **подсу́нуть**

подсозна́ние subconscious (mind). **подсозна́тельный** subconscious.

подсоли́ть (-со́ли́шь) *pf* (*impf* **подса́ливать**) add salt to.

подсо́лнечник sunflower. **подсо́лнечный** sunflower.

подсо́хнуть (-ну) *pf* (*impf* **подсыха́ть**) dry out a little.

подспо́рье help.

подста́вить (-влю) *pf*, **подставля́ть** *impf* put (under); bring up; expose; ~ **но́жку** +*dat* trip up. **подста́вка** stand; support. **подставно́й** false.

подстака́нник glass-holder.

подстелю́ *etc.*: *see* **подостла́ть**

подстерега́ть *impf*, **подстере́чь** (-егу́, -ежёшь; -рёг, -ла́) *pf* lie in wait for.

подстила́ть *impf of* **подостла́ть**. **подсти́лка** litter.

подстра́ивать *impf of* **подстро́ить**

подстрека́тель *m* instigator. **подстрека́тельство** instigation. **подстрека́ть** *impf*, **подстрекну́ть** (-ну́, -нёшь) *pf* instigate, incite.

подстре́ливать *impf*, **под-**

стрели́ть (-лю́, -лишь) *pf* wound.

подстригáть *impf*, **подстри́чь** (-игу́, -ижёшь; -и́г) *pf* cut; clip, trim; **~ся** have a hair-cut.

подстрóить *pf* (*impf* **подстрáивать**) build on; cook up.

подстрóчн|ый literal; **~ое примечáние** footnote.

пóдступ approach. **подступáть** *impf*, **подступи́ть** (-плю́, -пишь) *pf* approach; **~ся к**+*dat* approach.

подсуди́мый *sb* defendant; the accused. **подсу́дный**+*dat* under the jurisdiction of.

подсу́нуть (-ну) *pf* (*impf* **подсóвывать**) put, shove; palm off.

подсчёт calculation; count. **подсчитáть** *pf*, **подсчи́тывать** count (up); calculate.

подсылáть *impf of* **подослáть**.

подсыхáть *impf of* **подсóхнуть**. **подся́ду** *etc*.: *see* **подсéсть**. **подтáлкивать** *impf of* **подтолкну́ть**

подтáскивать *impf of* **подтащи́ть**

подтасовáть *pf*, **подтасóвывать** *impf* shuffle unfairly; juggle with.

подтáчивать *impf of* **подточи́ть**

подтащи́ть (-щу́, -щишь) *pf* (*impf* **подтáскивать**) drag up.

подтверди́ть (-ржу́) *pf*, **подтверждáть** *impf* confirm; corroborate. **подтверждéние** confirmation, corroboration.

подтёк bruise. **подтекáть** *impf of* **подтéчь**; leak.

подтерéть (-дотру́, -дотрёшь; подтёр) *pf* (*impf* **подтирáть**) wipe (up).

подтéчь (-ечёт; -тёк, -лá) *pf* (*impf* **подтекáть**) **под**+*acc* flow under.

подтирáть *impf of* **подтерéть**

подтолкну́ть (-ну́, -нёшь) *pf* (*impf* **подтáлкивать**) push; urge on.

подточи́ть (-чу́, -чишь) *pf* (*impf* **подтáчивать**) sharpen; eat away; undermine.

подтру́нивать *impf*, **подтруни́ть** *pf* **над**+*instr* tease.

подтя́гивать *impf*, **подтяну́ть** (-ну́, -нешь) *pf* tighten; pull up; move up; **~ся** tighten one's belt *etc*.; move up; pull o.s. together. **подтя́жки** (-жек) *pl* braces, suspenders. **подтя́нутый** smart.

по|ду́мать *pf* think (for a while). **поду́мывать** *impf*+*inf* *or* **о**+*prep* think about.

по|ду́ть (-у́ю) *pf*.

поду́шка pillow; cushion.

подхали́м *m* toady. **подхали́мство** grovelling.

подхвати́ть (-ачу́, -áтишь) *pf*, **подхвáтывать** *impf* catch (up), pick up, take up.

подхлестну́ть (-ну, -нёшь) *pf*, **подхлёстывать** *impf* whip up.

подхóд approach. **подходи́ть** (-ожу́, -óдишь) *impf of* **подойти́**. **подходя́щий** suitable.

подцепи́ть (-плю́, -пишь) *pf*, **подцепля́ть** *impf* hook on; pick up.

подчáс *adv* sometimes.

подчёркивать *impf*, **подчеркну́ть** (-ну́, -нёшь) *pf* underline; emphasize.

подчинéние subordination; submission. **подчинённый** subordinate. **подчини́ть** *pf*, **подчиня́ть** *impf* subordinate, subject; **~ся** +*dat* submit to.

подшивáть *impf of* **подши́ть**.

подши́вка hemming; lining; soling.

подши́пник bearing.

подши́ть (-дошью́, -дошьёшь) *pf* (*impf* **подшива́ть**) hem, line; sole.

подшути́ть (-учу́, -у́тишь) *pf*, **подшу́чивать** *impf* **над**+*instr* mock; play a trick on.

подъе́ду *etc.*: *see* **подъе́хать**

подъе́зд entrance, doorway; approach. **подъезжа́ть** *impf of* **подъе́хать**

подъём lifting; raising; ascent; climb; enthusiasm; instep; reveille. **подъёмник** lift, elevator, hoist. **подъёмный** lifting; ~ **кран** crane; ~ **мост** drawbridge.

подъе́хать (-е́ду) *pf* (*impf* **подъезжа́ть**) drive up.

подыма́ть(ся *impf of* **подня́ть(ся**

подыска́ть (-ыщу́, -ы́щешь) *pf*, **поды́скивать** *impf* seek (out).

подыто́живать *impf*, **подыто́жить** (-жу) *pf* sum up.

подыха́ть *impf of* **подо́хнуть**

подыша́ть (-шу́, -шишь) *pf* breathe.

поеда́ть *impf of* **пое́сть**

поеди́нок (-нка) duel.

по́езд (*pl* -а́) train. **пое́здка** trip.

пое́сть (-е́м, -е́шь, -е́ст, -еди́м; -е́л) *pf* (*impf* **поеда́ть**) eat, eat up; have a bite to eat.

по|е́хать (-е́ду) *pf* go; set off.

по|жале́ть (-е́ю) *pf.*

по|жа́ловать(ся *pf.* **пожа́луй** *adv* perhaps. **пожа́луйста** *partl* please; you're welcome.

пожа́р fire. **пожа́рище** scene of a fire. **пожа́рник, пожа́рный** *sb* fireman. **пожа́рн|ый** fire; **~ая кома́нда** fire-brigade; **~ая ле́стница** fire-escape; **~ая маши́на** fire-engine.

пожа́тие handshake. **пожа́ть**[1] (-жму́, -жмёшь) *pf* (*impf* **пожима́ть**) press; ~ **ру́ку**+*dat* shake hands with; ~ **плеча́ми** shrug one's shoulders.

пожа́ть[2] (-жну́, -жнёшь) *pf* (*impf* **пожина́ть**) reap.

пожела́ние wish, desire. **по|жела́ть** *pf.*

по|желте́ть (-е́ю) *pf.*

по|жени́ть (-ню́, -нишь) *pf.* **пожени́ться** (-же́нимся) *pf* get married.

поже́ртвование donation. **по|же́ртвовать** *pf.*

пожива́ть *impf* live; **как (вы) пожива́ете?** how are you (getting on)? **пожи́зненный** life(long).

пожило́й elderly.

пожима́ть *impf of* **пожа́ть**. **пожина́ть** *impf of* **пожа́ть**[2]. **пожира́ть** *impf of* **пожра́ть**

пожи́тки (-ов) *pl* belongings.

пожи́ть (-иву́, -ивёшь; по́жил, -а́, -о) *pf.* live for a while; stay.

пожму́ *etc.*: *see* **пожа́ть**[1]. **пожну́** *etc.*: *see* **пожа́ть**[2]

пожра́ть (-ру́, -рёшь; -а́л, -а́, -о) *pf* (*impf* **пожира́ть**) devour.

по́за pose.

по|забо́титься (-о́чусь) *pf.*

позабыва́ть *impf*, **позабы́ть** (-у́ду) *pf* forget all about.

по|зави́довать *pf.* **по|за́втракать** *pf.*

позавчера́ *adv* the day before yesterday.

позади́ *adv* & *prep*+*gen* behind.

по|заи́мствовать *pf.*

позапро́шлый before last.

по|зва́ть (-зову́, -зовёшь; -а́л, -а́, -о) *pf.*

позволе́ние permission. **поз-**

волительный permissible. **позволить** *pf*, **позволять** *impf* +*dat* allow, permit; **позволь(те)** allow me; excuse me.

по|звонить *pf.*

позвонок (-нка) vertebra. **позвоночник** spine. **позвоночн|ый** spinal; vertebrate; **~ые** *sb pl* vertebrates.

позднее *adv* later. **поздний** late; **поздно** it is late.

по|здороваться *pf.* **поздравить** (-влю) *pf*, **поздравлять** *impf* **с**+*instr* congratulate on. **поздравление** congratulation.

по|зеленеть (-еет) *pf.*

позже *adv* later (on).

позировать *impf* pose.

позитив positive. **позитивный** positive.

позиция position.

познавательный cognitive.

познавать (-наю, -наёшь) *impf of* **познать**

по|знакомить(ся (-млю(сь) *pf.*

познание cognition. **познать** *pf* (*impf* **познавать**) get to know.

позолота gilding. **по|золотить** (-лочу) *pf.*

позор shame, disgrace. **позорить** *impf* (*pf* **о~**) disgrace; **~ся** disgrace o.s. **позорный** shameful.

поиграть *pf* play (for a while).

поимённо *adv* by name.

поимка capture.

поинтересоваться *pf* be curious.

поискать (-ищу, -ищешь) *pf* look for. **поиски** (-ов) *pl* search.

поистине *adv* indeed.

поить (пою, поишь) *impf* (*pf* **на~**) give something to drink; water.

пойду *etc.*: *see* **пойти**

пойло swill.

поймать *pf of* **ловить**. **пойму** *etc.*: *see* **понять**

пойти (-йду, -йдёшь; пошёл, -шла) *pf of* **идти, ходить**; go, walk; begin to walk; +*inf* begin; **пошёл!** off you go! I'm off; **пошёл вон!** be off!

пока *adv* for the present; cheerio; **~ что** in the meanwhile. **пока** *conj* while; **~ не** until.

показ showing, demonstration.

показание testimony, evidence; reading. **показатель** *m* index.

показательный significant; model; demonstration. **показать** (-ажу, -ажешь) *pf*, **показывать** *impf* show. **по|казаться** (-ажусь, -ажешься) *pf*, **показываться** *impf* show o.s.; appear.

показной for show; ostentatious. **показуха** show.

по|калечить(ся (-чу(сь) *pf.*

покамест *adv* & *conj* for the present, while; meanwhile.

по|карать *pf.*

по|кататься *pf.*

покатить (-чу, -тишь) *pf* start (rolling); **~ся** start rolling.

покатый sloping; slanting.

покачать *pf* rock, swing; **~ головой** shake one's head. **покачивать** rock slightly; **~ся** rock; stagger. **покачнуть** (-ну, -нёшь) shake; rock; **~ся** sway, totter, lurch.

покашливать *impf* have a slight cough.

покаяние confession; repentance. **по|каяться** *pf.*

поквитаться *pf* be quits; get even.

покидать *impf*, **покинуть** (-ну)

pf leave; abandon. **покúнутый** deserted.

покладáя: **не ~ рук** untiringly.

поклáдистый complaisant, obliging.

поклóн bow; greeting; regards. **поклонéние** worship. **поклонúться** (-нюсь, -нишься) *pf of* **клáняться. поклóнник** admirer; worshipper. **поклоня́ться** *impf* +*dat* worship.

по|кля́сться (-янýсь, -нёшься; -я́лся, -лáсь) *pf*.

покóиться *impf* rest, repose. **покóй** rest, peace; room. **покóйник, -ица** the deceased. **покóйный** calm, quiet; deceased.

по|колебáть(ся (-éблю(сь) *pf*.

поколéние generation.

по|колотúть(ся (-очý(сь, -óтишь(ся) *pf*.

покóнчить (-чу) *pf* **с**+*instr* finish; put an end to; **~ с собóй** commit suicide.

покорéние conquest. **покорúть** *pf* (*impf* **покоря́ть**) subdue; conquer; **~ся** submit.

по|кормúть(ся (-млю(сь, -мишь(ся) *pf*.

покóрный humble; submissive, obedient.

по|корóбить(ся (-блю(сь) *pf*.

покоря́ть(ся *impf of* **покорúть(ся**

покóс mowing; meadow(-land).

покосúвшийся rickety, ramshackle. **по|косúть(ся** (-ошý(сь) *pf*.

по|крáсить (-áшу) *pf*. **покрáска** painting, colouring.

по|краснéть (-éю) *pf*. **по|кривúть(ся** (-влю(сь) *pf*.

покрóв cover. **покровúтель** *m*, **покровúтельница** patron; sponsor. **покровúтельственный** protective; patronizing. **покровúтельство** protection, patronage. **покровúтельствовать** *impf* +*dat* protect, patronize.

покрóй cut.

покрошúть (-шý, -шишь) *pf* crumble; chop.

покрутúть (-учý, -ýтишь) *pf* twist.

покрывáло cover; bedspread; veil. **покрывáть** *impf*, **по|кры́ть** (-рóю) *pf* cover; **~ся** cover o.s.; get covered. **покры́тие** covering; surfacing; payment. **покры́шка** cover; tyre.

покупáтель *m* buyer; customer. **покупáть** *impf of* **купúть. покýпка** purchase. **покупнóй** bought, purchased; purchase.

по|курúть (-рю́, -ришь) *pf* have a smoke.

по|кýшать *pf*.

покушéние +**на**+*acc* attempted assassination of.

пол[1] (*loc* -ý; *pl* -ы́) floor.

пол[2] sex.

пол- *in comb with n in gen, in oblique cases usu* **полу-**, half.

полá (*pl* -ы) flap; **из-под полы́** on the sly.

полагáть *impf* suppose, think. **полагáться** *impf of* **положúться; полагáется** *impers* one is supposed to; +*dat* it is due to.

по|лáкомить(ся (-млю(сь) *pf*.

полгóда (полугóда) *m* half a year.

пóлдень (-дня *or* -лýдня) *m* noon. **полднéвный** *adj*.

пóле (*pl* -я́, -éй) field; ground; margin; brim. **полев|óй** field; **~ы́е цветы́** wild flowers.

полежáть (-жý) *pf* lie down for a while.

полéзн|ый useful; helpful; good, wholesome; **~ая нагрýзка** payload.

по|лéзть (-зу; -лéз) *pf.*

полемизúровать *impf* debate, engage in controversy. **полéмика** controversy; polemics. **полемúческий** polemical.

по|ленúться (-ню́сь, -нишься) *pf.*

полéно (*pl* -énья, -ьев) log.

полёт flight. **по|летéть** (-лечý) *pf.*

пóлзать *indet impf*, **ползтú** (-зý, -зёшь; полз, -лá) *det impf* crawl, creep; ooze; fray. **ползýчий** creeping.

поли- *in comb* poly-.

поливáть(ся *impf of* **полúть(ся. полúвка** watering.

полигáмия polygamy.

полиглóт polyglot.

полиграфúческий printing. **полиграфúя** printing.

полигóн range.

поликлúника polyclinic.

полимéр polymer.

полиня́лый faded. **по|линя́ть** *pf.*

полиомиелúт poliomyelitis

полировáть *impf* (*pf* **от~**) polish. **полирóвка** polishing; polish.

полит- *abbr in comb* (*of* **политúческий**) political. **политзаключённый** *sb* political prisoner.

политехнúческий polytechnic.

полúтик politician. **полúтика** policy; politics. **политúческий** political; **политúчески коррéктнтый** politically correct.

полúть (-лью, -льёшь; пóлил, -á, -o) *pf* (*impf* **поливáть**) pour over; water; **~ся** *+instr* pour over o.s.

полицéйский police; *sb* policeman. **полúция** police.

полúчн|ое *sb*: **с ~ым** red-handed.

полк (-á, *loc* -ý) regiment.

пóлка shelf; berth.

полкóвник colonel. **полковóдец** (-дца) commander; general. **полковóй** regimental.

пол-лúтра half a litre.

полнéть (-éю) *impf* (*pf* **по~**) put on weight.

пóлно *adv* that's enough! stop it!

полно- *in comb* full; completely. **полнолýние** full moon. **~метрáжный** full-length. **~прáвный** enjoying full rights; competent. **~цéнный** of full value.

полномóчие (*usu pl*) authority, power. **полномóчный** plenipotentiary.

пóлностью *adv* in full; completely. **полнотá** completeness; corpulence.

пóлночь (-л(ý)ночи) midnight.

пóлный (-лон, -лнá, пóлнó) full; complete; plump.

половúк (-á) mat, matting.

половúна half; **два с половúной** two and a half; **~ шестóго** half-past five. **половúнка** half.

половúца floor-board.

половóдье high water.

половóй[1] floor.

половóй[2] sexual.

полóгий gently sloping.

положéние position; situation; status; regulations; thesis; provisions. **полóженный** agreed; determined. **полóжим** let us assume; suppose. **положúтельный** positive. **положúть** (-жý,

-жишь) *pf* (*impf* **класть**) put; lay (down); **~ся** (*impf* **полага́ться**) rely.

по́лоз (*pl* -о́зья, -ьев) runner.

по|лома́ть(ся *pf.* **поло́мка** breakage.

полоса́ (*acc* по́лосу́; *pl* по́лосы, -ло́с, -а́м) stripe; strip; band; region; belt; period. **полоса́тый** striped.

полоска́ть (-ощу́, -о́щешь) *impf* (*pf* **вы́~**, **от~**, **про~**) rinse; **~ го́рло** gargle; **~ся** paddle; flap.

по́лость[1] (*gen pl* -е́й) cavity.

по́лость[2] (*gen pl* -е́й) travelling rug.

полоте́нце (*gen pl* -нец) towel.

полотёр floor-polisher.

поло́тнище width; panel. **полотно́** (*pl* -а, -тен) linen; canvas. **полотня́ный** linen.

поло́ть (-лю́, -лешь) *impf* (*pf* **вы́~**) weed.

полощу́ *etc.*: *see* **полоска́ть**

полти́нник fifty copecks.

полтора́ (-лу́тора) *m* & *neut*, **полторы́** (-лу́тора) *f* one and a half. **полтора́ста** (полу́т-) a hundred and fifty.

полу-[1] *see* **пол-**

полу-[2] *in comb* half-, semi-, demi-. **полуботи́нок** (-нка; *gen pl* -нок) shoe. **~го́дие** half a year. **~годи́чный** six months', lasting six months. **~година́льный** six-month-old. **~годово́й** half-yearly, six-monthly. **~гра́мотный** semi-literate. **~защи́тник** half-back. **~кру́г** semicircle. **~кру́глый** semicircular. **~ме́сяц** crescent (moon). **~мра́к** semi-darkness. **~но́чный** midnight. **~о́стров** peninsula. **~откры́тый** ajar. **~проводни́к** (-а́) semi-conductor, transistor. **~ста́нок** (-нка) halt. **~тьма́** semi-darkness. **~фабрика́т** semi-finished product, convenience food. **~фина́л** semi-final. **~часово́й** half-hourly. **~ша́рие** hemisphere. **~шу́бок** (-бка) sheepskin coat.

полу́денный midday.

получа́тель *m* recipient. **получа́ть** *impf*, **получи́ть** (-чу́, -чишь) *pf* get, receive, obtain; **~ся** come, turn up; turn out; **из э́того ничего́ не получи́лось** nothing came of it. **получе́ние** receipt. **полу́чка** receipt; pay(-packet).

полу́чше *adv* a little better.

полчаса́ (получа́са) *m* half an hour.

по́лчище horde.

по́лый hollow; flood.

по|лысе́ть (-е́ю) *pf.*

по́льза use; benefit, profit; **в по́льзу**+*gen* in favour of, on behalf of. **по́льзование** use. **по́льзоваться** *impf* (*pf* **вос~**) +*instr* make use of, utilize; profit by; enjoy.

по́лька Pole; polka. **по́льский** Polish; *sb* polonaise.

по|льсти́ть(ся (-льщу́(сь)

полью́ *etc. see* **поли́ть**

По́льша Poland.

полюби́ть (-блю́, -бишь) *pf* come to like; fall in love with.

по|любова́ться (-бу́юсь) *pf.*

полюбо́вный amicable.

по|любопы́тствовать *pf.*

по́люс pole.

поля́к Pole.

поля́на glade, clearing.

поляриза́ция polarization. **поля́рник** polar explorer. **поля́рн|ый** polar; **~ая звезда́** pole-star.

пом- *abbr in comb* (*of* **помо́щ-**

ник) assistant. **~нáч** assistant chief, assistant head.
помáда pomade; lipstick.
помазáние anointment. **по|мá-зать(ся** (-áжу(сь) *pf.* **помазóк** (-зкá) small brush.
помалéньку *adv* gradually; gently; modestly; so-so.
помáлкивать *impf* hold one's tongue.
по|манúть (-нió, -нишь) *pf.*
помáрка blot; pencil mark; correction.
по|мáслить *pf.*
помахáть (-машý, -мáшешь) *pf*, **помáхивать** *impf* +*instr* wave; wag.
помéдлить *pf* +с+*instr* delay.
помéньше a little smaller; a little less.
по|менять(ся *pf.*
померéть (-мрý, -мрёшь; -мер, -лá, -ло) *pf* (*impf* **помирáть**) die.
по|мерéщиться (-щусь) *pf.*
по|мéрить *pf.*
помертвéлый deathly pale.
по|мертвéть (-éю) *pf.*
поместúть (-ещý) *pf* (*impf* **помещáть**) accommodate; place, locate; invest; **~ся** lodge; find room. **помéстье** (*gen pl* -тий, -тьям) estate.
пóмесь cross(-breed), hybrid.
помёт dung; droppings; litter, brood.
помéта, помéтка mark, note.
по|мéтить (-éчу) *pf* (*impf also* **помечáть**) mark; date; **~ гáлочкой** tick.
помéха hindrance; obstacle; *pl* interference.
помечáть *impf of* **помéтить**
помéшанный mad; *sb* lunatic. **помешáтелство** madness; craze. **по|мешáть** *pf.* **помешáться** *pf* go mad.
помещáть *impf of* **поместúть.**
помещáться *impf of* **поместúться**; be (situated); be accommodated, find room. **помещéние** premises; apartment, room, lodging; location; investment. **помéщик** landowner.
помидóр tomato.
помúлование forgiveness. **помúловать** *pf* forgive.
помúмо *prep*+*gen* apart from; besides; without the knowledge of.
поминáть *impf of* **помянýть; не ~ лúхом** remember kindly. **помúнки** (-нок) *pl* funeral repast.
помирáть *impf of* **померéть**
по|мирúть(ся *pf.*
пóмнить *impf* remember.
помогáть *impf of* **помóчь**
по-мóему *adv* in my opinion.
помóи (-ев) *pl* slops. **помóйка** (*gen pl* -óек) rubbish dump. **помóйный** slop.
помóл grinding.
помóлвка betrothal.
по|молúться (-люсь, -лишься) *pf.* **по|молодéть** (-éю) *pf.*
помолчáть (-чý) *pf* be silent for a time.
помóрье: *see* **по-** II.
по|мóрщиться (-щусь) *pf.*
помóст dais; rostrum.
по|мочúться (-чýсь, -чишься) *pf.*
помóчь (-огý, -óжешь; -óг, -лá) *pf* (*impf* **помогáть**) (+*dat*) help. **помóщник, помóщница** assistant. **пóмощь** help; **на ~!** help!
помóю *etc.*: *see* **помы́ть**
пóмпа pump.
помутнéние dimness, clouding.
помчáться (-чýсь) *pf* rush; dart off.

помыка́ть *impf* *+instr* order about.
по́мысел (-сла) intention; thought.
по|мы́ть(ся (-мо́ю(сь) *pf*.
помяну́ть (-ну́, -нешь) *pf* (*impf* **помина́ть**) mention; pray for.
помя́тый crumpled. **по|мя́ться** (-мнётся) *pf*.
по|наде́яться (-е́юсь) *pf* count, rely.
пона́добиться (-блюсь) *pf* be *or* become necessary; **если пона́добится** if necessary.
понапра́сну *adv* in vain.
понаслы́шке *adv* by hearsay.
по-настоя́щему *adv* properly, truly.
поннача́лу *adv* at first.
понево́ле *adv* willynilly; against one's will.
понеде́льник Monday.
понемно́гу, понемно́жку *adv* little by little.
по|нести́(сь (-су́(сь, -сёшь(ся; -нёс(ся, -ла́(сь) *pf*.
понижа́ть *impf*, **пони́зить** (-ни́жу) *pf* lower; reduce; **~ся** fall, drop, go down. **пониже́ние** fall; lowering; reduction.
поника́ть *impf*, **по|ни́кнуть** (-ну; -ни́к) *pf* droop, wilt.
понима́ние understanding. **понима́ть** *impf of* **поня́ть**
по-но́вому *adv* in a new fashion.
поно́с diarrhoea.
поноси́ть[1] (-ошу́, -о́сишь) *pf* carry; wear.
поноси́ть[2] (-ошу́, -о́сишь) *impf* abuse (*verbally*).
поно́шенный worn; threadbare.
по|нра́виться (-влюсь) *pf*.
понто́н pontoon.
пону́дить (-у́жу) *pf*, **понужда́ть** *impf* compel.
понука́ть *impf* urge on.
пону́рить *pf*: **~ го́лову** hang one's head. **пону́рый** downcast.
по|ню́хать *pf*. **понюшка: ~ табаку́** pinch of snuff.
поня́тие concept; notion, idea. **поня́тливый** bright, quick. **поня́тн|ый** understandable, comprehensible; clear; **~о** naturally; **~о?** (do you) see? **поня́ть** (пойму́, -мёшь; по́нял, -а́, -о) *pf* (*impf* **понима́ть**) understand; realize.
по|обе́дать *pf*. **по|обеща́ть** *pf*.
поо́даль *adv* at some distance.
поодино́чке *adv* one by one.
поочерёдно *adv* in turn.
поощре́ние encouragement. **поощри́ть** *pf*, **поощря́ть** *impf* encourage.
поп (-а́) priest.
попада́ние hit. **попада́ть(ся** *impf of* **попа́сть(ся**
попадья́ priest's wife.
попа́ло: *see* **попа́сть. по|па́риться** *pf*.
попа́рно *adv* in pairs, two by two.
попа́сть (-аду́, -адёшь; -а́л) *pf* (*impf* **попада́ть**) **+в+***acc* hit; get (in)to, find o.s. in; **+на+***acc* hit upon, come on; **не туда́ ~** get the wrong number; **~ся** be caught; find o.s.; turn up; **что попадётся** anything. **попа́ло** *with prons & advs*: **где ~** anywhere; **как ~** anyhow; **что ~** the first thing to hand.
поперёк *adv* & *prep+gen* across.
попереме́нно *adv* in turns.
попере́чник diameter. **попере́чн|ый** transverse, diamet-

rical, cross; **~ый разре́з, ~ое сече́ние** cross-section.
поперхну́ться (-ну́сь, -нёшься) *pf* choke.
по|пе́рчить (-чу́) *pf.*
попече́ние care; charge; **на попече́нии**+*gen* in the care of. **попечи́тель** *m* guardian, trustee.
попира́ть *impf* (*pf* **попра́ть**) trample on; flout.
попи́ть (-пью́, -пьёшь; по́пил, -ла, по́пи́ло) *pf* have a drink.
поплаво́к (-вка́) float.
попла́кать (-а́чу) *pf* cry a little.
по|плати́ться (-чу́сь, -тишься) *pf.*
поплы́ть (-ыву́, -ывёшь; -ы́л, -ыла́, -о) *pf.* start swimming.
попо́йка drinking-bout.
попола́м *adv* in two, in half; half-and-half.
поползнове́ние half a mind; pretension(s).
пополне́ние replenishment; reinforcement. **по|полне́ть** (-е́ю) *pf.* **попо́лнить** *pf*, **пополня́ть** *impf* replenish; re-stock; reinforce.
пополу́дни *adv* in the afternoon; p.m.
попо́на horse-cloth.
по|по́тчевать (-чую) *pf.*
поправи́мый rectifiable. **попра́вить** (-влю) *pf*, **поправля́ть** *impf* repair; correct, put right; set straight; **~ся** correct o.s.; get better, recover; improve. **попра́вка** correction; repair; adjustment; recovery.
попра́ть *pf of* **попира́ть**
по-пре́жнему *adv* as before.
попрёк reproach. **попрека́ть** *impf*, **попрекну́ть** (-ну́, -нёшь) *pf* reproach.
по́прище field; walk of life.
по|про́бовать *pf.* **по|проси́ть(ся** (-ошу́(сь, -о́сишь(ся) *pf.*
по́просту *adv* simply; without ceremony.
попроша́йка *m* & *f* cadger. **попроша́йничать** *impf* cadge.
попроща́ться *pf* (+с+*instr*) say goodbye (to).
попры́гать *pf* jump, hop.
попуга́й parrot.
популя́рность popularity. **популя́рный** popular.
попусти́тельство connivance.
по-пусто́му, по́пусту *adv* in vain.
попу́тно *adv* at the same time; in passing. **попу́тный** passing. **попу́тчик** fellow-traveller.
по|пыта́ться *pf.* **попы́тка** attempt.
по|пя́титься (-я́чусь) *pf.* **попя́тный** backward; **идти́ на ~** go back on one's word.
по́ра[1] pore.
пора́[2] (*acc* -у; *pl* -ы, пор, -а́м) time; it is time; **до каки́х пор?** till when?; **до сих пор** till now; **с каки́х пор?** since when?
порабо́тать *pf* do some work.
поработи́ть (-ощу́) *pf*, **порабоща́ть** *impf* enslave. **порабоще́ние** enslavement.
поравня́ться *pf* come alongside.
по|ра́довать(ся *pf.*
поража́ть *impf*, **по|рази́ть** (-ажу́) *pf* hit; strike; defeat; affect; astonish; **~ся** be astounded. **пораже́ние** defeat.
порази́тельный striking; astonishing.
по-ра́зному *adv* differently.
пора́нить *pf* wound; injure.
порва́ть (-ву́, -вёшь; -ва́л, -а́, -о) *pf* (*impf* **порыва́ть**) tear (up);

break, break off; **~ся** tear; break (off).
по|редéть (-éет) *pf.*
порéз cut. **порéзать** (-éжу) *pf* cut; **~ся** cut o.s.
порéй leek.
по|рекомендовáть *pf.*
по|ржавéть (-éет) *pf.*
пóристый porous.
порицáние reprimand. **порицáть** *impf* reprimand.
пóрка flogging.
пóровну *adv* equally.
порóг threshold; rapids.
порóда breed, race, species; (*also* **гóрная порóда**) rock. **порóдистый** thoroughbred. **породи́ть** (-ожý) *pf* (*impf* **порождáть**) give birth to; give rise to.
по|родни́ть(ся *pf.* **порóдный** pedigree.
порождáть *impf of* **породи́ть**
пóрознь *adv* separately, apart.
порóй, порóю *adv* at times.
порóк vice; defect.
поросёнок (-нка; *pl* -сята, -сят) piglet.
пóросль shoots; young wood.
порóть[1] (-рю, -решь) *impf* (*pf* **вы́~**) thrash; whip.
порóть[2] (-рю, -решь) *impf* (*pf* **рас~**) undo, unpick; **~ся** come unstitched.
пóрох (*pl* ~á) gunpowder, powder. **пороховóй** powder.
порóчить (-чу) *impf* (*pf* **о~**) discredit; smear. **порóчный** vicious, depraved; faulty.
пороши́ть (-ши́т) *impf* snow slightly.
порошóк (-шкá) powder.
порт (*loc* -ý; *pl* -ы, -óв) port.
портати́вный portable; **~ компью́тер** laptop; **~ телефóн** mobile phone.
портвéйн port (wine).
пóртить (-чу) *impf* (*pf* **ис~**) spoil; corrupt; **~ся** deteriorate; go bad.
портни́ха dressmaker. **портнóвский** tailor's. **портнóй** *sb* tailor.
портóвый port.
портрéт portrait.
портсигáр cigarette-case.
португáлец (-льца), **-лка** Portuguese. **Португáлия** Portugal. **португáльский** Portuguese.
портфéль *m* brief-case; portfolio.
портьéра curtain(s), portière.
портя́нка foot-binding; puttee
поругáние desecration.
порýганный desecrated; outraged. **поругáть** *pf* scold, swear at; **~ся** swear; fall out.
порýка bail; guarantee; surety; **на порýки** on bail.
по-рýсски *adv* (in) Russian.
поручáть *impf of* **поручи́ть. поручéние** assignment; errand; message.
пóручень (-чня) *m* handrail.
поручи́тельство guarantee; bail.
поручи́ть (-чý, -чишь) *pf* (*impf* **поручáть**) entrust; instruct.
поручи́ться (-чýсь, -чишься) *pf of* **ручáться**
порхáть *impf*, **порхнýть** (-нý, -нёшь) *pf* flutter, flit.
пóрция portion; helping.
пóрча spoiling; damage; curse.
пóршень (-шня) *m* piston.
поры́в[1] gust; rush; fit
поры́в[2] breaking. **порывáть(ся**[1] *impf of* **порвáть(ся**
порывáться[2] *impf* make jerky movements; endeavour. **поры́вистый** gusty; jerky; impetuous; fitful.

поря́дковый ordinal. **поря́док** (-дка) order; sequence; manner, way; procedure; **всё в поря́дке** everything is alright; **~ дня** agenda, order of the day. **поря́дочный** decent; honest; respectable; fair, considerable.

посади́ть (-ажу́, -а́дишь) *pf of* **сади́ть, сажа́ть. поса́дка** planting; embarkation; boarding; landing. **поса́дочный** planting; landing.

посажу́ *etc.*: *see* **посади́ть.**

по|сва́тать(ся *pf.* **по|свеже́ть** (-е́ет) *pf.* **по|свети́ть** (-ечу́, -е́тишь) *pf.* **по|светле́ть** (-е́ет) *pf.*

посви́стывать *impf* whistle.

по-сво́ему *adv* (in) one's own way.

посвяти́ть (-ящу́) *pf,* **посвяща́ть** *impf* devote; dedicate; let in; ordain. **посвяще́ние** dedication; initiation; ordination.

посе́в sowing; crops. **посевн|о́й** sowing; **~а́я пло́щадь** area under crops.

по|седе́ть (-е́ю) *pf.*

поселе́нец (-нца) settler; exile. **поселе́ние** settlement; exile. **по|сели́ть** *pf,* **поселя́ть** *impf* settle; lodge; arouse; **~ся** settle, take up residence. **посёлок** (-лка) settlement; housing estate.

посеребрённый (-рён, -а́) silver-plated. **по|серебри́ть** *pf.*

посереди́не *adv* & *prep+gen* in the middle (of).

посети́тель *m* visitor. **посети́ть** (-ещу́) *pf* (*impf* **посеща́ть**) visit; attend.

по|се́товать *pf.*

посеща́емость attendance. **посеща́ть** *impf of* **посети́ть. посеще́ние** visit.

по|се́ять (-е́ю) *pf.*

посиде́ть (-ижу́) *pf* sit (for a while).

поси́льный within one's powers; feasible.

посине́лый gone blue. **по|сине́ть** (-е́ю) *pf.*

по|скака́ть (-ачу́, -а́чешь) *pf.*

поскользну́ться (-ну́сь, -нёшься) *pf* slip.

поско́льку *conj* as far as, (in) so far as.

по|скро́мничать *pf.* **по|скупи́ться** (-плю́сь) *pf.*

посла́нец (-нца) messenger, envoy. **посла́ние** message; epistle. **посла́нник** envoy, minister. **посла́ть** (-шлю́, -шлёшь) *pf* (*impf* **посыла́ть**) send.

по́сле *adv* & *prep+gen* after; afterwards.

после- *in comb* post-; after-. **послевое́нный** post-war. **~за́втра** *adv* the day after tomorrow. **~родово́й** post-natal. **~сло́вие** epilogue; concluding remarks.

после́дний last; recent; latest; latter. **после́дователь** *m* follower. **после́довательность** sequence; consistency. **после́довательный** consecutive; consistent. **по|сле́довать** *pf.* **после́дствие** consequence. **после́дующий** subsequent; consequent.

посло́вица proverb, saying.

по|служи́ть (-жу́, -жишь) *pf.* **послужно́й** service.

послуша́ние obedience. **по|слу́шать(ся** *pf.* **послу́шный** obedient.

по|слы́шаться (-шится) *pf.*

посма́тривать *impf* look from time to time.

посме́иваться *impf* chuckle.

посме́ртный posthumous.

по|сме́ть (-е́ю) *pf.*
посмея́ние ridicule. **по-сме́яться** (-ею́сь, -еёшься) *pf* laugh; +**над**+*instr* laugh at.
по|смотре́ть(ся (-рю́(сь, -ришь(ся) *pf.*
посо́бие aid; allowance, benefit; textbook. **посо́бник** accomplice.
по|сове́товать(ся *pf.* **по|со-де́йствовать** *pf.*
посо́л (-сла́) ambassador.
по|соли́ть (-олю́, -о́ли́шь) *pf.*
посо́льство embassy.
поспа́ть (-сплю́; -а́л, -а́, -о) *pf* sleep; have a nap.
поспева́ть[1] *impf*, **по|спе́ть**[1] (-е́ет) *pf* ripen.
поспева́ть[2] *impf*, **поспе́ть**[2] (-е́ю) *pf* have time; be in time (**к**+*dat*, **на**+*acc* for); +**за**+*instr* keep up with.
по|спеши́ть (-шу́) *pf.* **поспе́шный** hasty, hurried.
по|спо́рить *pf.* **по|спосо́бствовать** *pf.*
посрами́ть (-млю́) *pf*, **посрамля́ть** *impf* disgrace.
посреди́, посреди́не *adv* & *prep+gen* in the middle (of). **посре́дник** mediator. **посре́дничество** mediation. **посре́дственный** mediocre. **посре́дством** *prep+gen* by means of.
по|ссо́рить(ся *pf.*
пост[1] (-а́, *loc* -у́) post.
пост[2] (-а́, *loc* -у́) fast(ing).
по|ста́вить[1] (-влю) *pf.*
поста́вить[2] (-влю) *pf*, **поставля́ть** *impf* supply. **поста́вка** delivery. **поставщи́к** (-а́) supplier.
постаме́нт pedestal.
постанови́ть (-влю́, -вишь) *pf* (*impf* **постановля́ть**) decree; decide.
постано́вка production; arrangement; putting, placing.
постановле́ние decree; decision. **постановля́ть** *impf of* **постанови́ть**
постано́вщик producer; (film) director.
по|стара́ться *pf.*
по|старе́ть (-е́ю) *pf.*
по-ста́рому *adv* as before.
посте́ль bed. **постелю́** *etc.*: *see* **постла́ть**
постепе́нный gradual.
по|стесня́ться *pf.*
постига́ть *impf of* **пости́чь. пости́гнуть:** *see* **пости́чь. постиже́ние** comprehension, grasp. **постижи́мый** comprehensible.
постила́ть *impf of* **постла́ть**
постира́ть *pf* do some washing.
пости́ться (-щу́сь) *impf* fast.
пости́чь, пости́гнуть (-и́гну; -и́г(нул)) *pf* (*impf* **постига́ть**) comprehend, grasp; befall.
по|стла́ть (-стелю́, -сте́лешь) *pf* (*impf also* **постила́ть**) spread; make (*bed*).
по́стн|ый lenten; lean; glum; **~ое ма́сло** vegetable oil.
постово́й on point duty.
посто́й billeting.
посто́льку: ~, поско́льку *conj* to that extent, insofar as.
по|сторони́ться (-ню́сь, -нишься) *pf.* **посторо́нний** strange; foreign; extraneous, outside; *sb* stranger, outsider.
постоя́нный permanent; constant; continual; **~ый ток** direct current. **постоя́нство** constancy.
по|стоя́ть (-ою́) *pf* stand (for a while); +**за**+*acc* stand up for.
пострада́вший *sb* victim.
по|страда́ть *pf.*

постригáться *impf*, **постри́чься** (-игу́сь, -ижёшься; -и́гся) *pf* take monastic vows; get one's hair cut.
построéние construction; building; formation. **по|стрóить(ся** (-рóю(сь) *pf*. **пострóйка** building.
постскри́птум postscript.
постули́ровать *impf* & *pf* postulate.
поступáтельный forward. **поступáть** *impf*, **поступи́ть** (-плю́, -пишь) *pf* act; do; be received; +**в** *or* **на**+*acc* enter, join; +**с**+*instr* treat; **~ся** +*instr* waive, forgo. **поступлéние** entering, joining; receipt. **посту́пок** (-пка) act, deed. **пóступь** gait; step.
по|стучáть(ся (-чу́(сь) *pf*.
по|стыди́ться (-ыжу́сь) *pf*. **посты́дный** shameful.
посу́да crockery; dishes. **посу́дный** china; dish.
по|сули́ть *pf*.
посчастли́виться *pf impers* (+*dat*) be lucky; **ей посчастли́вилось** +*inf* she had the luck to.
посчитáть *pf* count (up). **по|считáться** *pf*.
посылáть *impf of* **послáть**. **посы́лка** sending; parcel; errand; premise. **посы́льный** *sb* messenger.
посы́пать (-плю, -плешь) *pf*, **посыпáть** *impf* strew. **посы́паться** (-плется) *pf* begin to fall; rain down.
посягáтельство encroachment; infringement. **посягáть** *impf*, **посягну́ть** (-ну́, -нёшь) *pf* encroach, infringe.
пот (*loc* -у́; *pl* -ы́) sweat.
потайнóй secret.
потакáть *impf* +*dat* indulge.
потасóвка brawl.
потáш (-á) potash.
по-твóему *adv* in your opinion.
потвóрствовать *impf* (+*dat*) be indulgent (towards), pander (to).
потёк damp patch.
потёмки (-мок) *pl* darkness.
по|темнéть (-éет) *pf*.
потенциáл potential. **потенциáльный** potential.
по|теплéть (-éет) *pf*.
потерпéвший *sb* victim.
по|терпéть (-плю́, -пишь) *pf*.
потéря loss; waste; *pl* casualties.
по|терять(ся *pf*.
по|тесни́ть *pf*. **по|тесни́ться** *pf* sit closer, squeeze up.
потéть (-éю) *impf* (*pf* **вс~, за~**) sweat; mist over.
потéха fun. **по|тéшить(ся** (-шу(сь) *pf*. **потéшный** amusing.
потéчь (-чёт, -тёк, -лá) *pf* begin to flow.
потирáть *impf* rub.
потихóньку *adv* softly; secretly; slowly.
пóтный (-тен, -тнá, -тно) sweaty.
потóк stream; torrent; flood.
потолóк (-лкá) ceiling.
по|толстéть (-éю) *pf*.
потóм *adv* later (on); then. **потóмок** (-мка) descendant. **потóмство** posterity.
потомý *adv* that is why; **~ что** *conj* because.
по|тонýть (-нý, -нешь) *pf*. **потóп** flood, deluge. **по|топи́ть** (-плю́, -пишь) *pf*, **потопля́ть** *impf* sink.
по|топтáть (-пчý, -пчешь) *pf*.
по|торопи́ть(ся (-плю́(сь, -пишь(ся) *pf*.

пото́чный continuous; production-line.

по|тра́тить (-а́чу) *pf.*

потреби́тель *m* consumer, user. **потреби́тельский** consumer; consumers'. **потреби́ть** (-блю́) *pf*, **потребля́ть** *impf* consume. **потребле́ние** consumption. **потре́бность** need, requirement. **по|тре́бовать(ся** *pf.*

по|трево́жить(ся (-жу(сь) *pf.*

потрёпанный shabby; tattered. **по|трепа́ть(ся** (-плю́(сь, -плешь(ся) *pf.*

по|тре́скаться *pf.* **потре́скивать** *impf* crackle.

потро́гать *pf* touch, feel, finger.

потроха́ (-о́в) *pl* giblets. **потроши́ть** (-шу́) *impf* (*pf* **вы**~) disembowel, clean.

потруди́ться (-ужу́сь, -у́дишься) *pf* do some work; take the trouble.

потрясáть *impf*, **потрясти́** (-су́, -сёшь; -я́с, -ла́) *pf* shake; rock; stagger; +*acc or instr* brandish, shake. **потряса́ющий** staggering, tremendous. **потрясе́ние** shock.

поту́ги *f pl* vain attempts; **родовы́е** ~ labour.

поту́пить (-плю) *pf*, **потупля́ть** *impf* lower; ~**ся** look down.

по|тускне́ть (-е́ет) *pf.*

потусторо́ний мир the next world.

потуха́ть *impf*, **по|ту́хнуть** (-нет, -у́х) *pf* go out; die out. **поту́хший** extinct; lifeless.

по|туши́ть (-шу́, -шишь) *pf.*

по́тчевать (-чую) *impf* (*pf* **по**~) +*instr* treat to.

потя́гиваться *impf*, **по|тяну́ться** (-ну́сь, -нешься) *pf* stretch o.s. **по|тяну́ть** (-ну́, -нешь) *pf.*

по|у́жинать *pf.* **по|умне́ть** (-е́ю) *pf.*

поуча́ть *impf* preach at.

поучи́тельный instructive.

поха́бный obscene.

похвала́ praise. **по|хвали́ть(ся** (-лю́(сь, -лишь(ся) *pf.* **похва́льный** laudable; laudatory.

по|хва́стать(ся *pf.*

похити́тель *m* kidnapper; abductor; thief. **похи́тить** (-хи́щу) *pf*, **похища́ть** *impf* kidnap; abduct; steal. **похище́ние** theft; kidnapping; abduction.

похлёбка broth, soup.

похло́пать *pf* slap; clap.

по|хлопота́ть (-очу́, -о́чешь) *pf.*

похме́лье hangover.

похо́д campaign; march; hike; excursion.

по|хода́тайствовать *pf.*

походи́ть (-ожу́, -о́дишь) *impf* **на**+*acc* resemble.

похо́дка gait, walk. **похо́дный** mobile, field; marching. **похожде́ние** adventure.

похо́жий alike; ~ **на** like.

похолода́ние drop in temperature.

по|хорони́ть (-ню́, -нишь) *pf.* **похоро́нный** funeral. **по́хороны** (-ро́н, -рона́м) *pl* funeral.

по|хороше́ть (-е́ю) *pf.*

по́хоть lust.

по|худе́ть (-е́ю) *pf.*

по|целова́ть(ся *pf.* **поцелу́й** kiss.

поча́ток (-тка) ear; (corn) cob.

по́чва soil; ground; basis. **по́чвенный** soil; ~ **покро́в** topsoil.

почём *adv* how much; how; ~ **знать?** who can tell?; ~ **я зна́ю?**

how should I know?

почему́ *adv* why. **почему́-либо, -нибудь** *advs* for some reason or other. **почему́-то** *adv* for some reason.

по́черк hand(writing).

почерне́лый blackened, darkened. **по|черне́ть** (-е́ю) *pf.*

почерпну́ть (-ну́, -нёшь) *pf* draw, scoop up; glean.

по|черстве́ть (-е́ю) *pf.* **по|чеса́ть(ся** (-ешу́(сь, -е́шешь(ся) *pf.*

по́честь honour. **почёт** honour; respect. **почётный** of honour; honourable; honorary.

по́чечный renal; kidney.

почива́ть *impf of* **почи́ть**

почи́н initiative.

по|чини́ть (-ню́, -нишь) *pf*, **починя́ть** *impf* repair, mend. **почи́нка** repair.

по|чи́стить(ся (-ищу(сь) *pf.*

почита́ть[1] *impf* honour; revere.

почита́ть[2] *pf* read for a while.

почи́ть (-и́ю, -и́ешь) *pf* (*impf* **почива́ть**) rest; pass away; ~ **на ла́врах** rest on one's laurels.

по́чка[1] bud.

по́чка[2] kidney.

по́чта post, mail; post-office. **почтальо́н** postman. **почта́мт** (*main*) post-office.

почте́ние respect. **почте́нный** venerable; considerable.

почти́ *adv* almost.

почти́тельный respectful. **почти́ть** (-чту́) *pf* honour.

почто́в|ый postal; **~ая ка́рточка** postcard; **~ый перево́д** postal order; **~ый я́щик** letterbox.

по|чу́вствовать *pf.*

по|чу́диться (-ишься) *pf.*

пошатну́ть (-ну́, -нёшь) *pf* shake; **~ся** shake; stagger.

по|шевели́ть(ся (-елю́(сь, -е́лишь(ся) *pf.* **пошёл** *etc.*: *see* **пойти́**

поши́вочный sewing.

по́шлина duty.

по́шлость vulgarity; banality.

по́шлый vulgar; banal.

штучный

поштучный by the piece.

по|шути́ть (-учу́, -у́тишь) *pf.*

поща́да mercy. **по|щади́ть** (-ажу́) *pf.*

по|щекота́ть (-очу́, -о́чешь) *pf.*

пощёчина slap in the face.

по|щу́пать *pf.*

поэ́зия poetry. **поэ́ма** poem. **поэ́т** poet. **поэти́ческий** poetic.

поэ́тому *adv* therefore.

пою́ *etc.*: *see* **петь, пои́ть**

появи́ться (-влю́сь, -вишься) *pf*, **появля́ться** *impf* appear. **появле́ние** appearance.

по́яс (*pl* -а́) belt; girdle; waistband; waist; zone.

поясне́ние explanation. **поясни́тельный** explanatory. **поясни́ть** *pf* (*impf* **поясня́ть**) explain, elucidate.

поясни́ца small of the back.

поясно́й waist; to the waist; zonal.

поясня́ть *impf of* **поясни́ть**

пра- *pref* first; great-. **праба́бушка** great-grandmother.

пра́вда (the) truth. **правди́вый** true; truthful. **правдоподо́бный** likely; plausible. **пра́ведный** righteous; just.

пра́вило rule; principle.

пра́вильн|ый right, correct; regular; **~о!** that's right!

прави́тель *m* ruler. **прави́тельственный** government(al). **прави́тельство** government. **пра́вить**[1] (-влю) +*instr* rule, govern; drive.

пра́вить² (-влю) *impf* correct. **пра́вка** correcting.

правле́ние board; administration; government.

пра́|внук, ~внучка great-grandson, -granddaughter.

пра́во¹ (*pl* -а́) law; right; **(води́тельские) права́** driving licence; **на права́х**+*gen* in the capacity of, as.

пра́во² *adv* really.

право-¹ *in comb* law; right. **правове́рный** orthodox. **~ме́рный** lawful, rightful. **~мо́чный** competent. **~наруше́ние** infringement of the law, offence. **~наруши́тель** *m* offender, delinquent. **~писа́ние** spelling, orthography. **~сла́вный** orthodox; *sb* member of the Orthodox Church. **~су́дие** justice.

право-² *in comb* right, right-hand. **правосторо́нний** right; right-hand.

правово́й legal.

правота́ rightness; innocence.

пра́вый¹ right; right-hand; right-wing.

пра́вый² (прав, -а́, -о) right, correct; just.

пра́вящий ruling.

пра́дед great-grandfather; *pl* ancestors. **праде́душка** *m* great-grandfather.

пра́здник (public) holiday. **пра́здничный** festive. **пра́зднование** celebration. **пра́здновать** *impf* (*pf* **от~**) celebrate. **пра́здность** idleness. **пра́здный** idle; useless.

пра́ктика practice; practical work. **практикова́ть** *impf* practise; **~ся** (*pf* **на~ся**) be practised; **+в**+*prep* practise. **практи́ческий, практи́чный** practical.

пра́отец (-тца) forefather.

пра́порщик ensign.

прапра́дед great-great-grandfather. **прароди́тель** *m* forefather.

прах dust; remains.

пра́чечная *sb* laundry. **пра́чка** laundress.

пребыва́ние stay. **пребыва́ть** *impf* be; reside.

превзойти́ (-йду́, -йдёшь; -ошёл, -шла́) *pf* (*impf* **превосходи́ть**) surpass; excel.

превозмога́ть *impf*, **превозмо́чь** (-огу́, -о́жешь; -о́г, -ла́) *pf* overcome.

превознести́ (-су́, -сёшь; -ёс, -ла́) *pf*, **превозноси́ть** (-ошу́, -о́сишь) *impf* extol, praise.

превосходи́тельство Excellency. **превосходи́ть** (-ожу́, -о́дишь) *impf of* **превзойти́**. **превосхо́дный** superlative; superb, excellent. **превосхо́дство** superiority. **превосходя́щий** superior.

преврати́ть (-ащу́) *pf*, **превраща́ть** *impf* convert, turn, reduce; **~ся** turn, change. **превра́тный** wrong; changeful. **превраще́ние** transformation.

превы́сить (-ы́шу) *pf*, **превыша́ть** *impf* exceed. **превыше́ние** exceeding, excess.

прегра́да obstacle; barrier. **прегради́ть** (-ажу́) *pf*, **прегражда́ть** *impf* bar, block.

пред *prep*+*instr*: *see* **пе́ред**

предава́ть(ся (-даю́(сь, -даёшь(ся) *impf of* **преда́ть(ся**

преда́ние legend; tradition; handing over, committal. **пре́данность** devotion. **пре́данный** devoted. **преда́тель** *m*, **~ница** betrayer, traitor. **преда́тельский** treacherous. **пре-**

да́тельство treachery. **преда́ть** (-а́м, -а́шь, -а́ст, -ади́м; пре́дал, -а́, -о) *pf* (*impf* **предава́ть**) hand over, commit; betray; **~ся** abandon o.s.; give way, indulge.

предаю́ *etc.*: *see* **предава́ть**

предвари́тельный preliminary; prior. **предвари́ть** *pf*, **предваря́ть** *impf* forestall, anticipate.

предве́стник forerunner; harbinger. **предвеща́ть** *impf* portend; augur.

предвзя́тый preconceived; biased.

предви́деть (-и́жу) *impf* foresee.

предвкуси́ть (-ушу́, -у́сишь) *pf*, **предвкуша́ть** *impf* look forward to.

предводи́тель *m* leader. **предводи́тельствовать** *impf* +*instr* lead.

предвое́нный pre-war.

предвосхи́тить (-и́щу) *pf*, **предвосхища́ть** *impf* anticipate.

предвы́борный (pre-)election.

предго́рье foothills.

предде́рие threshold.

преде́л limit; bound. **преде́льный** boundary; maximum; utmost.

предзнаменова́ние omen, augury.

предисло́вие preface.

предлага́ть *impf of* **предложи́ть**. **предло́г**[1] pretext.

предло́г[2] preposition.

предложе́ние[1] sentence; clause.

предложе́ние[2] offer; proposition; proposal; motion; suggestion; supply. **предложи́ть** (-жу́, -жишь) *pf* (*impf* **предлага́ть**) offer; propose; suggest; order.

предло́жный prepositional.

предме́стье suburb.

предме́т object; subject.

предназнача́ть *impf*, **предназна́чить** (-чу) *pf* destine, intend; earmark.

преднаме́ренный premeditated.

пре́до: *see* **пе́ред**

пре́док (-дка) ancestor.

предопределе́ние predetermination. **предопредели́ть** *pf*, **предопределя́ть** *impf* predetermine, predestine.

предоста́вить (-влю) *pf*, **предоставля́ть** *impf* grant; leave; give.

предостерега́ть *impf*, **предостере́чь** (-егу́, -ежёшь; -ёг, -ла́) *pf* warn. **предостереже́ние** warning. **предосторо́жность** precaution.

предосуди́тельный reprehensible.

предотврати́ть (-ащу́) *pf*, **предотвраща́ть** *impf* avert, prevent.

предохране́ние protection; preservation. **предохрани́тель** *m* guard; safety device, safety-catch; fuse. **предохрани́тельный** preservative; preventive; safety. **предохрани́ть** *pf*, **предохраня́ть** *impf* preserve, protect.

предписа́ние order; *pl* directions, instructions. **предписа́ть** (-ишу́, -и́шешь) *pf*, **предпи́сывать** *impf* order, direct; prescribe.

предпле́чье forearm.

предполага́емый supposed. **предполага́ется** *impers* it is proposed. **предполага́ть** *impf*, **предположи́ть** (-жу́, -о́жишь) *pf* suppose, assume. **предположе́ние** supposition, assumption. **предположи́тельный** conjectural; hypothetical.

предпосле́дний penultimate, last-but-one.

предпосы́лка precondition; premise.

предпоче́сть (-чту́, -чтёшь; -чёл, -чла́) *pf*, **предпочита́ть** *impf* prefer. **предпочте́ние** preference. **предпочти́тельный** preferable.

предприи́мчивый enterprising.

предпринима́тель *m* owner; entrepreneur; employer. **предпринима́тельство**: **свобо́дное** ~ free enterprise. **предпринима́ть** *impf*, **предприня́ть** (-иму́, -и́мешь; -и́нял, -а́, -о) *pf* undertake. **предприя́тие** undertaking, enterprise.

предрасположе́ние predisposition.

предрассу́док (-дка) prejudice.

предрека́ть *impf*, **предре́чь** (-еку́, -ечёшь; -рёк, -ла́) *pf* foretell.

предреша́ть *impf*, **предреши́ть** (-шу́) *pf* decide beforehand; predetermine.

председа́тель *m* chairman.

предсказа́ние prediction. **предсказа́ть** (-ажу́, -а́жешь) *pf*, **предска́зывать** *impf* predict; prophesy.

предсме́ртный dying.

представа́ть (-таю́, -таёшь) *impf of* **предста́ть**

представи́тель *m* representative. **представи́тельный** representative; imposing. **представи́тельство** representation; representatives.

предста́вить (-влю) *pf*, **представля́ть** *impf* present; submit; introduce; represent; ~ **себе́** imagine; **представля́ть собо́й** represent, be; ~**ся** present itself, occur; seem; introduce o.s.; +*instr* pretend to be. **представле́ние** presentation; performance; idea, notion.

предста́ть (-а́ну) *pf* (*impf* **представа́ть**) appear.

предстоя́ть (-ои́т) *impf* be in prospect, lie ahead. **предстоя́щий** forthcoming; imminent.

предте́ча *m* & *f* forerunner, precursor.

предубежде́ние prejudice.

предугада́ть *pf*, **предуга́дывать** *impf* guess; foresee.

предупреди́тельный preventive; warning; courteous, obliging. **предупреди́ть** (-ежу́) *pf*, **предупрежда́ть** *impf* warn; give notice; prevent; anticipate. **предупрежде́ние** notice; warning; prevention.

предусма́тривать *impf*, **предусмотре́ть** (-рю́, -ришь) *pf* envisage, foresee; provide for. **предусмотри́тельный** prudent; farsighted.

предчу́вствие presentiment; foreboding. **предчу́вствовать** *impf* have a presentiment (about).

предше́ственник predecessor. **предше́ствовать** *impf* +*dat* precede.

предъяви́тель *m* bearer. **предъяви́ть** (-влю́, -вишь) *pf*, **предъявля́ть** *impf* show, produce; bring (*lawsuit*); ~ **пра́во на**+*acc* lay claim to.

предыду́щий previous.

преéмник successor. **преéмственность** succession; continuity.

пре́жде *adv* first; formerly; *prep+gen* before; **~ всего́** first of all; first and foremost; **~ чем** *conj* before. **преждевре́менный** premature. **пре́жний** previous, former.

презервати́в condom.

президе́нт president. **президе́нтский** presidential. **прези́диум** presidium.

презира́ть *impf* despise. **презре́ние** contempt. **презре́нный** contemptible. **презри́тельный** scornful.

преиму́щественно *adv* mainly, chiefly, principally. **преиму́щественный** main, primary; preferential. **преиму́щество** advantage; preference; **по преиму́ществу** for the most part.

преиспо́дняя *sb* the underworld.

прейскура́нт price list, catalogue.

преклоне́ние admiration. **преклони́ть** *pf*, **преклоня́ть** *impf* bow, bend; **~ся** bow down; *+dat or* **перед***+instr* admire, worship. **преклóнный: ~ во́зраст** old age.

прекра́сный beautiful; fine; excellent.

прекрати́ть (-ащу́) *pf*, **прекраща́ть** *impf* stop, discontinue; **~ся** cease, end. **прекраще́ние** halt; cessation.

преле́стный delightful. **пре́лесть** charm, delight.

преломи́ть (-млю́, -мишь) *pf*, **преломля́ть** *impf* refract. **преломле́ние** refraction.

прельсти́ть (-льщу́) *pf*, **прельща́ть** *impf* attract; entice; **~ся** be attracted; fall (*+instr* for).

прелюбоде́яние adultery.

прелю́дия prelude.

преми́нуть (-ну) *pf with neg* not fail.

премирова́ть *impf & pf* award a prize to; give a bonus. **пре́мия** prize; bonus; premium.

премье́р prime minister; lead(ing actor). **премье́ра** première. **премье́р-мини́стр** prime minister. **премье́рша** leading lady.

пренебрега́ть *impf*, **пренебре́чь** (-егу́, -ежёшь; -ёг, -ла́) *pf +instr* scorn; neglect. **пренебреже́ние** scorn; neglect. **пренебрежи́тельный** scornful.

пре́ния (-ий) *pl* debate.

преоблада́ние predominance. **преоблада́ть** *impf* predominate; prevail.

преобража́ть *impf*, **преобрази́ть** (-ажу́) *pf* transform. **преображе́ние** transformation; Transfiguration. **преобразова́ние** transformation; reform. **преобразова́ть** *pf*, **преобразóвывать** *impf* transform; reform, reorganize.

преодолева́ть *impf*, **преодоле́ть** (-е́ю) *pf* overcome.

препара́т preparation.

препина́ние: зна́ки препина́ния punctuation marks.

препира́тельство altercation, wrangling.

преподава́ние teaching. **преподава́тель** *m*, **~ница** teacher. **преподава́тельский** teaching. **преподава́ть** (-даю́, -даёшь) *impf* teach.

преподнести́ (-су́, -сёшь; -ёс, -ла́) *pf*, **преподноси́ть** (-ошу́, -óсишь) present with, give.

препроводи́ть (-вожу́, -вóдишь) *pf*, **препровожда́ть** *impf* send, forward.

препя́тствие obstacle; hurdle. **препя́тствовать** *impf* (*pf* **вос~**) +*dat* hinder.

прерва́ть (-ву́, -вёшь; -а́л, -а́, -о) *pf* (*impf* **прерыва́ть**) interrupt; break off; **~ся** be interrupted; break.

перека́ние argument. **пререка́ться** *impf* argue.

прерыва́ть(ся *impf of* **прерва́ть(ся**

пресека́ть *impf*, **пресе́чь** (-еку́, -ечёшь; -ёк, -екла́) *pf* stop; put an end to; **~ся** stop; break.

пресле́дование pursuit; persecution; prosecution. **пресле́довать** *impf* pursue; haunt; persecute; prosecute.

преслову́тый notorious.

пресмыка́ться *impf* grovel. **пресмыка́ющееся** *sb* reptile.

пресново́дный freshwater.

пре́сный fresh; unleavened; insipid; bland.

пресс press. **пре́сса** the press. **пресс-конфере́нция** press-conference.

престаре́лый aged.

прести́ж prestige.

престо́л throne.

преступле́ние crime. **престу́пник** criminal. **престу́пность** criminality; crime, delinquency. **престу́пный** criminal.

пресы́титься (-ы́щусь) *pf*, **пресыща́ться** *impf* be satiated. **пресыще́ние** surfeit, satiety.

претвори́ть *pf*, **претворя́ть** *impf* (**в**+*acc*) turn, change, convert; **~ в жизнь** realize, carry out.

претенде́нт claimant; candidate; pretender. **претендова́ть** *impf* **на**+*acc* lay claim to; have pretensions to. **прете́нзия** claim; pretension; **быть в прете́нзии на**+*acc* have a grudge, a grievance, against.

претерпева́ть *impf*, **претерпе́ть** (-плю́, -пишь) *pf* undergo; suffer.

пре́ть (пре́ет) *impf* (*pf* **со~**) rot.

преувеличе́ние exaggeration. **преувели́чивать** *impf*, **преувели́чить** (-чу) *pf* exaggerate.

преуменьша́ть *impf*, **преуме́ньшить** (-е́ньшу́) *pf* underestimate; understate.

преуспева́ть *impf*, **преуспе́ть** (-е́ю) *pf* be successful; thrive.

преходя́щий transient.

прецеде́нт precedent.

при *prep* +*prep* by, at; in the presence of; attached to, affiliated to; with; about; on; in the time of; under; during; when, in case of; **~ всём том** for all that.

приба́вить (-влю) *pf*, **прибавля́ть** add; increase; **~ся** increase; rise; wax; **день приба́вился** the days are getting longer. **приба́вка** addition; increase. **прибавле́ние** addition; supplement, appendix. **приба́вочный** additional; surplus.

Приба́лтика the Baltic States.

прибау́тка humorous saying.

прибега́ть[1] *impf of* **прибежа́ть**

прибега́ть[2] *impf*, **прибе́гнуть** (-ну; -бе́г) *pf* +**к**+*dat* resort to.

прибежа́ть (-егу́) *pf* (*impf* **прибега́ть**) come running.

прибе́жище refuge.

приберега́ть *impf*, **прибере́чь** (-егу́, -ежёшь; -ёг, -ла́) *pf* save (up), reserve.

приберу́ *etc.*: *see* **прибра́ть.**

прибива́ть *impf of* **приби́ть.**

прибира́ть *impf of* **прибра́ть**

приби́ть (-бью́, -бьёшь) *pf* (*impf* **прибива́ть**) nail; flatten; drive.

приближа́ть *impf*, **прибли́зить** (-и́жу) *pf* bring *or* move nearer; **~ся** approach; draw nearer. **приближе́ние** approach. **приблизи́тельный** approximate.

прибо́й surf, breakers.

прибо́р instrument, device, apparatus; set. **прибо́рная доска́** instrument panel; dashboard.

прибра́ть (-беру́, -берёшь; -а́л, -а́, -о) *pf* (*impf* **прибира́ть**) tidy (up); put away.

прибре́жный coastal; offshore.

прибыва́ть *impf*, **прибы́ть** (-бу́ду; при́был, -а́, -о) *pf* arrive; increase, grow; rise; wax. **при́быль** profit, gain; increase, rise. **при́быльный** profitable. **прибы́тие** arrival.

прибью́ *etc.*: *see* **приби́ть**

прива́л halt.

прива́ривать *impf*, **привари́ть** (-рю́, -ришь) *pf* weld on.

приватиза́ция privatization. **приватизи́ровать** *impf* & *pf* privatize.

приведу́ *etc.*: *see* **привести́**

привезти́ (-зу́, -зёшь; -ёз, -ла́) (*impf* **привози́ть**) bring.

привере́дливый pernickety.

приве́рженец (-нца) adherent. **приве́рженный** devoted.

приве́сить (-е́шу) *pf* (*impf* **приве́шивать**) hang up, suspend.

привести́ (-еду́, -едёшь; -ёл, -а́) *pf* (*impf* **приводи́ть**) bring; lead; take; reduce; cite; put in(to), set.

приве́т greeting(s); regards; hi! **приве́тливый** friendly; affable. **приве́тствие** greeting; speech of welcome. **приве́тствовать** *impf* & *pf* greet, salute; welcome.

приве́шивать *impf of* **приве́сить**

привива́ть(ся *impf of* **приви́ть(ся**. **приви́вка** inoculation.

привиде́ние ghost; apparition.

при|ви́деться (-дится) *pf*.

привилегиро́ванный privileged. **привиле́гия** privilege.

привинти́ть (-нчу́) *pf*, **приви́нчивать** *impf* screw on.

приви́ть (-вью́, -вьёшь; -и́л, -а́, -о) *pf* (*impf* **привива́ть**) inoculate; graft; inculcate; foster; **~ся** take; become established.

при́вкус after-taste; smack.

привлека́тельный attractive. **привлека́ть** *impf*, **привле́чь** (-еку́, -ечёшь; -ёк, -ла́) *pf* attract; draw; draw in, win over; (*law*) have up; **~ к суду́** sue. **привлече́ние** attraction.

приво́д drive, gear. **приводи́ть** (-ожу́, -о́дишь) *impf of* **привести́**. **приводно́й** driving.

привожу́ *etc.*: *see* **приводи́ть, привози́ть**

приво́з bringing; importation; load. **привози́ть** (-ожу́, -о́зишь) *impf of* **привезти́**. **привозно́й, приво́зный** imported.

приво́льный free.

привстава́ть (-таю́, -таёшь) *impf*, **привста́ть** (-а́ну) *pf* half-rise; rise.

привыка́ть *impf*, **привы́кнуть** (-ну; -ы́к) *pf* get accustomed. **привы́чка** habit. **привы́чный** habitual, usual.

привью́ *etc.*: *see* **приви́ть**

привя́занность attachment; affection. **привяза́ть** (-яжу́, -я́жешь) *pf*, **привя́зывать** *impf* attach; tie, bind; **~ся** become attached; attach o.s.; **+к+*dat*** pester. **привя́зчивый** annoying; affectionate. **при́вязь** tie;

lead, leash; tether.

пригибáть *impf of* **пригнýть**

пригласи́ть (-ашý) *pf*, **приглашáть** *impf* invite. **приглашéние** invitation.

пригляде́ться (-яжýсь) *pf*, **пригля́дываться** *impf* look closely; +**к**+*dat* scrutinize; get used to.

пригнáть (-гоню́, -гóнишь; -áл, -á, -о) *pf* (*impf* **пригоня́ть**) bring in; fit, adjust.

пригнýть (-нý, -нёшь) *pf* (*impf* **пригибáть**) bend down.

приговáривать[1] *impf* keep saying.

приговáривать[2] *impf*, **приговори́ть** *pf* sentence, condemn. **приговóр** verdict, sentence.

пригоди́ться (-ожýсь) *pf* prove useful. **пригóдный** fit, suitable.

пригоня́ть *impf of* **пригнáть**

пригорáть *impf*, **пригорéть** (-ри́т) *pf* be burnt.

при́город suburb. **при́городный** suburban.

пригóрок (-рка) hillock.

при́горшня (*gen pl* -ей) handful.

приготови́тельный preparatory. **приготóвить** (-влю) *pf*, **приготовля́ть** *impf* prepare; **∼ся** prepare. **приготовлéние** preparation.

пригревáть *impf*, **пригрéть** (-éю) *pf* warm; cherish.

при|грози́ть (-ожý) *pf*.

придавáть (-даю́, -даёшь) *impf*, **придáть** (-áм, -áшь, -áст, -ади́м; при́дал, -á, -о) *pf* add; give; attach. **придáча** adding; addition; **в придáчу** into the bargain.

придави́ть (-влю́, -вишь) *pf*, **придáвливать** *impf* press (down).

придáное *sb* dowry. **придáток** (-тка) appendage.

придвигáть *impf*, **придви́нуть** (-ну) *pf* move up, draw up; **∼ся** move up, draw near.

придвóрный court.

придéлать *pf*, **придéлывать** *impf* attach.

придéрживаться *impf* hold on, hold; +*gen* keep to.

придерýсь *etc.*: *see* **придрáться**. **придирáться** *impf of* **придрáться**. **приди́рка** quibble; fault-finding. **приди́рчивый** fault-finding.

придорóжный roadside.

придрáться (-дерýсь, -дерёшься; -áлся, -áсь, -áлóсь) *pf* (*impf* **придирáться**) find fault.

придý *etc.*: *see* **прийти́**

придýмать *pf*, **придýмывать** *impf* think up, invent.

приéду *etc.*: *see* **приéхать**. **приéзд** arrival. **приезжáть** *impf of* **приéхать**. **приéзжий** newly arrived; *sb* newcomer.

приём receiving; reception; surgery; welcome; admittance; dose; go; movement; method, way; trick. **приéмлемый** acceptable. **приёмная** *sb* waiting-room; reception room. **приёмник** (radio) receiver. **приёмный** receiving; reception; entrance; foster, adopted.

приéхать (-éду) *pf* (*impf* **приезжáть**) arrive, come.

прижáть (-жмý, -жмёшь) *pf* (*impf* **прижимáть**) press; clasp; **∼ся** nestle up.

прижéчь (-жгý, -жжёшь; -жёг, -жглá) *pf* (*impf* **прижигáть**) cauterize.

приживáться *impf of* **прижи́ться**

прижигáние cauterization.

прижига́ть *impf of* **приже́чь**
прижима́ть(ся *impf of* **прижа́ть(ся**
прижи́ться (-иву́сь, -ивёшься; -жи́лся, -а́сь) *pf* (*impf* **прижива́ться**) become acclimatized.
прижму́ *etc.*: *see* **прижа́ть**
приз (*pl* -ы́) prize.
призва́ние vocation. **призва́ть** (-зову́, -зовёшь; -а́л, -а́, -о) *pf* (*impf* **призыва́ть**) call; call upon; call up.
призе́мистый stocky, squat.
приземле́ние landing. **приземли́ться** *pf*, **приземля́ться** *impf* land.
призёр prizewinner.
при́зма prism.
признава́ть (-на́ю, -наёшь) *impf*, **призна́ть** *pf* recognize; admit; **~ся** confess. **при́знак** sign, symptom; indication. **призна́ние** confession, declaration; acknowledgement; recognition. **при́знанный** acknowledged, recognized. **призна́тельный** grateful.
призову́ *etc.*: *see* **призва́ть**
при́зрак spectre, ghost. **при́зрачный** ghostly; illusory, imagined.
призы́в call, appeal; slogan; call-up. **призыва́ть** *impf of* **призва́ть**. **призывно́й** conscription.
при́иск mine.
прийти́ (приду́, -дёшь; пришёл, -шла́) *pf* (*impf* **приходи́ть**) come; arrive; **~ в себя́** regain consciousness; **~сь +по+***dat* fit; suit; **+на+***acc* fall on; *impers+dat* have to; happen (to), fall to the lot (of).
прика́з order, command. **приказа́ние** order, command. **приказа́ть** (-ажу́, -а́жешь) *pf*, **прика́зывать** *impf* order, command.
прика́лывать *impf of* **приколо́ть**. **прикаса́ться** *impf of* **прикосну́ться**
прика́нчивать *impf of* **прико́нчить**
прикати́ть (-ачу́, -а́тишь) *pf*, **прика́тывать** *impf* roll up.
прики́дывать *impf*, **прики́нуть** (-ну) *pf* throw in, add; weigh; estimate; **~ся** *+instr* pretend (to be).
прикла́д[1] butt.
прикла́д[2] trimmings. **прикладно́й** applied. **прикла́дывать(ся** *impf of* **приложи́ть(ся**
прикле́ивать *impf*, **прикле́ить** *pf* stick; glue.
приключа́ться *impf*, **приключи́ться** *pf* happen, occur. **приключе́ние** adventure. **приключе́нческий** adventure.
прикова́ть (-кую́, -куёшь) *pf*, **прико́вывать** *impf* chain; rivet.
прикола́чивать *impf*, **приколоти́ть** (-очу́, -о́тишь) *pf* nail.
приколо́ть (-лю́, -лешь) *pf* (*impf* **прика́лывать**) pin; stab.
прикомандирова́ть *pf*, **прикомандиро́вывать** *impf* attach.
прико́нчить (-чу) *pf* (*impf* **прика́нчивать**) use up; finish off.
прикоснове́ние touch; concern. **прикосну́ться** (-ну́сь, -нёшься) *pf* (*impf* **прикаса́ться**) **к+***dat* touch.
прикрепи́ть (-плю́) *pf*, **прикрепля́ть** *impf* fasten, attach. **прикрепле́ние** fastening; registration.
прикрыва́ть *impf*, **прикры́ть** (-ро́ю) *pf* cover; screen; shelter. **прикры́тие** cover; escort.
прику́ривать *impf*, **прикури́ть**

(-рю́, -ришь) *pf* get a light.
прикуси́ть (-ушу́, -у́сишь) *pf*, **прику́сывать** *impf* bite.
прила́вок (-вка) counter.
прилага́тельное *sb* adjective.
прилага́ть *impf of* **приложи́ть**
прила́дить (-а́жу) *pf*, **прила́живать** *impf* fit, adjust.
приласка́ть *pf* caress, pet; **~ся** snuggle up.
прилега́ть *impf* (*pf* **приле́чь**) к+*dat* fit; adjoin. **прилега́ющий** close-fitting; adjoining, adjacent.
приле́жный diligent.
прилепи́ть(ся (-плю́(сь, -пишь(ся) *pf*, **прилепля́ть(ся** *impf* stick.
прилёт arrival. **прилета́ть** *impf*, **прилете́ть** (-ечу́) *pf* arrive, fly in; come flying.
приле́чь (-ля́гу, -ля́жешь; -ёг, -гла́) *pf* (*impf* **прилега́ть**) lie down.
прили́в flow, flood; rising tide; surge. **прилива́ть** *impf of* **прили́ть. прили́вный** tidal.
прилипа́ть *impf*, **прили́пнуть** (-нет; -ли́п) *pf* stick.
прили́ть (-льёт; -и́л, -а́, -о) *pf* (*impf* **прилива́ть**) flow; rush.
прили́чие decency. **прили́чный** decent.
приложе́ние application; enclosure; supplement; appendix.
приложи́ть (-жу́, -жишь) *pf* (*impf* **прикла́дывать, прилага́ть**) put; apply; affix; add; enclose; **~ся** take aim; +*instr* put, apply; +к+*dat* kiss.
прильёт *etc.*: *see* **прили́ть.**
при|льну́ть (-ну́, -нёшь) *pf.* **приля́гу** *etc.*: *see* **приле́чь**
прима́нивать *impf*, **премани́ть** (-ню́, -нишь) *pf* lure; entice. **прима́нка** bait, lure.

примене́ние application; use.
примени́ть (-ню́, -нишь) *pf*, **применя́ть** *impf* apply; use; **~ся** adapt o.s., conform.
приме́р example.
при|ме́рить *pf* (*impf also* **примеря́ть**) try on. **приме́рка** fitting.
приме́рно *adv* approximately.
приме́рный exemplary; approximate.
примеря́ть *impf of* **приме́рить**
при́месь admixture.
приме́та sign, token. **приме́тный** perceptible; conspicuous.
примеча́ние note, footnote; *pl* comments. **примеча́тельный** notable.
примеша́ть *pf*, **приме́шивать** *impf* add, mix in.
примина́ть *impf of* **примя́ть**
примире́ние reconciliation.
примири́тельный conciliatory.
при|мири́ть *pf*, **примиря́ть** *impf* reconcile; conciliate; **~ся** be reconciled.
примити́вный primitive.
примкну́ть (-ну́, -нёшь) *pf* (*impf* **примыка́ть**) join; fix, attach.
примну́ *etc.*: *see* **примя́ть**
примо́рский seaside; maritime.
примо́рье seaside.
примо́чка wash, lotion.
приму́ *etc.*: *see* **приня́ть**
примча́ться (-чу́сь) *pf* come tearing along.
примыка́ть *impf of* **примкну́ть;** +к+*dat* adjoin. **примыка́ющий** affiliated.
примя́ть (-мну́, -мнёшь) *pf* (*impf* **примина́ть**) crush; trample down.
принадлежа́ть (-жу́) *impf* belong. **принадле́жность** belonging; membership; *pl* acces-

sories; equipment.
принести́ (-су́, -сёшь; -нёс, -ла́) *pf* (*impf* **приноси́ть**) bring; fetch.
принижа́ть *impf*, **прини́зить** (-и́жу) *pf* humiliate; belittle.
принима́ть(ся *impf of* **приня́ть(ся**
приноси́ть (-ошу́, -о́сишь) *impf of* **принести́. приноше́ние** gift, offering.
при́нтер (*comput*) printer.
принуди́тельный compulsory. **прину́дить** (-у́жу) *pf*, **принужда́ть** *impf* compel. **принужде́ние** compulsion, coercion. **принуждённый** constrained, forced.
принц prince. **принце́сса** princess.
при́нцип principle. **принципиа́льно** *adv* on principle; in principle. **принципиа́льный** of principle; general.
приня́тие taking; acceptance; admission. **при́нято** it is accepted, it is usual; **не** ~ it is not done. **приня́ть** (-иму́, -и́мешь; при́нял, -а́, -о) *pf* (*impf* **принима́ть**) take; accept; take over; receive; **+за**+*acc* take for; ~ **уча́стие** take part; ~**ся** begin; take; take root; ~ **за рабо́ту** set to work.
приободри́ть *pf*, **приободря́ть** *impf* cheer up; ~**ся** cheer up.
приобрести́ (-ету́, -етёшь; -рёл, -а́) *pf*, **приобрета́ть** *impf* acquire. **приобрете́ние** acquisition.
приобща́ть *impf*, **приобщи́ть** (-щу́) *pf* join, attach, unite; ~**ся** **к**+*dat* join in.
приорите́т priority.
приостана́вливать *impf*, **приостанови́ть** (-влю́, -вишь) *pf* stop, suspend; ~**ся** stop. **приостано́вка** halt, suspension.
приоткрыва́ть *impf*, **приоткры́ть** (-ро́ю) *pf* open slightly.
припа́док (-дка) fit; attack.
припа́сы (-ов) *pl* supplies.
припе́в refrain.
приписа́ть (-ишу́, -и́шешь) *pf*, **припи́сывать** *impf* add; attribute. **припи́ска** postscript; codicil.
припло́д offspring; increase.
приплыва́ть *impf*, **приплы́ть** (-ыву́, -ывёшь; -ы́л, -а́, -о) *pf* swim up; sail up.
приплю́снуть (-ну) *pf*, **приплю́щивать** *impf* flatten.
приподнима́ть *impf*, **приподня́ть** (-ниму́, -ни́мешь; -о́днял, -а́, -о) *pf* raise (a little); ~**ся** raise o.s. (a little).
припо́й solder.
приполза́ть *impf*, **приползти́** (-зу́, -зёшь; -полз, -ла́) *pf* creep up, crawl up.
припомина́ть *impf*, **припо́мнить** *pf* recollect.
припра́ва seasoning, flavouring. **припра́вить** (-влю) *pf*, **приправля́ть** *impf* season, flavour.
припря́тать (-я́чу) *pf*, **припря́тывать** *impf* secrete, put by.
припу́гивать *impf*, **припугну́ть** (-ну́, -нёшь) *pf* scare.
прираба́тывать *impf*, **прирабо́тать** *pf* earn ... extra. **при́работок** (-тка) additional earnings.
прира́внивать *impf*, **приравня́ть** *pf* equate (with **к**+*dat*).
прираста́ть *impf*, **прирасти́** (-тёт; -ро́с, -ла́) *pf* adhere; take; increase; accrue.
приро́да nature. **приро́дный**

natural; by birth; innate. **прирождённый** innate; born.

приро́с *etc.*: *see* **прирасти́. приро́ст** increase.

приуча́ть *impf*, **приручи́ть** (-чу́) *pf* tame; domesticate.

приса́живаться *impf of* **присе́сть**

присва́ивать *impf*, **присво́ить** *pf* appropriate; award.

приседа́ть *impf*, **присе́сть** (-ся́ду) *pf* (*impf also* **приса́живаться**) sit down, take a seat.

прискака́ть (-ачу́, -а́чешь) *pf* come galloping.

приско́рбный sorrowful.

присла́ть (-ишлю́, -ишлёшь) *pf* (*impf* **присыла́ть**) send.

прислони́ть(ся (-оню́(сь, -о́нишь(ся) *pf*, **прислоня́ть(ся** *impf* lean, rest.

прислу́га servant; crew. **прислу́живать** *impf* (**к**+*dat*) wait (on), attend.

прислу́шаться *pf*, **прислу́шиваться** *impf* listen; +**к**+*dat* listen to; heed.

присма́тривать *impf*, **присмотре́ть** (-рю́, -ришь) *pf* +**за** +*instr* look after, keep an eye on; **~ся** (**к**+*dat*) look closely (at). **присмо́тр** supervision.

при|сни́ться *pf*.

присоедине́ние joining; addition; annexation. **присоедини́ть** *pf*, **присоединя́ть** *impf* join; add; annex; **~ся к**+*dat* join; subscribe to (*an opinion*).

приспосо́бить (-блю) *pf*, **приспособля́ть** *impf* fit, adjust, adapt; **~ся** adapt o.s. **приспособле́ние** adaptation; device; appliance. **приспособля́емость** adaptability.

пристава́ть (-таю́, -таёшь) *impf of* **приста́ть**

приста́вить (-влю) *pf* (*impf* **приставля́ть**) **к**+*dat* place, set, *or* lean against; add; appoint to look after.

приста́вка prefix.

приставля́ть *impf of* **приста́вить**

при́стальный intent.

приста́нище refuge, shelter.

при́стань (*gen pl* -е́й) landing-stage; pier; wharf.

приста́ть (-а́ну) *pf* (*impf* **пристава́ть**) stick, adhere (**к**+*dat* to); pester.

пристёгивать *impf*, **пристегну́ть** (-ну́, -нёшь) *pf* fasten.

присто́йный decent, proper.

пристра́ивать(ся *impf of* **пристро́ить(ся**

пристра́стие predilection, passion; bias. **пристра́стный** biased.

пристре́ливать *impf*, **пристрели́ть** *pf* shoot (down).

пристро́ить (-о́ю) *pf* (*impf* **пристра́ивать**) add, build on; fix up; **~ся** be fixed up, get a place. **пристро́йка** annexe, extension.

при́ступ assault; fit, attack.

приступа́ть *impf*, **приступи́ть** (-плю́, -пишь) *pf* **к**+*dat* set about, start.

при|стыди́ть (-ыжу́) *pf*.

при|стыкова́ться *pf*.

присуди́ть (-ужу́, -у́дишь) *pf*, **присужда́ть** *impf* sentence, condemn; award; confer. **присужде́ние** awarding; conferment.

прису́тствие presence. **прису́тствовать** *impf* be present, attend. **прису́тствующие** *sb pl* those present.

прису́щий inherent; characteristic.

присыла́ть *impf of* **присла́ть**

прися́га oath. **присяга́ть** *impf*, **присягну́ть** (-ну́, -нёшь) *pf* swear.
прися́ду *etc.*: *see* **присе́сть**
прися́жный *sb* juror.
прита́йться *pf* hide.
прита́птывать *impf of* **притопта́ть**
прита́скивать *impf*, **притащи́ть** (-ащу́, -а́щишь) *pf* bring, drag, haul; **~ся** drag o.s.
притвори́ться *pf*, **притворя́ться** *impf* +*instr* pretend to be. **притво́рный** pretended, feigned. **притво́рство** pretence, sham. **притво́рщик** sham; hypocrite.
притека́ть *impf of* **прите́чь**
притесне́ние oppression. **притесни́ть** *pf*, **притесня́ть** *impf* oppress.
прите́чь (-ечёт, -еку́т; -ёк, -ла́) *pf* (*impf* **притека́ть**) pour in.
притиха́ть *impf*, **прити́хнуть** (-ну; -и́х) *pf* quiet down.
прито́к tributary; influx.
при́толока lintel.
прито́м *conj* (and) besides.
прито́н den, haunt.
притопта́ть (-пчу́, -пчешь) *pf* (*impf* **прита́птывать**) trample down.
при́торный sickly-sweet, luscious, cloying.
притра́гиваться *impf*, **притро́нуться** (-нусь) *pf* touch.
притупи́ть (-плю́, -пишь) *pf*, **притупля́ть** *impf* blunt, dull; deaden; **~ся** become blunt *or* dull.
при́тча parable.
притяга́тельный attractive, magnetic. **притя́гивать** *impf of* **притяну́ть**
притяжа́тельный possessive.
притяже́ние attraction.
притяза́ние claim, pretension. **притяза́тельный** demanding.
притя́нутый far-fetched. **притяну́ть** (-ну́, -нешь) *pf* (*impf* **притя́гивать**) attract; drag (up).
приуро́чивать *impf*, **приуро́чить** (-чу) *pf* **к**+*dat* time for.
приуса́дебный: **~ уча́сток** individual plot (*in kolkhoz*).
приуча́ть *impf*, **приучи́ть** (-чу́, -чишь) *pf* train, school.
прихлеба́тель *m* sponger.
прихо́д coming, arrival; receipts; parish. **приходи́ть(ся** (-ожу́(сь, -о́дишь(ся) *impf of* **прийти́(сь. прихо́дный** receipt. **приходя́щий** non-resident; **~ больно́й** outpatient. **прихожа́нин** (*pl* -а́не, -а́н), **-а́нка** parishioner.
прихо́жая *sb* hall, lobby.
прихотли́вый capricious; fanciful, intricate. **при́хоть** whim, caprice.
прихра́мывать limp (slightly).
прице́л sight; aiming. **прице́ливаться** *impf*, **прице́литься** *pf* take aim.
прице́ниваться *impf*, **прицени́ться** (-ню́сь, -нишься) *pf* (**к**+*dat*) ask the price (of).
прице́п trailer. **прицепи́ть** (-плю́, -пишь) *pf*, **прицепля́ть** *impf* hitch, hook on; **~ся к**+*dat* stick to, cling to. **прице́пка** hitching, hooking on; quibble. **прицепно́й**: **~ ваго́н** trailer.
прича́л mooring; mooring line. **прича́ливать** *impf*, **прича́лить** *pf* moor.
прича́стие[1] participle. **прича́стие**[2] communion. **причасти́ть** (-ащу́) *pf* (*impf* **причаща́ть**) give communion to; **~ся** receive communion.

причáстный[1] participial. **причáстный**[2] concerned; privy.
причащáть *impf of* **причасти́ть**
причём *conj* moreover, and.
причесáть (-ешу́, -éшешь) *pf*, **причёсывать** *impf* comb; do the hair (of); **~ся** do one's hair, have one's hair done. **причёска** hair-do; haircut.
причи́на cause; reason. **причини́ть** *pf*, **причиня́ть** *impf* cause.
причи́слить *pf*, **причисля́ть** *impf* number, rank (**к**+*dat* among); add on.
причитáние lamentation. **причитáть** *impf* lament.
причитáться *impf* be due.
причмóкивать *impf*, **причмóкнуть** (-ну) *pf* smack one's lips.
причу́да caprice, whim.
при|чу́диться *pf*.
причу́дливый odd; fantastic; whimsical.
при|швартовáть *pf*. **пришёл** *etc.*: *see* **прийти́**
пришéлец (-ьца) newcomer.
пришéствие coming; advent.
пришивáть *impf*, **приши́ть** (-шью́, -шьёшь) *pf* sew on.
пришлю́ *etc.*: *see* **прислáть**
пришпи́ливать *impf*, **пришпи́лить** *pf* pin on.
пришпóривать *impf*, **пришпóрить** *pf* spur (on).
прищеми́ть (-млю́) *pf*, **прищемля́ть** *impf* pinch.
прищéпка clothes-peg.
прищу́риваться *impf*, **прищу́риться** *pf* screw up one's eyes.
прию́т shelter, refuge. **приюти́ть** (-ючу́) *pf* shelter; **~ся** take shelter.
прия́тель *m*, **прия́тельница** friend. **прия́тельский** friendly.
прия́тный nice, pleasant.
про *prep+acc* about; for; **~ себя́** to o.s.
про|анализи́ровать *pf*.
прóба test; hallmark; sample.
пробéг run; race. **пробегáть** *impf*, **пробежáть** (-егу́) *pf* run; cover; run past. **пробéжка** run.
пробéл blank, gap; flaw.
проберу́ *etc.*: *see* **пробрáть.**
пробивáть(ся *impf of* **пробúть(ся.** **пробирáть(ся** *impf of* **пробрáть(ся**
проби́рка test-tube. **проби́ровать** *impf* test, assay.
про|би́ть (-бью́, -бьёшь) *pf* (*impf also* **пробивáть**) make a hole in; pierce; punch; **~ся** force, make, one's way.
прóбка cork; stopper; fuse; (traffic) jam, congestion. **прóбковый** cork.
проблéма problem.
прóблеск flash; gleam, ray.
прóбный trial, test; **~ кáмень** touchstone. **прóбовать** *impf* (*pf* **ис~, по~**) try; attempt.
пробóина hole.
пробóр parting.
про|бормотáть (-очу́, -óчешь) *pf*.
пробрáть (-беру́, -берёшь; -áл, -á, -о) *pf* (*impf* **пробирáть**) penetrate; scold; **~ся** make *or* force one's way.
пробу́ду *etc.*: *see* **пробы́ть**
про|буди́ть (-ужу́, -у́дишь) *pf*, **пробуждáть** *impf* wake (up); arouse; **~ся** wake up. **пробуждéние** awakening.
про|бурáвить (-влю) *pf*, **пробурáвливать** *impf* bore (through), drill.
про|бури́ть *pf*.
пробы́ть (-бу́ду; прóбыл, -á, -о) *pf* stay; be.

пробью *etc.*: *see* **пробúть**
провáл failure; downfall; gap. **провáливать** *impf*, **провалúть** (-лю́, -лишь) *pf* bring down; ruin; reject, fail; **~ся** collapse; fall in; fail; disappear.
провéдать *pf*, **провéдывать** *impf* call on; learn.
проведéние conducting; construction; installation.
провезтú (-зу́, -зёшь; -ёз, -лá) *pf* (*impf* **провозúть**) convey, transport.
провéрить *pf*, **проверя́ть** *impf* check; test. **провéрка** checking, check; testing.
про|вестú (-еду́, -едёшь; -ёл, -á) *pf* (*impf also* **проводúть**) lead, take; build; install; carry out; conduct; pass; draw; spend; *+instr* pass over.
провéтривать *impf*, **провéтрить** *pf* air.
про|вéять (-éю) *pf*.
провидéние Providence.
провúзия provisions.
провинúться *pf* be guilty; do wrong.
провинциáльный provincial. **провúнция** province; the provinces.
прóвод (*pl* -á) wire, lead, line. **проводúмость** conductivity. **проводúть**¹ (-ожу́, -óдишь) *impf of* **провестú**; conduct.
проводúть² (-ожу́, -óдишь) *pf* (*impf* **провожáть**) accompany; see off.
провóдка leading, taking; building; installation; wiring, wires.
проводнúк¹ (-á) guide; conductor.
проводнúк² (-á) conductor; bearer; transmitter.
прóводы (-ов) *pl* send-off. **провожáтый** *sb* guide, escort. **провожáть** *impf of* **проводúть**
провóз conveyance, transport.
провозгласúть (-ашу́) *pf*, **провозглашáть** *impf* proclaim; propose. **провозглашéние** proclamation.
провозúть (-ожу́, -óзишь) *impf of* **провезтú**
провокáтор agent provocateur. **провокáция** provocation.
прóволока wire. **прóволочный** wire.
провóрный quick; agile. **провóрство** quickness; agility.
провоцúровать *impf* & *pf* (*pf* **с~**) provoke.
прогадáть *pf*, **прогáдывать** *impf* miscalculate.
прогáлина glade; space.
прогибáть(ся *impf of* **прогну́ть(ся**
проглáтывать *impf*, **проглотúть** (-очу́, -óтишь) *pf* swallow.
проглядéть (-яжу́) *pf*, **прогля́дывать**¹ *impf* overlook; look through. **проглянýть** (-я́нет) *pf*, **прогля́дывать**² *impf* show, peep through, appear.
прогнáть (-гоню́, -гóнишь; -áл, -á, -о) *pf* (*impf* **прогоня́ть**) drive away; banish; drive; sack.
прогнивáть *impf*, **прогнúть** (-ниёт; -úл, -á, -о) *pf* rot through.
прогнóз prognosis; (weather) forecast.
прогну́ть (-ну́, -нёшь) *pf* (*impf* **прогибáть**) cause to sag; **~ся** sag, bend.
проговáривать *impf*, **проговорúть** *pf* say, utter; talk; **~ся** let the cat out of the bag.
проголодáться *pf* get hungry.
про|голосовáть *pf*.
прогóн purlin; girder; stairwell.

прогоня́ть *impf of* **прогна́ть**
прогора́ть *impf*, **прогоре́ть** (-рю́) *pf* burn (through); burn out; go bankrupt.
прого́рклый rancid, rank.
програ́мма programme; syllabus. **программи́ровать** *impf* (*pf* **за~**) programme. **программи́ст** (computer) programmer.
прогрева́ть *impf*, **прогре́ть** (-е́ю) *pf* heat; warm up; **~ся** warm up.
про|греме́ть (-млю́) *pf*.
про|грохота́ть (-очу́, -о́чешь) *pf*.
прогре́сс progress. **прогресси́вный** progressive. **прогресси́ровать** *impf* progress.
прогрыза́ть *impf*, **прогры́зть** (-зу́, -зёшь; -ы́з) *pf* gnaw through.
про|гуде́ть (-гужу́) *pf*.
прогу́л truancy; absenteeism. **прогу́ливать** *impf*, **прогуля́ть** *pf* play truant, be absent, (from); miss; take for a walk; **~ся** take a walk. **прогу́лка** walk, stroll; outing. **прогу́льщик** absentee, truant.
продава́ть (-даю́, -даёшь) *impf*, **прода́ть** (-а́м, -а́шь, -а́ст, -ади́м; про́дал, -а́, -о) *pf* sell. **продава́ться** (-даётся) *impf* be for sale; sell. **продаве́ц** (-вца́) seller, vendor; salesman. **продавщи́ца** seller, vendor; saleswoman. **прода́жа** sale. **прода́жный** for sale; corrupt.
продвига́ть *impf*, **продви́нуть** (-ну) *pf* move on, push forward; advance; **~ся** advance; move forward; push on. **продвиже́ние** advancement.
продева́ть *impf of* **проде́ть**
про|деклами́ровать *pf*.
проде́лать *pf*, **проде́лывать** *impf* do, perform, make. **проде́лка** trick; prank.
продемонстри́ровать *pf* demonstrate, show.
продёргивать *impf of* **продёрнуть**
продержа́ть (-жу́, -жишь) *pf* hold; keep; **~ся** hold out.
продёрнуть (-ну, -нешь) *pf* (*impf* **продёргивать**) pass, run; criticize severely.
проде́ть (-е́ну) *pf* (*impf* **продева́ть**) pass; **~ ни́тку в иго́лку** thread a needle.
продешеви́ть (-влю́) *pf* sell too cheap.
про|диктова́ть *pf*.
продлева́ть *impf*, **продли́ть** *pf* prolong. **продле́ние** extension.
про|дли́ться *pf*.
продма́г grocery. **продово́льственный** food. **продово́льствие** food; provisions.
продолгова́тый oblong.
продолжа́тель *m* continuer. **продолжа́ть** *impf*, **продо́лжить** (-жу) *pf* continue; prolong; **~ся** continue, last, go on. **продолже́ние** continuation; sequel; **в ~**+*gen* in the course of. **продолжи́тельность** duration. **продолжи́тельный** long; prolonged.
продо́льный longitudinal.
продро́гнуть (-ну; -о́г) *pf* be chilled to the bone.
продтова́ры (-ов) *pl* food products.
продува́ть *impf* **проду́ть**
проду́кт product; *pl* food-stuffs. **продукти́вность** productivity. **продукти́вный** productive. **продукто́вый** food. **проду́кция** production.
проду́манный well thought-out. **проду́мать** *pf*, **проду́мы-**

вать *impf* think over; think out.
продýть (-ýю, -ýешь) *pf* (*impf* **продувáть**) blow through.
продырявить (-влю) *pf* make a hole in.
проедáть *impf of* **проéсть. проéду** *etc.*: *see* **проéхать**
проéзд passage, thoroughfare; trip. **проéздить** (-зжу) *pf* (*impf* **проезжáть**) spend travelling. **проездн|óй** travelling; **~óй билéт** ticket; **~áя плáта** fare; **~ые** *sb pl* travelling expenses. **проезжáть** *impf of* **проéздить, проéхать. проéзжий** passing (by); *sb* passer-by.
проéкт project, plan, design; draft. **проектúровать** *impf* (*pf* **с~**) project; plan. **проéктный** planning; planned. **проéктор** projector.
проекциóнный фонáрь projector. **проéкция** projection.
проéсть (-éм, -éшь, -éст, -едúм; -éл) *pf* (*impf* **проедáть**) eat through, corrode; spend on food.
проéхать (-éду) *pf* (*impf* **проезжáть**) pass, ride, drive (by, through); cover.
прожáренный (*cul*) well-done.
прожевáть (-жую, -жуёшь) *pf*, **прожёвывать** *impf* chew well.
прожéктор (*pl* -ы *or* -á) searchlight.
прожéчь (-жгý, -жжёшь; -жёг, -жглá) *pf* (*impf* **прожигáть**) burn (through).
проживáть *impf of* **прожúть. прожигáть** *impf of* **прожéчь**
прожúточный мúнимум living wage. **прожúть** (-ивý, -ивёшь; -óжил, -á, -о) *pf* (*impf* **проживáть**) live; spend.
прожóрливый gluttonous.
прóза prose. **прозаúческий** prose; prosaic.
прозвáние, прóзвище nickname. **прозвáть** (-зовý, -зовёшь; -áл, -á, -о) *pf* (*impf* **прозывáть**) nickname, name.
про|звучáть *pf.*
про|зевáть *pf.* **про|зимовáть** *pf.* **прозовý** *etc.*: *see* **прозвáть**
прозорлúвый perspicacious.
прозрáчный transparent.
прозревáть *impf*, **прозрéть** *pf* regain one's sight; see clearly. **прозрéние** recovery of sight; insight.
прозывáть *impf of* **прозвáть**
прозябáние vegetation. **прозябáть** *impf* vegetate.
проигрáть *pf*, **проúгрывать** *impf* lose; play; **~ся** gamble away all one's money. **проигрывáтель** *m* record-player. **прóигрыш** loss.
произведéние work; production; product. **произвестú** (-едý, -едёшь; -ёл, -á) *pf*, **производúть** (-ожý, -óдишь) *impf* make; carry out; produce; +**в**+*acc*/*nom pl* promote to (the rank of). **производúтель** *m* producer. **производúтельность** productivity. **производúтельный** productive. **производный** derivative. **произвóдственный** industrial; production. **произвóдство** production.
произвóл arbitrariness; arbitrary rule. **произвóльный** arbitrary.
произнестú (-сý, -сёшь; -ёс, -лá) *pf*, **произносúть** (-ошý, -óсишь) *impf* pronounce; utter. **произношéние** pronunciation.
произойтú (-ойдёт; -ошёл, -шлá) *pf* (*impf* **происходúть**) happen,

occur; result; be descended.
произраста́ть *impf*, **произрасти́** (-ту́; -тёшь; -рос, -ла́) *pf* sprout; grow.
про́иски (-ов) *pl* intrigues.
проистека́ть *impf*, **происте́чь** (-ечёт; -ёк, -ла́) *pf* spring, result.
происходи́ть (-ожу́, -о́дишь) *impf of* **произойти́**. **происхожде́ние** origin; birth.
происше́ствие event, incident.
пройдо́ха *m* & *f* sly person.
пройти́ (-йду́, -йдёшь; -ошёл, -шла́) *pf* (*impf* **проходи́ть**) pass; go; go past; cover; study; get through; **~сь** (*impf* **проха́живаться**) take a stroll.
прок use, benefit.
прокажённый *sb* leper. **прока́за**[1] leprosy.
прока́за[2] mischief, prank. **прока́зничать** *impf* (*pf* **на~**) be up to mischief. **прока́зник** prankster.
прока́лывать *impf of* **проколо́ть**
прока́пывать *impf of* **прокопа́ть**
прока́т hire.
прокати́ться (-ачу́сь, -а́тишься) *pf* roll; go for a drive.
прока́тный rolling; rolled.
прокипяти́ть (-ячу́) *pf* boil (thoroughly).
прокиса́ть *impf*, **про|ки́снуть** (-нет) *pf* turn (sour).
прокла́дка laying; construction; washer; packing. **прокла́дывать** *impf of* **проложи́ть**
проклама́ция leaflet.
проклина́ть *impf*, **прокля́сть** (-яну́, -янёшь; -о́клял, -а́, -о) *pf* curse, damn. **прокля́тие** curse; damnation. **прокля́тый** (-я́т, -а́, -о) damned.
проко́л puncture.
проколо́ть (-лю́, -лешь) *pf* (*impf* **прока́лывать**) prick, pierce.
прокомменти́ровать *pf* comment (upon).
про|компости́ровать *pf*.
про|конспекти́ровать *pf*.
про|консульти́ровать(ся *pf*.
про|контроли́ровать *pf*.
прокопа́ть *pf* (*impf* **прока́пывать**) dig, dig through.
прoко́рм nourishment, sustenance. **про|корми́ть(ся** (-млю́(сь, -мишь(ся) *pf*.
про|корректи́ровать *pf*.
прокра́дываться *impf*, **прокра́сться** (-аду́сь, -адёшься) *pf* steal in.
прокурату́ра office of public prosecutor. **прокуро́р** public prosecutor.
прокуси́ть (-ушу́, -у́сишь) *pf*, **проку́сывать** *impf* bite through.
прокути́ть (-учу́, -у́тишь) *pf*, **проку́чивать** *impf* squander; go on a binge.
пролага́ть *impf of* **проложи́ть**
прола́мывать *impf of* **пролома́ть**
пролега́ть *impf* lie, run.
пролеза́ть *impf*, **проле́зть** (-зу; -ле́з) *pf* get through, climb through.
про|лепета́ть (-ечу́, -е́чешь) *pf*.
пролёт span; stairwell; bay.
пролетариа́т proletariat. **пролета́рий** proletarian. **пролета́рский** proletarian.
пролета́ть *impf*, **пролете́ть** (-ечу́) *pf* fly; cover; fly by, past, through.
проли́в strait. **пролива́ть** *impf*, **проли́ть** (-лью́, -льёшь; -о́лил, -а́, -о) *pf* spill, shed; **~ся** be spilt.

проло́г prologue.
проложи́ть (-жу́, -жишь) *pf* (*impf* **прокла́дывать, пролага́ть**) lay; build; interlay.
проло́м breach, break. **пролома́ть, проломи́ть** (-млю́, -мишь) *pf* (*impf* **пролáмывать**) break (through).
пролью́ *etc.*: *see* **проли́ть**
про|ма́зать (-а́жу) *pf*. **прома́тывать(ся** *impf of* **промота́ть(ся**
про́мах miss; slip, blunder. **прома́хиваться** *impf*, **промахну́ться** (-ну́сь, -нёшься) *pf* miss; make a blunder.
прома́чивать *impf of* **промочи́ть**
промедле́ние delay. **проме́длить** *pf* delay; procrastinate.
промежу́ток (-тка) interval; space. **промежу́точный** intermediate
промелькну́ть (-ну́, -нёшь) *pf* flash (past, by).
проме́нивать *impf*, **промени́ть** *pf* exchange.
промерза́ть *impf*, **промёрзнуть** (-ну; -ёрз) *pf* freeze through. **промёрзлый** frozen.
промока́ть *impf*, **промо́кнуть** (-ну; -мо́к) *pf* get soaked; let water in.
промо́лвить (-влю) *pf* say, utter.
промолча́ть (-чу́) *pf* keep silent.
про|мота́ть *pf* (*impf also* **прома́тывать**) squander.
промочи́ть (-чу́, -чишь) *pf* (*impf* **прома́чивать**) soak, drench.
промо́ю *etc.*: *see* **промы́ть**
промтова́ры (-ов) *pl* manufactured goods.
промча́ться (-чу́сь) *pf* rush by.
промыва́ть *impf of* **промы́ть**
про́мысел (-сла) trade, business; *pl* works. **промысло́вый** producers'; business; game.
промы́ть (-мо́ю) *pf* (*impf* **промыва́ть**) wash (thoroughly); bathe; ~ **мозги́**+*dat* brainwash.
про|мыча́ть (-чу́) *pf*.
промы́шленник industrialist. **промы́шленность** industry. **промы́шленный** industrial.
пронести́ (-су́, -сёшь; -ёс, -ла́) *pf* (*impf* **проноси́ть**) carry (past, through); pass (over); **~сь** rush past, through; scud (past); fly; spread.
пронза́ть *impf*, **пронзи́ть** (-нжу́) *pf* pierce, transfix. **пронзи́тельный** piercing.
пронизáть (-ижу́, -и́жешь) *pf*, **прони́зывать** *impf* pierce; permeate.
проника́ть *impf*, **прони́кнуть** (-ну; -и́к) *pf* penetrate; percolate; **~ся** be imbued. **проникнове́ние** penetration; feeling. **проникнове́нный** heartfelt.
проница́емый permeable. **проница́тельный** perspicacious.
проноси́ть(ся (-ошу́(сь, -о́сишь(ся) *impf of* **пронести́(сь.**
про|нумерова́ть *pf*.
пронюхать *pf*, **пронюхивать** *impf* smell out, get wind of.
прообраз prototype.
пропага́нда propaganda. **пропаганди́ст** propagandist.
пропада́ть *impf of* **пропа́сть.**
пропа́жа loss.
пропа́лывать *impf of* **пропо́ло́ть**
про́пасть precipice; abyss; lots of.
пропа́сть (-аду́, -адёшь) *pf* (*impf*

пропада́ть) be missing; be lost; disappear; be done for, die; be wasted. **пропа́щий** lost; hopeless.

пропека́ть(ся *impf of* **пропе́чь(ся**. **про|пе́ть** (-пою́, -поёшь) *pf.*

пропе́чь (-еку́, -ечёшь; -ёк, -ла́) *pf* (*impf* **пропека́ть**) bake thoroughly; **~ся** get baked through.

пропива́ть *impf of* **пропи́ть**

прописа́ть (-ишу́, -и́шешь) *pf*, **пропи́сывать** *impf* prescribe; register; **~ся** register. **пропи́ска** registration; residence permit. **прописн|о́й: ~а́я бу́ква** capital letter; **~а́я и́стина** truism. **про́писью** *adv* in words.

пропита́ние subsistence, sustenance. **пропита́ть** *pf*, **пропи́тывать** *impf* impregnate, saturate.

пропи́ть (-пью́, -пьёшь; -о́пил, -а́, -о) *pf* (*impf* **пропива́ть**) spend on drink.

проплыва́ть *impf*, **проплы́ть** (-ыву́, -ывёшь; -ы́л, -а́, -о) *pf* swim, sail, *or* float past *or* through.

пропове́дник preacher; advocate. **пропове́довать** *impf* preach; advocate. **про́поведь** sermon; advocacy.

прополза́ть *impf*, **проползти́** (-зу́, -зёшь; -по́лз, -ла́) *pf* crawl, creep.

пропо́лка weeding. **прополо́ть** (-лю́, -лешь) *pf* (*impf* **пропа́лывать**) weed.

про|полоска́ть (-ощу́, -о́щешь) *pf.*

пропорциона́льный proportional, proportionate. **пропо́рция** proportion.

про́пуск (*pl* -а́ *or* -и, -о́в *or* -ов) pass, permit; password; admission; omission; non-attendance; blank, gap. **пропуска́ть** *impf*, **пропусти́ть** (-ущу́, -у́стишь) *pf* let pass; let in; pass; leave out; miss. **пропускно́й** admission.

про|пылесо́сить *pf.*

пропью́ *etc.*: *see* **пропи́ть**

прора́б works superintendent.

праба́тывать *impf*, **прорабо́тать** *pf* work (through, at); study; pick holes in.

прораста́ние germination; sprouting. **прораста́ть** *impf*, **прорасти́** (-тёт; -ро́с, -ла́) *pf* germinate, sprout.

прорва́ть (-ву́, -вёшь; -а́л, -а́, -о) *pf* (*impf* **прорыва́ть**) break through; **~ся** burst open; break through.

про|реаги́ровать *pf.*

прореди́ть (-ежу́) *pf*, **проре́живать** *impf* thin out.

проре́з cut; slit, notch. **про|ре́зать** (-е́жу) *pf*, **прореза́ть** *impf* (*impf also* **проре́зывать**) cut through; **~ся** be cut, come through.

проре́зывать(ся *impf of* **проре́зать(ся**. **про|репети́ровать** *pf.*

проре́ха tear, slit; flies; deficiency.

про|рецензи́ровать *pf.*

проро́к prophet.

पророни́ть *pf* utter.

проро́с *etc.*: *see* **прорасти́**

проро́ческий prophetic. **проро́чество** prophecy.

проро́ю *etc.*: *see* **проры́ть**

проруба́ть *impf*, **проруби́ть** (-блю́, -бишь) *pf* cut *or* hack through. **про́рубь** ice-hole.

проры́в break; break-through; hitch. **прорыва́ть**[1]**(ся** *impf of* **прорва́ть(ся**

прорывáть[2] *impf*, **проры́ть** (-рóю) *pf* dig through; **~ся** dig one's way through.

просáчиваться *impf of* **просочи́ться**

просвéрливать *impf*, **просверли́ть** *pf* drill, bore; perforate.

просвéт (clear) space; shaft of light; ray of hope; opening. **просвети́тельный** educational. **просвети́ть**[1] (-ещý) *pf* (*impf* **просвещáть**) enlighten.

просвети́ть[2] (-ечý, -éтишь) *pf* (*impf* **просвéчивать**) X-ray.

просветлéние brightening (up); lucidity. **про|светлéть** (-éет) *pf*.

просвéчивание radioscopy. **просвéчивать** *impf of* **просвети́ть**; be translucent; be visible.

просвещáть *impf of* **просвети́ть**. **просвещéние** enlightenment.

просви́ра communion bread.

прóседь streak(s) of grey.

просéивать *impf of* **просéять**

прóсека cutting, ride.

просёлок (-лка) country road.

просéять (-éю) *pf* (*impf* **просéивать**) sift.

про|сигнализи́ровать *pf*.

просидéть (-ижý) *pf*, **просиживать** *impf* sit.

проси́тельный pleading. **проси́ть** (-ошý, -óсишь) *impf* (*pf* **по~**) ask; beg; invite; **~ся** ask; apply.

проскáкивать *impf of* **проскочи́ть**

проскáльзывать *impf*, **проскользнýть** (-нý, -нёшь) *pf* slip, creep.

проскочи́ть (-чý, -чишь) *pf* (*impf* **проскáкивать**) rush by; slip through; creep in.

прослáвить (-влю) *pf*, **прославля́ть** *impf* glorify; make famous; **~ся** become famous. **прослáвленный** renowned.

проследи́ть (-ежý) *pf*, **прослéживать** *impf* track (down); trace.

прослези́ться (-ежýсь) *pf* shed a few tears.

прослóйка layer, stratum.

прослужи́ть (-жý, -жишь) *pf* serve (for a certain time).

про|слýшать *pf*, **прослýшивать** *impf* hear; listen to; miss, not catch.

про|слы́ть (-ывý, -ывёшь; -ы́л, -á, -о) *pf*.

просмáтривать *impf*, **просмотрéть** (-рю́, -ришь) *pf* look over; overlook. **просмóтр** survey; view, viewing; examination.

проснýться (-нýсь, -нёшься) *pf* (*impf* **просыпáться**) wake up.

прóсо millet.

просóвывать(ся *impf of* **просýнуть(ся**

про|сóхнуть (-ну; -óх) *pf* (*impf also* **просыхáть**) dry out.

просочи́ться (-и́тся) *pf* (*impf* **просáчиваться**) percolate; seep (out); leak (out).

проспáть (-плю́; -áл, -á, -о) *pf* (*impf* **просыпáть**) sleep (through); oversleep.

проспéкт avenue.

про|спрягáть *pf*.

просрóченный overdue; expired. **просрóчить** (-чу) *pf* allow to run out; be behind with; overstay. **просрóчка** delay; expiry of time limit.

простáивать *impf of* **простоя́ть**

простáк (-á) simpleton.

простéнок (-нка) pier (*between windows*).

простерéться (-трётся; -тёрся) *pf*, **простирáться** *impf* extend.

простúтельный pardonable, excusable. **простúть** (-ощý) *pf* (*impf* **прощáть**) forgive; excuse; **~ся** (с+*instr*) say goodbye (to).

проститýтка prostitute. **проститýция** prostitution.

прóсто *adv* simply.

простоволóсый bare-headed.

простодýшный simple-hearted; ingenuous.

простóй[1] downtime.

прост|óй[2] simple; plain; mere; **~ы́м глáзом** with the naked eye; **~óе числó** prime number.

простоквáша thick sour milk.

прóсто-нáпросто *adv* simply.

простонарóдный of the common people.

простóр spaciousness; space. **простóрный** spacious.

просторéчие popular speech.

простосердéчный simple-hearted.

простотá simplicity.

простоя́ть (-ою́) *pf* (*impf* **простáивать**) stand (idle).

прострáнный extensive, vast. **прострáнственный** spatial. **прострáнство** space.

прострéл lumbago. **прострéливать** *impf*, **прострелúть** (-лю́, -лишь) *pf* shoot through.

про|строчúть (-очý, -óчишь) *pf*.

простýда cold. **простудúться** (-ужýсь, -ýдишься) *pf*, **простужáться** *impf* catch (a) cold.

проступáть *impf*, **проступúть** (-ит) *pf* appear.

простýпок (-пка) misdemeanour.

простыня́ (*pl* прóстыни, -ы́нь, -ня́м) sheet.

просты́ть (-ы́ну) *pf* get cold.

просýнуть (-ну) *pf* (*impf* **просóвывать**) push, thrust.

просýшивать *impf*, **просушúть** (-шý, -шишь) *pf* dry out; **~ся** (get) dry.

просуществовáть *pf* exist; endure.

просчёт error. **просчитáться** *pf*, **просчúтываться** *impf* miscalculate.

просы́пать (-плю) *pf*, **просыпáть**[1] *impf* spill; **~ся** get spilt.

просыпáть[2] *impf of* **проспáть**.

просыпáться *impf of* **проснýться**. **просыхáть** *impf of* **просóхнуть**

прóсьба request.

протáлкивать(ся *impf of* **протолкнýть(ся**. **протáпливать** *impf of* **протопúть**

протáптывать *impf of* **протоптáть**

протáскивать *impf*, **протащúть** (-щý, -щишь) *pf* drag, push (through).

протéз artificial limb, prosthesis; **зубнóй ~** denture.

протеúн protein.

протекáть *impf of* **протéчь**

протéкция patronage.

протерéть (-трý, -трёшь; -тёр) *pf* (*impf* **протирáть**) wipe (over); wear (through).

протéст protest. **протестáнт**, **~ка** Protestant. **протестовáть** *impf* protest.

протéчь (-ечёт; -тёк, -лá) *pf* (*impf* **протекáть**) flow; leak; seep; pass; take its course.

прóтив *prep*+*gen* against; opposite; contrary to, as against.

прóтивень (-вня) *m* baking-tray; meat-pan.

протúвиться (-влюсь) *impf* (*pf* **вос~**) +*dat* oppose; resist. **про-**

тúвник opponent; the enemy. **протúвный**[1] opposite; contrary. **протúвный**[2] nasty, disgusting.

противо- *in comb* anti-, contra-, counter-. **противовéс** counterbalance. **~воздýшный** anti-aircraft. **~гáз** gas-mask. **~дéйствие** opposition. **~дéйствовать** *impf* +*dat* oppose, counteract. **~естéственный** unnatural. **~закóнный** illegal. **~зачáточный** contraceptive. **~полóжность** opposite; opposition, contrast. **~полóжный** opposite; contrary. **~постáвить** (-влю) *pf*, **~поставлять** *impf* oppose; contrast. **~речúвый** contradictory; conflicting. **~рéчие** contradiction. **~рéчить** (-чу) *impf* +*dat* contradict. **~стоять** (-ою) *impf* +*dat* resist, withstand. **~тáнковый** anti-tank. **~ядие** antidote.

протирáть *impf of* **протерéть**

протúскивать *impf*, **протúснуть** (-ну) *pf* force, squeeze (through, into).

проткнýть (-нý, -нёшь) *pf* (*impf* **протыкáть**) pierce.

протокóл minutes; report; protocol.

протолкнýть (-нý, -нёшь) *pf* (*impf* **протáлкивать**) push through; **~ся** push one's way through.

протóн proton.

протопúть (-плю, -пишь) *pf* (*impf* **протáпливать**) heat (thoroughly).

протоптáть (-пчý, -пчешь) *pf* (*impf* **протáптывать**) tread; wear out.

проторённый beaten, well-trodden.

прототúп prototype.

протóчный flowing, running.

про|трáлить *pf*. **протрý** *etc.*: *see* **протерéть**. **про|трубúть** (-блю) *pf*.

протрезвúться (-влюсь) *pf*, **протрезвляться** *impf* sober up.

протухáть *impf*, **протýхнуть** (-нет; -ýх) *pf* become rotten; go bad.

протыкáть *impf of* **проткнýть**

протягивать *impf*, **протянýть** (-нý, -нешь) *pf* stretch; extend; hold out; **~ся** stretch out; extend; last. **протяжéние** extent, stretch; period. **протяжный** long-drawn-out; drawling.

проýчивать *impf*, **проучúть** (-чý, -чишь) *pf* study; teach a lesson.

профáн ignoramus.

профанáция profanation.

профессионáл professional. **профессионáльный** professional; occupational. **профéссия** profession. **профéссор** (*pl* -á) professor.

профилáктика prophylaxis; preventive measures.

прóфиль *m* profile; type.

про|фильтровáть *pf*.

профсоюз trade-union.

прохáживаться *impf of* **пройтúсь**

прохвóст scoundrel.

прохлáда coolness. **прохладúтельный** refreshing, cooling. **прохлáдный** cool, chilly.

прохóд passage; gangway, aisle; duct. **проходúмец** (-мца) rogue. **проходúмый** passable. **проходúть** (-ожý, -óдишь) *impf of* **пройтú**. **проходнóй** entrance; communicating. **проходящий** passing. **прохóжий**

passing, in transit; *sb* passer-by.
процвета́ние prosperity. **процвета́ть** *impf* prosper, flourish.
процеди́ть (-ежу́, -е́дишь) *pf* (*impf* **проце́живать**) filter, strain.
процеду́ра procedure; (*usu in pl*) treatment.
проце́живать *pf of* **процеди́ть**
проце́нт percentage; per cent; interest.
проце́сс process; trial; legal proceedings. **проце́ссия** procession.
про|цити́ровать *pf.*
прочёска screening; combing.
проче́сть (-чту́, -чтёшь; -чёл, -чла́) *pf of* **чита́ть**
про́чий other.
прочи́стить (-и́щу) *pf* (*impf* **прочища́ть**) clean; clear.
про|чита́ть *pf*, **прочи́тывать** *impf* read (through).
прочища́ть *impf of* **прочи́стить**
про́чность firmness, stability, durability. **про́чный** (-чен, -чна́, -о) firm, sound, solid; durable.
прочте́ние reading. **прочту́** *etc.*: *see* **проче́сть**
прочу́вствовать *pf* feel deeply; experience, go through.
прочь *adv* away, off; averse to.
проше́дший past; last. **прошёл** *etc.*: *see* **пройти́**
проше́ние application, petition.
прошепта́ть (-пчу́, -пчешь) *pf* whisper.
проше́ствие: **по проше́ствии** +*gen* after.
прошива́ть *impf*, **проши́ть** (-шью́, -шьёшь) *pf* sew, stitch.
прошлого́дний last year's. **про́шл|ый** past; last; **~ое** *sb* the past.
про|шнурова́ть *pf.* **про|штуди́ровать** *pf.* **прошью́** *etc.*: *see* **проши́ть**
проща́й(те) goodbye. **проща́льный** parting; farewell. **проща́ние** farewell; parting. **проща́ть(ся** *impf of* **прости́ть(ся**
про́ще simpler, plainer.
проще́ние forgiveness, pardon.
прощу́пать *pf*, **прощу́пывать** *impf* feel.
про|экзаменова́ть *pf.*
прояви́тель *m* developer. **прояви́ть** (-влю́, -вишь) *pf*, **проявля́ть** *impf* show, display; develop; **~ся** reveal itself. **проявле́ние** display; manifestation; developing.
проясни́ться *pf*, **проясня́ться** *impf* clear, clear up.
пруд (-а́, *loc* -у́) pond. **пруди́ть** (-ужу́, -у́дишь) *impf* (*pf* **за~**) dam.
пружи́на spring. **пружи́нистый** springy. **пружи́нный** spring.
пру́сский Prussian.
прут (-а *or* -а́; *pl* -тья) twig.
пры́гать *impf*, **пры́гнуть** (-ну) *pf* jump, leap; bounce; **~ с шесто́м** pole-vault. **прыгу́н** (-а́), **прыгу́нья** (*gen pl* -ний) jumper. **прыжо́к** (-жка́) jump; leap; **прыжки́** jumping; **прыжки́ в во́ду** diving; **~ в высоту́** high jump; **~ в длину́** long jump.
пры́скать *impf*, **пры́снуть** (-ну) *pf* spurt; sprinkle; burst out laughing.
прыть speed; energy.
прыщ (-а́), **пры́щик** pimple.
пряди́льный spinning. **пряди́льня** (*gen pl* -лен) (spinning-)mill. **пряди́льщик** spinner. **пряду́** *etc.*: *see* **прясть.**

прядь lock; strand. **пря́жа** yarn, thread.
пря́жка buckle, clasp.
пря́лка distaff; spinning-wheel.
прямáя *sb* straight line. **пря́мо** *adv* straight; straight on; frankly; really.
прямоду́шие directness, straightforwardness. **~ду́шный** direct, straightforward.
прямо́й (-ям, -á, -о) straight; upright, erect; through; direct; straightforward; real.
прямолине́йный rectilinear; straightforward. **прямоуго́льник** rectangle. **прямоуго́льный** rectangular.
пря́ник spice cake. **пря́ность** spice. **пря́ный** spicy; heady.
прясть (-яду́, -ядёшь; -ял, -ялá, -о) *impf* (*pf* **с~**) spin.
пря́тать (-я́чу) *impf* (*pf* **с~**) hide; **~ся** hide. **пря́тки** (-ток) *pl* hide-and-seek.
пса *etc.*: *see* **пёс**
псало́м (-лмá) psalm. **псалты́рь** Psalter.
псевдони́м pseudonym.
псих madman, lunatic. **психиатри́я** psychiatry. **пси́хика** psyche; psychology. **психи́ческий** mental, psychical.
психоана́лиз psychoanalysis. **психо́з** psychosis. **психо́лог** psychologist. **психологи́ческий** psychological. **психоло́гия** psychology. **психопа́т** psychopath. **психопати́ческий** psychopathic. **психосомати́ческий** psychosomatic. **психотерапе́вт** psychotherapist. **психотерапи́я** psychotherapy. **психоти́ческий** psychotic.
птене́ц (-нцá) nestling; fledgeling. **пти́ца** bird. **птицефе́рма** poultry-farm. **пти́чий** bird, bird's, poultry. **пти́чка** bird; tick.
пу́блика public; audience. **публикáция** publication; notice, advertisement. **публиковáть** *impf* (*pf* **о~**) publish. **публици́стика** writing on current affairs. **публи́чность** publicity. **публи́чный** public; **~ дом** brothel.
пу́гало scarecrow. **пугáть** *impf* (*pf* **ис~, на~**) frighten, scare; **~ся** (+*gen*) be frightened (of). **пугáч** (-á) toy pistol. **пугли́вый** fearful.
пу́говица button.
пуд (*pl* -ы́) pood (= *16.38 kg*). **пудово́й, пудо́вый** one pood in weight.
пу́дель *m* poodle.
пу́динг blancmange.
пу́дра powder. **пу́дреница** powder compact. **пу́дреный** powdered. **пу́дриться** *impf* (*pf* **на~**) powder one's face.
пузáтый pot-bellied.
пузырёк (-рькá) vial; bubble. **пузы́рь** (-я́) *m* bubble; blister; bladder.
пук (*pl* -и́) bunch, bundle; tuft.
пу́кать *impf*, **пу́кнуть** *pf* fart.
пулемёт machine-gun. **пулемётчик** machine-gunner. **пуленепробивáемый** bullet-proof.
пульверизáтор atomizer; spray.
пульс pulse. **пульсáр** pulsar. **пульси́ровать** *impf* pulsate.
пульт desk, stand; control panel.
пу́ля bullet.
пункт point; spot; post; item. **пункти́р** dotted line. **пункти́рный** dotted, broken.
пункту́альный punctual.

пунктуа́ция punctuation.

пунцо́вый crimson.

пуп (-а́) navel. **пупови́на** umbilical cord. **пупо́к** (-пка́) navel; gizzard.

пурга́ blizzard.

пурита́нин (*pl* -та́не, -та́н), **-а́нка** Puritan.

пу́рпур purple, crimson. **пурпу́р|ный, ~овый** purple.

пуск starting (up). **пуска́й** *see* **пусть. пуска́ть(ся** *impf of* **пусти́ть(ся. пусково́й** starting.

пусте́ть (-е́ет) *impf* (*pf* **о~**) empty; become deserted.

пусти́ть (пущу́, пу́стишь) *pf* (*impf* **пуска́ть**) let go; let in; let; start; send; set in motion; throw; put forth; **~ся** set out; start.

пустова́ть *impf* be *or* stand empty. **пусто́й** (-ст, -а́, -о) empty; uninhabited; idle; shallow. **пустота́** (*pl* -ы) emptiness; void; vacuum; futility. **пустоте́лый** hollow.

пусты́нный uninhabited; deserted; desert. **пусты́ня** desert. **пусты́рь** (-я́) *m* waste land; vacant plot.

пусты́шка blank; hollow object; dummy.

пусть, пуска́й *partl* let; all right; though, even if.

пустя́к (-а́) trifle. **пустяко́вый** trivial.

пу́таница muddle, confusion. **пу́таный** muddled, confused. **пу́тать** *impf* (*pf* **за~, пере~, с~**) tangle; confuse; mix up; **~ся** get confused *or* mixed up.

путёвка pass; place on a group tour. **путеводи́тель** *m* guide, guide-book. **путево́й** travelling; road. **путём** *prep+gen* by means of. **путеше́ственник** traveller. **путеше́ствие** journey; voyage.

путеше́ствовать *impf* travel; voyage.

пу́ты (пут) *pl* shackles.

путь (-и́, *instr* -ём, *prep* -и́) way; track; path; course; journey; voyage; means; **в пути́** en route, on one's way.

пух (*loc* -у́) down; fluff.

пу́хлый (-хл, -а́, -о) plump. **пу́хнуть** (-ну; пух) *impf* (*pf* **вс~, о~**) swell.

пухови́к (-а́) feather-bed. **пухо́вка** powder-puff. **пухо́вый** downy.

пучи́на abyss; the deep.

пучо́к (-чка́) bunch, bundle.

пу́шечный gun, cannon.

пуши́нка bit of fluff. **пуши́стый** fluffy.

пу́шка gun, cannon.

пушни́на furs, pelts. **пушно́й** fur; fur-bearing.

пу́ще *adv* more; **~ всего́** most of all.

пущу́ *etc.*: *see* **пусти́ть**

пчела́ (*pl* -ёлы) bee. **пчели́ный** bee, bees'. **пчелово́д** bee-keeper. **пче́льник** apiary.

пшени́ца wheat. **пшени́чный** wheat(en).

пшённый millet. **пшено́** millet.

пыл (*loc* -у́) heat, ardour. **пыла́ть** *impf* blaze; burn.

пылесо́с vacuum cleaner. **пылесо́сить** *impf* (*pf* **про~**) vacuum(-clean). **пыли́нка** speck of dust. **пыли́ть** *impf* (*pf* **за~, на~**) raise a dust; cover with dust; **~ся** get dusty.

пы́лкий ardent; fervent.

пыль (*loc* -и́) dust. **пы́льный** (-лен, -льна́, -о) dusty. **пыльца́** pollen.

пыре́й couch grass.

пырну́ть (-ну́, -нёшь) *pf* jab.

пыта́ть *impf* torture. **пыта́ться** *impf* (*pf* **по~**) try. **пы́тка** torture, torment. **пытли́вый** inquisitive.

пыхте́ть (-хчу́) *impf* puff, pant.

пы́шка bun.

пы́шность splendour. **пы́шный** (-шен, -шна́, -шно) splendid; lush.

пьедеста́л pedestal.

пье́са play; piece.

пью *etc.*: *see* **пить**

пьяне́ть (-е́ю) *impf* (*pf* **о~**) get drunk. **пьяни́ть** *impf* (*pf* **о~**) intoxicate, make drunk. **пья́ница** *m* & *f* drunkard. **пья́нство** drunkenness. **пья́нствовать** *impf* drink heavily. **пья́ный** drunk.

пюпи́тр lectern; stand.

пюре́ *neut indecl* purée.

пядь (*gen pl* -е́й) span; **ни пя́ди** not an inch.

пя́льцы (-лец) *pl* embroidery frame.

пята́ (*pl* -ы, -а́м) heel.

пята́к (-а́), **пятачо́к** (-чка́) five-copeck piece. **пятёрка** five; figure 5; No. 5; fiver (5-*rouble note*).

пяти- *in comb* five; penta-. **пятибо́рье** pentathlon. **~десятиле́тие** fifty years; fiftieth anniversary, birthday. **П~деся́тница** Pentecost. **~деся́тый** fiftieth; **~деся́тые го́ды** the fifties. **~коне́чный** five-pointed. **~ле́тие** five years; fifth anniversary. **~ле́тка** five-year plan. **~со́тый** five-hundredth. **~уго́льник** pentagon. **~уго́льный** pentagonal.

пя́титься (пя́чусь) *impf* (*pf* **по~**) move backwards; back.

пя́тка heel.

пятна́дцатый fifteenth. **пятна́дцать** fifteen.

пятна́ть *impf* (*pf* **за~**) spot, stain. **пятна́шки** (-шек) *pl* tag.

пятни́стый spotted.

пя́тница Friday.

пятно́ (*pl* -а, -тен) stain; spot; blot; **роди́мое ~** birth-mark.

пя́тый fifth. **пять** (-и́, *instr* -ью) five. **пятьдеся́т** (-и́десяти, *instr* -ью́десятью) fifty. **пятьсо́т** (-тисо́т, -тиста́м) five hundred. **пя́тью** *adv* five times.

Р

раб (-а́), **раба́** slave. **рабовладе́лец** (-льца) slave-owner. **раболе́пие** servility. **раболе́пный** servile. **раболе́пствовать** cringe, fawn.

рабо́та work; job; functioning. **рабо́тать** *impf* work; function; be open; **~ над**+*instr* work on. **рабо́тник, -ица** worker. **работоспосо́бность** capacity for work, efficiency. **работоспосо́бный** able-bodied, hard-working. **работя́щий** hard-working. **рабо́чий** *sb* worker. **рабо́ч|ий** worker's; working; **~ая си́ла** manpower.

ра́бский slave; servile. **ра́бство** slavery. **рабы́ня** female slave.

равви́н rabbi.

ра́венство equality. **равне́ние** alignment. **равни́на** plain.

равно́ *adv* alike; equally; **~ как** as well as. **равно́** *predic*: *see* **ра́вный**

равно- *in comb* equi-, iso-. **равнобе́дренный** isosceles. **~ве́сие** equilibrium; balance. **~де́нствие** equinox. **~ду́шие**

indifference. **~ду́шный** indifferent. **~ме́рный** even; uniform. **~пра́вие** equality of rights. **~пра́вный** having equal rights. **~си́льный** of equal strength; equal, equivalent, tantamount. **~сторо́нний** equilateral. **~це́нный** of equal value; equivalent.

ра́вный (-вен, -вна́) equal. **равно́** *predic* make(s), equals; **всё ~о́** (it is) all the same. **равня́ть** *impf* (*pf* **с~**) make even; treat equally; +**с**+*instr* compare with, treat as equal to; **~ся** compete, compare; be equal; be tantamount.

рад (-а, -о) *predic* glad.

рада́р radar.

ра́ди *prep*+*gen* for the sake of.

радиа́тор radiator. **радиа́ция** radiation.

ра́дий radium.

радика́льный radical.

ра́дио *neut indecl* radio.

радио- *in comb* radio-; radioactive. **радиоакти́вный** radioactive. **~веща́ние** broadcasting. **~волна́** radio-wave. **~гра́мма** radio-telegram. **радио́лог** radiologist. **~ло́гия** radiology. **~лока́тор** radar (set). **~люби́тель** *m* radio amateur, ham. **~мая́к** (-а́) radio beacon. **~переда́тчик** transmitter. **~переда́ча** broadcast. **~приёмник** radio (set). **~свя́зь** radio communication. **~слу́шатель** *m* listener. **~ста́нция** radio station. **~электро́ника** radioelectronics.

радио́ла radiogram.

ради́ровать *impf* & *pf* radio. **ради́ст** radio operator.

ра́диус radius.

ра́довать *impf* (*pf* **об~, по~**) gladden, make happy; **~ся** be glad, rejoice. **ра́достный** joyful. **ра́дость** gladness, joy.

ра́дуга rainbow. **ра́дужн|ый** iridescent; cheerful; **~ая оболо́чка** iris.

раду́шие cordiality. **раду́шный** cordial.

ражу́ *etc.*: *see* **рази́ть**

раз (*pl* -ы́, раз) time, occasion; one; **ещё ~** (once) again; **как ~** just, exactly; **не ~** more than once; **ни ~у** not once. **раз** *adv* once, one day. **раз** *conj* if; since.

разба́вить (-влю) *pf*, **разбавля́ть** *impf* dilute.

разбаза́ривать *impf*, **разбаза́рить** *pf* squander.

разба́лтывать(ся *impf of* **разболта́ть(ся**

разбе́г running start. **разбега́ться** *impf*, **разбежа́ться** (-егусь) *pf* take a run, run up; scatter.

разберу́ *etc.*: *see* **разобра́ть**

разбива́ть(ся *impf of* **разби́ть(ся**. **разби́вка** laying out; spacing (out).

разбинтова́ть *pf*, **разбинто́вывать** *impf* unbandage.

разбира́тельство investigation. **разбира́ть** *impf of* **разобра́ть**; **~ся** *impf of* **разобра́ться**

разби́ть (-зобью, -зобьёшь) *pf* (*impf* **разбива́ть**) break; smash; divide (up); damage; defeat; mark out; space (out); **~ся** break, get broken; hurt o.s. **разби́тый** broken; jaded.

раз|богате́ть (-е́ю) *pf*.

разбо́й robbery. **разбо́йник** robber. **разбо́йничий** robber.

разболе́ться[1] (-ли́тся) *pf* begin to ache badly.

разболе́ться[2] (-е́юсь) *pf* become ill.

разболта́ть[1] *pf* (*impf* **разба́лтывать**) divulge, give away.

разболта́ть[2] *pf* (*impf* **разба́лтывать**) shake up; loosen; **~ся** work loose; get out of hand.

разбомби́ть (-блю́) *pf* bomb, destroy by bombing.

разбо́р analysis; critique; discrimination; investigation. **разбо́рка** sorting out; dismantling. **разбо́рный** collapsible. **разбо́рчивый** legible; discriminating.

разбра́сывать *impf of* **разброса́ть**

разбреда́ться *impf*, **разбрести́сь** (-едётся; -ёлся, -ла́сь) *pf* disperse; straggle. **разбро́д** disorder.

разбро́санный scattered; disconnected, incoherent. **разброса́ть** *pf* (*impf* **разбра́сывать**) throw about; scatter.

раз|буди́ть (-ужу́, -у́дишь) *pf*.

разбуха́ть *impf*, **разбу́хнуть** (-нет; -бу́х) *pf* swell.

разбушева́ться (-шу́юсь) *pf* fly into a rage; blow up; rage.

разва́л breakdown, collapse. **разва́ливать** *impf*, **развали́ть** (-лю́, -лишь) *pf* pull down; mess up; **~ся** collapse; go to pieces; tumble down; sprawl. **разва́лина** ruin; wreck.

ра́зве *partl* really?; **~ (то́лько)**, **~ (что)** except that, only.

развева́ться *impf* fly, flutter.

разве́дать *pf* (*impf* **разве́дывать**) find out; reconnoitre.

разведе́ние breeding; cultivation.

разведённ|ый divorced; **~ый**, **~ая** *sb* divorcee.

разве́дка intelligence (service); reconnaissance; prospecting. **разве́дочный** prospecting, exploratory.

разведу́ *etc.*: *see* **развести́**

разве́дчик intelligence officer; scout; prospector. **разве́дывать** *impf of* **разве́дать**

развезти́ (-зу́, -зёшь; -ёз, -ла́) *pf* (*impf* **развози́ть**) convey, transport; deliver.

разве́ивать(ся *impf of* **разве́ять(ся**. **развёл** *etc.*: *see* **развести́**

развенча́ть *pf*, **разве́нчивать** *impf* dethrone; debunk.

развёрнутый extensive, all-out; detailed. **разверну́ть** (-ну́, -нёшь) *pf* (*impf* **развёртывать, развора́чивать**) unfold, unwrap; unroll; unfurl; deploy; expand; develop; turn; scan; display; **~ся** unfold, unroll, come unwrapped; deploy; develop; spread; turn.

развёрстка allotment, apportionment.

развёртывать(ся *impf of* **разверну́ть(ся**

раз|весели́ть *pf* cheer up, amuse; **~ся** cheer up.

разве́сить[1] (-е́шу) *pf* (*impf* **разве́шивать**) spread; hang (out).

разве́сить[2] (-е́шу) *pf* (*impf* **разве́шивать**) weigh out. **разве́ска** weighing. **развесно́й** sold by weight.

развести́ (-еду́, -едёшь; -ёл, -а́) *pf* (*impf* **разводи́ть**) take; separate; divorce; dilute; dissolve; start; breed; cultivate; **~сь** get divorced; breed, multiply.

разветви́ться (-ви́тся) *pf*, **разветвля́ться** *impf* branch; fork. **разветвле́ние** branching, forking; branch; fork.

развéшать *pf*, **развéшивать** *impf* hang.
развéшивать *impf of* **развéсить, развéшать. развéшу** *etc.*: *see* **развéсить**
развéять (-éю) *pf* (*impf* **развéивать**) scatter, disperse; dispel; **~ся** disperse; be dispelled.
развивáть(ся *impf of* **развúть(ся**
развúлка fork.
развинтúть (-нчý) *pf*, **развúнчивать** *impf* unscrew.
развúтие development. **развитóй** (рáзвит, -á, -о) developed; mature. **развúть** (-зовью; -зовьёшь; -úл, -á, -о) *pf* (*impf* **развивáть**) develop; unwind; **~ся** develop.
развлекáть *impf*, **развлéчь** (-екý, -ечёшь; -ёк, -лá) *pf* entertain, amuse; **~ся** have a good time; amuse o.s. **развлечéние** entertainment, amusement.
развóд divorce. **разводúть(ся** (-ожý(сь, -óдишь(ся) *impf of* **развестú(сь. развóдка** separation. **разводнóй: ~ ключ** adjustable spanner; **~ мост** drawbridge.
развозúть (-ожý, -óзишь) *impf of* **развезтú**
разволновáть(ся *pf* get excited, be agitated.
разворáчивать(ся *impf of* **развернýть(ся**
разворовáть *pf*, **разворóвывать** *impf* loot; steal.
разворóт U-turn; turn; development.
разврáт depravity, corruption. **развратúть** (-ащý) *pf*, **развращáть** *impf* corrupt; deprave. **разврáтничать** *impf* lead a depraved life. **разврáтный** debauched, corrupt. **развращённый** (-ён, -á) corrupt.
развязáть (-яжý, -ýжешь) *pf*, **развязывать** *impf* untie; unleash; **~ся** come untied; **~ся с**+*instr* rid o.s. of. **развязка** dénouement; outcome. **развязный** overfamiliar.
разгадáть *pf*, **разгáдывать** *impf* solve, guess, interpret. **разгáдка** solution.
разгáр height, climax.
разгибáть(ся *impf of* **разогнýть(ся**
разглагóльствовать *impf* hold forth.
разглáдить (-áжу) *pf*, **разглáживать** *impf* smooth out; iron (out).
разгласúть (-ашý) *pf*, **разглашáть** *impf* divulge; **+о**+*prep* trumpet. **разглашéние** disclosure.
разглядéть (-яжý) *pf*, **разглядывать** *impf* make out, discern.
разгнéвать *pf* anger. **раз|гнéваться** *pf.*
разговáривать *impf* talk, converse. **разговóр** conversation. **разговóрник** phrase-book. **разговóрный** colloquial. **разговóрчивый** talkative.
разгóн dispersal; running start; distance. **разгонять(ся** *impf of* **разогнáть(ся**
разгорáживать *impf of* **разгородúть**
разгорáться *impf*, **разгорéться** (-рюсь) *pf* flare up.
разгородúть (-ожý, -óдишь) *pf* (*impf* **разгорáживать**) partition off.
раз|горячúть(ся (-чý(сь) *pf.*
разгрáбить (-блю) *pf* plunder, loot. **разграблéние** plunder, looting.
разграничéние demarcation;

differentiation. **разграни́чивать** *impf*, **разграни́чить** (-чу) *pf* delimit; differentiate.

разгреба́ть *impf*, **разгрести́** (-ебу́, -ебёшь; -ёб, -ла́) *pf* rake *or* shovel (away).

разгро́м crushing defeat; devastation; havoc. **разгроми́ть** (-млю́) *pf* rout, defeat.

разгружа́ть *impf*, **разгрузи́ть** (-ужу́, -у́зишь) *pf* unload; relieve; **~ся** unload; be relieved. **разгру́зка** unloading; relief.

разгрыза́ть *impf*, **раз|гры́зть** (-зу́, -зёшь; -ы́з) *pf* crack.

разгу́л revelry; outburst. **разгу́ливать** *impf* stroll about. **разгу́ливаться** *impf*, **разгуля́ться** *pf* spread o.s.; become wide awake; clear up. **разгу́льный** wild, rakish.

раздава́ть(ся (-даю́(сь, -даёшь(ся) *impf of* **разда́ть(ся**

раз|дави́ть (-влю́, -вишь) *pf*, **разда́вливать** *impf* crush; run over.

разда́ть (-а́м, -а́шь, -а́ст, -адим́; ро́з- *or* разда́л, -а́, -о) *pf* (*impf* **раздава́ть**) distribute, give out; **~ся** be heard; resound; ring out; make way; expand; put on weight. **разда́ча** distribution.

раздаю́ *etc.*: *see* **раздава́ть**

раздва́ивать(ся *impf of* **раздвои́ть(ся**

раздвига́ть *impf*, **раздви́нуть** (-ну) *pf* move apart; **~ся** move apart. **раздвижно́й** expanding; sliding.

раздвое́ние division; split; **~ ли́чности** split personality. **раздво́енный** forked; cloven; split. **раздвои́ть** *pf* (*impf* **раздва́ивать**) divide into two; bisect; **~ся** fork; split.

раздева́лка cloakroom. **раздева́ть(ся** *impf of* **разде́ть(ся**

разде́л division; section.

разде́латься *pf* +с+*instr* finish with; settle accounts with.

разделе́ние division. **раздели́мый** divisible. **раз|дели́ть** (-лю́, -лишь) *pf*, **разделя́ть** *impf* divide; separate; share; **~ся** divide; be divided; be divisible; separate. **разде́льный** separate.

разде́ну *etc.*: *see* **разде́ть**. **раздеру́** *etc.*: *see* **разодра́ть**

разде́ть (-де́ну) *pf* (*impf* **раздева́ть**) undress; **~ся** undress; take off one's coat.

раздира́ть *impf of* **разодра́ть**

раздобыва́ть *impf*, **раздобы́ть** (-бу́ду) *pf* get, get hold of.

раздо́лье expanse; liberty. **раздо́льный** free.

раздо́р discord.

раздоса́довать *pf* vex.

раздража́ть *impf*, **раздражи́ть** (-жу́) *pf* irritate; annoy; **~ся** get annoyed. **раздраже́ние** irritation. **раздражи́тельный** irritable.

раз|дроби́ть (-блю́) *pf*, **раздробля́ть** *impf* break; smash to pieces.

раздува́ть(ся *impf of* **разду́ть(ся**

разду́мать *pf*, **разду́мывать** *impf* change one's mind; ponder. **разду́мье** meditation; thought.

разду́ть (-у́ю) *pf* (*impf* **раздува́ть**) blow; fan; exaggerate; whip up; swell; **~ся** swell.

разева́ть *impf of* **рази́нуть**

разжа́лобить (-блю) *pf* move (to pity).

разжа́ловать *pf* demote.

разжа́ть (-зожму́, -мёшь) *pf* (*impf* **разжима́ть**) unclasp, open; release.

разжева́ть (-жую́, -жуёшь) *pf*, **разжёвывать** *impf* chew.

разже́чь (-зожгу́, -зожжёшь; -жёг, -зожгла́) *pf*, **разжига́ть** *impf* kindle; rouse.

разжима́ть *impf of* **разжа́ть**.

раз|жире́ть (-е́ю) *pf*.

рази́нуть (-ну) *pf* (*impf* **разева́ть**) open; ~ **рот** gape. **рази́ня** *m* & *f* scatter-brain.

рази́тельный striking. **рази́ть** (ражу́) *impf* (*pf* **по~**) strike.

разлага́ть(ся *impf of* **разложи́ть(ся**

разла́д discord; disorder.

разла́мывать(ся *impf of* **разлома́ть(ся**, **разломи́ть(ся**.

разлёгся *etc.*: *see* **разле́чься**

разлеза́ться *impf*, **разле́зться** (-зется; -ле́зся) *pf* come to pieces; fall apart.

разлета́ться *impf*, **разлете́ться** (-лечу́сь) *pf* fly away; scatter; shatter; rush.

разле́чься (-ля́гусь; -лёгся, -гла́сь) *pf* stretch out.

разли́в bottling; flood; overflow. **разлива́ть** *impf*, **разли́ть** (-золью́, -зольёшь; -и́л, -а́, -о) *pf* pour out; spill; flood (with); **~ся** spill; overflow; spread. **разливно́й** draught.

различа́ть *impf*, **различи́ть** (-чу́) *pf* distinguish; discern; **~ся** differ. **разли́чие** distinction; difference. **различи́тельный** distinctive, distinguishing. **разли́чный** different.

разложе́ние decomposition; decay; disintegration. **разложи́ть** (-жу́, -жишь) *pf* (*impf* **разлага́ть**, **раскла́дывать**) put away; spread (out); distribute; break down; decompose; resolve; corrupt; **~ся** decompose; become demoralized; be corrupted; disintegrate, go to pieces.

разло́м breaking; break. **разлома́ть**, **разломи́ть** (-млю́, -мишь) *pf* (*impf* **разла́мывать**) break to pieces; pull down; **~ся** break to pieces.

разлу́ка separation. **разлуча́ть** *impf*, **разлучи́ть** (-чу́) *pf* separate, part; **~ся** separate, part.

разлюби́ть (-блю́, -бишь) *pf* stop loving *or* liking.

разля́гусь *etc.*: *see* **разле́чься**

разма́зать (-а́жу) *pf*, **разма́зывать** *impf* spread, smear.

разма́лывать *impf of* **размоло́ть**

разма́тывать *impf of* **размота́ть**

разма́х sweep; swing; span; scope. **разма́хивать** *impf* +*instr* swing; brandish. **разма́хиваться** *impf*, **размахну́ться** (-ну́сь, -нёшься) *pf* swing one's arm. **разма́шистый** sweeping.

размежева́ние demarcation, delimitation. **размежева́ть** (-жу́ю) *pf*, **размежёвывать** *impf* delimit.

размёл *etc.*: *see* **размести́**

размельча́ть *impf*, **раз|мельчи́ть** (-чу́) *pf* crush, pulverize.

размелю́ *etc.*: *see* **размоло́ть**

разме́н exchange. **разме́нивать** *impf*, **разменя́ть** *pf* change; **~ся** +*instr* exchange; dissipate. **разме́нная моне́та** (small) change.

разме́р size; measurement; amount; scale, extent; *pl* proportions. **разме́ренный** measured. **разме́рить** *pf*, **размеря́ть** *impf* measure.

размести́ (-ету́, -етёшь; -мёл, -а́) *pf* (*impf* **размета́ть**) sweep clear; sweep away.

размести́ть (-ещу́) *pf* (*impf* **размеща́ть**) place, accommodate; distribute; **~ся** take one's seat. **размета́ть** *impf of* **размести́** **разме́тить** (-е́чу) *pf*, **размеча́ть** *impf* mark. **размеша́ть** *pf*, **разме́шивать** *impf* stir (in). **размеща́ть(ся** *impf of* **размести́ть(ся. размеще́ние** placing; accommodation; distribution. **размещу́** *etc.*: *see* **размести́ть** **размина́ть(ся** *impf of* **размя́ть(ся** **разми́нка** limbering up. **размину́ться** (-ну́сь, -нёшься) *pf* pass; +**с**+*instr* pass; miss. **размножа́ть** *impf*, **размно́жить** (-жу) *pf* multiply, duplicate; breed; **~ся** multiply; breed. **размозжи́ть** (-жу́) *pf* smash. **размо́лвка** tiff. **размоло́ть** (-мелю́, -ме́лешь) *pf* (*impf* **размалывать**) grind. **размора́живать** *impf*, **разморо́зить** (-о́жу) *pf* unfreeze, defrost; **~ся** unfreeze; defrost. **размота́ть** *pf* (*impf* **разма́тывать**) unwind. **размыва́ть** *impf*, **размы́ть** (-о́ет) *pf* wash away; erode. **размыка́ть** *impf of* **разомкну́ть** **размышле́ние** reflection; meditation. **размышля́ть** *impf* reflect, ponder. **размягча́ть** *impf*, **размягчи́ть** (-чу́) *pf* soften; **~ся** soften. **размяка́ть** *impf*, **размя́кнуть** (-ну; -мя́к) *pf* soften. **раз|мя́ть** (-зомну́, -зомнёшь) *pf* (*impf also* **размина́ть**) knead; mash; **~ся** stretch one's legs; limber up. **разна́шивать** *impf of* **разноси́ть**

разнести́ (-су́, -сёшь; -ёс, -ла́) *pf* (*impf* **разноси́ть**) carry; deliver; spread; note down; smash; scold; scatter; *impers* make puffy, swell. **разнима́ть** *impf of* **разня́ть** **ра́зниться** *impf* differ. **ра́зница** difference. **разно-** *in comb* different, vari-, hetero-. **разнобо́й** lack of co-ordination; difference. **~ви́дность** variety. **~гла́сие** disagreement; discrepancy. **~обра́зие** variety, diversity. **~обра́зный** various, diverse. **~речи́вый** contradictory. **~ро́дный** heterogeneous. **~сторо́нний** many-sided; versatile. **~цве́тный** variegated. **~шёрстный** of different colours; ill-assorted. **разноси́ть**[1] (-ошу́, -о́сишь) *pf* (*impf* **разна́шивать**) wear in. **разноси́ть**[2] (-ошу́, -о́сишь) *impf of* **разнести́. разно́ска** delivery. **ра́зность** difference. **разно́счик** pedlar. **разношу́** *etc.*: *see* **разноси́ть** **разну́зданный** unbridled. **ра́зн|ый** different; various; **~ое** *sb* various things. **разню́хать** *pf*, **разню́хивать** *impf* smell out. **разня́ть** (-ниму́, -ни́мешь; ро́з- *or* разня́л, -а́, -о) *pf* (*impf* **разнима́ть**) take to pieces; separate. **разоблача́ть** *impf*, **разоблачи́ть** (-чу́) *pf* expose. **разоблаче́ние** exposure. **разобра́ть** (-зберу́, -рёшь; -а́л, -а́, -о) *pf* (*impf* **разбира́ть**) take to pieces; buy up; sort out; investigate; analyse; understand; **~ся** sort things out; +**в**+*prep* investigate, look into; understand. **разобща́ть** *impf*, **разобщи́ть**

(-щу́) *pf* separate; estrange, alienate.
разобью́ *etc.*: *see* **разби́ть.**
разовью́ *etc.*: *see* **разви́ть**
ра́зовый single.
разогна́ть (-згоню́, -о́нишь; -гна́л, -а́, -о) *pf* (*impf* **разгоня́ть**) scatter; disperse; dispel; drive fast; **~ся** gather speed.
разогну́ть (-ну́, -нёшь) *pf* (*impf* **разгиба́ть**) unbend, straighten; **~ся** straighten up.
разогрева́ть *impf*, **разогре́ть** (-е́ю) *pf* warm up.
разоде́ть(ся (-е́ну(сь) *pf* dress up.
разодра́ть (-здеру́, -рёшь; -а́л, -а́, -о) *pf* (*impf* **раздира́ть**) tear (up); lacerate.
разожгу́ *etc.*: *see* **разже́чь.**
разожму́ *etc.*: *see* **разжа́ть**
разо|зли́ть *pf.*
разойти́сь (-йду́сь, -йдёшься; -ошёлся, -ошла́сь) *pf* (*impf* **расходи́ться**) disperse; diverge; radiate; differ; conflict; part; be spent; be sold out.
разолью́ *etc.*: *see* **разли́ть**
ра́зом *adv* at once, at one go.
разомкну́ть (-ну, -нёшь) *pf* (*impf* **размыка́ть**) open; break.
разомну́ *etc.*: *see* **размя́ть**
разорва́ть (-ву́, -вёшь; -а́л, -а́, -о) *pf* (*impf* **разрыва́ть**) tear; break (off); blow up; **~ся** tear; break; explode.
разоре́ние ruin; destruction. **разори́тельный** ruinous; wasteful. **разори́ть** *pf* (*impf* **разоря́ть**) ruin; destroy; **~ся** ruin o.s.
разоружа́ть *impf*, **разоружи́ть** (-жу́) *pf* disarm; **~ся** disarm. **разоруже́ние** disarmament.
разоря́ть(ся *impf of* **разори́ть(ся**
разосла́ть (-ошлю́, -ошлёшь) *pf* (*impf* **рассыла́ть**) distribute, circulate.
разостла́ть, расстели́ть (-стелю́, -те́лешь) *pf* (*impf* **расстила́ть**) spread (out); lay; **~ся** spread.
разотру́ *etc.*: *see* **растере́ть**
разочарова́ние disappointment.
разочарова́ть *pf*, **разочаро́вывать** *impf* disappoint; **~ся** be disappointed.
разочту́ *etc.*: *see* **расче́сть.**
разошёлся *etc.*: *see* **разойти́сь.**
разошлю́ *etc.*: *see* **разосла́ть.**
разошью́ *etc.*: *see* **расши́ть**
разраба́тывать *impf*, **разрабо́тать** *pf* cultivate; work, exploit; work out; develop. **разрабо́тка** cultivation; exploitation; working out; mining; quarry.
разража́ться *impf*, **разрази́ться** (-ажу́сь) *pf* break out; burst out.
разраста́ться *impf*, **разрасти́сь** (-тётся; -ро́сся, -ла́сь) *pf* grow; spread.
разрежённый (-ён, -а́) rarefied.
разре́з cut; section; point of view. **разре́зать** (-е́жу) *pf*, **разреза́ть** *impf* cut; slit.
разреша́ть *impf*, **разреши́ть** (-шу́) *pf* (+*dat*) allow; solve; settle; **~ся** be allowed; be solved; be settled. **разреше́ние** permission; permit; solution; settlement. **разреши́мый** solvable.
разро́зненный uncoordinated; odd; incomplete.
разро́сся *etc.*: *see* **разрасти́сь.**
разро́ю *etc.*: *see* **разры́ть**
разруба́ть *impf*, **разруби́ть** (-блю́, -бишь) *pf* cut; chop up.
разру́ха ruin, collapse. **разруша́ть** *impf*, **разру́шить** (-шу) *pf*

destroy; demolish; ruin; **~ся** go to ruin, collapse. **разруше́ние** destruction. **разруши́тельный** destructive.

разры́в break; gap; rupture; burst. **разрыва́ть**[1]**(ся** *impf of* **разорва́ть(ся**

разрыва́ть[2] *impf of* **разры́ть**

разрывно́й explosive.

разрыда́ться *pf* burst into tears.

разры́ть (-ро́ю) *pf* (*impf* **разрыва́ть**) dig (up).

раз|рыхли́ть *pf*, **разрыхля́ть** *impf* loosen; hoe.

разря́д[1] category; class.

разря́д[2] discharge. **разряди́ть** (-яжу́, -я́дишь) *pf* (*impf* **разряжа́ть**) unload; discharge; space out; **~ся** run down; clear, ease. **разря́дка** spacing (out); discharging; unloading; relieving.

разряжа́ть(ся *impf of* **разряди́ть(ся**

разубеди́ть (-ежу́) *pf*, **разубежда́ть** *impf* dissuade; **~ся** change one's mind.

разува́ться *impf of* **разу́ться**

разуве́рить *pf*, **разуверя́ть** *impf* dissuade, undeceive; **~ся** (**в**+*prep*) lose faith (in).

разузнава́ть (-наю́, -наёшь) *impf*, **разузна́ть** *pf* (try to) find out.

разукра́сить (-а́шу) *pf*, **разукра́шивать** *impf* adorn, embellish.

ра́зум reason; intellect. **разуме́ться** (-е́ется) *impf* be understood, be meant; **(само́ собо́й) разуме́ется** of course; it goes without saying. **разу́мный** rational, intelligent; sensible; reasonable; wise.

разу́ться (-у́юсь) *pf* (*impf* **разува́ться**) take off one's shoes.

разу́чивать *impf*, **разучи́ть** (-чу́, -чишь) *pf* learn (up). **разу́чиваться** *impf*, **разучи́ться** (-чу́сь, -чишься) *pf* forget (how to).

разъеда́ть *impf of* **разъе́сть**

разъедини́ть *pf*, **разъединя́ть** *impf* separate; disconnect.

разъе́дусь *etc.*: *see* **разъе́хаться**

разъе́зд departure; siding (track); mounted patrol; *pl* travel; journeys. **разъездно́й** travelling. **разъезжа́ть** *impf* drive *or* ride about; travel; **~ся** *impf of* **разъе́хаться**

разъе́сть (-е́ст, -едя́т; -е́л) *pf* (*impf* **разъеда́ть**) eat away; corrode.

разъе́хаться (-е́дусь) *pf* (*impf* **разъезжа́ться**) depart; separate; pass (one another); miss one another.

разъярённый (-ён, -а́) furious. **разъяри́ть** *pf*, **разъяря́ть** *impf* infuriate; **~ся** get furious.

разъясне́ние explanation; interpretation. **разъясни́тельный** explanatory.

разъясни́ть *pf*, **разъясня́ть** *impf* explain; interpret; **~ся** become clear, be cleared up.

разыгра́ть *pf*, **разы́грывать** *impf* perform; draw; raffle; play a trick on; **~ся** get up; run high.

разыска́ть (-ыщу́, -ы́щешь) *pf* find. **разы́скивать** *impf* search for.

рай (*loc* -ю́) paradise; garden of Eden.

райко́м district committee.

райо́н region. **райо́нный** district.

ра́йский heavenly.

рак crayfish; cancer; Cancer.

ракéта[1], **ракéтка** racket.
ракéта[2] rocket; missile; flare.
рáковина shell; sink.
рáковый cancer; cancerous.
ракýшка cockle-shell, mussel.
рáма frame. **рáмка** frame; *pl* framework.
рáмпа footlights.
рáна wound. **ранéние** wounding; wound. **рáненый** wounded; injured.
ранг rank.
рáнец (-нца) knapsack; satchel.
рáнить *impf* & *pf* wound; injure.
рáнний early. **рáно** *adv* early. **рáньше** *adv* earlier; before; formerly.
рапúра foil.
рáпорт report. **рапортовáть** *impf* & *pf* report.
рáса race. **расúзм**, racism. **расúстский** racist.
раскáиваться *impf of* **раскáяться**
раскалённый (-ён, -á) scorching; incandescent. **раскалúть** *pf* (*impf* **раскалять**) make red-hot; **~ся** become red-hot. **раскáлывать(ся** *impf of* **расколóть(ся**. **раскалять(ся** *impf of* **раскалúть(ся**. **раскáпывать** *impf of* **раскопáть**
раскáт roll, peal. **раскатáть** *pf*, **раскáтывать** *impf* roll (out), smooth out, level; drive *or* ride (about). **раскáтистый** rolling, booming. **раскатúться** (-ачýсь, -áтишься) *pf*, **раскáтываться** *impf* gather speed; roll away; peal, boom.
раскачáть *pf*, **раскáчивать** *impf* swing; rock; **~ся** swing, rock.
раскáяние repentance. **рас|кáяться** *pf* (*impf also* **раскáиваться**) repent.
расквитáться *pf* settle accounts.
раскúдывать *impf*, **раскúнуть** (-ну) *pf* stretch (out); spread; pitch; **~ся** spread out; sprawl.
раскладнóй folding. **раскладýшка** camp-bed. **расклáдывать** *impf of* **разложúть**
раскланяться *pf* bow; take leave.
расклéивать *impf*, **расклéить** *pf* unstick; stick (up); **~ся** come unstuck.
раскóл split; schism. **рас|колóть** (-лю́, -лешь) *pf* (*impf also* **раскáлывать**) split; break; disrupt; **~ся** split. **раскóльник** dissenter.
раскопáть *pf* (*impf* **раскáпывать**) dig up, unearth, excavate. **раскóпки** (-пок) *pl* excavations.
раскóсый slanting.
раскрáивать *impf of* **раскроúть**
раскрáсить (-áшу) *pf*, *impf* **раскрáшивать** paint, colour.
раскрепостúть (-ощý) *pf*, **раскрепощáть** *impf* liberate. **раскрепощéние** emancipation.
раскритиковáть *pf* criticize harshly.
раскроúть *pf* (*impf* **раскрáивать**) cut out.
раскрóю *etc.*: *see* **раскры́ть**
раскрутúть (-учý, -ýтишь) *pf*, **раскрýчивать** *impf* untwist; **~ся** come untwisted.
раскрывáть *impf*, **раскры́ть** (-óю) *pf* open; expose; reveal; discover; **~ся** open; uncover o.s.; come to light.
раскупáть *impf*, **раскупúть** (-ýпит) *pf* buy up.
раскýпоривать *impf*, **раскý-**

порить *pf* uncork, open.
раскуси́ть (-ушу́, -у́сишь) *pf*, **раску́сывать** *impf* bite through; see through.
ра́совый racial.
распа́д disintegration; collapse. **распада́ться** *impf of* **распа́сться**
распакова́ть *pf*, **распако́вывать** *impf* unpack.
распа́рывать(ся *impf of* **распоро́ть(ся**
распа́сться (-адётся) *pf* (*impf* **распада́ться**) disintegrate, fall to pieces.
распаха́ть (-ашу́, -а́шешь) *pf*, **распа́хивать**[1] *impf* plough up.
распа́хивать[2] *impf*, **распахну́ть** (-ну́, -нёшь) *pf* throw open; **~ся** fly open, swing open.
распашо́нка baby's vest.
распева́ть *impf* sing.
распеча́тать *pf*, **распеча́тывать** *impf* open; unseal.
распи́ливать *impf*, **распили́ть** (-лю́, -лишь) *pf* saw up.
распина́ть *impf of* **распя́ть**
расписа́ние time-table. **расписа́ть** (-ишу́, -и́шешь) *pf*, **распи́сывать** *impf* enter; assign; paint; **~ся** sign; register one's marriage; **+в**+*prep* sign for; acknowledge. **распи́ска** receipt. **расписно́й** painted, decorated.
распиха́ть *pf*, **распи́хивать** *impf* push, shove, stuff.
рас|пла́вить (-влю) *pf*, **расплавля́ть** *impf* melt, fuse. **распла́вленный** molten.
распла́каться (-а́чусь) *pf* burst into tears.
распласта́ть *pf*, **распла́стывать** *impf* spread; flatten; split; **~ся** sprawl.
распла́та payment; retribution. **расплати́ться** (-ачу́сь, -а́тишься) *pf*, **распла́чиваться** *impf* (**+с**+*instr*) pay off; get even; **+за**+*acc* pay for.
расплеска́ть(ся (-ещу́(сь, -е́щешь(ся) *pf*, **расплёскивать(ся** *impf* spill.
расплести́ (-ету́, -етёшь; -ёл, -а́) *pf*, **расплета́ть** *impf* unplait; untwist.
рас|плоди́ть(ся (-ожу́(сь) *pf*.
расплыва́ться *impf*, **расплы́ться** (-ывётся; -ы́лся, -а́сь) *pf* run. **расплы́вчатый** indistinct; vague.
расплю́щивать *impf*, **расплю́щить** (-щу) *pf* flatten out, hammer out.
распну́ *etc.*: *see* **распя́ть**
распознава́ть (-наю́, -наёшь) *impf*, **распозна́ть** *pf* recognize, identify; diagnose.
располага́ть *impf* +*instr* have at one's disposal. **располага́ться** *impf of* **расположи́ться**
располза́ться *impf*, **расползти́сь** (-зётся; -о́лзся, -зла́сь) *pf* crawl (away); give at the seams.
расположе́ние disposition; arrangement; situation; tendency; liking; mood. **располо́женный** disposed, inclined. **расположи́ть** (-жу́, -жишь) *pf* (*impf* **располага́ть**) dispose; set out; win over; **~ся** settle down.
распо́рка cross-bar, strut.
рас|поро́ть (-рю́, -решь) *pf* (*impf also* **распа́рывать**) unpick, rip; **~ся** rip, come undone.
распоряди́тель *m* manager. **распоряди́тельный** capable; efficient. **распоряди́ться** (-яжу́сь) *pf*, **распоряжа́ться** *impf* order, give orders; see; +*instr* manage, deal with. **распоря́док** (-дка) order; routine. **распоряже́ние** order; instruc-

tion; disposal, command.

распра́ва violence; reprisal.

распра́вить (-влю) *pf*, **расправля́ть** *impf* straighten; smooth out; spread.

распра́виться (-влюсь) *pf*, **расправля́ться** *impf* **с**+*instr* deal with severely; make short work of.

распределе́ние distribution; allocation. **распредели́тель** *m* distributor. **распредели́тельный** distributive, distributing; **~ щит** switchboard. **распредели́ть** *pf*, **распределя́ть** *impf* distribute; allocate.

распродава́ть (-даю, -даёшь) *impf*, **распрода́ть** (-а́м, -а́шь, -а́ст, -адим; -о́дал, -а́, -о) *pf* sell off; sell out of. **распрода́жа** (clearance) sale.

распростёртый outstretched; prostrate.

распростране́ние spreading; dissemination. **распространённый** (-ён, -а́) widespread, prevalent. **распространи́ть** *pf*, **распространя́ть** *impf* spread; **~ся** spread.

ра́спря (*gen pl* -ей) quarrel.

распряга́ть *impf*, **распря́чь** (-ягу́, -яжёшь; -я́г, -ла́) *pf* unharness.

распрями́ться *pf*, **распрямля́ться** *impf* straighten up.

распуска́ть *impf*, **распусти́ть** (-ущу́, -у́стишь) *pf* dismiss; dissolve; let out; relax; let get out of hand; melt; spread; **~ся** open; come loose; dissolve; melt; get out of hand; let o.s. go.

распу́тать *pf* (*impf* **распу́тывать**) untangle; unravel.

распу́тица season of bad roads.

распу́тный dissolute. **распу́тство** debauchery.

распу́тывать *impf of* **распу́тать**

распу́тье crossroads.

распуха́ть *impf*, **распу́хнуть** (-ну; -у́х) *pf* swell (up).

распу́щенный undisciplined; spoilt; dissolute.

распыли́тель *m* spray, atomizer. **распыли́ть** *pf*, **распыля́ть** *impf* spray; pulverize; disperse.

распя́тие crucifixion; crucifix. **распя́ть** (-пну́, -пнёшь) *pf* (*impf* **распина́ть**) crucify.

расса́да seedlings. **рассади́ть** (-ажу́, -а́дишь) *pf*, **расса́живать** *impf* plant out; seat; separate, seat separately.

расса́живаться *impf of* **рассе́сться**. **расса́сываться** *impf of* **рассоса́ться**

рассвести́ (-етёт; -ело́) *pf*, **рассвета́ть** *impf* dawn. **рассве́т** dawn.

рас|свирепе́ть (-е́ю) *pf*.

расседла́ть *pf* unsaddle.

рассе́ивание dispersal, scattering. **рассе́ивать(ся** *impf of* **рассе́ять(ся**

рассека́ть *impf of* **рассе́чь**

расселе́ние settling, resettlement; separation.

рассе́лина cleft, fissure.

рассели́ть *pf*, **расселя́ть** *impf* settle, resettle; separate.

рас|серди́ть(ся (-жу́(сь, -рдишь(ся) *pf*.

рассе́сться (-ся́дусь) *pf* (*impf* **расса́живаться**) take seats.

рассе́чь (-еку́, -ечёшь; -ёк, -ла́) *pf* (*impf* **рассека́ть**) cut (through); cleave.

рассе́янность absent-

mindedness; dispersion. **рассе́янный** absent-minded; diffused; scattered. **рассе́ять** (-е́ю) *pf* (*impf* **рассе́ивать**) disperse, scatter; dispel; **~ся** disperse, scatter; clear; divert o.s.
расска́з story; account. **рассказа́ть** (-ажу́, -а́жешь) *pf*, **расска́зывать** *impf* tell, recount. **расска́зчик** story-teller, narrator.
рассла́бить (-блю) *pf*, **расслабля́ть** *impf* weaken; **~ся** relax.
рассла́ивать(ся *impf of* **расслои́ть(ся**
рассле́дование investigation, examination; inquiry; **произвести́ ~**+*gen* hold an inquiry into. **рассле́довать** *impf* & *pf* investigate, look into, hold an inquiry into.
расслои́ть *pf* (*impf* **рассла́ивать**) divide into layers; **~ся** become stratified; flake off.
рассльı́шать (-шу) *pf* catch.
рассма́тривать *impf of* **рассмотре́ть**; examine; consider.
рас|смеши́ть (-шу́) *pf*.
рассмея́ться (-ею́сь, -еёшься) *pf* burst out laughing.
рассмотре́ние examination; consideration. **рассмотре́ть** (-рю́, -ришь) *pf* (*impf* **рассма́тривать**) examine, consider; discern, make out.
рассова́ть (-сую́, -суёшь) *pf*, **рассо́вывать** *impf* **по**+*dat* shove into.
рассо́л brine; pickle.
рассо́риться *pf* **с**+*instr* fall out with.
рас|сортирова́ть *pf*, **рассортиро́вывать** *impf* sort out.
рассоса́ться (-сётся) *pf* (*impf* **расса́сываться**) resolve.
рассо́хнуться (-нется; -о́хся) *pf* (*impf* **рассыха́ться**) crack.
расспра́шивать *impf*, **расспроси́ть** (-ошу́, -о́сишь) *pf* question; make inquiries of.
рассро́чить (-чу) *pf* spread (over a period). **рассро́чка** instalment.
расстава́ние parting. **расстава́ться** (-таю́сь, -таёшься) *impf of* **расста́ться**
расста́вить (-влю) *pf*, **расставля́ть** *impf* place, arrange; move apart. **расстано́вка** arrangement; pause.
расста́ться (-а́нусь) *pf* (*impf* **расстава́ться**) part, separate.
расстёгивать *impf*, **расстегну́ть** (-ну́, -нёшь) *pf* undo, unfasten; **~ся** come undone; undo one's coat.
расстели́ть(ся, *etc.*: *see* **разостла́ть(ся**. **расстила́ть(ся, -а́ю(сь** *impf of* **разостла́ть(ся**
расстоя́ние distance.
расстра́ивать(ся *impf of* **расстро́ить(ся**
расстре́л execution by firing squad. **расстре́ливать** *impf*, **расстреля́ть** *pf* shoot.
расстро́енный disordered; upset; out of tune. **расстро́ить** *pf* (*impf* **расстра́ивать**) upset; thwart; disturb; throw into confusion; put out of tune; **~ся** be upset; get out of tune; fall into confusion; fall through. **расстро́йство** upset; disarray; confusion; frustration.
расступа́ться *impf*, **расступи́ться** (-у́пится) *pf* part, make way.
рассуди́тельный reasonable; sensible. **рассуди́ть** (-ужу́, -у́дишь) *pf* judge; think; decide. **рассу́док** (-дка) reason; intellect. **рассужда́ть** *impf* reason; **+о**+*prep* discuss. **рассужде́ние**

reasoning; discussion; argument.

рассую́ *etc.*: *see* **рассова́ть**

рассчи́танный deliberate; intended. **рассчита́ть** *pf*, **рассчи́тывать** *impf*, **расче́сть** (разочту́, -тёшь; расчёл, разочла́) *pf* calculate; count; depend; **~ся** settle accounts.

рассыла́ть *impf of* **разосла́ть**. **рассы́лка** distribution. **рассы́льный** *sb* delivery man.

рассы́пать (-плю) *pf*, **рассыпа́ть** *impf* spill; scatter; **~ся** spill, scatter; spread out; crumble. **рассы́пчатый** friable; crumbly.

рассыха́ться *impf of* **рассо́хнуться**. **расся́дусь** *etc.*: *see* **рассе́сться**. **раста́лкивать** *impf of* **растолка́ть**. **раста́пливать(ся** *impf of* **растопи́ть(ся**

растаска́ть *pf*, **раста́скивать** *impf*, **растащи́ть** (-щу́, -щишь) *pf* pilfer, filch.

растащи́ть *see* **растаска́ть**.

рас|та́ять (-а́ю) *pf*.

раство́р² opening, span. **раство́р**¹ solution; mortar. **раствори́мый** soluble. **раствори́тель** *m* solvent. **раствори́ть**¹ *pf* (*impf* **растворя́ть**) dissolve; **~ся** dissolve.

раствори́ть² (-рю́, -ришь) *pf* (*impf* **растворя́ть**) open; **~ся** open.

растворя́ть(ся *impf of* **раствори́ть(ся**. **растека́ться** *impf of* **расте́чься**

расте́ние plant.

растере́ть (разотру́, -трёшь; растёр) *pf* (*impf* **растира́ть**) grind; spread; rub; massage.

растерза́ть *pf*, **расте́рзывать** *impf* tear to pieces.

расте́рянность confusion, dismay. **расте́рянный** confused, dismayed. **растеря́ть** *pf* lose; **~ся** get lost; lose one's head.

расте́чься (-ечётся, -еку́тся; -тёкся, -ла́сь) *pf* (*impf* **растека́ться**) run; spread.

расти́ (-ту́, -тёшь; рос, -ла́) *impf* grow; grow up.

растира́ние grinding; rubbing, massage. **растира́ть(ся** *impf of* **растере́ть(ся**

расти́тельность vegetation; hair. **расти́тельный** vegetable.

расти́ть (ращу́) *impf* bring up; train; grow.

растлева́ть *impf*, **растли́ть** *pf* seduce; corrupt.

растолка́ть *pf* (*impf* **раста́лкивать**) push apart; shake.

растолкова́ть *pf*, **растолко́вывать** *impf* explain.

рас|толо́чь (-лку́, -лчёшь; -ло́к, -лкла́) *pf*.

растолсте́ть (-е́ю) *pf* put on weight.

растопи́ть¹ (-плю́, -пишь) *pf* (*impf* **раста́пливать**) melt; thaw; **~ся** melt.

растопи́ть² (-плю́, -пишь) *pf* (*impf* **раста́пливать**) light, kindle; **~ся** begin to burn.

растопта́ть (-пчу́, -пчешь) *pf* trample, stamp on.

расторга́ть *impf*, **расто́ргнуть** (-ну; -о́рг) *pf* annul, dissolve. **расторже́ние** annulment, dissolution.

расторо́пный quick; efficient.

расточа́ть *impf*, **расточи́ть** (-чу́) *pf* squander, dissipate. **расточи́тельный** extravagant, wasteful.

растрави́ть (-влю́, -вишь) *pf*, **растравля́ть** *impf* irritate.

растра́та spending; waste; embezzlement. **растра́тить** (-а́чу)

pf, **растрáчивать** *impf* spend; waste; embezzle.
растрёпанный dishevelled; tattered. **рас|трепáть** (-плю́, -плешь) *pf* disarrange; tatter.
растрéскаться *pf*, **растрéскиваться** *impf* crack, chap.
растрóгать *pf* move, touch; **~ся** be moved.
растýщий growing.
растя́гивать *impf*, **растянýть** (-нý, -нешь) *pf* stretch (out); strain, sprain; drag out; **~ся** stretch; drag on; sprawl. **растяжéние** tension; strain, sprain. **растяжи́мый** tensile; stretchable. **растя́нутый** stretched; long-winded.
рас|фасовáть *pf*.
расформировáть *pf*, **расформирóвывать** *impf* break up; disband.
расхáживать *impf* walk about; pace up and down.
расхвáливать *impf*, **расхвали́ть** (-лю́, -лишь) *pf* lavish praises on.
расхватáть *pf*, **расхвáтывать** *impf* seize on, buy up.
расхити́тель *m* embezzler. **расхи́тить** (-и́щу) *pf*, **расхищáть** *impf* steal, misappropriate. **расхищéние** misappropriation.
расхля́банный loose; lax.
расхóд expenditure; consumption; *pl* expenses, outlay. **расходи́ться** (-ожýсь, -óдишься) *impf of* **разойти́сь**. **расхóдование** expense, expenditure. **расхóдовать** *impf* (*pf* **из~**) spend; consume. **расхождéние** divergence.
расхолáживать *impf*, **расхолоди́ть** (-ожý) *pf* damp the ardour of.
расхотéть (-очý, -óчешь, -оти́м) *pf* no longer want.
расхохотáться (-очýсь, -óчешься) *pf* burst out laughing.
расцарáпать *pf* scratch (all over).
расцвести́ (-етý, -етёшь; -ёл, -á) *pf*, **расцветáть** *impf* blossom; flourish. **расцвéт** blossoming (out); flowering, heyday.
расцвéтка colours; colouring.
расцéнивать *impf*, **расцени́ть** (-ню́, -нишь) *pf* estimate, value; consider. **расцéнка** valuation; price; (wage-)rate.
расцепи́ть (-плю́, -пишь) *pf*, **расцепля́ть** *impf* uncouple, unhook.
расчесáть (-ешý, -éшешь) *pf* (*impf* **расчёсывать**) comb; scratch. **расчёска** comb.
расчéсть *etc.*: *see* **рассчитáть**.
расчёсывать *impf of* **расчесáть**
расчёт[1] calculation; estimate; gain; settlement. **расчётливый** thrifty; careful. **расчётный** calculation; pay; accounts; calculated.
расчи́стить (-и́щу) *pf*, **расчищáть** *impf* clear; **~ся** clear. **расчи́стка** clearing.
рас|члени́ть *pf*, **расчленя́ть** *impf* dismember; divide.
расшатáть *pf*, **расшáтывать** *impf* shake loose, make rickety; impair.
расшевели́ть (-лю́, -éли́шь) *pf* stir; rouse.
расшибáть *impf*, **расшиби́ть** (-бý, -бёшь; -и́б) *pf* smash to pieces; hurt; stub; **~ся** hurt o.s.
расшивáть *impf of* **расши́ть**
расширéние widening; expansion; dilation, dilatation. **рас-**

ши́рить *pf*, **расширя́ть** *impf* widen; enlarge; expand; **~ся** broaden, widen; expand, dilate.
расши́ть (разошью́, -шьёшь) *pf* (*impf* **расшива́ть**) embroider; unpick.
расшифрова́ть *pf*, **расшифро́вывать** *impf* decipher.
расшнурова́ть *pf*, **расшнуро́вывать** *impf* unlace.
расще́лина crevice.
расщепи́ть (-плю́) *pf*, **расщепля́ть** *impf* split; **~ся** split. **расщепле́ние** splitting; fission.
ратифици́ровать *impf* & *pf* ratify.
рать army, battle.
ра́унд round.
рафини́рованный refined.
рацио́н ration.
рационализа́ция rationalization. **рационализи́ровать** *impf* & *pf* rationalize. **рациона́льный** rational; efficient.
ра́ция walkie-talkie.
рвану́ться (-ну́сь, -нёшься) *pf* dart, dash.
рва́ный torn; lacerated. **рвать**[1] (рву, рвёшь; рвал, -á, -о) *impf* tear (out); pull out; pick; blow up; break off; **~ся** break; tear; burst, explode; be bursting.
рвать[2] (рвёт; рва́ло) *impf* (*pf* **вы́~**) *impers+acc* vomit.
рвач (-á) self-seeker.
рве́ние zeal.
рво́та vomiting.
реабилита́ция rehabilitation. **реабилити́ровать** *impf* & *pf* rehabilitate.
реаги́ровать *impf* (*pf* **от~**, **про~**) react.
реакти́в reagent. **реакти́вный** reactive; jet-propelled. **реа́ктор** reactor.
реакционе́р reactionary. **реакцио́нный** reactionary. **реа́кция** reaction.
реализа́ция realization. **реали́зм** realism. **реализова́ть** *impf* & *pf* realize. **реали́ст** realist. **реалисти́ческий** realistic.
реа́льность reality; practicability. **реа́льный** real; practicable.
ребёнок (-нка; *pl* ребя́та, -я́т *and* де́ти, -е́й) child; infant.
ребро́ (*pl* рёбра, -бер) rib; edge.
ребя́та (-я́т) *pl* children; guys; lads. **ребя́ческий** child's; childish. **ребя́чество** childishness. **ребя́читься** (-чусь) *impf* be childish.
рёв roar; howl.
рева́нш revenge; return match.
ревера́нс curtsey.
реве́ть (-ву́, -вёшь) *impf* roar; bellow; howl.
ревизио́нный inspection; auditing. **реви́зия** inspection; audit; revision. **ревизо́р** inspector.
ревмати́зм rheumatism.
ревни́вый jealous. **ревнова́ть** *impf* (*pf* **при~**) be jealous. **ре́вностный** zealous. **ре́вность** jealousy.
револьве́р revolver.
революционе́р revolutionary. **революцио́нный** revolutionary. **револю́ция** revolution.
рега́та regatta.
ре́гби *neut indecl* rugby.
ре́гент regent.
регио́н region. **региона́льный** regional.
регистра́тор registrar. **регистрату́ра** registry. **регистра́ция** registration. **регистри́ровать** *impf* & *pf* (*pf also* **за~**)

register, record; **~ся** register; register one's marriage.
регла́мент standing orders; time-limit. **регламента́ция** regulation. **регламенти́ровать** *impf* & *pf* regulate.
регресси́ровать *impf* regress.
регули́ровать *impf* (*pf* **от~**, **у~**) regulate; adjust. **регули-ро́вщик** traffic controller. **регу-ля́рный** regular. **регуля́тор** regulator.
редакти́ровать *impf* (*pf* **от~**) edit. **реда́ктор** editor. **реда́к-торский** editorial. **редакцио́н-ный** editorial, editing. **реда́к-ция** editorial staff; editorial office; editing.
реде́ть (-е́ет) *impf* (*pf* **по~**) thin (out).
реди́с radishes. **реди́ска** radish.
ре́дкий (-док, -дка́, -о) thin; sparse; rare. **ре́дко** *adv* sparsely; rarely, seldom. **ре́дкость** rarity.
редколле́гия editorial board.
рее́стр register.
режи́м régime; routine; procedure; regimen; conditions.
режиссёр-(постано́вщик) producer; director.
ре́жущий cutting, sharp. **ре́-зать** (ре́жу) *impf* (*pf* **за~**, **про~**, **с~**) cut; engrave; kill, slaughter.
резви́ться (-влю́сь) *impf* gambol, play. **ре́звый** frisky, playful.
резе́рв reserve. **резе́рвный** reserve; back-up.
резервуа́р reservoir.
резе́ц (-зца́) cutter; chisel; incisor.
резиде́нция residence.
рези́на rubber. **рези́нка** rubber; elastic band. **рези́новый** rubber.
ре́зкий sharp; harsh; abrupt; shrill. **резно́й** carved. **резня́** carnage.
резолю́ция resolution.
резона́нс resonance; response.
результа́т result.
резьба́ carving, fretwork.
резюме́ *neut indecl* résumé.
рейд[1] roads, roadstead.
рейд[2] raid.
ре́йка lath, rod.
рейс trip; voyage; flight.
рейту́зы (-у́з) *pl* leggings; riding breeches.
река́ (*acc* ре́ку́; *pl* -и, ре́ка́м) river.
ре́квием requiem.
реквизи́т props.
рекла́ма advertising, advertisement. **реклами́ровать** *impf* & *pf* advertise. **рекла́мный** publicity.
рекоменда́тельный of recommendation. **рекоменда́ция** recommendation; reference. **ре-комендова́ть** *impf* & *pf* (*pf also* **от~**, **по~**) recommend; **~ся** introduce o.s.; be advisable.
реконструи́ровать *impf* & *pf* reconstruct. **реконстру́кция** reconstruction.
реко́рд record. **реко́рдный** record, record-breaking. **ре-кордсме́н, -е́нка** record-holder.
ре́ктор principal (*of university*).
реле́ (*electr*) *neut indecl* relay.
религио́зный religious. **рели́-гия** religion.
рели́квия relic.
релье́ф relief. **релье́фный** relief; raised, bold.

рельс rail.
рема́рка stage direction.
реме́нь (-мня́) *m* strap; belt.
реме́сленник artisan, craftsman. **реме́сленный** handicraft; mechanical. **ремесло́** (*pl* -ёсла, -ёсел) craft; trade.
ремо́нт repair(s); maintenance. **ремонти́ровать** *impf* & *pf* (*pf also* **от~**) repair; recondition. **ремо́нтный** repair.
ре́нта rent; income. **рента́бельный** paying, profitable.
рентге́н X-rays. **рентге́новский** X-ray. **рентгено́лог** radiologist. **рентгеноло́гия** radiology.
реорганиза́ция reorganization. **реорганизова́ть** *impf* & *pf* reorganize.
ре́па turnip.
репатрии́ровать *impf* & *pf* repatriate.
репертуа́р repertoire.
репети́ровать *impf* (*pf* **от~**, **про~**, **с~**) rehearse; coach. **репети́тор** coach. **репети́ция** rehearsal.
ре́плика retort; cue.
репорта́ж report; reporting. **репортёр** reporter.
репре́ссия repression.
репроду́ктор loud-speaker. **репроду́кция** reproduction.
репута́ция reputation.
ресни́ца eyelash.
респу́блика republic. **республика́нский** republican.
рессо́ра spring.
реставра́ция restoration. **реставри́ровать** *impf* & *pf* (*pf also* **от~**) restore.
рестора́н restaurant.
ресу́рс resort; *pl* resources.
ретрансля́тор (radio-)relay.
рефера́т synopsis, abstract; paper, essay.
рефере́ндум referendum.
рефле́кс reflex. **рефле́ктор** reflector.
рефо́рма reform. **реформи́ровать** *impf* & *pf* reform.
рефрижера́тор refrigerator.
рецензи́ровать *impf* (*pf* **про~**) review. **реце́нзия** review.
реце́пт prescription; recipe.
рециди́в relapse. **рецидиви́ст** recidivist.
речево́й speech; vocal.
ре́чка river. **речно́й** river.
речь (*gen pl* -е́й) speech.
реша́ть(ся *impf of* **реши́ть(ся**. **реша́ющий** decisive, deciding. **реше́ние** decision; solution.
решётка grating; grille, railing; lattice; trellis; fender, (fire-)guard; (fire-)grate; tail. **решето́** (*pl* -ёта) sieve. **решётчатый** lattice, latticed.
реши́мость resoluteness; resolve. **реши́тельно** *adv* resolutely; definitely; absolutely. **реши́тельность** determination. **реши́тельный** definite; decisive. **реши́ть** (-шу́) *pf* (*impf* **реша́ть**) decide; solve; **~ся** make up one's mind.
ржаве́ть (-е́ет) *impf* (*pf* **за~**, **по~**) rust. **ржа́вчина** rust. **ржа́вый** rusty.
ржано́й rye.
ржать (ржу, ржёшь) *impf* neigh.
ри́млянин (*pl* -яне, -ян), **ри́млянка** Roman. **ри́мский** Roman.
ринг boxing ring.
ри́нуться (-нусь) *pf* rush, dart.
рис rice.
риск risk. **риско́ванный** risky;

risqué. **рискова́ть** *impf*, **рискну́ть** *pf* run risks; *+instr or inf* risk.

рисова́ние drawing. **рисова́ть** *impf* (*pf* **на~**) draw; paint, depict; **~ся** be silhouetted; appear; pose.

ри́совый rice.

рису́нок (-нка) drawing; figure; pattern, design.

ритм rhythm. **ритми́ческий, ритми́чный** rhythmic.

ритуа́л ritual.

риф reef.

ри́фма rhyme. **рифмова́ть** *impf* rhyme; **~ся** rhyme.

робе́ть (-е́ю) *impf* (*pf* **о~**) be timid. **ро́бкий** (-бок, -бка́, -о) timid, shy. **ро́бость** shyness.

ро́бот robot.

ров (рва, *loc* -у) ditch.

рове́сник coeval. **ро́вно** *adv* evenly; exactly; absolutely. **ро́вный** flat; even; level; equable; exact; equal. **ровня́ть** *impf* (*pf* **с~**) even, level.

рог (*pl* -á, -о́в) horn; antler. **рога́тка** catapult. **рога́тый** horned. **рогови́ца** cornea. **рогово́й** horn; horny; horn-rimmed.

род (*loc* -у́; *pl* -ы́) family, kin, clan; birth, origin, stock; generation; genus; sort, kind. **роди́льный** maternity. **ро́дина** native land; homeland. **ро́динка** birth-mark. **роди́тели** (-ей) *pl* parents. **роди́тельный** genitive. **роди́тельский** parental. **роди́ть** (рожу́, -и́л, -ила́, -о) *impf* & *pf* (*impf also* **рожа́ть, рожда́ть**) give birth to; **~ся** be born.

родни́к (-á) spring.

родни́ть *impf* (*pf* **по~**) make related, link; **~ся** become related. **родн|о́й** own; native; home; **~о́й брат** brother; **~ы́е** *sb pl* relatives. **родня́** relative(s); kinsfolk. **родово́й** tribal; ancestral; generic; gender. **родонача́льник** ancestor; father. **родосло́вн|ый** genealogical; **~ая** *sb* genealogy, pedigree. **ро́дственник** relative. **ро́дственный** related. **родство́** relationship, kinship. **ро́ды** (-ов) *pl* childbirth; labour.

ро́жа (ugly) mug.

рожа́ть, рожда́ть(ся *impf of* **роди́ть(ся. рожда́емость** birthrate. **рожде́ние** birth. **рожде́ственский** Christmas. **Рождество́** Christmas.

рожь (ржи) rye.

ро́за rose.

ро́зга (*gen pl* -зог) birch.

ро́здал *etc.*: *see* **разда́ть**

розе́тка electric socket, power point; rosette.

ро́зница retail; **в ~у** retail. **ро́зничный** retail. **рознь** difference; dissension.

ро́знял *etc.*: *see* **разня́ть**

ро́зовый pink.

ро́зыгрыш draw; drawn game.

ро́зыск search; inquiry.

рои́ться swarm. **рой** (*loc* -ю́; *pl* -и́, -ёв) swarm.

рок fate.

рокиро́вка castling.

рок-му́зыка rock music.

рокова́й fateful; fatal.

ро́кот roar, rumble. **рокота́ть** (-о́чет) *impf* roar, rumble.

ро́лик roller; castor; *pl* roller skates.

роль (*gen pl* -е́й) role.

ром rum.

рома́н novel; romance. **романи́ст** novelist.

рома́нс (*mus*) romance.
рома́нтик romantic. **рома́нтика** romance. **романти́ческий, романти́чный** romantic.
рома́шка camomile.
ромб rhombus.
роня́ть *impf* (*pf* **урони́ть**) drop.
ро́пот murmur, grumble. **ропта́ть** (-пщу́, -пщешь) *impf* murmur, grumble.
рос *etc.*: *see* **расти́**
роса́ (*pl* -ы) dew. **роси́стый** dewy.
роско́шный luxurious; luxuriant. **ро́скошь** luxury; luxuriance.
ро́слый strapping.
ро́спись painting(s), mural(s).
ро́спуск dismissal; disbandment.
росси́йский Russian. **Росси́я** Russia.
ро́ссыпи *f pl* deposit.
рост growth; increase; height, stature.
ро́стбиф roast beef.
ростовщи́к (-а́) usurer, money-lender.
росто́к (-тка́) sprout, shoot.
ро́счерк flourish.
рот (рта, *loc* рту) mouth.
ро́та company.
рота́тор duplicator.
ро́тный company; *sb* company commander.
ротозе́й, -зе́йка gaper, rubberneck; scatter-brain.
ро́ща grove.
ро́ю *etc.*: *see* **рыть**
роя́ль *m* (grand) piano.
ртуть mercury.
руба́нок (-нка) plane.
руба́ха, руба́шка shirt.
рубе́ж (-а́) boundary, border(line); line; **за ~о́м** abroad.
рубе́ц (-бца́) scar; weal; hem; tripe.
руби́н ruby. **руби́новый** ruby; ruby-coloured.
руби́ть (-блю́, -бишь) *impf* (*pf* **с~**) fell; hew, chop; mince; build (of logs).
ру́бище rags.
ру́бка[1] felling; chopping; mincing.
ру́бка[2] deck house; **боева́я ~** conning-tower; **рулева́я ~** wheelhouse.
рублёвка one-rouble note.
рублёвый (one-)rouble.
ру́бленый minced, chopped; of logs.
рубль (-я́) *m* rouble.
ру́брика rubric, heading.
ру́бчатый ribbed. **ру́бчик** scar; rib.
ру́гань abuse, swearing. **руга́тельный** abusive. **руга́тельство** oath, swear-word. **руга́ть** *impf* (*pf* **вы́~, об~, от~**) curse, swear at; abuse; **~ся** curse, swear; swear at one another.
руда́ (*pl* -ы) ore. **рудни́к** (-а́) mine, pit. **рудни́чный** mine, pit; **~ газ** fire-damp. **рудоко́п** miner.
руже́йный rifle, gun. **ружьё** (*pl* -ья, -жей, -ьям) gun, rifle.
руи́на *usu pl* ruin.
рука́ (*acc* -у; *pl* -и, рук, -а́м) hand; arm; **идти́ по́д руку с**+*instr* walk arm in arm with; **под руко́й** at hand; **руко́й пода́ть** a stone's throw away; **э́то мне на́ руку** that suits me.
рука́в (-а́; *pl* -а́, -о́в) sleeve. **рукави́ца** mitten; gauntlet.
руководи́тель *m* leader; manager; instructor; guide. **руководи́ть** (-ожу́) *impf* +*instr* lead; guide; direct, manage. **руко-**

во́дство leadership; guidance; direction; guide; handbook, manual; leaders. **руково́дствоваться**+*instr* follow; be guided by. **руководя́щий** leading; guiding.
рукоде́лие needlework.
рукомо́йник washstand.
рукопа́шный hand-to-hand.
рукопи́сный manuscript. **ру́копись** manuscript.
рукоплеска́ние applause. **рукоплеска́ть** (-ещу́, -е́щешь) *impf* +*dat* applaud.
рукопожа́тие handshake.
рукоя́тка handle.
рулево́й steering; *sb* helmsman.
руле́тка tape-measure; roulette.
рули́ть *impf* (*pf* **вы~**) taxi.
руль (-я́) *m* rudder; helm; (steering-)wheel; handlebar.
румы́н (*gen pl* -ын), **~ка** Romanian. **Румы́ния** Romania. **румы́нский** Romanian.
румя́на (-я́н) *pl* rouge. **румя́нец** (-нца) (high) colour; flush; blush. **румя́ный** rosy, ruddy.
ру́пор megaphone; mouthpiece.
руса́к (-а́) hare.
руса́лка mermaid.
ру́сло river-bed; course.
ру́сский Russian; *sb* Russian.
ру́сый light brown.
Русь (*hist*) Russia.
рути́на routine.
ру́хлядь junk.
ру́хнуть (-ну) *pf* crash down.
руча́тельство guarantee. **руча́ться** *impf* (*pf* **поручи́ться**) +**за**+*acc* vouch for, guarantee.
руче́й (-чья́) brook.
ру́чка handle; (door-)knob; (chair-)arm; pen; **ручн|о́й** hand; arm; manual; tame; **~ы́е часы́** wrist-watch.

ру́шить (-у) *impf* (*pf* **об~**) pull down; **~ся** collapse.
РФ *abbr* (*of* **Росси́йская Федера́ция**) Russian Federation.
ры́ба fish. **рыба́к** (-а́) fisherman. **рыба́лка** fishing. **рыба́цкий, рыба́чий** fishing. **ры́бий** fish; fishy; **~ жир** cod-liver oil. **ры́бный** fish. **рыбoло́в** fisherman. **рыболо́вный** fishing.
рыво́к (-вка́) jerk.
рыда́ние sobbing. **рыда́ть** *impf* sob.
ры́жий (рыж, -а́, -е) red, red-haired; chestnut.
ры́ло snout; mug.
ры́нок (-нка) market; market-place. **ры́ночный** market.
рыса́к (-а́) trotter.
рысь[1] (*loc* -и́) trot; **~ю, на рыся́х** at a trot.
рысь[2] lynx.
ры́твина rut, groove. **ры́ть(ся** (ро́ю(сь) *impf* (*pf* **вы~, от~**) dig; rummage.
рыхли́ть *impf* (*pf* **вз~, раз~**) loosen. **ры́хлый** (-л, -а́, -о) friable; loose.
ры́царский chivalrous. **ры́царь** *m* knight.
рыча́г (-а́) lever.
рыча́ть (-чу́) *impf* growl, snarl.
рья́ный zealous.
рюкза́к (*gen* -а́) rucksack.
рю́мка wineglass.
ряби́на[1] rowan, mountain ash.
ряби́на[2] pit, pock. **ряби́ть** (-и́т) *impf* ripple; *impers*: **у меня́ ряби́т в глаза́х** I am dazzled. **рябо́й** pock-marked. **ря́бчик** hazel hen, hazel grouse. **рябь** ripples; dazzle.
ря́вкать *impf*, **ря́вкнуть** (-ну) *pf* bellow, roar.
ряд (*loc* -у́; *pl* -ы́) row; line; file,

rank; series; number. **рядово́й** ordinary; common; ~ **соста́в** rank and file; *sb* private. **ря́дом** *adv* alongside; close by; +**с**+*instr* next to.

ря́са cassock.

С

с, со *prep* **I.** +*gen* from; since; off; for, with; on; by; **с ра́дости** for joy; **с утра́** since morning. **II.** +*acc* about; the size of; **с неде́лю** for about a week. **III.** +*instr* with; and; **мы с ва́ми** you and I; **что с ва́ми?** what is the matter?

са́бля (*gen pl* -бель) sabre.

сабота́ж sabotage. **саботи́ровать** *impf* & *pf* sabotage.

са́ван shroud; blanket.

с|агити́ровать *pf.*

сад (*loc* -у́; *pl* -ы́) garden. **сади́ть** (сажу́, са́дишь) *impf* (*pf* **по~**) plant. **сади́ться** (сажу́сь) *impf of* **сесть. садо́вник, -ница** gardener. **садово́дство** gardening; horticulture. **садо́вый** garden; cultivated.

сади́зм sadism. **сади́ст** sadist. **сади́стский** sadistic.

са́жа soot.

сажа́ть *impf* (*pf* **посади́ть**) plant; seat; set, put. **са́женец** (-нца) seedling; sapling.

са́же́нь (*pl* -и, -жен *or* -же́не́й) sazhen (*2.13 metres*).

сажу́ *etc.*: *see* **сади́ть**

са́йка roll.

сайт (*comput*) (web)site.

саксофо́н saxophone.

сала́зки (-зок) *pl* toboggan.

сала́т lettuce; salad.

са́ло fat, lard; suet; tallow.

сало́н salon; saloon.

салфе́тка napkin.

са́льный greasy; tallow; obscene.

салю́т salute. **салютова́ть** *impf* & *pf* (*pf also* **от~**) +*dat* salute.

сам (-ого́) *m*, **сама́** (-о́й, *acc* -оё) *f*, **само́** (-ого́) *neut*, **са́ми** (-и́х) *pl*, *pron* -self, -selves; myself, *etc.*, ourselves, *etc.*; ~ **по себе́** in itself; by o.s.; ~ **собо́й** of itself, of its own accord; **~о́ собо́й (разуме́ется)** of course; it goes without saying.

са́мбо *neut indecl abbr* (*of* **самозащи́та без ору́жия**) unarmed combat.

саме́ц (-мца́) male. **са́мка** female.

само- *in comb* self-, auto-. **самобы́тный** original, distinctive. **~возгора́ние** spontaneous combustion. **~во́льный** wilful; unauthorized. **~де́льный** home-made. **~держа́вие** autocracy. **~держа́вный** autocratic. **~де́ятельность** amateur work, amateur performance; initiative. **~дово́льный** self-satisfied. **~ду́р** petty tyrant. **~ду́рство** high-handedness. **~забве́ние** selflessness. **~забве́нный** selfless. **~защи́та** self-defence. **~зва́нец** (-нца) impostor, pretender. **~ка́т** scooter. **~кри́тика** self-criticism. **~люби́вый** proud; touchy. **~лю́бие** pride, self-esteem. **~мне́ние** conceit, self-importance. **~наде́янный** presumptuous. **~облада́ние** self-control. **~обма́н** self-deception. **~оборо́на** self-defence. **~образова́ние** self-education. **~обслу́живание** self-service. **~определе́ние** self-determination. **~отве́р-**

женность selflessness. **~отве́рженный** selfless. **~поже́ртвование** self-sacrifice. **~ро́док** (-дка) nugget; person with natural talent. **~сва́л** tip-up lorry. **~созна́ние** (self-)consciousness. **~сохране́ние** self-preservation. **~стоя́тельность** independence. **~стоя́тельный** independent. **~су́д** lynch law, mob law. **~тёк** drift. **~тёком** *adv* by gravity; of its own accord. **~убийственный** suicidal. **~убийство** suicide. **~убийца** *m* & *f* suicide. **~уваже́ние** self-respect. **~уве́ренность** self-confidence. **~уве́ренный** self-confident. **~униже́ние** self-abasement. **~управле́ние** self-government. **~управля́ющийся** self-governing. **~упра́вный** arbitrary. **~учи́тель** *m* self-instructor, manual. **~у́чка** *m* & *f* self-taught person. **~хо́дный** self-propelled. **~чу́вствие** general state; **как ва́ше ~чу́вствие?** how do you feel?

самова́р samovar.

самого́н home-made vodka.

самолёт aeroplane.

самоцве́т semi-precious stone.

са́мый *pron* (the) very, (the) right; (the) same; (the) most.

сан dignity, office.

санато́рий sanatorium.

санда́лия sandal.

са́ни (-е́й) *pl* sledge, sleigh.

санита́р medical orderly; stretcher-bearer. **санитари́я** sanitation. **санита́рка** nurse. **санита́рн|ый** medical; health; sanitary; **~ая маши́на** ambulance; **~ый у́зел = сану́зел.**

са́нки (-нок) *pl* sledge; toboggan.

санкциони́ровать *impf* & *pf* sanction. **са́нкция** sanction.

сано́вник dignitary.

санпу́нкт medical centre.

санскри́т Sanskrit.

санте́хник plumber.

сантиме́тр centimetre; tape-measure.

сану́зел (-зла́) sanitary arrangements; WC.

санча́сть (*gen pl* -е́й) medical unit.

сапёр sapper.

сапо́г(-а́; *gen pl* -о́г) boot. **сапо́жник** shoemaker; cobbler. **сапо́жный** shoe.

сапфи́р sapphire.

сара́й shed; barn.

саранча́ locust(s).

сарафа́н sarafan; pinafore dress.

сарде́лька small fat sausage.

сарди́на sardine.

сарка́зм sarcasm. **саркасти́ческий** sarcastic.

сатана́ *m* Satan. **сатани́нский** satanic.

сателли́т satellite.

сати́н sateen.

сати́ра satire. **сати́рик** satirist. **сатири́ческий** satirical.

Сау́довская Ара́вия Saudi Arabia.

сафья́н morocco. **сафья́новый** morocco.

са́хар sugar. **сахари́н** saccharine. **са́харистый** sugary. **са́харница** sugar-basin. **са́харн|ый** sugar; sugary; **~ый заво́д** sugar-refinery; **~ый песо́к** granulated sugar; **~ая пу́дра** castor sugar; **~ая свёкла** sugar-beet.

сачо́к (-чка́) net.

сба́вить (-влю) *pf*, **сбавля́ть**

impf take off; reduce.
с|баланси́ровать *pf.*
сбе́гать[1] *pf* run; +**за**+*instr* run for. **сбега́ть**[2] *impf*, **сбежа́ть** (-егу́) *pf* run down (from); run away; disappear; **~ся** come running.
сберега́тельная ка́сса savings bank. **сберега́ть** *impf*, **сбере́чь** (-егу́, -ежёшь; -ёг, -ла́) *pf* save; save up; preserve. **сбереже́ние** economy; saving; savings. **сберка́сса** savings bank.
сбива́ть *impf*, **с|бить** (собью́, -бьёшь) *pf* bring down, knock down; knock off; distract; wear down; knock together; churn; whip, whisk; **~ся** be dislodged; slip; go wrong; be confused; **~ся с пути́** lose one's way; **~ся с ног** be run off one's feet. **сби́вчивый** confused; inconsistent.
сближа́ть *impf*, **сбли́зить** (-и́жу) *pf* bring (closer) together, draw together; **~ся** draw together; become good friends. **сближе́ние** rapprochement; closing in.
сбо́ку *adv* from one side; on one side.
сбор collection; duty; fee, toll; takings; gathering. **сбо́рище** crowd, mob. **сбо́рка** assembling, assembly; gather. **сбо́рник** collection. **сбо́рный** assembly; mixed, combined; prefabricated; detachable. **сбо́рочный** assembly. **сбо́рщик** collector; assembler.
сбра́сывать(ся *impf of* **сбро́сить(ся**
сбрива́ть *impf*, **сбрить** (сбре́ю) *pf* shave off.
сброд riff-raff.
сброс fault, break. **сбро́сить** (-о́шу) *pf* (*impf* **сбра́сывать**) throw down, drop; throw off; shed; discard.
сбру́я (*collect*) (riding) tack.
сбыва́ть *impf*, **сбыть** (сбу́ду; сбыл, -а́, -о) *pf* sell, market; get rid of; **~ся** come true, be realized. **сбыт** (*no pl*) sale; market.
св. *abbr* (*of* **свято́й**) Saint.
сва́дебный wedding. **сва́дьба** (*gen pl* -деб) wedding.
сва́ливать *impf*, **с|вали́ть** (-лю́, -лишь) *pf* throw down; overthrow; pile up; **~ся** fall (down), collapse. **сва́лка** dump; scuffle.
с|валя́ть *pf.*
сва́ривать *impf*, **с|вари́ть** (-рю́, -ришь) *pf* boil; cook; weld. **сва́рка** welding.
сварли́вый cantankerous.
сварно́й welded. **сва́рочный** welding. **сва́рщик** welder.
сва́стика swastika.
сва́тать *impf* (*pf* **по~**, **со~**) propose as a husband or wife; propose to; **~ся к**+*dat or* **за**+*acc* propose to.
сва́я pile.
све́дение piece of information; knowledge; *pl* information, intelligence; knowledge. **све́дущий** knowledgeable; versed.
сведу́ *etc.*: *see* **свести́**
свежезаморо́женный fresh-frozen; chilled. **све́жесть** freshness. **свеже́ть** (-е́ет) *impf* (*pf* **по~**) become cooler; freshen. **све́жий** (-еж, -а́, -о́, -и) fresh; new.
свезти́ (-зу́, -зёшь; свёз, -ла́) *pf* (*impf* **свози́ть**) take; bring *or* take down *or* away.
свёкла beet, beetroot.
свёкор (-кра) father-in-law. **свекро́вь** mother-in-law.
свёл *etc.*: *see* **свести́**
сверга́ть *impf*, **све́ргнуть** (-ну;

сверг) *pf* throw down, overthrow. **сверже́ние** overthrow.

свéрить *pf* (*impf* **сверя́ть**) collate.

сверка́ть *impf* sparkle, twinkle; glitter; gleam. **сверкну́ть** (-ну́, -нёшь) *pf* flash.

сверли́льный drill, drilling; boring. **сверли́ть** *impf* (*pf* **про~**) drill; bore (through); nag. **сверло́** drill. **сверля́щий** gnawing, piercing.

сверну́ть (-ну́, -нёшь) *pf* (*impf* **свёртывать, свора́чивать**) roll (up); turn; curtail, cut down; **~ шéю**+*dat* wring the neck of; **~ся** roll up, curl up; curdle, coagulate; contract.

свéрстник contemporary.

свёрток (-тка) package, bundle. **свёртывание** rolling (up); curdling; coagulation; curtailment, cuts. **свёртывать(ся** *impf of* **сверну́ть(ся**

сверх *prep*+*gen* over, above, on top of; beyond; in addition to; **~ того́** moreover.

сверх- *in comb* super-, over-, hyper-. **сверхзвуково́й** supersonic. **~пла́новый** over and above the plan. **~при́быль** excess profit. **~проводни́к** (-á) superconductor. **~секрéтный** top secret. **~уро́чный** overtime. **~уро́чные** *sb pl* overtime. **~человéк** superman. **~человéческий** superhuman. **~ъестéственный** supernatural.

свéрху *adv* from above; **~ до́низу** from top to bottom.

сверчо́к (-чка́) cricket.

сверше́ние achievement.

сверя́ть *impf of* **свéрить**

свéсить (-éшу) *pf* (*impf* **свéшивать**) let down, lower; **~ся** hang over, lean over.

свести́ (-еду́, -едёшь; -ёл, -á) *pf* (*impf* **своди́ть**) take; take down; take away; remove; bring together; reduce, bring; cramp.

свет[1] light; daybreak.

свет[2] world; society.

света́ть *impf impers* dawn. **свети́ло** luminary. **свети́ть** (-ечу́, -éтишь) *impf* (*pf* **по~**) shine; +*dat* light; light the way for; **~ся** shine, gleam. **светлéть** (-éет) *impf* (*pf* **по~, про~**) brighten (up); grow lighter. **свéтлость** brightness; Grace. **свéтлый** light; bright; joyous. **светлячо́к** (-чка́) glow-worm.

свето- *in comb* light, photo-. **светонепроница́емый** lightproof. **~фи́льтр** light filter. **~фо́р** traffic light(s).

светово́й light; luminous; **~ день** daylight hours.

светопреставлéние end of the world.

свéтский fashionable; refined; secular.

светя́щийся luminous, fluorescent. **свеча́** (*pl* -и, -éй) candle; (spark-)plug. **свечéние** luminescence, fluorescence. **свéчка** candle. **свечу́** *etc.*: *see* **свети́ть**

с|вéшать *pf*. **свéшивать(ся** *impf of* **свéсить(ся. свива́ть** *impf of* **свить**

свида́ние meeting; appointment; **до свида́ния!** goodbye!

свидéтель *m*, **-ница** witness. **свидéтельство** evidence; testimony; certificate. **свидéтельствовать** *impf* (*pf* **за~, о~**) give evidence, testify; be evidence (of); witness.

свина́рник pigsty.

свинéц (-нца́) lead.

свини́на pork. **сви́нка** mumps.

свино́й pig; pork. **сви́нство**

despicable act; outrage; squalor.

свинцо́вый lead; leaden.

свинья́ (*pl* -ньи, -не́й, -ньям) pig, swine.

свире́ль (reed-)pipe.

свирепе́ть (-е́ю) *impf* (*pf* **рас~**) grow savage; become violent. **свире́пствовать** *impf* rage; be rife. **свире́пый** fierce, ferocious.

свиса́ть *impf*, **сви́снуть** (-ну; -ис) *pf* hang down, dangle; trail.

свист whistle; whistling. **свиста́ть** (-ищу́, -и́щешь) *impf* whistle. **свисте́ть** (-ищу́) *impf*, **сви́стнуть** (-ну) *pf* whistle; hiss. **свисто́к** (-тка́) whistle.

сви́та suite; retinue.

сви́тер sweater.

сви́ток (-тка) roll, scroll. **с|вить** (совью́, совьёшь; -ил, -а́, -о) *pf* (*impf also* **свива́ть**) twist, wind; **~ся** roll up.

свихну́ться (-ну́сь, -нёшься) *impf* go mad; go astray.

свищ (-а́) flaw; (knot-)hole; fistula.

свищу́ *etc.*: *see* **свиста́ть, свисте́ть**

свобо́да freedom. **свобо́дно** *adv* freely; easily; fluently; loose(ly). **свобо́дный** free; easy; vacant; spare; loose; flowing. **свободолюби́вый** freedom-loving. **свободомы́слие** free-thinking.

свод code; collection; arch, vault.

своди́ть (-ожу́, -о́дишь) *impf of* **свести́**

сво́дка summary; report. **сво́дный** composite; step-.

сво́дчатый arched, vaulted.

своево́лие self-will, wilfulness.

своево́льный wilful.

своевре́менно *adv* in good time; opportunely. **своевре́менный** timely, opportune.

своенра́вие capriciousness. **своенра́вный** wilful, capricious.

своеобра́зие originality; peculiarity. **своеобра́зный** original; peculiar.

свожу́ *etc.*: *see* **своди́ть, свози́ть. свози́ть** (-ожу́, -о́зишь) *impf of* **свезти́**

свой (своего́) *m*, **своя́** (свое́й) *f*, **своё** (своего́) *neut*, **свои́** (свои́х) *pl*, *pron* one's (own); my, his, her, its; our, your, their. **сво́йственный** peculiar, characteristic. **сво́йство** property, attribute, characteristic.

сво́лочь swine; riff-raff.

сво́ра leash; pack.

свора́чивать *impf of* **сверну́ть, свороти́ть. с|ворова́ть** *pf*.

свороти́ть (-очу́, -о́тишь) *pf* (*impf* **свора́чивать**) dislodge, shift; turn; twist.

своя́к brother-in-law (*husband of wife's sister*). **своя́ченица** sister-in-law (*wife's sister*).

свыка́ться *impf*, **свы́кнуться** (-нусь; -ы́кся) *pf* get used.

свысока́ *adv* haughtily. **свы́ше** *adv* from above. **свы́ше** *prep+gen* over; beyond.

свя́занный constrained; combined; bound; coupled. **с|вяза́ть** (-яжу́, -я́жешь) *pf*, **свя́зывать** *impf* tie, bind; connect; **~ся** get in touch; get involved. **связи́ст, -и́стка** signaller; worker in communication services. **свя́зка** sheaf, bundle; ligament. **свя́зный** connected, coherent. **связь** (*loc* -и́) connection; link, bond; liaison;

communication(s).
святи́лище sanctuary. **свя́тки** (-ток) *pl* Christmas-tide. **свя́то** *adv* piously; religiously. **свят|о́й** (-ят, -á, -о) holy; **~о́й, ~а́я** *sb* saint. **святы́ня** sacred object *or* place. **свяще́нник** priest. **свяще́нный** sacred.

сгиб bend. **сгиба́ть** *impf of* **согну́ть**

сгла́дить (-а́жу) *pf*, **сгла́живать** *impf* smooth out; smooth over, soften.

сгла́зить (-а́жу) *pf* put the evil eye on.

сгнива́ть *impf*, **с|гнить** (-ию́, -иёшь; -ил, -á, -о) *pf* rot.

с|гнои́ться *pf*.

сгова́риваться *impf*, **сговори́ться** *pf* come to an arrangement; arrange. **сго́вор** agreement. **сгово́рчивый** compliant.

сгоня́ть *impf of* **согна́ть**

сгора́ние combustion; **дви́гатель вну́треннего сгора́ния** internal-combustion engine. **сгора́ть** *impf of* **сгоре́ть**

с|го́рбить(ся (-блю(сь) *pf*.

с|горе́ть (-рю́) *pf* (*impf also* **сгора́ть**) burn down; be burnt down; be used up; burn; burn o.s. out. **сгоряча́** *adv* in the heat of the moment.

с|гото́вить(ся (-влю(сь) *pf*.

сгреба́ть *impf*, **сгрести́** (-ебу́, -ебёшь; -ёб, -ла́) *pf* rake up, rake together.

сгружа́ть *impf*, **сгрузи́ть** (-ужу́, -у́зишь) *pf* unload.

с|группирова́ть(ся *pf*.

сгусти́ть (-ущу́) *pf*, **сгуща́ть** *impf* thicken; condense; **~ся** thicken; condense; clot. **сгу́сток** (-тка) clot. **сгуще́ние** thickening, condensation; clotting.

сдава́ть (сдаю́, сдаёшь) *impf of* **сдать**; **~ экза́мен** take an examination; **~ся** *impf of* **сда́ться**

сдави́ть (-влю́, -вишь) *pf*, **сда́вливать** *impf* squeeze.

сдать (-ам, -ашь, -аст, -ади́м; -ал, -á, -о) *pf* (*impf* **сдава́ть**) hand in, hand over; pass; let, hire out; surrender, give up; deal; **~ся** surrender, yield. **сда́ча** handing over; hiring out; surrender; change; deal.

сдвиг displacement; fault; change, improvement. **сдвига́ть** *impf*, **сдви́нуть** (-ну) *pf* shift, move; move together; **~ся** move, budge; come together.

с|де́лать(ся *pf*. **сде́лка** transaction; deal, bargain. **сде́льн|ый** piece-work; **~ая рабо́та** piece-work. **сде́льщина** piece-work.

сдёргивать *impf of* **сдёрнуть**

сде́ржанный restrained, reserved. **сдержа́ть** (-жу́, -жишь) *pf*, **сде́рживать** *impf* hold back; restrain; keep.

сдёрнуть (-ну) *pf* (*impf* **сдёргивать**) pull off.

сдеру́ *etc.*: *see* **содра́ть**. **сдира́ть** *impf of* **содра́ть**

сдо́ба shortening; fancy bread, bun(s). **сдо́бный** (-бен, -бна́, -о) rich, short.

с|до́хнуть (-нет; сдох) *pf* die; kick the bucket.

сдружи́ться (-жу́сь) *pf* become friends.

сдува́ть *impf*, **сду́нуть** (-ну) *pf*, **сдуть** (-у́ю) *pf* blow away *or* off.

сеа́нс performance; showing; sitting.

себесто́имость prime cost; cost (price).

себя́ (*dat & prep* **себе́**, *instr*

собой *or* собою) *refl pron* oneself; myself, yourself, himself, *etc.*; **ничего себе** not bad; **собой** -looking, in appearance.
себялюбие selfishness.
сев sowing.
се́вер north. **се́верный** north, northern; northerly. **се́веро-восто́к** north-east **се́веро-восто́чный** north-east(ern). **се́веро-за́пад** north-west. **се́веро-за́падный** north-west(ern). **северя́нин** (*pl* -я́не, -я́н) northerner.
севооборо́т crop rotation.
сего́ *see* **сей. сего́дня** *adv* today. **сего́дняшний** of today, today's.
седе́ть (-е́ю) *impf* (*pf* **по~**) turn grey. **седина́** (*pl* -ы) grey hair(s).
седла́ть *impf* (*pf* **о~**) saddle. **седло́** (*pl* сёдла, -дел) saddle.
седоборо́дый grey-bearded. **седоволо́сый** grey-haired. **седо́й** (сед, -á, -о) grey(-haired).
седо́к (-á) passenger; rider.
седьмо́й seventh.
сезо́н season. **сезо́нный** seasonal.
сей (сего́) *m*, **сия́** (сей) *f*, **сие́** (сего́) *neut*, **сии́** (сих) *pl*, *pron* this; these; **сию́ мину́ту** at once, instantly.
сейсми́ческий seismic.
сейф safe.
сейча́с *adv* (just) now; soon; immediately.
сёк *etc.*: *see* **сечь**
секре́т secret.
секретариа́т secretariat.
секрета́рский secretarial. **секрета́рша, секрета́рь** (-я́) *m* secretary.
секре́тный secret.
секс sex. **сексуа́льный** sexual; sexy.
сексте́т sextet.
се́кта sect. **секта́нт** sectarian.
се́ктор sector.
секу́ *etc.*: *see* **сечь**
секуляриза́ция secularization.
секу́нда second. **секунда́нт** second. **секу́ндный** second. **секундоме́р** stop-watch.
секцио́нный sectional. **се́кция** section.
селёдка herring.
селезёнка spleen.
се́лезень (-зня) *m* drake.
селе́кция breeding.
селе́ние settlement, village.
сели́тра saltpetre, nitre.
сели́ть(ся *impf* (*pf* **по~**) settle.
село́ (*pl* сёла) village.
сельдере́й celery.
сельдь (*pl* -и, -е́й) herring.
се́льск|ий rural; village; **~ое хозя́йство** agriculture. **сельскохозя́йственный** agricultural.
сельсове́т village soviet.
сема́нтика semantics. **семанти́ческий** semantic.
семафо́р semaphore; signal.
сёмга (smoked) salmon.
семе́йный family; domestic. **семе́йство** family.
се́мени *etc.*: *see* **се́мя**
семени́ть *impf* mince.
семени́ться *impf* seed. **семенни́к** (-á) testicle; seed-vessel. **семенно́й** seed; seminal.
семёрка seven; figure 7; No. 7.
се́меро (-ы́х) seven.
семе́стр term, semester.
се́мечко (*pl* -и) seed; *pl* sunflower seeds.
семидесятиле́тие seventy

years; seventieth anniversary, birthday. **семидеся́т|ый** seventieth; **~ые го́ды** the seventies. **семиле́тка** seven-year school. **семиле́тний** seven-year; seven-year-old.

семина́р seminar. **семина́рия** seminary.

семисо́тый seven-hundredth. **семна́дцатый** seventeenth. **семна́дцать** seventeen. **семь** (-ми́, -мью́) seven. **се́мьдесят** (-ми́десяти, -мью́десятью) seventy. **семьсо́т** (-мисо́т, *instr* -мьюста́ми) seven hundred. **се́мью** *adv* seven times.

семья́ (*pl* -мьи, -ме́й, -мьям) family. **семьяни́н** family man.

се́мя (-мени; *pl* -мена́, -мя́н, -мена́м) seed; semen, sperm.

сена́т senate. **сена́тор** senator.

се́ни (-е́й) *pl* (entrance-)hall.

се́но hay. **сенова́л** hayloft. **сеноко́с** haymaking; hayfield.

сенсацио́нный sensational. **сенса́ция** sensation.

сенте́нция maxim.

сентимента́льный sentimental.

сентя́брь (-я́) *m* September. **сентя́брьский** September.

се́псис sepsis.

се́ра sulphur; ear-wax.

серб, ~ка Serb. **Се́рбия** Serbia. **се́рбский** Serb(ian). **сербскохорва́тский** Serbo-Croat(ian).

серва́нт sideboard.

се́рвер (*comput*) server.

серви́з service, set. **сервирова́ть** *impf* & *pf* serve; lay (a table). **сервиро́вка** laying; table lay-out.

серде́чник core. **серде́чность** cordiality; warmth. **серде́чный** heart; cardiac; cordial; warm(-hearted). **серди́тый** angry. **серди́ть** (-ржу́, -рдишь) *impf* (*pf* рас~) anger; **~ся** be angry. **сердобо́льный** tender-hearted. **се́рдце** (*pl* -а́, -де́ц) heart; **в сердца́х** in anger; **от всего́ се́рдца** from the bottom of one's heart. **сердцебие́ние** palpitation. **сердцеви́дный** heart-shaped. **сердцеви́на** core, pith, heart.

серебрёный silver-plated. **серебри́стый** silvery. **серебри́ть** *impf* (*pf* **по~**) silver, silver-plate; **~ся** become silvery. **серебро́** silver. **сере́бряный** silver.

середи́на middle.

серёжка earring; catkin.

серена́да serenade.

се́ренький grey; dull.

сержа́нт sergeant.

сери́йный serial; mass. **се́рия** series; part.

се́рный sulphur; sulphuric.

серогла́зый grey-eyed.

се́рость uncouthness; ignorance.

серп (-а́) sickle; **~ луны́** crescent moon.

серпанти́н streamer.

сертифика́т certificate.

се́рый (сер, -а́, -о) grey; dull; uneducated.

серьга́ (*pl* -и, -рёг) earring.

серьёзность seriousness. **серьёзный** serious.

се́ссия session.

сестра́ (*pl* сёстры, сестёр, сёстрам) sister.

сесть (ся́ду) *pf* (*impf* **сади́ться**) sit down; land; set; shrink; **+на**+*acc* board, get on.

се́тка net, netting; (luggage-) rack; string bag; grid.

се́товать *impf* (*pf* **по~**) complain.

сетча́тка retina. **сеть** (*loc* -и́; *pl* -и, -е́й) net; network.

сече́ние section. **сечь** (секу́, сечёшь; сёк) *impf* (*pf* **вы́~**) cut to pieces; flog; **~ся** split.

се́ялка seed drill. **се́ять** (се́ю) *impf* (*pf* **по~**) sow.

сжа́литься *pf* take pity (**над** +*instr*) on.

сжа́тие pressure; grasp, grip; compression. **сжа́тый** compressed; compact; concise.

с|жать[1] (сожну́, -нёшь) *pf*.

сжать[2] (сожму́, -мёшь) *pf* (*impf* **сжима́ть**) squeeze; compress; grip; clench; **~ся** tighten, clench; shrink, contract.

с|жечь (сожгу́, сожжёшь; сжёг, сожгла́) *pf* (*impf* **сжига́ть**) burn (down); cremate.

сжива́ться *impf of* **сжи́ться**

сжига́ть *impf of* **сжечь**

сжима́ть(ся *impf of* **сжа́ть**[2]**(ся**

сжи́ться (-иву́сь, -ивёшься; -и́лся, -а́сь) *pf* (*impf* **сжива́ться**) **с**+*instr* get used to.

с|жу́льничать *pf*.

сза́ди *adv* from behind; behind. **сза́ди** *prep*+*gen* behind.

сзыва́ть *impf of* **созва́ть**

сиби́рский Siberian. **Сиби́рь** Siberia. **сибиря́к** (-а́), **сибиря́чка** Siberian.

сига́ра cigar. **сигаре́та** cigarette.

сигна́л signal. **сигнализа́ция** signalling. **сигнализи́ровать** *impf* & *pf* (*pf also* **про~**) signal. **сигна́льный** signal. **сигна́льщик** signal-man.

сиде́лка sick-nurse. **сиде́ние** sitting. **сиде́нье** seat. **сиде́ть** (-ижу́) *impf* sit; be; fit. **сидя́чий** sitting; sedentary.

сие́ *etc.*: *see* **сей**

си́зый (сиз, -а́, -о) (blue-)grey.

сий *see* **сей**

си́ла strength; force; power; **в си́лу** +*gen* on the strength of, because of; **не по ~ам** beyond one's powers; **си́лой** by force.

сила́ч (-а́) strong man. **си́литься** *impf* try, make efforts.

силово́й power; of force.

сило́к (-лка́) noose, snare.

си́лос silo; silage.

силуэ́т silhouette.

си́льно *adv* strongly, violently; very much, greatly. **си́льный** (-лен *or* -лён, -льна́, -о) strong; powerful; intense, hard.

симбио́з symbiosis.

си́мвол symbol. **символизи́ровать** *impf* symbolize. **символи́зм** symbolism. **символи́ческий** symbolic.

сим-ка́рта SIM (card).

симметри́я symmetry.

симпатизи́ровать *impf* +*dat* like, sympathize with. **симпати́чный** likeable, nice. **симпа́тия** liking; sympathy.

симпо́зиум symposium.

симпто́м symptom.

симули́ровать *impf* & *pf* simulate, feign. **симуля́нт** malingerer, sham. **симуля́ция** simulation, pretence.

симфо́ния symphony.

синаго́га synagogue.

синева́ blue. **синева́тый** bluish. **синегла́зый** blue-eyed. **сине́ть** (-е́ю) *impf* (*pf* **по~**) turn blue; show blue. **си́ний** (синь, -ня́, -не) (dark) blue.

сини́ца titmouse.

сино́д synod. **сино́ним** synonym. **си́нтаксис** syntax.

си́нтез synthesis. **синтези́ровать** *impf* & *pf* synthesize. **син-**

тети́ческий synthetic.
си́нус sine; sinus.
синхронизи́ровать *impf* & *pf* synchronize.
синь[1] blue. **синь**[2] *see* **си́ний**. **си́нька** blueing; blue-print.
синя́к (-á) bruise.
сиони́зм Zionism.
си́плый hoarse, husky. **си́пнуть** (-ну; сип) *impf* (*pf* **о~**) become hoarse, husky.
сире́на siren; hooter.
сире́невый lilac(-coloured). **сире́нь** lilac.
Си́рия Syria.
сиро́п syrup.
сирота́ (*pl* -ы) *m* & *f* orphan. **сиротли́вый** lonely.
систе́ма system. **систематизи́ровать** *impf* & *pf* systematize. **системати́ческий, системати́чный** systematic.
си́тец (-тца) (printed) cotton; chintz.
си́то sieve.
ситуа́ция situation.
си́тцевый print, chintz.
си́филис syphilis.
сифо́н siphon.
сия́ *see* **сей**
сия́ние radiance. **сия́ть** *impf* shine, beam.
сказ tale. **сказа́ние** story, legend. **сказа́ть** (-ажу́, -а́жешь) *pf* (*impf* **говори́ть**) say; speak; tell. **сказа́ться** (-ажу́сь, -а́жешься) *pf*, **ска́зываться** *impf* tell (on); declare o.s. **сказа́тель** *m* storyteller. **ска́зка** (fairy-)tale; fib. **ска́зочный** fairy-tale; fantastic. **сказу́емое** *sb* predicate.
скака́лка skipping-rope. **скака́ть** (-ачу́, -а́чешь) *impf* (*pf* **по~**) skip, jump; gallop. **скаково́й** race, racing.
скала́ (*pl* -ы) rock; cliff. **скали́стый** rocky.
ска́лить *impf* (*pf* **о~**); **~ зу́бы** bare one's teeth; grin; **~ся** bare one's teeth.
ска́лка rolling-pin.
скалола́з rock-climber.
ска́лывать *impf of* **сколо́ть**
скальп scalp.
ска́льпель *m* scalpel.
скаме́ечка footstool; small bench. **скаме́йка** bench. **скамья́** (*pl* ска́мьи, -е́й) bench; **~ подсуди́мых** dock.
сканда́л scandal; brawl, rowdy scene. **скандали́ст** troublemaker. **сканда́литься** *impf* (*pf* **о~**) disgrace o.s. **сканда́льный** scandalous.
скандина́вский Scandinavian.
сканди́ровать *impf* & *pf* declaim.
ска́нер (*comput, med*) scanner.
ска́пливать(ся *impf of* **скопи́ть(ся**
скарб goods and chattels.
ска́редный stingy.
скарлати́на scarlet fever.
скат slope; pitch.
ската́ть *pf* (*impf* **ска́тывать**) roll (up).
ска́терть (*pl* -и, -е́й) tablecloth.
скати́ть (-ачу́, -а́тишь) *pf*, **ска́тывать**[1] *impf* roll down; **~ся** roll down; slip, slide. **ска́тывать**[2] *impf of* **ската́ть**
скафа́ндр diving-suit; spacesuit.
ска́чка gallop, galloping. **ска́чки** (-чек) *pl* horse-race; races. **скачо́к** (-чка́) jump, leap.
ска́шивать *impf of* **скоси́ть**
сква́жина slit, chink; well.
сквер public garden.

скве́рно badly; bad. **скверносло́вить** (-влю) *impf* use foul language. **скве́рный** foul; bad.
сквози́ть *impf* be transparent; show through; **сквози́т** *impers* there is a draught. **сквозно́й** through; transparent. **сквозня́к** (-á) draught. **сквозь** *prep+acc* through.
скворе́ц (-рцá) starling.
скеле́т skeleton.
ске́птик sceptic. **скептици́зм** scepticism. **скепти́ческий** sceptical.
скетч sketch.
ски́дка reduction. **ски́дывать** *impf*, **ски́нуть** (-ну) *pf* throw off *or* down; knock off.
ски́петр sceptre.
скипида́р turpentine.
скирд (-á; *pl* -ы́), **скирда́** (*pl* -ы, -áм) stack, rick.
скиса́ть *impf*, **ски́снуть** (-ну; скис) *pf* go sour.
скита́лец (-льца) wanderer. **скита́ться** *impf* wander.
скиф Scythian.
склад[1] depot; store.
склад[2] mould; turn; logical connection; **~ ума́** mentality.
скла́дка fold; pleat; crease; wrinkle.
скла́дно *adv* smoothly.
складно́й folding, collapsible.
скла́дный (-ден, -дна, -о) well-knit, well-built; smooth, coherent.
скла́дчина: в скла́дчину by clubbing together. **скла́дывать(ся** *impf of* **сложи́ть(ся**
скле́ивать *impf*, **с|скле́ить** *pf* stick together; **~ся** stick together.
склеп (burial) vault, crypt.
склепа́ть *pf*, **склёпывать** *impf* rivet. **склёпка** riveting.
склеро́з sclerosis.
склóка squabble.
склон slope; **на ~е лет** in one's declining years. **склоне́ние** inclination; declension. **склони́ть** (-ню́, -нишь) *pf*, **склоня́ть** *impf* incline; bow; win over; decline; **~ся** bend, bow; yield; be declined. **скло́нность** inclination; tendency. **скло́нный** (-нен, -нна́, -нно) inclined, disposed. **склоня́емый** declinable.
скля́нка phial; bottle; (*naut*) bell.
скоба́ (*pl* -ы, -áм) cramp, clamp; staple.
ско́бка *dim of* **скоба́**; bracket; *pl* parenthesis, parentheses.
скобли́ть (-облю́, -о́бли́шь) *impf* scrape, plane.
ско́ванность constraint. **ско́ванный** constrained; bound. **скова́ть** (скую́, скуёшь) *pf* (*impf* **ско́вывать**) forge; chain; fetter; pin down, hold, contain.
сковорода́ (*pl* ско́вороды, -ро́д, -áм), **сковоро́дка** frying-pan.
ско́вывать *impf of* **скова́ть**
скола́чивать *impf*, **сколоти́ть** (-очу́, -о́тишь) *pf* knock together.
сколо́ть (-лю́, -лешь) *pf* (*impf* **ска́лывать**) chop off; pin together.
скольже́ние sliding, slipping; glide. **скользи́ть** (-льжу́) *impf*, **скользну́ть** (-ну́, -нёшь) *pf* slide; slip; glide. **ско́льзкий** (-зок, -зка́, -о) slippery. **скользя́щий** sliding.
ско́лько *adv* how much; how many; as far as.
с|кома́ндовать *pf*. **с|комбини́ровать** *pf*. **с|ко́мкать** *pf*. **с|ком-**

плектова́ть *pf.* **с|компромети́ровать** *pf.* **с|конструи́ровать** *pf.*

сконфу́женный embarrassed, confused, disconcerted. **с|конфу́зить(ся** (-у́жу(сь) *pf.*

с|концентри́ровать *pf.*

сконча́ться *pf* pass away, die.

с|копи́ровать *pf.*

скопи́ть (-плю́, -пишь) *pf* (*impf* **ска́пливать**) save (up); amass; **~ся** accumulate. **скопле́ние** accumulation; crowd.

ско́пом *adv* in a crowd, en masse.

скорбе́ть (-блю́) *impf* grieve. **ско́рбный** sorrowful. **скорбь** (*pl* -и, -е́й) sorrow.

скоре́е, скоре́й *comp of* **ско́ро, ско́рый**; *adv* rather, sooner; **как мо́жно ~** as soon as possible; **~ всего́** most likely.

скорлупа́ (*pl* -ы) shell.

скорня́к (-а́) furrier.

ско́ро *adv* quickly; soon.

скоро- *in comb* quick-, fast-. **скорова́рка** pressure-cooker. **~гово́рка** patter; tongue-twister. **ско́ропись** cursive; shorthand. **~по́ртящийся** perishable. **~пости́жный** sudden. **~спе́лый** early; fast-ripening; premature; hasty. **~сшива́тель** *m* binder, file. **~те́чный** transient, short-lived.

скоростно́й high-speed. **ско́рость** (*gen pl* -е́й) speed; gear.

скорпио́н scorpion; Scorpio.

с|корректи́ровать *pf.* **с|ко́рчить(ся** (-чу(сь) *pf.*

ско́р|ый (скор, -а́, -о) quick, fast; near; forthcoming; **~ая по́мощь** first-aid; ambulance.

с|коси́ть[1] (-ошу́, -о́сишь) *pf* (*impf also* **ска́шивать**) mow.

с|коси́ть[2] (-ошу́) *pf* (*impf also* **ска́шивать**) squint; cut on the cross.

скот (-а́), **скоти́на** cattle; livestock; beast. **ско́тный** cattle.

ското- *in comb* cattle. **ското-бо́йня** (*gen pl* -о́ен) slaughter-house. **~во́д** cattle-breeder. **~во́дство** cattle-raising.

ско́тский cattle; brutish. **ско́тство** brutish condition; brutality.

скра́сить (-а́шу) *pf*, **скра́шивать** *impf* smooth over; relieve.

скребо́к (-бка́) scraper. **скребу́** *etc.*: *see* **скрести́**

скре́жет grating; gnashing. **скрежета́ть** (-ещу́, -е́щешь) *impf* grate; +*instr* gnash.

скре́па clamp, brace; counter-signature.

скрепи́ть (-плю́) *pf*, **скрепля́ть** *impf* fasten (together), make fast; clamp; countersign, ratify; **скрепя́ се́рдце** reluctantly. **скре́пка** paper-clip. **скрепле́ние** fastening; clamping; tie, clamp.

скрести́ (-ебу́, -ебёшь; -ёб, -ла́) *impf* scrape; scratch; **~сь** scratch.

скрести́ть (-ещу́) *pf*, **скре́щивать** *impf* cross; interbreed. **скреще́ние** crossing. **скре́щивание** crossing; interbreeding.

с|криви́ть(ся (-влю́(сь) *pf.*

скрип squeak, creak. **скрипа́ч** (-а́) violinist. **скрипе́ть** (-плю́) *impf*, **скри́пнуть** (-ну) *pf* squeak, creak; scratch. **скрипи́чный** violin; **~ ключ** treble clef. **скри́пка** violin. **скрипу́чий** squeaky, creaking.

с|кройть *pf.*

скро́мничать *impf* (*pf* **по~**) be (too) modest. **скро́мность**

modesty. **скро́мный** (-мен, -мна́, -о) modest.

скро́ю *etc.*: *see* **скрыть. скрою́** *etc.*: *see* **скрои́ть**

скрупулёзный scrupulous.

с|крути́ть (-учу́, -у́тишь) *pf*, **скру́чивать** *impf* twist; roll; tie up.

скрыва́ть *impf*, **скрыть** (-о́ю) *pf* hide, conceal; **~ся** hide, go into hiding, be hidden; steal away; disappear. **скры́тничать** *impf* be secretive. **скры́тный** secretive. **скры́тый** secret, hidden; latent.

скря́га *m & f* miser.

ску́дный (-ден, -дна́, -о) scanty; meagre. **ску́дость** scarcity, paucity.

ску́ка boredom.

скула́ (*pl* -ы) cheek-bone. **скула́стый** with high cheek-bones.

скули́ть *impf* whine, whimper.

ску́льптор sculptor. **скульпту́ра** sculpture.

ску́мбрия mackerel.

скунс skunk.

скупа́ть *impf of* **скупи́ть**

скупе́ц (-пца́) miser.

скупи́ть (-плю́, -пишь) *pf* (*impf* **скупа́ть**) buy (up).

скупи́ться (-плю́сь) *impf* (*pf* **по~**) be stingy; skimp; be sparing (of +**на**+*acc*).

ску́пка buying (up).

ску́по *adv* sparingly. **скупо́й** (-п, -а́, -о) stingy, meagre. **ску́пость** stinginess.

ску́пщик buyer(-up).

ску́тер (*pl* -а́) outboard speed-boat.

скуча́ть *impf* be bored; **+по** *+dat* miss, yearn for.

ску́ченность density, overcrowding. **ску́ченный** dense, overcrowded. **ску́чить** (-чу) *pf* crowd (together); **~ся** cluster; crowd together.

ску́чный (-чен, -чна́, -о) boring; **мне ску́чно** I'm bored.

с|ку́шать *pf.* **скую́** *etc.*: *see* **скова́ть**

слабе́ть (-е́ю) *impf* (*pf* **о~**) weaken, grow weak. **слаби́тельн|ый** laxative; **~ое** *sb* laxative. **сла́бить** *impf impers*: **его́ сла́бит** he has diarrhoea.

слабо- *in comb* weak, feeble, slight. **слабово́лие** weakness of will. **~во́льный** weak-willed. **~не́рвный** nervy, nervous. **~ра́звитый** under-developed. **~у́мие** feeble-mindedness. **~у́мный** feeble-minded.

сла́бость weakness. **сла́бый** (-б, -а́, -о) weak.

сла́ва glory; fame; **на сла́ву** wonderfully well. **сла́вить** (-влю) *impf* celebrate, sing the praises of; **~ся** (+*instr*) be famous (for). **сла́вный** glorious, renowned; nice.

славяни́н (*pl* -я́не, -я́н), **славя́нка** Slav. **славянофи́л** Slavophil(e). **славя́нский** Slav, Slavonic.

слага́емое *sb* component, term, member. **слага́ть** *impf of* **сложи́ть**

сла́дить (-а́жу) *pf* **с**+*instr* cope with, handle; arrange.

сла́дк|ий (-док, -дка́, -о) sweet; **~ое** *sb* sweet course. **сладостра́стник** voluptuary. **сладостра́стный** voluptuous. **сла́дость** joy; sweetness; *pl* sweets.

сла́женность harmony. **сла́женный** co-ordinated, harmonious.

сла́мывать *impf of* **сломи́ть**

сла́нец (-нца) shale, slate.

сластёна *m* & *f* person with a sweet tooth. **сласть** (*pl* -и, -ей) delight; *pl* sweets, sweet things.

слать (шлю, шлёшь) *impf* send.

слаща́вый sugary, sickly-sweet. **сла́ще** *comp of* **сла́дкий**

сле́ва *adv* to *or* on the left; **~ напра́во** from left to right.

слёг *etc.*: *see* **слечь**

слегка́ *adv* slightly; lightly.

след (следа́, *dat* -у, *loc* -у́; *pl* -ы́) track; footprint; trace. **следи́ть**[1] (-ежу́) *impf* +**за**+*instr* watch; follow; keep up with; look after; keep an eye on. **следи́ть**[2] (-ежу́) *impf* (*pf* **на~**) leave footprints. **сле́дование** movement. **сле́дователь** *m* investigator. **сле́довательно** *adv* consequently. **сле́довать** *impf* (*pf* **по~**) **I.** +*dat or* **за**+*instr* follow; go, be bound; **II.** *impers* (+*dat*) ought; be owing, be owed; **вам сле́дует** +*inf* you ought to; **как сле́дует** properly; as it should be; **ско́лько с меня́ сле́дует?** how much do I owe (you)? **сле́дом** *adv* (**за**+*instr*) immediately after, close behind. **сле́дственный** investigation, inquiry. **сле́дствие**[1] consequence. **сле́дствие**[2] investigation. **сле́дующий** following, next. **сле́жка** shadowing.

слеза́ (*pl* -ёзы, -а́м) tear.

слеза́ть *impf of* **слезть**

слези́ться (-и́тся) *impf* water. **слезли́вый** tearful. **слёзный** tear; tearful. **слезоточи́вый** watering; **~ газ** tear-gas.

слезть (-зу; слез) *pf* (*impf* **слеза́ть**) climb *or* get down; dismount; get off; come off.

слепе́нь (-пня́) *m* horse-fly.

слепе́ц (-пца́) blind man. **слепи́ть**[1] *impf* blind; dazzle.

с|лепи́ть[2] (-плю́, -пишь) *pf* stick together.

сле́пнуть (-ну; слеп) *impf* (*pf* **о~**) go blind. **сле́по** *adv* blindly. **слеп|о́й** (-п, -а́, -о) blind; **~ы́е** *sb pl* the blind.

сле́пок (-пка) cast.

слепота́ blindness.

сле́сарь (*pl* -я́ *or* -и) *m* metalworker; locksmith.

слёт gathering; rally. **слета́ть** *impf*, **слете́ть** (-ечу́) *pf* fly down *or* away; fall down *or* off; **~ся** fly together; congregate.

слечь (сля́гу, -я́жешь; слёг, -гла́) *pf* take to one's bed.

сли́ва plum; plum-tree.

слива́ть(ся *impf of* **сли́ть(ся**.

сли́вки (-вок) *pl* cream. **сли́вочн|ый** cream; creamy; **~ое ма́сло** butter; **~ое моро́женое** dairy ice-cream.

сли́зистый slimy. **слизня́к** (-а́) slug. **слизь** mucus; slime.

с|линя́ть *pf*.

слипа́ться *impf*, **сли́пнуться** (-нется; -и́пся) *pf* stick together.

сли́тно together, as one word. **сли́ток** (-тка) ingot, bar. **с|лить** (солью́, -льёшь; -ил, -а́, -о) *pf* (*impf also* **слива́ть**) pour, pour out *or* off; fuse, amalgamate; **~ся** flow together; blend; merge.

слича́ть *impf*, **сличи́ть** (-чу́) *pf* collate; check. **сличе́ние** collation, checking.

сли́шком *adv* too; too much.

слия́ние confluence; merging; merger.

слова́к, -а́чка Slovak. **слова́цкий** Slovak.

слова́рный lexical; dictionary. **слова́рь** (-я́) *m* dictionary; vocabulary. **слове́сность** literature; philology. **слове́сный** verbal, oral. **сло́вно** *conj* as if; like, as. **сло́во** (*pl* -а́) word; **одни́м ~м** in a word. **сло́вом** *adv* in a word. **словообразова́ние** word-formation. **словоохо́тливый** talkative. **словосочета́ние** word combination, phrase. **словоупотребле́ние** usage.

слог[1] style.

слог[2] (*pl* -и, -о́в) syllable.

слоёный flaky.

сложе́ние composition; addition; build, constitution. **сложи́ть** (-жу́, -жишь) *pf* (*impf* **класть, скла́дывать, слага́ть**) put *or* lay (together); pile, stack; add, add up; fold (up); compose; take off, put down; lay down; **~ся** turn out; take shape; arise; club together. **сло́жность** complication; complexity. **сло́жный** (-жен, -жна́, -о) complicated; complex; compound.

слои́стый stratified; flaky. **слой** (*pl* -и́, -ёв) layer; stratum.

слом demolition, pulling down. **с|лома́ть(ся** *pf*. **сломи́ть** (-млю́, -мишь) *pf* (*impf* **сла́мывать**) break (off); overcome; **сломя́ го́лову** at breakneck speed; **~ся** break.

слон (-а́) elephant; bishop. **слони́ха** she-elephant. **слоно́в|ый** elephant; **~ая кость** ivory.

слоня́ться *impf* loiter, mooch (about).

слуга́ (*pl* -и) *m* (man) servant. **служа́нка** servant, maid. **слу́жащий** *sb* employee. **слу́жба** service; work. **служе́бный** office; official; auxiliary; secondary. **служе́ние** service, serving. **служи́ть** (-жу́, -жишь) *impf* (*pf* **по~**) serve; work.

с|лука́вить (-влю) *pf*.

слух hearing; ear; rumour; **по ~у** by ear. **слухов|о́й** acoustic, auditory, aural; **~о́й аппара́т** hearing aid; **~о́е окно́** dormer (window).

слу́чай incident, event; case; opportunity; chance; **ни в ко́ем слу́чае** in no circumstances. **случа́йно** *adv* by chance, accidentally; by any chance. **случа́йность** chance. **случа́йный** accidental; chance; incidental. **случа́ться** *impf*, **случи́ться** *pf* happen.

слу́шание listening; hearing. **слу́шатель** *m* listener; student; *pl* audience. **слу́шать** *impf* (*pf* **по~, про~**) listen (to); hear; attend lectures on; **(я) слу́шаю!** hello!; very well; **~ся** +*acc* obey, +*gen* heed.

слыть (-ыву́, -ывёшь; -ыл, -а́, -о) *impf* (*pf* **про~**) have the reputation (+*instr or* **за**+*acc* for).

слыха́ть *impf*, **слы́шать** (-шу) *impf* (*pf* **у~**) hear; sense. **слы́шаться** (-шится) *impf* (*pf* **по~**) be heard. **слы́шимость** audibility. **слы́шимый** audible. **слы́шный** (-шен, -шна́, -шно) audible.

слюда́ mica.

слюна́ (*pl* -и, -е́й) saliva; spit; *pl* spittle. **слюня́вый** dribbling.

сля́гу *etc.*: *see* **слечь**

сля́коть slush.

см. *abbr* (*of* **смотри́**) see, *vide*.

сма́зать (-а́жу) *pf*, **сма́зывать** *impf* lubricate; grease; slur over. **сма́зка** lubrication; greasing; grease. **сма́зочный** lubricating.

смак relish. **смакова́ть** *impf* relish; savour.

с|маневри́ровать *pf*.

сма́нивать *impf*, **смани́ть** (-ню́, -нишь) *pf* entice.

с|мастери́ть *pf*. **сма́тывать** *impf of* **смота́ть**

сма́хивать *impf*, **смахну́ть** (-ну́, -нёшь) *pf* brush away *or* off.

сма́чивать *impf of* **смочи́ть**

сме́жный adjacent.

смека́лка native wit.

смёл *etc.*: *see* **смести́**

смеле́ть (-е́ю) *impf* (*pf* **о~**) grow bolder. **сме́лость** boldness, courage. **сме́лый** (-л, -ла́, -ло) bold, courageous. **смельча́к** (-а́) daredevil.

смелю́ *etc.*: *see* **смоло́ть**

сме́на changing; change; replacement(s); relief; shift. **смени́ть** (-ню́, -нишь) *pf*, **сменя́ть**[1] *impf* change; replace; relieve; **~ся** hand over; be relieved; take turns; *+instr* give place to. **сме́нный** shift; changeable. **сме́нщик** relief; *pl* new shift. **сменя́ть**[2] *pf* exchange.

с|ме́рить *pf*.

смерка́ться *impf*, **сме́ркнуться** (-нется) *pf* get dark.

смерте́льный mortal, fatal, death; extreme. **сме́ртность** mortality. **сме́ртный** mortal; death; deadly, extreme. **смерть** (*gen pl* -е́й) death.

смерч whirlwind; waterspout.

смеси́тельный mixing. **с|меси́ть** (-ешу́, -е́сишь) *pf*.

смести́ (-ету́, -етёшь; -ёл, -а́) *pf* (*impf* **смета́ть**) sweep off, away.

смести́ть (-ещу́) *pf* (*impf* **смеща́ть**) displace; remove.

смесь mixture; medley.

сме́та estimate.

смета́на sour cream.

с|мета́ть[1] *pf* (*impf also* **смётывать**) tack (together).

смета́ть[2] *impf of* **смести́**

сме́тливый quick, sharp.

смету́ *etc.*: *see* **смести́**. **смётывать** *impf of* **смета́ть**

сметь (-е́ю) *impf* (*pf* **по~**) dare.

смех laughter; laugh. **смехотво́рный** laughable.

сме́шанный mixed; combined.

с|меша́ть *pf*, **сме́шивать** *impf* mix, blend; confuse; **~ся** mix, (inter)blend; get mixed up. **смеше́ние** mixture; mixing up.

смеши́ть (-шу́) *impf* (*pf* **на~**, **рас~**) make laugh. **смешли́вый** given to laughing. **смешно́й** (-шо́н, -шна́) funny; ridiculous.

смешу́ *etc.*: *see* **смеси́ть**, **смеши́ть**

смеща́ть(ся *impf of* **смести́ть(ся**. **смеще́ние** displacement, removal. **смещу́** *etc.*: *see* **смести́ть**

смея́ться (-ею́сь, -еёшься) *impf* laugh (at **+над**+*instr*).

смире́ние humility, meekness. **смире́нный** humble, meek. **смири́тельн|ый**: **~ая руба́шка** straitjacket. **смири́ть** *pf*, **смиря́ть** *impf* restrain, subdue; **~ся** submit; resign o.s. **сми́рно** *adv* quietly; **~!** attention! **сми́рный** quiet; submissive.

смогу́ *etc.*: *see* **смочь**

смола́ (*pl* -ы) resin; pitch, tar; rosin. **смоли́стый** resinous.

смолка́ть *impf*, **смо́лкнуть** (-ну; -олк) *pf* fall silent.

смо́лоду *adv* from one's youth.

с|молоти́ть (-очу́, -о́тишь) *pf*.

с|моло́ть (смелю́, сме́лешь) *pf*.

смоляно́й pitch, tar, resin.

с|монти́ровать *pf*.

сморка́ть *impf* (*pf* **вы~**) blow;

~ся blow one's nose.

смоpóдина (*no pl*; *usu collect*) currant; currants; currant-bush.

смóрщенный wrinkled. **с|мóрщить(ся** (-щу(сь) *pf*.

смотáть *pf* (*impf* **смáтывать**) wind, reel.

смотр (*loc* -ý; *pl* -óтры́) review, inspection. **смотрéть** (-рю́, -ришь) *impf* (*pf* **по~**) look (at **на**+*acc*); see; watch; look through; examine; +**за**+*instr* look after; +**в**+*acc*, **на**+*acc* look on to; +*instr* look (like); **смотри́(те)!** take care!; **смотря́** it depends; **смотря́ по**+*dat* depending on; **~ся** look at o.s. **смотрово́й** observation, inspection.

смочи́ть (-чу́, -чишь) *pf* (*impf* **смáчивать**) moisten.

с|мочь (-огу́, -óжешь; смог, -лá) *pf*.

с|моше́нничать *pf*. **смóю** *etc*.: *see* **смы́ть**

смрад stench. **смрáдный** stinking.

СМС-сообщéние text message.

смýглый (-гл, -á, -о) dark-complexioned, swarthy.

смути́ть (-ущу́) *pf*, **смущáть** *impf* embarrass, confuse; **~ся** be embarrassed, be confused. **смýтный** vague; dim; troubled. **смущéние** embarrassment, confusion. **смущённый** (-ён, -á) embarrassed, confused.

смывáть *impf of* **смыть**

смыкáть(ся *impf of* **сомкну́ть(ся**

смысл sense; meaning. **смы́слить** *impf* understand. **смыслово́й** semantic.

смыть (смóю) *pf* (*impf* **смывáть**) wash off, away.

смычóк (-чкá) bow.

смышлёный clever.

смягчáть *impf*, **смягчи́ть** (-чу́) *pf* soften; alleviate; **~ся** soften; relent; grow mild.

смятéние confusion; commotion. **с|мять(ся** (сомну́(сь, -нёшь(ся) *pf*.

снабди́ть (-бжу́) *pf*, **снабжáть** *impf* +*instr* supply with. **снабжéние** supply, supplying.

снáйпер sniper.

снарýжи *adv* on *or* from (the) outside.

снаря́д projectile, missile; shell; contrivance; tackle, gear. **снаряди́ть** (-яжу́) *pf*, **снаряжáть** *impf* equip, fit out. **снаряжéние** equipment, outfit.

снасть (*gen pl* -éй) tackle; *pl* rigging.

сначáла *adv* at first; all over again.

снáшивать *impf of* **сноси́ть**

СНГ *abbr* (*of* **Содрýжество незави́симых госудáрств**) CIS.

снег (*loc* -ý; *pl* -á) snow.

снеги́рь (-я́) bullfinch.

снегово́й snow. **снегопáд** snowfall. **Снегýрочка** Snow Maiden. **снежи́нка** snow-flake. **снéжн|ый** snow(y); **~ая бáба** snowman. **снежóк** (-жкá) light snow; snowball.

снести́[1] (-сý, -сёшь; -ёс, -лá) *pf* (*impf* **сноси́ть**) take; bring together; bring *or* fetch down; carry away; blow off; demolish; endure; **~сь** communicate (**с**+*instr* with).

с|нести́[2]**(сь** (-сý(сь, -сёшь(ся; снёс(ся, -слá(сь) *pf*.

снижáть *impf*, **сни́зить** (-и́жу) *pf* lower; bring down; reduce; **~ся** come down; fall. **снижéние** lowering; loss of height.

снизойти́ (-йду́, -йдёшь; -ошёл, -шла́) *pf* (*impf* **снисходи́ть**) condescend.

сни́зу *adv* from below.

снима́ть(ся *impf of* **сня́ть(ся.** **сни́мок** (-мка) photograph. **сниму́** *etc.*: *see* **снять**

сниска́ть (-ищу́, -и́щешь) *pf*, **сни́скивать** *impf* gain, win.

снисходи́тельность condescension; leniency. **снисходи́тельный** condescending; lenient. **снисходи́ть** (-ожу́, -о́дишь) *impf of* **снизойти́. снисхожде́ние** indulgence, leniency.

сни́ться *impf* (*pf* **при~**) *impers+dat* dream.

сноби́зм snobbery.

сно́ва *adv* again, anew.

снова́ть (сную́, снуёшь) *impf* rush about.

сновиде́ние dream.

сноп (-а́) sheaf.

сноро́вка knack, skill.

снос demolition; drift; wear. **сноси́ть**[1] (-ошу́, -о́сишь) *pf* (*impf* **сна́шивать**) wear out. **сноси́ть**[2]**(ся** (-ошу́(сь, -о́сишь(ся) *impf of* **снести́(сь. сно́ска** footnote. **сно́сно** *adv* tolerably, so-so. **сно́сный** tolerable; fair.

снотво́рный soporific.

сноха́ (*pl* -и) daughter-in-law.

сноше́ние intercourse; relations, dealings.

сношу́ *etc.*: *see* **сноси́ть**

сня́тие taking down; removal; making. **снять** (сниму́, -и́мешь; -ял, -а́, -о) *pf* (*impf* **снима́ть**) take off; take down; gather in; remove; rent; take; make; photograph; **~ся** come off; move off; be photographed.

со *see* **с** *prep.*

со- *pref* co-, joint. **соа́втор** co-author.

соба́ка dog. **соба́чий** dog's; canine. **соба́чка** little dog; trigger.

соберу́ *etc.*: *see* **собра́ть**

собе́с *abbr* (*of* **социа́льное обеспе́чение**) social security (department).

собесе́дник interlocutor, companion. **собесе́дование** conversation.

собира́тель *m* collector. **собира́ть(ся** *impf of* **собра́ть(ся**

собла́зн temptation. **соблазни́тель** *m*, **~ница** tempter; seducer. **соблазни́тельный** tempting; seductive. **соблазни́ть** *pf*, **соблазня́ть** *impf* tempt; seduce.

соблюда́ть *impf*, **со|блюсти́** (-юду́, -дёшь; -ю́л, -а́) *pf* observe; keep (to). **соблюде́ние** observance; maintenance.

собо́й, собо́ю *see* **себя́**

соболе́знование sympathy, condolence(s). **соболе́зновать** *impf +dat* sympathize *or* commiserate with.

со́боль (*pl* -и *or* -я́) *m* sable.

собо́р cathedral; council, synod. **собо́рный** cathedral.

собра́ние meeting; assembly; collection. **со́бранный** collected; concentrated.

собра́т (*pl* -ья, -ьев) colleague.

собра́ть (-беру́, -берёшь; -а́л, -а́, -о) *pf* (*impf* **собира́ть**) gather; collect; **~ся** gather; prepare; intend, be going; **+с+*instr*** collect.

со́бственник owner, proprietor. **со́бственнический** proprietary; proprietorial. **со́бственно** *adv*: **~ (говоря́)** strictly speaking, as a matter of fact. **собственнору́чно** *adv* personally, with one's own hand. **со́б-**

ственность property; ownership. **собственн|ый** (one's) own; proper; true; **имя ~ое** proper name; **~ой персоной** in person.

событие event.

собью *etc.*: *see* **сбить**

сова (*pl* -ы) owl.

совать (сую, -ёшь) *impf* (*pf* **сунуть**) thrust, shove; **~ся** push, push in; butt in.

совершать *impf*, **совершить** (-шу) *pf* accomplish; carry out; commit; complete; **~ся** happen; be accomplished. **совершение** accomplishment; perpetration. **совершенно** *adv* perfectly; absolutely, completely. **совершеннолетие** majority. **совершеннолетний** of age. **совершенный**[1] perfect; absolute, complete. **совершенный**[2] perfective. **совершенство** perfection. **совершенствование** perfecting; improvement.

совершенствовать *impf* (*pf* **у~**) perfect; improve; **~ся в**+*instr* perfect o.s. in; improve.

совестливый conscientious. **совестно** *impers*+*dat* be ashamed. **совесть** conscience.

совет advice, counsel; opinion; council; soviet, Soviet. **советник** adviser. **советовать** *impf* (*pf* **по~**) advise; **~ся с**+*instr* consult, ask advice of. **советолог** Kremlinologist. **советск|ий** Soviet; **~ая власть** the Soviet regime; **~ий Союз** the Soviet Union. **советчик** adviser.

совещание conference. **совещательный** consultative, deliberative. **совещаться** *impf* deliberate; consult.

совладать *pf* **с**+*instr* control, cope with.

совместимый compatible. **совместитель** *m* person holding more than one office. **совместить** (-ещу) *pf*, **совмещать** *impf* combine; **~ся** coincide; be combined, combine. **совместно** jointly. **совместный** joint, combined.

совок (-вка) shovel; scoop; dustpan.

совокупиться (-плюсь) *pf*, **совокупляться** *impf* copulate. **совокупление** copulation. **совокупно** *adv* jointly. **совокупность** aggregate, sum total.

совпадать *impf*, **совпасть** (-адёт) *pf* coincide; agree, tally. **совпадение** coincidence.

совратить (-ащу) *pf* (*impf* **совращать**) pervert, seduce.

со|врать (-вру, -врёшь; -ал, -á, -о) *pf*.

совращать(ся *impf of* **совратить(ся**. **совращение** perverting, seduction.

современник contemporary. **современность** the present (time); contemporaneity. **современный** contemporary; modern.

совру *etc.*: *see* **соврать**

совсем *adv* quite; entirely.

совхоз State farm.

совью *etc.*: *see* **свить**

согласие consent; assent; agreement; harmony. **согласиться** (-ашусь) *pf* (*impf* **соглашаться**) consent; agree. **согласно** *adv* in accord, in harmony; *prep*+*dat* in accordance with. **согласн|ый**[1] agreeable (to); in agreement; harmonious. **согласный**[2] consonant(al); *sb* consonant.

согласова́ние co-ordination; agreement. **согласо́ванность** co-ordination. **согласова́ть** *pf*, **согласо́вывать** *impf* co-ordinate; make agree; **~ся** conform; agree.

соглаша́ться *impf of* **согласи́ться**. **соглаше́ние** agreement. **соглашу́** *etc*.: *see* **согласи́ть**

согна́ть (сгоню́, сго́нишь; -а́л, -а́, -о) *pf* (*impf* **сгоня́ть**) drive away; drive together.

со|гну́ть (-ну́, -нёшь) *pf* (*impf also* **сгиба́ть**) bend, curve; **~ся** bend (down).

согрева́ть *impf*, **согре́ть** (-е́ю) *pf* warm, heat; **~ся** get warm; warm o.s.

со|греши́ть (-шу́) *pf*.

со́да soda.

соде́йствие assistance. **соде́йствовать** *impf* & *pf* (*pf also* **по~**) *+dat* assist; promote; contribute to.

содержа́ние maintenance, upkeep; content(s); pay. **содержа́тельный** rich in content; pithy. **содержа́ть** (-жу́, -жишь) *impf* keep; maintain; contain; **~ся** be kept; be maintained; be; be contained. **содержи́мое** *sb* contents.

со|дра́ть (сдеру́, -рёшь; -а́л, -а́, -о) *pf* (*impf also* **сдира́ть**) tear off, strip off; fleece.

содрога́ние shudder. **содрога́ться** *impf*, **содрогну́ться** (-ну́сь, -нёшься) *pf* shudder.

содру́жество concord; commonwealth.

соедине́ние joining, combination; joint; compound; formation. **Соединённое Короле́вство** United Kingdom. **Соединённые Шта́ты (Аме́рики)** *m pl* United States (of America). **соединённый** (-ён, -а́) united, joint. **соедини́тельный** connective, connecting. **соедини́ть** *pf*, **соединя́ть** *impf* join, unite; connect; combine; **~ся** join, unite; combine.

сожале́ние regret; pity; **к сожале́нию** unfortunately. **сожале́ть** (-е́ю) *impf* regret, deplore.

сожгу́ *etc*.: *see* **сжечь**. **сожже́ние** burning; cremation.

сожи́тель *m*, **~ница** room-mate, flat-mate; lover. **сожи́тельство** co-habitation.

сожму́ *etc*.: *see* **сжать²**. **сожну́** *etc*.: *see* **сжать¹**. **созва́ниваться** *impf of* **созвони́ться**

созва́ть (-зову́, -зовёшь; -а́л, -а́, -о) *pf* (*impf* **сзыва́ть, созыва́ть**) call together; call; invite.

созве́здие constellation.

созвони́ться *pf* (*impf* **созва́ниваться**) ring up; speak on the telephone.

созву́чие accord; assonance. **созву́чный** harmonious; *+dat* in keeping with.

создава́ть (-даю́, -даёшь) *impf*, **созда́ть** (-а́м, -а́шь, -а́ст, -ади́м; со́зда́л, -а́, -о) *pf* create; establish; **~ся** be created; arise, spring up. **созда́ние** creation; work; creature. **созда́тель** *m* creator; originator.

созерца́ние contemplation. **созерца́тельный** contemplative. **созерца́ть** *impf* contemplate.

созида́ние creation. **созида́тельный** creative.

сознава́ть (-наю́, -наёшь) *impf*, **созна́ть** *pf* be conscious of, realize; acknowledge; **~ся** confess. **созна́ние** consciousness; acknowledgement; confession.

сознáтельность awareness, consciousness. **сознáтельный** conscious; deliberate.

созову́ *etc.*: *see* **созвáть**

созревáть *impf*, **со|зрéть** (-éю) *pf* ripen, mature.

созы́в summoning, calling. **созывáть** *impf of* **созвáть**

соизмери́мый commensurable.

соискáние competition. **соискáтель** *m*, **~ница** competitor, candidate.

сойти́ (-йду́, -йдёшь; сошёл, -шлá) *pf* (*impf* **сходи́ть**) go *or* come down; get off; leave; come off; pass, go off; **~ с умá** go mad, go out of one's mind; **~сь** meet; gather; become friends; become intimate; agree.

сок (*loc* -у́) juice.

сóкол falcon.

сократи́ть (-ащу́) *pf*, **сокращáть** *impf* shorten; abbreviate; reduce; **~ся** grow shorter; decrease; contract. **сокращéние** shortening; abridgement; abbreviation; reduction.

сокровéнный secret; innermost. **сокрóвище** treasure. **сокрóвищница** treasure-house.

сокрушáть *impf*, **сокруши́ть** (-шу́) *pf* shatter; smash; distress; **~ся** grieve, be distressed. **сокрушéние** smashing; grief. **сокрушённый** (-ён, -á) grief-stricken. **сокруши́тельный** shattering.

сокры́тие concealment.

со|лгáть (-лгу́, -лжёшь; -áл, -á, -о) *pf*.

солдáт (*gen pl* -áт) soldier. **солдáтский** soldier's.

солéние salting; pickling. **солёный** (сóлон, -á, -о) salt(y); salted; pickled. **солéнье** salted food(s); pickles.

солидáрность solidarity. **соли́дный** solid; strong; reliable; respectable; sizeable.

соли́ст, соли́стка soloist.

соли́ть (-лю́, сóли́шь) *impf* (*pf* **по~**) salt; pickle.

сóлнечный sun; solar; sunny; **~ свет** sunlight; sunshine; **~ удáр** sunstroke. **сóлнце** sun. **солнцепёк: на ~е** in the sun. **солнцестоя́ние** solstice.

сóло *neut indecl* solo; *adv* solo.

соловéй (-вья́) nightingale.

сóлод malt.

солодкóвый liquorice.

солóма straw; thatch. **солóменный** straw; thatch. **солóминка** straw.

сóлон *etc.*: *see* **солёный. солони́на** corned beef. **солóнка** salt-cellar. **солончáк** (-á) saline soil; *pl* salt marshes. **соль** (*pl* -и, -éй) salt.

сóльный solo.

солью́ *etc.*: *see* **слить**

соляно́й, соля́ный salt, saline; **соля́ная кислотá** hydrochloric acid.

сóмкнутый close. **сомкну́ть** (-ну́, -нёшь) *pf* (*impf* **смыкáть**) close; **~ся** close.

сомневáться *impf* doubt, have doubts. **сомнéние** doubt. **сомни́тельный** doubtful.

сомну́ *etc.*: *see* **смять**

сон (сна) sleep; dream. **сонли́вость** sleepiness; somnolence. **сонли́вый** sleepy. **сóнный** sleepy; sleeping.

сонáта sonata.

сонéт sonnet.

соображáть *impf*, **сообрази́ть** (-ажу́) *pf* consider, think out;

weigh; understand. **соображе́ние** consideration; understanding; notion. **сообрази́тельный** quick-witted.

сообра́зный **с**+*instr* conforming to, in keeping with.

сообща́ *adv* together. **сообща́ть** *impf*, **сообщи́ть** (-щу́) *pf* communicate, report, announce; impart; +*dat* inform. **сообще́ние** communication, report; announcement. **соо́бщество** association. **соо́бщник** accomplice.

сооруди́**ть** (-ужу́) *pf*, **сооружа́ть** *impf* build, erect. **сооруже́ние** building; structure.

соотве́тственно *adv* accordingly, correspondingly; *prep* +*dat* according to, in accordance with. **соотве́тственный** corresponding. **соотве́тствие** accordance, correspondence. **соотве́тствовать** *impf* correspond, conform. **соотве́тствующий** corresponding; suitable.

сооте́чественник fellow-countryman.

соотноше́ние correlation.

сопе́рник rival. **сопе́рничать** *impf* compete, vie. **сопе́рничество** rivalry.

сопе́ть (-плю́) *impf* wheeze; snuffle.

со́пка hill, mound.

сопли́вый snotty.

сопоста́вить (-влю) *pf*, **сопоставля́ть** *impf* compare. **сопоставле́ние** comparison.

сопреде́льный contiguous.

со|пре́ть *pf*.

соприкаса́ться *impf*, **соприкосну́ться** (-ну́сь, -нёшься) *pf* adjoin; come into contact. **соприкоснове́ние** contact.

сопроводи́тельный accompanying. **сопроводи́ть** (-ожу́) *pf*, **сопровожда́ть** *impf* accompany; escort. **сопровожде́ние** accompaniment; escort.

сопротивле́ние resistance. **сопротивля́ться** *impf* +*dat* resist, oppose.

сопу́тствовать *impf* +*dat* accompany.

сопью́сь *etc.*: *see* **спи́ться**

сор litter, rubbish.

соразме́рить *pf*, **соразмеря́ть** *impf* balance, match. **соразме́рный** proportionate, commensurate.

сора́тник comrade-in-arms.

сорва́ть (-ву́, -вёшь; -а́л, -а́, -о) *pf* (*impf* **срыва́ть**) tear off, away, down; break off; pick; get; break; ruin, spoil; vent; **~ся** break away, break loose; fall, come down; fall through.

с|организова́ть *pf*.

соревнова́ние competition; contest. **соревнова́ться** *impf* compete.

сори́ть *impf* (*pf* **на~**) +*acc or instr* litter; throw about. **со́рн|ый** rubbish, refuse; **~ая трава́** weed(s). **сорня́к** (-а́) weed.

со́рок (-а́) forty.

соро́ка magpie.

сороков|о́й fortieth; **~ы́е го́ды** the forties.

соро́чка shirt; blouse; shift.

сорт (*pl* -а́) grade, quality; sort. **сортирова́ть** *impf* (*pf* **рас~**) sort, grade. **сортиро́вка** sorting. **сортиро́вочн|ый** sorting; **~ая** *sb* marshalling-yard. **сортиро́вщик** sorter. **со́ртный** high quality.

соса́ть (-су́, -сёшь) *impf* suck.

со|сва́тать *pf*.

сосе́д (*pl* -и, -ей, -ям), **сосе́дка** neighbour. **сосе́дний** neighbouring; adjacent, next. **сосе́дский** neighbours'. **сосе́дство** neighbourhood. **соси́ска** frankfurter, sausage.

со́ска (*baby's*) dummy.

соска́кивать *impf of* **соскочи́ть**

соска́льзывать *impf*, **соскользну́ть** (-ну́, -нёшь) *pf* slide down, slide off.

соскочи́ть (-чу́, -чишь) *pf* (*impf* **соска́кивать**) jump off *or* down; come off.

соску́читься (-чусь) *pf* get bored; ~ **по**+*dat* miss.

сослага́тельный subjunctive.

сосла́ть (сошлю́, -лёшь) *pf* (*impf* **ссыла́ть**) exile, deport; **~ся на**+*acc* refer to; cite; plead, allege.

сосло́вие estate; class.

сослужи́вец (-вца) colleague.

сосна́ (*pl* -ы, -сен) pine(-tree). **сосно́вый** pine; deal.

сосо́к (-ска́) nipple, teat.

сосредото́ченный concentrated. **сосредото́чивать** *impf*, **сосредото́чить** (-чу) *pf* concentrate; focus; **~ся** concentrate.

соста́в composition; structure; compound; staff; strength; train; **в ~е** +*gen* consisting of. **составитель** *m* compiler. **соста́вить** (-влю) *pf*, **составля́ть** *impf* put together; make (up); draw up; compile; be, constitute; total; **~ся** form, be formed. **составно́й** compound; component, constituent.

со|ста́рить(ся *pf*.

состоя́ние state, condition; fortune. **состоя́тельный** well-to-do; well-grounded. **состоя́ть** (-ою́) *impf* be; **+из**+*gen* consist of; **+в**+*prep* consist in, be. **состоя́ться** (-ои́тся) *pf* take place.

сострада́ние compassion. **сострада́тельный** compassionate.

с|остри́ть *pf*. **со|стря́пать** *pf*.

со|стыкова́ться *pf*, **состыко́вываться** *impf* dock.

состяза́ние competition, contest. **состяза́ться** *impf* compete.

сосу́д vessel.

сосу́лька icicle.

сосуществова́ние co-existence.

со|счита́ть *pf*. **сот** *see* **сто**.

сотворе́ние creation. **со|твори́ть** *pf*.

со|тка́ть (-ку́, -кёшь; -а́л, -ала́, -о) *pf*.

со́тня (*gen pl* -тен) a hundred.

со́товый cellular; ~ **телефо́н** mobile phone, cell phone.

сотру́ *etc.*: *see* **стере́ть**

сотру́дник collaborator; colleague; employee. **сотру́дничать** *impf* collaborate; **+в**+*prep* contribute to. **сотру́дничество** collaboration.

сотряса́ть *impf*, **сотрясти́** (-су́, -сёшь; -я́с, -ла́) *pf* shake; **~ся** tremble. **сотрясе́ние** shaking; concussion.

со́ты (-ов) *pl* honeycomb.

со́тый hundredth.

со́ус sauce; gravy; dressing.

соуча́стие participation; complicity. **соуча́стник** participant; accomplice.

софа́ (*pl* -ы) sofa.

соха́ (*pl* -и) (*wooden*) plough.

со́хнуть (-ну; сох) *impf* (*pf* **вы~**, **за~**, **про~**) (get) dry; wither.

сохране́ние preservation; conservation; (safe)keeping; retention. **сохрани́ть** *pf*, **сохраня́ть** *impf* preserve, keep; **~ся** remain (intact); last out; be well preserved. **сохра́нный** safe.

социа́л-демокра́т Social Democrat. **социа́л-демократи́ческий** Social Democratic. **социали́зм** socialism. **социали́ст** socialist. **социалисти́ческий** socialist. **социа́льн|ый** social; **~ое обеспече́ние** social security. **социо́лог** sociologist. **социоло́гия** sociology.

соцреали́зм socialist realism.

сочета́ние combination. **сочета́ть** *impf* & *pf* combine; **~ся** combine; harmonize; match.

сочине́ние composition; work. **сочини́ть** *pf*, **сочиня́ть** *impf* compose; write; make up.

сочи́ться (-и́тся) *impf* ooze (out), trickle; **~ кро́вью** bleed.

со́чный (-чен, -чна́, -о) juicy; rich.

сочту́ *etc.*: *see* **счесть**

сочу́вствие sympathy. **сочу́вствовать** *impf* +*dat* sympathize with.

сошёл *etc.*: *see* **сойти́. сошлю́** *etc.*: *see* **сосла́ть. сошью́** *etc.*: *see* **сшить**

сощу́ривать *impf*, **со|щу́рить** *pf* screw up, narrow; **~ся** screw up one's eyes; narrow.

сою́з¹ union; alliance; league. **сою́з²** conjunction. **сою́зник** ally. **сою́зный** allied; Union.

спад recession; abatement. **спада́ть** *impf of* **спасть**

спазм spasm.

спа́ивать *impf of* **спая́ть, спои́ть**

спа́йка soldered joint; solidarity, unity.

с|пали́ть *pf*.

спа́льн|ый sleeping; **~ый ваго́н** sleeping car; **~ое ме́сто** berth. **спа́льня** (*gen pl* -лен) bedroom.

спа́ржа asparagus.

спартакиа́да sports meeting.

спаса́тельный rescue; **~ жиле́т** life jacket; **~ круг** lifebuoy; **~ по́яс** lifebelt. **спаса́ть(ся** *impf of* **спасти́(сь. спасе́ние** rescue, escape; salvation. **спаси́бо** thank you. **спаси́тель** *m* rescuer; saviour. **спаси́тельный** saving; salutary.

спасти́ (-су́, -сёшь; спас, -ла́) *pf* (*impf* **спаса́ть**) save; rescue; **~сь** escape; be saved.

спасть (-адёт) *pf* (*impf* **спада́ть**) fall (down); abate.

спать (сплю; -ал, -а́, -о) *impf* sleep; **лечь ~** go to bed.

спа́янность cohesion, unity. **спа́янный** united. **спая́ть** *pf* (*impf* **спа́ивать**) solder, weld; unite.

спекта́кль *m* performance; show.

спектр spectrum.

спекули́ровать *impf* speculate. **спекуля́нт** speculator, profiteer. **спекуля́ция** speculation; profiteering.

спе́лый ripe.

сперва́ *adv* at first; first.

спе́реди *adv* in front, from the front; *prep*+*gen* (from) in front of.

спёртый close, stuffy.

спеси́вый arrogant, haughty. **спесь** arrogance, haughtiness.

спеть¹ (-е́ет) *impf* (*pf* **по~**) ripen.

с|петь² (спою́, споёшь) *pf*.

спец- *abbr in comb* (*of* **спе-**

циа́льный) special. **спецко́р** special correspondent. **~оде́жда** protective clothing; overalls.
специализа́ция specialization. **специализи́роваться** *impf* & *pf* specialize. **специали́ст, ~ка** specialist, expert. **специа́льность** speciality; profession. **специа́льный** special; specialist.
специ́фика specific character. **специфи́ческий** specific.
спе́ция spice.
спецо́вка protective clothing; overall(s).
спеши́ть (-шу́) *impf* (*pf* **по~**) hurry, be in a hurry; be fast.
спе́шка hurry, haste. **спе́шный** urgent.
спива́ться *impf of* **спи́ться**
СПИД *abbr* (*of* **синдро́м приобретённого иммýнного дефици́та**) Aids.
с|пики́ровать *pf.*
спи́ливать *impf*, **спили́ть** (-лю́, -лишь) *pf* saw down, off.
спина́ (*acc* -у; *pl* -ы) back. **спи́нка** back. **спинно́й** spinal; **~ мозг** spinal cord.
спира́ль spiral.
спирт alcohol, spirit(s). **спиртн|о́й** alcoholic; **~о́е** *sb* alcohol. **спирто́вка** spirit-stove. **спиртово́й** spirit, alcoholic.
списа́ть (-ишу́, -и́шешь) *pf*, **спи́сывать** *impf* copy; **~ся** exchange letters. **спи́сок** (-ска) list; record.
спи́ться (сопью́сь, -ьёшься; -и́лся, -а́сь) *pf* (*impf* **спива́ться**) take to drink.
спи́хивать *impf*, **спихну́ть** (-ну́, -нёшь) *pf* push aside, down.
спи́ца knitting-needle; spoke.
спи́чечн|ый match; **~ая коро́бка** match-box. **спи́чка** match.
спишу́ *etc.*: *see* **списа́ть**
сплав[1] floating. **сплав**[2] alloy. **спла́вить**[1] (-влю) *pf*, **сплавля́ть**[1] *impf* float; raft; get rid of. **спла́вить**[2] (-влю) *pf*, **сплавля́ть**[2] *impf* alloy; **~ся** fuse.
с|плани́ровать *pf.* **спла́чивать(ся** *impf of* **сплоти́ть(ся.**
сплёвывать *impf of* **сплю́нуть**
с|плести́ (-ету́, -етёшь; -ёл, -а́) *pf*, **сплета́ть** *impf* weave; plait; interlace. **сплете́ние** interlacing; plexus.
спле́тник, -ница gossip, scandalmonger. **спле́тничать** *impf* (*pf* **на~**) gossip. **спле́тня** (*gen pl* -тен) gossip, scandal.
сплоти́ть (-очу́) *pf* (*impf* **спла́чивать**) join; unite, rally; **~ся** unite, rally; close ranks. **сплоче́ние** uniting. **сплочённость** cohesion, unity. **сплочённый** (-ён, -а́) united; firm; unbroken.
сплошно́й solid; complete; continuous; utter. **сплошь** *adv* all over; completely; **~ да ря́дом** pretty often.
сплю *see* **спать**
сплю́нуть (-ну) *pf* (*impf* **сплёвывать**) spit; spit out.
сплю́щивать *impf*, **сплю́щить** (-щу) *pf* flatten; **~ся** become flat.
с|пляса́ть (-яшу́, -я́шешь) *pf.*
сподви́жник comrade-in-arms.
спои́ть (-ою́, -о́ишь) *pf* (*impf* **спа́ивать**) make a drunkard of.
споко́йн|ый quiet; calm; **~ой но́чи** good night! **споко́йствие** quiet; calm, serenity.
спола́скивать *impf of* **сполосну́ть**
сполза́ть *impf*, **сползти́** (-зу́,

-зёшь; -олз, -ла́) *pf* climb down; slip (down); fall away.

сполна́ *adv* in full.

сполосну́ть (-ну́, -нёшь) *pf* (*impf* **спола́скивать**) rinse.

спо́нсор sponsor, backer.

спор argument; controversy; dispute. **спо́рить** *impf* (*pf* **по~**) argue; dispute; debate. **спо́рный** debatable, questionable; disputed; moot.

спо́ра spore.

спорт sport. **спорти́вный** sports; **~ зал** gymnasium. **спортсме́н, ~ка** athlete, player.

спо́соб way, method; **таки́м ~ом** in this way. **спосо́бность** ability, aptitude; capacity. **спосо́бный** able; clever; capable. **спосо́бствовать** *impf* (*pf* **по~**) +*dat* assist; further.

споткну́ться (-ну́сь, -нёшься) *pf*, **спотыка́ться** *impf* stumble.

спохвати́ться (-ачу́сь, -а́тишься) *pf*, **спохва́тываться** *impf* remember suddenly.

спою́ *etc.*: *see* **спеть, спои́ть**

спра́ва *adv* to *or* on the right.

справедли́вость justice; fairness; truth. **справедли́вый** just; fair; justified.

спра́вить (-влю) *pf*, **справля́ть** *impf* celebrate. **спра́виться**[1] (-влюсь) *pf*, **справля́ться** *impf* **с**+*instr* cope with, manage. **спра́виться**[2] (-влюсь) *pf*, **справля́ться** *impf* inquire; +**в**+*prep* consult. **спра́вка** information; reference; certificate; **наводи́ть спра́вку** make inquiries. **спра́вочник** reference-book, directory. **спра́вочный** inquiry, information, reference.

спра́шивать(ся *impf of* **спроси́ть(ся**

спринт sprint. **спри́нтер** sprinter.

с|провоци́ровать *pf*. **с|проекти́ровать** *pf*.

спрос demand; asking; **без ~у** without permission. **спроси́ть** (-ошу́, -о́сишь) *pf* (*impf* **спра́шивать**) ask (for); inquire; **~ся** ask permission.

спрут octopus.

спры́гивать *impf*, **спры́гнуть** (-ну) *pf* jump off, jump down.

спры́скивать *impf*, **спры́снуть** (-ну) *pf* sprinkle.

спряга́ть *impf* (*pf* **про~**) conjugate. **спряже́ние** conjugation.

с|прясть (-яду́, -ядёшь; -ял, -я́ла́, -о) *pf*. **с|пря́тать(ся** (-я́чу(сь) *pf*.

спу́гивать *impf*, **спугну́ть** (-ну́, -нёшь) *pf* frighten off.

спуск lowering; descent; slope. **спуска́ть** *impf*, **спусти́ть** (-ущу́, -у́стишь) *pf* let down, lower; release; let out; send out; go down; forgive; squander; **~ кора́бль** launch a ship; **~ куро́к** pull the trigger; **~ пе́тлю** drop a stitch; **~ся** go down, descend. **спускно́й** drain. **спусково́й** trigger. **спустя́** *prep*+*acc* after; *adv* later.

с|пу́тать(ся *pf*.

спу́тник satellite, sputnik; (travelling) companion.

спущу́ *etc.*: *see* **спусти́ть**

спя́чка hibernation; sleepiness.

ср. *abbr* (*of* **сравни́**) cf.

сраба́тывать *impf*, **срабо́тать** *pf* make; work, operate.

сравне́ние comparison; simile. **сра́внивать** *impf of* **сравни́ть, сравня́ть. сравни́мый** comparable. **сравни́тельно** *adv* comparatively. **сравни́тельный** comparative. **сравни́ть** *pf* (*impf* **сра́внивать**) compare; **~ся**

с+*instr* compare with. **с|равня́ть** *pf* (*impf also* **срáвнивать**) make even, equal; level.

сражáть *impf*, **срази́ть** (-ажу́) *pf* strike down; overwhelm, crush; **~ся** fight. **сражéние** battle.

срáзу *adv* at once.

срам shame. **срами́ть** (-млю́) *impf* (*pf* **о~**) shame; **~ся** cover o.s. with shame. **срамотá** shame.

срастáние growing together. **срастáться** *impf*, **срасти́сь** (-тётся; срóсся, -лáсь) *pf* grow together; knit.

средá[1] (*pl* -ы) environment, surroundings; medium. **средá**[2] (*acc* -у; *pl* -ы, -áм *or* -ам) Wednesday. **среди́** *prep*+*gen* among; in the middle of; **~ бéла дня** in broad daylight. **средиземномóрский** Mediterranean. **срéдне** *adv* so-so. **средневекóвый** medieval. **средневекóвье** the Middle Ages. **срéдний** middle; medium; mean; average; middling; secondary; neuter; **~ее** *sb* mean, average. **средотóчие** focus. **срéдство** means; remedy.

срез cut; section; slice. **с|рéзать** (-éжу) *pf*, **срезáть** *impf* cut off; slice; fail; **~ся** fail.

с|репети́ровать *pf*.

срисовáть *pf*, **срисóвывать** *impf* copy.

с|ровня́ть *pf*.

сродствó affinity.

срок date; term; time, period; **в ~, к ~у** in time, to time.

срóсся *etc.*: *see* **срасти́сь**

срóчно *adv* urgently. **срóчность** urgency. **срóчный** urgent; for a fixed period.

срóю *etc.*: *see* **срыть**

сруб felling; framework. **срубáть** *impf*, **с|руби́ть** (-блю́, -бишь) *pf* cut down; build (*of logs*).

срыв disruption; breakdown; ruining. **срывáть**[1](**ся** *impf of* **сорвáть(ся**

срывáть[2] *impf*, **срыть** (срóю) *pf* raze to the ground.

сря́ду *adv* running.

ссáдина scratch. **ссади́ть** (-ажу́, -áдишь) *pf*, **ссáживать** *impf* set down; help down; turn off.

ссóра quarrel. **ссóрить** *impf* (*pf* **по~**) cause to quarrel; **~ся** quarrel.

СССР *abbr* (*of* **Сою́з Совéтских Социалисти́ческих Респу́блик**) USSR.

ссу́да loan. **ссуди́ть** (-ужу́, -у́дишь) *pf*, **ссужáть** *impf* lend, loan.

ссылáть(ся *impf of* **сослáть(ся.** **ссы́лка**[1] exile. **ссы́лка**[2] reference. **ссы́льный, ссы́льная** *sb* exile.

ссы́пать (-плю) *pf*, **ссыпáть** *impf* pour.

стабилизáтор stabilizer; tailplane. **стабилизи́ровать(ся** *impf* & *pf* stabilize. **стаби́льность** stability. **стаби́льный** stable, firm.

стáвень (-вня; *gen pl* -вней) *m*, **стáвня** (*gen pl* -вен) shutter.

стáвить (-влю) *impf* (*pf* **по~**) put, place, set; stand; station; erect; install; apply; present, stage. **стáвка**[1] rate; stake. **стáвка**[2] headquarters.

стáвня *see* **стáвень**

стади́он stadium.

стáдия stage.

стáдность herd instinct. **стáдный** gregarious. **стáдо** (*pl* -á) herd, flock.

стаж length of service; probation. **стажёр** probationer; student on a special non-degree course. **стажиро́вка** period of training.
стака́н glass.
сталелите́йный steel-founding; ~ **заво́д** steel foundry. **сталеплави́льный** steel-making; ~ **заво́д** steel works.
сталепрока́тный (steel-)rolling; ~ **стан** rolling-mill.
ста́лкивать(ся *impf of* **столкну́ть(ся**
ста́ло быть *conj* consequently.
сталь steel. **стально́й** steel.
стаме́ска chisel.
стан[1] figure, torso.
стан[2] camp.
стан[3] mill.
станда́рт standard. **станда́ртный** standard.
стани́ца Cossack village.
станкострое́ние machine-tool engineering.
станови́ться (-влю́сь, -вишься) *impf of* **стать**[1]
стано́к (-нка́) machine tool, machine.
ста́ну *etc.*: *see* **стать**[2]
станцио́нный station. **ста́нция** station.
ста́пель (*pl* -я́) *m* stocks.
ста́птывать(ся *impf of* **стопта́ть(ся**
стара́ние effort. **стара́тельность** diligence. **стара́тельный** diligent. **стара́ться** *impf* (*pf* **по~**) try.
старе́ть *impf* (*pf* **по~, у~**) grow old. **ста́рец** (-рца) elder, (*venerable*) old man. **стари́к** (-а́) old man. **старина́** antiquity, olden times; antique(s); old fellow.
стари́нный ancient; old; antique. **ста́рить** *impf* (*pf* **со~**) age, make old; **~ся** age, grow old.
старо- *in comb* old. **старове́р** Old Believer. **~жи́л** old resident. **~мо́дный** old-fashioned. **~славя́нский** Old Slavonic.
ста́роста head; monitor; churchwarden. **ста́рость** old age.
старт start; **на ~!** on your marks! **ста́ртёр** starter. **стартова́ть** *impf & pf* start. **ста́ртовый** starting.
стару́ха, стару́шка old woman. **ста́рческий** old man's; senile. **ста́рше** *comp of* **ста́рый**.
ста́рш|ий oldest, eldest; older, elder; senior; head; **~ие** *sb pl* (one's) elders; **~ий** *sb* chief; man in charge. **старшина́** *m* sergeant-major; petty officer; leader. **ста́рый** (-ар, -а́, -о) old. **старьё** old things, junk.
ста́скивать *impf of* **стащи́ть**
с|тасова́ть *pf.*
стати́ст extra.
стати́стика statistics. **статисти́ческий** statistical.
ста́тный stately.
ста́тский civil, civilian.
ста́тус status. **ста́тус-кво́** *neut indecl* status quo.
статуэ́тка statuette.
ста́туя statue.
стать[1] (-а́ну) *pf* (*impf* **станови́ться**) stand; take up position; stop; cost; begin; +*instr* become; +**c**+*instr* become of; **не ~** *impers*+*gen* cease to be; disappear; **его́ не ста́ло** he is no more; **~ на коле́ни** kneel.
стать[2] physique, build.
ста́ться (-а́нется) *pf* happen.
статья́ (*gen pl* -е́й) article;

clause; item; matter.

стациона́р permanent establishment; hospital. **стациона́рный** stationary; permanent; **~ больно́й** in-patient.

ста́чечник striker. **ста́чка** strike.

с|тащи́ть (-щу́, -щишь) *pf* (*impf also* **ста́скивать**) drag off, pull off.

ста́я flock; school, shoal; pack.

ствол (-а́) trunk; barrel.

ство́рка leaf, fold.

сте́бель (-бля; *gen pl* -бле́й) *m* stem, stalk.

стёган|ый quilted; **~ое одея́ло** quilt, duvet. **стега́ть**[1] *impf* (*pf* **вы́~**) quilt.

стега́ть[2] *impf*, **стегну́ть** (-ну́) *pf* (*pf also* **от~**) whip, lash.

стежо́к (-жка́) stitch.

стезя́ path, way.

стёк *etc.*: *see* **стечь. стека́ть(ся** *impf of* **сте́чь(ся**

стекло́ (*pl* -ёкла, -кол) glass; lens; (window-)pane.

стекло- *in comb* glass. **стекловолокно́** glass fibre. **~очисти́тель** *m* windscreen-wiper. **~ре́з** glass-cutter. **~тка́нь** fibreglass.

стекля́нный glass; glassy. **стеко́льщик** glazier.

стели́ть *see* **стлать**

стелла́ж (-а́) shelves, shelving.

сте́лька insole.

стелю́ *etc.*: *see* **стлать**

с|темне́ть (-е́ет) *pf.*

стена́ (*acc* -у; *pl* -ы, -а́м) wall. **стенгазе́та** wall newspaper.

стенд stand.

сте́нка wall; side. **стенно́й** wall.

стеногра́мма shorthand record. **стено́граф, стенографи́ст, ~ка** stenographer. **стенографи́ровать** *impf & pf* take down in shorthand. **стенографи́ческий** shorthand. **стеногра́фия** shorthand.

стенокарди́я angina.

степе́нный staid; middle-aged.

сте́пень (*gen pl* -е́й) degree; extent; power.

степно́й steppe. **степь** (*loc* -и́; *gen pl* -е́й) steppe.

стервя́тник vulture.

стерегу́ *etc.*: *see* **стере́чь**

сте́рео *indecl adj* stereo.

сте́рео- *in comb* stereo. **стереоти́п** stereotype. **стереоти́пный** stereotype(d). **стереофони́ческий** stereo(phonic). **~фо́ния** stereo(phony).

стере́ть (сотру́, сотрёшь; стёр) *pf* (*impf* **стира́ть**[1]) wipe off; rub out, rub sore; **~ся** rub off; wear down; be effaced.

стере́чь (-регу́, -режёшь; -ёг, -ла́) *impf* guard; watch for.

сте́ржень (-жня) *m* pivot; rod; core.

стерилизова́ть *impf & pf* sterilize. **стери́льный** sterile.

сте́рлинг sterling.

сте́рлядь (*gen pl* -е́й) sterlet.

стерпе́ть (-плю́, -пишь) *pf* bear, endure.

стёртый worn, effaced.

стесне́ние constraint. **стесни́тельный** shy; inconvenient. **с|тесни́ть** *pf*, **стесня́ть** *impf* constrain; hamper; inhibit. **с|тесни́ться** *pf*, **стесня́ться** *impf* (*pf also* **по~**) +*inf* feel too shy (to), be ashamed to.

стече́ние confluence; gathering; combination. **стечь** (-чёт; -ёк, -ла́) *pf* (*impf* **стека́ть**) flow down; **~ся** flow together; gather.

стилисти́ческий stylistic.

стиль *m* style. **сти́льный** stylish; period.
сти́мул stimulus, incentive. **стимули́ровать** *impf* & *pf* stimulate.
стипе́ндия grant.
стира́льный washing.
стира́ть[1](**ся** *impf of* **стере́ть(ся**
стира́ть[2] *impf* (*pf* **вы́~**) wash, launder; **~ся** wash. **сти́рка** washing, wash, laundering.
сти́скивать *impf*, **сти́снуть** (-ну) *pf* squeeze; clench; hug.
стих (-а́) verse; line; *pl* poetry.
стиха́ть *impf of* **сти́хнуть**
стихи́йный elemental; spontaneous. **стихи́я** element.
сти́хнуть (-ну; стих) *pf* (*impf* **стиха́ть**) subside; calm down.
стихотворе́ние poem. **стихотво́рный** in verse form.
стлать, стели́ть (стелю́, сте́лешь) *impf* (*pf* **по~**) spread; **~ посте́ль** make a bed; **~ся** spread; creep.
сто (ста; *gen pl* сот) a hundred.
стог (*loc* -е & -у́; *pl* -а́) stack, rick.
сто́имость cost; value. **сто́ить** *impf* cost; be worth(while); deserve.
стой *see* **стоя́ть**
сто́йка counter, bar; prop; upright; strut. **сто́йкий** firm; stable; steadfast. **сто́йкость** firmness, stability; steadfastness. **сто́йло** stall. **стоймя́** *adv* upright.
сток flow; drainage; drain, gutter; sewer.
стол (-а́) table; desk; cuisine.
столб (-а́) post, pole, pillar, column. **столбене́ть** (-е́ю) *impf* (*pf* **о~**) be rooted to the ground. **столбня́к** (-а́) stupor; tetanus.
столе́тие century; centenary. **столе́тний** hundred-year-old; of a hundred years.
столи́ца capital; metropolis. **столи́чный** (of the) capital.
столкнове́ние collision; clash. **столкну́ть** (-ну́, -нёшь) *pf* (*impf* **ста́лкивать**) push off, away; cause to collide; bring together; **~ся** collide, clash; **+с+***instr* run into.
столо́вая *sb* dining-room; canteen. **столо́вый** table.
столп (-а́) pillar.
столпи́ться *pf* crowd.
столь *adv* so. **сто́лько** *adv* so much, so many.
столя́р (-а́) joiner, carpenter. **столя́рный** joiner's.
стомато́лог dentist.
стометро́вка (the) hundred metres.
стон groan. **стона́ть** (-ну́, -нешь) *impf* groan.
стоп! *int* stop!
стопа́[1] foot.
стопа́[2] (*pl* -ы) ream; pile.
сто́пка[1] pile.
сто́пка[2] small glass.
сто́пор stop, catch. **сто́пориться** *impf* (*pf* **за~**) come to a stop.
стопроце́нтный hundred-percent.
стоп-сигна́л brake-light.
стопта́ть (-пчу́, -пчешь) *pf* (*impf* **ста́птывать**) wear down; **~ся** wear down.
с|торгова́ть(ся *pf.*
сто́рож (*pl* -а́) watchman, guard. **сторожево́й** watch; patrol-. **сторожи́ть** (-жу́) *impf* guard, watch (over).
сторона́ (*acc* сто́рону; *pl* сто́роны, -ро́н, -а́м) side; direction; hand; feature; part; land; **в сто-**

рону aside; **с моéй стороны́** for my part; **с однóй стороны́** on the one hand. **сторони́ться** (-ню́сь, -ни́шься) *impf* (*pf* **по~**) stand aside; +*gen* avoid. **сторо́нник** supporter, advocate.

сто́чный sewage, drainage.

стоя́нка stop; parking; stopping place, parking space; stand; rank. **стоя́ть** (-ою́) *impf* (*pf* **по~**) stand; be; stay; stop; have stopped; +**за**+*acc* stand up for; **~ на колéнях** kneel. **стоя́чий** standing; upright; stagnant.

сто́ящий deserving; worthwhile.

стр. *abbr* (*of* **страни́ца**) page.

страда́ (*pl* -ды) (hard work at) harvest time.

страда́лец (-льца) sufferer. **страда́ние** suffering. **страда́тельный** passive. **страда́ть** (-а́ю *or* -ра́жду) *impf* (*pf* **по~**) suffer; **~ за** +*gen* feel for.

стра́жа guard, watch; **под стра́жей** under arrest, in custody; **стоя́ть на стра́же** +*gen* guard.

страна́ (*pl* -ы) country; land; **~ све́та** cardinal point.

страни́ца page.

стра́нник, стра́нница wanderer.

стра́нно *adv* strangely. **стра́нность** strangeness; eccentricity. **стра́нн|ый** (-а́нен, -анна́, -о) strange.

стра́нствие wandering. **стра́нствовать** *impf* wander.

Страстн|о́й of Holy Week; **~а́я пя́тница** Good Friday.

стра́стный (-тен, -тна́, -о) passionate. **страсть**[1] (*gen pl* -е́й) passion. **страсть**[2] *adv* awfully, frightfully.

стратеги́ческий strategic(al). **страте́гия** strategy.

стратосфе́ра stratosphere.

стра́ус ostrich.

страх fear.

страхова́ние insurance; **~ жи́зни** life insurance. **страхова́ть** *impf* (*pf* **за~**) insure (от+*gen* against); **~ся** insure o.s. **страхо́вка** insurance.

страши́ться (-шу́сь) *impf* +*gen* be afraid of. **стра́шно** *adv* awfully. **стра́шный** (-шен, -шна́, -о) terrible, awful.

стрекоза́ (*pl* -ы) dragonfly.

стрекота́ть (-очу́, -о́чешь) *impf* chirr.

стрела́ (*pl* -ы) arrow; boom. **стреле́ц** (-льца́) Sagittarius. **стре́лка** pointer; hand; needle; arrow; spit; points. **стрелко́вый** rifle; shooting; infantry. **стрело́к** (-лка́) shot; rifleman, gunner. **стре́лочник** pointsman. **стрельба́** (*pl* -ы) shooting, firing. **стре́льчатый** lancet; arched. **стреля́ть** *impf* shoot; fire; **~ся** shoot o.s.; fight a duel.

стремгла́в *adv* headlong.

стреми́тельный swift; impetuous. **стреми́ться** (-млю́сь) *impf* strive. **стремле́ние** striving, aspiration. **стремни́на** rapid(s).

стре́мя (-мени; *pl* -мена́, -мя́н, -а́м) *neut* stirrup. **стремя́нка** step-ladder.

стресс stress. **стре́ссовый** stressful, stressed.

стри́женый short; short-haired, cropped; shorn. **стри́жка** hair-cut; shearing. **стричь** (-игу́, -ижёшь; -иг) *impf* (*pf* **о~**) cut, clip; cut the hair of; shear; **~ся** have one's hair cut.

строга́ть *impf* (*pf* **вы́~**) plane, shave.

стро́гий strict; severe. **стро́-**

гость strictness.
строево́й combatant; line; drill. **строе́ние** building; structure; composition.
строжа́йший, стро́же *superl & comp of* **стро́гий**
строи́тель *m* builder. **строи́тельный** building, construction. **строи́тельство** building, construction; building site.
стро́ить *impf* (*pf* **по~**) build; construct; make; base; draw up; **~ся** be built, be under construction; draw up; **стро́йся!** fall in! **строй** (*loc* -ю́; *pl* -и *or* -и́, -ев *or* -ёв) system; régime; structure; pitch; formation. **стро́йка** building; building-site. **стро́йность** proportion; harmony; balance, order. **стро́йный** (-óен, -ойна́, -o) harmonious, orderly, well-proportioned, shapely.
строка́ (*acc* -óку́; *pl* -и, -áм) line; **кра́сная ~** new paragraph.
строп, стро́па sling; shroud line.
стропи́ло rafter, beam.
строптúвый refractory.
строфа́ (*pl* -ы, -áм) stanza.
строчи́ть (-чу́, -óчи́шь) *impf* (*pf* **на~, про~**) stitch; scribble, dash off. **стро́чка** stitch; line.
стро́ю *etc.*: *see* **стро́ить**
струга́ть *impf* (*pf* **вы́~**) plane. **стру́жка** shaving.
струи́ться *impf* stream.
структу́ра structure.
струна́ (*pl* -ы) string. **стру́нный** stringed.
струп (*pl* -пья, -пьев) scab.
с|тру́сить (-у́шу) *pf.*
стручо́к (-чка́) pod.
струя́ (*pl* -и, -уй) jet, spurt, stream.
стря́пать *impf* (*pf* **с~**) cook; concoct. **стряпня́** cooking.
стря́хивать *impf*, **стряхну́ть** (-ну́, -нёшь) *pf* shake off.
студени́стый jelly-like.
студе́нт, студе́нтка student. **студе́нческий** student.
сту́день (-дня) *m* jelly; aspic.
студи́ть (-ужу́, -у́дишь) *impf* (*pf* **о~**) cool.
сту́дия studio.
сту́жа severe cold, hard frost.
стук knock; clatter. **сту́кать** *impf*, **сту́кнуть** (-ну) *pf* knock; bang; strike; **~ся** knock (o.s.), bang. **стука́ч** (-á) informer.
стул (*pl* -лья, -льев) chair. **стульча́к** (-á) (*lavatory*) seat. **сту́льчик** stool.
сту́па mortar.
ступа́ть *impf*, **ступи́ть** (-плю́, -пишь) *pf* step; tread. **ступе́нчатый** stepped, graded. **ступе́нь** (*gen pl* -е́не́й) step, rung; stage, grade. **ступе́нька** step. **ступня́** foot; sole.
стуча́ть (-чу́) *impf* (*pf* **по~**) knock; chatter; pound; **~ся в**+*acc* knock at.
стушева́ться (-шу́юсь) *pf*, **стушёвываться** *impf* efface o.s.
с|туши́ть (-шу́, -шишь) *pf.*
стыд (-á) shame. **стыди́ть** (-ыжу́) *impf* (*pf* **при~**) put to shame; **~ся** (*pf* **по~ся**) be ashamed. **стыдли́вый** bashful. **сты́дн|ый** shameful; **~о!** shame! **~о** *impers*+*dat* **ему́ ~о** he is ashamed; **как тебе́ не ~о!** you ought to be ashamed of yourself!
стык joint; junction. **стыкова́ть** *impf* (*pf* **со~**) join end to end; **~ся** (*pf* **при~ся**) dock. **стыко́вка** docking.
сты́нуть, стыть (-ы́ну; стыл) *impf* cool; get cold.

сты́чка skirmish; squabble.
стюарде́сса stewardess.
стя́гивать *impf*, **стяну́ть** (-ну́, -нешь) *pf* tighten; pull together; assemble; pull off; steal; **~ся** tighten; assemble.
стяжа́тель (-я) *m* money-grubber. **стяжа́ть** *impf* & *pf* gain, win.
суббо́та Saturday.
субсиди́ровать *impf* & *pf* subsidize. **субси́дия** subsidy.
субъе́кт subject; ego; person; character, type. **субъекти́вный** subjective.
сувени́р souvenir.
суверените́т sovereignty. **сувере́нный** sovereign.
сугли́нок (-нка) loam.
сугро́б snowdrift.
сугу́бо *adv* especially.
суд (-а́) court; trial; verdict.
суда́ *etc.*: *see* **суд, су́дно¹**
суда́к (-а́) pike-perch.
суде́бный judicial; legal; forensic. **суде́йский** judge's; referee's, umpire's. **суди́мость** previous convictions. **суди́ть** (сужу́, су́дишь) *impf* judge; try; referee, umpire; foreordain; **~ся** go to law.
су́дно¹ (*pl* -да́, -о́в) vessel, craft.
су́дно² (*gen pl* -ден) bed-pan.
судово́й ship's; marine.
судомо́йка kitchen-maid; scullery.
судопроизво́дство legal proceedings.
су́дорога cramp, convulsion. **су́дорожный** convulsive.
судострое́ние shipbuilding. **судострои́тельный** shipbuilding. **судохо́дный** navigable; shipping.
судьба́ (*pl* -ы, -деб) fate, destiny.
судья́ (*pl* -дьи, -де́й, -дьям) *m* judge; referee; umpire.
суеве́рие superstition. **суеве́рный** superstitious.
суета́ bustle, fuss. **суети́ться** (-ечу́сь) *impf* bustle, fuss. **суетли́вый** fussy, bustling.
сужде́ние opinion; judgement.
суже́ние narrowing; constriction. **су́живать** *impf*, **су́зить** (-у́жу) *pf* narrow, contract; **~ся** narrow; taper.
сук (-а́, *loc* -у́; *pl* су́чья, -ьев *or* -и́, -о́в) bough.
су́ка bitch. **су́кин** *adj*: **~ сын** son of a bitch.
сукно́ (*pl* -а, -кон) cloth; **положи́ть под ~** shelve. **суко́нный** cloth; clumsy, crude.
сули́ть *impf* (*pf* **по~**) promise.
султа́н plume.
сумасбро́д, сумасбро́дка nutcase. **сумасбро́дный** wild, mad. **сумасбро́дство** wild behaviour. **сумасше́дш|ий** mad; **~ий** *sb*, **~ая** *sb* lunatic. **сумасше́ствие** madness.
сумато́ха turmoil; bustle.
сумбу́р confusion. **сумбу́рный** confused.
су́меречный twilight. **су́мерки** (-рек) *pl* twilight, dusk.
суме́ть (-е́ю) *pf* +*inf* be able to, manage to.
су́мка bag.
су́мма sum. **сумма́рный** summary; total. **сумми́ровать** *impf* & *pf* add up; summarize.
су́мрак twilight; murk. **су́мрачный** gloomy.
су́мчатый marsupial.
сунду́к (-а́) trunk, chest.
су́нуть(ся (-ну(сь) *pf of* **сова́ть(ся**
суп (*pl* -ы́) soup.

супермáркет supermarket. **суперoблóжка** dust-jacket.

супрýг husband, spouse; *pl* husband and wife, (*married*) couple. **супрýга** wife, spouse. **супрýжеский** conjugal. **супрýжество** matrimony.

сургýч (-á) sealing-wax.

сурдúнка mute; **под сурдúнку** on the sly.

сурóвость severity, sternness. **сурóвый** severe, stern; bleak; unbleached.

сурóк (-рка́) marmot.

суррогáт substitute.

сýслик ground-squirrel.

суcтáв joint, articulation.

сýтки (-ток) *pl* twenty-four hours; a day.

сýтолока commotion.

сýточн|ый daily; round-the-clock; **~ые** *sb pl* per diem allowance.

сутýлиться *impf* stoop. **сутýлый** round-shouldered.

суть essence, main point.

суфлёр prompter. **суфлúровать** *impf +dat* prompt.

сýффикс suffix.

сухáрь (-я́) *m* rusk; *pl* breadcrumbs. **сýхо** *adv* drily; coldly.

сухожúлие tendon.

сухóй (сух, -á, -о) dry; cold. **сухопýтный** land. **сýхость** dryness; coldness. **сухощáвый** lean, skinny.

сучковáтый knotty; gnarled. **сучóк** (-чка́) twig; knot.

сýша (dry) land. **сýше** *comp of* **сухóй. сушёный** dried. **сушúлка** dryer; drying-room. **сушúть** (-шу́, -шишь) *impf* (*pf* **вы́~**) dry, dry out, up; **~ся** (get) dry.

сущéственный essential, vital. **существúтельное** *sb* noun.

существó being, creature; essence. **существовáние** existence. **существовáть** *impf* exist. **сýщий** absolute, downright. **сýщность** essence.

сую́ *etc.*: *see* **совáть. с|фабриковáть** *pf.* **с|фальшúвить** (-влю) *pf.*

с|фантазúровать *pf.*

сфéра sphere. **сферúческий** spherical.

сфинкс sphinx.

с|формировáть(ся *pf.* **с|формовáть** *pf.* **с|формулúровать** *pf.* **с|фотографúровать(ся** *pf.*

схватúть (-ачу́, -áтишь) *pf*, **схвáтывать** *impf* (*impf also* **хватáть**) seize; catch; grasp; **~ся** snatch, catch; grapple. **схвáтка** skirmish; *pl* contractions.

схéма diagram; outline, plan; circuit. **схематúческий** schematic; sketchy. **схематúчный** sketchy.

с|хитрúть *pf.*

схлы́нуть (-нет) *pf* (break and) flow back; subside.

сход coming off; descent; gathering. **сходúть**[1]**(ся** (-ожу́(сь, -óдишь(ся) *impf of* **сойтú(сь. сходúть**[2] (-ожу́, -óдишь) *pf* go; **+за+***instr* go to fetch. **схóдка** gathering, meeting. **схóдный** (-ден, -днá, -о) similar; reasonable. **схóдня** (*gen pl* -ей) (*usu pl*) gang-plank. **схóдство** similarity.

с|хоронúть(ся (-ню́(сь, -нишь(ся) *pf.*

сцедúть (-ежу́, -éдишь) *pf*, **сцéживать** *impf* strain off, decant.

сцéна stage; scene. **сценáрий** scenario; script. **сценарúст** script-writer. **сценúческий** stage.

сцепи́ть (-плю́, -пишь) *pf*, **сцепля́ть** *impf* couple; **~ся** be coupled; grapple. **сце́пка** coupling. **сцепле́ние** coupling; clutch.

счастли́вец (-вца), **счастли́вчик** lucky man. **счастли́вица** lucky woman. **счастли́в|ый** (сча́стли́в) happy; lucky; **~о!** all the best!; **~ого пути́** bon voyage. **сча́стье** happiness; good fortune.

сче́сть(ся (сочту́(сь, -тёшь(ся; счёл(ся, сочла́(сь) *pf of* **счита́ть(ся. счёт** (*loc* -у́; *pl* -а́) bill; account; counting, calculation; score; expense. **счётный** calculating; accounts. **счетово́д** book-keeper, accountant. **счётчик** counter; meter. **счёты** (-ов) *pl* abacus.

счи́стить (-ищу) *pf* (*impf* **счища́ть**) clean off; clear away.

счита́ть *impf* (*pf* **со~, счесть**) count; reckon; consider; **~ся** (*pf also* **по~ся**) settle accounts; be considered; **+с+***instr* take into consideration; reckon with.

счища́ть *impf of* **счи́стить**

США *pl indecl abbr* (*of* **Соединённые Шта́ты Аме́рики**) USA.

сшиба́ть *impf*, **сшиби́ть** (-бу́, -бёшь; сшиб) *pf* strike, hit, knock (off); **~ с ног** knock down; **~ся** collide; come to blows.

сшива́ть *impf*, **с|шить** (сошью́, -ьёшь) *pf* sew (together).

съеда́ть *impf of* **съесть. съедо́бный** edible; nice.

съе́ду *etc.*: *see* **съе́хать**

съёживаться *impf*, **съ|ёжиться** (-жусь) *pf* shrivel, shrink.

съезд congress; conference; arrival. **съе́здить** (-зжу) *pf* go, drive, travel.

съезжа́ть(ся *impf of* **съе́хать(ся. съел** *etc.*: *see* **съесть**

съёмка removal; survey, surveying; shooting. **съёмный** detachable, removable. **съёмщик, съёмщица** tenant; surveyor.

съестно́й food; **~о́е** *sb* food (supplies). **съ|есть** (-ем, -ешь, -ест, -еди́м; съел) *pf* (*impf also* **съеда́ть**)

съе́хать (-е́ду) *pf* (*impf* **съезжа́ть**) go down; come down; move; **~ся** meet; assemble.

съ|язви́ть (-влю́) *pf*.

сы́воротка whey; serum.

сыгра́ть *pf of* **игра́ть; ~ся** play (well) together.

сын (*pl* сыновья́, -ве́й, -вья́м *or* -ы́, -о́в) son. **сыно́вний** filial. **сыно́к** (-нка́) little son; sonny.

сы́пать (-плю) *impf* pour; pour forth; **~ся** fall; pour out; rain down; fray. **сыпно́й тиф** typhus. **сыпу́чий** friable; free-flowing; shifting. **сыпь** rash, eruption.

сыр (*loc* -у́; *pl* -ы́) cheese.

сыре́ть (-е́ю) *impf* (*pf* **от~**) become damp.

сыре́ц (-рца́) raw product.

сыр|о́й (сыр, -а́, -о) damp; raw; uncooked; unboiled; unfinished; unripe. **сы́рость** dampness. **сырьё** raw material(s).

сыска́ть (сыщу́, сы́щешь) *pf* find.

сы́тный (-тен, -тна́, -о) filling. **сы́тость** satiety. **сы́тый** (сыт, -а́, -о) full.

сыч (-а́) little owl.

сы́щик detective.

с|эконо́мить (-млю) *pf*.

сэр sir.

сюда́ *adv* here, hither.
сюже́т subject; plot; topic. **сюже́тный** subject; having a theme.
сюи́та suite.
сюрпри́з surprise.
сюрреали́зм surrealism. **сюрреалисти́ческий** surrealist.
сюрту́к (-á) frock-coat.
сяк *adv*: *see* **так. сям** *adv*: *see* **там**

Т

та *see* **тот**
таба́к (-á) tobacco. **табаке́рка** snuff-box. **таба́чный** tobacco.
та́бель (-я; *pl* -и, -ей *or* -я́, -е́й) *m* table, list. **та́бельный** table; time.
табле́тка tablet.
табли́ца table; ~ **умноже́ния** multiplication table.
та́бор (gipsy) camp.
табу́н (-á) herd.
табуре́т, табуре́тка stool.
тавро́ (*pl* -а, -а́м) brand.
тавтоло́гия tautology.
таджик, -и́чка Tadzhik.
Таджикиста́н Tadzhikistan.
таёжный taiga.
таз (*loc* -у́; *pl* -ы) basin; pelvis. **тазобе́дренный** hip. **та́зовый** pelvic.
таи́нственный mysterious; secret. **таи́ть** *impf* hide, harbour; **~ся** hide; lurk.
Тайва́нь *m* Taiwan.
тайга́ taiga.
тайко́м *adv* secretly, surreptitiously; ~ **от**+*gen* behind the back of.
тайм half; period of play.
та́йна secret; mystery. **тайни́к** (-á) hiding-place; *pl* recesses. **та́йный** secret; privy.
тайфу́н typhoon.
так *adv* so; like this; as it should be; just like that; **и** ~ even so; as it is; **и** ~ **да́лее** and so on; ~ **и сяк** this way and that; **не** ~ wrong; ~ **же** in the same way; ~ **же... как** as ... as; ~ **и есть** I thought so!; ~ **ему́ и на́до** serves him right; ~ **или ина́че** one way or another; ~ **себе́** so-so. **так** *conj* then; so; ~ **как** as, since; ~ **что** so.
такела́ж rigging.
та́кже *adv* also, too, as well.
тако́в *m* (-á *f*, -о́ *neut*, -ы́ *pl*) *pron* such.
так|о́й *pron* such (a); **в ~о́м слу́чае** in that case; **кто он ~о́й?** who is he?; **~о́й же** the same; **~и́м о́бразом** in this way; **что э́то ~о́е?** what is this? **тако́й-то** *pron* so-and-so; such-and-such.
та́кса fixed rate; tariff.
таксёр taxi-driver. **такси́** *neut indecl* taxi. **такси́ст** taxi-driver. **таксопа́рк** taxi depot.
такт time; bar; beat; tact.
та́к-таки after all, really.
та́ктика tactics. **такти́ческий** tactical.
такти́чность tact. **такти́чный** tactful.
та́ктов|ый time, timing; **~ая черта́** bar-line.
тала́нт talent. **тала́нтливый** talented.
талисма́н talisman.
та́лия waist.
тало́н, тало́нчик coupon.
та́лый thawed, melted.
тальк talc; talcum powder.
там *adv* there; ~ **и сям** here and

there; ~ **же** in the same place; ibid.

тамада́ *m* toast-master.

та́мбур[1] tambour; lobby; platform. **та́мбур**[2] chain-stitch.

тамо́женник customs official. **тамо́женный** customs. **тамо́жня** custom-house.

та́мошний of that place, local.

тампо́н tampon.

та́нгенс tangent.

та́нго *neut indecl* tango.

та́нец (-нца) dance; dancing.

тани́н tannin.

танк tank. **та́нкер** tanker. **танки́ст** member of a tank crew. **та́нковый** tank, armoured.

танцева́льный dancing; ~ **ве́чер** dance. **танцева́ть** (-цу́ю) *impf* dance. **танцо́вщик, танцо́вщица** (ballet) dancer. **танцо́р, танцо́рка** dancer.

та́пка, та́почка slipper.

та́ра packing; tare.

тарака́н cockroach.

тара́н battering-ram.

тара́нтул tarantula.

таре́лка plate; cymbal; satellite dish.

тари́ф tariff.

таска́ть *impf* drag, lug; carry; pull; take; pull out; swipe; wear; **~ся** drag; hang about.

тасова́ть *impf* (*pf* **с~**) shuffle.

ТАСС *abbr* (*of* **Телегра́фное аге́нтство Сове́тского Сою́за**) Tass (Telegraph Agency of the Soviet Union).

тата́рин, тата́рка Tatar.

татуиро́вка tattooing, tattoo.

тафта́ taffeta.

тахта́ ottoman.

та́чка wheelbarrow.

тащи́ть (-щу́, -щишь) *impf* (*pf* **вы́~, с~**) pull; drag, lug; carry; take; pull out; swipe; **~ся** drag o.s. along; drag.

та́ять (та́ю) *impf* (*pf* **рас~**) melt; thaw; dwindle.

ТВ *abbr* (*of* **телеви́дение**) TV, television.

тварь creature(s); wretch.

тверде́ть (-е́ет) *impf* (*pf* **за~**) harden, become hard. **тверди́ть** (-ржу́) *impf* (*pf* **вы́~**) repeat, say again and again; memorize. **твёрдо** *adv* hard; firmly, firm. **твердоло́бый** thick-skulled; diehard. **твёрдый** hard; firm; solid; steadfast; ~ **знак** hard sign, ъ; **~ое те́ло** solid. **тверды́ня** stronghold.

твой (-его́) *m*, **твоя́** (-е́й) *f*, **твоё** (-его́) *neut*, **твои́** (-и́х) *pl* your, yours.

творе́ние creation, work; creature. **творе́ц** (-рца́) creator. **твори́тельный** instrumental. **твори́ть** *impf* (*pf* **со~**) create; do; make; **~ся** happen.

творо́г (-а́) curds; cottage cheese.

тво́рческий creative. **тво́рчество** creation; creative work; works.

те *see* **тот**

т.е. *abbr* (*of* **то есть**) that is, i.e.

теа́тр theatre. **театра́льный** theatre; theatrical.

тебя́ *etc.*: *see* **ты**

те́зис thesis.

тёзка *m & f* namesake.

тёк *see* **течь**

текст text; libretto, lyrics.

тексти́ль *m* textiles. **тексти́льный** textile.

тексту́ра texture.

теку́чий fluid; unstable. **теку́щий** current; routine.

теле- *in comb* tele-; television.

телеви́дение television. **~визио́нный** television. **~ви́зор** television (set). **~гра́мма** telegram. **~гра́ф** telegraph (office). **~графи́ровать** *impf* & *pf* telegraph. **~гра́фный** telegraph(ic). **~зри́тель** *m* (television) viewer. **~объекти́в** telephoto lens. **~пати́ческий** telepathic. **~па́тия** telepathy. **~ско́п** telescope. **~ста́нция** television station. **~сту́дия** television studio. **~фо́н** telephone; (telephone) number; **(по)звони́ть по ~фо́ну** *+dat* ring up. **~фон-автома́т** public telephone, call-box. **~фони́ст, -и́стка** (telephone) operator. **~фо́нный** telephone; **~фо́нная кни́га** telephone directory; **~фо́нная ста́нция** telephone exchange; **~фо́нная тру́бка** receiver. **~фон-отве́тчик** answering machine. **~це́нтр** television centre.

теле́га cart, wagon. **теле́жка** small cart; trolley.

те́лекс telex.

телёнок (-нка; *pl* -я́та, -я́т) calf.

теле́сн|ый bodily; corporal; **~ого цве́та** flesh-coloured.

Теле́ц (-льца́) Taurus.

тели́ться *impf* (*pf* **о~**) calve.

тёлка heifer.

те́ло (*pl* -а́) body. **телогре́йка** padded jacket. **телосложе́ние** build. **телохрани́тель** *m* bodyguard.

теля́та *etc.*: *see* **телёнок. теля́тина** veal. **теля́чий** calf; veal.

тем *conj* (so much) the; **~ лу́чше** so much the better; **~ не ме́нее** nevertheless.

тем *see* **тот, тьма**

те́ма subject; theme. **тема́тика** subject-matter; themes. **темати́ческий** subject; thematic.

тембр timbre.

темне́ть (-е́ет) *impf* (*pf* **по~, с~**) become dark. **темни́ца** dungeon. **темно́** *predic* it is dark. **темноко́жий** dark-skinned, swarthy. **тёмно-си́ний** dark blue. **темнота́** darkness. **тёмный** dark.

темп tempo; rate.

темпера́мент temperament. **темпера́ментный** temperamental.

температу́ра temperature.

те́мя (-мени) *neut* crown, top of the head.

тенде́нция tendency; bias.

тенево́й, тени́стый shady.

те́ннис tennis. **тенниси́ст, -и́стка** tennis-player. **те́ннисн|ый** tennis; **~ая площа́дка** tennis-court.

те́нор (*pl* -а́) tenor.

тент awning.

тень (*loc* -и́; *pl* -и, -е́й) shade; shadow; phantom; ghost; particle, vestige, atom; suspicion; **те́ни для век** *pl* eyeshadow.

тео́лог theologian. **теологи́ческий** theological. **теоло́гия** theology.

теоре́ма theorem. **теоре́тик** theoretician. **теорети́ческий** theoretical. **тео́рия** theory.

тепе́решн|ий present. **тепе́рь** *adv* now; today.

тепле́ть (-е́ет) *impf* (*pf* **по~**) get warm. **те́плиться** (-ится) *impf* flicker; glimmer. **тепли́ца** greenhouse, conservatory. **тепли́чный** hothouse. **тепло́** heat; warmth. **тепло́** *adv* warmly; *predic* it is warm.

тепло- *in comb* heat; thermal; thermo-. **теплово́з** diesel locomotive. **~кро́вный** warm-blooded. **~обмéн** heat exchange. **~провóдный** heat-conducting. **~стóйкий** heat-resistant. **~хóд** motor ship. **~централь** heat and power station.

тепловóй heat; thermal. **теплотá** heat; warmth. **тёплый** (-пел, -плá, тёпло́) warm.

терáкт terrorist act.

терапéвт therapeutist. **терапи́я** therapy.

тереби́ть (-блю) *impf* pull (at); pester.

терéть (тру, трёшь; тёр) *impf* rub; grate; **~ся** rub o.s.; **~ся óколо**+*gen* hang about, hang around; **~ся среди́ +***gen* mix with.

терзáть *impf* tear to pieces; torment; **~ся** +*instr* suffer; be a prey to.

тёрка grater.

тéрмин term. **терминолóгия** terminology.

терми́ческий thermic, thermal. **термóметр** thermometer. **тéрмос** thermos (flask). **термостáт** thermostat. **термоя́дерный** thermonuclear.

тернóвник sloe, blackthorn. **терни́стый** thorny.

терпели́вый patient. **терпéние** patience. **терпéть** (-плю, -пишь) *impf* (*pf* **по~**) suffer; bear, endure. **терпéться** (-пится) *impf impers*+*dat*: **емý не тéрпится** +*inf* he is impatient to. **терпи́мость** tolerance. **терпи́мый** tolerant; tolerable.

тéрпкий (-пок, -пкá, -о) astringent; tart.

террáса terrace.

территориáльный territorial. **террито́рия** territory.

террóр terror. **терроризи́ровать** *impf* & *pf* terrorize. **террори́ст** terrorist.

тёртый grated; experienced.

терьéр terrier.

теря́ть *impf* (*pf* **по~, у~**) lose; shed; **~ся** get lost; disappear; fail, decline; become flustered.

тёс boards, planks. **тесáть** (тешý, тéшешь) *impf* cut, hew.

тесёмка ribbon, braid.

тесни́ть *impf* (*pf* **по~, с~**) crowd; squeeze, constrict; be too tight; **~ся** press through; move up; crowd, jostle. **теснотá** crowded state; crush. **тéсн|ый** crowded; (too) tight; close; compact; **~о** it is crowded.

тесóвый board, plank.

тест test.

тéсто dough; pastry.

тесть *m* father-in-law.

тесьмá ribbon, braid.

тéтерев (*pl* -á) black grouse. **тетёрка** grey hen.

тётка aunt.

тетрáдка, тетрáдь exercise book.

тётя (*gen pl* -ей) aunt.

тех- *abbr in comb* (*of* **техни́ческий**) technical.

тéхник technician. **тéхника** technical equipment; technology; technique. **тéхникум** technical college. **техни́ческ|ий** technical; **~ие услóвия** specifications. **технóлог** technologist. **технологи́ческий** technological. **технолóгия** technology. **техперсонáл** technical personnel.

течéние flow; course; current, stream; trend.

течь[1] (-чёт; тёк, -лá) *impf* flow; stream; leak. **течь**[2] leak.

тéшить (-шу) *impf* (*pf* **по~**)

amuse; gratify; **~ся** (+*instr*) amuse o.s. (with).

тешу́ *etc.*: *see* **теса́ть**

тёща mother-in-law.

тигр tiger. **тигри́ца** tigress.

тик[1] tic.

тик[2] teak.

ти́на slime, mud.

тип type. **типи́чный** typical. **типово́й** standard; model. **типогра́фия** printing-house, press. **типогра́фский** typographical.

тир shooting-range, -gallery.

тира́ж (-а́) draw; circulation; edition.

тира́н tyrant. **тира́нить** *impf* tyrannize. **тирани́ческий** tyrannical. **тирани́я** tyranny.

тире́ *neut indecl* dash.

ти́скать *impf*, **ти́снуть** (-**ну**) *pf* press, squeeze. **тиски́** (-о́в) *pl* vice; **в тиска́х** +*gen* in the grip of. **тисне́ние** stamping; imprint; design. **тиснёный** stamped.

тита́н[1] titanian.

тита́н[2] boiler.

тита́н[3] titan.

титр title, sub-title.

ти́тул title; title-page. **ти́тульный** title.

тиф (*loc* -у́) typhus.

ти́хий (тих, -а́, -о) quiet; silent; calm; slow. **тихоокеа́нский** Pacific. **ти́ше** *comp of* **ти́хий, ти́хо**; **ти́ше!** quiet! **тишина́** quiet, silence.

т. к. *abbr* (*of* **так как**) as, since.

тка́ный woven. **ткань** fabric, cloth; tissue. **ткать** (тку, ткёшь; -ал, -а́ла́, -о) *impf* (*pf* **со~**) weave. **тка́цкий** weaving; **~ стано́к** loom. **ткач, ткачи́ха** weaver.

ткну́ть(ся (-у(сь, -ёшь(ся) *pf of* **ты́кать(ся**

тле́ние decay; smouldering. **тлеть** (-е́ет) *impf* rot, decay; smoulder; **~ся** smoulder.

тля aphis.

тмин caraway(-seeds).

то *pron* that; **а не то́** or else, otherwise; **(да) и то́** and even then, and that; **то́ есть** that is (to say); **то и де́ло** every now and then. **то** *conj* then; **не то..., не то** either … or; half …, half; **то..., то** now …, now; **то ли..., то ли** whether … or.

-то *partl* just, exactly; **в то́м-то и де́ло** that's just it.

тобо́й *see* **ты**

това́р goods; commodity.

това́рищ comrade; friend; colleague. **това́рищеский** comradely; friendly.

това́рищество comradeship; company; association.

това́рный goods; commodity.

товаро- *in comb* commodity; goods. **товарообме́н** barter. **~оборо́т** (sales) turnover. **~отправи́тель** *m* consignor. **~получа́тель** *m* consignee.

тогда́ *adv* then; **~ как** whereas. **тогда́шний** of that time.

того́ *see* **тот**

тожде́ственный identical. **то́ждество** identity.

то́же *adv* also, too.

ток (*pl* -и) current.

тока́рный turning; **~ стано́к** lathe. **то́карь** (*pl* -я́, -е́й *or* -и, -ей) *m* turner, lathe operator.

токси́ческий toxic.

толк sense; use; **бе́з ~у** senselessly; **знать ~ в**+*prep* know well; **сбить с ~у** confuse; **с ~ом** intelligently.

толка́ть *impf* (*pf* **толкну́ть**) push, shove; jog; **~ся** jostle.

то́лки (-ов) *pl* rumours, gossip. **толкну́ть(ся** (-ну́(сь, -нёшь(ся) *pf of* **толка́ть(ся**

толкова́ние interpretation; *pl* commentary. **толкова́ть** *impf* interpret; explain; talk. **толко́вый** intelligent; clear; ~ **слова́рь** defining dictionary. **то́лком** *adv* plainly; seriously.

толкотня́ crush, squash.

толку́ *etc.*: *see* **толо́чь**

толку́чка crush, squash; second-hand market.

толокно́ oatmeal.

толо́чь (-лку́, -лчёшь; -ло́к, -лкла́) *impf* (*pf* **ис~, рас~**) pound, crush.

толпа́ (*pl* -ы) crowd. **толпи́ться** *impf* crowd; throng.

толсте́ть (-е́ю) *impf* (*pf* **по~**) grow fat; put on weight. **толстоко́жий** thick-skinned; pachydermatous. **то́лстый** (-а́, -о) fat; thick. **толстя́к** (-а́) fat man *or* boy.

толчёный crushed; ground. **толчёт** *etc.*: *see* **толо́чь**

толчея́ crush, squash.

толчо́к (-чка́) push, shove; (*sport*) put; jolt; shock, tremor.

то́лща thickness; thick. **то́лще** *comp of* **то́лстый. толщина́** thickness; fatness.

толь *m* roofing felt.

то́лько *adv* only, merely; ~ **что** (only) just; *conj* only, but; **(как)** ~, **(лишь)** ~ as soon as; ~ **бы** if only.

том (*pl* ~а́) volume. **то́мик** small volume.

тома́т tomato. **тома́тный** tomato.

томи́тельный tedious, wearing; agonizing. **томи́ть (-млю́)** *impf* (*pf* **ис~**) tire; torment; **~ся** languish; be tormented. **томле́ние** languor. **то́мный** (-мен, -мна́, -о) languid, languorous.

тон (*pl* -а́ *or* -ы, -о́в) tone; note; shade; form. **тона́льность** key.

то́ненький thin; slim. **то́нкий** (-нок, -нка́, -о) thin; slim; fine; refined; subtle; keen. **то́нкость** thinness; slimness; fineness; subtlety.

то́нна ton.

тонне́ль *see* **тунне́ль**

то́нус tone.

тону́ть (-ну́, -нешь) *impf* (*pf* **по~, у~**) sink; drown.

то́ньше *comp of* **то́нкий**

то́пать *impf* (*pf* **то́пнуть**) stamp.

топи́ть[1] (-плю́, -пишь) *impf* (*pf* **по~, у~**) sink; drown; ruin; **~ся** drown o.s.

топи́ть[2] (-плю́, -пишь) *impf* stoke; heat; melt (down); **~ся** burn; melt. **то́пка** stoking; heating; melting (down); furnace.

то́пкий boggy, marshy.

то́пливный fuel. **то́пливо** fuel.

то́пнуть (-ну) *pf of* **то́пать**

топографи́ческий topographical. **топогра́фия** topography.

то́поль (*pl* -я́ *or* -и) *m* poplar.

топо́р (-а́) axe. **топо́рик** hatchet. **топори́ще** axe-handle. **топо́рный** axe; clumsy, crude.

то́пот tramp; clatter. **топта́ть** (-пчу́, -пчешь) *impf* (*pf* **по~**) trample (down); **~ся** stamp; **~ся на ме́сте** mark time.

топча́н (-а́) trestle-bed.

топь bog, marsh.

торг (*loc* -у́; *pl* -и́) trading; bargaining; *pl* auction. **торгова́ть** *impf* (*pf* **с~**) trade; **~ся** bargain, haggle. **торго́вец** (-вца) merchant; tradesman. **тор-гóвка** market-woman; stall-holder. **торгóвля** trade. **торгó-вый** trade, commercial; merchant. **торгпрéд** *abbr* trade representative.

торéц (-рцá) butt-end; wooden paving-block.

торжéственный solemn; ceremonial. **торжествó** celebration; triumph. **торжествовáть** *impf* celebrate; triumph.

торможéние braking. **тóрмоз** (*pl* -á *or* -ы) brake. **тормозúть** (-ожý) *impf* (*pf* **за~**) brake; hamper.

тормошúть (-шý) *impf* pester; bother.

торопúть (-плю, -пишь) *impf* (*pf* **по~**) hurry; hasten; **~ся** hurry. **тороплúвый** hasty.

торпéда torpedo.

торс torso.

торт cake.

торф peat. **торфянóй** peat.

торчáть (-чý) *impf* stick out; protrude; hang about.

торшéр standard lamp.

тоскá melancholy; boredom; nostalgia; **~ по**+*dat* longing for. **ransлúвый** melancholy; depressed; dreary. **тосковáть** *impf* be melancholy, depressed; long; **~ по**+*dat* miss.

тост toast.

тот *m* (та *f*, то *neut*, те *pl*) *pron* that; the former; the other; the one; the same; the right; **и ~ и другóй** both; **к томý же** moreover; **не ~** the wrong; **ни ~ ни другóй** neither; **тот, кто** the one who, the person who. **тóтчас** *adv* immediately.

тоталитарúзм totalitarianism. **тоталитáрный** totalitarian.

totáльный total.

точúлка sharpener; pencil-sharpener. **точúло** whetstone, grindstone. **точúльный** grinding, sharpening; **~ кáмень** whetstone, grindstone. **точúльщик** (knife-)grinder. **точúть** (-чý, -чишь) *impf* (*pf* **вы́~, на~**) sharpen; hone; turn; eat away; gnaw at.

тóчка spot; dot; full stop; point; **~ зрéния** point of view; **~ с запятóй** semicolon. **тóчно**[1] *adv* exactly, precisely; punctually. **тóчно**[2] *conj* as though, as if. **тóчность** punctuality; precision; accuracy; **в тóчности** exactly, precisely. **тóчный** (-чен, -чнá, -о) exact, precise; accurate; punctual. **тóчь-в-тóчь** *adv* exactly; word for word.

тошнúть *impf impers*: **меня́ тошнúт** I feel sick. **тошнотá** nausea. **тошнотвóрный** sickening, nauseating.

тóщий (тощ, -á, -е) gaunt, emaciated; skinny; empty; poor.

травá (*pl* -ы) grass; herb. **травúнка** blade of grass.

травúть (-влю, -вишь) *impf* (*pf* **вы́~, за~**) poison; exterminate, destroy; etch; hunt; torment; badger. **травлéние** extermination; etching. **трáвля** hunting; persecution; badgering.

трáвма trauma, injury.

травоя́дный herbivorous. **травянúстый, травянóй** grass; herbaceous; grassy.

трагéдия tragedy. **трáгик** tragedian. **трагúческий, трагúчный** tragic.

традициóнный traditional. **традúция** tradition.

траектóрия trajectory.

трактáт treatise; treaty.

трактúр inn, tavern.

трактова́ть *impf* interpret; treat, discuss. **тракто́вка** treatment; interpretation.

тра́ктор tractor. **трактори́ст** tractor driver.

трал trawl. **тра́лить** *impf* (*pf* **про~**) trawl; sweep. **тра́льщик** trawler; mine-sweeper.

трамбова́ть *impf* (*pf* **у~**) ram, tamp.

трамва́й tram. **трамва́йный** tram.

трампли́н spring-board; ski-jump.

транзи́стор transistor; transistor radio.

транзи́тный transit.

транс trance.

трансатланти́ческий transatlantic.

трансли́ровать *impf* & *pf* broadcast, transmit. **трансляцио́нный** transmission; broadcasting. **трансля́ция** broadcast, transmission.

тра́нспорт transport; consignment. **транспортёр** conveyor. **транспорти́р** protractor. **транспорти́ровать** *impf* & *pf* transport. **тра́нспортный** transport.

трансформа́тор transformer.

транше́я trench.

трап ladder.

тра́пеза meal.

трапе́ция trapezium; trapeze.

тра́сса line, course, direction; route, road.

тра́та expenditure; waste. **тра́тить** (-а́чу) *impf* (*pf* **ис~, по~**) spend, expend; waste.

тра́улер trawler.

тра́ур mourning. **тра́урный** mourning; funeral; mournful.

трафаре́т stencil; stereotype; cliché. **трафаре́тный** stencilled; conventional, stereotyped.

тра́чу *etc.*: *see* **тра́тить**

тре́бование demand; request; requirement; requisition, order; *pl* needs. **тре́бовательный** demanding. **тре́бовать** *impf* (*pf* **по~**) summon; +*gen* demand, require; need; **~ся** be needed, be required.

трево́га alarm; anxiety. **трево́жить** (-жу) *impf* (*pf* **вс~, по~**) alarm; disturb; worry; **~ся** worry, be anxious; trouble o.s. **трево́жный** worried, anxious; alarming; alarm.

тре́звенник teetotaller. **трезве́ть** (-е́ю) *impf* (*pf* **о~**) sober up.

трезво́н peal (*of bells*); rumours; row.

тре́звость sobriety. **тре́звый** (-зв, -а́, -о) sober; teetotal.

тре́йлер trailer.

трель trill; warble.

тре́нер trainer, coach.

тре́ние friction.

тренирова́ть *impf* (*pf* **на~**) train, coach; **~ся** be in training. **трениро́вка** training, coaching. **трениро́вочный** training.

трепа́ть (-плю́, -плешь) *impf* (*pf* **ис~, по~, рас~**) blow about; dishevel; wear out; pat; **~ся** fray; wear out; flutter. **тре́пет** trembling; trepidation. **трепета́ть** (-ещу́, -е́щешь) *impf* tremble; flicker; palpitate. **тре́петный** trembling; flickering; palpitating; timid.

треск crack; crackle; fuss.

треска́ cod.

тре́скаться[1] *impf* (*pf* **по~**) crack; chap.

тре́скаться[2] *impf of* **тре́снуться**

тре́снуть (-нет) *pf* snap, crackle; crack; chap; bang; **~ся** (*impf* **тре́скаться**) +*instr* bang.

трест trust.

тре́т|ий (-ья, -ье) third; **~ье** *sb* sweet (course).

трети́ровать *impf* slight.

треть (*gen pl* -е́й) third. **тре́тье** *etc.*: *see* **тре́тий. треуго́льник** triangle. **треуго́льный** triangular.

тре́фы (треф) *pl* clubs.

трёх- *in comb* three-, tri-. **трёхгоди́чный** three-year. **~голо́сный** three-part. **~гра́нный** three-edged; trihedral. **~колёсный** three-wheeled. **~ле́тний** three-year; three-year old. **~ме́рный** three-dimensional. **~ме́сячный** three-month; quarterly; three-month-old. **~по́лье** three-field system. **~со́тый** three-hundredth. **~сторо́нний** three-sided; trilateral; tripartite. **~эта́жный** three-storeyed.

треща́ть (-щу́) *impf* crack; crackle; creak; chirr; crack up; chatter. **тре́щина** crack, split; fissure; chap.

три (трёх, -ём, -емя́, -ёх) three.

трибу́на platform, rostrum; stand. **трибуна́л** tribunal.

тригономе́трия trigonometry.

тридцатиле́тний thirty-year; thirty-year old. **тридца́тый** thirtieth. **три́дцать** (-и́, *instr* -ью́) thirty. **три́жды** *adv* three times; thrice.

трико́ *neut indecl* tricot; tights; knickers. **трикота́ж** knitted fabric; knitwear. **трикота́жный** jersey, tricot; knitted.

трина́дцатый thirteenth. **трина́дцать** thirteen. **трио́ль** triplet.

три́ппер gonorrhoea.

три́ста (трёхсо́т, -ёмста́м, -емяста́ми, -ёхста́х) three hundred.

трито́н *zool* triton.

триу́мф triumph.

тро́гательный touching, moving. **тро́гать(ся** *impf of* **тро́нуть(ся**

тро́е (-и́х) *pl* three. **троебо́рье** triathlon. **троекра́тный** thrice-repeated. **Тро́ица** Trinity; **тро́ица** trio. **Тро́ицын день** Whit Sunday. **тро́йка** three; figure 3; troika; No. 3; three-piece suit. **тройно́й** triple, treble; three-ply. **тро́йственный** triple; tripartite.

тролле́йбус trolley-bus.

тромб blood clot.

тромбо́н trombone.

трон throne.

тро́нуть (-ну) *pf* (*impf* **тро́гать**) touch; disturb; affect; **~ся** start, set out; be touched; be affected.

тропа́ path.

тро́пик tropic.

тропи́нка path.

тропи́ческий tropical.

трос rope, cable.

тростни́к (-а́) reed, rush. **тро́сточка, трость** (*gen pl* ~е́й) cane, walking-stick.

тротуа́р pavement.

трофе́й trophy; *pl* spoils (*of war*), booty.

троюродн|ый: ~ый брат, ~ая сестра́ second cousin.

тру *etc.*: *see* **тере́ть**

труба́ (*pl* -ы) pipe; chimney; funnel; trumpet; tube. **труба́ч** (-а́) trumpeter; trumpet-player.

труби́ть (-блю́) *impf* (*pf* **про~**) blow, sound; blare. **тру́бка** tube; pipe; (*telephone*) receiver. **трубопрово́д** pipe-line; piping; manifold. **трубочи́ст** chimney-sweep. **тру́бочный** pipe. **тру́бчатый** tubular.

труд (-а́) labour; work; effort; **с ~о́м** with difficulty. **труди́ться** (-ужу́сь, -у́дишься) *impf* toil, labour, work; trouble. **тру́дно** *predic* it is difficult. **тру́дность** difficulty. **тру́дный** (-ден, -дна́, -о) difficult; hard.

трудо- *in comb* labour, work. **трудоде́нь** (-дня́) *m* work-day (*unit*). **~ёмкий** labour-intensive. **~люби́вый** industrious. **~лю́бие** industry. **~спосо́бность** ability to work. **~спосо́бный** able-bodied; capable of working.

трудово́й work; working; earned; hard-earned. **трудя́щ|ийся** working; **~иеся** *sb pl* the workers. **тру́женик, тру́женица** toiler.

труп corpse; carcass.

тру́ппа troupe, company.

трус coward.

тру́сики (-ов) *pl* shorts; trunks; pants.

труси́ть[1] (-ушу́) *impf* trot, jog along.

тру́сить[2] (-у́шу) *impf* (*pf* **с~**) be a coward; lose one's nerve; be afraid. **труси́ха** coward. **трусли́вый** cowardly. **тру́сость** cowardice.

трусы́ (-о́в) *pl* shorts; trunks; pants.

труха́ dust; trash.

трушу́ *etc.*: *see* **труси́ть**[1], **тру́сить**[2]

трущо́ба slum; godforsaken hole.

трюк stunt; trick.

трюм hold.

трюмо́ *neut indecl* pier-glass.

трю́фель (*gen pl* -ле́й) *m* truffle.

тря́пка rag; spineless creature; *pl* clothes. **тряпьё** rags; clothes.

тряси́на quagmire. **тря́ска** shaking, jolting. **трясти́** (-су́, -сёшь; -яс, -ла́) *impf*, **тряхну́ть** (-ну́, -нёшь) *pf* (*pf also* **вы~**) shake; shake out; jolt; **~сь** shake; tremble, shiver; jolt.

тсс *int* sh! hush!

туале́т dress; toilet. **туале́тный** toilet.

туберкулёз tuberculosis.

ту́го *adv* tight(ly), taut; with difficulty. **туго́й** (туг, -а́, -о) tight; taut; tightly filled; difficult.

туда́ *adv* there, thither; that way; to the right place; **ни ~ ни сюда́** neither one way nor the other; **~ и обра́тно** there and back.

ту́же *comp of* **ту́го, туго́й**

тужу́рка (double-breasted) jacket.

туз (-а́, *acc* -а́) ace; bigwig.

тузе́мец (-мца), **-мка** native.

ту́ловище trunk; torso.

тулу́п sheepskin coat.

тума́н fog; mist; haze. **тума́нить** *impf* (*pf* **за~**) dim, cloud, obscure; **~ся** grow misty; be befogged. **тума́нность** fog, mist; nebula; obscurity. **тума́нный** foggy; misty; hazy; obscure, vague.

ту́мба post; bollard; pedestal. **ту́мбочка** bedside table.

ту́ндра tundra.

тунея́дец (-дца) sponger.

туни́ка tunic.

тунне́ль *m*, **тонне́ль** *m* tunnel.

тупе́ть (-е́ю) *impf* (*pf* **о~**) become blunt; grow dull. **тупи́к** (-á) cul-de-sac, dead end; impasse; **поста́вить в ~** stump, nonplus. **тупи́ться** (-пится) *impf* (*pf* **за~, ис~**) become blunt. **тупи́ца** *m* & *f* blockhead, dimwit. **тупо́й** (туп, -á, -о) blunt; obtuse; dull; vacant, stupid. **ту́пость** bluntness; vacancy; dullness, slowness.

тур turn; round.

тура́ rook, castle.

турба́за holiday village, campsite.

турби́на turbine.

туре́цкий Turkish; **~ бараба́н** bass drum.

тури́зм tourism. **тури́ст, -и́стка** tourist. **тури́ст(и́че)ский** tourist.

туркме́н (*gen pl* **-ме́н**), **~ка** Turkmen. **Туркмениста́н** Turkmenistan.

турне́ *neut indecl* tour.

турне́пс swede.

турни́р tournament.

ту́рок (-рка) Turk. **турча́нка** Turkish woman. **Ту́рция** Turkey.

ту́склый dim, dull; lacklustre. **тускне́ть** (-е́ет) *impf* (*pf* **по~**) grow dim.

тут *adv* here; now; **~ же** there and then.

ту́фля shoe.

ту́хлый (-хл, -á, -о) rotten, bad. **ту́хнуть**[1] (-нет; тух) go bad.

ту́хнуть[2] (-нет; тух) *impf* (*pf* **по~**) go out.

ту́ча cloud; storm-cloud.

ту́чный (-чен, -чнá, -чно) fat; rich, fertile.

туш flourish.

ту́ша carcass.

тушева́ть (-шу́ю) *impf* (*pf* **за~**) shade.

тушёный stewed. **туши́ть**[1] (-шу́, -шишь) *impf* (*pf* **с~**) stew.

туши́ть[2] (-шу́, -шишь) *impf* (*pf* **за~, по~**) extinguish.

тушу́ю *etc.*: *see* **тушева́ть. тушь** Indian ink; **~ (для ресни́ц)** mascara.

тща́тельность care. **тща́тельный** careful; painstaking.

тщеду́шный feeble, frail.

тщесла́вие vanity, vainglory. **тщесла́вный** vain. **тщета́** vanity. **тщётный** vain, futile.

ты (тебя́, тебе́, тобо́й, тебе́) you; thou; **быть на ты с**+*instr* be on intimate terms with.

ты́кать (ты́чу) *impf* (*pf* **ткнуть**) poke; prod; stick.

ты́ква pumpkin; gourd.

тыл (*loc* -ý; *pl* -ы́) back; rear. **ты́льный** back; rear.

тын paling; palisade.

ты́сяча (*instr* -ей *or* -ью) thousand. **тысячеле́тие** millennium; thousandth anniversary. **ты́сячный** thousandth; of (many) thousands.

тычи́нка stamen.

тьма[1] dark, darkness.

тьма[2] host, multitude.

тюбете́йка skull-cap.

тю́бик tube.

тюк (-á) bale, package.

тюле́нь *m* seal.

тюльпа́н tulip.

тюре́мный prison. **тюре́мщик** gaoler. **тюрьма́** (*pl* -ы, -рем) prison, gaol.

тюфя́к (-á) mattress.

тя́га traction; thrust; draught; attraction; craving. **тяга́ться** *impf* vie, contend. **тяга́ч** (-á) tractor.

тя́гостный burdensome; painful. **тя́гость** burden. **тяготе́ние**

gravity, gravitation; bent, inclination. **тяготе́ть** (-е́ю) *impf* gravitate; be attracted; ~ **над** hang over. **тяготи́ть** (-ощу́) *impf* be a burden on; oppress.

тягу́чий malleable, ductile; viscous; slow.

тя́жба lawsuit; competition.

тяжело́ *adv* heavily; seriously. **тяжело́** *predic* it is hard; it is painful. **тяжелоатле́т** weightlifter. **тяжелове́с** heavyweight. **тяжелове́сный** heavy; ponderous. **тяжёлый** (-ёл, -а́) heavy; hard; serious; painful. **тя́жесть** gravity; weight; heaviness; severity. **тя́жкий** heavy; severe; grave.

тяну́ть (-ну́, -нешь) *impf* (*pf* **по~**) pull; draw; drag; drag out; weigh; *impers* attract; be tight; **~ся** stretch; extend; stretch out; stretch o.s.; drag on; crawl; drift; move along one after another; last out; reach.

тяну́чка toffee.

У

у *prep+gen* by; at; with; from, of; belonging to; **у меня́ (есть)** I have; **у нас** at our place; in our country.

уба́вить (-влю) *pf*, **убавля́ть** *impf* reduce, diminish.

у|баю́кать *pf*, **убаю́кивать** *impf* lull (to sleep).

убега́ть *impf of* **убежа́ть**

убеди́тельный convincing; earnest. **убеди́ть** (-и́шь) *pf* (*impf* **убежда́ть**) convince; persuade; **~ся** be convinced; make certain.

убежа́ть (-егу́) *pf* (*impf* **убега́ть**) run away; escape; boil over.

убежда́ть(ся *impf of* **убеди́ть(ся**. **убежде́ние** persuasion; conviction, belief. **убеждённость** conviction. **убеждённый** (-ён, -а́) convinced; staunch.

убе́жище refuge, asylum; shelter.

уберега́ть *impf*, **убере́чь** (-регу́, -режёшь; -рёг, -гла́) *pf* protect, preserve; **~ся от+***gen* protect o.s. against.

уберу́ *etc.*: *see* **убра́ть**

убива́ть(ся *impf of* **уби́ть(ся**. **уби́йственный** deadly; murderous; killing. **уби́йство** murder. **уби́йца** *m* & *f* murderer.

убира́ть(ся *impf of* **убра́ть(ся**; **убира́йся!** clear off!

уби́тый killed; crushed; *sb* dead man. **уби́ть** (убью́, -ьёшь) *pf* (*impf* **убива́ть**) kill; murder; **~ся** hurt o.s.

убо́гий wretched. **убо́жество** poverty; squalor.

убо́й slaughter.

убо́р dress, attire.

убо́рка harvesting; clearing up. **убо́рная** *sb* lavatory; dressing-room. **убо́рочн|ый** harvesting; **~ая маши́на** harvester. **убо́рщик, убо́рщица** cleaner.

убра́нство furniture. **убра́ть** (уберу́, -рёшь; -а́л, -а́, -о) *pf* (*impf* **убира́ть**) remove; take away; put away; harvest; clear up; decorate; **~ посте́ль** make a bed; **~ со стола́** clear the table; **~ся** tidy up, clean up; clear off.

убыва́ть *impf*, **убы́ть** (убу́ду; у́был, -а́, -о) *pf* diminish; subside; wane; leave. **у́быль** diminution; casualties. **убы́ток** (-тка) loss; *pl* damages. **убы́точный** unprofitable.

убью *etc.*: *see* **убить**
уважа́емый respected; dear. **уважа́ть** *impf* respect. **уваже́ние** respect; **с ~м** yours sincerely. **уважи́тельный** valid; respectful.
уве́домить (-млю) *pf*, **уведомля́ть** *impf* inform. **уведомле́ние** notification.
уведу́ *etc.*: *see* **увести**
увезти́ (-зу́, -зёшь; увёз, -ла́) *pf* (*impf* **увози́ть**) take (away); steal; abduct.
увекове́чивать *impf*, **увекове́чить** (-чу) *pf* immortalize; perpetuate.
увёл *etc.*: *see* **увести**
увеличе́ние increase; magnification; enlargement. **увели́чивать** *impf*, **увели́чить** (-чу) *pf* increase; magnify; enlarge; **~ся** increase, grow. **увеличи́тель** *m* enlarger. **увеличи́тельн|ый** magnifying; enlarging; **~ое стекло́** magnifying glass.
у|венча́ть *pf*, **уве́нчивать** *impf* crown; **~ся** be crowned.
уве́ренность confidence; certainty. **уве́ренный** confident; sure; certain. **уве́рить** *pf* (*impf* **уверя́ть**) assure; convince; **~ся** satisfy o.s.; be convinced.
уверну́ться (-ну́сь, -нёшься) *pf*, **увёртываться** *impf* **от**+*gen* evade. **увёртка** dodge, evasion; subterfuge; *pl* wiles. **увёртливый** evasive, shifty.
увертю́ра overture.
уверя́ть(ся *impf of* **уве́рить(ся**
увеселе́ние amusement, entertainment. **увесели́тельный** entertainment; pleasure. **увеселя́ть** *impf* amuse, entertain.
уве́систый weighty.
увести́ (-еду́, -едёшь; -ёл, -а́) *pf* (*impf* **уводи́ть**) take (away); walk off with.
уве́чить (-чу) *impf* maim, cripple. **уве́чный** maimed, crippled; *sb* cripple. **уве́чье** maiming; injury.
уве́шать *pf*, **уве́шивать** *impf* hang (+*instr* with).
увеща́ть *impf*, **увещева́ть** *impf* exhort, admonish.
у|вида́ть *pf* see. **у|ви́деть(ся** (-и́жу(сь) *pf*.
увиливать *impf*, **увильну́ть** (-ну́, -нёшь) *pf* **от**+*gen* dodge; evade.
увлажни́ть *pf*, **увлажня́ть** *impf* moisten.
увлека́тельный fascinating. **увлека́ть** *impf*, **увле́чь** (-еку́, -ечёшь; -ёк, -ла́) *pf* carry away; fascinate; **~ся** be carried away; become mad (+*instr* about). **увлече́ние** animation; passion; crush.
уво́д withdrawal; stealing. **уводи́ть** (-ожу́, -о́дишь) *impf of* **увести**
увози́ть (-ожу́, -о́дишь) *impf of* **увезти**
уво́лить *pf*, **увольня́ть** *impf* discharge, dismiss; retire; **~ся** be discharged, retire. **увольне́ние** discharge, dismissal.
увы́ *int* alas!
увяда́ть *impf of* **увя́нуть**. **увя́дший** withered.
увяза́ть[1] *impf of* **увя́знуть**
увяза́ть[2] (-яжу́, -я́жешь) *pf* (*impf* **увя́зывать**) tie up; pack up; co-ordinate; **~ся** pack; tag along. **увя́зка** tying up; co-ordination.
у|вя́знуть (-ну; -я́з) *pf* (*impf also* **увяза́ть**) get bogged down.
увя́зывать(ся *impf of* **увяза́ть(ся**

у|вя́нуть (-ну) *pf* (*impf also* **увяда́ть**) fade, wither.
угада́ть *pf*, **уга́дывать** *impf* guess.
уга́р carbon monoxide (poisoning); ecstasy. **уга́рный газ** carbon monoxide.
угаса́ть *impf*, **у|га́снуть** (-нет; -а́с) *pf* go out; die down.
угле- *in comb* coal; charcoal; carbon. **углево́д** carbohydrate. **~водоро́д** hydrocarbon. **~добы́ча** coal extraction. **~кислота́** carbonic acid; carbon dioxide. **~ки́слый** carbonate (of). **~ро́д** carbon.
углово́й corner; angular.
углуби́ть (-блю́) *pf*, **углубля́ть** *impf* deepen; **~ся** deepen; delve deeply; become absorbed. **углубле́ние** depression, dip; deepening. **углублённый** deepened; profound; absorbed.
угна́ть (угоню́, -о́нишь; -а́л, -а́, -о) *pf* (*impf* **угоня́ть**) drive away; despatch; steal; **~ся за**+*instr* keep pace with.
угнета́тель *m* oppressor. **угнета́ть** *impf* oppress; depress. **угнете́ние** oppression; depression. **угнетённый** oppressed; depressed.
угова́ривать *impf*, **уговори́ть** *pf* persuade; **~ся** arrange, agree. **угово́р** persuasion; agreement.
уго́да: **в уго́ду** +*dat* to please. **угоди́ть** (-ожу́) *pf*, **угожда́ть** *impf* fall, get; bang; (+*dat*) hit; +*dat or* **на**+*acc* please. **уго́дливый** obsequious. **уго́дно** *predic*+*dat*: **как вам ~** as you wish; **что вам ~?** what would you like?; *partl* **кто ~** anyone (you like); **что ~** anything (you like).
уго́дье (*gen pl* -ий) land.
у́гол (угла́, *loc* -у́) corner; angle.
уголо́вник criminal. **уголо́вный** criminal.
уголо́к (-лка́, *loc* -у́) corner.
у́голь (у́гля́; *pl* у́гли, -ей *or* -е́й) *m* coal; charcoal.
уго́льник set square.
у́гольный coal; carbon(ic).
угомони́ть *pf* calm down; **~ся** calm down.
уго́н driving away; stealing. **угоня́ть** *impf of* **угна́ть**
угора́ть *impf*, **угоре́ть** (-рю́) *pf* get carbon monoxide poisoning; be mad. **угоре́лый** mad; possessed.
у́горь¹ (угря́) *m* eel.
у́горь² (угря́) *m* blackhead.
угости́ть (-ощу́) *pf*, **угоща́ть** *impf* entertain; treat. **угоще́ние** entertaining, treating; refreshments.
угрожа́ть *impf* threaten. **угро́за** threat, menace.
угро́зыск *abbr* criminal investigation department.
угрызе́ние pangs.
угрю́мый sullen, morose.
удава́ться (удаётся) *impf of* **уда́ться**
у|дави́ть(ся (-влю́(сь, -вишь(ся) *pf*. **уда́вка** running-knot, half hitch.
удале́ние removal; sending away; moving off. **удали́ть** *pf* (*impf* **удаля́ть**) remove; send away; move away; **~ся** move off, away; retire.
удало́й, уда́лый (-а́л, -а́, -о) daring, bold. **у́даль, удальство́** daring, boldness.
удаля́ть(ся *impf of* **удали́ть(ся**
уда́р blow; stroke; attack; kick; thrust; seizure; bolt. **ударе́ние**

accent; stress; emphasis. **уда́рить** *pf*, **ударя́ть** *impf* (*impf also* **бить**) strike; hit; beat; **~ся** strike, hit; +**в**+*acc* break into; burst into. **уда́рник, -ница** shock-worker. **уда́рный** percussion; shock; stressed; urgent.

уда́ться (-а́стся, -аду́тся; -а́лся, -ла́сь) *pf* (*impf* **удава́ться**) succeed, be a success; *impers* +*dat* +*inf* succeed, manage; **мне удало́сь найти́ рабо́ту** I managed to find a job. **уда́ча** good luck; success. **уда́чный** successful; felicitous.

удва́ивать *impf*, **удво́ить** (-о́ю) *pf* double, redouble. **удвое́ние** (re)doubling.

уде́л lot, destiny.

удели́ть *pf* (*impf* **уделя́ть**) spare, give.

уделя́ть *impf of* **удели́ть**

удержа́ние deduction; retention, keeping. **удержа́ть** (-жу́, -жишь) *pf*, **уде́рживать** *impf* hold (on to); retain; restrain; suppress; deduct; **~ся** hold out; stand firm; refrain (from).

удеру́ *etc.*: *see* **удра́ть**

удешеви́ть (-влю́) *pf*, **удешевля́ть** *impf* reduce the price of.

удиви́тельный surprising, amazing; wonderful. **удиви́ть** (-влю́) *pf*, **удивля́ть** *impf* surprise, amaze; **~ся** be surprised, be amazed. **удивле́ние** surprise, amazement.

удила́ (-и́л) *pl* bit.

уди́лище fishing-rod.

удира́ть *impf of* **удра́ть**

уди́ть (ужу́, у́дишь) *impf* fish for; **~ ры́бу** fish; **~ся** bite.

удлине́ние lengthening; extension. **удлини́ть** *pf*, **удлиня́ть** *impf* lengthen; extend; **~ся** become longer; be extended.

удо́бно *adv* comfortably; conveniently. **удо́бный** comfortable; convenient.

удобовари́мый digestible.

удобре́ние fertilization; fertilizer. **удо́брить** *pf*, **удобря́ть** *impf* fertilize.

удо́бство comfort; convenience.

удовлетворе́ние satisfaction; gratification. **удовлетворённый** (-рён, -а́) satisfied. **удовлетвори́тельный** satisfactory. **удовлетвори́ть** *pf*, **удовлетворя́ть** *impf* satisfy; +*dat* meet; +*instr* supply with; **~ся** be satisfied.

удово́льствие pleasure. **у|дово́льствоваться** *pf*.

удо́й milk-yield; milking.

удоста́ивать(ся *impf of* **удосто́ить(ся**

удостовере́ние certification; certificate; **~ ли́чности** identity card. **удостове́рить** *pf*, **удостоверя́ть** *impf* certify, witness; **~ся** make sure (**в**+*prep* of), assure o.s.

удосто́ить *pf* (*impf* **удоста́ивать**) make an award to; +*gen* award; +*instr* favour with; **~ся** +*gen* be awarded; be favoured with.

у́дочка (fishing-)rod.

удра́ть (удеру́, -ёшь; удра́л, -а́, -о) *pf* (*impf* **удира́ть**) make off.

удруча́ть *impf*, **удручи́ть** (-чу́) *pf* depress. **удручённый** (-чён, -а́) depressed.

удуша́ть *impf*, **удуши́ть** (-шу́, -шишь) *pf* stifle, suffocate. **удуше́ние** suffocation. **у́душливый** stifling. **у́душье** asthma; asphyxia.

уедине́ние solitude; seclusion.

уединённый secluded; lonely. **уедини́ться** *pf*, **уединя́ться** *impf* seclude o.s.
уе́зд uyezd, District.
уезжа́ть *impf*, **уе́хать** (уе́ду) *pf* go away, depart.
уж[1] (-а́) grass-snake.
уж[2]: *see* **уже́**[2]. **уж**[3], **уже́**[3] *partl* indeed; really.
у|жа́лить *pf*.
у́жас horror, terror; *predic* it is awful. **ужаса́ть** *impf*, **ужасну́ть** (-ну́, -нёшь) *pf* horrify; **~ся** be horrified, be terrified. **ужа́сно** *adv* terribly; awfully. **ужа́сный** awful, terrible.
у́же[1] *comp of* **у́зкий**
уже́[2], **уж**[2] *adv* already; ~ **не** no longer. **уже́**[3]: *see* **уж**[3]
уже́ние fishing.
ужива́ться *impf of* **ужи́ться. ужи́вчивый** easy to get on with.
ужи́мка grimace.
у́жин supper. **у́жинать** *impf* (*pf* **по~**) have supper.
ужи́ться (-иву́сь, -ивёшься; -и́лся, -ла́сь) *pf* (*impf* **ужива́ться**) get on.
ужу́ *see* **уди́ть**
узако́нивать *impf*, **узако́нить** *pf* legalize.
узбе́к, -е́чка Uzbek. **Узбекиста́н** Uzbekistan.
узда́ (*pl* -ы) bridle.
у́зел (узла́) knot; junction; centre; node; bundle.
у́зкий (у́зок, узка́, -о) narrow; tight; narrow-minded. **узкоколе́йка** narrow-gauge railway.
узлова́тый knotty. **узлов|о́й** junction; main, key; **~а́я ста́нция** junction.
узнава́ть (-наю́, -наёшь) *impf*, **узна́ть** *pf* recognize; get to know; find out.
у́зник, у́зница prisoner.
узо́р pattern, design. **узо́рчатый** patterned.
у́зость narrowness; tightness.
узурпа́тор usurper. **узурпи́ровать** *impf & pf* usurp.
у́зы (уз) *pl* bonds, ties.
уйду́ *etc.*: *see* **уйти́.**
у́йма lots (of).
уйму́ *etc.*: *see* **уня́ть**
уйти́ (уйду́, -дёшь; ушёл, ушла́) *pf* (*impf* **уходи́ть**) go away, leave, depart; escape; retire; bury o.s.; be used up; pass away.
ука́з decree; edict. **указа́ние** indication; instruction. **ука́занный** appointed, stated. **указа́тель** *m* indicator; gauge; index; directory. **указа́тельный** indicating; demonstrative; ~ **па́лец** index finger. **указа́ть** (-ажу́, -а́жешь) *pf*, **ука́зывать** *impf* show; indicate; point; point out. **ука́зка** pointer; orders.
ука́лывать *impf of* **уколо́ть**
уката́ть *pf*, **ука́тывать**[1] *impf* roll; flatten; wear out. **укати́ть** (-ачу́, -а́тишь) *pf*, **ука́тывать**[2] *impf* roll away; drive off; **~ся** roll away.
укача́ть *pf*, **ука́чивать** *impf* rock to sleep; make sick.
укла́д structure; style; organization. **укла́дка** packing; stacking; laying; setting. **укла́дчик** packer; layer. **укла́дывать(ся**[1] *impf of* **уложи́ть(ся**
укла́дываться[2] *impf of* **уле́чься**
укло́н slope; incline; gradient; bias; deviation. **уклоне́ние** deviation; digression. **уклони́ться** *pf*, **уклоня́ться** *impf* deviate; **+от**+*gen* turn (off, aside); avoid; evade. **укло́нчивый** evasive.

уклю́чина rowlock.
уко́л prick; injection; thrust.
уколо́ть (-лю́, -лешь) *pf* (*impf* **ука́лывать**) prick; wound.
у|комплектова́ть *pf*, **укомплекто́вывать** *impf* complete; bring up to (full) strength; man; +*instr* equip with.
уко́р reproach.
укора́чивать *impf of* **укороти́ть**
укорени́ть *pf*, **укореня́ть** *impf* implant, inculcate; **~ся** take root.
укори́зна reproach. **укори́зненный** reproachful. **укори́ть** *pf* (*impf* **укоря́ть**) reproach (**в**+*prep* with).
укороти́ть (-очу́) *pf* (*impf* **укора́чивать**) shorten.
укоря́ть *impf of* **укори́ть**
уко́с (hay-)crop.
укра́дкой *adv* stealthily. **украду́** *etc.*: *see* **укра́сть**
Украи́на Ukraine. **украи́нец** (-нца), **украи́нка** Ukrainian. **украи́нский** Ukrainian.
укра́сить (-а́шу) *pf* (*impf* **украша́ть**) adorn, decorate; **~ся** be decorated; adorn o.s.
у|кра́сть (-аду́, -дёшь) *pf*.
украша́ть(ся *impf of* **укра́сить(ся**. **украше́ние** decoration; adornment.
укрепи́ть (-плю́) *pf*, **укрепля́ть** *impf* strengthen; fix; fortify; **~ся** become stronger; fortify one's position. **укрепле́ние** strengthening; reinforcement; fortification.
укро́мный secluded, cosy.
укро́п dill.
укроти́тель *m* (animal-)tamer. **укроти́ть** (-ощу́) *pf*, **укроща́ть** *impf* tame; curb; **~ся** become tame; calm down. **укроще́ние** taming.
укро́ю *etc.*: *see* **укры́ть**
укрупне́ние enlargement; amalgamation. **укрупни́ть** *pf*, **укрупня́ть** *impf* enlarge; amalgamate.
укрыва́тель *m* harbourer. **укрыва́тельство** harbouring; receiving. **укрыва́ть** *impf*, **укры́ть** (-ро́ю) *pf* cover; conceal, harbour; shelter; receive; **~ся** cover o.s.; take cover. **укры́тие** cover; shelter.
у́ксус vinegar.
уку́с bite; sting. **укуси́ть** (-ушу́, -у́сишь) *pf* bite; sting.
уку́тать *pf*, **уку́тывать** *impf* wrap up; **~ся** wrap o.s. up.
укушу́ *etc.*: *see* **укуси́ть**
ул. *abbr* (*of* **у́лица**) street, road.
ула́вливать *impf of* **улови́ть**
ула́дить (-а́жу) *pf*, **ула́живать** *impf* settle, arrange.
у́лей (у́лья) (bee)hive.
улета́ть *impf*, **улете́ть** (улечу́) *pf* fly (away). **улету́чиваться**, *impf*, **улету́читься** (-чусь) *pf* evaporate; vanish.
уле́чься (уля́гусь, -я́жешься; улёгся, -гла́сь) *pf* (*impf* **укла́дываться**) lie down; settle; subside.
ули́ка clue; evidence.
ули́тка snail.
у́лица street; **на у́лице** in the street; outside.
улича́ть *impf*, **уличи́ть** (-чу́) *pf* establish the guilt of.
у́личный street.
уло́в catch. **улови́мый** perceptible; audible. **улови́ть** (-влю́, -вишь) *pf* (*impf* **ула́вливать**) catch; seize. **уло́вка** trick, ruse.
уложе́ние code. **уложи́ть** (-жу́,

-жишь) *pf* (*impf* **укла́дывать**) lay; pack; pile; ~ **спать** put to bed; **~ся** pack (up); fit in.

улуча́ть *impf*, **улучи́ть** (-чу́) *pf* find, seize.

улучша́ть *impf*, **улу́чшить** (-шу) *pf* improve; better; **~ся** improve; get better. **улучше́ние** improvement.

улыба́ться *impf*, **улыбну́ться** (-ну́сь, -нёшься) *pf* smile. **улы́бка** smile.

ультима́тум ultimatum.

ультра- *in comb* ultra-. **ультразвуково́й** supersonic. **~фиоле́товый** ultra-violet.

улягусь *etc.*: *see* **уле́чься**

ум (-а́) mind, intellect; head; **сойти́ с ~а́** go mad.

умали́ть *pf* (*impf* **умаля́ть**) belittle.

умалишённый mad; *sb* lunatic.

ума́лчивать *impf of* **умолча́ть**

умаля́ть *impf of* **умали́ть**

уме́лец (-льца) skilled craftsman. **уме́лый** able, skilful. **уме́ние** ability, skill.

уменьша́ть *impf*, **уме́ньшить** (-шу) *pf* reduce, diminish, decrease; **~ся** diminish, decrease; abate. **уменьше́ние** decrease, reduction; abatement. **уменьши́тельный** diminutive.

уме́ренность moderation. **уме́ренный** moderate; temperate.

умере́ть (умру́, -рёшь; у́мер, -ла́, -о) *pf* (*impf* **умира́ть**) die.

уме́рить *pf* (*impf* **умеря́ть**) moderate; restrain.

умертви́ть (-рщвлю́, -ртви́шь) *pf*, **умерщвля́ть** *impf* kill, destroy; mortify. **у́мерший** dead; *sb* the deceased. **умерщвле́ние** killing, destruction; mortification.

умеря́ть *impf of* **уме́рить**

уместо́ить (-ещу́) *pf* (*impf* **умеща́ть**) fit in, find room for; **~ся** fit in. **уме́стный** appropriate; pertinent; timely.

уме́ть (-е́ю) *impf* be able, know how.

умеща́ть(ся *impf of* **умести́ть(ся**

умиле́ние tenderness; emotion. **умили́ть** *pf*, **умиля́ть** *impf* move, touch; **~ся** be moved.

умира́ние dying. **умира́ть** *impf of* **умере́ть**. **умира́ющий** dying; *sb* dying person.

умиротворе́ние pacification; appeasement. **умиротвори́ть** *pf*, **умиротворя́ть** *impf* pacify; appease.

умне́ть (-е́ю) *impf* (*pf* **по~**) grow wiser. **у́мница** good girl; *m* & *f* clever person.

умножа́ть *impf*, **у|мно́жить** (-жу) *pf* multiply; increase; **~ся** increase, multiply. **умноже́ние** multiplication; increase. **умножи́тель** *m* multiplier.

у́мный (умён, умна́, у́мно́) clever, wise, intelligent. **умозаключе́ние** deduction; conclusion.

умоли́ть *pf* (*impf* **умоля́ть**) move by entreaties.

умолка́ть *impf*, **умо́лкнуть** (-ну; -о́лк) *pf* fall silent; stop. **умолча́ть** (-чу́) *pf* (*impf* **ума́лчивать**) fail to mention; hush up.

умоля́ть *impf of* **умоли́ть**; beg, entreat.

умопомеша́тельство derangement.

умори́тельный incredibly funny, killing. **у|мори́ть** *pf* kill; exhaust.

умо́ю *etc.*: *see* **умы́ть. умру́** *etc.*: *see* **умере́ть**
у́мственный mental, intellectual.
умудри́ть *pf*, **умудря́ть** *impf* make wiser; **~ся** contrive.
умыва́льная *sb* wash-room. **умыва́льник** wash-stand, wash-basin. **умыва́ть(ся** *impf of* **умы́ть(ся**
у́мысел (-сла) design, intention.
умы́ть (умо́ю) *pf* (*impf* **умыва́ть**) wash; **~ся** wash (o.s.).
умы́шленный intentional.
у|насле́довать *pf*.
унести́ (-су́, -сёшь; -ёс, -ла́) *pf* (*impf* **уноси́ть**) take away; carry off, make off with; **~сь** speed away; fly by; be carried (away).
универма́г *abbr* department store. **универса́льн|ый** universal; all-round; versatile; all-purpose; **~ магази́н** department store; **~ое сре́дство** panacea. **универса́м** *abbr* supermarket.
университе́т university. **университе́тский** university.
унижа́ть *impf*, **уни́зить** (-и́жу) *pf* humiliate; **~ся** humble o.s.; stoop. **униже́ние** humiliation. **уни́женный** humble. **унизи́тельный** humiliating.
уника́льный unique.
унима́ть(ся *impf of* **уня́ть(ся**
унисо́н unison.
унита́з lavatory pan.
унифици́ровать *impf* & *pf* standardize.
уничижи́тельный pejorative.
уничтожа́ть *impf*, **уничто́жить** (-жу) *pf* destroy, annihilate; abolish; do away with. **уничтоже́ние** destruction, annihilation; abolition.
уноси́ть(ся (-ошу́(сь, -о́сишь(ся) *impf of* **унести́(сь**
у́нция ounce.
уныва́ть *impf* be dejected. **уны́лый** dejected; doleful, cheerless. **уны́ние** dejection, despondency.
уня́ть (уйму́, -мёшь; -я́л, -а́, -о) *pf* (*impf* **унима́ть**) calm, soothe; **~ся** calm down.
упа́док (-дка) decline; decay; **~ ду́ха** depression. **упа́дочнический** decadent. **упа́дочный** depressive; decadent. **упаду́** *etc.*: *see* **упа́сть**
у|упакова́ть *pf*, **упако́вывать** *impf* pack (up). **упако́вка** packing; wrapping. **упако́вщик** packer.
упа́сть (-аду́, -адёшь) *pf of* **па́дать**
упере́ть (упру́, -рёшь; -ёр) *pf*, **упира́ть** *impf* rest, lean; **~ на**+*acc* stress; **~ся** rest, lean; resist; +**в**+*acc* come up against.
упи́танный well-fed; fattened.
упла́та payment. **у|плати́ть** (-ачу́, -а́тишь) *pf*, **упла́чивать** *impf* pay.
уплотне́ние compression; condensation; consolidation; sealing. **уплотни́ть** *pf*, **уплотня́ть** *impf* condense; compress; pack more into.
уплыва́ть *impf*, **уплы́ть** (-ыву́, -ывёшь; -ы́л, -а́, -о) *pf* swim *or* sail away; pass.
упова́ть *impf* +**на**+*acc* put one's trust in.
уподо́биться (-блюсь) *pf*, **уподобля́ться** *impf* +*dat* become like.
упое́ние ecstasy, rapture. **упои́тельный** intoxicating, ravishing.
уполза́ть *impf*, **уползти́** (-зу́,

-зёшь; -о́лз, -зла́) *pf* creep away, crawl away.

уполномо́ченный *sb* (authorized) agent, representative; proxy. **уполнома́чивать, уполномо́чивать** *impf*, **уполномо́чить** (-чу) *pf* authorize, empower.

упомина́ние mention. **упомина́ть** *impf*, **упомяну́ть** (-ну́, -нешь) *pf* mention, refer to.

упо́р prop, support; **в ~** point-blank; **сде́лать ~ на**+*acc or prep* lay stress on. **упо́рный** stubborn; persistent. **упо́рство** stubbornness; persistence. **упо́рствовать** *impf* be stubborn; persist (**в**+*prep* in).

упоря́дочивать *impf*, **упоря́дочить** (-чу) *pf* regulate, put in order.

употреби́тельный (widely-) used; common. **употреби́ть** (-блю́) *pf*, **употребля́ть** *impf* use. **употребле́ние** use; usage.

упра́ва justice.

управдо́м *abbr* manager (*of block of flats*). **упра́виться** (-влюсь) *pf*, **управля́ться** *impf* cope, manage; **+с**+*instr* deal with. **управле́ние** management; administration; direction; control; driving, steering; government. **управля́емый снаря́д** guided missile. **управля́ть** *impf* +*instr* manage, direct, run; govern; be in charge of; operate; drive. **управля́ющий** *sb* manager.

упражне́ние exercise. **упражня́ть** *impf* exercise, train; **~ся** practise, train.

упраздни́ть *pf*, **упраздня́ть** *impf* abolish.

упра́шивать *impf of* **упроси́ть**

упрёк reproach. **упрека́ть** *impf*, **упрекну́ть** (-ну́, -нёшь) *pf* reproach.

упроси́ть (-ошу́, -о́сишь) *pf* (*impf* **упра́шивать**) entreat; prevail upon.

упрости́ть (-ощу́) *pf* (*impf* **упроща́ть**) (over-)simplify.

упро́чивать *impf*, **упро́чить** (-чу) *pf* strengthen, consolidate; **~ся** be firmly established.

упрошу́ *etc.*: *see* **упроси́ть**

упроща́ть *impf of* **упрости́ть**. **упрощённый** (-щён, -а́) (over-)simplified.

упру́ *etc.*: *see* **упере́ть**

упру́гий elastic; springy. **упру́гость** elasticity; spring. **упру́же** *comp of* **упру́гий**

упря́жка harness; team. **упряжно́й** draught. **у́пряжь** harness.

упря́миться (-млюсь) *impf* be obstinate; persist. **упря́мство** obstinacy. **упря́мый** obstinate; persistent.

упуска́ть *impf*, **упусти́ть** (-ущу́, -у́стишь) *pf* let go, let slip; miss. **упуще́ние** omission; slip; negligence.

ура́ *int* hurrah!

уравне́ние equalization; equation. **ура́внивать** *impf*, **уравня́ть** *pf* equalize. **уравни́тельный** equalizing, levelling. **уравнове́сить** (-е́шу) *pf*, **уравнове́шивать** *impf* balance; counterbalance. **уравнове́шенность** composure. **уравнове́шенный** balanced, composed.

урага́н hurricane; storm.

ура́льский Ural.

ура́н uranium; Uranus. **ура́новый** uranium.

урва́ть (-ву́, -вёшь; -а́л, -а́, -о) *pf* (*impf* **урыва́ть**) snatch.

урегули́рование regulation;

settlement. **у|регулúровать** *pf.*
урéзать (-éжу) *pf*, **урезáть, урéзывать** *impf* cut off; shorten; reduce.
ýрка *m* & *f* (*sl*) lag, convict.
ýрна urn; litter-bin.
ýровень (-вня) *m* level; standard.
урóд freak, monster.
уродúться (-ожýсь) *pf* ripen; grow.
урóдливость deformity; ugliness. **урóдливый** deformed; ugly; bad. **урóдовать** *impf* (*pf* **из~**) disfigure; distort. **урóдство** disfigurement; ugliness.
урожáй harvest; crop; abundance. **урожáйность** yield; productivity. **урожáйный** productive, high-yield.
урождённый née. **урожéнец** (-нца), **урожéнка** native. **урожýсь** *see* **уродúться**
урóк lesson.
урóн losses; damage. **уронúть** (-ню́, -нишь) *pf of* **ронять**
урчáть (-чý) *impf* rumble.
урывáть *impf of* **урвáть. урывками** *adv* in snatches, by fits and starts.
ус (*pl* -ы́) whisker; tendril; *pl* moustache.
усадúть (-ажý, -áдишь) *pf*, **усáживать** *impf* seat, offer a seat; plant. **усáдьба** (*gen pl* -деб *or* -дьб) country estate; farmstead. **усáживаться** *impf of* **усéсться**
усáтый moustached; whiskered.
усвáивать *impf*, **усвóить** *pf* master; assimilate; adopt. **усвоéние** mastering; assimilation; adoption.
усéрдие zeal; diligence. **усéрдный** zealous; diligent.
усéсться (уся́дусь; -éлся) *pf* (*impf* **усáживаться**) take a seat; settle down (to).
усидéть (-ижý) *pf* remain seated; hold down a job. **усúдчивый** assiduous.
ýсик tendril; runner; antenna; *pl* small moustache.
усилéние strengthening; reinforcement; intensification; amplification. **усúленный** intensified, increased; earnest.
усúливать *impf*, **усúлить** *pf* intensify, increase; amplify; strengthen, reinforce; **~ся** increase, intensify; become stronger. **усúлие** effort. **усилитель** *m* amplifier; booster.
ускакáть (-ачý, -áчешь) *pf* skip off; gallop off.
ускользáть *impf*, **ускользнýть** (-нý, -нёшь) *pf* slip off; steal away; escape.
ускорéние acceleration. **ускóренный** accelerated; rapid; crash. **ускорúтель** accelerator.
ускóрить *pf*, **ускоря́ть** *impf* quicken; accelerate; hasten; **~ся** accelerate, be accelerated; quicken.
услóвие condition. **условиться** (-влюсь) *pf*, **услóвливаться, услáвливаться** *impf* agree; arrange. **услóвленный** agreed, fixed. **услóвность** convention. **услóвный** conditional; conditioned; conventional; agreed; relative.
усложнéние complication. **усложнúть** *pf*, **усложня́ть** *impf* complicate; **~ся** become complicated.
услýга service; good turn. **услýжливый** obliging.
услыхáть (-ы́шу) *pf*, **у|слы́шать** (-ы́шу) *pf* hear; sense; scent.

усма́тривать *impf of* **усмотре́ть**

усмеха́ться *impf*, **усмехну́ться** (-ну́сь, -нёшься) *pf* smile; grin; smirk. **усме́шка** smile; grin; sneer.

усмире́ние pacification; suppression. **усмири́ть** *pf*, **усмиря́ть** *impf* pacify; calm; suppress.

усмотре́ние discretion, judgement. **усмотре́ть** (-рю́, -ришь) *pf* (*impf* **усма́тривать**) perceive; see; regard; +**за**+*instr* keep an eye on.

усну́ть (-ну́, -нёшь) *pf* go to sleep.

усоверше́нствование advanced studies; improvement, refinement. **у|соверше́нствовать(ся** *pf*.

усомни́ться *pf* doubt.

успева́емость progress. **успева́ть** *impf*, **успе́ть** (-е́ю) *pf* have time; manage; succeed. **успе́х** success; progress. **успе́шный** successful.

успока́ивать *impf*, **успоко́ить** *pf* calm, quiet, soothe; **~ся** calm down; abate. **успока́ивающий** calming, sedative. **успокое́ние** calming, soothing; calm; peace. **успокои́тельн|ый** calming; reassuring; **~ое** *sb* sedative, tranquillizer.

уста́ (-т, -та́м) *pl* mouth.

уста́в regulations, statutes; charter.

устава́ть (-таю́, -ёшь) *impf of* **уста́ть**; **не устава́я** incessantly.

уста́вить (-влю) *pf*, **уставля́ть** *impf* set, arrange; cover, fill; direct; **~ся** find room, go in; stare.

уста́лость tiredness. **уста́лый** tired.

устана́вливать *impf*, **установи́ть** (-влю́, -вишь) *pf* put, set up; install; set; establish; fix; **~ся** dispose o.s.; be established; set in. **устано́вка** putting, setting up; installation; setting; plant, unit; directions. **установле́ние** establishment. **устано́вленный** established, prescribed.

уста́ну *etc.*: *see* **уста́ть**

устарева́ть *impf*, **у|старе́ть** (-е́ю) *pf* become obsolete; become antiquated. **устаре́лый** obsolete; antiquated, out-of-date.

уста́ть (-а́ну) *pf* (*impf* **устава́ть**) get tired.

устила́ть *impf*, **устла́ть** (-телю́, -те́лешь) *pf* cover; pave.

у́стный oral, verbal.

усто́й abutment; foundation, support. **усто́йчивость** stability, steadiness. **усто́йчивый** stable, steady. **устоя́ть** (-ою́) *pf* keep one's balance; stand firm; **~ся** settle; become fixed.

устра́ивать(ся *impf of* **устро́ить(ся**

устране́ние removal, elimination. **устрани́ть** *pf*, **устраня́ть** *impf* remove; eliminate; **~ся** resign, retire.

устраша́ть *impf*, **устраши́ть** (-шу́) *pf* frighten; **~ся** be frightened.

устреми́ть (-млю́) *pf*, **устремля́ть** *impf* direct, fix; **~ся** rush; be directed; concentrate. **устремле́ние** rush; aspiration.

у́стрица oyster.

устро́йтель *m*, **~ница** organizer. **устро́ить** *pf* (*impf* **устра́ивать**) arrange, organize; make; cause; settle, put in order; place, fix up; get; suit; **~ся** work out; manage; settle down; be found,

get fixed up. **устройство** arrangement; construction; mechanism, device; system.
уступ shelf, ledge. **уступать** *impf*, **уступить** (-плю, -пишь) *pf* yield; give up; ~ **дорогу** make way. **уступка** concession. **уступчивый** pliable; compliant.
устыдиться (-ыжусь) *pf* (+*gen*) be ashamed (of).
устье (*gen pl* -ьев) mouth; estuary.
усугубить (-ублю) *pf*, **усугублять** *impf* increase; aggravate.
усы *see* **ус**
усыновить (-влю) *pf*, **усыновлять** *impf* adopt. **усыновление** adoption.
усыпать (-плю) *pf*, **усыпать** *impf* strew, scatter.
усыпительный soporific. **усыпить** (-плю) *pf*, **усыплять** *impf* put to sleep; lull; weaken.
усядусь *etc.*: *see* **усесться**
утаивать *impf*, **утаить** *pf* conceal; keep secret.
утаптывать *impf of* **утоптать**
утаскивать *impf*, **утащить** (-щу, -щишь) *pf* drag off.
утварь utensils.
утвердительный affirmative. **утвердить** (-ржу) *pf*, **утверждать** *impf* confirm; approve; ratify; establish; assert; ~**ся** gain a foothold; become established; be confirmed. **утверждение** approval; confirmation; ratification; assertion; establishment.
утекать *impf of* **утечь**
утёнок (-нка; *pl* утята, -ят) duckling.
утеплить *pf*, **утеплять** *impf* warm.
утереть (утру, -рёшь; утёр) *pf* (*impf* **утирать**) wipe (off, dry).
утерпеть (-плю, -пишь) *pf* restrain o.s.
утёс cliff, crag.
утечка leak, leakage; escape; loss. **утечь** (-еку, -ечёшь; утёк, -ла) *pf* (*impf* **утекать**) leak, escape; pass.
утешать *impf*, **утешить** (-шу) *pf* console; ~**ся** console o.s. **утешение** consolation. **утешительный** comforting.
утилизировать *impf* & *pf* utilize.
утиль *m*, **утильсырьё** scrap.
утиный duck, duck's.
утирать(ся *impf of* **утереть(ся**
утихать *impf*, **утихнуть** (-ну; -их) *pf* abate, subside; calm down.
утка duck; canard.
уткнуть (-ну, -нёшь) *pf* bury; fix; ~**ся** bury o.s.
утолить *pf* (*impf* **утолять**) quench; satisfy; relieve.
утолщение thickening; bulge.
утолять *impf of* **утолить**
утомительный tedious; tiring. **утомить** (-млю) *pf*, **утомлять** *impf* tire, fatigue; ~**ся** get tired. **утомление** weariness. **утомлённый** weary.
у|тонуть (-ну, -нешь) *pf* drown, be drowned; sink.
утончённый refined.
у|топить(ся (-плю(сь, -пишь(ся) *pf*. **утопленник** drowned man.
утопический utopian. **утопия** Utopia.
утоптать (-пчу, -пчешь) *pf* (*impf* **утаптывать**) trample down.
уточнение more precise definition; amplification. **уточнить** *pf*, **уточнять** *impf* define more precisely; amplify.
утраивать *impf of* **утроить**

у|трамбова́ть *pf*, **утрамбо́вывать** *impf* ram, tamp; **~ся** become flat.

утра́та loss. **утра́тить** (-а́чу) *pf*, **утра́чивать** *impf* lose.

у́тренний morning. **у́тренник** morning performance; early-morning frost.

утри́ровать *impf* & *pf* exaggerate.

у́тро (-а *or* -а́, -у *or* -у́; *pl* -а, -ам *or* -а́м) morning.

утро́ба womb; belly.

утро́ить *pf* (*impf* **утра́ивать**) triple, treble.

утру́ *etc.*: *see* **утере́ть, у́тро**

утружда́ть *impf* trouble, tire.

утю́г (-а́) iron. **утю́жить** (-жу) *impf* (*pf* **вы́~, от~**) iron.

ух *int* oh, ooh, ah.

уха́ fish soup.

уха́б pot-hole. **уха́бистый** bumpy.

уха́живать *impf* **за**+*instr* tend; look after; court.

ухвати́ть (-ачу́, -а́тишь) *pf*, **ухва́тывать** *impf* seize; grasp; **~ся за**+*acc* grasp, lay hold of; set to; seize; jump at. **ухва́тка** grip; skill; trick; manner.

ухитри́ться *pf*, **ухитря́ться** *impf* manage, contrive. **ухищре́ние** device, trick.

ухмы́лка smirk. **ухмыльну́ться** (-ну́сь, -нёшься) *pf*, **ухмыля́ться** *impf* smirk.

у́хо (*pl* у́ши, уше́й) ear; ear-flap.

ухо́д[1] **+за**+*instr* care of; tending, looking after.

ухо́д[2] leaving, departure. **уходи́ть** (-ожу́, -о́дишь) *impf of* **уйти́**

ухудша́ть *impf*, **уху́дшить** (-шу) *pf* make worse; **~ся** get worse. **ухудше́ние** deterioration.

уцеле́ть (-е́ю) *pf* remain intact; survive.

уце́нивать *impf*, **уцени́ть** (-ню́, -нишь) *pf* reduce the price of.

уцепи́ть (-плю́, -пишь) *pf* catch hold of, seize; **~ся за**+*acc* catch hold of, seize; jump at.

уча́ствовать *impf* take part; hold shares. **уча́ствующий** *sb* participant. **уча́стие** participation; share; sympathy.

участи́ть (-ащу́) *pf* (*impf* **учаща́ть**) make more frequent; **~ся** become more frequent, quicken.

уча́стливый sympathetic. **уча́стник** participant. **уча́сток** (-тка) plot; part, section; sector; district; field, sphere. **у́часть** lot, fate.

учаща́ть(ся *impf of* **участи́ть(ся**

уча́щийся *sb* student; pupil. **учёба** studies; course; training. **учёбник** text-book. **учёбный** educational; school; training. **уче́ние** learning; studies; apprenticeship; teaching; doctrine; exercise.

учени́к (-а́), **учени́ца** pupil; apprentice; disciple. **учени́ческий** pupil's(s); apprentice('s); unskilled; crude. **учёность** learning, erudition. **учён|ый** learned; scholarly; academic; scientific; **~ая сте́пень** (*university*) degree; **~ый** *sb* scholar; scientist.

уче́сть (учту́, -тёшь; учёл, учла́) *pf* (*impf* **учи́тывать**) take stock of; take into account; discount. **учёт** stock-taking; calculation; taking into account; registration; discount; **без ~а** +*gen* disregarding; **взять на ~** register. **учётный** registration; discount.

учи́лище (*specialist*) school.
у|чини́ть *pf*, **учиня́ть** *impf* make; carry out; commit.
учи́тель (*pl* -я́) *m*, **учи́тельница** teacher. **учи́тельск|ий** teacher's, teachers'; **~ая** *sb* staff-room.
учи́тывать *impf of* **уче́сть**
учи́ть (учу́, у́чишь) *impf* (*pf* **вы́~, на~, об~**) teach; be a teacher; learn; **~ся** be a student; +*dat or inf* learn, study.
учреди́тельный constituent.
учреди́ть (-ежу́) *pf*, **учрежда́ть** *impf* found, establish. **учрежде́ние** founding; establishment; institution.
учти́вый civil, courteous.
учту́ *etc.*: *see* **уче́сть**
уша́нка hat with ear-flaps.
ушёл *etc.*: *see* **уйти́. у́ши** *etc.*: *see* **у́хо**
уши́б injury; bruise. **ушиба́ть** *impf*, **ушиби́ть** (-бу́, -бёшь; уши́б) *pf* injure; bruise; hurt; **~ся** hurt o.s.
ушко́ (*pl* -и́, -о́в) eye; tab.
ушно́й ear, aural.
уще́лье ravine, gorge, canyon.
ущеми́ть (-млю́) *pf*, **ущемля́ть** *impf* pinch, jam; limit; encroach on; hurt. **ущемле́ние** pinching, jamming; limitation; hurting.
уще́рб detriment; loss; damage; prejudice. **уще́рбный** waning.
ущипну́ть (-ну́, -нёшь) *pf of* **щипа́ть**
Уэ́льс Wales. **уэ́льский** Welsh.
ую́т cosiness, comfort. **ую́тный** cosy, comfortable.
уязви́мый vulnerable. **уязви́ть** (-влю́) *pf*, **уязвля́ть** *impf* wound, hurt.
уясни́ть *pf*, **уясня́ть** *impf* understand, make out.

фа́брика factory. **фабрика́нт** manufacturer. **фабрика́т** finished product, manufactured product. **фабрикова́ть** *impf* (*pf* **с~**) fabricate, forge. **фабри́чн|ый** factory; manufacturing; factory-made; **~ая ма́рка, ~ое клеймо́** trade-mark.
фа́була plot, story.
фаго́т bassoon.
фа́за phase; stage.
фаза́н pheasant.
фа́зис phase.
файл (*comput*) file.
фа́кел torch, flare.
факс fax.
факси́миле *neut indecl* facsimile.
факт fact; **соверши́вшийся ~** fait accompli. **факти́чески** *adv* in fact; virtually. **факти́ческий** actual; real; virtual.
фа́ктор factor.
факту́ра texture; style, execution.
факультати́вный optional. **факульте́т** faculty, department.
фа́лда tail (*of coat*).
фальсифика́тор falsifier, forger. **фальсифика́ция** falsification; adulteration; forgery. **фальсифици́ровать** *impf* & *pf* falsify; forge; adulterate. **фальши́вить** (-влю) *impf* (*pf* **с~**) be a hypocrite; sing *or* play out of tune. **фальши́вка** forged document. **фальши́вый** false; spurious; forged; artificial; out of tune. **фальшь** deception; falseness.
фами́лия surname. **фамилья́рничать** be over-familiar.

фамилья́рность (over-)familiarity. **фамилья́рный** (over-)familiar; unceremonious.

фанати́зм fanaticism. **фана́тик** fanatic.

фане́ра veneer; plywood.

фантазёр dreamer, visionary. **фантази́ровать** *impf* (*pf* **с~**) dream; make up, dream up; improvise. **фанта́зия** fantasy; fancy; imagination; whim. **фанта́стика** fiction, fantasy. **фантасти́ческий, фантасти́чный** fantastic.

фа́ра headlight.

фарао́н pharaoh; faro.

фарва́тер fairway, channel.

фармазо́н freemason.

фармаце́вт pharmacist.

фарс farce.

фа́ртук apron.

фарфо́р china; porcelain. **фарфо́ровый** china.

фарцо́вщик currency speculator.

фарш stuffing; minced meat. **фарширова́ть** *impf* (*pf* **за~**) stuff.

фаса́д façade.

фасова́ть *impf* (*pf* **рас~**) package.

фасо́ль kidney bean(s), French bean(s); haricot beans.

фасо́н cut; fashion; style; manner. **фасо́нный** shaped.

фата́ veil.

фатали́зм fatalism. **фата́льный** fatal.

фаши́зм Fascism. **фаши́ст** Fascist. **фаши́стский** Fascist.

фая́нс faience, pottery.

февра́ль (-я́) *m* February. **февра́льский** February.

федера́льный federal. **федера́ция** federation.

феери́ческий fairy-tale.

фейерве́рк firework(s).

фе́льдшер (*pl* -а́), **-шери́ца** (*partly-qualified*) medical assistant.

фельето́н feuilleton, feature.

фемини́зм feminism. **феминисти́ческий, фемини́стский** feminist.

фен (hair-)dryer.

фено́мен phenomenon. **феномена́льный** phenomenal.

феода́л feudal lord. **феодали́зм** feudalism. **феода́льный** feudal.

ферзь (-я́) *m* queen.

фе́рма[1] farm.

фе́рма[2] girder, truss.

ферма́та (*mus*) pause.

ферме́нт ferment.

фе́рмер farmer.

фестива́ль *m* festival.

фетр felt. **фе́тровый** felt.

фехтова́льщик, -щица fencer. **фехтова́ние** fencing. **фехтова́ть** *impf* fence.

фе́я fairy.

фиа́лка violet.

фиа́ско *neut indecl* fiasco.

фи́бра fibre.

фигля́р buffoon.

фигу́ра figure; court-card; (chess-)piece. **фигура́льный** figurative, metaphorical. **фигури́ровать** *impf* figure, appear.

фигури́ст, -и́стка figure-skater.

фигу́рка figurine, statuette; figure. **фигу́рн|ый** figured; **~ое ката́ние** figure-skating.

фи́зик physicist. **фи́зика** physics. **физио́лог** physiologist. **физиологи́ческий** physiological. **физиоло́гия** physiology. **физионо́мия** physiognomy; face, expression. **физиотерапе́вт** physiotherapist. **физи́ческий** physical; physics. **физкульту́ра** *abbr* P.E., gymnastics. **физкульту́рный** *abbr* gymnastic; athletic; ~ **зал** gymnasium.

фикса́ж fixer. **фикса́ция** fixing. **фикси́ровать** *impf* & *pf* (*pf also* **за~**) fix; record.

фикти́вный fictitious. ~ **брак** marriage of convenience. **фи́кция** fiction.

филантро́п philanthropist. **филантро́пия** philanthropy.

филармо́ния philharmonic society; concert hall.

филатели́ст philatelist.

филе́ *neut indecl* sirloin; fillet.

филиа́л branch.

фили́стер philistine.

фило́лог philologist. **филологи́ческий** philological. **филоло́гия** philology.

фило́соф philosopher. **филосо́фия** philosophy. **филосо́фский** philosophical.

фильм film. **фильмоско́п** projector.

фильтр filter. **фильтрова́ть** *impf* (*pf* **про~**) filter.

фина́л finale; final. **фина́льный** final.

финанси́ровать *impf* & *pf* finance. **фина́нсовый** financial. **фина́нсы** (-ов) *pl* finance, finances.

фи́ник date.

фи́ниш finish; finishing post.

фи́нка Finn. **Финля́ндия** Finland. **финля́ндский** Finnish. **финн** Finn. **фи́нский** Finnish.

фиоле́товый violet.

фи́рма firm; company. **фи́рменное блю́до** speciality of the house.

фисгармо́ния harmonium.

фити́ль (-я́) *m* wick; fuse.

флаг flag. **фла́гман** flagship.

флако́н bottle, flask.

фланг flank; wing.

флане́ль flannel.

флегмати́чный phlegmatic.

фле́йта flute.

фле́ксия inflexion. **флекти́вный** inflected.

фли́гель (*pl* -я́) *m* wing; annexe.

флирт flirtation. **флиртова́ть** *impf* flirt.

флома́стер felt-tip pen.

фло́ра flora.

флот fleet. **фло́тский** naval.

флю́гер (*pl* -а́) weather-vane.

флюоресце́нтный fluorescent.

флюс[1] gumboil, abscess.

флюс[2] (*pl* -ы́) flux.

фля́га flask; churn. **фля́жка** flask.

фойе́ *neut indecl* foyer.

фо́кус[1] trick.

фо́кус[2] focus. **фокуси́ровать** *impf* focus.

фо́кусник conjurer, juggler.

фолиа́нт folio.

фольга́ foil.

фолькло́р folklore.

фон background.

фона́рик small lamp; torch. **фона́рный** lamp; ~ **столб** lamp-post. **фона́рь** (-я́) *m* lantern; lamp; light.

фонд fund; stock; reserves.

фоне́тика phonetics. **фонети́ческий** phonetic.

фонта́н fountain.

форе́ль trout.

фо́рма form; shape; mould, cast; uniform. **форма́льность** formality. **форма́льный** formal. **форма́т** format. **форма́ция** structure; stage; formation; mentality. **фо́рменный** uniform; proper, regular. **формирова́ние** forming; unit, formation. **формирова́ть** *impf* (*pf* **с~**) form; organize; **~ся** form, develop. **формова́ть** *impf* (*pf* **с~**) form, shape; mould, cast.

фо́рмула formula. **формули́ровать** *impf* & *pf* (*pf also* **с~**) formulate. **формулиро́вка** formulation; wording; formula. **формуля́р** log-book; library card.

форси́ровать *impf* & *pf* force; speed up.

форсу́нка sprayer; injector.

фортепья́но *neut indecl* piano.

фо́рточка small hinged (window-)pane.

форту́на fortune.

фо́рум forum

фо́сфор phosphorus.

фо́то *neut indecl* photo(graph).

фото- *in comb* photo-, photoelectric. **фотоаппара́т** camera. **~бума́га** photographic paper. **~гени́чный** photogenic. **фото́граф** photographer. **~графи́ровать** *impf* (*pf* **с~**) photograph. **~графи́роваться** be photographed, have one's photograph taken. **~графи́ческий** photographic. **~гра́фия** photography; photograph; photographer's studio. **~ко́пия** photocopy. **~люби́тель** *m* amateur photographer. **~объекти́в** (camera) lens. **~репортёр** press photographer. **~хро́ника** news in pictures. **~элеме́нт** photoelectric cell.

фрагме́нт fragment.

фра́за sentence; phrase. **фразеоло́гия** phraseology.

фрак tail-coat, tails.

фракцио́нный fractional; factional. **фра́кция** fraction; faction.

франк franc.

франкмасо́н Freemason.

франт dandy.

Фра́нция France. **францу́женка** Frenchwoman. **францу́з** Frenchman. **францу́зский** French.

фрахт freight. **фрахтова́ть** *impf* (*pf* **за~**) charter.

фрега́т frigate.

фре́ска fresco.

фронт (*pl* -ы, -о́в) front. **фронтови́к** (-а́) front-line soldier. **фронтово́й** front(-line).

фронто́н pediment.

фрукт fruit. **фрукто́вый** fruit; **~ сад** orchard.

ФСБ *abbr* (*of* **Федера́льная слу́жба безопа́сности**) Federal Security Service.

фтор fluorine. **фто́ристый** fluorine; fluoride. **~ ка́льций** calcium fluoride.

фу *int* ugh! oh!

фуга́нок (-нка) smoothing-plane.

фуга́с landmine. **фуга́сный** high-explosive.

фунда́мент foundation. **фундамента́льный** solid, sound; main; basic.

функциона́льный functional. **функциони́ровать** *impf* function. **фу́нкция** function.

фунт pound.

фура́ж (-а́) forage, fodder. **фура́жка** peaked cap, forage-cap.

фурго́н van; caravan.

фут foot; foot-rule. **футбо́л** football. **футболи́ст** footballer. **футбо́лка** T-shirt, sports shirt.

футбо́льный football; **~ мяч** football.
футля́р case, container.
футури́зм futurism.
фуфа́йка jersey; sweater.
фы́ркать *impf*, **фы́ркнуть** (-ну) *pf* snort.
фюзеля́ж fuselage.

Х

хала́т dressing-gown. **хала́тный** careless, negligent.
халту́ра pot-boiler; hackwork; money made on the side. **халту́рщик** hack.
хам boor, lout. **ха́мский** boorish, loutish. **ха́мство** boorishness, loutishness.
хамелео́н chameleon.
хан khan.
хандра́ depression. **хандри́ть** *impf* be depressed.
ханжа́ hypocrite. **ха́нжеский** sanctimonious, hypocritical.
хао́с chaos. **хаоти́чный** chaotic.
хара́ктер character. **характеризова́ть** *impf* & *pf* (*pf also* **о~**) describe; characterize; **~ся** be characterized. **характери́стика** reference; description. **характе́рный** characteristic; distinctive; character.
ха́ркать *impf*, **ха́ркнуть** (-ну) *pf* spit.
ха́ртия charter.
ха́та peasant hut.
хвала́ praise. **хвале́бный** laudatory. **хвалёный** highly-praised. **хвали́ть** (-лю́, -лишь) *impf* (*pf* **по~**) praise; **~ся** boast.
хва́стать(ся *impf* (*pf* **по~**) boast. **хвастли́вый** boastful. **хвастовство́** boasting. **хвасту́н** (-а́) boaster.
хвата́ть[1] *impf*, **хвати́ть** (-ачу́, -а́тишь) *pf* (*pf also* **схвати́ть**) snatch, seize; grab; **~ся** remember; *+gen* realize the absence of; **+за**+*acc* snatch at, clutch at; take up.
хвата́ть[2] *impf*, **хвати́ть** (-а́тит) *pf*, *impers* (*+gen*) suffice, be enough; last out; **вре́мени не хвата́ло** there was not enough time; **у нас не хвата́ет де́нег** we haven't enough money; **хва́тит!** that will do!; **э́того ещё не хвата́ло!** that's all we needed! **хва́тка** grasp, grip; method; skill.
хво́йн|ый coniferous; **~ые** *sb pl* conifers.
хвора́ть *impf* be ill.
хво́рост brushwood; (*pastry*) straws. **хворости́на** stick, switch.
хвост (-а́) tail; tail-end. **хво́стик** tail. **хвостово́й** tail.
хво́я needle(s); (*coniferous*) branch(es).
херуви́м cherub.
хиба́р(к)а shack, hovel.
хи́жина shack, hut.
хи́лый (-л, -а́, -о) sickly.
химе́ра chimera.
хи́мик chemist. **химика́т** chemical. **хими́ческий** chemical.
хи́мия chemistry.
химчи́стка dry-cleaning; dry-cleaner's.
хи́на, хини́н quinine.
хиру́рг surgeon. **хирурги́ческий** surgical. **хирурги́я** surgery.
хитре́ц (-а́) cunning person. **хитри́ть** *impf* (*pf* **с~**) use cunning, be crafty. **хи́трость** cun-

ning; ruse; skill; intricacy. **хи́трый** cunning; skilful; intricate.

хихи́кать *impf*, **хихи́кнуть** (-ну) *pf* giggle, snigger.

хище́ние theft; embezzlement.

хи́щник predator, bird *or* beast of prey. **хи́щнический** predatory. **хи́щн|ый** predatory; rapacious; **~ые пти́цы** birds of prey.

хладнокро́вие coolness, composure. **хладнокро́вный** cool, composed.

хлам rubbish.

хлеб (*pl* -ы, -ов *or* -а́, -о́в) bread; loaf; grain. **хлеба́ть** *impf*, **хлебну́ть** (-ну́, -нёшь) *pf* gulp down. **хле́бный** bread; baker's; grain. **хлебозаво́д** bakery. **хлебопека́рня** (*gen pl* -рен) bakery.

хлев (*loc* -у́; *pl* -а́) cow-shed.

хлеста́ть (-ещу́, -е́щешь) *impf*, **хлестну́ть** (-ну́, -нёшь) *pf* lash; whip.

хлоп *int* bang! **хло́пать** *impf* (*pf* **хло́пнуть**) bang; slap; **~ (в ладо́ши)** clap.

хлопково́дство cotton-growing. **хло́пковый** cotton.

хло́пнуть (-ну) *pf of* **хло́пать**

хлопо́к[1] (-пка́) clap.

хло́пок[2] (-пка) cotton.

хлопота́ть (-очу́, -о́чешь) *impf* (*pf* **по~**) busy o.s.; bustle about; take trouble; **+о**+*prep or* **за**+*acc* petition for. **хлопотли́вый** troublesome; exacting; busy, bustling. **хло́поты** (-о́т) *pl* trouble; efforts.

хлопчатобума́жный cotton.

хло́пья (-ьев) *pl* flakes.

хлор chlorine. **хло́ристый, хло́рный** chlorine; chloride. **хло́рка** bleach. **хлорофи́лл** chlorophyll. **хлорофо́рм** chloroform.

хлы́нуть (-нет) *pf* gush, pour.

хлыст (-а́) whip, switch.

хмеле́ть (-е́ю) *impf* (*pf* **за~, о~**) get tipsy. **хмель** (*loc* -ю́) *m* hop, hops; drunkenness; **во хмелю́** tipsy. **хмельно́й** (-лён, -льна́) drunk; intoxicating.

хму́рить *impf* (*pf* **на~**): **~ бро́ви** knit one's brows; **~ся** frown; become gloomy; be overcast. **хму́рый** gloomy; overcast.

хны́кать (-ы́чу *or* -аю) *impf* whimper, snivel.

хо́бби *neut indecl* hobby.

хо́бот trunk. **хoбото́к** (-тка́) proboscis.

ход (*loc* -у́; *pl* -ы, -ов *or* -ы́ *or* -а́, -о́в) motion; going; speed; course; operation; stroke; move; manoeuvre; entrance; passage; **в ~у́** in demand; **дать за́дний ~** reverse; **дать ~** set in motion; **на ~у́** in transit, on the move; in motion; in operation; **по́лным ~ом** at full speed; **пусти́ть в ~** start, set in motion; **три часа́ ~у** three hours' journey.

хода́тайство petitioning; application. **хода́тайствовать** *impf* (*pf* **по~**) petition, apply.

ходи́ть (хожу́, хо́дишь) *impf* walk; go; run; pass, go round; lead, play; move; **+в**+*prep* wear; **+за**+*instr* look after. **хо́дкий** (-док, -дка́, -о) fast; marketable; popular. **ходьба́** walking; walk. **ходя́чий** walking; able to walk; popular; current.

хозрасчёт *abbr* (*of* **хозя́йственный расчёт**) self-financing system.

хозя́ин (*pl* -я́ева, -я́ев) owner, proprietor; master; boss; landlord; host; **хозя́ева по́ля** home team. **хозя́йка** owner; mistress; hostess; landlady. **хозя́йничать** *impf* keep house; be in charge; lord it. **хозя́йственник** financial manager. **хозя́йственный** economic; household; economical. **хозя́йство** economy; housekeeping; equipment; farm; **дома́шнее ~** housekeeping; **се́льское ~** agriculture.

хокке́ист (ice-)hockey-player. **хокке́й** hockey, ice-hockey.

холе́ра cholera.

холестери́н cholesterol.

холл hall, vestibule.

холм (-а́) hill. **холми́стый** hilly.

хо́лод (*pl* -а́, -о́в) cold; coldness; cold weather. **холоди́льник** refrigerator. **хо́лодно** *adv* coldly. **холо́дн|ый** (хо́лоден, -дна́, -о) cold; inadequate, thin; **~ое ору́жие** cold steel.

холо́п serf.

холосто́й (хо́лост, -а́) unmarried, single; bachelor; idle; blank. **холостя́к** (-а́) bachelor.

холст (-а́) canvas; linen.

холу́й (-луя́) *m* lackey.

хому́т (-а́) (horse-)collar; burden.

хомя́к (-а́) hamster.

хор (*pl* хо́ры) choir; chorus.

хорва́т, ~ка Croat. **Хорва́тия** Croatia. **хорва́тский** Croatian.

хорёк (-рька́) polecat.

хореографи́ческий choreographic. **хореогра́фия** choreography.

хори́ст member of a choir or chorus.

хорони́ть (-ню́, -нишь) *impf* (*pf* **за~, по~, с~**) bury.

хоро́шенький pretty; nice. **хороше́нько** *adv* properly, thoroughly. **хороше́ть** (-е́ю) *impf* (*pf* **по~**) grow prettier. **хоро́ший** (-о́ш, -а́, -о́) good; nice; pretty, nice-looking; **хорошо́** *predic* it is good; it is nice. **хорошо́** *adv* well; nicely; all right! good.

хо́ры (хор *or* -ов) *pl* gallery.

хоте́ть (хочу́, хо́чешь, хоти́м) *impf* (*pf* **за~**) wish; *+gen, acc* want; **~ пить** be thirsty; **~ сказа́ть** mean; **~ся** *impers +dat* want; **мне хоте́лось бы** I should like; **мне хо́чется** I want.

хоть *conj* although; even if; *partl* at least, if only; for example; **~ бы** if only. **хотя́** *conj* although; **~ бы** even if; if only.

хо́хот loud laugh(ter). **хохота́ть** (-очу́, -о́чешь) *impf* laugh loudly.

хочу́ *etc.*: *see* **хоте́ть**

храбре́ц (-а́) brave man. **храбри́ться** make a show of bravery; pluck up courage. **хра́брость** bravery. **хра́брый** brave.

храм temple, church.

хране́ние keeping; storage; **ка́мера хране́ния** cloakroom, left-luggage office. **храни́лище** storehouse, depository. **храни́тель** *m* keeper, custodian; curator. **храни́ть** *impf* keep; preserve; **~ся** be, be kept.

храпе́ть (-плю́) *impf* snore; snort.

хребе́т (-бта́) spine; (mountain) range; ridge.

хрен horseradish.

хрестома́тия reader.

хрип wheeze. **хрипе́ть** (-плю́) *impf* wheeze. **хри́плый** (-пл, -а́, -о) hoarse. **хри́пнуть** (-ну; хрип) *impf* (*pf* **о~**) become hoarse. **хрипота́** hoarseness.

христиани́н (*pl* -а́не, -а́н), **христиа́нка** Christian. **христиа́нский** Christian. **христиа́нство** Christianity. **Христо́с** (-иста́) Christ.

хром chromium; chrome.

хромати́ческий chromatic.

хрома́ть *impf* limp; be poor. **хромо́й** (хром, -а́, -о) lame; *sb* lame person.

хромосо́ма chromosome.

хромота́ lameness.

хро́ник chronic invalid. **хро́ника** chronicle; news items; newsreel. **хрони́ческий** chronic.

хронологи́ческий chronological. **хроноло́гия** chronology.

хру́пкий (-пок, -пка́, -о) fragile; frail. **хру́пкость** fragility; frailness.

хруст crunch; crackle.

хруста́ль (-я́) *m* cut glass; crystal. **хруста́льный** cut-glass; crystal; crystal-clear.

хрусте́ть (-ущу́) *impf*, **хру́стнуть** (-ну) *pf* crunch; crackle.

хрю́кать *impf*, **хрю́кнуть** (-ну) *pf* grunt.

хрящ (-а́) cartilage, gristle. **хрящево́й** cartilaginous, gristly.

худе́ть (-е́ю) *impf* (*pf* **по~**) grow thin.

ху́до harm; evil. **ху́до** *adv* ill, badly.

худоба́ thinness.

худо́жественный art, arts; artistic; **~ фильм** feature film. **худо́жник** artist.

худо́й[1] (худ, -а́, -о) thin, lean.

худо́й[2] (худ, -а́, -о) bad; full of holes; worn; **ему́ ху́до** he feels bad.

худоща́вый thin, lean.

ху́дший *superl of* **худо́й, плохо́й** (the) worst. **ху́же** *comp of* **худо́й, ху́до, плохо́й, пло́хо** worse.

хула́ abuse, criticism.

хулига́н hooligan. **хулига́нить** *impf* behave like a hooligan. **хулига́нство** hooliganism.

ху́нта junta.

ху́тор (*pl* -а́) farm; small village.

Ц

ца́пля (*gen pl* -пель) heron.

цара́пать *impf*, **цара́пнуть** (-ну) *pf* (*pf also* **на~, о~**) scratch; scribble; **~ся** scratch; scratch one another. **цара́пина** scratch.

цари́зм tsarism. **цари́ть** *impf* reign, prevail. **цари́ца** tsarina; queen. **ца́рский** tsar's; royal; tsarist; regal. **ца́рство** kingdom, realm; reign. **ца́рствование** reign. **ца́рствовать** *impf* reign. **царь** (-я́) *m* tsar; king.

цвести́ (-ету́, -етёшь; -ёл, -а́) *impf* flower, blossom; flourish.

цвет[1] (*pl* -а́) colour; **~ лица́** complexion.

цвет[2] (*loc* -у́; *pl* -ы́) flower; prime; **в цвету́** in blossom. **цветни́к** (-а́) flower-bed, flower-garden.

цветн|о́й coloured; colour; non-ferrous; **~а́я капу́ста** cauliflower; **~о́е стекло́** stained glass.

цветов|о́й colour; **~а́я слепота́** colour-blindness.

цвето́к (-тка́; *pl* цветы́ *or* цветки́, -о́в) flower. **цвето́чный** flower.

цвету́щий flowering; prosperous.

цеди́ть (цежу́, це́дишь) *impf* strain, filter.
целе́бный curative, healing.
целево́й earmarked for a specific purpose. **целенапра́вленный** purposeful. **целесообра́зный** expedient. **целеустремлённый** (-ён, -ённа *or* -ена́) purposeful.
целико́м *adv* whole; entirely.
целина́ virgin lands, virgin soil. **цели́нн|ый** virgin; **~ые зе́мли** virgin lands.
цели́тельный healing, medicinal.
це́лить(ся *impf* (*pf* **на~**) aim, take aim.
целлофа́н cellophane.
целова́ть *impf* (*pf* **по~**) kiss; **~ся** kiss.
це́лое *sb* whole; integer. **целому́дренный** chaste. **целому́дрие** chastity. **це́лостность** integrity. **це́лый** (цел, -а́, -о) whole; safe, intact.
цель target; aim, object, goal.
це́льный (-лен, -льна́, -о) of one piece, solid; whole; integral; single. **це́льность** wholeness.
цеме́нт cement. **цементи́ровать** *impf* & *pf* cement. **цеме́нтный** cement.
цена́ (*acc* -у; *pl* -ы) price, cost; worth.
ценз qualification. **це́нзор** censor. **цензу́ра** censorship.
цени́тель *m* judge, connoisseur. **цени́ть** (-ню́, -нишь) *impf* value; appreciate. **це́нность** value; price; *pl* valuables; values. **це́нный** valuable.
цент cent. **це́нтнер** centner (*100kg*).
центр centre. **централиза́ция** centralization. **централизова́ть** *impf* & *pf* centralize. **центра́льный** central. **центробе́жный** centrifugal.
цепене́ть (-е́ю) *impf* (*pf* **о~**) freeze; become rigid. **це́пкий** tenacious; prehensile; sticky; obstinate. **це́пкость** tenacity. **цепля́ться** *impf* **за**+*acc* clutch at; cling to.
цепно́й chain. **цепо́чка** chain; file. **цепь** (*loc* -и́; *gen pl* -е́й) chain; series; circuit.
церемо́ниться *impf* (*pf* **по~**) stand on ceremony. **церемо́ния** ceremony.
церковнославя́нский Church Slavonic. **церко́вный** church; ecclesiastical. **це́рковь** (-кви; *pl* -и, -е́й, -а́м) church.
цех (*loc* -у́; *pl* -и *or* -а́) shop; section; guild.
цивилиза́ция civilization. **цивилизо́ванный** civilized. **цивилизова́ть** *impf* & *pf* civilize.
циге́йка beaver lamb.
цикл cycle.
цико́рий chicory.
цили́ндр cylinder; top hat. **цилиндри́ческий** cylindrical.
цимба́лы (-а́л) *pl* cymbals.
цинга́ scurvy.
цини́зм cynicism. **ци́ник** cynic. **цини́чный** cynical.
цинк zinc. **ци́нковый** zinc.
цино́вка mat.
цирк circus.
циркули́ровать *impf* circulate. **ци́ркуль** *m* (pair of) compasses; dividers. **циркуля́р** circular. **циркуля́ция** circulation.
цисте́рна cistern, tank.
цитаде́ль citadel.
цита́та quotation. **цити́ровать** *impf* (*pf* **про~**) quote.
ци́трус citrus. **ци́трусов|ый** citrous; **~ые** *sb pl* citrus plants.

циферблáт dial, face.
цúфра figure; number, numeral. **цифровóй** numerical, digital.
цóколь *m* socle, plinth.
цыгáн (*pl* -е, -áн *or* -ы, -ов), **цыгáнка** gipsy. **цыгáнский** gipsy.
цыплёнок (-нка *pl* -лята, -лят) chicken; chick.
цы́почки: на ~, на цы́почках on tip-toe.

Ч

чабáн (-á) shepherd.
чад (*loc* -ý) fumes, smoke.
чадрá yashmak.
чай (*pl* -и́, -ёв) tea. **чаевы́е** (-ы́х) *sb pl* tip.
чáйка (*gen pl* чáек) (sea-)gull.
чáйная *sb* tea-shop. **чáйник** teapot; kettle. **чáйный** tea. **чайханá** tea-house.
чалмá turban.
чан (*loc* -ý; *pl* -ы́) vat, tub.
чаровáть *impf* bewitch; charm.
час (*with numerals* -á, *loc* -ý; *pl* -ы́) hour; *pl* guard-duty; **котóрый час?** what's the time?; **~** one o'clock; **в два ~á** at two o'clock; **стоя́ть на ~áх** stand guard; **~ы́ пик** rush-hour. **часóвня** (*gen pl* -вен) chapel. **часовóй** *sb* sentry. **часовóй** clock, watch; of one hour, hour-long. **часовщи́к** (-á) watchmaker.
части́ца small part; particle. **чати́чно** *adv* partly, partially. **части́чный** partial.
чáстник private trader.
чáстность detail; **в чáстности** in particular. **чáстный** private; personal; particular, individual.
чáсто *adv* often; close, thickly.
частокóл paling, palisade. **частотá** (*pl* -ы) frequency. **частóтный** frequency. **частýшка** ditty. **чáстый** (част, -á, -о) frequent; close (together); dense; close-woven; rapid.
часть (*gen pl* -éй) part; department; field; unit.
часы́ (-óв) *pl* clock, watch.
чат (*comput*) IRC (Internet Relay Chat).
чáхлый stunted; sickly, puny.
чахóтка consumption.
чáша bowl; chalice; **~ весóв** scale, pan. **чáшка** cup; scale, pan.
чáща thicket.
чáще *comp of* **чáсто, чáстый; ~ всегó** most often, mostly.
чáяние expectation; hope. **чáять** (чáю) *impf* hope, expect.
чвáнство conceit, arrogance.
чегó *see* **что**
чей *m*, **чья** *f*, **чьё** *neut*, **чьи** *pl pron* whose. **чéй-либо, чéй-нибудь** anyone's. **чéй-то** someone's.
чек cheque; bill; receipt.
чекáнить *impf* (*pf* **вы~, от~**) mint, coin; stamp. **чекáнка** coinage, minting. **чекáнный** stamped, engraved.
чёлка fringe; forelock.
чёлн (-á; *pl* чёлны́) dug-out (canoe); boat. **челнóк** (-á) dug-out (canoe); shuttle.
человéк (*pl* лю́ди; with numerals, *gen* -вéк, -ам) man, person.
человеко- *in comb* man-, anthropo-. **человеколюби́вый** philanthropic. **~лю́бие** philanthropy. **~ненави́стнический** misanthropic. **человéко-чáс** (*pl* -ы́) man-hour.
человéчек (-чка) little man. **че-**

ловéческий human; humane. **человéчество** mankind. **человéчность** humaneness. **человéчный** humane.
чéлюсть jaw(-bone); dentures, false teeth.
чем, чём *see* **что. чем** *conj* than; **~..., тем...**+*comp* the more ..., the more.
чемодáн suitcase.
чемпиóн, ~ка champion, title-holder. **чемпионáт** championship.
чемý *see* **что**
чепухá nonsense; trifle.
чéпчик cap; bonnet.
чéрви (-éй), **чéрвы** (черв) *pl* hearts. **червóнн|ый** of hearts; **~ое зóлото** pure gold.
червь (-я́; *pl* -и, -éй) *m* worm; bug. **червя́к** (-á) worm.
чердáк (-á) attic, loft.
черёд (-á, *loc* -ý) turn; **идтú своúм ~óм** take its course. **чередовáние** alternation. **чередовáть** *impf* alternate; **~ся** alternate, take turns.
чéрез, чрез *prep+acc* across; over; through; via; in; after; every other.
черёмуха bird cherry.
черенóк (-нкá) handle; graft, cutting.
чéреп (*pl* -á) skull.
черепáха tortoise; turtle; tortoiseshell. **черепáховый** tortoise; turtle; tortoiseshell. **черепáший** tortoise, turtle; very slow.
черепúца tile. **черепúчный** tile; tiled.
черепóк (-пкá) potsherd, fragment of pottery.
чересчýр *adv* too; too much.
черéшневый cherry. **черéшня** (*gen pl* -шен) cherry(-tree).
черкéс, черкéшенка Circassian.
черкнýть (-нý, -нёшь) *pf* scrape; leave a mark on; scribble.
чернéть (-éю) *impf* (*pf* **по~**) turn black; show black. **чернúка** (*no pl*; *usu collect*) bilberry; bilberries. **чернúла** (-úл) *pl* ink. **чернúльный** ink. **чернúть** *impf* (*pf* **о~**) blacken; slander.
черно- *in comb* black; unskilled; rough. **чёрно-бéлый** black-and-white. **~бýрый** dark-brown; **~бýрая лисá** silver fox. **~волóсый** black-haired. **~глáзый** black-eyed. **~зём** chernozem, black earth. **~кóжий** black; *sb* black. **~мóрский** Black-Sea. **~рабóчий** *sb* unskilled worker, labourer. **~слив** prunes. **~сморóдинный** blackcurrant.
черновúк (-á) rough copy, draft. **черновóй** rough; draft.
чернотá blackness; darkness.
чёрн|ый (-рен, -рнá) black; back; unskilled; ferrous; gloomy; *sb* (*derog*) black person; **~ая сморóдина** (*no pl*; *usu collect*) blackcurrant(s).
черпáк (-á) scoop. **чéрпать** *impf*, **черпнýть** (-нý, -нёшь) *pf* draw; scoop; extract.
черствéть (-éю) *impf* (*pf* **за~, о~, по~**) get stale; become hardened. **чёрствый** (чёрств, -á, -о) stale; hard.
чёрт (*pl* чéрти, -éй) devil.
чертá line; boundary; trait, characteristic. **чертёж** (-á) drawing; blueprint, plan. **чертёжник** draughtsman. **чертёжный** drawing. **чертúть** (-рчý, -ртишь) *impf* (*pf* **на~**) draw.

чёртов *adj* devil's; devilish. **чертовский** devilish.
чертополох thistle.
чёрточка line; hyphen. **черчение** drawing. **черчу** *etc.*: *see* **чертить**
чесать (чешу, -шешь) *impf* (*pf* **по~**) scratch; comb; card; **~ся** scratch o.s.; itch; comb one's hair.
чеснок (-а) garlic.
чествование celebration. **чествовать** *impf* celebrate; honour. **честность** honesty. **честный** (-тен, -тна, -о) honest. **честолюбивый** ambitious. **честолюбие** ambition. **честь** (*loc* -и) honour; **отдать ~** +*dat* salute.
чета pair, couple.
четверг (-а) Thursday. **четвереньки: на ~, на четвереньках** on hands and knees. **четвёрка** four; figure 4; No. 4. **четверо** (-ых) four. **четвероног|ий** four-legged; **~ое** *sb* quadruped. **четверостишие** quatrain. **четвёртый** fourth. **четверть** (*gen pl* -ей) quarter; quarter of an hour; **без четверти час** a quarter to one. **четвертьфинал** quarter-final.
чёткий (-ток, -тка, -о) precise; clear-cut; clear; distinct. **чёткость** precision; clarity.
чётный even.
четыре (-рёх, -рьмя, -рёх) four. **четыреста** (-рёхсот, -ьмястами, -ёхстах) four hundred.
четырёх- *in comb* four-, tetra-. **четырёхкратный** fourfold. **~местный** four-seater. **~сотый** four-hundredth. **~угольник** quadrangle. **~угольный** quadrangular.
четырнадцатый fourteenth. **четырнадцать** fourteen.
чех Czech.
чехол (-хла) cover, case.
чечевица lentil; lens.
чешка Czech. **чешский** Czech.
чешу *etc.*: *see* **чесать**
чешуйка scale. **чешуя** scales.
чибис lapwing.
чиж (-а) siskin.
чин (*pl* -ы) rank.
чинить[1] (-ню, -нишь) *impf* (*pf* **по~**) repair, mend.
чинить[2] *impf* (*pf* **у~**) carry out; cause; **~ препятствия** +*dat* put obstacles in the way of.
чиновник civil servant; official.
чип (micro)chip.
чипсы (-ов) *pl* (potato) crisps.
чирикать *impf*, **чирикнуть** (-ну) *pf* chirp.
чиркать *impf*, **чиркнуть** (-ну) *pf* +*instr* strike.
численность numbers; strength. **численный** numerical. **числитель** *m* numerator. **числительное** *sb* numeral. **числить** *impf* count, reckon; **~ся** be; +*instr* be reckoned. **число** (*pl* -а, -сел) number; date, day; **в числе** +*gen* among; **в том числе** including; **единственное ~** singular; **множественное ~** plural. **числовой** numerical.
чистилище purgatory.
чистильщик cleaner. **чистить** (чищу) *impf* (*pf* **вы~, о~, по~**) clean; peel; clear. **чистка** cleaning; purge. **чисто** *adv* cleanly, clean; purely; completely. **чистовой** fair, clean. **чистокровный** thoroughbred. **чистописание** calligraphy. **чистоплотный** clean; neat; decent. **чистосердечный** frank, sincere. **чистота** cleanness; neat-

ness; purity. **чистый** clean; neat; pure; complete.

читаемый widely-read, popular. **читальный** reading. **читатель** *m* reader. **читать** *impf* (*pf* **про~, прочесть**) read; recite; **~ лекции** lecture; **~ся** be legible; be discernible. **читка** reading.

чихать *impf*, **чихнуть** (-ну́, -нёшь) *pf* sneeze.

чище *comp of* **чисто, чистый**

чищу *etc.*: *see* **чистить**

член member; limb; term; part; article. **членить** *impf* (*pf* **рас~**) divide; articulate. **член-корреспондент** corresponding member, associate. **членораздельный** articulate. **членский** membership. **членство** membership.

чмокать *impf*, **чмокнуть** (-ну) *pf* smack; squelch; kiss noisily; **~ губами** smack one's lips.

чокаться *impf*, **чокнуться** (-нусь) *pf* clink glasses.

чопорный prim; stand-offish.

чреватый *+instr* fraught with.

чрево belly, womb. **чревовещатель** *m* ventriloquist.

чрез *see* **через. чрезвычайн|ый** extraordinary; extreme; **~ое положение** state of emergency. **чрезмерный** excessive.

чтение reading. **чтец** (-а́) reader; reciter.

чтить (чту) *impf* honour.

что, чего, чему, чем, о чём *pron* what?; how?; why?; how much?; which, what, who; anything; **в чём дело?** what is the matter? **для чего?** what ... for? why?; **~ ему до этого?** what does it matter to him?; **~ с тобой?** what's the matter (with you)?; **~ за** what? what sort of?; what (a) ...!; **что** *conj* that. **что (бы) ни** *pron* whatever, no matter what.

чтоб, чтобы *conj* in order (to), so as; that; to. **что-либо, что-нибудь** *prons* anything. **что-то**[1] *pron* something. **что-то**[2] *adv* somewhat, slightly; somehow, for some reason.

чувственность sensuality. **чувствительность** sensitivity; perceptibility; sentimentality. **чувствительный** sensitive; perceptible; sentimental. **чувство** feeling; sense; senses; **прийти в ~** come round. **чувствовать** *impf* (*pf* **по~**) feel; realize; appreciate; **~ себя** *+adv or instr* feel a certain way; **~ся** be perceptible; make itself felt.

чугун (-а́) cast iron. **чугунный** cast-iron.

чудак (-а́), **чудачка** eccentric, crank. **чудачество** eccentricity.

чудеса *etc.*: *see* **чудо. чудесный** miraculous; wonderful.

чудиться (-ишься) *impf* (*pf* **по~, при~**) seem.

чудно *adv* wonderfully; wonderful! **чудной** (-дён, -дна́) odd, strange. **чудный** wonderful; magical. **чудо** (*pl* -деса́) miracle; wonder. **чудовище** monster. **чудовищный** monstrous. **чудодейственный** miracle-working; miraculous. **чудом** *adv* miraculously. **чудотворный** miraculous, miracle-working.

чужбина foreign land. **чуждаться** *impf* *+gen* avoid; stand aloof from. **чуждый** (-жд, -а́, -о) alien (to); *+gen* free from, devoid of. **чужеземец** (-мца), **-земка** foreigner. **чужеземный** foreign. **чужой** someone else's, others'; strange, alien; foreign.

чула́н store-room; larder.
чуло́к (-лка́; *gen pl* -ло́к) stocking.
чума́ plague.
чума́зый dirty.
чурба́н block. **чу́рка** block, lump.
чу́ткий (-ток, -тка́, -о) keen; sensitive; sympathetic; delicate. **чу́ткость** keenness; delicacy.
чу́точка: ни чу́точки not in the least; **чу́точку** a little (bit).
чу́тче *comp of* **чу́ткий**
чуть *adv* hardly; just; very slightly; **~ не** almost; **~-чуть** a tiny bit.
чутьё scent; flair.
чу́чело stuffed animal, stuffed bird; scarecrow.
чушь nonsense.
чу́ять (чу́ю) *impf* scent; sense.
чьё *etc.*: *see* **чей**

Ш

ша́баш sabbath.
шабло́н template; mould, stencil; cliché. **шабло́нный** stencil; trite; stereotyped.
шаг (with numerals -а́, *loc* -у́; *pl* -и́) step; footstep; pace. **шага́ть** *impf*, **шагну́ть** (-ну́, -нёшь) *pf* step; stride; pace; make progress. **ша́гом** *adv* at walking pace.
ша́йба washer; puck.
ша́йка[1] tub.
ша́йка[2] gang, band.
шака́л jackal.
шала́ш (-а́) cabin, hut.
шали́ть *impf* be naughty; play up. **шаловли́вый** mischievous, playful. **ша́лость** prank; *pl* mischief. **шалу́н** (-а́), **шалу́нья** (*gen pl* -ний) naughty child.
шаль shawl.
шально́й mad, crazy.
ша́мкать *impf* mumble.
шампа́нское *sb* champagne.
шампиньо́н field mushroom.
шампу́нь *m* shampoo.
шанс chance.
шанта́ж (-а́) blackmail. **шантажи́ровать** *impf* blackmail.
ша́пка hat; banner headline. **ша́почка** hat.
шар (with numerals -а́; *pl* -ы́) sphere; ball; balloon.
шара́хать *impf*, **шара́хнуть** (-ну) hit; **~ся** dash; shy.
шарж caricature.
ша́рик ball; corpuscle. **ша́рикови|ый: ~ая (авто)ру́чка** ball-point pen; **~ый подши́пник** ball-bearing. **шарикоподши́пник** ball-bearing.
ша́рить *impf* grope; sweep.
ша́ркать *impf*, **ша́ркнуть** (-ну) *pf* shuffle; scrape.
шарлата́н charlatan.
шарма́нка barrel-organ. **шарма́нщик** organ-grinder.
шарни́р hinge, joint.
шарова́ры (-а́р) *pl* (*wide*) trousers.
шарови́дный spherical. **шарово́й** ball; globular. **шарообра́зный** spherical.
шарф scarf.
шасси́ *neut indecl* chassis.
шата́ть *impf* rock, shake; *impers* +*acc* **его́ шата́ет** he is reeling; **~ся** sway; reel, stagger; come loose, be loose; be unsteady; loaf about.
шатёр (-тра́) tent; marquee.
ша́ткий unsteady; shaky.
шату́н (-а́) connecting-rod.
ша́фер (*pl* -а́) best man.

шах check; **~ и мат** checkmate. **шахмати́ст** chess-player. **ша́хматы** (-ат) *pl* chess; chessmen.

ша́хта mine, pit; shaft. **шахтёр** miner. **шахтёрский** miner's; mining.

ша́шка[1] draught; *pl* draughts.

ша́шка[2] sabre.

шашлы́к (-а́) kebab; barbecue.

шва *etc.*: *see* **шов**

шва́бра mop.

шваль rubbish; riff-raff.

швартóв mooring-line; *pl* moorings. **швартова́ть** *impf* (*pf* **при~**) moor; **~ся** moor.

швед, ~ка Swede. **шве́дский** Swedish.

швéйн|ый sewing; **~ая маши́на** sewing-machine.

швейца́р porter, doorman.

швейца́рец (-рца), **-ца́рка** Swiss. **Швейца́рия** Switzerland. **швейца́рский** Swiss.

Швéция Sweden.

швея́ seamstress.

швырну́ть (-ну́, -нёшь) *pf*, **швыря́ть** *impf* throw, fling; **~ся** *+instr* throw (about); treat carelessly.

шевели́ть (-елю́, -е́ли́шь) *impf*, **шевельну́ть** (-ну́, -нёшь) *pf* (*pf also* **по~**) (*+instr*) move, stir; **~ся** move, stir.

шедéвр masterpiece.

шéйка (*gen pl* шéек) neck.

шёл *see* **идти́**

шéлест rustle. **шелестéть** (-сти́шь) *impf* rustle.

шёлк (*loc* -у́; *pl* -а́) silk. **шелкови́стый** silky. **шелкови́ца** mulberry(-tree). **шелкови́чный** mulberry; **~ червь** silkworm. **шёлковый** silk.

шелохну́ть (-ну́, -нёшь) *pf* stir, agitate; **~ся** stir, move.

шелуха́ skin; peelings; pod. **шелуши́ть** (-шу́) peel; shell; **~ся** peel (off), flake off.

шепеля́вить (-влю) *impf* lisp. **шепеля́вый** lisping.

шепну́ть (-ну́, -нёшь) *pf*, **шепта́ть** (-пчу́, -пчешь) *impf* whisper; **~ся** whisper (together). **шёпот** whisper. **шёпотом** *adv* in a whisper.

шерéнга rank; file.

шерохова́тый rough; uneven.

шерсть wool; hair, coat. **шерстянóй** wool(len).

терша́вый rough.

шест (-а́) pole; staff.

шéствие procession. **шéствовать** process; march.

шестёрка six; figure 6; No. 6.

шестерня́ (*gen pl* -рён) gearwheel, cogwheel.

шéстеро (-ы́х) six.

шести- *in comb* six-, hexa-, sex(i)-. **шестигра́нник** hexahedron. **~днéвка** six-day (*working*) week. **~деся́тый** sixtieth. **~мéсячный** six-month; six-month-old. **~сóтый** six-hundredth. **~угóльник** hexagon.

шестнадцатилéтний sixteen-year; sixteen-year-old. **шестна́дцатый** sixteenth. **шестна́дцать** sixteen. **шестóй** sixth. **шесть** (-и́, *instr* -ью́) six. **шестьдеся́т** (-и́десяти, *instr* -ью́десятью) sixty. **шестьсóт** (-исóт, -иста́м, -ьюста́ми, -иста́х) six hundred. **шéстью** *adv* six times.

шеф boss, chief; patron, sponsor. **шеф-пóвар** chef. **шéфство** patronage, adoption. **шéфствовать** *impf* **+над+** *instr* adopt; sponsor.

шéя neck.

ши́ворот collar.
шика́рный chic, smart; splendid.
ши́ло (*pl* -ья, -ьев) awl.
шимпанзе́ *m indecl* chimpanzee.
ши́на tyre; splint.
шине́ль overcoat.
шинкова́ть *impf* shred, chop.
ши́нный tyre.
шип (-а́) thorn, spike, crampon; pin; tenon.
шипе́ние hissing; sizzling. **шипе́ть** (-плю́) *impf* hiss; sizzle; fizz.
шипо́вник dog-rose.
шипу́чий sparkling; fizzy. **шипу́чка** fizzy drink. **шипя́щий** sibilant.
ши́ре *comp of* **широ́кий, широко́.** **ширина́** width; gauge. **ши́рить** *impf* extend, expand; **~ся** spread, extend.
ши́рма screen.
широ́к|ий (-о́к, -а́, -о́ко́) wide, broad; **това́ры ~ого потребле́ния** consumer goods. **широ́ко́** *adv* wide, widely, broadly.
широко- *in comb* wide-, broad-. **широковеща́ние** broadcasting. **~веща́тельный** broadcasting. **~экра́нный** wide-screen.
широта́ (*pl* -ы) width, breadth; latitude. **широ́тный** of latitude; latitudinal. **широча́йший** *superl of* **широ́кий. ширпотре́б** *abbr* consumption; consumer goods. **ширь** (wide) expanse.
шить (шью, шьёшь) *impf* (*pf* **с~**) sew; make; embroider. **шитьё** sewing; embroidery.
ши́фер slate.
шифр cipher, code; shelf mark. **шифро́ванный** coded. **шифрова́ть** *impf* (*pf* **за~**) encipher. **шифро́вка** enciphering; coded communication.
ши́шка cone; bump; lump; (*sl*) big shot.
шкала́ (*pl* -ы) scale; dial.
шкату́лка box, casket, case.
шкаф (*loc* -у́; *pl* -ы́) cupboard; wardrobe. **шка́фчик** cupboard, locker.
шквал squall.
шкив (*pl* -ы) pulley.
шко́ла school. **шко́льник** schoolboy. **шко́льница** schoolgirl. **шко́льный** school.
шку́ра skin, hide, pelt. **шку́рка** skin; rind; sandpaper.
шла *see* **идти́**
шлагба́ум barrier.
шлак slag; dross; clinker. **шлакобло́к** breeze-block.
шланг hose.
шлейф train.
шлем helmet.
шлёпать *impf*, **шлёпнуть** (-ну) *pf* smack, spank; shuffle; tramp; **~ся** fall flat, plop down.
шли *see* **идти́**
шлифова́льный polishing; grinding. **шлифова́ть** *impf* (*pf* **от~**) polish; grind. **шлифо́вка** polishing.
шло *see* **идти́. шлю** *etc.*: *see* **слать**
шлюз lock, sluice.
шлю́пка boat.
шля́па hat. **шля́пка** hat; head.
шмель (-я́) *m* bumble-bee.
шмон *sl* search, frisking.
шмы́гать *impf*, **шмы́гну́ть** (-ыгну́, -ы́гнёшь) *pf* dart, rush; +*instr* rub, brush; **~ но́сом** sniff.
шни́цель *m* schnitzel.
шнур (-а́) cord; lace; flex, cable. **шнурова́ть** *impf* (*pf* **за~,**

про~) lace up; tie. **шнурóк** (-рка́) lace.
шов (шва) seam; stitch; joint.
шовини́зм chauvinism. **шовини́ст** chauvinist. **шовинисти́ческий** chauvinistic.
шок shock. **шоки́ровать** *impf* shock.
шокола́д chocolate. **шокола́дка** chocolate, bar of chocolate. **шокола́дный** chocolate.
шо́рох rustle.
шо́рты (шорт) *pl* shorts.
шо́ры (шор) *pl* blinkers.
шоссе́ *neut indecl* highway.
шотла́ндец (-дца) Scotsman, Scot. **Шотла́ндия** Scotland. **шотла́ндка**[1] Scotswoman. **шотла́ндка**[2] tartan. **шотла́ндский** Scottish, Scots.
шо́у *neut indecl* show; **~ -би́знес** show business.
шофёр driver; chauffeur. **шофёрский** driver's; driving.
шпа́га sword.
шпага́т cord; twine; string; splits.
шпаклева́ть (-лю́ю) *impf* (*pf* **за~**) caulk; fill, putty. **шпаклёвка** filling, puttying; putty.
шпа́ла sleeper.
шпана́ (*sl*) hooligan(s); riff-raff.
шпарга́лка crib.
шпа́рить *impf* (*pf* **о~**) scald.
шпат spar.
шпиль *m* spire; capstan. **шпи́лька** hairpin; hat-pin; tack; stiletto heel.
шпина́т spinach.
шпингале́т (vertical) bolt; catch, latch.
шпио́н spy. **шпиона́ж** espionage. **шпио́нить** *impf* spy (**за** +*instr* on). **шпио́нский** spy's; espionage.
шпо́ра spur.
шприц syringe.
шпро́та sprat.
шпу́лька spool, bobbin.
шрам scar.
шрапне́ль shrapnel.
шрифт (*pl* -ы́) type, print.
шт. *abbr* (*of* **шту́ка**) item, piece.
штаб (*pl* -ы́) staff; headquarters.
шта́бель (*pl* -я́) *m* stack.
штабно́й staff; headquarters.
штамп die, punch; stamp; cliché. **штампо́ванный** punched, stamped, pressed; trite; stock.
шта́нга bar, rod, beam; weight. **штанги́ст** weight-lifter.
штани́шки (-шек) *pl* (*child's*) shorts. **штаны́** (-о́в) trousers.
штат[1] State.
штат[2], **шта́ты** (-ов) *pl* staff, establishment.
штати́в tripod, base, stand.
шта́тный staff; established.
шта́тск|ий civilian; **~ое (пла́тье)** civilian clothes; **~ий** *sb* civilian.
ште́мпель (*pl* -я́) *m* stamp; **почто́вый ~** postmark.
ште́псель (*pl* -я́) *m* plug, socket.
штиль *m* calm.
штифт (-а́) pin, dowel.
што́льня (*gen pl* -лен) gallery.
што́пать *impf* (*pf* **за~**) darn. **што́пка** darning; darning wool.
што́пор corkscrew; spin.
што́ра blind.
шторм gale.
штраф fine. **штрафно́й** penal; penalty. **штрафова́ть** *impf* (*pf* **о~**) fine.
штрих (-а́) stroke; feature. **штрихова́ть** *impf* (*pf* **за~**) shade, hatch.

штуди́ровать *impf* (*pf* **про~**) study.
шту́ка item, one; piece; trick.
штукату́р plasterer. **штукату́рить** *impf* (*pf* **от~, о~**) plaster. **штукату́рка** plastering; plaster.
штурва́л (steering-)wheel, helm.
штурм storm, assault.
шту́рман (*pl* -ы *or* -á) navigator.
штурмова́ть *impf* storm, assault. **штурмов|о́й** assault; storming; **~а́я авиа́ция** ground-attack aircraft. **штурмовщи́на** rushed work.
шту́чный piece, by the piece.
штык (-á) bayonet.
штырь (-я́) *m* pintle, pin.
шу́ба fur coat.
шу́лер (*pl* -á) card-sharper.
шум noise; uproar, racket; stir. **шуме́ть** (-млю́) *impf* make a noise; row; make a fuss. **шу́мный** (-мен, -мна́, -о) noisy; loud; sensational.
шумов|о́й sound; **~ы́е эффе́кты** sound effects. **шумо́к** (-мка́) noise; **под ~** on the quiet.
шу́рин brother-in-law (*wife's brother*).
шурф prospecting shaft.
шурша́ть (-шу́) *impf* rustle.
шу́стрый (-тёр, -тра́, -о) smart, bright, sharp.
шут (-á) fool; jester. **шути́ть** (-чу́, -тишь) *impf* (*pf* **по~**) joke; play, trifle; **+над+***instr* make fun of. **шу́тка** joke, jest. **шутли́вый** humorous; joking, light-hearted. **шу́точный** comic; joking. **шутя́** *adv* for fun, in jest; easily.
шушу́каться *impf* whisper together.
шху́на schooner.
шью *etc.*: *see* **шить**

Щ

щаве́ль (-я́) *m* sorrel.
щади́ть (щажу́) *impf* (*pf* **по~**) spare.
щебёнка, ще́бень (-бня) *m* crushed stone, ballast; road-metal.
ще́бет twitter, chirp. **щебета́ть** (-ечу́, -е́чешь) *impf* twitter, chirp.
щего́л (-гла́) goldfinch.
щёголь *m* dandy, fop. **щегольну́ть** (-ну́, -нёшь) *pf*, **щеголя́ть** *impf* dress fashionably; strut about; *+instr* show off, flaunt. **щегольско́й** foppish.
ще́дрость generosity. **ще́дрый** (-др, -á, -о) generous; liberal.
щека́ (*acc* щёку; *pl* щёки, -а́м) cheek.
щеко́лда latch, catch.
щекота́ть (-очу́, -о́чешь) *impf* (*pf* **по~**) tickle. **щеко́тка** tickling, tickle. **щекотли́вый** ticklish, delicate.
щёлкать *impf*, **щёлкнуть** (-ну) *pf* crack; flick; trill; *+instr* click, snap, pop.
щёлок bleach. **щелочно́й** alkaline. **щёлочь** (*gen pl* -е́й) alkali.
щелчо́к (-чка́) flick; slight; blow.
щель (*gen pl* -е́й) crack; chink; slit; crevice; slit trench.
щеми́ть (-млю́) *impf* constrict; ache; oppress.
щено́к (-нка́; *pl* -нки́, -о́в *or* -ня́та, -я́т) pup; cub.
щепа́ (*pl* -ы, -а́м), **ще́пка** splinter, chip; kindling.
щепети́льный punctilious.

щéпка *see* **щепá**
щепóтка, щéпóть pinch.
щетúна bristle; stubble. **щетúнистый** bristly. **щетúниться** *impf* (*pf* **о~**) bristle. **щётка** brush; fetlock.
щи (щей *or* щец, щам, щáми) *pl* shchi, cabbage soup.
щúколотка ankle.
щипáть (-плю́, -плешь) *impf*, **щипну́ть** (-ну́, -нёшь) *pf* (*pf also* **об~, о~, ущипну́ть**) pinch, nip; sting, bite; burn; pluck; nibble; **~ся** pinch. **щипкóм** *adv* pizzicato. **щипóк** (-пкá) pinch, nip. **щипцы́** (-óв) *pl* tongs, pincers, pliers; forceps.
щит (-á) shield; screen; sluice-gate; (tortoise-)shell; board; panel. **щитовúдный** thyroid. **щитóк** (-ткá) dashboard.
щу́ка pike.
щуп probe. **щу́пальце** (*gen pl* -лец) tentacle; antenna. **щу́пать** *impf* (*pf* **по~**) feel, touch.
щу́плый (-пл, -á, -о) weak, puny.
щу́рить *impf* (*pf* **со~**) screw up, narrow; **~ся** screw up one's eyes; narrow.

Э

эбéновый ebony.
эвакуáция evacuation. **эвакуúрованный** *sb* evacuee. **эвакуúровать** *impf* & *pf* evacuate.
эвкалúпт eucalyptus.
эволюционúровать *impf* & *pf* evolve. **эволюциóнный** evolutionary. **эволю́ция** evolution.
эгúда aegis.
эгоúзм egoism, selfishness. **эгоúст, ~ка** egoist. **эгоистúческий, эгоистúчный** egoistic, selfish.
эй *int* hi! hey!
эйфорúя euphoria.
эквáтор equator.
эквивалéнт equivalent.
экзальтáция exaltation.
экзáмен examination; **выдержать, сдать ~** pass an examination. **экзаменáтор** examiner. **экзаменовáть** *impf* (*pf* **про~**) examine; **~ся** take an examination.
экзеку́ция (corporal) punishment.
экзéма eczema.
экземпля́р specimen; copy.
экзистенциалúзм existentialism.
экзотúческий exotic.
э́кий what (a).
экипáж[1] carriage.
экипáж[2] crew. **экипировáть** *impf* & *pf* equip. **экипирóвка** equipping; equipment.
эклектúзм eclecticism.
эклéр éclair.
экологúческий ecological. **эколóгия** ecology.
экономика economics; economy. **экономúст** economist. **экономить** (-млю) *impf* (*pf* **с~**) use sparingly; save; economize. **экономúческий** economic; economical. **экономúчный** economical. **эконóмия** economy; saving. **эконóмка** housekeeper. **эконóмный** economical; thrifty.
экрáн screen. **экранизáция** filming; film version.
экскавáтор excavator.
эксклюзúвный exclusive.
экскурсáнт tourist. **экскурсиóнный** excursion. **экску́рсия**

(conducted) tour; excursion. **экскурсово́д** guide.

экспанси́вный effusive.

экспатриа́нт expatriate.

экспеди́тор shipping agent. **экспеди́ция** expedition; dispatch; forwarding office.

экспериме́нт experiment. **эксперимента́льный** experimental. **эксперименти́ровать** *impf* experiment.

экспе́рт expert. **эксперти́за** (expert) examination; commission of experts.

эксплуата́тор exploiter. **эксплуатацио́нный** operating. **эксплуата́ция** exploitation; operation. **эксплуати́ровать** *impf* exploit; operate, run.

экспози́ция lay-out; exposition; exposure. **экспона́т** exhibit. **экспоно́метр** exposure meter.

э́кспорт export. **экспорти́ровать** *impf* & *pf* export. **э́кспортный** export.

экспре́сс express (*train etc.*).

экспро́мт impromptu. **экспро́мтом** *adv* impromptu.

экспроприа́ция expropriation. **экспроприи́ровать** *impf* & *pf* expropriate.

экста́з ectasy.

экстрава га́нтный eccentric, bizarre.

экстра́кт extract.

экстреми́ст extremist. **экстреми́стский** extremist.

э́кстренный urgent; emergency; special.

эксцентри́чный eccentric.

эксце́сс excess.

эласти́чный elastic; supple.

элева́тор grain elevator; hoist.

элега́нтный elegant, smart.

эле́гия elegy.

электризова́ть *impf* (*pf* **на~**) electrify. **эле́ктрик** electrician. **электрифика́ция** electrification. **электрифици́ровать** *impf* & *pf* electrify. **электри́ческий** electric(al). **электри́чество** electricity. **электри́чка** electric train.

электро- *in comb* electro-, electric, electrical. **электробытово́й** electrical. **~во́з** electric locomotive. **электро́лиз** electrolysis. **~магни́тный** electromagnetic. **~монтёр** electrician. **~одея́ло** electric blanket. **~по́езд** electric train. **~прибо́р** electrical appliance. **~про́вод** (*pl* -а́) electric cable. **~прово́дка** electric wiring. **~ста́нция** power-station. **~те́хник** electrical engineer. **~те́хника** electrical engineering. **~шо́к** electric shock, electric-shock treatment. **~эне́ргия** electrical energy.

электро́д electrode.

электро́н electron. **электро́ника** electronics.

электро́нн|ый electron; electronic; **~ая по́чта** email; **~ое письмо́** email (letter); **~ый а́дрес** email address.

элеме́нт element; cell; character. **элемента́рный** elementary.

эли́та élite.

э́ллипс elipse.

эма́левый enamel. **эмалирова́ть** *impf* enamel. **эма́ль** enamel.

эмансипа́ция emancipation.

эмба́рго *neut indecl* embargo.

эмбле́ма emblem.

эмбрио́н embryo.

эмигра́нт emigrant, émigré.

эмигра́ция emigration. **эмигри́ровать** *impf* & *pf* emigrate.

эмоциона́льный emotional. **эмо́ция** emotion.

эмпири́ческий empirical.

эму́льсия emulsion.

э́ндшпиль *m* end-game.

энерге́тика power engineering. **энергети́ческий** energy. **энерги́чный** energetic. **эне́ргия** energy.

энтомоло́гия entomology.

энтузиа́зм enthusiasm. **энтузиа́ст** enthusiast.

энциклопеди́ческий encyclopaedic. **энциклопе́дия** encyclopaedia.

эпигра́мма epigram. **эпи́граф** epigraph.

эпиде́мия epidemic.

эпизо́д episode. **эпизоди́ческий** episodic; sporadic.

эпиле́псия epilepsy. **эпиле́птик** epileptic.

эпило́г epilogue. **эпита́фия** epitaph. **эпи́тет** epithet. **эпице́нтр** epicentre.

эпопе́я epic.

эпо́ха epoch, era.

э́ра era; **до на́шей э́ры** BC; **на́шей э́ры** AD.

эре́кция erection.

эро́зия erosion.

эроти́зм eroticism. **эро́тика** sensuality. **эроти́ческий, эроти́чный** erotic, sensual.

эруди́ция erudition.

эска́дра (*naut*) squadron. **эскадри́лья** (*gen pl* -лий) (*aeron*) squadron. **эскадро́н** (*mil*) squadron.

эскала́тор escalator. **эскала́ция** escalation.

эски́з sketch; draft. **эски́зный** sketch; draft.

эскимо́с, эскимо́ска Eskimo.

эско́рт escort.

эсми́нец (-нца) *abbr* (*of* **эска́дренный миноно́сец**) destroyer.

эссе́нция essence.

эстака́да trestle bridge; overpass; pier, boom.

эста́мп print, engraving, plate.

эстафе́та relay race; baton.

эсте́тика aesthetics. **эстети́ческий** aesthetic.

эсто́нец (-нца), **эсто́нка** Estonian. **Эсто́ния** Estonia. **эсто́нский** Estonian.

эстра́да stage, platform; variety. **эстра́дный** stage; variety; **~ конце́рт** variety show.

эта́ж (-а́) storey, floor. **этаже́рка** shelves.

э́так *adv* so, thus; about. **э́такий** such (a), what (a).

этало́н standard.

эта́п stage; halting-place.

э́тика ethics.

этике́т etiquette.

этике́тка label.

эти́л ethyl.

этимоло́гия etymology.

эти́ческий, эти́чный ethical.

этни́ческий ethnic. **этногра́фия** ethnography.

э́то *partl* this (is), that (is), it (is). **э́тот** *m*, **э́та** *f*, **э́то** *neut*, **э́ти** *pl pron* this, these.

этю́д study, sketch; étude.

эфеме́рный ephemeral.

эфио́п, ~ка Ethiopian. **эфио́пский** Ethiopian.

эфи́р ether; air. **эфи́рный** ethereal; ether, ester.

эффе́кт effect. **эффекти́вность** effectiveness. **эффекти́вный** effective. **эффе́ктный** effective; striking.

эх *int* eh! oh!

э́хо echo.
эшафо́т scaffold.
эшело́н echelon; special train.

Ю

юбиле́й anniversary; jubilee. **юбиле́йный** jubilee.
ю́бка skirt. **ю́бочка** short skirt.
ювели́р jeweller. **ювели́рный** jeweller's, jewellery; fine, intricate.
юг south; **на ~е** in the south. **ю́го-восто́к** south-east. **ю́го-за́пад** south-west. **югосла́в, ~ка** Yugoslav. **Югосла́вия** Yugoslavia. **югосла́вский** Yugoslav.
юдофо́б anti-Semite. **юдофо́бство** anti-Semitism.
южа́нин (*pl* -а́не, -а́н), **южа́нка** southerner. **ю́жный** south, southern; southerly.
юла́ top; fidget. **юли́ть** *impf* fidget.
ю́мор humour. **юмори́ст** humourist. **юмористи́ческий** humorous.
ю́ность youth. **ю́ноша** (*gen pl* -шей) *m* youth. **ю́ношеский** youthful. **ю́ношество** youth; young people. **ю́ный** (юн, -а́, -о) young; youthful.
юпи́тер floodlight.
юриди́ческий legal, juridical. **юриско́нсульт** legal adviser. **юри́ст** lawyer.
ю́ркий (-рок, -рка́, -рко) quick-moving, brisk; smart.
юро́дивый crazy.
ю́рта yurt, nomad's tent.
юсти́ция justice.
юти́ться (ючу́сь) *impf* huddle (together).

Я

я (меня́, мне, мной (-о́ю), (обо) мне) *pron* I.
я́беда *m* & *f*, tell-tale; informer.
я́блоко (*pl* -и, -ок) apple; **глазно́е ~** eyeball. **я́блоневый, я́блочный** apple. **я́блоня** apple-tree.
яви́ться (явлю́сь, я́вишься) *pf*, **явля́ться** *impf* appear; arise; +*instr* be, serve as. **я́вка** appearance, attendance; secret rendezvous. **явле́ние** phenomenon; appearance; occurrence; scene. **я́вный** obvious; overt. **я́вственный** clear. **я́вствовать** be clear, be obvious.
ягнёнок (-нка; *pl* -ня́та, -я́т) lamb.
я́года berry; berries.
я́годица buttock(s).
ягуа́р jaguar.
яд poison; venom.
я́дерный nuclear.
ядови́тый poisonous; venomous.
ядрёный healthy; bracing; juicy. **ядро́** (*pl* -а, я́дер) kernel, core; nucleus; (cannon-) ball; shot.
я́зва ulcer, sore. **я́звенн|ый** ulcerous; **~ая боле́знь** ulcers. **язви́тельный** caustic, sarcastic. **язви́ть** (-влю́) *impf* (*pf* **съ~**) be sarcastic.
язы́к (-а́) tongue; clapper; language. **языкове́д** linguist. **языкове́дение, языкозна́ние** linguistics. **языково́й** linguistic. **языко́вый** tongue; lingual. **язычко́вый** reed. **язы́чник** heathen, pagan. **язычо́к** (-чка́) tongue; reed; catch.
яи́чко (*pl* -и, -чек) egg; testicle.

яи́чник ovary. **яи́чница** fried eggs. **яйцо́** (*pl* я́йца, яи́ц) egg; ovum.

я́кобы *conj* as if; *partl* supposedly.

я́корн|ый anchor; **~ая стоя́нка** anchorage. **я́корь** (*pl* -я́) *m* anchor.

я́лик skiff.

я́ма pit, hole.

ямщи́к (-а́) coachman.

янва́рский January. **янва́рь** (-я́) *m* January.

янта́рный amber. **янта́рь** (-я́) *m* amber.

япо́нец (-нца), **япо́нка** Japanese. **Япо́ния** Japan. **япо́нский** Japanese.

ярд yard.

я́ркий (я́рок, ярка́, -о) bright; colourful, striking.

ярлы́к (-а́) label; tag.

я́рмарка fair.

ярмо́ (*pl* -а) yoke.

ярово́й spring.

я́ростный furious, fierce. **я́рость** fury.

я́рус circle; tier; layer.

я́рче *comp of* **я́ркий**

я́рый fervent; furious; violent.

я́сень *m* ash(-tree).

я́сли (-ей) *pl* manger; crèche, day nursery.

ясне́ть (-е́ет) *impf* become clear, clear. **я́сно** *adv* clearly. **ясно-ви́дение** clairvoyance. **ясно-ви́дец** (-дца), **ясновидица** clairvoyant. **я́сность** clarity; clearness. **я́сный** (я́сен, ясна́, -о) clear; bright; fine.

я́ства (яств) *pl* victuals.

я́стреб (*pl* -а́) hawk.

я́хта yacht.

яче́йка cell.

ячме́нь[1] (-я́) *m* barley.

ячме́нь[2] (-я́) *m* stye.

я́щерица lizard.

я́щик box; drawer.

ящу́р foot-and-mouth (disease).

Phrasefinder/ Разгово́рник

Useful phrases / Поле́зные фра́зы

yes, please	да, пожа́луйста
no, thank you	нет, спаси́бо
sorry	прости́те
excuse me	извини́те (меня́)
I'm sorry, I don't understand	прости́те, я не понима́ю

Meeting people / Встре́ча

hello/goodbye	здра́вствуйте/до свида́ния
how are you?	как пожива́ете?
nice to meet you	рад/ра́да с ва́ми познако́миться

Asking questions / Вопро́сы

do you speak English/Russian?	вы говори́те по-англи́йски/по-ру́сски?
what's your name?	как вас зову́т?/как ва́ше и́мя?
where are you from?	отку́да вы?
how much is it?	ско́лько э́то сто́ит?
where is…?	где… ?
can I have…?	мо́жно мне… ?
would you like…?	не хоти́те ли… ?

Statements about yourself / Немно́го о себе́

my name is…	меня́ зову́т… , моё и́мя…
I'm American/Russian	я америка́нец/америка́нка/ру́сский/ру́сская
I don't speak Russian/English	я не говорю́ по-ру́сски/по-англи́йски
I live near Chester/Moscow	я живу́ недалеко́ от Че́стера/Москвы́
I'm a student	я студе́нт/студе́нтка
I work in an office	я рабо́таю на фи́рме

Emergencies / Э́кстренные слу́чаи

can you help me, please?	не могли́ бы вы мне помо́чь?
I'm lost	я заблуди́лся/заблуди́лась
I'm ill	я бо́лен/больна́
call an ambulance	вы́зовите ско́рую по́мощь

Reading signs / Чита́ем на́дписи

no entry	нет вхо́да
no smoking	не кури́ть
fire exit	запа́сный вы́ход
for sale	продаётся

❶ Going Places

On the road	На шоссе
Where's the nearest service station?	где ближáйшая бензозапрáвочная стáнция?/где ближáйший автосéрвис?
what's the best way to get there?	как быстрée тудá добрáться?
I've got a puncture	у меня́ прокóл ши́ны
I'd like to hire a bike/car	я хотéл/хотéла бы взять напрокáт велосипéд/автомоби́ль
there's been an accident	произошлá авáрия/произошлó ДТП
my car's broken down	у меня́ сломáлась маши́на
the car won't start	мотóр не завóдится

By rail	Пóезд
where can I buy a ticket?	где я могу́ купи́ть билéт?
what time is the next train to Orel/ Oxford?	когдá слéдующий пóезд на Орёл/ Óксфорд?
do I have to change?	ну́жно ли мне дéлать пересáдку?
can I take my bike on the train?	меня́ пу́стят в вагóн с велосипéдом?
which platform for the train to Kiev/ London?	с какóй платфóрмы идёт пóезд на Ки́ев/Лóндон?
there's a train to London at 10 o'clock	пóезд на Лóндон отправля́ется в 10 часóв
a single/return to Leeds/Zvenigorod, please	билéт в оди́н конéц/билéт тудá и обрáтно до Ли́дса/Звени́города, пожáлуйста
I'd like an all-day ticket	мне ну́жен билéт на су́тки
I'd like to reserve a seat	я хотéл/хотéла бы зарезерви́ровать мéсто

At the airport	В аэропорту́
when's the next flight to Vladivostok/ Manchester?	когда́ сле́дующий рейс во Владивосто́к/в Ма́нчестер?
where do I check in?	где регистра́ция пассажи́ров?
I'd like to confirm my flight	я хоте́л/хоте́ла бы подтверди́ть свой рейс
I'd like a window seat/an aisle seat	мне хоте́лось бы взять ме́сто у окна́/у прохо́да
I want to change/cancel my reservation	я хочу́ измени́ть/отмени́ть зака́з биле́та

Getting there	Как прое́хать?
could you tell me the way to the castle (*on foot/by transport*)?	не подска́жете мне, как пройти́/прое́хать к за́мку?
how long will it take to get there?	до́лго ли туда́ добира́ться?
how far is it from here?	как далеко́ э́то отсю́да?
which bus do I take for the cathedral?	како́й авто́бус идёт до собо́ра?
can you tell me where to get off?	вы ска́жете мне, где вы́йти?
what time is the last bus?	до како́го ча́са хо́дит авто́бус?
how do I get to the airport?	как мне прое́хать до аэропо́рта?
where's the nearest underground station, (*Amer.*) subway station?	где ближа́йшая ста́нция метро́?
I'll take a taxi	я возьму́ такси́
can you call me a taxi?	мо́жете мне вы́звать такси́?
take the first turning on the right	поверни́те на пе́рвом поворо́те напра́во
turn left at the traffic lights/just past the church	поверни́те нале́во у светофо́ра/ сра́зу за це́рковью

❷ Keeping in touch

On the phone	Говори́м по телефо́ну
may I use your phone?	мо́жно позвони́ть по ва́шему телефо́ну?
do you have a mobile, (*Amer.*) cell phone?	у вас есть моби́льный телефо́н?
what is the code for St Petersburg/ Edinburgh?	како́й код (телефо́на) в Санкт-Петербу́рг/Эдинбу́рг?
I want to make a phone call	мне ну́жно сде́лать звоно́к
I'd like to reverse the charges, (*Amer.*) call collect	мне ну́жно, что́бы звоно́к оплати́ла вызыва́емая сторона́
I need to top up my mobile, (*Amer.*) cell phone	мне ну́жно доплати́ть за моби́льный телефо́н
the line's engaged, (*Amer.*) busy	ли́ния занята́
there's no answer	отве́та нет
hello, this is John/Igor	алло́, э́то Джон/И́горь
is Oleg/Richard there, please?	пожа́луйста, позови́те Оле́га/ Ри́чарда
who's calling?	кто говори́т?
sorry, wrong number	извини́те, не туда́ попа́ли
just a moment, please	одну́ мину́тку, пожа́луйста
please hold the line	не ве́шайте тру́бку, пожа́луйста
please tell him/her I called	пожа́луйста, переда́йте ему́/ей, что я звони́л/звони́ла
I'd like to leave a message for him/her	я хоте́л/хоте́ла бы оста́вить сообще́ние для него́/неё
...I'll try again later	...я ещё поздне́е позвоню́
please tell him/her that Elena called	пожа́луйста, переда́йте ему́/ей, что звони́ла Еле́на
can he/she ring me back?	мо́жет он/она́ мне перезвони́ть?
my home number is...	мой дома́шний телефо́н...
my business number is...	мой рабо́чий телефо́н...
my mobile, (*Amer.*) cell phone number is...	но́мер моего́ моби́льного...
we were cut off	нас прерва́ли

Сре́дства свя́зи. Отноше́ния ❷

Writing	Пи́шем письмо́
what's your address?	ваш а́дрес?
where is the nearest post office?	где ближа́йшая по́чта?
could I have a stamp for Russia, please?	пожа́луйста, да́йте мне ма́рку для письма́ в Росси́ю
I'd like to send a parcel/a fax	я хоте́л/хоте́ла бы посла́ть посы́лку/факс

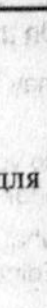

On line	Он-ла́йн
are you on the Internet?	вы подключены́ к Интерне́ту?
what's your email address?	како́й ваш электро́нный а́дрес?
we could send it by email	мы могли́ бы посла́ть э́то по электро́нной по́чте
I'll email it to you on Tuesday	я пошлю́ это вам по электро́нной по́чте во вто́рник
I looked it up on the Internet	я посмотре́л/посмотре́ла э́то по Интерне́ту
the information is on their website	информа́ция есть на их веб-са́йте

Meeting up	Встре́чи
what shall we do this evening?	что мы бу́дем де́лать сего́дня ве́чером?
where shall we meet?	где мы встре́тимся?
I'll see you outside the cafe at 6 o'clock	я вас встре́чу у кафе́ в 6 часо́в
see you later	до встре́чи
I can't today, I'm busy	сего́дня не могу́, я за́нят/занята́

❸ Food and Drink

Reservations	Заказ в ресторане
can you recommend a good restaurant?	можете ли порекомендовать хороший ресторан?
I'd like to reserve a table for four	я хотел/хотела бы заказать столик на четверых
a reservation for tomorrow evening at eight o'clock	заказ на завтра на восемь часов вечера

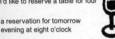

Ordering	Заказ блюд
could we see the menu/wine list, please?	можно нам меню/карту вин?
do you have a vegetarian/children's menu?	у вас есть вегетарианское/детское меню?
as a starter… and to follow…	на закуску… и затем…
could we have some more bread/rice?	можно ещё хлеба/риса?
what would you recommend?	что вы порекомендуете?
I'd like a	я хотел/хотела бы заказать
…white coffee, (*Amer.*) coffee with cream	…кофе с молоком
…black coffee	…чёрный кофе
…a decaffeinated coffee	…кофе без кофеина
…a liqueur	…ликёр
could I have the bill, (*Amer.*) check	счёт, пожалуйста

You will hear	Что вы слышите
вы готовы заказывать?	are you ready to order?
хотите заказать аперитив?	would you like an aperitif?
будете заказывать закуску?	would you like a starter?
какое блюдо будете заказывать?	what will you have for the main course?
заказываете десерт?	would you like a dessert?
кофе?/ликёр?	would you like coffee/liqueurs?
что ещё закажете?	anything else?
приятного аппетита!	enjoy your meal!
обслуживание (не) включено	service is (not) included

The menu	Меню́
starters	**заку́ски**
hors d'oeuvres	заку́ски
omelette	омле́т
soup	суп
fish	**ры́ба**
bass	морско́й о́кунь
cod	треска́
eel	у́горь
hake	хек
herring	се́льдь
monkfish	морско́й чёрт
mullet	кефа́ль
mussels	ми́дии
oyster	у́стрица
prawns	короле́вские креве́тки
salmon	лосо́сь, сёмга
sardines	сарди́ны
shrimps	креве́тки
sole	морско́й язы́к
squid	кальма́р
trout	форе́ль
tuna	туне́ц
turbot	па́лтус
meat	**мя́со**
beef	говя́дина
chicken	цыплёнок
chop	отбивна́я
duck	у́тка
goose	гусь
hare	за́яц
ham	ветчина́
kidneys	по́чки
lamb	(молода́я) бара́нина
liver	печёнка
pork	свини́на
rabbit	крольча́тина
sirloin	филе́
steak	бифште́кс, вы́резка
turkey	инде́йка
veal	теля́тина
venison	олени́на

Меню́	The menu
заку́ски	**starters**
заку́ски	hors d'oeuvres
омле́т	omelette
суп	soup
ры́ба	**fish**
кальма́р	squid
карп	carp
кефа́ль	mullet
креве́тки	prawns, shrimps
лосо́сь	salmon
ми́дии	mussels
морско́й о́кунь	bass
морско́й язы́к	sole
осетри́на	sturgeon
па́лтус	turbot
сарди́ны	sardines
се́льдь	herring
сёмга	salmon
треска́	cod
туне́ц	tuna
хек	hake
у́горь	eel
у́стрица	oyster
форе́ль	trout
мя́со	**meat**
(молода́я) бара́нина	lamb
бифште́кс	steak
ветчина́	ham
вы́резка	steak
говя́дина	beef
гусь	goose
колба́ски	sausages
олени́на	venison
отбивна́я	chop
печёнка	liver
по́чки	kidneys
свини́на	pork
теля́тина	veal
у́тка	duck
филе́	sirloin steak
цыплёнок	chicken

❸ Food and Drink

vegetables	**о́вощи**
asparagus	спа́ржа
aubergine	баклажа́н
beans	бобы́; фасо́ль
beetroot	свёкла
broccoli	бро́кколи
carrots	морко́вь
cabbage	капу́ста
celery	сельдере́й
courgettes (*Br.*)	цуки́ни
French beans (*Br.*)	стручко́вая фасо́ль
lettuce	сала́т-лату́к
mushrooms	грибы́
peas	горо́шек
(sweet) pepper	сла́дкий пе́рец
potatoes	карто́фель
runner beans	вьющаяся фасо́ль
tomato	помидо́р
sweet potato	сла́дкий карто́фель, бата́т
zucchini (*Amer.*)	цуки́ни

the way it's cooked	**как э́то пригото́влено**
baked	запечённый
boiled	отварно́й, варёный
fried	жа́реный
griddled	пригото́вленный на пло́ской сковороде́
grilled	(жа́реный) на гри́ле
poached	припу́щенный
pureed	пюре́, пюри́рованный
rare	с кро́вью (*о мясе*)
roast	жа́реный
stewed	тушёный
well done	хорошо́ прожа́ренный

о́вощи	**vegetables**
баклажа́н	aubergine
бобы́	beans
горо́шек	peas
грибы́	mushrooms
зелёный лук	spring onions
капу́ста	cabbage
карто́фель	potatoes
лук	onions
морко́вь	carrots
огуре́ц	cucumber
(сла́дкий) пе́рец	(sweet) pepper
помидо́р	tomato
реди́с	radish
свёкла	beetroot
сельдере́й	celery
спа́ржа	asparagus
фасо́ль	beans
цветна́я капу́ста	cauliflower

как э́то пригото́влено	**the way it's cooked**
варёный	boiled
в горшо́чке	casseroled (*в духовке*)
жа́реный	roast; (*на сковороде*) fried
жа́реный на гри́ле	grilled
запечённый	baked
отварно́й	boiled
пригото́вленный на пло́ской сковороде́	griddled
припу́щенный	poached
с кро́вью (*о мясе*)	rare
тушёный	stewed
хорошо́ прожа́ренный	well done

desserts	**десе́рты**
ice cream	моро́женое
fruit	фру́кты
gateau	торт
pie	пиро́г
other	**друго́е**
bread	хлеб
butter	сли́вочное ма́сло
cheese	сыр
cheeseboard	доска́/блю́до с сы́ром
garlic	чесно́к
mayonnaise	майоне́з
mustard	горчи́ца
olive oil	оли́вковое ма́сло
pepper	пе́рец
rice	рис
salt	соль
sauce	со́ус
seasoning	припра́ва
vinegar	у́ксус
drinks	**напи́тки**
beer	пи́во
bottle	буты́лка
carbonated	газиро́ванный
fizzy	шипу́чий
half-bottle	полбуты́лки
liqueur	ликёр
mineral water	минера́льная вода́
red wine	кра́сное вино́
rosé	ро́зовое вино́
soft drink	безалкого́льный напи́ток
still	негазиро́ванный
house wine	дома́шнее вино́
table wine	столо́вое вино́
tap water	водопрово́дная вода́
white wine	бе́лое вино́
wine	вино́

десе́рты	**desserts**
моро́женое	ice cream
пиро́г	pie
торт	gateau
фру́кты	fruit
друго́е	**other**
горчи́ца	mustard
майоне́з	mayonnaise
оли́вковое ма́сло	olive oil
пе́рец	pepper
припра́ва	seasoning
сли́вочное ма́сло	butter
соль	salt
со́ус	sauce
сыр	cheese
у́ксус	vinegar
хлеб	bread
хрен	horseradish
чесно́к	garlic
напи́тки	**drinks**
безалкого́льный напи́ток	soft drink
бе́лое вино́	white wine
буты́лка	bottle
вино́	wine
водопрово́дная вода́	tap water
газиро́ванный	carbonated
дома́шнее вино́	house wine
кра́сное вино́	red wine
ликёр	liqueur
минера́льная вода́	mineral water
негазиро́ванный	still
пи́во	beer
полбуты́лки	half-bottle
ро́зовое вино́	rosé
столо́вое вино́	table wine
шипу́чий	fizzy

❹ Places to stay

Camping	Ке́мпинг
can we pitch our tent here?	мы мо́жем здесь разби́ть пала́тку?
can we park our caravan here?	мо́жем здесь припаркова́ть наш карава́н?
what are the facilities like?	каки́е здесь усло́вия?
how much is it per night?	ско́лько здесь беру́т за су́тки?
where do we park the car?	где мо́жно припаркова́ть маши́ну?
we're looking for a campsite	мы и́щем ке́мпинг
this is a list of local campsites	вот спи́сок ме́стных ке́мпингов
we go on a camping holiday every year	мы ка́ждый год отдыха́ем в ке́мпинге

At the hotel	В гости́нице
I'd like a double/single room with bath	мне ну́жен двухме́стный/одноме́стный но́мер с ва́нной
we have a reservation in the name of Morris	мы зарезерви́ровали но́мер на фами́лию Мо́ррис
we'll be staying three nights, from Friday to Sunday	мы бу́дем здесь тро́е су́ток, с пя́тницы по воскресе́нье
how much does the room cost?	ско́лько сто́ит но́мер?
I'd like to see the room	я хоте́л/хоте́ла бы посмотре́ть но́мер
what time is breakfast?	когда́ здесь за́втрак?
can I leave this in your safe?	могу́ я э́то оста́вить в ва́шем се́йфе?
bed and breakfast	ночле́г и за́втрак
we'd like to stay another night	мы хоте́ли бы оста́ться ещё на су́тки
please call me at 7.30	пожа́луйста, позвони́те мне в 7.30
are there any messages for me?	есть ли мне сообще́ние?

Hostels	Молодёжные гости́ницы
could you tell me where the youth hostel is?	скажи́те мне, пожа́луйста, где молодёжная гости́ница?
what time does the hostel close?	когда́ молодёжную гости́ницу закрыва́ют?
I'll be staying in a hostel	я остановлю́сь в молодёжной гости́нице
the hostel we're staying in is great value	молодёжная гости́ница, где мы останови́лись, недорога́я и о́чень удо́бная
I know a really good hostel in Dublin	я зна́ю в Ду́блине весьма́ прили́чную молодёжную гости́ницу
I'd like to go backpacking in Australia	я хоте́л/хоте́ла бы попутеше́ствовать с рюкзако́м по Австра́лии

Rooms to rent	Жильё внаём
I'm looking for a room with a reasonable rent	я ищу́ ко́мнату за уме́ренную це́ну
I'd like to rent an apartment for a few weeks	я хоте́л/хоте́ла бы снять кварти́ру на не́сколько неде́ль
where do I find out about rooms to rent?	где мне узна́ть о ко́мнатах, кото́рые сдаю́тся?
what's the weekly rent?	ско́лько плати́ть за жильё в неде́лю?
I'm staying with friends at the moment	я сейча́с живу́ у друзе́й
I rent an apartment on the outskirts of town	я снима́ю кварти́ру на окра́ине го́рода
the room's fine—I'll take it	ко́мната мне подхо́дит—я сниму́ её
the deposit is one month's rent in advance	зада́ток вперёд в су́мме ме́сячной опла́ты

❺ Shopping and money

Banking	В бáнке
I'd like to change some money	я хотéл/хотéла бы поменя́ть дéньги
I want to change some dollars into euros	я хочу́ поменя́ть дóллары на éвро
do you need identification?	вам нýжно удостоверéние ли́чности?
what's the exchange rate today?	какóй курс обмéна на сегóдня?
Do you accept traveller's cheques, (*Amer.*) traveler's checks	вы принимáете дорóжные чéки?
I'd like to transfer some money from my account	я хотéл/хотéла бы перевести́ нéкоторую сýмму с моегó счёта
Where is there an ATM/a cash machine?	где здесь банкомáт?
I'd like high denomination notes, (*Amer.*) bills	мне нужны́ крýпные купю́ры
I'm with another bank	у меня́ счёт в другóм бáнке

Finding the right shop	Нýжный магази́н
where's the main shopping district?	где здесь торгóвый центр?
where can I buy batteries/postcards?	где я могу́ купи́ть батарéйки/откры́тки?
where's the nearest pharmacy/bookshop?	где ближáйшая аптéка/ближáйший кни́жный магази́н?
is there a good food shop around here?	есть здесь побли́зости хорóший продовóльственный магази́н?
what time do the shops open/close?	когдá магази́ны открывáются/закрывáются?
where did you get those?	где вы э́то купи́ли?
I'm looking for presents for my family	я ищу́ подáрки для мои́х родны́х
we'll do our shopping on Saturday	мы пойдём по магази́нам в суббóту
I love shopping	я люблю́ ходи́ть по магази́нам

Are you being served?	**Вас обслу́живают?**
how much does that cost?	ско́лько э́то сто́ит?
can I try it on?	могу́ я э́то приме́рить?
could you wrap it for me, please?	заверни́те, пожа́луйста
can I pay by credit card?	я могу́ плати́ть креди́тной ка́ртой?
do you have this in another colour, (*Amer.*) color?	есть у вас э́то друго́й расцве́тки?
could I have a bag, please?	бу́дьте добры́, да́йте мне паке́т
I'm just looking	я про́сто смотрю́
I'll think about it	я до́лжен/должна́ поду́мать
I'd like a receipt, please	мне нужна́ квита́нция/мне ну́жен чек
I need a bigger/smaller size	мне ну́жен бо́льший/ме́ньший разме́р
I take a size 10/a medium	ношу́ разме́р 10/сре́дний разме́р
it doesn't suit me	мне э́то не подхо́дит
I'm sorry, I don't have any change/ anything smaller	прости́те, у меня́ нет ме́лочи/ ме́лких де́нег
that's all, thank you	э́то всё, спаси́бо

Changing things	**Заме́на това́ра**
I'd like to change it, please	я хоте́л/хоте́ла бы э́то поменя́ть
I bought this here yesterday	я купи́л/купи́ла э́то здесь вчера́
can I have a refund?	могу́ я рассчи́тывать на возмеще́ние?/мне верну́т де́ньги?
can you mend it for me?	мо́жете э́то испра́вить/почини́ть?
it doesn't work	э́то не рабо́тает
can I speak to the manager?	могу́ я поговори́ть с ме́неджером?

❻ Sport and leisure

Keeping fit	Заня́тия спо́ртом
where can we play football/squash?	где мы мо́жем поигра́ть в футбо́л/сквош?
where is the local sports centre, (*Amer.*) center?	где здесь ме́стный спорти́вный центр?
what's the charge per day?	ско́лько сто́ит день заня́тий?
is there a reduction for children/ a student discount?	есть ли ски́дка для дете́й/ студе́нтов?
I'm looking for a swimming pool/ tennis court	я ищу́ бассе́йн/те́ннисный корт
you have to be a member	вы должны́ быть чле́ном (клу́ба)
I play tennis on Mondays	я игра́ю в те́ннис по понеде́льникам
I would like to go fishing/riding	я хоте́л/хоте́ла бы заня́ться ры́бной ло́влей/верхово́й ездо́й
I want to do aerobics	я хочу́ заня́ться аэро́бикой
I love swimming/rollerskating	я люблю́ пла́вание/ката́ние на ро́ликовых конька́х
we want to hire skis/snowboards	мы хоте́ли бы взять напрока́т лы́жи/сноубо́рды

Watching sport	Спорти́вные зре́лища
is there a football match on Saturday?	есть футбо́льный матч в воскресе́нье?
which teams are playing?	каки́е кома́нды игра́ют?
where can I get tickets?	где я могу́ купи́ть биле́ты?
I'd like to see a rugby/football match	я хоте́л/хоте́ла бы попа́сть на ре́гби/футбо́л
my favourite, (*Amer.*) favorite team is...	моя́ люби́мая кома́нда...
let's watch the game on TV	дава́йте посмо́трим игру́ по телеви́зору

Going out in the evening	В теа́тре, на конце́рте
what's on?	что идёт?
when does the box office open/close?	когда́ открыва́ется/закрыва́ется биле́тная ка́сса?
what time does the concert/ performance start?	когда́ нача́ло конце́рта/спекта́кля?
when does it finish?	когда́ конча́ется (спекта́кль)?
are there any seats left for tonight?	есть ли свобо́дные места́ на сего́дня?
how much are the tickets?	ско́лько сто́ят биле́ты?
where can I get a programme, (*Amer.*) program?	где я могу́ купи́ть програ́мму?
I want to book tickets for tonight's performance	я хочу́ заказа́ть биле́ты на сего́дняшний конце́рт/спекта́кль
I'll book seats in the circle	я закажу́ биле́ты на балко́н
I'd rather have seats in the stalls	я бы хоте́л/хоте́ла купи́ть биле́ты на места́ в парте́ре
somewhere in the middle, but not too far back	где-нибу́дь в середи́не, но не о́чень далеко́
four, please	четы́ре биле́та, пожа́луйста
for Saturday	на суббо́ту
we'd like to go to a club	мы бы хоте́ли сходи́ть в ночно́й клуб
I go clubbing every weekend	я хожу́ в ночно́й клуб ка́ждый уик-э́нд

Hobbies	Хо́бби
what do you do at the weekend?	что вы де́лаете по суббо́там и воскресе́ньям?
I like yoga/listening to music	мне нра́вится занима́ться йо́гой/ слу́шать му́зыку
I spend a lot of time surfing the Net	я мно́го вре́мени провожу́ в Интерне́те/я мно́го брожу́ по Интерне́ту
I read a lot	я мно́го чита́ю
I collect old coins	я собира́ю стари́нные моне́ты

❼ Time

Telling the time	Ско́лько вре́мени?
what time is it?	ско́лько вре́мени?
it's 2 o'clock	два часа́
at about 8 o'clock	о́коло 8 (восьми́) часо́в
from 10 o'clock onwards	по́сле 10 (десяти́) часо́в
at 5 o'clock in the morning/afternoon	в 5 (пять) (часо́в) утра́/ве́чера
it's five past/quarter past/half past one	пять мину́т/че́тверть/полови́на второ́го
it's twenty-five to/quarter to one	без двадцати́ пяти́/че́тверти час
a quarter/three quarters of an hour	че́тверть часа́/со́рок пять мину́т

Days and dates	Дни и чи́сла
Sunday, Monday, Tuesday, Wednesday, Thursday, Friday, Saturday	воскресе́нье, понеде́льник, вто́рник, среда́, четве́рг, пя́тница, суббо́та
January, February, March, April, May, June, July, August, September, October, November, December	янва́рь, февра́ль, март, апре́ль, май, ию́нь, ию́ль, а́вгуст, сентя́брь, октя́брь, ноя́брь, дека́брь
what's the date?	како́е сего́дня число́?
it's the second of June	сего́дня второ́е ию́ня
we meet up every Monday	мы ви́димся ка́ждый понеде́льник
we're going away in August	мы уезжа́ем в а́вгусте
on November 8th	восьмо́го ноября́

Public holidays and special days	Пра́здники, нерабо́чие дни
bank holiday	нерабо́чий день
bank holiday Monday	нерабо́чий понеде́льник
New Year's Day (*1 Jan.*)	Но́вый год (*1-е января́*)
Epiphany (*6 Jan.*)	Креще́ние Госпо́дне, Богоявле́ние (*19-е января́*)
St Valentine's Day (*14 Feb.*)	День свято́го Валенти́на (*14-е февраля́*)

Day of the Defender of the Fatherland	День защи́тника Отéчества (*23-е февраля́*)
Shrove Tuesday/Pancake Day	вто́рник на мáсленой недéле
Ash Wednesday	пéрвый день Вели́кого постá
International Woman's Day (*8 March*)	Восьмóе мáрта, Междунарóдный жéнский день (*8-е мáрта*)
Maundy Thursday	Вели́кий четвéрг (на Страстнóй недéле)
Good Friday	Страстнáя пя́тница
Easter	Пáсха
May Day (*1 May*)	Пéрвое мáя (*1-е мáя*)
VE Day (*8 May*)	День Побéды (*9-е мáя*)
Whit Sunday, Pentecost (*7th Sunday after Easter*)	Трóица, Трóицын день
Russian Defenders' Memorial Day (*marking the beginning of the Great Patriotic War (1941–45)*)	День пáмяти защи́тников Отéчества (*22-е ию́ня*)
Fourth of July/Independence Day (US)	День незави́симости
Assumption/Dormition of the Virgin Mary (*15 August*)	Успéние Пресвятóй Богорóдицы (*28-е áвгуста*)
Protecting Veil/Intercession of the Virgin Mary (*people pray for protection from evil and hardships and help in view of the long winter ahead*)	Покрóв Пресвятóй Богорóдицы (*14-е октября́*)
Halloween (*31 Oct.*)	Кáнун Дня Всех Святы́х
All Saints' Day (*1 Nov.*)	День Всех Святы́х
Guy Fawkes Day/Bonfire Night (*5 Nov., UK*)	день Гáя Фóкса, день годовщи́ны раскры́тия «пороховóго зáговора»
National Unity Day	День нарóдного еди́нства (*4-е ноября́*)
Remembrance Sunday (*anniversary of the armistice of 11 November 1918*)	Поминáльное воскресéнье
Thanksgiving (*4th Thursday in November, US*)	День благодарéния
Christmas Eve (*24 Dec.*)	Рождéственский сочéльник (*6-е января́*)
Christmas Day (*25 Dec.*)	Рождествó Христóво (*7-е января́*)
New Year's Eve (*31 Dec.*)	Новогóдняя ночь (*31-е декабря́*)

8 Weights and measures/ Ме́ры длины́, ве́са, объёма

Length/Длина́

inches/дюймы	0.39	3.9	7.8	11.7	15.6	19.5	39
centimetres/сантиме́тры	1	10	20	30	40	50	100

Distance/Расстоя́ние

miles/ми́ли	0.62	6.2	12.4	18.6	24.8	31	62
kilometres/киломе́тры	1	10	20	30	40	50	100

Weight/Вес

pounds/фу́нты	2.2	22	44	66	88	110	220
kilos/килогра́ммы	1	10	20	30	40	50	100

Capacity/Объём

(*Br.*) gallons/галло́ны	0.22	2.2	4.4	6.6	8.8	11	22
(*US*) gallons/галло́ны	0.26	2.64	5.28	7.92	10.56	13.2	26.4
litres/ли́тры	1	10	20	30	40	50	100

Temperature/Температу́ра

°C (Celsius)/ °C (по Це́льсию)	0	5	10	15	20	25	30	37	38	40
°F (Fahrenheit)/ °F (по Фаренге́йту)	32	41	50	59	68	77	86	98.4	100	104

Clothing and shoe sizes/Разме́ры оде́жды и о́буви

Women's clothing sizes/Же́нская оде́жда

UK	8	10	12	14	16	18
US	6	8	10	12	14	16
Russia	40	42	44	46	48	50

Men's clothing sizes (chest sizes)/Мужска́я оде́жда (костю́мы, пиджаки́)

UK/US	36	38	40	42	44	46
Russia	46	48	50	52	54	56

Women's shoes/Же́нская о́бувь

UK	2.5	3	3.5	4	4.5	5	5.5	6	6.5	7	7.5	8
US	5	5.5	6	6.5	7	7.5	8	8.5	9	9.5	10	10.5
Russia	35	35.5	36	37	37.5	38	39	39.5	40	40.5	41	42

Men's shoes/Мужска́я о́бувь

UK	6	6.5	7	7.5	8	8.5	9	9.5	10	10.5	11	11.5	12
US	6.5	7	7.5	8	8.5	9	9.5	10	10.5	11	11.5	12	12.5
Russia	39.5	40	40.5	41	42	42.5	43	44	44.5	45	46	46.5	47

A

a /ə, eɪ/, **an** /æn, ən/ *indef article, not usu translated*; **twice a week** два ра́за в неде́лю. **aback** /ə'bæk/ *adv*: **take ~** озада́чивать *impf*, озада́чить *pf*. **abacus** /'æbəkəs/ *n* счёты *m pl*. **abandon** /ə'bænd(ə)n/ *vt* покида́ть *impf*, поки́нуть *pf*; (*give up*) отка́зываться *impf*, отказа́ться *pf* от+*gen*; **~ o.s. to** предава́ться *impf*, преда́ться *pf* +*dat*. **abandoned** /ə'bænd(ə)nd/ *adj* поки́нутый; (*profligate*) распу́тный. **abase** /ə'beɪs/ *vt* унижа́ть *impf*, уни́зить *pf*. **abasement** /-mənt/ *n* униже́ние. **abate** /ə'beɪt/ *vi* затиха́ть *impf*, зати́хнуть *pf*. **abattoir** /'æbə,twɑ:(r)/ *n* скотобо́йня. **abbey** /'æbɪ/ *n* абба́тство. **abbreviate** /ə'bri:vɪ,eɪt/ *vt* сокраща́ть *impf*, сократи́ть *pf*. **abbreviation** /-'eɪʃ(ə)n/ *n* сокраще́ние. **abdicate** /'æbdɪ,keɪt/ *vi* отрека́ться *impf*, отре́чься *pf* от престо́ла. **abdication** /-'keɪʃ(ə)n/ *n* отрече́ние (от престо́ла). **abdomen** /'æbdəmən/ *n* брюшна́я по́лость. **abdominal** /-'dɒmɪn(ə)l/ *adj* брюшно́й. **abduct** /əb'dʌkt/ *vt* похища́ть *impf*, похи́тить *pf*. **abduction** /-'dʌkʃ(ə)n/ *n* похище́ние. **aberration** /,æbə'reɪʃ(ə)n/ *n* (*mental*) помутне́ние рассу́дка. **abet** /ə'bet/ *vt* подстрека́ть *impf*, подстрекну́ть *pf* (к соверше́нию преступле́ния *etc.*). **abhor** /əb'hɔ:(r)/ *vt* ненави́деть *impf*. **abhorrence** /-'hɒrəns/ *n* отвраще́ние. **abhorrent** /-'hɒrənt/ *adj* отврати́тельный. **abide** /ə'baɪd/ *vt* (*tolerate*) выноси́ть *impf*, вы́нести *pf*; **~ by** (*rules etc.*) сле́довать *impf*, по~ *pf*. **ability** /ə'bɪlɪtɪ/ *n* спосо́бность. **abject** /'æbdʒekt/ *adj* (*wretched*) жа́лкий; (*humble*) уни́женный; **~ poverty** кра́йняя нищета́. **ablaze** /ə'bleɪz/ *predic* охва́ченный огнём. **able** /'eɪb(ə)l/ *adj* спосо́бный, уме́лый; **be ~ to** мочь *impf*, с~ *pf*; (*know how to*) уме́ть *impf*, с~ *pf*. **abnormal** /æb'nɔ:m(ə)l/ *adj* ненорма́льный. **abnormality** /-'mælɪtɪ/ *n* ненорма́льность. **aboard** /ə'bɔ:d/ *adv* на борт(у́); (*train*) в по́езд(е). **abode** /ə'bəʊd/ *n* жили́ще; **of no fixed ~** без постоя́нного местожи́тельства. **abolish** /ə'bɒlɪʃ/ *vt* отменя́ть *impf*, отмени́ть *pf*. **abolition** /,æbə'lɪʃ(ə)n/ *n* отме́на. **abominable** /ə'bɒmɪnəb(ə)l/ *adj* отврати́тельный. **abomination** /-'neɪʃ(ə)n/ *n* ме́рзость. **aboriginal** /,æbə'rɪdʒɪn(ə)l/ *adj* коренно́й; *n* абориге́н, коренно́й жи́тель *m*. **aborigine** /-nɪ/ *n* абориге́н, коренно́й жи́тель *m*.

abort /ə'bɔːt/ *vi* (*med*) выки́дывать *impf*, вы́кинуть *pf*; *vt* (*terminate*) прекраща́ть *impf*, прекрати́ть *pf*. **abortion** /ə'bɔːʃ(ə)n/ *n* або́рт; **have an ~** де́лать *impf*, с~ *pf* або́рт. **abortive** /-tɪv/ *adj* безуспе́шный.

abound /ə'baʊnd/ *vi* быть в изоби́лии; **~ in** изоби́ловать *impf* +*instr*.

about /ə'baʊt/ *adv & prep* (*approximately*) о́коло+*gen*; (*concerning*) о+*prep*, насчёт+*gen*; (*up and down*) по+*dat*; (*in the vicinity*) круго́м; **be ~ to** собира́ться *impf*, собра́ться *pf* +*inf*.

above /ə'bʌv/ *adv* наверху́; (*higher up*) вы́ше; **from ~** све́рху; свы́ше; *prep* над+*instr*; (*more than*) свы́ше+*gen*. **aboveboard** *adj* че́стный. **abovementioned** *adj* вышеупомя́нутый.

abrasion /ə'breɪʒ(ə)n/ *n* истира́ние; (*wound*) сса́дина. **abrasive** /-sɪv/ *adj* абрази́вный; (*manner*) колю́чий; *n* абрази́вный материа́л.

abreast /ə'brest/ *adv* в ряд; **keep ~ of** идти́ в но́гу с+*instr*.

abridge /ə'brɪdʒ/ *vt* сокраща́ть *impf*, сократи́ть *pf*. **abridgement** /-mənt/ *n* сокраще́ние.

abroad /ə'brɔːd/ *adv* за грани́цей, за грани́цу; **from ~** из-за грани́цы.

abrupt /ə'brʌpt/ *adj* (*steep*) круто́й; (*sudden*) внеза́пный; (*curt*) ре́зкий.

abscess /'æbsɪs/ *n* абсце́сс.

abscond /əb'skɒnd/ *vi* скрыва́ться *impf*, скры́ться *pf*.

absence /'æbs(ə)ns/ *n* отсу́тствие. **absent** /-s(ə)nt/ *adj* отсу́тствующий; **be ~** отсу́тствовать *impf*; *vt*: **~ o.s.** отлуча́ться *impf*, отлучи́ться *pf*. **absentee** /ˌæbs(ə)n'tiː/ *n* отсу́тствующий *sb*. **absenteeism** *n* /-'tiːɪz(ə)m/ прогу́л. **absent-minded** *adj* рассе́янный.

absolute /'æbsəˌluːt/ *adj* абсолю́тный; (*complete*) по́лный, соверше́нный.

absolution /ˌæbsə'luːʃ(ə)n/ *n* отпуще́ние грехо́в. **absolve** /əb'zɒlv/ *vt* проща́ть *impf*, прости́ть *pf*.

absorb /əb'zɔːb/ *vt* впи́тывать *impf*, впита́ть *pf*. **absorbed** /əb'zɔːbd/ *adj* поглощённый. **absorbent** /əb'zɔːbənt/ *adj* всасыва́ющий. **absorption** /əb'zɔːpʃ(ə)n/ *n* впи́тывание; (*mental*) погружённость.

abstain /əb'steɪn/ *vi* возде́рживаться *impf*, воздержа́ться *pf* (**from** от+*gen*). **abstemious** /əb'stiːmɪəs/ *adj* возде́ржанный. **abstention** /əb'stenʃ(ə)n/ *n* воздержа́ние; (*person*) воздержа́вшийся *sb*. **abstinence** /'æbstɪnəns/ *n* воздержа́ние.

abstract /'æbstrækt/ *adj* абстра́ктный, отвлечённый; *n* рефера́т.

absurd /əb'sɜːd/ *adj* абсу́рдный. **absurdity** /-dɪtɪ/ *n* абсу́рд.

abundance /ə'bʌnd(ə)ns/ *n* оби́лие. **abundant** /-d(ə)nt/ *adj* оби́льный.

abuse *vt* /ə'bjuːz/(*insult*) руга́ть *impf*, вы́~, об~, от~ *pf*; (*misuse*) злоупотребля́ть *impf*, злоупотреби́ть *pf*; *n* /ə'bjuːs/ (*curses*) ру́гань, руга́тельства *neut pl*; (*misuse*) злоупотребле́ние. **abusive** /-sɪv/ *adj* оскорби́тельный, руга́тельный.

abut /ə'bʌt/ *vi* примыка́ть *impf* (**on** к+*dat*).

abysmal /ə'bɪzm(ə)l/ *adj* (*extreme*) безграни́чный; (*bad*) ужа́сный. **abyss** /ə'bɪs/ *n* бе́здна.

academic /ˌækə'demɪk/ *adj* академи́ческий. **academician** /əˌkædə'mɪʃ(ə)n/ *n* акаде́мик. **academy** /ə'kædəmɪ/ *n* акаде́мия.

accede /æk'si:d/ *vi* вступа́ть *impf*, вступи́ть *pf* (to в, на+*acc*); (*assent*) соглаша́ться *impf*, согласи́ться *pf*.

accelerate /ək'seləˌreɪt/ *vt* & *i* ускоря́ть(ся) *impf*, уско́рить(ся) *pf*; (*motoring*) дава́ть *impf*, дать *pf* газ. **acceleration** /-'reɪʃ(ə)n/ *n* ускоре́ние. **accelerator** /-ˌreɪtə(r)/ *n* ускори́тель *m*; (*pedal*) акселера́тор.

accent *n* /'æksent/ акце́нт; (*stress*) ударе́ние; *vt* /æk'sent/ де́лать *impf*, с~ *pf* ударе́ние на+*acc*. **accentuate** /æk'sentjʊˌeɪt/ *vt* акценти́ровать *impf* & *pf*.

accept /ək'sept/ *vt* принима́ть *impf*, приня́ть *pf*. **acceptable** /-təb(ə)l/ *adj* прие́млемый. **acceptance** /-t(ə)ns/ *n* приня́тие.

access /'ækses/ *n* до́ступ. **accessible** /ək'sesɪb(ə)l/ *adj* досту́пный. **accession** /ək'seʃ(ə)n/ *n* вступле́ние (на престо́л). **accessories** /ək'sesərɪz/ *n* принадле́жности *f pl*. **accessory** /ək'sesərɪ/ *n* (*accomplice*) соуча́стник, -ица.

accident /'æksɪd(ə)nt/ *n* (*chance*) случа́йность; (*mishap*) несча́стный слу́чай; (*crash*) ава́рия; **by** ~ случа́йно. **accidental** /-'dent(ə)l/ *adj* случа́йный.

acclaim /ə'kleɪm/ *vt* (*praise*) восхваля́ть *impf*, восхвали́ть *pf*; *n* восхвале́ние.

acclimatization /əˌklaɪmətaɪ'zeɪʃ(ə)n/ *n* акклиматиза́ция. **acclimatize** /ə'klaɪməˌtaɪz/ *vt* акклиматизи́ровать *impf* & *pf*.

accommodate /ə'kɒməˌdeɪt/ *vt* помеща́ть *impf*, помести́ть *pf*; (*hold*) вмеща́ть *impf*, вмести́ть *pf*. **accommodating** /-ˌdeɪtɪŋ/ *adj* услу́жливый. **accommodation** /-'deɪʃ(ə)n/ *n* (*hotel*) но́мер; (*home*) жильё.

accompaniment /ə'kʌmpənɪmənt/ *n* сопровожде́ние; (*mus*) аккомпанеме́нт. **accompanist** /-nɪst/ *n* аккомпаниа́тор. **accompany** /-nɪ/ *vt* сопровожда́ть *impf*, сопроводи́ть *pf*; (*escort*) провожа́ть *impf*, проводи́ть *pf*; (*mus*) аккомпани́ровать *impf* +*dat*.

accomplice /ə'kʌmplɪs/ *n* соуча́стник, -ица.

accomplish /ə'kʌmplɪʃ/ *vt* соверша́ть *impf*, соверши́ть *pf*. **accomplished** /-plɪʃt/ *adj* зако́нченный. **accomplishment** /-plɪʃmənt/ *n* выполне́ние; (*skill*) соверше́нство.

accord /ə'kɔ:d/ *n* согла́сие; **of one's own** ~ доброво́льно; **of its own** ~ сам собо́й, сам по себе́. **accordance** /-dəns/ *n*: **in** ~ **with** в соотве́тствии с+*instr*, согла́сно+*dat*. **according** /-dɪŋ/ *adv*: ~ **to** по+*dat*, ~ **to him** по его́ слова́м. **accordingly** /-dɪŋlɪ/ *adv* соотве́тственно.

accordion /ə'kɔ:dɪən/ *n* аккорде́он.

accost /ə'kɒst/ *vt* пристава́ть *impf*, приста́ть *pf* к+*dat*.

account /ə'kaʊnt/ *n* (*comm*) счёт; (*report*) отчёт; (*description*) описа́ние; **on no** ~ ни в ко́ем слу́чае; **on** ~ в счёт причита́ющейся су́ммы; **on** ~ **of** из-за+*gen*, по причи́не+*gen*; **take into** ~ принима́ть *impf*, приня́ть *pf* в расчёт; *vi*: ~ **for** объясня́ть *impf*, объясни́ть *pf*. **accountable** /-təb(ə)l/ *adj* отве́тственный.

accountancy /ə'kaʊntənsɪ/ *n* бухгалте́рия. **accountant** /-tənt/ *n* бухга́лтер.

accrue /ə'kru:/ *vi* нараста́ть *impf*, нарасти́ *pf*.

accumulate /ə'kju:mjʊˌleɪt/ *vt* & *i* нака́пливать(ся) *impf*, копи́ть(ся) *impf*, на~ *pf*. **accumulation** /-'leɪʃ(ə)n/ *n* накопле́ние. **accumulator** /-ˌleɪtə(r)/ *n* аккумуля́тор.

accuracy /'ækjʊrəsɪ/ *n* то́чность. **accurate** /-rət/ *adj* то́чный.

accusation /ˌækju:'zeɪʃ(ə)n/ *n* обвине́ние. **accusative** /ə'kju:zətɪv/ *adj* (*n*) вини́тельный (паде́ж). **accuse** /ə'kju:z/ *vt* обвиня́ть *impf*, обвини́ть *pf* (**of** в+*prep*); **the** ~**d** обвиня́емый *sb*.

accustom /ə'kʌstəm/ *vt* приуча́ть *impf*, приучи́ть *pf* (**to** к+*dat*). **accustomed** /-təmd/ *adj* привы́чный; **be, get** ~ привыка́ть *impf*, привы́кнуть *pf* (**to** к+*dat*).

ace /eɪs/ *n* туз; (*pilot*) ас.

ache /eɪk/ *n* боль; *vi* боле́ть *impf*.

achieve /ə'tʃi:v/ *vt* достига́ть *impf*, дости́чь & дости́гнуть *pf* +*gen*. **achievement** /-mənt/ *n* достиже́ние.

acid /'æsɪd/ *n* кислота́; *adj* ки́слый; ~ **rain** кисло́тный дождь. **acidity** /ə'sɪdɪtɪ/ *n* кислота́.

acknowledge /ək'nɒlɪdʒ/ *vt* признава́ть *impf*, призна́ть *pf*; (~ *receipt of*) подтвержда́ть *impf*, подтверди́ть *pf* получе́ние +*gen*. **acknowledgement** /-mənt/ *n* призна́ние; подтвержде́ние.

acne /'æknɪ/ *n* прыщи́ *m pl*.

acorn /'eɪkɔ:n/ *n* жёлудь *m*.

acoustic /ə'ku:stɪk/ *adj* акусти́ческий. **acoustics** /-stɪks/ *n pl* аку́стика.

acquaint /ə'kweɪnt/ *vt* знако́мить *impf*, по~ *pf*. **acquaintance** /-t(ə)ns/ *n* знако́мство; (*person*) знако́мый *sb*. **acquainted** /-tɪd/ *adj* знако́мый.

acquiesce /ˌækwɪ'es/ *vi* соглаша́ться *impf*, согласи́ться *pf*. **acquiescence** /-s(ə)ns/ *n* согла́сие.

acquire /ə'kwaɪə(r)/ *vt* приобрета́ть *impf*, приобрести́ *pf*. **acquisition** /ˌækwɪ'zɪʃ(ə)n/ *n* приобрете́ние. **acquisitive** /ə'kwɪzɪtɪv/ *adj* стяжа́тельский.

acquit /ə'kwɪt/ *vt* опра́вдывать *impf*, оправда́ть *pf*; ~ **o.s.** вести́ *impf* себя́. **acquittal** /-t(ə)l/ *n* оправда́ние.

acre /'eɪkə(r)/ *n* акр.

acrid /'ækrɪd/ *adj* е́дкий.

acrimonious /ˌækrɪ'məʊnɪəs/ *adj* язви́тельный.

acrobat /'ækrəˌbæt/ *n* акроба́т. **acrobatic** /-'bætɪk/ *adj* акробати́ческий.

across /ə'krɒs/ *adv* & *prep* че́рез+*acc*; (*athwart*) попере́к (+*gen*); (*to, on, other side*) на ту сто́рону (+*gen*), на той стороне́ (+*gen*); (*crosswise*) крестна́крест.

acrylic /ə'krɪlɪk/ *n* акри́л; *adj* акри́ловый.

act /ækt/ *n* (*deed*) акт, посту́пок; (*law*) акт, зако́н; (*of play*) де́йствие; (*item*) но́мер; *vi* поступа́ть *impf*, поступи́ть *pf*; де́йствовать *impf*, по~ *pf*; *vt* игра́ть *impf*, сыгра́ть *pf*. **acting** /'æktɪŋ/ *n* игра́; (*profession*) актёрство; *adj* исполня́ющий обя́занности+*gen.* **action** /'ækʃ(ə)n/ *n* де́йствие, посту́пок; (*law*) иск, проце́сс; (*battle*) бой; ~ **replay** повто́р; **be out of** ~ не рабо́тать *impf.* **activate** /'æktɪ,veɪt/ *vt* приводи́ть *impf*, привести́ *pf* в де́йствие. **active** /'æktɪv/ *adj* акти́вный; ~ **service** действи́тельная слу́жба; ~ **voice** действи́тельный зало́г. **activity** /æk'tɪvɪtɪ/ *n* де́ятельность. **actor** /'æktə(r)/ *n* актёр. **actress** /'æktrɪs/ *n* актри́са.

actual /'æktʃʊəl/ *adj* действи́тельный. **actuality** /-'ælɪtɪ/ *n* действи́тельность. **actually** /'æktʃʊəlɪ/ *adv* на са́мом де́ле, факти́чески.

acumen /'ækjʊmən/ *n* проница́тельность.

acupuncture /'ækju:,pʌŋktʃə(r)/ *n* иглоука́лывание.

acute /ə'kju:t/ *adj* о́стрый.

AD *abbr* н.э. (на́шей э́ры).

adamant /'ædəmənt/ *adj* непрекло́нный.

adapt /ə'dæpt/ *vt* приспособля́ть *impf*, приспосо́бить *pf*; (*theat*) инсцени́ровать *impf* & *pf*; ~ **o.s.** приспособля́ться *impf*, приспосо́биться *pf.* **adaptable** /-təb(ə)l/ *adj* приспособля́ющийся. **adaptation** /,ædæp'teɪʃ(ə)n/ *n* приспособле́ние; (*theat*) инсцениро́вка. **adapter** /-tə(r)/ *n* ада́птер.

add /æd/ *vt* прибавля́ть *impf*, приба́вить *pf*; (*say*) добавля́ть *impf*, доба́вить *pf*; ~ **together** скла́дывать *impf*, сложи́ть *pf*; ~ **up** сумми́ровать *impf* & *pf*; ~ **up to** составля́ть *impf*, соста́вить *pf*; (*fig*) своди́ться *impf*, свести́сь *pf* к+*dat.* **addenda** /ə'dendə/ *n* приложе́ния *pl.*

adder /'ædə(r)/ *n* гадю́ка.

addict /'ædɪkt/ *n* наркома́н, ~ка. **addicted** /ə'dɪktɪd/ *adj*: **be** ~ **to** быть рабо́м+*gen*; **become** ~ **to** пристрасти́ться *pf* к+*dat.* **addiction** /ə'dɪkʃ(ə)n/ *n* (*passion*) пристра́стие; (*to drugs*) наркома́ния.

addition /ə'dɪʃ(ə)n/ *n* прибавле́ние; дополне́ние; (*math*) сложе́ние; **in** ~ вдоба́вок, кро́ме того́. **additional** /-n(ə)l/ *adj* доба́вочный. **additive** /'ædɪtɪv/ *n* доба́вка.

address /ə'dres/ *n* а́дрес; (*speech*) речь; ~ **book** записна́я кни́жка; *vt* адресова́ть *impf* & *pf*; (*speak to*) обраща́ться *impf*, обрати́ться *pf* к+*dat*; ~ **a meeting** выступа́ть *impf*, вы́ступить *pf* на собра́нии. **addressee** /,ædre'si:/ *n* адреса́т.

adept /'ædept/ *adj* све́дущий; *n* ма́стер.

adequate /'ædɪkwət/ *adj* доста́точный.

adhere /əd'hɪə(r)/ *vi* прилипа́ть *impf*, прили́пнуть *pf* (**to** к+*dat*); (*fig*) приде́рживаться *impf* +*gen.* **adherence** /-rəns/ *n* приве́рженность. **adherent** /-rənt/ *n* приве́рженец. **adhesive** /əd'hi:sɪv/ *adj* ли́пкий; *n* кле́йкое вещество́.

ad hoc /æd 'hɒk/ *adj* специа́льный.

ad infinitum /æd ,ɪnfɪ'naɪtəm/ *adv* до бесконе́чности.

adjacent /ə'dʒeɪs(ə)nt/ *adj* сме́жный.

adjective /'ædʒɪktɪv/ *n* (и́мя) прилага́тельное.

adjoin /ə'dʒɔɪn/ *vt* прилега́ть *impf* к+*dat.*

adjourn /ə'dʒɜ:n/ *vt* откла́дывать *impf*, отложи́ть *pf*; *vi* объявля́ть *impf*, объяви́ть *pf*

переры́в; (*move*) переходи́ть *impf*, перейти́ *pf*.
adjudicate /ə'dʒu:dɪ,keɪt/ *vi* выноси́ть *impf*, вы́нести *pf* реше́ние (**in** по+*dat*); суди́ть *impf*.
adjust /ə'dʒʌst/ *vt* & *i* приспоса́бливать(ся) *impf*, приспосо́бить(ся) *pf*; *vt* пригоня́ть *impf*, пригна́ть *pf*; (*regulate*) регули́ровать *impf*, от~ *pf*. **adjustable** /-təb(ə)l/ *adj* регули́руемый. **adjustment** /-mənt/ *n* регули́рование, подго́нка.
ad lib /æd 'lɪb/ *vt* & *i* импровизи́ровать *impf*, сымпровизи́ровать *pf*.
administer /əd'mɪnɪstə(r)/ *vt* (*manage*) управля́ть *impf* +*instr*; (*give*) дава́ть *impf*, дать *pf*. **administration** /-'streɪʃ(ə)n/ *n* управле́ние; (*government*) прави́тельство. **administrative** /-strətɪv/ *adj* администрати́вный. **administrator** /-,streɪtə(r)/ *n* администра́тор.
admirable /'ædmərəb(ə)l/ *adj* похва́льный.
admiral /'ædmər(ə)l/ *n* адмира́л.
admiration /,ædmɪ'reɪʃ(ə)n/ *n* восхище́ние. **admire** /əd'maɪə(r)/ *vt* (*look at*) любова́ться *impf*, по~ *pf* +*instr*, на+*acc*; (*respect*) восхища́ться *impf*, восхити́ться *pf* +*instr*. **admirer** /əd'maɪərə(r)/ *n* покло́нник.
admissible /əd'mɪsɪb(ə)l/ *adj* допусти́мый. **admission** /əd'mɪʃ(ə)n/ *n* (*access*) до́ступ; (*entry*) вход; (*confession*) призна́ние. **admit** /əd'mɪt/ *vt* (*allow in*) впуска́ть *impf*, впусти́ть *pf*; (*confess*) признава́ть *impf*, призна́ть *pf*. **admittance** /əd'mɪt(ə)ns/ *n* до́ступ. **admittedly** /əd'mɪtɪdlɪ/ *adv* призна́ться.
admixture /æd'mɪkstʃə(r)/ *n* при́месь.
adolescence /,ædə'les(ə)ns/ *n* о́трочество. **adolescent** /-s(ə)nt/ *adj* подро́стковый; *n* подро́сток.
adopt /ə'dɒpt/ *vt* (*child*) усыновля́ть *impf*, усынови́ть *pf*; (*thing*) усва́ивать *impf*, усво́ить *pf*; (*accept*) принима́ть *impf*, приня́ть *pf*. **adoptive** /-tɪv/ *adj* приёмный. **adoption** /ə'dɒpʃ(ə)n/ *n* усыновле́ние; приня́тие.
adorable /ə'dɔ:rəb(ə)l/ *adj* преле́стный. **adoration** /,ædə'reɪʃ(ə)n/ *n* обожа́ние. **adore** /ə'dɔ:(r)/ *vt* обожа́ть *impf*.
adorn /ə'dɔ:n/ *vt* украша́ть *impf*, укра́сить *pf*. **adornment** /-mənt/ *n* украше́ние.
adrenalin /ə'drenəlɪn/ *n* адренали́н.
adroit /ə'drɔɪt/ *adj* ло́вкий.
adulation /,ædjʊ'leɪʃ(ə)n/ *n* преклоне́ние.
adult /'ædʌlt/ *adj* & *n* взро́слый (*sb*).
adulterate /ə'dʌltə,reɪt/ *vt* фальсифици́ровать *impf* & *pf*.
adultery /ə'dʌltərɪ/ *n* супру́жеская изме́на.
advance /əd'vɑ:ns/ *n* (*going forward*) продвиже́ние (вперёд); (*progress*) прогре́сс; (*mil*) наступле́ние; (*of pay etc.*) ава́нс; **in** ~ зара́нее; *pl* (*overtures*) ава́нсы *m pl*; *vi* (*go forward*) продвига́ться *impf*, продви́нуться *pf* вперёд; идти́ *impf* вперёд; (*mil*) наступа́ть *impf*; *vt* продвига́ть *impf*, продви́нуть *pf*; (*put forward*) выдвига́ть *impf*, вы́двинуть *pf*. **advanced** /əd'vɑ:nst/ *adj* (*modern*) передово́й. **advancement** /-mənt/ *n* продвиже́ние.

advantage /əd'vɑ:ntɪdʒ/ *n* преиму́щество; (*profit*) вы́года, по́льза; **take ~ of** по́льзоваться *impf*, вос~ *pf* +*instr*. **advantageous** /ˌædvən'teɪdʒəs/ *adj* вы́годный.

adventure /əd'ventʃə(r)/ *n* приключе́ние. **adventurer** /-rə(r)/ *n* иска́тель *m* приключе́ний. **adventurous** /-rəs/ *adj* предприи́мчивый.

adverb /'ædvɜ:b/ *n* наре́чие.

adversary /'ædvəsərɪ/ *n* проти́вник. **adverse** /'ædvɜ:s/ *adj* неблагоприя́тный. **adversity** /əd'vɜ:sɪtɪ/ *n* несча́стье.

advertise /'ædvəˌtaɪz/ *vt* (*publicize*) реклами́ровать *impf* & *pf*; *vt* & *i* (~ *for*) дава́ть *impf*, дать *pf* объявле́ние о+*prep*. **advertisement** /əd'vɜ:tɪsmənt/ *n* объявле́ние, рекла́ма.

advice /əd'vaɪs/ *n* сове́т. **advisable** /əd'vaɪzəb(ə)l/ *adj* жела́тельный. **advise** /əd'vaɪz/ *vt* сове́товать *impf*, по~ *pf* +*dat* & *inf*; (*notify*) уведомля́ть *impf*, уве́домить *pf*. **advisedly** /əd'vaɪzɪdlɪ/ *adv* наме́ренно. **adviser** /əd'vaɪzə(r)/ *n* сове́тник. **advisory** /əd'vaɪzərɪ/ *adj* совеща́тельный.

advocate *n* /'ædvəkət/ (*supporter*) сторо́нник; *vt* /'ædvəˌkeɪt/ выступа́ть *impf*, вы́ступить *pf* за+*acc*; (*advise*) сове́товать *impf*, по~ *pf*.

aegis /'i:dʒɪs/ *n* эги́да.

aerial /'eərɪəl/ *n* анте́нна; *adj* возду́шный.

aerobics /eə'rəʊbɪks/ *n* аэро́бика.

aerodrome /'eərəˌdrəʊm/ *n* аэродро́м. **aerodynamics** /-daɪ'næmɪks/ *n* аэродина́мика.

aeroplane /-ˌpleɪn/ *n* самолёт.

aerosol /-ˌsɒl/ *n* аэрозо́ль *m*.

aesthetic /i:s'θetɪk/ *adj* эстети́ческий. **aesthetics** /-tɪks/ *n pl* эсте́тика.

afar /ə'fɑ:(r)/ *adv*: **from ~** издалека́.

affable /'æfəb(ə)l/ *adj* приве́тливый.

affair /ə'feə(r)/ *n* (*business*) де́ло; (*love*) рома́н.

affect /ə'fekt/ *vt* влия́ть *impf*, по~ *pf* на+*acc*; (*touch*) тро́гать *impf*, тро́нуть *pf*; (*concern*) затра́гивать *impf*, затро́нуть *pf*; **affectation** /ˌæfek'teɪʃ(ə)n/ *n* жема́нство. **affected** /-tɪd/ *adj* жема́нный. **affection** /ə'fekʃ(ə)n/ *n* привя́занность. **affectionate** /ə'fekʃənət/ *adj* не́жный.

affiliated /ə'fɪlɪˌeɪtɪd/ *adj* свя́занный (**to** с+*instr*).

affinity /ə'fɪnɪtɪ/ *n* (*relationship*) родство́; (*resemblance*) схо́дство; (*attraction*) влече́ние.

affirm /ə'fɜ:m/ *vt* утвержда́ть *impf*. **affirmation** /ˌæfə'meɪʃ(ə)n/ *n* утвержде́ние. **affirmative** /ə'fɜ:mətɪv/ *adj* утверди́тельный.

affix /ə'fɪks/ *vt* прикрепля́ть *impf*, прикрепи́ть *pf*.

afflict /ə'flɪkt/ *vt* постига́ть *impf*, пости́чь *pf*; **be afflicted with** страда́ть *impf* +*instr*. **affliction** /ə'flɪkʃ(ə)n/ *n* боле́знь.

affluence /'æflʊəns/ *n* бога́тство. **affluent** /-ənt/ *adj* бога́тый.

afford /ə'fɔ:d/ *vt* позволя́ть *impf*, позво́лить *pf* себе́; (*supply*) предоставля́ть *impf*, предоста́вить *pf*.

affront /ə'frʌnt/ *n* оскорбле́ние; *vt* оскорбля́ть *impf*, оскорби́ть *pf*.

afield /ə'fi:ld/ *adv*: **far ~** далеко́; **farther ~** да́льше.

afloat /ə'fləʊt/ *adv* & *predic* на воде́.

afoot /ə'fʊt/ *predic*: **be ~** гото́виться *impf*.
aforesaid /ə'fɔ:sed/ *adj* вышеупомя́нутый.
afraid /ə'freɪd/ *predic*: **be ~** боя́ться *impf*.
afresh /ə'freʃ/ *adv* сно́ва.
Africa /'æfrɪkə/ *n* А́фрика. **African** /-kən/ *n* африка́нец, -ка́нка; *adj* африка́нский.
after /'ɑ:ftə(r)/ *adv* пото́м; *prep* по́сле +*gen*; (*time*) че́рез+*acc*; (*behind*) за+*acc*, *instr*; **~ all** в конце́ концо́в; *conj* по́сле того́, как.
aftermath /'ɑ:ftəmæθ/ *n* после́дствия *neut pl*. **afternoon** /-'nu:n/ *n* втора́я полови́на дня; **in the ~** днём. **aftershave** /-ʃeɪv/ *n* лосьо́н по́сле бритья́. **afterthought** /-θɔ:t/ *n* запозда́лая мысль.
afterwards /'ɑ:ftəwədz/ *adv* пото́м.
again /ə'gen/ *adv* опя́ть; (*once more*) ещё раз; (*anew*) сно́ва.
against /ə'genst/ *prep* (*opposing*) про́тив+*gen*; (*touching*) к+*dat*; (*hitting*) о+*acc*.
age /eɪdʒ/ *n* во́зраст; (*era*) век, эпо́ха; *vt* ста́рить *impf*, со~ *pf*; *vi* старе́ть *impf*, по~ *pf*. **aged** /'eɪdʒɪd/ *adj* престаре́лый.
agency /'eɪdʒənsɪ/ *n* аге́нтство. **agenda** /ə'dʒendə/ *n* пове́стка дня. **agent** /'eɪdʒ(ə)nt/ *n* аге́нт.
aggravate /'ægrə,veɪt/ *vt* ухудша́ть *impf*, уху́дшить *pf*; (*annoy*) раздража́ть *impf*, раздражи́ть *pf*.
aggregate /'ægrɪgət/ *adj* совоку́пный; *n* совоку́пность.
aggression /ə'greʃ(ə)n/ *n* агре́ссия. **aggressive** /-sɪv/ *adj* агресси́вный. **aggressor** /-sə(r)/ *n* агре́ссор.
aggrieved /ə'gri:vd/ *adj* оби́женный.
aghast /ə'gɑ:st/ *predic* в у́жасе (**at** от +*gen*).
agile /'ædʒaɪl/ *adj* прово́рный. **agility** /-'dʒɪlɪtɪ/ *n* прово́рство.
agitate /'ædʒɪ,teɪt/ *vt* волнова́ть *impf*, вз~ *pf*; *vi* агити́ровать *impf*. **agitation** /-'teɪʃ(ə)n/ *n* волне́ние; агита́ция.
agnostic /æg'nɒstɪk/ *n* агно́стик. **agnosticism** /-tɪ,sɪz(ə)m/ *n* агностици́зм.
ago /ə'gəʊ/ *adv* (тому́) наза́д; **long ~** давно́.
agonize /'ægə,naɪz/ *vi* му́читься *impf*. **agonizing** /-zɪŋ/ *adj* мучи́тельный. **agony** /'ægənɪ/ *n* аго́ния.
agrarian /ə'greərɪən/ *adj* агра́рный.
agree /ə'gri:/ *vi* соглаша́ться *impf*, согласи́ться *pf*; (*arrange*) догова́риваться *impf*, договори́ться *pf*. **agreeable** /-əb(ə)l/ *adj* (*pleasant*) прия́тный. **agreement** /-mənt/ *n* согла́сие; (*treaty*) соглаше́ние; **in ~** согла́сен (-сна).
agricultural /,ægrɪ'kʌltʃər(ə)l/ *adj* сельскохозя́йственный. **agriculture** /'ægrɪkʌltʃə(r)/ *n* се́льское хозя́йство.
aground /ə'graʊnd/ *predic* на мели́; *adv*: **run ~** сади́ться *impf*, сесть *pf* на мель.
ahead /ə'hed/ *adv* (*forward*) вперёд; (*in front*) впереди́; **~ of time** досро́чно.
aid /eɪd/ *vt* помога́ть *impf*, помо́чь *pf* +*dat*; *n* по́мощь; (*teaching*) посо́бие; **in ~ of** в по́льзу +*gen*.
Aids /eɪdz/ *n* СПИД.
ailing /'eɪlɪŋ/ *adj* (*ill*) больно́й.
ailment /'eɪlmənt/ *n* неду́г.
aim /eɪm/ *n* цель, наме́рение; **take ~** прице́ливаться *impf*,

прицéлиться *pf* (**at** в+*acc*); *vi* целиться *impf*, на~ *pf* (**at** в+*acc*); (*also fig*) мéтить *impf*, на~ *pf* (**at** в+*acc*); *vt* нацéливать *impf*, нацéлить *pf*; (*also fig*) наводи́ть *impf*, навести́ *pf*. **aimless** /'eɪmlɪs/ *adj* бесцéльный.

air /eə(r)/ *n* вóздух; (*look*) вид; **by ~** самолётом; **on the ~** в эфи́ре; *attrib* воздýшный; *vt* (*ventilate*) провéтривать *impf*, провéтрить *pf*; (*make known*) выставля́ть *impf*, вы́ставить *pf* напокáз. **air-conditioning** *n* кондициони́рование вóздуха. **aircraft** *n* самолёт. **aircraft-carrier** *n* авианóсец. **airfield** *n* аэродрóм. **air force** *n* ВВС (воéнно-воздýшные си́лы) *f pl*. **air hostess** *n* стюардéсса. **airless** /-l(ə)s/ *adj* дýшный. **airlift** *n* воздýшные перевóзки *f pl*; *vt* перевози́ть *impf*, перевезти́ *pf* по вóздуху. **airline** *n* авиакомпáния. **airlock** *n* воздýшная прóбка. **airmail** *n* áвиа(пóчта). **airman** *n* лётчик. **airport** *n* аэропóрт. **air raid** *n* воздýшный налёт. **airship** *n* дирижáбль *m*. **airstrip** *n* взлётно-посáдочная полосá. **airtight** *adj* гермети́чный. **air traffic controller** *n* диспéтчер. **airwaves** *n pl* радиовóлны *f pl*.

aisle /aɪl/ *n* боковóй неф; (*passage*) прохóд.

ajar /ə'dʒɑː(r)/ *predic* приоткры́тый.

akin /ə'kɪn/ *predic* (*similar*) похóжий; **be ~ to** быть сродни́ к+*dat*.

alabaster /'ælə,bæstə(r)/ *n* алебáстр.

alacrity /ə'lækrɪtɪ/ *n* быстротá.

alarm /ə'lɑːm/ *n* тревóга; *vt* тревóжить *impf*, вс~ *pf*; **~ clock** буди́льник. **alarming** /-mɪŋ/ *adj* тревóжный. **alarmist** /-mɪst/ *n* паникёр; *adj* паникёрский.

alas /ə'læs/ *int* увы́!

album /'ælbəm/ *n* альбóм.

alcohol /'ælkə,hɒl/ *n* алкогóль *m*, спирт; спиртны́е напи́тки *m pl*. **alcoholic** /,ælkə'hɒlɪk/ *adj* алкогóльный; *n* алкогóлик, -и́чка.

alcove /'ælkəʊv/ *n* алькóв.

alert /ə'lɜːt/ *adj* бди́тельный; *n* тревóга; *vt* предупреждáть *impf*, предупреди́ть *pf*.

algebra /'ældʒɪbrə/ *n* áлгебра.

alias /'eɪlɪəs/ *adv* инáче (называ́емый); *n* кли́чка, вы́мышленное и́мя *neut*.

alibi /'ælɪ,baɪ/ *n* áлиби *neut indecl*.

alien /'eɪlɪən/ *n* инострáнец, -нка; *adj* инострáнный; **~ to** чýждый +*dat*. **alienate** /-,neɪt/ *vt* отчуждáть *impf*. **alienation** /-'neɪʃ(ə)n/ *n* отчуждéние.

alight[1] /ə'laɪt/ *vi* сходи́ть *impf*, сойти́ *pf*; (*bird*) сади́ться *impf*, сесть *pf*.

alight[2] /ə'laɪt/ *predic*: **be ~** горéть *impf*; (*shine*) сия́ть *impf*.

align /ə'laɪn/ *vt* вырáвнивать *impf*, вы́ровнять *pf*. **alignment** /-mənt/ *n* вырáвнивание.

alike /ə'laɪk/ *predic* похóж; *adv* одинáково.

alimentary /,ælɪ'mentərɪ/ *adj*: **~ canal** пищевари́тельный канáл.

alimony /'ælɪmənɪ/ *n* алимéнты *m pl*.

alive /ə'laɪv/ *predic* жив, в живы́х.

alkali /'ælkə,laɪ/ *n* щёлочь. **alkaline** /-,laɪn/ *adj* щелочнóй.

all /ɔːl/ *adj* весь; *n* всё, *pl* все; *adv* совсéм, совершéнно; **~ along** всё врéмя; **~ right** хорошó, ла́дно; (*not bad*) та́к себе; непло́хо; **~ the same** всё равно́; **in ~** всего́; **two ~** по́ два; **not at ~** ниско́лько.

allay /ə'leɪ/ *vt* успока́ивать *impf*, успоко́ить *pf*.

allegation /,ælɪ'geɪʃ(ə)n/ *n* утвержде́ние. **allege** /ə'ledʒ/ *vt* утвержда́ть *impf*. **allegedly** /ə'ledʒɪdlɪ/ *adv* я́кобы.

allegiance /ə'li:dʒ(ə)ns/ *adv* ве́рность.

allegorical /,ælɪ'gɒrɪk(ə)l/ *adj* аллегори́ческий. **allegory** /'ælɪgərɪ/ *n* аллего́рия.

allergic /ə'lɜ:dʒɪk/ *adj* аллерги́ческий; **be ~ to** име́ть аллерги́ю к+*dat*. **allergy** /'ælədʒɪ/ *n* аллерги́я.

alleviate /ə'li:vɪ,eɪt/ *vt* облегча́ть *impf*, облегчи́ть *pf*. **alleviation** /-'eɪʃ(ə)n/ *n* облегче́ние.

alley /'ælɪ/ *n* переу́лок.

alliance /ə'laɪəns/ *n* сою́з. **allied** /'ælaɪd/ *adj* сою́зный.

alligator /'ælɪ,geɪtə(r)/ *n* аллига́тор.

allocate /'ælə,keɪt/ *vt* (*distribute*) распределя́ть *impf*, распредели́ть *pf*; (*allot*) выделя́ть *impf*, вы́делить *pf*. **allocation** /-'keɪʃ(ə)n/ *n* распределе́ние; выделе́ние.

allot /ə'lɒt/ *vt* выделя́ть *impf*, вы́делить *pf*; (*distribute*) распределя́ть *impf*, распредели́ть *pf*. **allotment** /-mənt/ *n* выделе́ние; (*land*) уча́сток.

allow /ə'laʊ/ *vt* разреша́ть *impf*, разреши́ть *pf*; (*let happen*; *concede*) допуска́ть *impf*, допусти́ть *pf*; **~ for** учи́тывать *impf*, уче́сть *pf*. **allowance** /-əns/ *n* (*financial*) посо́бие; (*deduction*, *also fig*) ски́дка; **make ~(s) for** учи́тывать *impf*, уче́сть *pf*.

alloy /'ælɔɪ/ *n* сплав.

all-round /'ɔ:lraʊnd/ *adj* разносторо́нний.

allude /ə'lu:d/ *vi* ссыла́ться *impf*, сосла́ться *pf* (**to** на+*acc*).

allure /ə'ljʊə(r)/ *vt* зама́нивать *impf*, замани́ть *pf*. **allure(ment)** (/-mənt/) *n* примáнка. **alluring** /-rɪŋ/ *adj* зама́нчивый.

allusion /ə'lu:ʒ(ə)n/ *n* ссы́лка.

ally *n* /'ælaɪ/ сою́зник; *vt* /ə'laɪ/ соединя́ть *impf*, соедини́ть *pf*; **~ oneself with** вступа́ть *impf*, вступи́ть *pf* в сою́з с+*instr*.

almighty /ɔ:l'maɪtɪ/ *adj* всемогу́щий.

almond /'ɑ:mənd/ *n* (*tree*; *pl collect*) минда́ль *m*; (*nut*) минда́льный оре́х.

almost /'ɔ:lməʊst/ *adv* почти́, едва́ не.

alms /ɑ:mz/ *n pl* ми́лостыня.

aloft /ə'lɒft/ *adv* наве́рх(-у́).

alone /ə'ləʊn/ *predic* оди́н; (*lonely*) одино́к; *adv* то́лько; **leave ~** оставля́ть *impf*, оста́вить *pf* в поко́е; **let ~** не говоря́ уже́ о+*prep*.

along /ə'lɒŋ/ *prep* по+*dat*, (*position*) вдоль+*gen*; *adv* (*onward*) да́льше; **all ~** всё вре́мя; **~ with** вме́сте с+*instr*. **alongside** /ə,lɒŋ'saɪd/ *adv* & *prep* ря́дом (с +*instr*).

aloof /ə'lu:f/ *predic* & *adv* (*distant*) сде́ржанный; (*apart*) в стороне́.

aloud /ə'laʊd/ *adv* вслух.

alphabet /'ælfə,bet/ *n* алфави́т. **alphabetical** /,ælfə'betɪk(ə)l/ *adj* алфави́тный.

alpine /'ælpaɪn/ *adj* альпи́йский.

already /ɔ:l'redɪ/ *adv* уже́.

also /'ɔ:lsəʊ/ *adv* та́кже, то́же.

altar /'ɔ:ltə(r)/ *n* алта́рь *m*.

alter /'ɔ:ltə(r)/ *vt* (*modify*) переде́лывать *impf*, переде́лать *pf*;

vt & i (*change*) изменя́ть(ся) *impf*, измени́ть(ся) *pf*. **alteration** /-'reɪʃ(ə)n/ *n* переде́лка; измене́ние.

alternate *adj* /ɔ:l'tɜ:nət/ чере́дующийся; *vt & i* /'ɔ:ltə,neɪt/ чередова́ть(ся) *impf*; **alternating current** переме́нный ток; **on ~ days** че́рез день. **alternation** /,ɔ:ltə'neɪʃ(ə)n/ *n* чередова́ние. **alternative** /ɔ:l'tɜ:nətɪv/ *n* альтернати́ва; *adj* альтернати́вный.

although /ɔ:l'ðəʊ/ *conj* хотя́.

altitude /'æltɪ,tju:d/ *n* высота́.

alto /'æltəʊ/ *n* альт.

altogether /,ɔ:ltə'geðə(r)/ *adv* (*fully*) совсе́м; (*in total*) всего́.

altruistic /,æltru:'ɪstɪk/ *adj* альтруисти́ческий.

aluminium /,æljʊ'mɪnɪəm/ *n* алюми́ний.

always /'ɔ:lweɪz/ *adv* всегда́; (*constantly*) постоя́нно.

Alzheimer's disease /'ælts ,haɪməz/ *n* боле́знь Альцге́ймера.

a.m. *abbr* (*morning*) утра́; (*night*) но́чи.

amalgamate /ə'mælgə,meɪt/ *vt & i* слива́ть(ся) *impf*, сли́ть(ся) *pf*; (*chem*) амальгами́ровать(ся) *impf & pf*. **amalgamation** /-'meɪʃ(ə)n/ *n* слия́ние; (*chem*) амальгами́рование.

amass /ə'mæs/ *vt* копи́ть *impf*, на~ *pf*.

amateur /'æmətə(r)/ *n* люби́тель *m*, ~ница; *adj* люби́тельский. **amateurish** /-rɪʃ/ *adj* дилета́нтский.

amaze /ə'meɪz/ *vt* изумля́ть *impf*, изуми́ть *pf*. **amazement** /-mənt/ *n* изумле́ние. **amazing** /-zɪŋ/ *adj* изуми́тельный.

ambassador /æm'bæsədə(r)/ *n* посо́л.

amber /'æmbə(r)/ *n* янта́рь *m*.

ambience /'æmbɪəns/ *n* среда́; атмосфе́ра.

ambiguity /,æmbɪ'gju:ɪtɪ/ *n* двусмы́сленность. **ambiguous** /æm'bɪgju:əs/ *adj* двусмы́сленный.

ambition /æm'bɪʃ(ə)n/ *n* (*quality*) честолю́бие; (*aim*) мечта́. **ambitious** /-'bɪʃəs/ *adj* честолюби́вый.

amble /'æmb(ə)l/ *vi* ходи́ть *indet*, идти́ *det* неторопли́вым ша́гом.

ambulance /'æmbjʊləns/ *n* маши́на ско́рой по́мощи.

ambush /'æmbʊʃ/ *n* заса́да; *vt* напада́ть *impf*, напа́сть *pf* из заса́ды на+*acc*.

ameliorate /ə'mi:lɪə,reɪt/ *vt & i* улучша́ть(ся) *impf*, улу́чшить(ся) *pf*. **amelioration** /-'reɪʃ(ə)n/ *n* улучше́ние.

amen /eɪ'men/ *int* ами́нь!

amenable /ə'mi:nəb(ə)l/ *adj* сгово́рчивый (**to** +*dat*)

amend /ə'mend/ *vt* (*correct*) исправля́ть *impf*, испра́вить *pf*; (*change*) вноси́ть *impf*, внести́ *pf* попра́вки в+*acc*. **amendment** /-mənt/ *n* попра́вка, исправле́ние. **amends** /ə'mendz/ *n pl*: **make ~ for** загла́живать *impf*, загла́дить *pf*.

amenities /ə'mi:nɪtɪz/ *n pl* удо́бства *neut pl*.

America /ə'merɪkə/ *n* Аме́рика. **American** /-kən/ *adj* америка́нский; *n* америка́нец, -нка. **Americanism** /-kə,nɪz(ə)m/ *n* американи́зм.

amiable /'eɪmɪəb(ə)l/ *adj* любе́зный. **amicable** /'æmɪkəb(ə)l/ *adj* дружелю́бный.

amid(st) /ə'mɪdst/ *prep* среди́+*gen*.

amino acid /ə,mi:nəʊ 'æsɪd/ *n* аминокислота́.

amiss /ə'mɪs/ *adv* нела́дный; **take ~** обижа́ться *impf*, оби́деться *pf* на+*acc*. **ammonia** /ə'məʊnɪə/ *n* аммиа́к; (*liquid* ~) нашаты́рный спирт. **ammunition** /ˌæmjʊ'nɪʃ(ə)n/ *n* боеприпа́сы *m pl*. **amnesia** /æm'ni:zɪə/ *n* амнези́я. **amnesty** /'æmnɪstɪ/ *n* амни́стия. **among(st)** /ə'mʌŋ(st)/ *prep* (*amidst*) среди́+*gen*, (*between*) ме́жду+*instr*. **amoral** /eɪ'mɒr(ə)l/ *adj* амора́льный. **amorous** /'æmərəs/ *adj* влю́бчивый. **amorphous** /ə'mɔ:fəs/ *adj* бесфо́рменный. **amortization** /əˌmɔ:taɪ'zeɪʃ(ə)n/ *n* амортиза́ция. **amount** /ə'maʊnt/ *n* коли́чество; *vi*: **~ to** составля́ть *impf*, соста́вить *pf*; (*be equivalent to*) быть равноси́льным+*dat*. **ampere** /'æmpeə(r)/ *n* ампе́р. **amphetamine** /æm'fetəmɪn/ *n* амфетами́н. **amphibian** /æm'fɪbɪən/ *n* амфи́бия. **amphibious** /-'fɪbɪəs/ *adj* земново́дный; (*mil*) пла́вающий. **amphitheatre** /'æmfɪˌθɪətə(r)/ *n* амфитеа́тр. **ample** /'æmp(ə)l/ *adj* доста́точный. **amplification** /ˌæmplɪfɪ'keɪʃ(ə)n/ *n* усиле́ние. **amplifier** /'æmplɪˌfaɪə(r)/ *n* усили́тель *m*. **amplify** /'æmplɪˌfaɪ/ *vt* уси́ливать *impf*, уси́лить *pf*. **amply** /'æmplɪ/ *adv* доста́точно. **amputate** /'æmpjʊˌteɪt/ *vt* ампути́ровать *impf* & *pf*. **amputation** /-'teɪʃ(ə)n/ *n* ампута́ция. **amuse** /ə'mju:z/ *vt* забавля́ть *impf*; развлека́ть *impf*, развле́чь *pf*. **amusement** /-mənt/ *n* заба́ва, развлече́ние; *pl* аттракцио́ны *m pl*. **amusing** /-zɪŋ/ *adj* заба́вный; (*funny*) смешно́й.

anachronism /ə'nækrəˌnɪz(ə)m/ *n* анахрони́зм. **anachronistic** /-'nɪstɪk/ *adj* анахрони́ческий. **anaemia** /ə'ni:mɪə/ *n* анеми́я. **anaemic** /-mɪk/ *adj* анеми́чный. **anaesthesia** /ˌænɪs'θi:zɪə/ *n* анестези́я. **anaesthetic** /-'θetɪk/ *n* обезбо́ливающее сре́дство. **anaesthetist** /ə'ni:sθətɪst/ *n* анестезио́лог. **anaesthetize** /ə'ni:sθəˌtaɪz/ *vt* анестези́ровать *impf* & *pf*. **anagram** /'ænəˌgræm/ *n* анагра́мма. **analogous** /ə'næləgəs/ *adj* аналоги́чный. **analogue** /'ænəˌlɒg/ *n* ана́лог. **analogy** /ə'nælədʒɪ/ *n* анало́гия. **analyse** /'ænəˌlaɪz/ *vt* анализи́ровать *impf* & *pf*. **analysis** /ə'nælɪsɪs/ *n* ана́лиз. **analyst** /'ænəlɪst/ *n* анали́тик; психоанали́тик. **analytical** /ˌænə'lɪtɪk(ə)l/ *adj* аналити́ческий. **anarchic** /ə'nɑ:kɪk/ *adj* анархи́ческий. **anarchist** /'ænəkɪst/ *n* анархи́ст, ~ка; *adj* анархи́стский. **anarchy** /'ænəkɪ/ *n* ана́рхия. **anathema** /ə'næθəmə/ *n* ана́фема. **anatomical** /ˌænə'tɒmɪk(ə)l/ *adj* анатоми́ческий. **anatomy** /ə'nætəmɪ/ *n* анато́мия. **ancestor** /'ænsestə(r)/ *n* пре́док. **ancestry** /-strɪ/ *n* происхожде́ние. **anchor** /'æŋkə(r)/ *n* я́корь *m*; *vt* ста́вить *impf*, по~ *pf* на я́корь; *vi* станови́ться *impf*, стать *pf* на я́корь. **anchorage** /'æŋkərɪdʒ/ *n* я́корная стоя́нка. **anchovy** /'æntʃəvɪ/ *n* анчо́ус.

ancient /'eɪnʃ(ə)nt/ *adj* дре́вний, стари́нный.
and /ænd, ənd/ *conj* и, (*but*) а; с+*instr*; **you ~ I** мы с ва́ми; **my wife ~ I** мы с жено́й.
anecdote /'ænɪk,dəʊt/ *n* анекдо́т.
anew /ə'nju:/ *adv* сно́ва.
angel /'eɪndʒ(ə)l/ *n* а́нгел. **angelic** /æn'dʒelɪk/ *adj* а́нгельский.
anger /'æŋgə(r)/ *n* гнев; *vt* серди́ть *impf*, рас~ *pf*.
angina /æn'dʒaɪnə/ *n* стенокарди́я.
angle[1] /'æŋg(ə)l/ *n* у́гол; (*fig*) то́чка зре́ния.
angle[2] /'æŋg(ə)l/ *vi* уди́ть *impf* ры́бу. **angler** /-glə(r)/ *n* рыболо́в.
angry /'æŋgrɪ/ *adj* серди́тый.
anguish /'æŋgwɪʃ/ *n* страда́ние, му́ка. **anguished** /-gwɪʃt/ *adj* отча́янный.
angular /'æŋgjʊlə(r)/ *adj* углово́й; (*sharp*) углова́тый.
animal /'ænɪm(ə)l/ *n* живо́тное *sb*; *adj* живо́тный. **animate** /-mət/ *adj* живо́й. **animated** /-meɪtɪd/ *adj* оживлённый; **~ cartoon** мультфи́льм. **animation** /-'meɪʃ(ə)n/ *n* оживле́ние.
animosity /,ænɪ'mɒsɪtɪ/ *n* вражде́бность.
ankle /'æŋk(ə)l/ *n* лоды́жка.
annals /'æn(ə)lz/ *n pl* ле́топись.
annex /ə'neks/ *vt* аннекси́ровать *impf* & *pf*. **annexation** /-'seɪʃ(ə)n/ *n* анне́ксия. **annexe** /'æneks/ *n* пристро́йка.
annihilate /ə'naɪə,leɪt/ *vt* уничтожа́ть *impf*, уничто́жить *pf*. **annihilation** /-'leɪʃ(ə)n/ *n* уничтоже́ние.
anniversary /,ænɪ'vɜ:sərɪ/ *n* годовщи́на.
annotate /'ænə,teɪt/ *vt* комменти́ровать *impf* & *pf*. **annotated** /-tɪd/ *adj* снабжённый коммента́риями. **annotation** /,ænə'teɪʃ(ə)n/ *n* аннота́ция.
announce /ə'naʊns/ *vt* объявля́ть *impf*, объяви́ть *pf*; заявля́ть *impf*, заяви́ть *pf*; (*radio*) сообща́ть *impf*, сообщи́ть *pf*. **announcement** /-mənt/ *n* объявле́ние; сообще́ние. **announcer** /-sə(r)/ *n* ди́ктор.
annoy /ə'nɔɪ/ *vt* досажда́ть *impf*, досади́ть *pf*; раздража́ть *impf*, раздражи́ть *pf*. **annoyance** /-əns/ *n* доса́да. **annoying** /-ɪŋ/ *adj* доса́дный.
annual /'ænjʊəl/ *adj* ежего́дный, (*of a given year*) годово́й; *n* (*book*) ежего́дник; (*bot*) одноле́тник. **annually** /-lɪ/ *adv* ежего́дно. **annuity** /ə'nju:ɪtɪ/ *n* (ежего́дная) ре́нта.
annul /ə'nʌl/ *vt* аннули́ровать *impf* & *pf*. **annulment** /-mənt/ *n* аннули́рование.
anoint /ə'nɔɪnt/ *vt* пома́зывать *impf*, пома́зать *pf*.
anomalous /ə'nɒmələs/ *adj* анома́льный. **anomaly** /-lɪ/ *n* анома́лия.
anonymous /ə'nɒnɪməs/ *adj* анони́мный. **anonymity** /,ænə'nɪmɪtɪ/ *n* анони́мность.
anorak /'ænə,ræk/ *n* ку́ртка.
anorexia /,ænə'reksɪə/ *n* аноре́ксия.
another /ə'nʌðə(r)/ *adj*, *pron* друго́й; **~ one** ещё (оди́н); **in ~ ten years** ещё че́рез де́сять лет.
answer /'ɑ:nsə(r)/ *n* отве́т; *vt* отвеча́ть *impf*, отве́тить *pf* (*person*) +*dat*, (*question*) на+*acc*; **~ the door** отворя́ть *impf*, отвори́ть *pf* дверь; **~ the phone** подходи́ть *impf*, подойти́ *pf* к

телефо́ну. **answerable** /-rəb(ə)l/ *adj* отве́тственный. **answering machine** *n* телефо́н-отве́тчик.

ant /ænt/ *n* мураве́й.

antagonism /æn'tægə͵nɪz(ə)m/ *n* антагони́зм. **antagonistic** /æn͵tægə'nɪstɪk/ *adj* антагонисти́ческий. **antagonize** /æn'tægə͵naɪz/ *vt* настра́ивать *impf*, настро́ить *pf* про́тив себя́.

Antarctic /æn'tɑːktɪk/ *n* Анта́рктика.

antelope /'æntɪ͵ləʊp/ *n* антило́па.

antenna /æn'tenə/ *n* у́сик; (*also radio*) анте́нна.

anthem /'ænθəm/ *n* гимн.

anthology /æn'θɒlədʒɪ/ *n* антоло́гия.

anthracite /'ænθrə͵saɪt/ *n* антраци́т.

anthropological /͵ænθrəpə'lɒdʒɪk(ə)l/ *adj* антропологи́ческий. **anthropologist** /͵ænθrə'pɒlədʒɪst/ *n* антропо́лог. **anthropology** /͵ænθrə'pɒlədʒɪ/ антрополо́гия.

anti-aircraft /͵æntɪ'eəkrɑːft/ *adj* зени́тный. **antibiotic** /͵æntɪbaɪ'ɒtɪk/ *n* антибио́тик. **antibody** /'æntɪ͵bɒdɪ/*n* антите́ло. **anticlimax** /-'klaɪmæks/*n* разочарова́ние. **anticlockwise** /-'klɒkwaɪz/ *adj* & *adv* про́тив часово́й стре́лки. **antidepressant** /-dɪ'pres(ə)nt/ *n* антидепресса́нт. **antidote** /'æntɪ͵dəʊt/ *n* противоя́дие. **antifreeze** /'æntɪ͵friːz/ *n* антифри́з.

antipathy /æn'tɪpəθɪ/ *n* антипа́тия. **anti-Semitic** /͵æntɪsɪ'mɪtɪk/ *adj* антисеми́тский. **anti-Semitism** /͵æntɪ'semɪ͵tɪz(ə)m/ *n* антисемити́зм. **antiseptic** /͵æntɪ'septɪk/ *adj* антисепти́ческий; *n* антисе́птик. **antisocial** /͵æntɪ'səʊʃ(ə)l/*adj* асоциа́льный. **anti-tank** /͵æntɪ'tæŋk/*adj* противота́нковый. **antithesis** /æn'tɪθɪsɪs/ *n* противополо́жность; (*philos*) антите́зис.

anticipate /æn'tɪsɪ͵peɪt/ *vt* ожида́ть *impf* +*gen*; (*with pleasure*) предвкуша́ть *impf*, предвкуси́ть *pf*; (*forestall*) предупрежда́ть *impf*, предупреди́ть *pf*. **anticipation** /-'peɪʃ(ə)n/ *n* ожида́ние; предвкуше́ние; предупрежде́ние.

antics /'æntɪks/ *n* вы́ходки *f pl*.

antiquarian /͵æntɪ'kweərɪən/ *adj* антиква́рный. **antiquated** /'æntɪ͵kweɪtɪd/ *adj* устаре́лый. **antique** /æn'tiːk/ *adj* стари́нный; *n* антиква́рная вещь; ~ **shop** антиква́рный магази́н. **antiquity** /æn'tɪkwɪtɪ/ *n* дре́вность.

antler /'æntlə(r)/ *n* оле́ний рог.

anus /'eɪnəs/ *n* за́дний прохо́д.

anvil /'ænvɪl/ *n* накова́льня.

anxiety /æŋ'zaɪətɪ/ *n* беспоко́йство. **anxious** /'æŋkʃ(ə)s/ *adj* беспоко́йный; **be** ~ беспоко́иться *impf*; трево́житься *impf*.

any /'enɪ/ *adj*, *pron* (*some*) како́й-нибудь; ско́лько-нибудь; (*every*) вся́кий, любо́й; (*anybody*) кто́-нибудь, (*anything*) что́-нибудь; (*with neg*) никако́й, ни оди́н; ниско́лько; никто́, ничто́; *adv* ско́лько-нибудь; (*with neg*) ниско́лько, ничу́ть. **anybody, anyone** *pron* кто́-нибудь; (*everybody*) вся́кий, любо́й; (*with neg*) никто́. **anyhow** *adv* ка́к-нибудь; ко́е-как; (*with neg*) ника́к; *conj* во вся́ком слу́чае; всё равно́. **anyone** *see* **anybody**. **anything** *pron* что́-нибудь; всё (что уго́дно); (*with neg*) ничего́. **anyway** *adv* во вся́ком слу́чае; как бы то ни́ было. **anywhere** *adv* где/куда́ уго́дно; (*with neg, interrog*) где́-нибудь, куда́-нибудь.

apart /ə'pɑ:t/ *adv* (*aside*) в стороне́, в сто́рону; (*separately*) врозь; (*distant*) друг от дру́га; (*into pieces*) на ча́сти; **~ from** кро́ме+*gen*.

apartheid /ə'pɑ:teɪt/ *n* апарте́йд.

apartment /ə'pɑ:tmənt/ *n* (*flat*) кварти́ра.

apathetic /ˌæpə'θetɪk/ *adj* апати́чный. **apathy** /'æpəθɪ/ *n* апа́тия.

ape /eɪp/ *n* обезья́на; *vt* обезья́нничать *impf*, с**~** *pf* с+*gen*.

aperture /'æpəˌtjʊə(r)/ *n* отве́рстие.

apex /'eɪpeks/ *n* верши́на.

aphorism /'æfəˌrɪz(ə)m/ *n* афори́зм.

apiece /ə'pi:s/ *adv* (*per person*) на ка́ждого; (*per thing*) за шту́ку; (*amount*) по+*dat or acc with numbers*.

aplomb /ə'plɒm/ *n* апло́мб.

Apocalypse /ə'pɒkəlɪps/ *n* Апока́липсис. **apocalyptic** /-'lɪptɪk/ *adj* апокалипти́ческий.

apologetic /əˌpɒlə'dʒetɪk/ *adj* извиня́ющийся; **be ~** извиня́ться *impf*. **apologize** /ə'pɒləˌdʒaɪz/ *vi* извиня́ться *impf*, извини́ться *pf* (**to** пе́ред +*instr*; **for** за+*acc*). **apology** /ə'pɒlədʒɪ/ *n* извине́ние.

apostle /ə'pɒs(ə)l/ *n* апо́стол.

apostrophe /ə'pɒstrəfɪ/ *n* апостро́ф.

appal /ə'pɔ:l/ *vi* ужаса́ть *impf*, ужасну́ть *pf*. **appalling** /-lɪŋ/ *adj* ужа́сный.

apparatus /ˌæpə'reɪtəs/ *n* аппара́т; прибо́р; (*gymnastic*) гимнасти́ческие снаря́ды *m pl*.

apparel /ə'pær(ə)l/ *n* одея́ние.

apparent /ə'pærənt/ *adj* (*seeming*) ви́димый; (*manifest*) очеви́дный. **apparently** /-lɪ/ *adv* ка́жется, по-ви́димому.

apparition /ˌæpə'rɪʃ(ə)n/ *n* виде́ние.

appeal /ə'pi:l/ *n* (*request*) призы́в, обраще́ние; (*law*) апелля́ция, обжа́лование; (*attraction*) привлека́тельность; **~ court** апелляцио́нный суд; *vi* (*request*) взыва́ть *impf*, воззва́ть *pf* (**to** к+*dat*; **for** о+*prep*); обраща́ться *impf*, обрати́ться *pf* (с призы́вом); (*law*) апелли́ровать *impf* & *pf*; **~ to** (*attract*) привлека́ть *impf*, привле́чь *pf*.

appear /ə'pɪə(r)/ *vi* появля́ться *impf*, появи́ться *pf*; (*in public*) выступа́ть *impf*, вы́ступить *pf*; (*seem*) каза́ться *impf*, по**~** *pf*. **appearance** /-rəns/ *n* появле́ние; выступле́ние; (*aspect*) вид.

appease /ə'pi:z/ *vt* умиротворя́ть *impf*, умиротвори́ть *pf*.

append /ə'pend/ *vt* прилага́ть *impf*, приложи́ть *pf*. **appendicitis** /əˌpendɪ'saɪtɪs/ *n* аппендици́т. **appendix** /ə'pendɪks/ *n* приложе́ние; (*anat*) аппенди́кс.

appertain /ˌæpə'teɪn/ *vi*: **~ to** относи́ться *impf* +*dat*.

appetite /'æpɪˌtaɪt/ *n* аппети́т. **appetizing** /-ˌtaɪzɪŋ/ *adj* аппети́тный.

applaud /ə'plɔ:d/ *vt* аплоди́ровать *impf* +*dat*. **applause** /-'plɔ:z/ *n* аплодисме́нты *m pl*.

apple /'æp(ə)l/ *n* я́блоко; *adj* я́блочный; **~ tree** я́блоня.

appliance /ə'plaɪəns/ *n* прибо́р. **applicable** /ə'plɪkəb(ə)l/ *adj* примени́мый. **applicant** /'æplɪkənt/ *n* кандида́т. **application** /ˌæplɪ'keɪʃ(ə)n/ *n* (*use*) примене́ние;

(*putting on*) наложе́ние; (*request*) заявле́ние. **applied** /ə'plaɪd/ *adj* прикладно́й. **apply** /ə'plaɪ/ *vt* (*use*) применя́ть *impf*, примени́ть *pf*; (*put on*) накла́дывать *impf*, наложи́ть *pf*; *vi* (*request*) обраща́ться *impf*, обрати́ться *pf* (**to** к+*dat*; **for** за +*acc*); **~ for** (*job*) подава́ть *impf*, пода́ть *pf* заявле́ние на+*acc*; **~ to** относи́ться *impf* к+*dat*.

appoint /ə'pɔɪnt/ *vt* назнача́ть *impf*, назна́чить *pf*. **appointment** /-mənt/ *n* назначе́ние; (*job*) до́лжность; (*meeting*) свида́ние.

apposite /'æpəzɪt/ *adj* уме́стный.

appraise /ə'preɪz/ *vt* оце́нивать *impf*, оцени́ть *pf*.

appreciable /ə'pri:ʃəb(ə)l/ *adj* заме́тный; (*considerable*) значи́тельный. **appreciate** /ə'pri:ʃɪˌeɪt/ *vt* цени́ть *impf*; (*understand*) понима́ть *impf*, поня́ть *pf*; *vi* повыша́ться *impf*, повы́ситься *pf* в цене́. **appreciation** /əˌpri:ʃɪ'eɪʃ(ə)n/ *n* (*estimation*) оце́нка; (*gratitude*) призна́тельность; (*rise in value*) повыше́ние цены́. **appreciative** /ə'pri:ʃətɪv/ *adj* призна́тельный (**of** за+*acc*).

apprehension /ˌæprɪ'henʃ(ə)n/ *n* (*fear*) опасе́ние. **apprehensive** /-'hensɪv/ *adj* опаса́ющийся.

apprentice /ə'prentɪs/ *n* учени́к; *vt* отдава́ть *impf*, отда́ть *pf* в уче́ние. **apprenticeship** /-ʃɪp/ *n* учени́чество.

approach /ə'prəʊtʃ/ *vt* & *i* подходи́ть *impf*, подойти́ *pf* (к+*dat*); приближа́ться *impf*, прибли́зиться *pf* (к+*dat*); *vt* (*apply to*) обраща́ться *impf*, обрати́ться *pf* к+*dat*; *n* приближе́ние; подхо́д; подъе́зд; (*access*) по́дступ.

approbation /ˌæprə'beɪʃ(ə)n/ *n* одобре́ние.

appropriate *adj* /ə'prəʊprɪət/ подходя́щий; *vt* /ə'prəʊprɪˌeɪt/ присва́ивать *impf*, присво́ить *pf*. **appropriation** /-'eɪʃ(ə)n/ *n* присвое́ние.

approval /ə'pru:v(ə)l/ *n* одобре́ние; **on ~** на про́бу. **approve** /ə'pru:v/ *vt* утвержда́ть *impf*, утверди́ть *pf*; *vt* & *i* (**~ of**) одобря́ть *impf*, одо́брить *pf*.

approximate *adj* /ə'prɒksɪmət/ приблизи́тельный; *vi* /ə'prɒksɪˌmeɪt/ приближа́ться *impf* (**to** к+*dat*). **approximation** /əˌprɒksɪ'meɪʃ(ə)n/ *n* приближе́ние.

apricot /'eɪprɪˌkɒt/ *n* абрико́с.

April /'eɪpr(ə)l/ *n* апре́ль *m*; *adj* апре́льский.

apron /'eɪprən/ *n* пере́дник.

apropos /'æprəˌpəʊ/ *adv*: **~ of** по по́воду+*gen*.

apt /æpt/ *adj* (*suitable*) уда́чный; (*inclined*) скло́нный. **aptitude** /'æptɪˌtju:d/ *n* спосо́бность.

aqualung /'ækwəˌlʌŋ/ *n* аквала́нг. **aquarium** /ə'kweərɪəm/ *n* аква́риум. **Aquarius** /ə'kweərɪəs/ *n* Водоле́й. **aquatic** /ə'kwætɪk/ *adj* водяно́й; (*of sport*) во́дный. **aqueduct** /'ækwɪˌdʌkt/ *n* акведу́к.

aquiline /'ækwɪˌlaɪn/ *adj* орли́ный.

Arab /'ærəb/ *n* ара́б, **~**ка; *adj* ара́бский. **Arabian** /ə'reɪbɪən/ *adj* арави́йский. **Arabic** /'ærəbɪk/ *adj* ара́бский.

arable /'ærəb(ə)l/ *adj* па́хотный.

arbitrary /'ɑ:bɪtrərɪ/ *adj* произво́льный. **arbitrate** /-ˌtreɪt/ *vi* де́йствовать *impf* в ка́честве трете́йского судьи́. **arbitration**

/-ˈtreɪʃ(ə)n/ *n* арбитра́ж, трете́йское реше́ние. **arbitrator** /-ˌtreɪtə(r)/ *n* арби́тр, трете́йский судья́ *m*.

arc /ɑ:k/ *n* дуга́. **arcade** /ɑ:ˈkeɪd/ *n* арка́да, (*shops*) пасса́ж.

arch¹ /ɑ:tʃ/ *n* а́рка, свод; (*of foot*) свод стопы́; *vt* & *i* выгиба́ть(ся) *impf*, вы́гнуть(ся) *pf*.

arch² /ɑ:tʃ/ *adj* игри́вый.

archaeological /ˌɑ:kɪəˈlɒdʒɪk(ə)l/ *adj* археологи́ческий. **archaeologist** /ˌɑ:kɪˈɒlədʒɪst/ *n* архео́лог. **archaeology** /ˌɑ:kɪˈɒlədʒɪ/ *n* археоло́гия.

archaic /ɑ:ˈkeɪɪk/ *adj* архаи́ческий.

archangel /ˈɑ:kˌeɪndʒ(ə)l/ *n* арха́нгел.

archbishop /ɑ:tʃˈbɪʃəp/ *n* архиепи́скоп.

arched /ɑ:tʃt/ *adj* сво́дчатый.

arch-enemy /ɑ:tʃˈenəmɪ/ *n* закля́тый враг.

archer /ˈɑ:tʃə(r)/ *n* стрело́к из лу́ка. **archery** /-rɪ/ *n* стрельба́ из лу́ка.

archipelago /ˌɑ:kɪˈpeləˌgəʊ/ *n* архипела́г.

architect /ˈɑ:kɪˌtekt/ *n* архите́ктор. **architectural** /-ˈtektʃər(ə)l/ *adj* архитекту́рный. **architecture** /ˈɑ:kɪˌtektʃə(r)/ *n* архитекту́ра.

archive(s) /ˈɑ:kaɪv(z)/ *n* архи́в.

archway /ˈɑ:tʃweɪ/*n* сво́дчатый прохо́д.

Arctic /ˈɑ:ktɪk/ *adj* аркти́ческий; *n* А́рктика.

ardent /ˈɑ:d(ə)nt/ *adj* горя́чий. **ardour** /ˈɑ:də(r)/ *n* пыл.

arduous /ˈɑ:djʊəs/ *adj* тру́дный.

area /ˈeərɪə/ *n* (*extent*) пло́щадь; (*region*) райо́н; (*sphere*) о́бласть.

arena /əˈri:nə/ *n* аре́на.

argue /ˈɑ:gju:/ *vt* (*maintain*) утвержда́ть *impf*; дока́зывать *impf*; *vi* спо́рить *impf*, по~ *pf*. **argument** /-mənt/ *n* (*dispute*) спор; (*reason*) до́вод. **argumentative** /ˌɑ:gju:ˈmentətɪv/ *adj* лю́бящий спо́рить.

aria /ˈɑ:rɪə/ *n* а́рия.

arid /ˈærɪd/ *adj* сухо́й.

Aries /ˈeəri:z/ *n* Ове́н.

arise /əˈraɪz/ *vi* возника́ть *impf*, возни́кнуть *pf*.

aristocracy /ˌærɪˈstɒkrəsɪ/ *n* аристокра́тия. **aristocrat** /ˈærɪstəˌkræt/ *n* аристокра́т, ~ка. **aristocratic** /ˌærɪstəˈkrætɪk/ *adj* аристократи́ческий.

arithmetic /əˈrɪθmətɪk/ *n* арифме́тика. **arithmetical** /ˌærɪθˈmetɪk(ə)l/ *adj* арифмети́ческий.

ark /ɑ:k/ *n* (Но́ев) ковче́г.

arm¹ /ɑ:m/ *n* (*of body*) рука́; (*of chair*) ру́чка; **~ in ~** под ру́ку; **at ~'s length** (*fig*) на почти́тельном расстоя́нии; **with open ~s** с распростёртыми объя́тиями.

arm² /ɑ:m/ *n pl* (*weapons*) ору́жие; *vt* вооружа́ть *impf*, вооружи́ть *pf*. **armaments** /ˈɑ:məmənts/ *n pl* вооруже́ние.

armchair /ˈɑ:mtʃeə(r)/ *n* кре́сло.

Armenia /ɑ:ˈmi:nɪə/ *n* Арме́ния. **Armenian** /-ən/ *n* армяни́н, армя́нка; *adj* армя́нский.

armistice /ˈɑ:mɪstɪs/ *n* переми́рие.

armour /ˈɑ:mə(r)/ *n* (*for body*) доспе́хи *m pl*; (*for vehicles*; *fig*) броня́. **armoured** /ˈɑ:məd/ *adj* брониро́ванный; (*vehicles etc.*) бронета́нковый, броне-; **~ car** броневи́к. **armoury** /ˈɑ:mərɪ/ *n* арсена́л.

armpit /ˈɑ:mpɪt/ *n* подмы́шка.

army /ˈɑ:mɪ/ *n* а́рмия; *adj* арме́йский.

aroma /ə'rəumə/ *n* арома́т. **aromatherapy** /ər,əumə'θerəpɪ/ *n* ароматерапи́я **aromatic** /,ærə'mætɪk/ *adj* аромати́чный.

around /ə'raund/ *adv* круго́м; *prep* вокру́г+*gen*; **all ~** повсю́ду.

arouse /ə'rauz/ *vt* (*wake up*) буди́ть *impf*, раз~ *pf*; (*stimulate*) возбужда́ть *impf*, возбуди́ть *pf*.

arrange /ə'reɪndʒ/ *vt* расставля́ть *impf*, расста́вить *pf*; (*plan*) устра́ивать *impf*, устро́ить *pf*; (*mus*) аранжи́ровать *impf* & *pf*; *vi*: **~ to** догова́риваться *impf*, договори́ться *pf* +*inf*. **arrangement** /-mənt/ *n* расположе́ние; устро́йство; (*agreement*) соглаше́ние; (*mus*) аранжиро́вка; *pl* приготовле́ния *neut pl*.

array /ə'reɪ/ *vt* выставля́ть *impf*, вы́ставить *pf*; *n* (*dress*) наря́д; (*display*) колле́кция.

arrears /ə'rɪəz/ *n pl* задо́лженность.

arrest /ə'rest/ *vt* аресто́вывать *impf*, арестова́ть *pf*; *n* аре́ст.

arrival /ə'raɪv(ə)l/ *n* прибы́тие, прие́зд; (*new* ~) вновь прибы́вший *sb*. **arrive** /ə'raɪv/ *vi* прибыва́ть *impf*, прибы́ть *pf*; приезжа́ть *impf*, прие́хать *pf*.

arrogance /'ærəgəns/ *n* высокоме́рие. **arrogant** /-gənt/ *adj* высокоме́рный.

arrow /'ærəu/ *n* стрела́; (*pointer*) стре́лка.

arsenal /'ɑ:sən(ə)l/ *n* арсена́л.

arsenic /'ɑ:sənɪk/ *n* мышья́к.

arson /'ɑ:s(ə)n/ *n* поджо́г.

art /ɑ:t/ *n* иску́сство; *pl* гуманита́рные нау́ки *f pl*; *adj* худо́жественный.

arterial /ɑ:'tɪərɪəl/ *adj*: **~ road** магистра́ль. **artery** /'ɑ:tərɪ/ *n* арте́рия.

artful /'ɑ:tfʊl/ *adj* хи́трый.

arthritis /ɑ:'θraɪtɪs/ *n* артри́т.

article /'ɑ:tɪk(ə)l/ *n* (*literary*) статья́; (*clause*) пункт; (*thing*) предме́т; (*gram*) арти́кль *m*.

articulate *vt* /ɑ:'tɪkjʊ,leɪt/ произноси́ть *impf*, произнести́ *pf*; (*express*) выража́ть *impf*, вы́разить *pf*; *adj* /ɑ:'tɪkjʊlət/ (*of speech*) членоразде́льный; **be ~** чётко выража́ть *impf* свои́ мы́сли. **articulated lorry** /ɑ:'tɪkjʊ,leɪtɪd 'lɒrɪ/ *n* грузово́й автомоби́ль с прице́пом.

artifice /'ɑ:tɪfɪs/ *n* хи́трость. **artificial** /,ɑ:tɪ'fɪʃ(ə)l/ *adj* иску́сственный.

artillery /ɑ:'tɪlərɪ/ *n* артилле́рия.

artisan /,ɑ:tɪ'zæn/ *n* ремéсленник.

artist /'ɑ:tɪst/ *n* худо́жник. **artiste** /ɑ:'ti:st/ *n* арти́ст, ~ка. **artistic** /ɑ:'tɪstɪk/ *adj* худо́жественный.

artless /'ɑ:tlɪs/ *adj* простоду́шный.

as /æz, əz/ *adv* как; *conj* (*when*) когда́; в то вре́мя как; (*because*) так как; (*manner*) как; (*though, however*) как ни; *rel pron* како́й; кото́рый; что; **as ... as** так (же)... как; **as for, to** относи́тельно+*gen*; что каса́ется +*gen*; **as if** как бу́дто; **as it were** ка́к бы; так сказа́ть; **as soon as** как то́лько; **as well** та́кже; то́же.

asbestos /æs'bestɒs/ *n* асбе́ст.

ascend /ə'send/ *vt* (*go up*) поднима́ться *impf*, подня́ться *pf* по+*dat*; (*throne*) всходи́ть *impf*, взойти́ *pf* на+*acc*; *vi* возноси́ться *impf*, вознести́сь *pf*. **ascendancy** /ə'send(ə)nsɪ/ *n*

власть. **Ascension** /ə'senʃ(ə)n/ *n* (*eccl*) Вознесе́ние. **ascent** /ə'sent/ *n* восхожде́ние (**of** на+*acc*).
ascertain /ˌæsə'teɪn/ *vt* устана́вливать *impf*, установи́ть *pf*.
ascetic /ə'setɪk/ *adj* аскети́ческий; *n* аске́т. **asceticism** /ə'setɪˌsɪz(ə)m/ *n* аскети́зм.
ascribe /ə'skraɪb/ *vt* припи́сывать *impf*, приписа́ть *pf* (**to** +*dat*).
ash[1] /æʃ/ *n* (*tree*) я́сень *m*.
ash[2] /æʃ/, **ashes** /'æʃɪz/ *n* зола́, пе́пел; (*human remains*) прах. **ashtray** *n* пе́пельница.
ashamed /ə'ʃeɪmd/ *predic*: **he is** ~ ему́ сты́дно; **be, feel,** ~ **of** стыди́ться *impf*, по~ *pf* +*gen*.
ashen /'æʃ(ə)n/ *adj* (*pale*) ме́ртвенно-бле́дный.
ashore /ə'ʃɔː(r)/ *adv* на бе́рег(ý).
Asia /'eɪʃə/ *n* А́зия. **Asian, Asiatic** /'eɪʃ(ə)n, ˌeɪʃɪ'ætɪk/ *adj* азиа́тский; *n* азиа́т, ~ка.
aside /ə'saɪd/ *adv* в сто́рону.
ask /ɑːsk/ *vt* & *i* (*enquire of*) спра́шивать *impf*, спроси́ть *pf*; (*request*) проси́ть *impf*, по~ *pf* (**for** *acc*, *gen*, о+*prep*); (*invite*) приглаша́ть *impf*, пригласи́ть *pf*; (*demand*) тре́бовать *impf* +*gen* (**of** от+*gen*); ~ **after** осведомля́ться *impf*, осве́домиться *pf* о+*prep*; ~ **a question** задава́ть *impf*, зада́ть *pf* вопро́с.
askance /ə'skɑːns/ *adv* ко́со.
askew /ə'skjuː/ *adv* кри́во.
asleep /ə'sliːp/ *predic* & *adv*: **be** ~ спать *impf*; **fall** ~ засыпа́ть *impf*, засну́ть *pf*.
asparagus /ə'spærəgəs/ *n* спа́ржа.
aspect /'æspekt/ *n* вид; (*side*) сторона́.
aspersion /ə'spɜːʃ(ə)n/ *n* клевета́.
asphalt /'æsfælt/ *n* асфа́льт.
asphyxiate /æs'fɪksɪˌeɪt/ *vt* удуша́ть *impf*, удуши́ть.
aspiration /ˌæspɪ'reɪʃ(ə)n/ *n* стремле́ние. **aspire** /ə'spaɪə(r)/ *vi* стреми́ться *impf* (**to** к+*dat*).
aspirin /'æsprɪn/ *n* аспири́н; (*tablet*) табле́тка аспири́на.
ass /æs/ *n* осёл.
assail /ə'seɪl/ *vt* напада́ть *impf*, напа́сть *pf* на+*acc*; (*with questions*) забра́сывать *impf*, заброса́ть *pf* вопро́сами. **assailant** /-lənt/ *n* напада́ющий *sb*.
assassin /ə'sæsɪn/ *n* уби́йца *m* & *f*. **assassinate** /-ˌneɪt/ *vt* убива́ть *impf*, уби́ть *pf*. **assassination** /-'neɪʃ(ə)n/ *n* уби́йство.
assault /ə'sɔːlt/ *n* нападе́ние; (*mil*) штурм; ~ **and battery** оскорбле́ние де́йствием; *vt* напада́ть *impf*, напа́сть *pf* на+*acc*.
assemblage /ə'semblɪdʒ/ *n* сбо́рка. **assemble** /ə'semb(ə)l/ *vt* & *i* собира́ть(ся) *impf*, собра́ть(ся) *pf*. **assembly** /ə'semblɪ/ *n* собра́ние; (*of machine*) сбо́рка.
assent /ə'sent/ *vi* соглаша́ться *impf*, согласи́ться *pf* (**to** на+*acc*); *n* согла́сие.
assert /ə'sɜːt/ *vt* утвержда́ть *impf*; ~ **o.s.** отста́ивать *impf*, отстоя́ть *pf* свои́ права́. **assertion** /ə'sɜːʃ(ə)n/ *n* утвержде́ние. **assertive** /ə'sɜːtɪv/ *adj* насто́йчивый.
assess /ə'ses/ *vt* (*amount*) определя́ть *impf*, определи́ть *pf*; (*value*) оце́нивать *impf*, оцени́ть *pf*. **assessment** /-mənt/ *n* определе́ние; оце́нка.
asset /'æset/ *n* це́нное ка́чество; (*comm*; *also pl*) акти́в.

assiduous /ə'sɪdjʊəs/ *adj* прилéжный.

assign /ə'saɪn/ *vt* (*appoint*) назначáть *impf*, назнáчить *pf*; (*allot*) отводи́ть *impf*, отвести́ *pf*. **assignation** /ˌæsɪg'neɪʃ(ə)n/ *n* свидáние. **assignment** /ə'saɪnmənt/ *n* (*task*) задáние; (*mission*) командирóвка.

assimilate /ə'sɪmɪˌleɪt/ *vt* усвáивать *impf*, усвóить *pf*. **assimilation** /-'leɪʃ(ə)n/ *n* усвоéние.

assist /ə'sɪst/ *vt* помогáть *impf*, помóчь *pf* +*dat*. **assistance** /-təns/ *n* пóмощь. **assistant** /-tənt/ *n* помóщник, ассистéнт.

associate *vt* /ə'səʊsɪˌeɪt/ ассоции́ровать *impf* & *pf*; *vi* общáться *impf* (**with** с+*instr*); *n* /ə'səʊʃɪət/ коллéга *m* & *f*. **association** /əˌsəʊsɪ'eɪʃ(ə)n/ *n* óбщество, ассоциáция.

assorted /ə'sɔːtɪd/ *adj* рáзный. **assortment** /ə'sɔːtmənt/ *n* ассортимéнт.

assuage /ə'sweɪdʒ/ *vt* (*calm*) успокáивать *impf*, успокóить *pf*; (*alleviate*) смягчáть *impf*, смягчи́ть *pf*.

assume /ə'sjuːm/ *vt* (*take on*) принимáть *impf*, приня́ть *pf*; (*suppose*) предпологáть *impf*, предположи́ть *pf*; **~d name** вы́мышленное и́мя *neut*; **let us ~** допу́стим. **assumption** /ə'sʌmpʃ(ə)n/ *n* (*taking on*) принятие на себé; (*supposition*) предположéние.

assurance /ə'ʃʊərəns/ *n* заверéние; (*self-~*) самоувéренность. **assure** /ə'ʃʊə(r)/ *vt* уверя́ть *impf*, увéрить *pf*.

asterisk /'æstərɪsk/ *n* звёздочка.

asthma /'æsmə/ *n* áстма. **asthmatic** /æs'mætɪk/ *adj* астматический.

astonish /ə'stɒnɪʃ/ *vt* удивля́ть *impf*, удиви́ть *pf*. **astonishing** /-ʃɪŋ/ *adj* удиви́тельный. **astonishment** /-mənt/ *n* удивлéние.

astound /ə'staʊnd/ *vt* изумля́ть *impf*, изуми́ть *pf*. **astounding** /-dɪŋ/ *adj* изуми́тельный.

astray /ə'streɪ/ *adv*: **go ~** сбивáться *impf*, сби́ться *pf* с пути́; **lead ~** сбивáть *impf*, сбить *pf* с пути́.

astride /ə'straɪd/ *prep* верхóм на+*prep*.

astringent /ə'strɪndʒ(ə)nt/ *adj* вя́жущий; тéрпкий.

astrologer /ə'strɒlədʒə(r)/ *n* астрóлог. **astrology** /-dʒɪ/ *n* астролóгия. **astronaut** /'æstrəˌnɔːt/ *n* астронáвт. **astronomer** /ə'strɒnəmə(r)/ *n* астронóм. **astronomical** /ˌæstrə'nɒmɪk(ə)l/ *adj* астрономи́ческий. **astronomy** /ə'strɒnəmɪ/ *n* астронóмия.

astute /ə'stjuːt/ *adj* проницáтельный.

asunder /ə'sʌndə(r)/ *adv* (*apart*) врозь; (*in pieces*) на чáсти.

asylum /ə'saɪləm/ *n* сумасшéдший дом; (*refuge*) убéжище; **~ seeker** претендéнт, **~**ка на получéние (полити́ческого) убéжища.

asymmetrical /ˌeɪsɪ'metrɪk(ə)l/ *adj* асимметри́чный.

at /æt, *unstressed* ət/ *prep* (*position*) на+*prep*, в+*prep*, у+*gen*: **at a concert** на концéрте; **at the cinema** в кинó; **at the window** у окнá; (*time*) в+*acc*: **at two o'clock** в два часá; на+*acc*: **at Easter** на Пáсху; (*price*) по+*dat*: **at 5p a pound** по пяти́ пéнсов за фунт; (*speed*): **at 60 mph** со скóростью шестьдеся́т миль в час; **~ first** снача́ла, сперва́; ~ **home** до́ма; ~ **last** наконе́ц; ~ **least** по кра́йней ме́ре; ~ **that** на том; (*moreover*) к тому́ же.

atheism /ˈeɪθɪˌɪz(ə)m/ *n* атеи́зм. **atheist** /-ɪst/ *n* атеи́ст, ~ка.

athlete /ˈæθliːt/ *n* спортсме́н, ~ка. **athletic** /æθˈletɪk/ *adj* атлети́ческий. **athletics** /æθˈletɪks/ *n* (лёгкая) атле́тика.

atlas /ˈætləs/ *n* а́тлас.

atmosphere /ˈætməsˌfɪə(r)/ *n* атмосфе́ра. **atmospheric** /ˌætməsˈferɪk/ *adj* атмосфе́рный.

atom /ˈætəm/ *n* а́том; ~ **bomb** а́томная бо́мба. **atomic** /əˈtɒmɪk/ *adj* а́томный.

atone /əˈtəʊn/ *vi* искупа́ть *impf*, искупи́ть *pf* (**for** +*acc*). **atonement** /-mənt/ *n* искупле́ние.

atrocious /əˈtrəʊʃəs/ *adj* ужа́сный. **atrocity** /əˈtrɒsɪtɪ/ *n* зве́рство.

attach /əˈtætʃ/ *vt* (*fasten*) прикрепля́ть *impf*, прикрепи́ть *pf*; (*append*) прилага́ть *impf*, приложи́ть *pf*; (*attribute*) придава́ть *impf*, прида́ть *pf*; **attached to** (*devoted*) привя́занный к+*dat*. **attaché** /əˈtæʃeɪ/ *n* атташе́ *m indecl*. **attachment** /əˈtætʃmənt/ *n* прикрепле́ние; привя́занность; (*tech*) принадле́жность.

attack /əˈtæk/ *vt* напада́ть *impf*, напа́сть *pf* на+*acc*; *n* нападе́ние; (*of illness*) припа́док.

attain /əˈteɪn/ *vt* достига́ть *impf*, дости́чь & дости́гнуть *pf* +*gen*. **attainment** /-mənt/ *n* достиже́ние.

attempt /əˈtempt/ *vt* пыта́ться *impf*, по~ *pf* +*inf*; *n* попы́тка.

attend /əˈtend/ *vt* & *i* (*be present at*) прису́тствовать *impf* (на +*prep*); *vt* (*accompany*) сопровожда́ть *impf*, сопроводи́ть *pf*; (*go to regularly*) посеща́ть *impf*, посети́ть *pf*; ~ **to** занима́ться *impf*, заня́ться *pf*. **attendance** /-dəns/ *n* (*presence*) прису́тствие; (*number*) посеща́емость. **attendant** /-dənt/ *adj* сопровожда́ющий; *n* дежу́рный *sb*; (*escort*) провожа́тый *sb*.

attention /əˈtenʃ(ə)n/ *n* внима́ние; **pay** ~ обраща́ть *impf*, обрати́ть *pf* внима́ние (**to** на+*acc*); *int* (*mil*) сми́рно! **attentive** /əˈtentɪv/ *adj* внима́тельный; (*solicitous*) забо́тливый.

attest /əˈtest/ *vt* & *i* (*also* ~ **to**) заверя́ть *impf*, заве́рить *pf*; свиде́тельствовать *impf*, за~ *pf* (о+*prep*).

attic /ˈætɪk/ *n* черда́к.

attire /əˈtaɪə(r)/ *vt* наряжа́ть *impf*, наряди́ть *pf*; *n* наря́д.

attitude /ˈætɪˌtjuːd/ *n* (*posture*) по́за; (*opinion*) отноше́ние (**towards** к+*dat*).

attorney /əˈtɜːnɪ/ *n* пове́ренный *sb*; **power of** ~ дове́ренность.

attract /əˈtrækt/ *vt* привлека́ть *impf*, привле́чь *pf*. **attraction** /əˈtrækʃ(ə)n/ *n* привлека́тельность; (*entertainment*) аттракцио́н. **attractive** /-tɪv/ *adj* привлека́тельный.

attribute *vt* /əˈtrɪbjuːt/ припи́сывать *impf*, приписа́ть *pf*; *n* /ˈætrɪˌbjuːt/ (*quality*) сво́йство. **attribution** /ˌætrɪˈbjuːʃ(ə)n/ *n* /ˈætrɪˌbjuːt/ припи́сывание. **attributive** /əˈtrɪbjuːtɪv/ *adj* атрибути́вный.

attrition /əˈtrɪʃ(ə)n/ *n*: **war of** ~ война́ на истоще́ние.

aubergine /ˈəʊbəˌʒiːn/ *n* баклажа́н.

auburn /ˈɔːbən/ *adj* тёмно-ры́жий.

auction /'ɔːkʃ(ə)n/ *n* аукцио́н; *vt* продава́ть *impf*, прода́ть *pf* с аукцио́на. **auctioneer** /ˌɔːkʃə'nɪə(r)/ *n* аукциони́ст.

audacious /ɔː'deɪʃəs/ *adj* (*bold*) сме́лый; (*impudent*) де́рзкий. **audacity** /ɔː'dæsɪtɪ/ *n* сме́лость; де́рзость.

audible /'ɔːdɪb(ə)l/ *adj* слы́шный. **audience** /'ɔːdɪəns/ *n* пу́блика, аудито́рия; (*listeners*) слу́шатели *m pl*, (*viewers, spectators*) зри́тели *m pl*; (*interview*) аудие́нция. **audit** /'ɔːdɪt/ *n* прове́рка счето́в, реви́зия; *vt* проверя́ть *impf*, прове́рить *pf* (счета́+*gen*). **audition** /ɔː'dɪʃ(ə)n/ *n* про́ба; *vt* устра́ивать *impf*, устро́ить *pf* про́бу +*gen*. **auditor** /'ɔːdɪtə(r)/ *n* ревизо́р. **auditorium** /ˌɔːdɪ'tɔːrɪəm/ *n* зри́тельный зал.

augment /ɔːg'ment/ *n* увели́чивать *impf*, увели́чить *pf*.

augur /'ɔːgə(r)/ *vt* & *i* предвеща́ть *impf*.

August /'ɔːgəst/ *n* а́вгуст; *adj* а́вгустовский. **august** /ɔː'gʌst/ *adj* вели́чественный.

aunt /ɑːnt/ *n* тётя, тётка.

au pair /əʊ 'peə(r)/ *n* домрабо́тница иностра́нного происхожде́ния.

aura /'ɔːrə/ *n* орео́л.

auspices /'ɔːspɪsɪz/ *n pl* покрови́тельство. **auspicious** /ɔː'spɪʃ(ə)s/ *adj* благоприя́тный.

austere /ɒ'stɪə(r)/ *adj* стро́гий. **austerity** /ɒ'sterɪtɪ/ *n* стро́гость.

Australia /ɒ'streɪlɪə/ *n* Австра́лия. **Australian** /-ən/ *n* австрали́ец, -и́йка; *adj* австрали́йский.

Austria /'ɒstrɪə/ *n* А́встрия. **Austrian** /-ən/ *n* австри́ец, -и́йка; *adj* австри́йский.

authentic /ɔː'θentɪk/ *adj* по́длинный. **authenticate** /-ˌkeɪt/ *vt* устана́вливать *impf*, установи́ть *pf* по́длинность+*gen*. **authenticity** /-'tɪsɪtɪ/ *n* по́длинность.

author /'ɔːθə(r)/ *n* а́втор.

authoritarian /ɔːˌθɒrɪ'teərɪən/ *adj* авторита́рный. **authoritative** /ɔː'θɒrɪtətɪv/ *adj* авторите́тный. **authority** /ɔː'θɒrɪtɪ/ *n* (*power*) власть, полномо́чие; (*weight; expert*) авторите́т; (*source*) авторите́тный исто́чник. **authorization** /ˌɔːθəraɪ'zeɪʃ(ə)n/ *n* уполномо́чивание; (*permission*) разреше́ние. **authorize** /'ɔːθəˌraɪz/ *vt* (*action*) разреша́ть *impf*, разреши́ть *pf*; (*person*) уполномо́чивать *impf*, уполномо́чить *pf*.

authorship /'ɔːθəʃɪp/ *n* а́вторство.

autobiographical /ˌɔːtəʊˌbaɪə'græfɪk(ə)l/ *adj* автобиографи́ческий. **autobiography** /ˌɔːtəʊbaɪ'ɒgrəfɪ/ *n* автобиогра́фия. **autocracy** /ɔː'tɒkrəsɪ/ *n* автокра́тия. **autocrat** /'ɔːtəˌkræt/ *n* автокра́т. **autocratic** /ˌɔːtə'krætɪk/ *adj* автократи́ческий. **autograph** /'ɔːtəˌgrɑːf/ *n* авто́граф. **automatic** /ˌɔːtə'mætɪk/ *adj* автомати́ческий. **automation** /ˌɔːtə'meɪʃ(ə)n/ *n* автоматиза́ция. **automaton** /ɔː'tɒmət(ə)n/ *n* автома́т. **automobile** /'ɔːtəməˌbiːl/ *n* автомоби́ль *m*. **autonomous** /ɔː'tɒnəməs/ *adj* автоно́мный. **autonomy** /ɔː'tɒnəmɪ/ *n* автоно́мия. **autopilot** /'ɔːtəʊˌpaɪlət/ *n* автопило́т. **autopsy** /'ɔːtɒpsɪ/ *n* вскры́тие; ауто́псия.

autumn /'ɔːtəm/ *n* о́сень. **autumn(al)** /ɔː'tʌmn(ə)l/ *adj* осе́нний.

auxiliary /ɔːg'zɪljərɪ/ *adj* вспомога́тельный; *n* помо́щник,

-ица.
avail /ə'veɪl/ *n*: **to no ~** напрáсно; *vt*: **~ o.s. of** пóльзоваться *impf*, вос~ *pf* +*instr*. **available** /-ləb(ə)l/ *adj* достýпный, налúчный.
avalanche /'ævə,lɑːntʃ/ *n* лавúна.
avant-garde /,ævɑ̃'gɑːd/ *n* авангáрд; *adj* авангáрдный.
avarice /'ævərɪs/ *n* жáдность. **avaricious** /-'rɪʃ(ə)s/ *adj* жáдный.
avenge /ə'vendʒ/ *vt* мстить *impf*, ото~ *pf* за+*acc*. **avenger** /-dʒə(r)/ *n* мстúтель *m*.
avenue /'ævə,njuː/ *n* (*of trees*) аллéя; (*wide street*) проспéкт; (*means*) путь *m*.
average /'ævərɪdʒ/ *n* срéднее числó, срéднее *sb*; **on ~** в срéднем; *adj* срéдний; *vt* дéлать *impf* в срéднем; *vt* & *i*: **~ (out at)** составлять *impf*, состáвить *pf* в срéднем.
averse /ə'vɜːs/ *adj*: **not ~ to** не прочь +*inf*, не прóтив+*gen*. **aversion** /ə'vɜːʃ(ə)n/ *n* отвращéние. **avert** /ə'vɜːt/ *vt* (*ward off*) предотвращáть *impf*, предотвратúть *pf*; (*turn away*) отводúть *impf*, отвестú *pf*.
aviary /'eɪvɪərɪ/ *n* птúчник.
aviation /,eɪvɪ'eɪʃ(ə)n/ *n* авиáция.
avid /'ævɪd/ *adj* жáдный; (*keen*) стрáстный.
avocado /,ævə'kɑːdəʊ/ *n* авокáдо *neut indecl*.
avoid /ə'vɔɪd/ *vt* избегáть *impf*, избежáть *pf* +*gen*; (*evade*) уклонáться *impf*, уклонúться *pf* от+*gen*. **avoidance** /-dəns/ *n* избежáние, уклонéние.
avowal /ə'vaʊ(ə)l/ *n* признáние. **avowed** /ə'vaʊd/ *adj* прúзнанный.
await /ə'weɪt/ *vt* ждать *impf* +*gen*.
awake /ə'weɪk/ *predic*: **be ~** не спать *impf*. **awake(n)** /-kən/ *vt* пробуждáть *impf*, пробудúть *pf*; *vi* просыпáться *impf*, проснýться *pf*.
award /ə'wɔːd/ *vt* присуждáть *impf*, присудúть *pf* (*person dat*, *thing acc*); награждáть *impf*, наградúть *pf* (*person acc*, *thing instr*); *n* нагрáда.
aware /ə'weə(r)/ *predic*: **be ~ of** сознавáть *impf*; знать *impf*. **awareness** /-n(ə)s/ *n* сознáние.
away /ə'weɪ/ *adv* прочь; **be ~** отсýтствовать *impf*; **far ~** (*from*) далекó (от+*gen*); **5 miles ~** в пятú мúлях отсюда; **~ game** игрá на чужóм пóле.
awe /ɔː/ *n* благоговéйный страх. **awful** /'ɔːfʊl/ *adj* ужáсный. **awfully** /'ɔːfʊlɪ/ *adv* ужáсно.
awhile /ə'waɪl/ *adv* нéкоторое врéмя.
awkward /'ɔːkwəd/ *adj* нелóвкий. **awkwardness** /-nɪs/ *n* нелóвкость.
awning /'ɔːnɪŋ/ *n* навéс, тент.
awry /ə'raɪ/ *adv* кóсо.
axe /æks/ *n* топóр; *vt* урéзывать, урезáть *impf*, урéзать *pf*.
axiom /'æksɪəm/ *n* аксиóма. **axiomatic** /-'mætɪk/ *adj* аксиоматúческий.
axis /'æksɪs/ *n* ось.
axle /'æks(ə)l/ *n* ось.
ay /aɪ/ *int* да!; *n* (*in vote*) гóлос «за».
Azerbaijan /,æzəbaɪ'dʒɑːn/ *n* Азербайджáн. **Azerbaijani** /-nɪ/ *n* азербайджáнец (-нца), -áнка; *adj* азербайджáнский.
azure /'æʒə(r)/ *n* лазýрь; *adj* лазýрный.

B

BA *abbr* (*univ*) бакала́вр.
babble /ˈbæb(ə)l/ *n* (*voices*) болтовня́; (*water*) журча́ние; *vi* болта́ть *impf*; (*water*) журча́ть *impf*.
baboon /bəˈbuːn/ *n* павиа́н.
baby /ˈbeɪbɪ/ *n* ребёнок; **~-sit** присма́тривать за детьми́ в отсу́тствие роди́телей; **~-sitter** приходя́щая ня́ня. **babyish** /ˈbeɪbɪɪʃ/ *adj* ребя́ческий.
bachelor /ˈbætʃələ(r)/ *n* холостя́к; (*univ*) бакала́вр.
bacillus /bəˈsɪləs/ *n* бацилла.
back /bæk/ *n* (*of body*) спина́; (*rear*) за́дняя часть; (*reverse*) оборо́т; (*of seat*) спи́нка; (*sport*) защи́тник; *adj* за́дний; *vt* (*support*) подде́рживать *impf*, поддержа́ть *pf*; (*car*) отодвига́ть *impf*, отодви́нуть *pf*; (*horse*) ста́вить *impf*, по~ *pf* на+*acc*; (*finance*) финанси́ровать *impf* & *pf*; *vi* отодвига́ться *impf*, отодви́нуться *pf* наза́д; **backed out of the garage** вы́ехал за́дом из гара́жа; **~ down** уступа́ть *impf*, уступи́ть *pf*; **~ out** уклоня́ться *impf*, уклони́ться *pf* (**of** от+*gen*); **~ up** (*support*) подде́рживать *impf*, поддержа́ть *pf*; (*confirm*) подкрепля́ть *impf*, подкрепи́ть *pf*. **backbiting** *n* спле́тня. **backbone** *n* позвоно́чник; (*support*) гла́вная опо́ра; (*firmness*) твёрдость хара́ктера. **backcloth, backdrop** *n* за́дник; (*fig*) фон. **backer** /ˈbækə(r)/ *n* спо́нсор; (*supporter*) сторо́нник. **backfire** *vi* дава́ть *impf*, дать *pf* отсе́чку. **background** *n* фон, за́дний план; (*person's*) происхожде́ние. **backhand(er)** *n* уда́р сле́ва. **backhanded** *adj* (*fig*) сомни́тельный. **backhander** *n* (*bribe*) взя́тка. **backing** /ˈbækɪŋ/ *n* подде́ржка. **backlash** *n* реа́кция. **backlog** *n* задо́лженность. **backside** *n* зад. **backstage** *adv* за кули́сами; *adj* закули́сный. **backstroke** *n* пла́вание на спине́. **backup** *n* подде́ржка; (*copy*) резе́рвная ко́пия; *adj* вспомога́тельный. **backward** /ˈbækwəd/ *adj* отста́лый. **backward(s)** /ˈbækwəd(z)/ *adv* наза́д. **backwater** *n* за́водь. **back yard** *n* за́дний двор.
bacon /ˈbeɪkən/ *n* беко́н.
bacterium /bækˈtɪərɪəm/ *n* бакте́рия.
bad /bæd/ *adj* плохо́й; (*food etc.*) испо́рченный; (*language*) гру́бый; **~-mannered** невоспи́танный; **~ taste** безвку́сица; **~-tempered** раздражи́тельный.
badge /bædʒ/ *n* значо́к.
badger /ˈbædʒə(r)/ *n* барсу́к; *vt* трави́ть *impf*, за~ *pf*.
badly /ˈbædlɪ/ *adv* пло́хо; (*very much*) о́чень.
badminton /ˈbædmɪnt(ə)n/ *n* бадминто́н.
baffle /ˈbæf(ə)l/ *vt* озада́чивать *impf*, озада́чить *pf*.
bag /bæg/ *n* (*handbag*) су́мка; (*plastic ~, sack, under eyes*) мешо́к; (*paper ~*) бума́жный паке́т; *pl* (*luggage*) бага́ж.
baggage /ˈbægɪdʒ/ *n* бага́ж.
baggy /ˈbægɪ/ *adj* мешкова́тый.
bagpipe /ˈbægpaɪp/ *n* волы́нка.
bail¹ /beɪl/ *n* (*security*) поручи́тельство; **release on ~** отпуска́ть *impf*, отпусти́ть *pf* на пору́ки; *vt* (**~ out**) брать *impf*, взять *pf* на пору́ки; (*help*) выруча́ть *impf*, вы́ручить *pf*.
bail² /beɪl/, **bale²** /beɪl/ *vt* вычер-

пывать *impf*, вы́черпнуть *pf* (во́ду из+*gen*); ~ **out** *vi* выбра́сываться *impf*, вы́броситься *pf* с парашю́том.
bailiff /ˈbeɪlɪf/ *n* суде́бный исполни́тель.
bait /beɪt/ *n* нажи́вка; прима́нка (*also fig*); *vt* (*torment*) трави́ть *impf*, за~ *pf*.
bake /beɪk/ *vt* & *i* пе́чь(ся) *impf*, ис~ *pf*. **baker** /ˈbeɪkə(r)/ *n* пе́карь *m*, бу́лочник. **bakery** /ˈbeɪkərɪ/ *n* пека́рня; (*shop*) бу́лочная *sb*.
balalaika /ˌbæləˈlaɪkə/ *n* балала́йка.
balance /ˈbæləns/ *n* (*scales*) весы́ *m pl*; (*equilibrium*) равнове́сие; (*econ*) бала́нс; (*remainder*) оста́ток; ~ **sheet** бала́нс; *vt* (*make equal*) уравнове́шивать *impf*, уравнове́сить *pf*; *vt* & *i* (*econ*; *hold steady*) баланси́ровать *impf*, с~ *pf*.
balcony /ˈbælkənɪ/ *n* балко́н.
bald /bɔːld/ *adj* лы́сый; ~ **patch** лы́сина. **balding** /ˈbɔːldɪŋ/ *adj* лысе́ющий. **baldness** /ˈbɔːldnɪs/ *n* плеши́вость.
bale[1] /beɪl/ *n* (*bundle*) ки́па.
bale[2] /beɪl/ *see* **bail**[2]
balk /bɔːlk/ *vi* арта́читься *impf*, за~ *pf*; **she balked at the price** цена́ её испуга́ла.
ball[1] /bɔːl/ *n* (*in games*) мяч; (*sphere*; *billiards*) шар; (*wool*) клубо́к; ~**-bearing** шарикоподши́пник; ~**-point (pen)** ша́риковая ру́чка.
ball[2] /bɔːl/ *n* (*dance*) бал.
ballad /ˈbæləd/ *n* балла́да.
ballast /ˈbæləst/ *n* балла́ст.
ballerina /ˌbæləˈriːnə/ *n* балери́на.
ballet /ˈbæleɪ/ *n* бале́т. **ballet-dancer** *n* арти́ст, ~ка, бале́та.
balloon /bəˈluːn/ *n* возду́шный шар.
ballot /ˈbælət/ *n* голосова́ние. **ballot-paper** *n* избира́тельный бюллете́нь *m*; *vt* держа́ть *impf* голосова́ние между́+*instr*.
balm /bɑːm/ *n* бальза́м. **balmy** /ˈbɑːmɪ/ *adj* (*soft*) мя́гкий.
Baltic /ˈbɔːltɪk/ *n* Балти́йское мо́ре; ~ **States** прибалти́йские госуда́рства, Приба́лтика.
balustrade /ˌbæləˈstreɪd/ *n* балюстра́да.
bamboo /bæmˈbuː/ *n* бамбу́к.
bamboozle /bæmˈbuːz(ə)l/ *vt* надува́ть *impf*, наду́ть *pf*.
ban /bæn/ *n* запре́т; *vt* запреща́ть *impf*, запрети́ть *pf*.
banal /bəˈnɑːl/ *adj* бана́льный. **banality** /bəˈnælɪtɪ/ *n* бана́льность.
banana /bəˈnɑːnə/ *n* бана́н.
band /bænd/ *n* (*stripe*, *strip*) полоса́; (*braid*, *tape*) тесьма́; (*category*) катего́рия; (*of people*) гру́ппа; (*gang*) ба́нда; (*mus*) орке́стр; (*radio*) диапазо́н; *vi*: ~ **together** объединя́ться *impf*, объедини́ться *pf*.
bandage /ˈbændɪdʒ/ *n* бинт; *vt* бинтова́ть *impf*, за~ *pf*.
bandit /ˈbændɪt/ *n* банди́т.
bandstand /ˈbændstænd/ *n* эстра́да для орке́стра.
bandwagon /ˈbændwægən/ *n*: **jump on the** ~ по́льзоваться *impf*, вос~ *pf* благоприя́тными обстоя́тельствами.
bandy-legged /ˈbændɪˌlegd/ *adj* кривоно́гий.
bane /beɪn/ *n* отра́ва.
bang /bæŋ/ *n* (*blow*) уда́р; (*noise*) стук; (*of gun*) вы́стрел; *vt* (*strike*) ударя́ть *impf*, уда́рить *pf*; *vi* хло́пать *impf*, хло́пнуть *pf*; (*slam shut*) захло́пываться *impf*, захло́пнуться *pf*; ~ **one's head** ударя́ться *impf*, уда́-

риться *pf* головóй; ~ **the door** хлóпать *impf*, хлóпнуть *pf* двéрью.

bangle /ˈbæŋg(ə)l/ *n* браслéт.

banish /ˈbænɪʃ/ *vt* изгонять *impf*, изгнáть *pf*.

banister /ˈbænɪstə(r)/ *n* перúла *neut pl*.

banjo /ˈbændʒəʊ/ *n* бáнджо *neut indecl*.

bank[1] /bæŋk/ *n* (*of river*) бéрег; (*of earth*) вал; *vt* сгребáть *impf*, сгрестú *pf* в кýчу; *vi* (*aeron*) накреня́ться *impf*, накренúться *pf*.

bank[2] /bæŋk/ *n* (*econ*) банк; ~ **account** счёт в бáнке; ~ **holiday** установленный прáздник; *vi* (*keep money*) держáть *impf* дéньги (в бáнке); *vt* (*put in* ~) класть *impf*, положúть *pf* в банк; ~ **on** полагáться *impf*, положúться *pf* на+*acc*. **banker** /ˈbæŋkə(r)/ *n* банкúр. **banknote** *n* банкнóта.

bankrupt /ˈbæŋkrʌpt/ *n* банкрóт; *adj* обанкрóтившийся; *vt* доводúть *impf*, довестú *pf* до банкрóтства. **bankruptcy** /-sɪ/ *n* банкрóтство.

banner /ˈbænə(r)/ *n* знáмя *neut*.

banquet /ˈbæŋkwɪt/ *n* банкéт, пир.

banter /ˈbæntə(r)/ *n* подшýчивание.

baptism /ˈbæptɪz(ə)m/ *n* крещéние. **baptize** /bæpˈtaɪz/ *vt* крестúть *impf*, о~ *pf*.

bar /bɑː(r)/ *n* (*beam*) брус; (*of cage*) решётка; (*of chocolate*) плúтка; (*of soap*) кусóк; (*barrier*) прегрáда; (*law*) адвокатýра; (*counter*) стóйка; (*room*) бар; (*mus*) такт; *vt* (*obstruct*) преграждáть *impf*, прегрáдúть *pf*; (*prohibit*) запрещáть *impf*, запретúть *pf*.

barbarian /bɑːˈbeərɪən/ *n* вáрвар. **barbaric** /bɑːˈbærɪk/, **barbarous** /ˈbɑːbərəs/ *adj* вáрварский.

barbecue /ˈbɑːbɪˌkjuː/ *n* (*party*) шашлы́к; *vt* жáрить *impf*, за~ *pf* на вéртеле.

barbed wire /ˌbɑːbd ˈwaɪə(r)/ *n* колю́чая прóволока.

barber /ˈbɑːbə(r)/ *n* парикмáхер; ~**'s shop** парикмáхерская *sb*.

bar code /ˈbɑː kəʊd/ *n* маркирóвка.

bard /bɑːd/ *n* бард.

bare /beə(r)/ *adj* (*naked*) гóлый; (*empty*) пустóй; (*small*) минимáльный; *vt* обнажáть *impf*, обнажúть *pf*; ~ **one's teeth** скáлить *impf*, о~ *pf* зýбы. **barefaced** *adj* нáглый. **barefoot** *adj* босóй. **barely** /ˈbeəlɪ/ *adv* едвá.

bargain /ˈbɑːgɪn/ *n* (*deal*) сдéлка; (*good buy*) вы́годная сдéлка; *vi* торговáться *impf*, с~ *pf*; ~ **for, on** (*expect*) ожидáть *impf* +*gen*.

barge /bɑːdʒ/ *n* бáржá; *vi*: ~ **into** (*room etc.*) врывáться *impf*, ворвáться *pf* в+*acc*.

baritone /ˈbærɪˌtəʊn/ *n* баритóн.

bark[1] /bɑːk/ *n* (*of dog*) лай; *vi* лáять *impf*.

bark[2] /bɑːk/ *n* (*of tree*) корá.

barley /ˈbɑːlɪ/ *n* ячмéнь *m*.

barmaid /ˈbɑːmeɪd/ *n* буфéтчица. **barman** /ˈbɑːmən/ *n* буфéтчик.

barmy /ˈbɑːmɪ/ *adj* трóнутый.

barn /bɑːn/ *n* амбáр.

barometer /bəˈrɒmɪtə(r)/ *n* барóметр.

baron /ˈbærən/ *n* барóн. **baroness** /-nɪs/ *n* баронéсса.

baroque /bəˈrɒk/ *n* барóкко *neut indecl*; *adj* барóчный.

barrack[1] /ˈbærək/ *n* казáрма.

barrack[2] /ˈbærək/ *vt* освúстывать *impf*, освистáть *pf*.

barrage /ˈbærɑːʒ/ *n* (*in river*) запрýда; (*gunfire*) огневóй вал; (*fig*) град.

barrel /ˈbær(ə)l/ *n* бóчка; (*of gun*) дýло.

barren /ˈbærən/ *adj* бесплóдный.

barricade *n* /ˈbærɪˌkeɪd/ баррикáда; *vt* /ˌbærɪˈkeɪd/ баррикадúровать *impf*, за~ *pf*.

barrier /ˈbærɪə(r)/ *n* барьéр.

barring /ˈbɑːrɪŋ/ *prep* исключáя.

barrister /ˈbærɪstə(r)/ *n* адвокáт.

barrow /ˈbærəʊ/ *n* телéжка.

barter /ˈbɑːtə(r)/ *n* бáртер, товарообмéн; *vi* обмéниваться *impf*, обменя́ться *pf* товáрами.

base¹ /beɪs/ *adj* нúзкий; (*metal*) неблагорóдный.

base² /beɪs/ *n* оснóва; (*also mil*) бáза; *vt* оснóвывать *impf*, основáть *pf*. **baseball** *n* бейсбóл. **baseless** /ˈbeɪslɪs/ *adj* необоснóванный. **basement** /ˈbeɪsmənt/ *n* подвáл.

bash /bæʃ/ *vt* трéснуть *pf*; *n*: **have a ~!** попрóбуй(те)!

bashful /ˈbæʃfʊl/ *adj* застéнчивый.

basic /ˈbeɪsɪk/ *adj* основнóй. **basically** /-kəlɪ/ *adv* в основнóм.

basin /ˈbeɪs(ə)n/ *n* таз; (*geog*) бассéйн.

basis /ˈbeɪsɪs/ *n* оснóва, бáзис.

bask /bɑːsk/ *vi* грéться *impf*; (*fig*) наслаждáться *impf*, насладúться *pf* (**in** +*instr*).

basket /ˈbɑːskɪt/ *n* корзúна. **basketball** *n* баскетбóл.

bass /beɪs/ *n* бас; *adj* басóвый.

bassoon /bəˈsuːn/ *n* фагóт.

bastard /ˈbɑːstəd/ *n* (*sl*) негодя́й.

baste /beɪst/ *vt* (*cul*) поливáть *impf*, полúть *pf* жúром.

bastion /ˈbæstɪən/ *n* бастиóн.

bat¹ /bæt/ *n* (*zool*) летýчая мышь.

bat² /bæt/ *n* (*sport*) битá; *vi* бить *impf*, по~ *pf* по мячý.

bat³ /bæt/ *vt*: **he didn't ~ an eyelid** он и глáзом не моргнýл.

batch /bætʃ/ *n* пáчка; (*of loaves*) вы́печка.

bated /ˈbeɪtɪd/ *adj*: **with ~ breath** затáив дыхáние.

bath /bɑːθ/ *n* (*vessel*) вáнна; *pl* плáвательный бассéйн; **have a bath** принимáть *impf*, приня́ть *pf* вáнну; *vt* купáть *impf*, вы́~, ис~ *pf*. **bathe** /beɪð/ *vi* купáться *impf*, вы́~, ис~ *pf*; *vt* омывáть *impf*, омы́ть *pf*. **bather** /ˈbeɪðə(r)/ *n* купáльщик, -ица. **bath-house** *n* бáня. **bathing** /ˈbeɪðɪŋ/ *n*: **~ cap** купáльная шáпочка; **~ costume** купáльный костю́м. **bathroom** *n* вáнная *sb*.

baton /ˈbæt(ə)n/ *n* (*staff of office*) жезл; (*sport*) эстафéта; (*mus*) (дирижёрская) пáлочка.

battalion /bəˈtælɪən/ *n* батальóн.

batten /ˈbæt(ə)n/ *n* рéйка.

batter /ˈbætə(r)/ *n* взбúтое тéсто; *vt* колотúть *impf*, по~ *pf*.

battery /ˈbætərɪ/ *n* батарéя.

battle /ˈbæt(ə)l/ *n* бúтва; (*fig*) борьбá; *vi* борóться *impf*. **battlefield** *n* пóле бóя. **battlement** /-mənt/ *n* зубчáтая стенá. **battleship** *n* линéйный корáбль *m*.

bawdy /ˈbɔːdɪ/ *adj* непристóйный.

bawl /bɔːl/ *vi* орáть *impf*.

bay¹ /beɪ/ *n* (*bot*) лáвр; *adj* лаврóвый.

bay² /beɪ/ *n* (*geog*) залúв.

bay³ /beɪ/ *n* (*recess*) пролёт; ~

window фона́рь *m*.
bay[4] /beɪ/ *vi* (*bark*) ла́ять *impf*; (*howl*) выть *impf*.
bay[5] /beɪ/ *adj* (*colour*) гнедо́й.
bayonet /ˈbeɪəˌnet/ *n* штык.
bazaar /bəˈzɑː(r)/ *n* база́р.
BC *abbr* до н.э. (до на́шей э́ры).
be[1] /biː/ *v* **1.** быть: *usually omitted in pres*: **he is a teacher** он учи́тель. **2.** (*exist*) существова́ть *impf*. **3.** (*frequentative*) быва́ть *impf*. **4.** (~ *situated*) находи́ться *impf*; (*stand*) стоя́ть *impf*; (*lie*) лежа́ть *impf*. **5.** (*in general definitions*) явля́ться *impf* +*instr*: **Moscow is the capital of Russia** столи́цей Росси́и явля́ется го́род Москва́. **6.: there is, are** име́ется, име́ются; (*emph*) есть.
be[2] /biː/ *v aux* **1.** *be+inf*, *expressing duty, plan*: до́лжен+*inf*. **2.** *be+past participle passive, expressing passive*: быть+*past participle passive in short form*: **it was done** бы́ло сде́лано; *impers construction of 3 pl+acc*: **I was beaten** меня́ би́ли; *reflexive construction*: **music was heard** слы́шалась му́зыка. **3.** *be+pres participle active, expressing continuous tenses*: *imperfective aspect*: **I am reading** я чита́ю.
beach /biːtʃ/ *n* пляж.
beacon /ˈbiːkən/ *n* мая́к, сигна́льный ого́нь *m*.
bead /biːd/ *n* бу́сина; (*drop*) ка́пля; *pl* бу́сы *f pl*.
beak /biːk/ *n* клюв.
beaker /ˈbiːkə(r)/ *n* (*child's*) ча́шка с но́сиком; (*chem*) менз́урка.
beam /biːm/ *n* ба́лка; (*ray*) луч; *vi* (*shine*) сия́ть *impf*.
bean /biːn/ *n* фасо́ль, боб.
bear[2] /beə(r)/ *n* медве́дь *m*.
bear[2] /beə(r)/ *vt* (*carry*) носи́ть *indet*, нести́ *det*, по~ *pf*; (*endure*) терпе́ть *impf*; (*child*) роди́ть *impf* & *pf*; ~ **out** подтвержда́ть *impf*, подтверди́ть *pf*; ~ **up** держа́ться *impf*. **bearable** /ˈbeərəb(ə)l/ *adj* терпи́мый.
beard /bɪəd/ *n* борода́. **bearded** /-dɪd/ *adj* борода́тый.
bearer /ˈbeərə(r)/ *n* носи́тель *m*; (*of cheque*) предъяви́тель *m*; (*of letter*) пода́тель *m*.
bearing /ˈbeərɪŋ/ *n* (*deportment*) оса́нка; (*relation*) отноше́ние; (*position*) пе́ленг; (*tech*) подши́пник; **get one's** ~**s** ориенти́роваться *impf* & *pf*; **lose one's** ~**s** потеря́ть *pf* ориенти́ровку.
beast /biːst/ *n* живо́тное *sb*; (*fig*) скоти́на *m* & *f*. **beastly** /ˈbiːstlɪ/ *adj* (*coll*) проти́вный.
beat /biːt/ *n* бой; (*round*) обхо́д; (*mus*) такт; *vt* бить *impf*, по~ *pf*; (*sport*) выи́грывать *impf*, вы́играть *pf* у+*gen*; (*cul*) взбива́ть *impf*, взбить *pf*; *vi* би́ться *impf*, ~ **off** отбива́ть *impf*, отби́ть *pf*; ~ **up** избива́ть *impf*, изби́ть *pf*. **beating** /ˈbiːtɪŋ/ *n* битьё; (*defeat*) пораже́ние; (*of heart*) бие́ние.
beautiful /ˈbjuːtɪfʊl/ *adj* краси́вый. **beautify** /-ˌfaɪ/ *vt* украша́ть *impf* укра́сить *pf*. **beauty** /ˈbjuːtɪ/ *n* красота́; (*person*) краса́вица.
beaver /ˈbiːvə(r)/ *n* бобр.
because /bɪˈkɒz/ *conj* потому́, что; так как; *adv*: ~ **of** из-за+*gen*.
beckon /ˈbekən/ *vt* мани́ть *impf*, по~ *pf* к себе́.
become /bɪˈkʌm/ *vi* станови́ться *impf*, стать *pf* +*instr*; ~ **of** ста́ться *pf* с+*instr*. **becom-**

ing /-mɪŋ/ *adj* (*dress*) идýщий к лицý+*dat*.

bed /bed/ *n* кровáть, постéль; (*garden*) грядка; (*sea*) дно; (*river*) рýсло; (*geol*) пласт; **go to ~** ложиться *impf*, лечь *pf* спать; **make the ~** стелить *impf*, по~ *pf* постéль. **bed and breakfast** *n* (*hotel*) мáленькая гостиница. **bedclothes** *n pl*, **bedding** /'bedɪŋ/ *n* постéльное бельё. **bedridden** /'bedrɪd(ə)n/ *adj* прикóванный к постéли. **bedroom** *n* спáльня. **bedside table** *n* тýмбочка. **bedsitter** /'bedsɪtə(r)/ *n* однокóмнатная квартира. **bedspread** *n* покрывáло. **bedtime** *n* врéмя *neut* ложиться спать.

bedlam /'bedləm/ *n* бедлáм.

bedraggled /bɪ'dræg(ə)ld/ *adj* растрёпанный.

bee /bi:/ *n* пчелá. **beehive** *n* ýлей.

beech /bi:tʃ/ *n* бук.

beef /bi:f/ *n* говядина. **beefburger** *n* котлéта.

beer /bɪə(r)/ *n* пиво.

beetle /'bi:t(ə)l/ *n* жук.

beetroot /'bi:tru:t/ *n* свёкла.

befall /bɪ'fɔ:l/ *vt* & *i* случáться *impf*, случиться *pf* (+*dat*).

befit /bɪ'fɪt/ *vt* подходить *impf*, подойти *pf* +*dat*.

before /bɪ'fɔ:(r)/ *adv* рáньше; *prep* пéред+*instr*, до+*gen*; *conj* до тогó как; прéжде чем; (*rather than*) скорée чем; **the day ~ yesterday** позавчерá. **beforehand** *adv* зарáнее.

befriend /bɪ'frend/ *vt* дружиться *impf*, по~ *pf* с+*instr*.

beg /beg/ *vt* (*ask*) óчень просить *impf*, по~ *pf* (*person*+*acc*; *thing*+*acc or gen*); *vi* нищенствовать *impf*; (*of dog*) служить *impf*; **~ for** просить *impf*, по~ *pf* +*acc or gen*; **~ pardon** просить *impf* прощéние.

beggar /'begə(r)/ *n* нищий *sb*.

begin /bɪ'gɪn/ *vt* (& *i*) начинáть(ся) *impf*, начáть(ся) *pf*. **beginner** /-'gɪnə(r)/ *n* начинáющий *sb*. **beginning** /-'gɪnɪŋ/ *n* начáло.

begrudge /bɪ'grʌdʒ/ *vt* (*give reluctantly*) жалéть *impf*, со~ *pf* о+*prep*.

beguile /bɪ'gaɪl/ *vt* (*charm*) очарóвывать *impf*, очаровáть *pf*; (*seduce, delude*) обольщáть *impf*, обольстить *pf*.

behalf /bɪ'hɑ:f/ *n*: **on ~ of** от имени +*gen*; (*in interest of*) в пóльзу +*gen*.

behave /bɪ'heɪv/ *vi* вести *impf* себя. **behaviour** /-'heɪvjə(r)/ *n* поведéние.

behest /bɪ'hest/ *n* завéт.

behind /bɪ'haɪnd/ *adv*, *prep* сзáди (+*gen*), позади (+*gen*), за (+*acc*, *instr*); *n* зад; **be, fall, ~** отставáть *impf*, отстáть *pf*.

behold /bɪ'həʊld/ *vt* смотрéть *impf*, по~ *pf*. **beholden** /-d(ə)n/ *predic*: **~ to** обязан+*dat*.

beige /beɪʒ/ *adj* бéжевый.

being /'bi:ɪŋ/ *n* (*existence*) бытиé; (*creature*) существó.

Belarus /ˌbelə'rʌs/ *n* Беларýсь.

belated /bɪ'leɪtɪd/ *adj* запоздáлый.

belch /beltʃ/ *vi* рыгáть *impf*, рыгнýть *pf*; *vt* извергáть *impf*, извéргнуть *pf*.

beleaguer /bɪ'li:gə(r)/ *vt* осаждáть *impf*, осадить *pf*.

belfry /'belfrɪ/ *n* колокóльня.

Belgian /'beldʒ(ə)n/ *n* бельгиец, -гийка; *adj* бельгийский. **Belgium** /-dʒəm/ *n* Бéльгия.

belie /bɪ'laɪ/ *vt* противорéчить *impf* +*dat*.

belief /bɪ'li:f/ *n* (*faith*) вéра;

(*confidence*) убеждéние. **believable** /-ˈliːvəb(ə)l/ *adj* правдоподóбный. **believe** /-ˈliːv/ *vt* вéрить *impf*, по~ *pf* +*dat*; ~ **in** вéрить *impf* в+*acc*. **believer** /-ˈliːvə(r)/ *n* вéрующий *sb*.

belittle /bɪˈlɪt(ə)l/ *vt* умаля́ть *impf*, умали́ть *pf*.

bell /bel/ *n* кóлокол; (*doorbell*) звонóк; ~ **tower** колокóльня.

bellicose /ˈbelɪˌkəʊz/ *adj* вои́нственный. **belligerence** /bɪˈlɪdʒər(ə)ns/ *n* вои́нственность. **belligerent** /bɪˈlɪdʒərənt/ *adj* вою́ющий; (*aggressive*) вои́нственный.

bellow /ˈbeləʊ/ *vt* & *i* ревéть *impf*.

bellows /ˈbeləʊz/ *n pl* мехи́ *m pl*.

belly /ˈbelɪ/ *n* живóт.

belong /bɪˈlɒŋ/ *vi* принадлежáть *impf* (**to** (к)+*dat*). **belongings** /-ɪŋz/ *n pl* пожи́тки (-ков) *pl*.

Belorussian /ˌbeləʊˈrʌʃ(ə)n/ *n* белору́с, ~ка; *adj* белору́сский.

beloved /bɪˈlʌvɪd/ *adj* & *sb* возлю́бленный.

below /bɪˈləʊ/ *adv* (*position*) внизу́; *prep* (*position*) под +*instr*; (*less than*) ни́же+*gen*.

belt /belt/ *n* (*strap*) пóяс, (*also tech*) ремéнь; (*zone*) зóна, полосá.

bench /bentʃ/ *n* скамéйка; (*for work*) станóк.

bend /bend/ *n* изги́б; *vt* (& *i*, *also* ~ **down**) сгибáть(ся) *impf*, согну́ть(ся) *pf*; ~ **over** склоня́ться *impf*, склони́ться *pf* над+*instr*.

beneath /bɪˈniːθ/ *prep* под+*instr*.

benediction /ˌbenɪˈdɪkʃ(ə)n/ *n* благословéние.

benefactor /ˈbenɪˌfæktə(r)/ *n* благодéтель *m*. **benefactress** /-ˌfæktrɪs/ *n* благодéтельница

beneficial /ˌbenɪˈfɪʃ(ə)l/ *adj* полéзный. **beneficiary** /-ˈfɪʃərɪ/ *n* получáтель *m*; (*law*) наслéдник. **benefit** /ˈbenɪfɪt/ *n* пóльза; (*allowance*) посóбие; (*theat*) бенефи́с; *vt* приноси́ть *impf*, принести́ *pf* пóльзу +*dat*; *vi* извлекáть *impf*, извлéчь *pf* вы́году.

benevolence /bɪˈnevəl(ə)ns/ *n* благожелáтельность. **benevolent** /-l(ə)nt/ *adj* благожелáтельный.

benign /bɪˈnaɪn/ *adj* дóбрый, мя́гкий; (*tumour*) доброкáчественный.

bent /bent/ *n* склóнность.

bequeath /bɪˈkwiːð/ *vt* завещáть *impf* & *pf* (**to**+*dat*). **bequest** /bɪˈkwest/ *n* посмéртный дар.

berate /bɪˈreɪt/ *vt* ругáть *impf*, вы́~ *pf*.

bereave /bɪˈriːv/ *vt* лишáть *impf*, лиши́ть *pf* (**of** +*gen*). **bereavement** /-mənt/ *n* тяжёлая утрáта.

berry /ˈberɪ/ *n* я́года.

berserk /bəˈsɜːk/ *adj*: **go** ~ взбеси́ться *pf*.

berth /bɜːθ/ *n* (*bunk*) кóйка; (*naut*) стоя́нка; *vi* причáливать *impf*, причáлить *pf*.

beseech /bɪˈsiːtʃ/ *vt* умоля́ть *impf*, умоли́ть *pf*.

beset /bɪˈset/ *vt* осаждáть *impf*, осади́ть *pf*.

beside /bɪˈsaɪd/ *prep* óколо+*gen*, ря́дом с+*instr*; ~ **the point** некстáти; ~ **o.s.** вне себя́. **besides** /bɪˈsaɪdz/ *adv* крóме тогó; *prep* крóме+*gen*.

besiege /bɪˈsiːdʒ/ *vt* осаждáть *impf*, осади́ть *pf*.

besotted /bɪˈsɒtɪd/ *adj* одурмáненный.

bespoke /bɪ'spəʊk/ *adj* сде́ланный на зака́з.

best /best/ *adj* лу́чший, са́мый лу́чший; *adv* лу́чше всего́, бо́льше всего́; **all the ~!** всего́ наилу́чшего! **at ~** в лу́чшем слу́чае; **do one's ~** де́лать *impf*, с~ *pf* всё возмо́жное; **~ man** ша́фер.

bestial /'bestɪəl/ *adj* зве́рский. **bestiality** /ˌbestɪ'ælɪtɪ/ *n* зве́рство.

bestow /bɪ'stəʊ/ *vt* дарова́ть *impf* & *pf*.

bestseller /ˌbest'selə(r)/ *n* бестсе́ллер.

bet /bet/ *n* пари́ *neut indecl*; (*stake*) ста́вка; *vi* держа́ть *impf* пари́ (**on** на+*acc*); *vt* (*stake*) ста́вить *impf*, по~ *pf*; **he bet me £5** он поспо́рил со мно́й на 5 фу́нтов.

betray /bɪ'treɪ/ *vt* изменя́ть *impf*, измени́ть *pf*+*dat*. **betrayal** /-'treɪəl/ *n* изме́на.

better /'betə(r)/ *adj* лу́чший; *adv* лу́чше; (*more*) бо́льше; *vt* улучша́ть *impf*, улу́чшить *pf*; **all the ~** тем лу́чше; **~ off** бо́лее состоя́тельный; **~ o.s.** выдвига́ться *impf*, вы́двинуться *pf*; **get ~** (*health*) поправля́ться *impf*, попра́виться *pf*; **get the ~ of** брать *impf*, взять *pf* верх над+*instr*; **had ~: you had ~ go** вам (*dat*) лу́чше бы пойти́; **think ~ of** переду́мывать *impf*, переду́мать *pf*. **betterment** /-mənt/ *n* улучше́ние.

between /bɪ'twiːn/ *prep* ме́жду +*instr*.

bevel /'bev(ə)l/ *vt* ска́шивать *impf*, скоси́ть *pf*.

beverage /'bevərɪdʒ/ *n* напи́ток.

bevy /'bevɪ/ *n* ста́йка.

beware /bɪ'weə(r)/ *vi* остерега́ться *impf*, остере́чься *pf* (**of** +*gen*).

bewilder /bɪ'wɪldə(r)/ *vt* сбива́ть *impf*, сбить *pf* с то́лку. **bewildered** /-dəd/ *adj* озада́ченный. **bewilderment** /-mənt/ *n* замеша́тельство.

bewitch /bɪ'wɪtʃ/ *vt* заколдо́вывать *impf*, заколдова́ть *pf*; (*fig*) очаро́вывать *impf*, очарова́ть *pf*. **bewitching** /-tʃɪŋ/ *adj* очарова́тельный.

beyond /bɪ'jɒnd/ *prep* за+*acc* & *instr*; по ту сто́рону+*gen*; (*above*) сверх+*gen*; (*outside*) вне+*gen*; **the back of ~** край све́та.

bias /'baɪəs/ *n* (*inclination*) укло́н; (*prejudice*) предубежде́ние. **biased** /'baɪəst/ *adj* предубеждённый.

bib /bɪb/ *n* нагру́дник.

Bible /'baɪb(ə)l/ *n* Би́блия. **biblical** /'bɪblɪk(ə)l/ *adj* библе́йский.

bibliographical /ˌbɪblɪə'græfɪk(ə)l/ *n* библиографи́ческий. **bibliography** /ˌbɪblɪ'ɒgrəfɪ/ *n* библиогра́фия.

bicarbonate (of soda) /baɪ'kɑːbənɪt/ *n* питьева́я со́да.

biceps /'baɪseps/ *n* би́цепс.

bicker /'bɪkə(r)/ *vi* препира́ться *impf*.

bicycle /'baɪsɪk(ə)l/ *n* велосипе́д.

bid /bɪd/ *n* предложе́ние цены́; (*attempt*) попы́тка; *vt* & *i* предлага́ть *impf*, предложи́ть *pf* (це́ну) (**for** за+*acc*); *vt* (*command*) прика́зывать *impf*, приказа́ть *pf* +*dat*. **bidding** /'bɪdɪŋ/ *n* предложе́ние цены́; (*command*) приказа́ние.

bide /baɪd/ *vt*: **~ one's time** ожида́ть *impf* благоприя́тного слу́чая.

biennial /baɪ'enɪəl/ *adj* двухле́т-

ний; *n* двухлéтник.
bier /bɪə(r)/ *n* катафáлк.
bifocals /baɪˈfəʊk(ə)lz/ *n pl* бифокáльные очки́ *pl.*
big /bɪg/ *adj* большóй; (*also important*) крýпный.
bigamist /ˈbɪgəmɪst/ *n* (*man*) двоежéнец; (*woman*) двумýжница. **bigamy** /-mɪ/ *n* двубрáчие.
bigwig /ˈbɪgwɪg/ *n* ши́шка.
bike /baɪk/ *n* велосипéд. **biker** /ˈbaɪkə(r)/ *n* мотоцикли́ст.
bikini /bɪˈkiːnɪ/ *n* бики́ни *neut indecl.*
bilateral /baɪˈlætər(ə)l/ *adj* двусторóнний.
bilberry /ˈbɪlbərɪ/ *n* черни́ка (*no pl*; *usu collect*).
bile /baɪl/ *n* жёлчь. **bilious** /ˈbɪljəs/ *adj* жёлчный.
bilingual /baɪˈlɪŋgw(ə)l/ *adj* двуязы́чный.
bill[1] /bɪl/ *n* счёт; (*parl*) законопроéкт; (**~** *of exchange*) вéксель; (*poster*) афи́ша; *vt* (*announce*) объявля́ть *impf*, объяви́ть *pf* в афи́шах; (*charge*) присылáть *impf*, прислáть *pf* счёт+*dat*.
bill[2] /bɪl/ *n* (*beak*) клюв.
billet /ˈbɪlɪt/ *vt* расквартирóвывать *impf*, расквартировáть *pf*.
billiards /ˈbɪljədz/ *n* бильярд.
billion /ˈbɪljən/ *n* биллиóн.
billow /ˈbɪləʊ/ *n* вал; *vi* вздымáться *impf*.
bin /bɪn/ *n* мýсорное ведрó.
bind /baɪnd/ *vt* (*tie*) свя́зывать *impf*, связáть *pf*; (*oblige*) обя́зывать *impf*, обязáть *pf*; (*book*) переплетáть *impf*, переплести́ *pf*. **binder** /ˈbaɪndə(r)/ *n* (*person*) переплётчик; (*for papers*) пáпка. **binding** /ˈbaɪndɪŋ/ *n* переплёт.
binge /bɪndʒ/ *n* кутёж; **~ drinking** попóйка.
binoculars /bɪˈnɒkjʊləz/ *n pl* бинóкль *m.*
biochemistry /ˌbaɪəʊˈkemɪstrɪ/ *n* биохи́мия. **biographer** /baɪˈɒgrəfə(r)/ *n* биóграф. **biographical** /ˌbaɪəˈgræfɪk(ə)l/ *adj* биографи́ческий. **biography** /baɪˈɒgrəfɪ/ *n* биогрáфия. **biological** /ˌbaɪəˈlɒdʒɪk(ə)l/ *adj* биологи́ческий. **biologist** /baɪˈɒlədʒɪst/ *n* биóлог. **biology** /baɪˈɒlədʒɪ/ *n* биолóгия.
bipartisan /ˌbaɪpɑːtɪˈzæn/ *adj* двухпарти́йный.
birch /bɜːtʃ/ *n* берёза; (*rod*) рóзга.
bird /bɜːd/ *n* пти́ца; **~ flu** пти́чий грипп; **~ of prey** хи́щная пти́ца.
birth /bɜːθ/ *n* рождéние; (*descent*) происхождéние; **~ certificate** мéтрика; **~ control** противозачáточные мéры *f pl.* **birthday** *n* день *m* рождéния; **fourth ~** четырёхлéтие. **birthplace** *n* мéсто рождéния. **birthright** *n* прáво по рождéнию.
biscuit /ˈbɪskɪt/ *n* печéнье.
bisect /baɪˈsekt/ *vt* разрезáть *impf*, разрéзать *pf* пополáм.
bisexual /baɪˈseksjʊəl/ *adj* бисексуáльный.
bishop /ˈbɪʃəp/ *n* епи́скоп; (*chess*) слон.
bit[1] /bɪt/ *n* (*piece*) кусóчек; **a ~** немнóго; **not a ~** ничуть.
bit[2] /bɪt/ *n* (*tech*) сверлó; (*bridle*) удилá (-л) *pl.*
bitch /bɪtʃ/ *n* (*coll*) стéрва. **bitchy** /ˈbɪtʃɪ/ *adj* стервóзный.
bite /baɪt/ *n* укýс; (*snack*) закýска; (*fishing*) клёв; *vt* кусáть *impf*, укуси́ть *pf*; *vi* (*fish*) клевáть *impf*, клю́нуть *pf*. **biting** /ˈbaɪtɪŋ/ *adj* éдкий.
bitter /ˈbɪtə(r)/ *adj* гóрький. **bit-**

terness /-nɪs/ *n* го́речь. **bitumen** /ˈbɪtjʊmɪn/ *n* биту́м. **bivouac** /ˈbɪvʊˌæk/ *n* бива́к. **bizarre** /bɪˈzɑ:(r)/ *adj* стра́нный. **black** /blæk/ *adj* чёрный; ~ **eye** подби́тый глаз; ~ **market** чёрный ры́нок; *v*: ~ **out** (*vt*) затемня́ть *impf*, затемни́ть *pf*; (*vi*) теря́ть *impf*, по~ *pf* созна́ние; *n* (*colour*) чёрный цвет; (~ *person*) негр, ~итя́нка; (*mourning*) тра́ур. **blackberry** *n* ежеви́ка (*no pl*; *usu collect*). **blackbird** *n* чёрный дрозд. **blackboard** *n* доска́. **blackcurrant** *n* чёрная сморо́дина (*no pl*; *usu collect*). **blacken** /ˈblækən/ *vt* (*fig*) черни́ть *impf*, о~ *pf*. **blackleg** *n* штрейкбре́хер. **blacklist** *n* вноси́ть *impf*, внести́ *pf* в чёрный спи́сок. **blackmail** *n* шанта́ж; *vt* шантажи́ровать *impf*. **blackout** *n* затемне́ние; (*faint*) потеря́ созна́ния. **blacksmith** *n* кузне́ц.

bladder /ˈblædə(r)/ *n* пузы́рь *m*.

blade /bleɪd/ *n* (*knife*) ле́звие; (*oar*) ло́пасть; (*grass*) были́нка.

blame /bleɪm/ *n* вина́, порица́ние; *vt* вини́ть *impf* (**for** в+*prep*); **be to** ~ быть винова́тым. **blameless** /ˈbleɪmlɪs/ *adj* безупре́чный.

blanch /blɑ:ntʃ/ *vt* (*vegetables*) ошпа́ривать *impf*, ошпа́рить *pf*; *vi* бледне́ть *impf*, по~ *pf*.

bland /blænd/ *adj* мя́гкий; (*dull*) пре́сный.

blandishments /ˈblændɪʃmənts/ *n pl* лесть.

blank /blæŋk/ *adj* (*look*) отсу́тствующий; (*paper*) чи́стый; *n* (*space*) про́пуск; (*form*) бланк; (*cartridge*) холосто́й патро́н; ~ **cheque** незапо́лненный чек.

blanket /ˈblæŋkɪt/ *n* одея́ло.

blare /bleə(r)/ *vi* труби́ть *impf*, про~ *pf*.

blasé /ˈblɑ:zeɪ/ *adj* пресы́щенный.

blasphemous /ˈblæsfəməs/ *adj* богоху́льный. **blasphemy** /-fəmɪ/ *n* богоху́льство.

blast /blɑ:st/ *n* (*wind*) поры́в ве́тра; (*explosion*) взрыв; *vt* взрыва́ть *impf*, взорва́ть *pf*; ~ **off** стартова́ть *impf* & *pf*. **blast-furnace** *n* до́мна.

blatant /ˈbleɪt(ə)nt/ *adj* я́вный.

blaze /bleɪz/ *n* (*flame*) пла́мя *neut*; (*fire*) пожа́р; *vi* пыла́ть *impf*.

blazer /ˈbleɪzə(r)/ *n* лёгкий пиджа́к.

bleach /bli:tʃ/ *n* хло́рка, отбе́ливатель *m*; *vt* отбе́ливать *impf*, отбели́ть *pf*.

bleak /bli:k/ *adj* пусты́нный; (*dreary*) уны́лый.

bleary-eyed /ˈblɪərɪˌaɪd/ *adj* с затума́ненными глаза́ми.

bleat /bli:t/ *vi* бле́ять *impf*.

bleed /bli:d/ *vi* кровоточи́ть *impf*.

bleeper /ˈbli:pə(r)/ *n* персона́льный сигнализа́тор.

blemish /ˈblemɪʃ/ *n* пятно́.

blend /blend/ *n* смесь; *vt* сме́шивать *impf*, смеша́ть *pf*; *vi* гармони́ровать *impf*. **blender** /ˈblendə(r)/ *n* ми́ксер.

bless /bles/ *vt* благословля́ть *impf*, благослови́ть *pf*. **blessed** /ˈblesɪd, blest/ *adj* благослове́нный. **blessing** /ˈblesɪŋ/ *n* (*action*) благослове́ние; (*object*) бла́го.

blight /blaɪt/ *vt* губи́ть *impf*, по~ *pf*.

blind /blaɪnd/ *adj* слепо́й; ~ **alley** тупи́к; *n* што́ра; *vt* ослепля́ть *impf*, ослепи́ть *pf*. **blindfold** *vt* завя́зывать *impf*, завяза́ть *pf* глаза́+*dat*. **blindness** /'blaındnıs/ *n* слепота́.

blink /blıŋk/ *vi* мига́ть *impf*, мигну́ть *pf*. **blinkers** /'blıŋkəz/ *n pl* шо́ры (-р) *pl*.

bliss /blıs/ *n* блаже́нство. **blissful** /'blısfʊl/ *adj* блаже́нный.

blister /'blıstə(r)/ *n* пузы́рь *m*, волды́рь *m*.

blithe /blaıð/ *adj* весёлый; (*carefree*) беспе́чный.

blitz /blıts/ *n* бомбёжка.

blizzard /'blızəd/ *n* мете́ль.

bloated /'bləʊtıd/ *adj* взду́тый.

blob /blɒb/ *n* (*liquid*) ка́пля; (*colour*) кля́кса.

bloc /blɒk/ *n* блок.

block /blɒk/ *n* (*wood*) чурба́н; (*stone*) глы́ба; (*flats*) жило́й дом; *vt* преграждáть *impf*, прегради́ть *pf*; **~ up** забива́ть *impf*, заби́ть *pf*.

blockade /blɒ'keıd/ *n* блока́да; *vt* блоки́ровать *impf* & *pf*.

blockage /'blɒkıdʒ/ *n* зато́р.

bloke /bləʊk/ *n* па́рень *m*.

blond /blɒnd/ *n* блонди́н, **~**ка; *adj* белоку́рый.

blood /blʌd/ *n* кровь; **~ donor** до́нор; **~-poisoning** *n* зараже́ние кро́ви; **~ pressure** кровяно́е давле́ние; **~ relation** бли́зкий ро́дственник, -ая ро́дственница; **~ transfusion** перелива́ние кро́ви. **bloodhound** *n* ище́йка. **bloodshed** *n* кровопроли́тие. **bloodshot** *adj* нали́тый кро́вью. **bloodthirsty** *adj* кровожа́дный. **bloody** /'blʌdı/ *adj* крова́вый.

bloom /blu:m/ *n* расцве́т; *vi* цвести́ *pf*.

blossom /'blɒsəm/ *n* цвет; **in ~** в цвету́.

blot /blɒt/ *n* кля́кса; пятно́; *vt* (*dry*) промока́ть *impf*, промокну́ть *pf*; (*smudge*) па́чкать *impf*, за**~** *pf*.

blotch /blɒtʃ/ *n* пятно́.

blotting-paper /'blɒtıŋ,peıpə(r)/ *n* промока́тельная бума́га.

blouse /blaʊz/ *n* ко́фточка, блу́зка.

blow[1] /bləʊ/ *n* уда́р.

blow[2] /bləʊ/ *vt* & *i* дуть *impf*, по**~** *pf*; **~ away** сноси́ть *impf*, снести́ *pf*; **~ down** вали́ть *impf*, по**~** *pf*; **~ one's nose** сморка́ться *impf*, сморкну́ться *pf*; **~ out** задува́ть *impf*, заду́ть *pf*; **~ over** (*fig*) проходи́ть *impf*, пройти́ *pf*; **~ up** взрыва́ть *impf*, взорва́ть *pf*; (*inflate*) надува́ть *impf*, наду́ть *pf*. **blow-lamp** *n* пая́льная ла́мпа.

blubber[1] /'blʌbə(r)/ *n* во́рвань.

blubber[2] /'blʌbə(r)/ *vi* реве́ть *impf*.

bludgeon /'blʌdʒ(ə)n/ *vt* (*compel*) вынужда́ть *impf*, вы́нудить *pf*.

blue /blu:/ *adj* (*dark*) си́ний; (*light*) голубо́й; *n* си́ний, голубо́й, цвет. **bluebell** *n* колоко́льчик. **bluebottle** *n* си́няя му́ха. **blueprint** *n* си́нька, светоко́пия; (*fig*) прое́кт.

bluff /blʌf/ *n* блеф; *vi* блефова́ть *impf*.

blunder /'blʌndə(r)/ *n* оплоша́ность; *vi* оплоша́ть *pf*.

blunt /blʌnt/ *adj* тупо́й; (*person*) прямо́й; *vt* тупи́ть *impf*, за**~**, ис**~** *pf*.

blur /blɜ:(r)/ *vt* затума́нивать *impf*, затума́нить *pf*. **blurred** /blɜ:d/ *adj* расплы́вчатый.

blurt /blɜ:t/ *vt*: **~ out** выба́лтывать *impf*, вы́болтать *pf*.

blush /blʌʃ/ *vi* красне́ть *impf*, по**~** *pf*.

bluster /'blʌstə(r)/ *vi* бушева́ть *impf*; *n* пусты́е слова́ *neut pl*.

boar /bɔ:(r)/ *n* бóров; (*wild*) кабáн.

board /bɔ:d/ *n* доскá; (*committee*) правлéние, совéт; **on ~** на борт(ý); *vt* садúться *impf*, сéсть *pf* (на корáбль, в пóезд и т.д.); **~ up** забивáть *impf*, забúть *pf*. **boarder** /'bɔ:də(r)/ *n* пансионéр. **boarding-house** /'bɔ:dɪŋ,haʊs/ *n* пансиóн. **boarding-school** *n* интернáт.

boast /bəʊst/ *vi* хвáстаться *impf*, по~ *pf*; *vt* гордúться *impf* +*instr*. **boaster** /'bəʊstə(r)/ *n* хвастýн. **boastful** /'bəʊstfʊl/ *adj* хвастлúвый.

boat /bəʊt/ *n* (*small*) лóдка; (*large*) корáбль *m*.

bob /bɒb/ *vi* подпрыгивать *impf*, подпры́гнуть *pf*.

bobbin /'bɒbɪn/ *n* катýшка.

bobsleigh /'bɒbsleɪ/ *n* бóбслéй.

bode /bəʊd/ *vt*: **~well/ill** предвещáть *impf* хорóшее/недóброе.

bodice /'bɒdɪs/ *n* лиф, корсáж.

bodily /'bɒdɪlɪ/ *adv* целикóм; *adj* телéсный.

body /'bɒdɪ/ *n* тéло, тýловище; (*corpse*) труп; (*group*) óрган; (*main part*) основнáя часть. **bodyguard** *n* телохранúтель *m*. **bodywork** *n* кýзов.

bog /bɒg/ *n* болóта; **get ~ged down** увязáть *impf*, увя́знуть *pf*. **boggy** /'bɒgɪ/ *adj* болóтистый.

bogus /'bəʊgəs/ *adj* поддéльный.

boil[1] /bɔɪl/ *n* (*med*) фурýнкул.

boil[2] /bɔɪl/ *vi* кипéть *impf*, вс~ *pf*; *vt* кипятúть *impf*, вс~ *pf*; (*cook*) варúть *impf*, с~ *pf*; **~ down to** сходúться *impf*, сойтúсь *pf* к томý, что; **~ over** выкипáть *impf*, вы́кипеть *pf*; *n* кипéние; **bring to the ~** доводúть *impf*, довестú *pf* до кипéния. **boiled** /bɔɪld/ *adj* варёный. **boiler** /'bɔɪlə(r)/ *n* котёл; **~ suit** комбинезóн. **boiling** /'bɔɪlɪŋ/ *adj* кипя́щий; **~ point** тóчка кипéния; **~ water** кипятóк.

boisterous /'bɔɪstərəs/ *adj* шумлúвый.

bold /bəʊld/ *adj* смéлый; (*type*) жúрный.

bollard /'bɒlɑ:d/ *n* (*in road*) столб; (*on quay*) пал.

bolster /'bəʊlstə(r)/ *n* вáлик; *vt*: **~ up** подпирáть *impf*, подперéть *pf*.

bolt /bəʊlt/ *n* засóв; (*tech*) болт; *vt* запирáть *impf*, заперéть *pf* на засóв; скрепля́ть *impf*, скрепúть *pf* болтáми; *vi* (*flee*) удирáть *impf*, удрáть *pf*; (*horse*) понестú *pf*.

bomb /bɒm/ *n* бóмба; *vt* бомбúть *impf*. **bombard** /bɒm'bɑ:d/ *vt* бомбардúровать *impf*. **bombardment** /bɒm'bɑ:dmənt/ *n* бомбардирóвка. **bomber** /'bɒmə(r)/ *n* бомбардирóвщик.

bombastic /bɒm'bæstɪk/ *adj* напы́щенный.

bond /bɒnd/ *n* (*econ*) облигáция; (*link*) связь; *pl* окóвы (-в) *pl*, (*fig*) ýзы (уз) *pl*.

bone /bəʊn/ *n* кость.

bonfire /'bɒn,faɪə(r)/ *n* костёр.

bonnet /'bɒnɪt/ *n* кáпор; (*car*) капóт.

bonus /'bəʊnəs/ *n* прéмия.

bony /'bəʊnɪ/ *adj* костúстый.

boo /bu:/ *vt* освúстывать *impf*, освистáть *pf*; *vi* улюлю́кать *impf*.

booby trap /'bu:bɪ ,træp/ *n* ловýшка.

book /bʊk/ *n* кнúга; *vt* (*order*) закáзывать *impf*, заказáть *pf*; (*reserve*) бронúровать *impf*, за~ *pf*. **bookbinder** *n* переплётчик. **bookcase** *n* кни́жный шкаф. **booking** /ˈbʊkɪŋ/ *n* зака́з; ~ **office** ка́сса. **bookkeeper** /ˈbʊkˌkiːpə(r)/ *n* бухга́лтер. **bookmaker** /ˈbʊkˌmeɪkə(r)/ *n* букме́кер. **bookshop** *n* кни́жный магази́н.

boom[1] /buːm/ *n* (*barrier*) бон.

boom[2] /buːm/ *n* (*sound*) гул; (*econ*) бум; *vi* гуде́ть *impf*; (*fig*) процвета́ть *impf*.

boorish /ˈbʊərɪʃ/ *adj* ха́мский.

boost /buːst/ *n* соде́йствие; *vt* увели́чивать *impf*, увели́чить *pf*.

boot /buːt/ *n* боти́нок; (*high*) сапо́г; (*football*) бу́тса; (*car*) бага́жник.

booth /buːð/ *n* кио́ск, бу́дка; (*polling*) каби́на.

booty /ˈbuːtɪ/ *n* добы́ча.

booze /buːz/ *n* вы́пивка; *vi* выпива́ть *impf*.

border /ˈbɔːdə(r)/ *n* (*frontier*) грани́ца; (*trim*) кайма́; (*gardening*) бордю́р; *vi* грани́чить *impf* (**on** с +*instr*). **borderline** *n* грани́ца.

bore[1] /bɔː(r)/ *n* (*calibre*) кана́л (ствола́); *vt* сверли́ть *impf*, про~ *pf*.

bore[2] /bɔː(r)/ *n* (*thing*) ску́ка; (*person*) ску́чный челове́к; *vt* надоеда́ть *impf*, надое́сть *pf* +*dat*. **bored** /bɔːd/ *impers*+*dat* +ску́чно: **I'm** ~ мне ску́чно; **we were** ~ нам бы́ло ску́чно. **boredom** /ˈbɔːdəm/ *n* ску́ка. **boring** /ˈbɔːrɪŋ/ *adj* ску́чный.

born /bɔːn/ *adj* прирождённый; **be** ~ роди́ться *impf* & *pf*.

borough /ˈbʌrə/ *n* райо́н.

borrow /ˈbɒrəʊ/ *vt* одолжа́ть *impf*, одолжи́ть *pf* (**from** у+*gen*).

Bosnia /ˈbɒznɪə/ *n* Бо́сния. **Bosnian** /-ən/ *n* босни́ец, -и́йка; *adj* босни́йский.

bosom /ˈbʊz(ə)m/ *n* грудь.

boss /bɒs/ *n* нача́льник; *vt* кома́ндовать *impf*, с~ *pf* +*instr*. **bossy** /ˈbɒsɪ/ *adj* команди́рский.

botanical /bəˈtænɪk(ə)l/ *adj* ботани́ческий. **botanist** /ˈbɒtənɪst/ *n* бота́ник. **botany** /ˈbɒtənɪ/ *n* бота́ника.

botch /bɒtʃ/ *vt* зала́тывать *impf*, залата́ть *pf*.

both /bəʊθ/ *adj* & *pron* о́ба *m* & *neut*, о́бе *f*; ~ ... **and** и... и.

bother /ˈbɒðə(r)/ *n* доса́да; *vt* беспоко́ить *impf*.

bottle /ˈbɒt(ə)l/ *n* буты́лка; *vt* разлива́ть *impf*, разли́ть *pf* по буты́лкам; ~ **up** сде́рживать *impf*, сдержа́ть *pf*.

bottom /ˈbɒtəm/ *n* (*of river, container, etc.*) дно; (*of mountain*) подно́жие; (*buttocks*) зад; **at the** ~ **of** (*stairs, page*) внизу́ +*gen*; **get to the** ~ **of** добира́ться *impf*, добра́ться *pf* до су́ти +*gen*; *adj* ни́жний. **bottomless** /-lɪs/ *adj* бездо́нный.

bough /baʊ/ *n* сук.

boulder /ˈbəʊldə(r)/ *n* валу́н.

bounce /baʊns/ *vi* подпры́гивать *impf*, подпры́гнуть *pf*; (*cheque*) верну́ться *pf*.

bound[1] /baʊnd/ *n* (*limit*) преде́л; *vt* ограни́чивать *impf*, ограни́чить *pf*.

bound[2] /baʊnd/ *n* (*spring*) прыжо́к; *vi* пры́гать *impf*, пры́гнуть *pf*.

bound[3] /baʊnd/ *adj*: **he is** ~ **to be there** он обяза́тельно там бу́дет.

bound[4] /baʊnd/ *adj*: **to be** ~ **for** направля́ться *impf* в+*acc*.

boundary /ˈbaʊndərɪ/ *n* грани́ца.

boundless /'baʊndlɪs/ *adj* безграни́чный.
bountiful /'baʊntɪfʊl/ *adj* (*generous*) ще́дрый; (*ample*) оби́льный. **bounty** /'baʊntɪ/ *n* ще́дрость; (*reward*) пре́мия.
bouquet /bu:'keɪ/ *n* буке́т.
bourgeois /'bʊəʒwɑ:/ *adj* буржуа́зный. **bourgeoisie** /ˌbʊəʒwɑ:'zi:/ *n* буржуази́я.
bout /baʊt/ *n* (*med*) при́ступ; (*sport*) схва́тка.
bow[1] /bəʊ/ *n* (*weapon*) лук; (*knot*) бант; (*mus*) смычо́к.
bow[2] /baʊ/ *n* (*obeisance*) покло́н; *vi* кла́няться *impf*, поклони́ться *pf*; *vt* склоня́ть *impf*, склони́ть *pf*.
bow[3] /baʊ/ *n* (*naut*) нос.
bowel /'baʊəl/ *n* кишка́; (*depths*) не́дра (-р) *pl*.
bowl[1] /bəʊl/ *n* ми́ска.
bowl[2] /bəʊl/ *n* (*ball*) шар; *vi* подава́ть *impf*, пода́ть *pf* мяч. **bowler** /'bəʊlə(r)/ *n* подаю́щий *sb* мяч; (*hat*) котело́к. **bowling-alley** /'bəʊlɪŋ 'ælɪ/ *n* кегельба́н. **bowls** /bəʊlz/ *n* игра́ в шары́.
box[1] /bɒks/ *n* коро́бка, я́щик; (*theat*) ло́жа; ~ **office** ка́сса.
box[2] /bɒks/ *vi* бокси́ровать *impf*. **boxer** /'bɒksə(r)/ *n* боксёр. **boxing** /'bɒksɪŋ/ *n* бокс. **Boxing Day** *n* второ́й день Рождества́.
boy /bɔɪ/ *n* ма́льчик. **boyfriend** *n* друг, молодо́й челове́к. **boyhood** /'bɔɪhʊd/*n* о́трочество. **boyish** /'bɔɪɪʃ/ *adj* мальчи́шеский.
boycott /'bɔɪkɒt/ *n* бойко́т; *vt* бойкоти́ровать *impf* & *pf*.
bra /brɑ:/ *n* ли́фчик.
brace /breɪs/ *n* (*clamp*) скре́па; *pl* подтя́жки *f pl*; (*dental*) ши́на; *vt* скрепля́ть *impf*, скрепи́ть *pf*; ~ **o.s.** собира́ться *impf*, собра́ться *pf* с си́лами.
bracelet /'breɪslɪt/ *n* брасле́т.
bracing /'breɪsɪŋ/ *adj* бодря́щий.
bracket /'brækɪt/ *n* (*support*) кронште́йн; *pl* ско́бки *f pl*; (*category*) катего́рия.
brag /bræg/ *vi* хва́статься *impf*, по~ *pf*.
braid /breɪd/ *n* тесьма́.
braille /breɪl/ *n* шрифт Бра́йля.
brain /breɪn/ *n* мозг. **brainstorm** *n* припа́док безу́мия. **brainwash** *vt* промыва́ть *impf*, промы́ть *pf* мозги́+*dat*. **brainwave** *n* блестя́щая иде́я.
braise /breɪz/ *vt* туши́ть *impf*, с~ *pf*.
brake /breɪk/ *n* то́рмоз; *vt* тормози́ть *impf*, за~ *pf*.
bramble /'bræmb(ə)l/ *n* ежеви́ка.
bran /bræn/ *n* о́труби (-бе́й) *pl*.
branch /brɑ:ntʃ/ *n* ве́тка; (*fig*) о́трасль; (*comm*) филиа́л; *vi* разветвля́ться *impf*, разветви́ться *pf*; ~ **out** (*fig*) расширя́ть *impf*, расши́рить *pf* де́ятельность.
brand /brænd/ *n* (*mark*) клеймо́; (*make*) ма́рка; (*sort*) сорт; *vt* клейми́ть *impf*, за~ *pf*.
brandish /'brændɪʃ/ *vt* разма́хивать *impf* +*instr*.
brandy /'brændɪ/ *n* конья́к.
brash /bræʃ/ *adj* наха́льный.
brass /brɑ:s/ *n* лату́нь, жёлтая медь; (*mus*) ме́дные инструме́нты *m pl*; *adj* лату́нный, ме́дный; ~ **band** ме́дный духово́й орке́стр; **top** ~ вы́сшее нача́льство.
brassière /'bræzɪə(r)/ *n* бюстга́лтер.
brat /bræt/ *n* чертёнок.
bravado /brə'vɑ:dəʊ/ *n* брава́да.

brave /breɪv/ *adj* хра́брый; *vt* покоря́ть *impf*, покори́ть *pf*. **bravery** /ˈbreɪvərɪ/ *n* хра́брость.

bravo /brɑːˈvəʊ/ *int* бра́во.

brawl /brɔːl/ *n* сканда́л; *vi* дра́ться *impf*, по~ *pf*.

brawny /ˈbrɔːnɪ/ *adj* му́скулистый.

bray /breɪ/ *n* крик осла́; *vi* крича́ть *impf*.

brazen /ˈbreɪz(ə)n/ *adj* бессты́дный.

brazier /ˈbreɪzɪə(r)/ *n* жаро́вня.

breach /briːtʃ/ *n* наруше́ние; (*break*) проло́м; (*mil*) брешь; *vt* прорыва́ть *impf*, прорва́ть *pf*; (*rule*) наруша́ть *impf*, нару́шить *pf*.

bread /bred/ *n* хлеб; (*white*) бу́лка. **breadcrumb** *n* кро́шка. **breadwinner** *n* корми́лец.

breadth /bredθ/ *n* ширина́; (*fig*) широта́.

break /breɪk/ *n* проло́м, разры́в; (*pause*) переры́в, па́уза; *vt* (& *i*) лома́ть(ся) *impf*, с~ *pf*; разбива́ть(ся) *impf*, разби́ть(ся) *pf*; *vt* (*violate*) наруша́ть *impf*, нару́шить *pf*; ~ **away** вырыва́ться *impf*, вы́рваться *pf*; ~ **down** (*vi*) (*tech*) лома́ться *impf*, с~ *pf*; (*talks*) срыва́ться *impf*, сорва́ться *pf*; (*vt*) (*door*) выла́мывать *impf*, вы́ломать *pf*; ~ **in(to)** вла́мываться *impf*, вломи́ться *pf* в+*acc*; ~ **off** (*vt* & *i*) отла́мывать(ся) *impf*, отломи́ть(ся) *pf*; (*vi*) (*speaking*) замолча́ть *pf*; (*vt*) (*relations*) порыва́ть *impf*, порва́ть *pf*; ~ **out** вырыва́ться *impf*, вы́рваться *pf*; (*fire, war*) вспы́хнуть *pf*; ~ **through** пробива́ться *impf*, проби́ться *pf*; ~ **up** (*vi*) (*marriage*) распада́ться *impf*, распа́сться *pf*; (*meeting*) прерыва́ться *impf*, прерва́ться *pf*; (*vt*) (*disperse*) разгоня́ть *impf*, разогна́ть *pf*; (*vt* & *i*) разбива́ть(ся) *impf*, разби́ть(ся) *pf*; ~ **with** порыва́ть *impf*, порва́ть *pf* с+*instr*. **breakage** /ˈbreɪkɪdʒ/ *n* поло́мка. **breakdown** *n* поло́мка; (*med*) не́рвный срыв. **breaker** /ˈbreɪkə(r)/ *n* буру́н. **breakfast** /ˈbrekfəst/ *n* за́втрак; *vi* за́втракать *impf*, по~ *pf*. **breakneck** *adj*: **at ~ speed** сломя́ го́лову. **breakthrough** *n* проры́в. **breakwater** *n* волноре́з.

breast /brest/ *n* грудь; **~-feeding** *n* кормле́ние гру́дью; **~ stroke** *n* брасс.

breath /breθ/ *n* дыха́ние; **be out of ~** запыха́ться *impf* & *pf*. **breathe** /briːð/ *vi* дыша́ть *impf*; **~ in** вдыха́ть *impf*, вдохну́ть *pf*; **~ out** выдыха́ть *impf*, вы́дохнуть *pf*. **breather** /ˈbriːðə(r)/ *n* переды́шка. **breathless** /ˈbreθlɪs/ *adj* запыха́вшийся.

breeches /ˈbriːtʃɪz/ *n pl* бри́джи (-жей) *pl*.

breed /briːd/ *n* поро́да; *vi* размножа́ться *impf*, размно́житься *pf*; *vt* разводи́ть *impf*, развести́ *pf*. **breeder** /ˈbriːdə(r)/ *n* -во́д: **cattle ~** скотово́д. **breeding** /ˈbriːdɪŋ/ *n* разведе́ние, -во́дство; (*upbringing*) воспи́танность.

breeze /briːz/ *n* ветеро́к; (*naut*) бриз. **breezy** /ˈbriːzɪ/ *adj* све́жий.

brevity /ˈbrevɪtɪ/ *n* кра́ткость.

brew /bruː/ *vt* (*beer*) вари́ть *impf*, с~ *pf*; (*tea*) зава́ривать *impf*, завари́ть *pf*; (*beer*) ва́рка; (*tea*) зава́рка. **brewer** /ˈbruːə(r)/ *n* пивова́р. **brewery** /ˈbruːərɪ/ *n* пивова́ренный заво́д.

bribe /braɪb/ *n* взя́тка; *vt* подкупа́ть *impf*, подкупи́ть *pf*. **bribery** /ˈbraɪbərɪ/ *n* по́дкуп.

brick /brɪk/ *n* кирпи́ч; *adj* кирпи́чный. **bricklayer** *n* ка́менщик.

bridal /ˈbraɪd(ə)l/ *adj* сва́дебный. **bride** /braɪd/ *n* неве́ста. **bridegroom** /ˈbraɪdgruːm/ *n* жени́х. **bridesmaid** /ˈbraɪdzmeɪd/ *n* подру́жка неве́сты.

bridge[1] /brɪdʒ/ *n* мост; (*of nose*) перено́сица; *vt* (*gap*) заполня́ть *impf*, запо́лнить *pf*; (*overcome*) преодолева́ть *impf*, преодоле́ть *pf*.

bridge[2] /brɪdʒ/ *n* (*game*) бридж.

bridle /ˈbraɪd(ə)l/ *n* узда́; *vi* возмуща́ться *impf*, возмути́ться *pf*.

brief /briːf/ *adj* недо́лгий; (*concise*) кра́ткий; *n* инстру́кция; *vt* инструкти́ровать *impf* & *pf*. **briefcase** *n* портфе́ль *m*. **briefing** /ˈbriːfɪŋ/ *n* инструкта́ж. **briefly** /ˈbriːflɪ/ *adv* кра́тко. **briefs** /briːfs/ *n pl* трусы́ (-со́в) *pl*.

brigade /brɪˈgeɪd/ *n* брига́да. **brigadier** /ˌbrɪgəˈdɪə(r)/ *n* генера́л-майо́р.

bright /braɪt/ *adj* я́ркий. **brighten** /ˈbraɪt(ə)n/ (*also* ~ **up**) *vi* проясня́ться *impf*, проясни́ться *pf*; *vt* оживля́ть *impf*, оживи́ть *pf*. **brightness** /ˈbraɪtnɪs/ *n* я́ркость.

brilliant /ˈbrɪlɪənt/ *adj* блестя́щий.

brim /brɪm/ *n* край; (*hat*) поля́ (-ле́й) *pl*.

brine /braɪn/ *n* рассо́л.

bring /brɪŋ/ *vt* (*carry*) приноси́ть *impf*, принести́ *pf*; (*lead*) приводи́ть *impf*, привести́ *pf*; (*transport*) привози́ть *impf*, привезти́ *pf*; ~ **about** приноси́ть *impf*, принести́ *pf*; ~ **back** возвраща́ть *impf*, возврати́ть *pf*; ~ **down** сва́ливать *impf*, свали́ть *pf*; ~ **round** (*unconscious person*) приводи́ть *impf*, привести́ *pf* в себя́; (*deliver*) привози́ть *impf*, привезти́ *pf*; ~ **up** (*educate*) воспи́тывать *impf*, воспита́ть *pf*; (*question*) поднима́ть *impf*, подня́ть *pf*.

brink /brɪŋk/ *n* край.

brisk /brɪsk/ *adj* (*air etc.*) све́жий; (*quick*) бы́стрый.

bristle /ˈbrɪs(ə)l/ *n* щети́на; *vi* щети́ниться *impf*, о~ *pf*.

Britain /ˈbrɪt(ə)n/ *n* Великобрита́ния, А́нглия. **British** /ˈbrɪtɪʃ/ *adj* брита́нский, англи́йский; ~ **Isles** Брита́нские острова́ *m pl*. **Briton** /ˈbrɪt(ə)n/ *n* брита́нец, -нка; англича́нин, -а́нка.

brittle /ˈbrɪt(ə)l/ *adj* хру́пкий.

broach /brəʊtʃ/ *vt* затра́гивать *impf*, затро́нуть *pf*.

broad /brɔːd/ *adj* широ́кий; **in ~ daylight** средь бе́ла дня; **in ~ outline** в о́бщих черта́х. **broadband** *n* (*comput*) широкополо́сная переда́ча да́нных. **broad-minded** /ˌbrɔːdˈmaɪndɪd/ *adj* с широ́кими взгля́дами. **broadly** /ˈbrɔːdlɪ/ *adv*: ~ **speaking** вообще́ говоря́.

broadcast /ˈbrɔːdkɑːst/ *n* переда́ча; *vt* передава́ть *impf*, переда́ть *pf* по ра́дио, по телеви́дению; (*seed*) се́ять *impf*, по~ *pf* вразбро́с. **broadcaster** /-stə(r)/ *n* ди́ктор. **broadcasting** /-stɪŋ/ *n* радио-, теле-, веща́ние.

brocade /brəˈkeɪd/ *n* парча́.

broccoli /ˈbrɒkəlɪ/ *n* бро́кколи *neut indecl*.

brochure /ˈbrəʊʃə(r)/ *n* брошю́ра.

broke /brəʊk/ *predic* без гроша́. **broken** /ˈbrəʊk(ə)n/ *adj* сло́манный; **~-hearted** с разби́тым се́рдцем.

broker /'brəʊkə(r)/ *n* бро́кер, ма́клер.

bronchitis /brɒŋ'kaɪtɪs/ *n* бронхи́т.

bronze /brɒnz/ *n* бро́нза; *adj* бро́нзовый.

brooch /brəʊtʃ/ *n* брошь, бро́шка.

brood /bru:d/ *n* вы́водок; *vi* мра́чно размышля́ть *impf*.

brook[1] /brʊk/ *n* руче́й.

brook[2] /brʊk/ *vt* терпе́ть *impf*.

broom /bru:m/ *n* метла́. **broomstick** *n* (*witches'*) помело́.

broth /brɒθ/ *n* бульо́н.

brothel /'brɒθ(ə)l/ *n* публи́чный дом.

brother /'brʌðə(r)/ *n* брат; **~-in-law** *n* (*sister's husband*) зять; (*husband's brother*) де́верь; (*wife's brother*) шу́рин; (*wife's sister's husband*) своя́к. **brotherhood** /'brʌðəhʊd/ *n* бра́тство. **brotherly** /'brʌðəlɪ/ *adj* бра́тский.

brow /braʊ/ *n* (*eyebrow*) бровь; (*forehead*) лоб; (*of hill*) гре́бень *m*. **browbeaten** /'braʊbi:t(ə)n/ *adj* запу́ганный.

brown /braʊn/ *adj* кори́чневый; (*eyes*) ка́рий; *n* кори́чневый цвет; *vt* (*cul*) подрумя́нивать *impf*, подрумя́нить *pf*.

browse /braʊz/ *vi* (*look around*) осма́триваться *impf*, осмотре́ться *pf*; (*in book*) просма́тривать *impf* просмотре́ть *pf* кни́гу.

bruise /bru:z/ *n* синя́к; *vt* ушиба́ть *impf*, ушиби́ть *pf*.

brunette /bru:'net/ *n* брюне́тка.

brunt /brʌnt/ *n* основна́я тя́жесть.

brush /brʌʃ/ *n* щётка; (*paint*) кисть; *vt* (*clean*) чи́стить *impf*, вы́~, по~ *pf* (щёткой); (*touch*) легко́ каса́ться *impf*, косну́ться *pf* +*gen*; (*hair*) расчёсывать *impf*, расчеса́ть *pf* щёткой; **~ aside, off** отма́хиваться *impf*, отмахну́ться *pf* от+*gen*; **~ up** смета́ть *impf*, смести́ *pf*; (*renew*) подчища́ть *impf*, подчи́стить *pf*.

brushwood /'brʌʃwʊd/ *n* хво́рост.

Brussels sprouts /ˌbrʌs(ə)lz 'spraʊts/ *n pl* брюссе́льская капу́ста.

brutal /'bru:t(ə)l/ *adj* жесто́кий. **brutality** /bru:'tælɪtɪ/ *n* жесто́кость. **brutalize** /'bru:təˌlaɪz/ *vt* ожесточа́ть *impf*, ожесточи́ть *pf*. **brute** /bru:t/ *n* живо́тное *sb*; (*person*) скоти́на. **brutish** /'bru:tɪʃ/ *adj* ха́мский.

B.Sc. *abbr* бакала́вр нау́к.

bubble /'bʌb(ə)l/ *n* пузы́рь *m*; *vi* пузы́риться *impf*; кипе́ть *impf*, вс~ *pf*.

buck /bʌk/ *n* саме́ц оле́ня, кро́лика *etc.*; *vi* брыка́ться *impf*.

bucket /'bʌkɪt/ *n* ведро́.

buckle /'bʌk(ə)l/ *n* пря́жка; *vt* застёгивать *impf*, застегну́ть *pf* (пря́жкой); *vi* (*warp*) коро́биться *impf*, по~, с~ *pf*.

bud /bʌd/ *n* по́чка.

Buddhism /'bʊdɪz(ə)m/ *n* будди́зм. **Buddhist** /'bʊdɪst/ *n* будди́ст; *adj* будди́йский.

budge /bʌdʒ/ *vt* & *i* шевели́ть(ся) *impf*, по~ *pf*.

budget /'bʌdʒɪt/ *n* бюдже́т; *vi*: **~ for** предусма́тривать *impf*, предусмотре́ть *pf* в бюдже́те.

buff /bʌf/ *adj* све́тло-кори́чневый.

buffalo /'bʌfəˌləʊ/ *n* бу́йвол.

buffet[1] /'bʊfeɪ/ *n* буфе́т.

buffet[2] /'bʌfɪt/ *vt* броса́ть *impf* (*impers*).

buffoon /bəˈfuːn/ *n* шут.

bug /bʌɡ/ *n* (*insect*) бука́шка; (*germ*) инфе́кция; (*comput*) оши́бка в програ́мме; (*microphone*) потайно́й микрофо́н; *vt* (*install* ~) устана́вливать *impf*, установи́ть *pf* аппарату́ру для подслу́шивания в+*prep*; (*listen*) подслу́шивать *impf*.

bugle /ˈbjuːɡ(ə)l/ *n* горн.

build /bɪld/ *n* (*of person*) телосложе́ние; *vt* стро́ить *impf*, по~ *pf*; ~ **on** пристра́ивать *impf*, пристро́ить *pf* (**to** к+*dat*); ~ **up** (*vt*) создава́ть *impf*, созда́ть *pf*; (*vi*) накопля́ться *impf*; накопи́ться *pf*. **builder** /ˈbɪldə(r)/ *n* строи́тель *m*. **building** /ˈbɪldɪŋ/ *n* (*edifice*) зда́ние; (*action*) строи́тельство; ~ **site** стро́йка; ~ **society** жили́щно-строи́тельный кооперати́в.

built-up area /ˈbɪltʌp ˈeərɪə/ *n* застро́енный райо́н.

bulb /bʌlb/ *n* лу́ковица; (*electric*) ла́мпочка. **bulbous** /ˈbʌlbəs/ *adj* лу́ковичный.

Bulgaria /bʌlˈɡeərɪə/ *n* Болга́рия. **Bulgarian** /-ən/ *n* болга́рин, -га́рка; *adj* болга́рский.

bulge /bʌldʒ/ *n* вы́пуклость; *vi* выпя́чиваться *impf*; выпира́ть *impf*. **bulging** /ˈbʌldʒɪŋ/ *adj* разбу́хший, оттопы́ривающийся.

bulk /bʌlk/ *n* (*size*) объём; (*greater part*) бо́льшая часть; **in** ~ гурто́м. **bulky** /ˈbʌlkɪ/ *adj* громо́здкий.

bull /bʊl/ *n* бык; (*male*) саме́ц. **bulldog** *n* бульдо́г. **bulldoze** /-dəʊz/ *vt* расчища́ть *impf*, расчи́стить *pf* бульдо́зером. **bulldozer** /-dəʊzə(r)/ *n* бульдо́зер. **bullfinch** *n* снеги́рь *m*. **bullock** /ˈbʊlək/ *n* вол. **bull's-eye** *n* я́блоко.

bullet /ˈbʊlɪt/ *n* пу́ля. **bullet-proof** *adj* пулесто́йкий.

bulletin /ˈbʊlɪtɪn/ *n* бюллете́нь *m*.

bullion /ˈbʊlɪən/ *n*: **gold** ~ зо́лото в сли́тках.

bully /ˈbʊlɪ/ *n* задира *m* & *f*; *vt* запу́гивать *impf*, запуга́ть *pf*.

bum /bʌm/ *n* зад.

bumble-bee /ˈbʌmb(ə)lˌbiː/ *n* шмель *m*.

bump /bʌmp/ *n* (*blow*) уда́р, толчо́к; (*swelling*) ши́шка; (*in road*) уха́б; *vi* ударя́ться *impf*, уда́риться *pf*; ~ **into** ната́лкиваться *impf*, натолкну́ться *pf* на+*acc*. **bumper** /ˈbʌmpə(r)/ *n* ба́мпер.

bumpkin /ˈbʌmpkɪn/ *n* дереве́нщина *m* & *f*.

bumptious /ˈbʌmpʃəs/ *adj* самоуве́ренный.

bumpy /ˈbʌmpɪ/ *adj* уха́бистый.

bun /bʌn/ *n* сдо́бная бу́лка; (*hair*) пучо́к.

bunch /bʌntʃ/ *n* (*of flowers*) буке́т; (*grapes*) гроздь; (*keys*) свя́зка.

bundle /ˈbʌnd(ə)l/ *n* у́зел; *vt* свя́зывать *impf*, связа́ть *pf* в у́зел; ~ **off** спрова́живать *impf*, спрова́дить *pf*.

bungalow /ˈbʌŋɡəˌləʊ/ *n* бу́нгало *neut indecl*.

bungle /ˈbʌŋɡ(ə)l/ *vt* по́ртить *impf*, ис~ *pf*.

bunk /bʌŋk/ *n* ко́йка.

bunker /ˈbʌŋkə(r)/ *n* бу́нкер.

buoy /bɔɪ/ *n* буй. **buoyancy** /ˈbɔɪənsɪ/ *n* плаву́честь; (*fig*) бо́дрость. **buoyant** /ˈbɔɪənt/ *adj* плаву́чий; (*fig*) бо́дрый.

burden /ˈbɜːd(ə)n/ *n* бре́мя *neut*; *vt* обременя́ть *impf*, обремени́ть *pf*.

bureau /ˈbjʊərəʊ/ *n* бюро́ *neut indecl*. **bureaucracy** /ˌbjːʊəˈrɒkrəsɪ/ *n* бюрокра́тия. **bur-**

eaucrat /ˈbjːʊərəˌkræt/ *n* бюрократ. **bureaucratic** /ˌbjːʊərəˈkrætɪk/ *adj* бюрократический.
burger /ˈbɜːgə(r)/ *n* котлета.
burglar /ˈbɜːglə(r)/ *n* взломщик. **burglary** /-rɪ/ *n* кража со взломом. **burgle** /ˈbɜːg(ə)l/ *vt* грабить *impf*, о~ *pf*.
burial /ˈberɪəl/ *n* погребение.
burly /ˈbɜːlɪ/ *adj* здоровенный.
burn /bɜːn/ *vt* жечь *impf*, с~ *pf*; *vt & i* (*injure*) обжигать(ся) *impf*, обжечь(ся) *pf*; *vi* гореть *impf*, с~ *pf*; (*by sun*) загорать *impf*, загореть *pf*; *n* ожог. **burner** /ˈbɜːnə(r)/ *n* горелка.
burnish /ˈbɜːnɪʃ/ *vt* полировать *impf*, от~ *pf*.
burp /bɜːp/ *vi* рыгать *impf*, рыгнуть *pf*.
burrow /ˈbʌrəʊ/ *n* нора; *vi* рыть *impf*, вы~ *pf* нору; (*fig*) рыться *impf*.
bursar /ˈbɜːsə/ *n* казначей. **bursary** /-rɪ/ *n* стипендия.
burst /bɜːst/ *n* разрыв, вспышка; *vi* разрываться *impf*, разорваться *pf*; (*bubble*) лопаться *impf*, лопнуть *pf*; *vt* разрывать *impf*, разорвать *pf*; ~ **into tears** расплакаться *pf*.
bury /ˈberɪ/ *vt* (*dead*) хоронить *impf*, по~ *pf*; (*hide*) зарывать *impf*, зарыть *pf*.
bus /bʌs/ *n* автобус; ~ **stop** автобусная остановка.
bush /bʊʃ/ *n* куст. **bushy** /ˈbʊʃɪ/ *adj* густой.
busily /ˈbɪzɪlɪ/ *adv* энергично.
business /ˈbɪznɪs/ *n* (*affair, dealings*) дело; (*firm*) предприятие; **mind your own** ~ не ваше дело; **on** ~ по делу. **businesslike** *adj* деловой. **businessman** *n* бизнесмен.
busker /ˈbʌskə(r)/ *n* уличный музыкант.
bust /bʌst/ *n* бюст; (*bosom*) грудь.
bustle /ˈbʌs(ə)l/ *n* суета; *vi* суетиться *impf*.
busy /ˈbɪzɪ/ *adj* занятой; *vt*: ~ **o.s.** заниматься *impf*, заняться *pf* (**with** +*instr*). **busybody** *n* назойливый человек.
but /bʌt/ *conj* но, а; ~ **then** зато; *prep* кроме+*gen*.
butcher /ˈbʊtʃə(r)/ *n* мясник; *vt* резать *impf*, за~ *pf*; ~**'s shop** мясная *sb*.
butler /ˈbʌtlə(r)/ *n* дворецкий *sb*.
butt[1] /bʌt/ *n* (*cask*) бочка.
butt[2] /bʌt/ *n* (*of gun*) приклад; (*cigarette*) окурок.
butt[3] /bʌt/ *n* (*target*) мишень.
butt[4] /bʌt/ *vt* бодать *impf*, за~ *pf*; ~ **in** вмешиваться *impf*, вмешаться *pf*.
butter /ˈbʌtə(r)/ *n* (сливочное) масло; *vt* намазывать *impf*, намазать *pf* маслом; ~ **up** льстить *impf*, по~ *pf*. **buttercup** *n* лютик. **butterfly** *n* бабочка.
buttock /ˈbʌtək/ *n* ягодица.
button /ˈbʌt(ə)n/ *n* пуговица; (*knob*) кнопка; *vt* застёгивать *impf*, застегнуть *pf*. **buttonhole** *n* петля.
buttress /ˈbʌtrɪs/ *n* контрфорс; *vt* подпирать *impf*, подпереть *pf*.
buxom /ˈbʌksəm/ *adj* полногрудая.
buy /baɪ/ *n* покупка; *vt* покупать *impf*, купить *pf*. **buyer** /ˈbaɪə(r)/ *n* покупатель *m*.
buzz /bʌz/ *n* жужжание; *vi* жужжать *impf*.
buzzard /ˈbʌzəd/ *n* канюк.
buzzer /ˈbʌzə(r)/ *n* зуммер.
by /baɪ/ *adv* мимо; *prep* (*near*) около+*gen*, у+*gen*; (*beside*)

ря́дом c+*instr*; (*past*) ми́мо +*gen*; (*time*) к+*dat*; (*means*) *instr without prep*; **~ and large** в це́лом.

bye /baɪ/ *int* пока́!

by-election /ˈbaɪɪ,lekʃ(ə)n/ *n* дополни́тельные вы́боры *m pl.*

Byelorussian /,bjeləʊˈrʌʃ(ə)n/ *see* **Belorussian**

bygone /ˈbaɪgɒn/ *adj* мину́вший; **let ~s be ~s** что прошло́, то прошло́. **by-law** *n* постановле́ние. **bypass** *n* обхо́д; *vt* обходи́ть *impf*, обойти́ *pf*. **by-product** *n* побо́чный проду́кт. **byroad** *n* небольша́я доро́га. **bystander** /ˈbaɪ ,stændə(r)/ *n* свиде́тель *m*. **byway** *n* просёлочная доро́га. **byword** *n* олицетворе́ние (**for** +*gen*).

Byzantine /bɪˈzæntaɪn/ *adj* византи́йский.

C

cab /kæb/ *n* (*taxi*) такси́ *neut indecl*; (*of lorry*) каби́на.

cabaret /ˈkæbə,reɪ/ *n* кабаре́ *neut indecl.*

cabbage /ˈkæbɪdʒ/ *n* капу́ста.

cabin /ˈkæbɪn/ *n* (*hut*) хи́жина; (*aeron*) каби́на; (*naut*) каю́та.

cabinet /ˈkæbɪnɪt/ *n* шкаф; (*Cabinet*) кабине́т; **~-maker** краснодере́вец; **~-minister** мини́стр-член кабине́та.

cable /ˈkeɪb(ə)l/ *n* (*rope*) кана́т; (*electric*) ка́бель *m*; (*cablegram*) телегра́мма; *vt* & *i* телеграфи́ровать *impf* & *pf*.

cache /kæʃ/ *n* потайно́й склад.

cackle /ˈkæk(ə)l/ *vi* горота́ть *impf.*

cactus /ˈkæktəs/ *n* ка́ктус.

caddy /ˈkædɪ/ *n* (*box*) ча́йница.

cadet /kəˈdet/ *n* новобра́нец.

cadge /kædʒ/ *vt* стреля́ть *impf*, стрельну́ть *pf.*

cadres /ˈkɑːdəz/ *n pl* ка́дры *m pl.*

Caesarean (section) /sɪˈzeərɪən (ˈsekʃ(ə)n)/ *n* ке́сарево сече́ние.

cafe /ˈkæfeɪ/ *n* кафе́ *neut indecl.* **cafeteria** /,kæfɪˈtɪərɪə/ *n* кафете́рий.

caffeine /ˈkæfiːn/ *n* кофеи́н.

cage /keɪdʒ/ *n* кле́тка.

cajole /kəˈdʒəʊl/ *vt* зада́бривать *impf*, задо́брить *pf.*

cake /keɪk/ *n* (*large*) торт, (*small*) пиро́жное *sb*; (*fruit-~*) кекс; *vt*: **~d** облéпленный (**in** +*instr*).

calamitous /kəˈlæmɪtəs/ *adj* бе́дственный. **calamity** /-ˈlæmɪtɪ/ *n* бе́дствие.

calcium /ˈkælsɪəm/ *n* ка́льций.

calculate /ˈkælkjʊ,leɪt/ *vt* вычисля́ть *impf*, вы́числить *pf*; *vi* рассчи́тывать *impf*, рассчита́ть *pf* (**on** на+*acc*). **calculation** /,kælkjʊˈleɪʃ(ə)n/ *n* вычисле́ние, расчёт. **calculator** /ˈkælkjʊ,leɪtə(r)/ *n* калькуля́тор.

calendar /ˈkælɪndə(r)/ *n* календа́рь *m*.

calf[1] /kɑːf/ *n* (*cow*) телёнок.

calf[2] /kɑːf/ *n* (*leg*) икра́.

calibrate /ˈkælɪ,breɪt/ *vt* калиброва́ть *impf.* **calibre** /-bə(r)/ *n* кали́бр.

call /kɔːl/ *v* звать *impf*, по~ *pf*; (*name*) называ́ть *impf*, назва́ть *pf*; (*cry*) крича́ть *impf*, кри́кнуть *pf*; (*wake*) буди́ть *impf*, раз~ *pf*; (*visit*) заходи́ть *impf*, зайти́ *pf* (**on** к+*dat*; **at** в+*acc*); (*stop at*) остана́вливаться *impf*, останови́ться *pf* (**at** в, на, +*prep*); (*summon*) вызыва́ть *impf*, вы́звать *pf*; (*ring up*) звони́ть *impf*, по~ *pf +dat*; ~ **for** (*require*) тре́бовать *impf*, по~ *pf +gen*; (*fetch*) заходи́ть *impf*, зайти́ *pf* за+*instr*; ~ **off** отменя́ть *impf*, отмени́ть *pf*; ~ **out** вскри́кивать *impf*, вскри́кнуть *pf*; ~ **up** призыва́ть *impf*, призва́ть *pf*; *n* (*cry*) крик; (*summons*) зов, призы́в; (*telephone*) (телефо́нный) вы́зов, разгово́р; (*visit*) визи́т; (*signal*) сигна́л; ~**-box** телефо́н-автома́т; ~ **centre** колл-це́нтр, информацио́нно-спра́вочная слу́жба; ~**-up** призы́в. **caller** /'kɔ:lə(r)/ *n* посети́тель *m*, ~ница; (*tel*) позвони́вший *sb*. **calling** /'kɔ:lɪŋ/ *n* (*vocation*) призва́ние.

callous /'kæləs/ *adj* (*person*) чёрствый.

callus /'kæləs/ *n* мозо́ль.

calm /kɑ:m/ *adj* споко́йный; *n* споко́йствие; *vt* & *i* (~ *down*) успока́ивать(ся) *impf*, успоко́ить(ся) *pf*.

calorie /'kælərɪ/ *n* кало́рия.

camber /'kæmbə(r)/ *n* скат.

camcorder /'kæm,kɔ:də(r)/ *n* камко́рдер.

camel /'kæm(ə)l/ *n* верблю́д.

camera /'kæmrə/ *n* фотоаппара́т. **cameraman** *n* кинооперáтор.

camouflage /'kæmə,flɑ:ʒ/ *n* камуфля́ж; *vt* маскирова́ть *impf*, за~ *pf*.

camp /kæmp/ *n* ла́герь *m*; *vi* (*set up* ~) располага́ться *impf*, расположи́ться *pf* ла́герем; (*go camping*) жить *impf* в пала́тках; ~**-bed** раскладу́шка; ~**-fire** костёр.

campaign /kæm'peɪn/ *n* кампа́ния; *vi* проводи́ть *impf*, провести́ *pf* кампа́нию.

campsite /'kæmpsaɪt/ *n* ла́герь *m*, ке́мпинг.

campus /'kæmpəs/ *n* университе́тский городо́к.

can[1] /kæn/ *n* ба́нка; *vt* консерви́ровать *impf*, за~ *pf*.

can[2] /kæn/ *v aux* (*be able*) мочь *impf*, с~ *pf +inf*; (*know how*) уме́ть *impf*, с~ *pf +inf*.

Canada /'kænədə/ *n* Кана́да. **Canadian** /kə'neɪdɪən/ *n* кана́дец, -дка; *adj* кана́дский.

canal /kə'næl/ *n* кана́л.

canary /kə'neərɪ/ *n* канаре́йка.

cancel /'kæns(ə)l/ *vt* (*make void*) аннули́ровать *impf* & *pf*; (*call off*) отменя́ть *impf*, отмени́ть *pf*; (*stamp*) гаси́ть *impf*, по~ *pf*. **cancellation** /,kænsə'leɪʃ(ə)n/ *n* аннули́рование; отме́на.

cancer /'kænsə(r)/ *n* рак; (**C**~) Рак. **cancerous** /'kænsərəs/ *adj* ра́ковый.

candelabrum /,kændɪ'lɑ:brəm/ *n* канделя́бр.

candid /'kændɪd/ *adj* открове́нный.

candidate /'kændɪdət/ *n* кандида́т.

candied /'kændɪd/ *adj* заса́харенный.

candle /'kænd(ə)l/ *n* свеча́. **candlestick** *n* подсве́чник.

candour /'kændə(r)/ *n* открове́нность.

candy /'kændɪ/ *n* сла́дости *f pl*.

cane /keɪn/ *n* (*plant*) тростни́к; (*stick*) трость, па́лка; *vt* бить *impf*, по~ *pf* па́лкой.

canine /'keɪnaɪn/ *adj* соба́чий; *n* (*tooth*) клык.

canister /'kænɪstə(r)/ *n* ба́нка.

cannabis /'kænəbɪs/ *n* гаши́ш.

cannibal /'kænɪb(ə)l/ *n* людое́д. **cannibalism** /-,lɪz(ə)m/ *n* людое́дство.

cannon /'kænən/ *n* пу́шка; ~**-ball** пу́шечное ядро́.

canoe /kə'nu:/ *n* кано́э *neut in-*

decl; *vi* пла́вать *indet*, плыть *det* на каноэ́.
canon /'kænən/ *n* кано́н; (*person*) кано́ник. **canonize** /-ˌnaɪz/ *vt* канонизова́ть *impf* & *pf*.
canopy /'kænəpɪ/ *n* балдахи́н.
cant /kænt/ *n* (*hypocrisy*) ха́нжество; (*jargon*) жарго́н.
cantankerous /kæn'tæŋkərəs/ *adj* сварли́вый.
cantata /kæn'tɑ:tə/ *n* канта́та.
canteen /kæn'ti:n/ *n* столо́вая *sb*.
canter /'kæntə(r)/ *n* лёгкий гало́п; *vi* (*rider*) е́здить *indet*, е́хать *det* лёгким гало́пом; (*horse*) ходи́ть *indet*, идти́ *det* лёгким гало́пом.
canvas /'kænvəs/ *n* (*art*) холст; (*naut*) паруси́на; (*tent material*) брезе́нт.
canvass /'kænvəs/ *vi* агити́ровать *impf*, с~ *pf* (**for** за+*acc*); *n* собира́ние голосо́в; агита́ция. **canvasser** /'kænvəsə(r)/ *n* собира́тель *m* голосо́в.
canyon /'kænjən/ *n* каньо́н.
cap /kæp/ *n* (*of uniform*) фура́жка; (*cloth*) ке́пка; (*woman's*) чепе́ц; (*lid*) кры́шка; *vt* превосходи́ть *impf*, превзойти́ *pf*.
capability /ˌkeɪpə'bɪlɪtɪ/ *n* спосо́бность. **capable** /'keɪpəb(ə)l/ *adj* спосо́бный (**of** на+*acc*).
capacious /kə'peɪʃəs/ *adj* вмести́тельный. **capacity** /kə'pæsɪtɪ/ *n* ёмкость; (*ability*) спосо́бность; **in the ~ of** в ка́честве +*gen*.
cape[1] /keɪp/ *n* (*geog*) мыс.
cape[2] /keɪp/ *n* (*cloak*) наки́дка.
caper /'keɪpə(r)/ *vi* скака́ть *impf*.
capers /'keɪpəz/ *n pl* (*cul*) ка́персы *m pl*.
capillary /kə'pɪlərɪ/ *adj* капилля́рный.
capital /'kæpɪt(ə)l/ *adj* (*letter*) прописно́й; **~ punishment** сме́ртная казнь; *n* (*town*) столи́ца; (*letter*) прописна́я бу́ква; (*econ*) капита́л. **capitalism** /-ˌlɪz(ə)m/ *n* капитали́зм. **capitalist** /-lɪst/ *n* капитали́ст; *adj* капиталисти́ческий. **capitalize** /-ˌlaɪz/ *vt* извлека́ть *impf*, извле́чь *pf* вы́году (**on** из+*gen*).
capitulate /kə'pɪtjʊˌleɪt/ *vi* капитули́ровать *impf* & *pf*. **capitulation** /-'leɪʃ(ə)n/ *n* капитуля́ция.
caprice /kə'pri:s/ *n* капри́з. **capricious** /-'prɪʃəs/ *adj* капри́зный.
Capricorn /'kæprɪˌkɔ:n/ *n* Козеро́г.
capsize /kæp'saɪz/ *vt* & *i* опроки́дывать(ся) *impf*, опроки́нуть(ся) *pf*.
capsule /'kæpsju:l/ *n* ка́псула.
captain /'kæptɪn/ *n* капита́н; *vt* быть капита́ном +*gen*.
caption /'kæpʃ(ə)n/ *n* по́дпись; (*cin*) титр.
captious /'kæpʃəs/ *adj* приди́рчивый.
captivate /'kæptɪˌveɪt/ *vt* пленя́ть *impf*, плени́ть *pf*. **captivating** /'kæptɪˌveɪtɪŋ/ *adj* плени́тельный. **captive** /'kæptɪv/ *adj* & *n* пле́нный. **captivity** /kæp'tɪvɪtɪ/ *n* нево́ля; (*esp mil*) плен. **capture** /'kæptʃə(r)/ *n* взя́тие, захва́т, поимка; *vt* (*person*) брать *impf*, взять *pf* в плен; (*seize*) захва́тывать *impf*, захвати́ть *pf*.
car /kɑ:(r)/ *n* маши́на; автомоби́ль *m*; **~ park** стоя́нка.
carafe /kə'ræf/ *n* графи́н.
caramel(s) /'kærəˌmel(z)/ *n* караме́ль.
carat /'kærət/ *n* кара́т.
caravan /'kærəˌvæn/ *n* фурго́н;

(*convoy*) карава́н.
caraway (seeds) /ˈkærəˌweɪ (siːdz)/ *n* тмин.
carbohydrate /ˌkɑːbəˈhaɪdreɪt/ *n* углево́д. **carbon** /ˈkɑːb(ə)n/ *n* углеро́д; ~ **copy** ко́пия; ~ **dioxide** углекислота́; ~ **monoxide** о́кись углеро́да; ~ **paper** копирова́льная бума́га.
carburettor /ˌkɑːbjʊˈretə(r)/ *n* карбюра́тор.
carcass /ˈkɑːkəs/ *n* ту́ша.
card /kɑːd/ *n* (*stiff paper*) карто́н; (*visiting* ~) ка́рточка; (*playing* ~) ка́рта; (*greetings* ~) откры́тка; (*ticket*) биле́т. **cardboard** *n* карто́н; *adj* карто́нный.
cardiac /ˈkɑːdɪˌæk/ *adj* серде́чный.
cardigan /ˈkɑːdɪgən/ *n* кардига́н.
cardinal /ˈkɑːdɪn(ə)l/ *adj* кардина́льный; ~ **number** коли́чественное числи́тельное *sb*; *n* кардина́л.
care /keə(r)/ *n* (*trouble*) забо́та; (*caution*) осторо́жность; (*tending*) ухо́д; **in the** ~ **of** на попече́нии +*gen*; **take** ~ осторо́жно!; смотри́(те)!; **take** ~ **of** забо́титься *impf*, по~ *pf* о+*prep*; *vi*: **I don't** ~ мне всё равно́; ~ **for** (*look after*) уха́живать *impf* за +*instr*; (*like*) нра́виться *impf*, по~ *pf impers* +*dat*.
career /kəˈrɪə(r)/ *n* карье́ра.
carefree /ˈkeəfriː/ *adj* беззабо́тный. **careful** /-fʊl/ *adj* (*cautious*) осторо́жный; (*thorough*) тща́тельный. **careless** /-lɪs/ *adj* (*negligent*) небре́жный; (*incautious*) неосторо́жный.
caress /kəˈres/ *n* ла́ска; *vt* ласка́ть *impf*.
caretaker /ˈkeəteɪkə(r)/ *n* смотри́тель *m*, ~ница; *attrib* вре́менный.
cargo /ˈkɑːgəʊ/ *n* груз.
caricature /ˈkærɪkətjʊə(r)/ *n* карикату́ра; *vt* изобража́ть *impf*, изобрази́ть *pf* в карикату́рном ви́де.
carnage /ˈkɑːnɪdʒ/ *n* резня́.
carnal /ˈkɑːn(ə)l/ *adj* пло́тский.
carnation /kɑːˈneɪʃ(ə)n/ *n* гвозди́ка.
carnival /ˈkɑːnɪv(ə)l/ *n* карнава́л.
carnivorous /kɑːˈnɪvərəs/ *adj* плотоя́дный.
carol /ˈkær(ə)l/ *n* (рожде́ственский) гимн.
carouse /kəˈraʊz/ *vi* кути́ть *impf*, кутну́ть *pf*.
carp[1] /kɑːp/ *n* карп.
carp[2] /kɑːp/ *vi* придира́ться *impf*, придра́ться *pf* (**at** к+*dat*).
carpenter /ˈkɑːpɪntə(r)/ *n* пло́тник. **carpentry** /-trɪ/ *n* пло́тничество.
carpet /ˈkɑːpɪt/ *n* ковёр; *vt* покрыва́ть *impf*, покры́ть *pf* ковро́м.
carping /ˈkɑːpɪŋ/ *adj* приди́рчивый.
carriage /ˈkærɪdʒ/ *n* (*vehicle*) каре́та; (*rly*) ваго́н; (*conveyance*) перево́зка; (*bearing*) оса́нка. **carriageway** *n* прое́зжая часть доро́ги. **carrier** /ˈkærɪə(r)/ *n* (*on bike*) бага́жник; (*firm*) тра́нспортная кампа́ния; (*med*) бациллоноси́тель *m*.
carrot /ˈkærət/ *n* морко́вка; *pl* морко́вь (*collect*).
carry /ˈkærɪ/ *vt* (*by hand*) носи́ть *indet*, нести́ *det*; переноси́ть *impf*, перенести́ *pf*; (*in vehicle*) вози́ть *indet*, везти́ *det*; (*sound*) передава́ть *impf*, переда́ть *pf*; *vi* (*sound*) быть слы́шен; **be carried away** увлека́ться *impf*,

увле́чься *pf*; ~ **on** (*continue*) продолжа́ть *impf*; ~ **out** выполня́ть *impf*, вы́полнить *pf*; ~ **over** переноси́ть *impf*, перенести́ *pf*.
cart /kɑːt/ *n* теле́га; *vt* (*lug*) тащи́ть *impf*.
cartilage /ˈkɑːtɪlɪdʒ/ *n* хрящ.
carton /ˈkɑːt(ə)n/ *n* карто́нка
cartoon /kɑːˈtuːn/ *n* карикату́ра; (*cin*) мультфи́льм. **cartoonist** /-nɪst/ *n* карикатури́ст, ~ка.
cartridge /ˈkɑːtrɪdʒ/ *n* патро́н; (*for printer*) ка́ртридж.
carve /kɑːv/ *vt* ре́зать *impf* по+*dat*; (*in wood*) выреза́ть *impf*, вы́резать *pf*; (*in stone*) высека́ть *impf*, вы́сечь; (*slice*) нареза́ть *impf*, наре́зать *pf*. **carving** /ˈkɑːvɪŋ/ *n* резьба́; ~ **knife** нож для нареза́ния мя́са.
cascade /kæsˈkeɪd/ *n* каска́д; *vi* па́дать *impf*.
case[1] /keɪs/ *n* (*instance*) слу́чай; (*law*) де́ло; (*med*) больно́й *sb*; (*gram*) паде́ж; **in** ~ (в слу́чае) е́сли; **in any** ~ во вся́ком слу́чае; **in no** ~ ни в ко́ем слу́чае; **just in** ~ на вся́кий слу́чай.
case[2] /keɪs/ *n* (*box*) я́щик; (*suitcase*) чемода́н; (*small box*) футля́р; (*cover*) чехо́л; (*display* ~) витри́на.
cash /kæʃ/ *n* нали́чные *sb*; (*money*) де́ньги *pl*; ~ **on delivery** нало́женным платежо́м; ~ **desk, register** ка́сса; ~ **machine** банкома́т; *vt*: ~ **a cheque** получа́ть *impf*, получи́ть *pf* де́ньги по че́ку. **cashier** /kæˈʃɪə(r)/ *n* касси́р.
casing /ˈkeɪsɪŋ/ *n* (*tech*) кожу́х.
casino /kəˈsiːnəʊ/ *n* казино́ *neut indecl*.
cask /kɑːsk/ *n* бо́чка.
casket /ˈkɑːskɪt/ *n* шкату́лка.
casserole /ˈkæsəˌrəʊl/ *n* (*pot*) ла́тка; (*stew*) рагу́ *neut indecl*.
cassette /kəˈset/ *n* кассе́та; ~ **recorder** кассе́тный магнитофо́н.
cassock /ˈkæsək/ *n* ря́са.
cast /kɑːst/ *vt* (*throw*) броса́ть *impf*, бро́сить *pf*; (*shed*) сбра́сывать *impf*, сбро́сить *pf*; (*theat*) распределя́ть *impf*, распредели́ть *pf* ро́ли +*dat*; (*found*) лить *impf*, с~ *pf*; ~ **off** (*knitting*) спуска́ть *impf*, спусти́ть *pf* пе́тли; (*naut*) отплыва́ть *impf*, отплы́ть *pf*; ~ **on** (*knitting*) набира́ть *impf*, набра́ть *pf* пе́тли; *n* (*of mind etc.*) склад; (*mould*) фо́рма; (*moulded object*) сле́пок; (*med*) ги́псовая повя́зка; (*theat*) де́йствующие ли́ца (-ц) *pl*. **castaway** /ˈkɑːstəweɪ/ *n* потерпе́вший *sb* кораблекруше́ние. **cast iron** *n* чугу́н. **cast-iron** *adj* чугу́нный. **cast-offs** *n pl* но́шеное пла́тье.
castanet /ˌkæstæˈnet/ *n* кастанье́та.
caste /kɑːst/ *n* ка́ста.
castigate /ˈkæstɪˌgeɪt/ *vt* бичева́ть *impf*.
castle /ˈkɑːs(ə)l/ *n* за́мок; (*chess*) ладья́.
castor /ˈkɑːstə(r)/ *n* (*wheel*) ро́лик; ~ **sugar** са́харная пу́дра.
castrate /kæˈstreɪt/ *vt* кастри́ровать *impf* & *pf*. **castration** /-ˈstreɪʃ(ə)n/ *n* кастра́ция.
casual /ˈkæʒʊəl/ *adj* (*chance*) случа́йный; (*offhand*) небре́жный; (*clothes*) обы́денный; (*unofficial*) неофициа́льный; (*informal*) лёгкий; (*labour*) подённый; ~ **labourer** подёнщик, -ица. **casualty** /ˈkæʒʊəltɪ/ *n* (*wounded*) ране-

ный *sb*; (*killed*) уби́тый *sb*; *pl* поте́ри (-рь) *pl*; ~ **ward** пала́та ско́рой по́мощи.

cat /kæt/ *n* ко́шка; (*tom*) кот; ~**'s-eye** (*on road*) (доро́жный) рефле́ктор.

catalogue /'kætəˌlɒg/ *n* катало́г; (*price list*) прейскура́нт; *vt* каталогизи́ровать *impf* & *pf*.

catalyst /'kætəlɪst/ *n* катализа́тор. **catalytic** /ˌkætə'lɪtɪk/ *adj* каталити́ческий.

catapult /'kætəˌpʌlt/ *n* (*toy*) рога́тка; (*hist*, *aeron*) катапу́льта; *vt* & *i* катапульти́ровать(ся) *impf* & *pf*.

cataract /'kætəˌrækt/ *n* (*med*) катара́кта.

catarrh /kə'tɑ:(r)/ *n* ката́р.

catastrophe /kə'tæstrəfɪ/ *n* катастро́фа. **catastrophic** /ˌkætə'strɒfɪk/ *adj* катастрофи́ческий.

catch /kætʃ/ *vt* (*ball*, *fish*, *thief*) лови́ть *impf*, пойма́ть *pf*; (*surprise*) застава́ть *impf*, заста́ть *pf*; (*disease*) заража́ться *impf*, зарази́ться *pf* +*instr*; (*be in time for*) успева́ть *impf*, успе́ть *pf* на+*acc*; *vt* & *i* (*snag*) зацепля́ть(ся) *impf*, зацепи́ть(ся) *pf* (**on** за+*acc*); ~ **on** (*become popular*) привива́ться *impf*, приви́ться *pf*; ~ **up with** догоня́ть *impf*, догна́ть *pf*; *n* (*of fish*) уло́в; (*trick*) уло́вка; (*on door etc.*) защёлка. **catching** /'kætʃɪŋ/ *adj* зара́зный. **catchword** *n* мо́дное слове́чко. **catchy** /'kætʃɪ/ *adj* прили́пчивый.

categorical /ˌkætɪ'gɒrɪk(ə)l/ *adj* категори́ческий. **category** /'kætɪgərɪ/ *n* катего́рия.

cater /'keɪtə(r)/ *vi*: ~ **for** поставля́ть *impf*, поста́вить *pf* прови́зию для+*gen*; (*satisfy*) удовлетворя́ть *impf*, удовлетвори́ть *pf*. **caterer** /'keɪtərə(r)/ *n* поставщи́к (прови́зии).

caterpillar /'kætəˌpɪlə(r)/ *n* гу́сеница.

cathedral /kə'θi:dr(ə)l/ *n* собо́р.

catheter /'kæθɪtə(r)/ *n* кате́тер.

Catholic /'kæθəlɪk/ *adj* католи́ческий; *n* като́лик, -ичка. **Catholicism** /kə'θɒlɪˌsɪz(ə)m/ *n* католи́чество.

cattle /'kæt(ə)l/ *n* скот.

Caucasus /'kɔ:kəsəs/ *n* Кавка́з.

cauldron /'kɔ:ldrən/ *n* котёл.

cauliflower /'kɒlɪˌflaʊə(r)/ *n* цветна́я капу́ста.

cause /kɔ:z/ *n* причи́на, по́вод; (*law etc.*) де́ло; *vt* причиня́ть *impf*, причини́ть *pf*; вызыва́ть *impf*, вы́звать *pf*; (*induce*) заставля́ть *impf*, заста́вить *pf*.

caustic /'kɔ:stɪk/ *adj* е́дкий.

cauterize /'kɔ:təˌraɪz/ *vt* прижига́ть *impf*, приже́чь *pf*.

caution /'kɔ:ʃ(ə)n/ *n* осторо́жность; (*warning*) предостереже́ние; *vt* предостерега́ть *impf*, предостере́чь *pf*. **cautious** /'kɔ:ʃəs/ *adj* осторо́жный. **cautionary** /'kɔ:ʃənərɪ/ *adj* предостерега́ющий.

cavalcade /ˌkævəl'keɪd/ *n* кавалька́да. **cavalier** /ˌkævə'lɪə(r)/ *adj* бесцеремо́нный. **cavalry** /'kævəlrɪ/ *n* кавале́рия.

cave /keɪv/ *n* пеще́ра; *vi*: ~ **in** обва́ливаться *impf*, обвали́ться *pf*; (*yield*) сдава́ться *impf*, сда́ться *pf*. **caveman** *n* пеще́рный челове́к. **cavern** /'kæv(ə)n/ *n* пеще́ра. **cavernous** /'kæv(ə)nəs/ *adj* пеще́ристый.

caviare /'kævɪˌɑ:(r)/ *n* икра́.

cavity /'kævɪtɪ/ *n* впа́дина, по́лость; (*in tooth*) дупло́.

cavort /kə'vɔ:t/ *vi* скака́ть *impf*.

caw /kɔ:/ *vi* ка́ркать *impf*, каркнуть *pf*.

CD *abbr* (*of* **compact disc**) компа́кт-ди́ск; **~ player** проигрыватель *m* компа́кт-ди́сков.

cease /siːs/ *vt* & *i* прекраща́ть(ся) *impf*, прекрати́ть(ся) *pf*; *vt* перестава́ть *impf*, переста́ть *pf* (+*inf*); **~-fire** прекраще́ние огня́. **ceaseless** /ˈsiːslɪs/ *adj* непреста́нный.

cedar /ˈsiːdə(r)/ *n* кедр.

cede /siːd/ *vt* уступа́ть *impf*, уступи́ть *pf*.

ceiling /ˈsiːlɪŋ/ *n* потоло́к; (*fig*) максима́льный у́ровень *m*.

celebrate /ˈselɪˌbreɪt/ *vt* & *i* пра́здновать *impf*, от~ *pf*; (*extol*) прославля́ть *impf*, просла́вить *pf*. **celebrated** /-tɪd/ *adj* знамени́тый. **celebration** /-ˈbreɪʃ(ə)n/ *n* пра́зднование. **celebrity** /sɪˈlebrɪtɪ/ *n* знамени́тость.

celery /ˈselərɪ/ *n* сельдере́й.

celestial /sɪˈlestɪəl/ *adj* небе́сный.

celibacy /ˈselɪbəsɪ/ *n* безбра́чие. **celibate** /ˈselɪbət/ *adj* холосто́й; *n* холостя́к.

cell /sel/ *n* (*prison*) ка́мера; (*biol*) кле́тка; **~ phone** со́товый телефо́н.

cellar /ˈselə(r)/ *n* подва́л.

cello /ˈtʃeləʊ/ *n* виолонче́ль.

cellophane /ˈseləˌfeɪn/ *n* целлофа́н. **cellular** /ˈseljʊlə(r)/ *adj* кле́точный.

Celt /kelt/ *n* кельт. **Celtic** /ˈkeltɪk/ *adj* ке́льтский.

cement /sɪˈment/ *n* цеме́нт; *vt* цементи́ровать *impf*, за~ *pf*.

cemetery /ˈsemɪtərɪ/ *n* кла́дбище.

censor /ˈsensə(r)/ *n* це́нзор; *vt* подверга́ть *impf*, подве́ргнуть *pf* цензу́ре. **censorious** /senˈsɔːrɪəs/ *adj* сверхкрити́ческий. **censorship** /ˈsensəʃɪp/ *n* цензу́ра. **censure** /ˈsensjə(r)/ *n* порица́ние; *vt* порица́ть *impf*.

census /ˈsensəs/ *n* пе́репись.

cent /sent/ *n* цент; **per ~** проце́нт.

centenary /senˈtiːnərɪ/ *n* столе́тие. **centennial** /-ˈtenɪəl/ *adj* столе́тний. **centigrade** /ˈsentɪˌgreɪd/ *adj*: **10° ~** 10° по Це́льсию. **centimetre** /ˈsentɪˌmiːtə(r)/ *n* сантиме́тр. **centipede** /ˈsentɪˌpiːd/ *n* сороконо́жка.

central /ˈsentr(ə)l/ *adj* центра́льный; **~ heating** центра́льное отопле́ние. **centralization** /ˌsentrəlaɪˈzeɪʃ(ə)n/ *n* централиза́ция. **centralize** /ˈsentrəˌlaɪz/ *vt* централизова́ть *impf* & *pf*.

centre /ˈsentə(r)/ *n* центр; середи́на; **~ forward** центр нападе́ния; *vi* & *i*: **~ on** сосредото́чивать(ся) *impf*, сосредото́чить(ся) *pf* на+*prep*. **centrifugal** /ˌsentrɪˈfjuːg(ə)l/ *adj* центробе́жный.

century /ˈsentʃərɪ/ *n* столе́тие, век.

ceramic /sɪˈræmɪk/ *adj* керами́ческий. **ceramics** /-mɪks/ *n pl* кера́мика.

cereals /ˈsɪərɪəlz/ *n pl* хле́бные зла́ки *m pl*; **breakfast ~** зерновы́е хло́пья (-ев) *pl*.

cerebral /ˈserɪbr(ə)l/ *adj* мозгово́й.

ceremonial /ˌserɪˈməʊnɪəl/ *adj* церемониа́льный; *n* церемониа́л. **ceremonious** /-nɪəs/ *adj* церемо́нный. **ceremony** /ˈserɪmənɪ/ *n* церемо́ния.

certain /ˈsɜːt(ə)n/ *adj* (*confident*) уве́рен (-нна); (*undoubted*) несомне́нный; (*unspecified*) изве́стный; (*inevitable*) ве́рный; **for ~** наверняка́. **certainly** /-lɪ/ *adv* (*of course*) коне́чно, безус-

ло́вно; (*without doubt*) несомне́нно; ~ **not!** ни в ко́ем слу́чае. **certainty** /-tɪ/ *n* (*conviction*) уве́ренность; (*fact*) несомне́нный факт.
certificate /sə'tɪfɪkət/ *n* свиде́тельство; сертифика́т. **certify** /'sɜːtɪfaɪ/ *vt* удостоверя́ть *impf*, удостове́рить *pf*.
cervical /sɜː'vaɪk(ə)l/ *n* ше́йный. **cervix** /'sɜːvɪks/ *n* ше́йка ма́тки.
cessation /se'seɪʃ(ə)n/ *n* прекраще́ние.
cf. *abbr* ср., сравни́.
CFCs *abbr* (*of* **chlorofluorocarbons**) хлори́рованные фторуглеро́ды *m pl*.
chafe /tʃeɪf/ *vt* (*rub*) тере́ть *impf*; (*rub sore*) натира́ть *impf*, натере́ть *pf*.
chaff /tʃɑːf/ *n* (*husks*) мяки́на; (*straw*) се́чка.
chaffinch /'tʃæfɪntʃ/ *n* зя́блик.
chagrin /'ʃægrɪn/ *n* огорче́ние.
chain /tʃeɪn/ *n* цепь; ~ **reaction** цепна́я реа́кция; ~ **smoker** зая́длый кури́льщик.
chair /tʃeə(r)/ *n* стул, (*armchair*) кре́сло; (*univ*) ка́федра; *vt* (*preside*) председа́тельствовать *impf* на+*prep*. **chairman, -woman** *n* председа́тель *m*, ~ница.
chalice /'tʃælɪs/ *n* ча́ша.
chalk /tʃɔːk/ *n* мел. **chalky** /'tʃɔːkɪ/ *adj* мелово́й.
challenge /'tʃælɪndʒ/ *n* (*summons, fig*) вы́зов; (*sentry's*) о́клик; (*law*) отво́д; *vt* вызыва́ть *impf*, вы́звать *pf*; (*sentry*) оклика́ть *impf*, окли́кнуть *pf*; (*law*) отводи́ть *impf*, отвести́ *pf*. **challenger** /-dʒə(r)/ *n* претенде́нт. **challenging** /-dʒɪŋ/ *adj* интригу́ющий.
chamber /'tʃeɪmbə(r)/ *n* (*cavity*) ка́мера; (*hall*) зал; (*parl*) пала́та; *pl* (*law*) адвока́тская конто́ра, (*judge's*) кабине́т (судьи́); ~ **music** ка́мерная му́зыка; ~ **pot** ночно́й горшо́к. **chambermaid** *n* го́рничная *sb*.
chameleon /kə'miːlɪən/ *n* хамелео́н.
chamois /'ʃæmwɑː/ *n* (*animal*) се́рна; (~-*leather*) за́мша.
champagne /ʃæm'peɪn/ *n* шампа́нское *sb*.
champion /'tʃæmpɪən/ *n* чемпио́н, ~ка; (*upholder*) побо́рник, -ица; *vt* боро́ться *impf* за +*acc*. **championship** *n* пе́рвенство, чемпиона́т.
chance /tʃɑːns/ *n* случа́йность; (*opportunity*) возмо́жность, (*favourable*) слу́чай; (*likelihood*) шанс (*usu pl*); **by** ~ случа́йно; *adj* случа́йный; *vi*: ~ **it** рискну́ть *pf*.
chancellery /'tʃɑːnsələrɪ/ *n* канцеля́рия. **chancellor** /'tʃɑːnsələ(r)/ *n* ка́нцлер; (*univ*) ре́ктор; **C~ of the Exchequer** ка́нцлер казначе́йства.
chancy /'tʃɑːnsɪ/ *adj* риско́ванный.
chandelier /ˌʃændɪ'lɪə(r)/ *n* лю́стра.
change /tʃeɪndʒ/ *n* переме́на; измене́ние; (*of clothes etc.*) сме́на; (*money*) сда́ча; (*of trains etc.*) переса́дка; **for a** ~ для разнообра́зия; *vt & i* меня́ть(ся) *impf*; изменя́ть(ся) *impf*, измени́ть(ся) *pf*; *vi* (*one's clothes*) переодева́ться *impf*, переоде́ться *pf*; (*trains etc.*) переса́живаться *impf*, пересе́сть *pf*; *vt* (*a baby*) перепелёнывать *impf*, перепелена́ть *pf*; (*money*) обме́нивать *impf*, обменя́ть *pf*; (*give ~ for*) разме́нивать *impf*, разменя́ть *pf*; ~ **into** превраща́ться *impf*,

превратиться *pf* в+*acc*; **~ over to** переходить *impf*, перейти *pf* на+*acc*. **changeable** /'tʃeɪndʒəb(ə)l/ *adj* изменчивый.

channel /'tʃæn(ə)l/ *n* (*water*) пролив; (*also TV*) канал; (*fig*) путь *m*; **the (English) C~** Ла-Манш; *vt* (*fig*) направлять *impf*.

chant /tʃɑ:nt/ *n* (*eccl*) песнопение; *vt* & *i* петь *impf*; (*slogans*) скандировать *impf* & *pf*.

chaos /'keɪɒs/ *n* хаос. **chaotic** /-'ɒtɪk/ *adj* хаотичный.

chap /tʃæp/ *n* (*person*) парень *m*.

chapel /'tʃæp(ə)l/ *n* часовня; (*Catholic*) капелла.

chaperone /'ʃæpəˌrəʊn/ *n* компаньонка.

chaplain /'tʃæplɪn/ *n* капеллан.

chapped /tʃæpt/ *adj* потрескавшийся.

chapter /'tʃæptə(r)/ *n* глава.

char /tʃɑ:(r)/ *vt* & *i* обугливать(ся) *impf*, обуглить(ся) *pf*.

character /'kærɪktə(r)/ *n* характер; (*theat*) действующее лицо; (*letter*) буква; (*Chinese etc.*) иероглиф. **characteristic** /ˌkærɪktə'rɪstɪk/ *adj* характерный; *n* свойство; (*of person*) черта характера. **characterize** /'kærɪktəˌraɪz/ *vt* характеризовать *impf* & *pf*.

charade /ʃə'rɑ:d/ *n* шарада.

charcoal /'tʃɑ:kəʊl/ *n* древесный уголь *m*.

charge /tʃɑ:dʒ/ *n* (*for gun*; *electr*) заряд; (*fee*) плата; (*person*) питомец, -мица; (*accusation*) обвинение; (*mil*) атака; **be in ~ of** заведовать *impf* +*instr*; **in the ~ of** на попечении +*gen*; *vt* (*gun*; *electr*) заряжать *impf*, зарядить *pf*; (*accuse*) обвинять *impf*, обвинить *pf* (**with** в+*prep*); (*mil*) атаковать *impf* & *pf*; *vi* бросаться *impf*, броситься *pf* в атаку; **~ (for)** брать *impf*, взять *pf* (за+*acc*); **~ to (the account of)** записывать *impf*, записать *pf* на счёт+*gen*.

chariot /'tʃærɪət/ *n* колесница.

charisma /kə'rɪzmə/ *n* обаяние. **charismatic** /ˌkærɪz'mætɪk/ *adj* обаятельный.

charitable /'tʃærɪtəb(ə)l/ *adj* благотворительный; (*kind, merciful*) милосердный. **charity** /'tʃærɪtɪ/ *n* (*kindness*) милосердие; (*organization*) благотворительная организация.

charlatan /'ʃɑ:lət(ə)n/ *n* шарлатан.

charm /tʃɑ:m/ *n* очарование; прелесть; (*spell*) заговор; *pl* чары (чар) *pl*; (*amulet*) талисман; (*trinket*) брелок; *vt* очаровывать *impf*, очаровать *pf*. **charming** /-mɪŋ/ *adj* очаровательный, прелестный.

chart /tʃɑ:t/ *n* (*naut*) морская карта; (*table*) график; *vt* наносить *impf*, нанести *pf* на график. **charter** /-tə(r)/ *n* (*document*) хартия; (*statutes*) устав; *vt* нанимать *impf*, нанять *pf*.

charwoman /'tʃɑ:wʊmən/ *n* приходящая уборщица.

chase /tʃeɪs/ *vt* гоняться *indet*, гнаться *det* за+*instr*; *n* погоня; (*hunting*) охота.

chasm /'kæz(ə)m/ *n* (*abyss*) бездна.

chassis /'ʃæsɪ/ *n* шасси *neut indecl*.

chaste /tʃeɪst/ *adj* целомудренный.

chastise /tʃæs'taɪz/ *vt* карать *impf*, по~ *pf*.

chastity /'tʃæstɪtɪ/ *n* целомудрие.

chat /tʃæt/ *n* бесéда; *vi* бесéдовать *impf*; ~ **room** (*comput*) раздéл чáта; ~ **show** телевизиóнная бесéда-интервью *f*.

chatter /ˈtʃætə(r)/ *n* болтовня́; *vi* болтáть *impf*; (*teeth*) стучáть *impf*. **chatterbox** *n* болтýн. **chatty** /ˈtʃætɪ/ *adj* разговóрчивый.

chauffeur /ˈʃəʊfə(r)/ *n* шофёр.

chauvinism /ˈʃəʊvɪˌnɪz(ə)m/ *n* шовини́зм. **chauvinist** /-nɪst/ *n* шовини́ст; *adj* шовинисти́ческий.

cheap /tʃiːp/ *adj* дешёвый. **cheapen** /ˈtʃiːpən/ *vt* (*fig*) опошля́ть *impf*, опошли́ть *pf*. **cheaply** /ˈtʃiːplɪ/ *adv* дёшево.

cheat /tʃiːt/ *vt* обмáнывать *impf*, обманýть *pf*; *vi* плутовáть *impf*, на~, с~ *pf*; *n* обмáнщик, -ица; плут.

check[1] /tʃek/ *n* контрóль *m*, провéрка; (*chess*) шах; ~**mate** шах и мат; *vt* (*examine*) проверя́ть *impf*, провéрить *pf*; контроли́ровать *impf*, про~ *pf*; (*restrain*) сдéрживать *impf*, сдержáть *pf*; ~ **in** регистри́роваться *impf*, за~ *pf*; ~ **out** вы́писываться *impf*, вы́писаться *pf*; ~**-out** кáсса; ~**-up** осмóтр.

check[2] /tʃek/ *n* (*pattern*) клéтка. **check(ed)** /tʃekt/ *adj* клéтчатый.

cheek /tʃiːk/ *n* щекá; (*impertinence*) нáглость. **cheeky** /tʃiːkɪ/ *adj* нáглый.

cheep /tʃiːp/ *vi* пищáть *impf*, пи́скнуть *pf*.

cheer /ˈtʃɪə(r)/ *n* ободря́ющий вóзглас; ~**s!** за (вáше) здорóвье!; *vt* (*applaud*) привéтствовать *impf* & *pf*; ~ **up** ободря́ть(ся) *impf*, ободри́ть(ся) *pf*. **cheerful** /ˈtʃɪəfʊl/ *adj* весёлый. **cheerio** /ˌtʃɪərɪˈəʊ/ *int* покá. **cheerless** /ˈtʃɪəlɪs/ *adj* уны́лый.

cheese /tʃiːz/ *n* сыр; ~**-cake** ватрýшка.

cheetah /ˈtʃiːtə/ *n* гепáрд.

chef /ʃef/ *n* (шеф-)пóвар.

chemical /ˈkemɪk(ə)l/ *adj* хими́ческий; *n* химикáт. **chemist** /ˈkemɪst/ *n* хи́мик; (*druggist*) аптéкарь *m*; ~**'s (shop)** аптéка. **chemistry** /ˈkemɪstrɪ/ *n* хи́мия.

cheque /tʃek/ *n* чек; ~**-book** чéковая кни́жка.

cherish /ˈtʃerɪʃ/ *vt* (*foster*) лелéять *impf*; (*hold dear*) дорожи́ть *impf* +*instr*; (*love*) нéжно люби́ть *impf*.

cherry /ˈtʃerɪ/ *n* ви́шня; *adj* вишнёвый.

cherub /ˈtʃerəb/ *n* херуви́м.

chess /tʃes/ *n* шáхматы (-т) *pl*; ~**-board** шáхматная доскá; ~**-men** *n* шáхматы (-т) *pl*.

chest /tʃest/ *n* сундýк; (*anat*) грудь; ~ **of drawers** комóд.

chestnut /ˈtʃesnʌt/ *n* каштáн; (*horse*) гнедáя *sb*.

chew /tʃuː/ *vt* жевáть *impf*. **chewing-gum** /ˈtʃuːɪŋ gʌm/ *n* жевáтельная рези́нка.

chic /ʃiːk/ *adj* элегáнтный.

chick /tʃɪk/ *n* цыплёнок. **chicken** /ˈtʃɪkɪn/ *n* кýрица; цыплёнок; *adj* трусли́вый; ~ **out** трýсить *impf*, с~ *pf*. **chicken-pox** /ˈtʃɪkɪn pɒks/ *n* ветря́нка.

chicory /ˈtʃɪkərɪ/ *n* цикóрий.

chief /tʃiːf/ *n* главá *m* & *f*; (*boss*) начáльник; (*of tribe*) вождь *m*; *adj* глáвный. **chiefly** /ˈtʃiːflɪ/ *adv* глáвным óбразом. **chieftain** /ˈtʃiːft(ə)n/ *n* вождь *m*.

chiffon /ˈʃɪfɒn/ *n* шифóн.

child /tʃaɪld/ *n* ребёнок; ~**-birth** рóды (-дов) *pl*. **childhood**

/'tʃaɪldhʊd/*n* детство. **childish** /'tʃaɪldɪʃ/ *adj* детский. **childless** /'tʃaɪldlɪs/ *adj* бездетный. **childlike** /'tʃaɪldlaɪk/ *adj* детский. **childrens'** /'tʃɪldr(ə)nz/ *adj* детский.

chili /'tʃɪlɪ/ *n* стручковый перец.

chill /tʃɪl/ *n* холод; (*ailment*) простуда; *vt* охлаждать *impf*, охладить *pf*. **chilly** /'tʃɪlɪ/ *adj* прохладный.

chime /tʃaɪm/ *n* (*set of bells*) набор колоколов; *pl* (*sound*) перезвон; (*of clock*) бой; *vt* & *i* (*clock*) бить *impf*, про~ *pf*; *vi* (*bell*) звонить *impf*, по~ *pf*.

chimney /'tʃɪmnɪ/ *n* труба; **~-sweep** трубочист.

chimpanzee /ˌtʃɪmpæn'ziː/ *n* шимпанзе *m indecl*.

chin /tʃɪn/ *n* подбородок.

china /'tʃaɪnə/ *n* фарфор.

China /'tʃaɪnə/ *n* Китай. **Chinese** /tʃaɪ'niːz/ *n* китаец, -аянка; *adj* китайский.

chink[1] /tʃɪŋk/ *n* (*sound*) звон; *vi* звенеть *impf*, про~ *pf*.

chink[2] /tʃɪŋk/ *n* (*crack*) щель.

chintz /tʃɪnts/ *n* ситец.

chip /tʃɪp/ *vt* & *i* откалывать(ся) *impf*, отколоть(ся) *pf*; *n* (*of wood*) щепка; (*in cup*) щербина; (*in games*) фишка; *pl* картофель-соломка (*collect*); (*electron*) чип, микросхема.

chiropodist /kɪ'rɒpədɪst/ *n* человек, занимающийся педикюром. **chiropody** /-'rɒpədɪ/ *n* педикюр.

chirp /tʃɜːp/ *vi* чирикать *impf*.

chisel /'tʃɪz(ə)l/ *n* (*wood*) стамеска; (*masonry*) зубило; *vt* высекать *impf*, высечь *pf*.

chit /tʃɪt/ *n* (*note*) записка.

chivalrous /'ʃɪvəlrəs/ *adj* рыцарский. **chivalry** /-rɪ/ *n* рыцарство.

chlorine /'klɔːriːn/ *n* хлор. **chlorophyll** /'klɒrəfɪl/ *n* хлорофилл.

chock-full /'tʃɒkfʊl/ *adj* битком набитый.

chocolate /'tʃɒkələt/ *n* шоколад; (*sweet*) шоколадная конфета; **~ bar** шоколадка.

choice /tʃɔɪs/ *n* выбор; *adj* отборный.

choir /'kwaɪə(r)/ *n* хор *m*; **~-boy** певчий *sb*.

choke /tʃəʊk/ *n* (*valve*) дроссель *m*; *vi* давиться *impf*, по~ *pf*; (*with anger etc.*) задыхаться *impf*, задохнуться *pf* (**with** от+*gen*); *vt* (*suffocate*) душить *impf*, за~ *pf*; (*of plants*) заглушать, глушить *impf*, заглушить *pf*.

cholera /'kɒlərə/ *n* холера.

cholesterol /kə'lestəˌrɒl/ *n* холестерин.

choose /tʃuːz/ *vt* (*select*) выбирать *impf*, выбрать *pf*; (*decide*) решать *impf*, решить *pf*. **choosy** /'tʃuːzɪ/ *adj* разборчивый.

chop /tʃɒp/ *vt* (*also ~ down*) рубить *impf*, рубнуть, рубануть *pf*; **~ off** отрубать *impf*, отрубить *pf*; *n* (*cul*) отбивная котлета.

chopper /'tʃɒpə(r)/ *n* топор. **choppy** /'tʃɒpɪ/ *adj* бурливый.

chop-sticks /'tʃɒpstɪks/ *n* палочки *f pl* для еды.

choral /'kɔːr(ə)l/ *adj* хоровой. **chorale** /kɔː'rɑːl/ *n* хорал.

chord /kɔːd/ *n* (*mus*) аккорд.

chore /tʃɔː(r)/ *n* обязанность.

choreographer /ˌkɒrɪ'ɒgrəfə(r)/ *n* хореограф. **choreography** /-grəfɪ/ *n* хореография.

chorister /'kɒrɪstə(r)/ *n* певчий *sb*.

chortle /ˈtʃɔːt(ə)l/ *vi* фы́ркать *impf*, фы́ркнуть *pf*. **chorus** /ˈkɔːrəs/ *n* хор; (*refrain*) припе́в. **christen** /ˈkrɪs(ə)n/ *vt* крести́ть *impf* & *pf*. **Christian** /ˈkrɪstɪən/ *n* христиани́н, -а́нка; *adj* христиа́нский; ~ **name** и́мя *neut*. **Christianity** /ˌkrɪstɪˈænɪtɪ/ *n* христиа́нство. **Christmas** /ˈkrɪsməs/ *n* Рождество́; ~ **Day** пе́рвый день Рождества́; ~ **Eve** сочéльник; ~ **tree** ёлка. **chromatic** /krəˈmætɪk/ *adj* хромати́ческий. **chrome** /krəʊm/ *n* хром. **chromium** /ˈkrəʊmɪəm/ *n* хром. **chromosome** /ˈkrəʊməˌsəʊm/ *n* хромосо́ма. **chronic** /ˈkrɒnɪk/ *adj* хрони́ческий. **chronicle** /ˈkrɒnɪk(ə)l/ *n* хро́ника, ле́топись. **chronological** /ˌkrɒnəˈlɒdʒɪk(ə)l/ *adj* хронологи́ческий. **chrysalis** /ˈkrɪsəlɪs/ *n* ку́колка. **chrysanthemum** /krɪˈsænθəməm/ *n* хризанте́ма. **chubby** /ˈtʃʌbɪ/ *adj* пу́хлый. **chuck** /tʃʌk/ *vt* броса́ть *impf*, бро́сить *pf*; ~ **out** вышиба́ть *impf*, вы́шибить *pf*. **chuckle** /ˈtʃʌk(ə)l/ *vi* посме́иваться *impf*. **chum** /tʃʌm/ *n* това́рищ. **chunk** /tʃʌŋk/ *n* ломо́ть *m*. **church** /tʃɜːtʃ/ *n* це́рковь. **churchyard** *n* кла́дбище. **churlish** /ˈtʃɜːlɪʃ/ *adj* гру́бый. **churn** /tʃɜːn/ *n* маслобо́йка; *vt* сбива́ть *impf*, сбить *pf*; *vi* (*foam*) пе́ниться *impf*, вс~ *pf*; (*stomach*) крути́ть *impf*; ~ **out** выпека́ть *impf*, вы́печь *pf*; ~ **up** взбить *pf*. **chute** /ʃuːt/ *n* жёлоб. **cider** /ˈsaɪdə(r)/ *n* сидр. **cigar** /sɪˈɡɑː(r)/ *n* сига́ра. **cigarette** /ˌsɪɡəˈret/ *n* сигаре́та; папиро́са; ~ **lighter** зажига́лка. **cinder** /ˈsɪndə(r)/ *n* шлак; *pl* зола́. **cine-camera** /ˈsɪnɪˌkæmrə/ *n* киноаппара́т. **cinema** /ˈsɪnɪˌmɑː/ *n* кино́ *neut indecl*. **cinnamon** /ˈsɪnəmən/ *n* кори́ца. **cipher** /ˈsaɪfə(r)/ *n* нуль *m*; (*code*) шифр. **circle** /ˈsɜːk(ə)l/ *n* круг; (*theatre*) я́рус; *vi* кружи́ться *impf*; *vt* (*walking*) обходи́ть *impf*, обойти́ *pf*; (*flying*) облета́ть *impf*, облете́ть *pf*. **circuit** /ˈsɜːkɪt/ *n* кругооборо́т; объе́зд, обхо́д; (*electron*) схе́ма; (*electr*) цепь. **circuitous** /sɜːˈkjuːɪtəs/ *adj* окружно́й. **circular** /ˈsɜːkjʊlə(r)/ *adj* кру́глый; (*moving in a circle*) кругово́й; *n* циркуля́р. **circulate** /ˈsɜːkjʊˌleɪt/ *vi* циркули́ровать *impf*; *vt* распространя́ть *impf*, распространи́ть *pf*. **circulation** /ˌsɜːkjuːˈleɪʃ(ə)n/ *n* (*air*) циркуля́ция; (*distribution*) распростране́ние; (*of newspaper*) тира́ж; (*med*) кровообраще́ние. **circumcise** /ˈsɜːkəmˌsaɪz/ *vt* обреза́ть *impf*, обре́зать *pf*. **circumcision** /-ˈsɪʒ(ə)n/ *n* обреза́ние. **circumference** /sɜːˈkʌmfərəns/ *n* окру́жность. **circumspect** /ˈsɜːkəmˌspekt/ *adj* осмотри́тельный. **circumstance** /ˈsɜːkəmst(ə)ns/ *n* обстоя́тельство; **under the ~s** при да́нных обстоя́тельствах, в тако́м слу́чае; **under no ~s** ни при каки́х обстоя́тельствах, ни в ко́ем слу́чае. **circumvent** /ˌsɜːkəmˈvent/ *vt* обходи́ть *impf*, обойти́ *pf*. **circus** /ˈsɜːkəs/ *n* цирк. **cirrhosis** /sɪˈrəʊsɪs/ *n* цирро́з.

CIS *abbr* (*of* **Commonwealth of Independent States**) СНГ.
cistern /'sɪst(ə)n/ *n* бачо́к.
citadel /'sɪtəd(ə)l/ *n* цитаде́ль.
cite /saɪt/ *vt* ссыла́ться *impf*, сосла́ться *pf* на+*acc*.
citizen /'sɪtɪz(ə)n/ *n* граждани́н, -а́нка. **citizenship** /'sɪtɪz(ə)nʃɪp/ *n* гражда́нство.
citrus /'sɪtrəs/ *n* ци́трус; *adj* ци́трусовый.
city /'sɪtɪ/ *n* го́род.
civic /'sɪvɪk/ *adj* гражда́нский. **civil** /-v(ə)l/ *adj* гражда́нский; (*polite*) ве́жливый; ~ **engineer** гражда́нский инжене́р; ~ **engineering** гражда́нское строи́тельство; **C~ Servant** госуда́рственный слу́жащий *sb*; чино́вник; **C~ Service** госуда́рственная слу́жба. **civilian** /sɪ'vɪlɪən/ *n* шта́тский *sb*; *adj* шта́тский. **civility** /sɪ'vɪlɪtɪ/ *n* ве́жливость. **civilization** /ˌsɪvɪlaɪ'zeɪʃ(ə)n/ *n* цивилиза́ция. **civilize** /'sɪvɪˌlaɪz/ *vt* цивилизова́ть *impf* & *pf*. **civilized** /'sɪvɪˌlaɪzd/ *adj* цивилизо́ванный.
clad /klæd/ *adj* оде́тый.
claim /kleɪm/ *n* (*demand*) тре́бование, притяза́ние; (*assertion*) утвержде́ние; *vt* (*demand*) тре́бовать *impf* +*gen*; (*assert*) утвержда́ть *impf*, утверди́ть *pf*. **claimant** /'kleɪmənt/ *n* претенде́нт.
clairvoyant /kleə'vɔɪənt/ *n* ясновидец, -дица; *adj* ясновидя́щий.
clam /klæm/ *n* моллю́ск; *vi*: ~ **up** отка́зываться *impf*, отказа́ться *pf* разгова́ривать.
clamber /'klæmbə(r)/ *vi* кара́бкаться *impf*, вс~ *pf*.
clammy /'klæmɪ/ *adj* вла́жный.
clamour /'klæmə(r)/ *n* шум; *vi*: ~ **for** шу́мно тре́бовать *impf*, по~ *pf* +*gen*.
clamp /klæmp/ *n* зажи́м; *vt* скрепля́ть *impf*, скрепи́ть *pf*; ~ **down on** прижа́ть *pf*.
clan /klæn/ *n* клан.
clandestine /klæn'destɪn/ *adj* та́йный.
clang, clank /klæŋ, klæŋk/ *n* лязг; *vt* & *i* ля́згать *impf*, ля́згнуть *pf* (+*instr*).
clap /klæp/ *vt* & *i* хло́пать *impf*, хло́пнуть *pf* +*dat*; *n* хлопо́к; (*thunder*) уда́р.
claret /'klærət/ *n* бордо́ *neut indecl*.
clarification /ˌklærɪfɪ'keɪʃ(ə)n/ *n* (*explanation*) разъясне́ние. **clarify** /'klærɪˌfaɪ/ *vt* разъясня́ть *impf*, разъясни́ть *pf*.
clarinet /ˌklærɪ'net/ *n* кларне́т.
clarity /'klærɪtɪ/ *n* я́сность.
clash /klæʃ/ *n* (*conflict*) столкнове́ние; (*disharmony*) дисгармо́ния; *vi* ста́лкиваться *impf*, столкну́ться *pf*; (*coincide*) совпада́ть *impf*, совпа́сть *pf*; не гармони́ровать *impf*.
clasp /klɑːsp/ *n* застёжка; (*embrace*) объя́тие; *vt* обхва́тывать *impf*, обхвати́ть *pf*; ~ **one's hands** сплести́ *pf* па́льцы рук.
class /klɑːs/ *n* класс; **~-room** класс; *vt* классифици́ровать *impf* & *pf*.
classic /'klæsɪk/ *adj* класси́ческий; *n* кла́ссик; *pl* (*literature*) кла́ссика; (*Latin and Greek*) класси́ческие языки́ *m pl*. **classical** /-k(ə)l/ *adj* класси́ческий.
classification /ˌklæsɪfɪ'keɪʃ(ə)n/ *n* классифика́ция. **classified** /'klæsɪˌfaɪd/ *adj* засекре́ченный. **classify** /'klæsɪˌfaɪ/ *vt* классифици́ровать *impf* & *pf*.
classy /'klɑːsɪ/ *adj* кла́ссный.

clatter /'klætə(r)/ *n* стук; *vi* стучáть *impf*, по~ *pf*.
clause /klɔ:z/ *n* статья́; (*gram*) предложéние.
claustrophobia /ˌklɔ:strə'fəʊbɪə/ *n* клаустрофóбия.
claw /klɔ:/ *n* кóготь; *vt* цара́пать *impf* когтя́ми.
clay /kleɪ/ *n* гли́на; *adj* гли́няный.
clean /kli:n/ *adj* чи́стый; *adv* (*fully*) совершéнно; **~-shaven** гла́дко вы́бритый; *vt* чи́стить *impf*, вы́~, по~ *pf*. **cleaner** /'kli:nə(r)/ *n* убóрщик, -ица. **cleaner's** /'kli:nəz/ *n* химчи́стка. **clean(li)ness** /'klenlɪnɪs/ *n* чистотá. **cleanse** /klenz/ *vt* очищáть *impf*, очи́стить *pf*.
clear /klɪə(r)/ *adj* я́сный; (*transparent*) прозра́чный; (*distinct*) отчётливый; (*free*) свобóдный (**of** от+*gen*); (*pure*) чи́стый; *vt* & *i* очищáть(ся) *impf*, очи́стить(ся) *pf*; *vt* (*jump over*) перепры́гивать *impf*, перепры́гнуть *pf*; (*acquit*) опра́вдывать *impf*, оправдáть *pf*; **~ away** убирáть *impf*, убрáть *pf* со столá; **~ off** (*go away*) убирáться *impf*, убрáться *pf*; **~ out** (*vt*) вычищáть *impf*, вы́чистить *pf*; (*vi*) (*make off*) убирáться *impf*, убрáться *pf*; **~ up** (*tidy* (*away*)) убирáть *impf*, убрáть *pf*; (*weather*) проясня́ться *impf*, проясни́ться *pf*; (*explain*) выясня́ть *impf*, вы́яснить *pf*. **clearance** /'klɪərəns/ *n* расчи́стка; (*permission*) разрешéние. **clearing** /'klɪərɪŋ/ *n* (*glade*) поля́на. **clearly** /'klɪəlɪ/ *adv* я́сно.
cleavage /'kli:vɪdʒ/ *n* разрéз груди́.
clef /klef/ *n* (*mus*) ключ.
cleft /kleft/ *n* трéщина.
clemency /'klemənsɪ/ *n* милосéрдие.
clench /klentʃ/ *vt* (*fist*) сжимáть *impf*, сжать *pf*; (*teeth*) сти́скивать *impf*, сти́снуть *pf*.
clergy /'klɜ:dʒɪ/ *n* духовéнство. **clergyman** *n* свящéнник. **clerical** /'klerɪk(ə)l/ *adj* (*eccl*) духóвный; (*of clerk*) канцеля́рский.
clerk /klɑ:k/ *n* контóрский слу́жащий *sb*.
clever /'klevə(r)/ *adj* у́мный. **cleverness** /-nɪs/ *n* умéние.
cliche /'kli:ʃeɪ/ *n* клишé *neut indecl*.
click /klɪk/ *vt* щёлкать *impf*, щёлкнуть *pf* +*instr*.
client /'klaɪənt/ *n* клиéнт. **clientele** /ˌkli:ɒn'tel/ *n* клиенту́ра.
cliff /klɪf/ *n* утёс.
climate /'klaɪmɪt/ *n* кли́мат. **climatic** /-'mætɪk/ *adj* климати́ческий.
climax /'klaɪmæks/ *n* кульминáция.
climb /klaɪm/ *vt* & *i* ла́зить *indet*, лезть *det* на+*acc*; влезáть *impf*, влезть *pf* на+*acc*; поднимáться *impf*, подня́ться *pf* на+*acc*; **~ down** (*tree*) слезáть *impf*, слезть *pf* (с+*gen*); (*mountain*) спускáться *impf*, спусти́ться *pf* (с+*gen*); (*give in*) отступáть *impf*, отступи́ть *pf*; *n* подъём. **climber** /-mə(r)/ *n* альпини́ст, ~ка; (*plant*) вью́щееся растéние. **climbing** /-mɪŋ/ *n* альпини́зм.
clinch /klɪntʃ/ *vt*: **~ a deal** закрепи́ть *pf* сдéлку.
cling /klɪŋ/ *vi* (*stick*) прилипáть *impf*, прили́пнуть *pf* (**to** к+*dat*); (*grasp*) цепля́ться *impf*, цепи́ться *pf* (**to** за+*acc*).
clinic /'klɪnɪk/ *n* кли́ника. **clinical** /-k(ə)l/ *adj* клини́ческий.
clink /klɪŋk/ *vt* & *i* звенéть *impf*,

про~ *pf* (+*instr*); **~ glasses** чо́каться *impf*, чо́кнуться *pf*; *n* звон.

clip[1] /klɪp/ *n* скре́пка; зажи́м; *vt* скрепля́ть *impf*, скрепи́ть *pf*.

clip[2] /klɪp/ *vt* (*cut*) подстрига́ть *impf*, подстри́чь *pf*. **clippers** /-pəz/ *n pl* но́жницы *f pl*. **clipping** /-pɪŋ/ *n* (*extract*) вы́резка.

clique /kliːk/ *n* кли́ка.

cloak /kləʊk/ *n* плащ. **cloakroom** *n* гардеро́б; (*lavatory*) убо́рная *sb*.

clock /klɒk/ *n* часы́ *m pl*; **~wise** /-waɪz/ по часово́й стре́лке; **~-work** часово́й механи́зм; *vi*: **~ in, out** отмеча́ться *impf*, отме́титься *pf* приходя́ на рабо́ту/уходя́ с рабо́ты.

clod /klɒd/ *n* ком.

clog /klɒg/ *vt*: **~ up** засоря́ть *impf*, засори́ть *pf*.

cloister /ˈklɔɪstə(r)/ *n* арка́да.

clone /kləʊn/ *n* клон.

close *adj* /kləʊs/ (*near*) бли́зкий; (*stuffy*) ду́шный; *vt* & *i* /kləʊz/ (*also* **~** *down*) закрыва́ть(ся) *impf*, закры́ть(ся) *pf*; (*conclude*) зака́нчивать *impf*, зако́нчить *pf*; *adv* бли́зко (**to** от+*gen*). **closed** /kləʊzd/ *adj* закры́тый. **closet** /ˈklɒzɪt/ *n* (стенно́й) шкаф. **close-up** *n* фотогра́фия сня́тая кру́пным пла́ном. **closing** /ˈkləʊzɪŋ/ *n* закры́тие; *adj* заключи́тельный. **closure** /ˈkləʊʒə(r)/ *n* закры́тие.

clot /klɒt/ *n* сгу́сток; *vi* сгуща́ться *impf*, сгусти́ться *pf*.

cloth /klɒθ/ *n* ткань; (*duster*) тря́пка; (*table-~*) ска́терть.

clothe /kləʊð/ *vt* одева́ть *impf*, оде́ть (**in** +*instr*, в+*acc*) *pf*. **clothes** /kləʊðz/ *n pl* оде́жда, пла́тье.

cloud /klaʊd/ *n* о́блако; (*rain* ~) ту́ча; *vt* затемня́ть *impf*, затемни́ть *pf*; омрача́ть *impf*, омрачи́ть *pf*; **~ over** покрыва́ться *impf*, покры́ться *pf* облака́ми, ту́чами. **cloudy** /-dɪ/ *adj* о́блачный; (*liquid*) му́тный.

clout /klaʊt/ *vt* ударя́ть *impf*, уда́рить *pf*; *n* затре́щина; (*fig*) влия́ние.

clove /kləʊv/ *n* гвозди́ка; (*of garlic*) зубо́к.

cloven /ˈkləʊv(ə)n/ *adj* раздво́енный.

clover /ˈkləʊvə(r)/ *n* кле́вер.

clown /klaʊn/ *n* кло́ун.

club /klʌb/ *n* (*stick*) дуби́нка; *pl* (*cards*) тре́фы (треф) *pl*; (*association*) клуб; *vt* колоти́ть *impf*, по~ *pf* дуби́нкой; *vi*: **~ together** скла́дываться *impf*, сложи́ться *pf*.

cluck /klʌk/ *vi* куда́хтать *impf*.

clue /kluː/ *n* (*evidence*) ули́ка; (*to puzzle*) ключ; (*hint*) намёк.

clump /klʌmp/ *n* гру́ппа.

clumsiness /ˈklʌmzɪnɪs/ *n* неуклю́жесть. **clumsy** /ˈklʌmzɪ/ *adj* неуклю́жий.

cluster /ˈklʌstə(r)/ *n* гру́ппа; *vi* собира́ться *impf*, собра́ться *pf* гру́ппами.

clutch /klʌtʃ/ *n* (*grasp*) хва́тка; ко́гти *m pl*; (*tech*) сцепле́ние; *vt* зажима́ть *impf*, зажа́ть *pf*; *vi*: **~ at** хвата́ться *impf*, хвати́ться *pf* за+*acc*.

clutter /ˈklʌtə(r)/ *n* беспоря́док; *vt* загроможда́ть *impf*, загромозди́ть *pf*.

c/o *abbr* (*of* **care of**) по а́дресу +*gen*; че́рез+*acc*.

coach /kəʊtʃ/ *n* (*horse-drawn*) каре́та; (*rly*) ваго́н; (*bus*) авто́бус; (*tutor*) репети́тор; (*sport*) тре́нер; *vt* репети́ровать *impf*; тренирова́ть *impf*, на~ *pf*.

coagulate /kəʊˈægjʊˌleɪt/ *vi* сгущаться *impf*, сгусти́ться *pf*.

coal /kəʊl/ *n* у́голь *m*; **~mine** у́гольная ша́хта.

coalition /ˌkəʊə'lɪʃ(ə)n/ *n* коали́ция.

coarse /kɔːs/ *adj* гру́бый.

coast /kəʊst/ *n* побере́жье, бе́рег; **~ guard** берегова́я охра́на; *vi* (*move without power*) дви́гаться *impf*, дви́нуться *pf* по ине́рции. **coastal** /-t(ə)l/ *adj* берегово́й, прибре́жный.

coat /kəʊt/ *n* пальто́ *neut indecl*; (*layer*) слой; (*animal*) шерсть, мех; **~ of arms** герб; *vt* покрыва́ть *impf*, покры́ть *pf*.

coax /kəʊks/ *vt* угова́ривать *impf*, уговори́ть *pf*.

cob /kɒb/ *n* (*corn-~*) поча́ток кукуру́зы.

cobble /'kɒb(ə)l/ *n* булы́жник (*also collect*). **cobbled** /-b(ə)ld/ *adj* булы́жный.

cobbler /'kɒblə(r)/ *n* сапо́жник.

cobweb /'kɒbweb/ *n* паути́на.

Coca-Cola /ˌkəʊkə'kəʊlə/ *n* (*propr*) ко́ка-ко́ла.

cocaine /kə'keɪn/ *n* кокаи́н.

cock /kɒk/ *n* (*bird*) пету́х; (*tap*) кран; (*of gun*) куро́к; *vt* (*gun*) взводи́ть *impf*, взвести́ *pf* куро́к+*gen*.

cockerel /'kɒkər(ə)l/ *n* петушо́к.

cockle /'kɒk(ə)l/ *n* сердцеви́дка.

cockpit /'kɒkpɪt/ *n* (*aeron*) каби́на.

cockroach /'kɒkrəʊtʃ/ *n* тарака́н.

cocktail /'kɒkteɪl/ *n* кокте́йль *m*.

cocky /'kɒkɪ/ *adj* ча́нный.

cocoa /'kəʊkəʊ/ *n* кака́о *neut indecl*.

coco(a)nut /'kəʊkəˌnʌt/ *n* коко́с.

cocoon /kə'kuːn/ *n* ко́кон.

cod /kɒd/ *n* треска́.

code /kəʊd/ *n* (*of laws*) ко́декс; (*cipher*) код; *vt* шифрова́ть *impf*, за~ *pf*. **codify** /'kəʊdɪˌfaɪ/ *vt* кодифици́ровать *impf* & *pf*.

co-education /ˌkəʊedjuː'keɪʃ(ə)n/ *n* совме́стное обуче́ние.

coefficient /ˌkəʊɪ'fɪʃ(ə)nt/ *n* коэффицие́нт.

coerce /kəʊ'ɜːs/ *vt* принужда́ть *impf*, прину́дить *pf*. **coercion** /kəʊ'ɜːʃ(ə)n/ *n* принужде́ние.

coexist /ˌkəʊɪg'zɪst/ *vi* сосуществова́ть *impf*. **coexistence** /-'zɪstəns/ *n* сосуществова́ние.

coffee /'kɒfɪ/ *n* ко́фе *m indecl*; **~-mill** *n* кофе́йница; **~-pot** *n* кофе́йник.

coffer /'kɒfə(r)/ *n pl* казна́.

coffin /'kɒfɪn/ *n* гроб.

cog /kɒg/ *n* зубе́ц. **cogwheel** *n* зубча́тое колесо́.

cogent /'kəʊdʒ(ə)nt/ *adj* убеди́тельный.

cohabit /kəʊ'hæbɪt/ *vi* сожи́тельствовать *impf*.

coherent /kəʊ'hɪərənt/ *adj* свя́зный. **cohesion** /kəʊ'hiːʒ(ə)n/ *n* сплочённость. **cohesive** /kəʊ'hiːsɪv/ *adj* сплочённый.

coil /kɔɪl/ *vt* & *i* свёртывать(ся) *impf*, сверну́ть(ся) *pf* кольцо́м; *n* кольцо́; (*electr*) кату́шка.

coin /kɔɪn/ *n* моне́та; *vt* чека́нить *impf*, от~ *pf*.

coincide /ˌkəʊɪn'saɪd/ *vi* совпада́ть *impf*, совпа́сть *pf*. **coincidence** /kəʊ'ɪnsɪdəns/ *n* совпаде́ние. **coincidental** /kəʊˌɪnsɪ'dent(ə)l/ *adj* случа́йный.

coke /kəʊk/ *n* кокс.

colander /'kʌləndə(r)/ *n* дуршла́г.

cold /kəʊld/ *n* хо́лод; (*med*) просту́да, на́сморк; *adj* холо́дный; **~-blooded** *adj* жесто́кий; (*zool*) холоднокро́вный.

colic /'kɒlɪk/ *n* ко́лики *f pl.*

collaborate /kə'læbə,reɪt/ *vi* сотру́дничать *impf.* **collaboration** /kə,læbə'reɪʃ(ə)n/ *n* сотру́дничество. **collaborator** /kə'læbə,reɪtə(r)/ *n* сотру́дник, -ица; (*traitor*) коллаборациони́ст, -и́стка.

collapse /kə'læps/ *vi* ру́хнуть *pf*; *n* паде́ние; круше́ние.

collar /'kɒlə(r)/ *n* воротни́к; (*dog's*) оше́йник; **~-bone** ключи́ца.

colleague /'kɒli:g/ *n* колле́га *m* & *f*.

collect /kə'lekt/ *vt* собира́ть *impf*, собра́ть *pf*; (*as hobby*) коллекциони́ровать *impf*; (*fetch*) забира́ть *impf*, забра́ть *pf.* **collected** /-'lektɪd/ *adj* (*calm*) со́бранный; **~ works** собра́ние сочине́ний. **collection** /-'lekʃ(ə)n/ *n* (*stamps etc.*) колле́кция; (*church etc.*) сбор; (*post*) вы́емка. **collective** /-'lektɪv/ *n* коллекти́в; *adj* коллекти́вный; **~ farm** колхо́з; **~ noun** собира́тельное существи́тельное *sb.* **collectivization** /kə,lektɪvaɪ'zeɪʃ(ə)n/ *n* коллективиза́ция. **collector** /-'lektə(r)/ *n* сбо́рщик; коллекционе́р.

college /'kɒlɪdʒ/ *n* колле́дж, учи́лище.

collide /kə'laɪd/ *vi* ста́лкиваться *impf*, столкну́ться *pf.* **collision** /-'lɪʒ(ə)n/ *n* столкнове́ние.

colliery /'kɒlɪərɪ/ *n* каменноу́гольная ша́хта.

colloquial /kə'ləʊkwɪəl/ *adj* разгово́рный. **colloquialism** /-,lɪz(ə)m/ *n* разгово́рное выраже́ние.

collusion /kə'lu:ʒ(ə)n/ *n* та́йный сго́вор.

colon[1] /'kəʊlən/ *n* (*anat*) то́лстая кишка́.

colon[2] /'kəʊlən/ *n* (*gram*) двоето́чие.

colonel /'kɜ:n(ə)l/ *n* полко́вник.

colonial /kə'ləʊnɪəl/ *adj* колониа́льный. **colonialism** /-,lɪz(ə)m/ *n* колониали́зм. **colonize** /'kɒlə,naɪz/ *vt* колонизова́ть *impf* & *pf.* **colony** /'kɒlənɪ/ *n* коло́ния.

colossal /kə'lɒs(ə)l/ *adj* колосса́льный.

colour /'kʌlə(r)/ *n* цвет, кра́ска; (*pl*) (*flag*) зна́мя *neut*; **~-blind** страда́ющий дальтони́змом; **~ film** цветна́я плёнка; *vt* раскра́шивать *impf*, раскра́сить *pf*; *vi* красне́ть *impf*, по**~** *pf.* **coloured** /-ləd/ *adj* цветно́й. **colourful** /-fʊl/ *adj* я́ркий. **colourless** /-lɪs/ *adj* бесцве́тный.

colt /kəʊlt/ *n* жеребёнок.

column /'kɒləm/ *n* (*archit, mil*) коло́нна; (*of smoke etc.*) столб; (*of print*) столбе́ц. **columnist** /'kɒləmnɪst/ *n* журнали́ст.

coma /'kəʊmə/ *n* ко́ма.

comb /kəʊm/ *n* гребёнка; *vt* причёсывать *impf*, причеса́ть *pf.*

combat /'kɒmbæt/ *n* бой; *vt* боро́ться *impf* с+*instr*, про́тив+*gen*.

combination /,kɒmbɪ'neɪʃ(ə)n/ *n* сочета́ние; комбина́ция. **combine** *n* /'kɒmbaɪn/ комбина́т; (**~**-*harvester*) комба́йн; *vt* & *i* /kəm'baɪn/ совмеща́ть(ся) *impf*, совмести́ть(ся) *pf.* **combined** /kəm'baɪnd/ *adj* совме́стный.

combustion /kəm'bʌstʃ(ə)n/ *n* горе́ние.

come /kʌm/ *vi* (*on foot*) приходи́ть *impf*, прийти́ *pf*; (*by transport*) приезжа́ть *impf*, прие́хать *pf*; **~ about** случа́ться *impf*, случи́ться *pf*; ~ **across** случа́йно ната́лкиваться *impf*, натолкну́ться *pf* на+*acc*; ~ **back** возвраща́ться *impf*, возврати́ться *pf*; ~ **in** входи́ть *impf*, войти́ *pf*; ~ **out** выходи́ть *impf*, вы́йти *pf*; ~ **round** (*revive*) приходи́ть *impf*, прийти́ *pf* в себя́; (*visit*) заходи́ть *impf*, зайти́ *pf*; (*agree*) соглаша́ться *impf*, согласи́ться *pf*; ~ **up to** (*approach*) подходи́ть *impf*, подойти́ *pf* к+*dat*; (*reach*) доходи́ть *impf*, дойти́ *pf* до+*gen*. **come-back** *n* возвраще́ние. **come-down** *n* униже́ние.

comedian /kə'mi:dıən/ *n* комедиа́нт. **comedy** /'kɒmıdı/ *n* коме́дия.

comet /'kɒmıt/ *n* коме́та.

comfort /'kʌmfət/ *n* комфо́рт; (*convenience*) удо́бство; (*consolation*) утеше́ние; *vt* утеша́ть *impf*, уте́шить *pf*. **comfortable** /'kʌmftəb(ə)l/ *adj* удо́бный.

comic /'kɒmık/ *adj* коми́ческий; *n* ко́мик; (*magazine*) ко́микс. **comical** /-k(ə)l/ *adj* смешно́й.

coming /'kʌmıŋ/ *adj* сле́дующий.

comma /'kɒmə/ *n* запята́я *sb*.

command /kə'mɑ:nd/ *n* (*order*) прика́з; (*order, authority*) кома́нда; **have** ~ **of** (*master*) владе́ть *impf* +*instr*; *vt* прика́зывать *impf*, приказа́ть *pf* +*dat*; (*mil*) кома́ндовать *impf*, с~ *pf* +*instr*. **commandant** /,kɒmən'dænt/ *n* коменда́нт. **commandeer** /,kɒmən'dıə(r)/ *vt* реквизи́ровать *impf* & *pf*. **commander** /kə'mɑ:ndə(r)/ *n* команди́р; **~-in-chief** главнокома́ндующий *sb*. **commandment** /kə'mɑ:ndmənt/ *n* за́поведь. **commando** /kə'mɑ:ndəʊ/ *n* деса́нтник.

commemorate /kə'memə,reıt/ *vt* ознамено́вывать *impf*, ознаменова́ть *pf*. **commemoration** /kə,memə'reıʃ(ə)n/ *n* ознаменова́ние. **commemorative** /kə'memərə,tıv/ *adj* па́мятный.

commence /kə'mens/ *vt* & *i* начина́ть(ся) *impf*, нача́ть(ся) *pf*. **commencement** /-mənt/ *n* нача́ло.

commend /kə'mend/ *vt* хвали́ть *impf*, по~ *pf*; (*recommend*) рекомендова́ть *impf* & *pf*. **commendable** /-dəb(ə)l/ *adj* похва́льный. **commendation** /,kɒmen'deıʃ(ə)n/ *n* похвала́.

commensurate /kə'menʃərət/ *adj* соразме́рный.

comment /'kɒment/ *n* замеча́ние; *vi* де́лать *impf*, с~ *pf* замеча́ния; ~ **on** комменти́ровать *impf* & *pf*, про~ *pf*. **commentary** /-məntərı/ *n* коммента́рий. **commentator** /-,teıtə(r)/ *n* коммента́тор.

commerce /'kɒmɜ:s/ *n* комме́рция. **commercial** /kə'mɜ:ʃ(ə)l/ *adj* торго́вый; *n* рекла́ма.

commiserate /kə'mızə,reıt/ *vi*: ~ **with** соболе́зновать *impf* +*dat*. **commiseration** /-'reıʃ(ə)n/ *n* соболе́знование.

commission /kə'mıʃ(ə)n/ *n* (*order for work*) зака́з; (*agent's fee*) комиссио́нные *sb*; (*of inquiry etc.*) коми́ссия; (*mil*) офице́рское зва́ние; *vt* зака́зывать *impf*, заказа́ть *pf*. **commissionaire** /kə,mıʃ(ə)'neə(r)/ *n* швейца́р. **commissioner** /kə'mıʃənə(r)/ *n* комисса́р.

commit /kə'mıt/ *vt* соверша́ть *impf*, соверши́ть *pf*; ~ **o.s.** обя́зываться *impf*, обяза́ться *pf*. **commitment** /-mənt/ *n* обяза́тельство.

committee /kə'mɪtɪ/ *n* комитéт. **commodity** /kə'mɒdɪtɪ/ *n* товáр. **commodore** /'kɒmə,dɔː(r)/ *n* (*officer*) коммодóр.
common /'kɒmən/ *adj* óбщий; (*ordinary*) простóй; *n* общúнная землЯ́; ~ **sense** здрáвый смысл. **commonly** /-lɪ/ *adv* обы́чно. **commonplace** *adj* банáльный. **commonwealth** *n* содрýжество.
commotion /kə'məʊʃ(ə)n/ *n* суматóха.
communal /'kɒmjʊn(ə)l/ *adj* общúнный, коммунáльный. **commune** *n* /'kɒmjuːn/ коммýна; *vi* /kə'mjuːn/ общáться *impf*.
communicate /kə'mjuːnɪ,keɪt/ *vt* передавáть *impf*, передáть *pf*; сообщáть *impf*, сообщúть *pf*. **communication** /-'keɪʃ(ə)n/ *n* сообщéние; связь. **communicative** /kə'mjuːnɪkətɪv/ *adj* разговóрчивый.
communion /kə'mjuːnɪən/ *n* (*eccl*) причáстие.
communiqué /kə'mjuːnɪ,keɪ/ *n* коммюникé *neut indecl*.
Communism /'kɒmjʊ,nɪz(ə)m/ *n* коммунúзм. **Communist** /'kɒmjʊnɪst/ *n* коммунúст, ~ка; *adj* коммунистúческий.
community /kə'mjuːnɪtɪ/ *n* óбщúна.
commute /kə'mjuːt/ *vt* заменя́ть *impf*, заменúть *pf*; (*travel*) добирáться *impf*, добрáться *pf* трáнспортом. **commuter** /-tə(r)/ *n* регуля́рный пассажúр.
compact[1] /'kɒmpækt/ *n* (*agreement*) соглашéние.
compact[2] /kəm'pækt/ *adj* компáктный; ~ **disc** /'kɒmpækt dɪsk/компáкт-дúск; *n* /'kɒmpækt/ пýдреница.
companion /kəm'pænjən/ *n* товáрищ; (*handbook*) спрáвочник. **companionable** /-nəb(ə)l/ *adj* общúтельный. **companionship** /-ʃɪp/*n* дрýжеское общéние. **company** /'kʌmpənɪ/ *n* óбщество, (*also firm*) компáния; (*theat*) трýппа; (*mil*) рóта.
comparable /'kɒmpərəb(ə)l/ *adj* сравнúмый. **comparative** /kəm'pærətɪv/ *adj* сравнúтельный; *n* сравнúтельная стéпень. **compare** /kəm'peə(r)/ *vt* & *i* срáвнивать(ся) *impf*, сравнúть(ся) *pf* (**to, with** с+*instr*). **comparison** /kəm'pærɪs(ə)n/ *n* сравнéние.
compartment /kəm'pɑːtmənt/ *n* отделéние; (*rly*) купé *neut indecl*.
compass /'kʌmpəs/ *n* кóмпас; *pl* цúркуль *m*.
compassion /kəm'pæʃ(ə)n/ *n* сострадáние. **compassionate** /-nət/ *adj* сострадáтельный.
compatibility /kəm,pætə'bɪlɪtɪ/ *n* совместúмость. **compatible** /kəm'pætəb(ə)l/ *adj* совместúмый.
compatriot /kəm'pætrɪət/ *n* соотéчественник, -ица.
compel /kəm'pel/ *vt* заставля́ть *impf*, застáвить *pf*.
compensate /'kɒmpen,seɪt/ *vt* компенсúровать *impf* & *pf* (**for** за+*acc*). **compensation** /-'seɪʃ(ə)n/ *n* компенсáция.
compete /kəm'piːt/ *vi* конкурúровать *impf*; соревновáться *impf*.
competence /'kɒmpɪtəns/ *n* компетéнтность. **competent** /-tənt/ *adj* компетéнтный.
competition /,kɒmpə'tɪʃ(ə)n/ *n* (*contest*) соревновáние, состязáние; (*rivalry*) конкурéнция. **competitive** /kəm'petɪtɪv/ *adj*

(*comm*) конкурентоспосо́бный. **competitor** /kəm'petɪtə(r)/ *n* конкуре́нт, ~ка.

compilation /ˌkɒmpɪ'leɪʃ(ə)n/ *n* (*result*) компиля́ция; (*act*) составле́ние. **compile** /kəm'paɪl/ *vt* составля́ть *impf*, соста́вить *pf*. **compiler** /kəm'paɪlə(r)/ *n* составитель *m*, ~ница.

complacency /kəm'pleɪsənsɪ/ *n* самодово́льство. **complacent** /kəm'pleɪs(ə)nt/ *adj* самодово́льный.

complain /kəm'pleɪn/ *vi* жа́ловаться *impf*, по~ *pf*. **complaint** /-'pleɪnt/ *n* жа́лоба.

complement /'kɒmplɪmənt/ *n* дополне́ние; (*full number*) (ли́чный) соста́в; *vt* дополня́ть *impf*, допо́лнить *pf*. **complementary** /ˌkɒmplɪ'mentərɪ/ *adj* дополни́тельный.

complete /kəm'pli:t/ *vt* заверша́ть *impf*, заверши́ть *pf*; *adj* (*entire, thorough*) по́лный; (*finished*) зако́нченный. **completion** /-'pli:ʃ(ə)n/ *n* заверше́ние.

complex /'kɒmpleks/ *adj* сло́жный; *n* ко́мплекс. **complexity** /kəm'pleksɪtɪ/ *n* сло́жность.

complexion /kəm'plekʃ(ə)n/ *n* цвет лица́.

compliance /kəm'plaɪəns/ *n* усту́пчивость. **compliant** /-'plaɪənt/ *adj* усту́пчивый.

complicate /'kɒmplɪˌkeɪt/ *vt* осложня́ть *impf*, осложни́ть *pf*. **complicated** /-tɪd/ *adj* сло́жный. **complication** /ˌkɒmplɪ'keɪʃ(ə)n/ *n* осложне́ние.

complicity /kəm'plɪsɪtɪ/ *n* соуча́стие.

compliment /'kɒmplɪmənt/ *n* комплиме́нт; *pl* приве́т; *vt* говори́ть *impf* комплиме́нт(ы) +*dat*; хвали́ть *impf*, по~ *pf*. **complimentary** /ˌkɒmplɪ'mentərɪ/ *adj* ле́стный; (*free*) беспла́тный.

comply /kəm'plaɪ/ *vi*: ~ **with** (*fulfil*) исполня́ть *impf*, испо́лнить *pf*; (*submit to*) подчиня́ться *impf*, подчини́ться *pf* +*dat*.

component /kəm'pəʊnənt/ *n* дета́ль; *adj* составно́й.

compose /kəm'pəʊz/ *vt* (*music etc.*) сочиня́ть *impf*, сочини́ть *pf*; (*draft; constitute*) составля́ть *impf*, соста́вить *pf*. **composed** /-'pəʊzd/ *adj* споко́йный; **be** ~ **of** состоя́ть *impf* из+*gen*. **composer** /-'pəʊzə(r)/ *n* компози́тор. **composition** /ˌkɒmpə'zɪʃ(ə)n/ *n* сочине́ние; (*make-up*) соста́в.

compost /'kɒmpɒst/ *n* компо́ст.

composure /kəm'pəʊʒə(r)/ *n* самооблада́ние.

compound[1] /'kɒmpaʊnd/ *n* (*chem*) соедине́ние; *adj* сло́жный.

compound[2] /'kɒmpaʊnd/ *n* (*enclosure*) огоро́женное ме́сто.

comprehend /ˌkɒmprɪ'hend/ *vt* понима́ть *impf*, поня́ть *pf*. **comprehensible** /-'hensɪb(ə)l/ *adj* поня́тный. **comprehension** /-'henʃ(ə)n/ *n* понима́ние. **comprehensive** /-'hensɪv/ *adj* всеобъе́млющий; ~ **school** общеобразова́тельная шко́ла.

compress /kəm'pres/ *vt* сжима́ть *impf*, сжать *pf*. **compressed** /-'prest/ *adj* сжа́тый.

comprise /kəm'praɪz/ *vt* состоя́ть *impf* из+*gen*.

compromise /'kɒmprəˌmaɪz/ *n* компроми́сс; *vt* компромети́ровать *impf*, с~ *pf*; *vi* идти́ *impf*, пойти́ *pf* на компроми́сс.

compulsion /kəm'pʌlʃ(ə)n/ *n* принужде́ние. **compulsory**

/-'pʌlsərɪ/ *adj* обязáтельный. **compunction** /kəm'pʌŋkʃ(ə)n/ *n* угрызéние сóвести.

computer /kəm'pju:tə(r)/ *n* компью́тер. ~ **game** компью́терная игрá; ~ **science** электрóнно-вычисли́тельная наýка.

comrade /'kɒmreɪd/ *n* товáрищ. **comradeship** *n* товáрищество.

con[1] /kɒn/ *see* **pro**[1]

con[2] /kɒn/ *vt* надувáть *impf*, надýть *pf*.

concave /'kɒnkeɪv/ *adj* вóгнутый.

conceal /kən'si:l/ *vt* скрывáть *impf*, скрыть *pf*.

concede /kən'si:d/ *vt* уступáть *impf*, уступи́ть *pf*; (*admit*) признавáть *impf*, признáть *pf*; (*goal*) пропускáть *impf*, пропусти́ть *pf*.

conceit /kən'si:t/ *n* самомнéние. **conceited** /kən'si:tɪd/ *adj* самовлюблённый.

conceivable /kən'si:vəb(ə)l/ *adj* мы́слимый. **conceive** /kən'si:v/ *vt* (*plan, imagine*) задýмывать *impf*, задýмать *pf*; (*biol*) зачинáть *impf* зачáть *pf*; *vi* заберéменеть *pf*.

concentrate /'kɒnsən,treɪt/ *vt* & *i* сосредотóчивать(ся) *impf*, сосредотóчить(ся) *pf* (**on** на +*prep*); *vt* (*also chem*) концентри́ровать *impf*, с~ *pf*. **concentration** /,kɒnsən'treɪʃ(ə)n/ *n* сосредотóченность, концентрáция.

concept /'kɒnsept/ *n* поня́тие. **conception** /kən'sepʃ(ə)n/ *n* поня́тие; (*biol*) зачáтие.

concern /kən'sɜ:n/ *n* (*worry*) забóта; (*comm*) предприя́тие; *vt* касáться *impf* +*gen*; ~ **o.s. with** занимáться *impf*, заня́ться *pf* +*instr*. **concerned** /-'sɜ:nd/ *adj* озабóченный; **as far as I'm** ~ что касáется меня́. **concerning** /-'sɜ:nɪŋ/ *prep* относи́тельно+*gen*.

concert /'kɒnsət/ *n* концéрт. **concerted** /kən'sɜ:tɪd/ *adj* согласóванный.

concertina /,kɒnsə'ti:nə/ *n* гармóника.

concession /kən'seʃ(ə)n/ *n* устýпка; (*econ*) концéссия. **concessionary** /-nərɪ/ *adj* концессиóнный.

conciliation /kən,sɪlɪ'eɪʃ(ə)n/ *n* примирéние. **conciliatory** /kən'sɪlɪətərɪ/ *adj* примири́тельный.

concise /kən'saɪs/ *adj* крáткий. **conciseness** /-nɪs/ *n* крáткость.

conclude /kən'klu:d/ *vt* заключáть *impf*, заключи́ть *pf*. **concluding** /-dɪŋ/ *adj* заключи́тельный. **conclusion** /-'klu:ʒ(ə)n/ *n* заключéние; (*deduction*) вы́вод. **conclusive** /-'klu:sɪv/ *adj* решáющий.

concoct /kən'kɒkt/ *vt* стря́пать *impf*, со~ *pf*. **concoction** /-'kɒkʃ(ə)n/ *n* стряпня́.

concourse /'kɒŋkɔ:s/ *n* зал.

concrete /'kɒŋkri:t/ *n* бетóн; *adj* бетóнный; (*fig*) конкрéтный.

concur /kən'kɜ:(r)/ *vi* соглашáться *impf*, согласи́ться *pf*. **concurrent** /-'kʌrənt/ *adj* одноврéмéнный.

concussion /kən'kʌʃ(ə)n/ *n* сотрясéние.

condemn /kən'dem/ *vt* осуждáть *impf*, осуди́ть *pf*; (*as unfit for use*) бракoвáть *impf*, за~ *pf*. **condemnation** /,kɒndem'neɪʃ(ə)n/ *n* осуждéние.

condensation /,kɒnden'seɪʃ(ə)n/ *n* конденсáция. **condense** /kən'dens/ *vt* (*liquid etc.*) конденси́ровать *impf* & *pf*; (*text etc.*) со-

сокраща́ть *impf*, сократи́ть *pf*. **condensed** /kən'denst/ *adj* сжа́тый; (*milk*) сгущённый. **condenser** /kən'densə(r)/ *n* конденса́тор.

condescend /ˌkɒndɪ'send/ *vi* снисходи́ть *impf*, снизойти́ *pf*. **condescending** /-'sendɪŋ/ *adj* снисходи́тельный. **condescension** /-'senʃ(ə)n/ *n* снисхожде́ние.

condiment /'kɒndɪmənt/ *n* припра́ва.

condition /kən'dɪʃ(ə)n/ *n* усло́вие; (*state*) состоя́ние; *vt* (*determine*) обусло́вливать *impf*, обусло́вить *pf*; (*psych*) приуча́ть *impf*, приучи́ть *pf*. **conditional** /-'dɪʃən(ə)l/ *adj* усло́вный.

condolence /kən'dəʊləns/ *n*: *pl* соболе́знование.

condom /'kɒndɒm/ *n* презервати́в.

condone /kən'dəʊn/ *vt* закрыва́ть *impf*, закры́ть *pf* глаза́ на+*acc*.

conducive /kən'dju:sɪv/ *adj* спосо́бствующий (**to** +*dat*).

conduct *n* /'kɒndʌkt/ (*behaviour*) поведе́ние; *vt* /kən'dʌkt/ вести́ *impf*, по~, про~ *pf*; (*mus*) дирижи́ровать *impf* +*instr*; (*phys*) проводи́ть *impf*. **conduction** /kən'dʌkʃ(ə)n/ *n* проводи́мость. **conductor** /kən'dʌktə(r)/ *n* (*bus*) конду́ктор; (*phys*) проводни́к; (*mus*) дирижёр.

conduit /'kɒndɪt/ *n* трубопро́во́д.

cone /kəʊn/ *n* ко́нус; (*bot*) ши́шка.

confectioner /kən'fekʃənə(r)/ *n* конди́тер; ~**'s** (*shop*) конди́терская *sb*. **confectionery** /-nərɪ/ *n* конди́терские изде́лия *neut pl*.

confederation /kənˌfedə'reɪʃ(ə)n/ *n* конфедера́ция.

confer /kən'fɜ:(r)/ *vt* присужда́ть *impf*, присуди́ть (**on** +*dat*) *pf*; *vi* совеща́ться *impf*. **conference** /'kɒnfərəns/ *n* совеща́ние; конфере́нция.

confess /kən'fes/ *vt* & *i* (*acknowledge*) признава́ть(ся) *impf*, призна́ть(ся) *pf* (**to** в+*prep*); (*eccl*) испове́довать(ся) *impf* & *pf*. **confession** /-'feʃ(ə)n/ *n* призна́ние; и́споведь. **confessor** /-'fesə(r)/ *n* духовни́к.

confidant(e) /ˌkɒnfɪ'dænt/ *n* бли́зкий собесе́дник. **confide** /kən'faɪd/ *vt* доверя́ть *impf*, дове́рить *pf*; ~ **in** дели́ться *impf*, по~ *pf* с+*instr*. **confidence** /'kɒnfɪd(ə)ns/ *n* (*trust*) дове́рие; (*certainty*) уве́ренность; (*self-*~) самоуве́ренность. **confident** /'kɒnfɪd(ə)nt/ *adj* уве́ренный. **confidential** /ˌkɒnfɪ'denʃ(ə)l/ *adj* секре́тный.

confine /kən'faɪn/ *vt* ограни́чивать *impf*, ограни́чить *pf*; (*shut in*) заключа́ть *impf*, заключи́ть *pf*. **confinement** /-mənt/ *n* заключе́ние. **confines** /'kɒnfaɪnz/ *n pl* преде́лы *m pl*.

confirm /kən'fɜ:m/ *vt* подтвержда́ть *impf*, подтверди́ть *pf*. **confirmation** /ˌkɒnfə'meɪʃ(ə)n/ *n* подтвержде́ние; (*eccl*) конфирма́ция. **confirmed** /-'fɜ:md/ *adj* закорене́лый.

confiscate /'kɒnfɪˌskeɪt/ *vt* конфискова́ть *impf* & *pf*. **confiscation** /ˌkɒnfɪ'skeɪʃ(ə)n/ *n* конфиска́ция.

conflict *n* /'kɒnflɪkt/ конфли́кт; противоре́чие; *vi*: /kən'flɪkt/ ~ **with** противоре́чить *impf* +*dat*. **conflicting** /kən'flɪktɪŋ/ *adj* противоречи́вый.

conform /kən'fɔːm/ *vi*: ~ **to** подчиня́ться *impf*, подчини́ться *pf* +*dat*. **conformity** /-'fɔːmɪtɪ/ *n* соотве́тствие; (*compliance*) подчине́ние.

confound /kən'faʊnd/ *vt* сбива́ть *impf*, сбить *pf* с то́лку. **confounded** /-dɪd/ *adj* прокля́тый.

confront /kən'frʌnt/ *vt* стоя́ть *impf* лицо́м к лицу́ с+*instr*; ~ (*person*) **with** ста́вить *impf*, по~ *pf* лицо́м к лицу́ с+*instr*. **confrontation** /ˌkɒnfrʌn'teɪʃ(ə)n/ *n* конфронта́ция.

confuse /kən'fjuːz/ *vt* смуща́ть *impf*, смути́ть *pf*; (*also mix up*) пу́тать *impf*, за~, с~ *pf*. **confusion** /-'fjuːʒ(ə)n/ *n* смуще́ние; пу́таница.

congeal /kən'dʒiːl/ *vt* густе́ть *impf*, за~ *pf*; (*blood*) свёртываться *impf*, сверну́ться *pf*.

congenial /kən'dʒiːnɪəl/ *adj* прия́тный.

congenital /kən'dʒenɪt(ə)l/ *adj* врождённый.

congested /kən'dʒestɪd/ *adj* перепо́лненный. **congestion** /-'dʒestʃ(ə)n/ *n* (*traffic*) зато́р.

congratulate /kən'grætjʊˌleɪt/ *vt* поздравля́ть *impf*, поздра́вить *pf* (**on** с+*instr*). **congratulation** /-'leɪʃ(ə)n/ *n* поздравле́ние; ~**s!** поздравля́ю!

congregate /'kɒŋgrɪˌgeɪt/ *vi* собира́ться *impf*, собра́ться *pf*. **congregation** /-'geɪʃ(ə)n/ *n* (*eccl*) прихожа́не (-н) *pl*.

congress /'kɒŋgres/ *n* съезд. **Congressman** *n* конгрессме́н.

conic(al) /'kɒnɪk(ə)l/ *adj* кони́ческий.

conifer /'kɒnɪfə(r)/ *n* хво́йное де́рево. **coniferous** /kə'nɪfərəs/ *adj* хво́йный.

conjecture /kən'dʒektʃə(r)/ *n* дога́дка; *vt* гада́ть *impf*.

conjugal /'kɒndʒʊg(ə)l/ *adj* супру́жеский.

conjugate /'kɒndʒʊˌgeɪt/ *vt* спряга́ть *impf*, про~ *pf*. **conjugation** /-'geɪʃ(ə)n/ *n* спряже́ние.

conjunction /kən'dʒʌŋkʃ(ə)n/ *n* (*gram*) сою́з; **in ~ with** совме́стно с+*instr*.

conjure /'kʌndʒə(r)/ *vi*: ~ **up** (*in mind*) вызыва́ть *impf*, вы́звать *pf* в воображе́нии. **conjurer** /-rə(r)/ *n* фо́кусник. **conjuring trick** /-rɪŋ/ *n* фо́кус.

connect /kə'nekt/ *vt & i* свя́зывать(ся) *impf*, связа́ть(ся) *pf*; соединя́ть(ся) *impf*, соедини́ть(ся) *pf*. **connected** /-'nektɪd/ *adj* свя́занный. **connection, -exion** /-'nekʃ(ə)n/ *n* связь; (*rly etc.*) переса́дка.

connivance /kə'naɪv(ə)ns/ *n* попусти́тельство. **connive** /kə'naɪv/ *vi*: ~ **at** попусти́тельствовать *impf* +*dat*.

connoisseur /ˌkɒnə'sɜː(r)/ *n* знато́к.

conquer /'kɒŋkə(r)/ *vt* (*country*) завоёвывать *impf*, завоева́ть *pf*; (*enemy*) побежда́ть *impf*, победи́ть *pf*; (*habit*) преодолева́ть *impf*, преодоле́ть *pf*. **conqueror** /'kɒŋkərə(r)/ *n* завоева́тель *m*. **conquest** /'kɒŋkwest/ *n* завоева́ние.

conscience /'kɒnʃ(ə)ns/ *n* со́весть. **conscientious** /ˌkɒnʃɪ'enʃ(ə)s/ *adj* добросо́вестный. **conscious** /'kɒnʃ(ə)s/ *adj* созна́тельный; *predic* в созна́нии; **be ~ of** сознава́ть *impf* +*acc*. **consciousness** /'kɒnʃəsnɪs/ *n* созна́ние.

conscript *vt* /kən'skrɪpt/ призыва́ть *impf*, призва́ть *pf* на вое́нную слу́жбу; *n* /'kɒnskrɪpt/ призывни́к. **conscription** /kən

'skrɪpʃ(ə)n/ *n* вóинская повúнность.
consecrate /'kɒnsɪˌkreɪt/ *vt* освящáть *impf*, освятúть *pf*. **consecration** /-'kreɪʃ(ə)n/ *n* освящéние.
consecutive /kən'sekjʊtɪv/ *adj* послéдовательный.
consensus /kən'sensəs/ *n* соглáсие.
consent /kən'sent/ *vi* соглашáться *impf*, согласúться *pf* (**to** +*inf*, на+*acc*); *n* соглáсие.
consequence /'kɒnsɪkwəns/ *n* послéдствие; **of great** ~ большóго значéния; **of some** ~ довóльно вáжный. **consequent** /-kwənt/ *adj* вытекáющий. **consequential** /ˌkɒnsɪ'kwenʃ(ə)l/ *adj* вáжный. **consequently** /'kɒnsɪˌkwəntlɪ/ *adv* слéдовательно.
conservation /ˌkɒnsə'veɪʃ(ə)n/ *n* сохранéние; (*of nature*) охрáна прирóды. **conservative** /kən'sɜːvətɪv/ *adj* консерватúвный; *n* консервáтор. **conservatory** /kən'sɜːvətərɪ/ *n* оранжерéя. **conserve** /kən'sɜːv/ *vt* сохранять *impf*, сохранúть *pf*.
consider /kən'sɪdə(r)/ *vt* (*think over*) обдýмывать *impf*, обдýмать *pf*; (*examine*) рассмáтривать *impf*, рассмотрéть *pf*; (*regard as, be of opinion that*) считáть *impf*, счесть *pf* +*instr*, за+*acc*, что; (*take into account*) считáться *impf* с+*instr*. **considerable** /-'sɪdərəb(ə)l/ *adj* значúтельный. **considerate** /-'sɪdərət/ *adj* внимáтельный. **consideration** /kənˌsɪdə'reɪʃ(ə)n/ *n* рассмотрéние; внимáние; (*factor*) фáктор; **take into** ~ принимáть *impf*, принять *pf* во внимáние. **considering** /-'sɪdərɪŋ/ *prep* принимáя +*acc* во внимáние.
consign /kən'saɪn/ *vt* передавáть *impf*, передáть *pf*. **consignment** /-'saɪnmənt/ *n* (*goods*) пáртия; (*consigning*) отпрáвка товáров.
consist /kən'sɪst/ *vi*: ~ **of** состоять *impf* из+*gen*. **consistency** /-'sɪstənsɪ/ *n* послéдовательность; (*density*) консистéнция. **consistent** /-'sɪstənt/ *adj* послéдовательный; ~ **with** совместúмый с+*instr*.
consolation /ˌkɒnsə'leɪʃ(ə)n/ *n* утешéние. **console**[1] /kən'səʊl/ *vt* утешáть *impf*, утéшить *pf*.
console[2] /'kɒnsəʊl/ *n* (*control panel*) пульт управлéния.
consolidate /kən'sɒlɪˌdeɪt/ *vt* укреплять *impf*, укрепúть *pf*. **consolidation** /-'deɪʃ(ə)n/ *n* укреплéние.
consonant /'kɒnsənənt/ *n* соглáсный *sb*.
consort /'kɒnsɔːt/ *n* супрýг, ~a.
conspicuous /kən'spɪkjʊəs/ *adj* замéтный.
conspiracy /kən'spɪrəsɪ/ *n* заговор. **conspirator** /-'spɪrətə(r)/ *n* заговóрщик, -ица. **conspiratorial** /-ˌspɪrə'tɔːrɪəl/ *adj* заговóрщицкий. **conspire** /-'spaɪə(r)/ *vi* устрáивать *impf*, устрóить *pf* заговор.
constable /'kʌnstəb(ə)l/ *n* полицéйский *sb*.
constancy /'kɒnstənsɪ/ *n* постоянство. **constant** /-st(ə)nt/ *adj* постоянный. **constantly** /-st(ə)ntlɪ/ *adv* постоянно.
constellation /ˌkɒnstə'leɪʃ(ə)n/ *n* созвéздие.
consternation /ˌkɒnstə'neɪʃ(ə)n/ *n* тревóга.
constipation /ˌkɒnstɪ'peɪʃ(ə)n/ *n* запóр.
constituency /kən'stɪtjʊənsɪ/ *n*

избира́тельный о́круг. **constituent** /-'stɪtjʊənt/ *n* (*component*) составна́я часть; (*voter*) избира́тель *m*; *adj* составно́й. **constitute** /'kɒnstɪ,tju:t/ *vt* составля́ть *impf*, соста́вить *pf*. **constitution** /,kɒnstɪ'tju:ʃ(ə)n/ *n* (*polit*, *med*) конститу́ция; (*composition*) составле́ние. **constitutional** /,kɒnstɪ'tju:ʃən(ə)l/ *adj* (*polit*) конституцио́нный.

constrain /kən'streɪn/ *vt* принужда́ть *impf*, прину́дить *pf*. **constrained** /-'streɪnd/ *adj* (*inhibited*) стеснённый. **constraint** /-'streɪnt/ *n* принужде́ние; (*inhibition*) стесне́ние.

constrict /kən'strɪkt/ *vt* (*compress*) сжима́ть *impf*, сжать *pf*; (*narrow*) су́живать *impf*, су́зить *pf*. **constriction** /-'strɪkʃ(ə)n/ *n* сжа́тие; суже́ние.

construct /kən'strʌkt/ *vt* стро́ить *impf*, по~ *pf*. **construction** /-'strʌkʃ(ə)n/ *n* строи́тельство; (*also gram*) констру́кция; (*interpretation*) истолкова́ние; ~ **site** стро́йка. **constructive** /-'strʌktɪv/ *adj* конструкти́вный.

construe /kən'stru:/ *vt* истолко́вывать *impf*, истолкова́ть *pf*.

consul /'kɒns(ə)l/ *n* ко́нсул. **consulate** /'kɒnsjʊlət/ *n* ко́нсульство.

consult /kən'sʌlt/ *vt* сове́товаться *impf*, по~ *pf* с+*instr*. **consultant** /-'sʌlt(ə)nt/ *n* консульта́нт. **consultation** /,kɒnsəl'teɪʃ(ə)n/ *n* консульта́ция.

consume /kən'sju:m/ *vt* потребля́ть *impf*, потреби́ть *pf*; (*eat or drink*) съеда́ть *impf*, съесть *pf*. **consumer** /-'sju:mə(r)/ *n* потреби́тель *m*; ~ **goods** това́ры *m pl* широ́кого потребле́ния.

consummate /'kɒnsjʊ,meɪt/ *vt* заверша́ть *impf*, заверши́ть *pf*; ~ **a marriage** осуществля́ть *impf*, осуществи́ть *pf* бра́чные отноше́ния. **consummation** /-'meɪʃ(ə)n/ *n* заверше́ние; (*of marriage*) осуществле́ние.

consumption /kən'sʌmpʃ(ə)n/ *n* потребле́ние.

contact /'kɒntækt/ *n* конта́кт; (*person*) связь; ~ **lens** конта́ктная ли́нза; *vt* свя́зываться *impf*, связа́ться *pf* с+*instr*.

contagious /kən'teɪdʒəs/ *adj* зара́зный.

contain /kən'teɪn/ *vt* содержа́ть *impf*; (*restrain*) сде́рживать *impf*, сдержа́ть *pf*. **container** /-nə(r)/ *n* (*vessel*) сосу́д; (*transport*) конте́йнер.

contaminate /kən'tæmɪ,neɪt/ *vt* загрязня́ть *impf*, загрязни́ть *pf*. **contamination** /-'neɪʃ(ə)n/ *n* загрязне́ние.

contemplate /'kɒntəm,pleɪt/ *vt* (*gaze*) созерца́ть *impf*; размышля́ть *impf*; (*consider*) предполага́ть *impf*, предположи́ть *pf*. **contemplation** /-'pleɪʃ(ə)n/ *n* созерца́ние; размышле́ние. **contemplative** /kən'templətɪv/ *adj* созерца́тельный.

contemporary /kən'tempərərɪ/ *n* совреме́нник; *adj* совреме́нный.

contempt /kən'tempt/ *n* презре́ние; ~ **of court** неуваже́ние к суду́; **hold in** ~ презира́ть *impf*. **contemptible** /-'temptɪb(ə)l/ *adj* презре́нный. **contemptuous** /-'temptjʊəs/ *adj* презри́тельный.

contend /kən'tend/ *vi* (*compete*) состяза́ться *impf*; ~ **for** оспа́ривать *impf*; ~ **with** справля́ться *impf*, спра́виться *pf* с+*instr*; *vt* утвержда́ть *impf*.

contender /-də(r)/ *n* претендéнт.

content[1] /'kɒntent/ *n* содержáние; *pl* содержи́мое *sb*; **(table of) ~s** содержáние.

content[2] /kən'tent/ *predic* довóлен (-льна); *vt*: **~ o.s. with** довóльствоваться *impf*, у~ *pf* +*instr*. **contented** /-'tentɪd/ *adj* довóльный.

contention /kən'tenʃ(ə)n/ *n* (*claim*) утверждéние. **contentious** /-'tenʃəs/ *adj* спóрный.

contest *n* /'kɒntest/ состязáние; *vt* /kən'test/ (*dispute*) оспáривать *impf*, оспóрить *pf*. **contestant** /kən'test(ə)nt/ *n* учáстник, -ица, состязáния.

context /'kɒntekst/ *n* контéкст.

continent /'kɒntɪnənt/ *n* матери́к. **continental** /ˌkɒntɪ'nent(ə)l/ *adj* материкóвый.

contingency /kən'tɪndʒənsɪ/ *n* возмóжный слýчай; **~ plan** вариáнт плáна. **contingent** /-'tɪndʒənt/ *adj* случáйный; *n* контингéнт.

continual /kən'tɪnjʊəl/ *adj* непрестáнный. **continuation** /-ˌtɪnjʊ'eɪʃ(ə)n/ *n* продолжéние. **continue** /-'tɪnju:/ *vt* & *i* продолжáть(ся) *impf*, продóлжить(ся) *pf*. **continuous** /-'tɪnjʊəs/ *adj* непреры́вный.

contort /kən'tɔ:t/ *vt* искажáть *impf*, искази́ть *pf*. **contortion** /-'tɔ:ʃ(ə)n/ *n* искажéние.

contour /'kɒntʊə(r)/ *n* кóнтур; **~ line** горизонтáль.

contraband /'kɒntrəˌbænd/ *n* контрабáнда.

contraception /ˌkɒntrə'sepʃ(ə)n/ *n* предупреждéние зачáтия. **contraceptive** /-'septɪv/ *n* противозачáточное срéдство; *adj* противозачáточный.

contract *n* /'kɒntrækt/ контрáкт, дóговóр; *vi* /kən'trækt/ (*make a* ~) заключáть *impf*, заключи́ть *pf* контрáкт; *vt* & *i* /kən'trækt/ (*shorten, reduce*) сокращáть(ся) *impf*, сократи́ть(ся) *pf*; *vt* (*illness*) заболевáть *impf*, заболéть *pf* +*instr*. **contraction** /kən'trækʃ(ə)n/ *n* сокращéние; *pl* (*med*) схвáтки *f pl*. **contractor** /kən'træktə(r)/ *n* подря́дчик.

contradict /ˌkɒntrə'dɪkt/ *vt* противорéчить *impf* +*dat*. **contradiction** /-'dɪkʃ(ə)n/ *n* противорéчие. **contradictory** /-'dɪktərɪ/ *adj* противоречи́вый.

contraflow /'kɒntrəfləʊ/ *n* встрéчное движéние.

contralto /kən'træltəʊ/ *n* контрáльто (*voice*) *neut* & (*person*) *f indecl*.

contraption /kən'træpʃ(ə)n/ *n* приспособлéние.

contrary *adj* (*opposite*) /'kɒntrərɪ/ противоположный; **~ to** вопреки́ +*dat*; (*perverse*) /kən'treərɪ/ капри́зный; *n* /'kɒntrərɪ/: **on the ~** наоборóт.

contrast /'kɒntrɑ:st/ *n* контрáст, противоположность; *vt* противопоставля́ть *impf*, противопостáвить *pf* (**with** +*dat*); *vi* контрасти́ровать *impf*.

contravene /ˌkɒntrə'vi:n/ *vt* нарушáть *impf*, нарýшить *pf*. **contravention** /-'venʃ(ə)n/ *n* нарушéние.

contribute /kən'trɪbju:t/ *vt* (*to fund etc.*) жéртвовать *impf*, по~ *pf* (**to** в+*acc*); **~ to** (*further*) содéйствовать *impf* & *pf*, по~ *pf* +*dat*; (*write for*) сотрýдничать *impf* в+*prep*. **contribution** /ˌkɒntrɪ'bju:ʃ(ə)n/ *n* (*money*) пожéртвование; (*fig*) вклад. **contributor** /kən'trɪbjʊtə(r)/ *n* (*donor*) жéртвователь *m*;

(*writer*) сотру́дник.
contrite /'kɒntraɪt/ *adj* ка́ющийся.
contrivance /kən'traɪv(ə)ns/ *n* приспособле́ние. **contrive** /kən'traɪv/ *vt* ухитря́ться *impf*, ухитри́ться *pf +inf.*
control /kən'trəʊl/ *n* (*mastery*) контро́ль *m*; (*operation*) управле́ние; *pl* управле́ния *pl*; *vt* (*dominate*; *verify*) контроли́ровать *impf*, про~ *pf*; (*regulate*) управля́ть *impf +instr*; ~ **o.s.** сде́рживаться *impf*, сдержа́ться *pf.*
controversial /ˌkɒntrə'vɜːʃ(ə)l/ *adj* спо́рный. **controversy** /'kɒntrəˌvɜːsɪ/ *n* спор.
convalesce /ˌkɒnvə'les/ *vi* выздора́вливать *impf.* **convalescence** /-'les(ə)ns/ *n* выздоровле́ние.
convection /kən'vekʃ(ə)n/ *n* конве́кция. **convector** /-'vektə(r)/ *n* конве́ктор.
convene /kən'viːn/ *vt* созыва́ть *impf*, созва́ть *pf.*
convenience /kən'viːnɪəns/ *n* удо́бство; (*public* ~) убо́рная *sb.* **convenient** /-'viːnɪənt/ *adj* удо́бный.
convent /'kɒnv(ə)nt/ *n* же́нский монасты́рь *m.*
convention /kən'venʃ(ə)n/ *n* (*assembly*) съезд; (*agreement*) конве́нция; (*custom*) обы́чай; (*conventionality*) усло́вность. **conventional** /-ʃən(ə)l/ *adj* общепри́нятый; (*also mil*) обы́чный.
converge /kən'vɜːdʒ/ *vi* сходи́ться *impf*, сойти́сь *pf.* **convergence** /-dʒəns/ *n* сходи́мость.
conversant /kən'vɜːs(ə)nt/ *predic*: ~ **with** знако́м с+*instr.*
conversation /ˌkɒnvə'seɪʃ(ə)n/ *n* разгово́р. **conversational** /-'seɪʃən(ə)l/ *adj* разгово́рный.
converse[1] /kən'vɜːs/ *vi* разгова́ривать *impf.*
converse[2] /'kɒnvɜːs/ *n* обра́тное *sb.* **conversely** /'kɒnvɜːslɪ/ *adv* наоборо́т. **conversion** /kən'vɜːʃ(ə)n/ *n* (*change*) превраще́ние; (*of faith*) обраще́ние; (*of building*) перестро́йка. **convert** /kən'vɜːt/ *vt* (*change*) превраща́ть *impf*, преврати́ть *pf* (**into** в+*acc*); (*to faith*) обраща́ть *impf*, обрати́ть *pf* (**to** в+*acc*); (*a building*) перестра́ивать *impf*, перестро́ить *pf.* **convertible** /kən'vɜːtɪb(ə)l/ *adj* обрати́мый; *n* автомоби́ль *m* со снима́ющейся кры́шей.
convex /'kɒnveks/ *adj* вы́пуклый.
convey /kən'veɪ/ *vt* (*transport*) перевози́ть *impf*, перевезти́ *pf*; (*communicate*) передава́ть *impf*, переда́ть *pf.* **conveyance** /-'veɪəns/ *n* перево́зка; переда́ча. **conveyancing** /-'veɪənsɪŋ/ *n* нотариа́льная переда́ча. **conveyor belt** /-'veɪə(r)/ *n* транспортёрная ле́нта.
convict /'kɒnvɪkt/ *n* осуждённый *sb*; *vt* /kən'vɪkt/ осужда́ть *impf*, осуди́ть *pf.* **conviction** /kən'vɪkʃ(ə)n/ *n* (*law*) осужде́ние; (*belief*) убежде́ние. **convince** /kən'vɪns/ *vt* убежда́ть *impf*, убеди́ть *pf.* **convincing** /kən'vɪnsɪŋ/ *adj* убеди́тельный.
convivial /kən'vɪvɪəl/ *adj* весёлый.
convoluted /'kɒnvəˌluːtɪd/ *adj* изви́листый; (*fig*) запу́танный.
convoy /'kɒnvɔɪ/ *n* конво́й.
convulse /kən'vʌls/ *vt*: **be ~d with** содрога́ться *impf*, содрог-

нуться *pf* от+*gen.* **convulsion** /-'vʌlʃ(ə)n/ *n* (*med*) конву́льсия.

cook /kʊk/ *n* куха́рка, по́вар; *vt* гото́вить *impf*; *vi* вари́ться *impf*; с~ *pf.* **cooker** /'kʊkə(r)/ *n* плита́, печь. **cookery** /'kʊkərɪ/ *n* кулина́рия.

cool /ku:l/ *adj* прохла́дный; (*calm*) хладнокро́вный; (*unfriendly*) холо́дный; *vt* охлажда́ть *impf*, охлади́ть *pf*; ~ **down, off** остыва́ть *impf*, осты́(ну)ть *pf.* **coolness** /'ku:lnɪs/ *n* прохла́да; (*calm*) хладнокро́вие; (*manner*) холодо́к.

coop /ku:p/ *n* куря́тник; *vt*: ~ **up** держа́ть *impf* взаперти́.

cooperate /kəʊ'ɒpə,reɪt/ *vi* сотру́дничать *impf.* **cooperation** /kəʊ,ɒpə'reɪʃ(ə)n/ *n* сотру́дничество. **cooperative** /kəʊ'ɒpərətɪv/ *n* кооперати́в; *adj* кооперати́вный; (*helpful*) услу́жливый.

co-opt /kəʊ'ɒpt/ *vt* коопти́ровать *impf* & *pf.*

coordinate *vt* /kəʊ'ɔ:dɪ,neɪt/ координи́ровать *impf* & *pf*; *n* /kəʊ'ɔ:dɪnət/ координа́та. **coordination** /kəʊ,ɔ:dɪ'neɪʃ(ə)n/ *n* координа́ция.

cope /kəʊp/ *vi*: ~ **with** справля́ться *impf*, спра́виться *pf* с+*instr.*

copious /'kəʊpɪəs/ *adj* оби́льный.

copper /'kɒpə(r)/ *n* (*metal*) медь; *adj* ме́дный.

coppice, copse /'kɒpɪs, kɒps/ *n* ро́щица.

copulate /'kɒpjʊ,leɪt/ *vi* совокупля́ться *impf*, совокупи́ться *pf.*

copy /'kɒpɪ/ *n* ко́пия; (*book*) экземпля́р; *vt* (*reproduce*) копи́ровать *impf*, с~ *pf*; (*transcribe*) перепи́сывать *impf*, переписа́ть *pf*; (*imitate*) подража́ть *impf* +*dat.* **copyright** *n* а́вторское пра́во.

coral /'kɒr(ə)l/ *n* кора́лл.

cord /kɔ:d/ *n* (*string*) верёвка; (*electr*) шнур.

cordial /'kɔ:dɪəl/ *adj* серде́чный.

corduroy /'kɔ:də,rɔɪ/ *n* ру́бчатый вельве́т.

core /kɔ:(r)/ *n* сердцеви́на; (*fig*) суть.

cork /kɔ:k/ *n* (*material*; *stopper*) про́бка; (*float*) поплаво́к. **corkscrew** *n* што́пор.

corn¹ /kɔ:n/ *n* зерно́; (*wheat*) пшени́ца; (*maize*) кукуру́за. **cornflakes** *n pl* кукуру́зные хло́пья (-пьев) *pl.* **cornflour** *n* кукуру́зная мука́. **corny** /'kɔ:nɪ/ *adj* (*coll*) бана́льный.

corn² /kɔ:n/ *n* (*med*) мозо́ль.

cornea /'kɔ:nɪə/ *n* рогова́я оболо́чка.

corner /'kɔ:nə(r)/ *n* у́гол; ~**-stone** *n* краеуго́льный ка́мень *m*; *vt* загоня́ть *impf*, загна́ть *pf* в у́гол.

cornet /'kɔ:nɪt/ *n* (*mus*) корне́т; (*ice-cream*) рожо́к.

cornice /'kɔ:nɪs/ *n* карни́з.

coronary (thrombosis) /'kɒrənərɪ (θrɒm'bəʊsɪs)/ *n* коронаротромбо́з. **coronation** /,kɒrə'neɪʃ(ə)n/ *n* корона́ция.

coroner /'kɒrənə(r)/ *n* ме́дик суде́бной эксперти́зы.

corporal¹ /'kɔ:pr(ə)l/ *n* капра́л.

corporal² /'kɔ:pr(ə)l/ *adj* теле́сный; ~ **punishment** теле́сное наказа́ние.

corporate /'kɔ:pərət/ *adj* корпорати́вный. **corporation** /,kɔ:pə'reɪʃ(ə)n/ *n* корпора́ция.

corps /kɔ:(r)/ *n* ко́рпус.

corpse /kɔ:ps/ *n* труп.

corpulent /'kɔ:pjʊlənt/ *adj* ту́чный.

corpuscle /'kɔ:pʌs(ə)l/ *n* кровя-

но́й ша́рик.
correct /kə'rekt/ *adj* пра́вильный; (*conduct*) корре́ктный; *vt* исправля́ть *impf*, испра́вить *pf*. **correction** /-'rekʃ(ə)n/ *n* исправле́ние.
correlation /ˌkɒrə'leɪʃ(ə)n/ *n* соотноше́ние.
correspond /ˌkɒrɪ'spɒnd/ *vi* соотве́тствовать *impf* (**to, with** +*dat*); (*by letter*) перепи́сываться *impf*. **correspondence** /-dəns/ *n* соотве́тствие; (*letters*) корреспонде́нция. **correspondent** /-dənt/ *n* корреспонде́нт. **corresponding** /-dɪŋ/ *adj* соотве́тствующий (**to** +*dat*).
corridor /'kɒrɪˌdɔː(r)/ *n* коридо́р.
corroborate /kə'rɒbəˌreɪt/ *vt* подтвержда́ть *impf*, подтверди́ть *pf*.
corrode /kə'rəʊd/ *vt* разъеда́ть *impf*, разъе́сть *pf*. **corrosion** /-'rəʊʒ(ə)n/ *n* корро́зия. **corrosive** /-'rəʊsɪv/ *adj* е́дкий.
corrugated iron /'kɒrʊˌgeɪtɪd 'aɪən/ *n* рифлёное желе́зо.
corrupt /kə'rʌpt/ *adj* (*person*) развращённый; (*government*) прода́жный; *vt* развраща́ть *impf*, разврати́ть *pf*. **corruption** /-'rʌpʃ(ə)n/ *n* развраще́ние; корру́пция.
corset /'kɔːsɪt/ *n* корсе́т.
cortège /kɔː'teɪʒ/ *n* корте́ж.
cortex /'kɔːteks/ *n* кора́.
corundum /kə'rʌndəm/ *n* кору́нд.
cosmetic /kɒz'metɪk/ *adj* космети́ческий. **cosmetics** /-tɪks/ *n pl* косме́тика.
cosmic /'kɒzmɪk/ *adj* косми́ческий. **cosmonaut** /'kɒzməˌnɔːt/ *n* космона́вт.
cosmopolitan /ˌkɒzmə'pɒlɪt(ə)n/ *adj* космополити́ческий.
cosmos /'kɒzmɒs/ *n* ко́смос.
Cossack /'kɒsæk/ *n* каза́к, -а́чка.
cosset /'kɒsɪt/ *vt* не́жить *impf*.
cost /kɒst/ *n* сто́имость, цена́; *vt* сто́ить *impf*.
costly /'kɒstlɪ/ *adj* дорого́й.
costume /'kɒstjuːm/ *n* костю́м.
cosy /'kəʊzɪ/ *adj* ую́тный.
cot /kɒt/ *n* де́тская крова́тка.
cottage /'kɒtɪdʒ/ *n* котте́дж; ~ **cheese** творо́г.
cotton /'kɒt(ə)n/ *n* хло́пок; (*cloth*) хлопчатобума́жная ткань; (*thread*) ни́тка; ~ **wool** ва́та; *adj* хло́пковый; хлопчатобума́жный.
couch /kaʊtʃ/ *n* дива́н.
couchette /kuː'ʃet/ *n* спа́льное ме́сто.
cough /kɒf/ *n* ка́шель *m*; *vi* ка́шлять *impf*.
council /'kaʊns(ə)l/ *n* сове́т; ~ **tax** ме́стный нало́г; ~ **house** жильё из обще́ственного фо́нда. **councillor** /'kaʊnsələ(r)/ *n* член сове́та.
counsel /'kaʊns(ə)l/ *n* (*advice*) сове́т; (*lawyer*) адвока́т; *vt* сове́товать *impf*, по~ *pf* +*dat*.
count[1] /kaʊnt/ *vt* счита́ть *impf*, со~, счесть *pf*; ~ **on** рассчи́тывать *impf* на+*acc*; *n* счёт. **countdown** *n* отсчёт вре́мени.
count[2] /kaʊnt/ *n* (*title*) граф.
countenance /'kaʊntɪnəns/ *n* лицо́; *vt* одобря́ть *impf*, одо́брить *pf*.
counter /'kaʊntə(r)/ *n* прила́вок; (*token*) фи́шка; *adv*: **run ~ to** идти́ *impf* вразре́з с+*instr*; *vt* пари́ровать *impf*, от~ *pf*. **counteract** *vt* противоде́йствовать *impf* +*dat*. **counterbalance** *n* противове́с; *vt* уравнове́шивать *impf*, уравнове́сить *pf*. **counterfeit** /-fɪt/ *adj*

поддéльный. **counterpart** *n* соответственная часть. **counterpoint** *n* контрапýнкт. **counter-revolutionary** *n* контрреволюционéр; *adj* контрреволюциóнный. **countersign** *vt* стáвить *impf*, по~ *pf* вторýю пóдпись на+*prep*.

countess /'kaʊntɪs/ *n* графи́ня.

countless /'kaʊntlɪs/ *adj* бесчи́сленный.

country /'kʌntrɪ/ *n* (*nation*) странá; (*native land*) рóдина; (*rural areas*) дерéвня; *adj* деревéнский, сéльский. **countryman** *n* (*compatriot*) соотéчественник; сéльский жи́тель *m*. **countryside** *n* прирóдный ландшáфт.

county /'kaʊntɪ/ *n* грáфство.

coup /ku:/ *n* (*polit*) переворóт.

couple /'kʌp(ə)l/ *n* пáра; (*a few*) нéсколько +*gen*; *vt* сцеплять *impf*, сцепи́ть *pf*.

coupon /'ku:pɒn/ *n* купóн; талóн; вáучер.

courage /'kʌrɪdʒ/ *n* хрáбрость. **courageous** /kə'reɪdʒəs/ *adj* хрáбрый.

courier /'kʊrɪə(r)/ *n* (*messenger*) курьéр; (*guide*) гид.

course /kɔ:s/ *n* курс; (*process*) ход, течéние; (*of meal*) блюдо; **of ~** конéчно.

court /kɔ:t/ *n* двор; (*sport*) корт, площáдка; (*law*) суд; **~ martial** воéнный суд; *vt* ухáживать *impf* за+*instr*. **courteous** /'kɜ:tɪəs/ *adj* вéжливый. **courtesy** /'kɜ:tɪsɪ/ *n* вéжливость. **courtier** /'kɔ:tɪə(r)/ *n* придвóрный *sb*. **courtyard** *n* двор.

cousin /'kʌz(ə)n/ *n* двоюрóдный брат, -ная сестрá.

cove /kəʊv/ *n* бýхточка.

covenant /'kʌvənənt/ *n* договóр.

cover /'kʌvə(r)/ *n* (*covering*; *lid*) покры́шка; (*shelter*) укры́тие; (*chair ~*; *soft case*) чехóл; (*bed*) покрывáло; (*book*) переплёт, облóжка; **under separate ~** в отдéльном конвéрте; *vt* покрывáть *impf*, покры́ть *pf*; (*hide*, *protect*) закрывáть *impf*, закры́ть *pf*. **coverage** /-rɪdʒ/ *n* освещéние. **covert** /'kəʊvɜ:t/ *adj* скры́тый.

covet /'kʌvɪt/ *vt* пожелáть *pf* +*gen*.

cow[1] /kaʊ/ *n* корóва. **cowboy** *n* ковбóй. **cowshed** *n* хлев.

cow[2] /kaʊ/ *vt* запýгивать *impf*, запугáть *pf*.

coward /'kaʊəd/ *n* трус. **cowardice** /-dɪs/ *n* трýсость. **cowardly** /-lɪ/ *adj* трусли́вый.

cower /'kaʊə(r)/ *vi* съёживаться *impf*, съёжиться *pf*.

cox(swain) /'kɒks(weɪn)/ *n* рулевóй *m*.

coy /kɔɪ/ *adj* жемáнно стыдли́вый.

crab /kræb/ *n* краб.

crack /kræk/ *n* (*in cup*, *ice*) трéщина; (*in wall*) щель; (*noise*) треск; *adj* первоклáссный; *vt* (*break*) колóть *impf*, рас~ *pf*; (*china*) дéлать *impf*, с~ *pf* трéщину в+*acc*; *vi* трéснуть *pf*. **crackle** /'kræk(ə)l/ *vi* потрéскивать *impf*.

cradle /'kreɪd(ə)l/ *n* колыбéль.

craft /krɑ:ft/ *n* (*trade*) ремеслó; (*boat*) сýдно. **craftiness** /'krɑ:ftɪnɪs/ *n* хи́трость. **craftsman** *n* ремéсленник. **crafty** /'krɑ:ftɪ/ *adj* хи́трый.

crag /kræg/ *n* утёс. **craggy** /'krægɪ/ *adj* скали́стый.

cram /kræm/ *vt* (*fill*) набивáть *impf*, наби́ть *pf*; (*stuff in*) впи́хивать *impf*, впихнýть *pf*; *vi* (*study*) зубри́ть *impf*.

cramp[1] /kræmp/ *n* (*med*) су́дорога.

cramp[2] /kræmp/ *vt* стесня́ть *impf*, стесни́ть *pf*. **cramped** /kræmpt/ *adj* те́сный.

cranberry /'krænbərɪ/ *n* клю́ква.

crane /kreɪn/ *n* (*bird*) жура́вль *m*; (*machine*) кран; *vt* (*one's neck*) вытя́гивать *impf*, вы́тянуть *pf* (ше́ю).

crank[1] /kræŋk/ *n* заводна́я ру́чка; **~-shaft** коле́нчатый вал; *vt* заводи́ть *impf*, завести́ *pf*.

crank[2] /kræŋk/ *n* (*eccentric*) чуда́к.

cranny /'krænɪ/ *n* щель.

crash /kræʃ/ *n* (*noise*) гро́хот, треск; (*accident*) ава́рия; (*financial*) крах; **~ course** ускоре́нный курс; **~ helmet** защи́тный шлем; **~ landing** авари́йная поса́дка; *vi* (**~** *into*) вреза́ться *impf*, вре́заться *pf* в+*acc*; (*aeron*) разбива́ться *impf*, разби́ться *pf*; (*fall with* **~**) гро́хнуться *pf*; (*comput*) зависа́ть *impf*, зави́снуть *pf*; *vt* (*bang down*) гро́хнуть *pf*.

crass /kræs/ *adj* гру́бый.

crate /kreɪt/ *n* я́щик.

crater /'kreɪtə(r)/ *n* кра́тер.

crave /kreɪv/ *vi*: **~ for** жа́ждать *impf* +*gen*. **craving** /'kreɪvɪŋ/ *n* стра́стное жела́ние.

crawl /krɔːl/ *vi* по́лзать *indet*, ползти́ *det*; **~ with** кише́ть +*instr*; *n* (*sport*) кроль *m*.

crayon /'kreɪən/ *n* цветно́й каранда́ш.

craze /kreɪz/ *n* ма́ния. **crazy** /'kreɪzɪ/ *adj* поме́шанный (**about** на+*prep*).

creak /kriːk/ *n* скрип; *vi* скрипе́ть *impf*.

cream /kriːm/ *n* сли́вки (-вок) *pl*; (*cosmetic*; *cul*) крем; **~ cheese** сли́вочный сыр; **soured ~** смета́на; *vt* сбива́ть *impf*, сбить *pf*; *adj* (*of cream*) сли́вочный; (*colour*) кре́мовый. **creamy** /'kriːmɪ/ *adj* сли́вочный, кре́мовый.

crease /kriːs/ *n* скла́дка; *vt* мять *impf*, из~, с~ *pf*. **creased** /kriːst/ *adj* мя́тый.

create /kriː'eɪt/ *vt* создава́ть *impf*, созда́ть *pf*. **creation** /-'eɪʃ(ə)n/ *n* созда́ние. **creative** /-'eɪtɪv/ *adj* тво́рческий. **creator** /-'eɪtə(r)/ *n* созда́тель *m*. **creature** /'kriːtʃə(r)/ *n* созда́ние.

crêche /kreʃ/ *n* (де́тские) я́сли (-лей) *pl*.

credence /'kriːd(ə)ns/ *n* ве́ра; **give ~** ве́рить *impf* (**to** +*dat*).

credentials /krɪ'denʃ(ə)lz/ *n pl* удостовере́ние; (*diplomacy*) вери́тельные гра́моты *f pl*.

credibility /ˌkredɪ'bɪlɪtɪ/ *n* правдоподо́бие; (*of person*) спосо́бность вызыва́ть дове́рие. **credible** /'kredɪb(ə)l/ *adj* (*of thing*) правдоподо́бный; (*of person*) заслу́живающий дове́рия.

credit /'kredɪt/ *n* дове́рие; (*comm*) креди́т; (*honour*) честь; **give ~** кредитова́ть *impf* & *pf* +*acc*; отдава́ть *impf*, отда́ть *pf* до́лжное+*dat*; **~ card** креди́тная ка́рточка; *vt*: **~ with** припи́сывать *impf*, приписа́ть *pf* +*dat*. **creditable** /-təb(ə)l/ *adj* похва́льный. **creditor** /-tə(r)/ *n* кредито́р.

credulity /krɪ'djuːlɪtɪ/ *n* легкове́рие. **credulous** /'kredjʊləs/ *adj* легкове́рный.

creed /kriːd/ *n* убежде́ния *neut pl*; (*eccl*) вероисповеда́ние.

creep /kriːp/ *vi* по́лзать *indet*, ползти́ *det*. **creeper** /'kriːpə(r)/ *n*

(*plant*) ползу́чее расте́ние.
cremate /krɪˈmeɪt/ *vt* креми́ровать *impf* & *pf*. **cremation** /-ˈmeɪʃ(ə)n/ *n* крема́ция. **crematorium** /ˌkreməˈtɔːrɪəm/ *n* кремато́рий.
crêpe /kreɪp/ *n* креп.
crescendo /krɪˈʃendəʊ/ *adv*, *adj*, & *n* креще́ндо *indecl*.
crescent /ˈkrez(ə)nt/ *n* полуме́сяц.
crest /krest/ *n* гре́бень *m*; (*heraldry*) герб.
crevasse, crevice /krəˈvæs, ˈkrevɪs/ *n* расще́лина, рассе́лина.
crew /kruː/ *n* брига́да; (*of ship, plane*) экипа́ж.
crib /krɪb/ *n* (*bed*) де́тская крова́тка; *vi* спи́сывать *impf*, списа́ть *pf*.
crick /krɪk/ *n* растяже́ние мышц.
cricket[1] /ˈkrɪkɪt/ *n* (*insect*) сверчо́к.
cricket[2] /ˈkrɪkɪt/ *n* (*sport*) кри́кет; ~ **bat** бита́.
crime /kraɪm/ *n* преступле́ние.
Crimea /kraɪˈmɪə/ *n* Крым. **Crimean** /-ən/ *adj* кры́мский.
criminal /ˈkrɪmɪn(ə)l/ *n* престу́пник; *adj* престу́пный; (*of crime*) уголо́вный.
crimson /ˈkrɪmz(ə)n/ *adj* мали́новый.
cringe /krɪndʒ/ *vi* (*cower*) съёживаться *impf*, съёжиться *pf*.
crinkle /ˈkrɪŋk(ə)l/ *n* морщи́на; *vt* & *i* мо́рщить(ся) *impf*, на~, с~ *pf*.
cripple /ˈkrɪp(ə)l/ *n* кале́ка *m* & *f*; *vt* кале́чить *impf*, ис~ *pf*; (*fig*) расша́тывать *impf*, расшата́ть *pf*.
crisis /ˈkraɪsɪs/ *n* кри́зис.
crisp /krɪsp/ *adj* (*brittle*) хрустя́щий; (*fresh*) све́жий. **crisps** /krɪsps/ *n pl* хрустя́щий карто́фель *m*.
criss-cross /ˈkrɪskrɒs/ *adv* крест-на́крест.
criterion /kraɪˈtɪərɪən/ *n* крите́рий.
critic /ˈkrɪtɪk/ *n* кри́тик. **critical** /-k(ə)l/ *adj* крити́ческий. **critically** /-kəlɪ/ *adv* (*ill*) тяжело́. **criticism** /-tɪˌsɪz(ə)m/ *n* кри́тика. **criticize** /-tɪˌsaɪz/ *vt* критикова́ть *impf*. **critique** /krɪˈtiːk/ *n* кри́тика.
croak /krəʊk/ *vi* ква́кать *impf*, ква́кнуть *pf*; хрипе́ть *impf*.
Croat /ˈkrəʊæt/ *n* хорва́т, ~ка. **Croatia** /krəʊˈeɪʃə/ *n* Хорва́тия. **Croatian** /krəʊˈeɪʃ(ə)n/ *adj* хорва́тский.
crochet /ˈkrəʊʃeɪ/ *n* вяза́ние крючко́м; *vt* вяза́ть *impf*, с~ *pf* (крючко́м).
crockery /ˈkrɒkərɪ/ *n* посу́да.
crocodile /ˈkrɒkəˌdaɪl/ *n* крокоди́л.
crocus /ˈkrəʊkəs/ *n* кро́кус.
crony /ˈkrəʊnɪ/ *n* закады́чный друг.
crook /krʊk/ *n* (*staff*) по́сох; (*swindler*) моше́нник. **crooked** /ˈkrʊkɪd/ *adj* криво́й; (*dishonest*) нече́стный.
crop /krɒp/ *n* (*yield*) урожа́й; *pl* культу́ры *f pl*; (*bird's*) зоб; *vt* (*cut*) подстрига́ть *impf*, подстри́чь *pf*; ~ **up** возника́ть *impf*, возни́кнуть *pf*.
croquet /ˈkrəʊkeɪ/ *n* кроке́т.
cross /krɒs/ *n* крест; (*biol*) по́месь; *adj* (*angry*) злой; *vt* (*on foot*) переходи́ть *impf*, перейти́ *pf* (че́рез) +*acc*; (*by transport*) переезжа́ть *impf*, перее́хать *pf* (че́рез) +*acc*; (*biol*) скре́щивать *impf*, скрести́ть *pf*; ~ **off**, **out** вычёркивать *impf*, вы́черкнуть *pf*; ~ **o.s.** крести́ться

impf, пере~ *pf*; ~ **over** переходи́ть *impf*, перейти́ *pf* (че́рез) +*acc*. ~**bar** попере́чина. ~**-breed** по́месь; ~**-country race** кросс; ~**-examination** перекрёстный допро́с; ~**-examine,** ~**-question** подверга́ть *impf*, подве́ргнуть *pf* перекрёстному допро́су; ~**-eyed** косогла́зый; ~**-legged: sit** ~ сиде́ть *impf* по-туре́цки; ~**-reference** перекрёстная ссы́лка; ~**road(s)** перекрёсток; ~**-section** перекрёстное сече́ние; ~**word (puzzle)** кроссво́рд. **crossing** /'krɒsɪŋ/ *n* (*intersection*) перекрёсток; (*foot*) перехо́д; (*transport*; *rly*) перее́зд.

crotch /krɒtʃ/ *n* (*anat*) проме́жность.

crotchet /'krɒtʃɪt/ *n* (*mus*) четвертна́я но́та.

crotchety /'krɒtʃɪtɪ/ *adj* раздражи́тельный.

crouch /kraʊtʃ/ *vi* приседа́ть *impf*, присе́сть *pf*.

crow /krəʊ/ *n* воро́на; **as the** ~ **flies** по прямо́й ли́нии; *vi* кукаре́кать *impf*. **crowbar** *n* лом.

crowd /kraʊd/ *n* толпа́; *vi* тесни́ться *impf*, с~ *pf*; ~ **into** вти́скиваться *impf*, вти́снуться *pf*. **crowded** /'kraʊdɪd/ *adj* перепо́лненный.

crown /kraʊn/ *n* коро́на; (*tooth*) коро́нка; (*head*) те́ма; (*hat*) тулья́; *vt* коронова́ть *impf* & *pf*.

crucial /'kru:ʃ(ə)l/ *adj* (*important*) о́чень ва́жный; (*decisive*) реша́ющий; (*critical*) крити́ческий.

crucifix /'kru:sɪˌfɪks/ *n* распя́тие. **crucifixion** /-'fɪkʃ(ə)n/ *n* распя́тие. **crucify** /'kru:sɪˌfaɪ/ *vt* распина́ть *impf*, распя́ть *pf*.

crude /kru:d/ *adj* (*rude*) гру́бый; (*raw*) сыро́й. **crudity** /'kru:dɪtɪ/ *n* гру́бость.

cruel /'kru:əl/ *adj* жесто́кий. **cruelty** /-tɪ/ *n* жесто́кость.

cruise /kru:z/ *n* круи́з; *vi* крейси́ровать *impf*. **cruiser** /'kru:zə(r)/ *n* кре́йсер.

crumb /krʌm/ *n* кро́шка.

crumble /'krʌmb(ə)l/ *vt* кроши́ть *impf*, рас~ *pf*; *vi* обва́ливаться *impf*, обвали́ться *pf*. **crumbly** /'krʌmblɪ/ *adj* рассы́пчатый.

crumple /'krʌmp(ə)l/ *vt* мять *impf*, с~ *pf*; (*intentionally*) ко́мкать *impf*, с~ *pf*.

crunch /krʌntʃ/ *n* (*fig*) реша́ющий моме́нт; *vt* грызть *impf*, раз~ *pf*; *vi* хрусте́ть *impf*, хру́стнуть *pf*.

crusade /kru:'seɪd/ *n* кресто́вый похо́д; (*fig*) кампа́ния. **crusader** /-'seɪdə(r)/ *n* крестоно́сец; (*fig*) боре́ц (**for** за+*acc*).

crush /krʌʃ/ *n* да́вка; (*infatuation*) си́льное увлече́ние; *vt* дави́ть *impf*, за~, раз~ *pf*; (*crease*) мять *impf*, с~ *pf*; (*fig*) подавля́ть *impf*, подави́ть *pf*.

crust /krʌst/ *n* (*of earth*) кора́; (*bread etc.*) ко́рка.

crutch /krʌtʃ/ *n* косты́ль *m*.

crux /krʌks/ *n*: ~ **of the matter** суть де́ла.

cry /kraɪ/ *n* крик; **a far** ~ **from** далеко́ от+*gen*; *vi* (*weep*) пла́кать *impf*; (*shout*) крича́ть *impf*, кри́кнуть *pf*.

crypt /krɪpt/ *n* склеп. **cryptic** /'krɪptɪk/ *adj* зага́дочный.

crystal /'krɪst(ə)l/ *n* криста́лл; (*glass*) хруста́ль *m*. **crystallize** /-laɪz/ *vt* & *i* кристаллизова́ть(ся) *impf* & *pf*.

cub /kʌb/ *n* детёныш; **bear** ~ медвежо́нок; **fox** ~ лисёнок; **lion** ~ львёнок; **wolf** ~

волчóнок

cube /kju:b/ *n* куб. **cubic** /'kju:bɪk/ *adj* куби́ческий.

cubicle /'kju:bɪk(ə)l/ *n* каби́на.

cuckoo /'kʊku:/ *n* куку́шка.

cucumber /'kju:kʌmbə(r)/ *n* огурéц.

cuddle /'kʌd(ə)l/ *vt* обнима́ть *impf*, обня́ть *pf*; *vi* обнима́ться *impf*, обня́ться *pf*; ~ **up** прижима́ться *impf*, прижа́ться *pf* (**to** к+ *dat*).

cudgel /'kʌdʒ(ə)l/ *n* дуби́нка.

cue[1] /kju:/ *n* (*theat*) ре́плика.

cue[2] /kju:/ *n* (*billiards*) кий.

cuff[1] /kʌf/ *n* манже́та; **off the** ~ экспро́мтом; ~**-link** за́понка.

cuff[2] /kʌf/ *vt* (*hit*) шлёпать *impf*, шлёпнуть *pf*.

cul-de-sac /'kʌldə,sæk/ *n* тупи́к.

culinary /'kʌlɪnərɪ/ *adj* кулина́рный.

cull /kʌl/ *vt* (*select*) отбира́ть *impf*, отобра́ть *pf*; (*slaughter*) бить *impf*.

culminate /'kʌlmɪ,neɪt/ *vi* конча́ться *impf*, ко́нчиться *pf* (**in** +*instr*). **culmination** /-'neɪʃ(ə)n/ *n* кульминацио́нный пункт.

culpability /,kʌlpə'bɪlɪtɪ/ *n* вино́вность. **culpable** /'kʌlpəb(ə)l/ *adj* вино́вный. **culprit** /'kʌlprɪt/ *n* вино́вник.

cult /kʌlt/ *n* культ.

cultivate /'kʌltɪ,veɪt/ *vt* (*land*) обраба́тывать *impf*, обрабо́тать *pf*; (*crops*) выра́щивать *impf*; вы́растить *impf*; (*develop*) развива́ть *impf*, разви́ть *pf*.

cultural /'kʌltʃər(ə)l/ *adj* культу́рный. **culture** /'kʌltʃə(r)/ *n* культу́ра. **cultured** /'kʌltʃəd/ *adj* культу́рный.

cumbersome /'kʌmbəsəm/ *adj* громо́здкий.

cumulative /'kju:mjʊlətɪv/ *adj* кумуляти́вный.

cunning /'kʌnɪŋ/ *n* хи́трость; *adj* хи́трый.

cup /kʌp/ *n* ча́шка; (*prize*) ку́бок.

cupboard /'kʌbəd/ *n* шкаф.

cupola /'kju:pələ/ *n* ку́пол.

curable /'kjʊərəb(ə)l/ *adj* излечи́мый.

curative /'kjʊərətɪv/ *adj* целéбный.

curator /kjʊə'reɪtə(r)/ *n* храни́тель *m*.

curb /kɜ:b/ *vt* обу́здывать *impf*, обузда́ть *pf*.

curd /kɜ:d/ *n* (*cheese*) творо́г. **curdle** /'kɜ:d(ə)l/ *vt* & *i* свёртывать(ся) *impf*, сверну́ть(ся) *pf*.

cure /'kjʊə(r)/ *n* сре́дство (**for** про́тив+*gen*); *vt* выле́чивать *impf*, вы́лечить *pf*; (*smoke*) копти́ть *impf*, за~ *pf*; (*salt*) соли́ть *impf*, по~ *pf*.

curfew /'kɜ:fju:/ *n* коменда́нтский час.

curiosity /,kjʊərɪ'ɒsɪtɪ/ *n* любопы́тство. **curious** /'kjʊərɪəs/ *adj* любопы́тный.

curl /kɜ:l/ *n* ло́кон; *vt* завива́ть *impf*, зави́ть *pf*; ~ **up** свёртываться *impf*, сверну́ться *pf*. **curly** /'kɜ:lɪ/ *adj* кудря́вый.

currants /'kʌrənts/ *n pl* (*dried*) изю́м (*collect*).

currency /'kʌrənsɪ/ *n* валю́та; (*prevalence*) хожде́ние. **current** /'kʌrənt/ *adj* теку́щий; *n* тече́ние; (*air*) струя́; (*water*; *electr*) ток.

curriculum /kə'rɪkjʊləm/ *n* курс обуче́ния; ~ **vitae** /'vi:taɪ/ автобиогра́фия.

curry[1] /'kʌrɪ/ *n* кэ́рри *neut indecl*.

curry[2] /'kʌrɪ/ *vt*: ~ **favour with** заи́скивать *impf* пе́ред+*instr*.

curse /kɜ:s/ *n* прокля́тие; (*oath*) руга́тельство; *vt* проклина́ть

impf, проклясть *pf*; *vi* ругаться *impf*, по~ *pf*.
cursor /'kɜ:sə(r)/ *n* (*comput*) курсор.
cursory /'kɜ:sərɪ/ *adj* беглый.
curt /kɜ:t/ *adj* резкий.
curtail /kɜ:'teɪl/ *vt* сокращать *impf*, сократить *pf*.
curtain /'kɜ:t(ə)n/ *n* занавеска.
curts(e)y /'kɜ:tsɪ/ *n* реверанс; *vi* делать *impf*, с~ *pf* реверанс.
curve /kɜ:v/ *n* изгиб; (*line*) кривая *sb*; *vi* изгибаться *impf*, изогнуться *pf*.
cushion /'kʊʃ(ə)n/ *n* подушка; *vt* смягчать *impf*, смягчить *pf*.
custard /'kʌstəd/ *n* сладкий заварной крем.
custodian /kʌ'stəʊdɪən/ *n* хранитель *m*. **custody** /'kʌstədɪ/ *n* опека; (*of police*) арест; **to take into ~** арестовать *pf*.
custom /'kʌstəm/ *n* обычай; (*comm*) клиентура; *pl* (*duty*) таможенные пошлины *f pl*; **go through ~s** проходить *impf*, пройти *pf* таможенный осмотр; **~-house** таможня; **~ officer** таможенник. **customary** /'kʌstəmərɪ/ *adj* обычный. **customer** /'kʌstəmə(r)/ *n* клиент; покупатель *m*.
cut /kʌt/ *vt* резать *impf*, по~ *pf*; (*hair*) стричь *impf*, о~ *pf*; (*mow*) косить *impf*, с~ *pf*; (*price*) снижать *impf*, снизить *pf*; (*cards*) снимать *impf*, снять *pf* колоду; **~ back** (*prune*) подрезать *impf*, подрезать *pf*; (*reduce*) сокращать *impf*, сократить *pf*; **~ down** срубать *impf*, срубить *pf*; **~ off** отрезать *impf*, отрезать *pf*; (*interrupt*) прерывать *impf*, прервать *pf*; (*disconnect*) отключать *impf*, отключить *pf*; **~ out** вырезывать *impf*, вырезать *pf*; **~ out for** созданный для+*gen*; **~ up** разрезать *impf*, разрезать *pf*; *n* (*gash*) порез; (*clothes*) покрой; (*reduction*) снижение; **~ glass** хрусталь *m*.
cute /kju:t/ *adj* симпатичный.
cutlery /'kʌtlərɪ/ *n* ножи, вилки и ложки *pl*.
cutlet /'kʌtlɪt/ *n* отбивная котлета.
cutting /'kʌtɪŋ/ *n* (*press*) вырезка; (*plant*) черенок; *adj* резкий.
CV *abbr* (*of* **curriculum vitae**) автобиография.
cycle /'saɪk(ə)l/ *n* цикл; (*bicycle*) велосипед; *vi* ездить *impf* на велосипеде. **cyclic(al)** /'sɪklɪk((ə)l)/ *adj* циклический. **cyclist** /'saɪklɪst/ *n* велосипедист.
cylinder /'sɪlɪndə(r)/ *n* цилиндр. **cylindrical** /sɪ'lɪndrɪk(ə)l/ *adj* цилиндрический.
cymbals /'sɪmb(ə)lz/ *n pl* тарелки *f pl*.
cynic /'sɪnɪk/ *n* циник. **cynical** /-k(ə)l/ *adj* циничный. **cynicism** /'sɪnɪsɪz(ə)m/ *n* цинизм.
cypress /'saɪprəs/ *n* кипарис.
Cyrillic /sɪ'rɪlɪk/ *n* кириллица.
cyst /sɪst/ *n* киста.
Czech /tʃek/ *n* чех, чешка; *adj* чешский; **~ Republic** Чешская Республика.

D

dab /dæb/ *n* мазок; *vt* (*eyes etc.*) прикладывать *impf* платок к+*dat*; **~ on** накладывать *impf*, наложить *pf* мазками.
dabble /'dæb(ə)l/ *vi*: **~ in** поверхностно заниматься *impf*, заняться *pf* +*instr*.

dachshund /'dækshʊnd/ *n* та́кса.

dad, daddy /dæd, 'dædɪ/ *n* па́па; **~-long-legs** *n* долгоно́жка.

daffodil /'dæfədɪl/ *n* жёлтый нарци́сс.

daft /dɑːft/ *adj* глу́пый.

dagger /'dægə(r)/ *n* кинжа́л.

dahlia /'deɪlɪə/ *n* георги́н.

daily /'deɪlɪ/ *adv* ежедне́вно; *adj* ежедне́вный; *n* (*charwoman*) приходя́щая убо́рщица; (*newspaper*) ежедне́вная газе́та.

dainty /'deɪntɪ/ *adj* изя́щный.

dairy /'deərɪ/ *n* маслобо́йня; (*shop*) моло́чная *sb*; *adj* моло́чный.

dais /'deɪɪs/ *n* помо́ст.

daisy /'deɪzɪ/ *n* маргари́тка.

dale /deɪl/ *n* доли́на.

dally /'dælɪ/ *vi* (*dawdle*) ме́шкать *impf*; (*toy*) игра́ть *impf* +*instr*; (*flirt*) флиртова́ть *impf*.

dam /dæm/ *n* (*barrier*) плоти́на; *vt* запру́живать *impf*, запруди́ть *pf*.

damage /'dæmɪdʒ/ *n* поврежде́ние; *pl* убы́тки *m pl*; *vt* поврежда́ть *impf*, повреди́ть *pf*.

damn /dæm/ *vt* (*curse*) проклина́ть *impf*, прокля́сть *pf*; (*censure*) осужда́ть *impf*, осуди́ть *pf*; *int* чёрт возьми́!; **I don't give a ~** мне наплева́ть. **damnation** /-'neɪʃ(ə)n/ *n* прокля́тие. **damned** /dæmd/ *adj* прокля́тый.

damp /dæmp/ *n* сы́рость; *adj* сыро́й; *vt* (*also* **dampen**) смачи́вать *impf*, смочи́ть *pf*; (*fig*) охлажда́ть *impf*, охлади́ть *pf*.

dance /dɑːns/ *vi* танцева́ть *impf*; *n* та́нец; (*party*) танцева́льный ве́чер. **dancer** /-sə(r)/ *n* танцо́р, **~**ка; (*ballet*) танцо́вщик, -ица; балери́на.

dandelion /'dændɪ,laɪən/ *n* одува́нчик.

dandruff /'dændrʌf/ *n* пе́рхоть.

Dane /deɪn/ *n* датча́нин, -а́нка; **Great ~** дог. **Danish** /'deɪnɪʃ/ *adj* да́тский.

danger /'deɪndʒə(r)/ *n* опа́сность. **dangerous** /-rəs/ *adj* опа́сный.

dangle /'dæŋg(ə)l/ *vt* & *i* пока́чивать(ся) *impf*.

dank /dæŋk/ *adj* промо́зглый.

dapper /'dæpə(r)/ *adj* вы́холенный.

dare /deə(r)/ *vi* (*have courage*) осме́ливаться *impf*, осме́литься *pf*; (*have impudence*) сметь *impf*, по~ *pf*; *vt* вызыва́ть *impf*, вы́звать *pf*; *n* вы́зов. **daredevil** *n* liха́ч; *adj* отча́янный. **daring** /'deərɪŋ/ *n* отва́га; *adj* отча́янный.

dark /dɑːk/ *adj* тёмный; **~ blue** тёмно-си́ний; *n* темнота́. **darken** /-kən/ *vt* затемня́ть *impf*, затемни́ть *pf*; *vi* темне́ть *impf*, по~ *pf*. **darkly** /-lɪ/ *adv* мра́чно. **darkness** /-nɪs/ *n* темнота́.

darling /'dɑːlɪŋ/ *n* дорого́й *sb*, ми́лый *sb*; *adj* дорого́й.

darn /dɑːn/ *vt* што́пать *impf*, за~ *pf*.

dart /dɑːt/ *n* стрела́; (*for game*) мета́тельная стрела́; (*tuck*) вы́тачка; *vi* брос́иться *pf*.

dash /dæʃ/ *n* (*hyphen*) тире́ *neut indecl*; (*admixture*) при́месь; *vt* швыря́ть *impf*, швырну́ть *pf*; *vi* броса́ться *impf*, бро́ситься *pf*. **dashboard** *n* прибо́рная доска́. **dashing** /'dæʃɪŋ/ *adj* лихо́й.

data /'deɪtə/ *n pl* да́нные *sb pl*. **database** *n* ба́за да́нных.

date[1] /deɪt/ *n* (*fruit*) фи́ник.

date[2] /deɪt/ *n* число́, да́та; (*engagement*) свида́ние; **out of ~**

устаре́лый; **up to ~** совреме́нный; в ку́рсе де́ла; *vt* дати́ровать *impf* & *pf*; (*go out with*) встреча́ться *impf* с+*instr*; *vi* (*originate*) относи́ться *impf* (**from** к+*instr*).

dative /'deɪtɪv/ *adj* (*n*) да́тельный (паде́ж).

daub /dɔ:b/ *vt* ма́зать *impf*, на~ *pf* (**with** +*instr*).

daughter /'dɔ:tə(r)/ *n* дочь; **~-in-law** неве́стка (*in relation to mother*), сноха́ (*in relation to father*).

daunting /'dɔ:ntɪŋ/ *adj* угрожа́ющий.

dawdle /'dɔ:d(ə)l/ *vi* ме́шкать *impf*.

dawn /dɔ:n/ *n* рассве́т; (*also fig*) заря́; *vi* (*day*) рассвета́ть *impf*, рассвести́ *pf impers*; **~ (up)on** осеня́ть *impf*, осени́ть *pf*; **it ~ed on me** меня́ осени́ло.

day /deɪ/ *n* день *m*; (*24 hours*) су́тки *pl*; *pl* (*period*) пери́од, вре́мя *neut*; **~ after ~** изо дня́ в де́нь; **the ~ after tomorrow** послеза́втра; **the ~ before** накану́не; **the ~ before yesterday** позавчера́; **the other ~** на днях; **by ~** днём; **every other ~** че́рез день; **~ off** выходно́й день *m*; **one ~** одна́жды; **these ~s** в на́ши дни. **daybreak** *n* рассве́т. **day-dreams** *n pl* мечты́ *f pl*. **daylight** *n* дневно́й свет; **in broad ~** средь бе́ла дня́. **day-time** *n*: **in the ~** днём.

daze /deɪz/ *n*: **in a ~**, **dazed** /deɪzd/ *adj* оглушён (-ена́).

dazzle /'dæz(ə)l/ *vt* ослепля́ть *impf*, ослепи́ть *pf*.

deacon /'di:kən/ *n* дья́кон.

dead /ded/ *adj* мёртвый; (*animals*) до́хлый; (*plants*) увя́дший; (*numb*) онеме́вший; *n*: **the ~** мёртвые *sb pl*; **at ~ of night** глубо́кой но́чью; *adv* соверше́нно; **~ end** тупи́к; **~ heat** одновре́ме́нный фи́ниш; **~line** преде́льный срок; **~lock** тупи́к.

deaden /'ded(ə)n/ *vt* заглуша́ть *impf*, заглуши́ть *pf*.

deadly /'dedlɪ/ *adj* смерте́льный.

deaf /def/ *adj* глухо́й; **~ and dumb** глухонемо́й. **deafen** /-f(ə)n/ *vt* оглуша́ть *impf*, оглуши́ть *pf*. **deafness** /-nɪs/ *n* глухота́.

deal[1] /di:l/ *n*: **a great, good, ~** мно́го (+*gen*); (*with comp*) гора́здо.

deal[2] /di:l/ *n* (*bargain*) сде́лка; (*cards*) сда́ча; *vt* (*cards*) сдава́ть *impf*, сдать *pf*; (*blow*) наноси́ть *impf*, нанести́ *pf*; **~ in** торгова́ть *impf* +*instr*; **~ out** распределя́ть *impf*, распредели́ть *pf*; **~ with** (*take care of*) занима́ться *impf*, заня́ться *pf* +*instr*; (*handle a person*) поступа́ть *impf*, поступи́ть *pf* с+*instr*; (*treat a subject*) рассма́тривать *impf*, рассмотре́ть *pf*; (*cope with*) справля́ться *impf*, спра́виться *pf* с+*instr*. **dealer** /'di:lə(r)/ *n* торго́вец (**in** +*instr*).

dean /di:n/ *n* дека́н.

dear /dɪə(r)/ *adj* дорого́й; (*also n*) ми́лый (*sb*).

dearth /dɜ:θ/ *n* недоста́ток.

death /deθ/ *n* смерть; **put to ~** казни́ть *impf* & *pf*; **~bed** *n* сме́ртное ло́же; **~ certificate** свиде́тельство о сме́рти; **~ penalty** сме́ртная казнь. **deathly** /'deθlɪ/ *adj* смерте́льный.

debar /dɪ'bɑ:(r)/ *vt*: **~ from** не допуска́ть *impf* до+*gen*.

debase /dɪ'beɪs/ *vt* унижа́ть

impf, уни́зить *pf*; (*coinage*) понижа́ть *impf*, пони́зить *pf* ка́чество +*gen*.

debatable /dɪ'beɪtəb(ə)l/ *adj* спо́рный. **debate** /dɪ'beɪθ/ *n* пре́ния (-ий) *pl*; *vt* обсужда́ть *impf*, обсуди́ть *pf*.

debauched /dɪ'bɔːtʃt/ *adj* развращённый. **debauchery** /-'bɔːtʃərɪ/ *n* развра́т.

debilitate /dɪ'bɪlɪˌteɪt/ *vt* ослабля́ть; *impf*, осла́бить *pf*. **debility** /-'bɪlɪtɪ/ *n* сла́бость.

debit /'debɪt/ *n* де́бет; *vt* дебетова́ть *impf* & *pf*.

debris /'debriː/ *n* обло́мки *m pl*.

debt /det/ *n* долг. **debtor** /'detə(r)/ *n* должни́к.

début /'deɪbjuː/ *n* дебю́т; **make one's ~** дебюти́ровать *impf* & *pf*.

decade /'dekeɪd/ *n* десятиле́тие.

decadence /'dekəd(ə)ns/ *n* декаде́нтство. **decadent** /-d(ə)nt/ *adj* декаде́нтский.

decaffeinated /diː'kæfɪˌneɪtɪd/ *adj* без кофеина.

decant /dɪ'kænt/ *vt* перелива́ть *impf*, перели́ть *pf*. **decanter** /-'kæntə(r)/ *n* графи́н.

decapitate /dɪ'kæpɪˌteɪt/ *vt* обезгла́вливать *impf*, обезгла́вить *pf*.

decay /dɪ'keɪ/ *vi* гнить *impf*, с~ *pf*; (*tooth*) разруша́ться *impf*, разру́шиться *pf*; *n* гние́ние; (*tooth*) разруше́ние.

decease /dɪ'siːs/ *n* кончи́на. **deceased** /-'siːst/ *adj* поко́йный; *n* поко́йник, -ица.

deceit /dɪ'siːt/ *n* обма́н. **deceitful** /-'siːtfʊl/ *adj* лжи́вый. **deceive** /-'siːv/ *vt* обма́нывать *impf*, обману́ть *pf*.

deceleration /diːˌselə'reɪʃ(ə)n/ *n* замедле́ние.

December /dɪ'sembə(r)/ *n* дека́брь *m*; *adj* дека́брьский.

decency /'diːsənsɪ/ *n* прили́чие. **decent** /-s(ə)nt/ *adj* прили́чный.

decentralization /diːˌsentrəlaɪ'zeɪʃ(ə)n/ *n* децентрализа́ция. **decentralize** /diː'sentrəˌlaɪz/ *vt* децентрализова́ть *impf* & *pf*.

deception /dɪ'sepʃ(ə)n/ *n* обма́н. **deceptive** /-'septɪv/ *adj* обма́нчивый.

decibel /'desɪˌbel/ *n* децибе́л.

decide /dɪ'saɪd/ *vt* реша́ть *impf*, реши́ть *pf*. **decided** /-'saɪdɪd/ *adj* реши́тельный.

deciduous /dɪ'sɪdjʊəs/ *adj* листопа́дный.

decimal /'desɪm(ə)l/ *n* десяти́чная дробь; *adj* десяти́чный; **~ point** запята́я *sb*.

decimate /'desɪˌmeɪt/ *vt* (*fig*) коси́ть *impf*, с~ *pf*.

decipher /dɪ'saɪfə(r)/ *vt* расшифро́вывать *impf*, расшифрова́ть *pf*.

decision /dɪ'sɪʒ(ə)n/ *n* реше́ние. **decisive** /dɪ'saɪsɪv/ *adj* (*firm*) реши́тельный, (*deciding*) реша́ющий.

deck /dek/ *n* па́луба; (*bus etc.*) эта́ж; **~-chair** *n* шезло́нг; *vt*: **~ out** украша́ть *impf*, укра́сить *pf*.

declaim /dɪ'kleɪm/ *vt* деклами́ровать *impf*, про~ *pf*.

declaration /ˌdeklə'reɪʃ(ə)n/ *n* объявле́ние; (*document*) деклара́ция. **declare** /dɪ'kleə(r)/ *vt* (*proclaim*) объявля́ть *impf*, объяви́ть *pf*; (*assert*) заявля́ть *impf*, заяви́ть *pf*.

declension /dɪ'klenʃ(ə)n/ *n* склоне́ние. **decline** /dɪ'klaɪn/ *n* упа́док; *vi* приходи́ть *impf*, прийти́ *pf* в упа́док; *vt* отклоня́ть *impf*, отклони́ть *pf*;

(*gram*) склоня́ть *impf*, про~ *pf*.

decode /diːˈkəʊd/ *vt* расшифро́вывать *impf*, расшифрова́ть *pf*.

decompose /ˌdiːkəmˈpəʊz/ *vi* разлага́ться *impf*, разложи́ться *pf*.

décor /ˈdeɪkɔː(r)/ *n* эстети́ческое оформле́ние. **decorate** /ˈdekəˌreɪt/ *vt* украша́ть *impf*, укра́сить *pf*; (*room*) ремонти́ровать *impf*, от~ *pf*; (*with medal etc.*) награжда́ть *impf*, награди́ть *pf*. **decoration** /ˌdekəˈreɪʃ(ə)n/ *n* украше́ние; (*medal*) о́рден. **decorative** /ˈdekərətɪv/ *adj* декорати́вный. **decorator** /ˈdekəˌreɪtə(r)/ *n* маля́р.

decorous /ˈdekərəs/ *adj* прили́чный. **decorum** /dɪˈkɔːrəm/ *n* прили́чие.

decoy /ˈdiːkɔɪ/ *n* (*bait*) прима́нка; *vt* зама́нивать *impf*, замани́ть *pf*.

decrease *vt* & *i* /dɪˈkriːs/ уменьша́ть(ся) *impf*, уме́ньшить(ся) *pf*; *n* /ˈdiːkriːs/ уменьше́ние.

decree /dɪˈkriː/ *n* ука́з; *vt* постановля́ть *impf*, постанови́ть *pf*.

decrepit /dɪˈkrepɪt/ *adj* дря́хлый.

dedicate /ˈdedɪˌkeɪt/ *vt* посвяща́ть *impf*, посвяти́ть *pf*. **dedication** /ˌdedɪˈkeɪʃ(ə)n/ *n* посвяще́ние.

deduce /dɪˈdjuːs/ *vt* заключа́ть *impf*, заключи́ть *pf*.

deduct /dɪˈdʌkt/ *vt* вычита́ть *impf*, вы́честь *pf*. **deduction** /-ˈdʌkʃ(ə)n/ *n* (*subtraction*) вы́чет; (*inference*) вы́вод.

deed /diːd/ *n* посту́пок; (*heroic*) по́двиг; (*law*) акт.

deem /diːm/ *vt* счита́ть *impf*, счесть *pf* +*acc* & *instr*.

deep /diːp/ *adj* глубо́кий; (*colour*) тёмный; (*sound*) ни́зкий; ~ **freeze** морози́льник. **deepen** /-pən/ *vt* & *i* углубля́ть(ся) *impf*, углуби́ть(ся) *pf*.

deer /dɪə(r)/ *n* оле́нь *m*.

deface /dɪˈfeɪs/ *vt* обезобра́живать *impf*, обезобра́зить *pf*.

defamation /ˌdefəˈmeɪʃ(ə)n/ *n* диффама́ция. **defamatory** /dɪˈfæmətərɪ/ *adj* клеветни́ческий.

default /dɪˈfɔːlt/ *n* (*failure to pay*) неупла́та; (*failure to appear*) нея́вка; (*comput*) автомати́ческий вы́бор; *vi* не выполня́ть *impf* обяза́тельств.

defeat /dɪˈfiːt/ *n* пораже́ние; *vt* побежда́ть *impf*, победи́ть *pf*. **defeatism** /-tɪz(ə)m/ *n* пораже́нчество. **defeatist** /-tɪst/ *n* пораже́нец; *adj* пораже́нческий.

defecate /ˈdefɪˌkeɪt/ *vi* испражня́ться *impf*, испражни́ться *pf*.

defect *n* /ˈdiːfekt/ дефе́кт; *vi* /dɪˈfekt/ перебега́ть *impf*, перебежа́ть *pf*. **defective** /dɪˈfektɪv/ *adj* неиспра́вный. **defector** /dɪˈfektə(r)/ *n* перебе́жчик.

defence /dɪˈfens/ *n* защи́та. **defenceless** /-ˈfenslɪs/ *adj* беззащи́тный. **defend** /-ˈfend/ *vt* защища́ть *impf*, защити́ть *pf*. **defendant** /-ˈfend(ə)nt/ *n* подсуди́мый *sb*. **defender** /-ˈfendə(r)/ *n* защи́тник. **defensive** /-ˈfensɪv/ *adj* оборони́тельный.

defer[1] /dɪˈfɜː(r)/ *vt* (*postpone*) отсро́чивать *impf*, отсро́чить *pf*.

defer[2] /dɪˈfɜː(r)/ *vi*: ~ **to** подчиня́ться *impf* +*dat*. **deference** /ˈdefərəns/ *n* уваже́ние. **deferential** /ˌdefəˈrenʃ(ə)l/ *adj* почти́тельный.

defiance /dɪˈfaɪəns/ *n* неповинове́ние; **in ~ of** вопреки́+*dat*. **defiant** /-ˈfaɪənt/ *adj* вызыва́ющий.

deficiency /dɪ'fɪʃənsɪ/ *n* недостáток. **deficient** /-'fɪʃ(ə)nt/ *adj* недостáточный. **deficit** /'defɪsɪt/ *n* дефици́т.
defile /dɪ'faɪl/ *vt* осквернять *impf*, осквернить *pf*.
define /dɪ'faɪn/ *vt* определять *impf*, определить *pf*. **definite** /'defɪnɪt/ *adj* определённый **definitely** /'defɪnɪtlɪ/ *adv* несомнéнно. **definition** /ˌdefɪ'nɪʃ(ə)n/ *n* определéние. **definitive** /dɪ'fɪnɪtɪv/ *adj* окончáтельный.
deflate /dɪ'fleɪt/ *vt* & *i* спускáть *impf*, спусти́ть *pf*; *vt* (*person*) сбивáть *impf*, сбить *pf* спесь с+*gen*. **deflation** /-'fleɪʃ(ə)n/ *n* дефля́ция.
deflect /dɪ'flekt/ *vt* отклоня́ть *impf*, отклони́ть *pf*.
deforestation /diːˌfɒrɪ'steɪʃ(ə)n/ *n* обезлéсение.
deformed /dɪ'fɔːmd/ *adj* урóдливый. **deformity** /-'fɔːmɪtɪ/ *n* урóдство.
defraud /dɪ'frɔːd/ *vt* обмáнывать *impf*, обманýть *pf*; ~ **of** вымáнивать *impf*, вы́манить *pf* +*acc* & у+*gen* (*of person*).
defray /dɪ'freɪ/ *vt* оплáчивать *impf*, оплати́ть *pf*.
defrost /diː'frɒst/ *vt* разморáживать *impf*, разморóзить *pf*.
deft /deft/ *adj* лóвкий.
defunct /dɪ'fʌŋkt/ *adj* бóльше не существýющий.
defy /dɪ'faɪ/ *vt* (*challenge*) вызывáть *impf*, вы́звать *pf*; (*disobey*) идти́ *impf*, по~ *pf* прóтив+*acc*; (*fig*) не поддавáться *impf* +*dat*.
degenerate *vi* / dɪ'dʒenəˌreɪt/ вырождáться *impf*, вы́родиться *pf*; *adj* /dɪ'dʒenərət/ вы́родившийся.
degradation /ˌdegrə'deɪʃ(ə)n/ *n* унижéние. **degrade** /dɪ'greɪd/ *vt* унижáть *impf*, уни́зить *pf*. **degrading** /dɪ'greɪdɪŋ/ *adj* унизи́тельный.
degree /dɪ'griː/ *n* стéпень; (*math etc.*) грáдус; (*univ*) учёная стéпень.
dehydrate /diː'haɪdreɪt/ *vt* обезвóживать *impf*, обезвóдить *pf*. **dehydration** /-'dreɪʃ(ə)n/ *n* обезвóживание.
deign /deɪn/ *vi* снисходи́ть *impf*, снизойти́ *pf*.
deity /'diːɪtɪ/ *n* божествó.
dejected /dɪ'dʒektɪd/ *adj* удручённый.
delay /dɪ'leɪ/ *n* задéржка; **without** ~ немéдленно; *vt* задéрживать *impf*, задержáть *pf*.
delegate *n* /'delɪgət/ делегáт; *vt* /'delɪˌgeɪt/ делеги́ровать *impf* & *pf*. **delegation** /-'geɪʃ(ə)n/ *n* делегáция.
delete /dɪ'liːt/ *vt* вычёркивать *impf*, вы́черкнуть *pf*.
deliberate *adj* /dɪ'lɪbərət/ (*intentional*) преднамéренный; (*careful*) осторóжный; *vt* & *i* /dɪ'lɪbəˌreɪt/ размышля́ть *impf*, размы́слить *pf* (о+*prep*); (*discuss*) совещáться *impf* (о+*prep*). **deliberation** /dɪˌlɪbə'reɪʃ(ə)n/ *n* размышлéние; (*discussion*) совещáние.
delicacy /'delɪkəsɪ/ *n* (*tact*) деликáтность; (*dainty*) лáкомство. **delicate** /-kət/ *adj* тóнкий; (*tactful, needing tact*) деликáтный; (*health*) болéзненный.
delicatessen /ˌdelɪkə'tes(ə)n/ *n* гастронóм.
delicious /dɪ'lɪʃəs/ *adj* óчень вкýсный.
delight /dɪ'laɪt/ *n* наслаждéние; (*delightful thing*) прéлесть. **delightful** /-fʊl/ *adj* прелéстный.
delinquency /dɪ'lɪŋkwənsɪ/ *n* преступность. **delinquent**

/-wənt/ *n* правонаруши́тель *m*, ~ница; *adj* вино́вный.

delirious /dɪ'lɪrɪəs/ *adj*: **be ~** бре́дить *impf*. **delirium** /-rɪəm/ *n* бред.

deliver /dɪ'lɪvə(r)/ *vt* (*goods*) доставля́ть *impf*, доста́вить *pf*; (*save*) избавля́ть *impf*, изба́вить *pf* (**from** от+*gen*); (*lecture*) прочита́ть *impf*, проче́сть *pf*; (*letters*) разноси́ть *impf*, разнести́ *pf*; (*speech*) произноси́ть *impf*, произнести́ *pf*; (*blow*) наноси́ть *impf*, нанести́ *pf*. **deliverance** /-'lɪvərəns/ *n* избавле́ние. **delivery** /-'lɪvərɪ/ *n* доста́вка.

delta /'deltə/ *n* де́льта.

delude /dɪ'lu:d/ *vt* вводи́ть *impf*, ввести́ *pf* в заблужде́ние.

deluge /'delju:dʒ/ *n* (*flood*) пото́п; (*rain*) ли́вень *m*; (*fig*) пото́к

delusion /dɪ'lu:ʒ(ə)n/ *n* заблужде́ние; **~s of grandeur** ма́ния вели́чия.

de luxe /də 'lʌks/ *adj* -люкс (*added to noun*).

delve /delv/ *vi* углубля́ться *impf*, углуби́ться *pf* (**into** в+*acc*).

demand /dɪ'mɑ:nd/ *n* тре́бование; (*econ*) спрос (**for** на+*acc*); *vt* тре́бовать *impf*, по~ *pf* +*gen*. **demanding** /-dɪŋ/ *adj* тре́бовательный.

demarcation /ˌdi:mɑ:'keɪʃ(ə)n/ *n* демарка́ция.

demean /dɪ'mi:n/ *vt*: **~ o.s.** унижа́ться *impf*, уни́зиться *pf*.

demeanour /dɪ'mi:nə(r)/ *n* мане́ра вести́ себя́.

demented /dɪ'mentɪd/ *adj* сумасше́дший. **dementia** /-'menʃə/ *n* слабоу́мие.

demise /dɪ'maɪz/ *n* кончи́на.

demobilize /di:'məʊbɪˌlaɪz/ *vt* демобилизова́ть *impf* & *pf*.

democracy /dɪ'mɒkrəsɪ/ *n* демокра́тия. **democrat** /'deməˌkræt/ *n* демокра́т. **democratic** /ˌdemə'krætɪk/ *adj* демократи́ческий. **democratization** /dɪˌmɒkrətaɪ'zeɪʃ(ə)n/ *n* демократиза́ция.

demolish /dɪ'mɒlɪʃ/ *vt* (*destroy*) разруша́ть *impf*, разру́шить *pf*; (*building*) сноси́ть *impf*, снести́ *pf*; (*refute*) опроверга́ть *impf*, опрове́ргнуть *pf*. **demolition** /ˌdemə'lɪʃ(ə)n/ *n* разруше́ние; снос.

demon /'di:mən/ *n* де́мон.

demonstrable /'demɒnstrəb(ə)l/ *adj* доказу́емый. **demonstrably** /dɪ'mɒnstrəblɪ/ *adv* нагля́дно. **demonstrate** /'demənˌstreɪt/ *vt* демонстри́ровать *impf* & *pf*; *vi* уча́ствовать *impf* в демонстра́ции. **demonstration** /ˌdemən'streɪʃ(ə)n/ *n* демонстра́ция. **demonstrative** /dɪ'mɒnstrətɪv/ *adj* экспанси́вный; (*gram*) указа́тельный. **demonstrator** /'demənˌstreɪtə(r)/ *n* демонстра́тор; (*polit*) демонстра́нт.

demoralize /dɪ'mɒrəˌlaɪz/ *vt* деморализова́ть *impf* & *pf*.

demote /dɪ'məʊt/ *vt* понижа́ть *impf*, пони́зить *pf* в до́лжности.

demure /dɪ'mjʊə(r)/ *adj* скро́мный.

den /den/ *n* берло́га.

denial /dɪ'naɪəl/ *n* отрица́ние; (*refusal*) отка́з.

denigrate /'denɪˌgreɪt/ *vt* черни́ть *impf*, о~ *pf*.

denim /'denɪm/ *adj* джинсо́вый; *n* джинсо́вая ткань.

Denmark /'denmɑ:k/ *n* Да́ния.

denomination /dɪˌnɒmɪ'neɪʃ(ə)n/ *n* (*money*) досто́инство; (*relig*) вероисповеда́ние. **denominator** /dɪ'nɒmɪˌneɪtə(r)/ *n* знаме-

на́тель *m*.
denote /dɪ'nəʊt/ *vt* означа́ть *impf*, озна́чить *pf*.
denounce /dɪ'naʊns/ *vt* (*condemn*) осужда́ть *impf*, осуди́ть *pf*; (*inform on*) доноси́ть *impf*, донести́ *pf* на+*acc*.
dense /dens/ *adj* густо́й; (*stupid*) тупо́й. **density** /'densɪtɪ/ *n* пло́тность.
dent /dent/ *n* вмя́тина; *vt* де́лать *impf*, с~ *pf* вмя́тину в+*prep*.
dental /'dent(ə)l/ *adj* зубно́й. **dentist** /'dentɪst/ *n* зубно́й врач. **dentures** /'dentʃəz/ *n pl* зубно́й проте́з.
denunciation /dɪˌnʌnsɪ'eɪʃ(ə)n/ *n* (*condemnation*) осужде́ние; (*informing*) доно́с.
deny /dɪ'naɪ/ *vt* отрица́ть *impf*; (*refuse*) отка́зывать *impf*, отказа́ть *pf* +*dat* (*person*) в+*prep*.
deodorant /diː'əʊdərənt/ *n* дезодора́нт.
depart /dɪ'pɑːt/ *vi* отбыва́ть *impf*, отбы́ть *pf*; (*deviate*) отклоня́ться *impf*, отклони́ться *pf* (**from** от+*gen*).
department /dɪ'pɑːtmənt/ *n* отде́л; (*univ*) ка́федра; ~ **store** универма́г.
departure /dɪ'pɑːtʃə(r)/ *n* отбы́тие; (*deviation*) отклоне́ние.
depend /dɪ'pend/ *vi* зави́сеть *impf* (**on** от+*gen*); (*rely*) полага́ться *impf*, положи́ться *pf* (**on** на+*acc*). **dependable** /-'pendəb(ə)l/ *adj* надёжный. **dependant** /-'pend(ə)nt/ *n* иждиве́нец. **dependence** /-'pend(ə)ns/ *n* зави́симость. **dependent** /-'pend(ə)nt/ *adj* зави́симый.
depict /dɪ'pɪkt/ *vt* изобража́ть *impf*, изобрази́ть *pf*.
deplete /dɪ'pliːt/ *vt* истоща́ть *impf*, истощи́ть *pf*. **depleted** /-'pliːtɪd/ *adj* истощённый. **depletion** /-'pliːʃ(ə)n/ *n* истоще́ние.
deplorable /dɪ'plɔːrəb(ə)l/ *adj* плаче́вный. **deplore** /dɪ'plɔː(r)/ *vt* сожале́ть *impf* о+*prep*.
deploy /dɪ'plɔɪ/ *vt* развёртывать *impf*, разверну́ть *pf*. **deployment** /-mənt/ *n* развёртывание.
deport /dɪ'pɔːt/ *vt* депорти́ровать *impf* & *pf*; высыла́ть *impf*, вы́слать *pf*. **deportation** /ˌdiːpɔː'teɪʃ(ə)n/ *n* депорта́ция; вы́сылка.
deportment /dɪ'pɔːtmənt/ *n* оса́нка.
depose /dɪ'pəʊz/ *vt* сверга́ть *impf*, све́ргнуть *pf*. **deposit** /-'pɒzɪt/ *n* (*econ*) вклад; (*advance*) зада́ток; (*sediment*) оса́док; (*coal etc.*) месторожде́ние; *vt* (*econ*) вноси́ть *impf*, внести́ *pf*.
depot /'depəʊ/ *n* (*transport*) депо́ *neut indecl*; (*store*) склад.
deprave /dɪ'preɪv/ *vt* развраща́ть *impf*, разврати́ть *pf*. **depraved** /-'preɪvd/ *adj* развращённый. **depravity** /-'prævɪtɪ/ *n* развра́т.
deprecate /'deprɪˌkeɪt/ *vt* осужда́ть *impf*, осуди́ть *pf*.
depreciate /dɪ'priːʃɪˌeɪt/ *vt* & *i* (*econ*) обесце́нивать(ся) *impf*, обесце́нить(ся) *pf*. **depreciation** /-'eɪʃ(ə)n/ *n* обесце́нение.
depress /dɪ'pres/ *vt* (*dispirit*) удруча́ть *impf*, удручи́ть *pf*. **depressed** /-'prest/ *adj* удручённый. **depressing** /-'presɪŋ/ *adj* угнета́ющий. **depression** /-'preʃ(ə)n/ *n* (*hollow*) впа́дина; (*econ*, *med*, *meteorol*, *etc.*) депре́ссия.
deprivation /ˌeprɪ'veɪʃ(ə)n/ *n*

лишéние. **deprive** /dɪ'praɪv/ *vt* лишáть *impf*, лишúть *pf* (**of** +*gen*)

depth /depθ/ *n* глубинá; **in the ~ of winter** в разгáре зимы́.

deputation /ˌdepjʊ'teɪʃ(ə)n/ *n* депутáция. **deputize** /'depjʊˌtaɪz/ *vi* замещáть *impf*, заместúть *pf* (**for** +*acc*). **deputy** /'depjʊtɪ/ *n* заместúтель *m*; (*parl*) депутáт.

derail /dɪ'reɪl/ *vt*: **be derailed** сходúть *impf*, сойтú *pf* с рéльсов. **derailment** /-mənt/ *n* сход с рéльсов.

deranged /dɪ'reɪndʒd/ *adj* сумасшéдший.

derelict /'derəlɪkt/ *adj* забрóшенный.

deride /dɪ'raɪd/ *vt* высмéивать *impf*, вы́смеять *pf*. **derision** /-'rɪʒ(ə)n/ *n* высмéивание. **derisive** /-'raɪsɪv/ *adj* (*mocking*) насмéшливый. **derisory** /-'raɪsərɪ/ *adj* (*ridiculous*) смехотвóрный.

derivation /ˌderɪ'veɪʃ(ə)n/ *n* происхождéние. **derivative** /də'rɪvətɪv/ *n* произвóдное *sb*; *adj* произвóдный. **derive** /dɪ'raɪv/ *vt* извлекáть *impf*, извлéчь *pf*; *vi*: **~ from** происходúть *impf*, произойтú *pf* от+*gen*.

derogatory /dɪ'rɒgətərɪ/ *adj* отрицáтельный.

descend /dɪ'send/ *vi* (& *t*) (*go down*) спускáться *impf*, спустúться *pf* (с+*gen*); **be descended from** происходúть *impf*, произойтú *pf* из, от, +*gen*. **descendant** /-'send(ə)nt/ *n* потóмок. **descent** /-'sent/ *n* спуск; (*lineage*) происхождéние.

describe /dɪ'skraɪb/ *vt* опúсывать *impf*, описáть *pf*. **description** /-'skrɪpʃ(ə)n/ *n* описáние. **descriptive** /-'skrɪptɪv/ *adj* описáтельный.

desecrate /'desɪˌkreɪt/ *vt* осквернять *impf*, осквернúть *pf*. **desecration** /ˌdesɪ'kreɪʃ(ə)n/ *n* осквернéние.

desert[1] /'dezət/ *n* (*waste*) пусты́ня.

desert[2] /dɪ'zɜːt/ *vt* покидáть *impf*, покúнуть *pf*; (*mil*) дезертúровать *impf* & *pf*. **deserter** /-'zɜːtə(r)/ *n* дезертúр. **desertion** /-'zɜːʃ(ə)n/ *n* дезертúрство.

deserts /dɪ'zɜːts/ *n pl* заслу́ги *f pl*. **deserve** /-'zɜːv/ *vt* заслу́живать *impf*, заслужúть *pf*. **deserving** /-'zɜːvɪŋ/ *adj* достóйный (**of** +*gen*).

design /dɪ'zaɪn/ *n* (*pattern*) узóр; (*of car etc.*) констру́кция, проéкт; (*industrial*) дизáйн; (*aim*) у́мысел; *vt* проектúровать *impf*, с~ *pf*; (*intend*) предназначáть *impf*, предназначить *pf*.

designate /'dezɪgˌneɪt/ *vt* (*indicate*) обозначáть *impf*, обознáчить *pf*; (*appoint*) назначáть *impf*, назнáчить *pf*.

designer /dɪ'zaɪnə(r)/ *n* (*tech*) констру́ктор; (*industrial*) дизáйнер; (*of clothes*) модельéр.

desirable /dɪ'zaɪərəb(ə)l/ *adj* желáтельный. **desire** /-'zaɪə(r)/ *n* желáние; *vt* желáть *impf*, по~ *pf* +*gen*.

desist /dɪ'zɪst/ *vi* (*refrain*) воздéрживаться *impf*, воздержáться *pf* (**from** от+*gen*).

desk /desk/ *n* пúсьменный стол; (*school*) пáрта.

desolate /'desələt/ *adj* забрóшенный. **desolation** /ˌdesə'leɪʃ(ə)n/ *n* забрóшенность.

despair /dɪ'speə(r)/ *n* отчáяние; *vi* отчáиваться *impf*, отчáяться *pf*. **desperate** /'despərət/ *adj* отчáянный. **desperation**

/ˌdespəˈreɪʃ(ə)n/ *n* отчáяние. **despicable** /dɪˈspɪkəb(ə)l/ *adj* презрéнный. **despise** /dɪˈspaɪz/ *vt* презирáть *impf*, презрéть *pf*. **despite** /dɪˈspaɪt/ *prep* несмотря́ на+*acc*. **despondency** /dɪˈspɒndənsɪ/ *n* уны́ние. **despondent** /-d(ə)nt/ *adj* уны́лый. **despot** /ˈdespɒt/ *n* дéспот. **dessert** /dɪˈzɜːt/ *n* десéрт. **destination** /ˌdestɪˈneɪʃ(ə)n/ *n* (*of goods*) мéсто назначéния; (*of journey*) цель. **destiny** /ˈdestɪnɪ/ *n* судьбá. **destitute** /ˈdestɪˌtjuːt/ *adj* без вся́ких средств. **destroy** /dɪˈstrɔɪ/ *vt* разрушáть *impf*, разру́шить *pf*. **destroyer** /-ˈstrɔɪə(r)/ *n* (*naut*) эсми́нец. **destruction** /-ˈstrʌkʃ(ə)n/ *n* разрушéние. **destructive** /-ˈstrʌktɪv/ *adj* разруши́тельный. **detach** /dɪˈtætʃ/ *vt* отделя́ть *impf*, отдели́ть *pf*. **detached** /-ˈtætʃt/ *adj* отдéльный; (*objective*) беспристрáстный; ~ **house** особня́к. **detachment** /-ˈtætʃmənt/ *n* (*objectivity*) беспристрáстие; (*mil*) отря́д. **detail** /ˈdiːteɪl/ *n* детáль, подрóбность; **in detail** подрóбно; *vt* подрóбно рассказывать *impf*, рассказáть *pf*. **detailed** /-teɪld/ *adj* подрóбный. **detain** /dɪˈteɪn/ *vt* задéрживать *impf*, задержáть *pf*. **detainee** /ˌdiːteɪˈniː/ *n* задéржанный *sb*. **detect** /dɪˈtekt/ *vt* обнару́живать *impf*, обнару́жить *pf*. **detection** /-ˈtekʃ(ə)n/ *n* обнаружéние; (*crime*) расслéдование. **detective** /-ˈtektɪv/ *n* детекти́в; ~ **film, story,** *etc*. детекти́в. **detector** /-ˈtektə(r)/ *n* детéктор.

detention /dɪˈtenʃ(ə)n/ *n* задержáние; (*school*) задéржка в наказáние. **deter** /dɪˈtɜː(r)/ *vt* удéрживать *impf*, удержáть *pf* (**from** от+*gen*). **detergent** /dɪˈtɜːdʒ(ə)nt/ *n* мóющее срéдство. **deteriorate** /dɪˈtɪərɪəˌreɪt/ *vi* ухудшáться *impf*, ухýдшиться *pf*. **deterioration** /-ˈreɪʃ(ə)n/ *n* ухудшéние. **determination** /dɪˌtɜːmɪˈneɪʃ(ə)n/ *n* реши́мость. **determine** /dɪˈtɜːmɪn/ *vt* (*ascertain*) устанáвливать *impf*, установи́ть *pf*; (*be decisive factor*) определя́ть *impf*, определи́ть *pf*; (*decide*) решáть *impf*, реши́ть *pf*. **determined** /dɪˈtɜːmɪnd/ *adj* реши́тельный. **deterrent** /dɪˈterənt/ *n* срéдство устрашéния. **detest** /dɪˈtest/ *vt* ненави́деть *impf*. **detestable** /-ˈtestəb(ə)l/ *adj* отврати́тельный. **detonate** /ˈdetəˌneɪt/ *vt* & *i* взрывáть(ся) *impf*, взорвáть(ся) *pf*. **detonator** /-tə(r)/ *n* детонáтор. **detour** /ˈdiːtʊə(r)/ *n* объéзд. **detract** /dɪˈtrækt/ *vi*: ~ **from** умаля́ть *impf*, умали́ть *pf* +*acc*. **detriment** /ˈdetrɪmənt/ *n* ущéрб. **detrimental** /-ˈment(ə)l/ *adj* врéдный. **deuce** /djuːs/ *n* (*tennis*) рáвный счёт. **devaluation** /diːˌvæljuːˈeɪʃ(ə)n/ *n* девальвáция. **devalue** /diːˈvæljuː/ *vt* девальви́ровать *impf* & *pf*. **devastate** /ˈdevəˌsteɪt/ *vt* опустошáть *impf*, опустоши́ть *pf*. **devastated** /-ˌsteɪtɪd/ *adj* потрясённый. **devastating** /-ˌsteɪtɪŋ/ *adj* уничтожáющий.

devastation /-'steɪʃ(ə)n/ *n* опустошение.
develop /dɪ'veləp/ *vt* & *i* развивать(ся) *impf*, развить(ся) *pf*; *vt* (*phot*) проявлять *impf*, проявить *pf*. **developer** /-pə(r)/ *n* (*of land etc.*) застройщик. **development** /-mənt/ *n* развитие.
deviant /'di:vɪənt/ *adj* ненормальный. **deviate** /-vɪeɪt/ *vi* отклоняться *impf*, отклониться *pf* (**from** от+*gen*). **deviation** /ˌdi:vɪ'eɪʃ(ə)n/ *n* отклонение.
device /dɪ'vaɪs/ *n* прибор.
devil /'dev(ə)l/ *n* чёрт. **devilish** /'devəlɪʃ/ *adj* чертовский.
devious /'di:vɪəs/ *adj* (*circuitous*) окружной; (*person*) непорядочный.
devise /dɪ'vaɪz/ *vt* придумывать *impf*, придумать *pf*.
devoid /dɪ'vɔɪd/ *adj* лишённый (**of** +*gen*).
devolution /ˌdi:və'lu:ʃ(ə)n/ *n* передача (власти).
devote /dɪ'vəʊt/ *vt* посвящать *impf*, посвятить *pf*. **devoted** /-'vəʊtɪd/ *adj* преданный. **devotee** /ˌdevə'ti:/ *n* поклонник. **devotion** /dɪ'vəʊʃ(ə)n/ *n* преданность.
devour /dɪ'vaʊə(r)/ *vt* пожирать *impf*, пожрать *pf*.
devout /dɪ'vaʊt/ *adj* набожный.
dew /dju:/ *n* роса.
dexterity /dek'sterɪtɪ/ *n* ловкость. **dext(e)rous** /'dekstrəs/ *adj* ловкий.
diabetes /ˌdaɪə'bi:ti:z/ *n* диабет. **diabetic** /ˌdaɪə'betɪk/ *n* диабетик; *adj* диабетический.
diabolic(al) /ˌdaɪə'bɒlɪk((ə)l)/ *adj* дьявольский.
diagnose /'daɪəgˌnəʊz/ *vt* диагностировать *impf* & *pf*. **diagnosis** /ˌdaɪəg'nəʊsɪs/ *n* диагноз.
diagonal /daɪ'ægən(ə)l/ *n* диагональ; *adj* диагональный. **diagonally** /-'ægənəlɪ/ *adv* по диагонали.
diagram /'daɪəˌgræm/ *n* диаграмма.
dial /'daɪ(ə)l/ *n* (*clock*) циферблат; (*tech*) шкала; *vt* набирать *impf*, набрать *pf*.
dialect /'daɪəˌlekt/ *n* диалект.
dialogue /'daɪəˌlɒg/ *n* диалог.
diameter /daɪ'æmɪtə(r)/ *n* диаметр. **diametric(al)** /ˌdaɪə'metrɪk((ə)l)/ *adj* диаметральный; **~ly opposed** диаметрально противоположный.
diamond /'daɪəmənd/ *n* алмаз; (*shape*) ромб; *pl* (*cards*) бубны (-бён, -бнам) *pl*.
diaper /'daɪəpə(r)/ *n* пелёнка.
diaphragm /'daɪəˌfræm/ *n* диафрагма.
diarrhoea /ˌdaɪə'rɪə/ *n* понос.
diary /'daɪərɪ/ *n* дневник.
dice /daɪs/ *see* **die**[1]
dicey /'daɪsɪ/ *adj* рискованный.
dictate /dɪk'teɪt/ *vt* диктовать *impf*, про~ *pf*. **dictation** /-'teɪʃ(ə)n/ *n* диктовка. **dictator** /-'teɪtə(r)/ *n* диктатор. **dictatorial** /ˌdɪktə'tɔ:rɪəl/ *adj* диктаторский. **dictatorship** /dɪk'teɪtəʃɪp/ *n* диктатура.
diction /'dɪkʃ(ə)n/ *n* дикция.
dictionary /'dɪkʃənrɪ/ *n* словарь *m*.
didactic /daɪ'dæktɪk/ *adj* дидактический.
die[1] /daɪ/ *n* (*pl* **dice** /daɪs/) игральная кость; (*pl* **dies** /daɪz/) (*stamp*) штамп.
die[2] /daɪ/ *vi* (*person*) умирать *impf*, умереть *pf*; (*animal*) дохнуть *impf*, из~, по~ *pf*; (*plant*) вянуть *impf*, за~ *pf*; **be dying to** очень хотеть *impf*; **~ down** (*fire, sound*) угасать *impf*,

уга́снуть *pf*; ~ **out** вымира́ть *impf*, вы́мереть *pf*.
diesel /'di:z(ə)l/ *n* (*engine*) ди́зель *m*; *attrib* ди́зельный.
diet /'daɪət/ *n* дие́та; (*habitual food*) пи́ща; *vi* быть на дие́те. **dietary** /'daɪətrɪ/ *adj* диети́ческий.
differ /'dɪfə(r)/ *vi* отлича́ться *impf*; различа́ться *impf*; (*disagree*) расходи́ться *impf*, разойти́сь *pf*. **difference** /'dɪfrəns/ *n* ра́зница; (*disagreement*) разногла́сие. **different** /'dɪfrənt/ *adj* разли́чный, ра́зный. **differential** /ˌdɪfə'renʃ(ə)l/ *n* (*difference*) ра́зница. **differentiate** /ˌdɪfə'renʃɪˌeɪt/ *vt* различа́ть *impf*, различи́ть *pf*.
difficult /'dɪfɪkəlt/ *adj* тру́дный. **difficulty** /-kəltɪ/ *n* тру́дность; (*difficult situation*) затрудне́ние; **without** ~ без труда́.
diffidence /'dɪfɪdəns/ *n* неуве́ренность в себе́. **diffident** /-d(ə)nt/ *adj* неуве́ренный в себе́.
diffused /dɪ'fju:zd/ *adj* рассе́янный.
dig /dɪg/ *n* (*archaeol*) раско́пки *f pl*; (*poke*) тычо́к; (*gibe*) шпи́лька; *pl* (*lodgings*) кварти́ра; **give a ~ in the ribs** ткнуть *pf* ло́ктем под ребро́; *vt* копа́ть *impf*, вы́~ *pf*; рыть *impf*, вы́~ *pf*; ~ **up** (*bone*) выка́пывать *impf*, вы́копать *pf*; (*land*) вска́пывать *impf*, вскопа́ть *pf*.
digest /daɪ'dʒest/ *vt* перева́ривать *impf*, перевари́ть *pf*. **digestible** /-'dʒestɪb(ə)l/ *adj* удобовари́мый. **digestion** /-'dʒestʃ(ə)n/ *n* пищеваре́ние.
digger /'dɪgə(r)/ *n* (*tech*) экскава́тор.
digit /'dɪdʒɪt/ *n* (*math*) знак.
digital /'dɪdʒɪt(ə)l/ *adj* цифрово́й.
dignified /'dɪgnɪˌfaɪd/ *adj* велича́вый. **dignitary** /-nɪtərɪ/ *n* сано́вник. **dignity** /-nɪtɪ/ *n* досто́инство.
digress /daɪ'gres/ *vi* отклоня́ться *impf*, отклони́ться *pf*. **digression** /-'greʃ(ə)n/ *n* отклоне́ние.
dike /daɪk/ *n* да́мба; (*ditch*) ров.
dilapidated /dɪ'læpɪˌdeɪtɪd/ *adj* ве́тхий.
dilate /daɪ'leɪt/ *vt & i* расширя́ть(ся) *impf*, расши́рить(ся) *pf*.
dilemma /daɪ'lemə/ *n* диле́мма.
dilettante /ˌdɪlɪ'tæntɪ/ *n* дилета́нт.
diligence /'dɪlɪdʒ(ə)ns/ *n* прилежа́ние. **diligent** /-lɪdʒ(ə)nt/ *adj* приле́жный.
dilute /daɪ'lju:t/ *vt* разбавля́ть *impf*, разба́вить *pf*.
dim /dɪm/ *adj* (*not bright*) ту́склый; (*vague*) сму́тный; (*stupid*) тупо́й.
dimension /daɪ'menʃ(ə)n/ *n* (*pl*) разме́ры *m pl*; (*math*) измере́ние. **-dimensional** /-'menʃən(ə)l/ *in comb* -ме́рный; **three-~** трёхме́рный.
diminish /dɪ'mɪnɪʃ/ *vt & i* уменьша́ть(ся) *impf*, уме́ньшить(ся) *pf*. **diminutive** /-'mɪnjʊtɪv/ *adj* ма́ленький; *n* уменьши́тельное *sb*.
dimness /'dɪmnɪs/ *n* ту́склость.
dimple /'dɪmp(ə)l/ *n* я́мочка.
din /dɪn/ *n* гро́хот; (*voices*) гам.
dine /daɪn/ *vi* обе́дать *impf*, по~ *pf*. **diner** /'daɪnə(r)/ *n* обе́дающий *sb*.
dinghy /'dɪŋgɪ/ *n* шлю́пка; (*rubber* ~) надувна́я ло́дка.
dingy /'dɪndʒɪ/ *adj* (*drab*) ту́склый; (*dirty*) гря́зный.
dining-car /'daɪnɪŋ kɑ:/ *n* ваго́н-рестора́н. **dining-room** *n* сто-

ло́вая *sb.* **dinner** /'dınə(r)/ *n* обе́д; **~-jacket** смо́кинг.

dinosaur /'daınə,sɔ:(r)/ *n* диноза́вр.

diocese /'daıəsıs/ *n* епа́рхия.

dip /dıp/ *vt* (*immerse*) окуна́ть *impf*, окуну́ть *pf*; (*partially*) обма́кивать *impf*, обмакну́ть *pf*; *vi* (*slope*) понижа́ться *impf*, пони́зиться *pf*; *n* (*depression*) впа́дина; (*slope*) укло́н; **have a ~** (*bathe*) купа́ться *impf*, вы́~ *pf*.

diphtheria /dıf'θıərıə/ *n* дифтери́я.

diphthong /'dıfθɒŋ/ *n* дифто́нг.

diploma /dı'pləʊmə/ *n* дипло́м. **diplomacy** /-'pləʊməsı/ *n* диплома́тия. **diplomat** /'dıplə,mæt/ *n* диплома́т. **diplomatic** /,dıplə'mætık/ *adj* дипломати́ческий.

dire /'daıə(r)/ *adj* стра́шный; (*ominous*) злове́щий.

direct /daı'rekt/ *adj* прямо́й; **~ current** постоя́нный ток; *vt* направля́ть *impf*, напра́вить *pf*; (*guide, manage*) руководи́ть *impf* +*instr*; (*film*) режисси́ровать *impf*. **direction** /-'rekʃ(ə)n/ *n* направле́ние; (*guidance*) руково́дство; (*instruction*) указа́ние; (*film*) режиссу́ра; **stage ~** рема́рка. **directive** /-'rektıv/ *n* директи́ва. **directly** /-'rektlı/ *adv* пря́мо; (*at once*) сра́зу. **director** /-'rektə(r)/ *n* дире́ктор; (*film etc.*) режиссёр(-постано́вщик). **directory** /-'rektərı/ *n* спра́вочник, указа́тель *m*; (*tel*) телефо́нная кни́га.

dirt /dɜ:t/ *n* грязь. **dirty** /'dɜ:tı/ *adj* гря́зный; *vt* па́чкать *impf*, за~ *pf*.

disability /,dısə'bılıtı/ *n* физи́ческий/психи́ческий недоста́ток; (*disablement*) инвали́дность. **disabled** /dıs'eıb(ə)ld/ *adj*: **he is ~** он инвали́д.

disadvantage /,dısəd'vɑ:ntıdʒ/ *n* невы́годное положе́ние; (*defect*) недоста́ток. **disadvantageous** /dıs,ædvən'teıdʒəs/ *adj* невы́годный.

disaffected /,dısə'fektıd/ *adj* недово́льный.

disagree /,dısə'gri:/ *vi* не соглаша́ться *impf*, согласи́ться *pf*; (*not correspond*) не соотве́тствовать *impf* +*dat*. **disagreeable** /-'gri:əb(ə)l/ *adj* неприя́тный. **disagreement** /-'gri:mənt/ *n* разногла́сие; (*quarrel*) ссо́ра.

disappear /,dısə'pıə(r)/ *vi* исчеза́ть *impf*, исче́знуть *pf*. **disappearance** /-'pıərəns/ *n* исчезнове́ние.

disappoint /,dısə'pɔınt/ *vt* разочаро́вывать *impf*, разочарова́ть *pf*. **disappointed** /-'pɔıntıd/ *adj* разочаро́ванный. **disappointing** /-'pɔıntıŋ/ *adj* разочаро́вывающий. **disappointment** /-'pɔıntmənt/ *n* разочарова́ние.

disapproval /,dısə'pru:v(ə)l/ *n* неодобре́ние. **disapprove** /,dısə'pru:v/ *vt* & *i* не одобря́ть *impf*.

disarm /dıs'ɑ:m/ *vt* (*mil*) разоружа́ть *impf.*, разоружи́ть *pf*; (*criminal; also fig*) обезору́живать *impf*, обезору́жить *pf*. **disarmament** /-'ɑ:məmənt/ *n* разоруже́ние.

disarray /,dısə'reı/ *n* беспоря́док.

disaster /dı'zɑ:stə(r)/ *n* бе́дствие. **disastrous** /-'zɑ:strəs/ *adj* катастрофи́ческий.

disband /dıs'bænd/ *vt* распуска́ть *impf*, распусти́ть *pf*; *vi* расходи́ться *impf*, разойти́сь *pf*.

disbelief /,dısbı'li:f/ *n* неве́рие.

disc, disk /dɪsk/ *n* диск; ~ **drive** (*comput*) дисково́д; ~ **jockey** диск-жоке́й, дидже́й.
discard /dɪ'skɑ:d/ *vt* отбра́сывать *impf*, отбро́сить *pf*.
discern /dɪ'sɜ:n/ *vt* различа́ть *impf*, различи́ть *pf*. **discernible** /-'sɜ:nɪb(ə)l/ *adj* различи́мый. **discerning** /-'sɜ:nɪŋ/ *adj* проница́тельный.
discharge *vt* / dɪs'tʃɑ:dʒ/ (*gun*; *electr*) разряжа́ть *impf*, разряди́ть *pf*; (*dismiss*) увольнять *impf*, уво́лить *pf*; (*prisoner*) освобожда́ть *impf*, освободи́ть *pf*; (*debt*; *duty*) выполня́ть *impf*, вы́полнить *pf*; (*from hospital*) выпи́сывать *impf*, вы́писать *pf*; *n* /'dɪstʃɑ:dʒ/ разгру́зка; (*electr*) разря́д; увольне́ние; освобожде́ние; выполне́ние; (*med*) выделе́ния *neut pl*.
disciple /dɪ'saɪp(ə)l/ *n* учени́к.
disciplinarian /ˌdɪsɪplɪ'neərɪən/ *n* сторо́нник дисципли́ны. **disciplinary** /ˌdɪsɪ'plɪnərɪ/ *adj* дисциплина́рный. **discipline** /'dɪsɪplɪn/ *n* дисципли́на; *vt* дисциплини́ровать *impf* & *pf*.
disclaim /dɪs'kleɪm/ *vt* (*deny*) отрица́ть *impf*; ~ **responsibility** слага́ть *impf*, сложи́ть *pf* с себя́ отве́тственность.
disclose /dɪs'kləʊz/ *vt* обнару́живать *impf*, обнару́жить *pf*. **disclosure** /-'kləʊʒə(r)/ *n* обнару́же́ние.
discoloured /dɪs'kʌləd/ *adj* обесцве́ченный.
discomfit /dɪs'kʌmfɪt/ *vt* смуща́ть *impf*, смути́ть *pf*. **discomfiture** /-'kʌmfɪtjə(r)/ *n* смуще́ние.
discomfort /dɪs'kʌmfət/ *n* неудо́бство.
disconcert /ˌdɪskən'sɜ:t/ *vt* смуща́ть *impf*, смути́ть *pf*.
disconnect /ˌdɪskə'nekt/ *vt* разъединя́ть *impf*, разъедини́ть *pf*; (*switch off*) выключа́ть *impf*, вы́ключить *pf*. **disconnected** /-tɪd/ *adj* (*incoherent*) бессвя́зный.
disconsolate /dɪs'kɒnsələt/ *adj* неуте́шный.
discontent /ˌdɪskən'tent/ *n* недово́льство. **discontented** /-'tentɪd/ *adj* недово́льный.
discontinue /ˌdɪskən'tɪnju:/ *vt* прекраща́ть *impf*, прекрати́ть *pf*.
discord /'dɪskɔ:d/ *n* разногла́сие; (*mus*) диссона́нс. **discordant** /dɪ'skɔ:d(ə)nt/ *adj* несогласу́ющийся; диссони́рующий.
discotheque /'dɪskəˌtek/ *n* дискоте́ка.
discount *n* /'dɪskaʊnt/ ски́дка; *vt* /dɪs'kaʊnt/ (*disregard*) не принима́ть *impf*, приня́ть *pf* в расчёт.
discourage /dɪ'skʌrɪdʒ/ *vt* обескура́живать *impf*, обескура́жить *pf*; (*dissuade*) отгова́ривать *impf*, отговори́ть *pf*.
discourse /'dɪskɔ:s/ *n* речь.
discourteous /dɪs'kɜ:tɪəs/ *adj* неве́жливый.
discover /dɪ'skʌvə(r)/ *vt* открыва́ть *impf*, откры́ть *pf*; (*find out*) обнару́живать *impf*, обнару́жить *pf*. **discovery** /-'skʌvərɪ/ *n* откры́тие.
discredit /dɪs'kredɪt/ *n* позо́р; *vt* дискредити́ровать *impf* & *pf*.
discreet /dɪ'skri:t/ *adj* такти́чный. **discretion** /-'skreʃ(ə)n/ *n* (*judgement*) усмотре́ние; (*prudence*) благоразу́мие; **at one's** ~ по своему́ усмотре́нию.
discrepancy /dɪs'krepənsɪ/ *n* не-

соотве́тствие.

discriminate /dɪ'skrɪmɪ,neɪt/ *vt* различа́ть *impf*, различи́ть *pf*; **~ against** дискримини́ровать *impf* & *pf*. **discrimination** /-'neɪʃ(ə)n/ *n* (*taste*) разбо́рчивость; (*bias*) дискримина́ция.

discus /'dɪskəs/ *n* диск.

discuss /dɪ'skʌs/ *vt* обсужда́ть *impf*, обсуди́ть *pf*. **discussion** /-'skʌʃ(ə)n/ *n* обсужде́ние.

disdain /dɪs'deɪn/ *n* презре́ние. **disdainful** /-fʊl/ *adj* презри́тельный.

disease /dɪ'zi:z/ *n* боле́знь. **diseased** /-'zi:zd/ *adj* больно́й.

disembark /,dɪsɪm'bɑ:k/ *vi* выса́живаться *impf*, вы́садиться *pf*.

disenchantment /,dɪsɪn'tʃɑ:ntmənt/ *n* разочарова́ние.

disengage /,dɪsɪn'geɪdʒ/ *vt* освобожда́ть *impf*, освободи́ть *pf*; (*clutch*) отпуска́ть *impf*, отпусти́ть *pf*.

disentangle /,dɪsɪn'tæŋg(ə)l/ *vt* распу́тывать *impf*, распу́тать *pf*.

disfavour /dɪs'feɪvə(r)/ *n* неми́лость.

disfigure /dɪs'fɪgə(r)/ *vt* уро́довать *impf*, из~ *pf*.

disgrace /dɪs'greɪs/ *n* позо́р; (*disfavour*) неми́лость; *vt* позо́рить *impf*, о~ *pf*. **disgraceful** /-'greɪsfʊl/ *adj* позо́рный.

disgruntled /dɪs'grʌnt(ə)ld/ *adj* недово́льный.

disguise /dɪs'gaɪz/ *n* маскиро́вка; *vt* маскирова́ть *impf*, за~ *pf*; (*conceal*) скрыва́ть *impf*, скрыть *pf*. **disguised** /-'gaɪzd/ *adj* замаскиро́ванный.

disgust /dɪs'gʌst/ *n* отвраще́ние; *vt* внуша́ть *impf*, внуши́ть *pf*. отвраще́ние +*dat*. **disgusting** /-'gʌstɪŋ/ *adj* отврати́тельный.

dish /dɪʃ/ *n* блю́до; *pl* посу́да *collect*; **~-washer** посу́домо́ечная маши́на; *vt*: **~ up** подава́ть *impf*, пода́ть *pf*.

dishearten /dɪs'hɑ:t(ə)n/ *vt* обескура́живать *impf*, обескура́жить *pf*.

dishevelled /dɪ'ʃev(ə)ld/ *adj* растрёпанный.

dishonest /dɪs'ɒnɪst/ *adj* нече́стный. **dishonesty** /-'ɒnɪstɪ/ *n* нече́стность. **dishonour** /-'ɒnə(r)/ *n* бесче́стье; *vt* бесче́стить *impf*, о~ *pf*. **dishonourable** /-'ɒnərəb(ə)l/ *adj* бесче́стный.

disillusion /,dɪsɪ'lu:ʒ(ə)n/ *vt* разочаро́вывать *impf*, разочарова́ть *pf*. **disillusionment** /-mənt/ *n* разочаро́ванность.

disinclination /,dɪsɪnklɪ'neɪʃ(ə)n/ *n* несклонность, неохо́та. **disinclined** /-'klaɪnd/ *adj* **be ~** не хоте́ться *impers* +*dat*.

disinfect /,dɪsɪn'fekt/ *vt* дезинфици́ровать *impf* & *pf*. **disinfectant** /-t(ə)nt/ *n* дезинфици́рующее сре́дство.

disingenuous /,dɪsɪn'dʒenjʊəs/ *adj* нейскренный.

disinherit /,dɪsɪn'herɪt/ *vt* лиша́ть *impf*, лиши́ть *pf* насле́дства.

disintegrate /dɪs'ɪntɪ,greɪt/ *vi* распада́ться *impf*, распа́сться *pf*. **disintegration** /-'greɪʃ(ə)n/ *n* распа́д.

disinterested /dɪs'ɪntrɪstɪd/ *adj* бескоры́стный.

disjointed /dɪs'dʒɔɪntɪd/ *adj* бессвя́зный.

disk /dɪsk/ *see* **disc**

dislike /dɪs'laɪk/ *n* нелюбо́вь (**for** к+*dat*); *vt* не люби́ть *impf*.

dislocate /'dɪslə,keɪt/ *vt* (*med*) вы́вихнуть *pf*.

dislodge /dɪs'lɒdʒ/ *vt* смеща́ть

impf, сместить *pf*.
disloyal /dɪs'lɔɪəl/ *adj* нелояльный. **disloyalty** /-tɪ/ *n* нелояльность.
dismal /'dɪzm(ə)l/ *adj* мрачный.
dismantle /dɪs'mænt(ə)l/ *vt* разбирать *impf*, разобрать *pf*.
dismay /dɪs'meɪ/ *vt* смущать *impf*, смутить *pf*; *n* смущение.
dismiss /dɪs'mɪs/ *vt* (*sack*) увольнять *impf*, уволить *pf*; (*disband*) распускать *impf*, распустить *pf*. **dismissal** /-səl/ *n* увольнение; роспуск.
dismount /dɪs'maʊnt/ *vi* спешиваться *impf*, спешиться *pf*.
disobedience /ˌdɪsə'biːdɪəns/ *n* непослушание. **disobedient** /-ənt/ *adj* непослушный. **disobey** /ˌdɪsə'beɪ/ *vt* не слушаться *impf* +*gen*.
disorder /dɪs'ɔːdə(r)/ *n* беспорядок. **disorderly** /-dəlɪ/ *adj* (*untidy*) беспорядочный; (*unruly*) буйный.
disorganized /dɪs'ɔːgəˌnaɪzd/ *adj* неорганизованный.
disorientation /dɪsˌɔːrɪən'teɪʃ(ə)n/ *n* дезориентация. **disoriented** /dɪs'ɔːrɪəntɪd/ *adj*: **I am/was ~** я потерял(а) направление.
disown /dɪs'əʊn/ *vt* отказываться *impf*, отказаться *pf* от+*gen*.
disparaging /dɪ'spærɪdʒɪŋ/ *adj* оскорбительный.
disparity /dɪ'spærɪtɪ/ *n* неравенство.
dispassionate /dɪ'spæʃənət/ *adj* беспристрастный.
dispatch /dɪ'spætʃ/ *vt* (*send*) отправлять *impf*, отправить *pf*; (*deal with*) расправляться *impf*, расправиться *pf* с+*instr*; *n* отправка; (*message*) донесение; (*rapidity*) быстрота; **~-rider** мотоциклист связи.
dispel /dɪ'spel/ *vt* рассеивать *impf*, рассеять *pf*.
dispensable /dɪ'spensəb(ə)l/ *adj* необязательный.
dispensary /dɪ'spensərɪ/ *n* аптека.
dispensation /ˌdɪspen'seɪʃ(ə)n/ *n* (*exemption*) освобождение (от обязательства). **dispense** /dɪ'spens/ *vt* (*distribute*) раздавать *impf*, раздать *pf*; **~ with** обходиться *impf*, обойтись *pf* без+*gen*.
dispersal /dɪ'spɜːsəl/ *n* распространение. **disperse** /-'spɜːs/ *vt* (*drive away*) разгонять *impf*, разогнать *pf*; (*scatter*) рассеивать *impf*, рассеять *pf*; *vi* расходиться *impf*, разойтись *pf*.
dispirited /dɪ'spɪrɪtɪd/ *adj* удручённый.
displaced /dɪs'pleɪst/ *adj*: **~ persons** перемещённые лица *neut pl*.
display /dɪ'spleɪ/ *n* показ; *vt* показывать *impf*, показать *pf*.
displeased /dɪs'pliːzd/ *predic* недоволен (-льна). **displeasure** /-'pleʒə(r)/ *n* недовольство.
disposable /dɪ'spəʊzəb(ə)l/ *adj* одноразовый. **disposal** /-'spəʊz(ə)l/ *n* удаление; **at your ~** в вашем распоряжении. **dispose** /-'spəʊz/ *vi*: **~ of** избавляться *impf*, избавиться *pf* от+*gen*. **disposed** /-'spəʊzd/ *predic*: **~ to** расположен (-ена) к+*dat* *or* +*inf*. **disposition** /ˌdɪspə'zɪʃ(ə)n/ *n* расположение; (*temperament*) нрав.
disproportionate /ˌdɪsprə'pɔːʃənət/ *adj* непропорциональный.
disprove /dɪs'pruːv/ *vt* опровергать *impf*, опровергнуть *pf*.
dispute /dɪ'spjuːt/ *n* (*debate*)

спор; (*quarrel*) ссóра; *vt* оспáривать *impf*, оспóрить *pf*.
disqualification /dɪsˌkwɒlɪfɪ'keɪʃ(ə)n/ *n* дисквалификáция. **disqualify** /dɪs'kwɒlɪˌfaɪ/ *vt* дисквалифицúровать *impf* & *pf*.
disquieting /dɪs'kwaɪətɪŋ/ *adj* тревóжный.
disregard /ˌdɪsrɪ'gɑːd/ *n* пренебрежéние +*instr*; *vt* игнорúровать *impf* & *pf*; пренебрегáть *impf*, пренебрéчь *pf* +*instr*.
disrepair /ˌdɪsrɪ'peə(r)/ *n* неисправность.
disreputable /dɪs'repjʊtəb(ə)l/ *adj* пóльзующийся дурнóй слáвой. **disrepute** /ˌdɪsrɪ'pjuːt/ *n* дурнáя слáва.
disrespect /ˌdɪsrɪ'spekt/ *n* неуважéние. **disrespectful** /-fʊl/ *adj* непочтúтельный.
disrupt /dɪs'rʌpt/ *vt* срывáть *impf*, сорвáть *pf*. **disruptive** /tɪv/ *adj* подрывнóй.
dissatisfaction /ˌdɪsætɪs'fækʃ(ə)n/ *n* недовóльство. **dissatisfied** /dɪ'sætɪsfaɪd/ *adj* недовóльный.
dissect /dɪ'sekt/ *vt* разрезáть *impf*, разрéзать *pf*; (*med*) вскрывáть *impf*, вскрыть *pf*.
disseminate /dɪ'semɪˌneɪt/ *vt* распространя́ть *impf*, распространúть *pf*; **dissemination** /-'neɪʃ(ə)n/ *n* распространéние.
dissension /dɪ'senʃ(ə)n/ *n* раздóр. **dissent** /-'sent/ *n* расхождéние; (*eccl*) раскóл.
dissertation /ˌdɪsə'teɪʃ(ə)n/ *n* диссертáция.
disservice /dɪs'sɜːvɪs/ *n* плохáя услýга.
dissident /'dɪsɪd(ə)nt/ *n* диссидéнт.
dissimilar /dɪ'sɪmɪlə(r)/ *adj* несхóдный.
dissipate /'dɪsɪˌpeɪt/ *vt* (*dispel*) рассéивать *impf*, рассéять *pf*; (*squander*) проматывать *impf*, промотáть *pf*. **dissipated** /-tɪd/ *adj* распýтный.
dissociate /ˌdɪ'səʊʃɪˌeɪt/ *vt*: ~ **o.s.** отмежёвываться *impf*, отмежевáться *pf* (**from** от+*gen*).
dissolute /'dɪsəˌluːt/ *adj* распýтный. **dissolution** /-'luːʃ(ə)n/ *n* расторжéние; (*parl*) рóспуск.
dissolve /dɪ'zɒlv/ *vt* & *i* (*in liquid*) растворя́ть(ся) *impf*, раствори́ть(ся) *pf*; *vt* (*annul*) расторгáть *impf*, растóргнуть *pf*; (*parl*) распускáть *impf*, распустúть *pf*.
dissonance /'dɪsənəns/ *n* диссонáнс. **dissonant** /-nənt/ *adj* диссонúрующий.
dissuade /dɪ'sweɪd/ *vt* отговáривать *impf*, отговорúть *pf*.
distance /'dɪst(ə)ns/ *n* расстоя́ние; **from a** ~ úздали; **in the** ~ вдалекé. **distant** /-'t(ə)nt/ *adj* далёкий, (*also of relative*) дáльний; (*reserved*) сдéржанный.
distaste /dɪs'teɪst/ *n* отвращéние. **distasteful** /-fʊl/ *adj* протúвный.
distended /dɪ'stendɪd/ *adj* надýтый.
distil /dɪ'stɪl/ *vt* (*whisky*) перегоня́ть *impf*, перегнáть *pf*; (*water*) дистиллúровать *impf* & *pf*. **distillation** /ˌdɪstɪ'leɪʃ(ə)n/ *n* перегóнка; дистилля́ция. **distillery** /dɪ'stɪlərɪ/ *n* перегóнный завóд.
distinct /dɪ'stɪŋkt/ *adj* (*different*) отли́чный; (*clear*) отчётливый; (*evident*) замéтный. **distinction** /-'stɪŋkʃ(ə)n/ *n* (*difference*; *excellence*) отли́чие; (*discrimination*) разли́чие. **distinctive** /-'stɪŋktɪv/ *adj* отличúтельный. **distinctly** /-'stɪŋktlɪ/ *adv* я́сно.
distinguish /dɪ'stɪŋgwɪʃ/ *vt* раз-

личáть *impf*, различи́ть *pf*; ~ **o.s.** отличáться *impf*, отличи́ться *pf*. **distinguished** /-'stɪŋgwɪʃt/ *adj* выдаю́щийся.

distort /dɪ'stɔːt/ *vt* искажáть *impf*, искази́ть *pf*; (*misrepresent*) извращáть *impf*, изврати́ть *pf*. **distortion** /-'stɔːʃ(ə)n/ *n* искажéние; извращéние.

distract /dɪ'strækt/ *vt* отвлекáть *impf*, отвлéчь *pf*. **distraction** /-'strækʃ(ə)n/ *n* (*amusement*) развлечéние; (*madness*) безу́мие.

distraught /dɪ'strɔːt/ *adj* обезу́мевший.

distress /dɪ'stres/ *n* (*suffering*) огорчéние; (*danger*) бéдствие; *vt* огорчáть *impf*, огорчи́ть *pf*.

distribute /dɪ'strɪbjuːt/ *vt* (*hand out*) раздавáть *impf*, раздáть *pf*; (*allocate*) распределя́ть *impf*, распредели́ть *pf*. **distribution** /ˌdɪstrɪ'bjuːʃ(ə)n/ *n* распределéние. **distributor** /dɪ'strɪbjʊtə(r)/ *n* распредели́тель *m*.

district /'dɪstrɪkt/ *n* райóн.

distrust /dɪs'trʌst/ *n* недовéрие; *vt* не доверя́ть *impf*. **distrustful** /-fʊl/ *adj* недовéрчивый.

disturb /dɪ'stɜːb/ *vt* беспокóить *impf*, о~ *pf*. **disturbance** /-bəns/ *n* нарушéние покóя; *pl* (*polit etc.*) беспоря́дки *m pl*.

disuse /dɪs'juːs/ *n* неупотреблéние; **fall into** ~ выходи́ть *impf*, вы́йти *pf* из употреблéния. **disused** /-'juːzd/ *adj* заброшенный.

ditch /dɪtʃ/ *n* канáва, ров.

dither /'dɪðə(r)/ *vi* колебáться *impf*.

ditto /'dɪtəʊ/ *n* то же сáмое; *adv* так же.

divan /dɪ'væn/ *n* дивáн.

dive /daɪv/ *vi* ныря́ть *impf*, нырну́ть *pf*; (*aeron*) пики́ровать *impf* & *pf*; *n* нырóк, прыжóк в вóду. **diver** /-və(r)/ *n* водолáз.

diverge /daɪ'vɜːdʒ/ *vi* расходи́ться *impf*, разойти́сь *pf*. **divergent** /-dʒ(ə)nt/ *adj* расходя́щийся.

diverse /daɪ'vɜːs/ *adj* разнообрáзный. **diversification** /-vɜːsɪfɪ'keɪʃ(ə)n/ *n* расширéние ассортимéнта. **diversify** /-'vɜːsɪˌfaɪ/ *vt* разнообрáзить *impf*. **diversion** /-'vɜːʃ(ə)n/ *n* (*detour*) объéзд; (*amusement*) развлечéние. **diversity** /-'vɜːsɪtɪ/ *n* разнообрáзие. **divert** /-'vɜːt/ *vt* отклоня́ть *impf*, отклони́ть *pf*; (*amuse*) развлекáть *impf*, развлéчь *pf*. **diverting** /-'vɜːtɪŋ/ *adj* забáвный.

divest /daɪ'vest/ *vt* (*deprive*) лишáть *impf*, лиши́ть *pf* (**of** +*gen*); ~ **o.s.** откáзываться *impf*, отказáться *pf* (**of** от+*gen*).

divide /dɪ'vaɪd/ *vt* (*share*; *math*) дели́ть *impf*, по~ *pf*; (*separate*) разделя́ть *impf*, раздели́ть *pf*. **dividend** /'dɪvɪˌdend/ *n* дивидéнд.

divine /dɪ'vaɪn/ *adj* божéственный.

diving /'daɪvɪŋ/ *n* ныря́ние; **~-board** трампли́н.

divinity /dɪ'vɪnɪtɪ/ *n* (*quality*) божéственность; (*deity*) божествó; (*theology*) богослóвие.

divisible /dɪ'vɪzɪb(ə)l/ *adj* дели́мый. **division** /-'vɪʒ(ə)n/ *n* (*dividing*) делéние, разделéние; (*section*) отдéл; (*mil*) диви́зия.

divorce /dɪ'vɔːs/ *n* развóд; *vi* разводи́ться *impf*, развести́сь *pf*. **divorced** /-'vɔːst/ *adj* разведённый.

divulge /daɪ'vʌldʒ/ *vt* разглашáть *impf*, разгласи́ть *pf*.

DIY *abbr* (*of* **do-it-yourself**): **he is good at ~** у него́ золоты́е ру́ки; **~ shop** магази́н «сде́лай сам».

dizziness /'dɪzɪnɪs/ *n* головокруже́ние. **dizzy** /'dɪzɪ/ *adj* (*causing dizziness*) головокружи́тельный; **I am ~** у меня́ кру́жится голова́.

DNA *abbr* (*of* **deoxyribonucleic acid**) ДНК.

do /du:/ *vt* де́лать *impf*, с~ *pf*; *vi* (*be suitable*) годи́ться *impf*; (*suffice*) быть доста́точным; **~-it-yourself** *see* **DIY**; **that will ~!** хва́тит!; **how ~ you ~?** здра́вствуйте!; как вы пожива́ете?; **~ away with** (*abolish*) уничтожа́ть *impf*, уничто́жить *pf*; **~ in** (*kill*) убива́ть *impf*, уби́ть *pf*; **~ up** (*restore*) ремонти́ровать *impf*, от~ *pf*; (*wrap up*) завёртывать *impf*, заверну́ть *pf*; (*fasten*) застёгивать *impf*, застегну́ть *pf*; **~ without** обходи́ться *impf*, обойти́сь *pf* без+*gen*

docile /'dəʊsaɪl/ *adj* поко́рный. **docility** /-'sɪlɪtɪ/ *n* поко́рность.

dock[1] /dɒk/ *n* (*naut*) док; *vt* ста́вить *impf*, по~ *pf* в док; *vi* входи́ть *impf*, войти́ *pf* в док; *vi* (*spacecraft*) стыкова́ться *impf*, со~ *pf*. **docker** /-kə(r)/ *n* до́кер. **dockyard** *n* верфь.

dock[2] /dɒk/ *n* (*law*) скамья́ подсуди́мых.

docket /'dɒkɪt/ *n* квита́нция; (*label*) ярлы́к.

doctor /'dɒktə(r)/ *n* врач; (*also univ*) до́ктор; *vt* (*castrate*) кастри́ровать *impf* & *pf*; (*spay*) удаля́ть *impf*, удали́ть *pf* яи́чники у+*gen*; (*falsify*) фальсифици́ровать *impf* & *pf*. **doctorate** /-rət/ *n* сте́пень до́ктора.

doctrine /'dɒktrɪn/ *n* доктри́на.

document /'dɒkjʊmənt/ *n* докуме́нт; *vt* документи́ровать *impf* & *pf*. **documentary** /ˌdɒkjʊ'mentərɪ/ *n* документа́льный фильм. **documentation** /ˌdɒkjʊmen'teɪʃ(ə)n/ *n* документа́ция.

doddery /'dɒdərɪ/ *adj* дря́хлый.

dodge /dɒdʒ/ *n* увёртка; *vt* уклоня́ться *impf*, уклони́ться *pf* от+*gen*; (*jump to avoid*) отска́кивать *impf*, отскочи́ть *pf* (от+*gen*). **dodgy** /'dɒdʒɪ/ *adj* ка́верзный.

doe /dəʊ/ *n* са́мка.

dog /dɒg/ *n* соба́ка, пёс; (*fig*) пресле́довать *impf*. **dog-eared** /'dɒgɪəd/ *adj* захва́танный.

dogged /'dɒgɪd/ *adj* упо́рный.

dogma /'dɒgmə/ *n* до́гма. **dogmatic** /-'mætɪk/ *adj* догмати́ческий.

doings /'du:ɪŋz/ *n pl* дела́ *neut pl*.

doldrums /'dɒldrəmz/ *n*: **be in the ~** хандри́ть *impf*.

dole /dəʊl/ *n* посо́бие по безрабо́тице; *vt* (**~ *out***) выдава́ть *impf*, вы́дать *pf*.

doleful /'dəʊlfʊl/ *adj* ско́рбный.

doll /'dɒl/ *n* ку́кла.

dollar /'dɒlə(r)/ *n* до́ллар.

dollop /'dɒləp/ *n* соли́дная по́рция.

dolphin /'dɒlfɪn/ *n* дельфи́н.

domain /də'meɪn/ *n* (*estate*) владе́ние; (*field*) о́бласть.

dome /dəʊm/ *n* ку́пол.

domestic /də'mestɪk/ *adj* (*of household*; *animals*) дома́шний; (*of family*) семе́йный; (*polit*) вну́тренний; *n* прислу́га. **domesticate** /-'mestɪˌkeɪt/ *vt* приуча́ть *impf*, приучи́ть *pf*. **domesticity** /ˌdɒmə'stɪsɪtɪ/ *n* дома́шняя, семе́йная, жизнь.

domicile /'dɒmɪˌsaɪl/ *n* местожительство.

dominance /ˈdɒmɪnəns/ *n* господство. **dominant** /-mɪnənt/ *adj* преобладающий; господствующий. **dominate** /-mɪˌneɪt/ *vt* господствовать *impf* над *+instr.* **domineering** /-mɪˈnɪərɪŋ/ *adj* властный.

dominion /dəˈmɪnɪən/ *n* владычество; (*realm*) владение.

domino /ˈdɒmɪˌnəʊ/ *n* кость домино; *pl* (*game*) домино *neut indecl.*

don /dɒn/ *vt* надевать *impf*, надеть *pf.*

donate /dəʊˈneɪt/ *vt* жертвовать *impf*, по~ *pf.* **donation** /-ˈneɪʃ(ə)n/ *n* пожертвование.

donkey /ˈdɒŋkɪ/ *n* осёл.

donor /ˈdəʊnə(r)/ *n* жертвователь *m*; (*med*) донор.

doom /duːm/ *n* (*ruin*) гибель; *vt* обрекать *impf*, обречь *pf.*

door /dɔː(r)/ *n* дверь. **doorbell** *n* (дверной) звонок. **doorman** *n* швейцар. **doormat** *n* половик. **doorstep** *n* порог. **doorway** *n* дверной проём.

dope /dəʊp/ *n* (*drug*) наркотик; *vt* дурманить *impf*, о~ *pf.*

dormant /ˈdɔːmənt/ *adj* (*sleeping*) спящий; (*inactive*) бездействующий.

dormer window /ˈdɔːmə ˈwɪndəʊ/ *n* слуховое окно.

dormitory /ˈdɔːmɪtərɪ/ *n* общая спальня.

dormouse /ˈdɔːmaʊs/ *n* соня.

dorsal /ˈdɔːs(ə)l/ *adj* спинной.

dosage /ˈdəʊsɪdʒ/ *n* дозировка. **dose** /dəʊs/ *n* доза.

dossier /ˈdɒsɪə(r)/ *n* досье *neut indecl.*

dot /dɒt/ *n* точка; *vt* ставить *impf*, по~ *pf* точки на+*acc*; (*scatter*) усеивать *impf*, усеять *pf* (**with** +*instr*); **~ted line** пунктир.

dote /dəʊt/ *vi*: **~ on** обожать *impf.*

double /ˈdʌb(ə)l/ *adj* двойной; (*doubled*) удвоенный; **~-bass** контрабас; **~ bed** двуспальная кровать; **~-breasted** двубортный; **~-cross** обманывать *impf*, обмануть *pf*; **~-dealing** двурушничество; **~-decker** двухэтажный автобус; **~-edged** обоюдоострый; **~ glazing** двойные рамы *f pl*; **~ room** комната на двоих; *adv* вдвое; (*two together*) вдвоём; *n* двойное количество; (*person's*) двойник; *pl* (*sport*) парная игра; *vt & i* удваивать(ся) *impf*, удвоить(ся) *pf*; **~ back** возвращаться *impf*, вернуться *pf* назад; **~ up** (*in pain*) скрючиваться *impf*, скрючиться *pf*; (*share a room*) помещаться *impf*, поместиться *pf* вдвоём в одной комнате; (**~** *up as*) работать *impf* + *instr* по совместительству.

doubt /daʊt/ *n* сомнение; *vt* сомневаться *impf* в+*prep.* **doubtful** /-fʊl/ *adj* сомнительный. **doubtless** /-lɪs/ *adv* несомненно.

dough /dəʊ/ *n* тесто. **doughnut** *n* пончик.

douse /daʊs/ *vt* (*drench*) заливать *impf*, залить *pf.*

dove /dʌv/ *n* голубь *m.* **dovetail** *n* ласточкин хвост.

dowdy /ˈdaʊdɪ/ *adj* неэлегантный.

down[1] /daʊn/ *n* (*fluff*) пух.

down[2] /daʊn/ *adv* (*motion*) вниз; (*position*) внизу; **be ~ with** (*ill*) болеть *impf* +*instr*; *prep* вниз с+*gen*, по+*dat*; (*along*) (вдоль) по+*dat*; *vt*: (*gulp*) опрокидывать *impf*, опрокинуть *pf*;

~-and-out бродя́га *m*; **~cast**, **~-hearted** уны́лый. **downfall** *n* ги́бель. **downhill** *adv* по́д гору. **download** *vt* (*comput*) загружа́ть *impf*, загрузи́ть *pf*. **downpour** *n* ли́вень *m*. **downright** *adj* я́вный; *adv* соверше́нно. **downstairs** *adv* (*motion*) вниз; (*position*) внизу́. **downstream** *adv* вниз по тече́нию. **down-to-earth** *adj* реалисти́ческий. **downtrodden** /'daʊn,trɒd(ə)n/ *adj* угнетённый.

dowry /'daʊərɪ/ *n* прида́ное *sb*.

doze /dəʊz/ *vi* дрема́ть *impf*.

dozen /'dʌz(ə)n/ *n* дю́жина.

drab /dræb/ *adj* бесцве́тный.

draft /drɑːft/ *n* (*outline, rough copy*) набро́сок; (*document*) прое́кт; (*econ*) тра́тта; *see also* **draught**; *vt* составля́ть *impf*, соста́вить *pf* план, прое́кт, +*gen*.

drag /dræg/ *vt* тащи́ть *impf*; (*river etc.*) драги́ровать *impf* & *pf*; **~ on** (*vi*) затя́гиваться *impf*, затяну́ться *pf*; *n* (*burden*) обу́за; (*on cigarette*) затя́жка; **in ~** в же́нской оде́жде.

dragon /'drægən/ *n* драко́н. **dragonfly** *n* стрекоза́.

drain /dreɪn/ *n* водосто́к; (*leakage*; *fig*) уте́чка; *vt* осуша́ть *impf*, осуши́ть *pf*; *vi* спуска́ться *impf*, спусти́ться *pf*. **drainage** /'dreɪnɪdʒ/ *n* дрена́ж; (*system*) канализа́ция.

drake /dreɪk/ *n* се́лезень *m*.

drama /'drɑːmə/ *n* дра́ма; (*quality*) драмати́зм. **dramatic** /drə'mætɪk/ *adj* драмати́ческий. **dramatist** /'dræmətɪst/ *n* драмату́рг. **dramatize** /'dræmə,taɪz/ *vt* драматизи́ровать *impf* & *pf*.

drape /dreɪp/ *vt* драпирова́ть *impf*, за~ *pf*; *n* драниро́вка.

drastic /'dræstɪk/ *adj* радика́льный.

draught /drɑːft/ *n* (*air*) сквозня́к; (*traction*) тя́га; *pl* (*game*) ша́шки *f pl*; *see also* **draft**; **there is a ~** сквози́т; **~ beer** пи́во из бо́чки. **draughtsman** /'drɑːftsmən/ *n* чертёжник. **draughty** /'drɑːftɪ/ *adj*: **it is ~ here** здесь ду́ет.

draw /drɔː/ *n* (*in lottery*) ро́зыгрыш; (*attraction*) прима́нка; (*drawn game*) ничья́; *vt* (*pull*) тяну́ть *impf*, по~ *pf*; таска́ть *indet*, тащи́ть *det*; (*curtains*) задёргивать *impf*, задёрнуть *pf* (занаве́ски); (*attract*) привлека́ть *impf*, привле́чь *pf*; (*pull out*) выта́скивать *impf*, вы́тащить *pf*; (*sword*) обнажа́ть *impf*, обнажи́ть *pf*; (*lots*) броса́ть *impf*, бро́сить *pf* (жре́бий); (*water*; *inspiration*) че́рпать *impf*, черпну́ть *pf*; (*evoke*) вызыва́ть *impf*, вы́звать *pf*; (*conclusion*) выводи́ть *impf*, вы́вести *pf* (заключе́ние); (*diagram*) черти́ть *impf*, на~ *pf*; (*picture*) рисова́ть *impf*, на~ *pf*; *vi* (*sport*) сыгра́ть *pf* вничью́; **~ aside** отводи́ть *impf*, отвести́ *pf* в сто́рону; **~ back** (*withdraw*) отступа́ть *impf*, отступи́ть *pf*; **~ in** втя́гивать *impf*, втяну́ть *pf*; (*train*) входи́ть *impf*, войти́ *pf* в ста́нцию; (*car*) подходи́ть *impf*, подойти́ *pf* (**to** к + *dat*); (*days*) стано́виться *impf* коро́че; **~ out** вытя́гивать *impf*, вы́тянуть *pf*; (*money*) выпи́сывать *impf*, вы́писать *pf*; (*train/car*) выходи́ть *impf*, вы́йти *pf* (со ста́нции/на доро́гу); **~ up** (*car*) подходи́ть *impf*, подойти́ *pf* (**to** к + *dat*); (*document*) составля́ть *impf*, соста́вить *pf*.

drawback *n* недоста́ток. **drawbridge** *n* подъёмный мост. **drawer** /'drɔːə(r)/ *n* я́щик. **drawing** /'drɔːɪŋ/ *n* (*action*) рисова́ние, черче́ние; (*object*) рису́нок, чертёж; **~-board** чертёжная доска́; **~-pin** кно́пка; **~-room** гости́ная *sb.*

drawl /drɔːl/ *n* протя́жное произноше́ние.

dread /dred/ *n* страх; *vt* боя́ться *impf* +*gen.* **dreadful** /'dredfʊl/ *adj* ужа́сный.

dream /driːm/ *n* сон; (*fantasy*) мечта́; *vi* ви́деть *impf*, у~ *pf* сон; **~ of** ви́деть *impf*, у~ *pf* во сне́; (*fig*) мечта́ть *impf* о+*prep.*

dreary /'drɪərɪ/ *adj* (*weather*) па́смурный; (*boring*) ску́чный.

dredge /dredʒ/ *vt* (*river etc.*) драги́ровать *impf* & *pf.* **dredger** /-dʒə(r)/ *n* дра́га.

dregs /dregz/ *n pl* оса́дки (-ков) *pl.*

drench /drentʃ/ *vt* прома́чивать *impf*, промочи́ть *pf*; **get ~ed** промока́ть *impf*, промо́кнуть *pf.*

dress /dres/ *n* пла́тье; (*apparel*) оде́жда; **~ circle** бельэта́ж; **~maker** портни́ха; **~ rehearsal** генера́льная репети́ция; *vt* & *i* одева́ть(ся) *impf*, оде́ть(ся) *pf*; *vt* (*cul*) приправля́ть *impf*, припра́вить *pf*; (*med*) перевя́зывать *impf*, перевяза́ть *pf*; **~ up** наряжа́ться *impf*, наряди́ться *pf* (**as** + *instr*).

dresser /'dresə(r)/ *n* ку́хонный шкаф.

dressing /'dresɪŋ/ *n* (*cul*) припра́ва; (*med*) перевя́зка; **~-gown** хала́т; **~-room** убо́рная *sb*; **~-table** туале́тный сто́лик.

dribble /'drɪb(ə)l/ *vi* (*person*) пуска́ть *impf*, пусти́ть *pf* слю́ни; (*sport*) вести́ *impf* мяч.

dried /draɪd/ *adj* сушёный. **drier** /draɪə(r)/ *n* суши́лка.

drift /drɪft/ *n* (*meaning*) смысл; (*snow*) сугро́б; *vi* плыть *impf* по тече́нию; (*naut*) дрейфова́ть *impf*; (*snow etc.*) скопля́ться *impf*, скопи́ться *pf*; **~ apart** расходи́ться *impf*, разойти́сь *pf.*

drill[1] /drɪl/ *n* сверло́; (*dentist's*) бур; *vt* сверли́ть *impf*, про~ *pf.*

drill[2] /drɪl/ *vt* (*mil*) обуча́ть *impf*, обучи́ть *pf* стро́ю; *vi* проходи́ть *impf*, пройти́ *pf* строеву́ю подгото́вку; *n* строева́я подгото́вка.

drink /drɪŋk/ *n* напи́ток; *vt* пить *impf*, вы́~ *pf*; **~-driving** вожде́ние в нетре́звом состоя́нии. **drinking-water** /'drɪŋkɪŋ 'wɔːtə(r)/ *n* питьева́я вода́.

drip /drɪp/ *n* (*action*) ка́панье; (*drop*) ка́пля; *vi* ка́пать *impf*, ка́пнуть *pf.*

drive /draɪv/ *n* (*journey*) езда́; (*excursion*) прогу́лка; (*campaign*) похо́д, камп́ания; (*energy*) эне́ргия; (*tech*) приво́д; (*driveway*) подъездна́я доро́га; *vt* (*urge*; *chase*) гоня́ть *indet*, гнать *det*; (*vehicle*) води́ть *indet*, вести́ *det*; управля́ть *impf* +*instr*; (*convey*) вози́ть *indet*, везти́ *det*, по~ *pf*; *vi* (*travel*) е́здить *indet*, е́хать *det*, по~ *pf*; *vt* доводи́ть *impf*, довести́ *pf* (**to** до+*gen*); (*nail etc.*) вбива́ть *impf*, вбить *pf* (**into** в+*acc*); **~ away** *vt* прогоня́ть *impf*, прогна́ть *pf*; *vi* уезжа́ть *impf*, уе́хать *pf*; **~ up** подъезжа́ть *impf*, подъе́хать *pf* (**to** к+*dat*).

driver /'draɪvə(r)/ *n* (*of vehicle*)

води́тель *m*, шофёр. **driving** /ˈdraɪvɪŋ/ *adj* (*force*) дви́жущий; (*rain*) проливно́й; **~-licence** води́тельские права́ *neut pl*; **~-test** экза́мен на получе́ние води́тельских прав; **~-wheel** веду́щее колесо́.

drizzle /ˈdrɪz(ə)l/ *n* ме́лкий до́ждь *m*; *vi* мороси́ть *impf.*

drone /drəʊn/ *n* (*bee*; *idler*) тру́тень *m*; (*of voice*) жужжа́ние; (*of engine*) гул; *vi* (*buzz*) жужжа́ть *impf*; (**~** *on*) бубни́ть *impf.*

drool /dru:l/ *vi* пуска́ть *impf*, пусти́ть *pf* слю́ни.

droop /dru:p/ *vi* поника́ть *impf*, пони́кнуть *pf.*

drop /drɒp/ *n* (*of liquid*) ка́пля; (*fall*) паде́ние, пониже́ние; *vt* & *i* (*price*) снижа́ть(ся) *impf*, сни́зить(ся) *pf*; *vi* (*fall*) па́дать *impf*, упа́сть *pf*; *vt* (*let fall*) роня́ть *impf*, урони́ть *pf*; (*abandon*) броса́ть *impf*, бро́сить *pf*; **~ behind** отстава́ть *impf*, отста́ть *pf*; **~ in** заходи́ть *impf*, зайти́ *pf* (**on** к+*dat*); **~ off** (*fall asleep*) засыпа́ть *impf*, засну́ть *pf*; (*from car*) выса́живать *impf*, вы́садить *pf*; **~ out** выбыва́ть *impf*, вы́быть *pf* (**of** из +*gen*). **droppings** /ˈdrɒpɪŋz/ *n pl* помёт.

drought /draʊt/ *n* за́суха.

droves /drəʊvz/ *n pl*: **in ~** то́лпами.

drown /draʊn/ *vt* топи́ть *impf*, у**~** *pf*; (*sound*) заглуша́ть *impf*, заглуши́ть *pf*; *vi* тону́ть *impf*, у**~** *pf.*

drowsy /ˈdraʊzɪ/ *adj* сонли́вый.

drudgery /ˈdrʌdʒərɪ/ *n* ну́дная рабо́та.

drug /drʌg/ *n* медикаме́нт; (*narcotic*) нарко́тик; **~ addict** наркома́н, **~**ка; *vt* дава́ть *impf*, дать *pf* нарко́тик+*dat.*

drum /drʌm/ *n* бараба́н; *vi* бить *impf* в бараба́н; бараба́нить *impf*; **~ sth into s.o.** вда́лбливать *impf*, вдолби́ть *pf* + *dat of person* в го́лову. **drummer** /ˈdrʌmə(r)/ *n* бараба́нщик.

drunk /drʌŋk/ *adj* пья́ный. **drunkard** /ˈdrʌŋkəd/ *n* пья́ница *m* & *f.* **drunken** /ˈdrʌŋkən/ *adj* пья́ный; **~ driving** вожде́ние в нетре́звом состоя́нии. **drunkenness** /ˈdrʌŋkənnɪs/ *n* пья́нство.

dry /draɪ/ *adj* сухо́й; **~ land** су́ша; *vt* суши́ть *impf*, вы́**~** *pf*; (*wipe dry*) вытира́ть *impf*, вы́тереть *pf*; *vi* со́хнуть *impf*, вы́**~**, про**~** *pf.* **dry-cleaning** /draɪˈkli:nɪŋ/ *n* химчи́стка. **dryness** /ˈdraɪnɪs/ *n* су́хость.

dual /ˈdju:əl/ *adj* двойно́й; (*joint*) совме́стный; **~-purpose** двойно́го назначе́ния.

dub[1] /dʌb/ *vt* (*nickname*) прозыва́ть *impf*, прозва́ть *pf.*

dub[2] /dʌb/ *vt* (*cin*) дубли́ровать *impf* & *pf.*

dubious /ˈdju:bɪəs/ *adj* сомни́тельный.

duchess /ˈdʌtʃɪs/ *n* герцоги́ня.

duchy /ˈdʌtʃɪ/ *n* ге́рцогство.

duck[1] /dʌk/ *n* (*bird*) у́тка.

duck[2] /dʌk/ *vt* (*immerse*) окуна́ть *impf*, окуну́ть *pf*; (*one's head*) нагну́ть *pf*; (*evade*) увёртываться *impf*, уверну́ться *pf* от+*gen*; *vi* (**~** *down*) наклоня́ться *impf*, наклони́ться *pf.*

duckling /ˈdʌklɪŋ/ *n* утёнок

duct /ˈdʌkt/ *n* прохо́д; (*anat*) прото́к.

dud /dʌd/ *n* (*forgery*) подде́лка; (*shell*) неразорва́вшийся снаря́д; *adj* подде́льный; (*worthless*) него́дный.

due /dju:/ *n* (*credit*) до́лжное *sb*; *pl* взно́сы *m pl*; *adj* (*proper*) до́лжный, надлежа́щий; *predic* (*expected*) до́лжен (-жна́); **in ~ course** со вре́менем; **~ south** пря́мо на юг; **~ to** благодаря́+*dat*.

duel /'dju:əl/ *n* дуэ́ль.

duet /dju:'et/ *n* дуэ́т.

duke /dju:k/ *n* ге́рцог.

dull /dʌl/ *adj* (*tedious*) ску́чный; (*colour*) ту́склый, (*weather*) па́смурный; (*not sharp*; *stupid*) тупо́й; *vt* притупля́ть *impf*, притупи́ть *pf*.

duly /'dju:lɪ/ *adv* надлежа́щим о́бразом; (*punctually*) своевре́менно.

dumb /dʌm/ *adj* немо́й. **dumbfounded** /'dʌmfəʊndɪd/ *adj* ошара́шенный.

dummy /'dʌmɪ/ *n* (*tailor's*) манеке́н; (*baby's*) со́ска; **~ run** испыта́тельный рейс.

dump /dʌmp/ *n* сва́лка; *vt* сва́ливать *impf*, свали́ть *pf*.

dumpling /'dʌmplɪŋ/ *n* клёцка.

dumpy /'dʌmpɪ/ *adj* призе́мистый.

dune /dju:n/ *n* дю́на.

dung /dʌŋ/ *n* наво́з.

dungarees /ˌdʌŋgə'ri:z/ *n pl* комбинезо́н.

dungeon /'dʌndʒ(ə)n/ *n* темни́ца.

duo /'dju:əʊ/ *n* па́ра; (*mus*) дуэ́т.

dupe /dju:p/ *vt* надува́ть *impf*, наду́ть *pf*; *n* простофи́ля *m* & *f*.

duplicate *n* /'dju:plɪkət/ ко́пия; **in ~** в двух экземпля́рах; *adj* запасно́й; *vt* /'dju:plɪkeɪt/ размножа́ть *impf*, размно́жить *pf* **duplicity** /dju:'plɪsɪtɪ/ *n* двули́чность.

durability /ˌdjʊərə'bɪlɪtɪ/ *n* про́чность. **durable** /'djʊərəb(ə)l/ *adj* про́чный. **duration** /djʊə'reɪʃ(ə)n/ *n* продолжи́тельность.

duress /djʊə'res/ *n* принужде́ние; **under ~** под давле́нием.

during /'djʊərɪŋ/ *prep* во вре́мя +*gen*; (*throughout*) в тече́ние +*gen*.

dusk /dʌsk/ *n* су́мерки (-рек) *pl*.

dust /dʌst/ *n* пыль; **~bin** му́сорный я́щик; **~-jacket** суперобло́жка; **~man** му́сорщик; **~pan** сово́к; *vt* & *i* (*clean*) стира́ть *impf*, стере́ть *pf* пыль (с+*gen*); (*sprinkle*) посыпа́ть *impf*, посы́пать *pf* *sth* +*acc*, *with* +*instr*. **duster** /'dʌstə(r)/ *n* пы́льная тря́пка. **dusty** /'dʌstɪ/ *adj* пы́льный.

Dutch /dʌtʃ/ *adj* голла́ндский; *n*: **the ~** голла́ндцы *m pl*. **Dutchman** *n* голла́ндец. **Dutchwoman** *n* голла́ндка.

dutiful /'dju:tɪˌfʊl/ *adj* послу́шный. **duty** /'dju:tɪ/ *n* (*obligation*) долг; обя́занность; (*office*) дежу́рство; (*tax*) по́шлина; **be on ~** дежу́рить *impf*; **~-free** *adj* беспо́шлинный.

duvet /'du:veɪ/ *n* стёганое одея́ло.

DVD *abbr* (*of* **digital versatile disk**) DVD; **~ player** DVD-пле́ер.

dwarf /dwɔ:f/ *n* ка́рлик; *vt* (*tower above*) возвыша́ться *impf*, возвы́ситься *pf* над+*instr*.

dwell /dwel/ *vi* обита́ть *impf*; **~ upon** остана́вливаться *impf* на+*prep*. **dweller** /'dwelə(r)/ *n* жи́тель *m*. **dwelling** /'dwelɪŋ/ *n* жили́ще.

dwindle /'dwɪnd(ə)l/ *vi* убыва́ть *impf*, убы́ть *pf*.

dye /daɪ/ *n* краси́тель *m*; *vt* ок-

ра́шивать *impf*, окра́сить *pf*.
dynamic /daɪ'næmɪk/ *adj* динами́ческий. **dynamics** /-mɪks/ *n pl* дина́мика.
dynamite /'daɪnə,maɪt/ *n* динами́т.
dynamo /'daɪnə,məʊ/ *n* дина́мо *neut indecl*.
dynasty /'dɪnəstɪ/ *n* дина́стия.
dysentery /'dɪsəntərɪ/ *n* дизентери́я.
dyslexia /dɪs'leksɪə/ *n* дисле́ксия. **dyslexic** /-'leksɪk/ *adj*: **he is ~** он дисле́ктик.

E

each /i:tʃ/ *adj & pron* ка́ждый; **~ other** друг дру́га (*dat* -гу, *etc.*).
eager /'i:gə(r)/ *adj* (*pupil*) усе́рдный; **I am ~ to** мне не те́рпится +*inf*; о́чень жела́ю +*inf*. **eagerly** /-lɪ/ *adv* с нетерпе́нием; жа́дно. **eagerness** /-nɪs/ *n* си́льное жела́ние.
eagle /'i:g(ə)l/ *n* орёл.
ear[1] /ɪə(r)/ *n* (*corn*) ко́лос.
ear[2] /ɪə(r)/ *n* (*anat*) у́хо; (*sense*) слух; **~-ache** боль в у́хе; **~drum** бараба́нная перепо́нка; **~mark** (*assign*) предназнача́ть *impf*, предназна́чить *pf*; **~phone** нау́шник; **~ring** серьга́; (*clip-on*) клипс; **~shot**: **within/out of ~** в преде́лах/вне преде́лов слы́шимости.
earl /ɜ:l/ *n* граф.
early /'ɜ:lɪ/ *adj* ра́нний; *adv* ра́но.
earn /ɜ:n/ *vt* зараба́тывать *impf*, зарабо́тать *pf*; (*deserve*) заслу́живать *impf*, заслужи́ть *pf*. **earnings** /'ɜ:nɪŋz/ *n pl* за́работок.
earnest /'ɜ:nɪst/ *adj* серьёзный; *n*: **in ~** всерьёз.
earth /ɜ:θ/ *n* земля́; (*soil*) по́чва; *vt* заземля́ть *impf*, заземли́ть *pf*. **earthenware** /'ɜ:θ(ə)n,weə(r)/ *adj* гли́няный. **earthly** /'ɜ:θlɪ/ *adj* земно́й. **earthquake** *n* землетрясе́ние. **earthy** /'ɜ:θɪ/ *adj* земли́стый; (*coarse*) гру́бый.
earwig /'ɪəwɪg/ *n* уховёртка.
ease /i:z/ *n* (*facility*) лёгкость; (*unconstraint*) непринуждённость; **with ~** легко́; *vt* облегча́ть *impf*, облегчи́ть *pf*; *vi* успока́иваться *impf*, успоко́иться *pf*.
easel /'i:z(ə)l/ *n* мольбе́рт.
east /i:st/ *n* восто́к; (*naut*) ост; *adj* восто́чный. **easterly** /'i:stəlɪ/ *adj* восто́чный. **eastern** /'i:st(ə)n/ *adj* восто́чный. **eastward(s)** /'i:stwəd(z)/ *adv* на восто́к, к восто́ку.
Easter /'i:stə(r)/ *n* Па́сха.
easy /'i:zɪ/ *adj* лёгкий; (*unconstrained*) непринуждённый; **~-going** ужи́вчивый.
eat /i:t/ *vt* есть *impf*, с~ *pf*; ку́шать *impf*, по~, с~ *pf*; **~ away** разъеда́ть *impf*, разъе́сть *pf*; **~ into** въеда́ться *impf*, въе́сться *pf* в+*acc*; **~ up** доеда́ть *impf*, дое́сть *pf*. **eatable** /i:təb(ə)l/ *adj* съедо́бный.
eaves /i:vz/ *n pl* стреха́. **eavesdrop** /'i:vzdrɒp/ *vi* подслу́шивать *impf*.
ebb /eb/ *n* (*tide*) отли́в; (*fig*) упа́док.
ebony /'ebənɪ/ *n* чёрное де́рево.
ebullient /ɪ'bʌlɪənt/ *adj* кипу́чий.
EC *abbr* (*of* **European Community**) Европе́йское соо́бщество.
eccentric /ɪk'sentrɪk/ *n* чуда́к; *adj* эксцентри́чный.
ecclesiastical /ɪ,kli:zɪ'æstɪk(ə)l/ *adj* церко́вный.

echo /ˈekəʊ/ *n* э́хо; *vi* (*resound*) отража́ться *impf*, отрази́ться *pf*; *vt* (*repeat*) повторя́ть *impf*, повтори́ть *pf*.

eclipse /ɪˈklɪps/ *n* затме́ние; *vt* затмева́ть *impf*, затми́ть *pf*.

ecological /ˌiːkəˈlɒdʒɪk(ə)l/ *adj* экологи́ческий. **ecology** /ɪˈkɒlədʒɪ/ *n* эколо́гия.

economic /ˌiːkəˈnɒmɪk/ *adj* экономи́ческий. **economical** /ˌiːkəˈnɒmɪk(ə)l/ *adj* эконо́мный. **economist** /ɪˈkɒnəmɪst/ *n* эконо-ми́ст. **economize** /ɪˈkɒnəˌmaɪz/ *vt & i* эконо́мить *impf*, с~ *pf*. **economy** /ɪˈkɒnəmɪ/ *n* эконо́мика; (*saving*) эконо́мия.

ecstasy /ˈekstəsɪ/ *n* экста́з. **ecstatic** /ekˈstætɪk/ *adj* экстати́ческий.

eddy /ˈedɪ/ *n* водоворо́т.

edge /edʒ/ *n* край; (*blade*) ле́звие; **on** ~ в не́рвном состоя́нии; **have the** ~ **on** име́ть *impf* преиму́щество над+*instr*; *vt* (*border*) окаймля́ть *impf*, окайми́ть *pf*; *vi* пробира́ться *impf*, пробра́ться *pf*. **edging** /ˈedʒɪŋ/ *n* кайма́. **edgy** /ˈedʒɪ/ *adj* раздражи́тельный.

edible /ˈedɪb(ə)l/ *adj* съедо́бный.

edict /ˈiːdɪkt/ *n* ука́з.

edifice /ˈedɪfɪs/ *n* зда́ние. **edifying** /ˈedɪˌfaɪɪŋ/ *adj* назида́тельный.

edit /ˈedɪt/ *vt* редакти́ровать *impf*, от~ *pf*; (*cin*) монти́ровать *impf*, с~ *pf*. **edition** /ɪˈdɪʃ(ə)n/ *n* изда́ние; (*number of copies*) тира́ж. **editor** /ˈedɪtə(r)/ *n* реда́ктор. **editorial** /ˌedɪˈtɔːrɪəl/ *n* передова́я статья́; *adj* реда́кторский, редакцио́нный.

educate /ˈedjʊˌkeɪt/ *vt* дава́ть *impf*, дать *pf* образова́ние +*dat*; **where was he educated?** где он получи́л образова́ние? **educated** /-ˌkeɪtɪd/ *adj* образо́ванный. **education** /-ˈkeɪʃ(ə)n/ *n* образова́ние. **educational** /-ˈkeɪʃən(ə)l/ *adj* образова́тельный; (*instructive*) уче́бный.

eel /iːl/ *n* у́горь *m*.

eerie /ˈɪərɪ/ *adj* жу́ткий.

effect /ɪˈfekt/ *n* (*result*) сле́дствие; (*validity*; *influence*) де́йствие; (*impression*; *theat*) эффе́кт; **in** ~ факти́чески; **take** ~ вступа́ть *impf*, вступи́ть *pf* в си́лу; (*medicine*) начина́ть *impf*, нача́ть *pf* де́йствовать; *vt* производи́ть *impf*, произвести́ *pf*. **effective** /-ˈfektɪv/ *adj* эффекти́вный; (*striking*) эффе́ктный; (*actual*) факти́ческий. **effectiveness** /-ˈfektɪvnɪs/ *n* эффекти́вность.

effeminate /ɪˈfemɪnət/ *adj* женоподо́бный.

effervesce /ˌefəˈves/ *vi* пузы́риться *impf*. **effervescent** /-ˈvesənt/ *adj* (*fig*) и́скря́щийся.

efficiency /ɪˈfɪʃənsɪ/ *n* эффекти́вность. **efficient** /-ˈfɪʃ(ə)nt/ *adj* эффекти́вный; (*person*) организо́ванный.

effigy /ˈefɪdʒɪ/ *n* изображе́ние.

effort /ˈefət/ *n* уси́лие.

effrontery /ɪˈfrʌntərɪ/ *n* на́глость.

effusive /ɪˈfjuːsɪv/ *adj* экспанси́вный.

e.g. *abbr* напр.

egalitarian /ɪˌgælɪˈteərɪən/ *adj* эгалита́рный.

egg[1] /eg/ *n* яйцо́; ~**cup** рю́мка для яйца́; ~**shell** яи́чная скорлупа́.

egg[2] /eg/ *vt*: ~ **on** подстрека́ть *impf*, подстрекну́ть *pf*.

ego /ˈiːgəʊ/ *n* «Я». **egocentric** /ˌiːgəʊˈsentrɪk/ *adj* эгоцентри́ческий. **egoism** /ˈiːgəʊˌɪz(ə)m/ *n* эгоизм. **ego(t)ist** /ˈiːgəʊ(t)ɪst/ *n* эгоист, ~ка. **ego(t)istical** /ˌiːgəˈ(t)ɪstɪk(ə)l/ *adj* эгоцентрический. **egotism** /ˈiːgəˌtɪz(ə)m/ *n* эготизм.

Egypt /ˈiːdʒɪpt/ *n* Египет. **Egyptian** /ɪˈdʒɪpʃ(ə)n/ *n* египтянин, -янка; *adj* египетский.

eiderdown /ˈaɪdəˌdaʊn/ *n* пуховое одеяло.

eight /eɪt/ *adj* & *n* восемь; (*number 8*) восьмёрка. **eighteen** /eɪˈtiːn/ *adj* & *n* восемнадцать. **eighteenth** /eɪˈtiːnθ/ *adj* & *n* восемнадцатый. **eighth** /eɪtθ/ *adj* & *n* восьмой; (*fraction*) восьмая *sb.* **eightieth** /ˈeɪtɪɪθ/ *adj* & *n* восьмидесятый. **eighty** /ˈeɪtɪ/ *adj* & *n* восемьдесят; *pl* (*decade*) восьмидесятые годы (-дов) *m pl.*

either /ˈaɪðə(r)/ *adj* & *pron* (*one of two*) один из двух, тот или другой; (*both*) и тот, и другой; оба; (*one or other*) любой; *adv* & *conj*: ~ ... **or** или… или, либо… либо.

eject /ɪˈdʒekt/ *vt* выбрасывать *impf*, выбросить *pf*; *vi* (*pilot*) катапультироваться *impf* & *pf*.

eke /iːk/ *vt*: ~ **out a living** перебиваться *impf*, перебиться *pf* кое-как.

elaborate *adj* /ɪˈlæbərət/ (*ornate*) витиеватый; (*detailed*) подробный; *vt* /ɪˈlæbəˌreɪt/ разрабатывать *impf*, разработать *pf*; (*detail*) уточнять *impf*, уточнить *pf*.

elapse /ɪˈlæps/ *vi* проходить *impf*, пройти *pf*; (*expire*) истекать *impf*, истечь *pf*.

elastic /ɪˈlæstɪk/ *n* резинка; *adj* эластичный, ~ **band** резинка. **elasticity** /-ˈstɪsɪtɪ/ *n* эластичность.

elated /ɪˈleɪtɪd/ *adj* в восторге. **elation** /ɪˈleɪʃ(ə)n/ *n* восторг.

elbow /ˈelbəʊ/ *n* локоть *m*; *vt*: ~ **(one's way) through** проталкиваться *impf*, протолкнуться *pf* через+*acc*.

elder[1] /ˈeldə(r)/ *n* (*tree*) бузина.

elder[2] /ˈeldə(r)/ *n* (*person*) старец; *pl* старшие *sb*; *adj* старший. **elderly** /ˈeldəlɪ/ *adj* пожилой. **eldest** /ˈeldɪst/ *adj* старший.

elect /ɪˈlekt/ *adj* избранный; *vt* избирать *impf*, избрать *pf*. **election** /ɪˈlekʃ(ə)n/ *n* выборы *m pl*. **elector** /ɪˈlektə(r)/ *n* избиратель *m*. **electoral** /ɪˈlektər(ə)l/ *adj* избирательный. **electorate** /ɪˈlektərət/ *n* избиратели *m pl*.

electric(al) /ɪˈlektrɪk((ə)l)/ *adj* электрический; ~ **shock** удар электрическим током. **electrician** /ˌɪlekˈtrɪʃ(ə)n/ *n* электрик. **electricity** /ˌɪlekˈtrɪsɪtɪ/ *n* электричество. **electrify** /ɪˈlektrɪˌfaɪ/ *vt* (*convert to electricity*) электрифицировать *impf* & *pf*; (*charge with electricity*; *fig*) электризовать *impf*, на~ *pf*. **electrode** /ɪˈlektrəʊd/ *n* электрод. **electron** /ɪˈlektrɒn/ *n* электрон. **electronic** /ˌɪlekˈtrɒnɪk/ *adj* электронный. **electronics** /ˌɪlekˈtrɒnɪks/ *n* электроника.

electrocute /ɪˈlektrəˌkjuːt/ *vt* убивать *impf*, убить *pf* электрическим током; (*execute*) казнить *impf* & *pf* на электрическом стуле. **electrolysis** /ˌɪlekˈtrɒlɪsɪs/ *n* электролиз.

elegance /ˈelɪgəns/ *n* элегантность. **elegant** /-gənt/ *adj* элегантный.

elegy /ˈelɪdʒɪ/ *n* элегия.

element /ˈelɪmənt/ *n* элемент;

(*earth, wind, etc.*) стихи́я; **be in one's ~** быть в свое́й стихи́и. **elemental** /-'ment(ə)l/ *adj* стихи́йный. **elementary** /-'mentərı/ *adj* элемента́рный; (*school etc.*) нача́льный.

elephant /'elıfənt/ *n* слон.

elevate /'elı,veıt/ *vt* поднима́ть *impf*, подня́ть *pf*. **elevated** /-,veıtıd/ *adj* возвы́шенный. **elevation** /-,veıʃ(ə)n/ *n* (*height*) высота́. **elevator** /-,veıtə(r)/ *n* (*lift*) лифт.

eleven /ı'lev(ə)n/ *adj* & *n* оди́ннадцать. **eleventh** /-'levənθ/ *adj* & *n* оди́ннадцатый; **at the ~ hour** в после́днюю мину́ту.

elf /elf/ *n* эльф.

elicit /ı'lısıt/ *vt* (*obtain*) выявля́ть *impf*, вы́явить *pf*; (*evoke*) вызыва́ть *impf*, вы́звать *pf*.

eligible /'elıdʒıb(ə)l/ *adj* име́ющий пра́во (**for** на+*acc*); (*bachelor*) подходя́щий.

eliminate /ı'lımı,neıt/ *vt* устраня́ть *impf*, устрани́ть *pf*; (*rule out*) исключа́ть *impf*, исключи́ть *pf*.

élite /eı'li:t/ *n* эли́та.

ellipse /ı'lıps/ *n* э́ллипс. **elliptic(al)** /ı'lıptık((ə)l)/ *adj* эллипти́ческий.

elm /elm/ *n* вяз.

elongate /'i:lɒŋ,geıt/ *vt* удлиня́ть *impf*, удлини́ть *pf*.

elope /ı'ləʊp/ *vi* бежа́ть *det* (с возлю́бленным).

eloquence /'eləkwəns/ *n* красноре́чие. **eloquent** /-kwənt/ *adj* красноречи́вый.

else /els/ *adv* (*besides*) ещё; (*instead*) друго́й; (*with neg*) бо́льше; **nobody ~** никто́ бо́льше; **or ~** и́наче; а (не) то; и́ли же; **s.o. ~** кто-нибу́дь друго́й; **something ~?** ещё что-нибудь? **elsewhere** *adv* (*place*) в друго́м ме́сте; (*direction*) в друго́е ме́сто.

elucidate /ı'lu:sı,deıt/ *vt* разъясня́ть *impf*, разъясни́ть *pf*.

elude /ı'lu:d/ *vt* избега́ть *impf* +*gen*. **elusive** /-'lu:sıv/ *adj* неулови́мый.

emaciated /ı'meısı,eıtıd/ *adj* истощённый.

email /'i:meıl/ *n* (*system, letters*) электро́нная по́чта; (*letter*) электро́нное письмо́; **~ address** электро́нный а́дрес

emanate /'emə,neıt/ *vi* исходи́ть *impf* (**from** из, от, +*gen*).

emancipate /ı'mænsı,peıt/ *vt* эмансипи́ровать *impf* & *pf*. **emancipation** /-'peıʃ(ə)n/ *n* эмансипа́ция.

embankment /ım'bæŋkmənt/ *n* (*river*) на́бережная *sb*; (*rly*) на́сыпь.

embargo /em'bɑ:gəʊ/ *n* эмба́рго *neut indecl*.

embark /ım'bɑ:k/ *vi* сади́ться *impf*, сесть *pf* на кора́бль; **~ upon** предпринима́ть *impf*, предприня́ть *pf*. **embarkation** /,embɑ:'keıʃ(ə)n/ *n* поса́дка (на кора́бль).

embarrass /ım'bærəs/ *vt* смуща́ть *impf*, смути́ть *pf*; **be ~ed** чу́вствовать *impf* себя́ неудо́бно. **embarrassing** /-sıŋ/ *adj* неудо́бный. **embarrassment** /-mənt/ *n* смуще́ние.

embassy /'embəsı/ *n* посо́льство.

embedded /ım'bedıd/ *adj* вре́занный.

embellish /ım'belıʃ/ *vt* (*adorn*) украша́ть *impf*, укра́сить *pf*; (*story*) прикра́шивать *impf*, прикра́сить *pf*. **embellishment** /-mənt/ *n* украше́ние.

embers /'embəz/ *n pl* тле́ющие

уго́льки́ *m pl.*
embezzle /ɪm'bez(ə)l/ *vt* растра́чивать *impf*, растра́тить *pf.* **embezzlement** /-mənt/ *n* растра́та.
embittered /ɪm'bɪtəd/ *adj* озло́бленный.
emblem /'embləm/ *n* эмбле́ма.
embodiment /ɪm'bɒdɪmənt/ *n* воплоще́ние. **embody** /ɪm'bɒdɪ/ *vt* воплоща́ть *impf*, воплоти́ть *pf.*
emboss /ɪm'bɒs/ *vt* чека́нить *impf*, вы́~, от~ *pf.*
embrace /ɪm'breɪs/ *n* объя́тие; *vi* обнима́ться *impf*, обня́ться *pf*; *vt* обнима́ть *impf*, обня́ть *pf*; (*accept*) принима́ть *impf*, приня́ть *pf*; (*include*) охва́тывать *impf*, охвати́ть *pf.*
embroider /ɪm'brɔɪdə(r)/ *vt* выши́вать *impf*, вы́шить *pf*; (*story*) прикра́шивать *impf*, прикра́сить *pf.* **embroidery** /-dərɪ/ *n* вы́шивка.
embroil /ɪm'brɔɪl/ *vt* впу́тывать *impf*, впу́тать *pf.*
embryo /'embrɪəʊ/ *n* эмбрио́н.
emerald /'emər(ə)ld/ *n* изумру́д.
emerge /ɪ'mɜːdʒ/ *vi* появля́ться *impf*, появи́ться *pf.* **emergence** /-dʒəns/ *n* появле́ние. **emergency** /-dʒənsɪ/ *n* кра́йняя необходи́мость; **state of ~** чрезвыча́йное положе́ние; **~ exit** запасно́й вы́ход.
emery paper /'emərɪ 'peɪpə(r)/ *n* нажда́чная бума́га.
emigrant /'emɪgrənt/ *n* эмигра́нт, ~ка. **emigrate** /'emɪgreɪt/ *vi* эмигри́ровать *impf* & *pf.* **emigration** /ˌemɪ'greɪʃ(ə)n/ *n* эмигра́ция.
eminence /'emɪnəns/ *n* (*fame*) знамени́тость. **eminent** /-nənt/ *adj* выдаю́щийся. **eminently** /-nəntlɪ/ *adv* чрезвыча́йно.
emission /ɪ'mɪʃ(ə)n/ *n* испуска́ние. **emit** /ɪ'mɪt/ *vt* испуска́ть *impf*, испусти́ть *pf*; (*light*) излуча́ть *impf*, излучи́ть *pf*; (*sound*) издава́ть *impf*, изда́ть *pf.*
emotion /ɪ'məʊʃ(ə)n/ *n* эмо́ция, чу́вство. **emotional** /-n(ə)l/ *adj* эмоциона́льный.
empathize /'empəˌθaɪz/ *vt* сопережива́ть *impf*, сопережи́ть *pf.* **empathy** /-pəθɪ/ *n* эмпа́тия.
emperor /'empərə(r)/ *n* импера́тор.
emphasis /'emfəsɪs/ *n* ударе́ние. **emphasize** /'emfəˌsaɪz/ *vt* подчёркивать *impf*, подчеркну́ть *pf.* **emphatic** /em'fætɪk/ *adj* вырази́тельный; категори́ческий.
empire /'empaɪə(r)/ *n* импе́рия.
empirical /ɪm'pɪrɪk(ə)l/ *adj* эмпири́ческий.
employ /ɪm'plɔɪ/ *vt* (*use*) по́льзоваться *impf* +*instr*; (*person*) нанима́ть *impf*, наня́ть *pf.* **employee** /ˌemplɔɪ'iː/ *n* сотру́дник, рабо́чий *sb.* **employer** /ɪm'plɔɪə(r)/ *n* работода́тель *m.* **employment** /ɪm'plɔɪmənt/ *n* рабо́та, слу́жба; (*use*) испо́льзование.
empower /ɪm'paʊə(r)/ *vt* уполномо́чивать *impf*, уполномо́чить *pf* (**to** на+*acc*).
empress /'emprɪs/ *n* императри́ца.
emptiness /'emptɪnɪs/ *n* пустота́. **empty** /'emptɪ/ *adj* пусто́й; **~-headed** пустоголо́вый; *vt* (*container*) опорожня́ть *impf*, опоро́жни́ть *pf*; (*solid*) высыпа́ть *impf*, вы́сыпать *pf*; (*liquid*) вылива́ть *impf*, вы́лить *pf*; *vi* пусте́ть *impf*, о~ *pf.*
emulate /'emjʊˌleɪt/ *vt* достига́ть *impf*, дости́гнуть, дости́чь *pf* +*gen*; (*copy*)

подража́ть *impf* +*dat*.
emulsion /ɪ'mʌlʃ(ə)n/ *n* эму́льсия.
enable /ɪ'neɪb(ə)l/ *vt* дава́ть *impf*, дать *pf* возмо́жность +*dat* & *inf*.
enact /ɪ'nækt/ *vt* (*law*) принима́ть *impf*, приня́ть *pf*; (*theat*) разы́грывать *impf*, разыгра́ть *pf*. **enactment** /-'næktmənt/ *n* (*law*) постановле́ние; (*theat*) игра́.
enamel /ɪ'næm(ə)l/ *n* эма́ль; *adj* эма́левый; *vt* эмалирова́ть *impf* & *pf*.
encampment /ɪn'kæmpmənt/ *n* ла́герь *m*.
enchant /ɪn'tʃɑːnt/ *vt* очаро́вывать *impf*, очарова́ть *pf*. **enchanting** /-tɪŋ/ *adj* очарова́тельный. **enchantment** /-mənt/ *n* очарова́ние.
encircle /ɪn'sɜːk(ə)l/ *vt* окружа́ть *impf*, окружи́ть *pf*.
enclave /'enkleɪv/ *n* анкла́в.
enclose /ɪn'kləʊz/ *vt* огора́живать *impf*, огороди́ть *pf*; (*in letter*) прикла́дывать *impf*, приложи́ть *pf*; **please find ~d** прилага́ется (-а́ются) +*nom*. **enclosure** /ɪn'kləʊʒə(r)/ *n* огоро́женное ме́сто; (*in letter*) приложе́ние.
encode /ɪn'kəʊd/ *vt* шифрова́ть *impf*, за~ *pf*.
encompass /ɪn'kʌmpəs/ *vt* (*encircle*) окружа́ть *impf*, окружи́ть *pf*; (*contain*) заключа́ть *impf*, заключи́ть *pf*.
encore /'ɒŋkɔː(r)/ *int* бис!; *n* вы́зов на бис.
encounter /ɪn'kaʊntə(r)/ *n* встре́ча; (*in combat*) столкнове́ние; *vt* встреча́ть *impf*, встре́тить *pf*; (*fig*) ста́лкиваться *impf*, столкну́ться *pf* с+*instr*.
encourage /ɪn'kʌrɪdʒ/ *vt* ободря́ть *impf*, ободри́ть *pf*. **encouragement** /-mənt/ *n* ободре́ние. **encouraging** /-dʒɪŋ/ *adj* ободри́тельный.
encroach /ɪn'krəʊtʃ/ *vt* вторга́ться *impf*, вто́ргнуться *pf* (**on** в+*acc*). **encroachment** /-mənt/ *n* вторже́ние.
encumber /ɪn'kʌmbə(r)/ *vt* обременя́ть *impf*, обремени́ть *pf*. **encumbrance** /-brəns/ *n* обу́за.
encyclopaedia /enˌsaɪklə'piːdɪə/ *n* энциклопе́дия. **encyclopaedic** /-'piːdɪk/ *adj* энциклопеди́ческий.
end /end/ *n* коне́ц; (*death*) смерть; (*purpose*) цель; **an ~ in itself** самоце́ль; **in the ~** в конце́ концо́в; **make ~s meet** своди́ть *impf*, свести́ *pf* концы́ с конца́ми; **no ~ of** ма́сса+*gen*; **on ~** (*upright*) стоймя́, ды́бом; (*continuously*) подря́д; **put an ~ to** класть *impf*, положи́ть *pf* коне́ц +*dat*; *vt* конча́ть *impf*, ко́нчить *pf*; (*halt*) прекраща́ть *impf*, прекрати́ть *pf*; *vi* конча́ться *impf*, ко́нчиться *pf*.
endanger /ɪn'deɪndʒə(r)/ *vt* подверга́ть *impf*, подве́ргнуть *pf* опа́сности.
endearing /ɪn'dɪərɪŋ/ *adj* привлека́тельный. **endearment** /-'dɪəmənt/ *n* ла́ска.
endeavour /ɪn'devə(r)/ *n* попы́тка; (*exertion*) уси́лие; (*undertaking*) де́ло; *vi* стара́ться *impf*, по~ *pf*.
endemic /en'demɪk/ *adj* эндеми́ческий.
ending /'endɪŋ/ *n* оконча́ние. **endless** /'endlɪs/ *adj* бесконе́чный.
endorse /ɪn'dɔːs/ *vt* (*document*) подпи́сывать *impf*, подписа́ть *pf*; (*support*) подде́рживать

impf, поддержáть *pf*. **endorsement** /-mənt/ *n* пóдпись; поддéржка; (*on driving licence*) прокóл.

endow /ɪn'daʊ/ *vt* обеспéчивать *impf*, обеспéчить *pf* постоя́нным дохóдом; (*fig*) одаря́ть *impf*, одари́ть *pf*. **endowment** /-mənt/ *n* пожéртвование; (*talent*) даровáние.

endurance /ɪn'djʊərəns/ *n* (*of person*) вынóсливость; (*of object*) прóчность. **endure** /-'djʊə(r)/ *vt* выноси́ть *impf*, вы́нести *pf*; терпéть *impf*, по~ *pf*; *vi* продолжáться *impf*, продóлжиться *pf*.

enemy /'enəmɪ/ *n* враг; *adj* врáжеский.

energetic /ˌenə'dʒetɪk/ *adj* энерги́чный. **energy** /'enədʒɪ/ *n* энéргия; *pl* си́лы *f pl*.

enforce /ɪn'fɔːs/ *vt* (*law etc.*) следи́ть *impf* за выполнéнием +*gen*. **enforcement** /-mənt/ *n* наблюдéние за выполнéнием +*gen*.

engage /ɪn'geɪdʒ/ *vt* (*hire*) нанимáть *impf*, наня́ть *pf*; (*tech*) зацепля́ть *impf*, зацепи́ть *pf*. **engaged** /-'geɪdʒd/ *adj* (*occupied*) зáнятый; **be ~ in** занимáться *impf*, заня́ться *pf* +*instr*; **become ~** обручáться *impf*, обручи́ться *pf* (**to** с+*instr*). **engagement** /-'geɪdʒmənt/ *n* (*appointment*) свидáние; (*betrothal*) обручéние; (*battle*) бой; **~ ring** обручáльное кольцó. **engaging** /-'geɪdʒɪŋ/ *adj* привлекáтельный.

engender /ɪn'dʒendə(r)/ *vt* порождáть *impf*, породи́ть *pf*.

engine /'endʒɪn/ *n* двигатель *m*; (*rly*) локомоти́в; **~-driver** (*rly*) машини́ст. **engineer** /ˌendʒɪ'nɪə(r)/ *n* инженéр; *vt* (*fig*) организовáть *impf* & *pf*. **engineering** /ˌendʒɪ'nɪərɪŋ/ *n* инженéрное дéло, тéхника.

England /'ɪŋglənd/ *n* Áнглия. **English** /'ɪŋglɪʃ/ *adj* англи́йский; *n*: **the ~** *pl* англичáне (-н) *pl*. **Englishman, -woman** *n* англичáнин, -áнка.

engrave /ɪn'greɪv/ *vt* гравировáть *impf*, вы́~ *pf*; (*fig*) врезáть *impf*, врéзать *pf*. **engraver** /-'greɪvə(r)/ *n* гравёр. **engraving** /-'greɪvɪŋ/ *n* гравю́ра.

engross /ɪn'grəʊs/ *vt* поглощáть *impf*, поглоти́ть *pf*; **be ~ed in** быть поглощённым +*instr*.

engulf /ɪn'gʌlf/ *vt* поглощáть *impf*, поглоти́ть *pf*.

enhance /ɪn'hɑːns/ *vt* увели́чивать *impf*, увели́чить *pf*.

enigma /ɪ'nɪgmə/ *n* загáдка. **enigmatic** /ˌenɪg'mætɪk/ *adj* загáдочный.

enjoy /ɪn'dʒɔɪ/ *vt* получáть *impf*, получи́ть *pf* удовóльствие от+*gen*; наслаждáться *impf*, насладиться *pf* +*instr*; (*health etc.*) обладáть *impf* +*instr*; **~ o.s.** хорошó проводи́ть *impf*, провести́ *pf* врéмя. **enjoyable** /-əb(ə)l/ *adj* прия́тный. **enjoyment** /-mənt/ *n* удовóльствие.

enlarge /ɪn'lɑːdʒ/ *vt* увели́чивать *impf*, увели́чить *pf*; **~ upon** распространя́ться *impf*, распространи́ться *pf* о+*prep*. **enlargement** /-mənt/ *n* увели́чéние.

enlighten /ɪn'laɪt(ə)n/ *vt* просвещáть *impf*, просвети́ть *pf*. **enlightenment** /-mənt/ *n* просвещéние.

enlist /ɪn'lɪst/ *vi* поступáть *impf*, поступи́ть *pf* на воéнную слу́жбу; *vt* (*mil*) вербовáть

impf, за∼ *pf*; (*support etc.*) заруча́ться *impf*, заручи́ться *pf* +*instr.*
enliven /ɪn'laɪv(ə)n/ *vt* оживля́ть *impf*, оживи́ть *pf.*
enmity /'enmɪtɪ/ *n* вражда́.
ennoble /ɪ'nəʊb(ə)l/ *vt* облагора́живать *impf*, облагоро́дить *pf.*
ennui /ɒn'wi:/ *n* тоска́.
enormity /ɪ'nɔ:mɪtɪ/ *n* чудо́вищность. **enormous** /-'nɔ:məs/ *adj* огро́мный. **enormously** /-'nɔ:məslɪ/ *adv* чрезвыча́йно.
enough /ɪ'nʌf/ *adj* доста́точно +*gen*; *adv* доста́точно, дово́льно; **be ∼** хвата́ть *impf*, хвати́ть *pf impers+gen.*
enquire, enquiry /ɪn'kwaɪə(r), ɪn 'kwaɪərɪ/ *see* **inquire, inquiry**
enrage /ɪn'reɪdʒ/ *vt* беси́ть *impf*, вз∼ *pf.*
enrapture /ɪn'ræptʃə(r)/ *vt* восхища́ть *impf*, восхити́ть *pf.*
enrich /ɪn'rɪtʃ/ *vt* обогаща́ть *impf*, обогати́ть *pf.*
enrol /ɪn'rəʊl/ *vt* & *i* запи́сывать(ся) *impf*, записа́ть(ся) *pf.* **enrolment** /-mənt/ *n* за́пись.
en route /ɑ̃ 'ru:t/ *adv* по пути́ (**to, for** в+*acc*).
ensconce /ɪn'skɒns/ *vt*: **∼ o.s.** заса́живаться *impf*, засе́сть *pf* (**with** за+*acc*).
ensemble /ɒn'sɒmb(ə)l/ *n* (*mus*) анса́мбль *m.*
enshrine /ɪn'ʃraɪn/ *vt* (*fig*) охраня́ть *impf*, охрани́ть *pf.*
ensign /'ensaɪn/ *n* (*flag*) флаг.
enslave /ɪn'sleɪv/ *vt* порабоща́ть *impf*, поработи́ть *pf.*
ensue /ɪn'sju:/ *vi* сле́довать *impf.* **ensuing** /-'sju:ɪŋ/ *adj* после́дующий.
ensure /ɪn'ʃʊə(r)/ *vt* обеспе́чивать *impf*, обеспе́чить *pf.*
entail /ɪn'teɪl/ *vt* (*necessitate*) влечь *impf* за собо́й.
entangle /ɪn'tæŋg(ə)l/ *vt* запу́тывать *impf*, запу́тать *pf.*
enter /'entə(r)/ *vt* & *i* входи́ть *impf*, войти́ *pf* в+*acc*; (*by transport*) въезжа́ть *impf*, въе́хать *pf* в+*acc*; *vt* (*join*) поступа́ть *impf*, поступи́ть *pf* в, на, +*acc*; (*competition*) вступа́ть *impf*, вступи́ть *pf* в+*acc*; (*in list*) вноси́ть *impf*, внести́ *pf* в+*acc.*
enterprise /'entəˌpraɪz/ *n* (*undertaking*) предприя́тие; (*initiative*) предприи́мчивость. **enterprising** /-zɪŋ/ *adj* предприи́мчивый.
entertain /ˌentə'teɪn/ *vt* (*amuse*) развлека́ть *impf*, развле́чь *pf*; (*guests*) принима́ть *impf*, приня́ть *pf*; угоща́ть *impf*, угости́ть *pf* (**to** +*instr*); (*hopes*) пита́ть *impf.* **entertaining** /-nɪŋ/ *adj* занима́тельный. **entertainment** /-mənt/ *n* развлече́ние; (*show*) представле́ние.
enthral /ɪn'θrɔ:l/ *vt* порабоща́ть *impf*, поработи́ть *pf.*
enthusiasm /ɪn'θju:zɪˌæz(ə)m/ *n* энтузиа́зм. **enthusiast** /-ˌæst/ *n* энтузиа́ст, **∼**ка. **enthusiastic** /-'æstɪk/ *adj* восто́рженный; по́лный энтузиа́зма.
entice /ɪn'taɪs/ *vt* зама́нивать *impf*, замани́ть *pf.* **enticement** /-mənt/ *n* прима́нка. **enticing** /-sɪŋ/ *adj* зама́нчивый.
entire /ɪn'taɪə(r)/ *adj* по́лный, це́лый, весь. **entirely** /-'taɪəlɪ/ *adv* вполне́, соверше́нно; (*solely*) исключи́тельно. **entirety** /-'taɪərətɪ/ *n*: **in its ∼** по́лностью.
entitle /ɪn'taɪt(ə)l/ *vt* (*authorize*) дава́ть *impf*, дать *pf* пра́во+*dat* (**to** на+*acc*); **be ∼d** (*book*) называ́ться *impf*; **be ∼d to** име́ть *impf* пра́во на+*acc.*

entity /'entɪtɪ/ *n* объéкт; феномéн.

entomology /ˌentə'mɒlədʒɪ/ *n* энтомолóгия.

entourage /ˌɒntʊə'rɑːʒ/ *n* свúта.

entrails /'entreɪlz/ *n pl* внýтренности (-тей) *pl.*

entrance[1] /'entrəns/ *n* вход, въезд; (*theat*) вы́ход; ~ **exam** вступúтельный экзáмен; ~ **hall** вестибю́ль *m.*

entrance[2] /ɪn'trɑːns/ *vt* (*charm*) очарóвывать *impf*, очаровáть *pf.* **entrancing** /-'trɑːnsɪŋ/ *adj* очаровáтельный.

entrant /'entrənt/ *n* учáстник (**for** +*gen*).

entreat /ɪn'triːt/ *vt* умоля́ть *impf*, умолúть *pf.* **entreaty** /-'triːtɪ/ *n* мольбá.

entrench /ɪn'trentʃ/ *vt* **be, become** ~**ed** (*fig*) укореня́ться *impf*, укоренúться *pf.*

entrepreneur /ˌɒntrəprə'nɜː(r)/ *n* предпринимáтель *m.*

entrust /ɪn'trʌst/ *vt* (*secret*) вверя́ть *impf*, вве́рить *pf* (**to** +*dat*); (*object*; *person*) поручáть *impf*, поручúть *pf* (**to** +*dat*).

entry /'entrɪ/ *n* вход, въезд; вступлéние; (*theat*) вы́ход; (*note*) зáпись; (*in reference book*) статья́.

entwine /ɪn'twaɪn/ *vt* (*interweave*) сплетáть *impf*, сплестú *pf*; (*wreathe*) обвивáть *impf*, обвúть *pf.*

enumerate /ɪ'njuːməˌreɪt/ *vt* перечисля́ть *impf*, перечúслить *pf.*

enunciate /ɪ'nʌnsɪˌeɪt/ *vt* (*express*) излагáть *impf*, изложúть *pf*; (*pronounce*) произносúть *impf*, произнестú *pf.* **enunciation** /-ˌeɪʃ(ə)n/ *n* изложéние; произношéние.

envelop /ɪn'veləp/ *vt* окýтывать *impf*, окýтать *pf.* **envelope** /'envəˌləʊp/ *n* конвéрт.

enviable /'envɪəb(ə)l/ *adj* завúдный. **envious** /'envɪəs/ *adj* завúстливый.

environment /ɪn'vaɪərənmənt/ *n* средá; (*the* ~) окружáющая средá. **environs** /-'vaɪərənz/ *n pl* окрéстности *f pl.*

envisage /ɪn'vɪzɪdʒ/ *vt* предусмáтривать *impf*, предусмотрéть *pf.*

envoy /'envɔɪ/ *n* послáнник, агéнт.

envy /'envɪ/ *n* зáвисть; *vt* завúдовать *impf*, по~ *pf* +*dat.*

enzyme /'enzaɪm/ *n* энзúм.

ephemeral /ɪ'femər(ə)l/ *adj* эфемéрный.

epic /'epɪk/ *n* эпопéя; *adj* эпúческий.

epidemic /ˌepɪ'demɪk/ *n* эпидéмия.

epilepsy /'epɪˌlepsɪ/ *n* эпилéпсия. **epileptic** /-'leptɪk/ *n* эпилéптик; *adj* эпилептúческий.

epilogue /'epɪˌlɒg/ *n* эпилóг.

episode /'epɪˌsəʊd/ *n* эпизóд. **episodic** /-'sɒdɪk/ *adj* эпизодúческий.

epistle /ɪ'pɪs(ə)l/ *n* послáние.

epitaph /'epɪˌtɑːf/ *n* эпитáфия.

epithet /'epɪˌθet/ *n* эпúтет.

epitome /ɪ'pɪtəmɪ/ *n* воплощéние. **epitomize** /-ˌmaɪz/ *vt* воплощáть *impf*, воплотúть *pf.*

epoch /'iːpɒk/ *n* эпóха.

equal /'iːkw(ə)l/ *adj* рáвный, одинáковый; (*capable of*) спосóбный (**to** на+*acc*, +*inf*); *n* рáвный *sb*; *vt* равня́ться *impf* +*dat.* **equality** /ɪ'kwɒlɪtɪ/ *n* рáвенство. **equalize** /'iːkwəˌlaɪz/ *vt* урáвнивать *impf*, уравня́ть *pf*; *vi* (*sport*) равня́ть *impf*, с~ *pf* счёт. **equally** /'iːkwəlɪ/ *adv* равнó, рáвным óбразом.

equanimity /ˌekwəˈnɪmɪtɪ/ *n* хладнокро́вие. **equate** /ɪˈkweɪt/ *vt* прира́внивать *impf*, приравня́ть *pf* (**with** к+*dat*). **equation** /ɪˈkweɪʒ(ə)n/ *n* (*math*) уравне́ние. **equator** /ɪˈkweɪtə(r)/ *n* эква́тор. **equatorial** /ˌekwəˈtɔːrɪəl/ *adj* экваториа́льный. **equestrian** /ɪˈkwestrɪən/ *adj* ко́нный. **equidistant** /ˌiːkwɪˈdɪst(ə)nt/ *adj* равностоя́щий. **equilibrium** /ˌiːkwɪˈlɪbrɪəm/ *n* равнове́сие. **equip** /ɪˈkwɪp/ *vt* обору́довать *impf* & *pf*; (*person*) снаряжа́ть *impf*, снаряди́ть *pf*; (*fig*) вооружа́ть *impf*, вооружи́ть *pf*. **equipment** /-mənt/ *n* обору́дование, снаряже́ние. **equitable** /ˈekwɪtəb(ə)l/ *adj* справедли́вый. **equity** /ˈekwɪtɪ/ *n* справедли́вость; *pl* (*econ*) обыкнове́нные а́кции *f pl*. **equivalent** /ɪˈkwɪvələnt/ *adj* эквивале́нтный; *n* эквивале́нт. **equivocal** /ɪˈkwɪvək(ə)l/ *adj* двусмы́сленный. **era** /ˈɪərə/ *n* э́ра. **eradicate** /ɪˈrædɪˌkeɪt/ *vt* искореня́ть *impf*, искорени́ть *pf*. **erase** /ɪˈreɪz/ *vt* стира́ть *impf*, стере́ть *pf*; (*from memory*) вычёркивать *impf*, вы́черкнуть *pf* (из па́мяти). **eraser** /-zə(r)/ *n* ла́стик. **erect** /ɪˈrekt/ *adj* прямо́й; *vt* сооружа́ть *impf*, сооруди́ть *pf*. **erection** /ɪˈrekʃ(ə)n/ *n* сооруже́ние; (*biol*) эре́кция. **erode** /ɪˈrəʊd/ *vt* разруша́ть *impf*, разру́шить *pf*. **erosion** /ɪˈrəʊʒ(ə)n/ *n* эро́зия; (*fig*) разруше́ние. **erotic** /ɪˈrɒtɪk/ *adj* эроти́ческий. **err** /ɜː(r)/ *vi* ошиба́ться *impf*, ошиби́ться *pf*; (*sin*) греши́ть *impf*, со~ *pf*. **errand** /ˈerənd/ *n* поруче́ние; **run ~s** быть на посы́лках (**for** у+*gen*). **erratic** /ɪˈrætɪk/ *adj* неро́вный. **erroneous** /ɪˈrəʊnɪəs/ *adj* оши́бочный. **error** /ˈerə(r)/ *n* оши́бка. **erudite** /ˈeruːˌdaɪt/ *adj* учёный. **erudition** /ˌeruːˈdɪʃ(ə)n/ *n* эруди́ция. **erupt** /ɪˈrʌpt/ *vi* взрыва́ться *impf*, взорва́ться *pf*; (*volcano*) изверга́ться *impf*, изве́ргнуться *pf*. **eruption** /ɪˈrʌpʃ(ə)n/ *n* изверже́ние. **escalate** /ˈeskəˌleɪt/ *vi* возраста́ть *impf*, возрасти́ *pf*; *vt* интенсифици́ровать *impf* & *pf*. **escalator** /ˈeskəˌleɪtə(r)/ *n* эскала́тор. **escapade** /ˈeskəˌpeɪd/ *n* вы́ходка. **escape** /ɪˈskeɪp/ *n* (*from prison*) побе́г; (*from danger*) спасе́ние; (*leak*) утёчка; **have a narrow ~** едва́ спасти́сь; *vi* (*flee*) бежа́ть *impf* & *pf*; убега́ть *impf*, убежа́ть *pf*; (*save o.s.*) спаса́ться *impf*, спасти́сь *pf*; (*leak*) утека́ть *impf*, уте́чь *pf*; *vt* избега́ть *impf*, избежа́ть *pf* +*gen*; (*groan*) вырыва́ться *impf*, вы́рваться *pf* из, у, +*gen*. **escort** *n* /ˈeskɔːt/ (*mil*) эско́рт; (*of lady*) кавале́р; *vt* /ɪˈskɔːt/ сопровожда́ть *impf*, сопроводи́ть *pf*; (*mil*) эскорти́ровать *impf* & *pf*. **Eskimo** /ˈeskɪˌməʊ/ *n* эскимо́с, ~ка. **esoteric** /ˌiːsəʊˈterɪk/ *adj* эзотери́ческий. **especially** /ɪˈspeʃəlɪ/ *adv* осо́бенно. **espionage** /ˈespɪəˌnɑːʒ/ *n* шпиона́ж.

espousal /ɪ'spaʊz(ə)l/ *n* поддéржка. **espouse** /ɪ'spaʊz/ *vt* (*fig*) поддéрживать *impf*, поддержáть *pf*.

essay /'eseɪ/ *n* óчерк; (*in school*) сочинéние.

essence /'es(ə)ns/ *n* (*philos*) сýщность; (*gist*) суть; (*extract*) эссéнция. **essential** /ɪ'senʃ(ə)l/ *adj* (*fundamental*) сущéственный; (*necessary*) необходи́мый; *n pl* (*necessities*) необходи́мое *sb*; (*crux*) суть; (*fundamentals*) оснóвы *f pl*. **essentially** /ɪ'senʃəlɪ/ *adv* по существý.

establish /ɪ'stæblɪʃ/ *vt* (*set up*) учреждáть *impf*, учреди́ть *pf*; (*fact etc.*) устанáвливать *impf*, установи́ть *pf*. **establishment** /-mənt/ *n* (*action*) учреждéние, установлéние; (*institution*) учреждéние.

estate /ɪ'steɪt/ *n* (*property*) имéние; (*after death*) наслéдство; (*housing* ~) жилóй масси́в; ~ **agent** агéнт по продáже недви́жимости; ~ **car** автомоби́ль *m* с кýзовом «универсáл».

esteem /ɪ'sti:m/ *n* уважéние; *vt* уважáть *impf*. **estimate** *n* /'estɪmət/ (*of quality*) оцéнка; (*of cost*) смéта; *vt* /'estɪˌmeɪt/ оцéнивать *impf*, оцени́ть *pf*. **estimation** /ˌestɪ'meɪʃ(ə)n/ *n* оцéнка, мнéние.

Estonia /ɪ'stəʊnɪə/ *n* Эстóния. **Estonian** /-nɪən/ *n* эстóнец, -нка; *adj* эстóнский.

estranged /ɪ'streɪndʒd/ *adj* отчуждённый.

estuary /'estjʊərɪ/ *n* ýстье.

etc. *abbr* и т.д. **etcetera** /et 'setərə/ и так дáлее.

etch /etʃ/ *vt* трави́ть *impf*, вы́~ *pf*. **etching** /'etʃɪŋ/ *n* (*action*) травлéние; (*object*) офóрт.

eternal /ɪ'tɜ:n(ə)l/ *adj* вéчный. **eternity** /-nɪtɪ/ *n* вéчность.

ether /'i:θə(r)/ *n* эфи́р. **ethereal** /ɪ'θɪərɪəl/ *adj* эфи́рный.

ethical /'eθɪk(ə)l/ *adj* эти́ческий, эти́чный. **ethics** /'eθɪks/ *n* э́тика.

ethnic /'eθnɪk/ *adj* этни́ческий.

etiquette /'etɪˌket/ *n* этикéт.

etymology /ˌetɪ'mɒlədʒɪ/ *n* этимолóгия.

EU *abbr* (*of* **European Union**) ЕС.

eucalyptus /ju:kə'lɪptəs/ *n* эвкали́пт.

Eucharist /'ju:kərɪst/ *n* причáстие.

eulogy /'ju:lədʒɪ/ *n* похвалá.

euphemism /'ju:fɪˌmɪz(ə)m/ *n* эвфеми́зм. **euphemistic** /-'mɪstɪk/ *adj* эвфемисти́ческий.

euro /'jʊərəʊ/ *n* éвро *neut indecl*.

Europe /'jʊərəp/ *n* Еврóпа. **European** /-'pɪən/ *n* европéец; *adj* европéйский; ~ **Community** Европéйское сооб́щество; ~ **Union** Европéйский сою́з.

evacuate /ɪ'vækjʊˌeɪt/ *vt* (*person, place*) эвакуи́ровать *impf* & *pf*. **evacuation** /-'eɪʃ(ə)n/ *n* эвакуáция.

evade /ɪ'veɪd/ *vt* уклоня́ться *impf*, уклони́ться *pf* от+*gen*.

evaluate /ɪ'væljʊˌeɪt/ *vt* оцéнивать *impf*, оцени́ть *pf*. **evaluation** /-'eɪʃ(ə)n/ *n* оцéнка.

evangelical /ˌi:væn'dʒelɪk(ə)l/ *adj* евáнгельский. **evangelist** /ɪ'vændʒəlɪst/ *n* евангели́ст.

evaporate /ɪ'væpəˌreɪt/ *vt* & *i* испаря́ть(ся) *impf*, испари́ть(ся) *pf*. **evaporation** /-'reɪʃ(ə)n/ *n* испарéние.

evasion /ɪ'veɪʒ(ə)n/ *n* уклонéние (**of** от+*gen*). **evasive** /ɪ'veɪsɪv/ *adj* уклóнчивый.

eve /iːv/ *n* канун; **on the ~** накануне.
even /'iːv(ə)n/ *adj* ровный; (*number*) чётный; **get ~** расквитаться *pf* (**with** с+*instr*); *adv* даже; (*just*) как раз; (*with comp*) ещё; **~ if** даже если; **~ though** хотя; **~ so** всё-таки; **not ~** даже не; *vt* выравнивать *impf*, выровнять *pf*.
evening /'iːvnɪŋ/ *n* вечер; *adj* вечерний; **~ class** вечерние курсы *m pl*.
evenly /'iːvənlɪ/ *adv* поровну, ровно. **evenness** /'iːvənnɪs/ *n* ровность.
event /ɪ'vent/ *n* событие, происшествие; **in the ~ of** в случае +*gen*; **in any ~** во всяком случае; **in the ~** в конечном счёте. **eventful** /ɪ'ventfʊl/ *adj* полный событий. **eventual** /ɪ'ventjʊəl/ *adj* конечный. **eventuality** /ɪˌventjʊ'ælɪtɪ/ *n* возможность. **eventually** /ɪ'ventjʊəlɪ/ *adv* в конце концов.
ever /'evə(r)/ *adv* (*at any time*) когда-либо, когда-нибудь; (*always*) всегда; (*emph*) же; **~ since** с тех пор (как); **~ so** очень; **for ~** навсегда; **hardly ~** почти никогда. **evergreen** *adj* вечнозелёный; *n* вечнозелёное растение. **everlasting** /ˌevə'lɑːstɪŋ/ *adj* вечный. **evermore** *adv*: **for ~** навсегда.
every /'evrɪ/ *adj* каждый, всякий, все (*pl*); **~ now and then** время от времени; **~ other** каждый второй; **~ other day** через день. **everybody, everyone** *pron* каждый, все (*pl*). **everyday** *adj* (*daily*) ежедневный; (*commonplace*) повседневный. **everything** *pron* всё. **everywhere** *adv* всюду, везде.
evict /ɪ'vɪkt/ *vt* выселять *impf*, выселить *pf*. **eviction** /ɪ'vɪkʃ(ə)n/ *n* выселение.
evidence /'evɪd(ə)ns/ *n* свидетельство, доказательство; **give ~** свидетельствовать *impf* (о+*prep*; +*acc*; +что). **evident** /-d(ə)nt/ *adj* очевидный.
evil /'iːv(ə)l/ *n* зло; *adj* злой.
evoke /ɪ'vəʊk/ *vt* вызывать *impf*, вызвать *pf*.
evolution /ˌiːvə'luːʃ(ə)n/ *n* эволюция. **evolutionary** /-nərɪ/ *adj* эволюционный. **evolve** /ɪ'vɒlv/ *vt & i* развивать(ся) *impf*, развить(ся) *pf*.
ewe /juː/ *n* овца.
ex- /eks/ *in comb* бывший.
exacerbate /ek'sæsəˌbeɪt/ *vt* обострять *impf*, обострить *pf*.
exact /ɪg'zækt/ *adj* точный; *vt* взыскивать *impf*, взыскать *pf* (**from, of** с+*gen*). **exacting** /-'zæktɪŋ/ *adj* требовательный. **exactitude, exactness** /-'zæktɪˌtjuːd, -'zæktnɪs/ *n* точность. **exactly** /-'zæktlɪ/ *adv* точно; (*just*) как раз; (*precisely*) именно.
exaggerate /ɪg'zædʒəˌreɪt/ *vt* преувеличивать *impf*, преувеличить *pf*. **exaggeration** /-'reɪʃ(ə)n/ *n* преувеличение.
exalt /ɪg'zɔːlt/ *vt* возвышать *impf*, возвысить *pf*; (*extol*) превозносить *impf*, превознести *pf*.
examination /ɪgˌzæmɪ'neɪʃ(ə)n/ *n* (*inspection*) осмотр; (*exam*) экзамен; (*law*) допрос. **examine** /ɪg'zæmɪn/ *vt* (*inspect*) осматривать *impf*, осмотреть *pf*; (*test*) экзаменовать *impf*, про~ *pf*; (*law*) допрашивать *impf*, допросить *pf*. **examiner** /ɪg'zæmɪnə(r)/ *n* экзаменатор.
example /ɪg'zɑːmp(ə)l/ *n* пример; **for ~** например.

exasperate /ɪg'zɑːspəˌreɪt/ *vt* раздража́ть *impf*, раздражи́ть *pf*. **exasperation** /-'reɪʃ(ə)n/ *n* раздраже́ние.

excavate /'ekskəˌveɪt/ *vt* раска́пывать *impf*, раскопа́ть *pf*. **excavations** /-'veɪʃ(ə)nz/ *n pl* раско́пки *f pl*. **excavator** /'ekskəˌveɪtə(r)/ *n* экскава́тор.

exceed /ɪk'siːd/ *vt* превыша́ть *impf*, превы́сить *pf*. **exceedingly** /-dɪŋlɪ/ *adv* чрезвыча́йно.

excel /ɪk'sel/ *vt* превосходи́ть *impf*, превзойти́ *pf*; *vi* отлича́ться *impf*, отличи́ться *pf* (**at, in** в+*prep*). **excellence** /'eksələns/ *n* превосхо́дство. **excellency** /'eksələnsɪ/ *n* превосходи́тельство. **excellent** /'eksələnt/ *adj* отли́чный.

except /ɪk'sept/ *vt* исключа́ть *impf*, исключи́ть *pf*; *prep* кро́ме+*gen*. **exception** /-'sepʃ(ə)n/ *n* исключе́ние; **take ~ to** возража́ть *impf*, возрази́ть *pf* про́тив+*gen*. **exceptional** /-'sepʃən(ə)l/ *adj* исключи́тельный.

excerpt /'eksɜːpt/ *n* отры́вок.

excess /ɪk'ses/ *n* избы́ток. **excessive** /-sɪv/ *adj* чрезме́рный.

exchange /ɪks'tʃeɪndʒ/ *n* обме́н (**of** +*instr*); (*of currency*) разме́н; (*building*) би́ржа; (*telephone*) центра́льная телефо́нная ста́нция; **~ rate** курс; *vt* обме́нивать *impf*, обменя́ть *pf* (**for** на+*acc*); обме́ниваться *impf*, обменя́ться *pf* +*instr*.

excise[1] /'eksaɪz/ *n* (*duty*) акци́з(ный сбор).

excise[2] /ek'saɪz/ *vt* (*cut out*) выреза́ть *impf*, вы́резать *pf*.

excitable /ɪk'saɪtəb(ə)l/ *adj* возбуди́мый. **excite** /-'saɪt/ *vt* (*cause, arouse*) возбужда́ть *impf*, возбуди́ть *pf*; (*thrill, agitate*) волнова́ть *impf*, вз~ *pf*. **excitement** /-'saɪtmənt/ *n* возбужде́ние; волне́ние.

exclaim /ɪk'skleɪm/ *vi* восклица́ть *impf*, воскли́кнуть *pf*. **exclamation** /ˌekskləˈmeɪʃ(ə)n/ *n* восклица́ние; **~ mark** восклица́тельный знак.

exclude /ɪk'skluːd/ *vt* исключа́ть *impf*, исключи́ть *pf*. **exclusion** /-'skluːʒ(ə)n/ *n* исключе́ние. **exclusive** /-'skluːsɪv/ *adj* исключи́тельный; (*high-class*) эксклюзи́вный.

excommunicate /ˌekskə'mjuːnɪˌkeɪt/ *vt* отлуча́ть *impf*, отлучи́ть *pf* (от це́ркви).

excrement /'ekskrɪmənt/ *n* экскреме́нты (-тов) *pl*.

excrete /ɪk'skriːt/ *vt* выделя́ть *impf*, вы́делить *pf*. **excretion** /-'skriːʃ(ə)n/ *n* выделе́ние.

excruciating /ɪk'skruːʃɪˌeɪtɪŋ/ *adj* мучи́тельный.

excursion /ɪk'skɜːʃ(ə)n/ *n* экску́рсия.

excusable /ɪk'skjuːzəb(ə)l/ *adj* прости́тельный. **excuse** /-'skjuːs/ *n* оправда́ние; (*pretext*) отгово́рка; /-'skjuːz/ *vt* (*forgive*) извиня́ть *impf*, извини́ть *pf*; (*justify*) опра́вдывать *impf*, оправда́ть *pf*; (*release*) освобожда́ть *impf*, освободи́ть *pf* (**from** от+*gen*); **~ me!** извини́те!; прости́те!

execute /'eksɪˌkjuːt/ *vt* исполня́ть *impf*, испо́лнить *pf*; (*criminal*) казни́ть *impf* & *pf*. **execution** /-'kjuːʃ(ə)n/ *n* исполне́ние; казнь. **executioner** /-'kjuːʃənə(r)/ *n* пала́ч. **executive** /ɪg'zekjʊtɪv/ *n* исполни́тельный о́рган; (*person*) руководи́тель *m*; *adj* исполни́тельный.

exemplary /ɪg'zemplərɪ/ *adj* примéрный. **exemplify** /-'zemplɪ,faɪ/ *vt* (*illustrate by example*) приводи́ть *impf*, привести́ *pf* примéр +*gen*; (*serve as example*) служи́ть *impf*, по~ *pf* примéром +*gen*.

exempt /ɪg'zempt/ *adj* освобождённый; *vt* освобождáть *impf*, освободи́ть *pf* (**from** от+*gen*). **exemption** /-'zempʃ(ə)n/ *n* освобождéние.

exercise /'eksə,saɪz/ *n* (*use*) применéние; (*physical* ~; *task*) упражнéние; **take** ~ упражня́ться *impf*; ~ **book** тетрáдь; *vt* (*use*) применя́ть *impf*, примени́ть *pf*; (*dog*) прогу́ливать *impf*; (*train*) упражня́ть *impf*.

exert /ɪg'zɜːt/ *vt* окáзывать *impf*, оказáть *pf*; ~ **o.s.** старáться *impf*, по~ *pf*. **exertion** /-'zɜːʃ(ə)n/ *n* напряжéние.

exhale /eks'heɪl/ *vt* выдыхáть *impf*, вы́дохнуть *pf*.

exhaust /ɪg'zɔːst/ *n* вы́хлоп; ~ **fumes** выхлопны́е гáзы *m pl*; ~ **pipe** выхлопнáя трубá; *vt* (*use up*) истощáть *impf*, истощи́ть *pf*; (*person*) изнуря́ть *impf*, изнури́ть *pf*; (*subject*) исчéрпывать *impf*, исчéрпать *pf*. **exhausted** /-stɪd/ *adj*: **be** ~ (*person*) быть измождённым. **exhausting** /-stɪŋ/ *adj* изнури́тельный. **exhaustion** /-stʃ(ə)n/ *n* изнурéние; (*depletion*) истощéние. **exhaustive** /-stɪv/ *adj* исчéрпывающий.

exhibit /ɪg'zɪbɪt/ *n* экспонáт; (*law*) вещéственное доказáтельство; *vt* (*manifest*) проявля́ть *impf*, прояви́ть *pf*; (*publicly*) выставля́ть *impf*, вы́ставить *pf*. **exhibition** /,eksɪ'bɪʃ(ə)n/ *n* вы́ставка. **exhibitor** /ɪg'zɪbɪtə(r)/ *n* экспонéнт.

exhilarated /ɪg'zɪlə,reɪtɪd/ *adj* в припóднятом настроéнии. **exhilarating** /-,reɪtɪŋ/ *adj* возбуждáющий. **exhilaration** /-'reɪʃ(ə)n/ *n* возбуждéние.

exhort /ɪg'zɔːt/ *vt* увещевáть *impf*. **exhortation** /,egzɔː'teɪʃ(ə)n/ *n* увещевáние.

exhume /eks'hjuːm/ *vt* выкáпывать *impf*, вы́копать *pf*.

exile /'eksaɪl/ *n* изгнáние; (*person*) изгнáнник; *vt* изгоня́ть *impf*, изгнáть *pf*.

exist /ɪg'zɪst/ *vi* существовáть *impf*. **existence** /-st(ən)s/ *n* существовáние. **existing** /-stɪŋ/ *adj* существу́ющий.

exit /'eksɪt/ *n* вы́ход; (*for vehicles*) вы́езд; (*theat*) ухóд (со сцéны); ~ **visa** выезднáя ви́за; *vi* уходи́ть *impf*, уйти́ *pf*.

exonerate /ɪg'zɒnə,reɪt/ *vt* опрáвдывать *impf*, оправдáть *pf*.

exorbitant /ɪg'zɔːbɪt(ə)nt/ *adj* непомéрный.

exorcize /'eksɔː,saɪz/ *vt* (*spirits*) изгоня́ть *impf*, изгнáть *pf*.

exotic /ɪg'zɒtɪk/ *adj* экзоти́ческий.

expand /ɪk'spænd/ *vt* & *i* расширя́ть(ся) *impf*, расши́рить(ся) *pf*; ~ **on** распространя́ться *impf*, распространи́ться *pf* о+*prep*. **expanse** /-'spæns/ *n* прострáнство. **expansion** /-'spænʃ(ə)n/ *n* расширéние. **expansive** /-'spænsɪv/ *adj* экспанси́вный.

expatriate /eks'pætrɪət/ *n* экспатриáнт, ~ка.

expect /ɪk'spekt/ *vt* (*await*) ожидáть *impf* +*gen*; ждать *impf* +*gen*, что; (*suppose*) полагáть *impf*; (*require*) трéбовать *impf* +*gen*, чтóбы. **expectant** /-t(ə)nt/ *adj* выжидáтельный; ~

mother беременная же́нщина. **expectation** /ˌekspekˈteɪʃ(ə)n/ *n* ожида́ние.

expediency /ɪkˈspiːdɪənsɪ/ *n* целесообра́зность. **expedient** /-ənt/ *n* приём; *adj* целесообра́зный. **expedite** /ˈekspɪˌdaɪt/ *vt* ускоря́ть *impf*, уско́рить *pf*. **expedition** /ˌekspɪˈdɪʃ(ə)n/ *n* экспеди́ция. **expeditionary** /ˌekspɪˈdɪʃənərɪ/ *adj* экспедицио́нный.

expel /ɪkˈspel/ *vt* (*drive out*) выгоня́ть *impf*, вы́гнать *pf*; (*from school etc.*) исключа́ть *impf*, исключи́ть *pf*; (*from country etc.*) изгоня́ть *impf*, изгна́ть *pf*.

expend /ɪkˈspend/ *vt* тра́тить *impf*, ис~, по~ *pf*. **expendable** /-ˈspendəb(ə)l/ *adj* необяза́тельный. **expenditure** /-ˈspendɪtʃə(r)/ *n* расхо́д. **expense** /-ˈspens/ *n* расхо́д; *pl* расхо́ды *m pl*, **at the ~ of** за счёт+*gen*; (*fig*) цено́ю+*gen*. **expensive** /-ˈspensɪv/ *adj* дорого́й.

experience /ɪkˈspɪərɪəns/ *n* о́пыт; (*incident*) пережива́ние; *vt* испы́тывать *impf*, испыта́ть *pf*; (*undergo*) пережива́ть *impf*, пережи́ть *pf*. **experienced** /-ənst/ *adj* о́пытный.

experiment /ɪkˈsperɪmənt/ *n* экспериме́нт; *vi* эксперименти́ровать *impf* (**on, with** над, с+*instr*). **experimental** /-ˈment(ə)l/ эксперимента́льный.

expert /ˈekspɜːt/ *n* экспе́рт; *adj* о́пытный. **expertise** /-ˈtiːz/ *n* специа́льные зна́ния *neut pl*.

expire /ɪkˈspaɪə(r)/ *vi* (*period*) истека́ть *impf*, исте́чь *pf*. **expiry** /-rɪ/ *n* истече́ние.

explain /ɪkˈspleɪn/ *vt* объясня́ть *impf*, объясни́ть *pf*. **explanation** /ˌekspləˈneɪʃ(ə)n/ *n* объясне́ние. **explanatory** /ɪkˈsplænətərɪ/ *adj* объясни́тельный.

expletive /ɪkˈspliːtɪv/ *n* (*oath*) бра́нное сло́во.

explicit /ɪkˈsplɪsɪt/ *adj* я́вный; (*of person*) прямо́й.

explode /ɪkˈspləʊd/ *vt & i* взрыва́ть(ся) *impf*, взорва́ть(ся) *pf*; *vt* (*discredit*) опроверга́ть *impf*, опрове́ргнуть *pf*; *vi* (*with anger etc.*) разража́ться *impf*, разрази́ться *pf*.

exploit *n* /ˈeksplɔɪt/ по́двиг; *vt* /ɪkˈsplɔɪt/ эксплуати́ровать *impf*; (*use to advantage*) испо́льзовать *impf & pf*. **exploitation** /ˌeksplɔɪˈteɪʃ(ə)n/ *n* эксплуата́ция. **exploiter** /ɪkˈsplɔɪtə(r)/ *n* эксплуата́тор.

exploration /ˌeksplәˈreɪʃ(ə)n/ *n* иссле́дование. **exploratory** /ɪkˈsplɒrətərɪ/ *adj* иссле́довательский. **explore** /ɪkˈsplɔː(r)/ *vt* иссле́довать *impf & pf*. **explorer** /ɪkˈsplɔːrə(r)/ *n* иссле́дователь *m*.

explosion /ɪkˈspləʊʒ(ə)n/ *n* взрыв. **explosive** /-ˈspləʊsɪv/ *n* взры́вчатое вещество́; *adj* взры́вчатый; (*fig*) взрывно́й.

exponent /ɪkˈspəʊnənt/ *n* (*interpreter*) истолкова́тель *m*; (*advocate*) сторо́нник.

export *n* /ˈekspɔːt/ вы́воз, э́кспорт; *vt* /ekˈspɔːt/ вывози́ть *impf*, вы́везти *pf*; экспорти́ровать *impf & pf*. **exporter** /ekˈspɔːtə(r)/ *n* экспортёр.

expose /ɪkˈspəʊz/ *vt* (*bare*) раскрыва́ть *impf*, раскры́ть *pf*; (*subject*) подверга́ть *impf*, подве́ргнуть *pf* (**to** +*dat*); (*discredit*) разоблача́ть *impf*, разоблачи́ть *pf*; (*phot*) экспони́ровать *impf & pf*.

exposition /ˌekspəˈzɪʃ(ə)n/ *n* изложéние. **exposure** /ɪk'spəʊʒə(r)/ *n* подвергáние (**to** +*dat*); (*phot*) вы́держка; (*unmasking*) разоблачéние; (*med*) хóлод.

expound /ɪk'spaʊnd/ *vt* излагáть *impf*, изложи́ть *pf*.

express /ɪk'spres/ *n* (*train*) экспрéсс; *adj* (*clear*) тóчный; (*purpose*) специáльный; (*urgent*) срóчный; *vt* выражáть *impf*, вы́разить *pf*. **expression** /-'spreʃ(ə)n/ *n* выражéние; (*expressiveness*) вырази́тельность. **expressive** /-'spresɪv/ *adj* вырази́тельный. **expressly** /-'spreslɪ/ *adv* (*clearly*) я́сно; (*specifically*) специáльно.

expropriate /eks'prəʊprɪˌeɪt/ *vt* экспроприи́ровать *impf* & *pf*. **expropriation** /-'eɪʃ(ə)n/ *n* экспроприáция.

expulsion /ɪk'spʌlʃ(ə)n/ *n* (*from school etc.*) исключéние; (*from country etc.*) изгнáние.

exquisite /'ekskwɪzɪt/ *adj* утончённый.

extant /ek'stænt/ *adj* сохрани́вшийся.

extempore /ɪk'stempərɪ/ *adv* экспрóмптом. **extemporize** /-'stempəˌraɪz/ *vt* & *i* импровизи́ровать *impf*, сымпровизи́ровать *pf*.

extend /ɪk'stend/ *vt* (*stretch out*) протя́гивать *impf*, протяну́ть *pf*; (*enlarge*) расширя́ть *impf*, расши́рить *pf*; (*prolong*) продлевáть *impf*, продли́ть *pf*; *vi* простирáться *impf*, простерéться *pf*. **extension** /-'stenʃ(ə)n/ *n* (*enlarging*) расширéние; (*time*) продлéние; (*to house*) пристрóйка; (*tel*) добáвочный. **extensive** /-'stensɪv/ *adj* обши́рный. **extent** /-'stent/ *n* (*degree*) стéпень.

extenuating /ɪk'stenjʊˌeɪtɪŋ/ *adj*: ~ **circumstances** смягчáющие вину́ обстоя́тельства *neut pl*.

exterior /ɪk'stɪərɪə(r)/ *n* вне́шность; *adj* вне́шний.

exterminate /ɪk'stɜːmɪˌneɪt/ *vt* истребля́ть *impf*, истреби́ть *pf*. **extermination** /-'neɪʃ(ə)n/ *n* истреблéние.

external /ɪk'stɜːn(ə)l/ *adj* вне́шний.

extinct /ɪk'stɪŋkt/ *adj* (*volcano*) поту́хший; (*species*) вы́мерший; **become** ~ вымирáть *impf*, вы́мереть *pf*. **extinction** /-'stɪŋkʃ(ə)n/ *n* вымирáние.

extinguish /ɪk'stɪŋgwɪʃ/ *vt* гаси́ть *impf*, по~ *pf*. **extinguisher** /-'stɪŋgwɪʃə(r)/ *n* огнетуши́тель *m*.

extol /ɪk'stəʊl/ *vt* превозноси́ть *impf*, превознести́ *pf*.

extort /ɪk'stɔːt/ *vt* вымогáть *impf* (**from** у+*gen*). **extortion** /-'stɔːʃ(ə)n/ *n* вымогáтельство. **extortionate** /-'stɔːʃənət/ *adj* вымогáтельский.

extra /'ekstrə/ *n* (*theat*) стати́ст, ~ка; (*payment*) приплáта; *adj* дополни́тельный; (*special*) осóбый; *adv* осóбенно.

extract *n* /'ekstrækt/ экстрáкт; (*from book etc.*) вы́держка; *vt* /ɪk'strækt/ извлекáть *impf*, извлéчь *pf*. **extraction** /ɪk'strækʃ(ə)n/ *n* извлечéние; (*origin*) происхождéние. **extradite** /'ekstrəˌdaɪt/ *vt* выдавáть *impf*, вы́дать *pf*. **extradition** /-'dɪʃ(ə)n/ *n* вы́дача.

extramarital /ˌekstrə'mærɪt(ə)l/ *adj* внебрáчный.

extraneous /ɪk'streɪnɪəs/ *adj* посторóнний.

extraordinary /ɪk'strɔːdɪnərɪ/ *adj* чрезвычáйный.

extrapolate /ɪk'stræpəˌleɪt/ *vt* & *i*

экстраполи́ровать *impf* & *pf.*
extravagance /ɪk'strævəgəns/ *n* расточи́тельность. **extravagant** /-gənt/ *adj* расточи́тельный, (*fantastic*) сумасбро́дный.
extreme /ɪk'stri:m/ *n* кра́йность; *adj* кра́йний. **extremity** /-'stremɪtɪ/ *n* (*end*) край; (*adversity*) кра́йность; *pl* (*hands & feet*) коне́чности *f pl.*
extricate /'ekstrɪ,keɪt/ *vt* выпу́тывать *impf*, вы́путать *pf.*
exuberance /ɪg'zju:bərəns/ *n* жизнера́достность. **exuberant** /-rənt/ *adj* жизнера́достный.
exude /ɪg'zju:d/ *vt* & *i* выделя́ть(ся) *impf*, вы́делить(ся) *pf*; (*fig*) излуча́ть(ся) *impf*, излучи́ть(ся) *pf.*
exult /ɪg'zʌlt/ *vi* ликова́ть *impf.* **exultant** /-tənt/ *adj* лику́ющий. **exultation** /ɪg,zʌl'teɪʃ(ə)n/ *n* ликова́ние.
eye /aɪ/ *n* глаз; (*needle etc.*) ушко́; *vt* разгля́дывать *impf*, разгляде́ть *pf.* **eyeball** *n* глазно́е я́блоко. **eyebrow** *n* бровь. **eyelash** *n* ресни́ца. **eyelid** *n* ве́ко. **eyeshadow** *n* те́ни *f pl* для век. **eyesight** *n* зре́ние. **eyewitness** *n* очеви́дец.

F

fable /'feɪb(ə)l/ *n* ба́сня.
fabric /'fæbrɪk/ *n* (*structure*) структу́ра; (*cloth*) ткань. **fabricate** /-,keɪt/ *vt* (*invent*) выду́мывать *impf*, вы́думать *pf.* **fabrication** /-'keɪʃ(ə)n/ *n* вы́думка.
fabulous /'fæbjʊləs/ *adj* ска́зочный.
façade /fə'sɑ:d/ *n* фаса́д.
face /feɪs/ *n* лицо́; (*expression*) выраже́ние; (*grimace*) грима́са; (*side*) сторона́; (*surface*) пове́рхность; (*clock etc.*) цифербла́т; **make ~s** ко́рчить *impf* ро́жи; **~ down** лицо́м вниз; **~ to ~** лицо́м к лицу́; **in the ~ of** пе́ред лицо́м+*gen*, вопреки́+*dat*; **on the ~ of it** на пе́рвый взгляд; *vt* (*be turned towards*) быть обращённым к+*dat*; (*of person*) стоя́ть *impf* лицо́м к+*dat*; (*meet firmly*) смотре́ть *impf* в лицо́+*dat*; (*cover*) облицо́вывать *impf*, облицева́ть *pf*; **I can't ~ it** я да́же ду́мать об э́том не могу́. **faceless** /'feɪslɪs/ *adj* безли́чный.
facet /'fæsɪt/ *n* грань; (*fig*) аспе́кт.
facetious /fə'si:ʃəs/ *adj* шутли́вый.
facial /'feɪʃ(ə)l/ *adj* лицево́й.
facile /'fæsaɪl/ *adj* пове́рхностный. **facilitate** /fə'sɪlɪ,teɪt/ *vt* облегча́ть *impf*, облегчи́ть *pf.* **facility** /fə'sɪlɪtɪ/ *n* (*ease*) лёгкость; (*ability*) спосо́бность; *pl* (*conveniences*) удо́бства *neut pl*, (*opportunities*) возмо́жности *f pl.*
facing /'feɪsɪŋ/ *n* облицо́вка; (*of garment*) отде́лка.
facsimile /fæk'sɪmɪlɪ/ *n* факси́миле *neut indecl.*
fact /fækt/ *n* факт; **the ~ is that** … де́ло в том, что…; **as a matter of ~** со́бственно говоря́; **in ~** на са́мом де́ле.
faction /'fækʃ(ə)n/ *n* фра́кция.
factor /'fæktə(r)/ *n* фа́ктор.
factory /'fæktərɪ/ *n* фа́брика, заво́д.
factual /'fæktjʊəl/ *adj* факти́ческий.
faculty /'fækəltɪ/ *n* спосо́бность; (*univ*) факульте́т.

fade /feɪd/ *vi* (*wither*) вя́нуть *impf*, за~ *pf*; (*colour*) выцвета́ть *impf*, вы́цвести *pf*; (*sound*) замира́ть *impf*, замере́ть *pf*.

faeces /'fi:si:z/ *n pl* кал.

fag /fæg/ *n* (*cigarette*) сигаре́тка.

fail /feɪl/ *n*: **without ~** обяза́тельно; *vi* (*weaken*) слабе́ть *impf*; (*break down*) отка́зывать *impf*, отказа́ть *pf*; (*not succeed*) терпе́ть *impf*, по~ *pf* неуда́чу; не удава́ться *impf*, уда́ться *pf impers*+*dat*; *vt* & *i* (*exam*) прова́ливать(ся) *impf*, провали́ть(ся) *pf*.; *vt* (*disappoint*) подводи́ть *impf*, подвести́ *pf*. **failing** /'feɪlɪŋ/ *n* недоста́ток; *prep* за неиме́нием +*gen*. **failure** /'feɪljə(r)/ *n* неуда́ча; (*person*) неуда́чник, -ица.

faint /feɪnt/ *n* о́бморок; *adj* (*weak*) сла́бый; (*pale*) бле́дный; **I feel ~** мне ду́рно; **~-hearted** малоду́шный; *vi* па́дать *impf*, упа́сть *pf* в о́бморок.

fair¹ /feə(r)/ *n* я́рмарка.

fair² /feə(r)/ *adj* (*hair, skin*) све́тлый; (*weather*) я́сный; (*just*) справедли́вый; (*average*) сно́сный; **a ~ amount** дово́льно мно́го +*gen*. **fairly** /'feəlɪ/ *adv* дово́льно.

fairy /'feərɪ/ *n* фе́я; **~-tale** ска́зка.

faith /feɪθ/ *n* ве́ра; (*trust*) дове́рие. **faithful** /'feɪθfʊl/ *adj* ве́рный; **yours ~ly** с уваже́нием.

fake /feɪk/ *n* подде́лка; *vt* подде́лывать *impf*, подде́лать *pf*.

falcon /'fɔ:lkən/ *n* со́кол.

fall /fɔ:l/ *n* паде́ние; *vi* па́дать *impf*, упа́сть *pf*; **~ apart** распада́ться *impf*, распа́сться *pf*; **~ asleep** засыпа́ть *impf*, засну́ть *pf*; **~ back on** прибега́ть *impf*, прибе́гнуть *pf* к+*dat*; **~ down** па́дать *impf*, упа́сть *pf*; **~ in** ру́хнуть *pf*; **~ in love with** влюбля́ться *impf*, влюби́ться *pf* в+*acc*; **~ off** отпада́ть *impf*, отпа́сть *pf*; **~ out** выпа́дать *impf*, вы́пасть *pf*; (*quarrel*) поссо́риться *pf*; **~ over** опроки́дываться *impf*, опроки́нуться *pf*; **~ through** прова́ливаться *impf*, провали́ться *pf*; **~-out** радиоакти́вные оса́дки (-ков) *pl*.

fallacy /'fæləsɪ/ *n* оши́бка.

fallible /'fælɪb(ə)l/ *adj* подве́рженный оши́бкам.

fallow /'fæləʊ/ *n*: **lie ~** лежа́ть *impf* под па́ром.

false /fɒls/ *adj* ло́жный; (*teeth*) иску́сственный; **~ start** неве́рный старт. **falsehood** /'fɒlshʊd/*n* ложь. **falsification** /,fɒlsɪfɪ'keɪʃ(ə)n/ *n* фальсифика́ция. **falsify** /'fɒlsɪ,faɪ/ *vt* фальсифици́ровать *impf* & *pf*. **falsity** /'fɒlsɪtɪ/ *n* ло́жность.

falter /'fɒltə(r)/ *vi* спотыка́ться *impf*, споткну́ться *pf*; (*stammer*) запина́ться *impf*, запну́ться *pf*.

fame /feɪm/ *n* сла́ва.

familiar /fə'mɪlɪə(r)/ *adj* (*well known*) знако́мый; (*usual*) обы́чный; (*informal*) фамилья́рный. **familiarity** /fə,mɪlɪ'ærɪtɪ/ *n* знако́мство; фамилья́рность. **familiarize** /fə'mɪlɪə,raɪz/ *vt* ознакомля́ть *impf*, ознако́мить *pf* (**with** с+*instr*).

family /'fæmɪlɪ/ *n* семья́; *attrib* семе́йный; **~ tree** родосло́вная *sb*.

famine /'fæmɪn/ *n* го́лод. **famished** /'fæmɪʃd/ *adj*: **be ~** голода́ть *impf*.

famous /'feɪməs/ *adj* знамени́тый.

fan¹ /fæn/ *n* ве́ер; (*ventilator*)

вентилятор; **~-belt** ремень *m* вентилятора; *vt* обмахивать *impf*, обмахнуть *pf*; (*flame*) раздувать *impf*, раздуть *pf*.

fan[2] /fæn/ *n* поклонник, ица; (*sport*) болельщик. **fanatic** /fə'nætɪk/ *n* фанатик. **fanatical** /fə'nætɪkəl/ *adj* фанатический.

fanciful /'fænsɪfʊl/ *adj* причудливый. **fancy** /'fænsɪ/ *n* фантазия; (*whim*) причуда; **take a ~ to** увлекаться *impf*, увлечься *pf* +*instr*; *adj* витиеватый; *vt* (*imagine*) представлять *impf*, представить *pf* себе; (*suppose*) полагать *impf*; (*like*) нравиться *impf*, по~ *pf impers*+*dat*; **~ dress** маскарадный костюм; **~-dress** костюмированный.

fanfare /'fænfeə(r)/ *n* фанфара.

fang /fæŋ/ *n* клык; (*serpent's*) ядовитый зуб.

fantasize /'fæntə,saɪz/ *vi* фантазировать *impf*. **fantastic** /fæn'tæstɪk/ *adj* фантастический. **fantasy** /'fæntəsɪ/ *n* фантазия.

far /fɑ:(r)/ *adj* дальний; **Russia is ~ away** Россия очень далеко; *adv* далёко; (*fig*) намного; **as ~ as** (*prep*) до+*gen*; (*conj*) поскольку; **by ~** намного; **(in) so ~ as** поскольку; **so ~** до сих пор; **~-fetched** притянутый за волосы; **~-reaching** далеко идущий; **~-sighted** дальновидный.

farce /fɑ:s/ *n* фарс. **farcical** /'fɑ:sɪk(ə)l/ *adj* смехотворный.

fare /feə(r)/ *n* (*price*) проездная плата; (*food*) пища; *vi* поживать *impf*. **farewell** /feə'wel/ *int* прощай(те)!; *n* прощание; *attrib* прощальный; **bid ~** прощаться *impf*, проститься *pf* (**to** с+*instr*).

farm /fɑ:m/ *n* ферма. **farmer** /'fɑ:mə(r)/ *n* фермер; **~s' market**; рынок сельскохозяйственной продукции. **farming** /'fɑ:mɪŋ/ *n* сельское хозяйство.

fart /fɑ:t/ *n* (*vulg*) пукание; *vi* пукать *impf*, пукнуть *pf*.

farther /'fɑ:ðə(r)/ *see* **further**. **farthest** /'fɑ:ðɪst/ *see* **furthest**.

fascinate /'fæsɪ,neɪt/ *vt* очаровывать *impf*, очаровать *pf*. **fascinating** /-,neɪtɪŋ/ *adj* очаровательный. **fascination** /-'neɪʃ(ə)n/ *n* очарование.

Fascism /'fæʃɪz(ə)m/ *n* фашизм. **Fascist** /-ʃɪst/ *n* фашист, ~ка; *adj* фашистский.

fashion /'fæʃ(ə)n/ *n* мода; (*manner*) манера; **after a ~** некоторым образом; *vt* придавать *impf*, придать *pf* форму +*dat*. **fashionable** /'fæʃnəb(ə)l/ *adj* модный.

fast[1] /fɑ:st/ *n* пост; *vi* поститься *impf*.

fast[2] /fɑ:st/ *adj* (*rapid*) скорый, быстрый; (*colour*) стойкий; (*shut*) плотно закрытый; **be ~** (*timepiece*) спешить *impf*.

fasten /'fɑ:s(ə)n/ *vt* (*attach*) прикреплять *impf*, прикрепить *pf* (**to** к+*dat*); (*tie*) привязывать *impf*, привязать *pf* (**to** к+*dat*); (*garment*) застёгивать *impf*, застегнуть *pf*. **fastener, fastening** /'fɑ:s(ə)nə(r), 'fɑ:snɪŋ/ *n* запор, задвижка; (*on garment*) застёжка.

fastidious /fæ'stɪdɪəs/ *adj* брезгливый.

fat /fæt/ *n* жир; *adj* (*greasy*) жирный; (*plump*) толстый; **get ~** толстеть *impf*, по~ *pf*.

fatal /'feɪt(ə)l/ *adj* роковой; (*deadly*) смертельный. **fatalism** /'feɪtə,lɪzəm/ *n* фатализм. **fatality** /fə'tælətɪ/ *n* (*death*) смерте́льный слу́чай. **fate** /feɪt/ *n* судьба́. **fateful** /'feɪtfʊl/ *adj* роково́й.

father /'fɑːðə(r)/ *n* оте́ц; **~-in-law** (*husband's* ~) свёкор; (*wife's* ~) тесть *m*. **fatherhood** *n* отцо́вство. **fatherland** *n* оте́чество. **fatherly** /'fɑːðəlɪ/ *adj* оте́ческий.

fathom /'fæð(ə)m/ *n* морска́я са́жень; *vt* (*fig*) понима́ть *impf*, поня́ть *pf*.

fatigue /fə'tiːg/ *n* утомле́ние; *vt* утомля́ть *impf*, утоми́ть *pf*.

fatten /'fæt(ə)n/ *vt* отка́рмливать *impf*, откорми́ть *pf*; *vi* толсте́ть *impf*, по~ *pf*. **fatty** /'fætɪ/ *adj* жи́рный.

fatuous /'fætjʊəs/ *adj* глу́пый.

fault /fɒlt/ *n* недоста́ток; (*blame*) вина́; (*geol*) сброс. **faultless** /-lɪs/ *adj* безупре́чный. **faulty** /-tɪ/ *adj* дефе́ктный.

fauna /'fɔːnə/ *n* фа́уна.

favour /'feɪvə(r)/ *n* (*kind act*) любе́зность; (*goodwill*) благоскло́нность; **in (s.o.'s)** ~ в по́льзу +*gen*; **be in ~ of** быть за+*acc*; *vt* (*support*) благоприя́тствовать *impf* +*dat*; (*treat with partiality*) ока́зывать *impf*, оказа́ть *pf* предпочте́ние +*dat*. **favourable** /-rəb(ə)l/ *adj* (*propitious*) благоприя́тный; (*approving*) благоскло́нный. **favourite** /-rɪt/ *n* люби́мец, -мица; (*also sport*) фавори́т, ~ка; *adj* люби́мый.

fawn[1] /fɔːn/ *n* оленёнок; *adj* желтова́то-кори́чневый.

fawn[2] /fɔːn/ *vi* подли́зываться *impf*, подлиза́ться *pf* (**on** к+*dat*).

fax /fæks/ *n* факс; *vt* посыла́ть *impf*, посла́ть *pf* по фа́ксу.

fear /fɪə(r)/ *n* страх, боя́знь, опасе́ние; *vt* & *i* боя́ться *impf* +*gen*; опаса́ться *impf* +*gen*. **fearful** /-fʊl/ *adj* (*terrible*) стра́шный; (*timid*) пугли́вый. **fearless** /-ɪs/ *adj* бесстра́шный. **fearsome** /-səm/ *adj* гро́зный.

feasibility /ˌfiːzɪ'bɪlɪtɪ/ *n* осуществи́мость. **feasible** /'fiːzɪb(ə)l/ *adj* осуществи́мый.

feast /fiːst/ *n* (*meal*) пир; (*festival*) пра́здник; *vi* пирова́ть *impf*.

feat /fiːt/ *n* по́двиг.

feather /'feðə(r)/ *n* перо́.

feature /'fiːtʃə(r)/ *n* черта́; (*newspaper*) (темати́ческая) статья́; ~ **film** худо́жественный фильм; *vt* помеща́ть *impf*, помести́ть *pf* на ви́дном ме́сте; (*in film*) пока́зывать *impf*, показа́ть *pf*; *vi* игра́ть *impf* сыгра́ть *pf* роль.

February /'februərɪ/ *n* февра́ль *m*; *adj* февра́льский.

feckless /'feklɪs/ *adj* безала́берный.

federal /'fedər(ə)l/ *adj* федера́льный. **federation** /-'reɪʃ(ə)n/ *n* федера́ция.

fee /fiː/ *n* гонора́р; (*entrance* ~ *etc.*) взнос; *pl* (*regular payment, school, etc.*) пла́та.

feeble /'fiːb(ə)l/ *adj* сла́бый.

feed /fiːd/ *n* корм; *vt* корми́ть *impf*, на~, по~ *pf*; *vi* корми́ться *impf*, по~ *pf*; ~ **up** отка́рмливать *impf*, откорми́ть *pf*; **I am fed up with** мне надое́л (-а, -о; -и) +*nom*. **feedback** *n* обра́тная связь.

feel /fiːl/ *vt* чу́вствовать *impf*, по~ *pf*; (*think*) счита́ть *impf*, счесть *pf*; *vi* (~ *bad etc.*) чу́вствовать *impf*, по~ *pf* себя́ +*adv*, +*instr*; ~ **like** хоте́ться *impf impers*+*dat*. **feeling** /-lɪŋ/ *n* (*sense*) ощуще́ние; (*emotion*) чу́вство; (*impression*) впечатле́-

ние; (*mood*) настрое́ние.

feign /feɪn/ *vt* притворя́ться *impf*, притвори́ться *pf* +*instr*. **feigned** /feɪnd/ *adj* притво́рный.

feline /'fi:laɪn/ *adj* коша́чий.

fell /fel/ *vt* (*tree*) сруба́ть *impf*, сруби́ть *pf*; (*person*) сбива́ть *impf*, сбить *pf* с ног.

fellow /'feləʊ/ *n* па́рень *m*; (*of society etc.*) член; **~ countryman** сооте́чественник. **fellowship** /-ʃɪp/ *n* това́рищество.

felt /felt/ *n* фетр; *adj* фе́тровый; **~-tip pen** флома́стер.

female /'fi:meɪl/ *n* (*animal*) са́мка; (*person*) же́нщина; *adj* же́нский. **feminine** /'femɪnɪn/ *adj* же́нский, же́нственный; (*gram*) же́нского ро́да. **femininity** /-'nɪnɪtɪ/ *n* же́нственность. **feminism** /'femɪˌnɪz(ə)m/ *n* фемини́зм. **feminist** /-nɪst/ *n* фемини́ст, **~**ка; *adj* феминистский.

fence /fens/ *n* забо́р; *vt*: **~ in** огора́живать *impf*, огороди́ть *pf*; **~ off** отгора́живать *impf*, отгороди́ть *pf*; *vi* (*sport*) фехтова́ть *impf*. **fencer** /-sə(r)/ *n* фехтова́льщик, -ица. **fencing** /-sɪŋ/ *n* (*enclosure*) забо́р; (*sport*) фехтова́ние.

fend /fend/ *vt*: **~ off** отража́ть *impf*, отрази́ть *pf*; *vi*: **~ for o.s.** забо́титься *impf*, по**~** *pf* о себе́. **fender** /-də(r)/ *n* решётка.

fennel /'fen(ə)l/ *n* фе́нхель *m*.

ferment *n* /'fɜ:ment/ броже́ние; *vi* /fə'ment/ броди́ть *impf*; *vt* ква́сить *impf*, за**~** *pf*; (*excite*) возбужда́ть *impf*, возбуди́ть *pf*. **fermentation** /ˌfɜ:men'teɪʃ(ə)n/ *n* броже́ние; (*excitement*) возбужде́ние.

fern /fɜ:n/ *n* па́поротник.

ferocious /fə'rəʊʃəs/ *adj* свире́пый. **ferocity** /-'rɒsɪtɪ/ *n* свире́пость.

ferret /'ferɪt/ *n* хорёк; *vt*: **~ out** (*search out*) разню́хивать *impf*, разню́хать *pf*; *vi*: **~ about** (*rummage*) ры́ться *impf*.

ferry /'ferɪ/ *n* паро́м; *vt* перевози́ть *impf*, перевезти́ *pf*.

fertile /'fɜ:taɪl/ *adj* плодоро́дный. **fertility** /fə'tɪlɪtɪ/ *n* плодоро́дие. **fertilize** /'fɜ:tɪˌlaɪz/ *vt* (*soil*) удобря́ть *impf*, удо́брить *pf*; (*egg*) оплодотворя́ть *impf*, оплодотвори́ть *pf*. **fertilizer** /'fɜ:tɪˌlaɪzə(r)/ *n* удобре́ние.

fervent /'fɜ:v(ə)nt/ *adj* горя́чий. **fervour** /-və(r)/ *n* жар.

fester /'festə(r)/ *vi* гнои́ться *impf*.

festival /'festɪv(ə)l/ *n* пра́здник, (*music etc.*) фестива́ль *m*. **festive** /'festɪv/ *adj* пра́здничный. **festivities** /fes'tɪvɪtɪz/ *n pl* торжества́ *neut pl*.

festoon /fe'stu:n/ *vt* украша́ть *impf*, укра́сить *pf*.

fetch /fetʃ/ *vt* (*carrying*) приноси́ть *impf*, принести́ *pf*; (*leading*) приводи́ть *impf*, привести́ *pf*; (*go and come back with*) (*on foot*) идти́ *impf*, по**~** *pf* за +*instr*; (*by vehicle*) заезжа́ть *impf*, зае́хать *pf* за+*instr*; (*price*) выруча́ть *impf*, вы́ручить *pf*. **fetching** /'fetʃɪŋ/ *adj* привлека́тельный.

fetid /'fetɪd/ *adj* злово́нный.

fetish /'fetɪʃ/ *n* фети́ш.

fetter /'fetə(r)/ *vt* ско́вывать *impf*, скова́ть *pf*; *n*: *pl* кандалы́ (-ло́в) *pl*; (*fig*) око́вы (-в) *pl*.

fettle /'fet(ə)l/ *n* состоя́ние.

feud /fju:d/ *n* кро́вная месть.

feudal /'fju:d(ə)l/ *adj* феода́льный. **feudalism** /-dəˌlɪz(ə)m/ *n* феодали́зм.

fever /'fi:və(r)/ *n* лихора́дка. **fe-**

verish /-rɪʃ/ *adj* лихора́дочный.
few /fjuː/ *adj* & *pron* немно́гие *pl*; ма́ло+*gen*; **a ~** не́сколько +*gen*; **quite a ~** нема́ло +*gen*.
fiancé /fɪ'ɒnseɪ/ *n* жени́х. **fiancée** /fɪ'ɒnseɪ/ *n* неве́ста.
fiasco /fɪ'æskəʊ/ *n* прова́л.
fib /fɪb/ *n* враньё; *vi* привира́ть *impf*, привра́ть *pf*.
fibre /'faɪbə(r)/ *n* волокно́. **fibreglass** *n* стекловолокно́. **fibrous** /-brəs/ *adj* волокни́стый.
fickle /'fɪk(ə)l/ *adj* непостоя́нный.
fiction /'fɪkʃ(ə)n/ *n* худо́жественная литерату́ра; (*invention*) вы́думка. **fictional** /'fɪkʃən(ə)l/ *adj* беллетристи́ческий. **fictitious** /fɪk'tɪʃəs/ *adj* вы́мышленный.
fiddle /'fɪd(ə)l/ *n* (*violin*) скри́пка; (*swindle*) обма́н; *vi*: **~ about** безде́льничать *impf*; **~ with** верте́ть *impf*; *vt* (*falsify*) подде́лывать *impf*, подде́лать *pf*; (*cheat*) жи́лить *impf*, у~ *pf*.
fidelity /fɪ'delɪtɪ/ *n* ве́рность.
fidget /'fɪdʒɪt/ *n* непосе́да *m* & *f*; *vi* ёрзать *impf*; не́рвничать *impf*. **fidgety** /-tɪ/ *adj* непосе́дливый.
field /fiːld/ *n* по́ле; (*sport*) площа́дка; (*sphere*) о́бласть; **~-glasses** полево́й бино́кль *m*. **~work** полевы́е рабо́ты *f pl*.
fiend /fiːnd/ *n* дья́вол. **fiendish** /'fiːndɪʃ/ *adj* дья́вольский.
fierce /'fɪəs/ *adj* свире́пый; (*strong*) си́льный.
fiery /'faɪərɪ/ *adj* о́гненный.
fifteen /fɪf'tiːn/ *adj* & *n* пятна́дцать. **fifteenth** /fɪf'tiːnθ/ *adj* & *n* пятна́дцатый. **fifth** /fɪfθ/ *adj* & *n* пя́тый; (*fraction*) пя́тая *sb*. **fiftieth** /'fɪftɪɪθ/ *adj* & *n* пятидеся́тый. **fifty** /'fɪftɪ/ *adj* & *n* пятьдеся́т; *pl* (*decade*) пятидеся́тые го́ды (-до́в) *m pl*.
fig /fɪg/ *n* инжи́р.
fight /faɪt/ *n* дра́ка; (*battle*) бой; (*fig*) борьба́; *vt* боро́ться *impf* с+*instr*; *vi* дра́ться *impf*; *vt* & *i* (*wage war*) воева́ть *impf* с+*instr*. **fighter** /-tə(r)/ *n* бое́ц; (*aeron*) истреби́тель *m*. **fighting** /-tɪŋ/ *n* бои́ *m pl*.
figment /'fɪgmənt/ *n* плод воображе́ния.
figurative /'fɪgjʊrətɪv/ *adj* перено́сный. **figure** /'fɪgə(r)/ *n* (*form, body, person*) фигу́ра; (*number*) ци́фра; (*diagram*) рису́нок; (*image*) изображе́ние; (*of speech*) оборо́т ре́чи; **~-head** (*naut*) носово́е украше́ние; (*person*) номина́льная глава́; *vt* (*think*) полага́ть *impf*; *vi* фигури́ровать *impf*; **~ out** вычисля́ть *impf*, вы́числить *pf*.
filament /'fɪləmənt/ *n* волокно́; (*electr*) нить.
file[1] /faɪl/ *n* (*tool*) напи́льник; *vt* подпи́ливать *impf*, подпили́ть *pf*.
file[2] /faɪl/ *n* (*folder*) па́пка; (*comput*) файл; *vt* подшива́ть *impf*, подши́ть *pf*; (*complaint*) подава́ть *impf*, пода́ть *pf*.
file[3] /faɪl/ *n* (*row*) ряд; **in (single) ~** гусько́м.
filigree /'fɪlɪˌgriː/ *adj* филигра́нный.
fill /fɪl/ *vt* & *i* (*also* **~ up**) наполня́ть(ся) *impf*, напо́лнить(ся) *pf*; *vt* заполня́ть *impf*, запо́лнить *pf*; (*tooth*) пломбирова́ть *impf*, за~ *pf*; (*occupy*) занима́ть *impf*, заня́ть *pf*; (*satiate*) насыща́ть *impf*, насы́тить *pf*; **~ in** (*vt*) заполня́ть *impf*, запо́лнить *pf*; (*vi*) замеща́ть *impf*,

заместить *pf.*
fillet /'fɪlɪt/ *n* (*cul*) филé *neut indecl.*
filling /'fɪlɪŋ/ *n* (*tooth*) плóмба; (*cul*) начи́нка.
filly /'fɪlɪ/ *n* кобы́лка.
film /fɪlm/ *n* (*layer*; *phot*) плёнка; (*cin*) фильм; **~ star** кинозвездá; *vt* снимáть *impf*, снять *pf*.
filter /'fɪltə(r)/ *n* фильтр; *vt* фильтровáть *impf*, про~ *pf*; **~ through, out** просáчиваться *impf*, просочи́ться *pf*.
filth /fɪlθ/ *n* грязь. **filthy** /-θɪ/ *adj* гря́зный.
fin /fɪn/ *n* плавни́к
final /'faɪn(ə)l/ *n* финáл; *pl* выпускны́е экзáмены *m pl*; *adj* послéдний; (*decisive*) окончáтельный. **finale** /fɪ'nɑ:lɪ/ *n* финáл. **finalist** /'faɪnəlɪst/ *n* финали́ст. **finality** /faɪ'nælɪtɪ/ *n* закóнченность. **finalize** /'faɪnə ˌlaɪz/ *vt* (*complete*) завершáть *impf*, заверши́ть *pf*; (*settle*) улáживать *impf*, улáдить *pf*. **finally** /'faɪnəlɪ/ *adv* (*at last*) наконéц; (*in the end*) в концé концóв.
finance /'faɪnæns/ *n* фина́нсы (-сов) *pl*; *vt* финанси́ровать *impf* & *pf*. **financial** /-'nænʃ(ə)l/ *adj* финáнсовый. **financier** /-'nænsɪə(r)/ *n* финанси́ст.
finch /fɪntʃ/ *n see comb, e.g.* **bullfinch**
find /faɪnd/ *n* нахóдка; *vt* находи́ть *impf*, найти́ *pf*; (*person*) заставáть *impf*, застáть *pf*; **~ out** узнавáть *impf*, узнáть *pf*; **~ fault with** придирáться *impf*, придрáться *pf* к+*dat*. **finding** /-dɪŋ/ *n pl* (*of inquiry*) вы́воды *m pl*.
fine[1] /faɪn/ *n* (*penalty*) штраф; *vt* штрафовáть *impf*, о~ *pf*.
fine[2] /faɪn/ *adj* (*weather*) я́сный; (*excellent*) прекрáсный; (*delicate*) тóнкий; (*of sand etc.*) мéлкий; **~ arts** изобрази́тельные искýсства *neut pl*; *adv* хорошó.
finery /-nərɪ/ *n* наря́д. **finesse** /fɪ'nes/ *n* тóнкость.
finger /'fɪŋgə(r)/ *n* пáлец; **~-nail** нóготь; **~-print** отпечáток пáльца; **~-tip** кóнчик пáльца; **have at (one's) ~s** знать *impf* как свой пять пáльцев; *vt* щýпать *impf*, по~ *pf*.
finish /'fɪnɪʃ/ *n* конéц; (*polish*) отдéлка; (*sport*) фи́ниш; *vt* & *i* кончáть(ся) *impf*, кóнчить(ся) *pf*; *vt* оканчивать *impf*, окóнчить *pf*.
finite /'faɪnaɪt/ *adj* конéчный.
Finland /'fɪnlənd/ *n* Финля́ндия.
Finn /fɪn/ *n* финн, фи́нка. **Finnish** /'fɪnɪʃ/ *adj* фи́нский.
fir /fɜ:(r)/ *n* ель, пи́хта.
fire /'faɪə(r)/ *vt* (*bake*) обжигáть *impf*, обжéчь *pf*; (*excite*) воспламеня́ть *impf*, воспламени́ть *pf*; (*gun*) стреля́ть *impf* из+*gen* (**at** в+*acc*, по+*dat*); (*dismiss*) увольня́ть *impf*, уво́лить *pf*; *n* огóнь *m*; (*grate*)ками́н; (*conflagration*) пожáр; (*bonfire*) костёр; (*fervour*) пыл; **be on ~** горéть *impf*; **catch ~** загорáться *impf*, загорéться *pf*; **set ~ to, set on ~** поджигáть *impf*, поджéчь *pf*; **~-alarm** пожáрная тревóга; **~arm(s)** огнестрéльное орýжие; **~ brigade** пожáрная комáнда; **~-engine** пожáрная маши́на; **~-escape** пожáрная лéстница; **~ extinguisher** огнетуши́тель *m*; **~-guard**ками́нная решётка; **~man** пожáрный *sb*; **~ place**ками́н; **~side** мéсто уками́на; **~ station** пожáрное депó *neut indecl*; **~wood** дровá (-в) *pl*;

~work фейерве́рк. **firing** /'faɪərɪŋ/ *n* (*shooting*) стрельба́.
firm¹ /fɜːm/ *n* (*business*) фи́рма.
firm² /fɜːm/ *adj* твёрдый. **firmness** /-nɪs/ *n* твёрдость.
first /fɜːst/ *adj* пе́рвый; *n* пе́рвый *sb*; *adv* сперва́, снача́ла; (*for the ~ time*) впервы́е; **in the ~ place** во-пе́рвых; **~ of all** пре́жде всего́; **at ~ sight** на пе́рвый взгляд; **~ aid** пе́рвая по́мощь; **~-class** первокла́ссный; **~-hand** из пе́рвых рук; **~-rate** первокла́ссный. **firstly** /-lɪ/ *adv* во-пе́рвых.
fiscal /'fɪsk(ə)l/ *adj* фина́нсовый.
fish /fɪʃ/ *n* ры́ба; *adj* ры́бный; *vi* лови́ть *impf* ры́бу; **~ out** выта́скивать *impf*, вы́таскать *pf*. **fisherman** /'fɪʃəmən/ *n* рыба́к. **fishery** /'fɪʃərɪ/ *n* ры́бный про́мысел. **fishing** /'fɪʃɪŋ/ *n* ры́бная ло́вля; **~ boat** рыболо́вное су́дно; **~ line** леса́; **~ rod** у́дочка. **fishmonger** /'fɪʃmʌŋgə(r)/ *n* торго́вец ры́бой. **fishmonger's** /'fɪʃmʌŋgəz/ *n* ры́бный магази́н. **fishy** /'fɪʃɪ/ *adj* ры́бный; (*dubious*) подозри́тельный.
fissure /'fɪʃə(r)/ *n* тре́щина.
fist /fɪst/ *n* кула́к.
fit¹ /fɪt/ *n*: **be a good ~** хорошо́ сиде́ть *impf*; *adj* (*suitable*) подходя́щий, го́дный; (*healthy*) здоро́вый; *vt* (*be suitable*) годи́ться *impf* +*dat*, на+*acc*, для +*gen*; *vt & i* (*be the right size* (*for*)) подходи́ть *impf*, подойти́ *pf* (+*dat*); (*adjust*) прила́живать *impf*, прила́дить *pf* (**to** к+*dat*); (*be small enough for*) входи́ть *impf*, войти́ *pf* в+*acc*; **~ out** снабжа́ть *impf*, снабди́ть *pf*.
fit² /fɪt/ *n* (*attack*) припа́док; (*fig*) поры́в. **fitful** /-fʊl/ *adj* поры́вистый.
fitter /'fɪtə(r)/ *n* монтёр. **fitting** /-tɪŋ/ *n* (*of clothes*) приме́рка; *pl* армату́ра; *adj* подходя́щий.
five /faɪv/ *adj & n* пять; (*number 5*) пятёрка; **~-year plan** пятиле́тка.
fix /fɪks/ *n* (*dilemma*) переде́лка; (*drugs*) уко́л; *vt* (*repair*) чини́ть *impf*, по~ *pf*; (*settle*) назнача́ть *impf*, назна́чить *pf*; (*fasten*) укрепля́ть *impf*, укрепи́ть *pf*; **~ up** (*organize*) организова́ть *impf & pf*; (*install*) устана́вливать *impf*, установи́ть *pf*. **fixation** /-'seɪʃ(ə)n/ *n* викса́ция. **fixed** /fɪkst/ *adj* устано́вленный. **fixture** /'fɪkstʃə(r)/ *n* (*sport*) предстоя́щее спорти́вное мероприя́тие; (*fitting*) приспособле́ние.
fizz, fizzle /fɪz, 'fɪz(ə)l/ *vi* шипе́ть *impf*; **fizzle out** выдыха́ться *impf*, вы́дохнуться *pf*. **fizzy** /'fɪzɪ/ *adj* шипу́чий.
flabbergasted /'flæbəˌgɑːstɪd/ *adj* ошеломлённый.
flabby /'flæbɪ/ *adj* дря́блый.
flag¹ /flæg/ *n* флаг, зна́мя *neut*; *vt*: **~ down** остана́вливать *impf*, останови́ть *pf*.
flag² /flæg/ *vi* (*weaken*) ослабева́ть *impf*, ослабе́ть *pf*.
flagon /'flægən/ *n* кувши́н.
flagrant /'fleɪgrənt/ *adj* вопию́щий.
flagship /'flægʃɪp/ *n* фла́гман.
flagstone /'flægstəʊn/ *n* плита́.
flair /'fleə(r)/ *n* чутьё.
flake /fleɪk/ *n* слой; *pl* хло́пья (-ьев) *pl*; *vi* шелуши́ться *impf*. **flaky** /'fleɪkɪ/ *adj* слои́стый.
flamboyant /flæm'bɔɪənt/ *adj* цвети́стый.
flame /fleɪm/ *n* пла́мя *neut*, ого́нь *m*; *vi* пыла́ть *impf*.

flange /flændʒ/ *n* фла́нец.
flank /flæŋk/ *n* (*of body*) бок; (*mil*) фланг; *vt* быть сбо́ку +*gen*.
flannel /ˈflæn(ə)l/ *n* флане́ль; (*for face*) моча́лка для лица́.
flap /flæp/ *n* (*board*) откидна́я доска́; (*pocket, tent* ~) кла́пан; (*panic*) па́ника; *vt* взма́хивать *impf*, взмахну́ть *pf* +*instr*; *vi* развева́ться *impf*.
flare /fleə(r)/ *n* вспы́шка; (*signal*) сигна́льная ракéта; *vi* вспы́хивать *impf*, вспы́хнуть *pf*; ~ **up** (*fire*) возгора́ться *impf*, возгоре́ться *pf*; (*fig*) вспыли́ть *pf*.
flash /flæʃ/ *n* вспы́шка; **in a** ~ ми́гом; *vi* сверка́ть *impf*, сверкну́ть *pf*. **flashback** *n* ретроспе́кция. **flashy** /ˈflæʃɪ/ *adj* показно́й.
flask /flɑːsk/ *n* фля́жка.
flat[1] /flæt/ *n* (*dwelling*) кварти́ра.
flat[2] /flæt/ *n* (*mus*) бемо́ль *m*; (*tyre*) спу́щенная ши́на; **on the** ~ на пло́скости; *adj* пло́ский; ~**-fish** ка́мбала. **flatly** /-lɪ/ *adv* наотре́з. **flatten** /-t(ə)n/ *vt* & *i* выра́внивать(ся) *impf*, вы́ровнять(ся) *pf*.
flatmate /ˈflætmeɪt/ *n* сосе́д, ~ка по кварти́ре.
flatter /ˈflætə(r)/ *vt* льсти́ть *impf*, по~ *pf* +*dat*. **flattering** /-rɪŋ/ *adj* льсти́вый. **flattery** /-rɪ/ *n* лесть.
flaunt /flɔːnt/ *vt* щеголя́ть *impf*, щегольну́ть *pf* +*instr*.
flautist /ˈflɔːtɪst/ *n* флейти́ст.
flavour /ˈfleɪvə(r)/ *n* вкус; (*fig*) при́вкус; *vt* приправля́ть *impf*, припра́вить *pf*.
flaw /flɔː/ *n* изъя́н.
flax /flæks/ *n* лён. **flaxen** /ˈflæks(ə)n/ *adj* (*colour*) соло́менный.
flea /fliː/ *n* блоха́; ~ **market** барахо́лка.
fleck /flek/ *n* кра́пинка.
flee /fliː/ *vi* бежа́ть *impf* & *pf* (**from** от+*gen*); *vt* бежа́ть *impf* из+*gen*.
fleece /fliːs/ *n* руно́; *vt* (*fig*) обдира́ть *impf*, ободра́ть *pf*. **fleecy** /-sɪ/ *adj* шерсти́стый.
fleet /fliːt/ *n* флот; (*vehicles*) парк.
fleeting /ˈfliːtɪŋ/ *adj* мимолётный.
flesh /fleʃ/ *n* (*as opposed to mind*) плоть; (*meat*) мя́со; **in the** ~ во плоти́. **fleshy** /-ʃɪ/ *adj* мяси́стый.
flex /fleks/ *n* шнур; *vt* сгиба́ть *impf*, согну́ть *pf*. **flexibility** /ˌfleksɪˈbɪlɪtɪ/ *adj* ги́бкость. **flexible** /ˈfleksɪb(ə)l/ *adj* ги́бкий.
flick /flɪk/ *vt* & *i* щёлкать *impf*, щёлкнуть *pf* (+*instr*); ~ **through** пролиста́ть *pf*.
flicker /ˈflɪkə(r)/ *n* мерца́ние; *vi* мерца́ть *impf*.
flier /ˈflaɪə(r)/ *see* **flyer**
flight[1] /flaɪt/ *n* (*fleeing*) бе́гство; **put (take) to** ~ обраща́ть(ся) *impf*, обрати́ть(ся) *pf* в бе́гство.
flight[2] /flaɪt/ *n* (*flying*) полёт; (*trip*) рейс; ~ **of stairs** ле́стничный марш. **flighty** /-tɪ/ *adj* ве́треный.
flimsy /ˈflɪmzɪ/ *adj* (*fragile*) непро́чный; (*dress*) лёгкий; (*excuse*) сла́бый.
flinch /flɪntʃ/ *vi* (*recoil*) отпря́дывать *impf*, отпря́нуть *pf*; (*fig*) уклоня́ться *impf*, уклони́ться *pf* (**from** от+*gen*).
fling /flɪŋ/ *vt* швыря́ть *impf*, швырну́ть *pf*; *vi* (*also* ~ *o.s.*) броса́ться *impf*, бро́ситься *pf*.
flint /flɪnt/ *n* креме́нь *m*.
flip /flɪp/ *vt* щёлкать *impf*,

щёлкнуть *pf* +*instr*.
flippant /'flɪpənt/ *adj* легкомы́сленный.
flipper /'flɪpə(r)/ *n* ласт.
flirt /flɜːt/ *n* коке́тка; *vi* флиртова́ть *impf* (**with** c+*instr*). **flirtation** /-'teɪʃ(ə)n/ *n* флирт.
flit /flɪt/ *vi* порха́ть *impf*, порхну́ть *pf*.
float /fləʊt/ *n* поплаво́к; *vi* пла́вать *indet*, плыть *det*; *vt* (*company*) пуска́ть *impf*, пусти́ть *pf* в ход.
flock /flɒk/ *n* (*animals*) ста́до; (*birds*) ста́я; *vi* стека́ться *impf*, стёчься *pf*.
flog /flɒg/ *vt* сечь *impf*, вы́~ *pf*.
flood /flʌd/ *n* наводне́ние; (*bibl*) пото́п; (*fig*) пото́к; *vi* (*river etc.*) выступа́ть *impf*, вы́ступить *pf* из берего́в; *vt* затопля́ть *impf*, затопи́ть *pf*. **floodgate** *n* шлюз. **floodlight** *n* проже́ктор.
floor /flɔː(r)/ *n* пол; (*storey*) эта́ж; **~board** полови́ца; *vt* (*confound*) ста́вить *impf*, по~ *pf* в тупи́к.
flop /flɒp/ *vi* (*fall*) плю́хаться *impf*, плю́хнуться *pf*; (*fail*) прова́ливаться *impf*, провали́ться *pf*.
flora /'flɔːrə/ *n* фло́ра. **floral** /-r(ə)l/ *adj* цвето́чный.
florid /'flɒrɪd/ *adj* цвети́стый; (*ruddy*) румя́ный. **florist** /'flɒrɪst/ *n* торго́вец цвета́ми.
flounce[1] /flaʊns/ *vi* броса́ться *impf*, бро́ситься *pf*.
flounce[2] /flaʊns/ *n* (*of skirt*) обо́рка.
flounder[1] /'flaʊndə(r)/ *n* (*fish*) ка́мбала.
flounder[2] /'flaʊndə(r)/ *vi* бара́хтаться *impf*.
flour /'flaʊə(r)/ *n* мука́.
flourish /'flʌrɪʃ/ *n* (*movement*) разма́хивание (+*instr*); (*of pen*) ро́счерк; *vi* (*thrive*) процвета́ть *impf*; *vt* (*wave*) разма́хивать *impf*, размахну́ть *pf* +*instr*.
flout /flaʊt/ *vt* попира́ть *impf*, попра́ть *pf*.
flow /fləʊ/ *vi* течь *impf*; ли́ться *impf*; *n* тече́ние.
flower /'flaʊə(r)/ *n* цвето́к; **~-bed** клу́мба; **~pot** цвето́чный горшо́к; *vi* цвести́ *impf*. **flowery** /-rɪ/ *adj* цвети́стый.
flu /fluː/ *n* грипп.
fluctuate /'flʌktjʊˌeɪt/ *vi* колеба́ться *impf*, по~ *pf*. **fluctuation** /-'eɪʃ(ə)n/ *n* колеба́ние.
flue /fluː/ *n* дымохо́д.
fluent /'fluːənt/ *adj* бе́глый. **fluently** /-lɪ/ *adv* свобо́дно.
fluff /flʌf/ *n* пух. **fluffy** /-fɪ/ *adj* пуши́стый.
fluid /'fluːɪd/ *n* жи́дкость; *adj* жи́дкий.
fluke /fluːk/ *n* случа́йная уда́ча.
fluorescent /flʊə'res(ə)nt/ *adj* флюоресце́нтный.
fluoride /'flʊəraɪd/ *n* фтори́д.
flurry /'flʌrɪ/ *n* (*squall*) шквал; (*fig*) волна́.
flush /flʌʃ/ *n* (*redness*) румя́нец; *vi* (*redden*) красне́ть *impf*, по~ *pf*; *vt* спуска́ть *impf*, спусти́ть *pf* во́ду в+*acc*.
flustered /'flʌstəd/ *adj* сконфу́женный.
flute /fluːt/ *n* фле́йта.
flutter /'flʌtə(r)/ *vi* (*flit*) порха́ть *impf*, порхну́ть *pf*; (*wave*) развева́ться *impf*.
flux /flʌks/ *n*: **in a state of ~** в состоя́нии измене́ния.
fly[1] /flaɪ/ *n* (*insect*) му́ха.
fly[2] /flaɪ/ *vi* лета́ть *indet*, лете́ть *det*, по~ *pf*; (*flag*) развева́ться *impf*; (*hasten*) нести́сь *impf*, по~ *pf*; *vt* (*aircraft*) управля́ть *impf* +*instr*; (*transport*) перево-

зи́ть *impf*, перевезти́ *pf* (самолётом); (*flag*) поднима́ть *impf*, подня́ть *pf*. **flyer, flier** /'flaɪə(r)/ *n* лётчик. **flying** /'flaɪɪŋ/ *n* полёт.

foal /fəʊl/ *n* (*horse*) жеребёнок

foam /fəʊm/ *n* пе́на; **~ plastic** пенопла́ст; **~ rubber** пенорези́на; *vi* пе́ниться *impf*, вс~ *pf*. **foamy** /-mɪ/ *adj* пе́нистый.

focal /'fəʊk(ə)l/ *adj* фо́кусный. **focus** /'fəʊkəs/ *n* фо́кус; (*fig*) центр; *vt* фокуси́ровать *impf*, с~ *pf*; (*concentrate*) сосредото́чивать *impf*, сосредото́чить *pf*.

fodder /'fɒdə(r)/ *n* корм.

foe /fəʊ/ *n* враг.

foetus /'fi:təs/ *n* заро́дыш.

fog /fɒg/ *n* тума́н. **foggy** /-gɪ/ *adj* тума́нный.

foible /'fɔɪb(ə)l/ *n* сла́бость.

foil[1] /fɔɪl/ *n* (*metal*) фольга́; (*contrast*) контра́ст.

foil[2] /fɔɪl/ *vt* (*thwart*) расстра́ивать *impf*, расстро́ить *pf*.

foil[3] /fɔɪl/ *n* (*sword*) рапи́ра.

foist /fɔɪst/ *vt* навя́зывать *impf*, навяза́ть *pf* (**on** *+dat*).

fold[1] /fəʊld/ *n* (*sheep-~*) овча́рня.

fold[2] /fəʊld/ *n* скла́дка, сгиб; *vt* скла́дывать *impf*, сложи́ть *pf*. **folder** /-də(r)/ *n* па́пка. **folding** /-dɪŋ/ *adj* складно́й.

foliage /'fəʊlɪɪdʒ/ *n* листва́.

folk /fəʊk/ *n* наро́д, лю́ди *pl*; *pl* (*relatives*) родня́ *collect*; *attrib* наро́дный. **folklore** /'fəʊklɔ:(r)/ *n* фолькло́р.

follow /'fɒləʊ/ *vt* сле́довать *impf*, по~ *pf* *+dat*, за*+instr*; (*walk behind*) идти́ *det* за*+instr*; (*fig*) следи́ть *impf* за*+instr*. **follower** /'fɒləʊwə(r)/ *n* после́дователь *m*. **following** /'fɒləʊwɪŋ/ *adj* сле́дующий.

folly /'fɒlɪ/ *n* глу́пость.

fond /fɒnd/ *adj* не́жный; **be ~ of** люби́ть *impf* *+acc*.

fondle /'fɒnd(ə)l/ *vt* ласка́ть *impf*.

fondness /'fɒndnɪs/ *n* любо́вь.

font /fɒnt/ *n* (*eccl*) купе́ль.

food /fu:d/ *n* пи́ща, еда́. **foodstuff** *n* пищево́й проду́кт.

fool /fu:l/ *n* дура́к, ду́ра; *vt* дура́чить *impf*, о~ *pf*; *vi*: **~ about** дура́читься *impf*. **foolhardy** /'fu:lˌhɑ:dɪ/ *adj* безрассу́дно хра́брый. **foolish** /'fu:lɪʃ/ *adj* глу́пый. **foolishness** /'fu:lɪʃnɪs/ *n* глу́пость. **foolproof** /'fu:lpru:f/ *adj* абсолю́тно надёжный.

foot /fʊt/ *n* нога́; (*measure*) фут; (*of hill etc.*) подно́жие; **on ~** пешко́м; **put one's ~ in it** сесть *pf* в лу́жу. **foot-and-mouth (disease)** *n* я́щур. **football** *n* футбо́л; *attrib* футбо́льный. **footballer** /'fʊtbɔ:lə(r)/ *n* футболи́ст. **foothills** *n pl* предго́рье. **footing** /'fʊtɪŋ/ *n* (*fig*) ба́зис; **lose one's ~** оступи́ться *pf*; **on an equal ~** на ра́вной ноге́. **footlights** *n pl* ра́мпа. **footman** *n* лаке́й. **footnote** *n* сно́ска. **footpath** *n* тропи́нка; (*pavement*) тротуа́р. **footprint** *n* след. **footstep** *n* (*sound*) шаг; (*footprint*) след. **footwear** *n* о́бувь.

for /fɔ:(r)/ *prep* (*of time*) в тече́ние *+gen*, на*+acc*; (*of purpose*) для*+gen*, за*+acc*, *+instr*; (*price*) за*+acc*; (*on account of*) из-за *+gen*; (*in place of*) вме́сто*+gen*; **~ the sake of** ра́ди *+gen*; **as ~** что каса́ется*+gen*; *conj* так как.

forage /'fɒrɪdʒ/ *n* фура́ж; *vi*: **~ for** разы́скивать *impf*.

foray /'fɒreɪ/ *n* набе́г.

forbearance /fɔːˈbeərəns/ *n* воздéржанность. **forbid** /fəˈbɪd/ *vt* запрещáть *impf*, запретúть *pf* (+*dat* (*person*) & *acc* (*thing*)). **forbidding** /-dɪŋ/ *adj* грóзный.

force /fɔːs/ *n* сúла; *pl* (*armed* ~) вооружённые сúлы *f pl*; **by** ~ сúлой; *vt* (*compel*) заставлять *impf*, застáвить *pf*; (*lock etc.*) взлáмывать *impf*, взломáть *pf*. **forceful** /-fʊl/ *adj* сúльный; (*speech*) убедúтельный. **forcible** /ˈfɔːsɪb(ə)l/ *adj* насúльственный.

forceps /ˈfɔːseps/ *n* щипцы́ (-цóв) *pl*.

ford /fɔːd/ *n* брод; *vt* переходúть *impf*, перейтú *pf* вброд+*acc*.

fore /fɔː(r)/ *n*: **come to the** ~ выдвигáться *impf*, вы́двинуться *pf* на перéдний плáн.

forearm *n* /ˈfɔːrɑːm/ предплéчье. **foreboding** /fɔːˈbəʊdɪŋ/ *n* предчýвствие. **forecast** /ˈfɔːkɑːst/ *n* предсказáние; (*of weather*) прогнóз; *vt* /fɔːrˈɑːm/ предскáзывать *impf*, предсказáть *pf*. **forecourt** *n* перéдний двор. **forefather** *n* прéдок. **forefinger** *n* указáтельный пáлец. **forefront** *n* (*foreground*) перéдний план; (*leading position*) авангáрд. **foregone** /ˈfɔːgɒn/ *adj*: ~ **conclusion** предрешённый исхóд. **foreground** *n* перéдний план. **forehead** /ˈfɒrɪd/ *n* лоб.

foreign /ˈfɒrɪn/ *adj* (*from abroad*) инострáнный; (*alien*) чýждый; (*external*) внéшний; ~ **body** инорóдное тéло; ~ **currency** валю́та. **foreigner** /ˈfɒrɪnə(r)/ *n* инострáнец, -нка.

foreman /ˈfɔːmən/ *n* мáстер.

foremost /ˈfɔːməʊst/ *adj* выдаю́щийся; **first and** ~ прéжде всегó.

forename /ˈfɔːneɪm/ *n* úмя.

forensic /fəˈrensɪk/ *adj* судéбный.

forerunner /ˈfɔːˌrʌnə(r)/ *n* предвéстник. **foresee** /fɔːˈsiː/ *vt* предвúдеть *impf*. **foreshadow** /fɔːˈʃædəʊ/ *vt* предвещáть *impf*. **foresight**/ˈfɔːsaɪt/ *n* предвúдение; (*caution*) предусмотрúтельность.

forest /ˈfɒrɪst/ *n* лес.

forestall /fɔːˈstɔːl/ *vt* предупреждáть *impf*, предупредúть *pf*.

forester /ˈfɒrɪstə(r)/ *n* леснúчий *sb*. **forestry** /ˈfɒrɪstrɪ/ *n* лесовóдство.

foretaste /ˈfɔːteɪst/ *n* предвкушéние; *vt* предвкушáть *impf*, предвкусúть *pf*. **foretell** /fɔːˈtel/ *vt* предскáзывать *impf*, предсказáть *pf*. **forethought** /ˈfɔːθɔːt/ *n* предусмотрúтельность. **forewarn** /fɔːˈwɔːn/ *vt* предостерегáть *impf*, предостерéчь *pf*. **foreword** /ˈfɔːwɜːd/ *n* предислóвие.

forfeit /ˈfɔːfɪt/ *n* (*in game*) фант; *vt* лишáться *impf*, лишúться *pf* +*gen*.

forge[1] /fɔːdʒ/ *n* (*smithy*) кýзница; (*furnace*) горн; *vt* ковáть *impf*, вы́~ *pf*; (*fabricate*) поддéлывать *impf*, поддéлать *pf*.

forge[2] /fɔːdʒ/ *vi*: ~ **ahead** продвигáться *impf*, продвúнуться *pf* вперёд.

forger /ˈfɔːdʒə(r)/ *n* фальшивомонéтчик. **forgery** /-rɪ/ *n* поддéлка.

forget /fəˈget/ *vt* забывáть *impf*, забы́ть *pf*. **forgetful** /-fʊl/ *adj* забы́вчивый.

forgive /fəˈgɪv/ *vt* прощáть *impf*, простúть *pf*. **forgiveness** /-nɪs/ *n* прощéние.

forgo /fɔːˈgəʊ/ *vt* воздéрживаться *impf*, воздержáться *pf* от+*gen*.

fork /fɔːk/ *n* (*eating*) ви́лка; (*digging*) ви́лы (-л) *pl*; (*in road*) разветвле́ние; *vi* (*road*) разветвля́ться *impf*, разветви́ться *pf*.
forlorn /fəˈlɔːn/ *adj* жа́лкий.
form /fɔːm/ *n* (*shape*; *kind*) фо́рма; (*class*) класс; (*document*) анке́та; *vt* (*make, create*) образо́вывать *impf*, образова́ть *pf*; (*develop*; *make up*) составля́ть *impf*, соста́вить *pf*; *vi* образо́вываться *impf*, образова́ться *pf*. **formal** /ˈfɔːm(ə)l/ *adj* форма́льный; (*official*) официа́льный. **formality** /fɔːˈmælɪtɪ/ *n* форма́льность. **format** /ˈfɔːmæt/ *n* форма́т. **formation** /fɔːˈmeɪʃ(ə)n/ *n* образова́ние. **formative** /ˈfɔːmətɪv/ *adj*: ~ **years** молоды́е го́ды (-до́в) *m pl*.
former /ˈfɔːmə(r)/ *adj* (*earlier*) пре́жний; (*ex*) бы́вший; **the** ~ (*of two*) пе́рвый. **formerly** /ˈfɔːməlɪ/ *adv* пре́жде.
formidable /ˈfɔːmɪdəb(ə)l/ *adj* (*dread*) гро́зный; (*arduous*) тру́дный.
formless /ˈfɔːmlɪs/ *adj* бесфо́рменный.
formula /ˈfɔːmjʊlə/ *n* фо́рмула. **formulate** /-ˌleɪt/ *vt* формули́ровать *impf*, с~ *pf*. **formulation** /-ˈleɪʃ(ə)n/ *n* формулиро́вка.
forsake /fəˈseɪk/ *vt* (*desert*) покида́ть *impf*, поки́нуть *pf*; (*renounce*) отка́зываться *impf*, отказа́ться *pf* от+*gen*.
fort /fɔːt/ *n* форт.
forth /fɔːθ/ *adv* вперёд, да́льше; **back and** ~ взад и вперёд; **and so** ~ и так да́лее. **forthcoming** /fɔːθˈkʌmɪŋ/ *adj* предстоя́щий; **be** ~ (*available*) поступа́ть *impf*, поступи́ть *pf*. **forthwith** /fɔːθˈwɪθ/ *adv* неме́дленно.
fortieth /ˈfɔːtɪɪθ/ *adj* & *n* сороково́й.
fortification /ˌfɔːtɪfɪˈkeɪʃ(ə)n/ *n* укрепле́ние. **fortify** /ˈfɔːtɪˌfaɪ/ *vt* укрепля́ть *impf*, укрепи́ть *pf*; (*fig*) подкрепля́ть *impf*, подкрепи́ть *pf*. **fortitude** /ˈfɔːtɪˌtjuːd/ *n* сто́йкость.
fortnight /ˈfɔːtnaɪt/ *n* две неде́ли *f pl*. **fortnightly** /-lɪ/ *adj* двухнеде́льный; *adv* раз в две неде́ли.
fortress /ˈfɔːtrɪs/ *n* кре́пость.
fortuitous /fɔːˈtjuːɪtəs/ *adj* случа́йный.
fortunate /ˈfɔːtjʊnət/ *adj* счастли́вый. **fortunately** /-lɪ/ *adv* к сча́стью. **fortune** /ˈfɔːtjuːn/ *n* (*destiny*) судьба́; (*good* ~) сча́стье; (*wealth*) состоя́ние.
forty /ˈfɔːtɪ/ *adj* & *n* со́рок; *pl* (*decade*) сороковы́е го́ды (-до́в) *m pl*.
forward /ˈfɔːwəd/ *adj* пере́дний; (*presumptuous*) развя́зный; *n* (*sport*) напада́ющий *sb*; *adv* вперёд; *vt* (*letter*) пересыла́ть *impf*, пересла́ть *pf*.
fossil /ˈfɒs(ə)l/ *n* ископа́емое *sb*; *adj* ископа́емый. **fossilized** /ˈfɒsɪˌlaɪzd/ *adj* ископа́емый.
foster /ˈfɒstə(r)/ *vt* (*child*) приюти́ть *pf*; (*idea*) вына́шивать *impf*, вы́носить *pf*; (*create*) создава́ть *impf*, созда́ть *pf*; (*cherish*) леле́ять *impf*; ~**-child** приёмыш.
foul /faʊl/ *adj* (*dirty*) гря́зный; (*repulsive*) отврати́тельный; (*obscene*) непристо́йный; *n* (*sport*) наруше́ние пра́вил; *vt* (*dirty*) па́чкать *impf*, за~, ис~ *pf*; (*entangle*) запу́тывать *impf*, запу́тать *pf*.
found /faʊnd/ *vt* осно́вывать *impf*, основа́ть *pf*.
foundation /faʊnˈdeɪʃ(ə)n/ *n* (*of*

building) фундáмент; (*basis*) оснóва; (*institution*) учреждéние; (*fund*) фонд. **founder**[1] /'faʊndə(r)/ *n* основáтель *m*.

founder[2] /'faʊndə(r)/ *vi* (*naut*, *fig*) тонýть *impf*, по~ *pf*.

foundry /'faʊndrɪ/ *n* литéйная *sb*.

fountain /'faʊntɪn/ *n* фонтáн; **~-pen** авторýчка.

four /fɔ:(r)/ *adj* & *n* четы́ре; (*number 4*) четвёрка; **on all ~s** на четверéньках. **fourteen** /fɔ:'ti:n/ *adj* & *n* четы́рнадцать. **fourteenth** /fɔ:'ti:nθ/ *adj* & *n* четы́рнадцатый. **fourth** /fɔ:θ/ *adj* & *n* четвёртый; (*quarter*) чéтверть.

fowl /faʊl/ *n* (*domestic*) домáшняя пти́ца; (*wild*) дичь *collect*.

fox /fɒks/ *n* лисá, лиси́ца; *vt* озадáчивать *impf*, озадáчить *pf*.

foyer /'fɔɪeɪ/ *n* фойé *neut indecl*.

fraction /'frækʃ(ə)n/ *n* (*math*) дробь; (*portion*) части́ца.

fractious /'frækʃəs/ *adj* раздражи́тельный.

fracture /'fræktʃə(r)/ *n* перелóм; *vt* & *i* ломáть(ся) *impf*, с~ *pf*.

fragile /'frædʒaɪl/ *adj* лóмкий.

fragment /'frægmənt/ *n* облóмок; (*of conversation*) отры́вок; (*of writing*) фрагмéнт. **fragmentary** /-tərɪ/ *adj* отры́вочный.

fragrance /'freɪgrəns/ *n* аромáт. **fragrant** /-grənt/ *adj* аромáтный, души́стый.

frail /freɪl/ *adj* хрýпкий.

frame /freɪm/ *n* óстов; (*build*) телосложéние; (*picture*) рáма; (*cin*) кадр; **~ of mind** настроéние; *vt* (*devise*) создавáть *impf*, создáть *pf*; (*formulate*) формули́ровать *impf*, с~ *pf*; (*picture*) вставля́ть *impf*, встáвить *pf* в рáму; (*incriminate*) фабриковáть *impf*, с~ *pf* обвинéние прóтив+*gen*. **framework** *n* óстов; (*fig*) рáмки *f pl*.

franc /fræŋk/ *n* франк.

France /frɑ:ns/ *n* Фрáнция.

franchise /'fræntʃaɪz/ *n* (*comm*) привилéгия; (*polit*) прáво гóлоса.

frank[1] /fræŋk/ *adj* откровéнный.

frank[2] /fræŋk/ *vt* (*letter*) франки́ровать *impf* & *pf*.

frantic /'fræntɪk/ *adj* нейстовый.

fraternal /frə'tɜ:n(ə)l/ *adj* брáтский. **fraternity** /-'tɜ:nɪtɪ/ *n* брáтство.

fraud /frɔ:d/ *n* обмáн; (*person*) обмáнщик. **fraudulent** /'frɔ:djʊlənt/ *adj* обмáнный.

fraught /frɔ:t/ *adj*: **~ with** чревáтый +*instr*.

fray[1] /freɪ/ *vt* & *i* обтрёпывать(ся) *impf*, обтрепáть(ся) *pf*.

fray[2] /freɪ/ *n* бой.

freak /fri:k/ *n* урóд; *attrib* необы́чный.

freckle /'frek(ə)l/ *n* веснýшка. **freckled** /'frekəld/ *adj* веснýшчатый.

free /fri:/ *adj* свобóдный; (*gratis*) бесплáтный; **~ kick** штрафнóй удáр; **~ speech** свобóда слóва; *vt* освобождáть *impf*, освободи́ть *pf*. **freedom** /'fri:dəm/ *n* свобóда. **freehold** *n* неограни́ченное прáво сóбственности на недви́жимость. **freelance** /'fri:lɑ:ns/ *adj* внештáтный. **Freemason** *n* франкмасóн.

freeze /fri:z/ *vi* замерзáть *impf*, мёрзнуть *impf*, замёрзнуть *pf*; *vt* заморáживать *impf*, заморóзить *pf*. **freezer** /-zə(r)/ *n* морози́льник; (*compartment*) морози́лка. **freezing** /-zɪŋ/ *adj* моро́зный; **below ~** ни́же нуля́.

freight /freɪt/ *n* фрахт. **freighter** /-tə(r)/ *n* (*ship*) грузово́е су́дно.

French /frentʃ/ *adj* францу́зский; **~ bean** фасо́ль; **~ horn** валто́рна; **~ windows** двуство́рчатое окно́ до по́ла. **Frenchman** *n* францу́з. **Frenchwoman** *n* францу́женка.

frenetic /frə'netɪk/ *adj* неисто́вый.

frenzied /'frenzɪd/ *adj* неи́стовый. **frenzy** /-zɪ/ *n* неи́стовство.

frequency /'fri:kwənsɪ/ *n* частота́. **frequent** *adj* /'fri:kwənt/ ча́стый; *vt* /frɪ'kwent/ ча́сто посеща́ть *impf.*

fresco /'freskəʊ/ *n* фре́ска.

fresh /freʃ/ *adj* све́жий; (*new*) но́вый; **~ water** пре́сная вода́. **freshen** /-ʃ(ə)n/ *vt* освежа́ть *impf*, освежи́ть *pf*; *vi* свеже́ть *impf*, по~ *pf.* **freshly** /-lɪ/ *adv* свежо́; (*recently*) неда́вно. **freshness** /-nɪs/ *n* све́жесть. **freshwater** *adj* пресново́дный.

fret¹ /fret/ *vi* му́читься *impf.* **fretful** /-fʊl/ *adj* раздражи́тельный.

fret² /fret/ *n* (*mus*) лад.

fretsaw /'fretsɔ:/ *n* ло́бзик.

friar /'fraɪə(r)/ *n* мона́х.

friction /'frɪkʃ(ə)n/ *n* тре́ние; (*fig*) тре́ния *neut pl.*

Friday /'fraɪdeɪ/ *n* пя́тница.

fridge /frɪdʒ/ *n* холоди́льник.

fried /fraɪd/ *adj*: **~ egg** яи́чница.

friend /frend/ *n* друг, подру́га; прия́тель *m*, ~ница. **friendly** /-lɪ/ *adj* дру́жеский. **friendship** *n* дру́жба.

frieze /fri:z/ *n* фриз.

frigate /'frɪgɪt/ *n* фрега́т.

fright /fraɪt/ *n* испу́г. **frighten** /-t(ə)n/ *vt* пуга́ть *impf*, ис~, на~ *pf.* **frightful** /-fʊl/ *adj* стра́шный.

frigid /'frɪdʒɪd/ *adj* холо́дный.

frill /frɪl/ *n* obо́рка.

fringe /frɪndʒ/ *n* бахрома́; (*of hair*) чёлка; (*edge*) край.

frisk /frɪsk/ *vi* (*frolic*) резви́ться *impf*; *vt* (*search*) шмона́ть *impf.* **frisky** /-kɪ/ *adj* ре́звый.

fritter /'frɪtə(r)/ *vt*: **~ away** растра́чивать *impf*, растра́тить *pf.*

frivolity /frɪ'vɒlɪtɪ/ *n* легкомы́сленность. **frivolous** /'frɪvələs/ *adj* легкомы́сленный.

fro /frəʊ/ *adv*: **to and ~** взад и вперёд.

frock /frɒk/ *n* пла́тье.

frog /frɒg/ *n* лягу́шка.

frolic /'frɒlɪk/ *vi* резви́ться *impf.*

from /frɒm/ *prep* от+*gen*; (*~ off, down ~; in time*) с+*gen*; (*out of*) из+*gen*; (*according to*) по+*dat*; (*because of*) из-за+*gen*; **~ above** све́рху; **~ abroad** из-за грани́цы; **~ afar** и́здали; **~ among** из числа́+*gen*; **~ behind** из-за+*gen*; **~ day to day** изо дня́ в день; **~ everywhere** отовсю́ду; **~ here** отсю́да; **~ memory** по па́мяти; **~ now on** отны́не; **~ there** отту́да; **~ time to time** вре́мя от вре́мени; **~ under** из-под+*gen.*

front /frʌnt/ *n* фаса́д, пере́дняя сторона́; (*mil*) фронт; **in ~ of** впереди́+*gen*, пе́ред+*instr*; *adj* пере́дний; (*first*) пе́рвый.

frontier /'frʌntɪə(r)/ *n* грани́ца.

frost /frɒst/ *n* моро́з; **~-bite** отмороже́ние; **~-bitten** отморо́женный. **frosted** /-tɪd/ *adj*: **~ glass** ма́товое стекло́. **frosty** /-tɪ/ *adj* моро́зный; (*fig*) ледяно́й.

froth /frɒθ/ *n* пена; *vi* пениться *impf*, вс~ *pf.* **frothy** /-θɪ/ *adj* пенистый.
frown /fraʊn/ *n* хмурый взгляд; *vi* хмуриться *impf*, на~ *pf.*
frugal /'fru:g(ə)l/ *adj* (*careful*) бережливый; (*scanty*) скудный.
fruit /fru:t/ *n* плод; *collect* фрукты *m pl*; *adj* фруктовый. **fruitful** /-fʊl/ *adj* плодотворный. **fruition** /fru:'ɪʃ(ə)n/ *n*: **come to ~** осуществиться *pf.* **fruitless** /'fru:tlɪs/ *adj* бесплодный.
frustrate /frʌ'streɪt/ *vt* фрустрировать *impf* & *pf.* **frustrating** /-'streɪtɪŋ/ *adj* фрустрирующий. **frustration** /-'streɪʃ(ə)n/ *n* фрустрация.
fry[1] /fraɪ/ *n*: **small ~** мелюзга.
fry[2] /fraɪ/ *vt* & *i* жарить(ся) *impf*, за~, из~ *pf.* **frying-pan** /'fraɪɪŋ pæn/ *n* сковорода.
fuel /'fju:əl/ *n* топливо.
fugitive /'fju:dʒɪtɪv/ *n* беглец.
fulcrum /'fʊlkrəm/ *n* точка опоры.
fulfil /fʊl'fɪl/ *vt* (*perform*) выполнять *impf*, выполнить *pf*; (*dreams*) осуществлять *impf*, осуществить *pf.* **fulfilling** /-lɪŋ/ *adj* удовлетворяющий. **fulfilment** /-mənt/ *n* выполнение; осуществление; удовлетворение.
full /fʊl/ *adj* полный (**of** +*gen*, *instr*); (*replete*) сытый; **~ stop** точка; **~ time: I work ~ time** я работаю на полную ставку; *n*: **in ~** полностью; **to the ~** в полной мере. **fullness** /'fʊlnɪs/ *n* полнота. **fully** /'fʊlɪ/ *adv* вполне.
fulsome /'fʊlsəm/ *adj* чрезмерный.
fumble /'fʌmb(ə)l/ *vi*: **~ for** нащупывать *impf* +*acc*; **~ with** возиться *impf* c+*instr.*
fume /fju:m/ *vi* (*with anger*) кипеть *impf*, вс~ *pf* гневом. **fumes** /fju:mz/ *n pl* испарения *neut pl.* **fumigate** /'fju:mɪˌgeɪt/ *vt* окуривать *impf*, окурить *pf.*
fun /fʌn/ *n* забава; **it was ~** было забавно; **have ~** забавляться *impf*; **make ~ of** смеяться *impf*, по~ *pf* над +*instr.*
function /'fʌŋkʃ(ə)n/ *n* функция; (*event*) вечер; *vi* функционировать *impf*; действовать *impf.* **functional** /-n(ə)l/ *adj* функциональный. **functionary** /-nərɪ/ *n* чиновник.
fund /fʌnd/ *n* фонд; (*store*) запас.
fundamental /ˌfʌndə'ment(ə)l/ *adj* основной; *n*: *pl* основы *f pl.*
funeral /'fju:nər(ə)l/ *n* похороны (-он, -онам) *pl.*
fungus /'fʌŋgəs/ *n* гриб.
funnel /'fʌn(ə)l/ *n* воронка; (*chimney*) дымовая труба.
funny /'fʌnɪ/ *adj* смешной; (*odd*) странный.
fur /fɜ:(r)/ *n* мех; **~ coat** шуба.
furious /'fjʊərɪəs/ *adj* бешеный.
furnace /'fɜ:nɪs/ *n* горн, печь.
furnish /'fɜ:nɪʃ/ *vt* (*provide*) снабжать *impf*, снабдить *pf* (**with** c+*instr*); (*house*) обставлять *impf*, обставить *pf.* **furniture** /'fɜ:nɪtʃə(r)/ *n* мебель.
furrow /'fʌrəʊ/ *n* борозда.
furry /'fɜ:rɪ/ *adj* пушистый.
further, farther /'fɜ:ðə(r), 'fɑ:ðə(r)/ *comp adj* дальнейший; *adv* дальше; *vt* продвигать *impf*, продвинуть *pf.* **furthermore** *adv* к тому же. **furthest, farthest** /'fɜ:ðɪst, 'fɑ:ðɪst/ *superl adj* самый дальний.
furtive /'fɜ:tɪv/ *adj* скрытый,

та́йный.

fury /ˈfjʊərɪ/ *n* я́рость.

fuse[1] /fjuːz/ *vt & i* (*of metal*) сплавля́ть(ся) *impf*, спла́вить(ся) *pf*.

fuse[2] /fjuːz/ *n* (*in bomb*) запа́л; (*detonating device*) взрыва́тель *m*.

fuse[3] /fjuːz/ *n* (*electr*) про́бка; *vi* перегора́ть *impf*, перегоре́ть *pf*.

fuselage /ˈfjuːzəˌlɑːʒ/ *n* фюзеля́ж.

fusion /ˈfjuːʒ(ə)n/ *n* пла́вка, слия́ние.

fuss /fʌs/ *n* суета́; *vi* суети́ться *impf*. **fussy** /-sɪ/ *adj* суетли́вый; (*fastidious*) разбо́рчивый.

futile /ˈfjuːtaɪl/ *adj* тще́тный. **futility** /-ˈtɪlɪtɪ/ *n* тще́тность.

future /ˈfjuːtʃə(r)/ *n* бу́дущее *sb*; (*gram*) бу́дущее вре́мя *neut*; *adj* бу́дущий. **futuristic** /ˌfjuːtʃəˈrɪstɪk/ *adj* футуристи́ческий.

fuzzy /ˈfʌzɪ/ *adj* (*hair*) пуши́стый; (*blurred*) расплы́вчатый.

G

gabble /ˈgæb(ə)l/ *vi* тарато́рить *impf*.

gable /ˈgeɪb(ə)l/ *n* щипе́ц.

gad /gæd/ *vi*: ~ **about** шата́ться *impf*.

gadget /ˈgædʒɪt/ *n* приспособле́ние.

gaffe /gæf/ *n* оплошность.

gag /gæg/ *n* кляп; *vt* засо́вывать *impf*, засу́нуть *pf* кляп в рот+*dat*.

gaiety /ˈgeɪətɪ/ *n* весёлость.

gaily /ˈgeɪlɪ/ *adv* ве́село.

gain /geɪn/ *n* при́быль; *pl* дохо́ды *m pl*; (*increase*) приро́ст; *vt* (*acquire*) получа́ть *impf*, получи́ть *pf*; ~ **on** нагоня́ть *impf*, нагна́ть *pf*.

gait /geɪt/ *n* похо́дка.

gala /ˈgɑːlə/ *n* пра́зднество; *adj* пра́здничный.

galaxy /ˈgæləksɪ/ *n* гала́ктика; (*fig*) плея́да.

gale /geɪl/ *n* бу́ря, што́рм.

gall[1] /gɔːl/ *n* (*bile*) жёлчь; (*cheek*) на́глость; **~-bladder** жёлчный пузы́рь *m*.

gall[2] /gɔːl/ *vt* (*vex*) раздража́ть *impf*, раздражи́ть *pf*.

gallant /ˈgælənt/ *adj* (*brave*) хра́брый; (*courtly*) гала́нтный. **gallantry** /-trɪ/ *n* хра́брость; гала́нтность.

gallery /ˈgælərɪ/ *n* галере́я.

galley /ˈgælɪ/ *n* (*ship*) гале́ра; (*kitchen*) ка́мбуз.

gallon /ˈgælən/ *n* галло́н.

gallop /ˈgæləp/ *n* гало́п; *vi* галопи́ровать *impf*.

gallows /ˈgæləʊz/ *n pl* ви́селица.

gallstone /ˈgɔːlstəʊn/ *n* жёлчный ка́мень *m*.

galore /gəˈlɔː(r)/ *adv* в изоби́лии.

galvanize /ˈgælvəˌnaɪz/ *vt* гальванизи́ровать *impf & pf*.

gambit /ˈgæmbɪt/ *n* гамби́т.

gamble /ˈgæmb(ə)l/ *n* (*undertaking*) риско́ванное предприя́тие; *vi* игра́ть *impf* в аза́ртные и́гры; (*fig*) рискова́ть *impf* (**with** +*instr*); ~ **away** прои́грывать *impf*, проигра́ть *pf*. **gambler** /-blə(r)/ *n* игро́к. **gambling** /-blɪŋ/ *n* аза́ртные и́гры *f pl*.

game /geɪm/ *n* игра́; (*single* ~) па́ртия; (*collect, animals*) дичь; *adj* (*ready*) гото́вый. **gamekeeper** /-ˌkiːpə(r)/ *n* лесни́к.

gammon /ˈgæmən/ *n* о́корок.

gamut /ˈgæmət/ *n* га́мма.

gang /gæŋ/ *n* бáнда; (*workmen*) бригáда.
gangrene /ˈgæŋgriːn/ *n* гангрéна.
gangster /ˈgæŋstə(r)/ *n* гáнгстер.
gangway /ˈgæŋweɪ/ *n* (*passage*) прохóд; (*naut*) схóдни (-ней) *pl.*
gaol /dʒeɪl/ *n* тюрьмá; *vt* заключáть *impf*, заключи́ть *pf* в тюрьмý. **gaoler** /-lə(r)/ *n* тюрéмщик.
gap /gæp/ *n* (*empty space*; *deficiency*) прóбел; (*in wall etc.*) брешь; (*fig*) разры́в.
gape /geɪp/ *vi* (*person*) зевáть *impf* (*at* на+*acc*); (*chasm*) зия́ть *impf.*
garage /ˈgærɑːdʒ/ *n* гарáж.
garb /gɑːb/ *n* одея́ние.
garbage /ˈgɑːbɪdʒ/ *n* мýсор.
garbled /ˈgɑːb(ə)ld/ *adj* искажённый.
garden /ˈgɑːd(ə)n/ *n* сад; *attrib* садóвый. **gardener** /ˈgɑːdnə(r)/ *n* садóвник. **gardening** /ˈgɑːdnɪŋ/ *n* садовóдство.
gargle /ˈgɑːg(ə)l/ *vi* полоскáть *impf*, про~ *pf* гóрло.
gargoyle /ˈgɑːgɔɪl/ *n* горгýлья.
garish /ˈgeərɪʃ/ *adj* кричáщий.
garland /ˈgɑːlənd/ *n* гирля́нда.
garlic /ˈgɑːlɪk/ *n* чеснóк.
garment /ˈgɑːmənt/ *n* предмéт одéжды.
garnish /ˈgɑːnɪʃ/ *n* гарни́р; *vt* гарни́ровать *impf* & *pf.*
garret /ˈgærɪt/ *n* мансáрда.
garrison /ˈgærɪs(ə)n/ *n* гарнизóн.
garrulous /ˈgærʊləs/ *adj* болтли́вый.
gas /gæs/ *n* газ; *attrib* гáзовый; *vt* отравля́ть *impf*, отрави́ть *pf* гáзом. **gaseous** /ˈgæsɪəs/ *adj* газообрáзный.
gash /gæʃ/ *n* порéз; *vt* порéзать *pf.*
gasket /ˈgæskɪt/ *n* проклáдка.
gasp /gɑːsp/ *vi* задыхáться *impf*, задохнýться *pf.*
gastric /ˈgæstrɪk/ *adj* желýдочный.
gate /geɪt/ *n* (*large*) ворóта (-т) *pl*; (*small*) кали́тка. **gateway** *n* (*gate*) ворóта (-т) *pl*; (*entrance*) вход.
gather /ˈgæðə(r)/ *vt* & *i* собирáть(ся) *impf*, собрáть(ся) *pf*; *vt* заключáть *impf*, заключи́ть *pf.* **gathering** /-rɪŋ/ *n* (*assembly*) собрáние.
gaudy /ˈgɔːdɪ/ *adj* кричáщий.
gauge /geɪdʒ/ *n* (*measure*) мéра; (*instrument*) кали́бр, измери́тельный прибóр; (*rly*) колея́; (*criterion*) критéрий; *vt* измеря́ть *impf*, измéрить *pf*; (*estimate*) оцéнивать *impf*, оцени́ть *pf.*
gaunt /gɔːnt/ *adj* тóщий.
gauntlet /ˈgɔːntlɪt/ *n* рукави́ца.
gauze /gɔːz/ *n* мáрля.
gay /geɪ/ *adj* весёлый; (*bright*) пёстрый; (*homosexual*) гомосексуáльный.
gaze /geɪz/ *n* при́стальный взгляд; *vt* при́стально глядéть *impf* (**at** на+*acc*).
gazelle /gəˈzel/ *n* газéль.
GCSE *abbr* (*of* **General Certificate of Secondary Education**) аттестáт о срéднем образовáнии.
gear /gɪə(r)/ *n* (*equipment*) принадлéжности *f pl*; (*in car*) скóрость; ~ **lever** рычáг; *vt* приспосабля́ть *impf*, приспосóбить *pf* (**to** к+*dat*). **gearbox** *n* корóбка передáч.
gel /dʒel/ *n* космети́ческое желé *neut indecl.* **gelatine** /ˈdʒelə,tiːn/ *n* желати́н.

gelding /'geldɪŋ/ *n* мéрин.
gelignite /'dʒelɪg,naɪt/ *n* гелигнит.
gem /dʒem/ *n* драгоцéнный кáмень *m*.
Gemini /'dʒemɪ,naɪ/ *n* Близнецы́ *m pl*.
gender /'dʒendə(r)/ *n* род.
gene /dʒi:n/ *n* ген.
genealogy /,dʒi:nɪ'ælədʒɪ/ *n* генеалóгия.
general /'dʒenər(ə)l/ *n* генерáл; *adj* óбщий; (*nationwide*) всеóбщий; **in ~** вообщé. **generalization** /,dʒenərəlaɪ'zeɪʃ(ə)n/ *n* обобщéние. **generalize** /'dʒenərə,laɪz/ *vi* обобщáть *impf*, обобщи́ть *pf*. **generally** /'dʒenərəlɪ/ *adv* (*usually*) обы́чно; (*in general*) вообщé.
generate /'dʒenə,reɪt/ *vt* порождáть *impf*, породи́ть *pf*. **generation** /-'reɪʃ(ə)n/ *n* (*in descent*) поколéние. **generator** /'dʒenə,reɪtə(r)/ *n* генерáтор.
generic /dʒɪ'nerɪk/ *adj* родовóй; (*general*) óбщий.
generosity /,dʒenə'rɒsɪtɪ/ *n* (*magnanimity*) великоду́шие; (*munificence*) щéдрость. **generous** /'dʒenərəs/ *adj* великоду́шный; щéдрый.
genesis /'dʒenɪsɪs/ *n* происхождéние; (**G~**) Кни́га Бытия́.
genetic /dʒɪ'netɪk/ *adj* генети́ческий. **genetics** /-tɪks/ *n* генéтика.
genial /'dʒi:nɪəl/ *adj* (*of person*) доброду́шный.
genital /'dʒenɪt(ə)l/ *adj* половóй. **genitals** /-t(ə)lz/ *n pl* половы́е óрганы *m pl*.
genitive /'dʒenɪtɪv/ *adj* (*n*) роди́тельный (падéж).
genius /'dʒi:nɪəs/ *n* (*person*) гéний; (*ability*) гениáльность.
genocide /'dʒenə,saɪd/ *n* геноци́д.
genome /'dʒi:nəʊm/ *n* генóм.
genre /'ʒɑ̃rə/ *n* жанр.
genteel /dʒen'ti:l/ *adj* благовоспи́танный.
gentile /'dʒentaɪl/ *n* нееврéй, ~ка.
gentility /dʒen'tɪlɪtɪ/ *n* благовоспи́танность.
gentle /'dʒent(ə)l/ *adj* (*mild*) мя́гкий; (*quiet*) ти́хий; (*light*) лёгкий. **gentleman** *n* джентльмéн. **gentleness** /-nɪs/ *n* мя́гкость. **gents** /dʒents/ *n pl* мужскáя убóрная *sb*.
genuine /'dʒenjʊɪn/ *adj* (*authentic*) пóдлинный; (*sincere*) и́скренний.
genus /'dʒi:nəs/ *n* род.
geographical /,dʒi:ə'græfɪk(ə)l/ *adj* географи́ческий. **geography** /dʒɪ'ɒgrəfɪ/ *n* геогрáфия. **geological** /,dʒi:ə'lɒdʒɪk(ə)l/ *adj* геологи́ческий. **geologist** /dʒɪ'ɒlədʒɪst/ *n* геóлог. **geology** /dʒɪ'ɒlədʒɪ/ *n* геолóгия. **geometric(al)** /,dʒɪə'metrɪk((ə)l)/ *adj* геометри́ческий. **geometry** /dʒɪ'ɒmɪtrɪ/ *n* геомéтрия.
Georgia /'dʒɔ:dʒɪə/ *n* Гру́зия. **Georgian** /-dʒɪən/ *n* грузи́н, ~ка; *adj* грузи́нский.
geranium /dʒə'reɪnɪəm/ *n* герáнь.
geriatric /,dʒerɪ'ætrɪk/ *adj* гериатри́ческий.
germ /dʒɜ:m/ *n* микрóб.
German /'dʒɜ:mən/ *n* нéмец, нéмка; *adj* немéцкий; **~ measles** красну́ха.
germane /dʒɜ:'meɪn/ *adj* умéстный.
Germanic /dʒɜ:'mænɪk/ *adj* германский.
Germany /'dʒɜ:mənɪ/ *n* Гермáния.
germinate /'dʒɜ:mɪ,neɪt/ *vi* прорастáть *impf*, прорасти́ *pf*.

gesticulate /dʒe'stɪkjʊ,leɪt/ *vi* жестикули́ровать *impf.* **gesture** /'dʒestʃə(r)/ *n* жест.

get /get/ *vt* (*obtain*) достава́ть *impf*, доста́ть *pf*; (*receive*) получа́ть *impf*, получи́ть *pf*; (*understand*) понима́ть *impf*, поня́ть *pf*; (*disease*) заража́ться *impf*, зарази́ться *pf* +*instr*; (*induce*) угова́ривать *impf*, уговори́ть *pf* (**to do** +*inf*); (*fetch*) приноси́ть *impf*, принести́ *pf*; *vi* (*become*) станови́ться *impf*, стать *pf* +*instr*; **have got** (*have*) име́ть *impf*; **have got to** быть до́лжен (-жна́) +*inf*; ~ **about** (*spread*) распространя́ться *impf*, распространи́ться *pf*; (*move around*) передвига́ться *impf*; (*travel*) разъезжа́ть *impf*; ~ **at** (*mean*) хоте́ть *impf* сказа́ть; ~ **away** (*slip off*) ускольза́ть *impf*, ускользну́ть *pf*; (*escape*) убега́ть *impf*, убежа́ть *pf*; (*leave*) уезжа́ть *impf*, уе́хать *pf*; ~ **away with** избега́ть *impf*, избежа́ть *pf* отве́тственности за+*acc*; ~ **back** (*recover*) получа́ть *impf*, получи́ть *pf* обра́тно; (*return*) возвраща́ться *impf*, верну́ться *pf*; ~ **by** (*manage*) справля́ться *impf*, спра́виться *pf*; ~ **down** сходи́ть *impf*, сойти́ *pf*; ~ **down to** принима́ться *impf*, приня́ться *pf* за+*acc*; ~ **off** слеза́ть *impf*, слезть *pf* с+*gen*; ~ **on** сади́ться *impf*, сесть *pf* в, на, +*acc*; (*prosper*) преуспева́ть *impf*, преуспе́ть *pf*; ~ **on with** (*person*) ужива́ться *impf*, ужи́ться *pf* с+*instr*; ~ **out of** (*avoid*) избавля́ться *impf*, изба́виться *pf* от+*gen*; (*car*) выходи́ть *impf*, вы́йти *pf* из+*gen*; ~ **round to** успева́ть *impf*, успе́ть *pf*; ~ **to** (*reach*) достига́ть *impf*, дости́гнуть & дости́чь *pf* +*gen*; ~ **up** (*from bed*) встава́ть *impf*, встать *pf*.

geyser /'gi:zə(r)/ *n* (*spring*) ге́йзер; (*water-heater*) коло́нка.

ghastly /'gɑ:stlɪ/ *adj* ужа́сный.

gherkin /'gɜ:kɪn/ *n* огуре́ц.

ghetto /'getəʊ/ *n* ге́тто *neut indecl.*

ghost /gəʊst/ *n* привиде́ние. **ghostly** /-lɪ/ *adj* при́зрачный.

giant /'dʒaɪənt/ *n* гига́нт; *adj* гига́нтский.

gibberish /'dʒɪbərɪʃ/ *n* тараба́рщина.

gibbet /'dʒɪbɪt/ *n* ви́селица.

gibe /dʒaɪb/ *n* насме́шка; *vi* насмеха́ться *impf* (**at** над+*instr*).

giblets /'dʒɪblɪts/ *n pl* потроха́ (-хо́в) *pl*.

giddiness /'gɪdɪnɪs/ *n* головокруже́ние. **giddy** /'gɪdɪ/ *predic*: **I feel** ~ у меня́ кру́жится голова́.

gift /gɪft/ *n* (*present*) пода́рок; (*donation*; *ability*) дар. **gifted** /-tɪd/ *adj* одарённый.

gig /gɪg/ *n* (*theat*) выступле́ние.

gigantic /dʒaɪ'gæntɪk/ *adj* гига́нтский.

giggle /'gɪg(ə)l/ *n* хихи́канье; *vi* хихи́кать *impf*, хихи́кнуть *pf*.

gild /gɪld/ *vt* золоти́ть *impf*, вы́~, по~ *pf*.

gill /gɪl/ *n* (*of fish*) жа́бра.

gilt /gɪlt/ *n* позоло́та; *adj* золочённый.

gimmick /'gɪmɪk/ *n* трюк.

gin /dʒɪn/ *n* (*spirit*) джин.

ginger /'dʒɪndʒə(r)/ *n* имби́рь *m*; *adj* (*colour*) ры́жий.

gingerly /'dʒɪndʒəlɪ/ *adv* осторо́жно.

gipsy /'dʒɪpsɪ/ *n* цыга́н, ~ка.

giraffe /dʒɪ'rɑ:f/ *n* жира́ф.

girder /'gɜ:də(r)/ *n* ба́лка. **girdle** /'gɜ:d(ə)l/ *n* по́яс.

girl /gɜːl/ *n* (*child*) де́вочка; (*young woman*) де́вушка. **girlfriend** *n* подру́га. **girlish** /-lɪʃ/ *adj* де́вичий.

girth /gɜːθ/ *n* обхва́т; (*on saddle*) подпру́га.

gist /dʒɪst/ *n* суть.

give /gɪv/ *vt* дава́ть *impf*, дать *pf*; **~ away** выдава́ть *impf*, вы́дать *pf*; **~ back** возвраща́ть *impf*, возврати́ть *pf*; **~ in** (*yield*, *vi*) уступа́ть *impf*, уступи́ть *pf* (**to** +*dat*); (*hand in*, *vt*) вруча́ть *impf*, вручи́ть *pf*; **~ out** (*emit*) издава́ть *impf*, изда́ть *pf*; (*distribute*) раздава́ть *impf*, разда́ть *pf*; **~ up** отка́зываться *impf*, отказа́ться *pf* от+*gen*; (*habit etc.*) броса́ть *impf*, бро́сить *pf*; **~ o.s. up** сдава́ться *impf*, сда́ться *pf*. **given** /ˈgɪv(ə)n/ *predic* (*inclined*) скло́нен (-онна́, -о́нно) (**to** к+*dat*).

glacier /ˈglæsɪə(r)/ *n* ледни́к.

glad /glæd/ *adj* ра́достный; *predic* рад. **gladden** /-d(ə)n/ *vt* ра́довать *impf*, об~ *pf*.

glade /gleɪd/ *n* поля́на.

gladly /ˈglædlɪ/ *adv* охо́тно.

glamorous /ˈglæmərəs/ *adj* я́ркий; (*attractive*) привлека́тельный.

glamour /ˈglæmə(r)/ *n* я́ркость; привлека́тельность.

glance /glɑːns/ *n* (*look*) бе́глый взгляд; *vi*: **~ at** взгля́дывать *impf*, взгляну́ть *pf* на+*acc*.

gland /glænd/ *n* железа́. **glandular** /-djʊlə(r)/ *adj* желе́зистый.

glare /gleə(r)/ *n* (*light*) ослепи́тельный блеск; (*look*) свире́пый взгляд; *vi* свире́по смотре́ть *impf* (**at** на+*acc*). **glaring** /-rɪŋ/ *adj* (*dazzling*) ослепи́тельный; (*mistake*) гру́бый.

glasnost /ˈglæznɒst/ *n* гла́сность.

glass /glɑːs/ *n* (*substance*) стекло́; (*drinking vessel*) стака́н; (*wine ~*) рю́мка; (*mirror*) зе́ркало; *pl* (*spectacles*) очки́ (-ко́в) *pl*; *attrib* стекля́нный. **glassy** /-sɪ/ *adj* (*look*) ту́склый.

glaze /gleɪz/ *n* глазу́рь; *vt* (*with glass*) застекля́ть *impf*, застекли́ть *pf*; (*pottery*) глазурова́ть *impf* & *pf*; (*cul*) глази́ровать *impf* & *pf*. **glazier** /-zjə(r)/ *n* стеко́льщик.

gleam /gliːm/ *n* про́блеск; *vi* свети́ться *impf*.

glean /gliːn/ *vt* собира́ть *impf*, собра́ть *pf* по крупи́цам.

glee /gliː/ *n* весе́лье. **gleeful** /-fʊl/ *adj* лику́ющий.

glib /glɪb/ *adj* бо́йкий.

glide /glaɪd/ *vi* скользи́ть *impf*; (*aeron*) плани́ровать *impf*, с~ *pf*. **glider** /-də(r)/ *n* планёр.

glimmer /ˈglɪmə(r)/ *n* мерца́ние; *vi* мерца́ть *impf*.

glimpse /glɪmps/ *vt* мелько́м ви́деть *impf*, у~ *pf*.

glint /glɪnt/ *n* блеск; *vi* блесте́ть *impf*.

glisten, glitter /ˈglɪs(ə)n, ˈglɪtə(r)/ *vi* блесте́ть *impf*.

gloat /gləʊt/ *vi* злора́дствовать *impf*.

global /ˈgləʊb(ə)l/ *adj* (*worldwide*) глоба́льный; (*total*) всео́бщий. **globe** /gləʊb/ *n* (*sphere*) шар; (*the earth*) земно́й шар; (*chart*) гло́бус. **globule** /ˈglɒbjuːl/ *n* ша́рик.

gloom /gluːm/ *n* мрак. **gloomy** /-mɪ/ *adj* мра́чный.

glorify /ˈglɔːrɪˌfaɪ/ *vt* прославля́ть *impf*, просла́вить *pf*. **glorious** /ˈglɔːrɪəs/ *adj* сла́вный; (*splendid*) великоле́пный. **glory** /ˈglɔːrɪ/ *n* сла́ва; *vi* торжествова́ть *impf*.

gloss /glɒs/ *n* лоск; *vi*: ~ **over** замáзывать *impf*, замáзать *pf*.

glossary /ˈglɒsərɪ/ *n* глоссáрий.

glove /glʌv/ *n* перчáтка.

glow /gləʊ/ *n* зáрево; (*of cheeks*) румя́нец; *vi* (*incandesce*) накаля́ться *impf*, накали́ться *pf*; (*shine*) сия́ть *impf*.

glucose /ˈglu:kəʊs/ *n* глюкóза.

glue /glu:/ *n* клей; *vt* приклéивать *impf*, приклéить *pf* (**to** к+*dat*).

glum /glʌm/ *adj* угрю́мый.

glut /glʌt/ *n* избы́ток.

glutton /ˈglʌt(ə)n/ *n* обжóра *m* & *f*. **gluttonous** /-nəs/ *adj* обжóрливый. **gluttony** /-nɪ/ *n* обжóрство.

GM *abbr* (*of* **genetically modified**) генети́чески модифици́рованный.

gnarled /nɑ:ld/ *adj* (*hands*) шишковáтый; (*tree*) сучковáтый.

gnash /næʃ/ *vt* скрежетáть *impf* +*instr*.

gnat /næt/ *n* комáр.

gnaw /nɔ:/ *vt* грызть *impf*.

gnome /nəʊm/ *n* гном.

go /gəʊ/ *n* (*try*) попы́тка; **be on the** ~ быть в движéнии; **have a** ~ пытáться *impf*, по~ *pf*; *vi* (*on foot*) ходи́ть *indet*, идти́ *det*, пойти́ *pf*; (*by transport*) éздить *indet*, éхать *det*, по~ *pf*; (*work*) рабóтать *impf*; (*become*) станови́ться *impf*, стать *pf* +*instr*; (*belong*) идти́ *impf*; **be** ~**ing** (*to do*) собирáться *impf*, собрáться *pf* (+*inf*); ~ **about** (*set to work at*) брáться *impf*, взя́ться *pf* за+*acc*; (*wander*) броди́ть *indet*; ~ **away** (*on foot*) уходи́ть *impf*, уйти́ *pf*; (*by transport*) уезжáть *impf*, уéхать *pf*; ~ **down** спускáться *impf*, спусти́ться *pf* (с+*gen*); ~ **in(to)** (*enter*) входи́ть *impf*, войти́ *pf* (в+*acc*); (*investigate*) расслéдовать *impf* & *pf*; ~ **off** (*go away*) уходи́ть *impf*, уйти́ *pf*; (*deteriorate*) пóртиться *impf*, ис~ *pf*; ~ **on** (*continue*) продолжáть(ся) *impf*, продóлжить(ся) *pf*; ~ **out** выходи́ть *impf*, вы́йти *pf*; (*flame etc.*) гáснуть *impf*, по~ *pf*; ~ **over** (*inspect*) пересмáтривать *impf*, пересмотрéть *pf*; (*rehearse*) повторя́ть *impf*, повтори́ть *pf*; (*change allegiance etc.*) переходи́ть *impf*, перейти́ *pf* (**to** в, на, +*acc*, к+*dat*); ~ **through** (*scrutinize*) разбирáть *impf*, разобрáть *pf*; ~ **through with** доводи́ть *impf*, довести́ *pf* до концá; ~ **without** обходи́ться *impf*, обойти́сь *pf* без+*gen*; ~**-ahead** предприи́мчивый; ~**-between** посрéдник.

goad /gəʊd/ *vt* (*provoke*) подстрекáть *impf*, подстрекну́ть *pf* (**into** к+*dat*).

goal /gəʊl/ *n* (*aim*) цель; (*sport*) ворóта (-т) *pl*; (*point won*) гол. **goalkeeper** *n* вратáрь *m*.

goat /gəʊt/ *n* козá; (*male*) козёл.

gobble /ˈgɒb(ə)l/ *vt* (*eat*) жрать *impf*; ~ **up** пожирáть *impf*, пожрáть *pf*.

goblet /ˈgɒblɪt/ *n* бокáл, ку́бок.

god /gɒd/ *n* бог; (**G**~) Бог. **godchild** *n* крéстник, -ица. **goddaughter** *n* крéстница. **goddess** /ˈgɒdɪs/ *n* боги́ня. **godfather** *n* крёстный *sb*. **God-fearing** /ˈgɒdfɪərɪŋ/ *adj* богобоя́зненный. **godless** /ˈgɒdlɪs/ *adj* безбóжный. **godly** /ˈgɒdlɪ/ *adj* нáбожный. **godmother** *n* крёстная *sb*. **godparent** *n* крёстный *sb*. **godsend** *n* бóжий дар. **godson** *n* крéстник.

goggle /ˈgɒg(ə)l/ *vi* тарáщить *impf* глазá (**at** на+*acc*); *n*: *pl* защи́тные очки́ (-ко́в) *pl.*

going /ˈgəʊɪŋ/ *adj* де́йствующий. **goings-on** /ˌgəʊɪŋˈzɒn/ *n pl* дела́ *neut pl.*

gold /gəʊld/ *n* зо́лото; *adj* золото́й; **~-plated** накладно́го зо́лота; **~-smith** золоты́х дел ма́стер. **golden** /-d(ə)n/ *adj* золото́й; **~ eagle** бе́ркут. **goldfish** *n* золота́я ры́бка.

golf /gɒlf/ *n* гольф; **~ club** (*implement*) клю́шка; **~ course** площа́дка для го́льфа. **golfer** /ˈgɒlfə(r)/ *n* игро́к в гольф.

gondola /ˈgɒndələ/ *n* гондо́ла.

gong /gɒŋ/ *n* гонг.

gonorrhoea /ˌgɒnəˈrɪə/ *n* три́ппер.

good /gʊd/ *n* добро́; *pl* (*wares*) това́р(ы); **do ~** (*benefit*) идти́ *impf*, пойти́ *pf* на по́льзу *+dat*; *adj* хоро́ший, до́брый; **~-humoured** доброду́шный; **~-looking** краси́вый; **~ morning** до́брое у́тро!; **~ night** споко́йной но́чи! **goodbye** /gʊdˈbaɪ/ *int* проща́й(те)!; до свида́ния! **goodness** /ˈgʊdnɪs/ *n* доброта́.

goose /guːs/ *n* гусь *m*; **~-flesh** гуси́ная ко́жа.

gooseberry /ˈgʊzbərɪ/ *n* крыжо́вник

gore[1] /gɔː(r)/ *n* (*blood*) запёкшаяся кровь.

gore[2] /gɔː(r)/ *vt* (*pierce*) бода́ть *impf*, за~ *pf*.

gorge /gɔːdʒ/ *n* (*geog*) уще́лье; *vi & t* объеда́ться *impf*, объе́сться *pf* (**on** *+instr*).

gorgeous /ˈgɔːdʒəs/ *adj* великоле́пный.

gorilla /gəˈrɪlə/ *n* гори́лла.

gorse /gɔːs/ *n* утёсник.

gory /ˈgɔːrɪ/ *adj* крова́вый.

gosh /gɒʃ/ *int* бо́же мой!

Gospel /ˈgɒsp(ə)l/ *n* Ева́нгелие.

gossip /ˈgɒsɪp/ *n* сплé́тня; (*person*) спле́тник, -ица; *vi* сплетни́чать *impf*, на~ *pf*.

Gothic /ˈgɒθɪk/ *adj* готи́ческий.

gouge /gaʊdʒ/ *vt*: **~ out** выда́лбливать *impf*, вы́долбить *pf*; (*eyes*) выка́лывать *impf*, вы́колоть *pf*.

goulash /ˈguːlæʃ/ *n* гуля́ш.

gourmet /ˈgʊəmeɪ/ *n* гурма́н.

gout /gaʊt/ *n* пода́гра.

govern /ˈgʌv(ə)n/ *vt* пра́вить *impf +instr*; (*determine*) определя́ть *impf*, определи́ть *pf*. **governess** /ˈgʌvənɪs/ *n* гуверна́нтка. **government** /ˈgʌvənmənt/ *n* прави́тельство. **governmental** /ˌgʌvənˈment(ə)l/ *adj* прави́тельственный. **governor** /ˈgʌvənə(r)/ *n* губерна́тор; (*of school etc.*) член правле́ния.

gown /gaʊn/ *n* пла́тье; (*official's*) ма́нтия.

grab /græb/ *vt* хвата́ть *impf*, схвати́ть *pf*.

grace /greɪs/ *n* (*gracefulness*) гра́ция; (*refinement*) изя́щество; (*favour*) ми́лость; (*at meal*) моли́тва; **have the ~ to** быть насто́лько такти́чен, что; **with bad ~** нелюбе́зно; **with good ~** с досто́инством; *vt* (*adorn*) украша́ть *impf*, укра́сить *pf*; (*favour*) удоста́ивать *impf*, удосто́ить *pf* (**with** *+gen*). **graceful** /-fʊl/ *adj* грацио́зный.

gracious /ˈgreɪʃəs/ *adj* ми́лостивый.

gradation /grəˈdeɪʃ(ə)n/ *n* града́ция.

grade /greɪd/ *n* (*level*) сте́пень; (*quality*) сорт; *vt* сортирова́ть *impf*, рас~ *pf*.

gradient /ˈgreɪdɪənt/ *n* укло́н.

gradual /ˈgrædjʊəl/ *adj* постепе́нный.

graduate *n* /ˈgrædjuət/ окóнчивший *sb* университéт, вуз; *vi* /ˈgrædjuˌeɪt/ кончáть *impf*, окóнчить *pf* (университéт, вуз); *vt* градуи́ровать *impf* & *pf*.
graffiti /grəˈfiːtiː/ *n* нáдписи *f pl*.
graft /grɑːft/ *n* (*bot*) черенóк; (*med*) пересáдка (живóй ткáни); *vt* (*bot*) прививáть *impf*, приви́ть *pf* (**to** +*dat*); (*med*) пересáживать *impf*, пересади́ть *pf*.
grain /greɪn/ *n* (*seed*; *collect*) зернó; (*particle*) крупи́нка; (*of sand*) песчи́нка; (*of wood*) (древéсное) волокнó; **against the ~** не по нутрý.
gram(me) /græm/ *n* грамм.
grammar /ˈgræmə(r)/ *n* граммáтика; **~ school** гимнáзия. **grammatical** /grəˈmætɪk(ə)l/ *adj* граммати́ческий.
gramophone /ˈgræməˌfəʊn/ *n* прои́грыватель *m*; **~ record** грампласти́нка.
granary /ˈgrænərɪ/ *n* амбáр.
grand /grænd/ *adj* великолéпный; **~ piano** рóяль *m*. **grandchild** *n* внук, внýчка. **granddaughter** *n* внýчка. **grandfather** *n* дéдушка *m*. **grandmother** *n* бáбушка. **grandparents** *n* бáбушка и дéдушка. **grandson** *n* внук. **grandstand** *n* трибýна.
grandeur /ˈgrændjə(r)/ *n* вели́чие.
grandiose /ˈgrændɪˌəʊs/ *adj* грандиóзный.
granite /ˈgrænɪt/ *n* грани́т.
granny /ˈgrænɪ/ *n* бáбушка.
grant /grɑːnt/ *n* (*financial*) грант, дотáция; (*univ*) стипéндия; *vt* даровáть *impf* & *pf*; (*concede*) допускáть *impf*, допусти́ть *pf*; **take for ~ed** (*assume*) считáть *impf*, счесть *pf* самó собóй разумéющимся; (*not appreciate*) принимáть *impf* как дóлжное.
granular /ˈgrænjʊlə(r)/ *adj* зерни́стый.
granulated /ˈgrænʊˌleɪtɪd/ *adj*: **~ sugar** сáхарный песóк.
granule /ˈgrænjuːl/ *n* зёрнышко.
grape /greɪp/ *n* (*single grape*) виногрáдина; *collect* виногрáд. **grapefruit** *n* грéйпфрут.
graph /grɑːf/ *n* грáфик.
graphic /ˈgræfɪk/ *adj* графи́ческий; (*vivid*) я́ркий.
graphite /ˈgræfaɪt/ *n* графи́т.
grapple /ˈgræp(ə)l/ *vi* (*struggle*) борóться *impf* (**with** с+*instr*).
grasp /grɑːsp/ *n* (*grip*) хвáтка; (*comprehension*) понимáние; *vt* (*clutch*) хватáть *impf*, схвати́ть *pf*; (*comprehend*) понимáть *impf*, поня́ть *pf*. **grasping** /-spɪŋ/ *adj* жáдный.
grass /grɑːs/ *n* травá. **grasshopper** /ˈgrɑːsˌhɒpə(r)/ *n* кузнéчик. **grassy** /ˈgrɑːsɪ/ *adj* травяни́стый.
grate[1] /greɪt/ *n* (*fireplace*) решётка.
grate[2] /greɪt/ *vt* (*rub*) терéть *impf*, на~ *pf*; *vi* (*sound*) скрипéть *impf*; **~ (up)on** (*irritate*) раздражáть *impf*, раздражи́ть *pf*.
grateful /ˈgreɪtfʊl/ *n* благодáрный.
grater /ˈgreɪtə(r)/ *n* тёрка.
gratify /ˈgrætɪˌfaɪ/ *vt* удовлетворя́ть *impf*, удовлетвори́ть *pf*.
grating /ˈgreɪtɪŋ/ *n* решётка.
gratis /ˈgrɑːtɪs/ *adv* бесплáтно.
gratitude /ˈgrætɪˌtjuːd/ *n* благодáрность.
gratuitous /grəˈtjuːɪtəs/ *adj* (*free*) даровóй; (*motiveless*) беспричи́нный.

gratuity /grəˈtjuːɪtɪ/ *n* (*tip*) чаевы́е *sb pl*.

grave[1] /greɪv/ *n* моги́ла. **gravedigger** /ˈgreɪvdɪgə(r)/ *n* моги́льщик. **gravestone** *n* надгро́бный ка́мень *m*. **graveyard** *n* кла́дбище.

grave[2] /greɪv/ *adj* серьёзный.

gravel /ˈgræv(ə)l/ *n* гра́вий.

gravitate /ˈgrævɪˌteɪt/ *vi* тяготе́ть *impf* (**towards** к+*dat*). **gravitational** /-ˈteɪʃən(ə)l/ *adj* гравитацио́нный. **gravity** /ˈgrævɪtɪ/ *n* (*seriousness*) серьёзность; (*force*) тя́жесть.

gravy /ˈgreɪvɪ/ *n* (мясна́я) подли́вка.

graze[1] /greɪz/ *vi* (*feed*) пасти́сь *impf*.

graze[2] /greɪz/ *n* (*abrasion*) цара́пина; *vt* (*touch*) задева́ть *impf*, заде́ть *pf*; (*abrade*) цара́пать *impf*, о~ *pf*.

grease /griːs/ *n* жир; (*lubricant*) сма́зка; **~-paint** грим; *vt* сма́зывать *impf*, сма́зать *pf*. **greasy** /-sɪ/ *adj* жи́рный.

great /greɪt/ *adj* (*large*) большо́й; (*eminent*) вели́кий; (*splendid*) замеча́тельный; **to a ~ extent** в большо́й сте́пени; **a ~ deal** мно́го (+*gen*); **a ~ many** мно́гие; **~-aunt** двоюро́дная ба́бушка; **~-granddaughter** пра́внучка; **~-grandfather** пра́дед; **~-grandmother** праба́бка; **~-grandson** пра́внук; **~-uncle** двоюро́дный де́душка *m*. **greatly** /-lɪ/ *adv* о́чень.

Great Britain /greɪt ˈbrɪt(ə)n/ *n* Великобрита́ния.

Greece /griːs/ *n* Гре́ция.

greed /griːd/ *n* жа́дность (**for** к+*dat*). **greedy** /-dɪ/ *adj* жа́дный (**for** к+*dat*).

Greek /griːk/ *n* грек, греча́нка; *adj* гре́ческий.

green /griːn/ *n* (*colour*) зелёный цвет; (*grassy area*) лужа́йка; *pl* зе́лень *collect*; *adj* зелёный. **greenery** /-nərɪ/ *n* зе́лень. **greenfly** *n* тля. **greengrocer** *n* зеленщи́к. **greengrocer's** *n* овощно́й магази́н. **greenhouse** *n* тепли́ца; **~ effect** парнико́вый эффе́кт.

greet /griːt/ *vt* здоро́ваться *impf*, по~ *pf* с+*instr*; (*meet*) встреча́ть *impf*, встре́тить *pf*. **greeting** /-tɪŋ/ *n* приве́т(ствие).

gregarious /grɪˈgeərɪəs/ *adj* общи́тельный.

grenade /grɪˈneɪd/ *n* грана́та.

grey /greɪ/ *adj* се́рый; (*hair*) седо́й.

greyhound /ˈgreɪhaʊnd/ *n* борза́я *sb*.

grid /grɪd/ *n* (*grating*) решётка; (*electr*) сеть; (*map*) координа́тная се́тка.

grief /griːf/ *n* го́ре; **come to ~** терпе́ть *impf*, по~ *pf* неуда́чу.

grievance /ˈgriːv(ə)ns/ *n* жа́лоба, оби́да.

grieve /griːv/ *vt* огорча́ть *impf*, огорчи́ть *pf*; *vi* горева́ть *impf* (**for** о+*prep*).

grievous /ˈgriːvəs/ *adj* тя́жкий.

grill /grɪl/ *n* ра́шпер; *vt* (*cook*) жа́рить *impf*, за~, из~ *pf* (на ра́шпере); (*question*) допра́шивать *impf*, допроси́ть *pf*.

grille /grɪl/ *n* (*grating*) решётка.

grim /grɪm/ *adj* (*stern*) суро́вый; (*unpleasant*) неприя́тный.

grimace /ˈgrɪməs/ *n* грима́са; *vi* грима́сничать *impf*.

grime /graɪm/ *n* грязь. **grimy** /-mɪ/ *adj* гря́зный.

grin /grɪn/ *n* усме́шка; *vi* усмеха́ться *impf*, усмехну́ться *pf*.

grind /graɪnd/ *vt* (*flour etc.*) моло́ть *impf*, с~ *pf*; (*axe*) точи́ть *impf*, на~ *pf*; ~ **one's teeth** скрежета́ть *impf* зуба́ми. **grip** /grɪp/ *n* хва́тка; *vt* схва́тывать *impf*, схвати́ть *pf*. **gripe** /graɪp/ *vi* ворча́ть *impf*. **gripping** /'grɪpɪŋ/ *adj* захва́тывающий. **grisly** /'grɪzlɪ/ *adj* жу́ткий. **gristle** /'grɪs(ə)l/ *n* хрящ. **grit** /grɪt/ *n* песо́к; (*for building*) гра́вий; (*firmness*) вы́держка. **grizzle** /'grɪz(ə)l/ *vi* хны́кать *impf*. **groan** /grəʊn/ *n* стон; *vi* стона́ть *impf*. **grocer** /'grəʊsə(r)/ *n* бакале́йщик; ~**'s (shop)** бакале́йная ла́вка, гастроно́м. **groceries** /-sərɪz/ *n pl* бакале́я *collect*. **groggy** /'grɒgɪ/ *adj* разби́тый. **groin** /grɔɪn/ *n* (*anat*) пах. **groom** /gru:m/ *n* ко́нюх; (*bridegroom*) жени́х; *vt* (*horse*) чи́стить *impf*, по~ *pf*; (*prepare*) гото́вить *impf*, под~ *pf* (**for** к+*dat*); **well-groomed** хорошо́ вы́глядящий. **groove** /gru:v/ *n* желобо́к. **grope** /grəʊp/ *vi* нащу́пывать *impf* (**for, after** +*acc*). **gross**[1] /grəʊs/ *n* (*12 dozen*) гросс. **gross**[2] /grəʊs/ *adj* (*fat*) ту́чный; (*coarse*) гру́бый; (*total*) вало-во́й; ~ **weight** вес бру́тто. **grotesque** /grəʊ'tesk/ *adj* гроте́скный. **grotto** /'grɒtəʊ/ *n* грот. **ground** /graʊnd/ *n* земля́; (*earth*) по́чва; *pl* (*dregs*) гу́ща; (*sport*) площа́дка; *pl* (*of house*) парк; (*reason*) основа́ние; ~ **floor** пе́рвый эта́ж; *vt* (*instruct*) обуча́ть *impf*, обучи́ть *pf* осно́вам (**in** +*gen*); (*aeron*) запреща́ть *impf*, запрети́ть *pf* полёты +*gen*; *vi* (*naut*) сади́ться *impf*, сесть *pf* на мель. **groundless** /-lɪs/ *adj* необосно́ванный. **groundwork** *n* фунда́мент. **group** /gru:p/ *n* гру́ппа; *vt* & *i* группирова́ть(ся) *impf*, с~ *pf*. **grouse**[1] /graʊs/ *n* шотла́ндская куропа́тка. **grouse**[2] /graʊs/ *vi* (*grumble*) ворча́ть *impf*. **grove** /grəʊv/ *n* ро́ща. **grovel** /'grɒv(ə)l/ *vi* пресмыка́ться *impf* (**before** пе́ред +*instr*). **grow** /grəʊ/ *vi* расти́ *impf*; (*become*) станови́ться *impf*, стать *pf* +*instr*; *vt* (*cultivate*) выра́щивать *impf*, вы́растить *pf*; (*hair*) отра́щивать *impf*, отрасти́ть *pf*; ~ **up** (*person*) выраста́ть *impf*, вы́расти *pf*; (*custom*) возника́ть *impf*, возни́кнуть *pf*. **growl** /graʊl/ *n* ворча́ние; *vi* ворча́ть *impf* (**at** на+*acc*). **grown-up** /grəʊn'ʌp/ *adj* взро́слый *sb*. **growth** /grəʊθ/ *n* рост; (*med*) о́пухоль. **grub** /grʌb/ *n* (*larva*) личи́нка; (*food*) жратва́; *vi*: ~ **about** ры́ться *impf*. **grubby** /'grʌbɪ/ *adj* запа́чканный. **grudge** /grʌdʒ/ *n* зло́ба; **have a** ~ **against** име́ть *impf* зуб про́тив+*gen*; *vt* жале́ть *impf*, по~ *pf* +*acc*, +*gen*. **grudgingly** /-dʒɪŋglɪ/ *adv* неохо́тно. **gruelling** /'gru:əlɪŋ/ *adj* изнури́тельный. **gruesome** /'gru:səm/ *adj* жу́ткий. **gruff** /grʌf/ *adj* (*surly*) грубова́тый; (*voice*) хри́плый. **grumble** /'grʌmb(ə)l/ *vi* ворча́ть *impf* (**at** на+*acc*). **grumpy** /'grʌmpɪ/ *adj* брюзгли́вый.

grunt /grʌnt/ *n* хрю́канье; *vi* хрю́кать *impf*, хрю́кнуть *pf*.

guarantee /ˌgærən'tiː/ *n* гара́нтия; *vt* гаранти́ровать *impf* & *pf* (**against** от+*gen*). **guarantor** /-'tɔː(r)/ *n* поручи́тель *m*.

guard /gɑːd/ *n* (*device*) предохрани́тель; (*watch*; *soldiers*) карау́л; (*sentry*) часово́й *sb*; (*watchman*) сто́рож; (*rly*) конду́ктор; *pl* (*prison*) надзира́тель *m*; *vt* охраня́ть *impf*, охрани́ть *pf*; *vi*: ~ **against** остерега́ться *impf*, остере́чься *pf* +*gen*, *inf*.

guardian /'gɑːdɪən/ *n* храни́тель *m*; (*law*) опеку́н.

guer(r)illa /gə'rɪlə/ *n* партиза́н; ~ **warfare** партиза́нская война́.

guess /ges/ *n* дога́дка; *vt* & *i* дога́дываться *impf*, догада́ться *pf* (о+*prep*); *vt* (~ *correctly*) уга́дывать *impf*, угада́ть *pf*. **guesswork** *n* дога́дки *f pl*.

guest /gest/ *n* гость *m*; ~ **house** ма́ленькая гости́ница.

guffaw /gʌ'fɔː/ *n* хо́хот; *vi* хохота́ть *impf*.

guidance /'gaɪd(ə)ns/ *n* руково́дство. **guide** /gaɪd/ *n* проводни́к, гид; (*guidebook*) путеводи́тель *m*; *vt* води́ть *indet*, вести́ *det*; (*direct*) руководи́ть *impf* +*instr*; ~**ed missile** управля́емая раке́та. **guidelines** *n pl* инстру́кции *f pl*; (*advice*) сове́т.

guild /gɪld/ *n* ги́льдия, цех.

guile /gaɪl/ *n* кова́рство. **guileless** /-lɪs/ *adj* простоду́шный.

guillotine /'gɪləˌtiːn/ *n* гильоти́на.

guilt /gɪlt/ *n* вина́; (*guiltiness*) вино́вность. **guilty** /-tɪ/ *adj* (*of crime*) вино́вный (**of** в+*prep*); (*of wrong*) винова́тый.

guinea-pig /'gɪnɪpɪg/ *n* морска́я сви́нка; (*fig*) подо́пытный кро́лик.

guise /gaɪz/ *n*: **under the** ~ **of** под ви́дом+*gen*.

guitar /gɪ'tɑː(r)/ *n* гита́ра. **guitarist** /-rɪst/ *n* гитари́ст.

gulf /gʌlf/ *n* (*geog*) зали́в; (*chasm*) про́пасть.

gull /gʌl/ *n* ча́йка.

gullet /'gʌlɪt/ *n* (*oesophagus*) пищево́д; (*throat*) го́рло.

gullible /'gʌlɪb(ə)l/ *adj* легкове́рный.

gully /'gʌlɪ/ *n* (*ravine*) овра́г.

gulp /gʌlp/ *n* глото́к; *vt* жа́дно глота́ть *impf*.

gum[1] /gʌm/ *n* (*anat*) десна́.

gum[2] /gʌm/ *n* каме́дь; (*glue*) клей; *vt* скле́ивать *impf*, скле́ить *pf*.

gumption /'gʌmpʃ(ə)n/ *n* инициати́ва.

gun /gʌn/ *n* (*piece of ordnance*) ору́дие, пу́шка; (*rifle etc.*) ружьё; (*pistol*) пистоле́т; *vt*: ~ **down** расстре́ливать *impf*, расстреля́ть *pf*. **gunner** /-nə(r)/ *n* артиллери́ст. **gunpowder** *n* по́рох.

gurgle /'gɜːg(ə)l/ *vi* бу́лькать *impf*.

gush /gʌʃ/ *vi* хлы́нуть *pf*.

gusset /'gʌsɪt/ *n* клин.

gust /gʌst/ *n* поры́в. **gusty** /-stɪ/ *adj* поры́вистый.

gusto /'gʌstəʊ/ *n* смак.

gut /gʌt/ *n* кишка́; *pl* (*entrails*) кишки́ *f pl*; *pl* (*bravery*) му́жество; *vt* потроши́ть *impf*, вы~ *pf*; (*devastate*) опустоша́ть *impf*, опустоши́ть *pf*.

gutter /'gʌtə(r)/ *n* (*of roof*) (водосто́чный) жёлоб; (*of road*) сто́чная кана́ва.

guttural /'gʌtər(ə)l/ *adj* горта́нный.

guy[1] /gaɪ/ *n* (*rope*) оття́жка.
guy[2] /gaɪ/ *n* (*fellow*) па́рень *m*.
guzzle /'gʌz(ə)l/ *vt* (*food*) пожира́ть *impf*, пожра́ть *pf*; (*liquid*) хлеба́ть *impf*, хлебну́ть *pf*.
gym /dʒɪm/ *n* (*gymnasium*) гимнасти́ческий зал; (*gymnastics*) гимна́стика. **gymnasium** /dʒɪm 'neɪzɪəm/ *n* гимнасти́ческий зал. **gymnast** /'dʒɪmnæst/ *n* гимна́ст. **gymnastic** /dʒɪm 'næstɪk/ *adj* гимнасти́ческий. **gymnastics** /dʒɪm'næstɪks/ *n* гимна́стика.
gynaecologist /,gaɪnɪ'kɒlədʒɪst/ *n* гинеко́лог. **gynaecology** /-dʒɪ/ *n* гинеколо́гия.
gyrate /,dʒaɪ'reɪt/ *vi* враща́ться *impf*.

H

haberdashery /'hæbə,dæʃərɪ/ *n* галантере́я; (*shop*) галантере́йный магази́н.
habit /'hæbɪt/ *n* привы́чка; (*monk's*) ря́са.
habitable /'hæbɪtəb(ə)l/ *adj* приго́дный для жилья́. **habitat** /-tæt/ *n* есте́ственная среда́. **habitation** /-'teɪʃ(ə)n/ *n*: **unfit for ~** неприго́дный для жилья́.
habitual /hə'bɪtjʊəl/ *adj* привы́чный.
hack[1] /hæk/ *vt* руби́ть *impf*; **~saw** ножо́вка.
hack[2] /hæk/ *n* (*hired horse*) наёмная ло́шадь; (*writer*) халту́рщик **hackneyed** /'hæknɪd/ *adj* изби́тый.
haddock /'hædək/ *n* пи́кша.
haemophilia /,hi:mə'fɪlɪə/ *n* гемофили́я. **haemorrhage** /'hemərɪdʒ/ *n* кровотече́ние. **haemorrhoids** /'hemə,rɔɪdz/ *n pl* геморро́й *collect*.
hag /hæg/ *n* карга́.
haggard /'hægəd/ *adj* измождённый.
haggle /'hæg(ə)l/ *vi* торгова́ться *impf*, с~ *pf*.
hail[1] /heɪl/ *n* град; *vi* **it is ~ing** идёт град. **hailstone** *n* гра́дина.
hail[2] /heɪl/ *vt* (*greet*) приве́тствовать *impf* (& *pf in past*); (*taxi*) подзыва́ть *impf*, подозва́ть *pf*.
hair /heə(r)/ *n* (*single ~*) во́лос; *collect* (*human*) во́лосы (-о́с, -оса́м) *pl*; (*animal*) шерсть. **hairbrush** *n* щётка для воло́с. **haircut** *n* стри́жка; **have a ~** постри́чься *pf*. **hair-do** /'heədu:/ *n* причёска. **hairdresser** /'heə ,dresə(r)/ *n* парикма́хер. **hairdresser's** /'heə,dresəz/ *n* парикма́херская *sb*. **hair-dryer** /'heə ,draɪə(r)/ *n* фен. **hairstyle** *n* причёска. **hairy** /'heərɪ/ *adj* волоса́тый.
hale /heɪl/ *adj*: **~ and hearty** здоро́вый и бо́дрый.
half /hɑ:f/ *n* полови́на; (*sport*) тайм; *adj* полови́нный; **in ~** попола́м; **one and a ~** полтора́; **~ past** (*one etc.*) полови́на (второ́го и т.д.); **~-hearted** равноду́шный; **~ an hour** полчаса́; **~-time** переры́в ме́жду та́ймами; **~way** на полпути́; **~-witted** слабоу́мный.
hall /hɔ:l/ *n* (*large room*) зал; (*entrance ~*) холл, вестибю́ль *m*; (*~ of residence*) общежи́тие. **hallmark** *n* проби́рное клеймо́; (*fig*) при́знак.
hallo /hə'ləʊ/ *int* здра́вствуй(те), приве́т; (*on telephone*) алло́.
hallucination /hə,lu:sɪ'neɪʃ(ə)n/ *n* галлюцина́ция.
halo /'heɪləʊ/ *n* (*around Saint*)

нимб.

halt /hɒlt/ *n* остано́вка; *vt & i* остана́вливать(ся) *impf*, останови́ть(ся) *pf*; *int* (*mil*) стой(те)! **halting** /-tɪŋ/ *adj* запина́ющий.

halve /hɑːv/ *vt* дели́ть *impf*, раз~ *pf* попола́м.

ham /hæm/ *n* (*cul*) ветчина́.

hamburger /'hæm,bɜːgə(r)/ *n* котле́та.

hamlet /'hæmlɪt/ *n* дереву́шка.

hammer /'hæmə(r)/ *n* молото́к; *vt* бить *impf* молотко́м.

hammock /'hæmək/ *n* гама́к.

hamper[1] /'hæmpə(r)/ *n* (*basket*) корзи́на с кры́шкой.

hamper[2] /'hæmpə(r)/ *vt* (*hinder*) меша́ть *impf*, по~ *pf* +*dat*.

hamster /'hæmstə(r)/ *n* хомя́к.

hand /hænd/ *n* рука́; (*worker*) рабо́чий *sb*; (*writing*) по́черк; (*clock* ~) стре́лка; **at** ~ под руко́й; **on** ~**s and knees** на четвере́ньках; *vt* передава́ть *impf*, переда́ть *pf*; ~ **in** подава́ть *impf*, пода́ть *pf*; ~ **out** раздава́ть *impf*, разда́ть *pf*. **handbag** *n* су́мка. **handbook** *n* руково́дство. **handcuffs** /-kʌfs/ *n pl* нару́чники *m pl*. **handful** /-fʊl/ *n* горсть.

handicap /'hændɪ,kæp/ *n* (*sport*) гандика́п; (*hindrance*) поме́ха. **handicapped** /-,kæpt/ *adj*: ~ **person** инвали́д.

handicraft /'hændɪ,krɑːft/ *n* ремесло́.

handiwork /'hændɪ,wɜːk/ *n* ручна́я рабо́та.

handkerchief /'hæŋkə,tʃiːf/ *n* носово́й плато́к.

handle /'hænd(ə)l/ *n* ру́чка, рукоя́тка; *vt* (*people*) обраща́ться *impf* с+*instr*; (*situations*) справля́ться *impf*, спра́виться *pf* с+*instr*; (*touch*) тро́гать *impf*, тро́нуть *pf* руко́й, рука́ми. **handlebar(s)** /'hændəl,bɑːz/ *n* руль *m*.

handmade /'hændmeɪd/ *adj* ручно́й рабо́ты.

handout /'hændaʊt/ *n* пода́чка; (*document*) лифле́т.

handrail /'hændreɪl/ *n* пери́ла (-л) *pl*.

handshake /'hændʃeɪk/ *n* рукопожа́тие.

handsome /'hænsəm/ *adj* краси́вый; (*generous*) ще́дрый.

handwriting /'hænd,raɪtɪŋ/ *n* по́черк.

handy /'hændɪ/ *adj* (*convenient*) удо́бный; (*skilful*) ло́вкий; **come in** ~ пригоди́ться *pf*.

hang /hæŋ/ *vt* ве́шать *impf*, пове́сить *pf*; *vi* висе́ть *impf*; ~ **about** слоня́ться *impf*; ~ **on** (*cling*) держа́ться *impf*; (*tel*) не ве́шать *impf* тру́бку; (*persist*) упо́рствовать *impf*; ~ **out** выве́шивать *impf*, вы́весить *pf*; (*spend time*) болта́ться *impf*; ~ **up** ве́шать *impf*, пове́сить *pf*; (*tel*) ве́шать *impf*, пове́сить *pf* тру́бку. **hanger** /'hæŋə(r)/ *n* ве́шалка. **hanger-on** /,hæŋə'rɒn/ *n* прилипа́ла *m & f*. **hangman** *n* пала́ч.

hangar /'hæŋə(r)/ *n* анга́р.

hangover /'hæŋəʊvə(r)/ *n* похме́лье.

hang-up /'hæŋʌp/ *n* ко́мплекс.

hanker /'hæŋkə(r)/ *vi*: ~ **after** мечта́ть *impf* о+*prep*.

haphazard /hæp'hæzəd/ *adj* случа́йный.

happen /'hæpən/ *vi* (*occur*) случа́ться *impf*, случи́ться *pf*; происходи́ть *impf*, произойти́ *pf*; ~ **upon** ната́лкиваться *impf*, натолкну́ться *pf* на+*acc*.

happiness /'hæpɪnɪs/ *n* сча́стье.

happy /'hæpɪ/ *adj* счастли́вый;

~-go-lucky беззабо́тный.
harass /'hærəs/ *vt* (*pester*) дёргать *impf*; (*persecute*) преследовать *impf*. **harassment** /-mənt/ *n* тра́вля; пресле́дование.
harbinger /'hɑ:bɪndʒə(r)/ *n* предве́стник.
harbour /'hɑ:bə(r)/ *n* га́вань, порт; *vt* (*person*) укрыва́ть *impf*, укры́ть *pf*; (*thoughts*) зата́ивать *impf*, затаи́ть *pf*.
hard /hɑ:d/ *adj* твёрдый; (*difficult*) тру́дный; (*difficult to bear*) тяжёлый; (*severe*) суро́вый; *adv* (*work*) мно́го; (*hit*) си́льно; (*try*) о́чень; **~-boiled egg** яйцо́ вкрутую; **~ disk** (*comput*) жёсткий диск; **~-headed** практи́чный; **~-hearted** жестокосе́рдный; **~-up** стеснённый в сре́дствах; **~-working** трудолюби́вый. **hardboard** *n* строи́тельный карто́н.
harden /'hɑ:d(ə)n/ *vi* затвердева́ть *impf*, затверде́ть *pf*; (*fig*) ожесточа́ться *impf*, ожесточи́ться *pf*.
hardly /'hɑ:dlɪ/ *adv* едва́ (ли).
hardship /'hɑ:dʃɪp/ *n* (*privation*) нужда́.
hardware /'hɑ:dweə(r)/ *n* скобяны́е изде́лия *neut pl*; (*comput*) аппарату́ра.
hardy /'hɑ:dɪ/ *adj* (*robust*) выно́сливый; (*plant*) морозосто́йкий.
hare /heə(r)/ *n* за́яц.
hark /hɑ:k/ *vi*: **~ back to** возвраща́ться *impf*, верну́ться *pf* к+*dat*; *int* слу́шай(те)!
harm /hɑ:m/ *n* вред; *vt* вреди́ть *impf*, по~ *pf* +*dat*. **harmful** /-fʊl/ *adj* вре́дный. **harmless** /-lɪs/ *adj* безвре́дный.
harmonic /hɑ:'mɒnɪk/ *adj* гармони́ческий. **harmonica** /-'mɒnɪkə/ *n* губна́я гармо́ника.
harmonious /-'məʊnɪəs/ *adj* гармони́чный. **harmonize** /'hɑ:mə,naɪz/ *vi* гармони́ровать *impf* (**with** с+*instr*). **harmony** /'hɑ:mənɪ/ *n* гармо́ния.
harness /'hɑ:nɪs/ *n* у́пряжь; *vt* запряга́ть *impf*, запря́чь *pf*; (*fig*) испо́льзовать *impf* & *pf*.
harp /hɑ:p/ *n* а́рфа; *vi*: **~ on** тверди́ть *impf* о+*prep*.
harpoon /hɑ:'pu:n/ *n* гарпу́н.
harpsichord /'hɑ:psɪ,kɔ:d/ *n* клавеси́н.
harrowing /'hærəʊɪŋ/ *adj* душераздира́ющий.
harsh /hɑ:ʃ/ *adj* (*sound*, *colour*) ре́зкий; (*cruel*) суро́вый.
harvest /'hɑ:vɪst/ *n* жа́тва, сбор (плодо́в); (*yield*) урожа́й; (*fig*) плоды́ *m pl*; *vt* & *abs* собира́ть *impf*, собра́ть *pf* (урожа́й).
hash /hæʃ/ *n*: **make a ~ of** напу́тать *pf* +*acc*, в+*prep*.
hashish /'hæʃi:ʃ/ *n* гаши́ш.
hassle /'hæs(ə)l/ *n* беспоко́йство.
hassock /'hæsək/ *n* поду́шечка.
haste /heɪst/ *n* спе́шка. **hasten** /'heɪs(ə)n/ *vi* спеши́ть *impf*, по~ *pf*; *vt* & *i* торопи́ть(ся) *impf*, по~ *pf*; *vt* ускоря́ть *impf*, ускорить *pf*. **hasty** /'heɪstɪ/ *adj* (*hurried*) поспе́шный; (*quick-tempered*) вспы́льчивый.
hat /hæt/ *n* ша́пка; (*stylish*) шля́па.
hatch[1] /hætʃ/ *n* люк; **~-back** маши́на-пика́п.
hatch[2] /hætʃ/ *vi* вылу́пливаться, вылупля́ться *impf*, вы́лупиться *pf*.
hatchet /'hætʃɪt/ *n* топо́рик.
hate /heɪt/ *n* не́нависть; *vt* ненави́деть *impf*. **hateful** /-fʊl/ *adj* ненави́стный. **hatred** /-trɪd/ *n*

ненависть.

haughty /ˈhɔːtɪ/ *adj* надменный.

haul /hɔːl/ *n* (*fish*) улóв; (*loot*) добы́ча; (*distance*) ездá; *vt* (*drag*) тяну́ть *impf*; таскáть *indet*, тащи́ть *det*. **haulage** /-lɪdʒ/ *n* перевóзка.

haunt /hɔːnt/ *n* люби́мое мéсто; *vt* (*ghost*) обитáть *impf*; (*memory*) преслéдовать *impf*. **haunted** /-tɪd/ *adj*: ~ **house** дом с привидéниями. **haunting** /-tɪŋ/ *adj* навя́зчивый.

have /hæv/ *vt* имéть *impf*; **I** ~ (*possess*) у меня́ (есть; был, -á, -о) +*nom*; **I** ~ **not** у меня́ нет (*past* нé было) +*gen*; **I** ~ **(got) to** я дóлжен +*inf*; **you had better** вам лу́чше бы +*inf*; ~ **on** (*wear*) быть одéтым в +*prep*; (*be engaged in*) быть зáнятым +*instr*.

haven /ˈheɪv(ə)n/ *n* (*refuge*) убéжище.

haversack /ˈhævəˌsæk/ *n* рюкзáк.

havoc /ˈhævək/ *n* (*devastation*) опустошéние; (*disorder*) беспоря́док.

hawk[1] /hɔːk/ *n* (*bird*) я́стреб.

hawk[2] /hɔːk/ *vt* (*trade*) торговáть *impf* вразнóс+*instr*. **hawker** /-kə(r)/ *n* разнóсчик.

hawser /ˈhɔːzə(r)/ *n* трос.

hawthorn /ˈhɔːθɔːn/ *n* боя́рышник.

hay /heɪ/ *n* сéно; **make** ~ коси́ть *impf*, с~ *pf* сéно; ~ **fever** сéнная лихорáдка. **haystack** *n* стог.

hazard /ˈhæzəd/ *n* риск; *vt* рисковáть *impf* +*instr*. **hazardous** /-dəs/ *adj* рискóванный.

haze /heɪz/ *n* ды́мка.

hazel /ˈheɪz(ə)l/ *n* лещи́на. **hazelnut** *n* леснóй орéх.

hazy /ˈheɪzɪ/ *adj* тумáнный; (*vague*) сму́тный.

he /hiː/ *pron* он.

head /hed/ *n* головá; (*mind*) ум; (~ *of coin*) лицевáя сторонá монéты; ~**s or tails?** орёл и́ли рéшка?; (*chief*) главá *m*, начáльник; *attrib* глáвный; *vt* (*lead*) возглавля́ть *impf*, возглáвить *pf*; (*ball*) забивáть *impf*, заби́ть *pf* головóй; *vi*: ~ **for** направля́ться *impf*, напрáвиться *pf* в, на, +*acc*, к+*dat*. **headache** *n* головнáя боль. **head-dress** *n* головнóй убóр. **header** /-də(r)/ *n* удáр головóй. **heading** /-dɪŋ/ *n* (*title*) заголóвок. **headland** *n* мыс. **headlight** *n* фáра. **headline** *n* заголóвок. **headlong** *adv* стремглáв. **headmaster, -mistress** *n* дирéктор шкóлы. **head-on** *adj* головóй; *adv* в лоб. **headphone** *n* нау́шник. **headquarters** *n* штаб-квarти́ра. **headscarf** *n* косы́нка. **headstone** *n* надгрóбный кáмень *m*. **headstrong** *adj* своевóльный. **headway** *n* движéние вперёд. **heady** /-dɪ/ *adj* опьяня́ющий.

heal /hiːl/ *vt* излéчивать *impf*, излечи́ть *pf*; *vi* заживáть *impf*, зажи́ть *pf*. **healing**/ -lɪŋ/ *adj* целéбный.

health /helθ/ *n* здорóвье; ~ **care** здравоохранéние. **healthy** /-θɪ/ *adj* здорóвый; (*beneficial*) полéзный.

heap /hiːp/ *n* ку́ча; *vt* нагромождáть *impf*, нагромозди́ть *pf*.

hear /hɪə(r)/ *vt* слы́шать *impf*, у~ *pf*; (*listen to*) слу́шать *impf*, по~ *pf*; ~ **out** выслу́шивать *impf*, вы́слушать *pf*. **hearing** /-rɪŋ/ *n* слух; (*law*) слу́шание. **hearsay** *n* слух.

hearse /hɜːs/ *n* катафáлк.

heart /hɑːt/ *n* се́рдце; (*essence*) суть; *pl* (*cards*) че́рви (-ве́й) *pl*; **by ~** наизу́сть; **~ attack** серде́чный при́ступ. **heartburn** *n* изжо́га. **hearten** /-t(ə)n/ *vt* ободря́ть *impf*, ободри́ть *pf*. **heartfelt** *adj* серде́чный. **heartless** /-lɪs/ *adj* бессерде́чный. **heart-rending** /-ˌrendɪŋ/ *adj* душераздира́ющий. **hearty** /-tɪ/ *adj* (*cordial*) серде́чный; (*vigorous*) здоро́вый.

hearth /hɑːθ/ *n* оча́г.

heat /hiːt/ *n* жара́; (*phys*) теплота́; (*of feeling*) пыл; (*sport*) забе́г, заéзд; *vt* & *i* (*heat up*) нагрева́ть(ся) *impf*, нагре́ть(ся) *pf*; *vt* (*house*) топи́ть *impf*. **heater** /-tə(r)/ *n* нагрева́тель *m*. **heating** /-tɪŋ/ *n* отопле́ние.

heath /hiːθ/ *n* пу́стошь.

heathen /ˈhiːð(ə)n/ *n* язы́чник; *adj* язы́ческий.

heather /ˈheðə(r)/ *n* ве́реск.

heave /hiːv/ *vt* (*lift*) поднима́ть *impf*, подня́ть *pf*; (*pull*) тяну́ть *impf*, по~ *pf*.

heaven /ˈhev(ə)n/ *n* (*sky*) не́бо; (*paradise*) рай; *pl* небеса́ *neut pl*. **heavenly** /-lɪ/ *adj* небе́сный; (*divine*) боже́ственный.

heavy /ˈhevɪ/ *adj* тяжёлый; (*strong, intense*) си́льный. **heavyweight** *n* тяжелове́с.

Hebrew /ˈhiːbruː/ *adj* (древне)евре́йский.

heckle /ˈhek(ə)l/ *vt* препира́ться *impf* с+*instr*.

hectic /ˈhektɪk/ *adj* лихора́дочный.

hedge /hedʒ/ *n* жива́я и́згородь. **hedgerow** *n* шпале́ра.

hedgehog /ˈhedʒhɒg/ *n* ёж.

heed /hiːd/ *vt* обраща́ть *impf*, обрати́ть *pf* внима́ние на+*acc*. **heedless** /-lɪs/ *adj* небре́жный.

heel[1] /hiːl/ *n* (*of foot*) пята́; (*of foot, sock*) пя́тка; (*of shoe*) каблу́к.

heel[2] /hiːl/ *vi* крени́ться *impf*, на~ *pf*.

hefty /ˈheftɪ/ *adj* дю́жий.

heifer /ˈhefə(r)/ *n* тёлка.

height /haɪt/ *n* высота́; (*of person*) рост. **heighten** /-t(ə)n/ *vt* (*strengthen*) уси́ливать *impf*, уси́лить *pf*.

heinous /ˈheɪnəs/ *adj* гну́сный.

heir /eə(r)/ *n* насле́дник. **heiress** /ˈeərɪs/ *n* насле́дница. **heirloom** /ˈeəluːm/ *n* фами́льная вещь.

helicopter /ˈhelɪˌkɒptə(r)/ *n* вертолёт.

helium /ˈhiːlɪəm/ *n* ге́лий.

hell /hel/ *n* ад. **hellish** /-lɪʃ/ *adj* а́дский.

hello /həˈləʊ/ *see* **hallo**

helm /helm/ *n* руль.

helmet /ˈhelmɪt/ *n* шлем.

help /help/ *n* по́мощь; *vt* помога́ть *impf*, помо́чь *pf* +*dat*; (*can't* ~) не мочь *impf* не +*inf*; **~ o.s.** брать *impf*, взять *pf* себе́; **~ yourself!** бери́те! **helpful** /-fʊl/ *adj* поле́зный; (*obliging*) услу́жливый. **helping** /-pɪŋ/ *n* (*of food*) по́рция. **helpless** /-lɪs/ *adj* беспо́мощный.

helter-skelter /ˌheltəˈskeltə(r)/ *adv* как попа́ло.

hem /hem/ *n* рубе́ц; *vt* подруба́ть *impf*, подруби́ть *pf*; **~ in** окружа́ть *impf*, окружи́ть *pf*.

hemisphere /ˈhemɪˌsfɪə(r)/ *n* полуша́рие.

hemp /hemp/ *n* (*plant*) конопля́; (*fibre*) пенька́.

hen /hen/ *n* (*female bird*) са́мка; (*domestic fowl*) ку́рица.

hence /hens/ *adv* (*from here*) отсю́да; (*as a result*) сле́довательно; **3 years ~** че́рез три го́да. **henceforth** /-ˈfɔːθ/ *adv* отны́не.

henchman /'hentʃmən/ *n* приспе́шник.
henna /'henə/ *n* хна.
hepatitis /ˌhepə'taɪtɪs/ *n* гепати́т.
her /hɜ:(r)/ *poss pron* её; свой.
herald /'her(ə)ld/ *n* ве́стник; *vt* возвеща́ть *impf*, возвести́ть *pf*.
herb /hɜ:b/ *n* трава́. **herbaceous** /hɜ:'beɪʃ(ə)s/ *adj* травяно́й; ~ **border** цвето́чный бордю́р. **herbal** /'hɜ:b(ə)l/ *adj* травяно́й.
herd /hɜ:d/ *n* ста́до; (*people*) толпи́ться *impf*, с~ *pf*; *vt* (*tend*) пасти́ *impf*; (*drive*) загоня́ть *impf*, загна́ть *pf* в ста́до.
here /hɪə(r)/ *adv* (*position*) здесь, тут; (*direction*) сюда́; ~ **is ...** вот (+*nom*); ~ **and there** там и сям; ~ **you are!** пожа́луйста. **hereabout(s)** /ˌhɪərə'baʊts/ *adv* побли́зости. **hereafter** /ˌhɪər'ɑ:ftə(r)/ *adv* в бу́дущем. **hereby** /ˌhɪə'baɪ/ *adv* э́тим. **hereupon** /ˌhɪərə'pɒn/ *adv* (*in consequence*) вследствие э́того; (*after*) по́сле э́того. **herewith** /hɪə'wɪð/ *adv* при сём.
hereditary /hɪ'redɪtərɪ/ *adj* насле́дственный. **heredity** /-'redɪtɪ/ *n* насле́дственность.
heresy /'herəsɪ/ *n* е́ресь. **heretic** /'herətɪk/ *n* ерети́к. **heretical** /hɪ'retɪk(ə)l/ *adj* ерети́ческий.
heritage /'herɪtɪdʒ/ *n* насле́дие.
hermetic /hɜ:'metɪk/ *adj* гермети́ческий.
hermit /'hɜ:mɪt/ *n* отше́льник.
hernia /'hɜ:nɪə/ *n* гры́жа.
hero /'hɪərəʊ/ *n* геро́й. **heroic** /hɪ'rəʊɪk/ *adj* герои́ческий.
heroin /'herəʊɪn/ *n* герои́н.
heroine /'herəʊɪn/ *n* герои́ня.
heroism /'herəʊɪz(ə)m/ *n* герои́зм.
heron /'herən/ *n* ца́пля.
herpes /'hɜ:pi:z/ *n* лиша́й.
herring /'herɪŋ/ *n* сельдь; (*food*) селёдка.
hers /hɜ:z/ *poss pron* её; свой.
herself /hə'self/ *pron* (*emph*) (она́) сама́; (*refl*) себя́.
hertz /hɜ:ts/ *n* герц.
hesitant /'hezɪt(ə)nt/ *adj* нереши́тельный. **hesitate** /-ˌteɪt/ *vi* колеба́ться *impf*, по~ *pf*; (*in speech*) запина́ться *impf*, запну́ться *pf*. **hesitation** /-'teɪʃ(ə)n/ *n* колеба́ние.
hessian /'hesɪən/ *n* мешкови́на.
heterogeneous /ˌhetərəʊ'dʒi:nɪəs/ *adj* разноро́дный.
heterosexual /ˌhetərəʊ'seksjʊəl/ *adj* гетеросексуа́льный.
hew /hju:/ *vt* руби́ть *impf*.
hexagon /'heksəgən/ *n* шестиуго́льник.
hey /heɪ/ *int* эй!
heyday /'heɪdeɪ/ *n* расцве́т.
hi /haɪ/ *int* приве́т!
hiatus /haɪ'eɪtəs/ *n* пробе́л.
hibernate /'haɪbəˌneɪt/ *vi* быть *impf* в спя́чке; впада́ть *impf*, впасть *pf* в спя́чку. **hibernation** /-'neɪʃ(ə)n/ *n* спя́чка.
hiccup /'hɪkʌp/ *vi* ика́ть *impf*, икну́ть *pf*; *n*: *pl* ико́та.
hide[1] /haɪd/ *n* (*skin*) шку́ра.
hide[2] /'hɪd(ə)n/ *vt* & *i* (*conceal*) пря́тать(ся) *impf*, с~ *pf*; скрыва́ть(ся) *impf*, скры́ть(ся) *pf*.
hideous /'hɪdɪəs/ *adj* отврати́тельный.
hideout /'haɪdaʊt/ *n* укры́тие.
hiding /'haɪdɪŋ/ *n* (*flogging*) по́рка.
hierarchy /'haɪəˌrɑ:kɪ/ *n* иера́рхия.
hieroglyphics /ˌhaɪərə'glɪfɪks/ *n pl* иеро́глифы *m pl*.
hi-fi /'haɪfaɪ/ *n* проигрыватель *m* с высокока́чественным воспроизведе́нием зву́ка за́писи.

higgledy-piggledy /ˌhɪgəldɪ 'pɪgəldɪ/ *adv* как придётся.

high /haɪ/ *adj* высо́кий; (*wind*) си́льный; (*on drugs*) в наркоти́ческом дурма́не; **~er education** вы́сшее образова́ние; **~-handed** своево́льный; **~-heeled** на высо́ких каблука́х; **~ jump** прыжо́к в высоту́; **~-minded** благоро́дный; иде́йный; **~-pitched** высо́кий; **~-rise** высо́тный. **highbrow** *adj* интеллектуа́льный. **highland(s)** *n* го́рная страна́. **highlight** *n* (*fig*) вы́сшая то́чка; *vt* обраща́ть *impf*, обрати́ть *pf* внима́ние на+*acc*. **highly** /-lɪ/ *adv* весьма́; **~-strung** легко́ возбужда́емый. **highness** /-nɪs/ *n* (*title*) высо́чество. **highstreet** *n* гла́вная у́лица. **highway** *n* магистра́ль.

hijack /'haɪdʒæk/ *vt* похища́ть *impf*, похи́тить *pf*. **hijacker** /-kə(r)/ *n* похити́тель *m*.

hike /haɪk/ *n* похо́д.

hilarious /hɪ'leərɪəs/ *adj* умори́тельный. **hilarity** /-'lærɪtɪ/ *n* весе́лье.

hill /hɪl/ *n* холм. **hillock** /'hɪlək/ *n* хо́лмик. **hillside** *n* склон холма́. **hilly** /'hɪlɪ/ *adj* холми́стый.

hilt /hɪlt/ *n* рукоя́тка.

himself /hɪm'self/ *pron* (*emph*) (он) сам; (*refl*) себя́.

hind /haɪnd/ *adj* (*rear*) за́дний.

hinder /'hɪndə(r)/ *vt* меша́ть *impf*, по~ *pf* +*dat*. **hindrance** /-drəns/ *n* поме́ха.

Hindu /'hɪndu:/ *n* инду́с; *adj* инду́сский.

hinge /hɪndʒ/ *n* шарни́р; *vi* (*fig*) зави́сеть *impf* от+*gen*.

hint /hɪnt/ *n* намёк; *vi* намека́ть *impf*, намекну́ть *pf* (**at** на+*acc*)

hip /hɪp/ *n* (*anat*) бедро́.

hippie /'hɪpɪ/ *n* хи́ппи *neut indecl*.

hippopotamus /ˌhɪpə'pɒtəməs/ *n* гиппопота́м.

hire /'haɪə(r)/ *n* наём, прока́т; **~-purchase** поку́пка в рассро́чку; *vt* нанима́ть *impf*, наня́ть *pf*; **~ out** сдава́ть *impf*, сдать *pf* напрока́т.

his /hɪz/ *poss pron* его́; свой.

hiss /hɪs/ *n* шипе́ние; *vi* шипе́ть *impf*; *vt* (*performer*) осви́стывать *impf*, освиста́ть *pf*.

historian /hɪ'stɔ:rɪən/ *n* исто́рик. **historic(al)** /hɪ'stɒrɪk(ə)l/ *adj* истори́ческий. **history** /'hɪstərɪ/ *n* исто́рия.

histrionic /ˌhɪstrɪ'ɒnɪk/ *adj* театра́льный.

hit /hɪt/ *n* (*blow*) уда́р; (*on target*) попада́ние (в цель); (*success*) успе́х; *vt* (*strike*) ударя́ть *impf*, уда́рить *pf*; (*target*) попада́ть *impf*, попа́сть *pf* (в цель); **~ (up)on** находи́ть *impf*, найти́ *pf*.

hitch /hɪtʃ/ *n* (*stoppage*) заде́ржка; *vt* (*fasten*) привя́зывать *impf*, привяза́ть *pf*; **~ up** подтя́гивать *impf*, подтяну́ть *pf*; **~-hike** е́здить *indet*, е́хать *det*, по~ *pf* автосто́пом.

hither /'hɪðə(r)/ *adv* сюда́. **hitherto** /'hɪðətu:/ *adv* до сих пор.

HIV *abbr* (*of* **human immunodeficiency virus**) ВИЧ.

hive /haɪv/ *n* у́лей.

hoard /hɔ:d/ *n* запа́с; *vt* скопля́ть *impf*, скопи́ть *pf*.

hoarding /'hɔ:dɪŋ/ *n* рекла́мный щит.

hoarse /hɔ:s/ *adj* хри́плый.

hoax /həʊks/ *n* надува́тельство.

hobble /'hɒb(ə)l/ *vi* ковыля́ть *impf*.

hobby /'hɒbɪ/ *n* хо́бби *neut in-*

decl.

hock /hɒk/ *n* (*wine*) рейнвейн.

hockey /ˈhɒkɪ/ *n* хоккей.

hoe /həʊ/ *n* мотыга; *vt* мотыжить *impf.*

hog /hɒg/ *n* боров.

hoist /hɔɪst/ *n* подъёмник; *vt* поднимать *impf*, поднять *pf.*

hold[1] /həʊld/ *n* (*naut*) трюм.

hold[2] /həʊld/ *n* (*grasp*) захват; (*influence*) влияние (**on** на+*acc*); **catch ~ of** ухватиться *pf* за+*acc*; *vt* (*grasp*) держать *impf*; (*contain*) вмещать *impf*, вместить *pf*; (*possess*) владеть *impf* +*instr*; (*conduct*) проводить *impf*, провести *pf*; (*consider*) считать *impf*, счесть *pf* (+*acc* & *instr*, за+*acc*); *vi* держаться *impf*; (*weather*) продерживаться *impf*, продержаться *pf*; **~ back** сдерживать(ся) *impf*, сдержать(ся) *pf*; **~ forth** разглагольствовать *impf*; **~ on** (*wait*) подождать *pf*; (*tel*) не вешать *impf* трубку; (*grip*) держаться *impf* (**to** за+*acc*); **~ out** (*stretch out*) протягивать *impf*, протянуть *pf*; (*resist*) не сдаваться *impf*; **~ up** (*support*) поддерживать *impf*, поддержать *pf*; (*impede*) задерживать *impf*, задержать *pf.* **holdall** *n* сумка. **hold-up** *n* (*robbery*) налёт; (*delay*) задержка.

hole /həʊl/ *n* дыра; (*animal's*) нора; (*golf*) лунка.

holiday /ˈhɒlɪˌdeɪ/ *n* (*day off*) выходной день; (*festival*) праздник; (*annual leave*) отпуск; *pl* (*school*) каникулы (-л) *pl*; **~-maker** турист; **on ~** в отпуске.

holiness /ˈhəʊlɪnɪs/ *n* святость.

Holland /ˈhɒlənd/ *n* Голландия.

hollow /ˈhɒləʊ/ *n* впадина; (*valley*) лощина; *adj* пустой; (*sunken*) впалый; (*sound*) глухой; *vt* (**~ *out***) выдалбливать *impf*, выдолбить *pf.*

holly /ˈhɒlɪ/ *n* остролист.

holocaust /ˈhɒləˌkɔːst/ *n* массовое уничтожение.

holster /ˈhəʊlstə(r)/ *n* кобура.

holy /ˈhəʊlɪ/ *adj* святой, священный.

homage /ˈhɒmɪdʒ/ *n* почтение; **pay ~ to** преклоняться *impf*, преклониться *pf* перед+*instr.*

home /həʊm/ *n* дом; (*also* **homeland**) родина; **at ~** дома; **feel at ~** чувствовать *impf* себя как дома; *adj* домашний; (*native*) родной; **H~ Affairs** внутренние дела *neut pl*; *adv* (*direction*) домой; (*position*) дома. **homeless** /-lɪs/ *adj* бездомный. **home-made** *adj* (*food*) домашний; (*object*) самодельный. **homesick** *adj*: **be ~** скучать *impf* по дому. **homewards** /-wədz/ *adv* домой. **homework** *n* домашние задания *neut pl.*

homely /ˈhəʊmlɪ/ *adj* простой.

homicide /ˈhɒmɪˌsaɪd/ *n* (*action*) убийство.

homogeneous /ˌhɒməʊˈdʒiːnɪəs/ *adj* однородный.

homosexual /ˌhɒməʊˈseksjʊəl/ *n* гомосексуалист; *adj* гомосексуальный.

honest /ˈɒnɪst/ *n* честный. **honesty** /-tɪ/ *n* честность.

honey /ˈhʌnɪ/ *n* мёд. **honeymoon** *n* медовый месяц. **honeysuckle** *n* жимолость.

honk /hɒŋk/ *vi* гудеть *impf.*

honorary /ˈɒnərərɪ/ *adj* почётный.

honour /ˈɒnə(r)/ *n* честь; *vt* (*respect*) почитать *impf*; (*confer*) удостаивать *impf*, удостоить *pf* (**with** +*gen*); (*fulfil*) выпол-

ня́ть *impf*, вы́полнить *pf*. **honourable** /-rəb(ə)l/ *adj* че́стный.
hood /hʊd/ *n* капюшо́н; (*tech*) капо́т.
hoodwink /'hʊdwɪŋk/ *vt* обма́нывать *impf*, обману́ть *pf*.
hoof /hu:f/ *n* копы́то.
hook /hʊk/ *n* крючо́к; *vt* (*hitch*) зацепля́ть *impf*, зацепи́ть *pf*; (*fasten*) застёгивать *impf*, застегну́ть *pf*.
hooligan /'hu:lɪgən/ *n* хулига́н.
hoop /hu:p/ *n* о́бруч.
hoot /hu:t/ *vi* (*owl*) у́хать *impf*, у́хнуть *pf*; (*horn*) гуде́ть *impf*. **hooter** /'hu:tə(r)/ *n* гудо́к.
hop[1] /hɒp/ *n* (*plant*; *collect*) хмель *m*.
hop[2] /hɒp/ *n* (*jump*) прыжо́к; *vi* пры́гать *impf*, пры́гнуть *pf* (на одно́й ноге́).
hope /həʊp/ *n* наде́жда; *vi* наде́яться *impf*, по~ *pf* (**for** на+*acc*). **hopeful** /-fʊl/ *adj* (*promising*) обнадёживающий; **I am** ~ я наде́юсь. **hopefully** /-fʊlɪ/ *adv* с наде́ждой; (*it is hoped*) надо наде́яться. **hopeless** /-lɪs/ *adj* безнадёжный.
horde /hɔ:d/ *n* (*hist*; *fig*) орда́.
horizon /hə'raɪz(ə)n/ *n* горизо́нт. **horizontal** /,hɒrɪ'zɒnt(ə)l/ *adj* горизонта́льный.
hormone /'hɔ:məʊn/ *n* гормо́н.
horn /hɔ:n/ *n* рог; (*French horn*) валто́рна; (*car*) гудо́к.
hornet /'hɔ:nɪt/ *n* шёршень *m*.
horny /'hɔ:nɪ/ *adj* (*calloused*) мозо́листый.
horoscope /'hɒrə,skəʊp/ *n* гороско́п.
horrible, horrid /'hɒrɪb(ə)l, 'hɒrɪd/ *adj* ужа́сный. **horrify** /'hɒrɪ,faɪ/ *vt* ужаса́ть *impf*, ужасну́ть *pf*. **horror** /'hɒrə(r)/ *n* у́жас.
hors-d'oeuvre /ɔ:'dɜ:v/ *n* заку́ска.
horse /hɔ:s/ *n* ло́шадь. **horse-chestnut** *n* ко́нский кашта́н. **horseman, -woman** *n* вса́дник, -ица. **horseplay** *n* возня́. **horsepower** *n* лошади́ная си́ла. **horse-racing** /'hɔ:s,reɪsɪŋ/ *n* ска́чки (-чек) *pl*. **horse-radish** *n* хрен. **horseshoe** *n* подко́ва.
horticulture /'hɔ:tɪ,kʌltʃə(r)/ *n* садово́дство.
hose /həʊz/ *n* (~*-pipe*) шланг.
hosiery /'həʊzɪərɪ/ *n* чуло́чные изде́лия *neut pl*.
hospitable /'hɒspɪtəb(ə)l/ *adj* гостеприи́мный.
hospital /'hɒspɪt(ə)l/ *n* больни́ца.
hospitality /,hɒspɪ'tælɪtɪ/ *n* гостеприи́мство.
host[1] /həʊst/ *n* (*multitude*) мно́жество.
host[2] /həʊst/ *n* (*entertaining*) хозя́ин.
hostage /'hɒstɪdʒ/ *n* зало́жник.
hostel /'hɒst(ə)l/ *n* общежи́тие.
hostess /'həʊstɪs/ *n* хозя́йка; (*air* ~) стюарде́сса.
hostile /'hɒstaɪl/ *adj* вражде́бный. **hostility** /hɒ'stɪlɪtɪ/ *n* вражде́бность; *pl* вое́нные де́йствия *neut pl*.
hot /hɒt/ *adj* горя́чий, жа́ркий; (*pungent*) о́стрый; **~-headed** вспы́льчивый; **~-water bottle** гре́лка. **hotbed** *n* (*fig*) оча́г. **hothouse** *n* тепли́ца. **hotplate** *n* пли́тка.
hotel /həʊ'tel/ *n* гости́ница.
hound /haʊnd/ *n* охо́тничья соба́ка; *vt* трави́ть *impf*, за~ *pf*.
hour /aʊə(r)/ *n* час. **hourly** /'aʊəlɪ/ *adj* ежеча́сный.
house *n* /haʊs/ дом; (*parl*) пала́та; *attrib* дома́шний; *vt* /haʊz/ помеща́ть *impf*, поме-

сти́ть *pf.* **household** *n* семья́; *adj* хозя́йственный; дома́шний. **house-keeper** /ˈhaʊsˌkiːpə(r)/ *n* эконо́мка. **house-warming** /ˈhaʊsˌwɔːmɪŋ/ *n* новосе́лье. **housewife** *n* хозя́йка. **housework** *n* дома́шняя рабо́та. **housing** /ˈhaʊzɪŋ/ *n* (*accommodation*) жильё; (*casing*) кожу́х; ~ **estate** жило́й масси́в.

hovel /ˈhɒv(ə)l/ *n* лачу́га.

hover /ˈhɒvə(r)/ *vi* (*bird*) пари́ть *impf*; (*helicopter*) висе́ть *impf*; (*person*) мая́чить *impf.* **hovercraft** *n* су́дно на возду́шной поду́шке, СВП.

how /haʊ/ *adv* как, каки́м о́бразом; ~ **do you do?** здра́вствуйте!; ~ **many**, ~ **much** ско́лько (+*gen*). **however** /haʊˈevə(r)/ *adv* как бы ни (+*past*); *conj* одна́ко, тем не ме́нее; ~ **much** ско́лько бы ни (+*gen* & *past*).

howl /haʊl/ *n* вой; *vi* выть *impf.* **howler** /ˈhaʊlə(r)/ *n* грубе́йшая оши́бка.

hub /hʌb/ *n* (*of wheel*) ступи́ца; (*fig*) центр, средото́чие.

hubbub /ˈhʌbʌb/ *n* шум, гам.

huddle /ˈhʌd(ə)l/ *vi*: ~ **together** прижима́ться *impf*, прижа́ться *pf* друг к дру́гу.

hue /hjuː/ *n* (*tint*) отте́нок.

huff /hʌf/ *n*: **in a** ~ оскорблённый.

hug /hʌg/ *n* объя́тие; *vt* (*embrace*) обнима́ть *impf*, обня́ть *pf.*

huge /hjuːdʒ/ *adj* огро́мный.

hulk /hʌlk/ *n* ко́рпус (корабля́). **hulking** /-kɪŋ/ *adj* (*bulky*) грома́дный; (*clumsy*) неуклю́жий.

hull /hʌl/ *n* (*of ship*) ко́рпус.

hum /hʌm/ *n* жужжа́ние; *vi* (*buzz*) жужжа́ть *impf*; *vt* & *i* (*person*) напева́ть *impf.*

human /ˈhjuːmən/ *adj* челове́ческий, людско́й; *n* челове́к. **humane, humanitarian** /hjuːˈmeɪn, hjuːˌmænɪˈteərɪən/ *adj* челове́чный. **humanity** /hjuːˈmænɪtɪ/ *n* (*human race*) челове́чество; (*humaneness*) гума́нность; **the Humanities** гуманита́рные нау́ки *f pl.*

humble /ˈhʌmb(ə)l/ *adj* (*person*) смире́нный; (*abode*) скро́мный; *vt* унижа́ть *impf*, уни́зить *pf.*

humdrum /ˈhʌmdrʌm/ *adj* однообра́зный.

humid /ˈhjuːmɪd/ *adj* вла́жный. **humidity** /hjuːˈmɪdɪtɪ/ *n* вла́жность.

humiliate /hjuːˈmɪlɪˌeɪt/ *vt* унижа́ть *impf*, уни́зить *pf.* **humiliation** /-ˈeɪʃ(ə)n/ *n* униже́ние.

humility /hjuːˈmɪlɪtɪ/ *n* смире́ние.

humorous /ˈhjuːmərəs/ *adj* юмористи́ческий. **humour** /ˈhjuːmə(r)/ *n* ю́мор; (*mood*) настрое́ние; *vt* потака́ть *impf* +*dat.*

hump /hʌmp/ *n* горб; (*of earth*) буго́р.

humus /ˈhjuːməs/ *n* перегно́й.

hunch /hʌntʃ/ *n* (*idea*) предчу́вствие; *vt* го́рбить *impf*, с~ *pf.* **hunchback** *n* (*person*) горбу́н, ~ья. **hunchbacked** /ˈhʌntʃbækt/ *adj* горба́тый.

hundred /ˈhʌndrəd/ *adj* & *n* сто; ~**s of** со́тни *f pl* +*gen*; **two** ~ две́сти; **three** ~ три́ста; **four** ~ четы́реста; **five** ~ пятьсо́т. **hundredth** /ˈhʌndrədθ/ *adj* & *n* со́тый.

Hungarian /hʌŋˈgeərɪən/ *n* венгр, венге́рка; *adj* венге́рский. **Hungary** /ˈhʌŋgərɪ/ *n* Ве́нгрия.

hunger /ˈhʌŋɡə(r)/ *n* гóлод; (*fig*) жáжда (**for** *+gen*); ~ **strike** голодóвка; *vi* голодáть *impf*; ~ **for** жáждать *impf +gen*. **hungry** /ˈhʌŋɡrɪ/ *adj* голóдный.

hunk /hʌŋk/ *n* ломóть *m*.

hunt /hʌnt/ *n* охóта; (*fig*) пóиски *m pl* (**for** *+gen*); *vt* охóтиться *impf* на*+acc*, за*+instr*; (*persecute*) травúть *impf*, за~ *pf*; ~ **down** вы́следить *pf*; ~ **for** искáть *impf +acc or gen*; ~ **out** отыскáть *pf*. **hunter** /-tə(r)/ *n* охóтник. **hunting** /-tɪŋ/ *n* охóта.

hurdle /ˈhɜːd(ə)l/ *n* (*sport*; *fig*) барьéр. **hurdler** /ˈhɜːdlə(r)/ *n* барьерúст. **hurdles** /ˈhɜːd(ə)lz/ *n pl* (*sport*) барьéрный бег.

hurl /hɜːl/ *vt* швырять *impf*, швырнýть *pf*.

hurly-burly /ˈhɜːlɪˌbɜːlɪ/ *n* суматóха.

hurrah, hurray /hʊˈrɑː, hʊˈreɪ/ *int* урá!

hurricane /ˈhʌrɪkən/ *n* урагáн.

hurried /ˈhʌrɪd/ *adj* торопли́вый. **hurry** /ˈhʌrɪ/ *n* спéшка; **be in a** ~ спешúть *impf*; *vt* & *i* торопúть(ся) *impf*, по~ *pf*; *vi* спешúть *impf*, по~ *pf*.

hurt /hɜːt/ *n* ущéрб; *vi* болéть *impf*; *vt* повреждáть *impf*, повредúть *pf*; (*offend*) обижáть *impf*, обúдеть *pf*.

hurtle /ˈhɜːt(ə)l/ *vi* нестúсь *impf*, по~ *pf*.

husband /ˈhʌzbənd/ *n* муж.

hush /hʌʃ/ *n* тишинá; *vt*: ~ **up** заминáть *impf*, замять *pf*; *int* тúше!

husk /hʌsk/ *n* шелухá.

husky /ˈhʌskɪ/ *adj* (*voice*) хрúплый.

hustle /ˈhʌs(ə)l/ *n* толкотня́; *vt* (*push*) затолкáть *impf*, затолкнýть *pf*; (*herd people*) загонять *impf*, загнáть *pf*; *vt* & *i* (*hurry*) торопúть(ся) *impf*, по~ *pf*.

hut /hʌt/ *n* хúжина.

hutch /hʌtʃ/ *n* клéтка.

hyacinth /ˈhaɪəsɪnθ/ *n* гиацúнт.

hybrid /ˈhaɪbrɪd/ *n* гибрúд; *adj* гибрúдный.

hydrangea /haɪˈdreɪndʒə/ *n* гортéнзия.

hydrant /ˈhaɪdrənt/ *n* гидрáнт.

hydraulic /haɪˈdrɒlɪk/ *adj* гидравлúческий.

hydrochloric acid /ˌhaɪdrəˈklɔːrɪk ˈæsɪd/ *n* соляная кислотá. **hydroelectric** /ˌhaɪdrəʊɪˈlektrɪk/ *adj* гидроэлектрúческий; ~ **power station** гидроэлектростáнция, ГЭС *f indecl*.

hydrofoil /ˈhaɪdrəˌfɔɪl/ *n* сýдно на подвóдных кры́льях, СПК.

hydrogen /ˈhaɪdrədʒ(ə)n/ *n* водорóд.

hyena /haɪˈiːnə/ *n* гиéна.

hygiene /ˈhaɪdʒiːn/ *n* гигиéна. **hygienic** /-ˈdʒiːnɪk/ *adj* гигиенúческий.

hymn /hɪm/ *n* гимн.

hyperbole /haɪˈpɜːbəlɪ/ *n* гипéрбола.

hyphen /ˈhaɪf(ə)n/ *n* дефúс. **hyphen(ate)** /ˈhaɪfəˌneɪt/ *vt* писáть *impf*, на~ *pf* чéрез дефúс.

hypnosis /hɪpˈnəʊsɪs/ *n* гипнóз. **hypnotic** /hɪpˈnɒtɪk/ *adj* гипнотúческий. **hypnotism** /ˈhɪpnəˌtɪz(ə)m/ *n* гипнотúзм. **hypnotist** /ˈhɪpnətɪst/ *n* гипнотизёр. **hypnotize** /ˈhɪpnəˌtaɪz/ *vt* гипнотизúровать *impf*, за~ *pf*.

hypochondria /ˌhaɪpəˈkɒndrɪə/ *n* ипохóндрия. **hypochondriac** /-rɪˌæk/ *n* ипохóндрик.

hypocrisy /hɪˈpɒkrɪsɪ/ *n* лицемéрие. **hypocrite** /ˈhɪpəkrɪt/ *n* лицемéр. **hypocritical** /ˌhɪpəˈkrɪtɪk(ə)l/ *adj* лицемéрный.

hypodermic /ˌhaɪpəˈdɜːmɪk/ *adj* подко́жный.

hypothesis /haɪˈpɒθɪsɪs/ *n* гипо́теза. **hypothesize** /-ˈpɒθɪˌsaɪz/ *vi* стро́ить *impf*, по~ *pf* гипоте́зу. **hypothetical** /ˌhaɪpəˈθetɪk(ə)l/ *adj* гипотети́ческий.

hysterectomy /ˌhɪstəˈrektəmɪ/ *n* гистерэктоми́я, удале́ние ма́тки.

hysteria /hɪˈstɪərɪə/ *n* истери́я. **hysterical** /-ˈsterɪk(ə)l/ *adj* истери́ческий. **hysterics** /-ˈsterɪks/ *n pl* исте́рика.

I

I /aɪ/ *pron* я.

ibid(em) /ˈɪbɪˌd(em)/ *adv* там-же.

ice /aɪs/ *n* лёд; **~-age** леднико́вый пери́од; **~-axe** ледору́б; **~-cream** моро́женое *sb*; **~ hockey** хокке́й (с ша́йбой); **~ rink** като́к; **~ skate** конёк; *vi* ката́ться *impf* на конька́х; *vt* (*chill*) замора́живать *impf*, заморо́зить *pf*; (*cul*) глазирова́ть *impf* & *pf*; *vi*: **~ over, up** обледенева́ть *impf*, обледене́ть *pf*. **iceberg** /ˈaɪsbɜːg/ *n* а́йсберг. **icicle** /ˈaɪsɪk(ə)l/ *n* сосу́лька. **icing** /ˈaɪsɪŋ/ *n* (*cul*) глазу́рь. **icy** /ˈaɪsɪ/ *adj* ледяно́й.

icon /ˈaɪkɒn/ *n* ико́на.

ID *abbr* (*of* **identification**) удостовере́ние ли́чности.

idea /aɪˈdɪə/ *n* иде́я, мысль; (*conception*) поня́тие.

ideal /aɪˈdiːəl/ *n* идеа́л; *adj* идеа́льный. **idealism** /-ˈdiːəˌlɪz(ə)m/ *n* идеали́зм. **idealist** /-ˈdɪəlɪst/ *n* идеали́ст. **idealize** /-ˈdɪəˌlaɪz/ *vt* идеализи́ровать *impf* & *pf*.

identical /aɪˈdentɪk(ə)l/ *adj* тожде́ственный, одина́ковый.

identification /aɪˌdentɪfɪˈkeɪʃ(ə)n/ *n* (*recognition*) опозна́ние; (*of person*) установле́ние ли́чности. **identify** /aɪˈdentɪˌfaɪ/ *vt* опознава́ть *impf*, опозна́ть *pf*.

identity /aɪˈdentɪtɪ/ *n* (*of person*) ли́чность; **~ card** удостовере́ние ли́чности.

ideological /ˌaɪdɪəˈlɒdʒɪk(ə)l/ *adj* идеологи́ческий. **ideology** /ˌaɪdɪˈɒlədʒɪ/ *n* идеоло́гия.

idiom /ˈɪdɪəm/ *n* идио́ма. **idiomatic** /-ˈmætɪk/ *adj* идиомати́ческий.

idiosyncrasy /ˌɪdɪəʊˈsɪŋkrəsɪ/ *n* идиосинкрази́я.

idiot /ˈɪdɪət/ *n* идио́т. **idiotic** /-ˈɒtɪk/ *adj* идио́тский.

idle /ˈaɪd(ə)l/ *adj* (*unoccupied*; *lazy*; *purposeless*) пра́здный; (*vain*) тще́тный; (*empty*) пусто́й; (*machine*) неде́йствующий; *vi* безде́льничать *impf*; (*engine*) рабо́тать *impf* вхолосту́ю; *vt*: **~ away** пра́здно проводи́ть *impf*, провести́ *pf*. **idleness** /-nɪs/ *n* пра́здность.

idol /ˈaɪd(ə)l/ *n* и́дол. **idolatry** /aɪˈdɒlətrɪ/ *n* идолопокло́нство; (*fig*) обожа́ние. **idolize** /ˈaɪdəˌlaɪz/ *vt* боготвори́ть *impf*.

idyll /ˈɪdɪl/ *n* иди́ллия. **idyllic** /ɪˈdɪlɪk/ *adj* идилли́ческий.

i.e. *abbr* т.е., то есть.

if /ɪf/ *conj* е́сли, е́сли бы; (*whether*) ли; **as ~** как бу́дто; **even ~** да́же е́сли; **~ only** е́сли бы то́лько.

ignite /ɪgˈnaɪt/ *vt* зажига́ть *impf*, заже́чь *pf*; *vi* загора́ться *impf*, загоре́ться *pf*. **ignition** /-ˈnɪʃ(ə)n/ *n* зажига́ние.

ignoble /ɪgˈnəʊb(ə)l/ *adj* ни́зкий.

ignominious /ˌɪɡnəˈmɪnɪəs/ *adj* позóрный. **ignoramus** /ˌɪɡnəˈreɪməs/ *n* невéжда *m.* **ignorance** /ˈɪɡnərəns/ *n* невéжество, (*of certain facts*) невéдение. **ignorant** /ˈɪɡnərənt/ *adj* невéжественный; (*uninformed*) несвéдущий (**of** в+*prep*).

ignore /ɪɡˈnɔː(r)/ *vt* не обращáть *impf* внимáния на+*acc*; игнорíровать *impf* & *pf*.

ilk /ɪlk/ *n*: **of that ~** такóго рóда.

ill /ɪl/ *n* (*evil*) зло; (*harm*) вред; *pl* (*misfortunes*) несчáстья (-тий) *pl*; *adj* (*sick*) больнóй; (*bad*) дурнóй; *adv* плóхо, дýрно; **fall ~** заболевáть *impf*, заболéть *pf*; **~-advised** неблагоразýмный; **~-mannered** невéжливый; **~-treat** *vt* плóхо обращáться *impf* с+*instr*.

illegal /ɪˈliːɡ(ə)l/ *adj* нелегáльный. **illegality** /ˌɪliːˈɡælɪtɪ/ *n* незакóнность, нелегáльность.

illegible /ɪˈledʒɪb(ə)l/ *adj* неразбóрчивый.

illegitimacy /ˌɪlɪˈdʒɪtɪməsɪ/ *n* незакóнность; (*of child*) незаконнорождённость. **illegitimate** /-mət/ *adj* незакóнный; незаконнорождённый.

illicit /ɪˈlɪsɪt/ *adj* незакóнный, недозвóленный.

illiteracy /ɪˈlɪtərəsɪ/ *n* неграмóтность. **illiterate** /-rət/ *adj* неграмóтный.

illness /ˈɪlnɪs/ *n* болéзнь.

illogical /ɪˈlɒdʒɪk(ə)l/ *adj* нелогíчный.

illuminate /ɪˈluːmɪˌneɪt/ *vt* освещáть *impf*, осветíть *pf*. **illumination** /-ˈneɪʃ(ə)n/ *n* освещéние.

illusion /ɪˈluːʒ(ə)n/ *n* иллю́зия. **illusory** /ɪˈluːsərɪ/ *adj* иллюзóрный.

illustrate /ˈɪləˌstreɪt/ *vt* иллюстрíровать *impf* & *pf*, про~ *pf*. **illustration** /-ˈstreɪʃ(ə)n/ *n* иллюстрáция. **illustrative** /ˈɪləstrətɪv/ *adj* иллюстратíвный.

illustrious /ɪˈlʌstrɪəs/ *adj* знаменíтый.

image /ˈɪmɪdʒ/ *n* (*phys*; *statue etc.*) изображéние; (*optical ~*) отражéние; (*likeness*) кóпия; (*metaphor*; *conception*) óбраз; (*reputation*) репутáция. **imagery** /-dʒərɪ/ *n* óбразность.

imaginable /ɪˈmædʒɪnəb(ə)l/ *adj* вообразíмый. **imaginary** /-ˈmædʒɪnərɪ/ *adj* воображáемый. **imagination** /-ˈneɪʃ(ə)n/ *n* воображéние. **imagine** /ɪˈmædʒɪn/ *vt* воображáть *impf*, вообразíть *pf*; (*conceive*) представля́ть *impf*, представить *pf* себé.

imbecile /ˈɪmbɪˌsiːl/ *n* слабоýмный *sb*; (*fool*) глупéц.

imbibe /ɪmˈbaɪb/ *vt* (*absorb*) впíтывать *impf*, впитáть *pf*.

imbue /ɪmˈbjuː/ *vt* внушáть *impf*, внушíть *pf* +*dat* (**with** +*acc*).

imitate /ˈɪmɪˌteɪt/ *vt* подражáть *impf* +*dat*. **imitation** /-ˈteɪʃ(ə)n/ *n* подражáние (**of** +*dat*); *attrib* искýсственный. **imitative** /ˈɪmɪtətɪv/ *adj* подражáтельный.

immaculate /ɪˈmækjʊlət/ *adj* безупрéчный.

immaterial /ˌɪməˈtɪərɪəl/ *adj* (*unimportant*) несущéственный.

immature /ˌɪməˈtjʊə(r)/ *adj* незрéлый.

immeasurable /ɪˈmeʒərəb(ə)l/ *adj* неизмерíмый.

immediate /ɪˈmiːdɪət/ *adj* (*direct*) непосрéдственный; (*swift*) немéдленный. **immediately** /-lɪ/

adv тóтчас, срáзу.

immemorial /ˌɪmɪ'mɔːrɪəl/ *adj*: **from time ~** с незапáмятных времён.

immense /ɪ'mens/ *adj* огрóмный.

immerse /ɪ'mɜːs/ *vt* погружáть *impf*, погрузи́ть *pf*. **immersion** /ɪ'mɜːʃ(ə)n/ *n* погружéние.

immigrant /'ɪmɪgrənt/ *n* иммигрáнт, **~**ка. **immigration** /-'greɪʃ(ə)n/ *n* иммигрáция.

imminent /'ɪmɪnənt/ *adj* надвигáющийся; (*danger*) грозя́щий.

immobile /ɪ'məʊbaɪl/ *adj* неподви́жный. **immobilize** /-bɪˌlaɪz/ *vt* парализовáть *impf* & *pf*.

immoderate /ɪ'mɒdərət/ *adj* умéренный.

immodest /ɪ'mɒdɪst/ *adj* нескрóмный.

immoral /ɪ'mɒr(ə)l/ *adj* безнрáвственный. **immorality** /ˌɪmə'rælɪtɪ/ *n* безнрáвственность.

immortal /ɪ'mɔːt(ə)l/ *adj* бессмéртный. **immortality** /-'tælɪtɪ/ *n* бессмéртие. **immortalize** /ɪ'mɔːtəˌlaɪz/ *vt* обессмéртить *pf*.

immovable /ɪ'muːvəb(ə)l/ *adj* неподви́жный; (*fig*) непоколеби́мый.

immune /ɪ'mjuːn/ *adj* (*to illness*) невосприи́мчивый (**to** к+*dat*); (*free from*) свобóдный (**from** от+*gen*). **immunity** /ɪ'mjuːnɪtɪ/ *n* иммунитéт (**from** к+*dat*); освобождéние (**from** от+*gen*). **immunize** /'ɪmjuːˌnaɪz/ *vt* иммунизи́ровать *impf* & *pf*.

immutable /ɪ'mjuːtəb(ə)l/ *adj* неизмéнный.

imp /ɪmp/ *n* бесёнок.

impact /'ɪmpækt/ *n* удáр; (*fig*) влия́ние.

impair /ɪm'peə(r)/ *vt* вреди́ть *impf*, по~ *pf*.

impale /ɪm'peɪl/ *vt* протыкáть *impf*, проткнýть *pf*.

impart /ɪm'pɑːt/ *vt* дели́ться *impf*, по~ *pf* +*instr* (**to** с+*instr*).

impartial /ɪm'pɑːʃ(ə)l/ *adj* беспристрáстный.

impassable /ɪm'pɑːsəb(ə)l/ *adj* непроходи́мый; (*for vehicles*) непроéзжий.

impasse /'æmpæs/ *n* тупи́к.

impassioned /ɪm'pæʃ(ə)nd/ *adj* стрáстный.

impassive /ɪm'pæsɪv/ *adj* бесстрáстный.

impatience /ɪm'peɪʃəns/ *n* нетерпéние. **impatient** /-ʃənt/ *adj* нетерпели́вый.

impeach /ɪm'piːtʃ/ *vt* обвиня́ть *impf*, обвини́ть *pf* (**for** в+*prep*).

impeccable /ɪm'pekəb(ə)l/ *adj* безупрéчный.

impecunious /ˌɪmpɪ'kjuːnɪəs/ *adj* безде́нежный.

impedance /ɪm'piːd(ə)ns/ *n* пóлное сопротивлéние. **impede** /-'piːd/ *vt* препя́тствовать *impf*, вос~ *pf* +*dat*. **impediment** /-'pedɪmənt/ *n* препя́тствие; (*in speech*) заикáние.

impel /ɪm'pel/ *vt* побуждáть *impf*, побуди́ть *pf* (**to** +*inf*, к+*dat*).

impending /ɪm'pendɪŋ/ *adj* предстоя́щий.

impenetrable /ɪm'penɪtrəb(ə)l/ *adj* непроницáемый.

imperative /ɪm'perətɪv/ *adj* необходи́мый; *n* (*gram*) повели́тельное наклонéние.

imperceptible /ˌɪmpə'septɪb(ə)l/ *adj* незамéтный.

imperfect /ɪm'pɜːfɪkt/ *n* имперфéкт; *adj* несовершéнный. **imperfection** /ˌɪmpə'fekʃ(ə)n/ *n* несовершéнство; (*fault*) недостáток. **imperfective** /ˌɪmpə

'fektıv/ *adj* (*n*) несоверше́нный (вид).
imperial /ım'pıərıəl/ *adj* импе́рский. **imperialism** /-'pıərıə,lız(ə)m/ *n* империали́зм. **imperialist** /-'pıərıəlıst/ *n* империали́ст; *attrib* империалисти́ческий.
imperil /ım'perıl/ *vt* подверга́ть *impf*, подве́ргнуть *pf* опа́сности.
imperious /ım'pıərıəs/ *adj* вла́стный.
impersonal /ım'pɜ:sən(ə)l/ *adj* безли́чный.
impersonate /ım'pɜ:sə,neıt/ *vt* (*imitate*) подража́ть *impf*; (*pretend to be*) выдава́ть *impf*, вы́дать *pf* себя́ за+*acc*. **impersonation** /-'neıʃ(ə)n/ *n* подража́ние.
impertinence /ım'pɜ:tınəns/ *n* де́рзость. **impertinent** /-nənt/ *adj* де́рзкий.
imperturbable /,ımpə'tɜ:bəb(ə)l/ *adj* невозмути́мый.
impervious /ım'pɜ:vıəs/ *adj* (*fig*) глухо́й (**to** к+*dat*).
impetuous /ım'petjʊəs/ *adj* стреми́тельный.
impetus /'ımpıtəs/ *n* дви́жущая си́ла.
impinge /ım'pındʒ/ *vi*: ~ **(up)on** ока́зывать *impf*, оказа́ть *pf* (отрица́тельный) эффе́кт на+*acc*.
implacable /ım'plækəb(ə)l/ *adj* неумоли́мый.
implant /'ımplɑ:nt/ *vt* вводи́ть *impf*, ввести́ *pf*; (*fig*) се́ять *impf*, по~ *pf*.
implement[1] /'ımplımənt/ *n* ору́дие, инструме́нт.
implement[2] /'ımplı,ment/ *vt* (*fulfil*) выполня́ть *impf*, вы́полнить *pf*.
implicate /'ımplı,keıt/ *vt* впу́тывать *impf*, впу́тать *pf*. **implication** /-'keıʃ(ə)n/ *n* (*inference*) намёк; *pl* значе́ние.
implicit /ım'plısıt/ *adj* подразумева́емый; (*absolute*) безогово́рочный.
implore /ım'plɔ:(r)/ *vt* умоля́ть *impf*.
imply /ım'plaı/ *vt* подразумева́ть *impf*.
impolite /,ımpə'laıt/ *adj* неве́жливый.
imponderable /ım'pɒndərəb(ə)l/ *adj* неопределённый.
import *n* /'ımpɔ:t/ (*meaning*) значе́ние; (*of goods*) и́мпорт; *vt* /ım'pɔ:t/ импорти́ровать *impf* & *pf*. **importer** /ım'pɔ:tə(r)/ *n* импортёр.
importance /ım'pɔ:t(ə)ns/ *n* ва́жность. **important** /-t(ə)nt/ *adj* ва́жный.
impose /ım'pəʊz/ *vt* (*tax*) облага́ть *impf*, обложи́ть *pf* +*instr* (**on** +*acc*); (*obligation*) налага́ть *impf*, наложи́ть *pf* (**on** на+*acc*); ~ **(o.s.) on** налега́ть *impf* на+*acc*. **imposing** /-'pəʊzıŋ/ *adj* внуши́тельный. **imposition** /,ımpə'zıʃ(ə)n/ *n* обложе́ние, наложе́ние.
impossibility /ım,pɒsı'bılıtı/ *n* невозмо́жность. **impossible** /ım'pɒsıb(ə)l/ *adj* невозмо́жный.
impostor /ım'pɒstə(r)/ *n* самозва́нец.
impotence /'ımpət(ə)ns/ *n* бесси́лие; (*med*) импоте́нция. **impotent** /-t(ə)nt/ *adj* бесси́льный; (*med*) импоте́нтный.
impound /ım'paʊnd/ *vt* (*confiscate*) конфискова́ть *impf* & *pf*.
impoverished /ım'pɒvərıʃt/ *adj* обедне́вший.
impracticable /ım'præktıkəb(ə)l/

adj невыполни́мый.
imprecise /ˌımprı'saıs/ *n* неточный.
impregnable /ım'pregnəb(ə)l/ *adj* непристу́пный.
impregnate /'ımpregˌneıt/ *vt* (*fertilize*) оплодотворя́ть *impf*, оплодотвори́ть *pf*; (*saturate*) пропи́тывать *impf*, пропита́ть *pf*.
impresario /ˌımprı'sɑ:rıəʊ/ *n* аге́нт.
impress *vt* /ım'pres/ производи́ть *impf*, произвести́ *pf* (како́е-либо) впечатле́ние на+*acc*; ~ **upon (s.o.)** внуша́ть *impf*, внуши́ть *pf* (+*dat*). **impression** /-'preʃ(ə)n/ *n* впечатле́ние; (*imprint*) отпеча́ток; (*reprint*) (стереоти́пное) изда́ние.
impressionism /ım'preʃəˌnız(ə)m/ *n* импрессиони́зм. **impressionist** /-nıst/ *n* импрессиони́ст.
impressive /ım'presıv/ *adj* впечатля́ющий.
imprint *n* /'ımprınt/ отпеча́ток; *vt* /ım'prınt/ отпеча́тывать *impf*, отпеча́тать *pf*; (*on memory*) запечатлева́ть *impf*, запечатле́ть *pf*.
imprison /ım'prız(ə)n/ *vt* заключа́ть *impf*, заключи́ть *pf* (в тюрьму́). **imprisonment** /-mənt/ *n* тюре́мное заключе́ние.
improbable /ım'prɒbəb(ə)l/ *adj* невероя́тный.
impromptu /ım'prɒmptju:/ *adj* импровизи́рованный; *adv* без подгото́вки, экспро́мтом.
improper /ım'prɒpə(r)/ *adj* (*incorrect*) непра́вильный; (*indecent*) неприли́чный. **impropriety** /ˌımprə'praıətı/ *n* неуме́стность.
improve /ım'pru:v/ *vt* & *i* улучша́ть(ся) *impf*, улу́чшить(ся) *pf*. **improvement** /-mənt/ *n* улучше́ние.
improvisation /ˌımprəvaı'zeıʃ(ə)n/ *n* импровиза́ция. **improvise** /'ımprəˌvaız/ *vt* импровизи́ровать *impf*, сымпровизи́ровать *pf*.
imprudent /ım'pru:d(ə)nt/ *adj* неосторо́жный.
impudence /'ımpjʊd(ə)ns/ *n* на́глость. **impudent** /-d(ə)nt/ *adj* на́глый.
impulse /'ımpʌls/ *n* толчо́к, и́мпульс; (*sudden tendency*) поры́в. **impulsive** /ım'pʌlsıv/ *adj* импульси́вный.
impunity /ım'pju:nıtı/ *n*: **with** ~ безнака́занно.
impure /ım'pjʊə(r)/ *adj* нечи́стый.
impute /ım'pju:t/ *vt* припи́сывать *impf*, приписа́ть *pf* (**to** +*dat*).
in /ın/ *prep* (*place*) в+*prep*, на +*prep*; (*into*) в+*acc*, на+*acc*; (*point in time*) в+*prep*, на+*prep*; **in the morning** (*etc.*) у́тром (*instr*); **in spring** (*etc.*) весно́й (*instr*); (*at some stage in*; *throughout*) во вре́мя +*gen*; (*duration*) за+*acc*; (*after interval of*) че́рез+*acc*; (*during course of*) в тече́ние+*gen*; (*circumstance*) в+*prep*, при+*prep*; *adv* (*place*) внутри́; (*motion*) внутрь; (*at home*) до́ма; (*in fashion*) в мо́де; **in here, there** (*place*) здесь, там; (*motion*) сюда́, туда́; *adj* вну́тренний; (*fashionable*) мо́дный; *n*: **the ins and outs** все ходы́ и вы́ходы.
inability /ˌınə'bılıtı/ *n* неспосо́бность.
inaccessible /ˌınæk'sesıb(ə)l/ *adj* недосту́пный.

inaccurate /ɪnˈækjʊrət/ *adj* нето́чный. **inaction** /ɪnˈækʃ(ə)n/ *n* безде́йствие. **inactive** /-ˈæktɪv/ *adj* безде́йственный. **inactivity** /ˌɪnækˈtɪvɪtɪ/ *n* безде́йственность.
inadequate /ɪnˈædɪkwət/ *adj* недоста́точный.
inadmissible /ˌɪnədˈmɪsɪb(ə)l/ *adj* недопусти́мый.
inadvertent /ˌɪnədˈvɜːt(ə)nt/ *adj* нечáянный.
inalienable /ɪnˈeɪlɪənəb(ə)l/ *adj* неотъе́млемый.
inane /ɪˈneɪn/ *adj* глу́пый.
inanimate /ɪnˈænɪmət/ *adj* неодушевлённый.
inappropriate /ˌɪnəˈprəʊprɪət/ *adj* неуме́стный.
inarticulate /ˌɪnɑːˈtɪkjʊlət/ *adj* (*person*) косноязы́чный; (*indistinct*) невня́тный.
inasmuch /ˌɪnəzˈmʌtʃ/ *adv*: ~ **as** так как; ввиду́ того́, что.
inattentive /ˌɪnəˈtentɪv/ *adj* невнима́тельный.
inaudible /ɪnˈɔːdɪb(ə)l/ *adj* неслы́шный.
inaugural /ɪˈnɔːgjʊr(ə)l/ *adj* вступи́тельный. **inaugurate** /-ˌreɪt/ *vt* (*admit to office*) торже́ственно вводи́ть *impf*, ввести́ *pf* в до́лжность; (*open*) открыва́ть *impf*, откры́ть *pf*; (*introduce*) вводи́ть *impf*, ввести́ *pf*. **inauguration** /-ˈreɪʃ(ə)n/ *n* введе́ние в до́лжность; откры́тие; нача́ло.
inauspicious /ˌɪnɔːˈspɪʃəs/ *adj* неблагоприя́тный.
inborn, inbred /ˈɪnbɔːn, ˈɪnbred/ *adj* врождённый.
incalculable /ɪnˈkælkjʊləb(ə)l/ *adj* неисчисли́мый.
incandescent /ˌɪnkænˈdes(ə)nt/ *adj* накалённый.
incantation /ˌɪnkænˈteɪʃ(ə)n/ *n* заклина́ние.
incapability /ɪnˌkeɪpəˈbɪlɪtɪ/ *n* неспосо́бность. **incapable** /ɪnˈkeɪpəb(ə)l/ *adj* неспосо́бный (**of** к+*dat*, на+*acc*).
incapacitate /ˌɪnkəˈpæsɪˌteɪt/ *vt* де́лать *impf*, с~ *pf* неспосо́бным. **incapacity** /-ˈpæsɪtɪ/ *n* неспосо́бность.
incarcerate /ɪnˈkɑːsəˌreɪt/ *vt* заключа́ть *impf*, заключи́ть *pf* (в тюрьму́). **incarceration** /-ˈreɪʃ(ə)n/ *n* заключе́ние (в тюрьму́).
incarnate /ɪnˈkɑːnət/ *adj* воплощённый. **incarnation** /-ˈneɪʃ(ə)n/ *n* воплоще́ние.
incendiary /ɪnˈsendɪərɪ/ *adj* зажига́тельный.
incense[1] /ˈɪnsens/ *n* фимиа́м, ла́дан.
incense[2] /ɪnˈsens/ *vt* разгнева́ть *pf*.
incentive /ɪnˈsentɪv/ *n* побужде́ние.
inception /ɪnˈsepʃ(ə)n/ *n* нача́ло.
incessant /ɪnˈses(ə)nt/ *adj* непреста́нный.
incest /ˈɪnsest/ *n* кровосмеше́ние.
inch /ɪntʃ/ *n* дюйм; ~ **by** ~ ма́ло-пома́лу; *vi* ползти́ *impf*.
incidence /ˈɪnsɪd(ə)ns/ *n* (*phys*) паде́ние; (*prevalence*) распростране́ние. **incident** /-d(ə)nt/ *n* слу́чай, инциде́нт. **incidental** /ˌɪnsɪˈdent(ə)l/ *adj* (*casual*) случа́йный; (*inessential*) несуще́ственный. **incidentally** /ˌɪnsɪˈdentəlɪ/ *adv* ме́жду про́чим.
incinerate /ɪnˈsɪnəˌreɪt/ *vt* испепеля́ть *impf*, испепели́ть *pf*. **incinerator** /-tə(r)/ *n* мусоросжига́тельная печь.
incipient /ɪnˈsɪpɪənt/ *adj* начина́ющийся.

incision /ɪn'sɪʒ(ə)n/ *n* надрéз (**in** на+*acc*). **incisive** /ɪn'saɪsɪv/ *adj* (*fig*) óстрый. **incisor** /ɪn'saɪzə(r)/ *n* резéц.

incite /ɪn'saɪt/ *vt* подстрекáть *impf*, подстрекнýть *pf* (**to** к+*dat*). **incitement** /-mənt/ *n* подстрекáтельство.

inclement /ɪn'klemənt/ *adj* сурóвый.

inclination /ˌɪnklɪ'neɪʃ(ə)n/ *n* (*slope*) наклóн; (*propensity*) склóнность (**for, to** к+*dat*). **incline** *n* /'ɪnklaɪn/ наклóн; *vt* & *i* /ɪn'klaɪn/ склонять(ся) *impf*, склонить(ся) *pf*. **inclined** /ɪn'klaɪnd/ *predic* (*disposed*) склóнен (-оннá, -óнно) (**to** к+*dat*).

include /ɪn'klu:d/ *vt* включáть *impf*, включить *pf* (**in** в+*acc*); (*contain*) заключáть *impf*, заключить *pf* в себé. **including** /-'klu:dɪŋ/ *prep* включáя+*acc*. **inclusion** /-'klu:ʃ(ə)n/ *n* включéние. **inclusive** /-'klu:sɪv/ *adj* включáющий (в себé); *adv* включительно.

incognito /ˌɪnkɒg'ni:təʊ/ *adv* инкóгнито.

incoherent /ˌɪnkəʊ'hɪərənt/ *adj* бессвязный.

income /'ɪnkʌm/ *n* дохóд; ~ **tax** подохóдный налóг.

incommensurate /ˌɪnkə'menʃərət/ *adj* несоразмéрный.

incomparable /ɪn'kɒmpərəb(ə)l/ *adj* несравнимый (**to, with** с+*instr*); (*matchless*) несравнéнный.

incompatible /ˌɪnkəm'pætɪb(ə)l/ *adj* несовместимый.

incompetence /ɪn'kɒmpɪt(ə)ns/ *n* некомпетéнтность. **incompetent** /-t(ə)nt/ *adj* некомпетéнтный.

incomplete /ˌɪnkəm'pli:t/ *adj* непóлный, незакóнченный.

incomprehensible /ɪnˌkɒmprɪ'hensɪb(ə)l/ *adj* непонятный.

inconceivable /ˌɪnkən'si:vəb(ə)l/ *adj* невообразимый.

inconclusive /ˌɪnkən'klu:sɪv/ *adj* (*evidence*) недостáточный; (*results*) неопределённый.

incongruity /ˌɪnkɒŋ'gru:ɪtɪ/ *n* несоответствие. **incongruous** /ɪn'kɒŋgrʊəs/ *adj* несоответствующий.

inconsequential /ɪnˌkɒnsɪ'kwenʃ(ə)l/ *adj* незначительный.

inconsiderable /ˌɪnkən'sɪdərəb(ə)l/ *adj* незначительный.

inconsiderate /ˌɪnkən'sɪdərət/ *adj* невнимáтельный.

inconsistency /ˌɪnkən'sɪst(ə)nsɪ/ *n* непослéдовательность. **inconsistent** /-t(ə)nt/ *adj* непослéдовательный.

inconsolable /ˌɪnkən'səʊləb(ə)l/ *adj* безутéшный.

inconspicuous /ˌɪnkən'spɪkjʊəs/ *adj* незамéтный.

incontinence /ɪn'kɒntɪnəns/ *n* (*med*) недержáние. **incontinent** /-nənt/ *adj*: **be** ~ страдáть *impf* недержáнием.

incontrovertible /ˌɪnkɒntrə'vɜ:tɪb(ə)l/ *adj* неопровержимый.

inconvenience /ˌɪnkən'vi:nɪəns/ *n* неудóбство; *vt* затруднять *impf*, затруднить *pf*. **inconvenient** /-ənt/ *adj* неудóбный.

incorporate /ɪn'kɔ:pəˌreɪt/ *vt* (*include*) включáть *impf*, включить *pf*; (*unite*) объединять *impf*, объединить *pf*.

incorrect /ˌɪnkə'rekt/ *adj* непрáвильный.

incorrigible /ɪn'kɒrɪdʒɪb(ə)l/ *adj* неисправимый.

incorruptible /ˌɪnkə'rʌptɪb(ə)l/

adj неподку́пный.
increase *n* /'ınkri:s/ рост, увеличе́ние; (*in pay etc.*) приба́вка; *vt* & *i* /ın'kri:s/ увели́чивать(ся) *impf*, увели́чить(ся) *pf*.
incredible /ın'kredıb(ə)l/ *adj* невероя́тный.
incredulous /ın'kredjʊləs/ *adj* недове́рчивый.
increment /'ınkrımənt/ *n* приба́вка.
incriminate /ın'krımı,neıt/ *vt* изоблича́ть *impf*, изобличи́ть *pf*.
incubate /'ıŋkjʊbeıt/ *vt* (*eggs*) выводи́ть *impf*, вы́вести *pf* (в инкуба́торе). **incubator** /-tə(r)/ *n* инкуба́тор.
inculcate /'ınkʌl,keıt/ *vt* внедря́ть *impf*, внедри́ть *pf*.
incumbent /ın'kʌmbənt/ *adj* (*in office*) стоя́щий у вла́сти; **it is ~ (up)on you** вы обя́заны.
incur /ın'kɜ:(r)/ *vt* навлека́ть *impf*, навле́чь *pf* на себя́.
incurable /ın'kjʊərəb(ə)l/ *adj* неизлечи́мый.
incursion /ın'kɜ:ʃ(ə)n/ *n* (*invasion*) вторже́ние; (*attack*) набе́г.
indebted /ın'detıd/ *predic* в долгу́ (**to** у+*gen*).
indecency /ın'di:s(ə)nsı/ *n* неприли́чие. **indecent** /-'di:s(ə)nt/ *adj* неприли́чный.
indecision /,ındı'sıʒ(ə)n/ *n* нереши́тельность. **indecisive** /-'saısıv/ *adj* нереши́тельный.
indeclinable /,ındı'klaınəb(ə)l/ *adj* несклоня́емый.
indeed /ın'di:d/ *adv* в са́мом де́ле, действи́тельно; (*interrog*) неуже́ли?
indefatigable /,ındı'fætıgəb(ə)l/ *adj* неутоми́мый.
indefensible /,ındı'fensıb(ə)l/ *adj* не име́ющий оправда́ния.
indefinable /,ındı'faınəb(ə)l/ *adj* неопредели́мый. **indefinite** /ın'definıt/ *adj* неопределённый.
indelible /ın'delıb(ə)l/ *adj* несмыва́емый.
indemnify /ın'demnı,faı/ *vt*: **~ against** страхова́ть *impf*, за~ *pf* от+*gen*; **~ for** (*compensate*) компенси́ровать *impf* & *pf*. **indemnity** /-'demnıtı/ *n* (*against loss*) гара́нтия от убы́тков; (*compensation*) компенса́ция.
indent /ın'dent/ *vt* (*printing*) писа́ть *impf*, с~ *pf* с о́тступом. **indentation** /-'teıʃ(ə)n/ *n* (*notch*) зубе́ц; (*printing*) о́тступ.
independence /,ındı'pend(ə)ns/ *n* незави́симость, самостоя́тельность. **independent** /-d(ə)nt/ *adj* незави́симый, самостоя́тельный.
indescribable /,ındı'skraıbəb(ə)l/ *adj* неопису́емый.
indestructible /,ındı'strʌktıb(ə)l/ *adj* неразруши́мый.
indeterminate /,ındı'tɜ:mınət/ *adj* неопределённый.
index /'ındeks/ *n* (*alphabetical*) указа́тель *m*; (*econ*) и́ндекс; (*pointer*) стре́лка; **~ finger** указа́тельный па́лец.
India /'ındıə/ *n* И́ндия. **Indian** /-ən/ *n* инди́ец, индиа́нка; (*American*) инде́ец, индиа́нка; *adj* инди́йский; (*American*) инде́йский; **~ summer** ба́бье ле́то.
indicate /'ındı,keıt/ *vt* ука́зывать *impf*, указа́ть *pf*; (*be a sign of*) свиде́тельствовать *impf* о+*prep*. **indication** /-'keıʃ(ə)n/ *n* указа́ние; (*sign*) при́знак. **indicative** /ın'dıkətıv/ *adj* ука́зывающий; (*gram*) изъяви́тельный; *n* изъяви́тельное наклоне́ние. **indicator** /'ındı,keıtə(r)/ *n* указа́тель *m*.
indict /ın'daıt/ *vt* обвиня́ть *impf*,

обвини́ть *pf* (**for** в+*prep*).

indifference /ɪn'dɪfrəns/ *n* равноду́шие. **indifferent** /-frənt/ *adj* равноду́шный; (*mediocre*) посре́дственный.

indigenous /ɪn'dɪdʒɪnəs/ *adj* тузе́мный.

indigestible /ˌɪndɪ'dʒestɪb(ə)l/ *adj* неудобовари́мый. **indigestion** /-'dʒestʃ(ə)n/ *n* несваре́ние желу́дка.

indignant /ɪn'dɪgnənt/ *adj* негоду́ющий; **be ~** негодова́ть *impf* (**with** на+*acc*). **indignation** /-'neɪʃ(ə)n/ *n* негодова́ние.

indignity /ɪn'dɪgnɪtɪ/ *n* оскорбле́ние.

indirect /ˌɪndaɪ'rekt/ *adj* непрямо́й; (*econ*; *gram*) ко́свенный.

indiscreet /ˌɪndɪ'skriːt/ *adj* нескро́мный. **indiscretion** /-'skreʃ(ə)n/ *n* нескро́мность.

indiscriminate /ˌɪndɪ'skrɪmɪnət/ *adj* неразбо́рчивый. **indiscriminately** /-lɪ/ *adv* без разбо́ра.

indispensable /ˌɪndɪ'spensəb(ə)l/ *adj* необходи́мый.

indisposed /ˌɪndɪ'spəʊzd/ *predic* (*unwell*) нездоро́в.

indisputable /ˌɪndɪ'spjuːtəb(ə)l/ *adj* бесспо́рный.

indistinct /ˌɪndɪ'stɪŋkt/ *adj* нея́сный.

indistinguishable /ˌɪndɪ'stɪŋgwɪʃəb(ə)l/ *adj* неразличи́мый.

individual /ˌɪndɪ'vɪdjʊəl/ *n* ли́чность; *adj* индивидуа́льный. **individualism** /-'vɪdjʊəˌlɪz(ə)m/ *n* индивидуали́зм. **individualist** /-'vɪdjʊəlɪst/ *n* индивидуали́ст. **individualistic** /ˌɪndɪˌvɪdjʊə'lɪstɪk/ *adj* индивидуалисти́ческий. **individuality** /ˌɪndɪˌvɪdjʊ'ælɪtɪ/ *n* индивидуа́льность.

indivisible /ˌɪndɪ'vɪzɪb(ə)l/ *adj* недели́мый.

indoctrinate /ɪn'dɒktrɪˌneɪt/ *vt* внуша́ть *impf*, внуши́ть *pf* +*dat* (**with** +*acc*).

indolence /'ɪndələns/ *n* ле́ность. **indolent** /-lənt/ *adj* лени́вый.

indomitable /ɪn'dɒmɪtəb(ə)l/ *adj* неукроти́мый.

Indonesia /ˌɪndəʊ'niːzɪə/ *n* Индоне́зия.

indoor /'ɪndɔː(r)/ *adj* ко́мнатный. **indoors** /ɪn'dɔːz/ *adv* (*position*) в до́ме; (*motion*) в дом.

induce /ɪn'djuːs/ *vt* (*prevail on*) убежда́ть *impf*, убеди́ть *pf*; (*bring about*) вызыва́ть *impf*, вы́звать *pf*. **inducement** /-mənt/ *n* побужде́ние.

induction /ɪn'dʌkʃ(ə)n/ *n* (*logic*, *electr*) инду́кция; (*in post*) введе́ние в до́лжность.

indulge /ɪn'dʌldʒ/ *vt* потво́рствовать *impf* +*dat*; *vi* предава́ться *impf*, преда́ться *pf* (**in** +*dat*). **indulgence** /-dʒ(ə)ns/ *n* потво́рство; (*tolerance*) снисходи́тельность. **indulgent** /-dʒ(ə)nt/ *adj* снисходи́тельный.

industrial /ɪn'dʌstrɪəl/ *adj* промы́шленный. **industrialist** /-'dʌstrɪəlɪst/ *n* промы́шленник. **industrious** /-'dʌstrɪəs/ *adj* трудолюби́вый. **industry** /'ɪndəstrɪ/ *n* промы́шленность; (*zeal*) трудолю́бие.

inebriated /ɪ'niːbrɪˌeɪtɪd/ *adj* пья́ный.

inedible /ɪn'edɪb(ə)l/ *adj* несъедо́бный.

ineffective, ineffectual /ˌɪnɪ'fektɪv, ˌɪnɪ'fektjʊəl/ *adj* безрезульта́тный; (*person*) неспосо́бный.

inefficiency /ˌɪnɪ'fɪʃ(ə)nsɪ/ *n* неэффекти́вность. **inefficient** /-'fɪʃ(ə)nt/ *adj* неэффекти́вный.

ineligible /ɪn'elɪdʒɪb(ə)l/ *adj* не

имéющий прáво (**for** на+*acc*).
inept /ɪ'nept/ *adj* неумéлый.
inequality /ˌɪnɪ'kwɒlɪtɪ/ *n* нерáвенство.
inert /ɪ'nɜːt/ *adj* инéртный. **inertia** /ɪ'nɜːʃə/ *n* (*phys*) инéрция; (*sluggishness*) инéртность.
inescapable /ˌɪnɪ'skeɪpəb(ə)l/ *adj* неизбéжный.
inevitability /ɪnˌevɪtə'bɪlɪtɪ/ *n* неизбéжность. **inevitable** /ɪn'evɪtəb(ə)l/ *adj* неизбéжный.
inexact /ˌɪnɪg'zækt/ *adj* нетóчный.
inexcusable /ˌɪnɪk'skjuːzəb(ə)l/ *adj* непростúтельный.
inexhaustible /ˌɪnɪg'zɔːstɪb(ə)l/ *adj* неистощúмый.
inexorable /ɪn'eksərəb(ə)l/ *adj* неумолúмый.
inexpensive /ˌɪnɪk'spensɪv/ *adj* недорогóй.
inexperience /ˌɪnɪk'spɪərɪəns/ *n* неóпытность. **inexperienced** /-ənst/ *adj* неóпытный.
inexplicable /ˌɪnɪk'splɪkəb(ə)l/ *adj* необъяснúмый.
infallible /ɪn'fælɪb(ə)l/ *adj* непогрешúмый.
infamous /'ɪnfəməs/ *adj* позóрный. **infamy** /-mɪ/ *n* позóр.
infancy /'ɪnfənsɪ/ *n* младéнчество. **infant** /'ɪnfənt/ *n* младéнец. **infantile** /'ɪnfənˌtaɪl/ *adj* дéтский.
infantry /'ɪnfəntrɪ/ *n* пехóта.
infatuate /ɪn'fætjʊˌeɪt/ *vt* вскружúть *pf* гóлову +*dat*. **infatuation** /-'eɪʃ(ə)n/ *n* увлечéние.
infect /ɪn'fekt/ *vt* заражáть *impf*, заразúть *pf* (**with** +*instr*). **infection** /-'fekʃ(ə)n/ *n* зарáза, инфéкция. **infectious** /-'fekʃəs/ *adj* зарáзный; (*fig*) заразúтельный.
infer /ɪn'fɜː(r)/ *vt* заключáть *impf*, заключúть *pf*. **inference** /'ɪnfərəns/ *n* заключéние.
inferior /ɪn'fɪərɪə(r)/ *adj* (*in rank*) нúзший; (*in quality*) хýдший, плохóй; *n* подчинённый *sb*. **inferiority** /ɪnˌfɪərɪ'ɒrɪtɪ/ *n* бóлее нúзкое кáчество; **~ complex** кóмплекс неполноцéнности.
infernal /ɪn'fɜːn(ə)l/ *adj* áдский.
inferno /-nəʊ/ *n* ад.
infertile /ɪn'fɜːtaɪl/ *adj* неплодорóдный.
infested /ɪn'festɪd/ *adj*: **be ~ with** кишéть *impf* +*instr*.
infidelity /ˌɪnfɪ'delɪtɪ/ *n* невéрность.
infiltrate /'ɪnfɪlˌtreɪt/ *vt* постепéнно проникáть *impf*, проникнуть *pf* в+*acc*.
infinite /'ɪnfɪnɪt/ *adj* бесконéчный. **infinitesimal** /ˌɪnfɪnɪ'tesɪməl/ *adj* бесконéчно мáлый. **infinitive** /ɪn'fɪnɪtɪv/ *n* инфинитúв. **infinity** /ɪn'fɪnɪtɪ/ *n* бесконéчность.
infirm /ɪn'fɜːm/ *adj* нéмощный. **infirmary** /-mərɪ/ *n* больнúца. **infirmity** /-mɪtɪ/ *n* нéмощь.
inflame /ɪn'fleɪm/ *vt* & *i* (*excite*) возбуждáть(ся) *impf*, возбудúть(ся) *pf*; (*med*) воспалять(ся) *impf*, воспалúть(ся) *pf*. **inflammable** /-'flæməb(ə)l/ *adj* огнеопáсный. **inflammation** /ˌɪnflə'meɪʃ(ə)n/ *n* воспалéние. **inflammatory** /ɪn'flæmətərɪ/ *adj* подстрекáтельский.
inflate /ɪn'fleɪt/ *vt* надувáть *impf*, надýть *pf*. **inflation** /-'fleɪʃ(ə)n/ *n* (*econ*) инфляция.
inflection /ɪn'flekʃ(ə)n/ *n* (*gram*) флéксия.
inflexible /ɪn'fleksɪb(ə)l/ *adj* негúбкий; (*fig*) непреклóнный.
inflict /ɪn'flɪkt/ *vt* (*blow*) наносúть *impf*, нанестú *pf* (**(up)on** +*dat*); (*suffering*) причинять *impf*, причинúть *pf* (**(up)on**

+*dat*); (*penalty*) налага́ть *impf*, наложи́ть *pf* (**(up)on** на+*acc*); ~ **o.s. (up)on** навя́зываться *impf*, навяза́ться *pf* +*dat*.

inflow /'ɪnfləʊ/ *n* втека́ние, прито́к.

influence /'ɪnflʊəns/ *n* влия́ние; *vt* влия́ть *impf*, по~ *pf* на+*acc*. **influential** /ˌɪnflʊ'enʃ(ə)l/ *adj* влия́тельный.

influenza /ˌɪnflʊ'enzə/ *n* грипп.

influx /'ɪnflʌks/ *n* (*fig*) наплы́в.

inform /ɪn'fɔːm/ *vt* сообща́ть *impf*, сообщи́ть *pf* +*dat* (**of, about** +*acc*, о+*prep*); *vi* доноси́ть *impf*, донести́ *pf* (**against** на+*acc*).

informal /ɪn'fɔːm(ə)l/ *adj* (*unofficial*) неофициа́льный; (*casual*) обы́денный.

informant /ɪn'fɔːmənt/ *n* осведоми́тель *m*. **information** /ˌɪnfə'meɪʃ(ə)n/ *n* информа́ция. **informative** /ɪn'fɔːmətɪv/ *adj* поучи́тельный. **informer** /ɪn'fɔːmə(r)/ *n* доно́счик.

infra-red /ˌɪnfrə'red/ *adj* инфракра́сный.

infrequent /ɪn'friːkwənt/ *adj* ре́дкий.

infringe /ɪn'frɪndʒ/ *vt* (*violate*) наруша́ть *impf*, нару́шить *pf*; *vi*: ~ **(up)on** посяга́ть *impf*, посягну́ть *pf* на+*acc*. **infringement** /-mənt/ *n* наруше́ние; посяга́тельство.

infuriate /ɪn'fjʊərɪˌeɪt/ *vt* разъяря́ть *impf*, разъяри́ть *pf*.

infuse /ɪn'fjuːz/ *vt* (*fig*) внуша́ть *impf*, внуши́ть *pf* (**into** +*dat*). **infusion** /-'fjuːʒ(ə)n/ *n* (*fig*) внуше́ние; (*herbs etc*) насто́й.

ingenious /ɪn'dʒiːnɪəs/ *adj* изобрета́тельный. **ingenuity** /ˌɪndʒɪ'njuːɪtɪ/ *n* изобрета́тельность.

ingenuous /ɪn'dʒenjʊəs/ *adj* бесхи́тростный.

ingot /'ɪŋgɒt/ *n* сли́ток.

ingrained /ɪn'greɪnd/ *adj* закорене́лый.

ingratiate /ɪn'greɪʃɪˌeɪt/ *vt* ~ **o.s.** вкра́дываться *impf*, вкра́сться *pf* в ми́лость (**with** +*dat*).

ingratitude /ɪn'grætɪˌtjuːd/ *n* неблагода́рность.

ingredient /ɪn'griːdɪənt/ *n* ингредие́нт, составля́ющее *sb*.

inhabit /ɪn'hæbɪt/ *vt* жить *impf* в, на, +*prep*; обита́ть *impf* в, на, +*prep*. **inhabitant** /-t(ə)nt/ *n* жи́тель *m*, ~ница.

inhalation /ˌɪnhə'leɪʃ(ə)n/ *n* вдыха́ние. **inhale** /ɪn'heɪl/ *vt* вдыха́ть *impf*, вдохну́ть *pf*.

inherent /ɪn'hɪərənt/ *adj* прису́щий (**in** +*dat*).

inherit /ɪn'herɪt/ *vt* насле́довать *impf* & *pf*, у~ *pf*. **inheritance** /-təns/ *n* насле́дство.

inhibit /ɪn'hɪbɪt/ *vt* стесня́ть *impf*, стесни́ть *pf*. **inhibited** /-tɪd/ *adj* стесни́тельный. **inhibition** /ˌɪnhɪ'bɪʃ(ə)n/ *n* стесне́ние.

inhospitable /ˌɪnhɒ'spɪtəb(ə)l/ *adj* негостеприи́мный; (*fig*) недружелю́бный.

inhuman(e) /ɪn'hjuːmən, ˌɪnhjuː'meɪn/ *adj* бесчелове́чный.

inimical /ɪ'nɪmɪk(ə)l/ *adj* вражде́бный; (*harmful*) вре́дный.

inimitable /ɪ'nɪmɪtəb(ə)l/ *adj* неподража́емый.

iniquity /ɪ'nɪkwɪtɪ/ *n* несправедли́вость.

initial /ɪ'nɪʃ(ə)l/ *adj* (перво)нача́льный; *n* нача́льная бу́ква; *pl* инициа́лы *m pl*; *vt* ста́вить *impf*, по~ *pf* инициа́лы на+*acc*. **initially** /-ʃəlɪ/ *adv* в нача́ле.

initiate /ɪ'nɪʃɪˌeɪt/ *vt* вводи́ть *impf*, ввести́ *pf* (**into** в+*acc*). **initiation** /-'eɪʃ(ə)n/ *n* введе́ние.

initiative /ɪ'nɪʃətɪv/ *n* инициатива.
inject /ɪn'dʒekt/ *vt* вводить *impf*, ввести *pf* (*person* +*dat*, *substance* +*acc*). **injection** /-'dʒekʃ(ə)n/ *n* укол; (*fig*) инъекция.
injunction /ɪn'dʒʌŋkʃ(ə)n/ *n* (*law*) судебный запрет.
injure /'ɪndʒə(r)/ *vt* повреждать *impf*, повредить *pf*. **injury** /'ɪndʒərɪ/ *n* рана.
injustice /ɪn'dʒʌstɪs/ *n* несправедливость.
ink /ɪŋk/ *n* чернила (-л).
inkling /'ɪŋklɪŋ/ *n* представление.
inland /'ɪnlənd/ *adj* внутренний; *adv* (*motion*) внутрь страны; (*place*) внутри страны; **I~ Revenue** управление налоговых сборов.
in-laws /'ɪnlɔːz/ *n pl* родственники *m pl* супруга, -ги.
inlay /'ɪnleɪ/ *n* инкрустация; /-'leɪ/ *vt* инкрустировать *impf* & *pf*.
inlet /'ɪnlet/ *n* (*of sea*) узкий залив.
inmate /'ɪnmeɪt/ *n* (*prison*) заключённый *sb*; (*hospital*) больной *sb*.
inn /ɪn/ *n* гостиница.
innate /ɪ'neɪt/ *adj* врождённый.
inner /'ɪnə(r)/ *adj* внутренний. **innermost** *adj* глубочайший; (*fig*) сокровеннейший.
innocence /'ɪnəs(ə)ns/ *n* невинность; (*guiltlessness*) невиновность. **innocent** /-s(ə)nt/ *adj* невинный; (*not guilty*) невиновный (**of** в+*prep*).
innocuous /ɪ'nɒkjʊəs/ *adj* безвредный.
innovate /'ɪnə,veɪt/ *vi* вводить *impf*, ввести *pf* новшества. **innovation** /-'veɪʃ(ə)n/ *n* нововведение. **innovative** /'ɪnəvətɪv/ *adj* новаторский. **innovator** /'ɪnə,veɪtə(r)/ *n* новатор.
innuendo /,ɪnjʊ'endəʊ/ *n* намёк, инсинуация.
innumerable /ɪ'njuːmərəb(ə)l/ *adj* бесчисленный.
inoculate /ɪ'nɒkjʊ,leɪt/ *vt* прививать *impf*, привить *pf* +*dat* (**against** +*acc*). **inoculation** /-'leɪʃ(ə)n/ *n* прививка.
inoffensive /,ɪnə'fensɪv/ *adj* безобидный.
inopportune /ɪn'ɒpə,tjuːn/ *adj* несвоевременный.
inordinate /ɪn'ɔːdɪnət/ *adj* чрезмерный.
inorganic /,ɪnɔː'gænɪk/ *adj* неорганический.
in-patient /'ɪn,peɪʃ(ə)nt/ *n* стационарный больной *sb*.
input /'ɪnpʊt/ *n* ввод.
inquest /'ɪnkwest/ *n* судебное следствие, дознание.
inquire /ɪn'kwaɪə(r)/ *vt* спрашивать *impf*, спросить *pf*; *vi* справляться *impf*, справиться *pf* (**about** о+*prep*); расследовать *impf* & *pf* (**into** +*acc*). **inquiry** /-'kwaɪərɪ/ *n* вопрос, справка; (*investigation*) расследование.
inquisition /,ɪnkwɪ'zɪʃ(ə)n/ *n* инквизиция. **inquisitive** /ɪn'kwɪzɪtɪv/ *adj* пытливый, любознательный.
inroad /'ɪnrəʊd/ *n* (*attack*) набег; (*fig*) посягательство (**on, into** на+*acc*).
insane /ɪn'seɪn/ *adj* безумный. **insanity** /-'sænɪtɪ/ *n* безумие.
insatiable /ɪn'seɪʃəb(ə)l/ *adj* ненасытный.
inscribe /ɪn'skraɪb/ *vt* надписывать *impf*, надписать *pf*; (*engrave*) вырезать *impf*, вырезать *pf*. **inscription** /-'skrɪpʃ(ə)n/ *n* надпись.
inscrutable /ɪn'skruːtəb(ə)l/ *adj*

непостижи́мый, непроница́емый.

insect /'ɪnsekt/ *n* насеко́мое *sb.* **insecticide** /ɪn'sektɪˌsaɪd/ *n* инсектици́д.

insecure /ˌɪnsɪ'kjʊə(r)/ *adj* (*unsafe*) небезопа́сный; (*not confident*) неуве́ренный (в себе́).

insemination /ɪnˌsemɪ'neɪʃ(ə)n/ *n* оплодотворе́ние.

insensible /ɪn'sensɪb(ə)l/ *adj* (*unconscious*) потеря́вший созна́ние.

insensitive /ɪn'sensɪtɪv/ *adj* нечувстви́тельный.

inseparable /ɪn'sepərəb(ə)l/ *adj* неотдели́мый; (*people*) неразлу́чный.

insert /ɪn'sɜ:t/ *vt* вставля́ть *impf*, вста́вить *pf*; вкла́дывать *impf*, вложи́ть *pf*; (*coin*) опуска́ть *impf*, опусти́ть *pf*. **insertion** /-'sɜ:ʃ(ə)n/ *n* (*inserting*) вставле́ние, вкла́дывание; (*thing inserted*) вста́вка.

inshore /ɪn'ʃɔ:(r)/ *adj* прибре́жный; *adv* бли́зко к бе́регу.

inside /ɪn'saɪd/ *n* вну́тренняя часть; *pl* (*anat*) вну́тренности *f pl*; **turn ~ out** вывёртывать *impf*, вы́вернуть *pf* наизна́нку; *adj* вну́тренний; *adv* (*place*) внутри́; (*motion*) внутрь; *prep* (*place*) внутри́+*gen*, в+*prep*; (*motion*) внутрь+*gen*, в+*acc*.

insidious /ɪn'sɪdɪəs/ *adj* кова́рный.

insight /'ɪnsaɪt/ *n* проница́тельность.

insignia /ɪn'sɪgnɪə/ *n* зна́ки *m pl* разли́чия.

insignificant /ˌɪnsɪg'nɪfɪkənt/ *adj* незначи́тельный.

insincere /ˌɪnsɪn'sɪə(r)/ *adj* нейскренний.

insinuate /ɪn'sɪnjʊˌeɪt/ *vt* (*hint*) намека́ть *impf*, намекну́ть *pf* на+*acc*. **insinuation** /-'eɪʃ(ə)n/ *n* инсинуа́ция.

insipid /ɪn'sɪpɪd/ *adj* пре́сный.

insist /ɪn'sɪst/ *vt* & *i* наста́ивать *impf*, настоя́ть *pf* (**on** на+*prep*). **insistence** /-t(ə)ns/ *n* насто́йчивость. **insistent** /-t(ə)nt/ *adj* насто́йчивый.

insolence /'ɪnsələns/ *n* на́глость. **insolent** /-lənt/ *adj* на́глый.

insoluble /ɪn'sɒljʊb(ə)l/ *adj* (*problem*) неразреши́мый; (*in liquid*) нераствори́мый.

insolvent /ɪn'sɒlv(ə)nt/ *adj* несостоя́тельный.

insomnia /ɪn'sɒmnɪə/ *n* бессо́нница.

inspect /ɪn'spekt/ *vt* инспекти́ровать *impf*, про~ *pf*. **inspection** /-'spekʃ(ə)n/ *n* инспе́кция. **inspector** /-'spektə(r)/ *n* инспе́ктор; (*ticket ~*) контролёр.

inspiration /ˌɪnspɪ'reɪʃ(ə)n/ *n* вдохнове́ние. **inspire** /ɪn'spaɪə(r)/ *vt* вдохновля́ть *impf*, вдохнови́ть *pf*; внуша́ть *impf*, внуши́ть *pf* +*dat* (**with** +*acc*).

instability /ˌɪnstə'bɪlɪtɪ/ *n* неусто́йчивость; (*of character*) неуравнове́шенность.

install /ɪn'stɔ:l/ *vt* (*person in office*) вводи́ть *impf*, ввести́ *pf* в до́лжность; (*apparatus*) устана́вливать *impf*, установи́ть *pf*. **installation** /ˌɪnstə'leɪʃ(ə)n/ *n* введе́ние в до́лжность; устано́вка; *pl* сооруже́ния *neut pl*.

instalment /ɪn'stɔ:lmənt/ *n* (*comm*) взнос; (*publication*) вы́пуск; часть; **by ~s** в расср́очку.

instance /'ɪnst(ə)ns/ *n* (*example*) приме́р; (*case*) слу́чай; **for ~** наприме́р.

instant /'ɪnst(ə)nt/ *n* мгнове́ние, моме́нт; *adj* неме́дленный;

(*coffee etc.*) растворимый. **instantaneous** /ˌɪnstən'teɪnɪəs/ *adj* мгновенный. **instantly** /'ɪnstəntlɪ/ *adv* немедленно, тотчас.

instead /ɪn'sted/ *adv* вместо (**of** +*gen*); ~ **of going** вместо того, чтобы пойти.

instep /'ɪnstep/ *n* подъём.

instigate /'ɪnstɪˌgeɪt/ *vt* подстрекать *impf*, подстрекнуть *pf* (**to** к+*dat*). **instigation** /-'geɪʃ(ə)n/ *n* подстрекательство. **instigator** /'ɪnstɪˌgeɪtə(r)/ *n* подстрекатель *m*, ~ница.

instil /ɪn'stɪl/ *vt* (*ideas etc.*) внушать *impf*, внушить *pf* (**into** +*dat*).

instinct /'ɪnstɪŋkt/ *n* инстинкт. **instinctive** /ɪn'stɪŋktɪv/ *adj* инстинктивный.

institute /'ɪnstɪˌtju:t/ *n* институт; *vt* (*establish*) устанавливать *impf*, установить *pf*; (*introduce*) вводить *impf*, ввести *pf*; (*reforms*) проводить *impf*, провести *pf*. **institution** /-'tju:ʃ(ə)n/ *n* учреждение.

instruct /ɪn'strʌkt/ *vt* (*teach*) обучать *impf*, обучить *pf* (**in** +*dat*); (*inform*) сообщать *impf*, сообщить *pf* +*dat*; (*command*) приказывать *impf*, приказать *pf* +*dat*. **instruction** /-'strʌkʃ(ə)n/ *n* (*in pl*) инструкция; (*teaching*) обучение. **instructive** /-'strʌktɪv/ *adj* поучительный. **instructor** /-'strʌktə(r)/ *n* инструктор.

instrument /'ɪnstrəmənt/ *n* орудие, инструмент. **instrumental** /-'ment(ə)l/ *adj* (*mus*) инструментальный; (*gram*) творительный; **be** ~ **in** способствовать *impf*, по~ *pf* +*dat*; *n* (*gram*) творительный падеж. **instrumentation** /ˌɪnstrəmen'teɪʃ(ə)n/ *n* (*mus*) инструментовка.

insubordinate /ˌɪnsə'bɔ:dɪnət/ *adj* неподчиняющийся.

insufferable /ɪn'sʌfərəb(ə)l/ *adj* невыносимый.

insular /'ɪnsjʊlə(r)/ *adj* (*fig*) ограниченный.

insulate /'ɪnsjʊˌleɪt/ *vt* изолировать *impf* & *pf*. **insulation** /-'leɪʃ(ə)n/ *n* изоляция. **insulator** /'ɪnsjʊˌleɪtə(r)/ *n* изолятор.

insulin /'ɪnsjʊlɪn/ *n* инсулин.

insult *n* /'ɪnsʌlt/ оскорбление; *vt* /ɪn'sʌlt/ оскорблять *impf*, оскорбить *pf*. **insulting** /ɪn'sʌltɪŋ/ *adj* оскорбительный.

insuperable /ɪn'su:pərəb(ə)l/ *adj* непреодолимый.

insurance /ɪn'ʃʊərəns/ *n* страхование; *attrib* страховой. **insure** /-'ʃʊə(r)/ *vt* страховать *impf*, за~ *pf* (**against** от+*gen*).

insurgent /ɪn'sɜ:dʒ(ə)nt/ *n* повстанец.

insurmountable /ˌɪnsə'maʊntəb(ə)l/ *adj* непреодолимый.

insurrection /ˌɪnsə'rekʃ(ə)n/ *n* восстание.

intact /ɪn'tækt/ *adj* целый.

intake /'ɪnteɪk/ *n* (*of persons*) набор; (*consumption*) потребление.

intangible /ɪn'tændʒɪb(ə)l/ *adj* неосязаемый.

integral /'ɪntɪgr(ə)l/ *adj* неотъемлемый. **integrate** /-ˌgreɪt/ *vt* & *i* интегрироваться *impf* & *pf*. **integration** /-'greɪʃ(ə)n/ *n* интеграция.

integrity /ɪn'tegrɪtɪ/ *n* (*honesty*) честность.

intellect /'ɪntɪˌlekt/ *n* интеллект. **intellectual** /-'lektjʊəl/ *n* интеллигент; *adj* интеллектуальный.

intelligence /ɪn'telɪdʒ(ə)ns/ *n* (*intellect*) ум; (*information*) свéдения *neut pl*; (~ *service*) развéдка. **intelligent** /-dʒ(ə)nt/ *adj* ýмный.

intelligentsia /ɪn,telɪ'dʒentsɪə/ *n* интеллигéнция.

intelligible /ɪn'telɪdʒɪb(ə)l/ *adj* понятный.

intemperate /ɪn'tempərət/ *adj* невоздéржанный.

intend /ɪn'tend/ *vt* собирáться *impf*, собрáться *pf*; (*design*) предназначáть *impf*, предназнáчить *pf* (**for** для+*gen*, на+*acc*).

intense /ɪn'tens/ *adj* сильный. **intensify** /-'tensɪ,faɪ/ *vt* & *i* усиливать(ся) *impf*, усилить(ся) *pf*. **intensity** /-'tensɪtɪ/ *n* интенсивность, сила. **intensive** /-'tensɪv/ *adj* интенсивный.

intent /ɪn'tent/ *n* намéрение; *adj* (*resolved*) стремящийся (**on** к+*dat*); (*occupied*) погружённый (**on** в+*acc*); (*earnest*) внимáтельный. **intention** /-'tenʃ(ə)n/ *n* намéрение. **intentional** /-'tenʃən(ə)l/ *adj* намéренный.

inter /ɪn'tɜ:(r)/ *vt* хоронить *impf*, по~ *pf*.

interact /,ɪntər'ækt/ *vi* взаимодéйствовать *impf*. **interaction** /-'ækʃ(ə)n/ *n* взаимодéйствие. **interactive** /-tɪv/ *adj* (*comput*) интерактивный.

intercede /,ɪntə'si:d/ *vi* ходáтайствовать *impf*, по~ *pf* (**for** за+*acc*; **with** пéред+*instr*).

intercept /,ɪntə'sept/ *vt* перехвáтывать *impf*, перехватить *pf*. **interception** /-'sepʃ(ə)n/ *n* перехвáт.

interchange /'ɪntə,tʃeɪndʒ/ *n* обмéн (**of** +*instr*); (*junction*) трáнспортная развязка; *vt* обмéниваться *impf*, обменяться *pf* +*instr*. **interchangeable** /-'tʃeɪndʒəb(ə)l/ *adj* взаимозаменяемый.

inter-city /,ɪntə'sɪtɪ/ *adj* междугорóдный.

intercom /'ɪntə,kɒm/ *n* селéктор; (*to get into house*) домофóн.

interconnected /,ɪntəkə'nektɪd/ *adj* взаимосвязанный.

intercourse /'ɪntə,kɔ:s/ *n* (*social*) общéние; (*trade*; *sexual*) сношéния *neut pl*.

interdisciplinary /,ɪntədɪsɪ'plɪnərɪ/ *adj* межотраслевóй.

interest /'ɪntrəst/ *n* интерéс (**in** к+*dat*); (*econ*) процéнты *m pl*; *vt* интересовáть *impf*; (~ *person in*) заинтересóвывать *impf*, заинтересовáть *pf* (**in** +*instr*); **be ~ed in** интересовáться *impf* +*instr*. **interesting** /-stɪŋ/ *adj* интерéсный.

interfere /,ɪntə'fɪə(r)/ *vi* вмéшиваться *impf*, вмешáться *pf* (**in** в+*acc*). **interference** /-'fɪərəns/ *n* вмешáтельство; (*radio*) помéхи *f pl*.

interim /'ɪntərɪm/ *n*: **in the ~** тем врéменем; *adj* промежýточный; (*temporary*) врéменный.

interior /ɪn'tɪərɪə(r)/ *n* (*of building*) интерьéр; (*of object*) внýтренность; *adj* внýтренний.

interjection /,ɪntə'dʒekʃ(ə)n/ *n* восклицáние; (*gram*) междомéтие.

interlock /,ɪntə'lɒk/ *vt* & *i* сцеплять(ся) *impf*, сцепить(ся) *pf*.

interloper /'ɪntə,ləʊpə(r)/ *n* незвáный гость *m*.

interlude /'ɪntə,lu:d/ *n* (*theat*) антрáкт; (*mus*, *fig*) интерлюдия.

intermediary /,ɪntə'mi:dɪərɪ/ *n* посрéдник.

intermediate /,ɪntə'mi:dɪət/ *adj* промежýточный.

interminable /ɪn'tɜ:mɪnəb(ə)l/ *adj* бесконе́чный.
intermission /ˌɪntə'mɪʃ(ə)n/ *n* (*theat*) антра́кт.
intermittent /ˌɪntə'mɪt(ə)nt/ *adj* преры́вистый.
intern /ɪn'tɜ:n/ *vt* интерни́ровать *impf* & *pf*.
internal /ɪn'tɜ:n(ə)l/ *adj* вну́тренний; ~ **combustion engine** дви́гатель *m* вну́треннего сгора́ния.
international /ˌɪntə'næʃən(ə)l/ *adj* междунаро́дный; *n* (*contest*) междунаро́дные состяза́ния *neut pl*.
Internet /'ɪntəˌnet/ *n* Интерне́т; **on the** ~ в Интерне́те.
internment /ɪn'tɜ:nmənt/ *n* интерни́рование.
interplay /'ɪntəˌpleɪ/ *n* взаимоде́йствие.
interpret /ɪn'tɜ:prɪt/ *vt* (*explain*) толкова́ть *impf*; (*understand*) истолко́вывать *impf*, истолкова́ть *pf*; *vi* переводи́ть *impf*, перевести́ *pf*. **interpretation** /-'teɪʃ(ə)n/ *n* толкова́ние. **interpreter** /ɪn'tɜ:prɪtə(r)/ *n* перево́дчик, -ица.
interrelated /ˌɪntərɪ'leɪtɪd/ *adj* взаимосвя́занный.
interrogate /ɪn'terəˌgeɪt/ *vt* допра́шивать *impf*, допроси́ть *pf*. **interrogation** /-'geɪʃ(ə)n/ *n* допро́с. **interrogative** /ˌɪntə'rɒgətɪv/ *adj* вопроси́тельный.
interrupt /ˌɪntə'rʌpt/ *vt* прерыва́ть *impf*, прерва́ть *pf*. **interruption** /-'rʌpʃ(ə)n/ *n* переры́в.
intersect /ˌɪntə'sekt/ *vt* & *i* пересека́ть(ся) *impf*, пересе́чь(ся) *pf*. **intersection** /-'sekʃ(ə)n/ *n* пересече́ние.
intersperse /ˌɪntə'spɜ:s/ *vt* (*scatter*) рассыпа́ть *impf*, рассы́пать *pf* (**between, among** ме́жду+*instr*, среди́+*gen*).
intertwine /ˌɪntə'twaɪn/ *vt* & *i* переплета́ть(ся) *impf*, переплести́(сь) *pf*.
interval /'ɪntəv(ə)l/ *n* интерва́л; (*theat*) антра́кт.
intervene /ˌɪntə'vi:n/ *vi* (*occur*) происходи́ть *impf*, произойти́ *pf*; ~ **in** вме́шиваться *impf*, вмеша́ться *pf* в+*acc*. **intervention** /-'venʃ(ə)n/ *n* вмеша́тельство; (*polit*) интерве́нция.
interview /'ɪntəˌvju:/ *n* интервью́ *neut indecl*; *vt* интервьюи́ровать *impf* & *pf*, про~ *pf*. **interviewer** /-ˌvju:ə(r)/ *n* интервьюе́р.
interweave /ˌɪntə'wi:v/ *vt* вотка́ть *pf*.
intestate /ɪn'testeɪt/ *adj* без завеща́ния.
intestine /ɪn'testɪn/ *n* кишка́; *pl* кише́чник.
intimacy /'ɪntɪməsɪ/ *n* инти́мность. **intimate**[1] /'ɪntɪmət/ *adj* инти́мный.
intimate[2] /'ɪntɪˌmeɪt/ *vt* (*hint*) намека́ть *impf*, намекну́ть *pf* на+*acc*. **intimation** /-'meɪʃ(ə)n/ *n* намёк.
intimidate /ɪn'tɪmɪˌdeɪt/ *vt* запу́гивать *impf*, запуга́ть *pf*.
into /'ɪntʊ/ *prep* в, во+*acc*, на+*acc*.
intolerable /ɪn'tɒlərəb(ə)l/ *adj* невыноси́мый. **intolerance** /-rəns/ *n* нетерпи́мость. **intolerant** /-rənt/ *adj* нетерпи́мый.
intonation /ˌɪntə'neɪʃ(ə)n/ *n* интона́ция.
intoxicated /ɪn'tɒksɪˌkeɪtɪd/ *adj* пья́ный. **intoxication** /-'keɪʃ(ə)n/ *n* опьяне́ние.
intractable /ɪn'træktəb(ə)l/ *adj* неподатливый.
intransigent /ɪn'trænsɪdʒ(ə)nt/

adj непримири́мый.
intransitive /ɪn'trænsɪtɪv/ *adj* непереходный.
intrepid /ɪn'trepɪd/ *adj* неустраши́мый.
intricacy /'ɪntrɪkəsɪ/ *n* запу́танность. **intricate** /'ɪntrɪkət/ *adj* запу́танный.
intrigue /'ɪntriːg/ *n* интри́га; *vi* интригова́ть *impf*; *vt* интригова́ть *impf*, за~ *pf*.
intrinsic /ɪn'trɪnzɪk/ *adj* прису́щий; (*value*) вну́тренний.
introduce /,ɪntrə'djuːs/ *vt* вводи́ть *impf*, ввести́ *pf*; (*person*) представля́ть *impf*, предста́вить *pf*. **introduction** /-'dʌkʃ(ə)n/ *n* введе́ние; представле́ние; (*to book*) предисло́вие. **introductory** /-'dʌktərɪ/ *adj* вступи́тельный.
introspection /,ɪntrə'spekʃ(ə)n/ *n* интроспе́кция.
intrude /ɪn'truːd/ *vi* вторга́ться *impf*, вто́ргнуться *pf* (**into** в+*acc*); (*disturb*) меша́ть *impf*, по~ *pf*. **intruder** /-'truːdə(r)/ *n* (*burglar*) граби́тель *m*. **intrusion** /-'truːʒ(ə)n/ *n* вторже́ние.
intuition /,ɪntjuː'ɪʃ(ə)n/ *n* интуи́ция. **intuitive** /ɪn'tjuːɪtɪv/ *adj* интуити́вный.
inundate /'ɪnən,deɪt/ *vt* наводня́ть *impf*, наводни́ть *pf*. **inundation** /-'deɪʃ(ə)n/ *n* наводне́ние.
invade /ɪn'veɪd/ *vt* вторга́ться *impf*, вто́ргнуться *pf* в+*acc*. **invader** /-də(r)/ *n* захва́тчик.
invalid[1] /'ɪnvəlɪd/ *n* (*person*) инвали́д.
invalid[2] /ɪn'vælɪd/ *adj* недействи́тельный. **invalidate** /-'vælɪ,deɪt/ *vt* де́лать *impf*, с~ *pf* недействи́тельным.
invaluable /ɪn'væljʊəb(ə)l/ *adj* неоцени́мый.
invariable /ɪn'veərɪəb(ə)l/ *adj* неизме́нный.
invasion /ɪn'veɪʒ(ə)n/ *n* вторже́ние.
invective /ɪn'vektɪv/ *n* брань.
invent /ɪn'vent/ *vt* изобрета́ть *impf*, изобрести́ *pf*; (*think up*) выду́мывать *impf*, вы́думать *pf*. **invention** /-'venʃ(ə)n/ *n* изобрете́ние; вы́думка. **inventive** /-'ventɪv/ *adj* изобрета́тельный. **inventor** /-'ventə(r)/ *n* изобрета́тель *m*.
inventory /'ɪnvəntərɪ/ *n* инвента́рь *m*.
inverse /'ɪnvɜːs/ *adj* обра́тный; *n* противополо́жность. **invert** /ɪn'vɜːt/ *vt* перевора́чивать *impf*, переверну́ть *pf*. **inverted commas** *n pl* кавы́чки *f pl*.
invest /ɪn'vest/ *vt* & *i* (*econ*) вкла́дывать *impf*, вложи́ть *pf* (де́ньги) (**in** в+*acc*).
investigate /ɪn'vestɪ,geɪt/ *vt* иссле́довать *impf* & *pf*; (*law*) рассле́довать *impf* & *pf*. **investigation** /-'geɪʃ(ə)n/ *n* иссле́дование; рассле́дование.
investment /ɪn'vestmənt/ *n* инвести́ция, вклад. **investor** /-'vestə(r)/ *n* вкла́дчик.
inveterate /ɪn'vetərət/ *adj* закорене́лый.
invidious /ɪn'vɪdɪəs/ *adj* оскорби́тельный.
invigorate /ɪn'vɪgə,reɪt/ *vt* оживля́ть *impf*, оживи́ть *pf*.
invincible /ɪn'vɪnsɪb(ə)l/ *adj* непобеди́мый.
inviolable /ɪn'vaɪələb(ə)l/ *adj* неруши́мый.
invisible /ɪn'vɪzɪb(ə)l/ *adj* неви́димый.
invitation /,ɪnvɪ'teɪʃ(ə)n/ *n* приглаше́ние. **invite** /ɪn'vaɪt/ *vt* приглаша́ть *impf*, пригласи́ть *pf*. **inviting** /ɪn'vaɪtɪŋ/ *adj* при-

влека́тельный.
invoice /'ɪnvɔɪs/ *n* факту́ра.
invoke /ɪn'vəʊk/ *vt* обраща́ться *impf*, обрати́ться *pf* к+*dat*.
involuntary /ɪn'vɒləntərɪ/ *adj* нево́льный.
involve /ɪn'vɒlv/ *vt* (*entangle*) вовлека́ть *impf*, вовле́чь *pf*; (*entail*) влечь *impf* за собо́й. **involved** /-'vɒlvd/ *adj* сло́жный.
invulnerable /ɪn'vʌlnərəb(ə)l/ *adj* неуязви́мый.
inward /'ɪnwəd/ *adj* вну́тренний. **inwardly** /-lɪ/ *adv* внутри́. **inwards** /'ɪnwədz/ *adv* внутрь.
iodine /'aɪə,di:n/ *n* йод.
iota /aɪ'əʊtə/ *n*: **not an ~** ни на йо́ту.
IOU /,aɪəʊ'ju:/ *n* долгова́я распи́ска.
Iran /ɪ'rɑ:n/ *n* Ира́н. **Iranian** /-'reɪnɪən/ *n* ира́нец, -нка; *adj* ира́нский.
Iraq /ɪ'rɑ:k/ *n* Ира́к. **Iraqi** /-kɪ/ *n* ира́кец; жи́тель *m*, **~** ница Ира́ка; *adj* ира́кский.
irascible /ɪ'ræsɪb(ə)l/ *adj* раздражи́тельный.
irate /aɪ'reɪt/ *adj* гне́вный.
Ireland /'aɪələnd/ *n* Ирла́ндия.
iris /'aɪərɪs/ *n* (*anat*) ра́дужная оболо́чка; (*bot*) каса́тик.
Irish /'aɪərɪʃ/ *adj* ирла́ндский. **Irishman** *n* ирла́ндец. **Irishwoman** *n* ирла́ндка.
irk /з:k/ *vt* раздража́ть *impf*, раздражи́ть *pf* +*dat*. **irksome** /-səm/ *adj* раздражи́тельный.
iron /'aɪən/ *n* желе́зо; (*for clothes*) утю́г; *adj* желе́зный; *vt* гла́дить *impf*, вы**~** *pf*.
ironic(al) /aɪ'rɒnɪkəl/ *adj* ирони́ческий. **irony** /'aɪrənɪ/ *n* иро́ния.
irradiate /ɪ'reɪdɪ,eɪt/ *vt* (*subject to radiation*) облуча́ть *impf*, облучи́ть *pf*. **irradiation** /-'eɪʃ(ə)n/ *n* облуче́ние.
irrational /ɪ'ræʃən(ə)l/ *adj* неразу́мный.
irreconcilable /ɪ'rekən,saɪləb(ə)l/ *adj* непримири́мый.
irrefutable /,ɪrɪ'fju:təb(ə)l/ *adj* неопровержи́мый.
irregular /ɪ'regjʊlə(r)/ *adj* нерегуля́рный; (*gram*) непра́вильный; (*not even*) неро́вный.
irrelevant /ɪ'relɪv(ə)nt/ *adj* неуме́стный.
irreparable /ɪ'repərəb(ə)l/ *adj* непоправи́мый.
irreplaceable /,ɪrɪ'pleɪsəb(ə)l/ *adj* незамени́мый.
irrepressible /,ɪrɪ'presɪb(ə)l/ *adj* неудержи́мый.
irreproachable /,ɪrɪ'prəʊtʃəb(ə)l/ *adj* безупре́чный.
irresistible /,ɪrɪ'zɪstɪb(ə)l/ *adj* неотрази́мый.
irresolute /ɪ'rezə,lu:t/ *adj* нереши́тельный.
irrespective /,ɪrɪ'spektɪv/ *adj*: **~ of** несмотря́ на+*acc*.
irresponsible /,ɪrɪ'spɒnsɪb(ə)l/ *adj* безотве́тственный.
irretrievable /,ɪrɪ'tri:vəb(ə)l/ *adj* непоправи́мый.
irreverent /ɪ'revərənt/ *adj* непочти́тельный.
irreversible /,ɪrɪ'vз:sɪb(ə)l/ *adj* необрати́мый.
irrevocable /ɪ'revəkəb(ə)l/ *adj* неотменя́емый.
irrigate /'ɪrɪ,geɪt/ *vt* ороша́ть *impf*, ороси́ть *pf*. **irrigation** /-'geɪʃ(ə)n/ *n* ороше́ние.
irritable /'ɪrɪtəb(ə)l/ *adj* раздражи́тельный. **irritate** /'ɪrɪ,teɪt/ *vt* раздража́ть *impf*, раздражи́ть *pf*. **irritation** /-'teɪʃ(ə)n/ *n* раздраже́ние.
Islam /'ɪzlɑ:m/ *n* исла́м. **Islamic** /-'læmɪk/ *adj* мусульма́нский.

island, isle /'aɪlənd, aɪl/ *n* óстров. **islander** /'aɪləndə(r)/ *n* островитя́нин, -я́нка.

isolate /'aɪsə,leɪt/ *vt* изоли́ровать *impf* & *pf.* **isolation** /-'leɪʃ(ə)n/ *n* изоля́ция.

Israel /'ɪzreɪl/ *n* Изра́иль *m.* **Israeli** /-'reɪlɪ/ *n* израильтя́нин, -я́нка; *adj* изра́ильский.

issue /'ɪʃu:/ *n* (*question*) (спóрный) вопрóс; (*of bonds etc.*) вы́пуск; (*of magazine*) нóмер; *vt* выпуска́ть *impf*, вы́пустить *pf*; (*give out*) выдава́ть *impf*, вы́дать *pf.*

isthmus /'ɪsməs/ *n* перешéек.

IT *abbr* (*of* **information technology**) информа́тика.

it /ɪt/ *pron* он, она́, онó; *demonstrative* э́то.

Italian /ɪ'tæljən/ *n* италья́нец, -нка; *adj* италья́нский.

italics /ɪ'tælɪks/ *n pl* курси́в; **in ~** курси́вом.

Italy /'ɪtəlɪ/ *n* Ита́лия.

itch /ɪtʃ/ *n* зуд; *vi* чеса́ться *impf.*

item /'aɪtəm/ *n* (*on list*) предмéт; (*in account*) статья́; (*on agenda*) пункт; (*in programme*) нóмер. **itemize** /-,maɪz/ *vt* перечисля́ть *impf*, перечи́слить *pf.*

itinerant /aɪ'tɪnərənt/ *adj* стра́нствующий. **itinerary** /aɪ'tɪnərərɪ/ *n* маршру́т.

its /ɪts/ *poss pron* его́, её; свой.

itself /ɪt'self/ *pron* (*emph*) (он(ó)) сам(ó), (она́) сама́; (*refl*) себя́; -ся (*suffixed to vt*).

IVF *abbr* (*of* **in vitro fertilization**) экстракорпора́льное оплодотворéние.

ivory /'aɪvərɪ/ *n* слонóвая кость.

ivy /'aɪvɪ/ *n* плющ.

J

jab /dʒæb/ *n* толчóк; (*injection*) укóл; *vt* ты́кать *impf*, ткнуть *pf.*

jabber /'dʒæbə(r)/ *vi* таратóрить *impf.*

jack /dʒæk/ *n* (*cards*) валéт; (*lifting device*) домкра́т; *vt* (**~** *up*) поднима́ть *impf*, подня́ть *pf* домкра́том.

jackdaw /'dʒækdɔ:/ *n* га́лка.

jacket /'dʒækɪt/ *n* (*tailored*) пиджа́к; (*anorak*) ку́ртка; (*on book*) (супер)облóжка.

jackpot /'dʒækpɒt/ *n* банк.

jade /dʒeɪd/ *n* (*mineral*) нефри́т.

jaded /'dʒeɪdɪd/ *adj* утомлённый.

jagged /'dʒægɪd/ *adj* зазу́бренный.

jaguar /'dʒægjʊə(r)/ *n* ягуа́р.

jail /dʒeɪl/ *see* **gaol**

jam[1] /dʒæm/ *n* (*crush*) да́вка; (*in traffic*) прóбка; *vt* (*thrust*) впи́хивать *impf*, впихну́ть *pf* (**into** в+*acc*); (*wedge open*; *block*) закли́нивать *impf*, заклини́ть *pf*; (*radio*) заглуша́ть *impf*, заглуши́ть *pf*; *vi* (*machine*) закли́нивать *impf*, заклини́ть *pf* *impers*+*acc.*

jam[2] /dʒæm/ *n* (*conserve*) варéнье, джем.

jangle /'dʒæŋg(ə)l/ *vi* (& *t*) звя́кать (+*instr*).

janitor /'dʒænɪtə(r)/ *n* привра́тник.

January /'dʒænjʊərɪ/ *n* янва́рь; *adj* янва́рский.

Japan /dʒə'pæn/ *n* Япóния. **Japanese** /,dʒæpə'ni:z/ *n* япóнец, -нка; *adj* япóнский.

jar[1] /dʒɑ:(r)/ *n* (*container*) ба́нка.

jar[2] /dʒɑ:(r)/ *vi* (*irritate*) раздража́ть *impf*, раздражи́ть *pf* (**upon** +*acc*).

jargon /ˈdʒɑːgən/ *n* жарго́н.

jasmin(e) /ˈdʒæzmɪn/ *n* жасми́н.

jaundice /ˈdʒɔːndɪs/ *n* желту́ха. **jaundiced** /-dɪst/ *adj* (*fig*) цини́чный.

jaunt /dʒɔːnt/ *n* прогу́лка.

jaunty /ˈdʒɔːntɪ/ *adj* бо́дрый.

javelin /ˈdʒævəlɪn/ *n* копьё.

jaw /dʒɔː/ *n* че́люсть; *pl* пасть, рот.

jay /dʒeɪ/ *n* со́йка.

jazz /dʒæz/ *n* джаз; *adj* джа́зовый.

jealous /ˈdʒeləs/ *adj* ревни́вый; (*envious*) зави́стливый; **be ~ of** (*person*) ревнова́ть *impf*; (*thing*) зави́довать *impf*, по~ *pf* +*dat*; (*rights*) ревни́во оберега́ть *impf*, обере́чь *pf*. **jealousy** /-sɪ/ *n* ре́вность; за́висть.

jeans /dʒiːnz/ *n pl* джи́нсы (-сов) *pl*.

jeer /dʒɪə(r)/ *n* насме́шка; *vt* & *i* насмеха́ться *impf* (**at** над+*instr*).

jelly /ˈdʒelɪ/ *n* (*sweet*) желе́ *neut indecl*; (*aspic*) сту́день *m*. **jellyfish** *n* меду́за.

jeopardize /ˈdʒepəˌdaɪz/ *vt* подверга́ть *impf*, подве́ргнуть *pf* опа́сности. **jeopardy** /-dɪ/ *n* опа́сность.

jerk /dʒɜːk/ *n* рыво́к; *vt* дёргать *impf* +*instr*; *vi* (*twitch*) дёргаться *impf*, дёрнуться *pf*. **jerky** /-kɪ/ *adj* неро́вный.

jersey /ˈdʒɜːzɪ/ *n* (*garment*) дже́мпер; (*fabric*) джерси́ *neut indecl*.

jest /dʒest/ *n* шу́тка; **in ~** в шу́тку; *vi* шути́ть *impf*, по~ *pf*. **jester** /-stə(r)/ *n* шут.

jet[1] /dʒet/ *n* (*stream*) струя́; (*nozzle*) сопло́; **~ engine** реакти́вный дви́гатель *m*; **~ plane** реакти́вный самолёт.

jet[2] /dʒet/ *n* (*mineralogy*) гага́т; **~-black** чёрный как смоль.

jettison /ˈdʒetɪs(ə)n/ *vt* выбра́сывать *impf*, вы́бросить *pf* за́ борт.

jetty /ˈdʒetɪ/ *n* при́стань.

Jew /dʒuː/ *n* евре́й, евре́йка. **Jewish** /-ɪʃ/ *adj* евре́йский.

jewel /ˈdʒuːəl/ *n* драгоце́нность, драгоце́нный ка́мень *m*. **jeweller** /-lə(r)/ *n* ювели́р. **jewellery** /-lərɪ/ *n* драгоце́нности *f pl*.

jib /dʒɪb/ *n* (*naut*) кли́вер; *vi*: **~ at** уклоня́ться *impf* от+*gen*.

jigsaw /ˈdʒɪgsɔː/ *n* (*puzzle*) моза́ика.

jingle /ˈdʒɪŋg(ə)l/ *n* звя́канье; *vi* (& *t*) звя́кать *impf*, звя́кнуть *pf* (+*instr*).

job /dʒɒb/ *n* (*work*) рабо́та; (*task*) зада́ние; (*position*) ме́сто. **jobless** /-lɪs/ *adj* безрабо́тный.

jockey /ˈdʒɒkɪ/ *n* жоке́й; *vi* оттира́ть *impf* друг дру́га.

jocular /ˈdʒɒkjʊlə(r)/ *adj* шутли́вый.

jog /dʒɒg/ *n* (*push*) толчо́к; *vt* подта́лкивать *impf*, подтолкну́ть *pf*; *vi* бе́гать *impf* трусцо́й. **jogger** /-gə(r)/ *n* занима́ющийся оздорови́тельным бе́гом. **jogging** /-gɪŋ/ *n* оздорови́тельный бег.

join /dʒɔɪn/ *vt* & *i* соединя́ть(ся) *impf*, соедини́ть(ся) *pf*; *vt* (*a group of people*) присоединя́ться *impf*, присоедини́ться *pf* к+*dat*; (*as member*) вступа́ть *impf*, вступи́ть *pf* в+*acc*; *vi*: **~ in** принима́ть *impf*, приня́ть *pf* уча́стие (в+*prep*); **~ up** вступа́ть *impf*, вступи́ть *pf* в а́рмию.

joiner /ˈdʒɔɪnə(r)/ *n* столя́р.

joint /dʒɔɪnt/ *n* соедине́ние; (*anat*) суста́в; (*meat*) кусо́к;

adj совме́стный; (*common*) о́бщий.

joist /dʒɔɪst/ *n* перекла́дина.

joke /dʒəʊk/ *n* шу́тка; *vi* шути́ть *impf*, по~ *pf*. **joker** /-kə(r)/ *n* шутни́к; (*cards*) джо́кер.

jollity /ˈdʒɒlɪtɪ/ *n* весе́лье. **jolly** /-lɪ/ *adj* весёлый; *adv* о́чень.

jolt /dʒəʊlt/ *n* толчо́к; *vt* & *i* трясти́(сь) *impf*.

jostle /ˈdʒɒs(ə)l/ *vt* & *i* толка́ть(ся) *impf*, толкну́ть(ся) *pf*.

jot /dʒɒt/ *n* йо́та; **not a ~** ни на йо́ту; *vt* (~ *down*) запи́сывать *impf*, записа́ть *pf*.

journal /ˈdʒɜːn(ə)l/ *n* журна́л; (*diary*) дневни́к. **journalese** /-ˈliːz/ *n* газе́тный язы́к. **journalism** /-lɪz(ə)m/ *n* журнали́стика. **journalist** /-lɪst/ *n* журнали́ст.

journey /ˈdʒɜːnɪ/ *n* путеше́ствие; *vi* путеше́ствовать *impf*.

jovial /ˈdʒəʊvɪəl/ *adj* весёлый.

joy /dʒɔɪ/ *n* ра́дость. **joyful, joyous** /-fʊl, -əs/ *adj* ра́достный. **joyless** /-lɪs/ *adj* безра́достный. **joystick** *n* рыча́г управле́ния; (*comput*) джо́йстик.

jubilant /ˈdʒuːbɪlənt/ *adj* лику́ющий; **be ~** ликова́ть *impf*. **jubilation** /-ˈleɪʃ(ə)n/ *n* ликова́ние.

jubilee /ˈdʒuːbɪˌliː/ *n* юбиле́й.

Judaism /ˈdʒuːdeɪˌɪz(ə)m/ *n* иудаи́зм.

judge /dʒʌdʒ/ *n* судья́ *m*; (*connoisseur*) цени́тель *m*; *vt* & *i* суди́ть *impf*. **judgement** /-mənt/ *n* (*legal decision*) реше́ние; (*opinion*) мне́ние; (*discernment*) рассуди́тельность.

judicial /dʒuːˈdɪʃ(ə)l/ *adj* суде́бный. **judiciary** /-ˈdɪʃɪərɪ/ *n* судьи́ *m pl*. **judicious** /-ˈdɪʃəs/ *adj* здравомы́слящий.

judo /ˈdʒuːdəʊ/ *n* дзюдо́ *neut indecl*.

jug /dʒʌg/ *n* кувши́н.

juggernaut /ˈdʒʌgəˌnɔːt/ *n* (*lorry*) многото́нный грузови́к; (*fig*) неумоли́мая си́ла.

juggle /ˈdʒʌg(ə)l/ *vi* жонгли́ровать *impf*. **juggler** /ˈdʒʌglə(r)/ *n* жонглёр.

jugular /ˈdʒʌgjʊlə(r)/ *n* яре́мная ве́на.

juice /dʒuːs/ *n* сок. **juicy** /-sɪ/ *adj* со́чный.

July /dʒuːˈlaɪ/ *n* ию́ль *m*; *adj* ию́льский.

jumble /ˈdʒʌmb(ə)l/ *n* (*disorder*) беспоря́док; (*articles*) барахло́; *vt* перепу́тывать *impf*, перепу́тать *pf*.

jump /dʒʌmp/ *n* прыжо́к, скачо́к; *vi* пры́гать *impf*, пры́гнуть *pf*; скака́ть *impf*; (*from shock*) вздра́гивать *impf*, вздро́гнуть *pf*; *vt* (~ *over*) перепры́гивать *impf*, перепры́гнуть *pf*; **~ at** (*offer*) ухва́тываться *impf*, ухвати́ться *pf* за+*acc*; **~ up** вска́кивать *impf*, вскочи́ть *pf*.

jumper /ˈdʒʌmpə(r)/ *n* дже́мпер.

jumpy /ˈdʒʌmpɪ/ *adj* не́рвный.

junction /ˈdʒʌŋkʃ(ə)n/ *n* (*rly*) у́зел; (*roads*) перекрёсток.

juncture /ˈdʒʌŋktʃə(r)/ *n*: **at this ~** в э́тот моме́нт.

June /dʒuːn/ *n* ию́нь *m*; *adj* ию́ньский.

jungle /ˈdʒʌŋg(ə)l/ *n* джу́нгли (-лей) *pl*.

junior /ˈdʒuːnɪə(r)/ *adj* мла́дший; **~ school** нача́льная шко́ла.

juniper /ˈdʒuːnɪpə(r)/ *n* можжеве́льник.

junk /dʒʌŋk/ *n* (*rubbish*) барахло́.

jurisdiction /ˌdʒʊərɪsˈdɪkʃ(ə)n/ *n* юрисди́кция.

jurisprudence /ˌdʒʊərɪsˈpruːd(ə)ns/ *n* юриспруде́нция.

juror /'dʒʊərə(r)/ *n* прися́жный *sb*. **jury** /'dʒʊərɪ/ *n* прися́жные *sb*; (*in competition*) жюри́ *neut indecl.*

just /dʒʌst/ *adj* (*fair*) справедли́вый; (*deserved*) заслу́женный; *adv* (*exactly*) как раз, и́менно; (*simply*) про́сто; (*barely*) едва́; (*very recently*) то́лько что; **~ in case** на вся́кий слу́чай.

justice /'dʒʌstɪs/ *n* (*proceedings*) правосу́дие; (*fairness*) справедли́вость; **do ~ to** отдава́ть *impf*, отда́ть *pf* до́лжное *+dat.*

justify /'dʒʌstɪ,faɪ/ *vt* опра́вдывать *impf*, оправда́ть *pf.* **justification** /-fɪ'keɪʃ(ə)n/ *n* оправда́ние.

jut /dʒʌt/ *vi* (**~** *out*) выдава́ться *impf*; выступа́ть *impf.*

juvenile /'dʒu:və,naɪl/ *n* & *adj* несовершенноле́тний *sb* & *adj.*

juxtapose /,dʒʌkstə'pəʊz/ *vt* помеща́ть *impf*, помести́ть *pf* ря́дом; (*for comparison*) сопоставля́ть *impf*, сопоста́вить *pf* (**with** c*+instr*).

K

kaleidoscope /kə'laɪdə,skəʊp/ *n* калейдоско́п.

kangaroo /,kæŋgə'ru:/ *n* кенгуру́ *m indecl.*

Kazakhstan /,kæzæk'stɑ:n/ *n* Казахста́н.

keel /ki:l/ *n* киль *m*; *vi*: **~ over** опроки́дываться *impf*, опроки́нуться *pf.*

keen /ki:n/ *adj* (*enthusiastic*) по́лный энтузиа́зма; (*sharp*) о́стрый; (*strong*) си́льный; **be ~ on** увлека́ться *impf*, увле́чься *pf +instr*; (*want to do*) о́чень хоте́ть *impf +inf.*

keep[1] /ki:p/ *n* (*tower*) гла́вная ба́шня; (*maintenance*) содержа́ние.

keep[2] /ki:p/ *vt* (*possess, maintain*) держа́ть *impf*; храни́ть *impf*; (*observe*) соблюда́ть *impf*, соблюсти́ *pf* (*the law*); сде́рживать *impf*, сдержа́ть *pf* (*one's word*); (*family*) содержа́ть *impf*; (*diary*) вести́ *impf*; (*detain*) заде́рживать *impf*, задержа́ть *pf*; (*retain, reserve*) сохраня́ть *impf*, сохрани́ть *pf*; *vi* (*remain*) остава́ться *impf*, оста́ться *pf*; (*of food*) не по́ртиться *impf*; **~ back** (*vt*) (*hold back*) уде́рживать *impf*, удержа́ть *pf*; (*vi*) держа́ться *impf* сза́ди; **~ doing sth** всё *+verb*: **she ~s giggling** она́ всё хихи́кает; **~ from** уде́рживаться *impf*, удержа́ться *pf* от*+gen*; **~ on** продолжа́ть *impf*, продо́лжить *pf* (*+inf*); **~ up (with)** (*vi*) не отстава́ть *impf* (от*+gen*).

keepsake /'ki:pseɪk/ *n* пода́рок на па́мять.

keg /keg/ *n* бочо́нок.

kennel /'ken(ə)l/ *n* конура́.

kerb /kɜ:b/ *n* край тротуа́ра.

kernel /'kɜ:n(ə)l/ *n* (*nut*) ядро́; (*grain*) зерно́; (*fig*) суть.

kerosene /'kerə,si:n/ *n* кероси́н.

kettle /'ket(ə)l/ *n* ча́йник.

key /ki:/ *n* ключ; (*piano, typewriter*) кла́виш(а); (*mus*) тона́льность; *attrib* веду́щий, ключево́й. **keyboard** *n* клавиату́ра. **keyhole** *n* замо́чная сква́жина.

KGB *abbr* КГБ.

khaki /'kɑ:kɪ/ *n* & *adj* ха́ки *neut*, *adj indecl.*

kick /kɪk/ *n* уда́р ного́й, пино́к; *vt* ударя́ть *impf*, уда́рить *pf* ного́й; пина́ть *impf*, пнуть *pf*; *vi* (*of horse etc.*) ляга́ться *impf.*

kick-off /ˈkɪkɒf/ *n* начáло (игры́).
kid[1] /kɪd/ *n* (*goat*) козлёнок; (*child*) малы́ш.
kid[2] /kɪd/ *vt* (*deceive*) обмáнывать *impf*, обмануть *pf*; *vi* (*joke*) шути́ть *impf*, по~ *pf*.
kidnap /ˈkɪdnæp/ *vt* похищáть *impf*, похи́тить *pf*.
kidney /ˈkɪdnɪ/ *n* пóчка.
kill /kɪl/ *vt* убивáть *impf*, уби́ть *pf*. **killer** /-lə(r)/ *n* уби́йца *m* & *f*. **killing** /-lɪŋ/ *n* уби́йство; *adj* (*murderous, fig*) уби́йственный; (*amusing*) умори́тельный.
kiln /kɪln/ *n* óбжиговая печь.
kilo /ˈkiːləʊ/ *n* киlо́ *neut indecl*. **kilohertz** /ˈkɪlə,hɜːts/ *n* килогéрц. **kilogram(me)** /ˈkɪlə,græm/ *n* килогрáмм. **kilometre** /ˈkɪlə,miːtə(r)/ *n* киломéтр. **kilowatt** /ˈkɪlə,wɒt/ *n* киловáтт.
kilt /kɪlt/ *n* шотлáндская ю́бка.
kimono /kɪˈməʊnəʊ/ *n* кимонó *neut indecl*.
kin /kɪn/ *n* (*family*) семья́; (*collect, relatives*) родня́.
kind[1] /kaɪnd/ *n* сорт, род; **a ~ of** что-то врóде+*gen*; **this ~ of** такóй; **what ~ of** что (э́то, он, *etc.*) за +*nom*; **~ of** (*adv*) как бу́дто, кáк-то.
kind[2] /kaɪnd/ *adj* дóбрый.
kindergarten /ˈkɪndə,gɑːt(ə)n/ *n* дéтский сад.
kindle /ˈkɪnd(ə)l/ *vt* зажигáть *impf*, зажéчь *pf*. **kindling** /-dlɪŋ/ *n* растóпка.
kindly /ˈkaɪndlɪ/ *adj* дóбрый; *adv* любéзно; (*with imper*) (*request*) бу́дьте добры́, +*imper*. **kindness** /ˈkaɪndnɪs/ *n* добротá.
kindred /ˈkɪndrɪd/ *adj*: **~ spirit** роднáя душá.
kinetic /kɪˈnetɪk/ *adj* кинети́ческий.
king /kɪŋ/ *n* корóль *m* (*also chess, cards, fig*); (*draughts*) дáмка. **kingdom** /ˈkɪŋdəm/ *n* королéвство; (*fig*) цáрство. **kingfisher** /ˈkɪŋfɪʃə(r)/ *n* зиморóдок.
kink /kɪŋk/ *n* переги́б.
kinship /ˈkɪnʃɪp/ *n* родствó; (*similarity*) схóдство. **kinsman, -woman** *n* рóдственник, -ица.
kiosk /ˈkiːɒsk/ *n* киóск; (*telephone*) бу́дка.
kip /kɪp/ *n* сон; *vi* дры́хнуть *impf*.
kipper /ˈkɪpə(r)/ *n* копчёная селёдка.
Kirghizia /kɜːˈgiːzɪə/ *n* Кирги́зия.
kiss /kɪs/ *n* поцелу́й; *vt* & *i* целовáть(ся) *impf*, по~ *pf*.
kit /kɪt/ *n* (*clothing*) снаряжéние; (*tools*) набóр, комплéкт; *vt*: **~ out** снаряжáть *impf*, снаряди́ть *pf*. **kitbag** *n* вещевóй мешóк.
kitchen /ˈkɪtʃɪn/ *n* ку́хня; *attrib* ку́хонный; **~ garden** огорóд.
kite /kaɪt/ *n* (*toy*) змей.
kitsch /kɪtʃ/ *n* дешёвка.
kitten /ˈkɪt(ə)n/ *n* котёнок.
knack /næk/ *n* сноро́вка.
knapsack /ˈnæpsæk/ *n* рюкзáк.
knead /niːd/ *vt* меси́ть *impf*, с~ *pf*.
knee /niː/ *n* колéно. **kneecap** *n* колéнная чáшка.
kneel /niːl/ *vi* стоя́ть *impf* на колéнях; (**~** *down*) станови́ться *impf*, стать *pf* на колéни.
knickers /ˈnɪkəz/ *n pl* тру́сики (-ов) *pl*.
knick-knack /ˈnɪknæk/ *n* безделу́шка.
knife /naɪf/ *n* нож; *vt* колóть *impf*, за~ *pf* ножóм.
knight /naɪt/ *n* (*hist*) ры́царь *m*; (*holder of order*) кавалéр; (*chess*) конь *m*. **knighthood** /-hʊd/ *n* ры́царское звáние.
knit /nɪt/ *vt* (*garment*) вязáть

impf, с~ *pf*; *vi* (*bones*) срастáться *impf*, срастись *pf*; ~ **one's brows** хмýрить *impf*, на~ *pf* брóви. **knitting** /-tɪŋ/ *n* (*action*) вязáние; (*object*) вязáнье; ~**-needle** спи́ца. **knitwear** *n* трикотáж.

knob /nɒb/ *n* ши́шка, кнóпка; (*door handle*) рýчка. **knobb(l)y** /'nɒb(l)ɪ/ *adj* шишковáтый.

knock /nɒk/ *n* (*noise*) стук; (*blow*) удáр; *vt* & *i* (*strike*) ударя́ть *impf*, удáрить *pf*; (*strike door etc.*) стучáть *impf*, по~ *pf* (**at** в+*acc*); ~ **about** (*treat roughly*) колоти́ть *impf*, по~ *pf*; (*wander*) шатáться *impf*; ~ **down** (*person*) сбивáть *impf*, сбить *pf* с ног; (*building*) сноси́ть *impf*, снести́ *pf*; ~ **off** сбивáть *impf*, сбить *pf*; (*stop work*) шабáшить *impf* (рабóту); (*deduct*) сбавля́ть *impf*, сбáвить *pf*; ~ **out** выбивáть *impf*, вы́бить *pf*; (*sport*) нокаути́ровать *impf* & *pf*; ~**-out** нокáут; ~ **over** опроки́дывать *impf*, опроки́нуть *impf*. **knocker** /'nɒkə(r)/ *n* двернóй молотóк.

knoll /nəʊl/ *n* бугóр.

knot /nɒt/ *n* ýзел; *vt* завя́зывать *impf*, завязáть *pf* узлóм. **knotty** /-tɪ/ *adj* (*fig*) запýтанный.

know /nəʊ/ *vt* знать *impf*; (~ *how to*) умéть *impf*, с~ *pf* +*inf*; ~**-how** умéние. **knowing** /'nəʊɪŋ/ *adj* многозначи́тельный. **knowingly** /'nəʊɪŋlɪ/ *adv* сознáтельно. **knowledge** /'nɒlɪdʒ/ *n* знáние; **to my** ~ наскóлько мне извéстно.

knuckle /'nʌk(ə)l/ *n* сустáв пáльца; *vi*: ~ **down to** впрягáться *impf*, впря́чься *pf* в+*acc*; ~ **under** уступáть *impf*, уступи́ть *pf* (**to** +*dat*).

Korea /kə'ri:ə/ *n* Корéя.

ko(w)tow /kaʊ'taʊ/ *vi* (*fig*) раболéпствовать *impf* (**to** пéред +*instr*).

Kremlin /'kremlɪn/ *n* Кремль *m*.

kudos /'kju:dɒs/ *n* слáва.

L

label /'leɪb(ə)l/ *n* этикéтка, ярлы́к; *vt* приклéивать *impf*, приклéить *pf* ярлы́к к+*dat*.

laboratory /lə'bɒrətərɪ/ *n* лаборатóрия.

laborious /lə'bɔ:rɪəs/ *adj* кропотли́вый.

labour /'leɪbə(r)/ *n* труд; (*med*) рóды (-дов) *pl*; *attrib* трудовóй; ~ **force** рабóчая си́ла; ~**-intensive** трудоёмкий; **L**~ **Party** лейбори́стская пáртия; *vi* труди́ться *impf*; *vt*: ~ **a point** входи́ть *impf*, войти́ *pf* в изли́шние подрóбности. **laboured** /-bəd/ *adj* затруднённый; (*style*) вы́мученный. **labourer** /-bərə(r)/ *n* чернорабóчий *sb*. **labourite** /-bə,raɪt/ *n* лейбори́ст.

labyrinth /'læbərɪnθ/ *n* лабири́нт.

lace /leɪs/ *n* (*fabric*) крýжево; (*cord*) шнурóк; *vt* (~ *up*) шноровáть *impf*, за~ *pf*.

lacerate /'læsə,reɪt/ *vt* (*also fig*) терзáть *impf*, ис~ *pf*. **laceration** /-'reɪʃ(ə)n/ *n* (*wound*) рвáная рáна.

lack /læk/ *n* недостáток (**of** +*gen*, в+*prep*), отсýтствие; *vt* & *i* не хватáть *impf*, хвати́ть *pf* *impers* +*dat* (*person*), +*gen* (*object*).

lackadaisical /,lækə'deɪzɪk(ə)l/ *adj* тóмный.

laconic /lə'kɒnɪk/ *adj* лакони́чный.

lacquer /'lækə(r)/ *n* лак; *vt* лакирова́ть *impf*, от~ *pf*.

lad /læd/ *n* па́рень *m*.

ladder /'lædə(r)/ *n* ле́стница.

laden /'leɪd(ə)n/ *adj* нагружённый.

ladle /'leɪd(ə)l/ *n* (*spoon*) поло́вник; *vt* че́рпать *impf*, черпну́ть *pf*.

lady /'leɪdɪ/ *n* да́ма, ле́ди *f indecl.* **ladybird** *n* бо́жья коро́вка.

lag[1] /læg/ *vi*: ~ **behind** отстава́ть *impf*, отста́ть *pf* (от+*gen*).

lag[2] /læg/ *vt* (*insulate*) изоли́ровать *impf* & *pf*.

lagoon /lə'gu:n/ *n* лагу́на.

lair /leə(r)/ *n* ло́говище.

laity /'leɪɪtɪ/ *n* (*in religion*) миря́не (-н) *pl*.

lake /leɪk/ *n* о́зеро.

lamb /læm/ *n* ягнёнок; (*meat*) бара́нина.

lame /leɪm/ *adj* хромо́й; **be** ~ хрома́ть *impf*; **go** ~ хроме́ть *impf*, о~ *pf*; *vt* кале́чить *impf*, о~ *pf*.

lament /lə'ment/ *n* плач; *vt* сожале́ть *impf* о+*prep*. **lamentable** /'læməntəb(ə)l/ *adj* приско́рбный.

laminated /'læmɪˌneɪtɪd/ *adj* слои́стый.

lamp /læmp/ *n* ла́мпа; (*in street*) фона́рь *m*. **lamp-post** *n* фона́рный столб. **lampshade** *n* абажу́р.

lance /lɑ:ns/ *n* пи́ка; *vt* (*med*) вскрыва́ть *impf*, вскрыть *pf* (ланце́том).

land /lænd/ *n* земля́; (*dry* ~) су́ша; (*country*) страна́; *vi* (*naut*) прича́ливать *impf*, прича́лить *pf*; *vt* & *i* (*aeron*) приземля́ть(ся) *impf*, приземли́ть(ся) *pf*; (*find o.s.*) попада́ть *impf*, попа́сть *pf*.

landing /-dɪŋ/ *n* (*aeron*) поса́дка; (*on stairs*) площа́дка; ~**-stage** при́стань. **landlady** *n* хозя́йка. **landlord** *n* хозя́ин. **landmark** *n* (*conspicuous object*) ориенти́р; (*fig*) ве́ха. **landowner** *n* землевладе́лец. **landscape** /'lændskeɪp/ *n* ландша́фт; (*also picture*) пейза́ж. **landslide** *n* о́ползень *m*.

lane /leɪn/ *n* (*in country*) доро́жка; (*street*) переу́лок; (*passage*) прохо́д; (*on road*) ряд; (*in race*) доро́жка.

language /'læŋgwɪdʒ/ *n* язы́к; (*style, speech*) речь.

languid /'læŋgwɪd/ *adj* то́мный.

languish /'læŋgwɪʃ/ *vi* томи́ться *impf*.

languor /'læŋgə(r)/ *n* то́мность.

lank /læŋk/ *adj* (*hair*) гла́дкий. **lanky** /-kɪ/ *adj* долговя́зый.

lantern /'lænt(ə)n/ *n* фона́рь *m*.

lap[1] /læp/ *n* (*of person*) коле́ни (-ней) *pl*; (*sport*) круг.

lap[2] /læp/ *vt* (*drink*) лака́ть *impf*, вы́~ *pf*; *vi* (*water*) плеска́ться *impf*.

lapel /lə'pel/ *n* отворо́т.

lapse /læps/ *n* (*mistake*) оши́бка; (*interval*) промежу́ток; (*expiry*) истече́ние; *vi* впада́ть *impf*, впасть *pf* (**into** в+*acc*); (*expire*) истека́ть *impf*, исте́чь *pf*.

laptop /'læptɒp/ *n* портати́вный компью́тер.

lapwing /'læpwɪŋ/ *n* чи́бис.

larch /lɑ:tʃ/ *n* ли́ственница.

lard /lɑ:d/ *n* свино́е са́ло.

larder /'lɑ:də(r)/ *n* кладова́я *sb*.

large /lɑ:dʒ/ *adj* большо́й; *n*: **at** ~ (*free*) на свобо́де; **by and** ~ вообще́ говоря́. **largely** /-lɪ/ *adj* в значи́тельной сте́пени.

largesse /lɑ:'ʒes/ *n* ще́дрость.

lark[1] /lɑ:k/ *n* (*bird*) жа́воронок.

lark² /lɑ:k/ *n* проказа; *vi* (~ *about*) резвиться *impf*.

larva /'lɑ:və/ *n* личинка.

laryngitis /ˌlærɪn'dʒaɪtɪs/ *n* ларингит. **larynx** /'lærɪŋks/ *n* гортань.

lascivious /lə'sɪvɪəs/ *adj* похотливый.

laser /'leɪzə(r)/ *n* лазер.

lash /læʃ/ *n* (*blow*) удар плетью; (*eyelash*) ресница; *vt* (*beat*) хлестать *impf*, хлестнуть *pf*; (*tie*) привязывать *impf*, привязать *pf* (**to** к+*dat*).

last¹ /lɑ:st/ *adj* (*final*) последний; (*most recent*) прошлый; **the year** (*etc.*) **before** ~ позапрошлый год (и т.д.); ~ **but one** предпоследний; ~ **night** вчера вечером; **at** ~ наконец; *adv* (*after all others*) после всех; (*on the last occasion*) в последний раз; (*lastly*) наконец.

last² /lɑ:st/ *vi* (*go on*) продолжаться *impf*, продолжиться *pf*; длиться *impf*, про~ *pf*; (*be preserved*) сохраняться *impf*, сохраниться *pf*; (*suffice*) хватать *impf*, хватить *pf*. **lasting** /-tɪŋ/ *adj* (*permanent*) постоянный; (*durable*) прочный.

lastly /'lɑ:stlɪ/ *adv* в заключение; наконец.

latch /lætʃ/ *n* щеколда.

late /leɪt/ *adj* поздний; (*recent*) недавний; (*dead*) покойный; **be** ~ **for** опаздывать *impf*, опоздать *pf* на+*acc*; *adv* поздно. **lately** /-lɪ/ *adv* в последнее время. **later** /-tə(r)/ *adv* (*after vv*) позже; **a year** ~ год спустя; **see you** ~! пока!

latent /'leɪt(ə)nt/ *adj* скрытый.

lateral /'lætər(ə)l/ *adj* боковой.

lath /lɑ:θ/ *n* рейка.

lathe /leɪð/ *n* токарный станок.

lather /'lɑ:ðə(r/ *n* (мыльная) пена; *vt* & *i* мылить(ся) *impf*, на~ *pf*.

Latin /'lætɪn/ *adj* латинский; *n* латинский язык; **~-American** латиноамериканский.

latitude /'lætɪˌtju:d/ *n* свобода; (*geog*) широта.

latter /'lætə(r)/ *adj* последний; **~-day** современный. **latterly** /-lɪ/ *adv* в последнее время.

lattice /'lætɪs/ *n* решётка.

Latvia /'lætvɪə/ *n* Латвия. **Latvian** /-ən/ *n* латвиец, -ийка; латыш, ~ка; *adj* латвийский, латышский.

laud /lɔ:d/ *vt* хвалить *impf*, по~ *pf*. **laudable** /-dəb(ə)l/ *adj* похвальный.

laugh /lɑ:f/ *n* смех; *vi* смеяться *impf* (**at** над+*instr*); ~ **it off** отшучиваться *impf*, отшутиться *pf*; **~ing-stock** посмешище. **laughable** /-fəb(ə)l/ *adj* смешной. **laughter** /-tə(r)/ *n* смех.

launch¹ /lɔ:ntʃ/ *vt* (*ship*) спускать *impf*, спустить *pf* на воду; (*rocket*) запускать *impf*, запустить *pf*; (*undertake*) начинать *impf*, начать *pf*; *n* спуск на воду; запуск. **launcher** /-tʃə(r)/ *n* (*for rocket*) пусковая установка. **launching pad** /'lɔ:ntʃɪŋ pæd/ *n* пусковая площадка.

launch² /lɔ:ntʃ/ *n* (*naut*) катер.

launder /'lɔ:ndə(r)/ *vt* стирать *impf*, вы~ *pf*. **laund(e)rette** /-'dret/ *n* прачечная *sb* самообслуживания. **laundry** /'lɔ:ndrɪ/ *n* (*place*) прачечная *sb*; (*articles*) бельё.

laurel /'lɒr(ə)l/ *n* лавр(овое дерево).

lava /'lɑ:və/ *n* лава.

lavatory /'lævətərɪ/ *n* уборная *sb*.

lavender /'lævɪndə(r)/ *n* лаванда.

lavish /'lævɪʃ/ *adj* щéдрый; (*abundant*) обúльный; *vt* расточáть *impf* (**upon** +*dat*).

law /lɔː/ *n* закóн; (*system*) прáво; ~ **and order** правопоря́док. **law-court** *n* суд. **lawful** /-fʊl/ *adj* закóнный. **lawless** /-lɪs/ *adj* беззакóнный.

lawn /lɔːn/ *n* газóн; **~-mower** газонокосúлка.

lawsuit /'lɔːsuːt/ *n* процéсс.

lawyer /'lɔɪə(r)/ *n* адвокáт, юрúст.

lax /læks/ *adj* слáбый. **laxative** /-sətɪv/ *n* слабúтельное *sb*. **laxity** /-sɪtɪ/ *n* слáбость.

lay[1] /leɪ/ *adj* (*non-clerical*) свéтский.

lay[2] /leɪ/ *vt* (*place*) класть *impf*, положúть *pf*; (*cable, pipes*) проклáдывать *impf*, проложúть *pf*; (*carpet*) стлать *impf*, по~ *pf*; (*trap etc.*) устрáивать *impf*, устрóить *pf*; (*eggs*) класть *impf*, положúть *pf*; *v abs* (*lay eggs*) нестúсь *impf*, с~ *pf*; ~ **aside** отклáдывать *impf*, отложúть *pf*; ~ **bare** раскрывáть *impf*, раскры́ть *pf*; ~ **a bet** держáть *impf* парú (**on** на+*acc*); ~ **down** (*relinquish*) откáзываться *impf*, отказáться *pf* от+*gen*; (*rule etc.*) устанáвливать *impf*, установúть *pf*; ~ **off** (*workmen*) увольня́ть *impf*, увóлить *pf*; ~ **out** (*spread*) выклáдывать *impf*, вы́ложить *pf*; (*garden*) разбивáть *impf*, разбúть *pf*; ~ **the table** накрывáть *impf*, накры́ть *pf* стол (**for** (*meal*) к+*dat*); ~ **up** запасáть *impf*, запастú *pf* +*acc*, +*gen*; **be laid up** быть прикóванным к постéли. **layabout** *n* бездéльник.

layer /'leɪə(r)/ *n* слой, пласт.

layman /'leɪmən/ *n* миря́нин; (*non-expert*) неспециалúст.

laze /leɪz/ *vi* бездéльничать *impf*. **laziness** /-zɪnɪs/ *n* лень. **lazy** /-zɪ/ *adj* ленúвый; **~-bones** лентя́й, ~ка.

lead[1] /liːd/ *n* (*example*) примéр; (*leadership*) руковóдство; (*position*) пéрвое мéсто; (*theat*) глáвная роль; (*electr*) прóвод; (*dog's*) поводóк; *vt* водúть *indet*, вестú *det*; (*be in charge of*) руководúть *impf* +*instr*; (*induce*) побуждáть *impf*, побудúть *pf*; *vt* & *i* (*cards*) ходúть *impf* (с+*gen*); *vi* (*sport*) занимáть *impf*, заня́ть *pf* пéрвое мéсто; ~ **away** уводúть *impf*, увестú *pf*; ~ **to** (*result in*) приводúть *impf*, привестú *pf* к+*dat*.

lead[2] /led/ *n* (*metal*) свинéц. **leaden** /'led(ə)n/ *adj* свинцóвый.

leader /'liːdə(r)/ *n* руководúтель *m*, ~ница, лúдер; (*mus*) пéрвая скрúпка; (*editorial*) передовáя статья́. **leadership** *n* руковóдство.

leading /'liːdɪŋ/ *adj* ведýщий, выдаю́щийся; ~ **article** передовáя статья́.

leaf /liːf/ *n* лист; (*of table*) откиднáя доскá; *vi*: ~ **through** перелúстывать *impf*, перелистáть *pf*. **leaflet** /'liːflɪt/ *n* листóвка.

league /liːg/ *n* лúга; **in ~ with** в союзе с +*instr*.

leak /liːk/ *n* течь, утéчка; *vi* (*escape*) течь *impf*; (*allow water to* ~) пропускáть *impf* вóду; ~ **out** просáчиваться *impf*, просочúться *pf*.

lean[1] /liːn/ *adj* (*thin*) худóй; (*meat*) пóстный.

lean[2] /liːn/ *vt* & *i* прислоня́ть(ся) *impf*, прислонúть(ся) *pf* (**against** к+*dat*); (*be inclined*) быть склóнным (**to(wards)** к+*dat*); ~ **back** откúдываться *impf*, откúнуться *pf*; ~ **out of** высóвываться *impf*, вы́сунуться *pf* в +*acc*. **leaning** /-nɪŋ/ *n* склóнность.

leap /li:p/ *n* прыжóк, скачóк; *vi* пры́гать *impf*, пры́гнуть *pf*; скакáть *impf*; ~ **year** високóсный год.

learn /lɜ:n/ *vt* (*a subject*) учúть *impf*, вы́~ *pf*; (*to do sth*) учúться *impf*, на~ *pf* +*inf*; (*find out*) узнавáть *impf*, узнáть *pf*. **learned** /-nɪd/ *adj* учёный. **learner** /-nə(r)/ *n* ученúк, -úца. **learning** /-nɪŋ/ *n* (*studies*) учéние; (*erudition*) учёность.

lease /li:s/ *n* арéнда; *vt* (*of owner*) сдавáть *impf*, сдать *pf* в арéнду; (*of tenant*) брать *impf*, взять *pf* в арéнду. **leaseholder** /-ˌhəʊldə(r)/ *n* арендáтор.

leash /li:ʃ/ *n* прúвязь.

least /li:st/ *adj* наимéньший, малéйший; *adv* мéнее всегó; **at** ~ по крáйней мéре; **not in the** ~ ничýть.

leather /ˈleðə(r)/ *n* кóжа; *attrib* кóжаный.

leave[1] /li:v/ *n* (*permission*) разрешéние; (*holiday*) óтпуск; **on** ~ в óтпуске; **take (one's)** ~ прощáться *impf*, простúться *pf* (**of** с+*instr*).

leave[2] /li:v/ *vt & i* оставля́ть *impf*, остáвить *pf*; (*abandon*) покидáть *impf*, покúнуть *pf*; (*go away*) уходúть *impf*, уйтú *pf* (**from** от+*gen*); уезжáть *impf*, уéхать *pf* (**from** от+*gen*); (*go out of*) выходúть *impf*, вы́йти *pf* из+*gen*; (*entrust*) предоставля́ть *impf*, предостáвить *pf* (**to** +*dat*); ~ **out** пропускáть *impf*, пропустúть *pf*.

lecherous /ˈletʃərəs/ *adj* разврáтный.

lectern /ˈlektз:n/ *n* аналóй; (*in lecture room*) пюпúтр.

lecture /ˈlektʃə(r)/ *n* (*discourse*) лéкция; (*reproof*) нотáция; *vi* (*deliver* ~(*s*)) читáть *impf*, про~ *pf* лéкцию (-ии) (**on** по+*dat*); *vt* (*admonish*) читáть *impf*, про~ *pf* нотáцию+*dat*; ~ **room** аудитóрия. **lecturer** /-tʃərə(r)/ *n* лéктор; (*univ*) преподавáтель *m*, ~ница.

ledge /ledʒ/ *n* вы́ступ; (*shelf*) пóлочка.

ledger /ˈledʒə(r)/ *n* глáвная кнúга.

lee /li:/ *n* защúта; *adj* подвéтренный.

leech /li:tʃ/ *n* (*worm*) пия́вка.

leek /li:k/ *n* лук-порéй.

leer /lɪə(r)/ *vi* кривúться *impf*, с~ *pf*.

leeward /ˈli:wəd/ *n* подвéтренная сторонá; *adj* подвéтренный.

leeway /ˈli:weɪ/ *n* (*fig*) свобóда дéйствий.

left /left/ *n* лéвая сторонá; (**the L**~; *polit*) лéвые *sb pl*; *adj* лéвый; *adv* налéво, слéва (**of** от+*gen*); ~**-hander** левшá *m & f*; ~**-wing** лéвый.

left-luggage office /left ˈlʌgɪdʒ ˈɒfɪs/ *n* кáмера хранéния.

leftovers /ˈleftˌəʊvəz/ *n pl* остáтки *m pl*; (*food*) объéдки (-ков) *pl*.

leg /leg/ *n* ногá; (*of furniture etc.*) нóжка; (*of journey etc.*) этáп.

legacy /ˈlegəsɪ/ *n* наслéдство.

legal /ˈli:g(ə)l/ *adj* (*of the law*) правовóй; (*lawful*) легáльный. **legality** /lɪˈgælɪtɪ/ *n* легáльность. **legalize** /ˈli:gəlaɪz/ *vt* легализúровать *impf & pf*.

legend /ˈledʒ(ə)nd/ *n* легéнда.

legendary /-dʒəndərɪ/ *adj* легендáрный. **leggings** /ˈlegɪŋz/ *n pl* вя́заные рейту́зы (-з) *pl.* **legible** /ˈledʒɪb(ə)l/ *adj* разбóрчивый. **legion** /ˈliːdʒ(ə)n/ *n* легиóн. **legislate** /ˈledʒɪsˌleɪt/ *vi* издавáть *impf*, издáть *pf* закóны. **legislation** /-ˈleɪʃ(ə)n/ *n* законодáтельство. **legislative** /ˈledʒɪslətɪv/ *adj* законодáтельный. **legislator** /ˈledʒɪsˌleɪtə(r)/ *n* законодáтель *m*. **legislature** /ˈledʒɪsˌlətʃə(r)/ *n* законодáтельные учреждéния *neut pl.*

legitimacy /lɪˈdʒɪtɪməsɪ/ *n* закóнность; (*of child*) законнорождённость. **legitimate** /-mət/ *adj* закóнный; (*child*) законнорождённый. **legitimize** /-ˌmaɪz/ *vt* узакóнивать *impf*, узакóнить *pf.*

leisure /ˈleʒə(r)/ *n* свобóдное врéмя, досу́г; **at ~** на досу́ге. **leisurely** /-lɪ/ *adj* неторопли́вый.

lemon /ˈlemən/ *n* лимóн. **lemonade** /ˌleməˈneɪd/ *n* лимонáд.

lend /lend/ *vt* давáть *impf*, дать *pf* взаймы́ (**to** +*dat*); одáлживать *impf*, одолжи́ть *pf* (**to** +*dat*).

length /leŋkθ/ *n* длинá; (*of time*) продолжи́тельность; (*of cloth*) отрéз; **at ~** подрóбно. **lengthen** /ˈleŋθ(ə)n/ *vt* & *i* удлиня́ть(ся) *impf*, удлини́ть(ся) *pf.* **lengthways** *adv* в длину́, вдоль. **lengthy** /ˈleŋθɪ/ *adj* дли́нный.

leniency /ˈliːnɪənsɪ/ *n* снисходи́тельность. **lenient** /-ənt/ *adj* снисходи́тельный.

lens /lenz/ *n* ли́нза; (*phot*) объекти́в; (*anat*) хрустáлик.

Lent /lent/ *n* вели́кий пост.

lentil /ˈlentɪl/ *n* чечеви́ца.

Leo /ˈliːəʊ/ *n* Лев.

leopard /ˈlepəd/ *n* леопáрд.

leotard /ˈliːəˌtɑːd/ *n* трикó *neut indecl.*

leper /ˈlepə(r)/ *n* прокажённый *sb.* **leprosy** /ˈleprəsɪ/ *n* прокáза.

lesbian /ˈlezbɪən/ *n* лесбия́нка; *adj* лесби́йский.

lesion /ˈliːʒ(ə)n/ *n* повреждéние.

less /les/ *adj* мéньший; *adv* мéньше, мéнее; *prep* за вы́четом +*gen.*

lessee /leˈsiː/ *n* арендáтор.

lessen /ˈles(ə)n/ *vt* & *i* уменьшáть(ся) *impf*, умéньшить(ся) *pf.*

lesser /ˈlesə(r)/ *adj* мéньший.

lesson /ˈles(ə)n/ *n* урóк.

lest /lest/ *conj* (*in order that not*) чтóбы не; (*that*) как бы не.

let /let/ *n* (*lease*) сдáча в наём; *vt* (*allow*) позволя́ть *impf*, позвóлить *pf* +*dat*; разрешáть *impf*, разреши́ть *pf* +*dat*; (*rent out*) сдавáть *impf*, сдать *pf* внаём (**to** +*dat*); *v aux* (*imperative*) (*1st person*) давáй(те); (*3rd person*) пусть; **~ alone** не говоря́ ужé о+*prep*; **~ down** (*lower*) опускáть *impf*, опусти́ть *pf*; (*fail*) подводи́ть *impf*, подвести́ *pf*; (*disappoint*) разочарóвывать *impf*, разочаровáть *pf*; **~ go** выпускáть *impf*, вы́пустить *pf*; **~'s go** пойдёмте!; пошли́!; поéхали!; **~ in(to)** (*admit*) впускáть *impf*, впусти́ть *pf* в+*acc*; (*into secret*) посвящáть *impf*, посвяти́ть *pf* в+*acc*; **~ know** давáть *impf*, дать *pf* знать +*dat*; **~ off** (*gun*) вы́стрелить *pf* из+*gen*; (*not punish*) отпускáть *impf*, отпусти́ть *pf* без наказáния; **~ out** (*release, loosen*) выпускáть *impf*, вы́пустить *pf*; **~ through** пропускáть *impf*, пропусти́ть *pf*; **~ up** затиха́ть *impf*, зати́хнуть *pf*.

lethal /'li:θ(ə)l/ *adj* (*fatal*) смерте́льный; (*weapon*) смертоно́сный.

lethargic /lɪ'θɑ:dʒɪk/ *adj* летарги́ческий. **lethargy** /'leθədʒɪ/ *n* летарги́я.

letter /'letə(r)/ *n* письмо́; (*symbol*) бу́ква; (*printing*) ли́тера; **~-box** почто́вый я́щик. **lettering** /-rɪŋ/ *n* шрифт.

lettuce /'letɪs/ *n* сала́т.

leukaemia /lu:'ki:mɪə/ *n* лейкеми́я.

level /'lev(ə)l/ *n* у́ровень; *adj* ро́вный; **~ crossing** (железнодоро́жный) перее́зд; **~-headed** уравнове́шенный; *vt* (*make* ~) выра́внивать *impf*, вы́ровнять *pf*; (*sport*) сра́внивать *impf*, сравня́ть *pf*; (*gun*) наводи́ть *impf*, навести́ *pf* (**at** в, на, +*acc*); (*criticism*) направля́ть *impf*, напра́вить *pf* (**at** про́тив+*gen*).

lever /'li:və(r)/ *n* рыча́г. **leverage** /-rɪdʒ/ *n* де́йствие рычага́; (*influence*) влия́ние.

levity /'levɪtɪ/ *n* легкомы́слие.

levy /'levɪ/ *n* (*tax*) сбор; *vt* (*tax*) взима́ть *impf* (**from** с+*gen*).

lewd /lju:d/ *adj* (*lascivious*) похотли́вый; (*indecent*) са́льный.

lexicon /'leksɪkən/ *n* слова́рь *m*.

liability /,laɪə'bɪlɪtɪ/ *n* (*responsibility*) отве́тственность (**for** за+*acc*); (*burden*) обу́за. **liable** /'laɪəb(ə)l/ *adj* отве́тственный (**for** за+*acc*); (*susceptible*) подве́рженный (**to** +*dat*).

liaise /lɪ'eɪz/ *vi* подде́рживать *impf* связь (с+*instr*). **liaison** /-'eɪzɒn/ *n* связь; (*affair*) любо́вная связь.

liar /'laɪə(r)/ *n* лгун, ~ья.

libel /'laɪb(ə)l/ *n* клевета́; *vt* клевета́ть *impf*, на~ *pf* на+*acc*.

libellous /-bələs/ *adj* клеветни́ческий.

liberal /'lɪbər(ə)l/ *n* либера́л; *adj* либера́льный; (*generous*) ще́дрый.

liberate /'lɪbə,reɪt/ *vt* освобожда́ть *impf*, освободи́ть *pf*. **liberation** /-'reɪʃ(ə)n/ *n* освобожде́ние. **liberator** /'lɪbə,reɪtə(r)/ *n* освободи́тель *m*.

libertine /'lɪbə,ti:n/ *n* распу́тник.

liberty /'lɪbətɪ/ *n* свобо́да; **at ~** на свобо́де.

Libra /'li:brə/ *n* Весы́ (-со́в) *pl*.

librarian /laɪ'breərɪən/ *n* библиоте́карь *m*. **library** /'laɪbrərɪ/ *n* библиоте́ка.

libretto /lɪ'bretəʊ/ *n* либре́тто *neut indecl*.

licence[1] /'laɪs(ə)ns/ *n* (*permission, permit*) разреше́ние, лице́нзия; (*liberty*) (изли́шняя) во́льность. **license, -ce**[2] /'laɪs(ə)ns/ *vt* (*allow*) разреша́ть *impf*, разреши́ть *pf* +*dat*; дава́ть *impf*, дать *pf* пра́во +*dat*.

licentious /laɪ'senʃəs/ *adj* распу́щенный.

lichen /'laɪkən/ *n* лиша́йник.

lick /lɪk/ *n* лиза́ние; *vt* лиза́ть *impf*, лизну́ть *pf*.

lid /lɪd/ *n* кры́шка; (*eyelid*) ве́ко.

lie[1] /laɪ/ *n* (*untruth*) ложь; *vi* лгать *impf*, со~ *pf*.

lie[2] /laɪ/ *n*: **~ of the land** (*fig*) положе́ние веще́й; *vi* лежа́ть *impf*; (*be situated*) находи́ться *impf*; **~ down** ложи́ться *impf*, лечь *pf*; **~ in** остава́ться *impf* в посте́ли.

lieu /lju:/ *n*: **in ~ of** вме́сто+*gen*.

lieutenant /lef'tenənt/ *n* лейтена́нт.

life /laɪf/ *n* жизнь; (*way of* ~) о́браз жи́зни; (*energy*) жи́-

вость. **lifebelt** *n* спаса́тельный по́яс. **lifeboat** *n* спаса́тельная ло́дка. **lifebuoy** *n* спаса́тельный круг. **lifeguard** *n* спаса́тель *m*, -ница. **life-jacket** *n* спаса́тельный жиле́т. **lifeless** /-lɪs/ *adj* безжи́зненный. **lifelike** /-laɪk/ *adj* реалисти́чный. **lifeline** *n* спаса́тельный коне́ц. **lifelong** *adj* пожи́зненный. **life-size(d)** /-saɪz(d)/ *adj* в натура́льную величину́. **lifetime** *n* жизнь.

lift /lɪft/ *n* (*machine*) лифт, подъёмник; (*force*) подъёмная си́ла; **give s.o. a ~** подвози́ть *impf*, подвезти́ *pf*; *vt* & *i* поднима́ть(ся) *impf*, подня́ть(ся) *pf*.

ligament /ˈlɪgəmənt/ *n* свя́зка.

light[1] /laɪt/ *n* свет, освеще́ние; (*source of ~*) ого́нь *m*, ла́мпа, фона́рь *m*; *pl* (*traffic ~*) светофо́р; **can I have a ~?** мо́жно прикури́ть?; **~-bulb** ла́мпочка; *adj* (*bright*) све́тлый; (*pale*) бле́дный; *vt* & *i* (*ignite*) зажига́ть(ся) *impf*, заже́чь(ся) *pf*; *vt* (*illuminate*) освеща́ть *impf*, освети́ть *pf*; **~ up** освеща́ть(ся) *impf*, освети́ть(ся) *pf*; (*begin to smoke*) закури́ть *pf*.

light[2] /laɪt/ *adj* (*not heavy*) лёгкий; **~-hearted** беззабо́тный.

lighten[1] /ˈlaɪt(ə)n/ *vt* (*make lighter*) облегча́ть *impf*, облегчи́ть *pf*; (*mitigate*) смягча́ть *impf*, смягчи́ть *pf*.

lighten[2] /ˈlaɪt(ə)n/ *vt* (*illuminate*) освеща́ть *impf*, освети́ть *pf*; *vi* (*grow bright*) светле́ть *impf*, по~ *pf*.

lighter /ˈlaɪtə(r)/ *n* зажига́лка.

lighthouse /ˈlaɪthaʊs/ *n* мая́к.

lighting /ˈlaɪtɪŋ/ *n* освеще́ние.

lightning /ˈlaɪtnɪŋ/ *n* мо́лния.

lightweight /ˈlaɪtweɪt/ *n* (*sport*) легкове́с; *adj* легкове́сный.

like[1] /laɪk/ *adj* (*similar*) похо́жий (на+*acc*); **what is he ~?** что он за челове́к?

like[2] /laɪk/ *vt* нра́виться *impf*, по~ *pf impers*+*dat*: **I ~ him** он мне нра́вится; люби́ть *impf*; *vi* (*wish*) хоте́ть *impf*; **if you ~** е́сли хоти́те; **I should ~** я хоте́л бы; мне хоте́лось бы. **likeable** /ˈlaɪkəb(ə)l/ *adj* симпати́чный.

likelihood /ˈlaɪklɪˌhʊd/ *n* вероя́тность. **likely** /ˈlaɪklɪ/ *adj* (*probable*) вероя́тный; (*suitable*) подходя́щий.

liken /ˈlaɪkən/ *vt* уподобля́ть *impf*, уподо́бить *pf* (**to** +*dat*).

likeness /ˈlaɪknɪs/ *n* (*resemblance*) схо́дство; (*portrait*) портре́т.

likewise /ˈlaɪkwaɪz/ *adv* (*similarly*) подо́бно; (*also*) то́же, та́кже.

liking /ˈlaɪkɪŋ/ *n* вкус (**for** к+*dat*).

lilac /ˈlaɪlək/ *n* сире́нь; *adj* сире́невый.

lily /ˈlɪlɪ/ *n* ли́лия; **~ of the valley** ла́ндыш.

limb /lɪm/ *n* член.

limber /ˈlɪmbə(r)/ *vi*: **~ up** размина́ться *impf*, размя́ться *pf*.

limbo /ˈlɪmbəʊ/ *n* (*fig*) состоя́ние неопределённости.

lime[1] /laɪm/ *n* (*mineralogy*) и́звесть. **limelight** *n*: **in the ~** (*fig*) в це́нтре внима́ния. **limestone** *n* известня́к.

lime[2] /laɪm/ *n* (*fruit*) лайм.

lime[3] /laɪm/ *n* (*~-tree*) ли́па.

limit /ˈlɪmɪt/ *n* грани́ца, преде́л; *vt* ограни́чивать *impf*, ограни́чить *pf*. **limitation** /-ˈteɪʃ(ə)n/ *n* ограниче́ние. **limitless** /ˈlɪmɪtlɪs/ *adj* безграни́чный.

limousine /ˈlɪməˌziːn/ *n* лимузи́н.

limp[1] /lɪmp/ *n* хромота́; *vi* хрома́ть *impf*.

limp[2] /lɪmp/ *adj* мя́гкий; (*fig*) вя́лый.

limpid /ˈlɪmpɪd/ *adj* прозра́чный.

linchpin /ˈlɪntʃpɪn/ *n* чека́.

line[1] /laɪn/ *n* (*long mark*) ли́ния, черта́; (*transport, tel*) ли́ния; (*cord*) верёвка; (*wrinkle*) морщи́на; (*limit*) грани́ца; (*row*) ряд; (*of words*) строка́; (*of verse*) стих; *vt* (*paper*) линова́ть *impf*, раз~ *pf*; *vt* & *i* (~ *up*) выстра́ивать(ся) *impf*, вы́строить(ся) *pf* в ряд.

line[2] /laɪn/ *vt* (*clothes*) класть *impf*, положи́ть *pf* на подкла́дку.

lineage /ˈlɪnɪɪdʒ/ *n* происхожде́ние.

linear /ˈlɪnɪə(r)/ *adj* лине́йный.

lined[1] /laɪnd/ *adj* (*paper*) лино́ванный; (*face*) морщи́нистый.

lined[2] /laɪnd/ *adj* (*garment*) на подкла́дке.

linen /ˈlɪnɪn/ *n* полотно́; *collect* бельё.

liner /ˈlaɪnə(r)/ *n* ла́йнер.

linesman /ˈlaɪnzmən/ *n* боково́й судья́ *m*.

linger /ˈlɪŋɡə(r)/ *vi* заде́рживаться *impf*, задержа́ться *pf*.

lingerie /ˈlæ̃ʒərɪ/ *n* да́мское бельё.

lingering /ˈlɪŋɡərɪŋ/ *adj* (*illness*) затяжно́й.

lingo /ˈlɪŋɡəʊ/ *n* жарго́н.

linguist /ˈlɪŋɡwɪst/ *n* лингви́ст. **linguistic** /-ˈɡwɪstɪk/ *adj* лингвисти́ческий. **linguistics** /-ˈɡwɪstɪks/ *n* лингви́стика.

lining /ˈlaɪnɪŋ/ *n* (*clothing etc.*) подкла́дка; (*tech*) облицо́вка.

link /lɪŋk/ *n* (*of chain*) звено́; (*connection*) связь; *vt* соединя́ть *impf*, соедини́ть *pf*; свя́зывать *impf*, связа́ть *pf*.

lino(leum) /lɪˈnəʊlɪəm/ *n* лино́леум.

lintel /ˈlɪnt(ə)l/ *n* перемы́чка.

lion /ˈlaɪən/ *n* лев. **lioness** /-nɪs/ *n* льви́ца.

lip /lɪp/ *n* губа́; (*of vessel*) край. **lipstick** *n* губна́я пома́да.

liquefy /ˈlɪkwɪˌfaɪ/ *vt* & *i* превраща́ть(ся) *impf*, преврати́ть(ся) *pf* в жи́дкое состоя́ние.

liqueur /lɪˈkjʊə(r)/ *n* ликёр.

liquid /ˈlɪkwɪd/ *n* жи́дкость; *adj* жи́дкий.

liquidate /ˈlɪkwɪˌdeɪt/ *vt* ликвиди́ровать *impf* & *pf*. **liquidation** /-ˈdeɪʃ(ə)n/ *n* ликвида́ция; **go into ~** ликвиди́роваться *impf* & *pf*.

liquor /ˈlɪkə(r)/ *n* (спиртно́й) напи́ток.

liquorice /ˈlɪkərɪs/ *n* лакри́ца.

list[1] /lɪst/ *n* спи́сок; *vt* составля́ть *impf*, соста́вить *pf* спи́сок +*gen*; (*enumerate*) перечисля́ть *impf*, перечи́слить *pf*.

list[2] /lɪst/ *vi* (*naut*) накреня́ться *impf*, крени́ться *impf*, накрени́ться *pf*.

listen /ˈlɪs(ə)n/ *vi* слу́шать *impf*, по~ *pf* (**to** +*acc*). **listener** /-nə(r)/ *n* слу́шатель *m*.

listless /ˈlɪstlɪs/ *adj* апати́чный.

litany /ˈlɪtənɪ/ *n* лита́ния.

literacy /ˈlɪtərəsɪ/ *n* гра́мотность.

literal /ˈlɪtər(ə)l/ *adj* буква́льный.

literary /ˈlɪtərərɪ/ *adj* литерату́рный.

literate /ˈlɪtərət/ *adj* гра́мотный.

literature /ˈlɪtərətʃə(r)/ *n* литерату́ра.

lithe /laɪð/ *adj* ги́бкий.

lithograph /ˈlɪθəˌɡrɑːf/ *n* литография.

Lithuania /ˌlɪθuːˈeɪnɪə/ *n* Литвá. **Lithuanian** /-nɪən/ *n* литóвец, -вка; *adj* литóвский.

litigation /ˌlɪtɪˈgeɪʃ(ə)n/ *n* тя́жба.

litre /ˈliːtə(r)/ *n* литр.

litter /ˈlɪtə(r)/ *n* (*rubbish*) сор; (*brood*) помёт; *vt* (*make untidy*) сори́ть *impf*, на∼ *pf* (**with** +*instr*).

little /ˈlɪt(ə)l/ *n* немнóгое; ∼ **by** ∼ мáло-помáлу; **a** ∼ немнóго +*gen*; *adj* мáленький, небольшóй; (*in height*) небольшóго рóста; (*in distance, time*) корóткий; *adv* мáло, немнóго.

liturgy /ˈlɪtədʒɪ/ *n* литурги́я.

live[1] /laɪv/ *adj* живóй; (*coals*) горя́щий; (*mil*) боевóй; (*electr*) под напряжéнием; (*broadcast*) прямóй.

live[2] /lɪv/ *vi* жить *impf*; ∼ **down** заглáживать *impf*, заглáдить *pf*; ∼ **on** (*feed on*) питáться *impf* +*instr*; ∼ **through** пережи-вáть *impf*, пережи́ть *pf*; ∼ **until, to see** доживáть *impf*, дожи́ть *pf* до+*gen*; ∼ **up to** жить *impf* соглáсно +*dat*.

livelihood /ˈlaɪvlɪˌhʊd/ *n* срéдства *neut pl* к жи́зни.

lively /ˈlaɪvlɪ/ *adj* живóй.

liven (up) /ˈlaɪv(ə)n (ʌp)/ *vt & i* оживля́ть(ся) *impf*, оживи́ть(ся) *pf*.

liver /ˈlɪvə(r)/ *n* пéчень; (*cul*) печёнка.

livery /ˈlɪvərɪ/ *n* ливрéя.

livestock /ˈlaɪvstɒk/ *n* скот.

livid /ˈlɪvɪd/ *adj* (*angry*) взбешённый.

living /ˈlɪvɪŋ/ *n* срéдства *neut pl* к жи́зни; **earn a** ∼ зарабáтывать *impf*, заработáть *pf* на жизнь; *adj* живóй; ∼**-room** гости́ная *sb*.

lizard /ˈlɪzəd/ *n* я́щерица.

load /ləʊd/ *n* груз; (*also fig*) брéмя *neut*; (*electr*) нагру́зка; *pl* (*lots*) ку́ча; *vt* (*goods*) грузи́ть *impf*, по∼ *pf*; (*vehicle*) грузи́ть *impf*, на∼ *pf*; (*fig*) обременя́ть *impf*, обремени́ть *pf*; (*gun, camera*) заряжáть *impf*, заряди́ть *pf*.

loaf[1] /ləʊf/ *n* бухáнка.

loaf[2] /ləʊf/ *vi* бездéльничать *impf*. **loafer** /ˈləʊfə(r)/ *n* бездéльник.

loan /ləʊn/ *n* заём; *vt* давáть *impf*, дать *pf* взаймы́.

loath, loth /ləʊθ/ *predic*: **be** ∼ **to** не хотéть *impf* +*inf*.

loathe /ləʊð/ *vt* ненави́деть *impf*. **loathing** /ˈləʊðɪŋ/ *n* отвращéние. **loathsome** *adj* отврати́тельный.

lob /lɒb/ *vt* высокó подбрáсывать *impf*, подбрóсить *pf*.

lobby /ˈlɒbɪ/ *n* вестибю́ль *m*; (*parl*) кулуáры (-ров) *pl*.

lobe /ləʊb/ *n* (*of ear*) мóчка.

lobster /ˈlɒbstə(r)/ *n* омáр.

local /ˈləʊk(ə)l/ *adj* мéстный.

locality /ləʊˈkælɪtɪ/ *n* мéстность.

localized /ˈləʊkəˌlaɪzd/ *adj* локализóванный.

locate /ləʊˈkeɪt/ *vt* (*place*) помещáть *impf*, помести́ть *pf*; (*find*) находи́ть *impf*, найти́ *pf*; **be** ∼**d** находи́ться *impf*.

location /ləʊˈkeɪʃ(ə)n/ *n* (*position*) местонахождéние; **on** ∼ (*cin*) на нату́ре.

locative /ˈlɒkətɪv/ *adj* (*n*) мéстный (падéж).

lock[1] /lɒk/ *n* (*of hair*) лóкон; *pl* вóлосы (-óс, -осáм) *pl*.

lock[2] /lɒk/ *n* замóк; (*canal*) шлюз; *vt & i* запирáть(ся) *impf*, заперéть(ся) *pf*; ∼ **out** не впускáть *impf*; ∼ **up** (*imprison*) сажáть *impf*, посади́ть *pf*;

(*close*) закрыва́ть(ся) *impf*, закры́ть(ся) *pf*.
locker /ˈlɒkə(r)/ *n* шка́фчик.
locket /ˈlɒkɪt/ *n* медальо́н.
locksmith /ˈlɒksmɪθ/ *n* сле́сарь *m*.
locomotion /ˌləʊkəˈməʊʃ(ə)n/ *n* передвиже́ние. **locomotive** /-ˈməʊtɪv/ *n* локомоти́в.
lodge /lɒdʒ/ *n* (*hunting*) (охо́тничий) до́мик; (*porter's*) сторо́жка; (*Masonic*) ло́жа; *vt* (*complaint*) подава́ть *impf*, пода́ть *pf*; *vi* (*reside*) жить *impf* (**with** у+*gen*); (*stick*) заса́живать *impf*, засе́сть *pf*. **lodger** /-dʒə(r)/ *n* жиле́ц, жили́ца. **lodging** /-dʒɪŋ/ *n* (*also pl*) кварти́ра, (снима́емая) ко́мната.
loft /lɒft/ *n* (*attic*) черда́к.
lofty /ˈlɒftɪ/ *adj* о́чень высо́кий; (*elevated*) возвы́шенный.
log /lɒg/ *n* бревно́; (*for fire*) поле́но; **~-book** (*naut*) ва́хтенный журна́л.; *vi*: **~ off** (*comput*) выходи́ть *impf*, вы́йти *pf* из систе́мы; **~ on** (*comput*) входи́ть *impf*, войти́ *pf* в систе́му.
logarithm /ˈlɒgəˌrɪð(ə)m/ *n* логари́фм.
loggerhead /ˈlɒgəˌhed/ *n*: **be at ~s** быть в ссо́ре.
logic /ˈlɒdʒɪk/ *n* ло́гика. **logical** /-k(ə)l/ *adj* (*of logic*) логи́ческий; (*consistent*) логи́чный.
logistics /ləˈdʒɪstɪks/ *n pl* организа́ция; (*mil*) материа́льно-техни́ческое обеспе́чение.
logo /ˈləʊgəʊ/ *n* эмбле́ма.
loin /lɔɪn/ *n* (*pl*) поясни́ца; (*cul*) филе́йная часть.
loiter /ˈlɔɪtə(r)/ *vi* слоня́ться *impf*.
lone, lonely /ləʊn, ˈləʊnlɪ/ *adj* одино́кий. **loneliness** /ˈləʊnlɪnɪs/ *n* одино́чество.
long¹ /lɒŋ/ *vi* (*want*) стра́стно жела́ть *impf*, по**~** *pf* (**for** +*gen*); (*miss*) тоскова́ть *impf* (**for** по+*dat*).
long² /lɒŋ/ *adj* (*space*) дли́нный; (*time*) до́лгий; (*in measurements*) длино́й в+*acc*; **in the ~ run** в коне́чном счёте; **~-sighted** дальнозо́ркий; **~-suffering** долготерпели́вый; **~-term** долгосро́чный; **~-winded** многоречи́вый; *adv* до́лго; **~ ago** (уже́) давно́; **as ~ as** пока́; **~ before** задо́лго до+*gen*.
longevity /lɒnˈdʒevɪtɪ/ *n* долгове́чность.
longing /ˈlɒŋɪŋ/ *n* стра́стное жела́ние (**for** +*gen*); тоска́ (**for** по+*dat*); *adj* тоску́ющий.
longitude /ˈlɒŋgɪˌtjuːd/ *n* долгота́.
longways /ˈlɒŋweɪz/ *adv* в длину́.
look /lʊk/ *n* (*glance*) взгляд; (*appearance*) вид; (*expression*) выраже́ние; *vi* смотре́ть *impf*, по**~** *pf* (**at** на, в, +*acc*); (*appear*) вы́глядеть *impf* +*instr*; (*face*) выходи́ть *impf* (**towards, onto** на+*acc*); **~ about** осма́триваться *impf*, осмотре́ться *pf*; **~ after** (*attend to*) присма́тривать *impf*, присмотре́ть *pf* за+*instr*; **~ down on** презира́ть *impf*; **~ for** иска́ть *impf* +*acc*, +*gen*; **~ forward to** предвкуша́ть *impf*, предвкуси́ть *pf*; **~ in on** загля́дывать *impf*, загляну́ть *pf* к+*dat*; **~ into** (*investigate*) рассма́тривать *impf*, рассмотре́ть *pf*; **~ like** быть похо́жим на+*acc*; **it ~s like rain** похо́же на (то, что бу́дет) дождь; **~ on** (*regard*) счита́ть *impf*, счесть *pf* (**as** +*instr*, за+*instr*); **~ out** выгля́дывать *impf*, вы́глянуть *pf* (в окно́); быть настороже́;

imper осторо́жно!; ~ **over, through** просма́тривать *impf*, просмотре́ть *pf*; ~ **round** (*inspect*) осма́тривать *impf*, осмотре́ть *pf*; ~ **up** (*raise eyes*) поднима́ть *impf*, подня́ть *pf* глаза́; (*in dictionary etc.*) иска́ть *impf*; (*improve*) улучша́ться *impf*, улу́чшиться *pf*; ~ **up to** уважа́ть *impf*.

loom[1] /lu:m/ *n* тка́цкий стано́к.

loom[2] /lu:m/ *vi* вырисо́вываться *impf*, вы́рисоваться; (*fig*) надвига́ться *impf*.

loop /lu:p/ *n* пе́тля; *vi* образо́вывать *impf*, образова́ть *pf* пе́тлю; (*fasten with loop*) закрепля́ть *impf*, закрепи́ть *pf* петлёй; (*wind*) обма́тывать *impf*, обмота́ть *pf* (**around** вокру́г+*gen*).

loophole /'lu:phəʊl/ *n* бойни́ца; (*fig*) лазе́йка.

loose /lu:s/ *adj* (*free*; *not tight*) свобо́дный; (*not fixed*) неприкреплённый; (*connection, screw*) сла́бый; (*lax*) распу́щенный; **at a ~ end** без де́ла. **loosen** /-s(ə)n/ *vt* & *i* ослабля́ть(ся) *impf*, осла́бить(ся) *pf*.

loot /lu:t/ *n* добы́ча; *vt* гра́бить *impf*, о~ *pf*.

lop /lɒp/ *vt* (*tree*) подреза́ть *impf*, подре́зать *pf*; (~ *off*) отруба́ть *impf*, отруби́ть *pf*.

lope /ləʊp/ *vi* бе́гать *indet*, бежа́ть *det* вприпры́жку.

lopsided /lɒp'saɪdɪd/ *adj* кривобо́кий.

loquacious /lɒ'kweɪʃəs/ *adj* болтли́вый.

lord /lɔ:d/ *n* (*master*) господи́н; (*eccl*) Госпо́дь; (*peer*; *title*) лорд; *vt*: ~ **it over** помыка́ть *impf* +*instr*. **lordship** *n* (*title*) све́тлость.

lore /lɔ:(r)/ *n* зна́ния *neut pl.*

lorry /'lɒrɪ/ *n* грузови́к.

lose /lu:z/ *vt* теря́ть *impf*, по~ *pf*; *vt* & *i* (*game etc.*) прои́грывать *impf*, проигра́ть *pf*; *vi* (*clock*) отстава́ть *impf*, отста́ть *pf*. **loss** /lɒs/ *n* поте́ря; (*monetary*) убы́ток; (*in game*) про́игрыш.

lot /lɒt/ *n* жре́бий; (*destiny*) у́часть; (*of goods*) па́ртия; **a ~, ~s** мно́го; **the ~** всё, все *pl.*

loth /ləʊθ/ *see* **loath**

lotion /'ləʊʃ(ə)n/ *n* лосьо́н.

lottery /'lɒtərɪ/ *n* лотере́я.

loud /laʊd/ *adj* (*sound*) гро́мкий; (*noisy*) шу́мный; (*colour*) крича́щий; **out ~** вслух. **loudspeaker** *n* громкоговори́тель *m*.

lounge /laʊndʒ/ *n* гости́ная *sb*; *vi* сиде́ть *impf* разваля́сь; (*idle*) безде́льничать *impf*.

louse /laʊs/ *n* вошь. **lousy** /'laʊzɪ/ *adj* (*coll*) парши́вый.

lout /laʊt/ *n* балбе́с, у́валень *m*.

lovable /'lʌvəb(ə)l/ *adj* ми́лый. **love** /lʌv/ *n* любо́вь (**of, for** к+*dat*); **in ~ with** влюблённый в+*acc*; *vt* люби́ть *impf*. **lovely** /'lʌvlɪ/ *adj* прекра́сный; (*delightful*) преле́стный. **lover** /'lʌvə(r)/ *n* любо́вник, -ица.

low /ləʊ/ *adj* ни́зкий, невысо́кий; (*quiet*) ти́хий.

lower[1] /'ləʊə(r)/ *vt* опуска́ть *impf*, опусти́ть *pf*; (*price, voice, standard*) понижа́ть *impf*, пони́зить *pf*.

lower[2] /'ləʊə(r)/ *adj* ни́жний.

lowland /'ləʊlənd/ *n* ни́зменность.

lowly /'ləʊlɪ/ *adj* скро́мный.

loyal /'lɔɪəl/ *adj* ве́рный. **loyalty** /-tɪ/ *n* ве́рность.

LP *abbr* (*of* **long-playing record**) долгоигра́ющая пласти́нка.

Ltd. *abbr* (*of* **Limited**) с ограни́ченной отве́тственностью.

lubricant /'lu:brɪkənt/ *n* сма́зка. **lubricate** /-ˌkeɪt/ *vt* сма́зывать *impf*, сма́зать *pf*. **lubrication** /-'keɪʃ(ə)n/ *n* сма́зка.

lucid /'lu:sɪd/ *adj* я́сный. **lucidity** /ˌlu:'sɪdɪtɪ/ *n* я́сность.

luck /lʌk/ *n* (*chance*) слу́чай; (*good* ~) сча́стье, уда́ча; (*bad* ~) неуда́ча. **luckily** /-kɪlɪ/ *adv* к сча́стью. **lucky** /-kɪ/ *adj* счастли́вый; **be** ~ везти́ *imp*, по~ *pf impers* +*dat*: **I was** ~ мне повезло́.

lucrative /'lu:krətɪv/ *adj* при́быльный.

ludicrous /'lu:dɪkrəs/ *adj* смехотво́рный.

lug /lʌg/ *vt* (*drag*) таска́ть *indet*, тащи́ть *det*.

luggage /'lʌgɪdʒ/ *n* бага́ж.

lugubrious /lʊ'gu:brɪəs/ *adj* печа́льный.

lukewarm /lu:k'wɔ:m/ *adj* теплова́тый; (*fig*) прохла́дный.

lull /lʌl/ *n* (*in storm*) зати́шье; (*interval*) переры́в; *vt* (*to sleep*) убаю́кивать *impf*, убаю́кать *pf*; (*suspicions*) усыпля́ть *impf*, усыпи́ть *pf*.

lullaby /'lʌləˌbaɪ/ *n* колыбе́льная пе́сня.

lumbar /'lʌmbə(r)/ *adj* поясни́чный.

lumber[1] /'lʌmbə(r)/ *vi* (*move*) брести́ *impf*.

lumber[2] /'lʌmbə(r)/ *n* (*domestic*) ру́хлядь; *vt* обременя́ть *impf*, обремени́ть *pf*. **lumberjack** /'lʌmbədʒæk/ *n* лесору́б.

luminary /'lu:mɪnərɪ/ *n* свети́ло.

luminous /'lu:mɪnəs/ *adj* светя́щийся.

lump /lʌmp/ *n* ком; (*swelling*) о́пухоль; *vt*: ~ **together** сме́шивать *impf*, смеша́ть *pf* (в одно́).

lunacy /'lu:nəsɪ/ *n* безу́мие.

lunar /'lu:nə(r)/ *adj* лу́нный.

lunatic /'lu:nətɪk/ *adj* (*n*) сумасше́дший (*sb*).

lunch /lʌntʃ/ *n* обе́д; ~**-hour**, ~**-time** обе́денный переры́в; *vi* обе́дать *impf*, по~ *pf*.

lung /lʌŋ/ *n* лёгкое *sb*.

lunge /lʌndʒ/ *vi* де́лать *impf*, с~ *pf* вы́пад (**at** про́тив+*gen*).

lurch[1] /lɜ:tʃ/ *n*: **leave in the** ~ покида́ть *impf*, поки́нуть *pf* в беде́.

lurch[2] /lɜ:tʃ/ *vi* (*stagger*) ходи́ть *indet*, идти́ *det* шата́ясь.

lure /ljʊə(r)/ *n* прима́нка; *vt* прима́нивать *impf*, примани́ть *pf*.

lurid /'ljʊərɪd/ *adj* (*gaudy*) крича́щий; (*details*) жу́ткий.

lurk /lɜ:k/ *vi* зата́иваться *impf*, затаи́ться *pf*.

luscious /'lʌʃəs/ *adj* со́чный.

lush /lʌʃ/ *adj* пы́шный, со́чный.

lust /lʌst/ *n* по́хоть (**of, for** к+*dat*); *vi* стра́стно жела́ть *impf*, по~ *pf* (**for** +*gen*). **lustful** /-fʊl/ *adj* похотли́вый.

lustre /'lʌstə(r)/ *n* гля́нец. **lustrous** /'lʌstrəs/ *adj* глянцеви́тый.

lusty /'lʌstɪ/ *adj* (*healthy*) здоро́вый; (*lively*) живо́й.

lute /lu:t/ *n* (*mus*) лю́тня.

luxuriant /lʌg'zjʊərɪənt/ *adj* пы́шный.

luxuriate /lʌg'zjʊərɪˌeɪt/ *vi* наслажда́ться *impf*, наслади́ться *pf* (**in** +*instr*).

luxurious /lʌg'zjʊərɪəs/ *adj* роско́шный. **luxury** /'lʌgʒərɪ/ *n* ро́скошь.

lymph /lɪmf/ *attrib* лимфати́ческий.

lynch /lɪntʃ/ *vt* линчева́ть *impf* & *pf*.

lyric /'lɪrɪk/ *n* ли́рика; *pl* слова́

neut pl пе́сни. **lyrical** /-k(ə)l/ *adj* лири́ческий.

M

MA *abbr* (*of* **Master of Arts**) маги́стр гуманита́рных нау́к.
macabre /məˈkɑːbr(ə)/ *adj* жу́ткий.
macaroni /ˌmækəˈrəʊnɪ/ *n* макаро́ны (-н) *pl*.
mace /meɪs/ *n* (*of office*) жезл.
machination /ˌmækɪˈneɪʃ(ə)n/ *n* махина́ция.
machine /məˈʃiːn/ *n* маши́на; (*state* ~) аппара́т; *attrib* маши́нный; **~-gun** пулемёт; **~ tool** стано́к; *vt* обраба́тывать *impf*, обрабо́тать *pf* на станке́; (*sew*) шить *impf*, с~ *pf* (на маши́не). **machinery** /-nərɪ/ *n* (*machines*) маши́ны *f pl*; (*of state*) аппара́т. **machinist** /-nɪst/ *n* машини́ст; (*sewing*) шве́йник, -ица, швея́.
mackerel /ˈmækr(ə)l/ *n* ску́мбрия, макре́ль.
mackintosh /ˈmækɪnˌtɒʃ/ *n* плащ.
mad /mæd/ *adj* сумасше́дший. **madden** /ˈmæd(ə)n/ *vt* беси́ть *impf*, вз~ *pf*. **madhouse** *n* сумасше́дший дом. **madly** /-lɪ/*adv* безу́мно. **madman** *n* сумасше́дший *sb*. **madness** /-nɪs/ *n* сумасше́ствие. **madwoman** *n* сумасше́дшая *sb*.
madrigal /ˈmædrɪg(ə)l/ *n* мадрига́л.
maestro /ˈmaɪstrəʊ/ *n* маэ́стро *m indecl*.
Mafia /ˈmæfɪə/ *n* ма́фия.
magazine /ˌmægəˈziːn/ *n* журна́л; (*of gun*) магази́н.
maggot /ˈmægət/ *n* личи́нка.
magic /ˈmædʒɪk/ *n* ма́гия, волшебство́; *adj* (*also* **magical**) волше́бный. **magician** /məˈdʒɪʃ(ə)n/ *n* волше́бник; (*conjurer*) фо́кусник.
magisterial /ˌmædʒɪˈstɪərɪəl/ *adj* авторите́тный.
magistrate /ˈmædʒɪstrət/ *n* судья́ *m*.
magnanimity /ˌmægnəˈnɪmɪtɪ/ *n* великоду́шие. **magnanimous** /mægˈnænɪməs/ *adj* великоду́шный.
magnate /ˈmægneɪt/ *n* магна́т.
magnesium /mægˈniːzɪəm/ *n* ма́гний.
magnet /ˈmægnɪt/ *n* магни́т. **magnetic** /-ˈnetɪk/ *adj* магни́тный; (*attractive*) притяга́тельный. **magnetism** /ˈmægnɪˌtɪz(ə)m/ *n* магнети́зм; притяга́тельность. **magnetize** /ˈmægnɪˌtaɪz/ *vt* намагни́чивать *impf*, намагни́тить *pf*.
magnification /ˌmægnɪfɪˈkeɪʃ(ə)n/ *n* увеличе́ние.
magnificence /mægˈnɪfɪs(ə)ns/ *n* великоле́пие. **magnificent** /-s(ə)nt/ *adj* великоле́пный.
magnify /ˈmægnɪˌfaɪ/ *vt* увели́чивать *impf*, увели́чить *pf*; (*exaggerate*) преувели́чивать *impf*, преувели́чить *pf*. **magnifying glass** /-ˌfaɪɪŋ glɑːs/ *n* увеличи́тельное стекло́.
magnitude /ˈmægnɪˌtjuːd/ *n* величина́; (*importance*) ва́жность.
magpie /ˈmægpaɪ/ *n* соро́ка.
mahogany /məˈhɒgənɪ/ *n* кра́сное де́рево.
maid /meɪd/ *n* прислу́га. **maiden** /ˈmeɪd(ə)n/ *adj* (*aunt etc.*) незаму́жняя; (*first*) пе́рвый; **~ name** де́вичья фами́лия.
mail /meɪl/ *n* (*letters*) по́чта; **~ order** почто́вый зака́з; *vt* по-

сыла́ть *impf*, посла́ть *pf* по по́чте.
maim /meɪm/ *vt* калéчить *impf*, ис~ *pf*.
main /meɪn/ *n* (*gas* ~; *pl*) магистра́ль; **in the** ~ в основно́м; *adj* основно́й, гла́вный; (*road*) магистра́льный. **mainland** *n* матери́к. **mainly** /-lɪ/ *adv* в основно́м. **mainstay** *n* (*fig*) гла́вная опо́ра.
maintain /meɪn'teɪn/ *vt* (*keep up*) поддéрживать *impf*, поддержа́ть *pf*; (*family*) содержа́ть *impf*; (*machine*) обслу́живать *impf*, обслужи́ть *pf*; (*assert*) утвержда́ть *impf*. **maintenance** /'meɪntənəns/ *n* поддéржка; содержа́ние; обслу́живание.
maize /meɪz/ *n* кукуру́за.
majestic /mə'dʒestɪk/ *adj* вели́чественный. **majesty** /'mædʒɪstɪ/ *n* вели́чественность; (*title*) вели́чество.
major[1] /'meɪdʒə(r)/ *n* (*mil*) майо́р.
major[2] /'meɪdʒə(r)/ *adj* (*greater*) бо́льший; (*more important*) бо́лее ва́жный; (*main*) гла́вный; (*mus*) мажо́рный; *n* (*mus*) мажо́р. **majority** /mə'dʒɒrɪtɪ/ *n* большинство́; (*full age*) совершенноле́тие.
make /meɪk/ *vt* дéлать *impf*, с~ *pf*; (*produce*) производи́ть *impf*, произвести́ *pf*; (*prepare*) гото́вить *impf*, при~ *pf*; (*amount to*) равня́ться *impf* +*dat*; (*earn*) зараба́тывать *impf*, зарабо́тать *pf*; (*compel*) заставля́ть *impf*, заста́вить *pf*; (*reach*) добира́ться *impf*, добра́ться *pf* до+*gen*; (*be in time for*) успева́ть *impf*, успе́ть *pf* на+*acc*; **be made of** состоя́ть *impf* из+*gen*; ~ **as if, though** дéлать *impf*, с~ *pf* вид, что; ~ **a bed** стели́ть *impf*, по~ *pf* постéль; ~ **believe** притворя́ться *impf*, притвори́ться *pf*; ~**-believe** притво́рство; ~ **do with** дово́льствоваться *impf*, у~ *pf* +*instr*; ~ **off** удира́ть *impf*, удра́ть *pf*; ~ **out** (*cheque*) выпи́сывать *impf*, вы́писать *pf*; (*assert*) утвержда́ть *impf*, утверди́ть *pf*; (*understand*) разбира́ть *impf*, разобра́ть *pf*; ~ **over** передава́ть *impf*, переда́ть *pf*; ~ **up** (*form, compose, complete*) составля́ть *impf*, соста́вить *pf*; (*invent*) выду́мывать *impf*, вы́думать *pf*; (*theat*) гримирова́ть(ся) *impf*, за~ *pf*; ~**-up** (*theat*) грим; (*cosmetics*) космéтика; (*composition*) соста́в; ~ **it up** мири́ться *impf*, по~ *pf* (**with** с+*instr*); ~ **up for** возмеща́ть *impf*, возмести́ть *pf*; ~ **up one's mind** реша́ться *impf*, реши́ться *pf*. **make** /meɪk/ *n* ма́рка. **makeshift** *adj* врéменный.
malady /'mælədɪ/ *n* болéзнь.
malaise /mə'leɪz/ *n* (*fig*) беспоко́йство.
malaria /mə'leərɪə/ *n* маляри́я.
male /meɪl/ *n* (*animal*) самéц; (*person*) мужчи́на *m*; *adj* мужско́й.
malevolence /mə'levələns/ *n* недоброжела́тельность. **malevolent** /-lənt/ *adj* недоброжела́тельный.
malice /'mælɪs/ *n* зло́ба. **malicious** /mə'lɪʃ(ə)s/ *adj* зло́бный.
malign /mə'laɪn/ *vt* клевета́ть *impf*, на~ *pf* на+*acc*. **malignant** /-'lɪgnənt/ *adj* (*harmful*) зловрéдный; (*malicious*) зло́бный; (*med*) злока́чественный.
malinger /mə'lɪŋgə(r)/ *vi* притворя́ться *impf*, притвори́ться *pf* больны́м. **malingerer** /-rə(r)/

n симулянт.
mallard /'mælɑ:d/ *n* кряква.
malleable /'mælɪəb(ə)l/ *adj* ковкий; (*fig*) податливый.
mallet /'mælɪt/ *n* (деревянный) молоток.
malnutrition /ˌmælnju:'trɪʃ(ə)n/ *n* недоедание.
malpractice /mæl'præktɪs/ *n* преступная небрежность.
malt /mɔ:lt/ *n* солод.
maltreat /mæl'tri:t/ *vt* плохо обращаться *impf* с+*instr.*
mammal /'mæm(ə)l/ *n* млекопитающее *sb.*
mammoth /'mæməθ/ *adj* громадный.
man /mæn/ *n* (*human, person*) человек; (*human race*) человечество; (*male*) мужчина *m*; (*labourer*) рабочий *sb*; *pl* (*soldiers*) солдаты *m pl*; *vt* (*furnish with men*) укомплектовывать *impf*, укомплектовать *pf* личным составом; ставить *impf*, по~ *pf* людей к+*dat*; (*stall etc.*) обслуживать *impf*, обслужить *pf*; (*gate, checkpoint*) стоять *impf* на+*prep.*
manacle /'mænək(ə)l/ *n* наручник; *vt* надевать *impf*, надеть *pf* наручники на+*acc.*
manage /'mænɪdʒ/ *vt* (*control*) управлять *impf* +*instr*; *vi*(& *t*) (*cope*) справляться *impf*, справиться *pf* (с+*instr*); (*succeed*) суметь *pf*. **management** /-mənt/ *n* управление (**of** +*instr*); (*the* ~) администрация. **manager** /-dʒə(r)/ *n* управляющий *sb* (**of** +*instr*); менеджер. **managerial** /-'dʒɪərɪəl/ *adj* административный. **managing director** /'mænɪdʒɪŋ daɪ'rektə(r)/ *n* директор-распорядитель *m.*
mandarin /'mændərɪn/ *n* мандарин.
mandate /'mændeɪt/ *n* мандат. **mandated** /-tɪd/ *adj* подмандатный. **mandatory** /-dətərɪ/ *adj* обязательный.
mane /meɪn/ *n* грива.
manful /'mænfʊl/ *adj* мужественный.
manganese /'mæŋgəˌni:z/ *n* марганец.
manger /'meɪndʒə(r)/ *n* ясли (-лей) *pl*; **dog in the** ~ собака на сене.
mangle /'mæŋg(ə)l/ *vt* (*mutilate*) калечить *impf*, ис~ *pf.*
mango /'mæŋgəʊ/ *n* манго *neut indecl.*
manhandle /'mænˌhænd(ə)l/ *vt* грубо обращаться *impf* с+*instr.*
manhole /'mænhəʊl/ *n* смотровой колодец.
manhood /'mænhʊd/ *n* возмужалость.
mania /'meɪnɪə/ *n* мания. **maniac** /'meɪnɪˌæk/ *n* маньяк, -ячка. **manic** /'mænɪk/ *adj* маниакальный.
manicure /'mænɪˌkjʊə(r)/ *n* маникюр; *vt* делать *impf*, с~ *pf* маникюр +*dat.* **manicurist** /-ˌkjʊərɪst/ *n* маникюрша.
manifest /'mænɪˌfest/ *adj* очевидный; *vt* (*display*) проявлять *impf*, проявить *pf*; *n* манифест. **manifestation** /-'teɪʃ(ə)n/ *n* проявление. **manifesto** /-'festəʊ/ *n* манифест.
manifold /'mænɪˌfəʊld/ *adj* разнообразный.
manipulate /mə'nɪpjʊˌleɪt/ *vt* манипулировать *impf* +*instr.* **manipulation** /-'leɪʃ(ə)n/ *n* манипуляция.
manly /'mænlɪ/ *adj* мужественный.
mankind /mæn'kaɪnd/ *n* человечество.

manner /ˈmænə(r)/ *n* (*way*) óбраз; (*behaviour*) манéра; *pl* манéры *f pl.* **mannerism** /ˈmænərɪz(ə)m/ *n* манéра.

mannish /ˈmænɪʃ/ *adj* мужеподóбный.

manoeuvrable /məˈnuːvrəb(ə)l/ *adj* манёвренный. **manoeuvre** /-ˈnuːvə(r)/ *n* манёвр; *vt* & *i* маневрúровать *impf.*

manor /ˈmænə(r)/ *n* помéстье; (*house*) помéщичий дом.

manpower /ˈmæn,paʊə(r)/ *n* человéческие ресýрсы *m pl.*

manservant /ˈmæn,sɜːv(ə)nt/ *n* слугá *m.*

mansion /ˈmænʃ(ə)n/ *n* особня́к.

manslaughter /ˈmæn,slɔːtə(r)/ *n* непредумы́шленное убúйство.

mantelpiece /ˈmænt(ə)l,piːs/ *n* камúнная доскá.

manual /ˈmænjʊəl/ *adj* ручнóй; *n* руковóдство. **manually** /-lɪ/ *adv* вручнýю.

manufacture /,mænjʊˈfæktʃə(r)/ *n* произвóдство; *vt* производúть *impf*, произвестú *pf.* **manufacturer** /-ˈfæktʃərə(r)/ *n* фабрикáнт.

manure /məˈnjʊə(r)/ *n* навóз.

manuscript /ˈmænjʊskrɪpt/ *n* рýкопись.

many /ˈmenɪ/ *adj* & *n* мнóго +*gen*, мнóгие *pl*; **how ~** скóлько +*gen.*

map /mæp/ *n* кáрта; (*of town*) план; *vt*: **~ out** намечáть *impf*, намéтить *pf.*

maple /ˈmeɪp(ə)l/ *n* клён.

mar /mɑː(r)/ *vt* пóртить *impf*, ис~ *pf.*

marathon /ˈmærəθ(ə)n/ *n* марафóн.

marauder /məˈrɔːdə(r)/ *n* мародёр. **marauding** /-dɪŋ/ *adj* мародёрский.

marble /ˈmɑːb(ə)l/ *n* мрáмор; (*toy*) шáрик; *attrib* мрáморный.

March /mɑːtʃ/ *n* март; *adj* мáртовский.

march /mɑːtʃ/ *vi* маршировáть *impf*, про~ *pf*; *n* марш.

mare /meə(r)/ *n* кобы́ла.

margarine /,mɑːdʒəˈriːn/ *n* маргарúн.

margin /ˈmɑːdʒɪn/ *n* (*on page*) пóле; (*edge*) край; **profit ~** прúбыль; **safety ~** запáс прóчности.

marigold /ˈmærɪ,gəʊld/ *n* ноготкú (-кóв) *pl.*

marijuana /,mærɪˈwɑːnə/ *n* марихуáна.

marina /məˈriːnə/ *n* марúна.

marinade /,mærɪˈneɪd/ *n* маринáд; *vt* маринoвáть *impf*, за~ *pf.*

marine /məˈriːn/ *adj* морскóй; *n* (*soldier*) солдáт морскóй пехóты; *pl* морскáя пехóта. **mariner** /ˈmærɪnə(r)/ *n* моря́к.

marital /ˈmærɪt(ə)l/ *adj* супрýжеский, брáчный.

maritime /ˈmærɪ,taɪm/ *adj* морскóй; (*near sea*) примóрский.

mark[1] /mɑːk/ *n* (*coin*) мáрка.

mark[2] /mɑːk/ *n* (*for distinguishing*) мéтка; (*sign*) знак; (*school*) отмéтка; (*trace*) след; **on your ~s** на стáрт!; *vt* (*indicate*; *celebrate*) отмечáть *impf*, отмéтить *pf*; (*school etc.*) проверя́ть *impf*, провéрить *pf*; (*stain*) пáчкать *impf*, за~ *pf*; (*sport*) закрывáть *impf*, закры́ть *pf*; **~ my words** попóмни(те) мои словá!; **~ out** размечáть *impf*, размéтить *pf.* **marker** /-kə(r)/ *n* знак; (*in book*) заклáдка.

market /ˈmɑːkɪt/ *n* ры́нок; **~ garden** огорóд; **~-place** базáрная площадь; *vt* продава́ть *impf*, прода́ть *pf*. **marketing** /-tɪŋ/ *n* маркети́нг.

marksman /ˈmɑːksmən/ *n* стрело́к.

marmalade /ˈmɑːməˌleɪd/ *n* апельси́новый джем.

maroon[1] /məˈruːn/ *adj* (*n*) (*colour*) тёмно-бордо́вый (цвет).

maroon[2] /məˈruːn/ *vt* (*put ashore*) выса́живать *impf*, вы́садить *pf* (на необита́емый о́стров); (*cut off*) отреза́ть *impf*, отре́зать *pf*.

marquee /mɑːˈkiː/ *n* тэнт.

marquis /ˈmɑːkwɪs/ *n* марки́з.

marriage /ˈmærɪdʒ/ *n* брак; (*wedding*) сва́дьба; *attrib* бра́чный. **marriageable** /-dʒəb(ə)l/ *adj*: ~ **age** бра́чный во́зраст. **married** /ˈmærɪd/ *adj* (*man*) жена́тый; (*woman*) заму́жняя, за́мужем; (*to each other*) жена́ты; (*of* ~ *persons*) супру́жеский.

marrow /ˈmærəʊ/ *n* ко́стный мозг; (*vegetable*) кабачо́к.

marry /ˈmærɪ/ *vt* (*of man*) жени́ться *impf* & *pf* на +*prep*; (*of woman*) выходи́ть *impf*, вы́йти *pf* за́муж за +*acc*; *vi* (*of couple*) пожени́ться *pf*.

marsh /mɑːʃ/ *n* боло́то. **marshy** /-ʃɪ/ *adj* боло́тистый.

marshal /ˈmɑːʃ(ə)l/ *n* ма́ршал; *vt* выстра́ивать *impf*, вы́строить *pf*; (*fig*) собира́ть *impf*, собра́ть *pf*.

marsupial /mɑːˈsuːpɪəl/ *n* су́мчатое живо́тное *sb*.

martial /ˈmɑːʃ(ə)l/ *adj* вое́нный; ~ **law** вое́нное положе́ние.

martyr /ˈmɑːtə(r)/ *n* му́ченик, -ица; *vt* му́чить *impf*, за~ *pf*. **martyrdom** /-dəm/ *n* му́ченичество.

marvel /ˈmɑːv(ə)l/ *n* чу́до; *vi* изумля́ться *impf*, изуми́ться *pf*. **marvellous** /-ləs/ *adj* чуде́сный.

Marxist /ˈmɑːksɪst/ *n* маркси́ст; *adj* маркси́стский. **Marxism** /-sɪz(ə)m/ *n* маркси́зм.

marzipan /ˈmɑːzɪˌpæn/ *n* марципа́н.

mascara /mæˈskɑːrə/ *n* тушь.

mascot /ˈmæskɒt/ *n* талисма́н.

masculine /ˈmæskjʊlɪn/ *adj* мужско́й; (*gram*) мужско́го ро́да; (*of woman*) мужепо-до́бный.

mash /mæʃ/ *n* карто́фельное пюре́ *neut indecl*; *vt* размина́ть *impf*, размя́ть *pf*.

mask /mɑːsk/ *n* ма́ска; *vt* маскирова́ть *impf*, за~ *pf*.

masochism /ˈmæsəˌkɪz(ə)m/ *n* мазохи́зм. **masochist** /-kɪst/ *n* мазохи́ст. **masochistic** /-ˈkɪstɪk/ *adj* мазохи́стский.

mason /ˈmeɪs(ə)n/ *n* ка́менщик; (**M~**) масо́н. **Masonic** /məˈsɒnɪk/ *adj* масо́нский. **masonry** /ˈmeɪʃənrɪ/ *n* ка́менная кла́дка.

masquerade /ˌmæskəˈreɪd/ *n* маскара́д; *vi*: ~ **as** выдава́ть *impf*, вы́дать *pf* себя́ за+*acc*.

Mass /mæs/ *n* (*eccl*) ме́сса.

mass /mæs/ *n* ма́сса; (*majority*) большинство́; *attrib* ма́ссовый; ~ **media** сре́дства *neut pl* ма́ссовой информа́ции; **~-produced** ма́ссового произво́дства; ~ **production** ма́ссовое произво́дство; *vt* масси́ровать *impf* & *pf*.

massacre /ˈmæsəkə(r)/ *n* резня́; *vt* выреза́ть *impf*, вы́резать *pf*.

massage /ˈmæsɑːʒ/ *n* масса́ж; *vt* масси́ровать *impf* & *pf*. **masseur, -euse** /mæˈsɜː(r), -ˈsɜːz/ *n* массажи́ст, ~ка.

massive /ˈmæsɪv/ *adj* масси́вный; (*huge*) огро́мный.
mast /mɑːst/ *n* ма́чта.
master /ˈmɑːstə(r)/ *n* (*owner*) хозя́ин; (*of ship*) капита́н; (*teacher*) учи́тель *m*; (**M~**, *univ*) маги́стр; (*workman*; *artist*) ма́стер; (*original*) по́длинник, оригина́л; **be ~ of** владе́ть *impf* +*instr*; **~-key** отмы́чка; *vt* (*overcome*) преодолева́ть *impf*, преодоле́ть *pf*; справля́ться *impf*, спра́виться *pf* с+*instr*; (*a subject*) овладева́ть *impf*, овладе́ть *pf* +*instr*. **masterful** /-fʊl/ *adj* вла́стный. **masterly** /-lɪ/ *adj* мастерско́й. **masterpiece** *n* шеде́вр. **mastery** /-rɪ/ *n* (*of a subject*) владе́ние (**of** +*instr*).
masturbate /ˈmæstəˌbeɪt/ *vi* мастурби́ровать *impf*.
mat /mæt/ *n* ко́врик, (*at door*) полови́к; (*on table*) подста́вка.
match[1] /mætʃ/ *n* спи́чка. **matchbox** *n* спи́чечная коро́бка.
match[2] /mætʃ/ *n* (*equal*) ро́вня *m* & *f*; (*contest*) матч, состяза́ние; (*marriage*) па́ртия; *vi* & *t* (*go well* (*with*)) гармони́ровать *impf* (с+*instr*); подходи́ть *impf*, подойти́ *pf* (к+*dat*).
mate[1] /meɪt/ *n* (*chess*) мат.
mate[2] /meɪt/ *n* (*one of pair*) саме́ц, са́мка; (*fellow worker*) това́рищ; (*naut*) помо́щник капита́на; *vi* (*of animals*) спа́риваться *impf*, спа́риться *pf*.
material /məˈtɪərɪəl/ *n* материа́л; (*cloth*) мате́рия; *pl* (*necessary articles*) принадле́жности *f pl*. **materialism** /-ˈtɪərɪəˌlɪz(ə)m/ *n* материали́зм. **materialistic** /-ˌtɪərɪəˈlɪstɪk/ *adj* материалисти́ческий. **materialize** /-ˈtɪərɪəˌlaɪz/ *vi* осуществля́ться *impf*, осуществи́ться *pf*.
maternal /məˈtɜːn(ə)l/ *adj* матери́нский; **~ grandfather** де́душка с матери́нской стороны́. **maternity** /-ˈtɜːnɪtɪ/ *n* матери́нство; **~ leave** декре́тный о́тпуск; **~ ward** роди́льное отделе́ние.
mathematical /ˌmæθɪˈmætɪk(ə)l/ *adj* математи́ческий. **mathematician** /ˌmæθɪməˈtɪʃ(ə)n/ *n* матема́тик. **mathematics, maths** /mæθəˈmætɪks, mæθs/ *n* матема́тика.
matinée /ˈmætɪˌneɪ/ *n* дневно́й спекта́кль *m*.
matriarchal /ˌmeɪtrɪˈɑːk(ə)l/ *adj* матриарха́льный. **matriarchy** /ˈmeɪtrɪˌɑːkɪ/ *n* матриарха́т.
matriculate /məˈtrɪkjʊˌleɪt/ *vi* быть при́нятым в вуз. **matriculation** /-ˈleɪʃ(ə)n/ *n* зачисле́ние в вуз.
matrimonial /ˌmætrɪˈməʊnɪəl/ *adj* супру́жеский. **matrimony** /ˈmætrɪmənɪ/ *n* брак.
matrix /ˈmeɪtrɪks/ *n* ма́трица.
matron /ˈmeɪtrən/ *n* ста́ршая сестра́.
matt /mæt/ *adj* ма́товый.
matted /ˈmætɪd/ *adj* спу́танный.
matter /ˈmætə(r)/ *n* (*affair*) де́ло; (*question*) вопро́с; (*substance*) вещество́; (*philos*; *med*) мате́рия; (*printed*) материа́л; **a ~ of life and death** вопро́с жи́зни и сме́рти; **a ~ of opinion** спо́рное де́ло; **a ~ of taste** де́ло вку́са; **as a ~ of fact** факти́чески; со́бственно говоря́; **what's the ~?** в чём де́ло?; **what's the ~ with him?** что с ним?; **~-of-fact** прозаи́чный; *vi* име́ть *impf* значе́ние; **it doesn't ~** э́то не име́ет значе́ния; **it ~s a lot to me** для меня́ э́то о́чень ва́жно.
matting /ˈmætɪŋ/ *n* рого́жа.
mattress /ˈmætrɪs/ *n* матра́с.
mature /məˈtjʊə(r)/ *adj* зре́лый;

vi зреть *impf*, со~ *pf*. **maturity** /-rɪtɪ/ *n* зре́лость.
maul /mɔːl/ *vt* терза́ть *impf*.
mausoleum /ˌmɔːsəˈliːəm/ *n* мавзоле́й.
mauve /məʊv/ *adj* (*n*) розова́то-лило́вый (цвет).
maxim /ˈmæksɪm/ *n* сенте́нция.
maximum /ˈmæksɪməm/ *n* ма́ксимум; *adj* максима́льный.
may /meɪ/ *v aux* (*possibility, permission*) мочь *impf*, с~ *pf*; (*possibility*) возмо́жно, что +*indicative*; (*wish*) пусть +*indicative*.
May /meɪ/ *n* (*month*) май; *adj* ма́йский ~ **Day** Пе́рвое *sb* ма́я.
maybe /ˈmeɪbiː/ *adv* мо́жет быть.
mayonnaise /ˌmeɪəˈneɪz/ *n* майоне́з.
mayor /meə(r)/ *n* мэр. **mayoress** /ˈmeərɪs/ *n* жена́ мэ́ра; же́нщина-мэр.
maze /meɪz/ *n* лабири́нт.
meadow /ˈmedəʊ/ *n* луг.
meagre /ˈmiːgə(r)/ *adj* ску́дный.
meal[1] /miːl/ *n* еда́; **at ~times** во вре́мя еды́.
meal[2] /miːl/ *n* (*grain*) мука́. **mealy** /ˈmiːlɪ/ *adj*: **~-mouthed** сладкоречи́вый.
mean[1] /miːn/ *adj* (*average*) сре́дний; *n* (*middle point*) середи́на; *pl* (*method*) сре́дство, спо́соб; *pl* (*resources*) сре́дства *neut pl*; **by all ~s** коне́чно, пожа́луйста; **by ~s of** при по́мощи +*gen*, посре́дством +*gen*; **by no ~s** совсе́м не; **~s test** прове́рка нужда́емости.
mean[2] /miːn/ *adj* (*ignoble*) по́длый; (*miserly*) скупо́й; (*poor*) убо́гий.
mean[3] /miːn/ *vt* (*have in mind*) име́ть *impf* в виду́; (*intend*) намерева́ться *impf* +*inf*; (*signify*) зна́чить *impf*.
meander /mɪˈændə(r)/ *vi* (*stream*) извива́ться *impf*; (*person*) броди́ть *impf*. **meandering** /-rɪŋ/ *adj* изви́листый.
meaning /ˈmiːnɪŋ/ *n* значе́ние. **meaningful** /-fʊl/ *adj* (много)значи́тельный. **meaningless** /-lɪs/ *adj* бессмы́сленный.
meantime, meanwhile /ˈmiːntaɪm, ˈmiːnwaɪl/ *adv* ме́жду тем.
measles /ˈmiːz(ə)lz/ *n* корь. **measly** /-zlɪ/ *adj* ничто́жный.
measurable /ˈmeʒərəb(ə)l/ *adj* измери́мый. **measure** /ˈmeʒə(r)/ *n* ме́ра; **made to ~** сши́тый по ме́рке; сде́ланный на зака́з; *vt* измеря́ть *impf*, изме́рить *pf*; (*for clothes*) снима́ть *impf*, снять *pf* ме́рку с+*gen*; *vi* име́ть *impf* +*acc*: **the room ~s 30 feet in length** ко́мната име́ет три́дцать фу́тов в длину́; **~ off, out** отмеря́ть *impf*, отме́рить *pf*; **~ up to** соотве́тствовать *impf* +*dat*. **measured** /ˈmeʒəd/ *adj* (*rhythmical*) ме́рный. **measurement** /ˈmeʒəmənt/ *n* (*action*) измере́ние; *pl* (*dimensions*) разме́ры *m pl*.
meat /miːt/ *n* мя́со. **meatball** *n* котле́та. **meaty** /-tɪ/ *adj* мяси́стый; (*fig*) содержа́тельный.
mechanic /mɪˈkænɪk/ *n* меха́ник. **mechanical** /-k(ə)l/ *adj* механи́ческий; (*fig; automatic*) машина́льный; **~ engineer** инжене́р-меха́ник; **~ engineering** машинострое́ние. **mechanics** /-nɪks/ *n* меха́ника. **mechanism** /ˈmekəˌnɪz(ə)m/ *n* механи́зм. **mechanization** /ˌmekənaɪˈzeɪʃ(ə)n/ *n* механиза́ция. **mechanize** /ˈmekəˌnaɪz/ *vt* механизи́-

рова́ть *impf* & *pf*.
medal /ˈmed(ə)l/ *n* меда́ль. **medallion** /mɪˈdæljən/ *n* медальо́н. **medallist** /ˈmedəlɪst/ *n* медали́ст.
meddle /ˈmed(ə)l/ *vi* вме́шиваться *impf*, вмеша́ться *pf* (**in, with** в+*acc*).
media /ˈmiːdɪə/ *pl of* **medium**
mediate /ˈmiːdɪˌeɪt/ *vi* посре́дничать *impf*. **mediation** /-ˈeɪʃ(ə)n/ *n* посре́дничество. **mediator** /-ˌeɪtə(r)/ *n* посре́дник.
medical /ˈmedɪk(ə)l/ *adj* медици́нский; ~ **student** ме́дик, -и́чка. **medicated** /ˈmedɪˌkeɪtɪd/ *adj* (*impregnated*) пропи́танный лека́рством. **medicinal** /mɪˈdɪsɪn(ə)l/ *adj* (*of medicine*) лека́рственный; (*healing*) целе́бный. **medicine** /ˈmedsɪn/ *n* медици́на; (*substance*) лека́рство.
medieval /ˌmedɪˈiːv(ə)l/ *adj* средневеко́вый.
mediocre /ˌmiːdɪˈəʊkə(r)/ *adj* посре́дственный. **mediocrity** /-ˈɒkrɪtɪ/ *n* посре́дственность.
meditate /ˈmedɪˌteɪt/ *vi* размышля́ть *impf*. **meditation** /-ˈteɪʃ(ə)n/ *n* размышле́ние. **meditative** /ˈmedɪtətɪv/ *adj* заду́мчивый.
Mediterranean /ˌmedɪtəˈreɪnɪən/ *adj* средиземномо́рский; *n* Средизе́мное мо́ре.
medium /ˈmiːdɪəm/ *n* (*means*) сре́дство; (*phys*) среда́; (*person*) ме́диум; *pl* (*mass media*) сре́дства *neut pl* ма́ссовой информа́ции; *adj* сре́дний; **happy** ~ золота́я середи́на.
medley /ˈmedlɪ/ *n* смесь; (*mus*) попурри́ *neut indecl*.
meek /miːk/ *adj* кро́ткий.
meet /miːt/ *vt* & *i* встреча́ть(ся) *impf*, встре́тить(ся) *pf*; *vt* (*make acquaintance*) знако́миться *impf*, по~ *pf* с+*instr*; *vi* (*assemble*) собира́ться *impf*, собра́ться *pf*. **meeting** /-tɪŋ/ *n* встре́ча; (*of committee*) заседа́ние, ми́тинг.
megalomania /ˌmegələˈmeɪnɪə/ *n* мегалома́ния.
megaphone /ˈmegəˌfəʊn/ *n* мегафо́н.
melancholic /ˌmelənˈkɒlɪk/ *adj* меланхоли́ческий. **melancholy** /ˈmelənkəlɪ/ *n* грусть; *adj* уны́лый, гру́стный.
mellow /ˈmeləʊ/ *adj* (*colour, sound*) со́чный; (*person*) дободу́шный; *vi* смягча́ться *impf*, смягчи́ться *pf*.
melodic /mɪˈlɒdɪk/ *adj* мелоди́ческий. **melodious** /-ˈləʊdɪəs/ *adj* мелоди́чный. **melody** /ˈmelədɪ/ *n* мело́дия.
melodrama /ˈmeləˌdrɑːmə/ *n* мелодра́ма. **melodramatic** /ˌmelədrəˈmætɪk/ *adj* мелодрамати́ческий.
melon /ˈmelən/ *n* ды́ня; (*water-*~) арбу́з.
melt /melt/ *vt* & *i* раста́пливать(ся) *impf*, растопи́ть(ся) *pf*; (*smelt*) пла́вить(ся) *impf*, рас~ *pf*; (*dissolve*) растворя́ть(ся) *impf*, раствори́ть(ся) *pf*; *vi* (*thaw*) та́ять *impf*, рас~ *pf*; ~**ing point** то́чка плавле́ния.
member /ˈmembə(r)/ *n* член. **membership** /-ʃɪp/ *n* чле́нство; (*number of* ~) коли́чество чле́нов; *attrib* чле́нский.
membrane /ˈmembreɪn/ *n* перепо́нка.
memento /mɪˈmentəʊ/ *n* сувени́р. **memoir** /ˈmemwɑː(r)/ *n pl* мемуа́ры (-ров) *pl*; воспомина́ния *neut pl*. **memorable** /ˈmemərəb(ə)l/ *adj* достопа́мят-

ный. **memorandum** /ˌmeməˈrændəm/ *n* записка. **memorial** /mɪˈmɔːrɪəl/ *adj* мемориальный; *n* памятник. **memorize** /ˈmeməˌraɪz/ *vt* запоминать *impf*, запомнить *pf*. **memory** /ˈmemərɪ/ *n* память; (*recollection*) воспоминание.

menace /ˈmenɪs/ *n* угроза; *vt* угрожать *impf* +*dat*. **menacing** /-sɪŋ/ *adj* угрожающий.

menagerie /mɪˈnædʒərɪ/ *n* зверинец.

mend /mend/ *vt* чинить *impf*, по~ *pf*; (*clothes*) штопать *impf*, за~ *pf*; ~ **one's ways** исправляться *impf*, исправиться *pf*.

menial /ˈmiːnɪəl/ *adj* низкий, чёрный.

meningitis /ˌmenɪnˈdʒaɪtɪs/ *n* менингит.

menopause /ˈmenəˌpɔːz/ *n* климакс.

menstrual /ˈmenstrʊəl/ *adj* менструальный. **menstruation** /-strʊˈeɪʃ(ə)n/ *n* менструация.

mental /ˈment(ə)l/ *adj* умственный; (*of* ~ *illness*) психический; ~ **arithmetic** счёт в уме. **mentality** /menˈtælɪtɪ/ *n* ум; (*character*) склад ума.

mention /ˈmenʃ(ə)n/ *vt* упоминать *impf*, упомянуть *pf*; **don't** ~ **it** не за что!; **not to** ~ не говоря уже о+*prep*.

menu /ˈmenjuː/ *n* меню *neut indecl*.

mercantile /ˈmɜːkənˌtaɪl/ *adj* торговый.

mercenary /ˈmɜːsɪnərɪ/ *adj* корыстный; (*hired*) наёмный; *n* наёмник.

merchandise /ˈmɜːtʃənˌdaɪz/ *n* товары *m pl*. **merchant** /ˈmɜːtʃənt/ *n* купец; торговец; ~ **navy** торговый флот.

merciful /ˈmɜːsɪˌfʊl/ *adj* милосердный. **mercifully** /-lɪ/ *adv* к счастью. **merciless** /ˈmɜːsɪlɪs/ *adj* беспощадный.

mercurial /mɜːˈkjʊərɪəl/ *adj* (*person*) изменчивый. **mercury** /ˈmɜːkjʊrɪ/ *n* ртуть.

mercy /ˈmɜːsɪ/ *n* милосердие; **at the** ~ **of** во власти +*gen*.

mere /mɪə(r)/ *adj* простой; **a** ~ **£40** всего лишь сорок фунтов. **merely** /ˈmɪəlɪ/ *adv* только, просто.

merge /mɜːdʒ/ *vt* & *i* сливать(ся) *impf*, слить(ся) *pf*. **merger** /-dʒə(r)/ *n* объединение.

meridian /məˈrɪdɪən/ *n* меридиан.

meringue /məˈræŋ/ *n* меренга.

merit /ˈmerɪt/ *n* заслуга, достоинство; *vt* заслуживать *impf*, заслужить *pf* +*gen*.

mermaid /ˈmɜːmeɪd/ *n* русалка.

merrily /ˈmerɪlɪ/ *adv* весело. **merriment** /ˈmerɪmənt/ *n* веселье. **merry** /ˈmerɪ/ *adj* весёлый; ~**-go-round** карусель; ~**-making** веселье.

mesh /meʃ/ *n* сеть; *vi* сцепляться *impf*, сцепиться *pf*.

mesmerize /ˈmezməˌraɪz/ *vt* гипнотизировать *impf*, за~ *pf*.

mess /mes/ *n* (*disorder*) беспорядок; (*trouble*) беда; (*eating-place*) столовая *sb*; *vi*: ~ **about** возиться *impf*; ~ **up** портить *impf*, ис~ *pf*.

message /ˈmesɪdʒ/ *n* сообщение. **messenger** /ˈmesɪndʒə(r)/ *n* курьер.

Messiah /mɪˈsaɪə/ *n* мессия *m*. **Messianic** /ˌmesɪˈænɪk/ *adj* мессианский.

Messrs /ˈmesəz/ *abbr* господа (*gen* -д) *m pl*.

messy /ˈmesɪ/ *adj* (*untidy*) беспорядочный; (*dirty*) грязный.

metabolism /mɪ'tæbəˌlɪz(ə)m/ *n* обме́н веще́ств.
metal /'met(ə)l/ *n* мета́лл; *adj* металли́ческий. **metallic** /mɪ'tælɪk/ *adj* металли́ческий. **metallurgy** /mɪ'tælədʒɪ/ *n* металлу́рги́я.
metamorphosis /ˌmetə'mɔːfəsɪs/ *n* метаморфо́за.
metaphor /'metəˌfɔː(r)/ *n* мета́фора. **metaphorical** /ˌmetə'fɒrɪk(ə)l/ *adj* метафори́ческий.
metaphysical /ˌmetə'fɪzɪk(ə)l/ *adj* метафизи́ческий. **metaphysics** /-'fɪzɪks/ *n* метафи́зика.
meteor /'miːtɪə(r)/ *n* метео́р. **meteoric** /ˌmiːtɪ'ɒrɪk/ *adj* метеори́ческий. **meteorite** /'miːtɪəˌraɪt/ *n* метеори́т. **meteorological** /ˌmiːtɪərə'lɒdʒɪk(ə)l/ *adj* метеорологи́ческий. **meteorology** /ˌmiːtɪə'rɒlədʒɪ/ *n* метеороло́гия.
meter /'miːtə(r)/ *n* счётчик; *vt* измеря́ть *impf*, изме́рить *pf*.
methane /'miːθeɪn/ *n* мета́н.
method /'meθəd/ *n* ме́тод. **methodical** /mɪ'θɒdɪk(ə)l/ *adj* методи́чный.
Methodist /'meθədɪst/ *n* методи́ст; *adj* методи́стский.
methodology /ˌmeθə'dɒlədʒɪ/ *n* методоло́гия.
methylated /'meθɪˌleɪtɪd/ *adj*: ~ **spirit(s)** денатура́т.
meticulous /mə'tɪkjʊləs/ *adj* тща́тельный.
metre /'miːtə(r)/ *n* ме́тр. **metric(al)** /'metrɪk((ə)l)/ *adj* метри́ческий.
metronome /'metrəˌnəʊm/ *n* метроно́м.
metropolis /mɪ'trɒpəlɪs/ *n* столи́ца. **metropolitan** /ˌmetrə'pɒlɪt(ə)n/ *adj* столи́чный; *n* (*eccl*) митрополи́т.
mettle /'met(ə)l/ *n* хара́ктер.
Mexican /'meksɪkən/ *adj* мексика́нский; *n* мексика́нец, -а́нка.
Mexico /'meksɪˌkəʊ/ *n* Ме́ксика.
mezzanine /'metsəˌniːn/ *n* антресо́ли *f pl*.
miaow /miː'aʊ/ *int* мя́у; *n* мяу́канье; *vi* мяу́кать *impf*, мяу́кнуть *pf*.
mica /'maɪkə/ *n* слюда́.
microbe /'maɪkrəʊb/ *n* микро́б. **microchip** /'maɪkrəʊˌtʃɪp/ *n* чип, микросхе́ма. **microcomputer** /'maɪkrəʊkəmˌpjuːtə(r)/ *n* микрокомпью́тер. **microcosm** /'maɪkrəˌkɒz(ə)m/ *n* микроко́см. **microfilm** /'maɪkrəʊˌfɪlm/ *n* микрофи́льм. **micro-organism** /ˌmaɪkrəʊ'ɔːgəˌnɪz(ə)m/ *n* микроорганизм. **microphone** /'maɪkrəˌfəʊn/ *n* микрофо́н. **microscope** *n* /'maɪkrəˌskəʊp/ микроско́п. **microscopic** /ˌmaɪkrə'skɒpɪk/ *adj* микроскопи́ческий. **microwave** /'maɪkrəʊˌweɪv/*n* микроволна́; ~ **oven** микрово́лновая печь.
mid /mɪd/ *adj*: ~ **May** середи́на ма́я. **midday** /'mɪddeɪ/ *n* по́лдень *m*; *attrib* полу́денный. **middle** /'mɪd(ə)l/ *n* середи́на; *adj* сре́дний; ~**-aged** сре́дних лет; **M~ Ages** сре́дние века́ *m pl*; ~**-class** буржуа́зный; ~**man** посре́дник; ~**-sized** сре́днего разме́ра. **middleweight** *n* сре́дний вес.
midge /mɪdʒ/ *n* мо́шка.
midget /'mɪdʒɪt/ *n* ка́рлик, -ица.
midnight /'mɪdnaɪt/ *n* по́лночь; *attrib* полу́но́чный. **midriff** /'mɪdrɪf/ *n* диафра́гма. **midst** /mɪdst/ *n* середи́на. **midsummer** *n* середи́на ле́та. **midway** *adv* на полпути́. **mid-week** *n* середи́на неде́ли. **midwinter** *n* середи́на зимы́.

midwife /ˈmɪdwaɪf/ *n* акушéрка. **midwifery** /ˌmɪdˈwɪfərɪ/ *n* акушéрство.

might /maɪt/ *n* мощь; **with all one's ~** изо всех сил. **mighty** /ˈmaɪtɪ/ *adj* мóщный.

migraine /ˈmiːgreɪn/ *n* мигрéнь.

migrant /ˈmaɪgrənt/ *adj* кочýющий; (*bird*) перелётный; *n* (*person*) переселéнец; (*bird*) перелётная птúца. **migrate** /maɪˈgreɪt/ *vi* мигрúровать *impf* & *pf.* **migration** /-ˈgreɪʃ(ə)n/ *n* миграция. **migratory** /-ˈgreɪtərɪ/ *adj* кочýющий; (*bird*) перелётный.

mike /maɪk/ *n* микрофóн.

mild /maɪld/ *adj* мя́гкий.

mildew /ˈmɪldjuː/ *n* плéсень.

mile /maɪl/ *n* ми́ля. **mileage** /-lɪdʒ/ *n* расстоя́ние в ми́лях; (*of car*) пробéг. **milestone** *n* верстовóй столб; (*fig*) вéха.

militancy /ˈmɪlɪt(ə)nsɪ/ *n* вои́нственность. **militant** /-t(ə)nt/ *adj* вою́ющий; *n* активи́ст. **military** /-tərɪ/ *adj* воéнный; *n* воéнные *sb pl.* **militate** /-ˌteɪt/ *vi*: **~ against** говори́ть *impf* прóтив+*gen.* **militia** /mɪˈlɪʃə/ *n* мили́ция. **militiaman** *n* милиционéр.

milk /mɪlk/ *n* молокó; *attrib* молóчный; *vt* дои́ть *impf*, по~ *pf.* **milkman** *n* продавéц молокá. **milky** /-kɪ/ *adj* молóчный; **M~ Way** Млéчный Путь *m.*

mill /mɪl/ *n* мéльница; (*factory*) фáбрика; *vt* (*grain etc.*) молóть *impf*, с~ *pf*; (*metal*) фрезеровáть *impf*, от~ *pf*; (*coin*) гурти́ть *impf*; *vi*: **~ around** толпи́ться *impf.* **miller** /ˈmɪlə(r)/ *n* мéльник.

millennium /mɪˈlenɪəm/ *n* тысячелéтие.

millet /ˈmɪlɪt/ *n* (*plant*) прóсо; (*grain*) пшенó.

milligram(me) /ˈmɪlɪˌgræm/ *n* миллигрáмм. **millimetre** /-ˌmiːtə(r)/ *n* миллимéтр.

million /ˈmɪljən/ *n* миллиóн. **millionaire** /-ˈneə(r)/ *n* миллионéр. **millionth** /-jənθ/ *adj* миллиóнный.

millstone /ˈmɪlstəʊn/ *n* жёрнов; (*fig*) кáмень *m* на шéе.

mime /maɪm/ *n* мим; (*dumbshow*) пантоми́ма; *vt* изображáть *impf*, изобрази́ть *pf* мими́чески. **mimic** /ˈmɪmɪk/ *n* ми́мист; *vt* передрáзнивать *impf*, передразни́ть *pf.* **mimicry** /ˈmɪmɪkrɪ/ *n* имитáция.

minaret /ˌmɪnəˈret/ *n* минарéт.

mince /mɪns/ *n* (*meat*) фарш; *vt* руби́ть *impf*; (*in machine*) пропускáть *impf*, пропусти́ть *pf* чéрез мясорýбку; *vi* (*walk*) семени́ть *impf*; **not ~ matters** говори́ть *impf* без обинякóв. **mincemeat** *n* начи́нка из изю́ма, миндаля́ и т.п.

mind /maɪnd/ *n* ум; **bear in ~** имéть *impf* в видý; **change one's ~** передýмывать *impf*, передýмать *pf*; **make up one's ~** решáться *impf*, реши́ться *pf*; **you're out of your ~** вы с умá сошли́; *vt* (*give heed to*) обращáть *impf*, обрати́ть *pf* внимáние на+*acc*; (*look after*) присмáтривать *impf*, присмотрéть *pf* за+*instr*; **I don't ~** я ничегó не имéю прóтив; **don't ~ me** не обращáй(те) внимáния на меня́!; **~ you don't forget** смотри́ не забýдь!; **~ your own business** не вмéшивайтесь в чужи́е делá!; **never ~** ничегó! **mindful** /-fʊl/ *adj* пóмнящий. **mindless** /-lɪs/ *adj* бессмы́сленный.

mine[1] /maɪn/ *poss pron* мой;

свой.

mine² /maɪn/ *n* ша́хта, рудни́к; (*fig*) исто́чник; (*mil*) ми́на; *vt* (*obtain from* ~) добыва́ть *impf*, добы́ть *pf*; (*mil*) мини́ровать *impf* & *pf*. **minefield** *n* ми́нное по́ле. **miner** /'maɪnə(r)/ *n* шахтёр.

mineral /'mɪnər(ə)l/ *n* минера́л; *adj* минера́льный; ~ **water** минера́льная вода́. **mineralogy** /-'rælədʒɪ/ *n* минерало́гия.

mingle /'mɪŋg(ə)l/ *vt* & *i* сме́шивать(ся) *impf*, смеша́ть(ся) *pf*.

miniature /'mɪnɪtʃə(r)/ *n* миниатю́ра; *adj* миниатю́рный.

minibus /'mɪnɪˌbʌs/ *n* микроавто́бус.

minim /'mɪnɪm/ *n* (*mus*) полови́нная но́та. **minimal** /-məl/ *adj* минима́льный. **minimize** /-ˌmaɪz/ *vt* (*reduce*) доводи́ть *impf*, довести́ *pf* до ми́нимума. **minimum** /-məm/ *n* ми́нимум; *adj* минима́льный.

mining /'maɪnɪŋ/ *n* го́рное де́ло.

minister /'mɪnɪstə(r)/ *n* мини́стр; (*eccl*) свяще́нник. **ministerial** /-'stɪərɪəl/ *adj* министе́рский. **ministration** /-'streɪʃ(ə)n/ *n* по́мощь. **ministry** /'mɪnɪstrɪ/ *n* (*polit*) министе́рство; (*eccl*) духове́нство.

mink /mɪŋk/ *n* но́рка; *attrib* но́рковый.

minor /'maɪnə(r)/ *adj* (*unimportant*) незначи́тельный; (*less important*) второстепе́нный; (*mus*) мино́рный; *n* (*person under age*) несовершенноле́тний *n*; (*mus*) мино́р. **minority** /-'nɒrɪtɪ/ *n* меньшинство́; (*age*) несовершенноле́тие.

minstrel /'mɪnstr(ə)l/ *n* менестре́ль *m*.

mint¹ /mɪnt/ *n* (*plant*) мя́та; (*peppermint*) пе́речная мя́та.

mint² /mɪnt/ *n* (*econ*) моне́тный двор; **in ~ condition** но́венький; *vt* чека́нить *impf*, от~, вы́~ *pf*.

minuet /ˌmɪnjʊ'et/ *n* менуэ́т.

minus /'maɪnəs/ *prep* ми́нус +*acc*; без+*gen*; *n* ми́нус.

minuscule /'mɪnəˌskjuːl/ *adj* малю́сенький.

minute¹ /'mɪnɪt/ *n* мину́та; *pl* протоко́л.

minute² /maɪ'njuːt/ *adj* ме́лкий. **minutiae** /-'njuːʃɪˌaɪ/ *n pl* ме́лочи (-че́й) *f pl*.

miracle /'mɪrək(ə)l/ *n* чу́до. **miraculous** /-'rækjʊləs/ *adj* чуде́сный.

mirage /'mɪrɑːʒ/ *n* мира́ж.

mire /'maɪə(r)/ *n* (*mud*) грязь; (*swamp*) боло́то.

mirror /'mɪrə(r)/ *n* зе́ркало; *vt* отража́ть *impf*, отрази́ть *pf*.

mirth /mɜːθ/ *n* весе́лье.

misadventure /ˌmɪsəd'ventʃə(r)/ *n* несча́стный слу́чай.

misapprehension /ˌmɪsæprɪ'henʃ(ə)n/ *n* недопонима́ние.

misappropriate /ˌmɪsə'prəʊprɪˌeɪt/ *vt* незако́нно присва́ивать *impf*, присво́ить *pf*. **misbehave** /ˌmɪsbɪ'heɪv/ *vi* ду́рно вести́ *impf* себя́. **misbehaviour** /ˌmɪsbɪ'heɪvɪə(r)/ *n* дурно́е поведе́ние.

miscalculate /ˌmɪs'kælkjʊˌleɪt/ *vt* непра́вильно рассчи́тывать *impf*, рассчита́ть *pf*; (*fig, abs*) просчи́тываться *impf*, просчита́ться *pf*. **miscalculation** /-'leɪʃ(ə)n/ *n* просчёт. **miscarriage** /'mɪsˌkærɪdʒ/ *n* (*med*) вы́кидыш; ~ **of justice** суде́бная оши́бка. **miscarry** /mɪs'kærɪ/ *vi* (*med*) име́ть *impf* вы́кидыш.

miscellaneous /ˌmɪsə'leɪnɪəs/ *adj* ра́зный, разнообра́зный. **miscellany** /mɪ'selənɪ/ *n* смесь.

mischief /ˈmɪstʃɪf/ *n* (*harm*) вред; (*naughtiness*) озорство́. **mischievous** /ˈmɪstʃɪvəs/ *adj* озорно́й. **misconception** /ˌmɪskənˈsepʃ(ə)n/ *n* непра́вильное представле́ние. **misconduct** /mɪsˈkɒndʌkt/ *n* дурно́е поведе́ние. **misconstrue** /ˌmɪskənˈstruː/ *vt* непра́вильно истолко́вывать *impf*, истолкова́ть *pf*.

misdeed, misdemeanour /mɪsˈdiːd, ˌmɪsdɪˈmiːnə(r)/ *n* просту́пок. **misdirect** /ˌmɪsdaɪˈrekt/ *vt* непра́вильно направля́ть *impf*, напра́вить *pf*; (*letter*) непра́вильно адресова́ть *impf* & *pf*.

miser /ˈmaɪzə(r)/ *n* скупе́ц. **miserable** /ˈmɪzərəb(ə)l/ *adj* (*unhappy, wretched*) несча́стный, жа́лкий; (*weather*) скве́рный. **miserly** /ˈmaɪzəlɪ/ *adj* скупо́й. **misery** /ˈmɪzərɪ/ *n* страда́ние.

misfire /mɪsˈfaɪə(r)/ *vi* дава́ть *impf*, дать *pf* осе́чку. **misfit** /ˈmɪsfɪt/ *n* (*person*) неуда́чник. **misfortune** /mɪsˈfɔːtjuːn/ *n* несча́стье. **misgiving** /mɪsˈgɪvɪŋ/ *n* опасе́ние. **misguided** /mɪsˈgaɪdɪd/ *adj* обма́нутый.

mishap /ˈmɪshæp/ *n* неприя́тность. **misinform** /ˌmɪsɪnˈfɔːm/ *vt* непра́вильно информи́ровать *impf* & *pf*. **misinterpret** /ˌmɪsɪnˈtɜːprɪt/ *vt* неве́рно истолко́вывать *impf*, истолкова́ть *pf*. **misjudge** /mɪsˈdʒʌdʒ/ *vt* неве́рно оце́нивать *impf*, оцени́ть *pf*. **misjudgement** /mɪsˈdʒʌdʒmənt/ *n* неве́рная оце́нка. **mislay** /mɪsˈleɪ/ *vt* затеря́ть *pf*. **mislead** /mɪsˈliːd/ *vt* вводи́ть *impf*, ввести́ *pf* в заблужде́ние. **mismanage** /mɪsˈmænɪdʒ/ *vt* пло́хо управля́ть *impf* +*instr*. **mismanagement** /mɪsˈmænɪdʒmənt/ *n* плохо́е управле́ние. **misnomer** /mɪsˈnəʊmə(r)/ *n* непра́вильное назва́ние.

misogynist /mɪˈsɒdʒɪnɪst/ *n* женоненави́стник. **misogyny** /-nɪ/ *n* женоненави́стничество.

misplaced /mɪsˈpleɪst/ *adj* неуме́стный. **misprint** /ˈmɪsprɪnt/ *n* опеча́тка. **misquote** /mɪsˈkwəʊt/ *vt* непра́вильно цити́ровать *impf*, про~ *pf*. **misread** /mɪsˈriːd/ *vt* (*fig*) непра́вильно истолко́вывать *impf*, истолкова́ть *pf*. **misrepresent** /ˌmɪsreprɪˈzent/ *vt* искажа́ть *impf*, искази́ть *pf*. **misrepresentation** /mɪsˌreprɪzenˈteɪʃ(ə)n/ *n* искаже́ние.

Miss /mɪs/ *n* (*title*) мисс.

miss /mɪs/ *n* про́мах; *vi* прома́хиваться *impf*, промахну́ться *pf*; *vt* (*fail to hit, see, hear*) пропуска́ть *impf*, пропусти́ть *pf*; (*train*) опа́здывать *impf*, опозда́ть *pf* на+*acc*; (*regret absence of*) скуча́ть *impf* по+*dat*; **~ out** пропуска́ть *impf*, пропусти́ть *pf*; **~ the point** не понима́ть *impf*, поня́ть *pf* су́ти.

misshapen /mɪsˈʃeɪpən/ *adj* уро́дливый.

missile /ˈmɪsaɪl/ *n* снаря́д, раке́та.

missing /ˈmɪsɪŋ/ *adj* отсу́тствующий, недостаю́щий; (*person*) пропа́вший бе́з вести.

mission /ˈmɪʃ(ə)n/ *n* ми́ссия; командиро́вка. **missionary** /ˈmɪʃənərɪ/ *n* миссионе́р. **missive** /ˈmɪsɪv/ *n* посла́ние.

misspell /mɪsˈspel/ *vt* непра́вильно писа́ть *impf*, на~ *pf*. **misspelling** /-lɪŋ/ *n* непра́вильное написа́ние.

mist /mɪst/ *n* тума́н; *vt* & *i* затума́нивать(ся) *impf*, затума́нить(ся) *pf*.

mistake /mɪ'steɪk/ *vt* непра́вильно понима́ть *impf*, поня́ть *pf*; ~ **for** принима́ть *impf*, приня́ть *pf* за+*acc*; *n* оши́бка; **make a** ~ ошиба́ться *impf*, ошиби́ться *pf*. **mistaken** /-kən/ *adj* оши́бочный; **be** ~ ошиба́ться *impf*, ошиби́ться *pf*.

mister /'mɪstə(r)/ *n* ми́стер, господи́н.

mistletoe /'mɪs(ə)l,təʊ/ *n* оме́ла.

mistress /'mɪstrɪs/ *n* хозя́йка; (*teacher*) учи́тельница; (*lover*) любо́вница.

mistrust /mɪs'trʌst/ *vt* не доверя́ть *impf* +*dat*; *n* недове́рие. **mistrustful** /-fʊl/ *adj* недове́рчивый.

misty /'mɪstɪ/ *adj* тума́нный.

misunderstand /,mɪsʌndə'stænd/ *vt* непра́вильно понима́ть *impf*, поня́ть *pf*. **misunderstanding** /-dɪŋ/ *n* недоразуме́ние.

misuse *vt* /mɪs'ju:z/ непра́вильно употребля́ть *impf*, употреби́ть *pf*; (*ill treat*) ду́рно обраща́ться *impf* с+*instr*; *n* /-'ju:s/ непра́вильное употребле́ние.

mite /maɪt/ *n* (*insect*) клещ.

mitigate /'mɪtɪ,geɪt/ *vt* смягча́ть *impf*, смягчи́ть *pf*. **mitigation** /-'geɪʃ(ə)n/ *n* смягче́ние.

mitre /'maɪtə(r)/ *n* ми́тра.

mitten /'mɪt(ə)n/ *n* рукави́ца.

mix /mɪks/ *vt* меша́ть *impf*, с~ *pf*; *vi* сме́шиваться *impf*, смеша́ться *pf*; (*associate*) обща́ться *impf*; ~ **up** (*confuse*) пу́тать *impf*, с~ *pf*; **get ~ed up in** заме́шиваться *impf*, замеша́ться *pf* в+*acc*; *n* смесь. **mixer** /'mɪksə(r)/ *n* смеси́тель *m*; (*cul*) ми́ксер. **mixture** /'mɪkstʃə(r)/ *n* смесь; (*medicine*) миксту́ра.

moan /məʊn/ *n* стон; *vi* стона́ть *impf*, про~ *pf*.

moat /məʊt/ *n* (крепостно́й) ров.

mob /mɒb/ *n* толпа́; *vt* (*attack*) напада́ть *impf*, напа́сть *pf* толпо́й на+*acc*. **mobster** /-stə(r)/ *n* бандит.

mobile /'məʊbaɪl/ *adj* подвижно́й, передвижно́й; ~ **phone** портати́вный телефо́н. **mobility** /mə'bɪlɪtɪ/ *n* подви́жность. **mobilize** /'məʊbɪ,laɪz/ *vt* & *i* мобилизова́ть(ся) *impf* & *pf*.

moccasin /'mɒkəsɪn/ *n* мокаси́н (*gen pl* -н).

mock /mɒk/ *vt* & *i* издева́ться *impf* над+*instr*; *adj* (*sham*) подде́льный; (*pretended*) мни́мый; **~-up** *n* маке́т. **mockery** /'mɒkərɪ/ *n* издева́тельство; (*travesty*) паро́дия.

mode /məʊd/ *n* (*manner*) о́браз; (*method*) ме́тод.

model /'mɒd(ə)l/ *n* (*representation*) моде́ль; (*pattern, ideal*) образе́ц; (*artist's*) нату́рщик, -ица; (*fashion*) манеке́нщик, -ица; (*make*) моде́ль; *adj* образцо́вый; *vt* лепи́ть *impf*, вы́~, с~ *pf*; (*clothes*) демонстри́ровать *impf* & *pf*; *vi* (*act as* ~) быть нату́рщиком, -ицей; быть манеке́нщиком, -ицей; ~ **after, on** создава́ть *impf*, созда́ть *pf* по образцу́ +*gen*.

modem /'məʊdem/ *n* моде́м.

moderate *adj* /'mɒdərət/ (*various senses; polit*) уме́ренный; (*medium*) сре́дний; *vt* /'mɒdə,reɪt/ умеря́ть *impf*, уме́рить *pf*; *vi* стиха́ть *impf*, сти́хнуть *pf*. **moderation** /,mɒdə'reɪʃ(ə)n/ *n* уме́ренность; **in** ~ уме́ренно.

modern /'mɒd(ə)n/ *adj* совреме́нный; (*language, history*) но́вый. **modernization** /ˌmɒdənaɪˈzeɪʃ(ə)n/ *n* модерниза́ция. **modernize** /ˈmɒdəˌnaɪz/ *vt* модернизи́ровать *impf* & *pf.*

modest /ˈmɒdɪst/ *adj* скро́мный. **modesty** /-stɪ/ *n* скро́мность.

modification /ˌmɒdɪfɪˈkeɪʃ(ə)n/ *n* модифика́ция. **modify** /ˈmɒdɪˌfaɪ/ *vt* модифици́ровать *impf* & *pf.*

modish /ˈməʊdɪʃ/ *adj* мо́дный.

modular /ˈmɒdjʊlə(r)/ *adj* мо́дульный. **modulate** /-ˌleɪt/ *vt* модули́ровать *impf.* **modulation** /-ˈleɪʃ(ə)n/ *n* модуля́ция. **module** /ˈmɒdjuːl/ *n* мо́дуль *m.*

mohair /ˈməʊheə(r)/ *n* мохе́р.

moist /mɔɪst/ *adj* вла́жный. **moisten** /ˈmɔɪs(ə)n/ *vt* & *i* увлажня́ть(ся) *impf*, увлажни́ть(ся) *pf.* **moisture** /ˈmɔɪstʃə(r)/ *n* вла́га.

molar /ˈməʊlə(r)/ *n* (*tooth*) коренно́й зуб.

mole[1] /məʊl/ *n* (*on skin*) ро́динка.

mole[2] /məʊl/ *n* (*animal*; *agent*) крот.

molecular /məˈlekjʊlə(r)/ *adj* молекуля́рный. **molecule** /ˈmɒlɪˌkjuːl/ *n* моле́кула.

molest /məˈlest/ *vt* пристава́ть *impf*, приста́ть *pf* к+*dat.*

mollify /ˈmɒlɪˌfaɪ/ *vt* смягча́ть *impf*, смягчи́ть *pf.*

mollusc /ˈmɒləsk/ *n* моллю́ск.

molten /ˈməʊlt(ə)n/ *adj* распла́вленный.

moment /ˈməʊmənt/ *n* моме́нт, миг; **at the ~** сейча́с; **at the last ~** в после́днюю мину́ту; **just a ~** сейча́с! **momentarily** /-ˈterɪlɪ/ *adv* на мгнове́ние. **momentary** /ˈməʊməntərɪ/ *adj* мгнове́нный. **momentous** /məˈmentəs/ *adj* ва́жный. **momentum** /məˈmentəm/ *n* коли́чество движе́ния; (*impetus*) дви́жущая си́ла; **gather ~** набира́ть *impf*, набра́ть *pf* ско́рость.

monarch /ˈmɒnək/ *n* мона́рх. **monarchy** /-kɪ/ *n* мона́рхия.

monastery /ˈmɒnəstərɪ/ *n* монасты́рь *m.* **monastic** /məˈnæstɪk/ *adj* мона́шеский.

Monday /ˈmʌndeɪ/ *n* понеде́льник.

monetary /ˈmʌnɪtərɪ/ *adj* де́нежный. **money** /ˈmʌnɪ/ *n* де́ньги (-нег, -ньга́м) *pl*; **~-lender** ростовщи́к.

mongrel /ˈmʌŋgr(ə)l/ *n* дворня́жка.

monitor /ˈmɒnɪt(ə)r/ *n* (*naut*; *TV*) монито́р; *vt* проверя́ть *impf*, прове́рить *pf.*

monk /mʌŋk/ *n* мона́х.

monkey /ˈmʌŋkɪ/ *n* обезья́на.

mono /ˈmɒnəʊ/ *n* мо́но *neut indecl.* **monochrome** *adj* одноцве́тный. **monogamous** /məˈnɒgəməs/ *adj* единобра́чный. **monogamy** /məˈnɒgəmɪ/ *n* единобра́чие. **monogram** /ˈmɒnəˌgræm/ *n* моногра́мма. **monograph** *n* моногра́фия. **monolith** /ˈmɒnəlɪθ/ *n* моноли́т. **monolithic** /ˌmɒnəˈlɪθɪk/ *adj* моноли́тный. **monologue** /ˈmɒnəˌlɒg/ *n* моноло́г. **monopolize** /məˈnɒpəˌlaɪz/ *vt* монополизи́ровать *impf* & *pf.* **monopoly** /məˈnɒpəlɪ/ *n* монопо́лия. **monosyllabic** /ˌmɒnəsɪˈlæbɪk/ *adj* односло́жный. **monosyllable** /ˈmɒnəˌsɪləb(ə)l/ *n* односло́жное сло́во. **monotone** *n* моното́нность; **in a ~** моното́нно. **monotonous** /məˈnɒtən(ə)s/ *adj* моното́нный. **monotony** /məˈnɒtənɪ/ *n* моното́нность.

monsoon /mɒnˈsuːn/ *n* (*wind*) муссо́н; (*rainy season*) дождли́-

вый сезо́н.

monster /ˈmɒnstə(r)/ *n* чудо́вище. **monstrosity** /mɒnˈstrɒsɪtɪ/ *n* чудо́вище. **monstrous** /ˈmɒnstrəs/ *adj* чудо́вищный; (*huge*) грома́дный.

montage /mɒnˈtɑːʒ/ *n* монта́ж.

month /mʌnθ/ *n* ме́сяц. **monthly** /-lɪ/ *adj* ме́сячный; *n* ежеме́сячник; *adv* ежеме́сячно.

monument /ˈmɒnjʊmənt/ *n* па́мятник. **monumental** /-ˈment(ə)l/ *adj* монумента́льный.

moo /muː/ *vi* мыча́ть *impf*.

mood[1] /muːd/ *n* (*gram*) наклоне́ние.

mood[2] /muːd/ *n* настрое́ние. **moody** /-dɪ/ *adj* капри́зный.

moon /muːn/ *n* луна́. **moonlight** *n* лу́нный свет; *vi* халту́рить *impf*. **moonlit** /-lɪt/ *adj* лу́нный.

moor[1] /mʊə(r)/ *n* ме́стность, поро́сшая ве́реском. **moorland** *n* ве́ресковая пу́стошь.

moor[2] /mʊə(r)/ *vt & i* швартова́ть(ся) *impf*, при~ *pf*. **mooring** /-rɪŋ/ *n* (*place*) прича́л; *pl* (*cables*) шварто́вы *m pl*.

Moorish /ˈmʊərɪʃ/ *adj* маврита́нский.

moose /muːs/ *n* америка́нский лось *m*.

moot /muːt/ *adj* спо́рный.

mop /mɒp/ *n* шва́бра; *vt* протира́ть *impf*, протере́ть *pf* (шва́брой); ~ **one's brow** вытира́ть *impf*, вы́тереть *pf* лоб; ~ **up** вытира́ть *impf*, вы́тереть *pf*.

mope /məʊp/ *vi* хандри́ть *impf*.

moped /ˈməʊped/ *n* мопе́д.

moraine /məˈreɪn/ *n* море́на.

moral /ˈmɒr(ə)l/ *adj* мора́льный; *n* мора́ль; *pl* нра́вы *m pl*. **morale** /məˈrɑːl/ *n* мора́льное состоя́ние. **morality** /məˈrælɪtɪ/ *n* нра́вственность, мора́ль. **moralize** /ˈmɒrəˌlaɪz/ *vi* морализи́ровать *impf*.

morass /məˈræs/ *n* боло́то.

moratorium /ˌmɒrəˈtɔːrɪəm/ *n* морато́рий.

morbid /ˈmɔːbɪd/ *adj* боле́зненный.

more /mɔː(r)/ *adj* (*greater quantity*) бо́льше +*gen*; (*additional*) ещё; *adv* бо́льше; (*forming comp*) бо́лее; **and what is** ~ и бо́льше того́; ~ **or less** бо́лее и́ли ме́нее; **once** ~ ещё раз. **moreover** /mɔːˈrəʊvə(r)/ *adv* сверх того́; кро́ме того́.

morgue /mɔːg/ *n* морг.

moribund /ˈmɒrɪˌbʌnd/ *adj* умира́ющий.

morning /ˈmɔːnɪŋ/ *n* у́тро; **in the** ~ у́тром; **in the** ~**s** по утра́м; *attrib* у́тренний.

moron /ˈmɔːrɒn/ *n* слабоу́мный *sb*.

morose /məˈrəʊs/ *adj* угрю́мый.

morphine /ˈmɔːfiːn/ *n* мо́рфий.

Morse (code) /mɔːs (kəʊd)/ *n* а́збука Мо́рзе.

morsel /ˈmɔːs(ə)l/ *n* кусо́чек.

mortal /ˈmɔːt(ə)l/ *adj* сме́ртный; (*fatal*) смерте́льный; *n* сме́ртный *sb*. **mortality** /-ˈtælɪtɪ/ *n* сме́ртность.

mortar /ˈmɔːtə(r)/ *n* (*vessel*) сту́п(к)а; (*cannon*) миномёт; (*cement*) (известко́вый) раство́р.

mortgage /ˈmɔːgɪdʒ/ *n* ссу́да на поку́пку до́ма; *vt* закла́дывать *impf*, заложи́ть *pf*.

mortify /ˈmɔːtɪˌfaɪ/ *vt* унижа́ть *impf*, уни́зить *pf*.

mortuary /ˈmɔːtjʊərɪ/ *n* морг.

mosaic /məʊˈzeɪɪk/ *n* моза́ика; *adj* моза́ичный.

mosque /mɒsk/ *n* мече́ть.

mosquito /mɒˈskiːtəʊ/ *n* кома́р.

moss /mɒs/ *n* мох. **mossy** /-sɪ/ *adj* мши́стый.
most /məʊst/ *adj* наибо́льший; *n* наибо́льшее коли́чество; *adj* & *n* (*majority*) большинство́ +*gen*; бо́льшая часть +*gen*; *adv* бо́льше всего́, наибо́лее; (*forming superl*) са́мый. **mostly** /-lɪ/ *adv* гла́вным о́бразом.
MOT (test) *n* техосмо́тр.
motel /məʊ'tel/ *n* моте́ль *m*.
moth /mɒθ/ *n* моты́лёк; (*clothes-*~) моль.
mother /'mʌðə(r)/ *n* мать; *vt* относи́ться *impf* по-матери́нски к +*dat*; **~-in-law** (*wife's* ~) тёща; (*husband's* ~) свекро́вь; **~-of-pearl** перламу́тр; *adj* перламу́тровый; ~ **tongue** родно́й язы́к. **motherhood** *n* матери́нство. **motherland** *n* ро́дина. **motherly** /-lɪ/ *adj* матери́нский.
motif /məʊ'ti:f/ *n* моти́в.
motion /'məʊʃ(ə)n/ *n* движе́ние; (*gesture*) жест; (*proposal*) предложе́ние; *vt* пока́зывать *impf*, показа́ть *pf* +*dat* же́стом, что́бы +*past*. **motionless** /-lɪs/ *adj* неподви́жный. **motivate** /'məʊtɪˌveɪt/ *vt* побужда́ть *impf*, побуди́ть *pf*. **motivation** /ˌməʊtɪ'veɪʃ(ə)n/ *n* побужде́ние. **motive** /'məʊtɪv/ *n* моти́в; *adj* дви́жущий.
motley /'mɒtlɪ/ *adj* пёстрый.
motor /'məʊtə(r)/ *n* дви́гатель *m*, мото́р; ~ **bike** мотоци́кл; ~ **boat** мото́рная ло́дка; ~ **car** автомоби́ль *m*; ~ **cycle** мотоци́кл; **~-cyclist** мотоцикли́ст; ~ **racing** автомоби́льные го́нки *f pl*; ~ **scooter** моторо́ллер; ~ **vehicle** автомаши́на. **motoring** /-rɪŋ/ *n* автомобили́зм. **motorist** /-rɪst/ *n* автомобили́ст, ~ка. **motorize** /-ˌraɪz/ *vt* моторизова́ть *impf* & *pf*. **motorway** *n* автостра́да.
mottled /'mɒtəld/ *adj* кра́пчатый.
motto /'mɒtəʊ/ *n* деви́з.
mould[1] /məʊld/ *n* (*shape*) фо́рма, фо́рмочка; *vt* формова́ть *impf*, с~ *pf*. **moulding** /-dɪŋ/ *n* (*archit*) лепно́е украше́ние.
mould[2] /məʊld/ *n* (*fungi*) пле́сень. **mouldy** /-dɪ/ *adj* заплесневе́лый.
moulder /'məʊldə(r)/ *vi* разлага́ться *impf*, разложи́ться *pf*.
moult /məʊlt/ *vi* линя́ть *impf*, вы́~ *pf*.
mound /maʊnd/ *n* холм; (*heap*) на́сыпь.
Mount /maʊnt/ *n* (*in names*) гора́.
mount /maʊnt/ *vt* (*ascend*) поднима́ться *impf*, подня́ться *pf* на+*acc*; (~ *a horse etc.*) сади́ться *impf*, сесть *pf* на+*acc*; (*picture*) накле́ивать *impf*, накле́ить *pf* на карто́н; (*gun*) устана́вливать *impf*, установи́ть *pf*; ~ **up** (*accumulate*) нака́пливаться *impf*, накопи́ться *pf*; *n* (*for picture*) карто́н; (*horse*) верхова́я ло́шадь.
mountain /'maʊntɪn/ *n* гора́; *attrib* го́рный. **mountaineer** /-'nɪə(r)/ *n* альпини́ст, ~ка. **mountaineering** /-'nɪərɪŋ/ *n* альпини́зм. **mountainous** /'maʊntɪnəs/ *adj* гори́стый.
mourn /mɔ:n/ *vt* опла́кивать *impf*, опла́кать *pf*; *vi* скорбе́ть *impf* (**over** о+*prep*). **mournful** /-fʊl/ *adj* ско́рбный. **mourning** /-nɪŋ/ *n* тра́ур.
mouse /maʊs/ *n* мышь.
mousse /mu:s/ *n* мусс.
moustache /mə'stɑ:ʃ/ *n* усы́ (усо́в) *pl*.

mousy /'maʊsɪ/ *adj* мыши́ный; (*timid*) ро́бкий.

mouth *n* /maʊθ/ рот; (*poetical*) уста́ (-т) *pl*; (*entrance*) вход; (*of river*) у́стье; *vt* /maʊð/ говори́ть *impf*, сказа́ть *pf* одни́ми губа́ми. **mouthful** /-fʊl/ *n* глото́к. **mouth-organ** *n* губна́я гармо́ника. **mouthpiece** *n* мундшту́к; (*person*) ру́пор.

movable /'mu:vəb(ə)l/ *adj* подвижно́й.

move /mu:v/ *n* (*in game*) ход; (*change of residence*) перее́зд; (*movement*) движе́ние; (*step*) шаг; *vt* & *i* дви́гать(ся) *impf*, дви́нуться *pf*; *vt* (*affect*) тро́гать *impf*, тро́нуть *pf*; (*propose*) вноси́ть *impf*, внести́ *pf*; *vi* (*develop*) развива́ться *impf*, разви́ться *pf*; (~ *house*) переезжа́ть *impf*, перее́хать *pf*; ~ **away** (*vt* & *i*) удаля́ть(ся) *impf*, удали́ть(ся) *pf*; (*vi*) уезжа́ть *impf*, уе́хать *pf*; ~ **in** въезжа́ть *impf*, въе́хать *pf*; ~ **on** идти́ *impf*, пойти́ *pf* да́льше; ~ **out** съезжа́ть *impf*, съе́хать *pf* (**of** с+*gen*). **movement** /-mənt/ *n* движе́ние; (*mus*) часть. **moving** /-vɪŋ/ *n* дви́жущийся; (*touching*) тро́гательный.

mow /məʊ/ *vt* (*also* ~ *down*) коси́ть *impf*, с~ *pf*. **mower** /'məʊə(r)/ *n* коси́лка.

MP *abbr* (*of* **Member of Parliament**) член парла́мента.

Mr /'mɪstə(r)/ *abbr* ми́стер, господи́н. **Mrs** /'mɪsɪz/ *abbr* ми́ссис *f indecl*, госпожа́.

Ms /mɪz/ *n* миз, госпожа́.

much /mʌtʃ/ *adj* & *n* мно́го +*gen*; мно́гое *sb*; *adv* о́чень; (*with comp adj*) гора́здо.

muck /mʌk/ *n* (*dung*) наво́з; (*dirt*) грязь; ~ **about** вози́ться *impf*; ~ **out** чи́стить *impf*, вы́~ *pf*; ~ **up** изга́живать *impf*, изга́дить *pf*.

mucous /'mju:kəs/ *adj* сли́зистый. **mucus** /'mju:kəs/ *n* слизь.

mud /mʌd/ *n* грязь. **mudguard** *n* крыло́.

muddle /'mʌd(ə)l/ *vt* пу́тать *impf*, с~ *pf*; *vi*: ~ **through** ко́е-ка́к справля́ться *impf*, спра́виться *pf*; *n* беспоря́док.

muddy /'mʌdɪ/ *adj* гря́зный; *vt* обры́згивать *impf*, обры́згать *pf* гря́зью.

muff /mʌf/ *n* му́фта.

muffle /'mʌf(ə)l/ *vt* (*for warmth*) заку́тывать *impf*, заку́тать *pf*; (*sound*) глуши́ть *impf*, за~ *pf*.

mug /mʌg/ *n* (*vessel*) кру́жка; (*face*) мо́рда.

muggy /'mʌgɪ/ *adj* сыро́й и тёплый.

mulch /mʌltʃ/ *n* му́льча; *vt* мульчи́ровать *impf* & *pf*.

mule /mju:l/ *n* мул.

mull /mʌl/ *vt*: ~ **over** обду́мывать *impf*, обду́мать *pf*. **mulled** /mʌld/ *adj*: ~ **wine** глинтве́йн.

mullet /'mʌlɪt/ *n* (*grey* ~) кефа́ль; (*red* ~) барабу́лька.

multicoloured /'mʌltɪ,kʌləd/ *adj* многокра́сочный. **multifarious** /,mʌltɪ'feərɪəs/ *adj* разнообра́зный. **multilateral** /,mʌltɪ'lætər(ə)l/ *adj* многосторо́нний. **multimillionaire** /,mʌltɪ,mɪljə'neə(r)/ *n* мультимиллионе́р. **multinational** /,mʌltɪ'næʃ(ə)n(ə)l/ *adj* многонациона́льный.

multiple /'mʌltɪp(ə)l/ *adj* составно́й; (*numerous*) многочи́сленный; ~ **sclerosis** рассе́янный склеро́з; *n* кра́тное число́; **least common** ~ о́бщее наиме́ньшее кра́тное *sb*. **multiplication** /,mʌltɪplɪ'keɪʃ(ə)n/ *n* умноже́ние. **multiplicity** /,mʌltɪ'plɪsɪtɪ/ *n*

многочи́сленность. **multiply** /ˈmʌltɪˌplaɪ/ *vt* (*math*) умножа́ть *impf*, умно́жить *pf*; *vi* размножа́ться *impf*, размно́житься *pf*.
multi-storey /ˌmʌltɪˈstɔːrɪ/ *adj* многоэта́жный.
multitude /ˈmʌltɪˌtjuːd/ *n* мно́жество; (*crowd*) толпа́.
mum[1] /mʌm/ *adj*: **keep ~** молча́ть *impf*.
mum[2] /mʌm/ *n* (*mother*) ма́ма.
mumble /ˈmʌmb(ə)l/ *vt* & *i* бормота́ть *impf*, про~ *pf*.
mummy[1] /ˈmʌmɪ/ *n* (*archaeol*) му́мия.
mummy[2] /ˈmʌmɪ/ *n* (*mother*) ма́ма, ма́мочка.
mumps /mʌmps/ *n* сви́нка.
munch /mʌntʃ/ *vt* жева́ть *impf*.
mundane /mʌnˈdeɪn/ *adj* земно́й.
municipal /mjuːˈnɪsɪp(ə)l/ *adj* муниципа́льный. **municipality** /-ˈpælɪtɪ/ *n* муниципалите́т.
munitions /mjuːˈnɪʃ(ə)ns/ *n pl* вое́нное иму́щество.
mural /ˈmjʊər(ə)l/ *n* стенна́я ро́спись.
murder /ˈmɜːdə(r)/ *n* уби́йство; *vt* убива́ть *impf*, уби́ть *pf*; (*language*) кове́ркать *impf*, ис~ *pf*. **murderer, murderess** /ˈmɜːdərə(r), ˈmɜːdərɪs/ *n* уби́йца *m* & *f*. **murderous** /ˈmɜːdərəs/ *adj* уби́йственный.
murky /ˈmɜːkɪ/ *adj* тёмный, мра́чный.
murmur /ˈmɜːmə(r)/ *n* шёпот; *vt* & *i* шепта́ть *impf*, шепну́ть *pf*.
muscle /ˈmʌs(ə)l/ *n* му́скул. **muscular** /ˈmʌskjʊlə(r)/ *adj* мы́шечный; (*person*) му́скулистый.
Muscovite /ˈmʌskəˌvaɪt/ *n* москви́ч, ~ка.
muse /mjuːz/ *vi* размышля́ть *impf*.
museum /mjuːˈzɪəm/ *n* музе́й.
mush /mʌʃ/ *n* ка́ша.
mushroom /ˈmʌʃrʊm/ *n* гриб.
music /ˈmjuːzɪk/ *n* му́зыка; (*sheet* ~) но́ты *f pl*; **~-hall** мю́зик-хо́лл; **~ stand** пюпи́тр. **musical** /-k(ə)l/ *adj* музыка́льный; *n* опере́тта. **musician** /mjuːˈzɪʃ(ə)n/ *n* музыка́нт.
musk /mʌsk/ *n* му́скус.
musket /ˈmʌskɪt/ *n* мушке́т.
Muslim /ˈmʊzlɪm/ *n* мусульма́нин, -а́нка; *adj* мусульма́нский.
muslin /ˈmʌzlɪn/ *n* мусли́н.
mussel /ˈmʌs(ə)l/ *n* ми́дия.
must /mʌst/ *v aux* (*obligation*) до́лжен (-жна́) *predic+inf*; на́до *impers+dat* & *inf*; (*necessity*) ну́жно *impers+dat* & *inf*; **~ not** (*prohibition*) нельзя́ *impers+dat* & *inf*.
mustard /ˈmʌstəd/ *n* горчи́ца.
muster /ˈmʌstə(r)/ *vt* собира́ть *impf*, собра́ть *pf*; (*courage etc.*) собира́ться *impf*, собра́ться *pf* c+*instr*.
musty /ˈmʌstɪ/ *adj* за́тхлый.
mutation /mjuːˈteɪʃ(ə)n/ *n* мута́ция.
mute /mjuːt/ *adj* немо́й; *n* немо́й *sb*; (*mus*) сурди́нка. **muted** /-tɪd/ *adj* приглушённый.
mutilate /ˈmjuːtɪˌleɪt/ *vt* уве́чить *impf*, из~ *pf*. **mutilation** /-ˈleɪʃ(ə)n/ *n* уве́чье.
mutineer /ˌmjuːtɪˈnɪə(r)/ *n* мяте́жник. **mutinous** /ˈmjuːtɪnəs/ *adj* мяте́жный. **mutiny** /ˈmjuːtɪnɪ/ *n* мяте́ж; *vi* бунтова́ть *impf*, взбунтова́ться *pf*.
mutter /ˈmʌtə(r)/ *vi* бормота́ть *impf*; *impf*; *n* бормота́ние.
mutton /ˈmʌt(ə)n/ *n* бара́нина.
mutual /ˈmjuːtʃʊəl/ *adj* взаи́мный; (*common*) о́бщий.

muzzle /'mʌz(ə)l/ *n* (*animal's*) мóрда; (*on animal*) намóрдник; (*of gun*) дýло; *vt* надевáть *impf*, надéть *pf* намóрдник на+*acc*; (*fig*) заставлять *impf*, застáвить *pf* молчáть.

my /maɪ/ *poss pron* мой; свой.

myopia /maɪ'əʊpɪə/ *n* близорýкость. **myopic** /-'ɒpɪk/ *adj* близорýкий.

myriad /'mɪrɪəd/ *n* мириáды (-д) *pl*; *adj* бесчи́сленный.

myrtle /'mɜːt(ə)l/ *n* мирт; *attrib* ми́ртовый.

myself /maɪ'self/ *pron* (*emph*) (я) сам, самá; (*refl*) себя́; -ся (*suffixed to vt*).

mysterious /mɪ'stɪərɪəs/ *adj* таи́нственный. **mystery** /'mɪstərɪ/ *n* тáйна.

mystic(al) /'mɪstɪk(ə)l/ *adj* мисти́ческий; *n* ми́стик. **mysticism** /'mɪstɪˌsɪz(ə)m/ *n* мистици́зм. **mystification** /ˌmɪstɪfɪ'keɪʃ(ə)n/ *n* озадáченность. **mystify** /'mɪstɪˌfaɪ/ *vt* озадáчивать *impf*, озадáчить *pf*.

myth /mɪθ/ *n* миф. **mythical** /'mɪθɪk(ə)l/ *adj* мифи́ческий. **mythological** /ˌmɪθə'lɒdʒɪk(ə)l/ *adj* мифологи́ческий. **mythology** /mɪ'θɒlədʒɪ/ *n* мифолóгия.

N

nag[1] /næg/ *n* (*horse*) лóшадь.

nag[2] /næg/ *vt* (*also* ~ *at*) пили́ть *impf* +*acc*; *vi* (*of pain*) ныть *impf*.

nail /neɪl/ *n* (*finger-*, *toe-*~) нóготь *m*; (*metal spike*) гвоздь *m*; **~ varnish** лак для ногтéй; *vt* прибивáть *impf*, приби́ть *pf* (гвоздя́ми).

naive /naɪ'iːv/ *adj* наи́вный. **naivety** /-tɪ/ *n* наи́вность.

naked /'neɪkɪd/ *adj* гóлый; **~ eye** невооружённый глаз. **nakedness** /-nɪs/ *n* наготá.

name /neɪm/ *n* назвáние; (*forename*) и́мя *neut*; (*surname*) фами́лия; (*reputation*) репутáция; **what is his ~?** как егó зовýт?; **~-plate** дощéчка с фами́лией; **~sake** тёзка *m* & *f*; *vt* называ́ть *impf*, назвáть *pf*; (*appoint*) назначáть *impf*, назнáчить *pf*. **nameless** /-lɪs/ *adj* безымя́нный. **namely** /-lɪ/ *adv* (а) и́менно; то есть.

nanny /'nænɪ/ *n* ня́ня.

nap /næp/ *n* корóткий сон; *vi* вздремнýть *pf*.

nape /neɪp/ *n* загри́вок.

napkin /'næpkɪn/ *n* салфéтка.

nappy /'næpɪ/ *n* пелёнка.

narcissus /nɑː'sɪsəs/ *n* нарци́сс.

narcotic /nɑː'kɒtɪk/ *adj* наркоти́ческий; *n* наркóтик.

narrate /nə'reɪt/ *vt* расскáзывать *impf*, рассказáть *pf*. **narration** /-'reɪʃ(ə)n/ *n* расскáз. **narrative** /'nærətɪv/ *n* расскáз; *adj* повествовáтельный. **narrator** /nə'reɪtə(r)/ *n* расскáзчик

narrow /'nærəʊ/ *adj* ýзкий; *vt* & *i* сýживать(ся) *impf*, сýзить(ся) *pf*. **narrowly** /-lɪ/ *adv* (*hardly*) чуть, éле-éле; **he ~ escaped drowning** он чуть не утонýл. **narrow-minded** /ˌnærəʊ'maɪndɪd/ *adj* ограни́ченный. **narrowness** /'nærəʊnɪs/ *n* ýзость.

nasal /'neɪz(ə)l/ *adj* носовóй; (*voice*) гнусáвый.

nasturtium /nə'stɜːʃəm/ *n* настýрция.

nasty /'nɑːstɪ/ *adj* неприя́тный, проти́вный; (*person*) злой.

nation /ˈneɪʃ(ə)n/ *n* (*people*) нарóд; (*country*) странá. **national** /ˈnæʃən(ə)l/ *adj* национáльный, нарóдный; (*of the state*) госудáрственный; *n* пóдданный *sb*. **nationalism** /ˈnæʃənə,lɪz(ə)m/ *n* национализм. **nationalist** /ˈnæʃənəlɪst/ *n* националист, ~ка. **nationalistic** /,næʃənəˈlɪstɪk/ *adj* националистический. **nationality** /,næʃəˈnælɪtɪ/ *n* национáльность; (*citizenship*) граждáнство, пóдданство. **nationalization** /,næʃənəlaɪˈzeɪʃ(ə)n/ *n* национализáция. **nationalize** /ˈnæʃənə,laɪz/ *vt* национализи́ровать *impf* & *pf*.

native /ˈneɪtɪv/ *n* (~ *of*) урожéнец, -нка (+*gen*); (*aborigine*) тузéмец, -мка; *adj* (*innate*) прирóдный; (*of one's birth*) роднóй; (*indigenous*) тузéмный; ~ **land** рóдина; ~ **language** роднóй язы́к; ~ **speaker** носи́тель *m* языкá.

nativity /nəˈtɪvɪtɪ/ *n* Рождествó (Христóво).

natter /ˈnætə(r)/ *vi* болтáть *impf*.

natural /ˈnætʃər(ə)l/ *adj* естéственный, прирóдный; ~ **resources** прирóдные богáтства *neut pl*; ~ **selection** естéственный отбóр; *n* (*mus*) бекáр. **naturalism** /-,lɪz(ə)m/ *n* натурали́зм. **naturalist** /-lɪst/ *n* натурали́ст. **naturalistic** /,nætʃərəˈlɪstɪk/ *adj* натуралисти́ческий. **naturalization** /,nætʃərəlaɪˈzeɪʃ(ə)n/ *n* натурализáция. **naturalize** /ˈnætʃərə,laɪz/ *vt* натурализи́ровать *impf* & *pf*. **naturally** /ˈnætʃərəlɪ/ *adv* естéственно. **nature** /ˈneɪtʃə(r)/ *n* прирóда; (*character*) харáктер; **by** ~ по прирóде.

naught /nɔːt/ *n*: **come to** ~ своди́ться *impf*, свести́сь *pf* к нулю́.

naughty /ˈnɔːtɪ/ *adj* шаловли́вый.

nausea /ˈnɔːzɪə/ *n* тошнотá. **nauseate** /-zɪ,eɪt/ *vt* тошни́ть *impf impers* от +*gen*. **nauseating** /-zɪ,eɪtɪŋ/ *adj* тошнотвóрный. **nauseous** /-zɪəs/ *adj*: **I feel** ~ меня́ тошни́т.

nautical /ˈnɔːtɪk(ə)l/ *n* морскóй.

naval /ˈneɪv(ə)l/ *adj* (воéнно-)морскóй.

nave /neɪv/ *n* неф.

navel /ˈneɪv(ə)l/ *n* пупóк.

navigable /ˈnævɪgəb(ə)l/ *adj* судохóдный. **navigate** /-,geɪt/ *vt* (*ship*) вести́ *impf*; (*sea*) плáвать *impf* по+*dat*. **navigation** /,nævɪˈgeɪʃ(ə)n/ *n* навигáция. **navigator** /ˈnævɪ,geɪtə(r)/ *n* штýрман.

navvy /ˈnævɪ/ *n* землекóп.

navy /ˈneɪvɪ/ *n* воéнно-морскóй флот; ~ **blue** тёмно-си́ний.

Nazi /ˈnɑːtsɪ/ *n* наци́ст, ~ка; *adj* наци́стский. **Nazism** /ˈnɑːtsɪz(ə)m/ *n* наци́зм.

NB *abbr* нотабéне.

near /nɪə(r)/ *adv* бли́зко; ~ **at hand** под рукóй; ~ **by** ря́дом; *prep* вóзле+*gen*, óколо+*gen*, у+*gen*; *adj* бли́зкий; ~**-sighted** близорýкий; *vt* & *i* приближáться *impf*, прибли́зиться *pf* к+*dat*. **nearly** /-lɪ/ *adv* почти́.

neat /niːt/ *adj* (*tidy*) опря́тный, аккурáтный; (*clear*) чёткий; (*undiluted*) неразбáвленный.

nebulous /ˈnebjʊləs/ *adj* нея́сный.

necessarily /ˈnesəsərɪlɪ/ *adv* обязáтельно. **necessary** /ˈnesəsərɪ/ *adj* необходи́мый; (*inevitable*) неизбéжный. **necessitate** /nɪˈsesɪ,teɪt/ *vt* дéлать *impf*, с~ *pf* необходи́мым. **necessity**

/-'sesıtı/ *n* необходи́мость; неизбе́жность; (*object*) предме́т пе́рвой необходи́мости.
neck /nek/ *n* ше́я; (*of garment*) вы́рез; ~ **and** ~ голова́ в го́лову. **necklace** /'neklıs/ *n* ожере́лье. **neckline** *n* вы́рез.
nectar /'nektə(r)/ *n* некта́р.
née /neı/ *adj* урождённая.
need /ni:d/ *n* нужда́; *vt* нужда́ться *impf* в+*prep*; **I** (*etc.*) ~ мне (*dat*) ну́жен (-жна́, -жно, -жны́) +*nom*; **I** ~ **five roubles** мне ну́жно пять рубле́й.
needle /'ni:d(ə)l/ *n* игла́, иго́лка; (*knitting*) спи́ца; (*pointer*) стре́лка; *vt* придира́ться *impf*, придра́ться *pf* к+*dat*.
needless /'ni:dlıs/ *adj* нену́жный; ~ **to say** разуме́ется. **needy** /'ni:dı/ *adj* нужда́ющийся.
negation /nı'geıʃ(ə)n/ *n* отрица́ние. **negative** /'negətıv/ *adj* отрица́тельный; *n* отрица́ние; (*phot*) негати́в.
neglect /nı'glekt/ *vt* пренебрега́ть *impf*, пренебре́чь *pf* +*instr*; не забо́титься *impf* о+*prep*; *n* пренебреже́ние; (*condition*) забро́шенность. **neglectful** /-fʊl/ *adj* небре́жный, невнима́тельный (**of** к+*dat*). **negligence** /'neglıdʒ(ə)ns/ *n* небре́жность. **negligent** /-dʒ(ə)nt/ *adj* небре́жный. **negligible** /-dʒıb(ə)l/ *adj* незначи́тельный.
negotiate /nı'gəʊʃı,eıt/ *vi* вести́ *impf* перегово́ры; *vt* (*arrange*) заключа́ть *impf*, заключи́ть *pf*; (*overcome*) преодолева́ть *impf*, преодоле́ть *pf*. **negotiation** /nı,gəʊʃı'eıʃ(ə)n/ *n* (*discussion*) перегово́ры *m pl*.
Negro /'ni:grəʊ/ *n* негр; *adj* негритя́нский.
neigh /neı/ *n* ржа́ние; *vi* ржать *impf*.
neighbour /'neıbə(r)/ *n* сосе́д, ~ка. **neighbourhood** /-hʊd/ *n* ме́стность; **in the** ~ **of** о́коло +*gen*. **neighbouring** /-rıŋ/ *adj* сосе́дний. **neighbourly** /-lı/ *adj* добрососе́дский.
neither /'naıðə(r)/ *adv* та́кже не, то́же не; *pron* ни тот, ни друго́й; ~ ... **nor** ни… ни.
neon /'ni:ɒn/ *n* нео́н; *attrib* нео́новый.
nephew /'nevju:/ *n* племя́нник.
nepotism /'nepə,tız(ə)m/ *n* кумовство́.
nerve /nɜ:v/ *n* нерв; (*courage*) сме́лость; (*impudence*) на́глость; **get on the** ~**s of** де́йствовать *impf*, по~ *pf* +*dat* на не́рвы. **nervous** /'nɜ:vəs/ *adj* не́рвный; ~ **breakdown** не́рвное расстро́йство. **nervy** /'nɜ:vı/ *adj* нерво́зный.
nest /nest/ *n* гнездо́; ~ **egg** сбереже́ния *neut pl*; *vi* гнезди́ться *impf*. **nestle** /'nes(ə)l/ *vi* льнуть *impf*, при~ *pf*.
net[1] /net/ *n* сеть, се́тка; *vt* (*catch*) лови́ть *impf*, пойма́ть *pf* сетя́ми.
net[2], **nett** /net/ *adj* чи́стый; *vt* получа́ть *impf*, получи́ть *pf* … чи́стого дохо́да.
Netherlands /'neðələndz/ *n* Нидерла́нды (-ов) *pl*.
nettle /'net(ə)l/ *n* крапи́ва.
network /'netwɜ:k/ *n* сеть.
neurologist /njʊə'rɒlədʒıst/ *n* невро́лог. **neurology** /-dʒı/ *n* невроло́гия. **neurosis** /-'rəʊsıs/ *n* невро́з. **neurotic** /-'rɒtık/ *adj* невроти́ческий.
neuter /'nju:tə(r)/ *adj* сре́дний, сре́днего ро́да; *n* сре́дний род; *vt* кастри́ровать *impf* & *pf*. **neutral** /-tr(ə)l/ *adj* нейтра́ль-

ный; *n* (*gear*) нейтра́льная ско́рость. **neutrality** /nju:'trælıtı/ *n* нейтралите́т. **neutralize** /'nju:trə,laız/ *vt* нейтрализова́ть *impf* & *pf.* **neutron** /'nju:trɒn/ *n* нейтро́н.

never /'nevə(r)/ *adv* никогда́; **~ again** никогда́ бо́льше; **~ mind** ничего́!; всё равно́!; **~ once** ни ра́зу. **nevertheless** /,nevəðə'les/ *conj*, *adv* тем не ме́нее.

new /nju:/ *adj* но́вый; (*moon, potatoes*) молодо́й. **new-born** *adj* новорождённый. **newcomer** /'nju:kʌmə(r)/ *n* прише́лец. **newfangled** /'nju:fæŋg(ə)ld/ *adj* новомо́дный. **newly** /'nju:lı/ *adv* то́лько что, неда́вно. **newness** /'nju:nıs/ *n* новизна́.

news /nju:z/ *n* но́вость, -ти *pl*, изве́стие, -ия *pl.* **newsagent** *n* продаве́ц газе́т. **newsletter** *n* информацио́нный бюллете́нь *m.* **newspaper** *n* газе́та. **newsprint** *n* газе́тная бума́га. **newsreel** *n* кинохро́ника.

newt /nju:t/ *n* трито́н.

New Zealand /nju: 'zi:lənd/ *n* Но́вая Зела́ндия; *adj* новозела́ндский.

next /nekst/ *adj* сле́дующий, бу́дущий; *adv* (**~** *time*) в сле́дующий раз; (*then*) пото́м, зате́м; **~ door** (*house*) в сосе́днем до́ме; (*flat*) в сосе́дней кварти́ре; **~ of kin** ближа́йший ро́дственник; **~ to** ря́дом с+*instr*; (*fig*) почти́. **next-door** *adj* сосе́дний; **~ neighbour** ближа́йший сосе́д.

nib /nıb/ *n* перо́.

nibble /'nıb(ə)l/ *vt* & *i* грызть *impf*; *vt* обгрыза́ть *impf*, обгры́зть *pf*; (*grass*) щипа́ть *impf*; (*fish*) клева́ть *impf.*

nice /naıs/ *adj* (*pleasant*) прия́тный, хоро́ший; (*person*) ми́лый. **nicety** /'naısıtı/ *n* то́нкость.

niche /ni:ʃ/ *n* ни́ша; (*fig*) своё ме́сто.

nick /nık/ *n* (*scratch*) цара́пина; (*notch*) зару́бка; **in the ~ of time** в са́мый после́дний моме́нт; *vt* (*scratch*) цара́пать *impf*, о**~** *pf*; (*steal*) сти́брить *pf.*

nickel /'nık(ə)l/ *n* ни́кель *m.*

nickname /'nıkneım/ *n* про́звище; *vt* прозыва́ть *impf*, прозва́ть *pf.*

nicotine /'nıkə,ti:n/ *n* никоти́н.

niece /ni:s/ *n* племя́нница.

niggardly /'nıgədlı/ *adj* скупо́й.

niggling /'nıglıŋ/ *adj* ме́лочный.

night /naıt/ *n* ночь; (*evening*) ве́чер; **at ~** но́чью; **last ~** вчера́ ве́чером; *attrib* ночно́й; **~-club** ночно́й клуб. **nightcap** *n* ночно́й колпа́к; (*drink*) стака́нчик спиртно́го на́ ночь. **nightdress** *n* ночна́я руба́шка. **nightfall** *n* наступле́ние но́чи. **nightingale** /'naıtıŋ,geıl/ *n* солове́й. **nightly** /'naıtlı/ *adj* ежено́щный; *adv* ежено́щно. **nightmare** /'naıtmeə(r)/*n* кошма́р. **nightmarish** /'naıtmeərıʃ/ *adj* кошма́рный.

nil /nıl/ *n* нуль *m.*

nimble /'nımb(ə)l/ *adj* прово́рный.

nine /naın/ *adj* & *n* де́вять; (*number 9*) девя́тка. **nineteen** /naın 'ti:n/ *adj* & *n* девятна́дцать. **nineteenth** /naın'ti:nθ/ *adj* & *n* девятна́дцатый. **ninetieth** /'naıntııəθ/ *adj* & *n* девяно́стый. **ninety** /'naıntı/ *adj* & *n* девяно́сто; *pl* (*decade*) девяно́стые го́ды (-до́в) *m pl.* **ninth** /'naınθ/ *adj* & *n* девя́тый.

nip /nıp/ *vt* (*pinch*) щипа́ть *impf*, щипну́ть *pf*; (*bite*) куса́ть *impf*,

укуси́ть *pf*; ~ **in the bud** пресека́ть *impf*, пресе́чь *pf* в заро́дыше; *n* щипо́к; уку́с; **there's a ~ in the air** во́здух па́хнет моро́зцем.
nipple /'nɪp(ə)l/ *n* сосо́к.
nirvana /nɪə'vɑːnə/ *n* нирва́на.
nit /nɪt/ *n* гни́да.
nitrate /'naɪtreɪt/ *n* нитра́т. **nitrogen** /'naɪtrədʒ(ə)n/ *n* азо́т.
no /nəʊ/ *adj* (*not any*) никако́й, не оди́н; (*not a* (*fool etc.*)) (совсе́м) не; *adv* нет; (нисколько) не+*comp*; *n* отрица́ние, отка́з; (*in vote*) го́лос «про́тив»; ~ **doubt** коне́чно, несомне́нно; ~ **longer** уже́ не, бо́льше не; **no one** никто́; ~ **wonder** не удиви́тельно.
Noah's ark /ˌnəʊəz 'ɑːk/ *n* Но́ев ковче́г.
nobility /nəʊ'bɪlɪtɪ/ *n* (*class*) дворя́нство; (*quality*) благоро́дство. **noble** /'nəʊb(ə)l/ *adj* дворя́нский; благоро́дный. **nobleman** *n* дворяни́н.
nobody /'nəʊbədɪ/ *pron* никто́; *n* ничто́жество.
nocturnal /nɒk'tɜːn(ə)l/ *adj* ночно́й.
nod /nɒd/ *vi* кива́ть *impf*, кивну́ть *pf* голово́й; *n* киво́к.
nodule /'nɒdjuːl/ *n* узело́к.
noise /nɔɪz/ *n* шум. **noiseless** /-lɪs/ *adj* бесшу́мный. **noisy** /'nɔɪzɪ/ *adj* шу́мный.
nomad /'nəʊmæd/ *n* коче́вник. **nomadic** /-'mædɪk/ *adj* кочево́й.
nomenclature /nəʊ'menklətʃə(r)/ *n* номенклату́ра.
nominal /'nɒmɪn(ə)l/ *adj* номина́льный. **nominate** /'nɒmɪˌneɪt/ *vt* (*propose*) выдвига́ть *impf*, вы́двинуть *pf*; (*appoint*) назнача́ть *impf*, назна́чить *pf*. **nomination** /ˌnɒmɪ'neɪʃ(ə)n/ *n* выдвиже́ние; назначе́ние. **nominative** /'nɒmɪnətɪv/ *adj* (*n*) имени́тельный (паде́ж). **nominee** /ˌnɒmɪ'niː/ *n* кандида́т.
non-alcoholic /ˌnɒnælkə'hɒlɪk/ *adj* безалкого́льный. **non-aligned** /ˌnɒnə'laɪnd/ *adj* неприсоедини́вшийся.
nonchalance /'nɒnʃələns/ *n* беззабо́тность. **nonchalant** /-lənt/ *n* беззабо́тный.
non-commissioned /ˌnɒnkə'mɪʃ(ə)nd/ *adj*: ~ **officer** у́нтер-офице́р. **non-committal** /-'mɪt(ə)l/ *adj* укло́нчивый.
non-conformist /ˌnɒnkən'fɔːmɪst/ *n* нонконформи́ст; *adj* нонконформи́стский.
nondescript /'nɒndɪskrɪpt/ *adj* неопределённый.
none /nʌn/ *pron* (*no one*) никто́; (*nothing*) ничто́; (*not one*) не оди́н; *adv* ниско́лько не; ~ **the less** тем не ме́нее.
nonentity /nɒ'nentɪtɪ/ *n* ничто́жество.
non-existent /ˌnɒnɪg'zɪst(ə)nt/ *adj* несуществу́ющий. **non-fiction** /nɒn'fɪkʃ(ə)n/ *adj* документа́льный. **non-intervention** /ˌnɒnɪntə'venʃ(ə)n/ *n* невмеша́тельство. **non-party** *adj* беспарти́йный. **non-payment** /nɒn'peɪmənt/ *n* неплатёж.
nonplus /nɒn'plʌs/ *vt* ста́вить *impf*, по~ *pf* в тупи́к.
non-productive /ˌnɒnprə'dʌktɪv/ *adj* непроизводи́тельный. **non-resident** /nɒn'rezɪd(ə)nt/ *adj* не прожива́ющий (где́-нибудь).
nonsense /'nɒns(ə)ns/ *n* ерунда́. **nonsensical** /nɒn'sensɪk(ə)l/ *adj* бессмы́сленный.
non-smoker /nɒn'sməʊkə(r)/ *n* (*person*) некуря́щий *sb*; (*compartment*) купе́ *neut indecl*, для некуря́щих. **non-stop** /nɒn

ˈstɒp/ *adj* безостано́вочный; (*flight*) беспоса́дочный; *adv* без остано́вок; без поса́док. **non-violent** /nɒnˈvaɪələnt/ *adj* ненаси́льственный.

noodles /ˈnuːd(ə)lz/ *n pl* лапша́.

nook /nʊk/ *n* уголо́к.

noon /nuːn/ *n* по́лдень *m*.

no one /ˈnəʊwʌn/ *see* **no**

noose /nuːs/ *n* пе́тля.

nor /nɔː(r)/ *conj* и не; то́же; **neither ... ~** ни... ни.

norm /nɔːm/ *n* но́рма. **normal** /ˈnɔːm(ə)l/ *adj* норма́льный. **normality** /nɔːˈmælɪtɪ/ *n* норма́льность. **normalize** /ˈnɔːməˌlaɪz/ *vt* нормализова́ть *impf* & *pf*.

north /nɔːθ/ *n* се́вер; (*naut*) норд; *adj* се́верный; *adv* к се́веру, на се́вер; **~-east** се́веро-восто́к; **~-easterly, -eastern** се́веро-восто́чный; **~-west** се́веро-за́пад; **~-westerly, -western** се́веро-за́падный. **northerly** /ˈnɔːðəlɪ/ *adj* се́верный. **northern** /ˈnɔːð(ə)n/ *adj* се́верный. **northerner** /ˈnɔːðənə(r)/ *n* северя́нин, -я́нка. **northward(s)** /ˈnɔːθwəd(z)/ *adv* на се́вер, к се́веру.

Norway /ˈnɔːweɪ/ *n* Норве́гия. **Norwegian** /nɔːˈwiːdʒ(ə)n/ *adj* норве́жский; *n* норве́жец, -жка.

nose /nəʊz/ *n* нос; *vt*: **~ about, out** разню́хивать *impf*, разню́хать *pf*. **nosebleed** *n* кровотече́ние из́ носу. **nosedive** *n* пике́ *neut indecl*.

nostalgia /nɒˈstældʒə/ *n* ностальги́я. **nostalgic** /-dʒɪk/ *adj* ностальги́ческий.

nostril /ˈnɒstrɪl/ *n* ноздря́.

not /nɒt/ *adv* не; нет; ни; **~ at all** ниско́лько, ничу́ть; (*reply to thanks*) не сто́ит (благода́рности); **~ once** ни ра́зу; **~ that** не то, что́бы; **~ too** дово́льно +*neg*; **~ to say** что́бы не сказа́ть; **~ to speak of** не говоря́ уже́ о+*prep*.

notable /ˈnəʊtəb(ə)l/ *adj* заме́тный; (*remarkable*) замеча́тельный. **notably** /-blɪ/ *adv* (*especially*) осо́бенно; (*perceptibly*) заме́тно.

notary (public) /ˈnəʊtərɪ (ˈpʌblɪk)/ *n* нота́риус.

notation /nəʊˈteɪʃ(ə)n/ *n* нота́ция; (*mus*) но́тное письмо́.

notch /nɒtʃ/ *n* зару́бка; *vt*: **~ up** выи́грывать *impf*, вы́играть *pf*.

note /nəʊt/ *n* (*record*) заме́тка, за́пись; (*annotation*) примеча́ние; (*letter*) запи́ска; (*banknote*) банкно́т; (*mus*) но́та; (*tone*) тон; (*attention*) внима́ние; *vt* отмеча́ть *impf*, отме́тить *pf*; **~ down** запи́сывать *impf*, записа́ть *pf*. **notebook** *n* записна́я кни́жка. **noted** /ˈnəʊtɪd/ *adj* знамени́тый; изве́стный (**for** +*instr*). **notepaper** *n* почто́вая бума́га. **noteworthy** /ˈnəʊtwɜːðɪ/ *adj* досто́йный внима́ния.

nothing /ˈnʌθɪŋ/ *n* ничто́, ничего́; **~ but** ничего́ кро́ме+*gen*, то́лько; **~ of the kind** ничего́ подо́бного; **come to ~** конча́ться *impf*, ко́нчиться *pf* ниче́м; **for ~** (*free*) да́ром; (*in vain*) зря, напра́сно; **have ~ to do with** не име́ть *impf* никако́го отноше́ния к+*dat*; **there is (was) ~ for it (but to)** ничего́ друго́го не остаётся (остава́лось) (как); **to say ~ of** не говоря́ уже́ о+*prep*.

notice /ˈnəʊtɪs/ *n* (*sign*) объявле́ние; (*warning*) предупрежде́-

ние; (*attention*) внима́ние; (*review*) о́тзыв; **give (in) one's ~** подава́ть *impf*, пода́ть *pf* заявле́ние об ухо́де с рабо́ты; **give s.o. ~** предупрежда́ть *impf*, предупреди́ть *pf* об увольне́нии; **take ~ of** обраща́ть *impf*, обрати́ть *pf* внима́ния на+*acc*; **~-board** доска́ для объявле́ний; *vt* замеча́ть *impf*, заме́тить *pf*. **noticeable** /-səb(ə)l/ *adj* заме́тный. **notification** /ˌnəʊtɪfɪ'keɪʃ(ə)n/ *n* извеще́ние. **notify** /'nəʊtɪˌfaɪ/ *vt* извеща́ть *impf*, извести́ть *pf* (**of** о+*prep*).

notion /'nəʊʃ(ə)n/ *n* поня́тие.

notoriety /ˌnəʊtə'raɪətɪ/ *n* дурна́я сла́ва. **notorious** /nəʊ'tɔːrɪəs/ *adj* пресловýтый.

notwithstanding /ˌnɒtwɪθ'stændɪŋ/ *prep* несмотря́ на+*acc*; *adv* тем не ме́нее.

nought /nɔːt/ *n* (*nothing*) *see* **naught**; (*zero*) нуль *m*; (*figure 0*) ноль *m*.

noun /naʊn/ *n* (и́мя *neut*) существи́тельное *sb*.

nourish /'nʌrɪʃ/ *vt* пита́ть *impf*, на~ *pf*. **nourishing** /-ʃɪŋ/ *adj* пита́тельный. **nourishment** /-mənt/ *n* пита́ние.

novel /'nɒv(ə)l/ *adj* но́вый; (*unusual*) необыкнове́нный; *n* рома́н. **novelist** /-lɪst/ *n* романи́ст. **novelty** /-tɪ/ *n* (*newness*) новизна́; (*new thing*) нови́нка.

November /nə'vembə(r)/ *n* ноя́брь *m*; *adj* ноя́брьский.

novice /'nɒvɪs/ *n* (*eccl*) послу́шник, -ица; (*beginner*) нови́чо́к.

now /naʊ/ *adv* тепе́рь, сейча́с; (*immediately*) то́тчас же; (*next*) тогда́; *conj*: **~ (that)** раз, когда́; **(every) ~ and again, then** вре́мя от вре́мени; **by ~** уже́; **from ~ on** впредь. **nowadays** /'naʊəˌdeɪz/ *adv* в на́ше вре́мя.

nowhere /'nəʊweə(r)/ *adv* (*place*) нигде́; (*direction*) никуда́; *pron*: **I have ~ to go** мне не́куда пойти́.

noxious /'nɒkʃəs/ *adj* вре́дный.

nozzle /'nɒz(ə)l/ *n* со́пло́.

nuance /'njuːɑ̃s/ *n* нюа́нс.

nuclear /'njuːklɪə(r)/ *adj* я́дерный. **nucleus** /-klɪəs/ *n* ядро́.

nude /njuːd/ *adj* обнажённый, наго́й; *n* обнажённая фигу́ра.

nudge /nʌdʒ/ *vt* подта́лкивать *impf*, подтолкну́ть *pf* ло́ктем; *n* толчо́к ло́ктем.

nudity /'njuːdɪtɪ/ *n* нагота́.

nugget /'nʌgɪt/ *n* саморо́док.

nuisance /'njuːs(ə)ns/ *n* доса́да; (*person*) раздража́ющий челове́к.

null /nʌl/ *adj*: **~ and void** недействи́тельный. **nullify** /'nʌlɪˌfaɪ/ *vt* аннули́ровать *impf* & *pf*. **nullity** /'nʌlɪtɪ/ *n* недействи́тельность.

numb /nʌm/ *adj* онеме́лый; (*from cold*) окочене́лый; **go ~** онеме́ть *pf*; (*from cold*) окочене́ть *pf*.

number /'nʌmbə(r)/ *n* (*total*) коли́чество; (*total*; *symbol*; *math*; *gram*) число́; (*identifying numeral*; *item*) но́мер; **~-plate** номерна́я доще́чка; *vt* (*assign ~ to*) нумерова́ть *impf*, за~, про~ *pf*; (*contain*) насчи́тывать *impf*; **~ among** причисля́ть *impf*, причи́слить *pf* к+*dat*; **his days are ~ed** его́ дни сочтены́.

numeral /'njuːmər(ə)l/ *n* ци́фра; (*gram*) (и́мя *neut*) числи́тельное *sb*. **numerical** /njuː'merɪk(ə)l/ *adj* числово́й. **numerous** /'njuːmərəs/ *adj* многочи́сленный; (*many*) мно́го +*gen pl*.

nun /nʌn/ *n* монáхиня. **nunnery** /'nʌnəri/ *n* (жéнский) монасты́рь *m*.
nuptial /'nʌpʃ(ə)l/ *adj* свáдебный; *n*: *pl* свáдьба.
nurse /nɜ:s/ *n* (*child's*) ня́ня; (*medical*) медсестрá; *vt* (*suckle*) корми́ть *impf*, на~, по~ *pf*; (*tend sick*) ухáживать *impf* за +*instr*; **nursing home** санатóрий; дом престарéлых. **nursery** /'nɜ:səri/ *n* (*room*) дéтская *sb*; (*day* ~) я́сли (-лей) *pl*; (*for plants*) питóмник; ~ **rhyme** дéтские прибаýтки *f pl*; ~ **school** дéтский сад.
nut /nʌt/ *n* орéх; (*for bolt etc.*) гáйка. **nutshell** *n*: **in a** ~ в двух словáх.
nutmeg /'nʌtmeg/ *n* мускáтный орéх.
nutrient /'nju:triənt/ *n* питáтельное веществó. **nutrition** /nju:'triʃ(ə)n/ *n* питáние. **nutritious** /-'triʃəs/ *adj* питáтельный.
nylon /'nailɒn/ *n* нейлóн; *pl* нейлóновые чулки́ (-лóк) *pl*.
nymph /nimf/ *n* ни́мфа.

O

O /əʊ/ *int* о!; ах!
oaf /əʊf/ *n* неуклю́жий человéк.
oak /əʊk/ *n* дуб; *attrib* дубóвый.
oar /ɔ:(r)/ *n* весло́. **oarsman** /'ɔ:zmən/ *n* гребéц.
oasis /əʊ'eisis/ *n* оáзис.
oath /əʊθ/ *n* прися́га; (*expletive*) ругáтельство.
oatmeal /'əʊtmi:l/ *n* овся́нка. **oats** /əʊts/ *n pl* овёс (овсá) *collect*.
obdurate /'ɒbdjʊrət/ *adj* упря́мый.
obedience /əʊ'bi:diəns/ *n* послушáние. **obedient** /-ənt/ *adj* послу́шный.
obese /əʊ'bi:s/ *n* ту́чный. **obesity** /-siti/ *n* ту́чность.
obey /əʊ'bei/ *vt* слу́шаться *impf*, по~ *pf* +*gen*; (*law, order*) подчиня́ться *impf*, подчини́ться *pf* +*dat*.
obituary /ə'bitjʊəri/ *n* некролóг.
object *n* /'ɒbdʒikt/ (*thing*) предмéт; (*aim*) цель; (*gram*) дополнéние; *vi* /əb'dʒekt/ возражáть *impf*, возрази́ть *pf* (**to** прóтив +*gen*); **I don't** ~ я не прóтив. **objection** /əb'dʒekʃ(ə)n/ *n* возражéние; **I have no** ~ я не возражáю. **objectionable** /əb'dʒekʃənəb(ə)l/ *adj* неприя́тный. **objective** /əb'dʒektiv/ *adj* объекти́вный; *n* цель. **objectivity** /,ɒbdʒek'tiviti/ *n* объекти́вность. **objector** /əb'dʒektə(r)/ *n* возражáющий *sb*.
obligation /,ɒbli'geiʃ(ə)n/ *n* обязáтельство; **I am under an** ~ я обя́зан(а). **obligatory** /ə'bligətəri/ *adj* обязáтельный. **oblige** /ə'blaidʒ/ *vt* обя́зывать *impf*, обязáть *pf*; **be** ~**d to** (*grateful*) быть обя́занным+*dat*. **obliging** /ə'blaidʒiŋ/ *adj* услу́жливый.
oblique /ə'bli:k/ *adj* косóй; (*fig*; *gram*) кóсвенный.
obliterate /ə'blitə,reit/ *vt* (*efface*) стирáть *impf*, стерéть *pf*; (*destroy*) уничтожáть *impf*, уничтóжить *pf*. **obliteration** /-'reiʃ(ə)n/ *n* стирáние; уничтожéние.
oblivion /ə'bliviən/ *n* забвéние. **oblivious** /-viəs/ *adj* (*forgetful*) забы́вчивый; **to be** ~ **of** не замечáть *impf* +*gen*.
oblong /'ɒblɒŋ/ *adj* продолго-

ва́тый.

obnoxious /əb'nɒkʃəs/ *adj* проти́вный.

oboe /'əʊbəʊ/ *n* гобо́й.

obscene /əb'siːn/ *adj* непристо́йный. **obscenity** /-'senɪtɪ/ *n* непристо́йность.

obscure /əb'skjʊə(r)/ *adj* (*unclear*) нея́сный; (*little known*) малоизве́стный; *vt* затемня́ть *impf*, затемни́ть *pf*; де́лать *impf*, с~ *pf* нея́сным. **obscurity** /-rɪtɪ/ *n* нея́сность; неизве́стность.

obsequious /əb'siːkwɪəs/ *adj* подобостра́стный.

observance /əb'zɜːv(ə)ns/ *n* соблюде́ние; (*rite*) обря́д. **observant** /-v(ə)nt/ *adj* наблюда́тельный. **observation** /ˌɒbzə'veɪʃ(ə)n/ *n* наблюде́ние; (*remark*) замеча́ние. **observatory** /əb'zɜːvətərɪ/ *n* обсервато́рия. **observe** /əb'zɜːv/ *vt* (*law etc.*) соблюда́ть *impf*, соблюсти́ *pf*; (*watch*) наблюда́ть *impf*; (*remark*) замеча́ть *impf*, заме́тить *pf*. **observer** /əb 'zɜːvə(r)/ *n* наблюда́тель *m*.

obsess /əb'ses/ *vt* пресле́довать *impf*; **obsessed by** одержи́мый +*instr*. **obsession** /-'seʃ(ə)n/ *n* одержи́мость; (*idea*) навя́зчивая иде́я. **obsessive** /-'sesɪv/ *adj* навя́зчивый.

obsolete /'ɒbsəˌliːt/ *adj* устаре́лый, вы́шедший из употребле́ния.

obstacle /'ɒbstək(ə)l/ *n* препя́тствие.

obstetrician /ˌɒbstə'trɪʃ(ə)n/ *n* акуше́р. **obstetrics** /əb'stetrɪks/ *n* акуше́рство.

obstinacy /'ɒbstɪnəsɪ/ *n* упря́мство. **obstinate** /'ɒbstɪnət/ *adj* упря́мый.

obstreperous /əb'strepərəs/ *adj* бу́йный.

obstruct /əb'strʌkt/ *vt* загражда́ть *impf*, загради́ть *pf*; (*hinder*) препя́тствовать *impf*, вос~ *pf* +*dat*. **obstruction** /-'strʌkʃ(ə)n/ *n* загражде́ние; (*obstacle*) препя́тствие. **obstructive** /-'strʌktɪv/ *adj* загражда́ющий; препя́тствующий.

obtain /əb'teɪn/ *vt* получа́ть *impf*, получи́ть *pf*; достава́ть *impf*, доста́ть *pf*.

obtrusive /əb'truːsɪv/ *adj* навя́зчивый; (*thing*) броса́ющийся в глаза́.

obtuse /əb'tjuːs/ *adj* тупо́й.

obviate /'ɒbvɪˌeɪt/ *vt* устраня́ть *impf*, устрани́ть *pf*.

obvious /'ɒbvɪəs/ *adj* очеви́дный.

occasion /ə'keɪʒ(ə)n/ *n* слу́чай; (*cause*) по́вод; (*occurrence*) собы́тие; *vt* причиня́ть *impf*, причини́ть *pf*. **occasional** /-nəl/ *adj* ре́дкий. **occasionally** /-nəlɪ/ *adv* иногда́, вре́мя от вре́мени.

occult /ɒ'kʌlt/ *adj* окку́льтный; *n*: **the ~** окку́льт.

occupancy /'ɒkjʊpənsɪ/ *n* заня́тие. **occupant** /-pənt/ *n* жи́тель *m*, ~ница. **occupation** /ˌɒkjʊ 'peɪʃ(ə)n/ *n* заня́тие; (*military* ~) оккупа́ция; (*profession*) профе́ссия. **occupational** /-'peɪʃən(ə)l/ *adj* профессиона́льный; ~ **therapy** трудотерапи́я. **occupy** /'ɒkjʊˌpaɪ/ *vt* занима́ть *impf*, заня́ть *pf*; (*mil*) оккупи́ровать *impf* & *pf*.

occur /ə'kɜː(r)/ *vi* (*happen*) случа́ться *impf*, случи́ться *pf*; (*be found*) встреча́ться *impf*; ~ **to** приходи́ть *impf*, прийти́ *pf* в го́лову+*dat*. **occurrence** /-'kʌrəns/ *n* слу́чай, происше́ствие.

ocean /'əʊʃ(ə)n/ *n* океа́н.

oceanic /ˌəʊʃɪ'ænɪk/ *adj* океа́нский.

o'clock /ə'klɒk/ *adv*: **(at) six ~** (в) шесть часо́в.

octagonal /ɒk'tægən(ə)l/ *adj* восьмиуго́льный.

octave /'ɒktɪv/ *n* (*mus*) окта́ва.

October /ɒk'təʊbə(r)/ *n* октя́брь *m*; *adj* октя́брьский.

octopus /'ɒktəpəs/ *n* осьмино́г.

odd /ɒd/ *adj* (*strange*) стра́нный; (*not in a set*) разро́зненный; (*number*) нечётный; (*not paired*) непа́рный; (*casual*) случа́йный; **five hundred ~** пятьсо́т с ли́шним; **~ job** случа́йная рабо́та. **oddity** /'ɒdɪtɪ/ *n* стра́нность; (*person*) чуда́к, -а́чка. **oddly** /'ɒdlɪ/ *adv* стра́нно; **~ enough** как э́то ни стра́нно. **oddment** /'ɒdmənt/ *n* оста́ток. **odds** /ɒdz/ *n pl* ша́нсы *m pl*; **be at ~ with** (*person*) не ла́дить с+*instr*; (*things*) не соотве́тствовать *impf* +*dat*; **long (short) ~** нера́вные (почти́ ра́вные) ша́нсы *m pl*; **the ~ are that** вероя́тнее всего́, что; **~ and ends** обры́вки *m pl*.

ode /əʊd/ *n* о́да.

odious /'əʊdɪəs/ *adj* ненави́стный.

odour /'əʊdə(r)/ *n* за́пах.

oesophagus /iː'sɒfəgəs/ *n* пищево́д.

of /ɒv/ *prep expressing* **1.** *origin*: из+*gen*: **he comes ~ a working-class family** он из рабо́чей семьи́; **2.** *cause*: от+*gen*: **he died ~ hunger** он у́мер от го́лода; **3.** *authorship*: *gen*: **the works ~ Pushkin** сочине́ния Пу́шкина; **4.** *material*: из +*gen*: **made ~ wood** сде́ланный из де́рева; **5.** *reference*: о+*prep*: **he talked ~ Lenin** он говори́л о Ле́нине; **6.** *partition*: *gen* (*often in* -у́(-ю)): **a glass ~ milk, tea** стака́н молока́, ча́ю; из+*gen*: **one ~ them** оди́н из них; **7.** *belonging*: *gen*: **the capital ~ England** столи́ца А́нглии.

off /ɒf/ *adv*: *in phrasal vv, see v, e.g.* **clear ~** убира́ться; *prep* (*from surface of*) с+*gen*; (*away from*) от+*gen*; **~ and on** вре́мя от вре́мени; **~-white** не совсе́м бе́лый.

offal /'ɒf(ə)l/ *n* требуха́.

offence /ə'fens/ *n* (*insult*) оби́да; (*against law*) просту́пок, преступле́ние; **take ~** обижа́ться *impf*, оби́деться *pf* (**at** на+*acc*). **offend** /ə'fend/ *vt* обижа́ть *impf*, оби́деть *pf*; **~ against** наруша́ть *impf*, нару́шить *pf*. **offender** /ə'fendə(r)/ *n* правонаруши́тель *m*, **~**ница. **offensive** /ə'fensɪv/ *adj* (*attacking*) наступа́тельный; (*insulting*) оскорби́тельный; (*repulsive*) проти́вный; *n* нападе́ние.

offer /'ɒfə(r)/ *vt* предлага́ть *impf*, предложи́ть *pf*; *n* предложе́ние; **on ~** в прода́же.

offhand /ɒf'hænd/ *adj* бесцеремо́нный.

office /'ɒfɪs/ *n* (*position*) до́лжность; (*place, room etc.*) бюро́ *neut indecl*, конто́ра, канцеля́рия. **officer** /'ɒfɪsə(r)/ *n* должностно́е лицо́; (*mil*) офице́р. **official** /ə'fɪʃ(ə)l/ *adj* служе́бный; (*authorized*) официа́льный; *n* должностно́е лицо́. **officiate** /ə'fɪʃɪˌeɪt/ *vi* (*eccl*) соверша́ть *impf*, соверши́ть *pf* богослуже́ние. **officious** /ə'fɪʃəs/ *adj* (*intrusive*) навя́зчивый.

offing /'ɒfɪŋ/ *n*: **be in the ~** предстоя́ть *impf*.

off-licence /ˈɒflaɪs(ə)ns/ *n* ви́нный магази́н. **off-load** *vt* разгружа́ть *impf*, разгрузи́ть *pf*. **off-putting** /ˈɒfpʊtɪŋ/ *adj* отта́лкивающий. **offset** *vt* возмеща́ть *impf*, возмести́ть *pf*. **offshoot** *n* о́тпрыск. **offshore** *adj* прибре́жный. **offside** *adv* вне игры́. **offspring** *n* потомо́к; (*collect*) пото́мки *m pl*.

often /ˈɒf(ə)n/ *adv* ча́сто.

ogle /ˈəʊg(ə)l/ *vt & i* смотре́ть *impf* с вожделе́нием на+*acc*.

ogre /ˈəʊgə(r)/ *n* велика́н-людое́д.

oh /əʊ/ *int* о!; ах!

ohm /əʊm/ *n* ом.

oil /ɔɪl/ *n* ма́сло; (*petroleum*) нефть; (*paint*) ма́сло, ма́сляные кра́ски *f pl*; *vt* сма́зывать *impf*, сма́зать *pf*; **~-painting** карти́на, напи́санная ма́сляными кра́сками; **~ rig** нефтяна́я вы́шка; **~-tanker** та́нкер; **~-well** нефтяна́я сква́жина. **oilfield** *n* месторожде́ние не́фти. **oilskin** *n* клеёнка; *pl* непромока́емый костю́м. **oily** /ˈɔɪlɪ/ *adj* масляни́стый.

ointment /ˈɔɪntmənt/ *n* мазь.

OK /əʊˈkeɪ/ *adv & adj* хорошо́, норма́льно; *int* ла́дно!; *vt* одобря́ть *impf*, одо́брить *pf*.

old /əʊld/ *adj* ста́рый; (*ancient*; *of long standing*) стари́нный; (*former*) бы́вший; **how ~ are you?** ско́лько тебе́, вам, (*dat*) лет?; **~ age** ста́рость; **~-age pension** пе́нсия по ста́рости; **old-fashioned** старомо́дный; **~ maid** ста́рая де́ва; **~ man** (*also father, husband*) стари́к; **~-time** стари́нный; **~ woman** стару́ха; (*coll*) стару́шка.

olive /ˈɒlɪv/ *n* (*fruit*) оли́вка; (*colour*) оли́вковый цвет; *adj* оли́вковый; **~ oil** оли́вковое ма́сло.

Olympic /əˈlɪmpɪk/ *adj* олимпи́йский; **~ games** Олимпи́йские и́гры *f pl*.

omelette /ˈɒmlɪt/ *n* омле́т.

omen /ˈəʊmən/ *n* предзнамено-ва́ние. **ominous** /ˈɒmɪnəs/ *adj* злове́щий.

omission /əˈmɪʃ(ə)n/ *n* про́пуск; (*neglect*) упуще́ние. **omit** /əˈmɪt/ *vt* (*leave out*) пропуска́ть *impf*, пропусти́ть *pf*; (*neglect*) упуска́ть *impf*, упусти́ть *pf*.

omnibus /ˈɒmnɪbəs/ *n* (*bus*) авто́бус; (*collection*) колле́кция.

omnipotence /ɒmˈnɪpət(ə)ns/ *n* всемогу́щество. **omnipotent** /-t(ə)nt/ *adj* всемогу́щий. **omnipresent** /ˌɒmnɪˈprez(ə)nt/ *adj* вездесу́щий. **omniscient** /ɒmˈnɪsɪənt/ *adj* всеве́дущий.

on /ɒn/ *prep* (*position*) на+*prep*; (*direction*) на+*acc*; (*time*) в+*acc*; **~ the next day** на сле́дующий день; **~ Mondays** (*repeated action*) по понеде́льникам (*dat pl*); **~ the first of June** пе́рвого ию́ня (*gen*); (*concerning*) по+*prep*, о+*prep*, на+*acc*; *adv* да́льше, вперёд; *in phrasal vv, see vv, e.g.* **move ~** идти́ да́льше; **and so ~** и так да́лее, и т.д.; **be ~** (*film etc.*) идти́ *impf*; **further ~** да́льше; **later ~** по́зже.

once /wʌns/ *adv* (оди́н) раз; (*on past occasion*) одна́жды; (*formerly*) не́когда; **all at ~** неожи́данно; **at ~** сра́зу, неме́дленно; (*if, when*) **~** как то́лько; **~ again, more** ещё раз; **~ and for all** раз и навсегда́; **~ or twice** не́сколько раз; **~ upon a time there lived ...** жил-бы́л... .

oncoming /ˈɒnˌkʌmɪŋ/ *adj*: **~ traffic** встре́чное движе́ние.

one /wʌn/ *adj* оди́н (одна́, -но́);

(*only*, *single*) еди́нственный; *n* оди́н; *pron*: *not usu translated*; *v translated in 2nd pers sg or by impers construction*: **~ never knows** никогда́ не зна́ешь; **where can ~ buy this book?** где мо́жно купи́ть э́ту кни́гу?; **~ after another** оди́н за други́м; **~ and all** все до одного́; все как оди́н; **~ and only** еди́нственный; **~ and the same** оди́н и тот же; **~ another** друг дру́га (*dat* -гу, *etc.*); **~ fine day** в оди́н прекра́сный день; **~ o'clock** час; **~-parent family** семья́ с одни́м роди́телем; **~-sided, -track, -way** односторо́нний; **~-time** бы́вший; **~-way street** у́лица односторо́ннего движе́ния.

onerous /'əʊnərəs/ *adj* тя́гостный.

oneself /wʌn'self/ *pron* себя́; -ся (*suffixed to vt*).

onion /'ʌnjən/ *n* (*plant*; *pl collect*) лук; (*single* ~) лу́ковица.

onlooker /'ɒn,lʊkə(r)/ *n* наблюда́тель *m*.

only /'əʊnlɪ/ *adj* еди́нственный; *adv* то́лько; **if ~** е́сли бы то́лько; **~ just** то́лько что; *conj* но.

onset /'ɒnset/ *n* нача́ло.

onslaught /'ɒnslɔ:t/ *n* на́тиск.

onus /'əʊnəs/ *n* отве́тственность.

onward(s) /'ɒnwəd(z)/ *adv* вперёд.

ooze /u:z/ *vt* & *i* сочи́ться *impf.*

opal /'əʊp(ə)l/ *n* опа́л.

opaque /əʊ'peɪk/ *adj* непрозра́чный.

open /'əʊpən/ *adj* откры́тый; (*frank*) открове́нный; **in the ~ air** на откры́том во́здухе; **~-minded** *adj* непредубеждённый; *vt* & *i* открыва́ть(ся) *impf*, откры́ть(ся) *pf*; *vi* (*begin*) начина́ться *impf*, нача́ться *pf*; (*flowers*) распуска́ться *impf*, распусти́ться *pf.*

opening /-ɪŋ/ *n* откры́тие; (*aperture*) отве́рстие; (*beginning*) нача́ло; *adj* нача́льный, пе́рвый; (*introductory*) вступи́тельный.

opera /'ɒpərə/ *n* о́пера; *attrib* о́перный; **~-house** о́перный теа́тр.

operate /'ɒpə,reɪt/ *vi* де́йствовать *impf* (**upon** на+*acc*); (*med*) опери́ровать *impf* & *pf* (**on** +*acc*); *vt* управля́ть *impf* +*instr.*

operatic /,ɒpə'rætɪk/ *adj* о́перный.

operating-theatre /'ɒpəreɪtɪŋ ,θɪətə(r)/ *n* операцио́нная *sb.*

operation /,ɒpə'reɪʃ(ə)n/ *n* де́йствие; (*med*; *mil*) опера́ция.

operational /-'reɪʃən(ə)l/ *adj* (*in use*) де́йствующий; (*mil*) операти́вный. **operative** /'ɒpərətɪv/ *adj* де́йствующий. **operator** /'ɒpə,reɪtə(r)/ *n* опера́тор; (*telephone* ~) телефони́ст, ~ка.

operetta /,ɒpə'retə/ *n* опере́тта.

ophthalmic /ɒf'θælmɪk/ *adj* глазно́й.

opinion /ə'pɪnjən/ *n* мне́ние; **in my ~** по-мо́ему; **~ poll** опро́с обще́ственного мне́ния. **opinionated** /-,neɪtɪd/ *adj* догмати́чный.

opium /'əʊpɪəm/ *n* о́пиум.

opponent /ə'pəʊnənt/ *n* проти́вник.

opportune /'ɒpə,tju:n/ *adj* своевре́менный. **opportunism** /-'tju:nɪz(ə)m/ *n* оппортуни́зм. **opportunist** /-'tju:nɪst/ *n* оппортуни́ст. **opportunistic** /-tju:'nɪstɪk/ *n* оппортунисти́ческий.

opportunity /-'tju:nɪtɪ/ *n* слу́чай, возмо́жность.

oppose /ə'pəʊz/ *vt* (*resist*) противиться *impf*, вос~ *pf* +*dat*; (*speak etc. against*) выступать *impf*, выступить *pf* против+*gen*. **opposed** /-'pəʊzd/ *adj* против (**to** +*gen*); **as ~ to** в противоположность+*dat*. **opposing** /-'pəʊzɪŋ/ *adj* противный; (*opposite*) противоположный. **opposite** /'ɒpəzɪt/ *adj* противоположный; (*reverse*) обратный; *n* противоположность; **just the ~** как раз наоборот; *adv* напротив; *prep* (на)против+*gen*. **opposition** /ˌɒpə'zɪʃ(ə)n/ *n* (*resistance*) сопротивление; (*polit*) оппозиция.

oppress /ə'pres/ *vt* угнетать *impf*. **oppression** /-'preʃ(ə)n/ *n* угнетение. **oppressive** /-'presɪv/ *adj* угнетающий. **oppressor** /-'presə(r)/ *n* угнетатель *m*.

opt /ɒpt/ *vi* выбирать *impf*, выбрать *pf* (**for** +*acc*); **~ out** не принимать *impf* участия (**of** в+*prep*).

optic /'ɒptɪk/ *adj* зрительный. **optical** /'ɒptɪk(ə)l/ *adj* оптический. **optician** /ɒp'tɪʃ(ə)n/ *n* оптик. **optics** /'ɒptɪks/ *n* оптика.

optimism /'ɒptɪˌmɪz(ə)m/ *n* оптимизм. **optimist** /-mɪst/ *n* оптимист. **optimistic** /-'mɪstɪk/ *adj* оптимистический. **optimum** /'ɒptɪməm/ *adj* оптимальный.

option /'ɒpʃ(ə)n/ *n* выбор. **optional** /-nəl/ *adj* необязательный.

opulence /'ɒpjʊləns/ *n* богатство. **opulent** /-lənt/ *adj* богатый.

opus /'əʊpəs/ *n* опус.

or /ɔ:(r)/ *conj* или; **~ else** иначе; **~ so** приблизительно.

oracle /'ɒrək(ə)l/ *n* оракул.

oral /'ɔ:r(ə)l/ *adj* устный; *n* устный экзамен.

orange /'ɒrɪndʒ/ *n* (*fruit*) апельсин; (*colour*) оранжевый цвет; *attrib* апельсиновый; *adj* оранжевый.

oration /ɔ:'reɪʃ(ə)n/ *n* речь. **orator** /'ɒrətə(r)/ *n* оратор.

oratorio /ˌɒrə'tɔ:rɪəʊ/ *n* оратория.

oratory /'ɒrətərɪ/ *n* (*speech*) красноречие.

orbit /'ɔ:bɪt/ *n* орбита; *vt* вращаться *impf* по орбите вокруг+*gen*. **orbital** /-təl/ *adj* орбитальный.

orchard /'ɔ:tʃəd/ *n* фруктовый сад.

orchestra /'ɔ:kɪstrə/ *n* оркестр. **orchestral** /-'kestr(ə)l/ *adj* оркестровый. **orchestrate** /'ɔ:kɪˌstreɪt/ *vt* оркестровать *impf* & *pf*. **orchestration** /ˌɔ:kɪ'streɪʃ(ə)n/ *n* оркестровка.

orchid /'ɔ:kɪd/ *n* орхидея.

ordain /ɔ:'deɪn/ *vt* предписывать *impf*, предписать *pf*; (*eccl*) посвящать *impf*, посвятить *pf* (в духовный сан).

ordeal /ɔ:'di:l/ *n* тяжёлое испытание.

order /'ɔ:də(r)/ *n* порядок; (*command*) приказ; (*for goods*) заказ; (*insignia, medal; fraternity*) орден; (*archit*) ордер; *pl* (*holy* ~) духовный сан; **in ~ to** (для того) чтобы +*inf*; *vt* (*command*) приказывать *impf*, приказать *pf* +*dat*; (*goods etc.*) заказывать *impf*, заказать *pf*. **orderly** /-lɪ/ *adj* аккуратный; (*quiet*) тихий; *n* (*med*) санитар; (*mil*) ординарец.

ordinance /'ɔ:dɪnəns/ *n* декрет.

ordinary /'ɔ:dɪnərɪ/ *adj* обыкновенный, обычный.

ordination /ˌɔ:dɪ'neɪʃ(ə)n/ *n* пос-

вяще́ние.
ore /ɔ:(r)/ *n* руда́.
organ /'ɔ:gən/ *n* о́рган; (*mus*) орга́н. **organic** /-'gænɪk/ *adj* органи́ческий. **organism** /'ɔ:gə,nɪz(ə)m/ *n* органи́зм. **organist** /-nɪst/ *n* органи́ст. **organization** /,ɔ:gənaɪ'zeɪʃ(ə)n/ *n* организа́ция. **organize** /'ɔ:gə,naɪz/ *vt* организо́вывать *impf* (*pres not used*), организова́ть *impf* (*in pres*) & *pf*; устра́ивать *impf*, устро́ить *pf*. **organizer** /-,naɪzə(r)/ *n* организа́тор.
orgy /'ɔ:dʒɪ/ *n* о́ргия.
Orient /'ɔ:rɪənt/ *n* Восто́к. **oriental** /,ɔ:rɪ'ent(ə)l/ *adj* восто́чный.
orient, orientate /'ɔ:rɪənt, 'ɔ:rɪən,teɪt/ *vt* ориенти́ровать *impf* & *pf* (**o.s.** -ся). **orientation** /,ɔ:rɪən'teɪʃ(ə)n/ *n* ориента́ция.
orifice /'ɒrɪfɪs/ *n* отве́рстие.
origin /'ɒrɪdʒɪn/ *n* происхожде́ние, нача́ло. **original** /ə'rɪdʒɪn(ə)l/ *adj* оригина́льный; (*initial*) первонача́льный; (*genuine*) по́длинный; *n* оригина́л. **originality** /ə,rɪdʒɪ'nælɪtɪ/ *n* оригина́льность. **originate** /ə'rɪdʒɪ,neɪt/ *vt* порожда́ть *impf*, породи́ть *pf*; *vi* брать *impf*, взять *pf* нача́ло (**from, in** в+*prep*, от+*gen*); (*arise*) возника́ть *impf*, возни́кнуть *pf*. **originator** /-'rɪdʒɪ,neɪtə(r)/ *n* а́втор, инициа́тор.
ornament *n* /'ɔ:nəmənt/ украше́ние; *vt* /'ɔ:nəment/ украша́ть *impf*, укра́сить *pf*. **ornamental** /-'ment(ə)l/ *adj* декорати́вный.
ornate /ɔ:'neɪt/ *adj* витиева́тый.
ornithologist /,ɔ:nɪ'θɒlədʒɪst/ *n* орнито́лог. **ornithology** /-dʒɪ/ *n* орнитоло́гия.
orphan /'ɔ:f(ə)n/ *n* сирота́ *m* & *f*; *vt*: **be ~ed** сироте́ть *impf*, о~ *pf*. **orphanage** /-nɪdʒ/ *n* сиро́тский дом. **orphaned** /'ɔ:f(ə)nd/ *adj* осироте́лый.
orthodox /'ɔ:θə,dɒks/ *adj* ортодокса́льный; (*eccl*, **O~**) правосла́вный. **orthodoxy** /-,dɒksɪ/ *n* ортодо́ксия; (**O~**) правосла́вие.
orthopaedic /,ɔ:θə'pi:dɪk/ *adj* ортопеди́ческий.
oscillate /'ɒsɪ,leɪt/ *vi* колеба́ться *impf*, по~ *pf*. **oscillation** /-'leɪʃ(ə)n/ *n* колеба́ние.
osmosis /ɒz'məʊsɪs/ *n* о́смос.
ostensible /ɒ'stensɪb(ə)l/ *adj* мни́мый. **ostensibly** /-blɪ/ *adv* я́кобы.
ostentation /,ɒsten'teɪʃ(ə)n/ *n* выставле́ние напока́з. **ostentatious** /-ʃəs/ *adj* показно́й.
osteopath /'ɒstɪə,pæθ/ *n* остеопа́т. **osteopathy** /,ɒstɪ'ɒpəθɪ/ *n* остеопа́тия.
ostracize /'ɒstrə,saɪz/ *vt* подверга́ть *impf*, подве́ргнуть *pf* остраки́зму.
ostrich /'ɒstrɪtʃ/ *n* стра́ус.
other /'ʌðə(r)/ *adj* друго́й, ино́й; тот; **every ~** ка́ждый второ́й; **every ~ day** че́рез день; **on the ~ hand** с друго́й стороны́; **on the ~ side** на той стороне́, по ту сто́рону; **one or the ~** тот и́ли ино́й; **the ~ day** на дня́х, неда́вно; **the ~ way round** наоборо́т; **the ~s** остальны́е *sb pl*. **otherwise** *adv* & *conj* и́наче, а то.
otter /'ɒtə(r)/ *n* вы́дра.
ouch /aʊtʃ/ *int* ой!, ай!
ought /ɔ:t/ *v aux* до́лжен (-жна́) (бы) +*inf*.
ounce /aʊns/ *n* у́нция.
our, ours /'aʊə(r), 'aʊəz/ *poss pron* наш; свой. **ourselves** /,aʊə'selvz/ *pron* (*emph*) (мы) са́ми; (*refl*) себя́; -ся (*suffixed to vt*).
oust /aʊst/ *vt* вытесня́ть *impf*,

вы́теснить *pf.*
out /aʊt/ *adv* **1.** *in phrasal vv often rendered by pref* вы-; **2.: to be ~** *in various senses*: **he is ~** (*not at home*) его́ нет до́ма; (*not in office etc.*) он вы́шел; (*sport*) выходи́ть *impf*, вы́йти *pf* из игры́; (*of fashion*) вы́йти *pf* из мо́ды; (*be published*) вы́йти *pf* из печа́ти; (*of candle etc.*) поту́хнуть *pf*; (*of flower*) распусти́ться *pf*; (*be unconscious*) потеря́ть *pf* созна́ние; **3.: ~-and-~** отъя́вленный; **4.: ~ of** из+*gen*, вне+*gen*; **~ of date** устаре́лый, старомо́дный; **~ of doors** на откры́том во́здухе; **~ of work** безрабо́тный.
outbid /aʊt'bɪd/ *vt* предлага́ть *impf*, предложи́ть *pf* бо́лее высо́кую це́ну, чем+*nom.* **outboard** *adj*: **~ motor** подвесно́й мото́р *m.* **outbreak** *n* (*of anger, disease*) вспы́шка; (*of war*) нача́ло. **outbuilding** *n* надво́рная постро́йка. **outburst** *n* взрыв. **outcast** *n* изгна́нник. **outcome** *n* результа́т. **outcry** *n* (шу́мные) проте́сты *m pl.* **outdated** /aʊt'deɪtɪd/ *adj* устаре́лый. **outdo** *vt* превосходи́ть *impf*, превзойти́ *pf.*
outdoor /'aʊtdɔː(r)/ *adj*, **outdoors** /-'dɔːz/ *adv* на откры́том во́здухе, на у́лице.
outer /'aʊtə(r)/ *adj* (*external*) вне́шний, нару́жный; (*far from centre*) да́льний. **outermost** *adj* са́мый да́льний.
outfit /'aʊtfɪt/ *n* (*equipment*) снаряже́ние; (*set of things*) набо́р; (*clothes*) наря́д. **outgoing** *adj* уходя́щий; (*sociable*) общи́тельный. **outgoings** *n pl* изде́ржки *f pl.* **outgrow** *vt* выраста́ть *impf*, вы́расти *pf* из+*gen.* **outhouse** *n* надво́рная постро́йка.
outing /'aʊtɪŋ/ *n* прогу́лка, экску́рсия.
outlandish /aʊt'lændɪʃ/ *adj* дико́винный. **outlaw** *n* лицо́ вне зако́на; банди́т; *vt* объявля́ть *impf*, объяви́ть *pf* вне зако́на. **outlay** *n* изде́ржки *f pl.* **outlet** /'aʊtlɪt/ *n* выходно́е отве́рстие; (*fig*) вы́ход; (*market*) ры́нок; (*shop*) торго́вая то́чка. **outline** *n* очерта́ние, ко́нтур; (*sketch, summary*) набро́сок; *vt* оче́рчивать *impf*, очерти́ть *pf*; (*plans etc.*) набра́сывать *impf*, наброса́ть *pf.* **outlive** *vt* пережи́ть *pf.* **outlook** *n* перспекти́вы *f pl*; (*attitude*) кругозо́р. **outlying** /'aʊt,laɪɪŋ/ *adj* перифери́йный. **outmoded** /aʊt'məʊdɪd/ *adj* старомо́дный. **outnumber** *vt* чи́сленно превосходи́ть *impf*, превзойти́ *pf.* **out-patient** *n* амбулато́рный больно́й *sb.* **outpost** *n* форпо́ст. **output** *n* вы́пуск, проду́кция.
outrage /'aʊtreɪdʒ/ *n* безобра́зие; (*indignation*) возмуще́ние; *vt* оскорбля́ть *impf*, оскорби́ть *pf.* **outrageous** /-'reɪdʒəs/ *adj* возмути́тельный.
outright /'aʊtraɪt/ *adv* (*entirely*) вполне́; (*once for all*) раз (и) навсегда́; (*openly*) откры́то; *adj* прямо́й. **outset** *n* нача́ло; **at the ~** внача́ле; **from the ~** с са́мого нача́ла.
outside /aʊt'saɪd/ *n* нару́жная сторона́; **at the ~** са́мое бо́льшее; **from the ~** извне́; **on the ~** снару́жи; *adj* нару́жный, вне́шний; (*sport*) кра́йний; *adv* (*on the ~*) снару́жи; (*to the ~*) нару́жу; (*out of doors*) на откры́том во́здухе, на у́лице; *prep* вне+*gen*; за преде́лами +*gen.* **outsider** /-də(r)/ *n* посто-

ро́нний *sb*; (*sport*) аутса́йдер. **outsize** /'aʊtsaɪz/ *adj* бо́льше станда́ртного разме́ра. **outskirts** *n pl* окра́ина. **outspoken** /aʊt'spəʊkən/ *adj* прямо́й. **outstanding** /aʊt'stændɪŋ/ *adj* (*remarkable*) выдаю́щийся; (*unpaid*) неупла́ченный. **outstay** *vt*: ~ **one's welcome** заси́живаться *impf*, засиде́ться *pf*. **outstretched** /'aʊtstretʃt/ *adj* распростёртый. **outstrip** *vt* обгоня́ть *impf*, обогна́ть *pf*.

outward /'aʊtwəd/ *adj* (*external*) вне́шний, нару́жный. **outwardly** /-lɪ/ *adv* вне́шне, на вид. **outwards** /-wədz/ *adv* нару́жу.

outweigh /aʊt'weɪ/ *vt* переве́шивать *impf*, переве́сить *pf*. **outwit** *vt* перехитри́ть *pf*.

oval /'əʊv(ə)l/ *adj* ова́льный; *n* ова́л.

ovary /'əʊvərɪ/ *n* яи́чник.

ovation /əʊ'veɪʃ(ə)n/ *n* ова́ция.

oven /'ʌv(ə)n/ *n* (*industrial*) печь; (*domestic*) духо́вка.

over /'əʊvə(r)/ *adv* & *prep with vv*: *see vv*; *prep* (*above*) над+*instr*; (*through*; *covering*) по+*dat*; (*concerning*) о+*prep*; (*across*) че́рез+*acc*; (*on the other side of*) по ту сто́рону+*gen*; (*more than*) свы́ше+*gen*; бо́лее+*gen*; (*with age*) за+*acc*; **all** ~ (*finished*) всё ко́нчено; (*everywhere*) повсю́ду; **all** ~ **the country** по всей стране́; ~ **again** ещё раз; ~ **against** по сравне́нию с+*instr*; ~ **and above** не говоря́ уже́ о+*prep*; ~ **the telephone** по телефо́ну; ~ **there** вон там.

overall /'əʊvər,ɔ:l/ *n* хала́т; *pl* комбинезо́н; *adj* о́бщий. **overawe** *vt* внуша́ть *impf*, внуши́ть *pf* благогове́йный страх+*dat*. **overbalance** *vi* теря́ть *impf*, по~ *pf* равнове́сие. **overbearing** /,əʊvə'beərɪŋ/ *adj* вла́стный. **overboard** *adv* (*motion*) за́ борт; (*position*) за бо́ртом. **overcast** *adj* о́блачный. **overcoat** *n* пальто́ *neut indecl*. **overcome** *vt* преодолева́ть *impf*, преодоле́ть *pf*; *adj* охва́ченный. **overcrowded** /,əʊvə'kraʊdɪd/ *adj* перепо́лненный. **overcrowding** /,əʊvə'kraʊdɪŋ/ *n* переполне́ние. **overdo** *vt* (*cook*) пережа́ривать *impf*, пережа́рить *pf*; ~ **it, things** (*work too hard*) переутомля́ться *impf*, переутоми́ться *pf*; (*go too far*) переба́рщивать *impf*, переборщи́ть *pf*.

overdose /'əʊvə,dəʊs/ *n* чрезме́рная до́за. **overdraft** *n* превыше́ние креди́та; (*amount*) долг ба́нку. **overdraw** *vi* превыша́ть *impf*, превы́сить *pf* креди́т (в ба́нке). **overdue** *adj* просро́ченный; **be** ~ (*late*) запа́здывать *impf*, запозда́ть *pf*. **overestimate** *vt* переоце́нивать *impf*, переоцени́ть *pf*. **overflow** *vi* перелива́ться *impf*, перели́ться *pf*; (*river etc.*) разлива́ться *impf*, разли́ться *pf*; (*outlet*) перели́в. **overgrown** /,əʊvə'grəʊn/ *adj* заро́сший. **overhang** *vt* & *i* выступа́ть *impf* над+*instr*; *n* свес, вы́ступ.

overhaul /'əʊvə,hɔ:l/ *vt* ремонти́ровать *impf* & *pf*; *n*: ремо́нт. **overhead** *adv* наверху́, над голово́й; *adj* возду́шный, подвесно́й; *n*: *pl* накладны́е расхо́ды *m pl*. **overhear** *vt* неча́янно слы́шать *impf*, у~ *pf*. **overheat** *vt* & *i* перегрева́ть(ся) *impf*, перегре́ть(ся) *pf*. **overjoyed** /,əʊvə'dʒɔɪd/ *adj* в восто́рге (**at** от+*gen*). **overland** *adj* сухопу́тный; *adv* по су́ше. **overlap** *vt* части́чно покрыва́ть *impf*, покры́ть *pf*; *vi* частично совпада́ть *impf*, совпа́сть *pf*.

overleaf /ˌəʊvəˈliːf/ *adv* на оборо́те. **overload** *vt* перегружа́ть *impf*, перегрузи́ть *pf*. **overlook** *vt* (*look down on*) смотре́ть *impf* све́рху на+*acc*; (*of window*) выходи́ть *impf* на, в, +*acc*; (*not notice*) не замеча́ть *impf*, заме́тить *pf* +*gen*; (~ *offence etc.*) проща́ть *impf*, прости́ть *pf*.

overly /ˈəʊvəlɪ/ *adv* сли́шком.

overnight /ˌəʊvəˈnaɪt/ *adv* (*during the night*) за́ ночь; (*suddenly*) неожи́данно; **stay** ~ ночева́ть *impf*, пере~ *pf*; *adj* ночно́й. **overpay** *vt* перепла́чивать *impf*, переплати́ть *pf*.

over-populated /ˌəʊvəˈpɒpjʊˌleɪtɪd/ *adj* перенаселённый. **over-population** *n* перенаселённость. **overpower** *vt* одолева́ть *impf*, одоле́ть *pf*. **overpriced** /ˌəʊvəˈpraɪst/ *adj* завы́шенный в цене́. **over-production** *n* перепроизво́дство. **overrate** /ˌəʊvəˈreɪt/ *vt* переоце́нивать *impf*, переоцени́ть *pf*. **override** *vt* (*fig*) отверга́ть *impf*, отве́ргнуть *pf*. **overriding** /ˌəʊvəˈraɪdɪŋ/ *adj* гла́вный, реша́ющий. **overrule** *vt* отверга́ть *impf*, отве́ргнуть *pf*. **overrun** *vt* (*conquer*) завоёвывать *impf*, завоева́ть *pf*; **be** ~ **with** кише́ть *impf* +*instr*.

overseas /ˌəʊvəˈsiːz/ *adv* за мо́рем, че́рез мо́ре; *adj* замо́рский. **oversee** /ˌəʊvəˈsiː/ *vt* надзира́ть *impf* за+*instr*. **overseer** /ˈəʊvəˌsiːə(r)/ *n* надзира́тель *m*, ~ница. **overshadow** *vt* затмева́ть *impf*, затми́ть *pf*. **overshoot** *vi* переходи́ть *impf*, перейти́ *pf* грани́цу. **oversight** *n* случа́йный недосмо́тр. **oversleep** *vi* просыпа́ть *impf*, проспа́ть *pf*. **overspend** *vi* тра́тить *impf* сли́шком мно́го. **overstate** *vt* преувели́чивать *impf*, преувели́чить *pf*. **overstep** *vt* переступа́ть *impf*, переступи́ть *pf* +*acc*, че́рез+*acc*.

overt /əʊˈvɜːt/ *adj* я́вный, откры́тый.

overtake /ˌəʊvəˈteɪk/ *vt* обгоня́ть *impf*, обогна́ть *pf*. **overthrow** *vt* сверга́ть *impf*, све́ргнуть *pf*. **overtime** *n* (*work*) сверхуро́чная рабо́та; (*payment*) сверхуро́чное *sb*; *adv* сверхуро́чно.

overtone /ˈəʊvəˌtəʊn/ *n* скры́тый намёк.

overture /ˈəʊvəˌtjʊə(r)/ *n* предложе́ние; (*mus*) увертю́ра.

overturn /ˌəʊvəˈtɜːn/ *vt* & *i* опроки́дывать(ся) *impf*, опроки́нуть(ся) *pf*. **overwhelm** /ˌəʊvəˈwelm/ *vt* подавля́ть *impf*, подави́ть *pf*. **overwhelming** /ˌəʊvəˈwelmɪŋ/ *adj* подавля́ющий. **overwork** *vt* & *i* переутомля́ть(ся) *impf*, переутоми́ть(ся) *pf*; *n* переутомле́ние.

owe /əʊ/ *vt* (~ *money*) быть до́лжным +*acc* & *dat*; (*be indebted*) быть обя́занным +*instr* & *dat*; **he, she,** ~**s me three roubles** он до́лжен, она́ должна́, мне три рубля́; **she** ~**s him her life** она́ обя́зана ему́ жи́знью. **owing** /ˈəʊɪŋ/ *adj*: **be** ~ причита́ться *impf* (**to** +*dat*); ~ **to** из-за+*gen*, по причи́не+*gen*.

owl /aʊl/ *n* сова́.

own /əʊn/ *adj* свой; (свой) со́бственный; **on one's** ~ самостоя́тельно; (*alone*) оди́н; *vt* (*possess*) владе́ть *impf* +*instr*; (*admit*) признава́ть *impf*, призна́ть *pf*; ~ **up** признава́ться *impf*, признáться *pf.* **owner** /ˈəʊnə(r)/ *n* владéлец. **ownership** /ˈəʊnəʃɪp/ *n* владéние (**of** +*instr*), сóбственность.

ox /ɒks/ *n* вол.

oxidation /ˌɒksɪˈdeɪʃ(ə)n/ *n* окислéние. **oxide** /ˈɒksaɪd/ *n* óкись. **oxidize** /ˈɒksɪˌdaɪz/ *vt* & *i* окислять(ся) *impf*, окислить(ся) *pf.* **oxygen** /ˈɒksɪdʒ(ə)n/ *n* кислорóд.

oyster /ˈɔɪstə(r)/ *n* ýстрица.

ozone /ˈəʊzəʊn/ *n* озóн.

P

pace /peɪs/ *n* шаг; (*fig*) темп; **keep ~ with** идти *impf* в нóгу с+*instr*; **set the ~** задавáть *impf*, задáть *pf* темп; *vi*: **~ up and down** ходить *indet* взад и вперёд. **pacemaker** *n* (*med*) электрóнный стимулятор.

pacifism /ˈpæsɪˌfɪz(ə)m/ *n* пацифизм. **pacifist** /-fɪst/ *n* пацифист. **pacify** /-ˌfaɪ/ *vt* усмирять *impf*, усмирить *pf.*

pack /pæk/ *n* ýзел, вьюк; (*soldier's*) рáнец; (*hounds*) свóра; (*wolves*) стáя; (*cards*) колóда; *vt* (& *i*) упакóвывать(ся) *impf*, упаковáть(ся) *pf*; (*cram*) набивáть *impf*, набить *pf.* **package** /ˈpækɪdʒ/ *n* посылка, пакéт; **~ holiday** организóванная туристическая поéздка. **packaging** /-dʒɪŋ/ *n* упакóвка. **packet** /ˈpækɪt/ *n* пакéт; пáчка; (*large sum of money*) кýча дéнег. **packing-case** /ˈpækɪŋ keɪs/ *n* ящик.

pact /pækt/ *n* пакт.

pad /pæd/ *n* (*cushion*) подýшечка; (*shin ~ etc.*) щитóк; (*of paper*) блокнóт; *vt* подбивáть *impf*, подбить *pf.* **padding** /ˈpædɪŋ/ *n* набивка.

paddle[1] /ˈpæd(ə)l/ *n* (*oar*) веслó; *vi* (*row*) грести *impf.*

paddle[2] /ˈpæd(ə)l/ *vi* (*wade*) ходить *indet*, идти *det*, пойти *pf* босикóм по водé.

paddock /ˈpædək/ *n* выгон.

padlock /ˈpædlɒk/ *n* висячий замóк; *vt* запирáть *impf*, заперéть *pf* на висячий замóк.

paediatric /ˌpiːdɪˈætrɪk/ *adj* педиатрический. **paediatrician** /ˌpiːdɪəˈtrɪʃ(ə)n/ *n* педиáтор.

pagan /ˈpeɪgən/ *n* язычник, -ица; *adj* языческий. **paganism** /-ˌnɪz(ə)m/ *n* язычество.

page[1] /peɪdʒ/ *n* (*~-boy*) паж; *vt* (*summon*) вызывáть *impf*, вызвать *pf.*

page[2] /peɪdʒ/ *n* (*of book*) странúца.

pageant /ˈpædʒ(ə)nt/ *n* пышная процéссия. **pageantry** /-trɪ/ *n* пышность.

pail /peɪl/ *n* ведрó.

pain /peɪn/ *n* боль; *pl* (*efforts*) усилия *neut pl*; **~-killer** болеутоляющее срéдство; *vt* (*fig*) огорчáть *impf*, огорчить *pf.* **painful** /-fʊl/ *adj* болéзненный; **be ~** (*part of body*) болéть *impf.* **painless** /-lɪs/ *adj* безболéзненный. **painstaking** /ˈpeɪnz ˌteɪkɪŋ/ *adj* старáтельный.

paint /peɪnt/ *n* крáска; *vt* крáсить *impf*, по~ *pf*; (*portray*) писáть *impf*, на~ *pf* крáсками. **paintbrush** *n* кисть. **painter** /-tə(r)/ *n* (*artist*) худóжник, -ица; (*decorator*) маляр. **painting** /-tɪŋ/ *n* (*art*) живопись; (*picture*) картина.

pair /peə(r)/ *n* пáра; *often not translated with nn denoting a single object, e.g.* **a ~ of scissors** нóжницы (-ц) *pl*; **a ~ of trousers**

па́ра брюк; *vt* спа́ривать *impf*, спа́рить *pf*; ~ **off** разделя́ться *impf*, раздели́ться *pf* по па́рам.

Pakistan /ˌpɑːkɪˈstɑːn/ *n* Пакиста́н. **Pakistani** /-nɪ/ *n* пакиста́нец, -а́нка; *adj* пакиста́нский.

pal /pæl/ *n* прия́тель *m*, ~ница.

palace /ˈpælɪs/ *n* дворе́ц.

palatable /ˈpælətəb(ə)l/ *adj* вку́сный; (*fig*) прия́тный. **palate** /ˈpælət/ *n* нёбо; (*fig*) вкус.

palatial /pəˈleɪʃ(ə)l/ *adj* великоле́пный.

palaver /pəˈlɑːvə(r)/ *n* (*trouble*) беспоко́йство; (*nonsense*) чепуха́.

pale[1] /peɪl/ *n* (*stake*) кол; **beyond the** ~ невообрази́мый.

pale[2] /peɪl/ *adj* бле́дный; *vi* бледне́ть *impf*, по~ *pf*.

palette /ˈpælɪt/ *n* пали́тра.

pall[1] /pɔːl/ *n* покро́в.

pall[2] /pɔːl/ *vi*: ~ **on** надоеда́ть *impf*, надое́сть *pf* +*dat*.

palliative /ˈpælɪətɪv/ *adj* паллиати́вный; *n* паллиати́в.

pallid /ˈpælɪd/ *adj* бле́дный. **pallor** /ˈpælə(r)/ *n* бле́дность.

palm[1] /pɑːm/ *n* (*tree*) па́льма; **P~ Sunday** Ве́рбное воскресе́нье.

palm[2] /pɑːm/ *n* (*of hand*) ладо́нь; *vt*: ~ **off** всу́чивать *impf*, всучи́ть *pf* (**on** +*dat*).

palpable /ˈpælpəb(ə)l/ *adj* осяза́емый.

palpitations /ˌpælpɪˈteɪʃ(ə)nz/ *n pl* сердцебие́ние.

paltry /ˈpɔːltrɪ/ *adj* ничто́жный.

pamper /ˈpæmpə(r)/ *vt* балова́ть *impf*, из~ *pf*.

pamphlet /ˈpæmflɪt/ *n* брошю́ра.

pan[1] /pæn/ *n* (*saucepan*) кастрю́ля; (*frying-*~) сковорода́; (*of scales*) ча́шка; *vt*: ~ **out** промыва́ть *impf*, промы́ть *pf*; (*fig*) выходи́ть *impf*, вы́йти *pf*.

pan[2] /pæn/ *vi* (*cin*) панорами́ровать *impf* & *pf*.

panacea /ˌpænəˈsiːə/ *n* панаце́я.

panache /pəˈnæʃ/ *n* рисо́вка.

pancake /ˈpæŋkeɪk/ *n* блин.

pancreas /ˈpæŋkrɪəs/ *n* поджелу́дочная железа́.

panda /ˈpændə/ *n* па́нда.

pandemonium /ˌpændɪˈməʊnɪəm/ *n* гвалт.

pander /ˈpændə(r)/ *vi*: ~ **to** потво́рствовать *impf* +*dat*.

pane /peɪn/ *n* око́нное стекло́.

panel /ˈpæn(ə)l/ *n* пане́ль; (*control-*~) щит управле́ния; (*of experts*) гру́ппа специали́стов; (*of judges*) жюри́ *neut indecl*. **panelling** /-lɪŋ/ *n* пане́льная общи́вка.

pang /pæŋ/ *n pl* му́ки (-к) *pl*.

panic /ˈpænɪk/ *n* па́ника; **~-stricken** охва́ченный па́никой; *vi* впада́ть *impf*, впасть *pf* в па́нику. **panicky** /-kɪ/ *adj* пани́ческий.

pannier /ˈpænɪə(r)/ *n* корзи́нка.

panorama /ˌpænəˈrɑːmə/ *n* панора́ма. **panoramic** /-ˈræmɪk/ *adj* панора́мный.

pansy /ˈpænzɪ/ *n* аню́тины гла́зки (-зок) *pl*.

pant /pænt/ *vi* дыша́ть *impf* с оды́шкой.

panther /ˈpænθə(r)/ *n* панте́ра.

panties /ˈpæntɪz/ *n pl* тру́сики (-ков) *pl*.

pantomime /ˈpæntəˌmaɪm/ *n* рожде́ственское представле́ние; (*dumb show*) пантоми́ма.

pantry /ˈpæntrɪ/ *n* кладова́я *sb*.

pants /pænts/ *n pl* трусы́ (-со́в) *pl*; (*trousers*) брю́ки (-к) *pl*.

papal /ˈpeɪp(ə)l/ *adj* па́пский.

paper /ˈpeɪpə(r)/ *n* бума́га; *pl* докуме́нты *m pl*; (*newspaper*) газе́та; (*wallpaper*) обо́и (-о́ев) *pl*; (*treatise*) докла́д; *adj* бума́жный; *vt* окле́ивать *impf*, окле́ить *pf* обо́ями. **paperback** *n* кни́га в бума́жной обло́жке. **paperclip** *n* скре́пка. **paperwork** *n* канцеля́рская рабо́та.

par /pɑ:(r)/ *n*: **feel below ~** чу́вствовать *impf* себя́ нева́жно; **on a ~ with** наравне́ с+*instr*.

parable /'pærəb(ə)l/ *n* при́тча.

parabola /pə'ræbələ/ *n* пара́бола.

parachute /'pærə,ʃu:t/ *n* парашю́т; *vi* спуска́ться *impf*, спусти́ться *pf* с парашю́том. **parachutist** /-tɪst/ *n* парашюти́ст.

parade /pə'reɪd/ *n* пара́д; *vi* шествова́ть *impf*; *vt* (*show off*) выставля́ть *impf*, вы́ставить *pf* напока́з.

paradise /'pærə,daɪs/ *n* рай.

paradox /'pærə,dɒks/ *n* парадо́кс. **paradoxical** /,pærə'dɒksɪk(ə)l/ *adj* парадокса́льный.

paraffin /'pærəfɪn/ *n* (**~** *oil*) кероси́н.

paragon /'pærəgən/ *n* образе́ц.

paragraph /'pærə,grɑ:f/ *n* абза́ц.

parallel /'pærə,lel/ *adj* паралле́льный; *n* паралле́ль.

paralyse /'pærə,laɪz/ *vt* парализова́ть *impf* & *pf*. **paralysis** /pə'rælɪsɪs/ *n* парали́ч.

paramedic /,pærə'medɪk/ *n* медрабо́тник (без вы́сшего образова́ния).

parameter /pə'ræmɪtə(r)/ *n* пара́метр.

paramilitary /,pærə'mɪlɪtərɪ/ *adj* полувое́нный.

paramount /'pærə,maʊnt/ *adj* первостепе́нный.

paranoia /,pærə'nɔɪə/ *n* парано́йя. **paranoid** /'pærə,nɔɪd/ *adj*: **he is ~** он парано́ик.

parapet /'pærəpɪt/ *n* (*mil*) бру́ствер.

paraphernalia /,pærəfə'neɪlɪə/ *n* принадле́жности *f pl*.

paraphrase /'pærə,freɪz/ *n* переска́з; *vt* переска́зывать *impf*, пересказа́ть *pf*.

parasite /'pærə,saɪt/ *n* парази́т. **parasitic** /,pærə'sɪtɪk/ *adj* паразити́ческий.

parasol /'pærə,sɒl/ *n* зо́нтик.

paratrooper /'pærə,tru:pə(r)/ *n* парашюти́ст-деса́нтник.

parcel /'pɑ:s(ə)l/ *n* паке́т, посы́лка.

parch /pɑ:tʃ/ *vt* иссуша́ть *impf*, иссуши́ть *pf*; **become ~ed** пересыха́ть *impf*, пересо́хнуть *pf*.

parchment /'pɑ:tʃmənt/ *n* перга́мент.

pardon /'pɑ:d(ə)n/ *n* проще́ние; (*law*) поми́лование; *vt* проща́ть *impf*, прости́ть *pf*; (*law*) поми́ловать *pf*.

pare /peə(r)/ *vt* (*fruit*) чи́стить *impf*, о**~** *pf*; **~ away, down** уре́зывать *impf*, уре́зать *pf*.

parent /'peərənt/ *n* роди́тель *m*, **~**ница. **parentage** /-tɪdʒ/ *n* происхожде́ние. **parental** /pə'rent(ə)l/ *adj* роди́тельский.

parentheses /pə'renθə,si:z/ *n pl* (*brackets*) ско́бки *f pl*.

parish /'pærɪʃ/ *n* прихо́д. **parishioner** /pə'rɪʃənə(r)/ *n* прихожа́нин, -а́нка.

parity /'pærɪtɪ/ *n* ра́венство.

park /pɑ:k/ *n* парк; (*for cars etc.*) стоя́нка; *vt* & *abs* ста́вить *impf*, по**~** *pf* (маши́ну). **parking** /-kɪŋ/ *n* стоя́нка.

parliament /'pɑ:ləmənt/ *n* парла́мент. **parliamentarian** /,pɑ:lәmen'teərɪən/ *n* парламента́рий. **parliamentary** /-'mentərɪ/ *adj* парла́ментский.

parlour /'pɑ:lə(r)/ *n* гости́ная *sb*.

parochial /pə'rəʊkɪəl/ *adj* прихо́дский; (*fig*) ограни́ченный. **parochialism** /-,lɪz(ə)m/ *n* ограни́ченность.

parody /'pærədɪ/ *n* паро́дия; *vt* пароди́ровать *impf* & *pf*.

parole /pə'rəʊl/ *n* че́стное сло́во; **on** ~ освобождённый под че́стное сло́во.

paroxysm /'pærək,sɪz(ə)m/ *n* пароксі́зм.

parquet /'pɑ:keɪ/ *n* парке́т; *attrib* парке́тный.

parrot /'pærət/ *n* попуга́й.

parry /'pærɪ/ *vt* пари́ровать *impf* & *pf*, от~ *pf*.

parsimonious /,pɑ:sɪ'məʊnɪəs/ *adj* скупо́й.

parsley /'pɑ:slɪ/ *n* петру́шка.

parsnip /'pɑ:snɪp/ *n* пастерна́к.

parson /'pɑ:s(ə)n/ *n* свяще́нник.

part /pɑ:t/ *n* часть; (*in play*) роль; (*mus*) па́ртия; **for the most** ~ бо́льшей ча́стью; **in** ~ ча́стью; **for my** ~ что каса́ется меня́; **take** ~ **in** уча́ствовать *impf* в+*prep*; **~-time** (за́нятый) непо́лный рабо́чий день; *vt* & *i* (*divide*) разделя́ть(ся) *impf*, раздели́ть(ся) *pf*; *vi* (*leave*) расстава́ться *impf*, расста́ться *pf* (**from, with** с+*instr*); ~ **one's hair** де́лать *impf*, с~ *pf* себе́ пробо́р.

partake /pɑ:'teɪk/ *vi* принима́ть *impf*, приня́ть *pf* уча́стие (**in, of** в+*prep*); (*eat*) есть *impf*, съ~ *pf* (**of** +*acc*).

partial /'pɑ:ʃ(ə)l/ *adj* части́чный; (*biased*) пристра́стный; ~ **to** неравноду́шный к+*dat*. **partiality** /,pɑ:ʃɪ'ælɪtɪ/ *n* (*bias*) пристра́стность. **partially** /'pɑ:ʃəlɪ/ *adv* части́чно.

participant /pɑ:'tɪsɪpənt/ *n* уча́стник, -ица (**in** +*gen*). **participate** /-,peɪt/ *vi* уча́ствовать *impf* (**in** в+*prep*). **participation** /-'peɪʃ(ə)n/ *n* уча́стие.

participle /'pɑ:tɪ,sɪp(ə)l/ *n* прича́стие.

particle /'pɑ:tɪk(ə)l/ *n* части́ца.

particular /pə'tɪkjʊlə(r)/ *adj* осо́бый, осо́бенный; (*fussy*) разбо́рчивый; *n* подро́бность; **in** ~ в ча́стности.

parting /'pɑ:tɪŋ/ *n* (*leave-taking*) проща́ние; (*of hair*) пробо́р.

partisan /'pɑ:tɪ,zæn/ *n* (*adherent*) сторо́нник; (*mil*) партиза́н; *attrib* (*biased*) пристра́стный; партиза́нский.

partition /pɑ:'tɪʃ(ə)n/ *n* (*wall*) перегоро́дка; (*polit*) разде́л; *vt* разделя́ть *impf*, раздели́ть *pf*; ~ **off** отгора́живать *impf*, отгороди́ть *pf*.

partly /'pɑ:tlɪ/ *adv* части́чно.

partner /'pɑ:tnə(r)/ *n* (*in business*) компаньо́н; (*in dance, game*) партнёр, ~ша. **partnership** *n* това́рищество.

partridge /'pɑ:trɪdʒ/ *n* куропа́тка.

party /'pɑ:tɪ/ *n* (*polit*) па́ртия; (*group*) гру́ппа; (*social gathering*) вечери́нка; (*law*) сторона́; **be a** ~ **to** принима́ть *impf*, приня́ть *pf* уча́стие в+*prep*; *attrib* парти́йный; ~ **line** (*polit*) ли́ния па́ртии; (*telephone*) о́бщий телефо́нный про́вод; ~ **wall** о́бщая стена́.

pass /pɑ:s/ *vt* & *i* (*go past; of time*) проходи́ть *impf*, пройти́ *pf* (**by** ми́мо+*gen*); (*travel past*) проезжа́ть *impf*, прое́хать *pf* (**by** ми́мо+*gen*); (~ *examination*) сдать *pf* (экза́мен); *vt* (*sport*) пасова́ть *impf*, пасну́ть *pf*; (*overtake*) обгоня́ть *impf*, обогна́ть *pf*; (*time*) проводи́ть *impf*, провести́ *pf*; (*hand on*) передава́ть *impf*, переда́ть *pf*; (*law, resolution*) утвержда́ть *impf*, утверди́ть *pf*; (*sentence*) выноси́ть *impf*, вы́нести *pf* (**upon** +*dat*); **~ as, for** слыть *impf*, про~ *pf* +*instr*, за+*acc*; **~ away** (*die*) сконча́ться *pf*; **~ o.s. off as** выдава́ть *impf*, вы́дать *pf* себя́ за+*acc*; **~ out** теря́ть *impf*, по~ *pf* созна́ние; **~ over** (*in silence*) обходи́ть *impf*, обойти́ *pf* молча́нием; **~ round** передава́ть *impf*, переда́ть *pf*; **~ up** подава́ть *impf*, пода́ть *pf*; (*miss*) пропуска́ть *impf*, пропусти́ть *pf*; *n* (*permit*) про́пуск; (*sport*) пас; (*geog*) перева́л; **come to ~** случа́ться *impf*, случи́ться *pf*; **make a ~ at** пристава́ть *impf*, приста́ть *pf* к+*dat*.

passable /'pɑːsəb(ə)l/ *adj* проходи́мый, прое́зжий; (*not bad*) неплохо́й.

passage /'pæsɪdʒ/ *n* прохо́д; (*of time*) тече́ние; (*sea trip*) рейс; (*in house*) коридо́р; (*in book*) отры́вок; (*mus*) пасса́ж.

passenger /'pæsɪndʒə(r)/ *n* пасса́жи́р.

passer-by /ˌpɑːsə'baɪ/ *n* прохо́жий *sb*.

passing /'pɑːsɪŋ/ *adj* (*transient*) мимолётный; *n*: **in ~** мимохо́дом.

passion /'pæʃ(ə)n/ *n* страсть (**for** к+*dat*). **passionate** /-nət/ *adj* стра́стный.

passive /'pæsɪv/ *adj* пасси́вный; (*gram*) страда́тельный; *n* страда́тельный зало́г. **passivity** /-'sɪvɪtɪ/ *n* пасси́вность.

Passover /'pɑːsəʊvə(r)/ *n* евре́йская Па́сха.

passport /'pɑːspɔːt/ *n* па́спорт.

password /'pɑːswɜːd/ *n* паро́ль *m*.

past /pɑːst/ *adj* про́шлый; (*gram*) проше́дший; *n* про́шлое *sb*; (*gram*) проше́дшее вре́мя *neut*; *prep* ми́мо+*gen*; (*beyond*) за+*instr*; *adv* ми́мо.

pasta /'pæstə/ *n* макаро́нные изде́лия *neut pl*.

paste /peɪst/ *n* (*of flour*) те́сто; (*creamy mixture*) па́ста; (*glue*) кле́й; (*jewellery*) страз; *vt* накле́ивать *impf*, накле́ить *pf*.

pastel /'pæst(ə)l/ *n* (*crayon*) пасте́ль; (*drawing*) рису́нок пасте́лью; *attrib* пасте́льный.

pasteurize /'pɑːstjəˌraɪz/ *vt* пастеризова́ть *impf* & *pf*.

pastime /'pɑːstaɪm/ *n* времяпрепровожде́ние.

pastor /'pɑːstə(r)/ *n* па́стор. **pastoral** /-r(ə)l/ *adj* (*bucolic*) пастора́льный; (*of pastor*) па́сторский.

pastry /'peɪstrɪ/ *n* (*dough*) те́сто; (*cake*) пиро́жное *sb*.

pasture /'pɑːstjə(r)/ *n* (*land*) па́стбище.

pasty[1] /'pæstɪ/ *n* пирожо́к.

pasty[2] /'peɪstɪ/ *adj* (**~-*faced***) бле́дный.

pat /pæt/ *n* шлепо́к; (*of butter etc.*) кусо́к; *vt* хлопа́ть *impf*, по~ *pf*.

patch /pætʃ/ *n* запла́та; (*over eye*) повя́зка (на глазу́); (*spot*) пятно́; (*of land*) уча́сток земли́; *vt* ста́вить *impf*, по~ *pf* запла́ту на+*acc*; **~ up** (*fig*) ула́живать *impf*, ула́дить *pf*. **patchwork** *n* лоску́тная рабо́та; *attrib* лоску́тный. **patchy** /'pætʃɪ/ *adj* неро́вный.

pâté /'pæteɪ/ *n* паште́т.

patent /'peɪt(ə)nt/ *adj* я́вный; **~ leather** лакиро́ванная ко́жа; *n* пате́нт; *vt* патентова́ть *impf*,

за~ *pf*.
paternal /pəˈtɜːn(ə)l/ *adj* отцо́вский. **paternity** /-ˈtɜːnɪtɪ/ *n* отцо́вство.
path /pɑːθ/ *n* тропи́нка, тропа́; (*way*) путь *m*.
pathetic /pəˈθetɪk/ *adj* жа́лкий.
pathological /ˌpæθəˈlɒdʒɪk(ə)l/ *adj* патологи́ческий. **pathologist** /pəˈθɒlədʒɪst/ *n* пато́лог.
pathos /ˈpeɪθɒs/ *n* па́фос.
pathway /ˈpæθweɪ/ *n* тропи́нка, тропа́.
patience /ˈpeɪʃ(ə)ns/ *n* терпе́ние; (*cards*) пасья́нс. **patient** /-ʃ(ə)nt/ *adj* терпели́вый; *n* больно́й *sb*, пацие́нт, ~ка.
patio /ˈpætɪəʊ/ *n* терра́са.
patriarch /ˈpeɪtrɪˌɑːk/ *n* патриа́рх. **patriarchal** /-ˈɑːk(ə)l/ *adj* патриарха́льный.
patriot /ˈpætrɪət/ *n* патрио́т, ~ка. **patriotic** /-trɪˈɒtɪk/ *adj* патриоти́ческий. **patriotism** /ˈpætrɪəˌtɪz(ə)m/ *n* патриоти́зм.
patrol /pəˈtrəʊl/ *n* патру́ль *m*; **on** ~ на дозо́ре; *vt & i* патрули́ровать *impf*.
patron /ˈpeɪtrən/ *n* покрови́тель *m*; (*of shop*) клие́нт. **patronage** /ˈpætrənɪdʒ/ *n* покрови́тельство. **patroness** /ˈpeɪtrənɪs/ *n* покрови́тельница. **patronize** /ˈpætrəˌnaɪz/ *vt* (*treat condescendingly*) снисходи́тельно относи́ться *impf*, к+*dat*. **patronizing** /ˈpætrəˌnaɪzɪŋ/ *adj* покрови́тельственный.
patronymic /ˌpætrəˈnɪmɪk/ *n* о́тчество.
patter /ˈpætə(r)/ *vi* (*sound*) бараба́нить *impf*; *n* посту́кивание.
pattern /ˈpæt(ə)n/ *n* (*design*) узо́р; (*model*) образе́ц; (*sewing*) вы́кройка.
paunch /pɔːntʃ/ *n* брюшко́.
pauper /ˈpɔːpə(r)/ *n* бедня́к.
pause /pɔːz/ *n* па́уза, переры́в; (*mus*) ферма́та; *vi* остана́вливаться *impf*, останови́ться *pf*.
pave /peɪv/ *vt* мости́ть *impf*, вы́~ *pf*; ~ **the way** подготовля́ть *impf*, подгото́вить *pf* по́чву (**for** для+*gen*). **pavement** /-mənt/ *n* тротуа́р.
pavilion /pəˈvɪljən/ *n* павильо́н.
paw /pɔː/ *n* ла́па; *vt* тро́гать *impf* ла́пой; (*horse*) бить *impf* копы́том.
pawn[1] /pɔːn/ *n* (*chess*) пе́шка.
pawn[2] /pɔːn/ *vt* закла́дывать *impf*, заложи́ть *pf*. **pawnbroker** /-ˌbrəʊkə(r)/ *n* ростовщи́к. **pawnshop** *n* ломба́рд.
pay /peɪ/ *vt* плати́ть *impf*, за~, у~ *pf* (**for** за+*acc*); (*bill etc.*) опла́чивать *impf*, оплати́ть *pf*; *vi* (*be profitable*) окупа́ться *impf*, окупи́ться *pf*; *n* жа́лованье, зарпла́та; ~ **packet** полу́чка; **~-roll** платёжная ве́домость. **payable** /ˈpeɪəb(ə)l/ *adj* подлежа́щий упла́те. **payee** /peɪˈiː/ *n* получа́тель *m*. **payment** /ˈpeɪmənt/ *n* упла́та, платёж.
PC *abbr* (*of* **personal computer**) ПК (персона́льный компью́тер); (*of* **politically correct**) полити́чески корре́ктный.
pea /piː/ *n* (*also pl*, *collect*) горо́х.
peace /piːs/ *n* мир; **in** ~ в поко́е; ~ **and quiet** мир и тишина́. **peaceable, peaceful** /ˈpiːsəb(ə)l, ˈpiːsfʊl/ *adj* ми́рный.
peach /piːtʃ/ *n* пе́рсик.
peacock /ˈpiːkɒk/ *n* павли́н.
peak /piːk/ *n* (*of cap*) козырёк; (*summit*; *fig*) верши́на; ~ **hour** часы́ *m pl* пик.
peal /piːl/ *n* (*sound*) звон, трезво́н; (*of laughter*) взрыв.
peanut /ˈpiːnʌt/ *n* ара́хис.

pear /peə(r)/ *n* гру́ша.

pearl /pɜ:l/ *n* (*also fig*) жемчу́жина; *pl* (*collect*) же́мчуг.

peasant /ˈpez(ə)nt/ *n* крестья́нин, -я́нка; *attrib* крестья́нский.

peat /pi:t/ *n* торф.

pebble /ˈpeb(ə)l/ *n* га́лька.

peck /pek/ *vt* & *i* клева́ть *impf*, клю́нуть *pf*; *n* клево́к.

pectoral /ˈpektər(ə)l/ *adj* грудно́й.

peculiar /pɪˈkju:lɪə(r)/ *adj* (*distinctive*) своеобра́зный; (*strange*) стра́нный; **~ to** сво́йственный +*dat*. **peculiarity** /-lɪˈærɪtɪ/ *n* осо́бенность; стра́нность.

pecuniary /pɪˈkju:nɪərɪ/ *adj* де́нежный.

pedagogical /ˌpedəˈgɒgɪk(ə)l/ *adj* педагоги́ческий.

pedal /ˈped(ə)l/ *n* педа́ль; *vi* нажима́ть *impf*, нажа́ть *pf* педа́ль; (*ride bicycle*) е́хать *impf*, по~ *pf* на велосипе́де.

pedant /ˈped(ə)nt/ *n* педа́нт. **pedantic** /pɪˈdæntɪk/ *adj* педанти́чный.

peddle /ˈped(ə)l/ *vt* торгова́ть *impf* вразно́с+*instr*.

pedestal /ˈpedɪst(ə)l/ *n* пьедеста́л.

pedestrian /pɪˈdestrɪən/ *adj* пешехо́дный; (*prosaic*) прозаи́ческий; *n* пешехо́д; **~ crossing** перехо́д.

pedigree /ˈpedɪˌgri:/ *n* родосло́вная *sb*; *adj* поро́дистый.

pedlar /ˈpedlə(r)/ *n* разно́счик.

pee /pi:/ *n* пи-пи́ *neut indecl*; *vi* мочи́ться *impf*, по~ *pf*.

peek /pi:k/ *vi* (**~** *in*) загля́дывать *impf*, загляну́ть *pf*; (**~** *out*) выгля́дывать *impf*, вы́глянуть *pf*.

peel /pi:l/ *n* кожура́; *vt* очища́ть *impf*, очи́стить *pf*; *vi* (*skin*) шелуши́ться *impf*; (*paint*, **~** *off*) сходи́ть *impf*, сойти́ *pf*. **peelings** /-lɪŋz/ *n pl* очи́стки (-ков) *pl*.

peep /pi:p/ *vi* (**~** *in*) загля́дывать *impf*, загляну́ть *pf*; (**~** *out*) выгля́дывать *impf*, вы́глянуть *pf*; *n* (*glance*) бы́стрый взгляд; **~-hole** глазо́к.

peer[1] /pɪə(r)/ *vi* всма́триваться *impf*, всмотре́ться *pf* (**at** в+*acc*).

peer[2] /pɪə(r)/ *n* (*noble*) пэр; (*person one's age*) све́рстник.

peeved /pi:vd/ *adj* раздражённый. **peevish** /ˈpi:vɪʃ/ *adj* раздражи́тельный.

peg /peg/ *n* ко́лышек; (*clothes* **~**) крючо́к; (*for hat etc.*) ве́шалка; **off the ~** гото́вый; *vt* прикрепля́ть *impf*, прикрепи́ть *pf* ко́лышком, -ками.

pejorative /pɪˈdʒɒrətɪv/ *adj* уничижи́тельный.

pelican /ˈpelɪkən/ *n* пелика́н.

pellet /ˈpelɪt/ *n* ша́рик; (*shot*) дроби́на.

pelt[1] /pelt/ *n* (*skin*) шку́ра.

pelt[2] /pelt/ *vt* забра́сывать *impf*, заброса́ть *pf*; *vi* (*rain*) бараба́нить *impf*.

pelvis /ˈpelvɪs/ *n* таз.

pen[1] /pen/ *n* (*for writing*) ру́чка; **~-friend** друг по перепи́ске.

pen[2] /pen/ *n* (*enclosure*) заго́н.

penal /ˈpi:n(ə)l/ *adj* уголо́вный. **penalize** /-ˌlaɪz/ *vt* штрафова́ть *impf*, о~ *pf*. **penalty** /ˈpenəltɪ/ *n* наказа́ние; (*sport*) штраф; **~ area** штрафна́я площа́дка; **~ kick** штрафно́й уда́р. **penance** /ˈpenəns/ *n* епитимья́.

penchant /ˈpɑ̃ʃɑ̃/ *n* скло́нность (**for** к+*dat*).

pencil /ˈpensɪl/ *n* каранда́ш; **~-sharpener** точи́лка.

pendant /ˈpend(ə)nt/ *n* подве́ска.

pending /ˈpendɪŋ/ *adj* (*awaiting decision*) ожида́ющий реше́ния; *prep* (*until*) в ожида́нии +*gen*, до+*gen*.

pendulum /ˈpendjʊləm/ *n* ма́ятник.

penetrate /ˈpenɪˌtreɪt/ *vt* проника́ть *impf*, прони́кнуть *pf* в+*acc*. **penetrating** /-ˌtreɪtɪŋ/ *adj* проница́тельный; (*sound*) пронзи́тельный. **penetration** /ˌpenɪˈtreɪʃ(ə)n/ *n* проникнове́ние; (*insight*) проница́тельность.

penguin /ˈpeŋgwɪn/ *n* пингви́н.

penicillin /ˌpenɪˈsɪlɪn/ *n* пеницилли́н.

peninsula /pɪˈnɪnsjʊlə/ *n* полуо́стров.

penis /ˈpiːnɪs/ *n* пе́нис.

penitence /ˈpenɪt(ə)ns/ *n* раска́яние. **penitent** /-t(ə)nt/ *adj* раска́ивающийся; *n* ка́ющийся гре́шник.

penknife /ˈpennaɪf/ *n* перочи́нный нож.

pennant /ˈpenənt/ *n* вы́мпел.

penniless /ˈpenɪlɪs/ *adj* без гроша́.

penny /ˈpenɪ/ *n* пе́нни *neut indecl*, пенс.

pension /ˈpenʃ(ə)n/ *n* пе́нсия; *vt*: ~ **off** увольня́ть *impf*, уво́лить *pf* на пе́нсию. **pensionable** /-nəb(ə)l/ *adj* (*age*) пенсио́нный. **pensioner** /-nə(r)/ *n* пенсионе́р, ~ка.

pensive /ˈpensɪv/ *adj* заду́мчивый.

pentagon /ˈpentəgən/ *n* пятиуго́льник; **the P~** Пентаго́н.

Pentecost /ˈpentɪˌkɒst/ *n* Пятидеся́тница.

penthouse /ˈpenthaʊs/ *n* шика́рная кварти́ра на ве́рхнем этаже́.

pent-up /ˈpentʌp/ *adj* (*anger etc.*) сде́рживаемый.

penultimate /pɪˈnʌltɪmət/ *adj* предпосле́дний.

penury /ˈpenjʊrɪ/ *n* нужда́.

peony /ˈpiːənɪ/ *n* пио́н.

people /ˈpiːp(ə)l/ *n pl* (*persons*) лю́ди *pl*; *sg* (*nation*) наро́д; *vt* населя́ть *impf*, насели́ть *pf*.

pepper /ˈpepə(r)/ *n* пе́рец; *vt* пе́рчить *impf*, на~, по~ *pf*. **peppercorn** *n* перчи́нка. **peppermint** /ˈpepəˌmɪnt/ *n* пе́речная мя́та; (*sweet*) мя́тная конфе́та.

per /pɜː(r)/ *prep* (*for each*) (*person*) на+*acc*; **as** ~ согла́сно+*dat*; ~ **annum** в год; ~ **capita** на челове́ка; ~ **hour** в час; ~ **se** сам по себе́.

perceive /pəˈsiːv/ *vt* воспринима́ть *impf*, восприня́ть *pf*.

per cent /pə ˈsent/ *adv* & *n* проце́нт. **percentage** /pəˈsentɪdʒ/ *n* проце́нт; (*part*) часть.

perceptible /pəˈseptɪb(ə)l/ *adj* заме́тный. **perception** /-ˈsepʃ(ə)n/ *n* восприя́тие; (*quality*) понима́ние. **perceptive** /-ˈseptɪv/ *adj* то́нкий.

perch[1] /pɜːtʃ/ *n* (*fish*) о́кунь *m*.

perch[2] /pɜːtʃ/ *n* (*roost*) насе́ст; *vi* сади́ться *impf*, сесть *pf*. **perched** /-d/ *adj* высоко́ сидя́щий, располо́женный.

percussion /pəˈkʌʃ(ə)n/ *n* (~ *instruments*) уда́рные инструме́нты *m pl*.

peremptory /pəˈremptərɪ/ *adj* повели́тельный.

perennial /pəˈrenɪəl/ *adj* (*enduring*) ве́чный; *n* (*bot*) многоле́тнее расте́ние.

perestroika /ˌperɪˈstrɔɪkə/ *n* перестро́йка.

perfect *adj* /ˈpɜːfɪkt/ соверше́нный; (*gram*) перфе́ктный; *n* перфе́кт; *vt* /pəˈfekt/ соверше́нствовать *impf*, у~ *pf*. **perfection** /pəˈfekʃ(ə)n/ *n* соверше́нство. **perfective** /-ˈfektɪv/ *adj* (*n*) соверше́нный (вид).

perforate /ˈpɜːfəˌreɪt/ *vt* перфори́ровать *impf* & *pf*. **perforation** /-ˈreɪʃ(ə)n/ *n* перфора́ция.

perform /pəˈfɔːm/ *vt* (*carry out*) исполня́ть *impf*, испо́лнить *pf*; (*theat*, *mus*) игра́ть *impf*, сыгра́ть *pf*; *vi* выступа́ть *impf*, вы́ступить *pf*; (*function*) рабо́тать *impf*. **performance** /-məns/ *n* исполне́ние; (*of person*, *device*) де́йствие; (*of play etc.*) представле́ние, спекта́кль *m*; (*of engine etc.*) эксплуатацио́нные ка́чества *neut pl*. **performer** /-mə(r)/ *n* исполни́тель *m*.

perfume /ˈpɜːfjuːm/ *n* духи́ (-хо́в) *pl*; (*smell*) арома́т.

perfunctory /pəˈfʌŋktərɪ/ *adj* пове́рхностный.

perhaps /pəˈhæps/ *adv* мо́жет быть.

peril /ˈperɪl/ *n* опа́сность, риск. **perilous** /-ləs/ *adj* опа́сный, риско́ванный.

perimeter /pəˈrɪmɪtə(r)/ *n* вне́шняя грани́ца; (*geom*) пери́метр.

period /ˈpɪərɪəd/ *n* пери́од; (*epoch*) эпо́ха; (*menstrual*) ме́сячные *sb pl*. **periodic** /ˌpɪərɪˈɒdɪk/ *adj* периоди́ческий. **periodical** /-ˈɒdɪk(ə)l/ *adj* периоди́ческий; *n* периоди́ческое изда́ние.

peripheral /pəˈrɪfər(ə)l/ *adj* перифери́йный. **periphery** /-ˈrɪfərɪ/ *n* перифери́я.

periscope /ˈperɪˌskəʊp/ *n* периско́п.

perish /ˈperɪʃ/ *vi* погиба́ть *impf*, поги́бнуть *pf*; (*spoil*) по́ртиться *impf*, ис~ *pf*. **perishable** /-ʃəb(ə)l/ *adj* скоропо́ртящийся.

perjure /ˈpɜːdʒə(r)/ *v*: ~ **o.s.** наруша́ть *impf*, нару́шить *pf* кля́тву. **perjury** /-dʒərɪ/ *n* лжесвиде́тельство.

perk[1] /pɜːk/ *n* льго́та.

perk[2] /pɜːk/ *vi*: ~ **up** оживля́ться *impf*, оживи́ться *pf*. **perky** /-kɪ/ *adj* бо́йкий.

perm /pɜːm/ *n* перманéнт. **permanence** /ˈpɜːmənəns/ *n* постоя́нство. **permanent** /-nənt/ *adj* постоя́нный.

permeable /ˈpɜːmɪəb(ə)l/ *adj* проница́емый. **permeate** /ˈpɜːmɪˌeɪt/ *vt* проника́ть *impf*, прони́кнуть *pf* в+*acc*.

permissible /pəˈmɪsɪb(ə)l/ *adj* допусти́мый. **permission** /-ˈmɪʃ(ə)n/ *n* разреше́ние. **permissive** /-ˈmɪsɪv/ *adj* (сли́шком) либера́льный; ~ **society** о́бщество вседозво́ленности. **permissiveness** /-ˈmɪsɪvnɪs/ *n* вседозво́ленность. **permit** /ˈpɜːmɪt/ *vt* разреша́ть *impf*, разреши́ть *pf* +*dat*; *n* про́пуск.

permutation /ˌpɜːmjʊˈteɪʃ(ə)n/ *n* перестано́вка.

pernicious /pəˈnɪʃəs/ *adj* па́губный.

perpendicular /ˌpɜːpənˈdɪkjʊlə(r)/ *adj* перпендикуля́рный; *n* перпендикуля́р.

perpetrate /ˈpɜːpɪˌtreɪt/ *vt* соверша́ть *impf*, соверши́ть *pf*. **perpetrator** /-ˌtreɪtə(r)/ *n* вино́вник.

perpetual /pəˈpetjʊəl/ *adj* ве́чный. **perpetuate** /-tjʊˌeɪt/ *vt* увекове́чивать *impf*, увекове́чить *pf*. **perpetuity** /ˌpɜːpɪˈtjuːɪtɪ/ *n* ве́чность; **in** ~ навсегда́, наве́чно.

perplex /pə'pleks/ *vt* озада́чивать *impf*, озада́чить *pf*. **perplexity** /-'pleksɪtɪ/ *n* озада́ченность.

persecute /'pɜːsɪ,kjuːt/ *vt* пресле́довать *impf*. **persecution** /-,kjuːʃ(ə)n/ *n* пресле́дование.

perseverance /,pɜːsɪ'vɪərəns/ *n* насто́йчивость. **persevere** /,pɜːsɪ'vɪə(r)/ *vi* насто́йчиво, продолжа́ть *impf* (**in, at** *etc*. +*acc*, *inf*).

Persian /'pɜːʃ(ə)n/ *n* перс, ~ия́нка; *adj* перси́дский.

persist /pə'sɪst/ *vi* упо́рствовать *impf* (**in** в+*prep*); насто́йчиво продолжа́ть *impf* (**in** +*acc*, *inf*). **persistence** /-t(ə)ns/ *n* упо́рство. **persistent** /-t(ə)nt/ *adj* упо́рный.

person /'pɜːs(ə)n/ *n* челове́к; (*in play*; *gram*) лицо́; **in** ~ ли́чно. **personable** /-nəb(ə)l/ *adj* привлека́тельный. **personage** /-nɪdʒ/ *n* ли́чность. **personal** /-n(ə)l/ *adj* ли́чный. **personality** /,pɜːsə'nælɪtɪ/ *n* ли́чность. **personally** /-nəlɪ/ *adv* ли́чно. **personification** /pə,sɒnɪfɪ'keɪʃ(ə)n/ *n* олицетворе́ние. **personify** /-'sɒnɪ,faɪ/ *vt* олицетворя́ть *impf*, олицетвори́ть *pf*.

personnel /,pɜːsə'nel/ *n* ка́дры (-ров) *pl*, персона́л; ~ **department** отде́л ка́дров.

perspective /pə'spektɪv/ *n* перспекти́ва.

perspiration /,pɜːspɪ'reɪʃ(ə)n/ *n* пот. **perspire** /pə'spaɪə(r)/ *vi* поте́ть *impf*, вс~ *pf*.

persuade /pə'sweɪd/ *vt* (*convince*) убежда́ть *impf*, убеди́ть *pf* (**of** в+*prep*); (*induce*) угова́ривать *impf*, уговори́ть *pf*. **persuasion** /-'sweɪʒ(ə)n/ *n* убежде́ние. **persuasive** /-'sweɪsɪv/ *adj* убеди́тельный.

pertain /pə'teɪn/ *vi*: ~ **to** относи́ться *impf* отнести́сь *pf* к+*dat*.

pertinent /'pɜːtɪnənt/ *adj* уме́стный.

perturb /pə'tɜːb/ *vt* трево́жить *impf*, вс~ *pf*.

peruse /pə'ruːz/ *vt* (*read*) внима́тельно чита́ть *impf*, про~ *pf*; (*fig*) рассма́тривать *impf*, рассмотре́ть *pf*.

pervade /pə'veɪd/ *vt* наполня́ть *impf*. **pervasive** /-'veɪsɪv/ *adj* распространённый.

perverse /pə'vɜːs/ *adj* капри́зный. **perversion** /-'vɜːʒ(ə)n/ *n* извраще́ние. **pervert** *vt* /pə'vɜːt/ извраща́ть *impf*, изврати́ть *pf*; *n* /'pɜːvɜːt/ извращённый челове́к.

pessimism /'pesɪ,mɪz(ə)m/ *n* пессими́зм. **pessimist** /-mɪst/ *n* пессими́ст. **pessimistic** /-'mɪstɪk/ *adj* пессимисти́ческий.

pest /pest/ *n* вреди́тель *m*; (*fig*) зану́да. **pester** /'pestə(r)/ *vt* пристава́ть *impf*, приста́ть *pf* к+*dat*. **pesticide** /'pestɪ,saɪd/ *n* пестици́д.

pet /pet/ *n* (*animal*) дома́шнее живо́тное *sb*; (*favourite*) люби́мец, -мица; ~ **shop** зоомагази́н; *vt* ласка́ть *impf*.

petal /'pet(ə)l/ *n* лепесто́к.

peter /'piːtə(r)/ *vi*: ~ **out** (*road*) исчеза́ть *impf*, исче́знуть *pf*; (*stream*; *enthusiasm*) иссяка́ть *impf*, исся́кнуть *pf*.

petite /pə'tiːt/ *adj* ма́ленькая.

petition /pɪ'tɪʃ(ə)n/ *n* пети́ция; *vt* подава́ть *impf*, пода́ть *pf* проше́ние +*dat*. **petitioner** /-nə(r)/ *n* проси́тель *m*.

petrified /'petrɪ,faɪd/ *adj* окамене́лый; **be** ~ (*fig*) оцепене́ть *pf* (**with** от+*gen*).

petrol /'petr(ə)l/ *n* бензи́н; ~ **pump** бензоколо́нка; ~ **station** бензозапра́вочная ста́нция; ~ **tank** бензоба́к. **petroleum** /pɪ'trəʊlɪəm/ *n* нефть.

petticoat /'petɪ,kəʊt/ *n* ни́жняя ю́бка.

petty /'petɪ/ *adj* ме́лкий; ~ **cash** де́ньги (де́нег, -ньга́м) *pl* на ме́лкие расхо́ды.

petulant /'petjʊlənt/ *adj* раздражи́тельный.

pew /pju:/ *n* (церко́вная) скамья́.

phallic /'fælɪk/ *adj* фалли́ческий. **phallus** /'fæləs/ *n* фа́ллос.

phantom /'fæntəm/ *n* фанто́м.

pharmaceutical /,fɑ:mə'sju:tɪk(ə)l/ *adj* фармацевти́ческий. **pharmacist** /'fɑ:məsɪst/ *n* фармаце́вт. **pharmacy** /-məsɪ/ *n* фармаци́я; (*shop*) апте́ка.

phase /feɪz/ *n* фа́за; *vt*: ~ **in, out** постепе́нно вводи́ть *impf*, упраздня́ть *impf*.

Ph.D. *abbr* (*of* **Doctor of Philosophy**) кандида́т нау́к.

pheasant /'fez(ə)nt/ *n* фаза́н.

phenomenal /fɪ'nɒmɪn(ə)l/ *adj* феномена́льный. **phenomenon** /fɪ'nɒmɪnən/ *n* фено́мен.

phial /'faɪəl/ *n* пузырёк.

philanderer /fɪ'lændərə(r)/ *n* волоки́та *m*.

philanthropic /,fɪlən'θrɒpɪk/ *adj* филантропи́ческий. **philanthropist** /fɪ'lænθrəpɪst/ *n* филантро́п. **philanthropy** /-'lænθrəpɪ/ *n* филантро́пия.

philately /fɪ'lætəlɪ/ *n* филатели́я.

philharmonic /,fɪlhɑ:'mɒnɪk/ *adj* филармони́ческий.

Philistine /'fɪlɪ,staɪn/ *n* (*fig*) фили́стер.

philosopher /fɪ'lɒsəfə(r)/ *n* фило́соф. **philosophical** /,fɪlə'sɒfɪk(ə)l/ *adj* филосо́фский. **philosophize** /fɪ'lɒsəfaɪz/ *vi* филосо́фствовать *impf*. **philosophy** /fɪ'lɒsəfɪ/ *n* филосо́фия.

phlegm /flem/ *n* мокрота́. **phlegmatic** /fleg'mætɪk/ *adj* флегмати́ческий.

phobia /'fəʊbɪə/ *n* фо́бия.

phone /fəʊn/ *n* телефо́н; *vt* & *i* звони́ть *impf*, по~ *pf* +*dat*. *See also* **telephone**

phonetic /fə'netɪk/ *adj* фонети́ческий. **phonetics** /-tɪks/ *n* фоне́тика.

phoney /'fəʊnɪ/ *n* подде́льный.

phosphorus /'fɒsfərəs/ *n* фо́сфор.

photo /'fəʊtəʊ/ *n* фо́то *neut indecl*. **photocopier** /'fəʊtə,kɒpɪə(r)/ *n* копирова́льная маши́на. **photocopy** /-,kɒpɪ/ *n* фотоко́пия; *vt* де́лать *impf*, с~ *pf* фотоко́пию +*gen*. **photogenic** /,fəʊtəʊ'dʒenɪk/ *adj* фотогени́чный. **photograph** /'fəʊtə,grɑ:f/ *n* фотогра́фия; *vt* фотографи́ровать *impf*, с~ *pf*. **photographer** /fə'tɒgrəfə(r)/ *n* фото́граф. **photographic** /,fəʊtə'græfɪk/ *adj* фотографи́ческий. **photography** /fə'tɒgrəfɪ/ *n* фотогра́фия.

phrase /freɪz/ *n* фра́за; *vt* формули́ровать *impf*, с~ *pf*.

physical /'fɪzɪk(ə)l/ *adj* физи́ческий; ~ **education** физкульту́ра; ~ **exercises** заря́дка. **physician** /fɪ'zɪʃ(ə)n/ *n* врач. **physicist** /'fɪzɪsɪst/ *n* фи́зик. **physics** /'fɪzɪks/ *n* фи́зика.

physiological /,fɪzɪə'lɒdʒɪk(ə)l/ *n* физиологи́ческий. **physiologist** /,fɪzɪ'ɒlədʒɪst/ *n* физио́лог. **physiology** /,fɪzɪ'ɒlədʒɪ/ *n* физиоло́гия. **physiotherapist** /,fɪzɪəʊ'θerəpɪst/ *n* физиотерапе́вт. **physiotherapy** /ˌfɪzɪəʊ'θerəpɪ/ *n* физиотерапи́я.

physique /fɪ'zi:k/ *n* телосложе́ние.

pianist /'pɪənɪst/ *n* пиани́ст, ~ка.

piano /pɪ'ænəʊ/ *n* фортепья́но *neut indecl*; (*grand*) роя́ль *m*; (*upright*) пиани́но *neut indecl*.

pick¹ /pɪk/ *vt* (*flower*) срыва́ть *impf*, сорва́ть *pf*; (*gather*) собира́ть *impf*, собра́ть *pf*; (*select*) выбира́ть *impf*, вы́брать *pf*; ~ **one's nose, teeth** ковыря́ть *impf*, ковырну́ть *pf* в носу́, в зуба́х; ~ **a quarrel** иска́ть *impf* ссо́ры (**with** с+*instr*); ~ **one's way** выбира́ть *impf*, вы́брать *pf* доро́гу; ~ **on** (*nag*) придира́ться *impf* к+*dat*; ~ **out** отбира́ть *impf*, отобра́ть *pf*; ~ **up** (*lift*) поднима́ть *impf*, подня́ть *pf*; (*acquire*) приобрета́ть *impf*, приобрести́ *pf*; (*fetch*) (*on foot*) заходи́ть *impf*, зайти́ *pf* за +*instr*; (*in vehicle*) заезжа́ть *impf*, зае́хать *pf* за+*instr*; (*a cold*; *a girl*) подцепля́ть *impf*, подцепи́ть *pf*; ~ **o.s. up** поднима́ться *impf*, подня́ться *pf*; **~-up** (*truck*) пика́п; (*electron*) звукоснима́тель *m*.

pick² /pɪk/ *n* вы́бор; (*best part*) лу́чшая часть; **take your** ~ выбира́й(те)!

pick³ /pɪk/, **pickaxe** /'pɪkæks/ *n* кирка́.

picket /'pɪkɪt/ *n* (*person*) пике́тчик, -ица; (*collect*) пике́т; *vt* пикети́ровать *impf*.

pickle /'pɪk(ə)l/ *n* соле́нье; *vt* соли́ть *impf*, по~ *pf*. **pickled** /-k(ə)ld/ *adj* солёный.

pickpocket /'pɪkpɒkɪt/ *n* карма́нник.

picnic /'pɪknɪk/ *n* пикни́к.

pictorial /pɪk'tɔ:rɪəl/ *adj* изобрази́тельный; (*illustrated*) иллюстри́рованный. **picture** /'pɪktʃə(r)/ *n* карти́на; (*of health etc.*) воплоще́ние; (*film*) фильм; **the ~s** кино́ *neut indecl*; *vt* (*to o.s.*) представля́ть *impf*, предста́вить *pf* себе́. **picturesque** /ˌpɪktʃə'resk/ *adj* живопи́сный.

pie /paɪ/ *n* пиро́г.

piece /pi:s/ *n* кусо́к, часть; (*one of set*) шту́ка; (*of paper*) листо́к; (*mus, literature*) произведе́ние; (*chess*) фигу́ра; (*coin*) моне́та; **take to ~s** разбира́ть *impf*, разобра́ть *pf* (на ча́сти); ~ **of advice** сове́т; ~ **of information** све́дение; ~ **of news** но́вость; **~-work** сде́льщина; **~-worker** сде́льщик; *vt*: ~ **together** воссоздава́ть *impf*, воссозда́ть *pf* карти́ну +*gen*. **piecemeal** *adv* по частя́м.

pier /pɪə(r)/ *n* (*mole*) мол; (*projecting into sea*) пирс; (*of bridge*) бык; (*between windows etc.*) просте́нок.

pierce /pɪəs/ *vt* пронза́ть *impf*, пронзи́ть *pf*; (*ears*) прока́лывать *impf*, проколо́ть *pf*. **piercing** /-sɪŋ/ *adj* пронзи́тельный.

piety /'paɪɪtɪ/ *n* на́божность.

pig /pɪg/ *n* свинья́. **pigheaded** /pɪg'hedɪd/ *adj* упря́мый. **piglet** /'pɪglɪt/ *n* поросёнок. **pigsty** /'pɪgˌstaɪ/ *n* свина́рник. **pigtail** *n* коси́чка.

pigeon /'pɪdʒɪn/ *n* го́лубь; **~-hole** отделе́ние для бума́г.

pigment /'pɪgmənt/ *n* пигме́нт. **pigmentation** /-'teɪʃ(ə)n/ *n* пигмента́ция.

pike /paɪk/ *n* (*fish*) щу́ка.

pilchard /'pɪltʃəd/ *n* сарди́н(к)а.

pile¹ /paɪl/ *n* (*heap*) ку́ча, ки́па; *vt*: ~ **up** сва́ливать *impf*, свали́ть *pf* в ку́чу; (*load*) нагружа́ть *impf*, нагрузи́ть *pf* (**with**

+*instr*); *vi*: ~ **in(to), on** забира́ться *impf*, забра́ться *pf* в+*acc*; ~ **up** накопля́ться, нака́пливаться *impf*, накопи́ться *pf*.

pile² /paɪl/ *n* (*on cloth etc.*) ворс.

piles /paɪlz/ *n pl* геморро́й *collect*.

pilfer /ˈpɪlfə(r)/ *vt* ворова́ть *impf*.

pilgrim /ˈpɪlgrɪm/ *n* пилигри́м. **pilgrimage** /-mɪdʒ/ *n* пало́мничество.

pill /pɪl/ *n* пилю́ля; **the** ~ противозача́точная пилю́ля.

pillage /ˈpɪlɪdʒ/ *vt* гра́бить *impf*, о~ *pf*; *v abs* мародёрствовать *impf*.

pillar /ˈpɪlə(r)/ *n* столб; ~**-box** стоя́чий почто́вый я́щик.

pillion /ˈpɪljən/ *n* за́днее сиде́нье (мотоци́кла).

pillory /ˈpɪlərɪ/ *n* позо́рный столб; *vt* (*fig*) пригвожда́ть *impf*, пригвозди́ть *pf* к позо́рному столбу́.

pillow /ˈpɪləʊ/ *n* поду́шка. **pillowcase** *n* на́волочка.

pilot /ˈpaɪlət/ *n* (*naut*) ло́цман; (*aeron*) пило́т; *adj* о́пытный, про́бный; *vt* пилоти́ровать *impf*.

pimp /pɪmp/ *n* сво́дник.

pimple /ˈpɪmp(ə)l/ *n* прыщ.

pin /pɪn/ *n* була́вка; (*peg*) па́лец; ~**-point** то́чно определя́ть *impf*, определи́ть *pf*; ~**-stripe** то́нкая поло́ска; *vt* прика́лывать *impf*, приколо́ть *pf*; (*press*) прижима́ть *impf*, прижа́ть *pf* (**against** к+*dat*).

pinafore /ˈpɪnəˌfɔː(r)/ *n* пере́дник.

pincers /ˈpɪnsəz/ *n pl* (*tool*) кле́щи (-ще́й) *pl*, пинце́т; (*claw*) клешни́ *f pl*.

pinch /pɪntʃ/ *vt* щипа́ть *impf*, (у)щипну́ть *pf*; (*finger in door etc.*) прищемля́ть *impf*, прищеми́ть *pf*; (*of shoe*) жать *impf*; (*steal*) стяну́ть *pf*; *n* щипо́к; (*of salt*) щепо́тка; **at a** ~ в кра́йнем слу́чае.

pine¹ /paɪn/ *vi* томи́ться *impf*; ~ **for** тоскова́ть *impf* по+*dat*, *prep*.

pine² /paɪn/ *n* (*tree*) сосна́.

pineapple /ˈpaɪnæp(ə)l/ *n* анана́с.

ping-pong /ˈpɪŋpɒŋ/ *n* пингпо́нг.

pink /pɪŋk/ *n* (*colour*) ро́зовый цвет; *adj* ро́зовый.

pinnacle /ˈpɪnək(ə)l/ *n* верши́на.

pint /paɪnt/ *n* пи́нта.

pioneer /ˌpaɪəˈnɪə(r)/ *n* пионе́р, ~ка; *vt* прокла́дывать *impf*, проложи́ть *pf* путь к+*dat*.

pious /ˈpaɪəs/ *adj* на́божный.

pip¹ /pɪp/ *n* (*seed*) зёрнышко.

pip² /pɪp/ *n* (*sound*) бип.

pipe /paɪp/ *n* труба́; (*mus*) ду́дка; (*for smoking*) тру́бка; ~**-dream** пуста́я мечта́; *vt* пуска́ть *impf*, пусти́ть *pf* по труба́м; *vi* ~ **down** затиха́ть *impf*, зати́хнуть *pf*. **pipeline** *n* трубопрово́д; (*oil* ~) нефтепрово́д.

piper /ˈpaɪpə(r)/ *n* волы́нщик.

piping /ˈpaɪpɪŋ/ *adj*: ~ **hot** с пылу.

piquant /ˈpiːkənt/ *adj* пика́нтный.

pique /piːk/ *n*: **in a fit of** ~ в поры́ве раздраже́ния.

pirate /ˈpaɪərət/ *n* пира́т.

pirouette /ˌpɪrʊˈet/ *n* пиру́эт; *vi* де́лать *impf*, с~ *pf* пиру́эт(ы).

Pisces /ˈpaɪsiːz/ *n* Ры́бы *f pl*.

pistol /ˈpɪst(ə)l/ *n* пистоле́т.

piston /ˈpɪst(ə)n/ *n* по́ршень *m*.

pit /pɪt/ *n* я́ма; (*mine*) ша́хта; (*orchestra* ~) орке́стр; (*motor-*

racing) запра́вочно-ремо́нтный пункт; *vt*: **~ against** выставля́ть *impf*, вы́ставить *pf* про́тив+*gen*.

pitch¹ /pɪtʃ/ *n* (*resin*) смола́; **~-black** чёрный как смоль; **~-dark** о́чень тёмный.

pitch² /pɪtʃ/ *vt* (*camp, tent*) разбива́ть *impf*, разби́ть *pf*; (*throw*) броса́ть *impf*, бро́сить *pf*; *vi* (*fall*) па́дать *impf*, (у)па́сть *pf*; (*ship*) кача́ть *impf*, *n* (*football ~ etc.*) по́ле; (*degree*) у́ровень *m*; (*mus*) высота́; (*slope*) укло́н.

pitcher /ˈpɪtʃə(r)/ *n* (*vessel*) кувши́н.

pitchfork /ˈpɪtʃfɔːk/ *n* ви́лы (-л) *pl*.

piteous /ˈpɪtɪəs/ *adj* жа́лкий.

pitfall /ˈpɪtfɔːl/ *n* западня́.

pith /pɪθ/ *n* сердеви́на; (*essence*) суть. **pithy** /ˈpɪθɪ/ *adj* (*fig*) содержа́тельный.

pitiful /ˈpɪtɪˌfʊl/ *adj* жа́лкий. **pitiless** /ˈpɪtɪlɪs/ *adj* безжа́лостный.

pittance /ˈpɪt(ə)ns/ *n* жа́лкие гроши́ (-ше́й) *pl*.

pity /ˈpɪtɪ/ *n* жа́лость; **it's a ~** жа́лко, жаль; **take ~ on** сжа́литься *pf* над+*instr*; **what a ~** как жа́лко!; *vt* жале́ть *impf*, по~ *pf*; **I ~ you** мне жаль тебя́.

pivot /ˈpɪvət/ *n* сте́ржень *m*; (*fig*) центр; *vi* враща́ться *impf*.

pixie /ˈpɪksɪ/ *n* эльф.

pizza /ˈpiːtsə/ *n* пи́цца.

placard /ˈplækɑːd/ *n* афи́ша, плака́т.

placate /pləˈkeɪt/ *vt* умиротворя́ть *impf*, умиротвори́ть *pf*.

place /pleɪs/ *n* ме́сто; **in ~ of** вме́сто+*gen*; **in the first, second, ~** во-пе́рвых, во-вторы́х; **out of ~** не на ме́сте; (*unsuitable*) неуме́стный; **take ~** случа́ться *impf*, случи́ться *pf*; (*pre-arranged event*) состоя́ться *pf*; **take the ~ of** заменя́ть *impf*, замени́ть *pf*; *vt* (*stand*) ста́вить *impf*, по~ *pf*; (*lay*) класть *impf*, положи́ть *pf*; (*an order etc.*) помеща́ть *impf*, помести́ть *pf*.

placenta /pləˈsentə/ *n* плаце́нта.

placid /ˈplæsɪd/ *adj* споко́йный.

plagiarism /ˈpleɪdʒəˌrɪz(ə)m/ *n* плагиа́т. **plagiarize** /-ˌraɪz/ *vt* заи́мствовать *impf* & *pf*.

plague /pleɪg/ *n* чума́; *vt* му́чить *impf*, за~, из~ *pf*.

plaice /pleɪs/ *n* ка́мбала.

plain /pleɪn/ *n* равни́на; *adj* (*clear*) я́сный; (*simple*) просто́й; (*ugly*) некраси́вый; **~-clothes policeman** переоде́тый полице́йский *sb*.

plaintiff /ˈpleɪntɪf/ *n* исте́ц, исти́ца.

plaintive /ˈpleɪntɪv/ *adj* жа́лобный.

plait /plæt/ *n* коса́; *vt* плести́ *impf*, с~ *pf*.

plan /plæn/ *n* план; *vt* плани́ровать *impf*, за~, с~ *pf*; (*intend*) намерева́ться *impf* +*inf*.

plane¹ /pleɪn/ *n* (*tree*) плата́н.

plane² /pleɪn/ *n* (*tool*) руба́нок; *vt* строга́ть *impf*, вы́~ *pf*.

plane³ /pleɪn/ *n* (*surface*) пло́скость; (*level*) у́ровень *m*; (*aeroplane*) самолёт.

planet /ˈplænɪt/ *n* плане́та.

plank /plæŋk/ *n* доска́.

plant /plɑːnt/ *n* расте́ние; (*factory*) заво́д; *vt* сажа́ть *impf*, посади́ть *pf*; (*fix firmly*) про́чно ста́вить *impf*, по~ *pf*; (*garden etc.*) заса́живать *impf*, засади́ть *pf* (**with** +*instr*).

plantation /plɑːnˈteɪʃ(ə)n/ *n* (*of trees*) (лесо)насажде́ние; (*of cotton etc.*) планта́ция.

plaque /plæk/ *n* дощечка.
plasma /'plæzmə/ *n* пла́зма.
plaster /'plɑ:stə(r)/ *n* пла́стырь *m*; (*for walls etc.*) штукату́рка; (*of Paris*) гипс; *vt* (*wall*) штукату́рить *impf*, от~, о~ *pf*; (*cover*) облепля́ть *impf*, облепи́ть *pf*. **plasterboard** *n* суха́я штукату́рка. **plasterer** /-rə(r)/ *n* штукату́р.
plastic /'plæstɪk/ *n* пластма́сса; *adj* (*malleable*) пласти́чный; (*made of* ~) пластма́ссовый; ~ **surgery** пласти́ческая хирурги́я.
plate /pleɪt/ *n* таре́лка; (*metal sheet*) лист; (*in book*) (вкладна́я) иллюстра́ция; (*name* ~ *etc.*) доще́чка.
plateau /'plætəʊ/ *n* плато́ *neut indecl*.
platform /'plætfɔ:m/ *n* платфо́рма; (*rly*) перро́н.
platinum /'plætɪnəm/ *n* пла́тина.
platitude /'plætɪ,tju:d/ *n* бана́льность.
platoon /plə'tu:n/ *n* взвод.
plausible /'plɔ:zɪb(ə)l/ *adj* правдоподо́бный.
play /pleɪ/ *vt* & *i* игра́ть *impf*, сыгра́ть *pf* (*game*) в+*acc*, (*instrument*) на+*prep*, (*record*) ста́вить *impf*, по~ *pf*; ~ **down** преуменьша́ть *impf*, преуме́ньшить *pf*; ~ **a joke, trick, on** подшу́чивать *impf*, подшути́ть *pf* над+*instr*; ~ **off** игра́ть *impf*, сыгра́ть *pf* реша́ющую па́ртию; ~**-off** реша́ющая встре́ча; ~ **safe** де́йствовать *impf* наверняка́; *n* игра́; (*theat*) пье́са. **player** /'pleɪə(r)/ *n* игро́к; (*actor*) актёр, актри́са; (*musician*) музыка́нт. **playful** /'pleɪfʊl/ *adj* игри́вый. **playground** *n* площа́дка для игр. **playgroup, playschool** *n* де́тский сад. **playing** /'pleɪɪŋ/ *n*: ~**-card** игра́льная ка́рта; ~**-field** игрова́я площа́дка. **playmate** *n* друг де́тства. **plaything** *n* игру́шка. **playwright** /'pleɪraɪt/ *n* драмату́рг.
plea /pli:/ *n* (*entreaty*) мольба́; (*law*) заявле́ние. **plead** /pli:d/ *vi* умоля́ть *impf* (**with** +*acc*; **for** о+*prep*); *vt* (*offer as excuse*) ссыла́ться *impf*, сосла́ться *pf* на+*acc*; ~ **(not) guilty** (не) признава́ть *impf*, призна́ть *pf* себя́ вино́вным.
pleasant /'plez(ə)nt/ *adj* прия́тный. **pleasantry** /-trɪ/ *n* любе́зность. **please** /pli:z/ *vt* нра́виться *impf*, по~ *pf* +*dat*; *imper* пожа́луйста; бу́дьте добры́. **pleased** /pli:zd/ *adj* дово́льный; *predic* рад. **pleasing, pleasurable** /'pli:zɪŋ, 'pleʒərəb(ə)l/ *adj* прия́тный. **pleasure** /'pleʒə(r)/ *n* удово́льствие.
pleat /pli:t/ *n* скла́дка; *vt* плиссирова́ть *impf*.
plebiscite /'plebɪsɪt/ *n* плебисци́т.
plectrum /'plektrəm/ *n* плектр.
pledge /pledʒ/ *n* (*security*) зало́г; (*promise*) заро́к, обеща́ние; *vt* отдава́ть *impf*, отда́ть *pf* в зало́г; ~ **o.s.** обя́зываться *impf*, обяза́ться *pf*; ~ **one's word** дава́ть *impf*, дать *pf* сло́во.
plentiful /'plentɪ,fʊl/ *adj* оби́льный. **plenty** /'plentɪ/ *n* изоби́лие; ~ **of** мно́го+*gen*.
plethora /'pleθərə/ *n* (*fig*) изоби́лие.
pleurisy /'plʊərɪsɪ/ *n* плеври́т.
pliable /'plaɪəb(ə)l/ *adj* ги́бкий.
pliers /'plaɪəz/ *n pl* плоскогу́бцы (-цев) *pl*.

plight /plaɪt/ *n* незави́дное положе́ние.

plimsolls /ˈplɪms(ə)lz/ *n pl* спорти́вные та́почки *f pl.*

plinth /plɪnθ/ *n* пли́нтус.

plod /plɒd/ *vi* тащи́ться *impf.*

plonk /plɒŋk/ *vt* плю́хнуть *pf.*

plot /plɒt/ *n* (*of land*) уча́сток; (*of book etc.*) фа́була; (*conspiracy*) за́говор; *vt* (*on graph, map, etc.*) наноси́ть *impf*, нанести́ на гра́фик, на ка́рту; *v abs* (*conspire*) составля́ть *impf*, соста́вить *pf* за́говор.

plough /plaʊ/ *n* плуг; *vt* паха́ть *impf*, вс~ *pf*; *vi*: ~ **through** пробива́ться *impf*, проби́ться *pf* сквозь+*acc*.

ploy /plɔɪ/ *n* уло́вка.

pluck /plʌk/ *n* (*courage*) сме́лость; *vt* (*chicken*) щипа́ть *impf*, об~ *pf*; (*mus*) щипа́ть *impf*; (*flower*) срыва́ть *impf*, сорва́ть *pf*; ~ **up courage** собира́ться *impf*, собра́ться *pf* с ду́хом; *vi*: ~ **at** дёргать *impf*, дёрнуть *pf*. **plucky** /ˈplʌkɪ/ *adj* сме́лый.

plug /plʌg/ *n* (*stopper*) про́бка; (*electr*) ви́лка; (*electr socket*) розе́тка; *vt* (~ *up*) затыка́ть *impf*, заткну́ть *pf*; ~ **in** включа́ть *impf*, включи́ть *pf*.

plum /plʌm/ *n* сли́ва.

plumage /ˈpluːmɪdʒ/ *n* опере́ние.

plumb /plʌm/ *n* лот; *adv* вертика́льно; (*fig*) то́чно; *vt* измеря́ть *impf*, изме́рить *pf* глубину́+*gen*; (*fig*) проника́ть *impf*, прони́кнуть *pf* в+*acc*; ~ **in** подключа́ть *impf*, подключи́ть *pf*.

plumber /ˈplʌmə(r)/ *n* водопрово́дчик. **plumbing** /-mɪŋ/ *n* водопрово́д.

plume /pluːm/ *n* (*feather*) перо́; (*on hat etc.*) султа́н.

plummet /ˈplʌmɪt/ *vi* па́дать *impf*, (у)па́сть *pf*.

plump[1] /plʌmp/ *adj* пу́хлый.

plump[2] /plʌmp/ *vi*: ~ **for** выбира́ть *impf*, вы́брать *pf*.

plunder /ˈplʌndə(r)/ *vt* гра́бить *impf*, о~ *pf*; *n* добы́ча.

plunge /plʌndʒ/ *vt* & *i* (*immerse*) погружа́ть(ся) *impf*, погрузи́ть(ся) *pf* (**into** в+*acc*); *vi* (*dive*) ныря́ть *impf*, нырну́ть *pf*; (*rush*) броса́ться *impf*, бро́ситься *pf*. **plunger** /ˈplʌndʒə(r)/ *n* плу́нжер.

pluperfect /pluːˈpɜːfɪkt/ *n* давнопроше́дшее вре́мя *neut.*

plural /ˈplʊər(ə)l/ *n* мно́жественное число́. **pluralism** /-ˌlɪz(ə)m/ *n* плюрали́зм. **pluralistic** /-ˈlɪstɪk/ *adj* плюралисти́ческий.

plus /plʌs/ *prep* плюс+*acc*; *n* (знак) плюс.

plushy /ˈplʌʃɪ/ *adj* шика́рный.

plutonium /pluːˈtəʊnɪəm/ *n* плуто́ний.

ply /plaɪ/ *vt* (*tool*) рабо́тать *impf* +*instr*; (*task*) занима́ться *impf* +*instr*; (*keep supplied*) потчева́ть *impf* (**with** +*instr*); ~ **with questions** засыпа́ть *impf*, засы́пать *pf* вопро́сами.

plywood /ˈplaɪwʊd/ *n* фане́ра.

p.m. *adv* по́сле полу́дня.

pneumatic /njuːˈmætɪk/ *adj* пневмати́ческий; ~ **drill** отбо́йный молото́к.

pneumonia /njuːˈməʊnɪə/ *n* воспале́ние лёгких.

poach[1] /pəʊtʃ/ *vt* (*cook*) вари́ть *impf*; ~**ed egg** яйцо́-пашо́т.

poach[2] /pəʊtʃ/ *vi* браконье́рствовать *impf*. **poacher** /-tʃə(r)/ *n* браконье́р.

pocket /ˈpɒkɪt/ *n* карма́н; **out of** ~ в убы́тке; ~ **money** карма́нные де́ньги (-нег, -ньга́м) *pl*; *vt* класть *impf*, положи́ть *pf*. в карма́н.

pock-marked /ˈpɒkmɑːkt/ *adj* рябо́й.

pod /pɒd/ *n* стручо́к.

podgy /ˈpɒdʒɪ/ *adj* то́лстенький.

podium /ˈpəʊdɪəm/ *n* трибу́на; (*conductor's*) пульт.

poem /ˈpəʊɪm/ *n* стихотворе́ние; (*longer* ~) поэ́ма. **poet** /ˈpəʊɪt/ *n* поэ́т. **poetess** /ˈpəʊɪtɪs/ *n* поэте́сса. **poetic(al)** /pəʊˈetɪk/ *adj* поэти́ческий. **poetry** /ˈpəʊɪtrɪ/ *n* поэ́зия, стихи́ *m pl*.

pogrom /ˈpɒgrəm/ *n* погро́м.

poignancy /ˈpɔɪnjənsɪ/ *n* острота́. **poignant** /ˈpɔɪnjənt/ *adj* о́стрый.

point[1] /pɔɪnt/ *n* то́чка; (*place*; *in list*) пункт; (*in score*) очко́; (*in time*) моме́нт; (*in space*) ме́сто; (*essence*) суть; (*sense*) смысл; (*sharp* ~) остриё; (*tip*) ко́нчик; (*power* ~) ште́псель *m*; *pl* (*rly*) стре́лка; **be on the ~ of** (*doing*) собира́ться *impf*, собра́ться *pf* +*inf*; **beside, off, the ~** некста́ти; **that is the ~** в э́том и де́ло; **the ~ is that** де́ло в том, что; **there is no ~** (*in doing*) не име́ет смы́сла (+*inf*); **to the ~** кста́ти; **~-blank** прямо́й; **~ of view** то́чка зре́ния.

point[2] /pɔɪnt/ *vt* (*wall*) расшива́ть *impf*, расши́ть *pf* швы +*gen*; (*gun etc.*) наводи́ть *impf*, навести́ *pf* (**at** на+*acc*); *vi* по-, у-, ка́зывать *impf*, по-, у-, каза́ть *pf* (**at, to** на+*acc*). **pointed** /ˈpɔɪntɪd/ *adj* (*sharp*) о́стрый. **pointer** /ˈpɔɪntə(r)/ *n* указа́тель *m*, стре́лка. **pointless** /ˈpɔɪntlɪs/ *adj* бессмы́сленный.

poise /pɔɪz/ *n* уравнове́шенность. **poised** /pɔɪzd/ *adj* (*composed*) уравнове́шенный; (*ready*) гото́вый (**to** к+*dat*).

poison /ˈpɔɪz(ə)n/ *n* яд; *vt* отравля́ть *impf*, отрави́ть *pf*. **poisonous** /ˈpɔɪzənəs/ *adj* ядови́тый.

poke /pəʊk/ *vt* (*prod*) ты́кать *impf*, ткнуть *pf*; **~ fun at** подшу́чивать *impf*, подшути́ть *pf* над+*instr*; (*thrust*) сова́ть *impf*, су́нуть *pf*; **~ the fire** меша́ть *impf*, по~ *pf* у́гли в ками́не; *n* тычо́к. **poker**[1] /ˈpəʊkə(r)/ *n* (*rod*) кочерга́.

poker[2] /ˈpəʊkə(r)/ *n* (*cards*) по́кер.

poky /ˈpəʊkɪ/ *adj* те́сный.

Poland /ˈpəʊlənd/ *n* По́льша.

polar /ˈpəʊlə(r)/ *adj* поля́рный; **~ bear** бе́лый медве́дь *m*. **polarity** /pəˈlærɪtɪ/ *n* поля́рность. **polarize** /ˈpəʊlə,raɪz/ *vt* поляризова́ть *impf* & *pf*. **pole**[1] /pəʊl/ *n* (*geog*; *phys*) по́люс; **~-star** Поля́рная звезда́.

pole[2] /pəʊl/ *n* (*rod*) столб, шест; **~-vaulting** прыжо́к с шесто́м.

Pole /pəʊl/ *n* поля́к, по́лька.

polecat /ˈpəʊlkæt/ *n* хорёк.

polemic /pəˈlemɪk/ *adj* полеми́ческий; *n* поле́мика.

police /pəˈliːs/ *n* поли́ция; (*as pl*) полице́йские *sb*; (*in Russia*) мили́ция; **~ station** полице́йский уча́сток. **policeman** *n* полице́йский *sb*, полисме́н; (*in Russia*) милиционе́р. **policewoman** *n* же́нщина-полице́йский *sb*; (*in Russia*) же́нщина-милиционе́р.

policy[1] /ˈpɒlɪsɪ/ *n* поли́тика.

policy[2] /ˈpɒlɪsɪ/ *n* (*insurance*) по́лис.

polio /ˈpəʊlɪəʊ/ *n* полиомиели́т.

Polish /ˈpəʊlɪʃ/ *adj* по́льский.

polish /ˈpɒlɪʃ/ *n* (*gloss, process*)

полиро́вка; (*substance*) политу́ра; (*fig*) лоск; *vt* полирова́ть *impf*, от~ *pf*; ~ **off** расправля́ться *impf*, распра́виться *pf* с+*instr*. **polished** /-lɪʃt/ *adj* отто́ченный.

polite /pəˈlaɪt/ *adj* ве́жливый. **politeness** /-nɪs/ *n* ве́жливость.

politic /ˈpɒlɪtɪk/ *adj* полити́чный. **political** /pəˈlɪtɪkəl/ *adj* полити́ческий; ~ **economy** политэконо́мика; ~ **prisoner** политзаключённый *sb*. **politician** /ˌpɒlɪˈtɪʃ(ə)n/ *n* поли́тик. **politics** /ˈpɒlɪtɪks/ *n* поли́тика.

poll /pəʊl/ *n* (*voting*) голосова́ние; (*opinion* ~) опро́с; **go to the** ~**s** голосова́ть *impf*, про~ *pf*; *vt* получа́ть *impf*, получи́ть *pf*.

pollen /ˈpɒlən/ *n* пыльца́. **pollinate** /ˈpɒlɪˌneɪt/ *vt* опыля́ть *impf*, опыли́ть *pf*.

polling /ˈpəʊlɪŋ/ *attrib*: ~ **booth** каби́на для голосова́ния; ~ **station** избира́тельный уча́сток.

pollutant /pəˈluːtənt/ *n* загрязни́тель *m*. **pollute** /-ˈluːt/ *vt* загрязня́ть *impf*, загрязни́ть *pf*. **pollution** /-ˈluːʃ(ə)n/ *n* загрязне́ние.

polo /ˈpəʊləʊ/ *n* по́ло *neut indecl*; ~**-neck sweater** водола́зка.

polyester /ˌpɒlɪˈestə(r)/ *n* полиэфи́р. **polyethylene** /ˌpɒlɪˈeθəliːn/ *n* полиэтиле́н. **polyglot** /ˈpɒlɪˌglɒt/ *n* полигло́т; *adj* многоязы́чный. **polygon** /ˈpɒlɪgɒn/ *n* многоуго́льник. **polymer** /ˈpɒlɪmə(r)/ *n* полиме́р. **polystyrene** /ˌpɒlɪˈstaɪəˌriːn/ *n* полистиро́л. **polytechnic** /ˌpɒlɪˈteknɪk/ *n* техни́ческий вуз. **polythene** /ˈpɒlɪθiːn/ *n* полиэтиле́н. **polyunsaturated** /ˌpɒlɪʌnˈsætʃəˌreɪtɪd/ *adj*: ~ **fats** полиненасы́щенные жиры́ *m pl*. **polyurethane** /ˌpɒlɪˈjʊərəˌθeɪn/ *n* полиурета́н.

pomp /pɒmp/ *n* пы́шность. **pomposity** /pɒmˈpɒsɪtɪ/ *n* напы́щенность. **pompous** /ˈpɒmpəs/ *adj* напы́щенный.

pond /pɒnd/ *n* пруд.

ponder /ˈpɒndə(r)/ *vt* обду́мывать *impf*, обду́мать *pf*; *vi* размышля́ть *impf*, размы́слить *pf*.

ponderous /ˈpɒndərəs/ *adj* тяжелове́сный.

pony /ˈpəʊnɪ/ *n* по́ни *m indecl*.

poodle /ˈpuːd(ə)l/ *n* пу́дель *m*.

pool[1] /puːl/ *n* (*of water*) прудо́к; (*puddle*) лу́жа; (*swimming* ~) бассе́йн.

pool[2] /puːl/ *n* (*collective stakes*) совоку́пность ста́вок; (*common fund*) о́бщий фонд; *vt* объединя́ть *impf*, объедини́ть *pf*.

poor /pʊə(r)/ *adj* бе́дный; (*bad*) плохо́й; *n*: **the** ~ бедняки́ *m pl*. **poorly** /ˈpʊəlɪ/ *predic* нездоро́в.

pop[1] /pɒp/ *vi* хло́пать *impf*, хло́пнуть *pf*; *vt* (*put*) бы́стро всу́нуть *pf* (**into** в+*acc*); ~ **in on** забега́ть *impf*, забежа́ть *pf* к+*dat*; *n* хлопо́к.

pop[2] /pɒp/ *adj* поп-; ~ **concert** поп-конце́рт; ~ **music** поп-му́зыка.

pope /pəʊp/ *n* Па́па *m*.

poplar /ˈpɒplə(r)/ *n* то́поль *m*.

poppy /ˈpɒpɪ/ *n* мак.

populace /ˈpɒpjʊləs/ *n* просто́й наро́д. **popular** /-lə(r)/ *adj* наро́дный; (*liked*) популя́рный. **popularity** /-ˈlærɪtɪ/ *n* популя́рность. **popularize** /ˈpɒpjʊləˌraɪz/ *vt* популяризи́ровать *impf* & *pf*. **populate** /ˈpɒpjʊˌleɪt/ *vt* населя́ть *impf*, насели́ть *pf*. **population** /-ˈleɪʃ(ə)n/ *n* населе́-

ние. **populous** /ˈpɒpjʊləs/ *adj* (много)лю́дный.

porcelain /ˈpɔːsəlɪn/ *n* фарфо́р.

porch /pɔːtʃ/ *n* крыльцо́.

porcupine /ˈpɔːkjʊˌpaɪn/ *n* дикобра́з.

pore[1] /pɔː(r)/ *n* по́ра.

pore[2] /pɔː(r)/ *vi*: **~ over** погружа́ться *impf*, погрузи́ться *pf* в+*acc*.

pork /pɔːk/ *n* свини́на.

pornographic /ˌpɔːnəˈgræfɪk/ *adj* порнографи́ческий. **pornography** /pɔːˈnɒgrəfɪ/ *n* порногра́фия.

porous /ˈpɔːrəs/ *adj* по́ристый.

porpoise /ˈpɔːpəs/ *n* морска́я свинья́.

porridge /ˈpɒrɪdʒ/ *n* овся́ная ка́ша.

port[1] /pɔːt/ *n* (*harbour*) порт; (*town*) порто́вый го́род.

port[2] /pɔːt/ *n* (*naut*) ле́вый борт.

port[3] /pɔːt/ *n* (*wine*) портве́йн.

portable /ˈpɔːtəb(ə)l/ *adj* портати́вный.

portend /pɔːˈtend/ *vt* предвеща́ть *impf*. **portent** /ˈpɔːt(ə)nt/ *n* предзнаменова́ние. **portentous** /-ˈtentəs/ *adj* злове́щий.

porter[1] /ˈpɔːtə(r)/ *n* (*at door*) швейца́р.

porter[2] /ˈpɔːtə(r)/ *n* (*carrier*) носи́льщик.

portfolio /pɔːtˈfəʊlɪəʊ/ *n* портфе́ль *m*; (*artist's*) па́пка.

porthole /ˈpɔːthəʊl/ *n* иллюмина́тор.

portion /ˈpɔːʃ(ə)n/ *n* часть, до́ля; (*of food*) по́рция.

portly /ˈpɔːtlɪ/ *adj* доро́дный.

portrait /ˈpɔːtrɪt/ *n* портре́т. **portray** /pɔːˈtreɪ/ *vt* изобража́ть *impf*, изобрази́ть *pf*. **portrayal** /-ˈtreɪəl/ *n* изображе́ние.

Portugal /ˈpɔːtjʊg(ə)l/ *n* Португа́лия. **Portuguese** /ˌpɔːtjʊˈgiːz/ *n* португа́лец, -лка; *adj* португа́льский.

pose /pəʊz/ *n* по́за; *vt* (*question*) ста́вить *impf*, по~ *pf*; (*a problem*) представля́ть *impf*, предста́вить *pf*; *vi* пози́ровать *impf*; **~ as** выдава́ть *impf*, вы́дать *pf* себя́ за+*acc*.

posh /pɒʃ/ *adj* шика́рный.

posit /ˈpɒzɪt/ *vt* постули́ровать *impf* & *pf*.

position /pəˈzɪʃ(ə)n/ *n* положе́ние, пози́ция; **in a ~ to** в состоя́нии +*inf*; *vt* ста́вить *impf*, по~ *pf*.

positive /ˈpɒzɪtɪv/ *adj* положи́тельный; (*convinced*) уве́ренный; (*proof*) несомне́нный; *n* (*phot*) позити́в.

possess /pəˈzes/ *vt* облада́ть *impf* +*instr*; владе́ть *impf* +*instr*; (*of feeling etc.*) овладева́ть *impf*, овладе́ть *pf* +*instr*. **possessed** /-ˈzest/ *adj* одержи́мый. **possession** /-ˈzeʃ(ə)n/ *n* владе́ние (**of** +*instr*); *pl* со́бственность. **possessive** /-ˈzesɪv/ *adj* со́бственнический. **possessor** /-ˈzesə(r)/ *n* облада́тель *m*.

possibility /ˌpɒsɪˈbɪlɪtɪ/ *n* возмо́жность. **possible** /ˈpɒsɪb(ə)l/ *adj* возмо́жный; **as much as ~** ско́лько возмо́жно; **as soon as ~** как мо́жно скоре́е. **possibly** /ˈpɒsɪblɪ/ *adv* возмо́жно, мо́жет (быть).

post[1] /pəʊst/ *n* (*pole*) столб; *vt* (*~ up*) выве́шивать *impf*, вы́весить *pf*.

post[2] /pəʊst/ *n* (*station*) пост; (*job*) до́лжность; *vt* (*station*) расставля́ть *impf*, расста́вить *pf*; (*appoint*) назнача́ть *impf*, назна́чить *pf*.

post[3] /pəʊst/ *n* (*letters, ~ office*) по́чта; **by ~** по́чтой; *attrib* почтóвый; **~-box** почтóвый я́щик; **~-code** почтóвый и́ндекс; **~ office** пóчта; *vt* (*send by* ~) отправля́ть *impf*, отпрáвить *pf* по пóчте; (*put in* ~-*box*) опускáть *impf*, опусти́ть *pf* в почтóвый я́щик. **postage** /'pəʊstɪdʒ/ *n* почтóвый сбор, почтóвые расхóды *m pl*; **~ stamp** почтóвая мáрка. **postal** /'pəʊst(ə)l/ *adj* почтóвый; **~-order** почтóвый перевóд. **postcard** *n* откры́тка.

poster /'pəʊstə(r)/ *n* афи́ша, плакáт.

poste restante /ˌpəʊst re'stɑ̃t/ *n* до востребования.

posterior /pɒ'stɪərɪə(r)/ *adj* зáдний; *n* зад.

posterity /pɒ'sterɪtɪ/ *n* потóмство.

post-graduate /pəʊst'grædjʊət/ *n* аспирáнт.

posthumous /'pɒstjʊməs/ *adj* посмéртный.

postman /'pəʊstmən/ *n* почтальóн. **postmark** *n* почтóвый штéмпель *m*.

post-mortem /pəʊst'mɔːtəm/ *n* вскры́тие трýпа.

postpone /pəʊst'pəʊn/ *vt* отсрóчивать *impf*, отсрóчить *pf*. **postponement** /-mənt/ *n* отсрóчка.

postscript /'pəʊstskrɪpt/ *n* постскри́птум.

postulate /'pɒstjʊˌleɪt/ *vt* постули́ровать *impf* & *pf*.

posture /'pɒstʃə(r)/ *n* пóза, положéние.

post-war /pəʊst'wɔː(r)/ *adj* послевоéнный.

posy /'pəʊzɪ/ *n* букéтик.

pot /pɒt/ *n* горшóк; (*cooking* ~) кастрю́ля; **~-shot** вы́стрел наугáд; *vt* (*food*) консерви́ровать *impf*, за~ *pf*; (*plant*) сажáть *impf*, посади́ть *pf* в горшóк; (*billiards*) загоня́ть *impf*, загнáть *pf* в лýзу.

potash /'pɒtæʃ/ *n* potáш.

potassium /pə'tæsɪəm/ *n* кáлий.

potato /pə'teɪtəʊ/ *n* (*also collect*) картóшка (*no pl*); (*plant*; *also collect*) картóфель *m* (*no pl*).

potency /'pəʊt(ə)nsɪ/ *n* си́ла. **potent** /'pəʊt(ə)nt/ *adj* си́льный.

potential /pə'tenʃ(ə)l/ *adj* потенциáльный; *n* потенциáл. **potentiality** /pəˌtenʃɪ'ælɪtɪ/ *n* потенциáльность.

pot-hole /'pɒthəʊl/ *n* (*in road*) вы́боина.

potion /'pəʊʃ(ə)n/ *n* зéлье.

potter[1] /'pɒtə(r)/ *vi*: **~ about** вози́ться *impf*.

potter[2] /'pɒtə(r)/ *n* гончáр. **pottery** /'pɒtərɪ/ *n* (*goods*) гончáрные издéлия *neut pl*; (*place*) гончáрная *sb*.

potty[1] /'pɒtɪ/ *adj* (*crazy*) помéшанный (**about** на+*prep*).

potty[2] /'pɒtɪ/ *n* ночнóй горшóк.

pouch /paʊtʃ/ *n* сýмка.

poultry /'pəʊltrɪ/ *n* домáшняя пти́ца.

pounce /paʊns/ *vi*: **~ (up)on** набрáсываться *impf*, наброси́ться *pf* на+*acc*.

pound[1] /paʊnd/ *n* (*measure*) фунт; **~ sterling** фунт стéрлингов.

pound[2] /paʊnd/ *vt* (*strike*) колоти́ть *impf*, по~ *pf* по+*dat*, в+*acc*; *vi* (*heart*) колоти́ться *impf*; **~ along** (*run*) мчáться *impf* с грóхотом.

pour /pɔː(r)/ *vt* лить *impf*; **~ out** наливáть *impf*, нали́ть *pf*; *vi* ли́ться *impf*; **it is ~ing (with rain)** дождь льёт как из ведрá.

pout /paʊt/ *vi* дýть(ся) *impf*, на~ *pf*.

poverty /'pɒvətɪ/ *n* бéдность;

~-stricken убо́гий.

POW *abbr* военнопле́нный *sb.*

powder /ˈpaʊdə(r)/ *n* порошо́к; (*cosmetic*) пу́дра; *vt* пу́дрить *impf*, на~ *pf*. **powdery** /-rɪ/ *adj* порошкообра́зный.

power /ˈpaʊə(r)/ *n* (*vigour*) си́ла; (*might*) могу́щество; (*ability*) спосо́бность; (*control*) власть; (*authorization*) полномо́чие; (*State*) держа́ва; ~ **cut** переры́в электропита́ния; ~ **point** розе́тка; ~ **station** электроста́нция. **powerful** /-fʊl/ *adj* си́льный. **powerless** /-lɪs/ *adj* бесси́льный.

practicable /ˈpræktɪkəb(ə)l/ *adj* осуществи́мый. **practical** /-tɪk(ə)l/ *adj* (*help, activities*) практи́ческий; (*person, object*) практи́чный. **practically** /-klɪ/ *adv* практи́чески. **practice** /ˈpræktɪs/ *n* пра́ктика; (*custom*) обы́чай; (*mus*) заня́тия *neut pl*; **in** ~ на пра́ктике; **put into** ~ осуществля́ть *impf*, осуществи́ть *pf*. **practise** /ˈpræktɪs/ *vt* (*also abs of doctor etc.*) практикова́ть *impf*; упражня́ться *impf* в+*prep*; (*mus*) занима́ться *impf*, заня́ться *pf* на+*prep*. **practised** /ˈpræktɪst/ *adj* о́пытный. **practitioner** /prækˈtɪʃənə(r)/ *n* (*doctor*) практику́ющий врач; **general** ~ врач о́бщей пра́ктики.

pragmatic /prægˈmætɪk/ *adj* прагмати́ческий. **pragmatism** /ˈprægməˌtɪz(ə)m/ *n* прагмати́зм. **pragmatist** /ˈprægmətɪst/ *n* прагма́тик.

prairie /ˈpreərɪ/ *n* пре́рия.

praise /preɪz/ *vt* хвали́ть *impf*, по~ *pf*; *n* похвала́. **praiseworthy** /ˈpreɪzˌwɜːðɪ/ *adj* похва́льный.

pram /præm/ *n* де́тская коля́ска.

prance /prɑːns/ *vi* гарцева́ть *impf*.

prank /præŋk/ *n* вы́ходка.

prattle /ˈpræt(ə)l/ *vi* лепета́ть; *n* ле́пет.

prawn /prɔːn/ *n* креве́тка.

pray /preɪ/ *vi* моли́ться *impf*, по~ *pf* (**to** +*dat*; **for** о+*prep*). **prayer** /ˈpreə(r)/ *n* моли́тва.

preach /priːtʃ/ *vt* & *i* пропове́дывать *impf*. **preacher** /ˈpriːtʃə(r)/ *n* пропове́дник.

preamble /priːˈæmb(ə)l/ *n* преа́мбула.

pre-arrange /ˌpriːəˈreɪndʒ/ *vt* зара́нее организо́вывать *impf*, организова́ть *pf*.

precarious /prɪˈkeərɪəs/ *adj* опа́сный.

precaution /prɪˈkɔːʃ(ə)n/ *n* предосторо́жность. **precautionary** /-ʃənərɪ/ *adj*: ~ **measures** ме́ры предосторо́жности.

precede /prɪˈsiːd/ *vt* предше́ствовать *impf* +*dat*. **precedence** /ˈpresɪd(ə)ns/ *n* предпочте́ние. **precedent** /ˈpresɪd(ə)nt/ *n* прецеде́нт. **preceding** /prɪˈsiːdɪŋ/ *adj* преды-ду́щий.

precept /ˈpriːsept/ *n* наставле́ние.

precinct /ˈpriːsɪŋkt/ *n* двор; *pl* окре́стности *f pl*. **pedestrian** ~ уча́сток для пешехо́дов; **shopping** ~ торго́вый пасса́ж.

precious /ˈpreʃəs/ *adj* драгоце́нный; (*style*) мане́рный; *adv* о́чень.

precipice /ˈpresɪpɪs/ *n* обры́в. **precipitate** *adj* /prɪˈsɪpɪtət/ (*person*) опроме́тчивый; *vt* /prɪˈsɪpɪˌteɪt/ (*throw down*) низверга́ть *impf*, низве́ргнуть *pf*; (*hurry*) ускоря́ть *impf*, уско́рить *pf*. **precipitation** /prɪˌsɪpɪˈteɪʃ(ə)n/ *n* (*meteorol*) оса́дки *m pl.* **precipitous** /prɪ'sɪpɪtəs/ *adj* обры́вистый.

précis /'preɪsiː/ *n* конспе́кт.

precise /prɪ'saɪs/ *adj* то́чный. **precisely** /-'saɪslɪ/ *adv* то́чно; (*in answer*) и́менно. **precision** /-'sɪʃ(ə)n/ *n* то́чность.

preclude /prɪ'kluːd/ *vt* предотвраща́ть *impf*, предотврати́ть *pf.*

precocious /prɪ'kəʊʃəs/ *adj* ра́но разви́вшийся.

preconceived /,priːkən'siːvd/ *adj* предвзя́тый. **preconception** /,priːkən'sepʃ(ə)n/ *n* предвзя́тое мне́ние.

pre-condition /,priːkən'dɪʃ(ə)n/ *n* предпосы́лка.

precursor /priː'kɜːsə(r)/ *n* предше́ственник.

predator /'predətə(r)/ *n* хи́щник. **predatory** /-tərɪ/ *adj* хи́щный.

predecessor /'priːdɪ,sesə(r)/ *n* предше́ственник.

predestination /priː,destɪ'neɪʃ(ə)n/ *n* предопределе́ние.

predetermine /,priːdɪ'tɜːmɪn/ *vt* предреша́ть *impf*, предреши́ть *pf.*

predicament /prɪ'dɪkəmənt/ *n* затрудни́тельное положе́ние.

predicate /'predɪkət/ *n* (*gram*) сказу́емое *sb.* **predicative** /prɪ'dɪkətɪv/ *adj* предикати́вный.

predict /prɪ'dɪkt/ *vt* предска́зывать *impf*, предсказа́ть *pf.* **predictable** /-'dɪktəb(ə)l/ *adj* предсказу́емый. **prediction** /-'dɪkʃ(ə)n/ *n* предсказа́ние.

predilection /,priːdɪ'lekʃ(ə)n/ *n* пристра́стие (**for** к+*dat*).

predispose /,priːdɪ'spəʊz/ *vt* предраспола́гать *impf*, предрасположи́ть *pf* (**to** к+*dat*). **predisposition** /,priːdɪspə'zɪʃ(ə)n/ *n* предрасположе́ние (**to** к+*dat*).

predominance /prɪ'dɒmɪnəns/ *n* преоблада́ние. **predominant** /-nənt/ *adj* преоблада́ющий. **predominate** /-,neɪt/ *vi* преоблада́ть *impf.*

pre-eminence /priː'emɪnəns/ *n* превосхо́дство. **pre-eminent** /-nənt/ *adj* выдаю́щийся.

pre-empt /priː'empt/ *vt* (*fig*) завладева́ть *impf*, завладе́ть *pf* +*instr* пре́жде други́х. **pre-emptive** /-tɪv/ *adj* (*mil*) упрежда́ющий.

preen /priːn/ *vt* (*of bird*) чи́стить *impf*, по~ *pf* клю́вом; ~ **o.s.** (*be proud*) горди́ться *impf* собо́й.

pre-fab /'priːfæb/ *n* сбо́рный дом. **pre-fabricated** /priː'fæbrɪ,keɪtɪd/ *adj* сбо́рный.

preface /'prefəs/ *n* предисло́вие.

prefect /'priːfekt/ *n* префе́кт; (*school*) ста́роста *m.*

prefer /prɪ'fɜː(r)/ *vt* предпочита́ть *impf*, предпоче́сть *pf.* **preferable** /'prefərəb(ə)l/ *adj* предпочти́тельный. **preference** /'prefərəns/ *n* предпочте́ние. **preferential** /,prefə'renʃ(ə)l/ *adj* предпочти́тельный.

prefix /'priːfɪks/ *n* приста́вка.

pregnancy /'pregnənsɪ/ *n* бере́менность. **pregnant** /'pregnənt/ *adj* бере́менная.

prehistoric /,priːhɪ'stɒrɪk/ *adj* доистори́ческий.

prejudice /'predʒʊdɪs/ *n* предубежде́ние; (*detriment*) уще́рб; *vt* наноси́ть *impf*, нанести́ *pf* уще́рб+*dat*; ~ **against** предубежда́ть *impf*, предубеди́ть *pf* про́тив+*gen*; **be** ~**d against** име́ть *impf* предубежде́ние про́тив +*gen.*

preliminary /prɪ'lɪmɪnərɪ/ *adj*

предвари́тельный.
prelude /'prelju:d/ *n* прелю́дия.
premarital /pri:'mærɪt(ə)l/ *adj* добра́чный.
premature /,premə'tjʊə(r)/ *adj* преждевре́менный.
premeditated /pri:'medɪ,teɪtɪd/ *adj* преднаме́ренный.
premier /'premɪə(r)/ *adj* пе́рвый; *n* премье́р-мини́стр. **première** /'premɪ,eə(r)/ *n* премье́ра.
premise, premiss /'premɪs/ *n* (*logic*) (пред)посы́лка. **premises** /'premɪsɪz/ *n pl* помеще́ние.
premium /'pri:mɪəm/ *n* пре́мия.
premonition /,premə'nɪʃ(ə)n/ *n* предчу́вствие.
preoccupation /pri:,ɒkjʊ'peɪʃ(ə)n/ *n* озабо́ченность; (*absorbing subject*) забо́та. **preoccupied** /-'ɒkjʊ,paɪd/ *adj* озабо́ченный. **preoccupy** /-'ɒkjʊ,paɪ/ *vt* поглоща́ть *impf*, поглоти́ть *pf*.
preparation /,prepə'reɪʃ(ə)n/ *n* приготовле́ние; *pl* подгото́вка (**for** к+*dat*); (*substance*) препара́т. **preparatory** /prɪ'pærətərɪ/ *adj* подготови́тельный. **prepare** /prɪ'peə(r)/ *vt* & *i* при-, под-, гота́вливать(ся) *impf*, при-, под-, гото́вить(ся) *pf* (**for** к+*dat*). **prepared** /prɪ'peəd/ *adj* гото́вый.
preponderance /prɪ'pɒndərəns/ *n* переве́с.
preposition /,prepə'zɪʃ(ə)n/ *n* предло́г.
prepossessing /,pri:pə'zesɪŋ/ *adj* привлека́тельный.
preposterous /prɪ'pɒstərəs/ *adj* неле́пый.
prerequisite /pri:'rekwɪzɪt/ *n* предпосы́лка.
prerogative /prɪ'rɒgətɪv/ *n* прерогати́ва.
presage /'presɪdʒ/ *vt* предвеща́ть *impf*.
Presbyterian /,prezbɪ'tɪərɪən/ *n* пресвитериа́нин, -а́нка; *adj* пресвитериа́нский.
prescribe /prɪ'skraɪb/ *vt* предпи́сывать *impf*, предписа́ть *pf*; (*med*) пропи́сывать *impf*, прописа́ть *pf*. **prescription** /prɪ'skrɪpʃ(ə)n/ *n* (*med*) реце́пт.
presence /'prez(ə)ns/ *n* прису́тствие; **~ of mind** прису́тствие ду́ха. **present** /'prez(ə)nt/ *adj* прису́тствующий; (*being dealt with*) да́нный; (*existing now*) ны́нешний; (*also gram*) настоя́щий; *predic* налицо́; **be ~** прису́тствовать *impf* (**at** на+*prep*); **~-day** ны́нешний; *n*: **the ~** настоя́щее *sb*; (*gram*) настоя́щее вре́мя *neut*; (*gift*) пода́рок; **at ~** в настоя́щее вре́мя *neut*; **for the ~** пока́; *vt* (*introduce*) представля́ть *impf*, предста́вить *pf* (**to** +*dat*); (*award*) вруча́ть *impf*, вручи́ть *pf*; (*a play*) ста́вить *impf*, по~ *pf*; (*a gift*) преподноси́ть *impf*, преподнести́ *pf* +*dat* (**with** +*acc*); **~ o.s.** явля́ться *impf*, яви́ться *pf*. **presentable** /prɪ'zentəb(ə)l/ *adj* прили́чный. **presentation** /,prezən'teɪʃ(ə)n/ *n* (*introducing*) представле́ние; (*awarding*) подноше́ние.
presentiment /prɪ'zentɪmənt/ *n* предчу́вствие.
presently /'prezəntlɪ/ *adv* вско́ре.
preservation /,prezə'veɪʃ(ə)n/ *n* сохране́ние. **preservative** /prɪ'zɜ:vətɪv/ *n* консерва́нт. **preserve** /prɪ'zɜ:v/ *vt* (*keep safe*) сохраня́ть *impf*, сохрани́ть *pf*; (*maintain*) храни́ть *impf*; (*food*) консерви́ровать *impf*, за~ *pf*; *n* (*for game etc*) запове́дник; (*jam*) варе́нье.

preside /prɪ'zaɪd/ *vi* председа́тельствовать *impf* (**at** на+*prep*). **presidency** /'prezɪdənsɪ/ *n* президе́нтство. **president** /'prezɪd(ə)nt/ *n* президе́нт. **presidential** /,prezɪ'denʃ(ə)l/ *adj* президе́нтский. **presidium** /prɪ'sɪdɪəm/ *n* прези́диум.

press /pres/ *n* (*machine*) пресс; (*printing firm*) типогра́фия; (*publishing house*) изда́тельство; (*the* ~) пре́сса, печа́ть; ~ **conference** пресс-конфере́нция; *vt* (*button etc*) нажима́ть *impf*, нажа́ть *pf*; (*clasp*) прижима́ть *impf*, прижа́ть *pf* (**to** к+*dat*); (*iron*) гла́дить *impf*, вы́~ *pf*; (*insist on*) наста́ивать *impf*, настоя́ть *pf* на+*prep*; (*urge*) угова́ривать *impf*; ~ **on** (*make haste*) торопа́пливаться *impf*.

pressing /'presɪŋ/ *adj* неотло́жный. **pressure** /'preʃə(r)/ *n* давле́ние; ~**-cooker** скорова́рка; ~ **group** инициати́вная гру́ппа. **pressurize** /'preʃə,raɪz/ *vt* (*fig*) ока́зывать *impf*, оказа́ть *pf* давле́ние на+*acc*. **pressurized** /'preʃə,raɪzd/ *adj* гермети́ческий.

prestige /pre'sti:ʒ/ *n* прести́ж. **prestigious** /pre'stɪdʒəs/ *adj* прести́жный.

presumably /prɪ'zju:məblɪ/ *adv* предположи́тельно. **presume** /-'zju:m/ *vt* полага́ть *impf*; (*venture*) позволя́ть *impf*, позво́лить *pf* себе́. **presumption** /-'zʌmpʃ(ə)n/ *n* предположе́ние; (*arrogance*) самонаде́янность. **presumptuous** /-'zʌmptjʊəs/ *adj* самонаде́янный.

presuppose /,pri:sə'pəʊz/ *vt* предполага́ть *impf*.

pretence /prɪ'tens/ *n* притво́рство. **pretend** /-'tend/ *vt* притворя́ться *impf*, притвори́ться *pf* (**to be** +*instr*); де́лать *impf*, с~ *pf* вид (что); *vi*: ~ **to** претендова́ть *impf* на+*acc*. **pretender** /-'tendə(r)/ *n* претенде́нт. **pretension** /-'tenʃ(ə)n/ *n* прете́нзия. **pretentious** /-'tenʃəs/ *adj* претенцио́зный.

pretext /'pri:tekst/ *n* предло́г.

prettiness /'prɪtɪnɪs/ *n* милови́дность. **pretty** /'prɪtɪ/ *adj* хоро́шенький; *adv* дово́льно.

prevail /prɪ'veɪl/ *vi* (*predominate*) преоблада́ть *impf*; ~ **(up)on** угова́ривать *impf*, уговори́ть *pf*. **prevalence** /'prevələns/ *n* распростране́ние. **prevalent** /'prevələnt/ *adj* распространённый.

prevaricate /prɪ'værɪ,keɪt/ *vi* увили́вать *impf* увильну́ть *pf*.

prevent /prɪ'vent/ *vt* (*stop from happening*) предупрежда́ть *impf*, предупреди́ть *pf*; (*stop from doing*) меша́ть *impf*, по~ *pf* +*dat*. **prevention** /-'venʃ(ə)n/ *n* предупрежде́ние. **preventive** /-'ventɪv/ *adj* предупреди́тельный.

preview /'pri:vju:/ *n* предвари́тельный просмо́тр.

previous /'pri:vɪəs/ *adj* преды́дущий; *adv*: ~ **to** до+*gen*; пре́жде чем +*inf*. **previously** /-lɪ/ *adv* ра́ньше.

pre-war /pri:'wɔ:(r)/ *adj* довое́нный.

prey /preɪ/ *n* (*animal*) добы́ча; (*victim*) же́ртва (**to** +*gen*); **bird of** ~ хи́щная пти́ца; *vi*: ~ **(up)on** (*emotion etc.*) му́чить *impf*.

price /praɪs/ *n* цена́; ~**-list** прейскура́нт; *vt* назнача́ть *impf*, назна́чить *pf* це́ну +*gen*. **priceless** /-lɪs/ *adj* бесце́нный.

prick /prɪk/ *vt* колóть *impf*, у~ *pf*; (*conscience*) мýчить *impf*; ~ **up one's ears** навострúть *pf* ýши; *n* укóл. **prickle** /'prɪk(ə)l/ *n* (*thorn*) колю́чка; (*spine*) иглá. **prickly** /-klɪ/ *adj* колю́чий.

pride /praɪd/ *n* гóрдость; ~ **o.s. on** гордúться *impf* +*instr*.

priest /pri:st/ *n* свящéнник; (*non-Christian*) жрец.

prig /prɪg/ *n* педáнт.

prim /prɪm/ *adj* чóпорный.

primarily /'praɪmərɪlɪ/ *adv* первоначáльно; (*above all*) прéжде всегó. **primary** /'praɪmərɪ/ *adj* основнóй; ~ **school** начáльная шкóла. **prime** /praɪm/ *n*: **in one's** ~ в расцвéте сил; *adj* (*chief*) глáвный; ~ **minister** премьéр-минúстр; *vt* (*engine*) заправля́ть *impf*, запрáвить *pf*; (*bomb*) активизúровать *impf* & *pf*; (*with facts*) инструктúровать *impf* & *pf*; (*with paint etc.*) грунтовáть *impf*, за~ *pf*. **primer** /'praɪmə(r)/ *n* (*paint etc.*) грунт. **prim(a)eval** /praɪ'mi:v(ə)l/ *adj* первобы́тный. **primitive** /'prɪmɪtɪv/ *adj* первобы́тный; (*crude*) примитúвный. **primordial** /praɪ'mɔ:dɪəl/ *adj* искóнный.

primrose /'prɪmrəʊz/ *n* первоцвéт; (*colour*) блéдно-жёлтый цвет.

prince /prɪns/ *n* принц; (*in Russia*) князь. **princely** /'prɪnslɪ/ *adj* кня́жеский; (*sum*) огрóмный. **princess** /'prɪnses/ *n* принцéсса; (*wife*) княгúня; (*daughter*) княжнá.

principal /'prɪnsɪp(ə)l/ *n* глáвный; *n* дирéктор. **principality** /,prɪnsɪ'pælɪtɪ/ *n* кня́жество. **principally** /'prɪnsɪpəlɪ/ *adv* глáвным óбразом.

principle /'prɪnsɪp(ə)l/ *n* прúнцип; **in** ~ в прúнципе; **on** ~ принципиáльно. **principled** /-p(ə)ld/ *adj* принципиáльный.

print /prɪnt/ *n* (*mark*) след; (*also phot*) отпечáток; (*printing*) печáть; (*picture*) óттиск; **in** ~ в продáже; **out of** ~ распрóданный; *vt* (*impress*) запечатлевáть *impf*, запечатлéть *pf*; (*book etc.*) печáтать *impf*, на~ *pf*; (*write*) писáть *impf*, на~ *pf* печáтными бýквами; (*phot*; ~ *out*, *off*) отпечáтывать *impf*, отпечáтать *pf*; ~ **out** (*of computer etc.*) распечáтывать *impf*, распечáтать *pf*; **~-out** распечáтка. **printer** /-tə(r)/ *n* (*person*) печáтник, типóгаф; (*of computer*) прúнтер. **printing** /-tɪŋ/ *n* печáтание; **~-press** печáтный станóк.

prior /'praɪə(r)/ *adj* прéжний; *adv*: ~ **to** до+*gen*. **priority** /praɪ'ɒrɪtɪ/ *n* приоритéт. **priory** /'praɪərɪ/ *n* монасты́рь *m*.

prise /praɪz/ *vt*: ~ **open** взлáмывать *impf*, взломáть *pf*.

prism /'prɪz(ə)m/ *n* прúзма.

prison /'prɪz(ə)n/ *n* тюрьмá; *attrib* тюрéмный; ~ **camp** лáгерь *m*. **prisoner** /-nə(r)/ *n* заключённый *sb*; (~ *of war*) (военно)плéнный *sb*.

pristine /'prɪsti:n/ *adj* нетрóнутый.

privacy /'prɪvəsɪ/ *n* уединéние; (*private life*) чáстная жизнь. **private** /'praɪvət/ *adj* (*personal*) чáстный, лúчный; (*confidential*) конфиденциáльный; **in** ~ наединé; в чáстной жúзни; *n* рядовóй *sb*.

privation /praɪ'veɪʃ(ə)n/ *n* лишéние.

privilege /'prɪvɪlɪdʒ/ *n* привилéгия. **privileged** /-lɪdʒd/ *adj* привелигирóванный.

privy /ˈprɪvɪ/ *adj*: ~ **to** посвящённый в+*acc*.
prize /praɪz/ *n* пре́мия, приз; **~-winner** призёр; *vt* высоко́ цени́ть *impf*.
pro[1] /prəʊ/ *n*: **~s and cons** до́воды *m pl* за и про́тив.
pro[2] /prəʊ/ *n* (*professional*) профессиона́л.
probability /ˌprɒbəˈbɪlɪtɪ/ *n* вероя́тность. **probable** /ˈprɒbəb(ə)l/ *adj* вероя́тный. **probably** /-blɪ/ *adv* вероя́тно.
probate /ˈprəʊbeɪt/ *n* утвержде́ние завеща́ния.
probation /prəˈbeɪʃ(ə)n/ *n* испыта́тельный срок; (*law*) усло́вный пригово́р; **got two years ~** получи́л два го́да усло́вно. **probationary** /-nərɪ/ *adj* испыта́тельный.
probe /prəʊb/ *n* (*med*) зонд; (*fig*) рассле́дование; *vt* зонди́ровать *impf*; (*fig*) рассле́довать *impf* & *pf*.
probity /ˈprəʊbɪtɪ/ *n* че́стность.
problem /ˈprɒbləm/ *n* пробле́ма, вопро́с; (*math*) зада́ча. **problematic** /-ˈmætɪk/ *adj* проблемати́чный.
procedural /prəˈsiːdjərəl/ *adj* процеду́рный. **procedure** /-ˈsiːdjə(r)/ *n* процеду́ра. **proceed** /-ˈsiːd/ *vi* (*go further*) идти́ *impf*, пойти́ *pf* да́льше; (*act*) поступа́ть *impf*, поступи́ть *pf*; (*abs*, ~ *to say*; *continue*) продолжа́ть *impf*, продо́лжить *pf*; (*of action*) продолжа́ться *impf*, продо́лжиться *pf*; **~ from** исходи́ть *impf*. из, от+*gen*; **~ to** (*begin to*) принима́ться *impf*, приня́ться *pf* +*inf*. **proceedings** /-ˈsiːdɪŋz/ *n pl* (*activity*) де́ятельность; (*legal* ~) судопроизво́дство; (*published report*) труды́ *m pl*, запи́ски *f pl*.
proceeds /ˈprəʊsiːdz/ *n pl* вы́ручка. **process** /ˈprəʊses/ *n* проце́сс; *vt* обраба́тывать *impf*, обрабо́тать *pf*. **procession** /prəˈseʃ(ə)n/ *n* проце́ссия, ше́ствие.
proclaim /prəˈkleɪm/ *vt* провозглаша́ть *impf*, провозгласи́ть *pf*. **proclamation** /ˌprɒkləˈmeɪʃ(ə)n/ *n* провозглаше́ние.
procure /prəˈkjʊə(r)/ *vt* достава́ть *impf*, доста́ть *pf*.
prod /prɒd/ *vt* ты́кать *impf*, ткнуть *pf*; *n* тычо́к.
prodigal /ˈprɒdɪg(ə)l/ *adj* расточи́тельный.
prodigious /prəˈdɪdʒəs/ *adj* огро́мный. **prodigy** /ˈprɒdɪdʒɪ/ *n*: **child ~** вундерки́нд.
produce *vt* /prəˈdjuːs/ (*evidence etc.*) представля́ть *impf*, предста́вить *pf*; (*ticket etc.*) предъявля́ть *impf*, предъяви́ть *pf*; (*play etc.*) ста́вить *impf*, по~ *pf*; (*manufacture*; *cause*) производи́ть *impf*, произвести́ *pf*; *n* /ˈprɒdjuːs/ (*collect*) проду́кты *m pl*. **producer** /prəˈdjuːsə(r)/ *n* (*econ*) производи́тель *m*; (*of play etc.*) режиссёр. **product** /ˈprɒdʌkt/ *n* проду́кт; (*result*) результа́т. **production** /prəˈdʌkʃ(ə)n/ *n* произво́дство; (*of play etc.*) постано́вка. **productive** /prəˈdʌktɪv/ *adj* продукти́вный; (*fruitful*) плодотво́рный. **productivity** /ˌprɒdʌkˈtɪvɪtɪ/ *n* производи́тельность.
profane /prəˈfeɪn/ *adj* све́тский; (*blasphemous*) богоху́льный. **profanity** /-ˈfænɪtɪ/ *n* богоху́льство.
profess /prəˈfes/ *vt* (*pretend*) притворя́ться *impf*, притвори́ться *pf* (**to be** +*instr*); (*declare*) заявля́ть *impf*, заяви́ть *pf*; (*faith*) испове́довать *impf*.

profession /-'feʃ(ə)n/ *n* (*job*) профе́ссия. **professional** /-'feʃən(ə)l/ *adj* профессиона́льный; *n* профессиона́л. **professor** /-'fesə(r)/ *n* профе́ссор.

proffer /'prɒfə(r)/ *vt* предлага́ть *impf*, предложи́ть *pf*.

proficiency /prə'fɪʃ(ə)nsɪ/ *n* уме́ние. **proficient** /-ʃ(ə)nt/ *adj* уме́лый.

profile /'prəʊfaɪl/ *n* про́филь *m*.

profit /'prɒfɪt/ *n* (*benefit*) по́льза; (*monetary*) при́быль; *vt* приноси́ть *impf*, принести́ *pf* по́льзу +*dat*; *vi*: ~ **from** по́льзоваться *impf*, вос~ *pf* +*instr*; (*financially*) получа́ть *impf*, получи́ть *pf* при́быль на +*prep*. **profitable** /'prɒfɪtəb(ə)l/ *adj* (*lucrative*) при́быльный; (*beneficial*) поле́зный. **profiteering** /-'tɪərɪŋ/ *n* спекуля́ция.

profligate /'prɒflɪgət/ *adj* распу́тный.

profound /prə'faʊnd/ *adj* глубо́кий.

profuse /prə'fju:s/ *adj* оби́льный. **profusion** /-'fju:ʒ(ə)n/ *n* изоби́лие.

progeny /'prɒdʒɪnɪ/ *n* пото́мство.

prognosis /prɒg'nəʊsɪs/ *n* прогно́з.

program(m)e /'prəʊgræm/ *n* програ́мма; *vt* программи́ровать *impf*, за~ *pf*. **programmer** /-mə(r)/ *n* программи́ст.

progress *n* /'prəʊgres/ прогре́сс; (*success*) успе́хи *m pl*; **make** ~ де́лать *impf*, с~ *pf* успе́хи; *vi* /prə'gres/ продвига́ться *impf*, продви́нуться *pf* вперёд. **progression** /prə'greʃ(ə)n/ *n* продвиже́ние. **progressive** /prə'gresɪv/ *adj* прогресси́вный.

prohibit /prə'hɪbɪt/ *vt* запреща́ть *impf*, запрети́ть *pf*. **prohibition** /ˌprəʊhɪ'bɪʃ(ə)n/ *n* запреще́ние; (*on alcohol*) сухо́й зако́н. **prohibitive** /prəʊ'hɪbɪtɪv/ *adj* запрети́тельный; (*price*) недосту́пный.

project *vt* /prə'dʒekt/ (*plan*) проекти́ровать *impf*, с~ *pf*; (*a film*) демонстри́ровать *impf*, про~ *pf*; *vi* (*jut out*) выступа́ть *impf*; *n* /'prɒdʒekt/ прое́кт. **projectile** /prə'dʒektaɪl/ *n* снаря́д. **projection** /prə'dʒekʃ(ə)n/ *n* (*cin*) прое́кция; (*protrusion*) вы́ступ; (*forecast*) прогно́з. **projector** /prə'dʒektə(r)/ *n* прое́ктор.

proletarian /ˌprəʊlɪ'teərɪən/ *adj* пролета́рский. **proletariat** /-rɪət/ *n* пролетариа́т.

proliferate /prə'lɪfəˌreɪt/ *vi* распространя́ться *impf*, распространи́ться *pf*. **proliferation** /-'reɪʃ(ə)n/ *n* распростране́ние.

prolific /prə'lɪfɪk/ *adj* плодови́тый.

prologue /'prəʊlɒg/ *n* проло́г.

prolong /prə'lɒŋ/ *vt* продлева́ть *impf*, продли́ть *pf*.

promenade /ˌprɒmə'nɑ:d/ *n* ме́сто для гуля́нья; (*at seaside*) на́бережная *sb*; *vi* прогу́ливаться *impf*, прогуля́ться *pf*.

prominence /'prɒmɪnəns/ *n* изве́стность. **prominent** /'prɒmɪnənt/ *adj* выступа́ющий; (*distinguished*) выдаю́щийся.

promiscuity /ˌprɒmɪ'skju:ɪtɪ/ *n* лёгкое поведе́ние. **promiscuous** /prə'mɪskjʊəs/ *adj* лёгкого поведе́ния.

promise /'prɒmɪs/ *n* обеща́ние; *vt* обеща́ть *impf* & *pf*. **promising** /-sɪŋ/ *adj* многообеща́ющий.

promontory /'prɒməntərɪ/ *n* мыс.

promote /prə'məʊt/ *vt* (*in rank*) продвига́ть *impf*, продви́нуть *pf*; (*assist*) спосо́бствовать *impf* & *pf* +*dat*; (*publicize*) реклами́ровать *impf*. **promoter** /-'məʊtə(r)/ *n* (*of event etc.*) аге́нт. **promotion** /-'məʊʃ(ə)n/ *n* (*in rank*) продвиже́ние; (*comm*) рекла́ма.

prompt /prɒmpt/ *adj* бы́стрый, неме́дленный; *adv* ро́вно; *vt* (*incite*) побужда́ть *impf*, побуди́ть *pf* (**to** к+*dat*; +*inf*); (*speaker*; *also fig*) подска́зывать *impf*, подсказа́ть *pf* +*dat*; (*theat*) суфли́ровать *impf* +*dat*; *n* подска́зка. **prompter** /-tə(r)/ *n* суфлёр.

prone /prəʊn/ *adj* (лежа́щий) ничко́м; *predic*: ~ **to** скло́нен (-онна́, -о́нно) к+*dat*.

prong /prɒŋ/ *n* зубе́ц.

pronoun /'prəʊnaʊn/ *n* местоиме́ние.

pronounce /prə'naʊns/ *vt* (*declare*) объявля́ть *impf*, объяви́ть *pf*; (*articulate*) произноси́ть *impf*, произнести́ *pf*. **pronounced** /-'naʊnst/ *adj* я́вный; заме́тный. **pronouncement** /-'naʊnsmənt/ *n* заявле́ние. **pronunciation** /prəˌnʌnsɪ'eɪʃ(ə)n/ *n* произноше́ние.

proof /pru:f/ *n* доказа́тельство; (*printing*) корректу́ра; **~-reader** корре́ктор; *adj* (*impenetrable*) непроница́емый (**against** для+*gen*); (*not yielding*) неподдаю́щийся (**against** +*dat*).

prop[1] /prɒp/ *n* (*support*) подпо́рка; (*fig*) опо́ра; *vt* (~ *open*, *up*) подпира́ть *impf*, подпере́ть *pf*; (*fig*) подде́рживать *impf*, поддержа́ть *pf*.

prop[2] /prɒp/ *n* (*theat*) *see* **props**

propaganda /ˌprɒpə'gændə/ *n* пропага́нда.

propagate /'prɒpəˌgeɪt/ *vt* & *i* размножа́ть(ся) *impf*, размно́жить(ся) *pf*; (*disseminate*) распространя́ть(ся) *impf*, распространи́ть(ся) *pf*. **propagation** /-'geɪʃ(ə)n/ *n* размноже́ние; распростране́ние.

propel /prə'pel/ *vt* приводи́ть *impf*, привести́ *pf* в движе́ние. **propeller** /-'pelə(r)/ *n* винт.

propensity /prə'pensɪtɪ/ *n* накло́нность (**to** к+*dat*; +*inf*).

proper /'prɒpə(r)/ *adj* (*correct*) пра́вильный; (*suitable*) подходя́щий; (*decent*) присто́йный; ~ **noun** и́мя со́бственное. **properly** /'prɒpəlɪ/ *adv* как сле́дует.

property /'prɒpətɪ/ *n* (*possessions*) со́бственность, иму́щество; (*attribute*) сво́йство; *pl* (*theat*) реквизи́т.

prophecy /'prɒfɪsɪ/ *n* проро́чество. **prophesy** /'prɒfɪˌsaɪ/ *vt* проро́чить *impf*, на~ *pf*. **prophet** /'prɒfɪt/ *n* проро́к. **prophetic** /prə'fetɪk/ *adj* проро́ческий.

propitious /prə'pɪʃəs/ *adj* благоприя́тный.

proponent /prə'pəʊnənt/ *n* сторо́нник.

proportion /prə'pɔ:ʃ(ə)n/ *n* пропо́рция; (*due relation*) соразме́рность; *pl* разме́ры *m pl*. **proportional** /-n(ə)l/ *adj* пропорциона́льный. **proportionate** /-'pɔ:ʃən(ə)t/ *adj* соразме́рный (**to** +*dat*; с+*instr*).

proposal /prə'pəʊz(ə)l/ *n* предложе́ние. **propose** /-'pəʊz/ *vt* предлага́ть *impf*, предложи́ть *pf*; (*intend*) предполага́ть *impf*; *vi* (~ *marriage*) де́лать *impf*, с~ *pf* предложе́ние (**to** +*dat*).

proposition /ˌprɒpə'zɪʃ(ə)n/ *n* предложе́ние.

propound /prəˈpaʊnd/ *vt* предлага́ть *impf*, предложи́ть *pf* на обсужде́ние.
proprietor /prəˈpraɪətə(r)/ *n* со́бственник, хозя́ин.
propriety /prəˈpraɪtɪ/ *n* прили́чие.
props /prɒps/ *n pl* (*theat*) реквизи́т.
propulsion /prəˈpʌlʃ(ə)n/ *n* движе́ние вперёд.
prosaic /prəˈzeɪɪk/ *adj* прозаи́ческий.
proscribe /prəˈskraɪb/ *vt* (*forbid*) запреща́ть *impf*, запрети́ть *pf*.
prose /prəʊz/ *n* про́за.
prosecute /ˈprɒsɪˌkjuːt/ *vt* пресле́довать *impf*. **prosecution** /-ˈkjuːʃ(ə)n/ *n* суде́бное пресле́дование; (*prosecuting party*) обвине́ние. **prosecutor** /ˈprɒsəˌkjuːtə(r)/ *n* обвини́тель *m*.
prospect *n* /ˈprɒspekt/ вид; (*fig*) перспекти́ва; *vi*: /prəˈspekt/ ~ **for** иска́ть *impf*. **prospective** /prəˈspektɪv/ *adj* бу́дущий. **prospector** /prəˈspektə(r)/ *n* разве́дчик. **prospectus** /prəˈspektəs/ *n* проспе́кт.
prosper /ˈprɒspə(r)/ *vi* процвета́ть *impf*. **prosperity** /prɒˈsperɪtɪ/ *n* процвета́ние. **prosperous** /ˈprɒspərəs/ *adj* процвета́ющий; (*wealthy*) зажи́точный.
prostate (gland) /ˈprɒsteɪt (glænd)/ *n* проста́та.
prostitute /ˈprɒstɪˌtjuːt/ *n* проститу́тка. **prostitution** /-ˈtjuːʃ(ə)n/ *n* проститу́ция.
prostrate /ˈprɒstreɪt/ *adj* распростёртый, (лежа́щий) ничко́м; (*exhausted*) обесси́ленный; (*with grief*) уби́тый (**with** +*instr*).
protagonist /prəʊˈtægənɪst/ *n* гла́вный геро́й; (*in contest*) протагони́ст.
protect /prəˈtekt/ *vt* защища́ть *impf*, защити́ть. **protection** /-ˈtekʃ(ə)n/ *n* защи́та. **protective** /-ˈtektɪv/ *adj* защи́тный. **protector** /-ˈtektə(r)/ *n* защи́тник.
protégé(e) /ˈprɒtɪˌʒeɪ/ *n* протеже́ *m* & *f indecl*.
protein /ˈprəʊtiːn/ *n* бело́к.
protest *n* /ˈprəʊtest/ проте́ст; *vi* /prəˈtest/ протестова́ть *impf*; *vt* (*affirm*) утвержда́ть *impf*.
Protestant /ˈprɒtɪst(ə)nt/ *n* протеста́нт, ~ка; *adj* протеста́нтский.
protestation /ˌprɒtɪˈsteɪʃ(ə)n/ *n* (торже́ственное) заявле́ние (о+*prep*; что); (*protest*) проте́ст.
protocol /ˌprəʊtəˈkɒl/ *n* протоко́л.
proton /ˈprəʊtɒn/ *n* прото́н.
prototype /ˈprəʊtəˌtaɪp/ *n* прототи́п.
protract /prəˈtrækt/ *vt* тяну́ть *impf*. **protracted** /-ˈtræktɪd/ *adj* дли́тельный.
protrude /prəˈtruːd/ *vi* выдава́ться *impf*, вы́даться *pf*.
proud /praʊd/ *adj* го́рдый; **be ~ of** горди́ться *impf* +*instr*.
prove /pruːv/ *vt* дока́зывать *impf*, доказа́ть *pf*; *vi* ока́зываться *impf*, оказа́ться *pf* (**to be** +*instr*). **proven** /ˈpruːv(ə)n/ *adj* дока́занный.
provenance /ˈprɒvɪnəns/ *n* происхожде́ние.
proverb /ˈprɒvɜːb/ *n* посло́вица. **proverbial** /prəˈvɜːbɪəl/ *adj* воше́дший в погово́рку; (*well-known*) общеизве́стный.
provide /prəˈvaɪd/ *vt* (*supply person*) снабжа́ть *impf*, снабди́ть *pf* (**with** +*instr*); (*supply thing*)

предоставля́ть *impf*, предоста́вить *pf* (**to, for** +*dat*); дава́ть *impf*, дать *pf* (**to, for** +*dat*); *vi*: ~ **for** предусма́тривать *impf*, предусмотре́ть *pf* +*acc*; (~ *for family etc.*) содержа́ть *impf* +*acc*. **provided (that)** /-'vaɪdɪd/ *conj* при усло́вии, что; е́сли то́лько. **providence** /'prɒvɪd(ə)ns/ *n* провиде́ние; (*foresight*) предусмотри́тельность. **provident** /'prɒvɪd(ə)nt/ *adj* предусмотри́тельный. **providential** /-'denʃ(ə)l/ *adj* счастли́вый. **providing** /prə'vaɪdɪŋ/ *see* **provided (that)**

province /'prɒvɪns/ *n* о́бласть; *pl* (*the* ~) прови́нция. **provincial** /prə'vɪnʃ(ə)l/ *adj* провинциа́льный.

provision /prə'vɪʒ(ə)n/ *n* снабже́ние; *pl* (*food*) прови́зия; (*in agreement etc.*) положе́ние; **make ~ against** принима́ть *impf*, приня́ть *pf* ме́ры про́тив+*gen*. **provisional** /-'vɪʒən(ə)l/ *adj* вре́менный.

proviso /-'vaɪzəʊ/ *n* усло́вие.

provocation /,prɒvə'keɪʃ(ə)n/ *n* провока́ция. **provocative** /prə'vɒkətɪv/ *adj* провокацио́нный. **provoke** /prə'vəʊk/ *vt* провоци́ровать *impf*, с~ *pf*; (*call forth, cause*) вызыва́ть *impf*, вы́звать *pf*.

prow /praʊ/ *n* нос.

prowess /'praʊɪs/ *n* уме́ние.

prowl /praʊl/ *vi* ры́скать *impf*.

proximity /prɒk'sɪmɪtɪ/ *n* бли́зость.

proxy /'prɒksɪ/ *n* полномо́чие; (*person*) уполномо́ченный *sb*, замести́тель *m*; **by** ~ по дове́ренности; **stand ~ for** быть *impf* замести́телем +*gen*.

prudence /'pru:d(ə)ns/ *n* благоразу́мие. **prudent** /-d(ə)nt/ *adj* благоразу́мный.

prudery /'pru:dərɪ/ *n* притво́рная стыдли́вость. **prudish** /-dɪʃ/ *adj* ни в ме́ру стыдли́вый.

prune[1] /pru:n/ *n* (*plum*) чернosли́в.

prune[2] /pru:n/ *vt* (*trim*) об-, под-, реза́ть *impf*, об-, под-, ре́зать *pf*.

pry /praɪ/ *vi* сова́ть *impf* нос (**into** в+*acc*).

PS *abbr* (*of* **postscript**) постскри́птум.

psalm /sɑ:m/ *n* псало́м.

pseudonym /'sju:dənɪm/ *n* псевдони́м.

psyche /'saɪkɪ/ *n* пси́хика. **psychiatric** /,saɪkɪ'ætrɪk/ *adj* психиатри́ческий. **psychiatrist** /saɪ'kaɪətrɪst/ *n* психиа́тр. **psychiatry** /saɪ'kaɪətrɪ/ *n* психиатри́я. **psychic** /'saɪkɪk/ *adj* ясновидя́щий. **psychoanalysis** /,saɪkəʊə'nælɪsɪs/ *n* психоана́лиз. **psychoanalyst** /,saɪkəʊ'ænəlɪst/ *n* психоанали́тик. **psychoanalytic(al)** /,saɪkəʊ,ænə'lɪtɪk((ə)l)/ *adj* психоаналити́ческий. **psychological** /,saɪkə'lɒdʒɪk(ə)l/ *adj* психологи́ческий. **psychologist** /saɪ'kɒlədʒɪst/ *n* психо́лог. **psychology** /saɪ'kɒlədʒɪ/ *n* психоло́гия. **psychopath** /'saɪkə,pæθ/ *n* психопа́т. **psychopathic** /,saɪkə'pæθɪk/ *adj* психопати́ческий. **psychosis** /saɪ'kəʊsɪs/ *n* психо́з. **psychotherapy** /,saɪkəʊ'θerəpɪ/ *n* психотерапи́я.

PTO *abbr* (*of* **please turn over**) см. на об., смотри́ на оборо́те.

pub /pʌb/ *n* пивна́я *sb*.

puberty /'pju:bətɪ/ *n* полова́я зре́лость.

public /'pʌblɪk/ *adj* обще́ственный; (*open*) публи́чный, откры́тый; ~ **school** ча́стная сре́дняя шко́ла; *n* пу́блика, обще́ственность; **in** ~ откры́то, публи́чно. **publication** /-'keɪʃ(ə)n/ *n* изда́ние. **publicity** /-'lɪsɪtɪ/ *n* рекла́ма. **publicize** /'pʌblɪˌsaɪz/ *vt* реклами́ровать *impf* & *pf*. **publicly** /pʌb'lɪsɪtɪ/ *adv* публи́чно, откры́то. **publish** /'pʌblɪʃ/ *vt* публикова́ть *impf*, о~ *pf*; (*book*) издава́ть *impf*, изда́ть *pf*. **publisher** /'pʌblɪʃə(r)/ *n* изда́тель *m*. **publishing** /'pʌblɪʃɪŋ/ *n* (*business*) изда́тельское де́ло; ~ **house** изда́тельство.

pucker /'pʌkə(r)/ *vt* & *i* мо́рщить(ся) *impf*, с~ *pf*.

pudding /'pʊdɪŋ/ *n* пу́динг, запека́нка; (*dessert*) сла́дкое *sb*.

puddle /'pʌd(ə)l/ *n* лу́жа.

puff /pʌf/ *n* (*of wind*) поры́в; (*of smoke*) дымо́к; ~ **pastry** слоёное те́сто; *vi* пыхте́ть *impf*; ~ **at** (*pipe etc.*) попы́хивать *impf* +*instr*; *vt*: ~ **up, out** (*inflate*) надува́ть *impf*, наду́ть *pf*.

pugnacious /pʌg'neɪʃəs/ *adj* драчли́вый.

puke /pju:k/ *vi* рвать *impf*, вы́~ *pf impers*+*acc*.

pull /pʊl/ *vt* тяну́ть *impf*, по~ *pf*; таска́ть *indet*, тащи́ть *det*, по~ *pf*; (*a muscle*) растя́гивать *impf*, растяну́ть *pf*; *vt* & *i* дёргать *impf*, дёрнуть *pf* (**at** (за)+*acc*); ~ **s.o's leg** разы́грывать *impf*, разыгра́ть *pf*; ~ **the trigger** спуска́ть *impf*, спусти́ть *pf* куро́к; ~ **apart, to pieces** разрыва́ть *impf*, разорва́ть *pf*; (*fig*) раскритикова́ть *pf*; ~ **down** (*demolish*) сноси́ть *impf*, снести́ *pf*; ~ **in** (*of train*) прибыва́ть *impf*, прибы́ть *pf*; (*of vehicle*) подъезжа́ть *impf*, подъе́хать *pf* к обо́чине (доро́ги); ~ **off** (*garment*) стя́гивать *impf*, стяну́ть *pf*; (*achieve*) успе́шно заверша́ть *impf*, заверши́ть *pf*; ~ **on** (*garment*) натя́гивать *impf*, натяну́ть *pf*; ~ **out** (*vt*) (*remove*) выта́скивать *impf*, вы́тащить *pf*; (*vi*) (*withdraw*) отка́зываться *impf*, отказа́ться *pf* от уча́стия (**of** в+*prep*); (*of vehicle*) отъезжа́ть *impf*, отъе́хать *pf* от обо́чины (доро́ги); (*of train*) отходи́ть *impf*, отойти́ *pf* (от ста́нции); ~ **through** выжива́ть *impf*, вы́жить *pf*; ~ **o.s. together** брать *impf*, взять *pf* себя́ в ру́ки; ~ **up** (*vt*) подтя́гивать *impf*, подтяну́ть *pf*; (*vt* & *i*) (*stop*) остана́вливать(ся) *impf*, останови́ть(ся) *pf*; *n* тя́га; (*fig*) блат.

pulley /'pʊlɪ/ *n* блок.

pullover /'pʊləʊvə(r)/ *n* пуло́вер.

pulp /pʌlp/ *n* пу́льпа.

pulpit /'pʊlpɪt/ *n* ка́федра.

pulsate /pʌl'seɪt/ *vi* пульси́ровать *impf*. **pulse** /pʌls/ *n* пульс.

pulses /'pʌlsɪz/ *n pl* (*food*) бобо́вые *sb*.

pulverize /'pʌlvəˌraɪz/ *vt* размельча́ть *impf*, размельчи́ть *pf*.

pummel /'pʌm(ə)l/ *vt* колоти́ть *impf*, по~ *pf*.

pump /pʌmp/ *n* насо́с; *vt* кача́ть *impf*; ~ **in(to)** вка́чивать *impf*, вкача́ть *pf*; ~ **out** выка́чивать *impf*, вы́качать *pf*; ~ **up** нака́чивать *impf*, накача́ть *pf*.

pumpkin /'pʌmpkɪn/ *n* ты́ква.

pun /pʌn/ *n* каламбу́р.

punch[1] /pʌntʃ/ *vt* (*with fist*) ударя́ть *impf*, уда́рить *pf* кулако́м; (*hole*) пробива́ть *impf*,

пробить *pf*; (*a ticket*) компостировать *impf*, про~ *pf*; **~-up** драка; *n* (*blow*) удар кулаком; (*for tickets*) компостер; (*for piercing*) перфоратор.
punch[2] /pʌntʃ/ *n* (*drink*) пунш.
punctilious /pʌŋk'tɪlɪəs/ *adj* щепетильный.
punctual /'pʌŋktjʊəl/ *adj* пунктуальный. **punctuality** /ˌpʌŋktjʊ'ælɪtɪ/ *n* пунктуальность.
punctuate /'pʌŋktjʊˌeɪt/ *vt* ставить *impf*, по~ *pf* знаки препинания в+*acc*; (*fig*) прерывать *impf*, прервать *pf*. **punctuation** /-'eɪʃ(ə)n/ *n* пунктуация; **~ marks** знаки *m pl* препинания.
puncture /'pʌŋktʃə(r)/ *n* прокол; *vt* прокалывать *impf*, проколоть *pf*.
pundit /'pʌndɪt/ *n* (*fig*) знаток.
pungent /'pʌndʒ(ə)nt/ *adj* едкий.
punish /'pʌnɪʃ/ *vt* наказывать *impf*, наказать *pf*. **punishable** /-ʃəb(ə)l/ *adj* наказуемый. **punishment** /-mənt/ *n* наказание. **punitive** /'pju:nɪtɪv/ *adj* карательный.
punter /'pʌntə(r)/ *n* (*gambler*) игрок; (*client*) клиент.
puny /'pju:nɪ/ *adj* хилый.
pupil /'pju:pɪl/ *n* ученик, -ица; (*of eye*) зрачок.
puppet /'pʌpɪt/ *n* марионетка, кукла.
puppy /'pʌpɪ/ *n* щенок.
purchase /'pɜ:tʃɪs/ *n* покупка; (*leverage*) точка опоры; *vt* покупать *impf*, купить *pf*. **purchaser** /-sə(r)/ *n* покупатель *m*.
pure /pjʊə(r)/ *adj* чистый.
purée /'pjʊəreɪ/ *n* пюре *neut indecl*.
purely /'pjʊəlɪ/ *adv* чисто.
purgatory /'pɜ:gətərɪ/ *n* чистилище; (*fig*) ад. **purge** /pɜ:dʒ/ *vt* очищать *impf*, очистить *pf*; *n* очищение; (*polit*) чистка.
purification /ˌpjʊərɪfɪ'keɪʃ(ə)n/ *n* очистка. **purify** /'pjʊərɪˌfaɪ/ *vt* очищать *impf*, очистить *pf*.
purist /'pjʊərɪst/ *n* пурист.
puritan, P., /'pjʊərɪt(ə)n/ *n* пуританин, -анка. **puritanical** /-'tænɪk(ə)l/ *adj* пуританский.
purity /'pjʊərɪtɪ/ *n* чистота.
purple /'pɜ:p(ə)l/ *adj* (*n*) пурпурный, фиолетовый (цвет).
purport /pə'pɔ:t/ *vt* претендовать *impf*.
purpose /'pɜ:pəs/ *n* цель, намерение; **on ~** нарочно; **to no ~** напрасно. **purposeful** /-fʊl/ *adj* целеустремлённый. **purposeless** /-lɪs/ *adj* бесцельный. **purposely** /-lɪ/ *adv* нарочно.
purr /pɜ:(r)/ *vi* мурлыкать *impf*.
purse /pɜ:s/ *n* кошелёк; *vt* поджимать *impf*, поджать *pf*.
pursue /pə'sju:/ *vt* преследовать *impf*. **pursuit** /-'sju:t/ *n* преследование; (*pastime*) занятие.
purveyor /pə'veɪə(r)/ *n* поставщик.
pus /pʌs/ *n* гной.
push /pʊʃ/ *vt* толкать *impf*, толкнуть *pf*; (*press*) нажимать *impf*, нажать *pf*; (*urge*) подталкивать *impf*, подтолкнуть *pf*; *vi* толкаться *impf*; **be ~ed for** иметь *impf* мало+*gen*; **he is ~ing fifty** ему скоро стукнет пятьдесят; **~ one's way** проталкиваться *impf*, протолкнуться *pf*; **~ around** (*person*) помыкать *impf* +*instr*; **~ aside** (*also fig*) отстранять *impf*, отстранить *pf*; **~ away** отталкивать *impf*, оттолкнуть *pf*; **~ off** (*vi*) (*in boat*) отталкиваться *impf*, оттолкнуться *pf* (от бе-

рега); (*go away*) убира́ться *impf*, убра́ться *pf*; ~ **on** (*vi*) продолжа́ть *impf* путь; *n* толчо́к; (*energy*) эне́ргия. **push-chair** *n* коля́ска. **pusher** /-ʃə(r)/ *n* (*drugs*) продаве́ц нарко́тиков. **pushy** /-ʃɪ/ *adj* напо́ристый.

puss, pussy(-cat) /pʊs, 'pʊsɪ(kæt)/ *n* ки́ска.

put /pʊt/ *vt* класть *impf*, положи́ть *pf*; (*upright*) ста́вить *impf*, по~ *pf*; помеща́ть *impf*, помести́ть *pf*; (*into specified state*) приводи́ть *impf*, привести́ *pf*; (*express*) выража́ть *impf*, вы́разить *pf*; (*a question*) задава́ть *impf*, зада́ть *pf*; ~ **an end, a stop, to** класть *impf*, положи́ть *pf* коне́ц +*dat*; ~ **o.s. in another's place** ста́вить *impf*, по~ *pf* себя́ на ме́сто +*gen*; ~ **about** (*rumour etc.*) распространя́ть *impf*, распространи́ть *pf*; ~ **away** (*tidy*) убира́ть *impf*, убра́ть *pf*; (*save*) откла́дывать *impf*, отложи́ть *pf*; ~ **back** (*in place*) ста́вить *impf*, по~ *pf* на ме́сто; (*clock*) переводи́ть *impf*, перевести́ *pf* наза́д; ~ **by** (*money*) откла́дывать *impf*, отложи́ть *pf*; ~ **down** класть *impf*, положи́ть *pf*; (*suppress*) подавля́ть *impf*, подави́ть *pf*; (*write down*) запи́сывать *impf*, записа́ть *pf*; (*passengers*) высա́живать *impf*, вы́садить *pf*; (*attribute*) припи́сывать *impf*, приписа́ть *pf* (**to** +*dat*); ~ **forward** (*proposal*) предлага́ть *impf*, предложи́ть *pf*; (*clock*) переводи́ть *impf*, перевести́ *pf* вперёд; ~ **in** (*install*) устана́вливать *impf*, установи́ть *pf*; (*a claim*) предъявля́ть *impf*, предъяви́ть *pf*; (*interpose*) вставля́ть *impf*, вста́вить *pf*; ~ **in an appearance** появля́ться *impf*, появи́ться *pf*; ~ **off** (*postpone*) откла́дывать *impf*, отложи́ть *pf*; (*repel*) отта́лкивать *impf*, оттолкну́ть *pf*; (*dissuade*) отгова́ривать *impf*, отговори́ть *pf* от+*gen*, +*inf*; ~ **on** (*clothes*) надева́ть *impf*, наде́ть *pf*; (*kettle, a record, a play*) ста́вить *impf*, по~ *pf*; (*turn on*) включа́ть *impf*, включи́ть *pf*; (*add to*) прибавля́ть *impf*, приба́вить *pf*; ~ **on airs** ва́жничать *impf*; ~ **on weight** толсте́ть *impf*, по~ *pf*; ~ **out** (*vex*) обижа́ть *impf*, оби́деть *pf*; (*inconvenience*) затрудня́ть *impf*, затрудни́ть *pf*; (*a fire etc.*) туши́ть *impf*, по~ *pf*; ~ **through** (*tel*) соединя́ть *impf*, соедини́ть *pf* по телефо́ну; ~ **up** (*building*) стро́ить *impf*, по~ *pf*; (*hang up*) ве́шать *impf*, пове́сить *pf*; (*price*) повыша́ть *impf*, повы́сить *pf*; (*a guest*) дава́ть *impf*, дать *pf* ночлег +*dat*; (*as guest*) ночева́ть *impf*, пере~ *pf*; ~ **up to** (*instigate*) подбива́ть *impf*, подби́ть *pf* на+*acc*; ~ **up with** терпе́ть *impf*.

putative /'pju:tətɪv/ *adj* предполага́емый.

putrefy /'pju:trɪ,faɪ/ *vi* гнить *impf*, с~ *pf*. **putrid** /'pju:trɪd/ *adj* гнило́й.

putty /'pʌtɪ/ *n* зама́зка.

puzzle /'pʌz(ə)l/ *n* (*enigma*) зага́дка; (*toy etc.*) головоло́мка; (*jigsaw*) моза́ика; *vt* озада́чивать *impf*, озада́чить *pf*; ~ **out** разгада́ть *pf*; *vi*: ~ **over** лома́ть *impf* себе́ го́лову над+*instr*.

pygmy /'pɪgmɪ/ *n* пигме́й.

pyjamas /pɪ'dʒɑ:məz/ *n pl* пижа́ма.

pylon /'paɪlən/ *n* пило́н.

pyramid /'pɪrəmɪd/ *n* пирами́да.

pyre /'paɪə(r)/ *n* погребáльный костёр.
python /'paɪθ(ə)n/ *n* питóн.

Q

quack[1] /kwæk/ *n* (*sound*) кря́канье; *vi* кря́кать *impf*, кря́кнуть *pf*.
quack[2] /kwæk/ *n* шарлатáн.
quad /kwɒd/ *n* (*court*) четырёхугóльный двор; *pl* (*quadruplets*) чéтверо близнецóв. **quadrangle** /'kwɒd,ræŋg(ə)l/ *n* (*figure*) четырёхугóльник; (*court*) четырёхугóльный двор. **quadrant** /'kwɒdrənt/ *n* квадрáнт.
quadruped /'kwɒdrʊ,ped/ *n* четвероногое живóтное *sb*.
quadruple /'kwɒdrʊp(ə)l/ *adj* четвернóй; *vt & i* учетверя́ть(ся) *impf*, учетвери́ть(ся) *pf*. **quadruplets** /'kwɒdrʊplɪts/ *n pl* чéтверо близнецóв.
quagmire /'kwɒg,maɪə(r)/ *n* болóто.
quail /kweɪl/ *n* (*bird*) пéрепел.
quaint /kweɪnt/ *adj* причýдливый.
quake /kweɪk/ *vi* дрожáть *impf* (**with** от+*gen*).
Quaker /'kweɪkə(r)/ *n* квáкер, ~ка.
qualification /,kwɒlɪfɪ'keɪʃ(ə)n/ *n* (*for post etc.*) квалификáция; (*reservation*) оговóрка. **qualified** /'kwɒlɪ,faɪd/ *adj* компетéнтный; (*limited*) ограни́ченный. **qualify** /'kwɒlɪ,faɪ/ *vt & i* (*prepare for job*) готóвить(ся) *impf* (**for** к+*dat*; +*inf*); *vt* (*render fit*) дéлать *impf*, с~ *pf* пригóдным; (*entitle*) давáть *impf*, дать *pf* прáво +*dat* (**to** на+*acc*); (*limit*): ~ **what one says** сдéлать *pf* оговóрку; *vi* получáть *impf*, получи́ть *pf* диплóм; ~ **for** (*be entitled to*) имéть *impf* прáво на+*acc*.
qualitative /'kwɒlɪtətɪv/ *adj* кáчественный. **quality** /'kwɒlɪtɪ/ *n* кáчество.
qualm /kwɑ:m/ *n* сомнéние; (*of conscience*) угрызéние сóвести.
quandary /'kwɒndərɪ/ *n* затрудни́тельное положéние.
quantify /'kwɒntɪ,faɪ/ *vt* определя́ть *impf*, определи́ть *pf* коли́чество +*gen*. **quantitative** /'kwɒntɪtətɪv/ *adj* коли́чественный. **quantity** /'kwɒntɪtɪ/ *n* коли́чество.
quarantine /'kwɒrən,ti:n/ *n* карантúн.
quarrel /'kwɒr(ə)l/ *n* ссóра; *vi* ссóриться *impf*, по~ *pf* (**with** с+*instr*; **about, for** из-за+*gen*). **quarrelsome** /-səm/ *adj* вздóрный.
quarry[1] /'kwɒrɪ/ *n* (*for stone etc.*) каменолóмня; *vt* добывáть *impf*, добы́ть *pf*.
quarry[2] /'kwɒrɪ/ *n* (*prey*) добы́ча.
quart /kwɔ:t/ *n* квáрта. **quarter** /'kwɔ:tə(r)/ *n* чéтверть; (*of year*; *of town*) квартáл; *pl* кварти́ры *f pl*; **a ~ to one** без чéтверти час; **~-final** чéтверть-финáл; *vt* (*divide*) дели́ть *impf*, раз~ *pf* на четы́ре чáсти; (*lodge*) расквартирóвывать *impf*, расквартировáть *pf*. **quarterly** /'kwɔ:təlɪ/ *adj* квартáльный; *adv* раз в квартáл. **quartet** /kwɔ:'tet/ *n* квартéт.
quartz /kwɔ:ts/ *n* кварц.
quash /kwɒʃ/ *vt* (*annul*) аннули́ровать *impf & pf*; (*crush*) подавля́ть *impf*, подави́ть *pf*.
quasi- /'kweɪzaɪ/ *in comb*

квази-.
quaver /'kweɪvə(r)/ *vi* дрожáть *impf*; *n* (*mus*) восьмáя *sb* нóты.
quay /ki:/ *n* нáбережная *sb*.
queasy /'kwi:zɪ/ *adj*: **I feel ~** меня́ тошни́т.
queen /kwi:n/ *n* королéва; (*cards*) дáма; (*chess*) ферзь *m*.
queer /kwɪə(r)/ *adj* стрáнный.
quell /kwel/ *vt* подавля́ть *impf*, подави́ть *pf*.
quench /kwentʃ/ *vt* (*thirst*) утоля́ть *impf*, утоли́ть *pf*; (*fire, desire*) туши́ть *impf*, по~ *pf*.
query /'kwɪərɪ/ *n* вопрóс; *vt* (*express doubt*) выражáть *impf* вы́разить *pf* сомнéние в+*prep*. **quest** /kwest/ *n* пóиски *m pl*; **in ~ of** в пóисках+*gen*. **question** /'kwestʃ(ə)n/ *n* вопрóс; **beyond ~** вне сомнéния; **it is a ~ of** э́то вопрóс+*gen*; **it is out of the ~** об э́том не мóжет быть и рéчи; **the person in ~** человéк, о котóром идёт речь; **the ~ is this** дéло в э́том; **~ mark** вопроси́тельный знак; *vt* расспрáшивать *impf*, распроси́ть *pf*; (*interrogate*) допрáшивать *impf* допроси́ть *pf*; (*doubt*) сомневáться *impf* в+*prep*. **questionable** /'kwestʃənəb(ə)l/ *adj* сомни́тельный. **questionnaire** /,kwestʃə'neə(r)/ *n* вопрóсник.
queue /kju:/ *n* óчередь; *vi* стоя́ть *impf* в óчереди.
quibble /'kwɪb(ə)l/ *n* софи́зм; (*minor criticism*) приди́рка; *vi* придирáться *impf*; (*argue*) спóрить *impf*.
quick /kwɪk/ *adj* скóрый, бы́стрый; **~-tempered** вспы́льчивый; **~-witted** нахóдчивый; *n*: **to the ~** за живóе; *adv* скóро, бы́стро; *as imper* скорéе! **quicken** /'kwɪkən/ *vt* & *i* ускоря́ть(ся) *impf*, ускóрить(ся) *pf*. **quickness** /'kwɪknɪs/ *n* быстротá. **quicksand** *n* зыбу́чий песóк. **quicksilver** *n* ртуть.
quid /kwɪd/ *n* фунт.
quiet /'kwaɪət/ *n* (*silence*) тишинá; (*calm*) спокóйствие; *adj* ти́хий; спокóйный; *int* ти́ше!; *vt* & *i* успокáивать(ся) *impf*, успокóить(ся) *pf*.
quill /kwɪl/ *n* перó; (*spine*) иглá.
quilt /kwɪlt/ *n* (стёганое) одея́ло; *vt* стегáть *impf*, вы́~ *pf*. **quilted** /'kwɪltɪd/ *adj* стёганый.
quintessential /,kwɪntɪ'senʃ(ə)l/ *adj* наибóлее сущéственный.
quintet /kwɪn'tet/ *n* квинтéт.
quins, quintuplets /kwɪnz, 'kwɪntjʊplɪts/ *n pl* пять близнецóв.
quip /kwɪp/ *n* острóта; *vi* остри́ть *impf*, с~ *pf*.
quirk /kwɜ:k/ *n* причу́да. **quirky** /-kɪ/ *adj* с причу́дами.
quit /kwɪt/ *vt* (*leave*) покидáть *impf*, поки́нуть *pf*; (*stop*) переставáть *impf*, перестáть *pf*; (*give up*) бросáть *impf*, брóсить *pf*; (*resign*) уходи́ть *impf*, уйти́ *pf* с+*gen*.
quite /kwaɪt/ *adv* (*wholly*) совсéм; (*rather*) довóльно; **~ a few** довóльно мнóго.
quits /kwɪts/ *predic*: **we are ~** мы с тобóй кви́ты; **I am ~ with him** я расквитáлся (*past*) с ним.
quiver /'kwɪvə(r)/ *vi* (*tremble*) трепетáть *impf*; *n* трéпет.
quiz /kwɪz/ *n* виктори́на. **quizzical** /'kwɪzɪk(ə)l/ *adj* насмéшливый.
quorum /'kwɔ:rəm/ *n* квóрум.
quota /'kwəʊtə/ *n* нóрма.
quotation /kwəʊ'teɪʃ(ə)n/ *n* цитáта; (*of price*) ценá; **~ marks** кавы́чки (-чек) *pl*. **quote**

/kwəʊt/ *vt* цити́ровать *impf*, про~ *pf*; ссыла́ться *impf*, сосла́ться *pf* на+*acc*; (*price*) назнача́ть *impf*, назна́чить *pf*.

R

rabbi /'ræbaɪ/ *n* равви́н.
rabbit /'ræbɪt/ *n* кро́лик.
rabble /'ræb(ə)l/ *n* сброд.
rabid /'ræbɪd/ *adj* бе́шеный. **rabies** /'reɪbi:z/ *n* бе́шенство.
race[1] /reɪs/ *n* (*ethnic* ~) ра́са; род.
race[2] /reɪs/ *n* (*contest*) (*on foot*) бег; (*of cars etc.*; *fig*) го́нка, го́нки *f pl*; (*of horses*) ска́чки *f pl*; **~-track** трек; (*for horse* ~) скакова́я доро́жка; *vi* (*compete*) состяза́ться *impf* в ско́рости; (*rush*) мча́ться *impf*; *vt* бежа́ть *impf* наперегонки́ с+*instr*. **racecourse** *n* ипподро́м. **racehorse** *n* скакова́я ло́шадь.
racial /'reɪʃ(ə)l/ *adj* ра́совый. **rac(ial)ism** /'reɪʃə,lɪz(ə)m, 'reɪsɪz(ə)m/ *n* раси́зм. **rac(ial)ist** /'reɪʃəlɪst, 'reɪsɪst/ *n* раси́ст, ~ка; *adj* раси́стский.
racing /'reɪsɪŋ/ *n* (*horses*) ска́чки *f pl*; (*cars*) го́нки *f pl*; ~ **car** го́ночный автомоби́ль *m*; ~ **driver** го́нщик.
rack /ræk/ *n* (*for hats etc.*) ве́шалка; (*for plates etc.*) стелла́ж; (*in train etc.*) се́тка; *vt*: ~ **one's brains** лома́ть *impf* себе́ го́лову.
racket[1] /'rækɪt/ *n* (*bat*) раке́тка.
racket[2] /'rækɪt/ *n* (*uproar*) шум; (*illegal activity*) рэ́кет. **racketeer** /,rækɪ'tɪə(r)/ *n* рэкети́р.
racy /'reɪsɪ/ *adj* колори́тный.
radar /'reɪdɑ:(r)/ *n* (*system*) радиолока́ция; (*apparatus*) радиолока́тор, рада́р; *attrib* рада́рный.
radiance /'reɪdɪəns/ *n* сия́ние. **radiant** /-dɪənt/ *adj* сия́ющий. **radiate** /-dɪ,eɪt/ *vt* & *i* излуча́ть(ся) *impf*, излучи́ться *pf*. **radiation** /-dɪ'eɪʃ(ə)n/ *n* излуче́ние. **radiator** /'reɪdɪ,eɪtə(r)/ *n* батаре́я; (*in car*) радиа́тор.
radical /'rædɪk(ə)l/ *adj* радика́льный; *n* радика́л.
radio /'reɪdɪəʊ/ *n* ра́дио *neut indecl*; (*set*) радиоприёмник; *vt* ради́ровать *impf* & *pf* +*dat*.
radioactive /,reɪdɪəʊ'æktɪv/ *adj* радиоакти́вный. **radioactivity** /-æk'tɪvɪtɪ/ *n* радиоакти́вность. **radiologist** /,reɪdɪ'ɒlədʒɪst/ *n* радио́лог; рентгено́лог. **radiotherapy** /,reɪdɪəʊ'θerəpɪ/ *n* радиотерапи́я.
radish /'rædɪʃ/ *n* реди́ска.
radius /'reɪdɪəs/ *n* ра́диус.
raffle /'ræf(ə)l/ *n* лотере́я; *vt* разы́грывать *impf*, разыгра́ть *pf* в лотере́е.
raft /rɑ:ft/ *n* плот.
rafter /'rɑ:ftə(r)/ *n* (*beam*) стропи́ло.
rag /ræg/ *n* тря́пка; *pl* (*clothes*) лохмо́тья (-ьев) *pl*.
rage /reɪdʒ/ *n* я́рость; **all the** ~ после́дний крик мо́ды; *vi* беси́ться *impf*; (*storm etc.*) бушева́ть *impf*.
ragged /'rægɪd/ *adj* (*jagged*) зазу́бренный; (*of clothes*) рва́ный.
raid /reɪd/ *n* налёт; (*by police*) обла́ва; *vt* де́лать *impf*, с~ *pf* налёт на+*acc*.
rail /reɪl/ *n* пери́ла (-л) *pl*; (*rly*) рельс; **by** ~ по́ездом. **railing** /'reɪlɪŋ/ *n* пери́ла (-л) *pl*.
railway /'reɪlweɪ/ *n* желе́зная доро́га; *attrib* железнодоро́жный. **railwayman** *n*

железнодоро́жник.

rain /reɪn/ *n* дождь *m*; *v impers*: **it is (was) ~ing** идёт (шёл) дождь; *vt* осыпа́ть *impf*, осы́пать *pf* +*instr* (**upon** +*acc*); *vi* осыпа́ться *impf*, осы́паться *pf*. **rainbow** *n* ра́дуга. **raincoat** *n* плащ. **raindrop** *n* дождева́я ка́пля. **rainfall** *n* (*amount of rain*) коли́чество оса́дков. **rainy** /'reɪnɪ/ *adj* дождли́вый; **~ day** чёрный день *m*.

raise /reɪz/ *vt* (*lift*) поднима́ть *impf*, подня́ть *pf*; (*heighten*) повыша́ть *impf*, повы́сить *pf*; (*provoke*) вызыва́ть *impf*, вы́звать *pf*; (*money*) собира́ть *impf*, собра́ть *pf*; (*children*) расти́ть *impf*.

raisin /'reɪz(ə)n/ *n* изю́минка; *pl* (*collect*) изю́м.

rake /reɪk/ *n* (*tool*) гра́бли (-бель & -блей) *pl*; *vt* грести́ *impf*; (**~ *together, up***) сгреба́ть *impf*, сгрести́ *pf*.

rally /'rælɪ/ *vt & i* спла́чивать(ся) *impf*, сплоти́ть(ся) *pf*; *vi* (*after illness etc.*) оправля́ться *impf*, опра́виться *pf*; *n* (*meeting*) слёт; ми́тинг; (*motoring* **~**) (авто)ра́лли *neut indecl*; (*tennis*) обме́н уда́рами.

ram /ræm/ *n* (*sheep*) бара́н; *vt* (*beat down*) трамбова́ть *impf*, у~ *pf*; (*drive in*) вбива́ть *impf*, вбить *pf*.

ramble /'ræmb(ə)l/ *vi* (*walk*) прогу́ливаться *impf*, прогуля́ться *pf*; (*speak*) бубни́ть *impf*; *n* прогу́лка. **rambling** /'ræmblɪŋ/ *adj* (*incoherent*) бессвя́зный.

ramification /,ræmɪfɪ'keɪʃ(ə)n/ *n* (*fig*) после́дствие.

ramp /ræmp/ *n* скат.

rampage /ræm'peɪdʒ/ *vi* бу́йствовать *impf*.

rampant /'ræmpənt/ *adj* (*plant*) бу́йный; (*unchecked*) безу́держный.

rampart /'ræmpɑ:t/ *n* вал.

ramshackle /'ræm,ʃæk(ə)l/ *adj* ве́тхий.

ranch /rɑ:ntʃ/ *n* ра́нчо *neut indecl*.

rancid /'rænsɪd/ *adj* прого́рклый.

rancour /'ræŋkə(r)/ *n* зло́ба.

random /'rændəm/ *adj* случа́йный; **at ~** наудачу.

range /reɪndʒ/ *n* (*of mountains*) цепь; (*artillery* **~**) полиго́н; (*of voice*) диапазо́н; (*scope*) круг, преде́лы *m pl*; (*operating distance*) да́льность; *vi* (*vary*) колеба́ться *impf*, по~ *pf*; (*wander*) броди́ть *impf*; **~ over** (*include*) охва́тывать *impf*, охвати́ть *pf*.

rank¹ /ræŋk/ *n* (*row*) ряд; (*taxi* **~**) стоя́нка такси́; (*grade*) зва́ние, чин, ранг; *vt* (*classify*) классифици́ровать *impf & pf*; (*consider*) счита́ть *impf* (**as** +*instr*); *vi*: **~ with** быть в числе́+*gen*.

rank² /ræŋk/ *adj* (*luxuriant*) бу́йный; (*in smell*) злово́нный; (*gross*) я́вный.

rankle /'ræŋk(ə)l/ *vi* боле́ть *impf*.

ransack /'rænsæk/ *vt* (*search*) обша́ривать *impf*, обша́рить *pf*; (*plunder*) гра́бить *impf*, о~ *pf*.

ransom /'rænsəm/ *n* вы́куп; *vt* выкупа́ть *impf*, вы́купить *pf*.

rant /rænt/ *vi* вопи́ть *impf*.

rap /ræp/ *n* стук; *vt* (ре́зко) ударя́ть *impf*, уда́рить *pf*; *vi* стуча́ть *impf*, сту́кнуть *pf*.

rape¹ /reɪp/ *vt* наси́ловать *impf*, из~ *pf*; *n* изнаси́лование.

rape² /reɪp/ *n* (*plant*) рапс.

rapid /'ræpɪd/ *adj* бы́стрый; *n*: *pl* поро́г, быстрина́. **rapidity**

/rə'pɪdɪtɪ/ *n* быстрота́.
rapt /ræpt/ *adj* восхищённый; (*absorbed*) поглощённый. **rapture** /'ræptʃə(r)/ *n* восто́рг. **rapturous** /'ræptʃərəs/ *adj* восто́рженный.
rare[1] /reə(r)/ *adj* (*of meat*) недожа́ренный.
rare[2] /reə(r)/ *adj* ре́дкий. **rarity** /'reərɪtɪ/ *n* ре́дкость.
rascal /'rɑːsk(ə)l/ *n* плут.
rash[1] /ræʃ/ *n* сыпь.
rash[2] /ræʃ/ *adj* опроме́тчивый.
rasher /'ræʃə(r)/ *n* ло́мтик (беко́на).
rasp /rɑːsp/ *n* (*file*) ра́шпиль *m*; (*sound*) скре́жет; *vt*: ~ **out** га́ркнуть *pf*.
raspberry /'rɑːzbərɪ/ *n* мали́на (*no pl*; *usu collect*).
rasping /'rɑːspɪŋ/ *adj* (*sound*) скрипу́чий.
rat /ræt/ *n* кры́са; ~ **race** го́нка за успе́хом.
ratchet /'rætʃɪt/ *n* храпови́к.
rate /reɪt/ *n* но́рма, ста́вка; (*speed*) ско́рость; *pl* ме́стные нало́ги *m pl*; **at any** ~ во вся́ком слу́чае; *vt* оце́нивать *impf*, оцени́ть *pf*; (*consider*) счита́ть *impf*; *vi* счита́ться *impf* (**as** +*instr*).
rather /'rɑːðə(r)/ *adv* скоре́е; (*somewhat*) дово́льно; **he (she) had (would)** ~ он (она́) предпочёл (-чла́) бы+*inf*.
ratification /,rætɪfɪ'keɪʃ(ə)n/ *n* ратифика́ция. **ratify** /'rætɪ,faɪ/ *vt* ратифици́ровать *impf* & *pf*.
rating /'reɪtɪŋ/ *n* оце́нка.
ratio /'reɪʃɪəʊ/ *n* пропо́рция.
ration /'ræʃ(ə)n/ *n* паёк, рацио́н; *vt* норми́ровать *impf* & *pf*; **be** ~**ed** выдава́ться *impf*, вы́даться *pf* по ка́рточкам.
rational /'ræʃən(ə)l/ *adj* разу́мный. **rationalism** /-,lɪz(ə)m/ *n* рационали́зм. **rationality** /,ræʃə'nælɪtɪ/ *n* разу́мность. **rationalize** /'ræʃənə,laɪz/ *vt* обосно́вывать *impf*, обоснова́ть *pf*; (*industry etc.*) рационализи́ровать *impf* & *pf*.
rattle /'ræt(ə)l/ *vi* & *t* (*sound*) греме́ть *impf* (+*instr*); ~ **along** (*move*) грохота́ть *impf*; ~ **off** (*utter*) отбараба́нить *pf*; *n* (*sound*) треск, гро́хот; (*toy*) погрему́шка. **rattlesnake** *n* грему́чая змея́.
raucous /'rɔːkəs/ *adj* ре́зкий.
ravage /'rævɪdʒ/ *vt* опустоша́ть *impf*, опустоши́ть *pf*; *n*: *pl* разруши́тельное де́йствие.
rave /reɪv/ *vi* бре́дить *impf*; ~ **about** быть в восто́рге от+*gen*.
raven /'reɪv(ə)n/ *n* во́рон.
ravenous /'rævənəs/ *adj* голо́дный как волк.
ravine /rə'viːn/ *n* уще́лье.
ravishing /'rævɪʃɪŋ/ *adj* восхити́тельный.
raw /rɔː/ *adj* сыро́й; (*inexperienced*) нео́пытный; ~ **material(s)** сырьё (*no pl*).
ray /reɪ/ *n* луч.
raze /reɪz/ *vt*: ~ **to the ground** ровня́ть *impf*, с~ *pf* с землёй.
razor /'reɪzə(r)/ *n* бри́тва; ~**-blade** ле́звие.
reach /riːtʃ/ *vt* (*attain, extend to, arrive at*) достига́ть *impf*, дости́чь & дости́гнуть *pf* +*gen*, до+*gen*; доходи́ть *impf*, дойти́ *pf* до+*gen*; (*with hand*) дотя́гиваться *impf*, дотяну́ться *pf* до+*gen*; *vi* (*extend*) простира́ться *impf*; *n* досяга́емость; (*pl, of river*) тече́ние.
react /rɪ'ækt/ *vi* реаги́ровать *impf*, от~, про~ *pf* (**to** на+*acc*). **reaction** /-'ækʃən/ *n* реа́кция. **reactionary**

/-'ækʃənərɪ/ *adj* реакцио́нный; *n* реакционе́р. **reactor** /-'æktə(r)/ *n* реа́ктор.

read /ri:d/ *vt* чита́ть *impf*, про~, проче́сть *pf*; (*mus*) разбира́ть *impf*, разобра́ть *pf*; (~ *a meter etc.*) снима́ть *impf*, снять *pf* показа́ния +*gen*; (*univ*) изуча́ть *impf*; (*interpret*) толкова́ть *impf*. **readable** /'ri:dəb(ə)l/ *adj* интере́сный. **reader** /'ri:də(r)/ *n* чита́тель *m*, ~ница; (*book*) хрестома́тия.

readily /'redɪlɪ/ *adv* (*willingly*) охо́тно; (*easily*) легко́. **readiness** /'redɪnɪs/ *n* гото́вность.

reading /'ri:dɪŋ/ *n* чте́ние; (*on meter*) показа́ние.

ready /'redɪ/ *adj* гото́вый (**for** к+*dat*, на+*acc*); **get** ~ гото́виться *impf*; **~-made** гото́вый; ~ **money** нали́чные де́ньги (-нег, -ньга́м) *pl*.

real /rɪəl/ *adj* настоя́щий, реа́льный; ~ **estate** недви́жимость. **realism** /-ˌlɪz(ə)m/ *n* реали́зм. **realist** /'rɪəlɪst/ *n* реали́ст. **realistic** /ˌrɪə'lɪstɪk/ *adj* реалисти́чный, -и́ческий. **reality** /rɪ'ælɪtɪ/ *n* действи́тельность; **in** ~ действи́тельно. **realization** /ˌrɪəlaɪ'zeɪʃ(ə)n/ *n* (*of plan etc.*) осуществле́ние; (*of assets*) реализа́ция; (*understanding*) осозна́ние. **realize** /'rɪəlaɪz/ *vt* (*plan etc.*) осуществля́ть *impf*, осуществи́ть *pf*; (*assets*) реализова́ть *impf* & *pf*; (*apprehend*) осознава́ть *impf*, осозна́ть *pf*. **really** /'rɪəlɪ/ *adv* действи́тельно, в са́мом де́ле.

realm /relm/ *n* (*kingdom*) короле́вство; (*sphere*) о́бласть.

reap /ri:p/ *vt* жать *impf*, сжать *pf*; (*fig*) пожина́ть *impf*, пожа́ть *pf*.

rear[1] /rɪə(r)/ *vt* (*lift*) поднима́ть *impf*, подня́ть *pf*; (*children*) воспи́тывать *impf*, воспита́ть *pf*; *vi* (*of horse*) станови́ться *impf*, стать *pf* на дыбы́.

rear[2] /rɪə(r)/ *n* за́дняя часть; (*mil*) тыл; **bring up the** ~ замыка́ть *impf*, замкну́ть *pf* ше́ствие; *adj* за́дний; (*also mil*) ты́льный. **rearguard** *n* арьерга́рд; ~ **action** арьерга́рдный бой.

rearmament /ri:'ɑ:məmənt/ *n* перевооруже́ние.

rearrange /ˌri:ə'reɪndʒ/ *vt* меня́ть *impf*.

reason /'ri:z(ə)n/ *n* (*cause*) причи́на, основа́ние; (*intellect*) ра́зум, рассу́док; *vi* рассужда́ть *impf*; ~ **with** (*person*) угова́ривать *impf* +*acc*. **reasonable** /-nəb(ə)l/ *adj* разу́мный; (*inexpensive*) недорого́й.

reassurance /ˌri:ə'ʃʊərəns/ *n* успока́ивание. **reassure** /-'ʃʊə(r)/ *vt* успока́ивать *impf*, успоко́ить *pf*.

rebate /'ri:beɪt/ *n* ски́дка.

rebel *n* /'reb(ə)l/ повста́нец; *vi* /rɪ'bel/ восстава́ть *impf*, восста́ть *pf*. **rebellion** /rɪ'beljən/ *n* восста́ние. **rebellious** /rɪ'beljəs/ *adj* мяте́жный.

rebound *vi* /rɪ'baʊnd/ отска́кивать *impf*, отскочи́ть *pf*; *n* /'ri:baʊnd/ рикоше́т.

rebuff /rɪ'bʌf/ *n* отпо́р; *vt* дава́ть *impf*, дать *pf* +*dat* отпо́р.

rebuild /ri:'bɪld/ *vt* перестра́ивать *impf*, перестро́ить *pf*.

rebuke /rɪ'bju:k/ *vt* упрека́ть *impf*, упрекну́ть *pf*; *n* упрёк.

rebuttal /rɪ'bʌtəl/ *n* опроверже́ние.

recalcitrant /rɪ'kælsɪtrənt/ *adj* непоко́рный.

recall *vt* /rɪ'kɔ:l/ (*an official*) отзыва́ть *impf*, отозва́ть *pf*; (*re-

member) вспомина́ть *impf*, вспо́мнить *pf*; *n* /ˈriːkɔːl/ о́тзыв; (*memory*) па́мять.
recant /rɪˈkænt/ *vi* отрека́ться *impf*, отре́чься *pf*.
recapitulate /ˌriːkəˈpɪtjʊˌleɪt/ *vt* резюми́ровать *impf* & *pf*.
recast /riːˈkɑːst/ *vt* переде́лывать *impf*, переде́лать *pf*.
recede /rɪˈsiːd/ *vi* отходи́ть *impf*, отойти́ *pf*.
receipt /rɪˈsiːt/ *n* (*receiving*) получе́ние; *pl* (*amount*) вы́ручка; (*written* ~) квита́нция; (*from till*) чек. **receive** /-ˈsiːv/ *vt* (*admit, entertain*) принима́ть *impf*, приня́ть *pf*; (*get, be given*) получа́ть *impf*, получи́ть *pf*. **receiver** /-ˈsiːvə(r)/ *n* (*radio, television*) приёмник; (*tel*) тру́бка.
recent /ˈriːs(ə)nt/ *adj* неда́вний; (*new*) но́вый. **recently** /-lɪ/ *adv* неда́вно.
receptacle /rɪˈseptək(ə)l/ *n* вмести́лище. **reception** /-ˈsepʃ(ə)n/ *n* приём; ~ **room** приёмная *sb*. **receptionist** /-ˈsepʃənɪst/ *n* секрета́рь *m*, -рша, в приёмной. **receptive** /-ˈseptɪv/ *adj* восприи́мчивый.
recess /rɪˈses/ *n* (*parl*) кани́кулы (-л) *pl*; (*niche*) ни́ша. **recession** /-ˈseʃ(ə)n/ *n* спад.
recipe /ˈresɪpɪ/ *n* реце́пт.
recipient /rɪˈsɪpɪənt/ *n* получа́тель *m*.
reciprocal /rɪˈsɪprək(ə)l/ *adj* взаи́мный. **reciprocate** /-ˌkeɪt/ *vt* отвеча́ть *impf* (взаи́мностью) на+*acc*.
recital /rɪˈsaɪt(ə)l/ *n* (со́льный) конце́рт. **recitation** /ˌresɪˈteɪʃ(ə)n/ *n* публи́чное чте́ние. **recite** /rɪˈsaɪt/ *vt* деклами́ровать *impf*, про~ *pf*; (*list*) перечисля́ть *impf*, перечи́слить *pf*.
reckless /ˈreklɪs/ *adj* (*rash*) опроме́тчивый; (*careless*) неосторо́жный.
reckon /ˈrekən/ *vt* подсчи́тывать *impf*, подсчита́ть *pf*; (*also regard as*) счита́ть *impf*, сче́сть *pf* (**to be** +*instr*); *vi*: ~ **on** рассчи́тывать *impf*, рассчита́ть *pf* на+*acc*; ~ **with** счита́ться *impf* с+*instr*. **reckoning** /ˈrekənɪŋ/ *n* счёт; **day of** ~ час распла́ты.
reclaim /rɪˈkleɪm/ *vt* тре́бовать *impf*, по~ *pf* обра́тно; (*land*) осва́ивать *impf*, осво́ить *pf*.
recline /rɪˈklaɪn/ *vi* полулежа́ть *impf*.
recluse /rɪˈkluːs/ *n* затво́рник.
recognition /ˌrekəgˈnɪʃ(ə)n/ *n* узнава́ние; (*acknowledgement*) призна́ние. **recognize** /ˈrekəgˌnaɪz/ *vt* узнава́ть *impf*, узна́ть *pf*; (*acknowledge*) признава́ть *impf*, призна́ть *pf*.
recoil /ˈriːkɔɪl/ *vi* отпря́дывать *impf*, отпря́нуть *pf*.
recollect /ˌrekəˈlekt/ *vt* вспомина́ть *impf*, вспо́мнить *pf*. **recollection** /-ˈlekʃ(ə)n/ *n* воспомина́ние.
recommend /ˌrekəˈmend/ *vt* рекомендова́ть *impf* & *pf*. **recommendation** /ˌrekəmenˈdeɪʃ(ə)n/ *n* рекоменда́ция.
recompense /ˈrekəmˌpens/ *n* вознагражде́ние; *vt* вознагражда́ть *impf*, вознагради́ть *pf*.
reconcile /ˈrekənˌsaɪl/ *vt* примиря́ть *impf*, примири́ть *pf*; ~ **o.s.** примиря́ться *impf*, примири́ться *pf* (**to** с+*instr*). **reconciliation** /ˌrekənˌsɪlɪˈeɪʃ(ə)n/ *n* примире́ние.
reconnaissance /rɪˈkɒnɪs(ə)ns/ *n* разве́дка. **reconnoitre** /ˌrekəˈnɔɪtə(r)/ *vt* разве́дывать *impf*, разве́дать *pf*.
reconstruct /ˌriːkənˈstrʌkt/ *vt* перестра́ивать *impf*, пере-

стро́ить *pf*. **reconstruction** /-'strʌkʃən/ *n* перестро́йка.

record *vt* /rɪ'kɔːd/ запи́сывать *impf*, записа́ть *pf*; *n* /'rekɔːd/ за́пись; (*minutes*) протоко́л; (*gramophone* ~) грампласти́нка; (*sport etc.*) реко́рд; **off the ~** неофициа́льно; *adj* реко́рдный; **~-breaker, -holder** рекордсме́н, ~ка; **~-player** прои́грыватель *m*. **recorder** /rɪ'kɔːdə(r)/ *n* (*mus*) блок-фле́йта. **recording** /-dɪŋ/ *n* за́пись.

recount[1] /rɪ'kaʊnt/ *vt* (*narrate*) переска́зывать *impf*, пересказа́ть *pf*.

re-count[2] /'riːkaʊnt/ *vt* (*count again*) пересчи́тывать *impf*, пересчита́ть *pf*; *n* пересчёт.

recoup /rɪ'kuːp/ *vt* возвраща́ть *impf*, верну́ть *pf* (**losses** поте́рянное).

recourse /rɪ'kɔːs/ *n*: **have ~ to** прибега́ть *impf*, прибе́гнуть *pf* к+*dat*.

recover /rɪ'kʌvə(r)/ *vt* (*regain possession*) получа́ть *impf*, получи́ть *pf* обра́тно; возвраща́ть *impf*, верну́ть *pf*; *vi* (~ *health*) поправля́ться *impf*, попра́виться *pf* (**from** по́сле +*gen*). **recovery** /-rɪ/ *n* возвраще́ние; выздоровле́ние.

recreate /ˌriːkrɪ'eɪt/ *vt* воссоздава́ть *impf*, воссозда́ть *pf*.

recreation /ˌrekrɪ'eɪʃ(ə)n/ *n* развлече́ние, о́тдых.

recrimination /rɪˌkrɪmɪ'neɪʃ(ə)n/ *n* взаи́мное обвине́ние.

recruit /rɪ'kruːt/ *n* новобра́нец; *vt* вербова́ть *impf*, за~ *pf*. **recruitment** /-mənt/ *n* вербо́вка.

rectangle /'rektæŋg(ə)l/ *n* прямоуго́льник. **rectangular** /rek'tæŋgjʊlə(r)/ *adj* прямоуго́льный.

rectify /'rektɪˌfaɪ/ *vt* исправля́ть *impf*, испра́вить *pf*.

rector /'rektə(r)/ *n* (*priest*) прихо́дский свяще́нник; (*univ*) ре́ктор. **rectory** /-rɪ/ *n* дом прихо́дского свяще́нника.

rectum /'rektəm/ *n* пряма́я кишка́.

recuperate /rɪ'kuːpəˌreɪt/ *vi* поправля́ться *impf*, попра́виться *pf*. **recuperation** /-ˌkuːpə'reɪʃ(ə)n/ *n* выздоровле́ние.

recur /rɪ'kɜː(r)/ *vi* повторя́ться *impf*, повтори́ться *pf*. **recurrence** /-'kʌrəns/ *n* повторе́ние. **recurrent** /-'kʌrənt/ *adj* повторя́ющийся.

recycle /riː'saɪk(ə)l/ *vt* перераба́тывать *impf*, перерабо́тать *pf*.

red /red/ *adj* кра́сный; (*of hair*) ры́жий; *n* кра́сный цвет; (*polit*) кра́сный *sb*; **in the ~** в долгу́; **~-handed** с поли́чным; **~ herring** ло́жный след; **~-hot** раскалённый до́красна́; **R~ Indian** инде́ец, индиа́нка; **~ tape** волоки́та. **redcurrant** *n* кра́сная сморо́дина (*no pl*; *usu collect*). **redden** /'red(ə)n/ *vt* окра́шивать *impf*, окра́сить *pf* в кра́сный цвет; *vi* красне́ть *impf*, по~ *pf*. **reddish** /'redɪʃ/ *adj* краснова́тый; (*hair*) рыжева́тый.

redecorate /riː'dekəˌreɪt/ *vt* отде́лывать *impf*, отде́лать *pf*.

redeem /rɪ'diːm/ *vt* (*buy back*) выкупа́ть *impf*, вы́купить *pf*; (*from sin*) искупа́ть *impf*, искупи́ть *pf*. **redeemer** /-'diːmə(r)/ *n* искупи́тель *m*. **redemption** /-'dempʃ(ə)n/ *n* вы́куп; искупле́ние.

redeploy /ˌriːdɪ'plɔɪ/ *vt* передислоци́ровать *impf & pf*.

redo /riː'duː/ *vt* переде́лывать *impf*, переде́лать *pf*.

redouble /riː'dʌb(ə)l/ *vt* удва́ивать *impf*, удво́ить *pf*.
redress /rɪ'dres/ *vt* исправля́ть *impf*, испра́вить *pf*; ~ **the balance** восстана́вливать *impf*, восстанови́ть *pf* равнове́сие; *n* возмеще́ние.
reduce /rɪ'djuːs/ *vt* (*decrease*) уменьша́ть *impf*, уме́ньшить *pf*; (*lower*) снижа́ть *impf*, сни́зить *pf*; (*shorten*) сокраща́ть *impf*, сократи́ть *pf*; (*bring to*) доводи́ть *impf*, довести́ *pf* (**to** в+*acc*). **reduction** /-'dʌkʃ(ə)n/ *n* уменьше́ние, сниже́ние, сокраще́ние; (*discount*) ски́дка.
redundancy /rɪ'dʌnd(ə)nsɪ/ *n* (*dismissal*) увольне́ние. **redundant** /-d(ə)nt/ *adj* изли́шний; **make** ~ увольня́ть *impf*, уво́лить *pf*.
reed /riːd/ *n* (*plant*) тростни́к; (*in oboe etc.*) язычо́к.
reef /riːf/ *n* риф.
reek /riːk/ *n* вонь; *vi*: ~ **(of)** воня́ть *impf* (+*instr*).
reel[1] /riːl/ *n* кату́шка; *vt*: ~ **off** (*story etc.*) отбараба́нить *pf*.
reel[2] /riːl/ *vi* (*stagger*) поша́тываться *impf*, пошатну́ться *pf*.
refectory /rɪ'fektərɪ/ *n* (*monastery*) тра́пезная *sb*; (*univ*) столо́вая *sb*.
refer /rɪ'fɜː(r)/ *vt* (*direct*) отсыла́ть *impf*, отосла́ть *pf* (**to** к+*dat*); *vi*: ~ **to** (*cite*) ссыла́ться *impf*, сосла́ться *pf* на+*acc*; (*mention*) упомина́ть *impf*, упомяну́ть *pf* +*acc*. **referee** /ˌrefə'riː/ *n* судья́ *m*; *vt* суди́ть *impf*. **reference** /'refərəns/ *n* (*to book etc.*) ссы́лка; (*mention*) упомина́ние; (*testimonial*) характери́стика; ~ **book** спра́вочник. **referendum** /ˌrefə'rendəm/ *n* рефере́ндум.
refine /rɪ'faɪn/ *vt* очища́ть *impf*, очи́стить *pf*. **refined** /-d/ *adj* (*in style etc.*) утончённый; (*in manners*) культу́рный. **refinement** /-mənt/ *n* утончённость. **refinery** /-nərɪ/ *n* (*oil* ~) нефтеочисти́тельный заво́д.
refit /riː'fɪt/ *vt* переоборудовать *impf* & *pf*.
reflect /rɪ'flekt/ *vt* отража́ть *impf*, отрази́ть *pf*; *vi* размышля́ть *impf*, размы́слить *pf* (**on** о+*prep*). **reflection** /-'flekʃ(ə)n/ *n* отраже́ние; размышле́ние; **on** ~ поду́мав. **reflective** /-'flektɪv/ *adj* (*thoughtful*) серьёзный. **reflector** /-'flektə(r)/ *n* рефле́ктор. **reflex** /'riːfleks/ *n* рефле́кс; *adj* рефле́кторный. **reflexive** /rɪ'fleksɪv/ *adj* (*gram*) возвра́тный.
reform /rɪ'fɔːm/ *vt* реформи́ровать *impf* & *pf*; *vt* & *i* (*of people*) исправля́ть(ся) *impf*, испра́вить(ся) *pf*; *n* рефо́рма; исправле́ние. **Reformation** /ˌrefə'meɪʃ(ə)n/ *n* Реформа́ция.
refract /rɪ'frækt/ *vt* преломля́ть *impf*, преломи́ть *pf*.
refrain[1] /rɪ'freɪn/ *n* припе́в.
refrain[2] /rɪ'freɪn/ *vi* возде́рживаться *impf*, воздержа́ться *pf* (**from** от+*gen*).
refresh /rɪ'freʃ/ *vt* освежа́ть *impf*, освежи́ть *pf*. **refreshments** /-mənts/ *n pl* напи́тки *m pl*.
refrigerate /rɪ'frɪdʒəˌreɪt/ *vt* охлажда́ть *impf*, охлади́ть *pf*. **refrigeration** /-'reɪʃ(ə)n/ *n* охлажде́ние. **refrigerator** /rɪ'frɪdʒəˌreɪtə(r)/ *n* холоди́льник.
refuge /'refjuːdʒ/ *n* убе́жище; **take** ~ находи́ть *impf*, найти́ *pf* убе́жище. **refugee** /ˌrefjʊ'dʒiː/ *n* бе́женец, -нка.
refund *vt* /rɪ'fʌnd/ возвраща́ть

impf, возврати́ть *pf*; (*expenses*) возмеща́ть *impf*, возмести́ть *pf*; *n* /'ri:fʌnd/ возвраще́ние (де́нег); возмеще́ние.

refusal /rɪ'fju:z(ə)l/ *n* отка́з. **refuse**[1] /rɪ'fju:z/ *vt* (*decline to accept*) отка́зываться *impf*, отказа́ться *pf* от+*gen*; (*decline to do sth*) отка́зываться *impf*, отказа́ться *pf* +*inf*; (*deny s.o. sth*) отка́зывать *impf*, отказа́ть *pf* +*dat*+в+*prep*.

refuse[2] /'refju:s/ *n* му́сор.

refute /rɪ'fju:t/ *vt* опроверга́ть *impf*, опрове́ргнуть *pf*.

regain /rɪ'geɪn/ *vt* возвраща́ть *impf*, верну́ть *pf*.

regal /'ri:g(ə)l/ *adj* короле́вский.

regalia /rɪ'geɪlɪə/ *n pl* рега́лии *f pl*.

regard /rɪ'gɑ:d/ *vt* смотре́ть *impf*, по~ *pf* на+*acc*; (*take into account*) счита́ться *impf* с+*instr*; ~ **as** счита́ть *impf* +*instr*, за+*instr*; **as ~s** что каса́ется+*gen*; *n* (*esteem*) уваже́ние; *pl* приве́т. **regarding** /-dɪŋ/ *prep* относи́тельно +*gen*. **regardless** /-lɪs/ *adv* не обраща́я внима́ния; ~ **of** не счита́ясь с+*instr*.

regatta /rɪ'gætə/ *n* рега́та.

regenerate /rɪ'dʒenə,reɪt/ *vt* перерожда́ть *impf*, переро-ди́ть *pf*.

regent /'ri:dʒ(ə)nt/ *n* ре́гент.

régime /reɪ'ʒi:m/ *n* режи́м.

regiment /'redʒɪmənt/ *n* полк. **regimental** /-'ment(ə)l/ *adj* полково́й. **regimentation** /,redʒɪmən'teɪʃ(ə)n/ *n* регламента́ция.

region /'ri:dʒ(ə)n/ *n* регио́н. **regional** /-nəl/ *adj* региона́льный.

register /'redʒɪstə(r)/ *n* рее́стр; (*also mus*) реги́стр; *vt* регистри́ровать *impf*, за~ *pf*; (*a letter*) отправля́ть *impf*, отпра́вить *pf* заказны́м. **registered** /-təd/ *adj* (*letter*) заказно́й. **registrar** /,redʒɪs'trɑ:(r)/ *n* регистра́тор. **registration** /,redʒɪ'streɪʃ(ə)n/ *n* регистра́ция; ~ **number** но́мер маши́ны. **registry** /'redʒɪstrɪ/ *n* регистрату́ра; ~ **office** загс.

regret /rɪ'gret/ *vt* сожале́ть *impf* о+*prep*; *n* сожале́ние. **regretful** /-fʊl/ *adj* по́лный сожале́ния. **regrettable** /-'gretəb(ə)l/ *adj* приско́рбный. **regrettably** /-'gretəblɪ/ *adv* к сожале́нию.

regular /'regjʊlə(r)/ *adj* регуля́рный; (*also gram*) пра́вильный; *n* (*coll*) завсегда́тай. **regularity** /,regjʊ'lærɪtɪ/ *n* регуля́рность. **regulate** /'regjʊ,leɪt/ *vt* регули́ровать *impf*, у~ *pf*. **regulation** /,regjʊ'leɪʃ(ə)n/ *n* регули́рование; *pl* пра́вила *neut pl*.

rehabilitate /,ri:hə'bɪlɪ,teɪt/ *vt* реабилити́ровать *impf* & *pf*. **rehabilitation** /-,bɪlɪ'teɪʃ(ə)n/ *n* реабилита́ция.

rehearsal /rɪ'hɜ:s(ə)l/ *n* репети́ция. **rehearse** /-'hɜ:s/ *vt* репети́ровать *impf*, от~ *pf*.

reign /reɪn/ *n* ца́рствование; *vi* ца́рствовать *impf*; (*fig*) цари́ть *impf*.

reimburse /,ri:ɪm'bɜ:s/ *vt* возмеща́ть *impf*, возмести́ть *pf* (+*dat of person*). **reimbursement** /-mənt/ *n* возмеще́ние.

rein /reɪn/ *n* по́вод.

reincarnation /,ri:ɪnkɑ:'neɪʃ(ə)n/ *n* перевоплоще́ние.

reindeer /'reɪndɪə(r)/ *n* се́верный оле́нь *m*.

reinforce /,ri:ɪn'fɔ:s/ *vt* подкрепля́ть *impf*, подкрепи́ть *pf*. **reinforcement** /-mənt/ *n* (*also pl*) подкрепле́ние.

reinstate /,ri:ɪn'steɪt/ *vt* восстанáвливать *impf*, восстановúть *pf*. **reinstatement** /-mənt/ *n* восстановлéние.

reiterate /ri:'ɪtə,reɪt/ *vt* повторя́ть *impf*, повторúть *pf*.

reject *vt* /rɪ'dʒekt/ отвергáть *impf*, отвéргнуть *pf*; (*as defective*) браковáть *impf*, за~ *pf*; *n* /'ri:dʒekt/ брак. **rejection** /-'dʒekʃ(ə)n/ *n* откáз (**of** от+*gen*).

rejoice /rɪ'dʒɔɪs/ *vi* рáдоваться *impf*, об~ *pf* (**in, at** +*dat*). **rejoicing** /-sɪŋ/ *n* рáдость.

rejoin /ri:'dʒɔɪn/ *vt* (вновь) присоединя́ться *impf*, присоединúться *pf* к+*dat*.

rejuvenate /rɪ'dʒu:vɪ,neɪt/ *vt* омолáживать *impf*, омолодúть *pf*.

relapse /rɪ'læps/ *n* рецидúв; *vi* снóва впадáть *impf*, впасть *pf* (**into** в+*acc*); (*into illness*) снóва заболевáть *impf*, заболéть *pf*.

relate /rɪ'leɪt/ *vt* (*tell*) рассказывать *impf*, рассказáть *pf*; (*connect*) свя́зывать *impf*, связáть *pf*; *vi* относúться *impf* (**to** к+*dat*). **related** /-tɪd/ *adj* рóдственный. **relation** /-'leɪʃ(ə)n/ *n* отношéние; (*person*) рóдственник, -ица. **relationship** *n* (*connection*; *liaison*) связь; (*kinship*) родствó. **relative** /'relətɪv/ *adj* относúтельный; *n* рóдственник, -ица. **relativity** /,relə'tɪvɪtɪ/ *n* относúтельность.

relax /rɪ'læks/ *vt* ослабля́ть *impf*, ослáбить *pf*; *vi* (*rest*) расслабля́ться *impf*, расслáбиться *pf*. **relaxation** /,ri:læk'seɪʃ(ə)n/ *n* ослаблéние; (*rest*) óтдых.

relay /'ri:leɪ/ *n* (*shift*) смéна; (*sport*) эстафéта; (*electr*) релé *neut indecl*; *vt* передавáть *impf*, передáть *pf*.

release /rɪ'li:s/ *vt* (*set free*) освобождáть *impf*, освободúть *pf*; (*unfasten, let go*) отпускáть *impf*, отпустúть *pf*; (*film etc.*) выпускáть *impf*, вы́пустить *pf*; *n* освобождéние; вы́пуск.

relegate /'relɪ,geɪt/ *vt* переводúть *impf*, перевестú *pf* (в нúзшую грýппу). **relegation** /-'geɪʃ(ə)n/ *n* перевóд (в нúзшую грýппу).

relent /rɪ'lent/ *vi* смягчáться *impf*, смягчúться *pf*. **relentless** /-lɪs/ *adj* непрестáнный.

relevance /'relɪv(ə)ns/ *n* умéстность. **relevant** /-v(ə)nt/ *adj* относя́щийся к дéлу; умéстный.

reliability /rɪ,laɪə'bɪlɪtɪ/ *n* надёжность. **reliable** /-'laɪəb(ə)l/ *adj* надёжный. **reliance** /-'laɪəns/ *n* довéрие. **reliant** /-'laɪənt/ *adj*: **be ~ upon** завúсеть *impf* от+*gen*.

relic /'relɪk/ *n* остáток, реликвия.

relief[1] /rɪ'li:f/ *n* (*art, geol*) рельéф.

relief[2] /rɪ'li:f/ *n* (*alleviation*) облегчéние; (*assistance*) пóмощь; (*in duty*) смéна. **relieve** /-'li:v/ *vt* (*alleviate*) облегчáть *impf*, облегчúть *pf*; (*replace*) сменя́ть *impf*, сменúть *pf*; (*unburden*) освобождáть *impf*, освободúть *pf* (**of** от+*gen*).

religion /rɪ'lɪdʒ(ə)n/ *n* релúгия. **religious** /-'lɪdʒəs/ *adj* религиóзный.

relinquish /rɪ'lɪŋkwɪʃ/ *vt* оставля́ть *impf*, остáвить *pf*; (*right etc.*) откáзываться *impf*, отказáться *pf* от+*gen*.

relish /'relɪʃ/ *n* (*enjoyment*) смак; (*cul*) припрáва; *vt* смаковáть *impf*.

relocate /,ri:ləʊ'keɪt/ *vt & i* перемещáть(ся) *impf*, переместúть(ся) *pf*.

reluctance /rɪ'lʌkt(ə)ns/ *n* неохóта. **reluctant** /-t(ə)nt/ *adj* неохóтный; **be ~ to** не желáть *impf* +*inf*.

rely /rɪ'laɪ/ *vi* полагáться *impf*, положúться *pf* (**on** на+*acc*).

remain /rɪ'meɪn/ *vi* оставáться *impf*, остáться *pf*. **remainder** /-'meɪndə(r)/ *n* остáток. **remains** /-'meɪnz/ *n pl* остáтки *m pl*; (*human* ~) остáнки (-ков) *pl*.

remand /rɪ'mɑːnd/ *vt* содержáть *impf* под стрáжей; **be on ~** содержáться *impf* под стрáжей.

remark /rɪ'mɑːk/ *vt* замечáть *impf*, замéтить *pf*; *n* замечáние. **remarkable** /-'mɑːkəb(ə)l/ *adj* замечáтельный.

remarry /riː'mærɪ/ *vi* вступáть *impf*, вступúть *pf* в нóвый брак.

remedial /rɪ'miːdɪəl/ *adj* лечéбный. **remedy** /'remɪdɪ/ *n* срéдство (**for** от, прóтив+*gen*); *vt* исправлять *impf*, испрáвить *pf*.

remember /rɪ'membə(r)/ *vt* пóмнить *impf*, вспоминáть *impf*, вспóмнить *pf*; (*greet*) передавáть *impf*, передáть *pf* привéт от+*gen* (**to** +*dat*). **remembrance** /-'membrəns/ *n* пáмять.

remind /rɪ'maɪnd/ *vt* напоминáть *impf*, напóмнить *pf* +*dat* (**of** +*acc*, о+*prep*). **reminder** /-də(r)/ *n* напоминáние.

reminiscence /,remɪ'nɪs(ə)ns/ *n* воспоминáние. **reminiscent** /-'nɪs(ə)nt/ *adj* напоминáющий.

remiss /rɪ'mɪs/ *predic* небрéжный. **remission** /-'mɪʃ(ə)n/ *n* (*pardon*) отпущéние; (*med*) ремúссия. **remit** /'riːmɪt/ *vt* пересылáть *impf*, переслáть *pf*. **remittance** /rɪ'mɪt(ə)ns/ *n* перевóд дéнег; (*money*) дéнежный перевóд.

remnant /'remnənt/ *n* остáток.

remonstrate /'remən,streɪt/ *vi*: ~ **with** увещевáть *impf* +*acc*.

remorse /rɪ'mɔːs/ *n* угрызéния *neut pl* сóвести. **remorseful** /-fʊl/ *adj* пóлный раскáяния. **remorseless** /-lɪs/ *adj* безжáлостный.

remote /rɪ'məʊt/ *adj* отдалённый; ~ **control** дистанциóнное управлéние.

removal /rɪ'muːv(ə)l/ *n* (*taking away*) удалéние; (*of obstacles*) устранéние. **remove** /-'muːv/ *vt* (*take away*) убирáть *impf*, убрáть *pf*; (*get rid of*) устранять *impf*, устранúть *pf*.

remuneration /rɪ,mjuːnə'reɪʃ(ə)n/ *n* вознаграждéние. **remunerative** /-'mjuːnərətɪv/ *adj* вы́годный.

renaissance /rɪ'neɪs(ə)ns/ *n* возрождéние; **the R~** Возрождéние.

render /'rendə(r)/ *vt* воздавáть *impf*, воздáть *pf*; (*help etc.*) окáзывать *impf*, оказáть *pf*; (*role etc.*) исполнять *impf*, испóлнить *pf*; (*stone*) штукатýрить *impf*, о~, от~ *pf*. **rendering** /-rɪŋ/ *n* исполнéние.

rendezvous /'rɒndɪ,vuː/ *n* (*meeting*) свидáние.

renegade /'renɪ,geɪd/ *n* ренегáт, ~ка.

renew /rɪ'njuː/ *vt* (*extend*; *continue*) возобновлять *impf*, возобновúть *pf*; (*replace*) обновлять *impf*, обновúть *pf*. **renewal** /-'njuːəl/ *n* (воз)обновлéние.

renounce /rɪ'naʊns/ *vt* отвергáть *impf*, отвéргнуть *pf*; (*claim*) откáзываться *impf*, отказáться *pf* от+*gen*.

renovate /ˈrenəˌveɪt/ *vt* ремонти́ровать *impf*, от~ *pf*. **renovation** /-ˈveɪʃ(ə)n/ *n* ремо́нт.

renown /rɪˈnaʊn/ *n* сла́ва. **renowned** /-ˈnaʊnd/ *adj* изве́стный; **be ~ for** сла́виться *impf* +*instr*.

rent /rent/ *n* (*for home*) квартпла́та; (*for premises*) (аре́ндная) пла́та; *vt* (*of tenant*) арендова́ть *impf* & *pf*; (*of owner*) сдава́ть *impf*, сдать *pf*.

renunciation /rɪˌnʌnsɪˈeɪʃ(ə)n/ *n* (*repudiation*) отрица́ние; (*of claim*) отка́з.

rep /rep/ *n* (*comm*) аге́нт.

repair /rɪˈpeə(r)/ *vt* ремонти́ровать *impf*, от~ *pf*; *n* (*also pl*) ремо́нт (*only sg*); почи́нка; **in good/bad ~** в хоро́шем/плохо́м состоя́нии.

reparations /ˌrepəˈreɪʃ(ə)nz/ *n pl* репара́ции *f pl*.

repatriate /riːˈpætrɪˌeɪt/ *vt* репатрии́ровать *impf* & *pf*. **repatriation** /-ˌpætrɪˈeɪʃ(ə)n/ *n* репатриа́ция.

repay /riːˈpeɪ/ *vt* отпла́чивать *impf*, отплати́ть *pf* (*person* +*dat*). **repayment** /-mənt/ *n* отпла́та.

repeal /rɪˈpiːl/ *vt* отменя́ть *impf*, отмени́ть *pf*; *n* отме́на.

repeat /rɪˈpiːt/ *vt* & *i* повторя́ть(ся) *impf*, повтори́ть(ся) *pf*; *n* повторе́ние. **repeatedly** /-tɪdlɪ/ *adv* неоднокра́тно.

repel /rɪˈpel/ *vt* отта́лкивать *impf*, оттолкну́ть *pf*; (*enemy*) отража́ть *impf*, отрази́ть *pf*.

repent /rɪˈpent/ *vi* раска́иваться *impf*, раска́яться *pf*. **repentance** /-ˈpent(ə)ns/ *n* раска́яние. **repentant** /-ˈpent(ə)nt/ *adj* раска́ивающийся.

repercussion /ˌriːpəˈkʌʃ(ə)n/ *n* после́дствие.

repertoire /ˈrepəˌtwɑː(r)/ *n* репертуа́р. **repertory** /ˈrepətərɪ/ *n* (*store*) запа́с; (*repertoire*) репертуа́р; **~ company** постоя́нная тру́ппа.

repetition /ˌrepɪˈtɪʃ(ə)n/ *n* повторе́ние. **repetitious, repetitive** /ˌrepɪˈtɪʃəs, rɪˈpetɪtɪv/ *adj* повторя́ющийся.

replace /rɪˈpleɪs/ *vt* (*put back*) класть *impf*, положи́ть *pf* обра́тно; (*substitute*) заменя́ть *impf*, замени́ть *pf* (**by** +*instr*). **replacement** /-mənt/ *n* заме́на.

replay /ˈriːpleɪ/ *n* переигро́вка.

replenish /rɪˈplenɪʃ/ *vt* пополня́ть *impf*, попо́лнить *pf*.

replete /rɪˈpliːt/ *adj* насы́щенный; (*sated*) сы́тый.

replica /ˈreplɪkə/ *n* ко́пия.

reply /rɪˈplaɪ/ *vt* & *i* отвеча́ть *impf*, отве́тить *pf* (**to** на+*acc*); *n* отве́т.

report /rɪˈpɔːt/ *vt* сообща́ть *impf*, сообщи́ть *pf*; *vi* докла́дывать *impf*, доложи́ть *pf*; (*present o.s.*) явля́ться *impf*, яви́ться *pf*; *n* сообще́ние; докла́д; (*school*) та́бель *m*; (*sound*) звук взры́ва, вы́стрела. **reporter** /-tə(r)/ *n* корреспонде́нт.

repose /rɪˈpəʊz/ *n* (*rest*) о́тдых; (*peace*) поко́й.

repository /rɪˈpɒzɪtərɪ/ *n* храни́лище.

repossess /ˌriːpəˈzes/ *vt* изыма́ть *impf*, изъя́ть *pf* за неплатёж.

reprehensible /ˌreprɪˈhensɪb(ə)l/ *adj* предосуди́тельный.

represent /ˌreprɪˈzent/ *vt* представля́ть *impf*; (*portray*) изобража́ть *impf*, изобрази́ть *pf*. **representation** /-zenˈteɪʃ(ə)n/ *n* (*being represented*) представи́тельство; (*statement of case*) представле́ние; (*portrayal*) изображе́ние. **representative** /'zentətɪv/ *adj* изобража́ющий (**of** +*acc*); (*typical*) типи́чный; *n* представи́тель *m.*

repress /rɪ'pres/ *vt* подавля́ть *impf*, подави́ть *pf.* **repression** /-'preʃ(ə)n/ *n* подавле́ние, репре́ссия. **repressive** /-'presɪv/ *adj* репресси́вный.

reprieve /rɪ'pri:v/ *vt* отсро́чивать *impf*, отсро́чить *pf* +*dat* приведе́ние в исполне́ние (сме́ртного) пригово́ра; *n* отсро́чка приведе́ния в исполне́ние (сме́ртного) пригово́ра; (*fig*) переды́шка.

reprimand /'reprɪ,mɑ:nd/ *n* вы́говор; *vt* де́лать *impf*, с~ *pf* вы́говор +*dat.*

reprint *vt* /ri:'prɪnt/ переиздава́ть *impf*, переизда́ть *pf*; *n* /'ri:prɪnt/ переизда́ние.

reprisal /rɪ'praɪz(ə)l/ *n* отве́тная ме́ра.

reproach /rɪ'prəʊtʃ/ *vt* упрека́ть *impf*, упрекну́ть *pf* (**with** в+*prep*). **reproachful** /-fʊl/ *adj* укори́зненный.

reproduce /,ri:prə'dju:s/ *vt* воспроизводи́ть *impf*, воспроизвести́ *pf*; *vi* размножа́ться *impf*, размно́житься *pf.* **reproduction** /-'dʌkʃ(ə)n/ *n* (*action*) воспроизведе́ние; (*object*) репроду́кция; (*of offspring*) размноже́ние. **reproductive** /-'dʌktɪv/ *adj* воспроизводи́тельный.

reproof /rɪ'pru:f/ *n* вы́говор. **reprove** /-'pru:v/ *vt* де́лать *impf* с~ *pf* вы́говор +*dat.*

reptile /'reptaɪl/ *n* пресмыка́ющееся *sb.*

republic /rɪ'pʌblɪk/ *n* респу́блика. **republican** /-kən/ *adj* республика́нский; *n* республика́нец, -нка.

repudiate /rɪ'pju:dɪ,eɪt/ *vt* (*renounce*) отка́зываться *impf*, отказа́ться *pf* от+*gen*; (*reject*) отверга́ть *impf*, отве́ргнуть *pf.* **repudiation** /-,pju:dɪ'eɪʃ(ə)n/ *n* отка́з (**of** от+*gen*).

repugnance /rɪ'pʌgnəns/ *n* отвраще́ние. **repugnant** /-nənt/ *adj* проти́вный.

repulse /rɪ'pʌls/ *vt* отража́ть *impf*, отрази́ть *pf.* **repulsion** /-'pʌlʃ(ə)n/ *n* отвраще́ние. **repulsive** /-'pʌlsɪv/ *adj* отврати́тельный.

reputable /'repjʊtəb(ə)l/ *adj* по́льзующийся хоро́шей репута́цией. **reputation, repute** /,repjʊ'teɪʃ(ə)n, rɪ'pju:t/ *n* репута́ция. **reputed** /-'pju:tɪd/ *adj* предполага́емый. **reputedly** /-'pju:tɪdlɪ/ *adv* по о́бщему мне́нию.

request /rɪ'kwest/ *n* про́сьба; **by, on,** ~ по про́сьбе; *vt* проси́ть *impf*, по~ *pf* +*acc*, +*gen* (*person* +*acc*).

requiem /'rekwɪ,em/ *n* ре́квием.

require /rɪ'kwaɪə(r)/ *vt* (*demand*; *need*) тре́бовать *impf*, по~ *pf* +*gen*; (*need*) нужда́ться *impf* в+*prep.* **requirement** /-mənt/ *n* тре́бование; (*necessity*) потре́бность. **requisite** /'rekwɪzɪt/ *adj* необходи́мый; *n* необходи́мая вещь. **requisition** /,rekwɪ'zɪʃ(ə)n/ *n* реквизи́ция; *vt* реквизи́ровать *impf* & *pf.*

resale /ri:'seɪl/ *n* перепрода́жа.

rescind /rɪ'sɪnd/ *vt* отменя́ть *impf*, отмени́ть *pf.*

rescue /'reskju:/ *vt* спаса́ть *impf*, спасти́ *pf*; *n* спасе́ние. **rescuer** /'reskju:ə(r)/ *n* спаси́тель *m.*

research /rɪ'sɜ:tʃ/ *n* иссле́дование (+*gen*); (*occupation*) иссле́довательская рабо́та; *vi*: ~ **into** иссле́довать *impf* & *pf*

+*acc.* **researcher** /-tʃə(r)/ *n* исследователь *m.*

resemblance /rɪ'zembləns/ *n* схо́дство. **resemble** /-'zemb(ə)l/ *vt* походи́ть *impf* на+*acc.*

resent /rɪ'zent/ *vt* возмуща́ться *impf*, возмути́ться *pf.* **resentful** /-fʊl/ *adj* возмущённый. **resentment** /-mənt/ *n* возмуще́ние.

reservation /ˌrezə'veɪʃ(ə)n/ *n* (*doubt*) огово́рка; (*booking*) предвари́тельный зака́з; (*land*) резерва́ция. **reserve** /rɪ'zɜ:v/ *vt* (*keep*) резерви́ровать *impf* & *pf*; (*book*) зака́зывать *impf*, заказа́ть *pf*; *n* (*stock*; *mil*) запа́с, резе́рв; (*sport*) запасно́й игро́к; (*nature* ~ *etc.*) запове́дник; (*proviso*) огово́рка; (*self-restraint*) сде́ржанность; *attrib* запасно́й. **reserved** /-'zɜ:vd/ *adj* (*person*) сде́ржанный. **reservist** /-'zɜ:vɪst/ *n* резерви́ст. **reservoir** /'rezəˌvwɑ:(r)/ *n* (*for water*) водохрани́лище; (*for other fluids*) резервуа́р.

resettle /ri:'set(ə)l/ *vt* переселя́ть *impf*, пересели́ть *pf.* **resettlement** /-mənt/ *n* переселе́ние.

reshape /ri:'ʃeɪp/ *vt* видоизменя́ть *impf*, видоизмени́ть *pf.*

reshuffle /ri:'ʃʌf(ə)l/ *n* перестано́вка.

reside /rɪ'zaɪd/ *vi* прожива́ть *impf.* **residence** /'rezɪd(ə)ns/ *n* (*residing*) прожива́ние; (*abode*) местожи́тельство; (*official* ~ *etc.*) резиде́нция. **resident** /'rezɪd(ə)nt/ *n* (постоя́нный) жи́тель *m*, ~ница; *adj* прожива́ющий; (*population*) постоя́нный. **residential** /ˌrezɪ'denʃ(ə)l/ *adj* жило́й.

residual /rɪ'zɪdjʊəl/ *adj* оста́точный. **residue** /'rezɪˌdju:/ *n* оста́ток.

resign /rɪ'zaɪn/ *vt* отка́зываться *impf*, отказа́ться *pf* от+*gen*; *vi* уходи́ть *impf*, уйти́ *pf* в отста́вку; ~ **o.s. to** покоря́ться *impf*, покори́ться *pf* +*dat.* **resignation** /ˌrezɪg'neɪʃ(ə)n/ *n* отста́вка, заявле́ние об отста́вке; (*being resigned*) поко́рность. **resigned** /rɪ'zaɪnd/ *adj* поко́рный.

resilient /rɪ'zɪlɪənt/ *adj* выно́сливый.

resin /'rezɪn/ *n* смола́.

resist /rɪ'zɪst/ *vt* сопротивля́ться *impf* +*dat*; (*temptation*) устоя́ть *pf* пе́ред+*instr.* **resistance** /-'zɪst(ə)ns/ *n* сопротивле́ние. **resistant** /-'zɪst(ə)nt/ *adj* сто́йкий.

resolute /'rezəˌlu:t/ *adj* реши́тельный. **resolution** /ˌrezə'lu:ʃ(ə)n/ *n* (*character*) реши́тельность; (*vow*) заро́к; (*at meeting etc.*) резолю́ция; (*of problem*) разреше́ние. **resolve** /rɪ'zɒlv/ *vt* (*decide*) реша́ть *impf*, реши́ть *pf*; (*settle*) разреша́ть *impf*, разреши́ть *pf*; *n* реши́тельность; (*decision*) реше́ние.

resonance /'rezənəns/ *n* резона́нс. **resonant** /'rezənənt/ *adj* зву́чный.

resort /rɪ'zɔ:t/ *vi*: ~ **to** прибега́ть *impf*, прибе́гнуть *pf* к+*dat*; *n* (*place*) куро́рт; **in the last** ~ в кра́йнем слу́чае.

resound /rɪ'zaʊnd/ *vi* (*of sound etc.*) раздава́ться *impf*, разда́ться *pf*; (*of place*) оглаша́ться *impf*, огласи́ться *pf* (**with** +*instr*).

resource /rɪ'sɔ:s/ *n* (*usu pl*) ресу́рс. **resourceful** /-fʊl/ *adj* нахо́дчивый.

respect /rɪ'spekt/ *n* (*relation*) отноше́ние; (*esteem*) уваже́ние; **with ~ to** что каса́ется+*gen*; *vt* уважа́ть *impf*. **respectability** /-ˌspektəˈbɪlɪtɪ/ *n* респекта́бельность. **respectable** /-ˈspektəb(ə)l/ *adj* прили́чный. **respectful** /-ˈspektfʊl/ *adj* почти́тельный. **respective** /-ˈspektɪv/ *adj* свой. **respectively** /-ˈspektɪvlɪ/ *adv* соотве́тственно.

respiration /ˌrespɪˈreɪʃ(ə)n/ *n* дыха́ние. **respirator** /ˈrespɪˌreɪtə(r)/ *n* респира́тор. **respiratory** /rɪˈspɪrətərɪ/ *adj* дыха́тельный.

respite /ˈrespaɪt/ *n* переды́шка.

resplendent /rɪˈsplend(ə)nt/ *adj* блиста́тельный.

respond /rɪˈspɒnd/ *vi*: **~ to** отвеча́ть *impf*, отве́тить *pf* на+*acc*; (*react*) реаги́ровать *impf*, про~, от~ *pf* на+*acc*. **response** /-ˈspɒns/ *n* отве́т; (*reaction*) о́тклик. **responsibility** /-ˌspɒnsɪˈbɪlɪtɪ/ *n* отве́тственность; (*duty*) обя́занность. **responsible** /-ˈspɒnsɪb(ə)l/ *adj* отве́тственный (**to** пе́ред +*instr*; **for** за+*acc*); (*reliable*) надёжный. **responsive** /-ˈspɒnsɪv/ *adj* отзы́вчивый.

rest[1] /rest/ *vi* отдыха́ть *impf*, отдохну́ть *pf*; *vt* (*place*) класть *impf*, положи́ть *pf*; (*allow to* ~) дава́ть *impf*, дать *pf* о́тдых+*dat*; *n* (*repose*) о́тдых; (*peace*) поко́й; (*mus*) па́уза; (*support*) опо́ра.

rest[2] /rest/ *n* (*remainder*) оста́ток; (*the others*) остальны́е *sb pl*.

restaurant /ˈrestəˌrɒnt/ *n* рестора́н.

restful /ˈrestfʊl/ *adj* успока́ивающий.

restitution /ˌrestɪˈtjuːʃ(ə)n/ *n* возвраще́ние.

restive /ˈrestɪv/ *adj* беспоко́йный.

restless /ˈrestlɪs/ *adj* беспоко́йный.

restoration /ˌrestəˈreɪʃ(ə)n/ *n* реставра́ция; (*return*) восстановле́ние. **restore** /rɪˈstɔː(r)/ *vt* реставри́ровать *impf* & *pf*; (*return*) восстана́вливать *impf*, восстанови́ть *pf*.

restrain /rɪˈstreɪn/ *vt* уде́рживать *impf*, удержа́ть *pf* (**from** от+*gen*). **restraint** /-ˈstreɪnt/ *n* сде́ржанность.

restrict /rɪˈstrɪkt/ *vt* ограни́чивать *impf*, ограни́чить *pf*. **restriction** /-ˈstrɪkʃ(ə)n/ *n* ограниче́ние. **restrictive** /-ˈstrɪktɪv/ *adj* ограничи́тельный.

result /rɪˈzʌlt/ *vi* сле́довать *impf*; происходи́ть *impf* (**from** из+*gen*); **~ in** конча́ться *impf*, ко́нчиться *pf* +*instr*; *n* результа́т; **as a ~** в результа́те (**of** +*gen*).

resume /rɪˈzjuːm/ *vt* & *i* возобновля́ть(ся) *impf*, возобнови́ть(ся) *pf*. **résumé** /ˈrezjʊˌmeɪ/ *n* резюме́ *neut indecl*. **resumption** /rɪˈzʌmpʃ(ə)n/ *n* возобновле́ние.

resurrect /ˌrezəˈrekt/ *vt* (*fig*) воскреша́ть *impf*, воскреси́ть *pf*. **resurrection** /-ˈrekʃ(ə)n/ *n* (*of the dead*) воскресе́ние; (*fig*) воскреше́ние.

resuscitate /rɪˈsʌsɪˌteɪt/ *vt* приводи́ть *impf*, привести́ *pf* в созна́ние.

retail /ˈriːteɪl/ *n* ро́зничная прода́жа; *attrib* ро́зничный; *adv* в ро́зницу; *vt* продава́ть *impf*, прода́ть *pf* в ро́зницу; *vi* продава́ться *impf* в ро́зницу. **retailer** /-lə(r)/ *n* ро́зничный торго́вец.

retain /rɪˈteɪn/ *vt* удéрживать *impf*, удержáть *pf*. **retaliate** /rɪˈtælɪˌeɪt/ *vi* отплáчивать *impf*, отплатить *pf* тем же. **retaliation** /-ˌtælɪˈeɪʃ(ə)n/ *n* отплáта, возмéздие. **retard** /rɪˈtɑːd/ *vt* замедлять *impf*, замéдлить *pf*. **retarded** /-dɪd/ *adj* отстáлый. **retention** /rɪˈtenʃ(ə)n/ *n* удержáние. **retentive** /-ˈtentɪv/ *adj* (*memory*) хорóший. **reticence** /ˈretɪs(ə)ns/ *n* сдéржанность. **reticent** /-s(ə)nt/ *adj* сдéржанный. **retina** /ˈretɪnə/ *n* сетчáтка. **retinue** /ˈretɪˌnjuː/ *n* свúта. **retire** /rɪˈtaɪə(r)/ *vi* (*withdraw*) удаляться *impf*, удалúться *pf*; (*from office etc.*) уходúть *impf*, уйтú *pf* в отстáвку. **retired** /-ˈtaɪəd/ *adj* в отстáвке. **retirement** /-ˈtaɪəmənt/ *n* отстáвка. **retiring** /-ˈtaɪrɪŋ/ *adj* скрóмный. **retort**[1] /rɪˈtɔːt/ *vt* отвечáть *impf*, отвéтить *pf* рéзко; *n* возражéние. **retort**[2] /rɪˈtɔːt/ *n* (*vessel*) ретóрта. **retrace** /rɪˈtreɪs/ *vt*: ~ **one's steps** возвращáться *impf*, возвратúться *pf*. **retract** /rɪˈtrækt/ *vt* (*draw in*) втягивать *impf*, втянýть *pf*; (*take back*) брать *impf*, взять *pf* назáд. **retreat** /rɪˈtriːt/ *vi* отступáть *impf*, отступúть *pf*; *n* отступлéние; (*withdrawal*) уединéние; (*place*) убéжище. **retrenchment** /rɪˈtrentʃmənt/ *n* сокращéние расхóдов. **retrial** /ˈriːtraɪəl/ *n* повтóрное слýшание дéла. **retribution** /ˌretrɪˈbjuːʃ(ə)n/ *n* возмéздие. **retrieval** /rɪˈtriːv(ə)l/ *n* возвращéние; (*comput*) пóиск (информáции); *vt* брать *impf*, взять *pf* обрáтно. **retrograde** /ˈretrəˌgreɪd/ *adj* (*fig*) реакциóнный. **retrospect** /ˈretrəˌspekt/ *n*: **in** ~ ретроспектúвно. **retrospective** /-ˈspektɪv/ *adj* (*law*) имéющий обрáтную сúлу.

return /rɪˈtɜːn/ *vt* & *i* (*give back*; *come back*) возвращáть(ся) *impf*, возвратúть(ся) *impf*, вернýть(ся) *pf*; *vt* (*elect*) избирáть *impf*, избрáть *pf*; *n* возвращéние; возврáт; (*profit*) прúбыль; **by** ~ обрáтной пóчтой; **in** ~ взамéн (**for** +*gen*); **many happy** ~**s!** с днём рождéния!; ~ **match** отвéтный матч; ~ **ticket** обрáтный билéт.

reunion /riːˈjuːnjən/ *n* встрéча (друзéй и т. п.); **family** ~ сбор всей семьú. **reunite** /ˌriːjuːˈnaɪt/ *vt* воссоединять *impf*, воссоединúть *pf*. **reuse** /riːˈjuːz/ *vt* снóва испóльзовать *impf* & *pf*. **rev** /rev/ *n* оборóт; *vt* & *i*: ~ **up** рванýть(ся) *pf*. **reveal** /rɪˈviːl/ *vt* обнарýживать *impf*, обнарýжить *pf*. **revealing** /-lɪŋ/ *adj* показáтельный. **revel** /ˈrev(ə)l/ *vi* пировáть *impf*; ~ **in** наслаждáться *impf* +*instr*. **revelation** /ˌrevəˈleɪʃ(ə)n/ *n* откровéние. **revenge** /rɪˈvendʒ/ *vt*: ~ **o.s.** мстить *impf*, ото~ *pf* (**for** за+*acc*; **on** +*dat*); *n* месть. **revenue** /ˈrevəˌnjuː/ *n* дохóд. **reverberate** /rɪˈvɜːbəˌreɪt/ *vi* отражáться *impf*. **reverberation** /-ˈreɪʃ(ə)n/ *n* отражéние; (*fig*) óтзвук. **revere** /rɪˈvɪə(r)/ *vt* почитáть *impf*. **reverence** /ˈrevərəns/ *n* почте́ние. **Reverend** /ˈreverənd/ *adj* (*in title*) (его́) преподо́бие. **reverent(ial)** /ˈrevərənt/, /ˌrevəˈrenʃ(ə)l/ *adj* почти́тельный.

reverie /ˈrevərɪ/ *n* мечта́ние.

reversal /rɪˈvɜːs(ə)l/ *n* (*change*) измене́ние; (*of decision*) отме́на. **reverse** /-ˈvɜːs/ *adj* обра́тный; **~ gear** за́дний ход; *vt* (*change*) изменя́ть *impf*, измени́ть *pf*; (*decision*) отменя́ть *impf*, отмени́ть *pf*; *vi* дава́ть *impf*, дать *pf* за́дний ход; *n* (*the* ~) обра́тное *sb*, противополо́жное *sb*; (~ *gear*) за́дний ход; (~ *side*) обра́тная сторона́. **reversible** /-ˈvɜːsɪb(ə)l/ *adj* обрати́мый; (*cloth*) двусторо́нний. **reversion** /-ˈvɜːʃ(ə)n/ *n* возвраще́ние. **revert** /-ˈvɜːt/ *vi* возвраща́ться *impf* (**to** в+*acc*, к+*dat*); (*law*) переходи́ть *impf*, перейти́ *pf* (**to** к+*dat*).

review /rɪˈvjuː/ *n* (*re-examination*) пересмо́тр; (*mil*) пара́д; (*survey*) обзо́р; (*criticism*) реце́нзия; *vt* (*re-examine*) пересма́тривать *impf*, пересмотре́ть *pf*; (*survey*) обозрева́ть *impf*, обозре́ть *pf*; (*troops etc.*) принима́ть *impf*, приня́ть *pf* пара́д+*gen*; (*book etc.*) рецензи́ровать *impf*, про~ *pf*. **reviewer** /-ˈvjuːə(r)/ *n* рецензе́нт.

revise /rɪˈvaɪz/ *vt* пересма́тривать *impf*, пересмотре́ть *pf*; исправля́ть *impf*, испра́вить *pf*; *vi* (*for exam*) гото́виться *impf* (**for** к+*dat*). **revision** /-ˈvɪʒ(ə)n/ *n* пересмо́тр, исправле́ние.

revival /rɪˈvaɪv(ə)l/ *n* возрожде́ние; (*to life etc.*) оживле́ние. **revive** /-ˈvaɪv/ *vt* возрожда́ть *impf*, возроди́ть *pf*; (*resuscitate*) оживля́ть *impf*, оживи́ть *pf*; *vi* ожива́ть *impf*, ожи́ть *pf*.

revoke /rɪˈvəʊk/ *vt* отменя́ть *impf*, отмени́ть *pf*.

revolt /rɪˈvəʊlt/ *n* бунт; *vt* вызыва́ть *impf*, вы́звать *pf* отвраще́ние у+*gen*; *vi* бунтова́ть *impf*, взбунтова́ться *pf*. **revolting** /-ˈvəʊltɪŋ/ *adj* отврати́тельный.

revolution /ˌrevəˈluːʃ(ə)n/ *n* (*single turn*) оборо́т; (*polit*) револю́ция. **revolutionary** /-ˈluːʃənərɪ/ *adj* революцио́нный; *n* революционе́р. **revolutionize** /-ˈluːʃəˌnaɪz/ *vt* революционизи́ровать *impf* & *pf*. **revolve** /rɪˈvɒlv/ *vt* & *i* враща́ть(ся) *impf*. **revolver** /rɪˈvɒlvə(r)/ *n* револьве́р.

revue /rɪˈvjuː/ *n* ревю́ *neut indecl.*

revulsion /rɪˈvʌlʃ(ə)n/ *n* отвраще́ние.

reward /rɪˈwɔːd/ *n* вознагражде́ние; *vt* (воз)награжда́ть *impf*, (воз)награди́ть *pf*.

rewrite /riːˈraɪt/ *vt* перепи́сывать *impf*, переписа́ть *pf*; (*recast*) переде́лывать *impf*, переде́лать *pf*.

rhapsody /ˈræpsədɪ/ *n* рапсо́дия.

rhetoric /ˈretərɪk/ *n* рито́рика. **rhetorical** /rɪˈtɒrɪk(ə)l/ *adj* ритори́ческий.

rheumatic /ruːˈmætɪk/ *adj* ревмати́ческий. **rheumatism** /ˈruːməˌtɪz(ə)m/ *n* ревмати́зм.

rhinoceros /raɪˈnɒsərəs/ *n* носоро́г.

rhododendron /ˌrəʊdəˈdendrən/ *n* рододе́ндрон.

rhubarb /ˈruːbɑːb/ *n* реве́нь *m.*

rhyme /raɪm/ *n* ри́фма; *pl* (*verse*) стихи́ *m pl*; *vt* & *i* рифмова́ть(ся) *impf*.

rhythm /ˈrɪð(ə)m/ *n* ритм. **rhyth-**

mic(al) /ˈrɪðmɪk(əl)/ *adj* ритми́ческий, -чный.

rib /rɪb/ *n* ребро́.

ribald /ˈrɪb(ə)ld/ *adj* непристо́йный.

ribbon /ˈrɪbən/ *n* ле́нта.

rice /raɪs/ *n* рис.

rich /rɪtʃ/ *adj* бога́тый; (*soil*) ту́чный; (*food*) жи́рный. **riches** /ˈrɪtʃɪz/ *n pl* бога́тство. **richly** /ˈrɪtʃlɪ/ *adv* (*fully*) вполне́.

rickety /ˈrɪkɪtɪ/ *adj* (*shaky*) расша́танный.

ricochet /ˈrɪkəˌʃeɪ/ *vi* рикошети́ровать *impf* & *pf*.

rid /rɪd/ *vt* освобожда́ть *impf*, освободи́ть *pf* (**of** от+*gen*); **get ~ of** избавля́ться *impf*, изба́виться *pf* от+*gen*. **riddance** /ˈrɪd(ə)ns/ *n*: **good ~!** ска́тертью доро́га!

riddle /ˈrɪd(ə)l/ *n* (*enigma*) зага́дка.

riddled /ˈrɪd(ə)ld/ *adj*: **~ with** изрешечённый; (*fig*) прони́занный.

ride /raɪd/ *vi* е́здить *indet*, е́хать *det*, по~ *pf* (**on horseback** верхо́м); *vt* е́здить *indet*, е́хать *det*, по~ *pf* в, на+*prep*; *n* пое́здка, езда́. **rider** /-də(r)/ *n* вса́дник, -ица; (*clause*) дополне́ние.

ridge /rɪdʒ/ *n* хребе́т; (*on cloth*) ру́бчик; (*of roof*) конёк.

ridicule /ˈrɪdɪˌkjuːl/ *n* насме́шка; *vt* осме́ивать *impf*, осмея́ть *pf*. **ridiculous** /rɪˈdɪkjʊləs/ *adj* смешно́й.

riding /ˈraɪdɪŋ/ *n* (*horse-~*) (верхова́я) езда́.

rife /raɪf/ *predic* распространённый.

riff-raff /ˈrɪfræf/ *n* подо́нки (-ков) *pl*.

rifle /ˈraɪf(ə)l/ *n* винто́вка; *vt* (*search*) обы́скивать *impf*, обыска́ть *pf*.

rift /rɪft/ *n* тре́щина (*also fig*).

rig /rɪg/ *vt* оснаща́ть *impf*, оснасти́ть *pf*; **~ out** наряжа́ть *impf*, наряди́ть *pf*; **~ up** скола́чивать *impf*, сколоти́ть *pf*; *n* бурова́я устано́вка. **rigging** /-gɪŋ/ *n* такела́ж.

right /raɪt/ *adj* (*position*; *justified*; *polit*) пра́вый; (*correct*) пра́вильный; (*the one wanted*) тот; (*suitable*) подходя́щий; **~ angle** прямо́й у́гол; *vt* исправля́ть *impf*, испра́вить *pf*; *n* пра́во; (*what is just*) справедли́вость; (*~ side*) пра́вая сторона́; (**the R~**; *polit*) пра́вые *sb pl*; **be in the ~** быть пра́вым; **by ~s** по пра́ву; **~ of way** пра́во прохо́да, прое́зда; *adv* (*straight*) пря́мо; (*exactly*) то́чно, как раз; (*to the full*) соверше́нно; (*correctly*) пра́вильно; как сле́дует; (*on the ~*) спра́во (**of** от+*gen*); (*to the ~*) напра́во; **~ away** сейча́с.

righteous /ˈraɪtʃəs/ *adj* (*person*) пра́ведный; (*action*) справедли́вый.

rightful /ˈraɪtfʊl/ *adj* зако́нный.

rigid /ˈrɪdʒɪd/ *adj* жёсткий; (*strict*) стро́гий. **rigidity** /rɪˈdʒɪdɪtɪ/ *n* жёсткость; стро́гость.

rigmarole /ˈrɪgməˌrəʊl/ *n* канитель.

rigorous /ˈrɪgərəs/ *adj* стро́гий. **rigour** /ˈrɪgə(r)/ *n* стро́гость.

rim /rɪm/ *n* (*of wheel*) о́бод; (*spectacles*) опра́ва. **rimless** /-lɪs/ *adj* без опра́вы.

rind /raɪnd/ *n* кожура́.

ring[1] /rɪŋ/ *n* кольцо́; (*circle*) круг; (*boxing*) ринг; (*circus*) (цирко́вая) аре́на; **~ road** кольцева́я доро́га; *vt* (*encircle*) окружа́ть *impf*, окружи́ть *pf*.

ring² /rɪŋ/ *vi* (*sound*) звонить *impf*, по~ *pf*; (*ring out, of shot etc.*) раздаваться *impf*, раздаться *pf*; (*of place*) оглашаться *impf*, огласиться *pf* (**with** +*instr*); *vt* звонить *impf*, по~ *pf* в+*acc*; ~ **back** перезванивать *impf*, перезвонить *pf*; ~ **off** повесить *pf* трубку; ~ **up** звонить *impf*, по~ *pf* +*dat*; *n* звон, звонок.

ringleader *n* главарь *m*.

ringtone *n* мелодия звонка, рингтон (в мобильном телефоне.

rink /rɪŋk/ *n* каток.

rinse /rɪns/ *vt* полоскать *impf*, вы~ *pf*; *n* полоскание.

riot /'raɪət/ *n* бунт; **run** ~ буйствовать *impf*; (*of plants*) буйно разрастаться *impf*, разрастись *pf*; *vi* бунтовать *impf*, взбунтоваться *pf*. **riotous** /'raɪətəs/ *adj* буйный.

rip /rɪp/ *vt* & *i* рвать(ся) *impf*; разо~ *pf*; ~ **up** разрывать *impf*, разорвать *pf*; *n* прореха, разрез.

ripe /raɪp/ *adj* зрелый, спелый. **ripen** /'raɪpən/ *vt* делать *impf*, с~ *pf* зрелым; *vi* созревать *impf*, созреть *pf*. **ripeness** /-nɪs/ *n* зрелость.

ripple /'rɪp(ə)l/ *n* рябь; *vt* & *i* покрывать(ся) *impf*, покрыть(ся) *pf* рябью.

rise /raɪz/ *vi* подниматься *impf*, подняться *pf*; повышаться *impf*, повыситься *pf*; (*get up*) вставать *impf*, встать *pf*; (*rebel*) восставать *impf*, восстать *pf*; (*sun etc.*) в(о)сходить *impf*, взойти; *n* подъём, возвышение; (*in pay*) прибавка; (*of sun etc.*) восход. **riser** /-zə(r)/ *n*: **he is an early** ~ он рано встаёт.

risk /rɪsk/ *n* риск; *vt* рисковать *impf*, рискнуть *pf* +*instr*. **risky** /-kɪ/ *adj* рискованный.

risqué /'rɪskeɪ/ *adj* непристойный.

rite /raɪt/ *n* обряд. **ritual** /'rɪtjʊəl/ *n* ритуал; *adj* ритуальный.

rival /'raɪv(ə)l/ *n* соперник, -ица; *adj* соперничающий; *vt* соперничать *impf* с+*instr*. **rivalry** /-rɪ/ *n* соперничество.

river /'rɪvə(r)/ *n* река. **riverside** *attrib* прибрежный.

rivet /'rɪvɪt/ *n* заклёпка; *vt* заклёпывать *impf*, заклепать *pf*; (*fig*) приковывать *impf*, приковать *pf* (**on** к+*dat*).

road /rəʊd/ *n* дорога; (*street*) улица; ~**-block** заграждение на дороге; ~**-map** (дорожная) карта; ~ **sign** дорожный знак. **roadside** *n* обочина; *attrib* придорожный. **roadway** *n* мостовая *sb*.

roam /rəʊm/ *vt* & *i* бродить *impf* (по+*dat*).

roar /rɔː(r)/ *n* (*animal's*) рёв; *vi* реветь *impf*.

roast /rəʊst/ *vt* & *i* жарить(ся) *impf*, за~, из~ *pf*; *adj* жареный; ~ **beef** ростбиф; *n* жаркое *sb*.

rob /rɒb/ *vt* грабить *impf*, о~ *pf*; красть *impf*, у~ *pf* у+*gen* (**of** +*acc*); (*deprive*) лишать *impf*, лишить *pf* (**of** +*gen*). **robber** /'rɒbə(r)/ *n* грабитель *m*. **robbery** /'rɒbərɪ/ *n* грабёж.

robe /rəʊb/ *n* (*also pl*) мантия.

robin /'rɒbɪn/ *n* малиновка.

robot /'rəʊbɒt/ *n* робот.

robust /rəʊ'bʌst/ *adj* крепкий.

rock¹ /rɒk/ *n* (*geol*) (горная) порода; (*cliff etc.*) скала; (*large stone*) большой камень *m*; **on the** ~**s** (*in difficulty*) на мели; (*drink*) со льдом.

rock² /rɒk/ *vt* & *i* качать(ся) *impf*, качнуть(ся) *pf*; *n* (*mus*) рок; **~ing-chair** кача́лка; **~ and roll** рок-н-ро́лл.

rockery /ˈrɒkərɪ/ *n* альпина́рий.

rocket /ˈrɒkɪt/ *n* раке́та; *vi* подска́кивать *impf*, подскочи́ть *pf*.

rocky /ˈrɒkɪ/ *adj* скали́стый; (*shaky*) ша́ткий.

rod /rɒd/ *n* (*stick*) прут; (*bar*) сте́ржень *m*; (*fishing-~*) у́дочка.

rodent /ˈrəʊd(ə)nt/ *n* грызу́н.

roe[1] /rəʊ/ *n* икра́; (*soft*) моло́ки (-о́к) *pl*.

roe[2] /rəʊ/ **(-deer)** // *n* косу́ля.

rogue /rəʊg/ *n* плут.

role /rəʊl/ *n* роль.

roll[1] /rəʊl/ *n* (*cylinder*) руло́н; (*register*) рее́стр; (*bread*) бу́лочка; **~-call** перекли́чка.

roll[2] /rəʊl/ *vt* & *i* ката́ть(ся) *indet*, кати́ть(ся) *det*, по~ *pf*; (~ *up*) свёртывать(ся) *impf*, сверну́ть(ся) *pf*; *vt* (~ *out*) (*dough*) раска́тывать *impf*, раската́ть *pf*; *vi* (*sound*) греме́ть *impf*; **~ over** перевора́чиваться *impf*, переверну́ться *pf*; *n* (*of drums*) бараба́нная дробь; (*of thunder*) раска́т.

roller /ˈrəʊlə(r)/ *n* (*small*) ро́лик; (*large*) като́к; (*for hair*) бигуди́ *neut indecl*; **~-skates** коньки́ *m pl* на ро́ликах.

rolling /ˈrəʊlɪŋ/ *adj* (*of land*) холми́стый; **~-pin** ска́лка. **~-stock** подвижно́й соста́в.

Roman /ˈrəʊmən/ *n* ри́млянин, -янка; *adj* ри́мский; **~ Catholic** (*n*) като́лик, -и́чка; (*adj*) ри́мско-католи́ческий.

romance /rəʊˈmæns/ *n* (*tale*; *love affair*) рома́н; (*quality*) рома́нтика.

Romanesque /ˌrəʊməˈnesk/ *adj* рома́нский.

Romania /rəʊˈmeɪnɪə/ *n* Румы́ния. **Romanian** /-nɪən/ *n* румы́н, **~**ка; *adj* румы́нский.

romantic /rəʊˈmæntɪk/ *adj* романти́чный, -ческий. **romanticism** /-tɪˌsɪz(ə)m/ *n* романти́зм.

romp /rɒmp/ *vi* вози́ться *impf*.

roof /ruːf/ *n* кры́ша; **~ of the mouth** нёбо; *vt* крыть *impf*, покры́ть *pf*.

rook[1] /rʊk/ *n* (*chess*) ладья́.

rook[2] /rʊk/ *n* (*bird*) грач.

room /ruːm/ *n* ко́мната; (*in hotel*) но́мер; (*space*) ме́сто. **roomy** /ˈruːmɪ/ *adj* просто́рный.

roost /ruːst/ *n* насе́ст.

root[1] /ruːt/ *n* ко́рень *m*; **take ~** укореня́ться *impf*, укорени́ться *pf*; *vi* пуска́ть *impf*, пусти́ть *pf* ко́рни; **~ out** вырыва́ть *impf*, вы́рвать *pf* с ко́рнем; **rooted to the spot** прико́ванный к ме́сту.

root[2] /ruːt/ *vi* (*rummage*) ры́ться *impf*; **~ for** боле́ть *impf* за +*acc*.

rope /rəʊp/ *n* верёвка; **~-ladder** верёвочная ле́стница; *vt*: **~ in** (*enlist*) втя́гивать *impf*, втяну́ть *pf*; **~ off** о(т)гора́живать *impf*, о(т)городи́ть *pf* верёвкой.

rosary /ˈrəʊzərɪ/ *n* чётки (-ток) *pl*.

rose /rəʊz/ *n* ро́за; (*nozzle*) се́тка.

rosemary /ˈrəʊzmərɪ/ *n* розмари́н.

rosette /rəʊˈzet/ *n* розе́тка.

rosewood /ˈrəʊzwʊd/ *n* ро́зовое де́рево.

roster /ˈrɒstə(r)/ *n* расписа́ние дежу́рств.

rostrum /ˈrɒstrəm/ *n* трибу́на.

rosy /ˈrəʊzɪ/ *adj* ро́зовый; (*cheeks*) румя́ный.

rot /rɒt/ *n* гниль; (*nonsense*) вздор; *vi* гнить *impf*, с~ *pf*; *vt* гноить *impf*, с~ *pf*.

rota /'rəʊtə/ *n* расписа́ние дежу́рств. **rotary** /'rəʊtərɪ/ *adj* враща́тельный, ротацио́нный. **rotate** /rəʊ'teɪt/ *vt & i* враща́ть(ся) *impf*. **rotation** /-'teɪʃ(ə)n/ *n* враще́ние; **in ~** по о́череди.

rote /rəʊt/ *n*: **by ~** наизу́сть.

rotten /'rɒt(ə)n/ *adj* гнило́й; (*fig*) отврати́тельный.

rotund /rəʊ'tʌnd/ *adj* (*round*) кру́глый; (*plump*) по́лный.

rouble /'ru:b(ə)l/ *n* рубль *m*.

rough /rʌf/ *adj* (*uneven*) неро́вный; (*coarse*) гру́бый; (*sea*) бу́рный; (*approximate*) приблизи́тельный; **~ copy** черно-ви́к; *n*: **the ~** тру́дности *f pl*; *vt*: **~ it** жить *impf* без удо́бств. **roughage** /'rʌfɪdʒ/ *n* гру́бая пи́ща. **roughly** /'rʌflɪ/ *adv* гру́бо; (*approximately*) приблизи́тельно.

roulette /ru:'let/ *n* руле́тка.

round /raʊnd/ *adj* кру́глый; **~-shouldered** суту́лый; *n* (*~ object*) круг; (*circuit*; *also pl*) обхо́д; (*sport*) тур, ра́унд; (*series*) ряд; (*ammunition*) патро́н; (*of applause*) взрыв; *adv* вокру́г; (*in a circle*) по кру́гу; **all ~** круго́м; **all the year ~** кру́глый год; *prep* вокру́г+*gen*; круго́м +*gen*; по+*dat*; **~ the corner** (*motion*) за́ угол, (*position*) за угло́м; *vt* (*go ~*) огиба́ть *impf*, обогну́ть *pf*; **~ off** (*complete*) заверша́ть *impf*, заверши́ть *pf*; **~ up** сгоня́ть *impf*, согна́ть *pf*; **~-up** заго́н; (*raid*) обла́ва. **roundabout** *n* (*merry-go-round*) карусе́ль; (*road junction*) кольцева́я тра́нспортная развя́зка; *adj* око́льный.

rouse /raʊz/ *vt* буди́ть *impf*, раз~ *pf*; (*to action etc.*) побужда́ть *impf*, побуди́ть *pf* (**to** к+*dat*). **rousing** /'raʊzɪŋ/ *adj* восто́рженный.

rout /raʊt/ *n* (*defeat*) разгро́м.

route /ru:t/ *n* маршру́т, путь *m*.

routine /ru:'ti:n/ *n* заведённый поря́док, режи́м; *adj* устано́вленный; очередно́й.

rove /rəʊv/ *vi* скита́ться *impf*.

row[1] /rəʊ/ *n* (*line*) ряд.

row[2] /rəʊ/ *vi* (*in boat*) грести́ *impf*.

row[3] /raʊ/ *n* (*dispute*) ссо́ра; (*noise*) шум; *vi* ссо́риться *impf*, по~ *pf*.

rowdy /'raʊdɪ/ *adj* бу́йный.

royal /'rɔɪəl/ *adj* короле́вский; (*majestic*) великоле́пный. **royalist** /-lɪst/ *n* роялист; *adj* роя-ли́стский. **royalty** /-tɪ/ *n* член, чле́ны *pl*, короле́вской семьи́; (*fee*) а́вторский гонора́р.

rub /rʌb/ *vt & i* тере́ть(ся) *impf*; *vt* (*polish*; *chafe*) натира́ть *impf*, натере́ть *pf*; (*~ dry*) вытира́ть *impf*, вы́тереть *pf*; **~ in, on** втира́ть *impf*, втере́ть *pf*; **~ out** стира́ть *impf*, стере́ть *pf*; **~ it in** растравля́ть *impf*, растрави́ть *pf* ра́ну.

rubber /'rʌbə(r)/ *n* рези́на; (*eraser*, *also ~ band*) рези́нка; *attrib* рези́новый; **~-stamp** (*fig*) штампова́ть *impf*.

rubbish /'rʌbɪʃ/ *n* му́сор; (*nonsense*) чепуха́.

rubble /'rʌb(ə)l/ *n* щёбень *m*.

rubella /ru:'belə/ *n* красну́ха.

ruby /'ru:bɪ/ *n* руби́н.

ruck /rʌk/ *vt* (*~ up*) мять *impf*, из~, с~ *pf*.

rucksack /'rʌksæk/ *n* рюкза́к.

rudder /'rʌdə(r)/ *n* руль *m*.

ruddy /'rʌdɪ/ *adj* (*face*) румя́ный; (*damned*) прокля́тый.

rude /ru:d/ *adj* грýбый. **rudeness** /-nɪs/ *n* грýбость.
rudimentary /ˌru:dɪ'mentərɪ/ *adj* рудиментáрный. **rudiments** /'ru:dɪmənts/ *n pl* оснóвы *f pl.*
rueful /'ru:fʊl/ *adj* печáльный.
ruff /rʌf/ *n* (*frill*) брыжи (-жей) *pl*; (*of feathers, hair*) кольцó (пéрьев, шéрсти) вокрýг шéи.
ruffian /'rʌfiən/ *n* хулигáн.
ruffle /'rʌf(ə)l/ *n* обóрка; *vt* (*hair*) ерóшить *impf*, взъ~ *pf*; (*water*) рябить *impf*; (*person*) смущáть *impf*, смутить *pf*.
rug /rʌg/ *n* (*mat*) ковёр; (*wrap*) плед.
rugby /'rʌgbɪ/ *n* рéгби *neut indecl.*
rugged /'rʌgɪd/ *adj* (*rocky*) скалистый.
ruin /'ru:ɪn/ *n* (*downfall*) гибель; (*building, ruins*) развáлины *f pl*, руины *f pl*; *vt* губить *impf*, по~ *pf*. **ruinous** /-nəs/ *adj* губительный.
rule /ru:l/ *n* прáвило; (*for measuring*) линéйка; (*government*) правлéние; **as a ~** как прáвило; *vt* & *i* прáвить *impf* (+*instr*); (*decree*) постановлять *impf*, постановить *pf*; **~ out** исключáть *impf*, исключить *pf*. **ruled** /ru:ld/ *adj* линóванный. **ruler** /'ru:lə(r)/ *n* (*person*) правитель *m*, ~ница; (*object*) линéйка. **ruling** /'ru:lɪŋ/ *n* (*of court etc.*) постановлéние.
rum /rʌm/ *n* (*drink*) ром.
Rumania(n) /rə'meɪnɪə(n)/ *see* **Romania(n)**
rumble /'rʌmb(ə)l/ *vi* громыхáть *impf*; *n* громыхáние.
ruminant /'ru:mɪnənt/ *n* жвáчное (живóтное) *sb.* **ruminate** /-ˌneɪt/ *vi* (*fig*) размышлять *impf* (**over, on** о+*prep*).
rummage /'rʌmɪdʒ/ *vi* рыться *impf*.
rumour /'ru:mə(r)/ *n* слух; *vt*: **it is ~ed that** хóдят слýхи (*pl*), что.
rump /rʌmp/ *n* крестéц; **~ steak** ромштéкс.
rumple /'rʌmp(ə)l/ *vt* мять *impf*, из~, с~ *pf*; (*hair*) ерóшить *impf*, взъ~ *pf*.
run /rʌn/ *vi* бéгать *indet*, бежáть *det*, по~ *pf*; (*work, of machines*) рабóтать *impf*; (*ply, of bus etc.*) ходить *indet*, идти *det*; (*seek election*) выставлять *impf*, выставить *pf* свою кандидатýру; (*of play etc.*) идти *impf*; (*of ink, dye*) расплывáться *impf*, расплыться *pf*; (*flow*) течь *impf*; (*of document*) гласить *impf*; *vt* (*manage; operate*) управлять *impf* +*instr*; (*a business etc.*) вести *impf*; **~ dry, low** иссякáть *impf*, иссякнуть *pf*; **~ risks** рисковáть *impf*; **~ across, into** (*meet*) встречáться *impf*, встрéтиться *pf* с+*instr*; **~ away** (*flee*) убегáть *impf*, убежáть *pf*; **~ down** (*knock down*) задавить *pf*; (*disparage*) принижáть *impf*, принизить *pf*; **be ~ down** (*of person*) переутомиться *pf* (*in past tense*); **~-down** (*decayed*) запýщенный; **~ in** (*engine*) обкáтывать *impf*, обкатáть *pf*; **~ into** *see* **~ across**; **~ out** кончáться *impf*, кóнчиться *pf*; **~ out of** истощáть *impf*, истощить *pf* свой запáс +*gen*; **~ over** (*glance over*) бéгло просмáтривать *impf*, просмотрéть *pf*; (*injure*) задавить *pf*; **~ through** (*pierce*) прокáлывать *impf*, проколóть *pf*; (*money*) промáтывать *impf*, промотáть *pf*; (*review*) повторять *impf*, повторить *pf*; **~ to** (*reach*) (*of money*) хватáть *impf*, хватить

pf impers+gen на+*acc*; **the money won't ~ to a car** этих денег не хватит на машину; **~ up against** наталкиваться *impf*, натолкнуться *pf* на+*acc*; *n* бег; (*sport*) перебежка; (*journey*) поездка; (*period*) полоса; **at a ~** бегом; **on the ~** в бегах; **~ on** большой спрос на+*acc*; **in the long ~** в конце концов.

rung /rʌŋ/ *n* ступенька.

runner /ˈrʌnə(r)/ *n* (*also tech*) бегун; (*of sledge*) полоз; (*bot*) побег; **~ bean** фасоль; **~-up** участник, занявший второе место. **running** /ˈrʌnɪŋ/ *n* бег; (*management*) управление (**of** +*instr*); **be in the ~** иметь шансы; *adj* бегущий; (*of* **~**) беговой; (*after pl n, in succession*) подряд; **~ commentary** репортаж; **~ water** водопровод. **runway** *n* взлётно-посадочная полоса.

rupee /ruːˈpiː/ *n* рупия.

rupture /ˈrʌptʃə(r)/ *n* разрыв; *vt* & *i* прорывать(ся) *impf*, прорвать(ся) *pf*.

rural /ˈrʊər(ə)l/ *adj* сельский.

ruse /ruːz/ *n* уловка.

rush[1] /rʌʃ/ *n* (*bot*) тростник.

rush[2] /rʌʃ/ *vt* & *i* (*hurry*) торопить(ся) *impf*, по~ *pf*; *vi* (*dash*) бросаться *impf*, броситься *pf*; (*of water*) нестись *impf*; по~ *pf*; *vt* (*to hospital etc.*) умчать *pf*; *n* (*of blood etc.*) прилив; (*hurry*) спешка; **be in a ~** торопиться *impf*; **~-hour(s)** часы *m pl* пик.

Russia /ˈrʌʃə/ *n* Россия. **Russian** /-ʃən/ *n* русский *sb*; *adj* (*of ~ nationality, culture*) русский; (*of ~ State*) российский.

rust /rʌst/ *n* ржавчина; *vi* ржаветь *impf*, за~, по~ *pf*.

rustic /ˈrʌstɪk/ *adj* деревенский.

rustle /ˈrʌs(ə)l/ *n* шелест, шорох, шуршание; *vi* & *t* шелестеть *impf* (+*instr*); **~ up** раздобывать *impf*; раздобыть *pf*.

rusty /ˈrʌstɪ/ *adj* ржавый.

rut /rʌt/ *n* колея.

ruthless /ˈruːθlɪs/ *adj* безжалостный.

rye /raɪ/ *n* рожь; *attrib* ржаной.

S

Sabbath /ˈsæbəθ/ *n* (*Jewish*) суббота; (*Christian*) воскресенье. **sabbatical** /səˈbætɪk(ə)l/ *n* годичный отпуск.

sable /ˈseɪb(ə)l/ *n* соболь.

sabotage /ˈsæbəˌtɑːʒ/ *n* диверсия; *vt* саботировать *impf* & *pf*. **saboteur** /ˌsæbəˈtɜː(r)/ *n* диверсант.

sabre /ˈseɪbə(r)/ *n* сабля.

sachet /ˈsæʃeɪ/ *n* упаковка.

sack[1] /sæk/ *vt* (*plunder*) разграбить *pf*.

sack[2] /sæk/ *n* мешок; (*dismissal*): **get the ~** быть уволенным; *vt* увольнять *impf*, уволить *pf*. **sacking** /-kɪŋ/ *n* (*hessian*) мешковина.

sacrament /ˈsækrəmənt/ *n* таинство; (*Eucharist*) причастие. **sacred** /ˈseɪkrɪd/ *adj* священный, святой. **sacrifice** /ˈsækrɪˌfaɪs/ *n* жертва; *vt* жертвовать *impf*, по~ *pf* +*instr*. **sacrilege** /ˈsækrɪlɪdʒ/ *n* святотатство. **sacrosanct** /ˈsækrəʊˌsæŋkt/ *adj* священный.

sad /sæd/ *adj* печальный, грустный. **sadden** /-d(ə)n/ *vt* печалить *impf*, о~ *pf*.

saddle /ˈsæd(ə)l/ *n* седло; *vt* седлать *impf*, о~ *pf*; (*burden*) обременя́ть *impf*, обремени́ть *pf* (**with** +*instr*).

sadism /'seɪdɪz(ə)m/ *n* сади́зм. **sadist** /-dɪst/ *n* сади́ст. **sadistic** /sə'dɪstɪk/ *adj* сади́стский.

sadness /'sædnɪs/ *n* печа́ль, грусть.

safe /seɪf/ *n* сейф; *adj* (*unharmed*) невреди́мый; (*out of danger*) в безопа́сности; (*secure*) безопа́сный; (*reliable*) надёжный; ~ **and sound** цел и невреди́м. **safeguard** *n* предохрани́тельная ме́ра; *vt* предохраня́ть *impf*, предохрани́ть *pf*. **safety** /-tɪ/ *n* безопа́сность; ~**-belt** реме́нь *m* безопа́сности; ~ **pin** англи́йская була́вка; ~**-valve** предохрани́тельный кла́пан.

sag /sæg/ *vi* (*of rope, curtain*) провиса́ть *impf*, прови́снуть *pf*; (*of ceiling*) прогиба́ться *impf*, прогну́ться *pf*.

saga /'sɑːgə/ *n* са́га.

sage[1] /seɪdʒ/ *n* (*herb*) шалфе́й.

sage[2] /seɪdʒ/ *n* (*person*) мудре́ц; *adj* му́дрый.

Sagittarius /ˌsædʒɪ'teərɪəs/ *n* Стреле́ц.

sail /seɪl/ *n* па́рус; *vt* (*a ship*) управля́ть *impf* +*instr*; *vi* пла́вать *indet*, плыть *det*; (*depart*) отплыва́ть *impf*, отплы́ть *pf*. **sailing** /-lɪŋ/ *n* (*sport*) па́русный спорт; ~**-ship** па́русное су́дно. **sailor** /-lə(r)/ *n* матро́с, моря́к.

saint /seɪnt/ *n* свято́й *sb.* **saintly** /-lɪ/ *adj* свято́й.

sake /seɪk/ *n*: **for the** ~ **of** ра́ди+*gen.*

salad /'sæləd/ *n* сала́т; ~**-dressing** припра́ва к сала́ту.

salami /sə'lɑːmɪ/ *n* саля́ми *f indecl.*

salary /'sælərɪ/ *n* жа́лованье.

sale /seɪl/ *n* прода́жа; (*also amount sold*) сбыт (*no pl*); (*with reduced prices*) распрода́жа; **be for** ~ продава́ться *impf*. **saleable** /-ləb(ə)l/ *adj* хо́дкий. **salesman** /'seɪlzmən/ *n* продаве́ц. **saleswoman** /'seɪlzˌwʊmən/ *n* продавщи́ца.

salient /'seɪlɪənt/ *adj* основно́й.

saliva /sə'laɪvə/ *n* слюна́.

sallow /'sæləʊ/ *adj* желтова́тый.

salmon /'sæmən/ *n* ло́сось *m*.

salon /'sælɒn/ *n* сало́н. **saloon** /sə'luːn/ *n* (*on ship*) сало́н; (*car*) седа́н; (*bar*) бар.

salt /sɔːlt/ *n* соль; ~**-cellar** соло́нка; ~ **water** морска́я вода́; ~**-water** морско́й; *adj* солёный; *vt* соли́ть *impf*, по~ *pf*. **salty** /-tɪ/ *adj* солёный.

salutary /'sæljʊtərɪ/ *adj* благотво́рный. **salute** /sə'luːt/ *n* отда́ча че́сти; (*with guns*) салю́т; *vt* & *i* отдава́ть *impf*, отда́ть *pf* честь (+*dat*).

salvage /'sælvɪdʒ/ *n* спасе́ние; *vt* спаса́ть *impf*, спасти́ *pf*.

salvation /sæl'veɪʃ(ə)n/ *n* спасе́ние; **S**~ **Army** А́рмия спасе́ния.

salve /sælv/ *n* мазь; *vt*: ~ **one's conscience** успока́ивать *impf*, успоко́ить *pf* со́весть.

salvo /'sælvəʊ/ *n* залп.

same /seɪm/ *adj*: **the** ~ тот же (са́мый); (*applying to both or all*) оди́н; (*identical*) одина́ковый; *pron*: **the** ~ одно́ и то́ же, то же са́мое; *adv*: **the** ~ таки́м же о́бразом, так же; **all the** ~ всё-таки, тем не ме́нее. **sameness** /-nɪs/ *n* однообра́зие.

samovar /'sæməˌvɑː(r)/ *n* самова́р.

sample /'sɑːmp(ə)l/ *n* образе́ц; *vt* про́бовать *impf*, по~ *pf*.

sanatorium /ˌsænə'tɔːrɪəm/ *n* санато́рий.

sanctify /'sæŋktɪ,faɪ/ *vt* освящáть *impf*, освятúть *pf*. **sanctimonious** /,sæŋktɪ'məʊnɪəs/ *adj* хáнжеский. **sanction** /'sæŋkʃ(ə)n/ *n* сáнкция; *vt* санкционúровать *impf* & *pf*. **sanctity** /'sæŋktɪtɪ/ *n* (*holiness*) свя́тость; (*sacredness*) свящéнность. **sanctuary** /'sæŋktjʊərɪ/ *n* святúлище; (*refuge*) убéжище; (*for wild life*) заповéдник.

sand /sænd/ *n* песóк; *vt* (~ *down*) шкýрить *impf*, по~ *pf*; **~-dune** дю́на.

sandal /'sænd(ə)l/ *n* сандáлия.

sandalwood /'sænd(ə)lwʊd/ *n* сандáловое дéрево.

sandbank /'sændbæŋk/ *n* óтмель.

sandpaper /'sænd,peɪpə(r)/ *n* шкýрка; *vt* шлифовáть *impf*, от~ *pf* шкýркой.

sandstone /'sændstəʊn/ *n* песчáник.

sandwich /'sænwɪdʒ/ *n* бутербрóд; *vt*: ~ **between** втúскивать *impf*, встúснуть *pf* мéжду +*instr.*

sandy /'sændɪ/ *adj* (*of sand*) песчáный; (*like sand*) песóчный; (*hair*) рыжевáтый.

sane /seɪn/ *adj* нормáльный; (*sensible*) разýмный.

sang-froid /sɑ̃'frwɑː/ *n* самообладáние.

sanguine /'sæŋgwɪn/ *adj* оптимистúческий.

sanitary /'sænɪtərɪ/ *adj* санитáрный; гигиенúческий; ~ **towel** гигиенúческая подýшка. **sanitation** /,sænɪ'teɪʃ(ə)n/ *n* (*conditions*) санитáрные услóвия *neut pl*; (*system*) водопровóд и канализáция. **sanity** /'sænɪtɪ/ *n* психúческое здорóвье; (*good sense*) здрáвый смысл.

sap /sæp/ *n* (*bot*) сок; *vt* (*exhaust*) истощáть *impf*, истощúть *pf*.

sapling /'sæplɪŋ/ *n* сáженец.

sapphire /'sæfaɪə(r)/ *n* сапфúр.

sarcasm /'sɑː,kæz(ə)m/ *n* саркáзм. **sarcastic** /sɑː'kæstɪk/ *adj* саркастúческий.

sardine /sɑː'diːn/ *n* сардúна.

sardonic /sɑː'dɒnɪk/ *adj* сардонúческий.

sash[1] /sæʃ/ *n* (*scarf*) кушáк.

sash[2] /sæʃ/ *n* (*frame*) скользя́щая рáма; **~-window** подъёмное окнó.

satanic /sə'tænɪk/ *adj* сатанúнский.

satchel /'sætʃ(ə)l/ *n* рáнец, сýмка.

satellite /'sætə,laɪt/ *n* спýтник, сателлúт (*also fig*); ~ **dish** параболúческая антéнна; тарéлка (*coll*); ~ **TV** спýтниковое телевúдение.

satiate /'seɪʃɪ,eɪt/ *vt* насыщáть *impf*, насы́тить *pf*.

satin /'sætɪn/ *n* атлáс.

satire /'sætaɪə(r)/ *n* сатúра. **satirical** /sə'tɪrɪk(ə)l/ *adj* сатирúческий. **satirist** /'sætərɪst/ *n* сатúрик. **satirize** /-,raɪz/ *vt* высмéивать *impf*, вы́смеять *pf*.

satisfaction /,sætɪs'fækʃ(ə)n/ *n* удовлетворéние. **satisfactory** /-'fæktərɪ/ *adj* удовлетворúтельный. **satisfy** /'sætɪs,faɪ/ *vt* удовлетворя́ть *impf*, удовлетворúть *pf*; (*hunger*, *curiosity*) утоля́ть *impf*, утолúть *pf*.

saturate /'sætʃə,reɪt/ *vt* насыщáть *impf*, насы́тить *pf*; **I got ~d** (*by rain*) я промóк до нúтки. **saturation** /,sætʃə'reɪʃ(ə)n/ *n* насыщéние.

Saturday /'sætə,deɪ/ *n* суббóта.

sauce /sɔːs/ *n* сóус; (*cheek*) нáглость. **saucepan** *n* кастрю́ля. **saucer** /'sɔːsə(r)/ *n* блю́дце.

saucy /ˈsɔːsɪ/ *adj* на́глый.
Saudi /ˈsaʊdɪ/ *n* сау́довец, -вка; *adj* сау́довский. **Saudi Arabia** /ˌsaʊdɪ əˈreɪbɪə/ *n* Сау́довская Ара́вия.
sauna /ˈsɔːnə/ *n* фи́нская ба́ня.
saunter /ˈsɔːntə(r)/ *vi* прогу́ливаться *impf*.
sausage /ˈsɒsɪdʒ/ *n* соси́ска; (*salami-type*) колбаса́.
savage /ˈsævɪdʒ/ *adj* ди́кий; (*fierce*) свире́пый; (*cruel*) жесто́кий; *n* дика́рь *m*; *vt* искуса́ть *pf*. **savagery** /-rɪ/ *n* ди́кость; жесто́кость.
save /seɪv/ *vt* (*rescue*) спаса́ть *impf*, спасти́ *pf*; (*money*) копи́ть *impf*, на~ *pf*; (*put aside, keep*) бере́чь *impf*; (*avoid using*) эконо́мить *impf*, с~ *pf*; *vi*: ~ **up** копи́ть *impf*, на~ *pf* де́ньги. **savings** /-vɪŋz/ *n pl* сбереже́ния *neut pl*; ~ **bank** сберега́тельная ка́сса. **saviour** /-vjə(r)/ *n* спаси́тель *m*.
savour /ˈseɪvə(r)/ *vt* смакова́ть *impf*.
savoury /ˈseɪvərɪ/ *adj* пика́нтный; (*fig*) поря́дочный.
saw /sɔː/ *n* пила́; *vt* пили́ть *impf*; ~ **up** распи́ливать *impf*, распили́ть *pf*. **sawdust** *n* опи́лки (-лок) *pl*.
saxophone /ˈsæksəˌfəʊn/ *n* саксофо́н.
say /seɪ/ *vt* говори́ть *impf*, сказа́ть *pf*; **to ~ nothing of** не говоря́ уже́ о+*prep*; **that is to ~** то есть; (*let us*) ~ ска́жем; **it is said (that)** говоря́т (что); *n* (*opinion*) мне́ние; (*influence*) влия́ние; **have one's ~** вы́сказаться *pf*. **saying** /ˈseɪɪŋ/ *n* погово́рка.
scab /skæb/ *n* (*on wound*) струп; (*polit*) штрейкбре́хер.
scabbard /ˈskæbəd/ *n* но́жны (*gen* -жен) *pl*.
scaffold /ˈskæfəʊld/ *n* эшафо́т. **scaffolding** /-dɪŋ/ *n* леса́ (-со́в) *pl*.
scald /skɔːld/ *vt* обва́ривать *impf*, обвари́ть *pf*.
scale /skeɪl/ *n* (*ratio*) масшта́б; (*grading*) шкала́; (*mus*) га́мма; *vt* (*climb*) взбира́ться *impf*, взобра́ться *pf* на+*acc*; ~ **down** понижа́ть *impf*, пони́зить *pf*.
scales[1] /skeɪlz/ *n pl* (*of fish*) чешуя́ (*collect*).
scales[2] /skeɪlz/ *n pl* весы́ (-со́в) *pl*.
scallop /ˈskɒləp/ *n* гребешо́к; (*decoration*) фесто́н.
scalp /skælp/ *n* ко́жа головы́.
scalpel /ˈskælp(ə)l/ *n* ска́льпель *m*.
scaly /ˈskeɪlɪ/ *adj* чешу́йчатый; (*of boiler etc.*) покры́тый на́кипью.
scamper /ˈskæmpə(r)/ *vi* бы́стро бе́гать *impf*; (*frolic*) резви́ться *impf*.
scan /skæn/ *vt* (*intently*) рассма́тривать *impf*; (*quickly*) просма́тривать *impf*, просмотре́ть *pf*; (*med*) просве́чивать *impf*, просвети́ть *pf*; *n* просве́чивание.
scandal /ˈskænd(ə)l/ *n* сканда́л; (*gossip*) спле́тни (-тен) *pl*. **scandalize** /-ˌlaɪz/ *vt* шоки́ровать *impf* & *pf*. **scandalous** /-ləs/ *adj* сканда́льный.
Scandinavia /ˌskændɪˈneɪvɪə/ *n* Скандина́вия. **Scandinavian** /-vɪən/ *adj* скандина́вский.
scanner /ˈskænə(r)/ *n* (*comput, med*) ска́нер.
scanty /ˈskæntɪ/ *adj* ску́дный.
scapegoat /ˈskeɪpɡəʊt/ *n* козёл отпуще́ния.
scar /skɑː(r)/ *n* шрам; *vt* оставля́ть *impf*, оста́вить *pf* шрам на+*prep*.
scarce /skeəs/ *adj* дефици́тный;

(*rare*) ре́дкий. **scarcely** /-lɪ/ *adv* едва́. **scarcity** /-sɪtɪ/ *n* дефици́т; ре́дкость.

scare /skeə(r)/ *vt* пуга́ть *impf*, ис~, на~ *pf*; ~ **away, off** отпу́гивать *impf*, отпугну́ть *pf*; *n* па́ника. **scarecrow** *n* пу́гало.

scarf /skɑːf/ *n* шарф.

scarlet /ˈskɑːlɪt/ *adj* (*n*) а́лый (цвет).

scathing /ˈskeɪðɪŋ/ *adj* уничтожа́ющий.

scatter /ˈskætə(r)/ *vt* & *i* рассыпа́ть(ся) *impf*, рассы́пать(ся) *pf*; (*disperse*) рассе́ивать(ся) *impf*, рассе́ять(ся) *pf*; **~-brained** ве́треный. **scattered** /-təd/ *adj* разбро́санный; (*sporadic*) отде́льный.

scavenge /ˈskævɪndʒ/ *vi* ры́ться *impf* в отбро́сах. **scavenger** /-dʒə(r)/ *n* (*person*) му́сорщик; (*animal*) живо́тное *sb*, пита́ющееся па́далью.

scenario /sɪˈnɑːrɪəʊ/ *n* сцена́рий. **scene** /siːn/ *n* (*place of disaster etc.*) ме́сто; (*place of action*) ме́сто де́йствия; (*view*) вид, пейза́ж; (*picture*) карти́на; (*theat*) сце́на, явле́ние; (*incident*) сце́на; **behind the ~s** за кули́сами; **make a ~** устра́ивать *impf*, устро́ить *pf* сце́ну. **scenery** /ˈsiːnərɪ/ *n* (*theat*) декора́ция; (*landscape*) пейза́ж. **scenic** /ˈsiːnɪk/ *adj* живопи́сный.

scent /sent/ *n* (*smell*) арома́т; (*perfume*) духи́ (-хо́в) *pl*; (*trail*) след. **scented** /-tɪd/ *adj* души́стый.

sceptic /ˈskeptɪk/ *n* ске́птик. **sceptical** /-k(ə)l/ *adj* скепти́ческий. **scepticism** /-tɪˌsɪz(ə)m/ *n* скептици́зм.

schedule /ˈʃedjuːl/ *n* (*timetable*) расписа́ние; *vt* составля́ть *impf*, соста́вить *pf* расписа́ние +*gen*.

schematic /skɪˈmætɪk/ *adj* схемати́ческий. **scheme** /skiːm/ *n* (*plan*) прое́кт; (*intrigue*) махина́ция; *vi* интригова́ть *impf*.

schism /ˈskɪz(ə)m/ *n* раско́л.

schizophrenia /ˌskɪtsəˈfriːnɪə/ *n* шизофрени́я. **schizophrenic** /-ˈfrenɪk/ *adj* шизофрени́ческий; *n* шизофре́ник.

scholar /ˈskɒlə(r)/ *n* учёный *sb*: **scholarly** /-lɪ/ *adj* учёный. **scholarship** *n* учёность; (*payment*) стипе́ндия.

school /skuːl/ *n* шко́ла; *attrib* шко́льный; *vt* (*train*) приуча́ть *impf*, приучи́ть *pf* (**to** к+*dat*, +*inf*). **school-book** *n* уче́бник. **schoolboy** *n* шко́льник. **schoolgirl** *n* шко́льница. **schooling** /-lɪŋ/ *n* обуче́ние. **school-leaver** /-ˌliːvə(r)/ *n* выпускни́к, -и́ца. **school teacher** *n* учи́тель *m*, ~ница.

schooner /ˈskuːnə(r)/ *n* шху́на.

sciatica /saɪˈætɪkə/ *n* и́шиас.

science /ˈsaɪəns/ *n* нау́ка; ~ **fiction** нау́чная фанта́стика. **scientific** /ˌsaɪənˈtɪfɪk/ *adj* нау́чный. **scientist** /ˈsaɪəntɪst/ *n* учёный *sb*.

scintillating /ˈsɪntɪˌleɪtɪŋ/ *adj* блиста́тельный.

scissors /ˈsɪzəz/ *n pl* но́жницы (-ц) *pl*.

scoff /skɒf/ *vi* (*mock*) смея́ться *impf* (**at** над+*instr*).

scold /skəʊld/ *vt* брани́ть *impf*, вы́~ *pf*.

scoop /skuːp/ *n* (*large*) черпа́к; (*ice-cream* ~) ло́жка для моро́женого; *vt* (~ *out, up*) вычё́рпывать *impf*, вы́черпать *pf*.

scooter /ˈskuːtə(r)/ *n* (*motor* ~) моторо́ллер.

scope /skəʊp/ *n* (*range*) преде́лы

m pl; (*chance*) возмо́жность.

scorch /skɔ:tʃ/ *vt* (*fingers*) обжига́ть *impf*, обже́чь *pf*; (*clothes*) сжига́ть *impf*, сжечь *pf*.

score /skɔ:(r)/ *n* (*of points etc.*) счёт; (*mus*) партиту́ра; *pl* (*great numbers*) мно́жество; *vt* (*notch*) де́лать *impf*, с~ *pf* зару́бки на+*prep*; (*points etc.*) получа́ть *impf*, получи́ть *pf*; (*mus*) оркестрова́ть *impf* & *pf*; *vi* (*keep* ~) вести́ *impf*, с~ *pf* счёт. **scorer** /-rə(r)/ *n* счётчик.

scorn /skɔ:n/ *n* презре́ние; *vt* презира́ть *impf* презре́ть *pf*. **scornful** /-fʊl/ *adj* презри́тельный.

Scorpio /'skɔ:pɪəʊ/ *n* Скорпио́н.

scorpion /'skɔ:pɪən/ *n* скорпио́н.

Scot /skɒt/ *n* шотла́ндец, -дка. **Scotch** /skɒtʃ/ *n* (*whisky*) шотла́ндское ви́ски *neut indecl*. **Scotland** *n* Шотла́ндия. **Scots, Scottish** /skɒts, 'skɒtɪʃ/ *adj* шотла́ндский.

scoundrel /'skaʊndr(ə)l/ *n* подле́ц.

scour¹ /'skaʊə(r)/ *vt* (*cleanse*) отчища́ть *impf*, отчи́стить *pf*.

scour² /'skaʊə(r)/ *vt* & *i* (*rove*) ры́скать *impf* (по+*dat*).

scourge /skɜ:dʒ/ *n* бич.

scout /skaʊt/ *n* разве́дчик; (**S**~) бойска́ут; *vi*: ~ **about** разы́скивать *impf* (**for** +*acc*).

scowl /skaʊl/ *vi* хму́риться *impf*, на~ *pf*; *n* хму́рый взгляд.

scrabble /'skræb(ə)l/ *vi*: ~ **about** ры́ться *impf*.

scramble /'skræmb(ə)l/ *vi* кара́бкаться *impf*, вс~ *pf*; (*struggle*) дра́ться *impf* (**for** за+*acc*); ~**d eggs** яи́чница-болту́нья.

scrap¹ /skræp/ *n* (*fragment etc.*) кусо́чек; *pl* оста́тки *m pl*; *pl* (*of food*) объе́дки (-ков) *pl*; ~ **metal** металлоло́м; *vt* сдава́ть *impf*, сдать *pf* в ути́ль.

scrap² /skræp/ *n* (*fight*) дра́ка; *vi* дра́ться *impf*.

scrape /skreɪp/ *vt* скрести́ *impf*; (*graze*) цара́пать *impf*, о~ *pf*; ~ **off** отскреба́ть *impf*, отскрести́ *pf*; ~ **through** (*exam*) с трудо́м выде́рживать *impf*, вы́держать *pf*; ~ **together** наскреба́ть *impf*, наскрести́ *pf*.

scratch /skrætʃ/ *vt* цара́пать *impf*, о~ *pf*; *vt* & *i* (*when itching*) чеса́ть(ся) *impf*, по~ *pf*; *n* цара́пина.

scrawl /skrɔ:l/ *n* кара́кули *f pl*; *vt* писа́ть *impf*, на~ *pf* кара́кулями.

scrawny /'skrɔ:nɪ/ *adj* сухопа́рый.

scream /skri:m/ *n* крик; *vi* крича́ть *impf*, кри́кнуть *pf*.

screech /skri:tʃ/ *n* визг; *vi* визжа́ть *impf*.

screen /skri:n/ *n* ши́рма; (*cin, TV*) экра́н; ~**-play** сцена́рий; *vt* (*protect*) защища́ть *impf*, защити́ть *pf*; (*hide*) укрыва́ть *impf*, укры́ть *pf*; (*show film etc.*) демонстри́ровать *impf* & *pf*; (*check on*) проверя́ть *impf*, прове́рить *pf*; ~ **off** отгора́живать *impf*, отгороди́ть *pf* ши́рмой.

screw /skru:/ *n* винт; *vt* (~ *on*) приви́нчивать *impf*, привинти́ть *pf*; (~ *up*) зави́нчивать *impf*, завинти́ть *pf*; (*crumple*) ко́мкать *impf*, с~ *pf*; ~ **up one's eyes** щу́риться *impf*, со~ *pf*. **screwdriver** *n* отвёртка.

scribble /'skrɪb(ə)l/ *vt* строчи́ть *impf*, на~ *pf*; *n* кара́кули *f pl*.

script /skrɪpt/ *n* (*of film etc.*) сцена́рий; (*of speech etc.*) текст; (*writing system*) письмо́; **~-writer** сценари́ст.

Scripture /ˈskrɪptʃə(r)/ *n* свяще́нное писа́ние.

scroll /skrəʊl/ *n* сви́ток; (*design*) завито́к; *vi* (*comput*) прокру́чивать *impf*, прокрути́ть *pf*.

scrounge /skraʊndʒ/ *vt* (*cadge*) стреля́ть *impf*, стрельну́ть *pf*; *vi* попроша́йничать *impf*.

scrub[1] /skrʌb/ *n* (*brushwood*) куста́рник; (*area*) за́росли *f pl*.

scrub[2] /skrʌb/ *vt* мыть *impf*, вы́~ *pf* щёткой.

scruff /skrʌf/ *n*: **by the ~ of the neck** за ши́ворот.

scruffy /ˈskrʌfɪ/ *adj* обо́дранный.

scrum /skrʌm/ *n* схва́тка вокру́г мяча́.

scruple /ˈskruːp(ə)l/ *n* (*also pl*) колеба́ния *neut pl*; угрызе́ния *neut pl* со́вести. **scrupulous** /-pjʊləs/ *adj* скрупулёзный.

scrutinize /ˈskruːtɪˌnaɪz/ *vt* рассма́тривать *impf*. **scrutiny** /ˈskruːtɪnɪ/ *n* рассмотре́ние.

scuffed /skʌft/ *adj* поцара́панный.

scuffle /ˈskʌf(ə)l/ *n* потасо́вка.

sculpt /skʌlpt/ *vt* вая́ть *impf*, из~ *pf*. **sculptor** /-tə(r)/ *n* ску́льптор. **sculpture** /-tʃə(r)/ *n* скульпту́ра.

scum /skʌm/ *n* на́кипь.

scurrilous /ˈskʌrɪləs/ *adj* непристо́йный.

scurry /ˈskʌrɪ/ *vi* поспе́шно бе́гать *indet*, бежа́ть *det*.

scuttle /ˈskʌt(ə)l/ *vi* (*run away*) удира́ть *impf*, удра́ть *pf*.

scythe /saɪð/ *n* коса́.

sea /siː/ *n* мо́ре; *attrib* морско́й; **~ front** на́бережная *sb*; **~-gull** ча́йка; **~-level** у́ровень *m* мо́ря; **~-lion** морско́й лев; **~-shore** побере́жье. **seaboard** *n* побере́жье. **seafood** *n* проду́кты *m pl* мо́ря.

seal[1] /siːl/ *n* (*on document etc.*) печа́ть; *vt* скрепля́ть *impf*, скрепи́ть *pf* печа́тью; (*close*) запеча́тывать *impf*, запеча́тать *pf*; **~ up** заде́лывать *impf*, заде́лать *pf*

seal[2] /siːl/ *n* (*zool*) тюле́нь *m*; (*fur-~*) ко́тик.

seam /siːm/ *n* шов; (*geol*) пласт.

seaman /ˈsiːm(ə)n/ *n* моря́к, матро́с.

seamless /ˈsiːmlɪs/ *adj* без шва.

seamstress /ˈsemstrɪs/ *n* швея́.

seance /ˈseɪɑ̃s/ *n* спирити́ческий сеа́нс.

seaplane /ˈsiːpleɪn/ *n* гидросамолёт.

searing /ˈsɪərɪŋ/ *adj* паля́щий.

search /sɜːtʃ/ *vt* обы́скивать *impf*, обыска́ть *pf*; *vi* иска́ть *impf* (**for** +*acc*); *n* по́иски *m pl*; о́быск; **~-party** по́исковая гру́ппа. **searching** /-tʃɪŋ/ *adj* (*look*) испыту́ющий. **searchlight** *n* прожéктор.

seasick /ˈsiːsɪk/ *adj*: **I was ~** меня́ укача́ло. **seaside** *n* бéрег мо́ря.

season /ˈsiːz(ə)n/ *n* сезо́н; (*one of four*) вре́мя *neut* го́да; **~ ticket** сезо́нный биле́т; *vt* (*flavour*) приправля́ть *impf*, припра́вить *pf*. **seasonable** /-nəb(ə)l/ *adj* по сезо́ну; (*timely*) своевре́менный. **seasonal** /-n(ə)l/ *adj* сезо́нный. **seasoning** /-nɪŋ/ *n* припра́ва.

seat /siːt/ *n* (*place*) ме́сто; (*of chair*) сиде́нье; (*chair*) стул; (*bench*) скаме́йка; (*of trousers*) зад; **~ belt** привязно́й реме́нь *m*; *vt* сажа́ть *impf*, посади́ть *pf*;

(*of room etc.*) вмещáть *impf*, вмести́ть *pf*; **be ~ed** сади́ться *impf*, сесть *pf*.
seaweed /'si:wi:d/ *n* морскáя вóдоросль.
secateurs /ˌsekə'tɜ:z/ *n pl* секáтор.
secede /sɪ'si:d/ *vi* откáлываться *impf*, отколóться *pf*. **secession** /-'seʃ(ə)n/ *n* откóл.
secluded /sɪ'klu:dɪd/ *adj* укрóмный. **seclusion** /-'klu:ʒ(ə)n/ *n* укрóмность.
second[1] /'sekənd/ *adj* вторóй; **~-class** второклáссный; **~-hand** подéржанный; (*of information*) из вторы́х рук; **~-rate** второразря́дный; **~ sight** яснови́дение; **on ~ thoughts** взвéсив всё ещё раз; **have ~ thoughts** передýмывать *impf*, передýмать *pf* (**about** +*acc*); *n* вторóй *sb*; (*date*) вторóе (числó) *sb*; (*time*) секýнда; *pl* (*comm*) товáр вторóго сóрта; **~ hand** (*of clock*) секýндная стрéлка; *vt* (*support*) поддéрживать *impf*, поддержáть *pf*; (*transfer*) откомандирóвывать *impf* откомандировáть *pf*. **secondary** /-dərɪ/ *adj* втори́чный, второстепéнный; (*education*) срéдний. **secondly** /-lɪ/ *adv* во-вторы́х.
secrecy /'si:krɪsɪ/ *n* секрéтность. **secret** /'si:krɪt/ *n* тáйна, секрéт; *adj* тáйный, секрéтный; (*hidden*) потайнóй.
secretarial /ˌsekrɪ'teərɪəl/ *adj* секретáрский. **secretariat** /-'teərɪət/ *n* секретариáт. **secretary** /'sekrɪtərɪ/ *n* секретáрь *m*, -рша; (*minister*) мини́стр.
secrete /sɪ'kri:t/ *vt* (*conceal*) укрывáть *impf*, укры́ть *pf*; (*med*) выделя́ть *impf*, вы́делить *pf*. **secretion** /-'kri:ʃ(ə)n/ *n* укрывáние; (*med*) выделéние.
secretive /'si:krɪtɪv/ *adj* скры́тный.
sect /sekt/ *n* сéкта. **sectarian** /sek'teərɪən/ *adj* сектáнтский.
section /'sekʃ(ə)n/ *n* сéкция; (*of book*) раздéл; (*geom*) сечéние.
sector /'sektə(r)/ *n* сéктор.
secular /'sekjʊlə(r)/ *adj* свéтский. **secularization** /ˌsekjʊlərai'zeɪʃ(ə)n/ *n* секуляризáция.
secure /sɪ'kjʊə(r)/ *adj* (*safe*) безопáсный; (*firm*) надёжный; (*emotionally*) увéренный; *vt* (*fasten*) закрепля́ть *impf*, закрепи́ть *pf*; (*guarantee*) обеспéчивать *impf*, обеспéчить *pf*; (*obtain*) доставáть *impf*, достáть *pf*. **security** /-'kjʊərɪtɪ/ *n* безопáсность; (*guarantee*) залóг; *pl* цéнные бумáги *f pl*.
sedate /sɪ'deɪt/ *adj* степéнный.
sedation /sɪ'deɪʃ(ə)n/ *n* успокоéние. **sedative** /'sedətɪv/ *n* успокáивающее срéдство.
sedentary /'sedəntərɪ/ *adj* сидя́чий.
sediment /'sedɪmənt/ *n* осáдок.
seduce /sɪ'dju:s/ *vt* соблазня́ть *impf*, соблазни́ть *pf*. **seduction** /-'dʌkʃ(ə)n/ *n* обольщéние. **seductive** /-'dʌktɪv/ *adj* соблазни́тельный.
see /si:/ *vt & i* ви́деть *impf*, у~ *pf*; *vt* (*watch, look*) смотрéть *impf*, по~ *pf*; (*find out*) узнавáть *impf*, узнáть *pf*; (*understand*) понимáть *impf*, поня́ть *pf*; (*meet*) ви́деться *impf*, у~ *pf* с+*instr*; (*imagine*) представля́ть *impf*, предстáвить *pf* себé; (*escort*, **~ off**) провожáть *impf*, проводи́ть *pf*; **~ about** (*attend to*) забóтиться *impf*, по~ *pf* о+*prep*; **~ through** (*fig*) ви́деть *impf*, наскво́зь+*acc*.

seed /siːd/ *n* се́мя *neut*. **seedling** /-lɪŋ/ *n* сея́нец; *pl* расса́да. **seedy** /-dɪ/ *adj* (*shabby*) потрёпанный.

seeing (that) /ˈsiːɪŋ (ðæt)/ *conj* ввиду́ того́, что.

seek /siːk/ *vt* иска́ть *impf* +*acc*, *gen*.

seem /siːm/ *vi* каза́ться *impf*, по~ *pf* (+*instr*). **seemingly** /-mɪŋlɪ/ *adv* по-ви́димому.

seemly /ˈsiːmlɪ/ *adj* прили́чный.

seep /siːp/ *vi* проса́чиваться *impf*, просочи́ться *pf*.

seethe /siːð/ *vi* кипе́ть *impf*, вс~ *pf*.

segment /ˈsegmənt/ *n* отре́зок; (*of orange etc.*) до́лька; (*geom*) сегме́нт.

segregate /ˈsegrɪˌgeɪt/ *vt* отделя́ть *impf*, отдели́ть *pf*. **segregation** /ˌsegrɪˈgeɪʃ(ə)n/ *n* сегрега́ция.

seismic /ˈsaɪzmɪk/ *adj* сейсми́ческий.

seize /siːz/ *vt* хвата́ть *impf*, схвати́ть *pf*; *vi*: ~ **up** заеда́ть *impf*, зае́сть *pf impers*+*acc*; ~ **upon** ухва́тываться *impf*, ухвати́ться *pf* за+*acc*. **seizure** /ˈsiːʒə(r)/ *n* захва́т; (*med*) припа́док.

seldom /ˈseldəm/ *adv* ре́дко.

select /sɪˈlekt/ *adj* и́збранный; *vt* отбира́ть *impf*, отобра́ть *pf*. **selection** /-ˈlekʃ(ə)n/ *n* (*choice*) вы́бор. **selective** /-ˈlektɪv/ *adj* разбо́рчивый.

self /self/ *n* со́бственное «я» *neut indecl*.

self- /self/ *in comb* само-; ~-**absorbed** эгоцентри́чный; ~-**assured** самоуве́ренный; ~-**catering (accommodation)** жильё с ку́хней; ~-**centred** эгоцентри́чный; ~-**confessed** открове́нный; ~-**confidence** самоуве́ренность; ~-**confident** самоуве́ренный; ~-**conscious** засте́нчивый; ~-**contained** (*person*) незави́симый; (*flat etc.*) отде́льный; ~-**control** самооблада́ние; ~-**defence** самозащи́та; ~-**denial** самоотрече́ние; ~-**determination** самоопределе́ние; ~-**effacing** скро́мный; ~-**employed person** незави́симый предпринима́тель *m*; ~-**esteem** самоуваже́ние; ~-**evident** очеви́дный; ~-**governing** самоуправля́ющий; ~-**help** самопо́мощь; ~-**importance** самомне́ние; ~-**imposed** доброво́льный; ~-**indulgent** изба́лованный; ~-**interest** со́бственный интере́с; ~-**pity** жа́лость к себе́; ~-**portrait** автопортре́т; ~-**preservation** самосохране́ние; ~-**reliance** самостоя́тельность; ~-**respect** самоуваже́ние; ~-**righteous** *adj* ха́нжеский; ~-**sacrifice** самопоже́ртвование; ~-**satisfied** самодово́льный; ~-**service** самообслу́живание (*attrib*: *in gen after n*); ~-**styled** самозва́нный; ~-**sufficient** самостоя́тельный.

selfish /ˈselfɪʃ/ *adj* эгоисти́чный. **selfless** /ˈselflɪs/ *adj* самоотве́рженный.

sell /sel/ *vt & i* продава́ть(ся) *impf*, прода́ть(ся) *pf*; *vt* (*deal in*) торгова́ть *impf* +*instr*; ~ **out of** распродава́ть *impf*, распрода́ть *pf*. **seller** /-lə(r)/ *n* продаве́ц. **selling** /-lɪŋ/ *n* прода́жа. **sell-out** /-aʊt/ *n*: **the play was a** ~ пье́са прошла́ с аншла́гом.

Sellotape /ˈseləˌteɪp/ *n* (*propr*) ли́пкая ле́нта.

semantic /sɪˈmæntɪk/ *adj* семанти́ческий. **semantics** /-tɪks/ *n*

семáнтика.
semblance /'sembləns/ *n* вúдимость.
semen /'si:mən/ *n* сéмя *neut.*
semi- /'semɪ/ *in comb* полу-; **~-detached house** дом, разделённый óбщей стенóй. **semibreve** /-ˌbri:v/ *n* цéлая нóта. **semicircle** *n* полукрýг. **semicircular** /-'sɜ:kjʊlə(r)/ *adj* полукрýглый. **semicolon** /-'kəʊlɒn/ *n* тóчка с запятóй. **semiconductor** /-kənˌdʌktə(r)/ *n* полупроводнúк. **semifinal** /-'faɪnəl/ *n* полуфинáл.
seminar /'semɪˌnɑ:(r)/ *n* семинáр. **seminary** /-nərɪ/ *n* семинáрия.
semiquaver /'semɪˌkweɪvə(r)/ *n* шестнáдцатая нóта.
semitone /'semɪˌtəʊn/ *n* полутóн.
senate /'senɪt/ *n* сенáт; (*univ*) совéт. **senator** /'senətə(r)/ *n* сенáтор.
send /send/ *vt* посылáть *impf*, послáть *pf* (**for** за+*instr*); **~ off** отправлять *impf*, отпрáвить *pf*; **~-off** прóводы (-дов) *pl*. **sender** /-də(r)/ *n* отправúтель *m*.
senile /'si:naɪl/ *adj* стáрческий. **senility** /sɪ'nɪlɪtɪ/ *n* стáрческое слабоýмие.
senior /'si:nɪə(r)/ *adj* (*n*) стáрший (*sb*); **~ citizen** старúк, старýха. **seniority** /ˌsi:nɪ'ɒrɪtɪ/ *n* старшинствó.
sensation /sen'seɪʃ(ə)n/ *n* сенсáция; (*feeling*) ощущéние. **sensational** /-'seɪʃən(ə)l/ *adj* сенсациóнный.
sense /sens/ *n* чýвство; (*good* **~**) здрáвый смысл; (*meaning*) смысл; *pl* (*sanity*) ум; *vt* чýвствовать *impf*. **senseless** /-lɪs/ *adj* бессмы́сленный.
sensibility /ˌsensɪ'bɪlɪtɪ/ *n* чувствúтельность; *pl* самолю́бие.
sensible /'sensɪb(ə)l/ *adj* благоразýмный. **sensitive** /'sensɪtɪv/ *adj* чувствúтельный; (*touchy*) обúдчивый. **sensitivity** /ˌsensɪ'tɪvɪtɪ/ *n* чувствúтельность.
sensory /'sensərɪ/ *adj* чувствúтельный.
sensual, sensuous /'sensjʊəl, 'sensjʊəs/ *adj* чýвственный.
sentence /'sent(ə)ns/ *n* (*gram*) предложéние; (*law*) приговóр; *vt* приговáривать *impf*, приговорúть *pf* (**to** к+*dat*).
sentiment /'sentɪmənt/ *n* (*feeling*) чýвство; (*opinion*) мнéние. **sentimental** /ˌsentɪ'ment(ə)l/ *adj* сентиментáльный. **sentimentality** /ˌsentɪmen'tælɪtɪ/ *n* сентиментáльность.
sentry /'sentrɪ/ *n* часовóй *sb*.
separable /'sepərəb(ə)l/ *adj* отделúмый. **separate** /'sepərət/ *adj* отдéльный; *vt* & *i* отделя́ть(ся) *impf*, отделúть(ся) *pf*. **separation** /ˌsepə'reɪʃ(ə)n/ *n* отделéние. **separatism** /'sepərəˌtɪz(ə)m/ *n* сепаратúзм. **separatist** /'sepərətɪst/ *n* сепаратúст.
September /sep'tembə(r)/ *n* сентя́брь *m*; *adj* сентя́брьский.
septic /'septɪk/ *adj* септúческий.
sepulchre /'sepəlkə(r)/ *n* могúла.
sequel /'si:kw(ə)l/ *n* (*result*) послéдствие; (*continuation*) продолжéние. **sequence** /-kwəns/ *n* послéдовательность; **~ of events** ход собы́тий.
sequester /sɪ'kwestə(r)/ *vt* секвестровáть *impf* & *pf*.
sequin /'si:kwɪn/ *n* блёстка.
Serb(ian) /'sɜ:b(ɪən)/ *adj* сéрбский; *n* серб, **~**ка. **Serbia** /'sɜ:bɪə/ *n* Сéрбия. **Serbo-**

Croat(ian) /ˌsɜːbəʊˈkrəʊæt, ˌsɜːbəʊkrəʊˈeɪʃ(ə)n/ *adj* сербскохорва́тский.
serenade /ˌserəˈneɪd/ *n* серена́да.
serene /sɪˈriːn/ *adj* споко́йный. **serenity** /-ˈrenɪtɪ/ *n* споко́йствие.
serf /sɜːf/ *n* крепостно́й *sb.* **serfdom** /-dəm/ *n* крепостно́е пра́во.
sergeant /ˈsɑːdʒ(ə)nt/ *n* серже́нт.
serial /ˈsɪərɪəl/ *adj*: ~ **number** сери́йный но́мер; *n* (*story*) рома́н с продолже́нием; (*broadcast*) сери́йная постано́вка. **serialize** /-ˌlaɪz/ *vt* ста́вить *impf*, по~ *pf* в не́скольких частя́х. **series** /ˈsɪəriːz/ *n* (*succession*) ряд; (*broadcast*) се́рия переда́ч.
serious /ˈsɪərɪəs/ *adj* серьёзный. **seriousness** /-nɪs/ *n* серьёзность.
sermon /ˈsɜːmən/ *n* про́поведь.
serpent /ˈsɜːpənt/ *n* змея́.
serrated /seˈreɪtɪd/ *adj* зазу́бренный.
serum /ˈsɪərəm/ *n* сы́воротка.
servant /ˈsɜːv(ə)nt/ *n* слуга́ *m*, служа́нка. **serve** /sɜːv/ *vt* служи́ть *impf*, по~ *pf* +*dat* (**as, for** +*instr*); (*attend to*) обслу́живать *impf*, обслужи́ть *pf*; (*food; ball*) подава́ть *impf*, пода́ть *pf*; (*sentence*) отбыва́ть *impf*, отбы́ть *pf*; (*writ etc.*) вруча́ть *impf*, вручи́ть *pf* (**on** +*dat*); *vi* (*be suitable*) годи́ться (**for** на +*acc*, для+*gen*); (*sport*) подава́ть *impf*, пода́ть *pf* мяч; **it ~s him right** подело́м ему́ (*dat*). **server** /ˈsɜːvə(r)/ *n* (*comput*) се́рвер. **service** /ˈsɜːvɪs/ *n* (*act of serving; branch of public work; eccl*) слу́жба; (*quality of* ~) обслу́живание; (*of car etc.*) техобслу́живание; (*set of dishes*) серви́з; (*sport*) пода́ча; (*transport*) сообще́ние; **at your** ~ к ва́шим услу́гам; *vt* (*car*) проводи́ть *impf*, провести́ *pf* техобслу́живание +*gen*; ~ **charge** пла́та за обслу́живание; ~ **station** ста́нция обслу́живания. **serviceable** /-səb(ə)l/ *n* (*useful*) поле́зный; (*durable*) про́чный. **serviceman** *n* военнослу́жащий *sb.*
serviette /ˌsɜːvɪˈet/ *n* салфе́тка.
servile /ˈsɜːvaɪl/ *adj* раболе́пный.
session /ˈseʃ(ə)n/ *n* заседа́ние, се́ссия.
set[1] /set/ *vt* (*put*; ~ *clock, trap*) ста́вить *impf*, по- *pf*; (*table*) накрыва́ть *impf*, накры́ть *pf*; (*bone*) вправля́ть *impf*, впра́вить *pf*; (*hair*) укла́дывать *impf*, уложи́ть *pf*; (*bring into state*) приводи́ть *impf*, привести́ *pf* (**in, to** в+*acc*); (*example*) подава́ть *impf*, пода́ть *pf*; (*task*) задава́ть *impf*, зада́ть *pf*; *vi* (*solidify*) тверде́ть *impf*, за~ *pf*; застыва́ть *impf*, засты́(ну)ть *pf*; (*sun etc.*) заходи́ть *impf*, зайти́ *pf*; сади́ться *impf*, сесть *pf*; ~ **about** (*begin*) начина́ть *impf*, нача́ть *pf*; (*attack*) напада́ть *impf*, напа́сть *pf* на+*acc*; ~ **back** (*impede*) препя́тствовать *impf*, вос~ *pf* +*dat*; **~-back** неуда́ча; ~ **in** наступа́ть *impf*, наступи́ть *pf*; ~ **off** (*on journey*) отправля́ться *impf*, отпра́виться *pf*; (*enhance*) оттеня́ть *impf*, оттени́ть *pf*; ~ **out** (*state*) излага́ть *impf*, изложи́ть *pf*; (*on journey*) *see* ~ **off**; ~ **up** (*business*) осно́вывать *impf*, основа́ть *pf*.
set[2] /set/ *n* набо́р, компле́кт; (*of*

dishes) сервиз; (*radio*) приёмник; (*television*) телевизор; (*tennis*) сет; (*theat*) декорация; (*cin*) съёмочная площадка.

set[3] /set/ *adj* (*established*) установленный.

settee /se'ti:/ *n* диван.

setting /'setɪŋ/ *n* (*frame*) оправа; (*surroundings*) обстановка; (*of mechanism etc.*) установка; (*of sun etc.*) заход.

settle /'set(ə)l/ *vt* (*decide*) решать *impf*, решить *pf*; (*reconcile*) улаживать *impf*, уладить *pf*; (*a bill etc.*) оплачивать *impf*, оплатить *pf*; (*calm*) успокаивать *impf*, успокоить *pf*; *vi* поселяться *impf*, поселиться *pf*; (*subside*) оседать *impf*, осесть *pf*; ~ **down** усаживаться *impf*, усесться *pf* (**to** за+*acc*). **settlement** /-mənt/ *n* поселение; (*agreement*) соглашение; (*payment*) уплата. **settler** /'setlə(r)/ *n* поселенец.

seven /'sev(ə)n/ *adj* & *n* семь; (*number 7*) семёрка. **seventeen** /,sev(ə)n'ti:n/ *adj* & *n* семнадцать. **seventeenth** /,sev(ə)n'ti:nθ/ *adj* & *n* семнадцатый. **seventh** /'sev(ə)nθ/ *adj* & *n* седьмой; (*fraction*) седьмая *sb*. **seventieth** /'sev(ə)ntɪɪθ/ *adj* & *n* семидесятый. **seventy** /'sev(ə)ntɪ/ *adj* & *n* семьдесят; *pl* (*decade*) семидесятые годы (-дов) *m pl*.

sever /'sevə(r)/ *vt* (*cut off*) отрезать *impf*, отрезать *pf*; (*relations*) разрывать *impf*, разорвать *pf*.

several /'sevr(ə)l/ *pron* (*adj*) несколько (+*gen*).

severance /'sevərəns/ *n* разрыв; ~ **pay** выходное пособие.

severe /sɪ'vɪə(r)/ *adj* строгий, суровый; (*pain*, *frost*) сильный; (*illness*) тяжёлый. **severity** /-'verɪtɪ/ *n* строгость, суровость.

sew /səʊ/ *vt* шить *impf*, с~ *pf*; ~ **on** пришивать *impf*, пришить *pf*; ~ **up** зашивать *impf*, зашить *pf*.

sewage /'su:ɪdʒ/ *n* сточные воды *f pl*; ~**-farm** поля *neut pl* орошения. **sewer** /'su:ə(r)/ *n* сточная труба. **sewerage** /-rɪdz/ *n* канализация.

sewing /'səʊɪŋ/ *n* шитьё; ~**-machine** швейная машина.

sex /seks/ *n* (*gender*) пол; (*sexual activity*) секс; **have** ~ иметь *impf* сношение. **sexual** /'seksjʊəl/ *adj* половой, сексуальный; ~ **intercourse** половое сношение. **sexuality** /,seksjʊ'ælɪtɪ/ *n* сексуальность. **sexy** /'seksɪ/ *adj* эротический.

sh /ʃ/ *int* тише!; тсс!

shabby /'ʃæbɪ/ *adj* ветхий.

shack /ʃæk/ *n* лачуга.

shackles /'ʃæk(ə)lz/ *n pl* оковы (-в) *pl*.

shade /ʃeɪd/ *n* тень; (*of colour, meaning*) оттенок; (*lamp*-~) абажур; **a** ~ чуть-чуть; *vt* затенять *impf*, затенить *pf*; (*eyes etc.*) заслонять *impf* заслонить *pf*; (*drawing*) тушевать *impf*, за~ *pf*. **shadow** /'ʃædəʊ/ *n* тень; *vt* (*follow*) тайно следить *impf* за+*instr*. **shadowy** /'ʃædəʊɪ/ *adj* тёмный. **shady** /'ʃeɪdɪ/ *adj* тенистый; (*suspicious*) подозрительный.

shaft /ʃɑ:ft/ *n* (*of spear*) древко; (*arrow*; *fig*) стрела; (*of light*) луч; (*of cart*) оглобля; (*axle*) вал; (*mine, lift*) шахта.

shaggy /'ʃægɪ/ *adj* лохматый.

shake /'ʃeɪk(ə)n/ *vt* & *i* трясти(сь) *impf*; *vi* (*tremble*) дрожа́ть *impf*; *vt* (*weaken*) колеба́ть *impf*, по~ *pf*; (*shock*) потряса́ть *impf* потрясти́ *pf*; ~ **hands** пожима́ть *impf*, пожа́ть *pf* ру́ку (**with** +*dat*); ~ **one's head** покача́ть *pf* голово́й; ~ **off** стря́хивать *impf*, стряхну́ть *pf*; (*fig*) избавля́ться *impf*, изба́виться *pf* от+*gen*.

shaky /'ʃeɪkɪ/ *adj* ша́ткий.

shallow /'ʃæləʊ/ *adj* ме́лкий; (*fig*) пове́рхностный.

sham /ʃæm/ *vt* & *i* притворя́ться *impf*, притвори́ться *pf* +*instr*; *n* притво́рство; (*person*) притво́рщик, -ица; *adj* притво́рный.

shambles /'ʃæmb(ə)lz/ *n* хао́с.

shame /ʃeɪm/ *n* (*guilt*) стыд; (*disgrace*) позо́р; **what a ~!** как жаль!; *vt* стыди́ть *impf*, при~ *pf*. **shameful** /-fʊl/ *adj* позо́рный. **shameless** /-lɪs/ *adj* бессты́дный.

shampoo /ʃæm'pu:/ *n* шампу́нь *m*.

shanty[1] /'ʃæntɪ/ *n* (*hut*) хиба́рка; ~ **town** трущо́ба.

shanty[2] /'ʃæntɪ/ *n* (*song*) матро́сская пе́сня.

shape /ʃeɪp/ *n* фо́рма; *vt* придава́ть *impf*, прида́ть *pf* фо́рму+*dat*; *vi*: ~ **up** скла́дываться *impf*, сложи́ться *pf*. **shapeless** /-lɪs/ *adj* бесфо́рменный. **shapely** /-lɪ/ *adj* стро́йный.

share /ʃeə(r)/ *n* до́ля; (*econ*) а́кция; *vt* дели́ть *impf*, по~ *pf*; (*opinion etc.*; ~ *out*) разделя́ть *impf*, раздели́ть *pf*. **shareholder** /-ˌhəʊldə(r)/ *n* акционе́р.

shark /ʃɑ:k/ *n* аку́ла.

sharp /ʃɑ:p/ *adj* о́стрый; (*steep*) круто́й; (*sudden*; *harsh*) ре́зкий; *n* (*mus*) дие́з; *adv* (*with time*) ро́вно; (*of angle*) кру́то. **sharpen** /-pən/ *vt* точи́ть *impf*, на~ *pf*.

shatter /'ʃætə(r)/ *vt* & *i* разбива́ть(ся) *impf*, разби́ть(ся) *pf* вдре́безги; *vt* (*hopes etc.*) разруша́ть *impf*, разру́шить *pf*.

shave /ʃeɪv/ *vt* & *i* бри́ть(ся) *impf*, по~ *pf*; *n* бритьё. **shaver** /-və(r)/ *n* электри́ческая бри́тва.

shawl /ʃɔ:l/ *n* шаль.

she /ʃi:/ *pron* она́.

sheaf /ʃi:f/ *n* сноп; (*of papers*) свя́зка.

shear /ʃɪə(r)/ *vt* стричь *impf*, о~ *pf*. **shears** /ʃɪəz/ *n pl* но́жницы (-ц) *pl*.

sheath /ʃi:θ/ *n* но́жны (*gen* -жен) *pl*.

shed[1] /ʃed/ *n* сара́й.

shed[2] /ʃed/ *vt* (*tears, blood, light*) пролива́ть *impf*, проли́ть *pf*; (*skin, clothes*) сбра́сывать *impf*, сбро́сить *pf*.

sheen /ʃi:n/ *n* блеск.

sheep /ʃi:p/ *n* овца́. **sheepish** /-pɪʃ/ *adj* сконфу́женный. **sheepskin** *n* овчи́на; ~ **coat** дублёнка.

sheer /ʃɪə(r)/ *adj* (*utter*) су́щий; (*textile*) прозра́чный; (*rock etc.*) отве́сный.

sheet /ʃi:t/ *n* (*on bed*) простыня́; (*of glass, paper, etc.*) лист.

sheikh /ʃeɪk/ *n* шейх.

shelf /ʃelf/ *n* по́лка.

shell /ʃel/ *n* (*of mollusc*) ра́ковина; (*seashell*) раку́шка; (*of tortoise*) щит; (*of egg, nut*) скорлупа́; (*of building*) о́стов; (*explosive* ~) снаря́д; *vt* (*peas etc.*) лущи́ть *impf*, об~ *pf*; (*bombard*) обстре́ливать *impf*, обстреля́ть *pf*.

shellfish /'ʃelfɪʃ/ *n* (*mollusc*) моллю́ск; (*crustacean*) ракообра́зное *sb*.

shelter /'ʃeltə(r)/ *n* убе́жище; *vt*

(*provide with refuge*) приюти́ть *pf*; *vt* & *i* укрыва́ть(ся) *impf*, укры́ть(ся) *pf*.

shelve[1] /ʃelv/ *vt* (*defer*) откла́дывать *impf*, отложи́ть *pf*.

shelve[2] /ʃelv/ *vi* (*slope*) отло́го спуска́ться *impf*.

shelving /'ʃelvɪŋ/ *n* (*shelves*) стелла́ж.

shepherd /'ʃepəd/ *n* пасту́х; *vt* проводи́ть *impf*, провести́ *pf*.

sherry /'ʃerɪ/ *n* хе́рес.

shield /ʃi:ld/ *n* щит; *vt* защища́ть *impf*, защити́ть *pf*.

shift /ʃɪft/ *vt* & *i* (*change position*) перемеща́ть(ся) *impf*, перемести́ть(ся) *pf*; (*change*) меня́ть(ся) *impf*; *n* перемеще́ние; переме́на; (*of workers*) сме́на; ~ **work** сме́нная рабо́та. **shifty** /-tɪ/ *adj* ско́льзкий.

shimmer /'ʃɪmə(r)/ *vi* мерца́ть *impf*; *n* мерца́ние.

shin /ʃɪn/ *n* го́лень.

shine /ʃaɪn/ *vi* свети́ть(ся) *impf*; (*glitter*) блесте́ть *impf*; (*excel*) блиста́ть *impf*; (*sun*, *eyes*) сия́ть *impf*; *vt* (*a light*) освеща́ть *impf*, освети́ть *pf* фонарём (**on** +*acc*); *n* гля́нец.

shingle /'ʃɪŋg(ə)l/ *n* (*pebbles*) га́лька.

shingles /'ʃɪŋg(ə)lz/ *n* опоя́сывающий лиша́й.

shiny /'ʃaɪnɪ/ *adj* блестя́щий.

ship /ʃɪp/ *n* кора́бль *m*; су́дно; *vt* (*transport*) перевози́ть *impf*, перевезти́ *pf*; (*dispatch*) отправля́ть *impf*, отпра́вить *pf*. **shipbuilding** *n* судострои́тельство. **shipment** /-mənt/ *n* (*dispatch*) отпра́вка; (*goods*) па́ртия. **shipping** /-pɪŋ/ *n* суда́ (-до́в) *pl*. **shipshape** *adv* в по́лном поря́дке. **shipwreck** *n* кораблекруше́ние; **be** ~**ed** терпе́ть *impf*, по~ *pf* кораблекруше́ние. **shipyard** *n* верфь.

shirk /ʃɜ:k/ *vt* увиливать *impf*, увильну́ть *pf* от+*gen*.

shirt /ʃɜ:t/ *n* руба́шка.

shit /ʃɪt/ *n* (*vulg*) говно́; *vi* срать *impf*, по~ *pf*.

shiver /'ʃɪvə(r)/ *vi* (*tremble*) дрожа́ть *impf*; *n* дрожь.

shoal /ʃəʊl/ *n* (*of fish*) стая.

shock /ʃɒk/ *n* (*emotional*) потрясе́ние; (*impact*) уда́р, толчо́к; (*electr*) уда́р то́ком; (*med*) шок; *vt* шоки́ровать *impf*. **shocking** /-kɪŋ/ *adj* (*outrageous*) сканда́льный; (*awful*) ужа́сный.

shoddy /'ʃɒdɪ/ *adj* халту́рный.

shoe /ʃu:/ *n* ту́фля; *vt* подко́вывать *impf*, подкова́ть *pf*. **shoelace** *n* шнуро́к. **shoemaker** /-ˌmeɪkə(r)/ *n* сапо́жник. **shoestring** *n*: **on a** ~ с небольши́ми сре́дствами.

shoo /ʃu:/ *int* кш!; *vt* прогоня́ть *impf*, прогна́ть *pf*.

shoot /ʃu:t/ *vt* & *i* стреля́ть *impf*, вы́стрелить *pf* (*a gun* из +*gen*; **at** в+*acc*); (*arrow*) пуска́ть *impf*, пусти́ть *pf*; (*kill*) застрели́ть *pf*; (*execute*) расстре́ливать *impf*, расстреля́ть *pf*; (*hunt*) охо́титься *impf* на+*acc*; (*football*) бить *impf* (по воро́там); (*cin*) снима́ть *impf*, снять *pf* (фильм); *vi* (*go swiftly*) проноси́ться *impf*, пронести́сь *pf*; ~ **down** (*aircraft*) сбива́ть *impf*, сбить *pf*; ~ **up** (*grow*) бы́стро расти́ *impf*, по~ *pf*; (*prices*) подска́кивать *impf*, подскочи́ть *pf*; *n* (*branch*) росто́к, побе́г; (*hunt*) охо́та. **shooting** /-tɪŋ/ *n* стрельба́; (*hunting*) охо́та; ~**-gallery** тир.

shop /ʃɒp/ *n* магази́н; (*workshop*) мастерска́я *sb*, цех; ~ **assistant** продаве́ц, -вщи́ца;

~-lifter магази́нный вор; **~-lifting** воровство́ в магази́нах; **~ steward** цехово́й ста́роста *m*; **~-window** витри́на; *vi* де́лать *impf*, с~ *pf* поку́пки (*f pl*). **shopkeeper** /-ˌki:pə(r)/ *n* ла́вочник. **shopper** /ˈʃɒpə(r)/ *n* покупа́тель *m*, ~ница. **shopping** /ˈʃɒpɪŋ/ *n* поку́пки *f pl*; **go, do one's ~** де́лать *impf*, с~ *pf* поку́пки; **~ centre** торго́вый центр.

shore[1] /ʃɔ:(r)/ *n* бе́рег.

shore[2] /ʃɔ:(r)/ *vt*: **~ up** подпира́ть *impf*, подпере́ть *pf*.

short /ʃɔ:t/ *adj* коро́ткий; (*not tall*) ни́зкого ро́ста; (*deficient*) недоста́точный; **be ~ of** испы́тывать *impf*, испыта́ть *pf* недоста́ток в+*prep*; (*curt*) ре́зкий; **in ~** одни́м сло́вом; **~-change** обсчи́тывать *impf*, обсчита́ть *pf*; **~ circuit** коро́ткое замыка́ние; **~ cut** коро́ткий путь *m*; **~ list** оконча́тельный спи́сок; **~-list** включа́ть *impf*, включи́ть *pf* в оконча́тельный спи́сок; **~-lived** недолгове́чный; **~-sighted** близору́кий; (*fig*) недальнови́дный; **~ story** расска́з; **in ~ supply** дефици́тный; **~-tempered** вспы́льчивый; **~-term** краткосро́чный; **~-wave** коротковолно́вый. **shortage** /-tɪdʒ/ *n* недоста́ток. **shortcoming** /-ˌkʌmɪŋ/ *n* недоста́ток. **shorten** /-t(ə)n/ *vt & i* укора́чивать(ся) *impf*, укороти́ть(ся) *pf*. **shortfall** *n* дефици́т. **shorthand** *n* стеногра́фия; **~ typist** машини́стка-стенографи́стка. **shortly** /-lɪ/ *adv*: **~ after** вско́ре (по́сле+*gen*); **~ before** незадо́лго (до+*gen*). **shorts** /ʃɔ:ts/ *n pl* шо́рты (-т) *pl*.

shot /ʃɒt/ *n* (*discharge of gun*) вы́стрел; (*pellets*) дробь; (*person*) стрело́к; (*attempt*) попы́тка; (*phot*) сни́мок; (*cin*) кадр; (*sport*) (*stroke*) уда́р; (*throw*) бросо́к; **like a ~** неме́дленно; **~-gun** дробови́к.

should /ʃʊd/ *v aux* (*ought*) до́лжен (бы) +*inf*: **you ~ know that** вы должны́ э́то знать; **he ~ be here soon** он до́лжен бы быть тут ско́ро; (*conditional*) бы +*past*: **I ~ say** я бы сказа́л(а); **I ~ like** я бы хоте́л(а).

shoulder /ˈʃəʊldə(r)/ *n* плечо́; **~-blade** лопа́тка; **~-strap** брете́лька; взва́ливать *impf*, взвали́ть *pf* на пле́чи; (*fig*) брать *impf*, взять *pf* на себя́.

shout /ʃaʊt/ *n* крик; *vi* крича́ть *impf*, кри́кнуть *pf*; **~ down** перекри́кивать *impf*, перекрича́ть *pf*.

shove /ʃʌv/ *n* толчо́к; *vt & i* толка́ть(ся) *impf*, толкну́ть *pf*; **~ off** (*coll*) убира́ться *impf*, убра́ться *pf*.

shovel /ˈʃʌv(ə)l/ *n* лопа́та; *vt* (**~ up**) сгреба́ть *impf*, сгрести́ *pf*.

show /ʃəʊ/ *vt* пока́зывать *impf*, показа́ть *pf*; (*exhibit*) выставля́ть *impf*, вы́ставить *pf*; (*film etc.*) демонстри́ровать *impf*, про~ *pf*; *vi* (*also* **~ up**) быть ви́дным, заме́тным; **~ off** (*vi*) привлека́ть *impf*; привле́чь *pf* к себе́ внима́ние; **~ up** *see vi*; (*appear*) появля́ться *impf*; появи́ться *pf*; *n* (*exhibition*) вы́ставка; (*theat*) спекта́кль *m*, шо́у *neut indecl*; (*effect*) ви́димость; **~ of hands** голосова́ние подня́тием руки́; **~ business** шо́у-би́знес; **~-case** витри́на; **~-jumping** соревнова́ние по скачка́м; **~-room** сало́н. **showdown** *n* развя́зка.

shower /ˈʃauə(r)/ *n* (*rain*) дóждик; (*hail*; *fig*) град; (~*-bath*) душ; *vt* осыпáть *impf*, осы́пать *pf* +*instr* (**on** +*acc*); *vi* принимáть *impf*, приня́ть *pf* душ. **showery** /-rɪ/ *adj* дождли́вый.

showpiece /ˈʃəupi:s/ *n* образéц.

showy /ˈʃəuɪ/ *adj* показнóй.

shrapnel /ˈʃræpn(ə)l/ *n* шрапнéль.

shred /ʃred/ *n* клочóк; **not a** ~ ни кáпли; *vt* мельчи́ть *impf*, из~ *pf*.

shrewd /ʃru:d/ *adj* проницáтельный.

shriek /ʃri:k/ *vi* визжáть *impf*; взви́гнуть *pf*.

shrill /ʃrɪl/ *adj* пронзи́тельный.

shrimp /ʃrɪmp/ *n* кревéтка.

shrine /ʃraɪn/ *n* святы́ня.

shrink /ʃrɪŋk/ *vi* сади́ться *impf*, сесть *pf*; (*recoil*) отпря́нуть *pf*; *vt* вызывáть *impf*, вы́звать *pf* усáдку у+*gen*; ~ **from** избегáть *impf* +*gen*. **shrinkage** /-kɪdʒ/ *n* усáдка.

shrivel /ˈʃrɪv(ə)l/ *vi* смóрщиваться *impf*, смóрщиться *pf*.

shroud /ʃraud/ *n* сáван; *vt* (*fig*) окýтывать *impf*, окýтать *pf* (**in** +*instr*).

Shrove Tuesday /ʃrəuv/ *n* втóрник на мáсленой недéле.

shrub /ʃrʌb/ *n* куст. **shrubbery** /-bərɪ/ *n* кустáрник.

shrug /ʃrʌg/ *vt* & *i* пожимáть *impf*, пожáть *pf* (плечáми).

shudder /ˈʃʌdə(r)/ *n* содрогáние; *vi* содрогáться *impf*, содрогнýться *pf*.

shuffle /ˈʃʌf(ə)l/ *vt* & *i* (*one's feet*) шáркать *impf* (ногáми); *vt* (*cards*) тасовáть *impf*, с~ *pf*.

shun /ʃʌn/ *vt* избегáть *impf* +*gen*.

shunt /ʃʌnt/ *vi* (*rly*) маневри́ровать *impf*, с~ *pf*; *vt* (*rly*) переводи́ть *impf*, перевести́ *pf* на запаснóй путь.

shut /ʃʌt/ *vt* & *i* (*also* ~ *down*) закрывáть(ся) *impf*, закры́ть(ся) *pf*; ~ **out** (*exclude*) исключáть *impf*, исключи́ть *pf*; (*fence off*) загорáживать *impf*, загороди́ть *pf*; (*keep out*) не пускáть *impf*, пусти́ть *pf*; ~ **up** (*vi*) замолчáть *pf*; (*imper*) заткни́сь!

shutter /ˈʃʌtə(r)/ *n* стáвень *m*; (*phot*) затвóр.

shuttle /ˈʃʌt(ə)l/ *n* челнóк.

shy[1] /ʃaɪ/ *adj* застéнчивый.

shy[2] /ʃaɪ/ *vi* (*in alarm*) отпря́дывать *impf*, отпря́нуть *pf*.

Siberia /saɪˈbɪərɪə/ *n* Сиби́рь. **Siberian** /-rɪən/ *adj* сиби́рский; *n* сибиря́к, -я́чка.

sick /sɪk/ *adj* больнóй; **be** ~ (*vomit*) рвать *impf*, вы́~ *pf impers* +*acc*: **he was** ~ егó вы́рвало; **feel** ~ тошни́ть *impf impers* +*acc*; **be** ~ **of** надоедáть *impf*, надоéсть *pf* +*nom* (*object*) & *dat* (*subject*): **I'm** ~ **of her** онá мне надоéла; ~**-leave** óтпуск по болéзни. **sicken** /-kən/ *vt* вызывáть *impf*, вы́звать *pf* тошнотý, (*disgust*) отвращéние, у+*gen*; *vi* заболевáть *impf*, заболéть *pf*. **sickening** /-kənɪŋ/ *adj* отврати́тельный.

sickle /ˈsɪk(ə)l/ *n* серп.

sickly /ˈsɪklɪ/ *adj* болéзненный; (*nauseating*) тошнотвóрный.

sickness /ˈsɪknɪs/ *n* болéзнь; (*vomiting*) тошнотá.

side /saɪd/ *n* сторонá; (*of body*) бок; ~ **by** ~ ря́дом (**with** с+*instr*); **on the** ~ на сторонé; *vi*: ~ **with** вставáть *impf*, встать *pf* на стóрону+*gen*; ~**-effect** побóчное дéйствие; ~**-step** (*fig*) уклоня́ться *impf*, уклони́ться *pf* от+*gen*; ~**-track** (*distract*) отвлекáть *impf*, отвлéчь *pf.* **sideboard** *n* буфе́т; *pl* ба́ки (-к) *pl.* **sidelight** *n* боково́й фона́рь *m.* **sideline** *n* (*work*) побо́чная рабо́та.

sidelong /'saɪdlɒŋ/ *adj* (*glance*) косо́й.

sideways /'saɪdweɪz/ *adv* бо́ком.

siding /'saɪdɪŋ/ *n* запасно́й путь *m.*

sidle /'saɪd(ə)l/ *vi*: ~ **up to** подходи́ть *impf*, подойти́ *pf* к (+*dat*) бочко́м.

siege /siːdʒ/ *n* оса́да; **lay ~ to** осажда́ть *impf*, осади́ть *pf*; **raise the ~ of** снима́ть *impf*, снять *pf* оса́ду с+*gen.*

sieve /sɪv/ *n* си́то; *vt* просе́ивать *impf*, просе́ять *pf.*

sift /sɪft/ *vt* просе́ивать *impf*, просе́ять *pf*; (*fig*) тща́тельно рассма́тривать *impf*, рассмотре́ть *pf.*

sigh /saɪ/ *vi* вздыха́ть *impf*, вздохну́ть *pf*; *n* вздох.

sight /saɪt/ *n* (*faculty*) зре́ние; (*view*) вид; (*spectacle*) зре́лище; *pl* достопримеча́тельности *f pl*; (*on gun*) прице́л; **at first ~** с пе́рвого взгля́да; **catch ~ of** уви́деть *pf*; **know by ~** знать *impf* в лицо́; **lose ~ of** теря́ть *impf*, по~ *pf* из виду; (*fig*) упуска́ть *impf*, упусти́ть *pf* из виду.

sign /saɪn/ *n* знак; (*indication*) при́знак; (~*board*) вы́веска; *vt* & *abs* подпи́сывать(ся) *impf*, подписа́ть(ся) *pf*; *vi* (*give* ~) подава́ть *impf*, пода́ть *pf* знак; ~ **on** (*as unemployed*) записываться *impf*, записа́ться *pf* в спи́ски безрабо́тных; (~ *up*) нанима́ться *impf*, наня́ться *pf.*

signal /'sɪgn(ə)l/ *n* сигна́л; *vt* & *i* сигнализи́ровать *impf* & *pf.* **signal-box** *n* сигна́льная бу́дка.

signatory /'sɪgnətərɪ/ *n* подписа́вший *sb*; (*of treaty*) сторона́, подписа́вшая до́говор.

signature /'sɪgnətʃə(r)/ *n* по́дпись.

significance /sɪg'nɪfɪkəns/ *n* значе́ние. **significant** /-kənt/ *adj* значи́тельный. **signify** /'sɪgnɪ,faɪ/ *vt* означа́ть *impf.*

signpost /'saɪnpəʊst/ *n* указа́тельный столб.

silage /'saɪlɪdʒ/ *n* си́лос.

silence /'saɪləns/ *n* молча́ние, тишина́; *vt* заста́вить *pf* замолча́ть. **silencer** /-sə(r)/ *n* глуши́тель *m.* **silent** /'saɪlənt/ *adj* (*not speaking*) безмо́лвный; (*of film*) немо́й; (*without noise*) ти́хий; **be ~** молча́ть *impf.*

silhouette /,sɪluː'et/ *n* силуэ́т; *vt*: **be ~d** вырисо́вываться *impf*, вы́рисоваться *pf* (**against** на фо́не+*gen*).

silicon /'sɪlɪkən/ *n* кре́мний. **silicone** /-,kəʊn/ *n* силико́н.

silk /sɪlk/ *n* шёлк; *attrib* шёлковый. **silky** /-kɪ/ *adj* шелкови́стый.

sill /sɪl/ *n* подоко́нник.

silly /'sɪlɪ/ *adj* глу́пый.

silo /'saɪləʊ/ *n* си́лос.

silt /sɪlt/ *n* ил.

silver /'sɪlvə(r)/ *n* серебро́; (*cutlery*) столо́вое серебро́; *adj* (*of* ~) сере́бряный; (*silvery*) серебри́стый; **~-plated** посеребрённый. **silversmith** *n* сере́бряных дел ма́стер. **silverware** /'sɪlvə,weə(r)/ *n* столо́вое серебро́. **silvery** /'sɪlvərɪ/ *adj* серебри́стый.

SIM (card) /sɪm/ *n* сим-ка́рта.

similar /'sɪmɪlə(r)/ *adj* подо́бный (**to** +*dat*). **similarity** /,sɪmɪ'lærɪtɪ/ *n* схо́дство. **similarly** /'sɪmɪləlɪ/ *adv* подо́бным о́бразом.

simile /'sɪmɪlɪ/ *n* сравне́ние.
simmer /'sɪmə(r)/ *vt* кипяти́ть *impf* на ме́дленном огне́; *vi* кипе́ть *impf* на ме́дленном огне́; **~ down** успока́иваться *impf*, успоко́иться *pf*.
simper /'sɪmpə(r)/ *vi* жема́нно улыба́ться *impf*, улыбну́ться *pf*.
simple /'sɪmp(ə)l/ *adj* просто́й; **~-minded** тупова́тый. **simplicity** /sɪm'plɪsɪtɪ/ *n* простота́. **simplify** /'sɪmplɪ,faɪ/ *vt* упроща́ть *impf*, упрости́ть *pf*. **simply** /'sɪmplɪ/ *adv* про́сто.
simulate /'sɪmjʊ,leɪt/ *vt* притворя́ться *impf*, притвори́ться *pf* +*instr*; (*conditions etc.*) модели́ровать *impf* & *pf*. **simulated** /-,leɪtɪd/ *adj* (*pearls etc.*) иску́сственный.
simultaneous /,sɪməl'teɪnɪəs/ *adj* одновре́ме́нный.
sin /sɪn/ *n* грех; *vi* греши́ть *impf*, со~ *pf*.
since /sɪns/ *adv* с тех пор; *prep* с+*gen*; *conj* с тех пор как; (*reason*) так как.
sincere /sɪn'sɪə(r)/ *adj* и́скренний. **sincerely** /-'sɪəlɪ/ *adv* и́скренне; **yours ~** и́скренне Ваш. **sincerity** /-'serɪtɪ/ *n* и́скренность.
sinew /'sɪnju:/ *n* сухожи́лие.
sinful /'sɪnfʊl/ *adj* гре́шный.
sing /sɪŋ/ *vt* & *i* петь *impf*, про~, с~ *pf*.
singe /sɪndʒ/ *vt* пали́ть *impf*, о~ *pf*.
singer /'sɪŋə(r)/ *n* певе́ц, -ви́ца.
single /'sɪŋg(ə)l/ *adj* оди́н; (*unmarried*) (*of man*) нежена́тый; (*of woman*) незаму́жняя; (*bed*) односпа́льный; **~-handed** без посторо́нней по́мощи; **~-minded** целеустремлённый; **~ parent** мать/оте́ц-одино́чка; **~ room** ко́мната на одного́; *n* (*ticket*) биле́т в оди́н коне́ц; *pl* (*tennis etc.*) одино́чная игра́ *vt*: **~ out** выделя́ть *impf*, вы́делить *pf*. **singly** /'sɪŋglɪ/ *adv* по-одному́.
singular /'sɪŋgjʊlə(r)/ *n* еди́нственное число́; *adj* еди́нственный; (*unusual*) необыча́йный. **singularly** /-ləlɪ/ *adv* необыча́йно.
sinister /'sɪnɪstə(r)/ *adj* злове́щий.
sink /sɪŋk/ *vi* (*descend slowly*) опуска́ться *impf*, опусти́ться *pf*; (*in mud etc.*) погружа́ться *impf*, погрузи́ться *pf*; (*in water*) тону́ть *impf*, по~ *pf*; *vt* (*ship*) топи́ть *impf*, по~ *pf*; (*pipe, post*) вка́пывать *impf*, вкопа́ть *pf*; *n* ра́ковина.
sinner /'sɪnə(r)/ *n* гре́шник, -ица.
sinus /'saɪnəs/ *n* па́зуха.
sip /sɪp/ *vt* пить *impf*, ма́ленькими глотка́ми; *n* ма́ленький глото́к.
siphon /'saɪf(ə)n/ *n* сифо́н; **~ off** (*also fig*) перека́чивать *impf*, перекача́ть *pf*.
sir /sɜ:(r)/ *n* сэр.
siren /'saɪərən/ *n* сире́на.
sister /'sɪstə(r)/ *n* сестра́; **~-in-law** (*husband's sister*) золо́вка; (*wife's sister*) своя́ченица; (*brother's wife*) неве́стка.
sit /sɪt/ *vi* (*be sitting*) сиде́ть *impf*; (**~** *down*) сади́ться *impf*, сесть *pf*; (*parl, law*) заседа́ть *impf*; *vt* уса́живать *impf*, усади́ть *pf*; (*exam*) сдава́ть *impf*; **~ back** отки́дываться *impf*, отки́нуться *pf*; **~ down** сади́ться *impf*, сесть *pf*; **~ up** приподнима́ться *impf*, приподня́ться *pf*; (*not go to bed*) не ложи́ться *impf* спать.

site /saɪt/ *n* (*where a thing takes place*) ме́сто; (*where a thing is*) местоположе́ние.

sitting /'sɪtɪŋ/ *n* (*parl etc.*) заседа́ние; (*for meal*) сме́на; **~-room** гости́ная *sb.*

situated /'sɪtjʊˌeɪtɪd/ *adj*: **be ~** находи́ться *impf.* **situation** /ˌsɪtjʊ'eɪʃ(ə)n/ *n* местоположе́ние; (*circumstances*) положе́ние; (*job*) ме́сто.

six /sɪks/ *adj & n* шесть; (*number 6*) шестёрка. **sixteen** /ˌsɪks'tiːn/ *adj & n* шестна́дцать. **sixteenth** /-'tiːnθ/ *adj & n* шестна́дцатый. **sixth** /sɪksθ/ *adj & n* шесто́й; (*fraction*) шеста́я *sb.* **sixtieth** /'sɪkstɪɪθ/ *adj & n* шестидеся́тый. **sixty** /'sɪkstɪ/ *adj & n* шестьдеся́т; *pl* (*decade*) шестидеся́тые го́ды (-до́в) *m pl.*

size /saɪz/ *n* разме́р; *vt*: **~ up** оце́нивать *impf*, оцени́ть *pf.* **sizeable** /'saɪzəb(ə)l/ *adj* значи́тельный.

sizzle /'sɪz(ə)l/ *vi* шипе́ть *impf.*

skate[1] /skeɪt/ *n* (*fish*) скат.

skate[2] /skeɪt/ *n* (*ice-~*) конёк; (*roller-~*) конёк на ро́ликах; *vi* ката́ться *impf* на конька́х; **skating-rink** като́к.

skeleton /'skelɪt(ə)n/ *n* скеле́т.

sketch /sketʃ/ *n* зарисо́вка; (*theat*) скетч; *vt & i* зарисо́вывать *impf*, зарисова́ть *pf.* **sketchy** /-tʃɪ/ *adj* схемати́ческий; (*superficial*) пове́рхностный.

skew /skjuː/ *adj* косо́й; **on the ~** ко́со.

skewer /'skjuːə(r)/ *n* ве́ртел.

ski /skiː/ *n* лы́жа; **~-jump** трампли́н; *vi* ходи́ть *impf* на лы́жах.

skid /skɪd/ *n* зано́с; *vi* заноси́ть *impf*, занести́ *pf impers+acc.*

skier /'skiːə(r)/ *n* лы́жник. **skiing** /'skiːɪŋ/ *n* лы́жный спорт.

skilful /'skɪlfʊl/ *adj* иску́сный.

skill /skɪl/ *n* мастерство́; (*countable*) поле́зный на́вык. **skilled** /skɪld/ *adj* иску́сный; (*trained*) квалифици́рованный.

skim /skɪm/ *vt* снима́ть *impf*, снять *pf* (*cream* сли́вки *pl*, *scum* на́кипь) с+*gen*; *vi* скользи́ть *impf* (**over, along** по+*dat*); **~ through** бе́гло просма́тривать *impf*, просмотре́ть *pf*; *adj*: **~ milk** сня́тое молоко́.

skimp /skɪmp/ *vt & i* скупи́ться *impf* (на+*acc*). **skimpy** /-pɪ/ *adj* ску́дный.

skin /skɪn/ *n* ко́жа; (*hide*) шку́ра; (*of fruit etc.*) кожура́; (*on milk*) пе́нка; *vt* сдира́ть *impf*, содра́ть *pf* ко́жу, шку́ру, с+*gen*; (*fruit*) снима́ть *impf*, снять *pf* кожуру́ с+*gen.* **skinny** /-nɪ/ *adj* то́щий.

skip[1] /skɪp/ *vi* скака́ть *impf*; (*with rope*) пры́гать *impf* че́рез скака́лку; *vt* (*omit*) пропуска́ть *impf*, пропусти́ть *pf.*

skip[2] /skɪp/ *n* (*container*) скип.

skipper /'skɪpə(r)/ *n* (*naut*) шки́пер.

skirmish /'skɜːmɪʃ/ *n* схва́тка.

skirt /skɜːt/ *n* ю́бка; *vt* обходи́ть *impf*, обойти́ *pf* стороно́й; **~ing-board** пли́нтус.

skittle /'skɪt(ə)l/ *n* ке́гля; *pl* ке́гли *f pl.*

skulk /skʌlk/ *vi* (*hide*) скрыва́ться *impf*; (*creep*) кра́сться *impf.*

skull /skʌl/ *n* че́реп.

skunk /skʌŋk/ *n* ску́нс.

sky /skaɪ/ *n* не́бо. **skylark** *n* жа́воронок. **skylight** *n* окно́ в кры́ше. **skyline** *n* горизо́нт. **skyscraper** /-ˌskreɪpə(r)/ *n* небоскрёб.

slab /slæb/ *n* плитá; (*of cake etc.*) кусóк.
slack /slæk/ *adj* (*loose*) слáбый; (*sluggish*) вя́лый; (*negligent*) небрéжный; *n* (*of rope*) слабинá; *pl* брю́ки (-к) *pl.* **slacken** /-kən/ *vt* ослабля́ть *impf*, ослáбить *pf*; *vt* & *i* (*slow down*) замедля́ть(ся) *impf*, замéдлить(ся) *pf*; *vi* ослабевáть *impf*, ослабéть *pf.*
slag /slæg/ *n* шлак.
slam /slæm/ *vt* & *i* захлóпывать(ся) *impf*, захлóпнуть(ся) *pf.*
slander /ˈslɑːndə(r)/ *n* клеветá; *vt* клеветáть *impf*, на~ *pf* на+*acc.* **slanderous** /-rəs/ *adj* клеветни́ческий.
slang /slæŋ/ *n* жаргóн. **slangy** /slæŋɪ/ *adj* жаргóнный.
slant /slɑːnt/ *vt* & *i* наклоня́ть(ся) *impf*, наклони́ть(ся) *pf*; *n* уклóн. **slanting** /-tɪŋ/ *adj* косóй.
slap /slæp/ *vt* шлёпать *impf*, шлёпнуть *pf*; *n* шлепóк; *adv* пря́мо. **slapdash** *adj* небрéжный. **slapstick** *n* фарс.
slash /slæʃ/ *vt* (*cut*) порóть *impf*, рас~ *pf*; (*fig*) урéзывать *impf*, урéзать *pf*; *n* разрéз; (*sign*) дробь.
slat /slæt/ *n* плáнка.
slate[1] /sleɪt/ *n* слáнец; (*for roofing*) (крóвельная) пли́тка.
slate[2] /sleɪt/ *vt* (*criticize*) разноси́ть *impf*, разнести́ *pf.*
slaughter /ˈslɔːtə(r)/ *n* (*of animals*) убóй; (*massacre*) резня́; *vt* (*animals*) рéзать *impf*, за~ *pf*; (*people*) убивáть *impf*, уби́ть *pf.* **slaughterhouse** *n* бóйня.
Slav /slɑːv/ *n* славяни́н, -я́нка; *adj* славя́нский.
slave /sleɪv/ *n* раб, рабы́ня; *vi* рабóтать *impf* как раб. **slavery** /-vərɪ/ *n* рáбство.
Slavic /ˈslɑːvɪk/ *adj* славя́нский.
slavish /ˈsleɪvɪʃ/ *adj* рáбский.
Slavonic /sləˈvɒnɪk/ *adj* славя́нский.
slay /sleɪ/ *vt* убивáть *impf*, уби́ть *pf.*
sleazy /ˈsliːzɪ/ *adj* убóгий.
sledge /sledʒ/ *n* сáни (-нéй) *pl.*
sledge-hammer /ˈsledʒˌhæmə(r)/ *n* кувáлда.
sleek /sliːk/ *adj* глáдкий.
sleep /sliːp/ *n* сон; **go to ~** засыпáть *impf*, засну́ть *pf*; *vi* спать *impf*; (*spend the night*) ночевáть *impf*, пере~ *pf.* **sleeper** /-pə(r)/ *n* спя́щий *sb*; (*on track*) шпáла; (*sleeping-car*) спáльный вагóн. **sleeping** /-pɪŋ/ *adj* спя́щий; **~-bag** спáльный мешóк; **~-car** спáльный вагóн; **~-pill** снотвóрная таблéтка. **sleepless** /-lɪs/ *adj* бессóнный. **sleepy** /-pɪ/ *adj* сóнный.
sleet /sliːt/ *n* мóкрый снег.
sleeve /sliːv/ *n* рукáв; (*of record*) конвéрт.
sleigh /sleɪ/ *n* сáни (-нéй) *pl.*
sleight-of-hand /ˌslaɪtəvˈhænd/ *n* лóвкость рук.
slender /ˈslendə(r)/ *adj* (*slim*) тóнкий; (*meagre*) ску́дный; (*of hope etc.*) слáбый.
sleuth /sluːθ/ *n* сы́щик.
slice /slaɪs/ *n* кусóк; *vt* (~ *up*) нарезáть *impf*, нарéзать *pf.*
slick /slɪk/ *adj* (*dextrous*) лóвкий; (*crafty*) хи́трый; *n* нефтянáя плёнка.
slide /slaɪd/ *vi* скользи́ть *impf*; *vt* (*drawer etc.*) задвигáть *impf*, задви́нуть *pf*; *n* (*children's* ~) гóрка; (*microscope* ~) предмéтное стеклó; (*phot*) диапозити́в, слайд; (*for hair*) закóлка. **sliding** /-dɪŋ/ *adj*

(*door*) задвижно́й.

slight[1] /slaɪt/ *adj* (*slender*) то́нкий; (*inconsiderable*) небольшо́й; (*light*) лёгкий; **not the ~est** ни мале́йшего, -шей (*gen*); **not in the ~est** ничу́ть.

slight[2] /slaɪt/ *vt* пренебрега́ть *impf*, пренебре́чь *pf* +*instr*; *n* оби́да.

slightly /'slaɪtlɪ/ *adv* слегка́, немно́го.

slim /slɪm/ *adj* то́нкий; (*chance etc.*) сла́бый; *vi* худе́ть *impf*, по~ *pf*.

slime /slaɪm/ *n* слизь. **slimy** /-mɪ/ *adj* слизи́стый; (*person*) ско́льзкий.

sling /slɪŋ/ *vt* (*throw*) швыря́ть *impf*, швырну́ть *pf*; (*suspend*) подве́шивать *impf*, подве́сить *pf*; *n* (*med*) пе́ревязь.

slink /slɪŋk/ *vi* кра́сться *impf*.

slip /slɪp/ *n* (*mistake*) оши́бка; (*garment*) комбина́ция; (*pillowcase*) на́волочка; (*paper*) листо́чек; **~ of the tongue** обмо́лвка; **give the ~** ускользну́ть *pf* от+*gen*; *vi* скользи́ть *impf*, скользну́ть *pf*; (*fall over*) поскользну́ться *pf*; (*from hands etc.*) выска́льзывать *impf*, вы́скользнуть *pf*; *vt* (*insert*) сова́ть *impf*, су́нуть *pf*; **~ off** (*depart*) ускольза́ть *impf*, ускользну́ть *pf*; **~ up** (*make mistake*) ошиба́ться *impf*, ошиби́ться *pf*. **slipper** /-pə(r)/ *n* та́пка. **slippery** /-pərɪ/ *adj* ско́льзкий.

slit /slɪt/ *vt* разреза́ть *impf*, разре́зать *pf*; (*throat*) перере́зать *pf*; *n* щель; (*cut*) разре́з.

slither /'slɪðə(r)/ *vi* скользи́ть *impf*.

sliver /'slɪvə(r)/ *n* ще́пка.

slob /slɒb/ *n* неря́ха *m* & *f*.

slobber /'slɒbə(r)/ *vi* пуска́ть *impf*, пусти́ть *pf* слю́ни.

slog /slɒg/ *vt* (*hit*) си́льно ударя́ть *impf*, уда́рить *pf*; (*work*) упо́рно рабо́тать *impf*.

slogan /'sləʊgən/ *n* ло́зунг.

slop /slɒp/ *n*: *pl* помо́и (-о́ев) *pl*; *vt* & *i* выплёскивать(ся) *impf*, вы́плескать(ся) *pf*.

slope /sləʊp/ *n* (*artificial*) накло́н; (*geog*) склон; *vi* име́ть *impf* накло́н. **sloping** /-pɪŋ/ *adj* накло́нный.

sloppy /'slɒpɪ/ *adj* (*work*) неря́шливый; (*sentimental*) сентимента́льный.

slot /slɒt/ *n* отве́рстие; **~-machine** автома́т; *vt*: **~ in** вставля́ть *impf*, вста́вить *pf*.

sloth /sləʊθ/ *n* лень.

slouch /slaʊtʃ/ *vi* (*stoop*) суту́литься *impf*.

slovenly /'slʌvənlɪ/ *adj* неря́шливый.

slow /sləʊ/ *adj* ме́дленный; (*tardy*) медли́тельный; (*stupid*) тупо́й; (*business*) вя́лый; **be ~** (*clock*) отстава́ть *impf*, отста́ть *pf*; *adv* ме́дленно; *vt* & *i* (**~ down, up**) замедля́ть(ся) *impf*, заме́длить(ся) *pf*.

sludge /slʌdʒ/ *n* (*mud*) грязь; (*sediment*) отсто́й.

slug /slʌg/ *n* (*zool*) слизня́к.

sluggish /'slʌgɪʃ/ *adj* вя́лый.

sluice /slu:s/ *n* шлюз.

slum /slʌm/ *n* трущо́ба.

slumber /'slʌmbə(r)/ *n* сон; *vi* спать *impf*.

slump /slʌmp/ *n* спад; *vi* ре́зко па́дать *impf*, (у)па́сть *pf*; (*of person*) сва́ливаться *impf*, свали́ться *pf*.

slur /slɜ:(r)/ *vt* говори́ть *impf* невня́тно; *n* (*stigma*) пятно́.

slush /slʌʃ/ *n* сля́коть.

slut /slʌt/ *n* (*sloven*) неря́ха; (*trollop*) потаску́ха.

sly /slaɪ/ *adj* хи́трый; **on the ~** тайко́м.
smack[1] /smæk/ *vi*: **~ of** па́хнуть *impf* +*instr.*
smack[2] /smæk/ *n* (*slap*) шлепо́к; *vt* шлёпать *impf*, шлёпнуть *pf.*
small /smɔ:l/ *adj* ма́ленький, небольшо́й, ма́лый; (*of agent, particles; petty*) ме́лкий; **~ change** ме́лочь; **~-scale** мелкомасшта́бный; **~ talk** све́тская бесе́да.
smart[1] /smɑ:t/ *vi* са́днить *impf impers.*
smart[2] /smɑ:t/ *adj* элега́нтный; (*brisk*) бы́стрый; (*cunning*) ло́вкий; (*sharp*) смека́листый (*coll*).
smash /smæʃ/ *vt* & *i* разбива́ть(ся) *impf*, разби́ть(ся) *pf*; *vi*: **~ into** вреза́ться *impf*, вре́заться *pf* в+*acc*; *n* (*crash*) гро́хот; (*collision*) столкнове́ние; (*blow*) си́льный уда́р.
smattering /ˈsmætərɪŋ/ *n* пове́рхностное зна́ние.
smear /smɪə(r)/ *vt* сма́зывать *impf*, сма́зать *pf*; (*dirty*) па́чкать *impf*, за~, ис~ *pf*; (*discredit*) поро́чить *impf*, о~ *pf*; *n* (*spot*) пятно́; (*slander*) клевета́; (*med*) мазо́к.
smell /smel/ *n* (*sense*) обоня́ние; (*odour*) за́пах; *vt* чу́вствовать *impf* за́пах+*gen*; (*sniff*) ню́хать *impf*, по~ *pf*; *vi*: **~ of** па́хнуть *impf* +*instr*. **smelly** /-lɪ/ *adj* воню́чий.
smelt /smelt/ *vt* (*ore*) пла́вить *impf*; (*metal*) выплавля́ть *impf*, вы́плавить *pf.*
smile /smaɪl/ *vi* улыба́ться *impf*, улыбну́ться *pf*; *n* улы́бка.
smirk /smɜ:k/ *vi* ухмыля́ться *impf*, ухмыльну́ться *pf*; *n* ухмы́лка.
smith /smɪθ/ *n* кузне́ц.
smithereens /ˌsmɪðəˈri:nz/ *n*: **(in)to ~** вдре́безги.
smithy /ˈsmɪðɪ/ *n* ку́зница.
smock /smɒk/ *n* блу́за.
smog /smɒg/ *n* тума́н (с ды́мом).
smoke /sməʊk/ *n* дым; **~-screen** дымова́я заве́са; *vt* & *i* (*cigarette etc.*) кури́ть *impf*, по~ *pf*; *vt* (*cure; colour*) копти́ть *impf*, за~ *pf*; *vi* (*abnormally*) дыми́ть *impf*; (*of fire*) дыми́ться *impf.* **smoker** /-kə(r)/ *n* кури́льщик, -ица, куря́щий *sb.* **smoky** /-kɪ/ *adj* ды́мный.
smooth /smu:ð/ *adj* (*surface etc.*) гла́дкий; (*movement etc.*) пла́вный; *vt* пригла́живать *impf*, пригла́дить *pf*; **~ over** сгла́живать *impf*, сгла́дить *pf.*
smother /ˈsmʌðə(r)/ *vt* (*stifle, also fig*) души́ть *impf*, за~ *pf*; (*cover*) покрыва́ть *impf*, покры́ть *pf.*
smoulder /ˈsməʊldə(r)/ *vi* тлеть *impf.*
smudge /smʌdʒ/ *n* пятно́; *vt* сма́зывать *impf*, сма́зать *pf.*
smug /smʌg/ *adj* самодово́льный.
smuggle /ˈsmʌg(ə)l/ *vt* провози́ть *impf*, провезти́ *pf* контраба́ндой; (*convey secretly*) проноси́ть *impf*, пронести́ *pf.* **smuggler** /-glə(r)/ *n* контрабанди́ст. **smuggling** /-glɪŋ/ *n* контраба́нда.
smut /smʌt/ *n* са́жа; (*indecency*) непристо́йность. **smutty** /-tɪ/ *adj* гря́зный; непристо́йный.
snack /snæk/ *n* заку́ска; **~ bar** заку́сочная *sb*, (*within institution*) буфе́т.
snag /snæg/ *n* (*fig*) загво́здка; *vt* зацепля́ть *impf*, зацепи́ть *pf.*
snail /sneɪl/ *n* ули́тка.
snake /sneɪk/ *n* змея́.

snap /snæp/ *vi* (*of dog or person*) огрызáться *impf*, огрызнýться *pf* (**at** на+*acc*); *vt* & *i* (*break*) обрывáть(ся) *impf*, оборвáть(ся) *pf*; *vt* (*make sound*) щёлкать *impf*, щёлкнуть *pf* +*instr*; **~ up** (*buy*) расхвáтывать *impf*, расхватáть *pf*; *n* (*sound*) щёлк; (*photo*) снúмок; *adj* (*decision*) скоропалúтельный. **snappy** /-pɪ/ *adj* (*brisk*) живóй; (*stylish*) шикáрный. **snapshot** /ˈsnæp ʃɒt/ *n* снúмок.

snare /sneə(r)/ *n* ловýшка.

snarl /snɑːl/ *vi* рычáть *impf*, за~ *pf*; *n* рычáние.

snatch /snætʃ/ *vt* хватáть *impf*, (с)хватúть *pf*; *vi*: **~ at** хватáться *impf*, (с)хватúться *pf* за+*acc*; *n* (*fragment*) обрывок.

sneak /sniːk/ *vi* (*slink*) крáсться *impf*; *vt* (*steal*) стащúть *pf*; *n* ябедник, -ица (*coll*). **sneaking** /-kɪŋ/ *adj* тáйный. **sneaky** /-kɪ/ *adj* лукáвый.

sneer /snɪə(r)/ *vi* насмехáться *impf* (**at** над+*instr*).

sneeze /sniːz/ *vi* чихáть *impf*, чихнýть *pf*; *n* чихáнье.

snide /snaɪd/ *adj* ехúдный.

sniff /snɪf/ *vi* шмыгать *impf*, шмыгнýть *pf* нóсом; *vt* нюхать *impf*, по~ *pf*.

snigger /ˈsnɪgə(r)/ *vi* хихúкать *impf*, хихúкнуть *pf*; *n* хихúканье.

snip /snɪp/ *vt* рéзать *impf* (нóжницами); **~ off** срезáть *impf*, срéзать *pf*.

snipe /snaɪp/ *vi* стрелять *impf* из укрытия (**at** в+*acc*); (*fig*) нападáть *impf*, напáсть *pf* на+*acc*. **sniper** /-pə(r)/ *n* снáйпер.

snippet /ˈsnɪpɪt/ *n* отрéзок; *pl* (*of news etc.*) обрывки *m pl*.

snivel /ˈsnɪv(ə)l/ *vi* (*run at nose*) распускáть *impf*, распустúть *pf* сóпли; (*whimper*) хныкать *impf*.

snob /snɒb/ *n* сноб. **snobbery** /-bərɪ/ *n* снобúзм. **snobbish** /-bɪʃ/ *adj* снобúстский.

snoop /snuːp/ *vi* шпиóнить *impf*; **~ about** разнюхивать *impf*, разнюхать *pf*.

snooty /ˈsnuːtɪ/ *adj* чвáнный.

snooze /snuːz/ *vi* вздремнýть *pf*; *n* корóткий сон.

snore /snɔː(r)/ *vi* храпéть *impf*.

snorkel /ˈsnɔːk(ə)l/ *n* шнóркель *m*.

snort /snɔːt/ *vi* фыркать *impf*, фыркнуть *pf*.

snot /snɒt/ *n* сóпли (-лéй) *pl*.

snout /snaʊt/ *n* рыло, мóрда.

snow /snəʊ/ *n* снег; **~-white** белоснéжный; *vi*: **it is ~ing, it snows** идёт снег; **~ed under** завáленный рабóтой; **we were ~ed up, in** нас занеслó снéгом. **snowball** *n* снежóк. **snowdrop** *n* подснéжник. **snowflake** *n* снежúнка. **snowman** *n* снéжная бáба. **snowstorm** *n* метéль. **snowy** /-ɪ/ *adj* снéжный; (*snow-white*) белоснéжный.

snub /snʌb/ *vt* игнорúровать *impf* & *pf*.

snuff[1] /snʌf/ *n* (*tobacco*) нюхательный табáк.

snuff[2] /snʌf/ *vt*: **~ out** тушúть *impf*, по~ *pf*.

snuffle /ˈsnʌf(ə)l/ *vi* сопéть *impf*.

snug /snʌg/ *adj* уютный.

snuggle /ˈsnʌg(ə)l/ *vi*: **~ up to** прижимáться *impf*, прижáться *pf* к+*dat*.

so /səʊ/ *adv* так; (*in this way*) так; (*thus, at beginning of sentence*) итáк; (*also*) тáкже, тóже; *conj* (*therefore*) так что, поэтому; **and ~ on** и так дáлее; **if**

~ в тако́м слу́чае; ~ **... as** так(о́й)... как; ~ **as to** с тем что́бы; ~**-called** так называ́емый; **(in)** ~ **far as** насто́лько; ~ **long!** пока́!; ~ **long as** поско́льку; ~ **much** насто́лько; ~ **much** ~ до тако́й сте́пени; ~ **much the better** тем лу́чше; ~ **that** что́бы; ~**... that** так... что; ~ **to say, speak** так сказа́ть; ~ **what?** ну и что?

soak /səʊk/ *vt* мочи́ть *impf*, на~ *pf*; (*drench*) прома́чивать *impf*, промочи́ть *pf*; ~ **up** впи́тывать *impf*, впита́ть *pf*; *vi*: ~ **through** проса́чиваться *impf*, просочи́ться *pf*; **get** ~**ed** промока́ть *impf*, промо́кнуть *pf*.

soap /səʊp/ *n* мы́ло; *vt* мы́лить *impf*, на~ *pf*; ~ **opera** многосери́йная переда́ча; ~ **powder** стира́льный порошо́к. **soapy** /-pɪ/ *adj* мы́льный.

soar /sɔ:(r)/ *vi* пари́ть *impf*; (*prices*) подска́кивать *impf*, подскочи́ть *pf*.

sob /sɒb/ *vi* рыда́ть *impf*; *n* рыда́ние.

sober /ˈsəʊbə(r)/ *adj* тре́звый; *vt* & *i*: ~ **up** отрезвля́ть(ся) *impf*, отрезви́ть(ся) *pf*. **sobriety** /səˈbraɪətɪ/ *n* тре́звость.

soccer /ˈsɒkə(r)/ *n* футбо́л.

sociable /ˈsəʊʃəb(ə)l/ *adj* общи́тельный. **social** /ˈsəʊʃ(ə)l/ *adj* обще́ственный, социа́льный; **S~ Democrat** социа́л-демокра́т; ~ **sciences** обще́ственные нау́ки *f pl*; ~ **security** социа́льное обеспе́чение. **socialism** /-ˌlɪz(ə)m/ *n* социали́зм. **socialist** /-lɪst/ *n* социали́ст; *adj* социалисти́ческий. **socialize** /-ˌlaɪz/ *vt* обща́ться *impf*. **society** /səˈsaɪətɪ/ *n* о́бщество. **sociological** /ˌsəʊsɪəˈlɒdʒɪk(ə)l/ *adj* социологи́ческий. **sociologist** /ˌsəʊsɪˈɒlɪdʒɪst/ *n* социо́лог. **sociology** /ˌsəʊsɪˈɒlədʒɪ/ *n* социоло́гия.

sock /sɒk/ *n* носо́к.

socket /ˈsɒkɪt/ *n* (*eye*) впа́дина; (*electr*) ште́псель *m*; (*for bulb*) патро́н.

soda /ˈsəʊdə/ *n* со́да; ~**-water** со́довая вода́.

sodden /ˈsɒd(ə)n/ *adj* промо́кший.

sodium /ˈsəʊdɪəm/ *n* на́трий.

sodomy /ˈsɒdəmɪ/ *n* педера́стия.

sofa /ˈsəʊfə/ *n* дива́н.

soft /sɒft/ *adj* мя́гкий; (*sound*) ти́хий; (*colour*) нея́ркий; (*malleable*) ко́вкий; (*tender*) не́жный; ~ **drink** безалкого́льный напи́ток. **soften** /ˈsɒf(ə)n/ *vt* & *i* смягча́ть(ся) *impf*, смягчи́ть(ся) *pf*. **softness** /ˈsɒftnɪs/ *n* мя́гкость. **software** /-weə(r)/ *n* програ́ммное обеспе́чение.

soggy /ˈsɒgɪ/ *adj* сыро́й.

soil[1] /sɔɪl/ *n* по́чва.

soil[2] /sɔɪl/ *vt* па́чкать *impf*, за~, ис~ *pf*.

solace /ˈsɒləs/ *n* утеше́ние.

solar /ˈsəʊlə(r)/ *adj* со́лнечный.

solder /ˈsəʊldə(r)/ *n* припо́й; *vt* пая́ть *impf*; (~ *together*) спа́ивать *impf*, спая́ть *pf*. **soldering iron** /-rɪŋ ˈaɪən/ *n* пая́льник.

soldier /ˈsəʊldʒə(r)/ *n* солда́т.

sole[1] /səʊl/ *n* (*of foot, shoe*) подо́шва.

sole[2] /səʊl/ *n* (*fish*) морско́й язы́к.

sole[3] /səʊl/ *adj* еди́нственный.

solemn /ˈsɒləm/ *adj* торже́ственный. **solemnity** /səˈlemnɪtɪ/ *n* торже́ственность.

solicit /səˈlɪsɪt/ *vt* проси́ть *impf*, по~ *pf* +*acc*, *gen*, о+*prep*; *vi* (*of prostitute*) истава́ть *impf* к мужчи́нам. **solicitor** /-ˈlɪsɪtə(r)/

n адвокат. **solicitous** /-'lɪsɪtəs/ *adj* заботливый.

solid /'sɒlɪd/ *adj* (*not liquid*) твёрдый; (*not hollow; continuous*) сплошной; (*firm*) прочный; (*pure*) чистый; *n* твёрдое тело; *pl* твёрдая пища. **solidarity** /ˌsɒlɪ'dærɪtɪ/ *n* солидарность. **solidify** /sə'lɪdɪˌfaɪ/ *vi* затвердевать *impf*, затвердеть *pf*. **solidity** /-'lɪdɪtɪ/ *n* твёрдость; прочность.

soliloquy /sə'lɪləkwɪ/ *n* монолог.

solitary /'sɒlɪtərɪ/ *adj* одинокий, уединённый; **~ confinement** одиночное заключение. **solitude** /'sɒlɪˌtju:d/ *n* одиночество, уединение.

solo /'səʊləʊ/ *n* соло *neut indecl*; *adj* сольный; *adv* соло. **soloist** /-ɪst/ *n* солист, ~ка.

solstice /'sɒlstɪs/ *n* солнцестояние.

soluble /'sɒljʊb(ə)l/ *adj* растворимый. **solution** /sə'lu:ʃ(ə)n/ *n* раствор; (*of puzzle etc.*) решение. **solve** /sɒlv/ *vt* решать *impf*, решить *pf*. **solvent** /'sɒlv(ə)nt/ *adj* растворяющий; (*financially*) платёжеспособный; *n* растворитель *m*.

sombre /'sɒmbə(r)/ *adj* мрачный.

some /sʌm/ *adj* & *pron* (*any*) какой-нибудь; (*a certain*) какой-то; (*a certain amount or number of*) некоторый, *or often expressed by noun in* (*partitive*) *gen*; (*several*) несколько+*gen*; (*~ people, things*) некоторые *pl*; **~ day** когда-нибудь; **~ more** ещё; **~ ... others** одни... другие. **somebody, someone** /'sʌmbədɪ, 'sʌmwʌn/ *n, pron* (*def*) кто-то; (*indef*) кто-нибудь. **somehow** /'sʌmhaʊ/ *adv* как-то; как-нибудь; (*for some reason*) почему-то; **~ or other** так или иначе.

somersault /'sʌməˌsɒlt/ *n* сальто *neut indecl*; *vi* кувыркаться *impf*, кувыр(к)нуться *pf*.

something /'sʌmθɪŋ/ *n* & *pron* (*def*) что-то; (*indef*) что-нибудь; **~ like** (*approximately*) приблизительно; (*a thing like*) что-то вроде+*gen*. **sometime** /'sʌmtaɪm/ *adv* некогда; *adj* бывший. **sometimes** /-taɪmz/ *adv* иногда. **somewhat** /'sʌmwɒt/ *adv* несколько, довольно. **somewhere** /'sʌmweə(r)/ *adv* (*position*) (*def*) где-то; (*indef*) где-нибудь; (*motion*) куда-то; куда-нибудь.

son /sʌn/ *n* сын; **~-in-law** зять *m*.

sonata /sə'nɑ:tə/ *n* соната.

song /sɒŋ/ *n* песня.

sonic /'sɒnɪk/ *adj* звуковой.

sonnet /'sɒnɪt/ *n* сонет.

soon /su:n/ *adv* скоро; (*early*) рано; **as ~ as** как только; **as ~ as possible** как можно скорее; **~er or later** рано или поздно; **the ~er the better** чем раньше, тем лучше.

soot /sʊt/ *n* сажа, копоть.

soothe /su:ð/ *vt* успокаивать *impf*, успокоить *pf*; (*pain*) облегчать *impf*, облегчить *pf*.

sophisticated /sə'fɪstɪˌkeɪtɪd/ *adj* (*person*) искушённый; (*equipment*) сложный.

soporific /ˌsɒpə'rɪfɪk/ *adj* снотворный.

soprano /sə'prɑ:nəʊ/ *n* сопрано (*voice*) *neut* & (*person*) *f indecl*.

sorcerer /'sɔ:sərə(r)/ *n* колдун. **sorcery** /'sɔ:sərɪ/ *n* колдовство.

sordid /'sɔ:dɪd/ *adj* грязный.

sore /sɔ:(r)/ *n* болячка; *adj* больно́й; **my throat is ~** у меня́ боли́т го́рло.

sorrow /ˈsɒrəʊ/ *n* печа́ль. **sorrowful** /-fʊl/ *adj* печа́льный.

sorry /ˈsɒrɪ/ *adj* жа́лкий; *predic*: **be ~** жале́ть *impf* (**about** о+*prep*); жаль *impers*+*dat* (**for** +*gen*); **~!** извини́(те)!

sort /sɔːt/ *n* род, вид, сорт; *vt* (*also* **~** *out*) сортирова́ть *impf*, рас**~** *pf*; (*also fig*) разбира́ть *impf*, разобра́ть *pf*.

sortie /ˈsɔːtɪ/ *n* вы́лазка.

SOS *n* (радио)сигна́л бе́дствия.

soul /səʊl/ *n* душа́.

sound[1] /saʊnd/ *adj* (*healthy, thorough*) здоро́вый; (*in good condition*) испра́вный; (*logical*) здра́вый, разу́мный; (*of sleep*) кре́пкий.

sound[2] /saʊnd/ *n* (*noise*) звук, шум; *attrib* звуково́й; **~ effects** звуковы́е эффе́кты *m pl*; *vi* звуча́ть *impf*, про**~** *pf*.

sound[3] /saʊnd/ *vt* (*naut*) измеря́ть *impf*, изме́рить *pf* глубину́ +*gen*; **~ out** (*fig*) зонди́ровать *impf*, по**~** *pf*; *n* зонд.

sound[4] /saʊnd/ *n* (*strait*) проли́в.

soup /suːp/ *n* суп; *vt*: **~ed up** форси́рованный.

sour /ˈsaʊə(r)/ *adj* ки́слый; **~ cream** смета́на; *vt* & *i* (*fig*) озлобля́ть(ся) *impf*, озло́бить(ся) *pf*.

source /sɔːs/ *n* исто́чник; (*of river*) исто́к

south /saʊθ/ *n* юг; (*naut*) зюйд; *adj* ю́жный; *adv* к ю́гу, на юг; **~-east** ю́го-восто́к; **~-west** ю́го-за́пад. **southerly** /ˈsʌðəlɪ/ *adj* ю́жный. **southern** /ˈsʌð(ə)n/ *adj* ю́жный. **southerner** /ˈsʌðənə(r)/ *n* южа́нин, -а́нка.

southward(s) /ˈsaʊθwədz/ *adv* на юг, к ю́гу.

souvenir /ˌsuːvəˈnɪə(r)/ *n* сувени́р.

sovereign /ˈsɒvrɪn/ *adj* сувере́нный; *n* мона́рх. **sovereignty** /-tɪ/ *n* суверените́т.

soviet /ˈsəʊvɪət/ *n* сове́т; **S~ Union** Сове́тский Сою́з; *adj* (**S~**) сове́тский.

sow[1] /saʊ/ *n* свинья́.

sow[2] /səʊ/ *vt* (*seed*) се́ять *impf*, по**~** *pf*; (*field*) засе́ивать *impf*, засе́ять *pf*.

soya /ˈsɔɪə/ *n*: **~ bean** со́евый боб.

spa /spɑː/ *n* куро́рт.

space /speɪs/ *n* (*place, room*) ме́сто; (*expanse*) простра́нство; (*interval*) промежу́ток; (*outer* **~**) ко́смос; *attrib* косми́ческий; *vt* расставля́ть *impf*, расста́вить *pf* с промежу́тками. **spacecraft, -ship** *n* косми́ческий кора́бль *m*.

spacious /ˈspeɪʃəs/ *adj* просто́рный.

spade /speɪd/ *n* (*tool*) лопа́та; *pl* (*cards*) пи́ки (пик) *pl*.

spaghetti /spəˈgetɪ/ *n* спаге́тти *neut indecl*.

Spain /speɪn/ *n* Испа́ния.

span /spæn/ *n* (*of bridge*) пролёт; (*aeron*) разма́х; *vt* (*of bridge*) соединя́ть *impf*, соедини́ть *pf* сто́роны +*gen*, (*river*) берега́ +*gen*; (*fig*) охва́тывать *impf*, охвати́ть *pf*.

Spaniard /ˈspænjəd/ *n* испа́нец, -нка. **Spanish** /ˈspænɪʃ/ *adj* испа́нский.

spank /spæŋk/ *vt* шлёпать *impf*, шлёпнуть *pf*.

spanner /ˈspænə(r)/ *n* га́ечный ключ.

spar[1] /spɑː(r)/ *n* (*aeron*) лонжеро́н.

spar² /spɑː(r)/ *vi* боксировать *impf*; (*fig*) препираться *impf*. **spare** /speə(r)/ *adj* (*in reserve*) запасной; (*extra, to* ~) лишний; (*of seat, time*) свободный; ~ **parts** запасные части *f pl*; ~ **room** комната для гостей; *n*: *pl* запчасти *f pl*; *vt* (*grudge*) жалеть *impf*, по~ *pf* +*acc*, *gen*; **he** ~**d no pains** он не жалел трудов; (*do without*) обходиться *impf*, обойтись *pf* без+*gen*; (*time*) уделять *impf*, уделить *pf*; (*show mercy towards*) щадить *impf*, по~ *pf*; (*save from*) избавлять *impf*, избавить *pf* от+*gen*: ~ **me the details** избавьте меня от подробностей.

spark /spɑːk/ *n* искра; ~**-plug** запальная свеча; *vt* (~ *off*) вызывать *impf*, вызвать *pf*.

sparkle /'spɑːk(ə)l/ *vi* сверкать *impf*.

sparrow /'spærəʊ/ *n* воробей.

sparse /spɑːs/ *adj* редкий.

Spartan /'spɑːt(ə)n/ *adj* спартанский.

spasm /'spæz(ə)m/ *n* спазм. **spasmodic** /spæz'mɒdɪk/ *adj* спазмодический.

spastic /'spæstɪk/ *n* паралитик.

spate /speɪt/ *n* разлив; (*fig*) поток.

spatial /'speɪʃ(ə)l/ *adj* пространственный.

spatter, splatter /'spætə(r), 'splætə(r)/ *vt* (*liquid*) брызгать *impf* +*instr*; (*person etc.*) забрызгивать *impf*, забрызгать *pf* (**with** +*instr*); *vi* плескать(ся) *impf*, плеснуть *pf*.

spatula /'spætjʊlə/ *n* шпатель *m*.

spawn /spɔːn/ *vt* & *i* метать *impf* (икру); *vt* (*fig*) порождать *impf*, породить *pf*.

speak /spiːk/ *vt* & *i* говорить *impf*, сказать *pf*; *vi* (*make speech*) выступать *impf*, выступить *pf* (с речью); (~ *out*) высказываться *impf*, высказаться *pf* (**for** за+*acc*; **against** против+*gen*). **speaker** /-kə(r)/ *n* говорящий *sb*; (*giving speech*) выступающий *sb*; (*orator*) оратор; (**S**~, *parl*) спикер; (*loud*-~) громкоговоритель *m*.

spear /'spɪə(r)/ *n* копьё; *vt* пронзать *impf*, пронзить *pf* копьём. **spearhead** *vt* возглавлять *impf*, возглавить *pf*.

special /'speʃ(ə)l/ *adj* особый, специальный. **specialist** /'speʃəlɪst/ *n* специалист, ~ка. **speciality** /ˌspeʃɪ'ælɪtɪ/ *n* (*dish*) фирменное блюдо; (*subject*) специальность. **specialization** /ˌspeʃəlaɪ'zeɪʃ(ə)n/ *n* специализация. **specialize** /'speʃəˌlaɪz/ *vt* & *i* специализировать(ся) *impf* & *pf*. **specially** /'speʃəlɪ/ *adv* особенно.

species /'spiːʃɪz/ *n* вид.

specific /spɪ'sɪfɪk/ *adj* особенный. **specification(s)** /ˌspesɪfɪ'keɪʃ(ə)nz/ *n* спецификация. **specify** /'spesɪˌfaɪ/ *vt* уточнять *impf*, уточнить *pf*.

specimen /'spesɪmən/ *n* образец, экземпляр.

speck /spek/ *n* крапинка, пятнышко. **speckled** /-k(ə)ld/ *adj* крапчатый.

spectacle /'spektək(ə)l/ *n* зрелище; *pl* очки (-ков) *pl*.

spectacular /spek'tækjʊlə(r)/ *adj* эффектный; (*amazing*) потрясающий.

spectator /spek'teɪtə(r)/ *n* зритель *m*.

spectre /'spektə(r)/ *n* призрак.

spectrum /'spektrəm/ *n* спектр.

speculate /ˈspekjʊˌleɪt/ *vi* (*meditate*) размышля́ть *impf*, размы́слить *pf* (**on** о+*prep*); (*conjecture*) гада́ть *impf*; (*comm*) спекули́ровать *impf*. **speculation** /ˌspekjʊˈleɪʃ(ə)n/ *n* (*conjecture*) дога́дка; (*comm*) спекуля́ция. **speculative** /ˈspekjʊlətɪv/ *adj* гипотети́ческий; спекуляти́вный. **speculator** /ˈspekjʊˌleɪtə(r)/ *n* спекуля́нт.

speech /spiːtʃ/ *n* речь. **speechless** /-lɪs/ *adj* (*fig*) онеме́вший.

speed /spiːd/ *n* ско́рость; *vi* мча́ться *impf*, про~ *pf*; (*illegally*) превыша́ть *impf*, превы́сить *pf* ско́рость; ~ **up** ускоря́ть(ся) *impf*, уско́рить(ся) *pf*. **speedboat** *n* быстрохо́дный ка́тер. **speedometer** /spiːˈdɒmɪtə(r)/ *n* спидо́метр. **speedy** /ˈspiːdɪ/ *adj* бы́стрый.

spell[1] /spel/ *n* (*charm*) загово́р.

spell[2] /spel/ *vt* (*say*) произноси́ть *impf*, произнести́ *pf* по бу́квам; (*write*) пра́вильно писа́ть *impf*, на~ *pf*; **how do you ~ that word?** как пи́шется э́то сло́во?

spell[3] /spel/ *n* (*period*) пери́од.

spellbound /ˈspelbaʊnd/ *adj* зачаро́ванный.

spelling /ˈspelɪŋ/ *n* правописа́ние.

spend /spend/ *vt* (*money*; *effort*) тра́тить *impf*, ис~, по~ *pf*; (*time*) проводи́ть *impf*, провести́ *pf*.

sperm /spɜːm/ *n* спе́рма.

sphere /sfɪə(r)/ *n* сфе́ра; (*ball*) шар. **spherical** /ˈsferɪk(ə)l/ *adj* сфери́ческий.

spice /spaɪs/ *n* пря́ность; *vt* приправля́ть *impf*, припра́вить *pf*. **spicy** /-sɪ/ *adj* пря́ный; (*fig*) пика́нтный.

spider /ˈspaɪdə(r)/ *n* пау́к.

spike /spaɪk/ *n* (*point*) остриё; (*on fence*) зубе́ц; (*on shoes*) шип.

spill /spɪl/ *vt* & *i* (*liquid*) пролива́ть(ся) *impf*, проли́ть(ся) *pf*; (*dry substance*) рассыпа́ть(ся) *impf*, рассы́пать(ся) *pf*.

spin /spɪn/ *vt* (*thread etc.*) прясть *impf*, с~ *pf*; (*coin*) подбра́сывать *impf*, подбро́сить *pf*; *vt* & *i* (*turn*) кружи́ть(ся) *impf*; ~ **out** (*prolong*) затя́гивать *impf*, затяну́ть *pf*.

spinach /ˈspɪnɪdʒ/ *n* шпина́т.

spinal /ˈspaɪn(ə)l/ *adj* спинно́й; ~ **column** спинно́й хребе́т; ~ **cord** спинно́й мозг.

spindle /ˈspɪnd(ə)l/ *n* ось *m*. **spindly** /-dlɪ/ *adj* дли́нный и то́нкий.

spine /spaɪn/ *n* (*anat*) позвоно́чник, хребе́т; (*prickle*) игла́; (*of book*) корешо́к. **spineless** /-lɪs/ *adj* (*fig*) бесхара́ктерный.

spinning /ˈspɪnɪŋ/ *n* пряде́ние; ~**-wheel** пря́лка.

spinster /ˈspɪnstə(r)/ *n* незаму́жняя же́нщина.

spiral /ˈspaɪər(ə)l/ *adj* спира́льный; (*staircase*) винтово́й; *n* спира́ль; *vi* (*rise sharply*) ре́зко возраста́ть *impf*, возрасти́ *pf*.

spire /ˈspaɪə(r)/ *n* шпиль *m*.

spirit /ˈspɪrɪt/ *n* дух, душа́; *pl* (*mood*) настрое́ние; *pl* (*drinks*) спиртно́е *sb*; ~**-level** ватерпа́с; *vt*: ~ **away** та́йно уноси́ть *impf*, унести́ *pf*. **spirited** /-tɪd/ *adj* живо́й. **spiritual** /-tjʊəl/ *adj* духо́вный. **spiritualism** /-tjʊəˌlɪz(ə)m/ *n* спирити́зм. **spiritualist** /-tjʊəlɪst/ *n* спири́т.

spit[1] /spɪt/ *n* (*skewer*) ве́ртел.

spit[2] /spɪt/ *vi* плева́ть *impf*, плю́нуть *pf*; (*of rain*) мороси́ть *impf*; (*of fire*) разбры́згивать *impf*, разбры́згать *pf* и́скры; (*sizzle*) шипе́ть *impf*; *vt*: ~ **out** выплёвывать *impf*, вы́плюнуть *pf*; ~**ing image** то́чная ко́пия; *n* слюна́.

spite /spaɪt/ *n* зло́ба; **in ~ of** несмотря́ на+*acc*. **spiteful** /-fʊl/ *adj* зло́бный.

spittle /'spɪt(ə)l/ *n* слюна́.

splash /splæʃ/ *vt* (*person*) забры́згивать *impf*, забры́згать *pf* (**with** +*instr*); (~ *liquid*) бры́згать *impf* +*instr*; *vi* плеска́ть(ся) *impf*, плесну́ть *pf*; (*move*) шлёпать *impf*, шлёпнуть *pf* (**through** по+*dat*); *n* (*act*, *sound*) плеск; (*mark made*) пятно́.

splatter /'splætə(r)/ *see* **spatter**

spleen /spliːn/ *n* селезёнка.

splendid /'splendɪd/ *adj* великоле́пный. **splendour** /'splendə(r)/ *n* великоле́пие.

splice /splaɪs/ *vt* (*ropes etc.*) сра́щивать *impf*, срасти́ть *pf*; (*film*, *tape*) склеи́вать *impf*, скле́ить *pf* концы́+*gen*.

splint /splɪnt/ *n* ши́на.

splinter /'splɪntə(r)/ *n* оско́лок; (*in skin*) зано́за; *vt* & *i* расщепля́ть(ся) *impf*, расщепи́ть(ся) *pf*.

split /splɪt/ *n* расще́лина, расще́п; (*schism*) раско́л; *pl* шпага́т; *vt* & *i* расщепля́ть(ся) *impf*, расщепи́ть(ся) *pf*; раска́лывать(ся) *impf*, расколо́ть(ся) *pf*; *vt* (*divide*) дели́ть *impf*, раз~ *pf*; ~ **second** мгнове́ние о́ка; ~ **up** (*part company*) расходи́ться *impf*, разойти́сь *pf*.

splutter /'splʌtə(r)/ *vi* бры́згать *impf* слюно́й; *vt* (*utter*) говори́ть *impf* захлёбываясь.

spoil /spɔɪl/ *n* (*booty*) добы́ча; *vt* & *i* (*damage*; *decay*) по́ртить(ся) *impf*, ис~ *pf*; *vt* (*indulge*) балова́ть *impf*, из~ *pf*.

spoke /spəʊk/ *n* спи́ца.

spokesman, -woman /'spəʊksmən, -ˌwʊmən/ *n* представи́тель *m*, ~ница.

sponge /spʌndʒ/ *n* гу́бка; ~ **cake** бискви́т; *vt* (*wash*) мыть *impf*, вы́~, по~ *pf* гу́бкой; *vi*: ~ **on** жить *impf* на счёт+*gen*. **sponger** /-dʒə(r)/ *n* приживальщик. **spongy** /-dʒɪ/ *adj* гу́бчатый.

sponsor /'spɒnsə(r)/ *n* спо́нсор; *vt* финанси́ровать *impf* & *pf*.

spontaneity /ˌspɒntə'niːɪtɪ/ *n* спонта́нность. **spontaneous** /spɒn'teɪnɪəs/ *adj* спонта́нный.

spoof /spuːf/ *n* паро́дия.

spooky /'spuːkɪ/ *adj* жу́ткий.

spool /spuːl/ *n* кату́шка.

spoon /spuːn/ *n* ло́жка; *vt* че́рпать *impf*, черпну́ть *pf* ло́жкой. **spoonful** /-fʊl/ *n* ло́жка.

sporadic /spə'rædɪk/ *adj* споради́ческий.

sport /spɔːt/ *n* спорт; ~**s car** спорти́вный автомоби́ль *m*; *vt* щеголя́ть *impf*, щегольну́ть *pf* +*instr*. **sportsman** *n* спортсме́н. **sporty** /-tɪ/ *adj* спорти́вный.

spot /spɒt/ *n* (*place*) ме́сто; (*mark*) пятно́; (*pimple*) пры́щик; **on the ~** на ме́сте; (*at once*) сра́зу; ~ **check** вы́борочная прове́рка; *vt* (*notice*) замеча́ть *impf*, заме́тить *pf*. **spotless** /-lɪs/ *adj* абсолю́тно чи́стый. **spotlight** *n* проже́ктор; (*fig*) внима́ние. **spotty** /-tɪ/ *adj* прыщева́тый.

spouse /spaʊz/ *n* супру́г, ~а.

spout /spaʊt/ *vi* бить *impf* струёй; хлы́нуть *pf*; (*pontificate*) ора́торствовать *impf*; *vt* изверга́ть *impf*, изве́ргнуть *pf*; (*verses etc.*) деклами́ровать *impf*, про~ *pf*; *n* (*tube*) но́сик; (*jet*) струя́.

sprain /spreɪn/ *vt* растя́гивать *impf*, растяну́ть *pf*; *n* растяже́ние.

sprawl /sprɔːl/ *vi* (*of person*) разва́ливаться *impf*, развали́ться *pf*; (*of town*) раски́дываться *impf*, раски́нуться *pf*.

spray[1] /spreɪ/ *n* (*flowers*) ве́т(оч)ка.

spray[2] /spreɪ/ *n* бры́зги (-г) *pl*; (*atomizer*) пульверизáтор; *vt* опры́скивать *impf*, опры́скать *pf* (**with** +*instr*); (*cause to scatter*) распыля́ть *impf*, распыли́ть *pf*.

spread /spred/ *vt* & *i* (*news, disease, etc.*) распространя́ть(ся) *impf*, распространи́ть(ся) *pf*; *vt* (~ *out*) расстила́ть *impf*, разостла́ть *pf*; (*unfurl, unroll*) развёртывать *impf*, разверну́ть *pf*; (*bread etc.* +*acc*; *butter etc.* +*instr*) нама́зывать *impf*, нама́зать *pf*; *n* (*expansion*) распростране́ние; (*span*) разма́х; (*feast*) пир; (*paste*) па́ста.

spree /spriː/ *n* кутёж; **go on a** ~ кути́ть *impf*, кутну́ть *pf*.

sprig /sprɪg/ *n* ве́точка.

sprightly /'spraɪtlɪ/ *adj* бо́дрый.

spring /sprɪŋ/ *vi* (*jump*) пры́гать *impf*, пры́гнуть *pf*; *vt* (*tell unexpectedly*) неожи́данно сообща́ть *impf*, сообщи́ть *pf* (**on** +*dat*); ~ **a leak** дава́ть *impf*, дать *pf* течь; ~ **from** (*originate*) происходи́ть *impf*, произойти́ *pf* из+*gen*; *n* (*jump*) прыжо́к; (*season*) весна́, *attrib* весе́нний; (*water*) исто́чник; (*elasticity*) упру́гость; (*coil*) пружи́на; **~-clean** генера́льная убо́рка. **springboard** *n* трампли́н.

sprinkle /'sprɪŋk(ə)l/ *vt* (*with liquid*) опры́скивать *impf*, опры́скать *pf* (**with** +*instr*); (*with solid*) посыпа́ть *impf*, посы́пать *pf* (**with** +*instr*). **sprinkler** /-klə(r)/ *n* разбры́згиватель *m*.

sprint /sprɪnt/ *vi* бежа́ть *impf* на коро́ткую диста́нцию; (*rush*) рвану́ться *pf*; *n* спринт. **sprinter** /-tə(r)/ *n* спри́нтер.

sprout /spraʊt/ *vi* пуска́ть *impf*, пусти́ть *pf* ростки́; *n* росто́к; *pl* брюссе́льская капу́ста.

spruce[1] /spruːs/ *adj* наря́дный, элега́нтный; *vt*: ~ **o.s. up** приводи́ть *impf*, привести́ *pf* себя́ в поря́док.

spruce[2] /spruːs/ *n* ель.

spur /spɜː(r)/ *n* шпо́ра; (*fig*) сти́мул; **on the ~ of the moment** под влия́нием мину́ты; *vt*: ~ **on** подхлёстывать *impf*, подхлестну́ть *pf*.

spurious /'spjʊərɪəs/ *adj* подде́льный.

spurn /spɜːn/ *vt* отверга́ть *impf*, отве́ргнуть *pf*.

spurt /spɜːt/ *n* (*jet*) струя́; (*effort*) рыво́к; *vi* бить *impf* струёй; (*make an effort*) де́лать *impf*, с~ *pf* рыво́к.

spy /spaɪ/ *n* шпио́н; *vi* шпио́нить *impf* (**on** за+*instr*). **spying** /-ɪŋ/ *n* шпиона́ж.

squabble /'skwɒb(ə)l/ *n* перебра́нка; *vi* вздо́рить *impf*, по~ *pf*.

squad /skwɒd/ *n* кома́нда, гру́ппа.

squadron /'skwɒdrən/ *n* (*mil*) эскадро́н; (*naut*) эска́дра; (*aeron*) эскадри́лья.

squalid /'skwɒlɪd/ *adj* убо́гий.

squall /skwɔːl/ *n* шквал.

squalor /'skwɒlə(r)/ *n* убо́жество.

squander /'skwɒndə(r)/ *vt* растра́чивать *impf*, растра́-

тить *pf.*

square /skweə(r)/ *n* (*shape*) квадра́т; (*in town*) пло́щадь; (*on paper, material*) кле́тка; (*instrument*) науго́льник; *adj* квадра́тный; (*meal*) пло́тный; **~ root** квадра́тный ко́рень *m*; *vt* (*accounts*) своди́ть *impf*, свести́ *pf*; (*math*) возводи́ть *impf*, возвести́ *pf* в квадра́т; *vi* (*correspond*) соотве́тствовать *impf* (**with** +*dat*).

squash /skwɒʃ/ *n* (*crowd*) толку́чка; (*drink*) сок; *vt* разда́вливать *impf*, раздави́ть *pf*; (*suppress*) подавля́ть *impf*, подави́ть *pf*; *vi* вти́скиваться *impf*, вти́снуться *pf*.

squat /skwɒt/ *adj* призе́мистый; *vi* сиде́ть *impf* на ко́рточках; **~ down** сади́ться *impf*, сесть *pf* на ко́рточки.

squatter /'skwɒtə(r)/ *n* незако́нный жиле́ц.

squawk /skwɔːk/ *n* клёкот; *vi* клекота́ть *impf*.

squeak /skwiːk/ *n* писк; (*of object*) скрип; *vi* пища́ть *impf*, пи́скнуть *pf*; (*of object*) скрипе́ть *impf*, скри́пнуть *pf*. **squeaky** /-kɪ/ *adj* пискли́вый, скрипу́чий.

squeal /skwiːl/ *n* визг; *vi* визжа́ть *impf*, ви́згнуть *pf*.

squeamish /'skwiːmɪʃ/ *adj* брезгли́вый.

squeeze /skwiːz/ *n* (*crush*) да́вка; (*pressure*) сжа́тие; (*hand*) пожа́тие; *vt* дави́ть *impf*; сжима́ть *impf*, сжать *pf*; **~ in** впи́хивать(ся) *impf*, впихну́ть(ся) *pf*; вти́скивать(ся) *impf*, вти́снуть(ся) *pf*; **~ out** выжима́ть *impf*, вы́жать *pf*; **~ through** проти́скивать(ся) *impf*, проти́снуть(ся) *pf*.

squelch /skweltʃ/ *vi* хлю́пать *impf*, хлю́пнуть *pf*.

squid /skwɪd/ *n* кальма́р.

squint /skwɪnt/ *n* косогла́зие; *vi* коси́ть *impf*; (*screw up eyes*) щу́риться *impf*.

squire /'skwaɪə(r)/ *n* сквайр, поме́щик.

squirm /skwɜːm/ *vi* (*wriggle*) извива́ться *impf*, изви́ться *pf*.

squirrel /'skwɪr(ə)l/ *n* бе́лка.

squirt /skwɜːt/ *n* струя́; *vi* бить *impf* струёй; *vt* пуска́ть *impf*, пусти́ть *pf* струю́ (*substance* +*gen*; **at** на+*acc*).

St. *abbr* (*of* **Street**) ул., у́лица; (*of* **Saint**) св., Свято́й, -а́я.

stab /stæb/ *n* уда́р (ножо́м *etc.*); (*pain*) внеза́пная о́страя боль; *vt* наноси́ть *impf*, нанести́ *pf* уда́р (ножо́м *etc.*) (*person* +*dat*).

stability /stə'bɪlɪtɪ/ *n* усто́йчивость, стаби́льность. **stabilize** /'steɪbɪˌlaɪz/ *vt* стабилизи́ровать *impf* & *pf*.

stable /'steɪb(ə)l/ *adj* усто́йчивый, стаби́льный; (*psych*) уравнове́шенный; *n* коню́шня.

staccato /stə'kɑːtəʊ/ *n* стаккáто *neut indecl*; *adv* стаккáто; *adj* отры́вистый.

stack /stæk/ *n* ку́ча; *vt* скла́дывать *impf*, сложи́ть *pf* в ку́чу.

stadium /'steɪdɪəm/ *n* стадио́н.

staff /stɑːf/ *n* (*personnel*) штат, сотру́дники *m pl*; (*stick*) посо́х, жезл; *adj* шта́тный; (*mil*) штабно́й.

stag /stæg/ *n* саме́ц-оле́нь *m*.

stage /steɪdʒ/ *n* (*theat*) сце́на; (*period*) ста́дия; *vt* (*theat*) ста́вить *impf*, по~ *pf*; (*organize*) организова́ть *impf* & *pf*; **~-manager** режиссёр.

stagger /'stægə(r)/ *vi* шата́ться *impf*, шатну́ться *pf*; *vt* (*hours of* *work etc.*) распределя́ть *impf*, распредели́ть *pf*. **be staggered** /-gəd/ *vi* поража́ться *impf*, порази́ться *pf*. **staggering** /-gərɪŋ/ *adj* потряса́ющий.

stagnant /ˈstæɡnənt/ *adj* (*water*) стоя́чий; (*fig*) засто́йный. **stagnate** /stæɡˈneɪt/ *vi* заста́иваться *impf*, застоя́ться *pf*; (*fig*) косне́ть *impf*, за~ *pf*.

staid /steɪd/ *adj* степе́нный.

stain /steɪn/ *n* пятно́; (*dye*) кра́ска; *vt* па́чкать *impf*, за~, ис~ *pf*; (*dye*) окра́шивать *impf*, окра́сить *pf*; **~ed glass** цветно́е стекло́. **stainless** /-lɪs/ *adj*: **~ steel** нержаве́ющая сталь.

stair /steə(r)/ *n* ступе́нька. **staircase, stairs** /ˈsteəkeɪs, steəz/ *n pl* ле́стница.

stake /steɪk/ *n* (*stick*) кол; (*bet*) ста́вка; (*comm*) до́ля; **be at ~** быть поста́вленным на ка́рту; *vt* (*mark out*) огора́живать *impf*, огороди́ть *pf* ко́льями; (*support*) укрепля́ть *impf*, укрепи́ть *pf* коло́м; (*risk*) ста́вить *impf*, по~ *pf* на ка́рту.

stale /steɪl/ *adj* несве́жий; (*musty, damp*) за́тхлый; (*hackneyed*) изби́тый.

stalemate /ˈsteɪlmeɪt/ *n* пат; (*fig*) тупи́к.

stalk /stɔːk/ *n* сте́бель *m*; *vt* высле́живать *impf*; *vi* (& *t*) (*stride*) ше́ствовать *impf* (по+*dat*).

stall /stɔːl/ *n* сто́йло; (*booth*) ларёк; *pl* (*theat*) партéр; *vi* (*of engine*) гло́хнуть *impf*, за~ *pf*; (*play for time*) оття́гивать *impf*, оттяну́ть *pf* вре́мя; *vt* (*engine*) нечá янно заглуша́ть *impf*, заглуши́ть *pf*.

stallion /ˈstæljən/ *n* жеребе́ц.

stalwart /ˈstɔːlwət/ *adj* сто́йкий; *n* сто́йкий приве́рженец.

stamina /ˈstæmɪnə/ *n* выно́сливость.

stammer /ˈstæmə(r)/ *vi* заика́ться *impf*; *n* заика́ние.

stamp /stæmp/ *n* печа́ть; (*postage*) (почто́вая) ма́рка; *vt* штампова́ть *impf*; *vi* то́пать *impf*, то́пнуть *pf* (нога́ми); **~ out** поборо́ть *pf*.

stampede /stæmˈpiːd/ *n* пани́ческое бе́гство; *vi* обраща́ться *impf* в пани́ческое бе́гство.

stance /stɑːns/ *n* пози́ция.

stand /stænd/ *n* (*hat, coat*) ве́шалка; (*music*) пюпи́тр; (*umbrella, support*) подста́вка; (*booth*) ларёк; (*taxi*) стоя́нка; (*at stadium*) трибу́на; (*position*) пози́ция; (*resistance*) сопротивле́ние; *vi* стоя́ть *impf*; (**~** *up*) встава́ть *impf*, встать *pf*; (*remain in force*) остава́ться *impf*, оста́ться в си́ле; *vt* (*put*) ста́вить *impf*, по~ *pf*; (*endure*) терпе́ть *impf*, по~ *pf*; **~ back** отходи́ть *impf*, отойти́ *pf* (**from** от+*gen*); (*not go forward*) держа́ться *impf* позади́; **~ by** (*vi*) (*not interfere*) не вме́шиваться *impf*, вмеша́ться *pf*; (*be ready*) быть *impf* на гото́ве; (*vt*) (*support*) подде́рживать *impf*, поддержа́ть *pf*; (*stick to*) приде́рживаться *impf* +*gen*; **~ down** (*resign*) уходи́ть *impf*, уйти́ *pf* с по́ста (**as** +*gen*); **~ for** (*signify*) означа́ть *impf*; (*tolerate*): **I shall not ~ for it** я не потерплю́; **~-in** замести́тель *m*; **~ in** (*for*) замеща́ть *impf*, замести́ть *pf*; **~ out** выделя́ться *impf*, вы́делиться *pf*; **~ up** встава́ть *impf*, встать *pf*; **~ up for** (*defend*) отста́ивать *impf*, отстоя́ть *pf*; **~ up to** (*endure*) выде́рживать *impf*, вы́держать *pf*; (*not give in to*) противостоя́ть *impf* +*dat*.

standard /'stændəd/ *n* (*norm*) стандáрт, норм; (*flag*) знáмя *neut*; **~ of living** жи́зненный ýровень *m*; *adj* нормáльный, стандáртный. **standardization** /ˌstændədaɪ'zeɪʃ(ə)n/ *n* нормализáция, стандартизáция. **standardize** /'stændəˌdaɪz/ *vt* стандартизи́ровать *impf* & *pf*; нормализовáть *impf* & *pf*.

standing /'stændɪŋ/ *n* положéние; *adj* (*upright*) стоя́чий; (*permanent*) постоя́нный.

standpoint /'stændpɔɪnt/ *n* тóчка зрéния.

standstill /'stændstɪl/ *n* останóвка, застóй, пáуза; **be at a ~** стоя́ть *impf* на мёртвой тóчке; **bring (come) to a ~** остáнавливать(ся) *impf*, останови́ть(ся) *pf*.

stanza /'stænzə/ *n* строфá.

staple¹ /'steɪp(ə)l/ *n* (*metal bar*) скобá; (*for paper*) скрéпка; *vt* скрепля́ть *impf*, скрепи́ть *pf*.

staple² /'steɪp(ə)l/ *n* (*product*) глáвный продýкт; *adj* оснoвнóй.

star /stɑː(r)/ *n* звездá; (*asterisk*) звёздочка; *vi* игрáть *impf*, сыгрáть *pf* глáвную роль. **starfish** *n* морскáя звездá.

starboard /'stɑːbəd/ *n* прáвый борт.

starch /stɑːtʃ/ *n* крахмáл; *vt* крахмáлить *impf*, на~ *pf*. **starchy** /-tʃɪ/ *adj* крахмáлистый; (*prim*) чóпорный.

stare /steə(r)/ *n* при́стальный взгляд; *vi* при́стально смотрéть *impf* (**at** на+*acc*).

stark /stɑːk/ *adj* (*bare*) гóлый; (*desolate*) пусты́нный; (*sharp*) рéзкий; *adv* совершéнно.

starling /'stɑːlɪŋ/ *n* скворéц.

starry /'stɑːrɪ/ *adj* звёздный.

start /stɑːt/ *n* начáло; (*sport*) старт; *vi* начинáться *impf*, начáться *pf*; (*engine*) заводи́ться *impf*, завести́сь *pf*; (*set out*) отправля́ться *impf*, отпрáвиться *pf*; (*shudder*) вздрáгивать *impf*, вздрóгнуть *pf*; (*sport*) стартовáть *impf* & *pf*; *vt* начинáть *impf*, начáть *pf* (*gerund*, *inf*, +*inf*; *by*, +*gerund* с тогó, что...; **with** +*instr*, с+*gen*); (*car*, *engine*) заводи́ть *impf*, завести́ *pf*; (*fire*, *rumour*) пускáть *impf*, пусти́ть *pf*; (*found*) оснóвывать *impf*, основáть *pf*. **starter** /-tə(r)/ *n* (*tech*) стáртёр; (*cul*) закýска. **starting-point** /-tɪŋ pɔɪnt/ *n* отправнóй пункт.

startle /'stɑːt(ə)l/ *vt* испугáть *pf*.

starvation /stɑː'veɪʃ(ə)n/ *n* гóлод. **starve** /stɑːv/ *vi* голодáть *impf*; (*to death*) умирáть *impf*, умерéть с гóлоду; *vt* мори́ть *impf*, по~, у~ *pf* гóлодом. **starving** /'stɑːvɪŋ/ *adj* голодáющий; (*hungry*) óчень голóдный.

state /steɪt/ *n* (*condition*) состоя́ние; (*polit*) госудáрство, штат; *adj* (*ceremonial*) торжéственный; парáдный; (*polit*) госудáрственный; *vt* (*announce*) заявля́ть *impf*, заяви́ть *pf*; (*expound*) излагáть *impf*, изложи́ть *pf*. **stateless** /-lɪs/ *adj* не имéющий граждáнства. **stately** /-lɪ/ *adj* вели́чественный. **statement** /-mənt/ *n* заявлéние; (*comm*) отчёт. **statesman** *n* госудáрственный дéятель *m*.

static /'stætɪk/ *adj* неподви́жный.

station /'steɪʃ(ə)n/ *n* (*rly*) вокзáл, стáнция; (*social*) общéственное положéние; (*meteorological*, *hydro-electric power*, *radio etc.*) стáнция; (*post*) пост;

vt размещáть *impf*, разместúть *pf*.

stationary /'steɪʃənərɪ/ *adj* неподвúжный.

stationery /'steɪʃənərɪ/ *n* канцеля́рские принадлéжности *f pl*; (*writing-paper*) почтóвая бумáга; ~ **shop** канцеля́рский магазúн.

statistic /stə'tɪstɪk/ *n* статистúческое дáнное. **statistical** /-'tɪstɪk(ə)l/ *adj* статистúческий. **statistician** /ˌstætɪ'stɪʃ(ə)n/ *n* статúстик. **statistics** /stə'tɪstɪks/ *n* статúстика.

statue /'stætju:/ *n* стáтуя. **statuette** /ˌstætjʊ'et/ *n* статуэ́тка.

stature /'stætʃə(r)/ *n* рост; (*merit*) калúбр.

status /'steɪtəs/ *n* стáтус. **status quo** /ˌsteɪtəs 'kwəʊ/ *n* стáтус-квó *neut indecl*.

statute /'stætju:t/ *n* статýт. **statutory** /-tərɪ/ *adj* установлéнный закóном.

staunch /stɔ:ntʃ/ *adj* вéрный.

stave /steɪv/ *vt*: ~ **off** предотвращáть *impf*, предотвратúть *pf*.

stay /steɪ/ *n* (*time spent*) пребывáние; *vi* (*remain*) оставáться *impf*, остáться *pf* (**to dinner** обéдать); (*put up*) останáвливаться *impf*, остановúться *pf* (**at** (*place*) в+*prep*; **at** (*friends' etc;*) у+*gen*); (*live*) жить; ~ **behind** оставáться *impf*, остáться *pf*; ~ **in** оставáться *impf*, остáться *pf* дóма; ~ **up** не ложúться *impf* спать; (*trousers*) держáться *impf*. **staying-power** /'steɪɪŋ ˌpaʊə(r)/ *n* вынóсливость.

stead /sted/ *n*: **stand s.o. in good** ~ окáзываться *impf*, оказáться *pf* полéзным комý-л.

steadfast /'stedfɑ:st/ *adj* стóйкий, непоколебúмый.

steady /'stedɪ/ *adj* (*firm*) устóйчивый; (*continuous*) непреры́вный; (*wind, temperature*) рóвный; (*speed*) постоя́нный; (*unshakeable*) непоколебúмый; *vt* (*boat etc.*) приводúть *impf*, привестú *pf* в равновéсие.

steak /steɪk/ *n* бифштéкс.

steal /sti:l/ *vt* & *abs* воровáть *impf*, с~ *pf*; красть *impf*, у~ *pf*; *vi* (*creep*) крáсться *impf*; подкрáдываться *impf*, подкрáсться *pf*. **stealth** /stelθ/ *n*: **by** ~ укрáдкой. **stealthy** /-θɪ/ *adj* воровáтый, тáйный, скры́тый.

steam /sti:m/ *n* пар; **at full** ~ на всех парáх; **let off** ~ (*fig*) давáть *impf*, дать *pf* вы́ход своúм чýвствам; *vt* пáрить *impf*; *vi* пáриться *impf*, по~ *pf*; (*vessel*) ходúть *indet*, идтú *det* на парáх; ~ **up** (*mist over*) запотевáть *impf*, запотéть *pf*; потéть *impf*, за~, от~ *pf*; ~ **engine** паровáя машúна. **steamer, steamship** /-mə(r), -ʃɪp/ *n* парохóд. **steamy** /-mɪ/ *adj* напóлненный пáром; (*passionate*) горя́чий.

steed /sti:d/ *n* конь *m*.

steel /sti:l/ *n* сталь; *adj* стальнóй; *vt*: ~ **o.s.** ожесточáться *impf*, ожесточúться *pf*; ~ **works** сталелитéйный завóд. **steely** /-lɪ/ *adj* стальнóй.

steep[1] /sti:p/ *adj* крутóй; (*excessive*) чрезмéрный.

steep[2] /sti:p/ *vt* (*immerse*) погружáть *impf*, погрузúть *pf* (**in** в+*acc*); (*saturate*) пропúтывать *impf*, пропитáть *pf* (**in** +*instr*).

steeple /'sti:p(ə)l/ *n* шпиль *m*. **steeplechase** *n* скáчки *f pl* с препя́тствиями.

steer /stɪə(r)/ *vt* управля́ть *impf*, пра́вить *impf* +*instr*; *v abs* рули́ть *impf*; ~ **clear of** избега́ть *impf*, избежа́ть *pf* +*gen*. **steering-wheel** /ˈstɪərɪŋ,wi:l/ *n* руль *m*.

stem[1] /stem/ *n* сте́бель *m*; (*of wine-glass*) но́жка; (*ling*) осно́ва; *vi*: ~ **from** происходи́ть *impf*, произойти́ *pf* от+*gen*.

stem[2] /stem/ *vt* (*stop*) остана́вливать *impf*, останови́ть *pf*.

stench /stentʃ/ *n* злово́ние.

stencil /ˈstensɪl/ *n* трафаре́т; (*tech*) шабло́н; *vt* наноси́ть *impf*, нанести́ *pf* по трафаре́ту. **stencilled** /-sɪld/ *adj* трафаре́тный.

step /step/ *n* (*pace, action*) шаг; (*dance*) па *neut indecl*; (*of stairs, ladder*) ступе́нь; ~ **by** ~ шаг за ша́гом; **in** ~ в но́гу; **out of** ~ не в но́гу; **take** ~**s** принима́ть *impf*, приня́ть *pf* ме́ры *vi* шага́ть *impf*, шагну́ть *pf*; ступа́ть *impf*, ступи́ть *pf*; ~ **aside** сторони́ться *impf*, по~ *pf*; ~ **back** отступа́ть *impf*, отступи́ть *pf*; ~ **down** (*resign*) уходи́ть *impf*, уйти́ *pf* в отста́вку; ~ **forward** выступа́ть *impf*, вы́ступить *pf*; ~ **in** (*intervene*) вме́шиваться *impf*, вмеша́ться *pf*; ~ **on** наступа́ть *impf*, наступи́ть *pf* на+*acc* (**s.o.'s foot** кому́-л. на́ ногу); ~ **over** перешагивать *impf*, перешагну́ть *pf* +*acc*, че́рез+*acc*; ~ **up** (*increase*) повыша́ть *impf*, повы́сить *pf*. **step-ladder** *n* стремя́нка. **stepping-stone** /ˈstepɪŋ,stəʊn/ *n* ка́мень *m* для перехо́да; (*fig*) сре́дство. **steps** /steps/ *n pl* ле́стница.

stepbrother /ˈstep,brʌθə(r)/ *n* сво́дный брат. **stepdaughter** /ˈstep,dɔ:tə(r)/ *n* па́дчерица. **stepfather** /ˈstep,fɑ:ðə(r)/ *n* о́тчим. **stepmother** /ˈstep,mʌðə(r)/ *n* ма́чеха. **stepsister** /ˈstep,sɪstə(r)/ *n* сво́дная сестра́. **stepson** /ˈstepsʌn/ *n* па́сынок.

steppe /step/ *n* степь.

stereo /ˈsterɪəʊ/ *n* (*system*) стереофони́ческая систе́ма; (*stereophony*) стереофо́ния; *adj* (*recorded in* ~) сте́рео *indecl*. **stereophonic** /-ˈfɒnɪk/ *adj* стереофони́ческий. **stereotype** /-,taɪp/ *n* стереоти́п. **stereotyped** /-,taɪpt/ *adj* стереоти́пный.

sterile /ˈsteraɪl/ *adj* стери́льный. **sterility** /stəˈrɪlɪtɪ/ *n* стери́льность. **sterilization** /,sterɪlaɪˈzeɪʃ(ə)n/ *n* стерилиза́ция. **sterilize** /ˈsterɪ,laɪz/ *vt* стерилизова́ть *impf* & *pf*.

sterling /ˈstɜ:lɪŋ/ *n* сте́рлинг; **pound** ~ фунт сте́рлингов; *adj* сте́рлинговый.

stern[1] /stɜ:n/ *n* корма́.

stern[2] /stɜ:n/ *adj* суро́вый, стро́гий.

stethoscope /ˈsteθə,skəʊp/ *n* стетоско́п.

stew /stju:/ *n* (*cul*) мя́со тушёное вме́сте с овоща́ми; *vt* & *i* (*cul*) туши́ть(ся) *impf*, с~ *pf*; (*fig*) томи́ть(ся) *impf*.

steward /ˈstju:əd/ *n* бортпроводни́к. **stewardess** /-dɪs/ *n* стюарде́сса.

stick[1] /stɪk/ *n* па́лка; (*of chalk etc.*) па́лочка; (*hockey*) клю́шка.

stick[2] /stɪk/ *vt* (*spear*) зака́лывать *impf*, заколо́ть *pf*; (*make adhere*) прикле́ивать *impf*, прикле́ить *pf* (**to** к+*dat*); (*coll*) (*put*) ста́вить *impf*, по~ *pf*; (*lay*) класть *impf*, положи́ть *pf*; (*endure*) терпе́ть *impf*, вы́~ *pf*; *vi* (*adhere*) ли́пнуть *impf* (**to**

к+*dat*); прилипа́ть *impf*, прили́пнуть *pf* (**to** к+*dat*); ~ **in** (*thrust in*) втыка́ть *impf*, воткну́ть *pf*; (*into opening*) всо́вывать *impf*, всу́нуть *pf*; ~ **on** (*glue on*) накле́ивать *impf*, накле́ить *pf*; ~ **out** (*thrust out*) высо́вывать *impf*, вы́сунуть *pf* (**from** из+*gen*); (*project*) торча́ть *impf*; ~ **to** (*keep to*) приде́рживаться *impf*, придержа́ться *pf* +*gen*; (*remain at*) не отвлека́ться *impf* от+*gen*; ~ **together** держа́ться *impf* вме́сте; ~ **up for** защища́ть *impf*, защити́ть *pf*; **be, get, stuck** застрева́ть *impf*, застря́ть *pf*. **sticker** /-kə(r)/ *n* накле́йка.

sticky /'stɪkɪ/ *adj* ли́пкий.

stiff /stɪf/ *adj* жёсткий, негибкий; (*prim*) чо́порный; (*difficult*) тру́дный; (*penalty*) суро́вый; **be** ~ (*ache*) боле́ть *impf*. **stiffen** /-f(ə)n/ *vt* де́лать *impf*, с~ *pf* жёстким; *vi* станови́ться *impf*, стать *pf* жёстким. **stiffness** /-nɪs/ *n* жёсткость; (*primness*) чо́порность.

stifle /'staɪf(ə)l/ *vt* души́ть *impf*, за~ *pf*; (*suppress*) подавля́ть *impf*, подави́ть *pf*; (*sound*) заглуша́ть *impf*, заглуши́ть *pf*; *vi* задыха́ться *impf*, задохну́ться *pf*. **stifling** /-lɪŋ/ *adj* уду́шливый.

stigma /'stɪgmə/ *n* клеймо́.

stile /staɪl/ *n* перела́з (*coll*).

stilettos /stɪ'letəʊz/ *n pl* ту́фли *f pl* на шпи́льках.

still /stɪl/ *adv* (всё) ещё; (*nevertheless*) тем не ме́нее; (*motionless*) неподви́жно; **stand** ~ не дви́гаться *impf*, дви́нуться *pf*; *n* (*quiet*) тишина́; *adj* ти́хий; (*immobile*) неподви́жный. **stillborn** *adj* мертворождённый. **still life** *n* натюрмо́рт. **stillness** /-nɪs/ *n* тишина́.

stilted /'stɪltɪd/ *adj* ходу́льный.

stimulant /'stɪmjʊlənt/ *n* возбужда́ющее сре́дство. **stimulate** /-ˌleɪt/ *vt* возбужда́ть *impf*, возбуди́ть *pf*. **stimulating** /-ˌleɪtɪŋ/ *adj* возбуди́тельный. **stimulation** /-'leɪʃ(ə)n/ *n* возбужде́ние. **stimulus** /'stɪmjʊləs/ *n* сти́мул.

sting /stɪŋ/ *n* (*wound*) уку́с; (*stinger*; *fig*) жа́ло; *vt* жа́лить *impf*, у~ *pf*; *vi* (*burn*) жечь *impf*. **stinging** /'stɪŋɪŋ/ *adj* (*caustic*) язви́тельный.

stingy /'stɪndʒɪ/ *adj* скупо́й.

stink /stɪŋk/ *n* вонь; *vi* воня́ть *impf* (**of** +*instr*). **stinking** /-kɪŋ/ *adj* воню́чий.

stint /stɪnt/ *n* срок; *vi*: ~**on** скупи́ться *impf*, по~ *pf* на+*acc*.

stipend /'staɪpend/ *n* (*salary*) жа́лование; (*grant*) стипе́ндия.

stipulate /'stɪpjʊˌleɪt/ *vt* обусло́вливать *impf*, обусло́вить *pf*. **stipulation** /-'leɪʃ(ə)n/ *n* усло́вие.

stir /stɜː(r)/ *n* (*commotion*) шум; *vt* (*mix*) меша́ть *impf*, по~ *pf*; (*excite*) волнова́ть *impf*, вз~ *pf*; *vi* (*move*) шевели́ться *impf*, шевельну́ться *pf*; ~ **up** возбужда́ть *impf*, возбуди́ть *pf*. **stirring** /-rɪŋ/ *adj* волну́ющий.

stirrup /'stɪrəp/ *n* стре́мя *neut*.

stitch /stɪtʃ/ *n* стежо́к; (*knitting*) пе́тля; (*med*) шов; (*pain*) ко́лики *f pl*; *vt* (*embroider*, *make line of* ~*es*) строчи́ть *impf*, про~ *pf*; (*join by sewing*, *make*, *suture*) сшива́ть *impf*, сшить *pf*; ~ **up** зашива́ть *impf*, заши́ть *pf*. **stitching** /-tʃɪŋ/ *n* (*stitches*) стро́чка.

stoat /stəʊt/ *n* горноста́й.

stock /stɒk/ *n* (*store*) запа́с; (*of shop*) ассортиме́нт; (*live*~)

скот; (*cul*) бульо́н; (*lineage*) семья́; (*fin*) а́кции *f pl*; **in ~** в нали́чии; **out of ~** распро́дан; **take ~ of** крити́чески оце́нивать *impf*, оцени́ть *pf*; *adj* станда́ртный; *vt* име́ть в нали́чии; **~ up** запаса́ться *impf*, запасти́сь *pf* (**with** +*instr*). **stockbroker** *n* биржево́й ма́клер. **stock-exchange** *n* би́ржа. **stockpile** *n* запа́с; *vt* нака́пливать *impf*, накопи́ть *pf*. **stock-taking** *n* переучёт.

stocking /'stɒkɪŋ/ *n* чуло́к

stocky /'stɒkɪ/ *adj* призе́мистый.

stodgy /'stɒdʒɪ/ *adj* тяжёлый.

stoic(al) /'stəʊɪk((ə)l)/ *adj* сто́йческий. **stoicism** /'stəʊɪˌsɪz(ə)m/ *n* стоици́зм.

stoke /stəʊk/ *vt* топи́ть *impf*.

stolid /'stɒlɪd/ *adj* флегмати́чный.

stomach /'stʌmək/ *n* желу́док, (*also surface of body*) живо́т; *vt* терпе́ть *impf*, по~ *pf*. **stomach ache** /'stʌmək eɪk/ *n* боль в животе́.

stone /stəʊn/ *n* ка́мень *m*; (*of fruit*) ко́сточка; *adj* ка́менный; *vt* побива́ть *impf*, поби́ть *pf* камня́ми; (*fruit*) вынима́ть *impf*, вы́нуть *pf* ко́сточки из+*gen*. **Stone Age** *n* ка́менный век **stone-deaf** *adj* соверше́нно глухо́й. **stone-mason** *n* ка́менщик. **stonily** /-nɪlɪ/ *adv* с ка́менным выраже́нием, хо́лодно. **stony** /-nɪ/ *adj* камени́стый; (*fig*) ка́менный.

stool /stu:l/ *n* табуре́т, табуре́тка.

stoop /stu:p/ *n* суту́лость; *vt & i* суту́лить(ся) *impf*, с~ *pf*; (*bend (down)*) наклоня́ть(ся) *impf*, наклони́ть(ся) *pf*; **~ to** (*abase o.s.*) унижа́ться *impf*, унизи́ться *pf* до+*gen*; (*condescend*) снисходи́ть *impf*, снизойти́ *pf* до+*gen*. **stooped, stooping** /stu:pt, 'stu:pɪŋ/ *adj* суту́лый.

stop /stɒp/ *n* остано́вка; **put a ~ to** положи́ть *pf* коне́ц +*dat*; *vt* остана́вливать *impf*, останови́ть *pf*; (*discontinue*) прекраща́ть *impf*, прекрати́ть *pf*; (*restrain*) уде́рживать *impf*, удержа́ть *pf* (**from** от+*gen*); *vi* остана́вливаться *impf*, останови́ться *pf*; (*discontinue*) прекраща́ться *impf*, прекрати́ться *pf*; (*cease*) перестава́ть *impf*, переста́ть *pf* (+*inf*); **~ up** *vt* затыка́ть *impf*, заткну́ть *pf*. **stoppage** /-pɪdʒ/ *n* остано́вка; (*strike*) забасто́вка. **stopper** /-pə(r)/ *n* про́бка. **stop-press** *n* э́кстренное сообще́ние в газе́те. **stop-watch** *n* секундоме́р.

storage /'stɔ:rɪdʒ/ *n* хране́ние.

store /stɔ:(r)/ *n* запа́с; (*storehouse*) склад; (*shop*) магази́н; **set ~ by** цени́ть *impf*; **what is in ~ for me?** что ждёт меня́ впереди́?; *vt* запаса́ть *impf*, запасти́ *pf*; (*put into storage*) сдава́ть *impf*, сдать *pf* на хране́ние. **storehouse** *n* склад. **store-room** кладова́я *sb*.

storey /'stɔ:rɪ/ *n* эта́ж.

stork /stɔ:k/ *n* а́ист.

storm /stɔ:m/ *n* бу́ря, (*thunder ~*) гроза́; *vt* (*mil*) штурмова́ть *impf*; *vi* бушева́ть *impf*. **stormy** /-mɪ/ *adj* бу́рный.

story /'stɔ:rɪ/ *n* расска́з, по́весть; (*anecdote*) анекдо́т; (*plot*) фа́була; **~-teller** расска́зчик.

stout /staut/ *adj* (*strong*) кре́пкий; (*staunch*) сто́йкий; (*portly*) доро́дный.

stove /stəʊv/ *n* (*with fire inside*)

печь; (*cooker*) плита́.

stow /stəʊ/ *vt* укла́дывать *impf*, уложи́ть *pf*. **stowaway** /'stəʊə,weɪ/ *n* безбиле́тный пассажи́р.

straddle /'stræd(ə)l/ *vt* (*sit astride*) сиде́ть *impf* верхо́м на+*prep*; (*stand astride*) стоя́ть *impf*, расста́вив но́ги над +*instr*.

straggle /'stræg(ə)l/ *vi* отстава́ть *impf*, отста́ть *pf*. **straggler** /-glə(r)/ *n* отста́вший *sb*. **straggling** /-glɪŋ/ *adj* разбро́санный. **straggly** /-glɪ/ *adj* растрёпанный.

straight /streɪt/ *adj* прямо́й; (*undiluted*) неразба́вленный; *predic* (*in order*) в поря́дке; *adv* пря́мо; ~ **away** сра́зу. **straighten** /-t(ə)n/ *vt* & *i* выпрямля́ть(ся) *impf*, вы́прямить(ся) *pf*; *vt* (*put in order*) поправля́ть *impf*, попра́вить *pf*. **straightforward** *adj* прямо́й; (*simple*) просто́й.

strain[1] /streɪn/ *n* (*tension*) натяже́ние; (*sprain*) растяже́ние; (*effort, exertion*) напряже́ние; (*tendency*) скло́нность; (*sound*) звук; *vt* (*stretch*) натя́гивать *impf*, натяну́ть *pf*; (*sprain*) растя́гивать *impf*, растяну́ть *pf*; (*exert*) напряга́ть *impf*, напря́чь *pf*; (*filter*) проце́живать *impf*, процеди́ть *pf*; *vi* (*also exert o.s.*) напряга́ться *impf*, напря́чься *pf*. **strained** /streɪnd/ *adj* натя́нутый. **strainer** /-nə(r)/ *n* (*tea* ~) си́течко; (*sieve*) си́то.

strain[2] /streɪn/ *n* (*breed*) поро́да.

strait(s) /streɪt(s)/ *n* (*geog*) проли́в. **strait-jacket** *n* смири́тельная руба́шка. **straits** *n pl* (*difficulties*) затрудни́тельное положе́ние.

strand[1] /strænd/ *n* (*hair, rope*) прядь; (*thread, also fig*) нить.

strand[2] /strænd/ *vt* сажа́ть *impf*, посади́ть *pf* на мель. **stranded** /-dɪd/ *adj* на мели́.

strange /streɪndʒ/ *adj* стра́нный; (*unfamiliar*) незнако́мый; (*alien*) чужо́й. **strangely** /-lɪ/ *adv* стра́нно. **strangeness** /-nɪs/ *n* стра́нность. **stranger** /'streɪndʒə(r)/ *n* незнако́мец.

strangle /'stræŋg(ə)l/ *vt* души́ть *impf*, за~ *pf*. **stranglehold** *n* мёртвая хва́тка. **strangulation** /,stræŋgjʊ'leɪʃ(ə)n/ *n* удуше́ние.

strap /stræp/ *n* реме́нь *m*; *vt* (*tie up*) стя́гивать *impf*, стяну́ть *pf* ремнём. **strapping** /-pɪŋ/ *adj* ро́слый.

stratagem /'strætədʒəm/ *n* хи́трость. **strategic** /strə'tiːdʒɪk/ *adj* стратеги́ческий. **strategist** /'strætɪdʒɪst/ *n* страте́г. **strategy** /'strætɪdʒɪ/ *n* страте́гия.

stratum /'strɑːtəm/ *n* слой.

straw /strɔː/ *n* соло́ма; (*drinking*) соло́минка; **the last** ~ после́дняя ка́пля; *adj* соло́менный.

strawberry /'strɔːbərɪ/ *n* клубни́ка (*no pl*; *usu collect*); (*wild* ~) земляни́ка (*no pl*; *usu collect*).

stray /streɪ/ *vi* сбива́ться *impf*, сби́ться *pf*; (*digress*) отклоня́ться *impf*, отклони́ться *pf*; *adj* (*lost*) заблуди́вшийся; (*homeless*) бездо́мный; *n* (*from flock*) отби́вшееся от ста́да живо́тное *sb*; ~ **bullet** шальна́я пу́ля.

streak /striːk/ *n* полоса́ (**of luck** везе́ния); (*tendency*) жи́лка; *vi* (*rush*) проноси́ться *impf*, пронести́сь *pf*. **streaked** /striːkt/ *adj* с полоса́ми (**with** +*gen*). **streaky** /-kɪ/ *adj* полоса́тый; (*meat*) с просло́йками жи́ра.

stream /striːm/ *n* (*brook*, *tears*) ручей; (*brook*, *flood*, *tears*, *people etc.*) пото́к; (*current*) тече́ние; **up/down ~** вверх/вниз по тече́нию; *vi* течь *impf*; струи́ться *impf*; (*rush*) проноси́ться *impf*, пронести́сь *pf*; (*blow*) развева́ться *impf*. **streamer** /-mə(r)/ *n* вы́мпел. **stream-lined** *adj* обтека́емый; (*fig*) хорошо́ нала́женный.

street /striːt/ *n* у́лица; *adj* у́личный; **~ lamp** у́личный фона́рь *m*.

strength /streŋθ/ *n* си́ла; (*numbers*) чи́сленность; **on the ~ of** в си́лу+*gen*. **strengthen** /-θ(ə)n/ *vt* уси́ливать *impf*, уси́лить *pf*.

strenuous /ˈstrenjʊəs/ *adj* (*work*) тру́дный; (*effort*) напряжённый.

stress /stres/ *n* напряже́ние; (*mental*) стресс; (*emphasis*) ударе́ние; *vt* (*accent*) ста́вить *impf*, по~ *pf* ударе́ние на+*acc*; (*emphasize*) подчёркивать *impf* подчеркну́ть *pf*. **stressful** /-fʊl/ *adj* стре́ссовый.

stretch /stretʃ/ *n* (*expanse*) отре́зок; **at a ~** (*in succession*) подря́д; *vt* & *i* (*widen*, *spread out*) растя́гивать(ся) *impf*, растяну́ть(ся) *pf*; (*in length*, **~** *out limbs*) вытя́гивать(ся) *impf*, вы́тянуть(ся) *pf*; (*tauten*) натя́гивать(ся) *impf*, натяну́ть(ся) *pf*; (*extend*, *e.g. rope*, **~** *forth limbs*) протя́гивать(ся) *impf*, протяну́ть(ся) *pf*; *vi* (*material*, *land*) тяну́ться *impf*; **~ one's legs** (*coll*) размина́ть *impf*, размя́ть *pf* но́ги. **stretcher** /-tʃə(r)/ *n* носи́лки (-лок) *pl*.

strew /struː/ *vt* разбра́сывать *impf*, разброса́ть *pf*; **~ with** посыпа́ть *impf*, посы́пать *pf* +*instr*.

stricken /ˈstrɪkən/ *adj* поражённый.

strict /strɪkt/ *adj* стро́гий. **stricture(s)** /ˈstrɪktʃəz/ *n* (стро́гая) кри́тика.

stride /ˈstraɪd/ *n* (большо́й) шаг; *pl* (*fig*) успе́хи *m pl*; **to take sth in one's ~** преодолева́ть *impf*, преодоле́ть *pf* что-л. без уси́лий; *vi* шага́ть *impf*.

strident /ˈstraɪd(ə)nt/ *adj* ре́зкий.

strife /straɪf/ *n* раздо́р.

strike /straɪk/ *n* (*refusal to work*) забасто́вка; (*mil*) уда́р; *vi* (*be on* **~**) бастова́ть *impf*; (*go on* **~**) забастова́ть *pf*; (*attack*) ударя́ть *impf*, уда́рить *pf*; (*the hour*) бить *impf*, про~ *pf*; *vt* (*hit*) ударя́ть *impf*, уда́рить *pf*; (*impress*) поража́ть *impf*, порази́ть *pf*; (*discover*) открыва́ть *impf*, откры́ть *pf*; (*match*) зажига́ть *impf*, заже́чь *pf*; (*the hour*) бить *impf*, про~ *pf*; (*occur to*) приходи́ть *impf*, прийти́ *pf* в го́лову+*dat*; **~ off** вычёркивать *impf*, вы́черкнуть *pf*; **~ up** начина́ть *impf*, нача́ть *pf*. **striker** /-kə(r)/ *n* забасто́вщик. **striking** /-kɪŋ/ *adj* порази́тельный.

string /strɪŋ/ *n* бечёвка; (*mus*) струна́; (*series*) ряд; *pl* (*mus*) стру́нные инструме́нты *m pl*; **~ bag**, **~ vest** се́тка; *vt* (*thread*) низа́ть *impf*, на~ *pf*; **~ along** (*coll*) води́ть *impf* за нос; **~ out** (*prolong*) растя́гивать *impf*, растяну́ть *pf*; **strung up** (*tense*) напряжённый. **stringed** /strɪŋd/ *adj* стру́нный. **stringy** /ˈstrɪŋɪ/ *adj* (*fibrous*) волокни́стый; (*meat*) жи́листый.

stringent /ˈstrɪndʒ(ə)nt/ *adj* стро́гий.

strip[1] /strɪp/ *n* полоса́, поло́ска.

strip² /strɪp/ *vt* (*undress*) раздева́ть *impf*, разде́ть *pf*; (*deprive*) лиша́ть *impf*, лиши́ть *pf* (**of** +*gen*); ~ **off** (*tear off*) сдира́ть *impf*, содра́ть *pf*; *vi* раздева́ться *impf*, разде́ться *pf*. **strip-tease** *n* стрипти́з.

stripe /straɪp/ *n* полоса́. **striped** /straɪpt/ *adj* полоса́тый.

strive /'straɪv(ə)n/ *vi* (*endeavour*) стреми́ться *impf* (**for** к+*dat*); (*struggle*) боро́ться *impf* (**for** за+*acc*; **against** про́тив+*gen*).

stroke /strəʊk/ *n* (*blow*, *med*) уда́р; (*of oar*) взмах; (*swimming*) стиль *m*; (*of pen etc.*) штрих; (*piston*) ход; *vt* гла́дить *impf*, по~ *pf*.

stroll /strəʊl/ *n* прогу́лка; *vi* прогу́ливаться *impf*, прогуля́ться *pf*.

strong /strɒŋ/ *adj* си́льный; (*stout*; *of drinks*) кре́пкий; (*healthy*) здоро́вый; (*opinion etc.*) твёрдый. **stronghold** *n* кре́пость. **strong-minded, strong-willed** /-'maɪndɪd, -'wɪld/ *adj* реши́тельный.

structural /'strʌktʃər(ə)l/ *adj* структу́рный. **structure** /'strʌktʃə(r)/ *n* структу́ра; (*building*) сооруже́ние; *vt* организова́ть *impf* & *pf*.

struggle /'strʌg(ə)l/ *n* борьба́; *vi* боро́ться *impf* (**for** за+*acc*; **against** про́тив+*gen*); (*writhe*, ~ *with* (*fig*)) би́ться (**with** над +*instr*).

strum /strʌm/ *vi* бренча́ть *impf* (**on** на+*prep*).

strut¹ /strʌt/ *n* (*vertical*) сто́йка; (*horizontal*) распо́рка.

strut² /strʌt/ *vi* ходи́ть *indet*, идти́ *det* го́голем.

stub /stʌb/ *n* огры́зок; (*cigarette*) оку́рок; (*counterfoil*) корешо́к; *vt*: ~ **one's toe** ударя́ться *impf*, уда́риться *pf* ного́й (**on** на+*acc*); ~ **out** гаси́ть *impf*, по~ *pf*.

stubble /'stʌb(ə)l/ *n* жнивьё; (*hair*) щети́на.

stubborn /'stʌbən/ *adj* упря́мый. **stubbornness** /-nɪs/ *n* упря́мство.

stucco /'stʌkəʊ/ *n* штукату́рка.

stud¹ /stʌd/ *n* (*collar*, *cuff*) за́понка; (*nail*) гвоздь *m* с большо́й шля́пкой; *vt* (*bestrew*) усе́ивать *impf*, усе́ять *pf* (**with** +*instr*).

stud² /stʌd/ *n* (*horses*) ко́нный заво́д.

student /'stju:d(ə)nt/ *n* студе́нт, ~ка.

studied /'stʌdɪd/ *adj* напускно́й.

studio /'stju:dɪəʊ/ *n* сту́дия.

studious /'stju:dɪəs/ *adj* любя́щий нау́ку; (*diligent*) стара́тельный.

study /'stʌdɪ/ *n* изуче́ние; *pl* заня́тия *neut pl*; (*investigation*) иссле́дование; (*art*, *mus*) этю́д; (*room*) кабине́т; *vt* изуча́ть *impf*, изучи́ть *pf*; учи́ться *impf*, об~ *pf* +*dat*; (*scrutinize*) рассма́тривать *impf*, рассмотре́ть *pf*; *vi* (*take lessons*) учи́ться *impf*, об~ *pf*; (*do one's studies*) занима́ться *impf*.

stuff /stʌf/ *n* (*material*) материа́л; (*things*) ве́щи *f pl*; *vt* набива́ть *impf*, наби́ть *pf*; (*cul*) начиня́ть *impf*, начини́ть *pf*; (*cram into*) запи́хивать *impf*, запиха́ть *pf* (**into** в+*acc*); (*shove into*) сова́ть *impf*, су́нуть *pf* (**into** в+*acc*); *vi* (*overeat*) объеда́ться *impf*, объе́сться *pf*. **stuffiness** /-fɪnɪs/ *n* духота́. **stuffing** /-fɪŋ/ *n* наби́вка; (*cul*) начи́нка. **stuffy** /-fɪ/ *adj* ду́шный.

stumble /'stʌmb(ə)l/ *vi* (*also fig*)

спотыка́ться *impf*, споткну́ться *pf* (**over** о+*acc*); **~ upon** натыка́ться *impf*, наткну́ться *pf* на+*acc*. **stumbling-block** *n* ка́мень *m* преткнове́ния.

stump /stʌmp/ *n* (*tree*) пень *m*; (*pencil*) огры́зок; (*limb*) культя́; *vt* (*perplex*) ста́вить *impf*, по**~** *pf* в тупи́к

stun /stʌn/ *vt* (*also fig*) оглуша́ть *impf*, оглуши́ть *pf*. **stunning** /-nɪŋ/ *adj* потряса́ющий.

stunt¹ /stʌnt/ *n* трюк.

stunt² /stʌnt/ *vt* заде́рживать *impf*, задержа́ть *pf* рост+*gen*. **stunted** /-tɪd/ *adj* низкоро́слый.

stupefy /ˈstjuːpɪˌfaɪ/ *vt* оглуша́ть *impf*, оглуши́ть *pf*. **stupendous** /stjuːˈpendəs/ *adj* колосса́льный. **stupid** /ˈstjuːpɪd/ *adj* глу́пый. **stupidity** /stjuːˈpɪdɪtɪ/ *n* глу́пость. **stupor** /ˈstjuːpə(r)/ *n* оцепене́ние.

sturdy /ˈstɜːdɪ/ *adj* кре́пкий.

stutter /ˈstʌtə(r)/ *n* заика́ние; *vi* заика́ться *impf*.

sty¹ /staɪ/ *n* (*pig***~**) свина́рник.

sty² /staɪ/ *n* (*on eye*) ячме́нь *m*.

style /staɪl/ *n* стиль *m*; (*taste*) вкус; (*fashion*) мо́да; (*sort*) род; (*of hair*) приче́ска. **stylish** /-lɪʃ/ *adj* мо́дный. **stylist** /-lɪst/ *n* (*of hair*) парикма́хер. **stylistic** /-ˈlɪstɪk/ *adj* стилисти́ческий. **stylize** /-laɪz/ *vt* стилизова́ть *impf* & *pf*.

stylus /ˈstaɪləs/ *n* игла́ звукоснима́теля.

suave /swɑːv/ *adj* обходи́тельный.

subconscious /sʌbˈkɒnʃəs/ *adj* подсозна́тельный; *n* подсозна́ние. **subcontract** *vt* дава́ть *impf*, дать *pf* подря́дчику. **subcontractor** *n* подря́дчик. **subdivide** *vt* подразделя́ть *impf*, подраздели́ть *pf*. **subdivision** *n* подразделе́ние. **subdue** /səbˈdjuː/ *vt* покоря́ть *impf*, покори́ть *pf*. **subdued** /səbˈdjuːd/ *adj* (*suppressed, dispirited*) пода́вленный; (*soft*) мя́гкий; (*indistinct*) приглушённый. **sub-editor** *n* помо́щник реда́ктора.

subject *n* /ˈsʌbdʒɪkt/ (*theme*) те́ма; (*discipline, theme*) предме́т; (*question*) вопро́с; (*thing on to which action is directed*) объе́кт; (*gram*) подлежа́щее *sb*; (*national*) по́дданный *sb*; *adj*: **~ to** (*susceptible to*) подве́рженный+*dat*; (*on condition that*) при усло́вии, что…; е́сли; **be ~ to** (*change etc.*) подлежа́ть *impf* +*dat*; *vt*: /səbˈdʒekt/ **~ to** подверга́ть *impf*, подве́ргнуть *pf* +*dat*. **subjection** /səbˈdʒekʃ(ə)n/ *n* подчине́ние. **subjective** /səbˈdʒektɪv/ *adj* субъекти́вный. **subjectivity** /ˌsʌbdʒekˈtɪvɪtɪ/ *n* субъекти́вность. **subject-matter** *n* (*of book, lecture*) содержа́ние, те́ма; (*of discussion*) предме́т.

subjugate /ˈsʌbdʒʊˌgeɪt/ *vt* покоря́ть *impf*, покори́ть *pf*. **subjugation** /ˌsʌbdʒʊˈgeɪʃ(ə)n/ *n* покоре́ние.

subjunctive (mood) /səbˈdʒʌŋktɪv (muːd)/ *n* сослага́тельное наклоне́ние.

sublet /ˈsʌblet/ *vt* передава́ть *impf*, переда́ть *pf* в субаре́нду.

sublimate /ˈsʌblɪˌmeɪt/ *vt* сублими́ровать *impf* & *pf*. **sublimation** /ˌsʌblɪˈmeɪʃ(ə)n/ *n* сублима́ция. **sublime** /səˈblaɪm/ *adj* возвы́шенный.

subliminal /səbˈlɪmɪn(ə)l/ *adj* подсозна́тельный. **sub-machine-gun** /ˌsʌbməˈʃiːn,gʌn/ *n* автома́т. **submarine** /ˌsʌbməˈriːn/ *n* подво́дная ло́дка. **submerge** /səbˈmɜːdʒ/ *vt* погружа́ть *impf*, погрузи́ть *pf*. **submission** /-ˈmɪʃ(ə)n/ *n* подчине́ние; (*for inspection*) представле́ние. **submissive** /-ˈmɪsɪv/ *adj* поко́рный. **submit** /-ˈmɪt/ *vi* подчиня́ться *impf*, подчини́ться *pf* (**to** +*dat*); *vt* представля́ть *impf*, предста́вить *pf*. **subordinate** *n* /səˈbɔːdɪnət/ подчинённый *sb*; *adj* подчинённый; (*secondary*) второстепе́нный; (*gram*) прида́точный; *vt* /səˈbɔːdɪˌneɪt/ подчиня́ть *impf*, подчини́ть *pf*. **subscribe** /səbˈskraɪb/ *vi* подпи́сываться *impf*, подписа́ться *pf* (**to** на+*acc*); **~ to** (*opinion*) присоединя́ться *impf*, присоедини́ться *pf* к+*dat*. **subscriber** /-ˈskraɪbə(r)/ *n* подпи́счик; абоне́нт. **subscription** /-ˈskrɪpʃ(ə)n/ *n* подпи́ска, абонеме́нт; (*fee*) взнос. **subsection** /ˈsʌbˌsekʃ(ə)n/ *n* подразде́л. **subsequent** /ˈsʌbsɪkwənt/ *adj* после́дующий. **subsequently** /ˈsʌbsɪkwəntlɪ/ *adv* впосле́дствии. **subservient** /səbˈsɜːvɪənt/ *adj* раболе́пный. **subside** /səbˈsaɪd/ *vi* убыва́ть *impf*, убы́ть *pf*; (*soil*) оседа́ть *impf*, осе́сть *pf*. **subsidence** /səbˈsaɪd(ə)ns/ *n* (*soil*) оседа́ние. **subsidiary** /səbˈsɪdɪərɪ/ *adj* вспомога́тельный; (*secondary*) второстепе́нный; *n* филиа́л. **subsidize** /ˈsʌbsɪˌdaɪz/ *vt* субсиди́ровать *impf* & *pf*. **subsidy** /ˈsʌbsɪdɪ/ *n* субси́дия. **subsist** /səbˈsɪst/ *vi* (*live*) жить *impf* (**on** +*instr*). **substance** /ˈsʌbst(ə)ns/ *n* вещество́; (*essence*) су́щность, суть; (*content*) содержа́ние. **substantial** /səbˈstænʃ(ə)l/ *adj* (*durable*) про́чный; (*considerable*) значи́тельный; (*food*) пло́тный. **substantially** /səbˈstænʃəlɪ/ *adv* (*basically*) в основно́м; (*considerably*) значи́тельно. **substantiate** /səbˈstænʃɪˌeɪt/ *vt* обосно́вывать *impf*, обоснова́ть *pf*. **substitute** /ˈsʌbstɪˌtjuːt/ *n* (*person*) замести́тель *m*; (*thing*) заме́на; *vt* заменя́ть *impf*, замени́ть *pf* +*instr* (**for** +*acc*); **I ~ water for milk** заменя́ю молоко́ водо́й. **substitution** /ˌsʌbstɪˈtjuːʃ(ə)n/ *n* заме́на. **subsume** /səbˈsjuːm/ *vt* относи́ть *impf*, отнести́ *pf* к како́й-л. катего́рии. **subterfuge** /ˈsʌbtəˌfjuːdʒ/ *n* увёртка. **subterranean** /ˌsʌbtəˈreɪnɪən/ *adj* подзе́мный. **subtitle** /ˈsʌbˌtaɪt(ə)l/ *n* подзаголо́вок; (*cin*) субти́тр.

subtle /ˈsʌt(ə)l/ *adj* то́нкий. **subtlety** /ˈsʌtəltɪ/ *n* то́нкость.

subtract /səbˈtrækt/ *vt* вычита́ть *impf*, вы́честь *pf*. **subtraction** /-ˈtrækʃ(ə)n/ *n* вычита́ние. **suburb** /ˈsʌbɜːb/ *n* при́город. **suburban** /səˈbɜːbən/ *adj* при́городный. **subversion** /səbˈvɜːʃ(ə)n/ *n* подрывна́я де́ятельность. **subversive** /səbˈvɜːsɪv/ *adj* подрывно́й. **subway** /ˈsʌbweɪ/ *n* подзе́мный перехо́д.

succeed /səkˈsiːd/ *vi* удава́ться *impf*, уда́ться *pf*; **the plan will ~** план уда́стся; **he ~ed in buying the book** ему́ удало́сь купи́ть кни́гу; (*be successful*) преуспева́ть *impf*, преуспе́ть *pf* (**in** в+*prep*); (*follow*) сменя́ть *impf*, смени́ть *pf*; (*be heir*) насле́довать *impf* & *pf* (**to** +*dat*). **succeeding** /-dɪŋ/ *adj* после́дующий. **success** /səkˈses/ *n* успе́х. **successful** /sək 'sesfʊl/ *adj* успе́шный. **succession** /sək'seʃ(ə)n/ *n* (*series*) ряд; (*to throne*) престолонасле́дие; **right of ~** пра́во насле́дования; **in ~** подря́д, оди́н за други́м. **successive** /sək'sesɪv/ *adj* (*consecutive*) последова́тельный. **successor** /sək'sesə(r)/ *n* пре-е́мник.

succinct /sək'sɪŋkt/ *adj* сжа́тый.

succulent /'sʌkjʊlənt/ *adj* со́чный.

succumb /sə'kʌm/ *vi* (*to pressure*) уступа́ть *impf*, уступи́ть *pf* (**to** +*dat*); (*to temptation*) поддава́ться *impf*, подда́ться *pf* (**to** +*dat*).

such /sʌtʃ/ *adj* тако́й; **~ people** таки́е лю́ди; **~ as** (*for example*) так наприме́р; (*of ~ a kind as*) тако́й как; **~ beauty as yours** така́я красота́ как ва́ша; (*that which*) тот, кото́рый; **I shall read ~ books as I like** я бу́ду чита́ть те кни́ги, кото́рые мне нра́вятся; **~ as to** тако́й, что́бы; **his illness was not ~ as to cause anxiety** его́ боле́знь была́ не тако́й (серьёзной), что́бы вы́звать беспоко́йство; **~ and ~** тако́й-то; *pron* тако́в; **~ was his character** тако́в был его́ хара́ктер; **as ~** сам по себе́; **~ is not the case** э́то не так. **suchlike** *pron* (*inanimate*) тому́ подо́бное; (*people*) такие лю́ди *pl*.

suck /sʌk/ *vt* соса́ть *impf*; **~ in** вса́сывать *impf*, всоса́ть *pf*; (*engulf*) заса́сывать *impf*, засоса́ть *pf*; **~ out** выса́сывать *impf*, вы́сосать *pf*; **~ up to** (*coll*) подли́зываться *impf*, подлиза́ться *pf* к+*dat*. **sucker** /-kə(r)/ *n* (*biol*, *rubber device*) присо́ска; (*bot*) корнево́й побе́г. **suckle** /-k(ə)l/ *vt* корми́ть *impf*, на~ *pf* гру́дью. **suction** /'sʌkʃ(ə)n/ *n* вса́сывание.

sudden /'sʌd(ə)n/ *adj* внеза́пный. **suddenly** /-lɪ/ *adv* вдруг. **suddenness** /-nɪs/ *n* внеза́пность.

sue /su:/ *vt* & *i* подава́ть *impf*, пода́ть *pf* в суд (на+*acc*); **~ s.o. for damages** предъявля́ть *impf*, предъяви́ть *pf* (к) кому́-л. иск о возмеще́нии уще́рба.

suede /sweɪd/ *n* за́мша; *adj* за́мшевый.

suet /'su:ɪt/ *n* нутряно́е са́ло.

suffer /'sʌfə(r)/ *vt* страда́ть *impf*, по~ *pf* +*instr*, от+*gen*; (*loss*, *defeat*) терпе́ть *impf*, по~ *pf*; (*tolerate*) терпе́ть *impf*; *vi* страда́ть *impf*, по~ *pf* (**from** +*instr*, от+*gen*). **sufferance** /-rəns/ *n*: **he is here on ~** его́ здесь те́рпят. **suffering** /-rɪŋ/ *n* страда́ние.

suffice /sə'faɪs/ *vi* & *t* быть доста́точным (для+*gen*); хвата́ть *impf*, хвати́ть *pf* *impers*+*gen* (+*dat*). **sufficient** /-fɪʃ(ə)nt/ *adj* доста́точный.

suffix /'sʌfɪks/ *n* су́ффикс.

suffocate /'sʌfə,keɪt/ *vt* удуша́ть *impf*, удуши́ть *pf*; *vi* задыха́ться *impf*, задохну́ться *pf*. **suffocating** /-tɪŋ/ *adj* уду́шливый. **suffocation** /,sʌfə'keɪʃ(ə)n/ *n* удуше́ние.

suffrage /'sʌfrɪdʒ/ *n* избира́тельное пра́во.

suffuse /sə'fju:z/ *vt* залива́ть *impf*, зали́ть *pf* (**with** +*instr*).

sugar /'ʃʊgə(r)/ *n* са́хар; *adj* са́харный; *vt* подсла́щивать *impf*, подсласти́ть *pf*; **~ basin** са́харница; **~ beet** са́харная свёкла; **~ cane** са́харный тро́стник. **sugary** /-rɪ/ *adj* са́харный; (*fig*) слаща́вый.

suggest /sə'dʒest/ *vt* предлага́ть *impf*, предложи́ть *pf*; (*evoke*) напоминáть *impf*, напóмнить *pf*; (*imply*) намекáть *impf*, намекнýть *pf* на+*acc*; (*indicate*) говорить *impf* о+*prep*. **suggestion** /-'dʒestʃ(ə)n/ *n* предложéние; (*psych*) внушéние. **suggestive** /-'dʒestɪv/ *adj* вызывáющий мы́сли (**of** о+*prep*); (*indecent*) соблазни́тельный.

suicidal /ˌsuːɪ'saɪd(ə)l/ *adj* самоуби́йственный; (*fig*) губи́тельный. **suicide** /'suːɪˌsaɪd/ *n* самоуби́йство; **commit ~** совершáть *impf*, соверши́ть *pf* самоуби́йство.

suit /suːt/ *n* (*clothing*) костю́м; (*law*) иск; (*cards*) масть; **follow ~** (*fig*) слéдовать *impf*, по~ *pf* примéру; *vt* (*be convenient for*) устрáивать *impf*, устрóить *pf*; (*adapt*) приспосáбливать *impf*, приспосóбить *pf*; (*be ~able for, match*) подходи́ть *impf*, подойти́ *pf* (+*dat*); (*look attractive on*) идти́ *impf* +*dat*. **suitability** /ˌsuːtə'bɪlɪtɪ/ *n* пригóдность. **suitable** /'suːtəb(ə)l/ *adj* (*fitting*) подходя́щий; (*convenient*) удóбный. **suitably** /'suːtəblɪ/ *adv* соотвéтственно. **suitcase** *n* чемодáн.

suite /swiːt/ *n* (*retinue*) сви́та; (*furniture*) гарнитýр; (*rooms*) апартáменты *m pl*; (*mus*) сю́ита.

suitor /'suːtə(r)/ *n* поклóнник.

sulk /sʌlk/ *vi* дýться *impf*. **sulky** /-kɪ/ *adj* надýтый.

sullen /'sʌlən/ *adj* угрю́мый.

sully /'sʌlɪ/ *vt* пятнáть *impf*, за~ *pf*.

sulphur /'sʌlfə(r)/ *n* сéра. **sulphuric** /sʌl'fjʊərɪk/ *adj*: **~ acid** сéрная кислотá.

sultana /sʌl'tɑːnə/ *n* (*raisin*) изю́минка; *pl* кишми́ш (*collect*).

sultry /'sʌltrɪ/ *adj* знóйный.

sum /sʌm/ *n* сýмма; (*arithmetical problem*) арифмети́ческая задáча; *pl* арифмéтика; *v*: **~ up** *vi* & *t* (*summarize*) подводи́ть *impf*, подвести́ *pf* итóги (+*gen*); *vt* (*appraise*) оцéнивать *impf*, оцени́ть *pf*.

summarize /'sʌməˌraɪz/ *vt* сумми́ровать *impf* & *pf*. **summary** /'sʌmərɪ/ *n* резюмé *neut indecl*, свóдка; *adj* суммáрный; (*dismissal*) бесцеремóнный.

summer /'sʌmə(r)/ *n* лéто; *attrib* лéтний. **summer-house** *n* бесéдка.

summit /'sʌmɪt/ *n* верши́на; **~ meeting** встрéча на верхáх.

summon /'sʌmən/ *vt* вызывáть *impf*, вы́звать *pf*; **~ up one's courage** собирáться *impf*, собрáться *pf* с дýхом. **summons** /-mənz/ *n* вы́зов; (*law*) повéстка в суд; *vt* вызывáть *impf*, вы́звать *pf* в суд.

sumptuous /'sʌmptjʊəs/ *adj* рoскóшный.

sun /sʌn/ *n* сóлнце; **in the ~** на сóлнце. **sunbathe** *vi* загорáть *impf*. **sunbeam** *n* сóлнечный луч. **sunburn** *n* загáр; (*inflammation*) сóлнечный ожóг. **sunburnt** /-bɜːnt/ *adj* загорéлый; **become ~** загорáть *impf*, загорéть *pf*.

Sunday /'sʌndeɪ/ *n* воскресéнье.

sundry /'sʌndrɪ/ *adj* рáзный; **all and ~** всё и вся.

sunflower /'sʌnflaʊə(r)/ *n* подсóлнечник. **sun-glasses** *n pl* очки́ (-кóв) *pl* от сóлнца.

sunken /'sʌŋkən/ *adj* (*cheeks, eyes*) впáлый; (*submerged*) погружённый; (*ship*) затóпленный; (*below certain level*) ни́же (какóго-л. ýровня).

sunlight /'sʌnlaɪt/ *n* сóлнечный

свет. **sunny** /ˈsʌnɪ/ *adj* со́лнечный. **sunrise** *n* восхо́д со́лнца. **sunset** *n* зака́т. **sunshade** *n* (*parasol*) зо́нтик; (*awning*) наве́с. **sunshine** *n* со́лнечный свет. **sunstroke** *n* со́лнечный уда́р. **suntan** *n* зага́р. **suntanned** /ˈsʌntænd/ *adj* загоре́лый.

super /ˈsuːpə(r)/ *adj* замеча́тельный. **superb** /suːˈpɜːb/ *adj* превосхо́дный. **supercilious** /ˌsuːpəˈsɪlɪəs/ *adj* высокоме́рный. **superficial** /-ˈfɪʃ(ə)l/ *adj* пове́рхностный. **superficiality** /-ˌfɪʃɪˈælɪtɪ/ *n* пове́рхностность. **superfluous** /suːˈpɜːflʊəs/ *adj* ли́шний. **superhuman** /ˌsuːpəˈhjuːmən/ *adj* сверхчелове́ческий. **superintendent** /ˌsuːpərɪnˈtendənt/ *n* заве́дующий *sb* (**of** +*instr*); (*police*) ста́рший полице́йский офице́р. **superior** /suːˈpɪərɪə(r)/ *n* ста́рший *sb*; *adj* (*better*) превосхо́дный; (*in rank*) ста́рший; (*haughty*) высокоме́рный. **superiority** /suːˌpɪərɪˈɒrɪtɪ/ *n* превосхо́дство. **superlative** /suːˈpɜːlətɪv/ *adj* превосхо́дный; *n* (*gram*) превосхо́дная сте́пень. **superman** *n* сверхчелове́к. **supermarket** *n* универса́м. **supernatural** *adj* сверхъесте́ственный. **superpower** *n* сверхдержа́ва. **supersede** /ˌsuːpəˈsiːd/ *vt* заменя́ть *impf*, замени́ть *pf*. **supersonic** *adj* сверхзвуково́й. **superstition** /ˌsuːpəˈstɪʃ(ə)n/ *n* суеве́рие. **superstitious** /ˌsuːpəˈstɪʃ(ə)s/ *adj* суеве́рный. **superstructure** *n* надстро́йка. **supervise** /ˈsuːpəˌvaɪz/ *vt* наблюда́ть *impf* за +*instr*. **supervision** /ˌsuːpəˈvɪʒ(ə)n/ *n* надзо́р. **supervisor** /ˈsuːpəˌvaɪzə(r)/ *n* нача́льник; (*of studies*) руководи́тель *m*.

supper /ˈsʌpə(r)/ *n* у́жин; **have ~** у́жинать *impf*, по~ *pf*.

supple /ˈsʌp(ə)l/ *adj* ги́бкий. **suppleness** /-nɪs/ *n* ги́бкость.

supplement *n* /ˈsʌplɪmənt/ (*to book*) дополне́ние; (*to periodical*) приложе́ние; *vt* /ˈsʌplɪˌment/ дополня́ть *impf*, допо́лнить *pf*. **supplementary** /ˌsʌplɪˈmentərɪ/ *adj* дополни́тельный.

supplier /səˈplaɪə(r)/ *n* поставщи́к **supply** /səˈplaɪ/ *n* (*stock*) запа́с; (*econ*) предложе́ние; *pl* (*mil*) припа́сы (-ов) *pl*, *vt* снабжа́ть *impf*, снабди́ть *pf* (**with** +*instr*).

support /səˈpɔːt/ *n* подде́ржка; *vt* подде́рживать *impf*, поддержа́ть *pf*; (*family*) содержа́ть *impf*. **supporter** /-tə(r)/ *n* сторо́нник; (*sport*) боле́льщик. **supportive** /-tɪv/ *adj* уча́стливый.

suppose /səˈpəʊz/ *vt* (*think*) полага́ть *impf*; (*presuppose*) предполага́ть *impf*, предположи́ть *pf*; (*assume*) допуска́ть *impf*, допусти́ть *pf*. **supposed** /-ˈpəʊzd/ *adj* (*assumed*) предполага́емый. **supposition** /ˌsʌpəˈzɪʃ(ə)n/ *n* предположе́ние.

suppress /səˈpres/ *vt* подавля́ть *impf*, подави́ть *pf*. **suppression** /-ˈpreʃ(ə)n/ *n* подавле́ние.

supremacy /suːˈpreməsɪ/ *n* госпо́дство. **supreme** /-ˈpriːm/ *adj* верхо́вный.

surcharge /ˈsɜːtʃɑːdʒ/ *n* наце́нка.

sure /ʃʊə(r)/ *adj* уве́ренный (**of** в+*prep*; **that** что); (*reliable*) ве́рный; **~ enough** действи́тельно; **he is ~ to come** он обяза́тельно придёт; **make ~ of** (*convince o.s.*) убежда́ться *impf*, убеди́ться *pf* в+*prep*; **make ~ that** (*check up*) проверя́ть *impf*, прове́рить *pf* что. **surely** /ˈʃʊəlɪ/ *adv* наверняка́. **surety** /ˈʃʊərɪtɪ/ *n* пору́ка; **stand ~ for** руча́ться *impf*, поручи́ться *pf* за+*acc.*

surf /sɜːf/ *n* прибо́й; *vi* занима́ться *impf*, заня́ться *pf* се́рфингом.

surface /ˈsɜːfɪs/ *n* пове́рхность; (*exterior*) вне́шность; **on the ~** (*fig*) вне́шне; **under the ~** (*fig*) по существу́; *adj* пове́рхностный; *vi* всплыва́ть *impf*, всплы́ть *pf*.

surfeit /ˈsɜːfɪt/ *n* (*surplus*) изли́шек.

surge /sɜːdʒ/ *n* волна́; *vi* (*rise, heave*) вздыма́ться *impf*; (*emotions*) нахлы́нуть *pf*; **~ forward** ри́нуться *pf* вперёд.

surgeon /ˈsɜːdʒ(ə)n/ *n* хиру́рг. **surgery** /ˈsɜːdʒərɪ/ *n* (*treatment*) хирурги́я; (*place*) кабине́т; (**~** *hours*) приёмные часы́ *m pl* (врача́). **surgical** /ˈsɜːdʒɪk(ə)l/ *adj* хирурги́ческий.

surly /ˈsɜːlɪ/ *adj* (*morose*) угрю́мый; (*rude*) гру́бый.

surmise /səˈmaɪz/ *vt* & *i* предполага́ть *impf*, предположи́ть *pf*.

surmount /səˈmaʊnt/ *vt* преодолева́ть *impf*, преодоле́ть *pf*.

surname /ˈsɜːneɪm/ *n* фами́лия.

surpass /səˈpɑːs/ *vt* превосходи́ть *impf*, превзойти́ *pf*.

surplus /ˈsɜːpləs/ *n* изли́шек; *adj* изли́шний.

surprise /səˈpraɪz/ *n* (*astonishment*) удивле́ние; (*surprising thing*) сюрпри́з; *vt* удивля́ть *impf*, удиви́ть *pf*; (*come upon suddenly*) застава́ть *impf*, заста́ть *pf* враспло́х; **be ~d** (*at*) удивля́ться *impf*, удиви́ться *pf* (+*dat*). **surprising** /-zɪŋ/ *adj* удиви́тельный.

surreal /səˈrɪəl/ *adj* сюрреалисти́ческий. **surrealism** /-lɪz(ə)m/ *n* сюрреали́зм. **surrealist** /-lɪst/ *n* сюрреали́ст; *adj* сюрреалисти́ческий.

surrender /səˈrendə(r)/ *n* сда́ча; (*renunciation*) отка́з; *vt* сдава́ть *impf*, сдать *pf*; (*give up*) отка́зываться *impf*, отказа́ться *pf* от+*gen*; *vi* сдава́ться *impf*, сда́ться *pf*; **~ o.s. to** предава́ться *impf*, преда́ться *pf* +*dat*.

surreptitious /ˌsʌrəpˈtɪʃəs/ *adj* та́йный.

surrogate /ˈsʌrəgət/ *n* замени́тель *m*.

surround /səˈraʊnd/ *vt* окружа́ть *impf*, окружи́ть *pf* (**with** +*instr*). **surrounding** /-dɪŋ/ *adj* окружа́ющий. **surroundings** /-dɪŋz/ *n* (*environs*) окре́стности *f pl*; (*milieu*) среда́.

surveillance /sɜːˈveɪləns/ *n* надзо́р.

survey *n* /ˈsɜːveɪ/ (*review*) обзо́р; (*inspection*) инспе́кция; (*poll*) опро́с; *vt* /səˈveɪ/ (*review*) обозрева́ть *impf*, обозре́ть *pf*; (*inspect*) инспекти́ровать *impf*, про~ *pf*; (*poll*) опра́шивать *impf*, опроси́ть *pf*. **surveyor** /səˈveɪə(r)/ *n* инспе́ктор.

survival /səˈvaɪv(ə)l/ *n* (*surviving*) выжива́ние; (*relic*) пережи́ток. **survive** /-ˈvaɪv/ *vt* пережива́ть *impf*, пережи́ть *pf*; *vi* выжива́ть *impf*, вы́жить *pf*. **survivor** /-ˈvaɪvə(r)/ *n* уцеле́вший *sb*; (*fig*) боре́ц.

susceptible /səˈseptɪb(ə)l/ *adj* подве́рженный (**to** влия́нию +*gen*); (*sensitive*) чувстви́тельный (**to** к+*dat*); (*impressionable*) впечатли́тельный.

suspect *n* /ˈsʌspekt/ подозрева́емый *sb*; *adj* подозри́тельный; *vt* /səˈspekt/ подозрева́ть *impf* (**of** в+*prep*); (*assume*) полага́ть *impf*.

suspend /sə'spend/ *vt* (*hang*) подве́шивать *impf*, подве́сить *pf*; (*delay*) приостана́вливать *impf*, приостанови́ть *pf*; (*debar temporarily*) вре́менно отстраня́ть *impf*, отстрани́ть *pf*; **~ed sentence** усло́вный пригово́р. **suspender** /-'spendə(r)/ *n* (*stocking*) подвя́зка. **suspense** /-'spens/ *n* неизве́стность. **suspension** /-'spenʃ(ə)n/ *n* (*halt*) приостано́вка; (*of car*) рессо́ры *f pl*; **~ bridge** вися́чий мост.

suspicion /sə'spɪʃ(ə)n/ *n* подозре́ние; **on ~** по подозре́нию (**of** в+*loc*); (*trace*) отте́нок. **suspicious** /-'spɪʃəs/ *adj* подозри́тельный.

sustain /sə'steɪn/ *vt* (*support*) подде́рживать *impf*, поддержа́ть *pf*; (*suffer*) потерпе́ть *pf*. **sustained** /-'steɪnd/ *adj* непреры́вный. **sustenance** /'sʌstɪnəns/ *n* пи́ща.

swab /swɒb/ *n* (*mop*) шва́бра; (*med*) тампо́н; (*specimen*) мазо́к.

swagger /'swægə(r)/ *vi* расха́живать *impf* с ва́жным ви́дом.

swallow[1] /'swɒləʊ/ *n* глото́к; *vt* прогла́тывать *impf*, проглоти́ть *pf*; **~ up** поглоща́ть *impf*, поглоти́ть *pf*.

swallow[2] /'swɒləʊ/ *n* (*bird*) ла́сточка.

swamp /swɒmp/ *n* боло́та; *vt* залива́ть *impf*, зали́ть *pf*; (*fig*) зава́ливать *impf*, завали́ть *pf* (**with** +*instr*). **swampy** /-pɪ/ *adj* боло́тистый.

swan /swɒn/ *n* ле́бедь *m*.

swap /swɒp/ *n* обме́н; *vt* (*for different thing*) меня́ть *impf*, об~, по~ *pf* (**for** на+*acc*); (*for similar thing*) обме́ниваться *impf*, обменя́ться *pf* +*instr*.

swarm /swɔːm/ *n* рой; (*crowd*) толпа́; *vi* рои́ться *impf*; толпи́ться *impf*; (*teem*) кише́ть *impf* (**with** +*instr*).

swarthy /'swɔːðɪ/ *adj* сму́глый.

swastika /'swɒstɪkə/ *n* сва́стика.

swat /swɒt/ *vt* прихло́пывать *impf*, прихло́пнуть *pf*.

swathe /sweɪð/ *n* (*expanse*) простра́нство; *vt* (*wrap*) заку́тывать *impf*, заку́тать *pf*.

sway /sweɪ/ *n* (*influence*) влия́ние; (*power*) власть *vt & i* кача́ть(ся) *impf*, качну́ть(ся) *pf*; *vt* (*influence*) име́ть *impf* влия́ние на+*acc*.

swear /sweə(r)/ *vi* (*vow*) кля́сться *impf*, по~ *pf*; (*curse*) руга́ться *impf*, ругну́ться *pf*; **~-word** руга́тельство.

sweat /swet/ *n* пот; *vi* поте́ть *impf*, вс~ *pf*. **sweater** /-tə(r)/ *n* сви́тер. **sweatshirt** *n* тёплая футбо́лка с дли́нными рука́вами. **sweaty** /-tɪ/ *adj* по́тный.

swede /swiːd/ *n* брю́ква.

Swede /swiːd/ *n* швед, **~**дка. **Sweden** /-d(ə)n/ *n* Шве́ция. **Swedish** /-dɪʃ/ *adj* шве́дский.

sweep /swiːp/ *n* (*span*) разма́х; (*chimney-~*) трубочи́ст; *vt* подмета́ть *impf*, подмести́ *pf*; *vi* (*go majestically*) ходи́ть *indet*, идти́ *det*, пойти́ *pf* велича́во; (*move swiftly*) мча́ться *impf*; **~ away** смета́ть *impf*, смести́ *pf*. **sweeping** /-pɪŋ/ *adj* (*changes*) радика́льный; (*statement*) огу́льный.

sweet /swiːt/ *n* (*sweetmeat*) конфе́та; (*dessert*) сла́дкое *sb*; *adj* сла́дкий; (*fragrant*) души́стый; (*dear*) ми́лый. **sweeten** /-t(ə)n/ *vt* подсла́щивать *impf*, подласти́ть *pf*. **sweetheart** *n* возлю́бленный, -нная *sb.* **sweetness** /-nɪs/ *n* сла́дость.

swell /swel/ *vi* (*up*) опуха́ть *impf*, опу́хнуть *pf*; *vt* & *i* (*a sail*) надува́ть(ся) *impf*, наду́ть(ся) *pf*; *vt* (*increase*) увели́чивать *impf*, увели́чить *pf*; *n* (*of sea*) зыбь. **swelling** /-lɪŋ/ *n* о́пухоль.

swelter /'sweltə(r)/ *vi* изнемога́ть *impf* от жары́. **sweltering** /-rɪŋ/ *adj* зно́йный.

swerve /swɜːv/ *vi* ре́зко свёртывать, свора́чивать *impf*, сверну́ть *pf*.

swift /swɪft/ *adj* бы́стрый.

swig /swɪg/ *n* глото́к; *vt* хлеба́ть *impf*.

swill /swɪl/ *n* по́йло; *vt* (*rinse*) полоска́ть *impf*, вы́~ *pf*.

swim /swɪm/ *vi* пла́вать *indet*, плыть *det*; *vt* (*across*) переплыва́ть *impf*, переплы́ть *pf* +*acc*, че́рез+*acc*. **swimmer** /-mə(r)/ *n* плове́ц, пловчи́ха. **swimming** /-mɪŋ/ *n* пла́вание. **swimming-pool** *n* бассе́йн для пла́вания. **swim-suit** *n* купа́льный костю́м.

swindle /'swɪnd(ə)l/ *vt* обма́нывать *impf*, обману́ть *pf*; *n* обма́н. **swindler** /-dlə(r)/ *n* моше́нник.

swine /swaɪn/ *n* свинья́.

swing /swɪŋ/ *vi* кача́ться *impf*, качну́ться *pf*; *vt* кача́ть *impf*, качну́ть *pf* +*acc*, *instr*; (*arms*) разма́хивать *impf* +*instr*; *n* кача́ние; (*shift*) крен; (*seat*) каче́ли (-лей) *pl*; **in full ~** в по́лном разга́ре.

swingeing /'swɪndʒɪŋ/ *adj* (*huge*) грома́дный; (*forcible*) си́льный.

swipe /swaɪp/ *n* си́льный уда́р; *vt* с сило́й ударя́ть *impf*, уда́рить *pf*.

swirl /swɜːl/ *vi* крути́ться *impf*; *n* (*of snow*) вихрь *m*.

swish /swɪʃ/ *vi* (*cut the air*) рассека́ть *impf*, рассе́чь *pf* во́здух со сви́стом; (*rustle*) шелесте́ть *impf*; *vt* (*tail*) взма́хивать *impf*, взмахну́ть *pf* +*instr*; (*brandish*) разма́хивать *impf* +*instr*; *n* (*of whip*) свист; (*rustle*) ше́лест.

Swiss /swɪs/ *n* швейца́рец, -ца́рка; *adj* швейца́рский.

switch /swɪtʃ/ *n* (*electr*) выключа́тель *m*; (*change*) измене́ние; *vt* & *i* (*also ~ over*) переключа́ть(ся) *impf*, переключи́ть(ся) *pf*; *vt* (*swap*) меня́ться *impf*, об~, по~ *pf* +*instr*; **~ off** выключа́ть *impf*, вы́ключить *pf*; **~ on** включа́ть *impf*, включи́ть *pf*. **switchboard** *n* коммута́тор.

Switzerland /'swɪtsələnd/ *n* Швейца́рия.

swivel /'swɪv(ə)l/ *vt* & *i* враща́ть(ся) *impf*.

swollen /'swəʊlən/ *adj* взду́тый.

swoon /swuːn/ *n* о́бморок; *vi* па́дать *impf*, упа́сть *pf* в о́бморок.

swoop /swuːp/ *vi*: **~ down** налета́ть *impf*, налете́ть *pf* (**on** на+*acc*); *n* налёт; **at one fell ~** одни́м уда́ром.

sword /sɔːd/ *n* меч.

sycophantic /ˌsɪkə'fæntɪk/ *adj* льсти́вый.

syllable /'sɪləb(ə)l/ *n* слог.

syllabus /'sɪləbəs/ *n* програ́мма.

symbol /'sɪmb(ə)l/ *n* си́мвол. **symbolic(al)** /sɪm'bɒlɪ(k(ə)l)/ *adj* символи́ческий. **symbolism** /'sɪmbəˌlɪz(ə)m/ *n* символи́зм. **symbolize** /'sɪmbəˌlaɪz/ *vt* символизи́ровать *impf*.

symmetrical /sɪ'metrɪk(ə)l/ *adj* симметри́ческий. **symmetry** /'sɪmɪtrɪ/ *n* симметри́я.

sympathetic /ˌsɪmpə'θetɪk/ *adj* сочу́вственный. **sympathize** /'sɪmpəˌθaɪz/ *vi* сочу́вствовать *impf* (**with** *+dat*). **sympathizer** /'sɪmpəˌθaɪzə(r)/ *n* сторо́нник. **sympathy** /'sɪmpəθɪ/ *n* сочу́вствие.

symphony /'sɪmfənɪ/ *n* симфо́ния.

symposium /sɪm'pəʊzɪəm/ *n* симпо́зиум.

symptom /'sɪmptəm/ *n* симпто́м. **symptomatic** /ˌsɪmptə'mætɪk/ *adj* симтомати́чный.

synagogue /'sɪnəˌgɒg/ *n* синаго́га.

synchronization /ˌsɪŋkrənaɪ'zeɪʃ(ə)n/ *n* синхрониза́ция. **synchronize** /'sɪŋkrəˌnaɪz/ *vt* синхронизи́ровать *impf & pf*.

syndicate /'sɪndɪkət/ *n* синдика́т.

syndrome /'sɪndrəʊm/ *n* синдро́м.

synonym /'sɪnənɪm/ *n* сино́ним. **synonymous** /sɪ'nɒnɪməs/ *adj* синоними́ческий.

synopsis /sɪ'nɒpsɪs/ *n* конспе́кт.

syntax /'sɪntæks/ *n* си́нтаксис.

synthesis /'sɪnθɪsɪs/ *n* си́нтез. **synthetic** /sɪn'θetɪk/ *adj* синтети́ческий.

syphilis /'sɪfɪlɪs/ *n* си́филис.

Syria /'sɪrɪə/ *n* Си́рия. **Syrian** /-rɪən/ *n* сири́ец, сири́йка; *adj* сири́йский.

syringe /sɪ'rɪndʒ/ *n* шприц; *vt* спринцева́ть *impf*.

syrup /'sɪrəp/ *n* сиро́п; (*treacle*) па́тока.

system /'sɪstəm/ *n* систе́ма; (*network*) сеть; (*organism*) органи́зм. **systematic** /ˌsɪstə'mætɪk/ *adj* системати́ческий. **systematize** /'sɪstəməˌtaɪz/ *vt* систематизи́ровать *impf & pf*.

T

tab /tæb/ *n* (*loop*) пе́телька; (*on uniform*) петли́ца; (*of boot*) ушко́; **keep ~s on** следи́ть *impf* за+*instr*.

table /'teɪb(ə)l/ *n* стол; (*chart*) табли́ца; **~cloth** ска́терть; **~spoon** столо́вая ло́жка; **~ tennis** насто́льный те́ннис; *vt* (*for discussion*) предлага́ть *impf*, предложи́ть *pf* на обсужде́ние.

tableau /'tæbləʊ/ *n* жива́я карти́на.

tablet /'tæblɪt/ *n* (*pill*) табле́тка; (*of stone*) плита́; (*memorial ~*) мемориа́льная доска́; (*name plate*) доще́чка.

tabloid /'tæblɔɪd/ *n* (*newspaper*) малоформа́тная газе́та; (*derog*) бульва́рная газе́та.

taboo /tə'bu:/ *n* табу́ *neut indecl*; *adj* запрещённый.

tacit /'tæsɪt/ *adj* молчали́вый. **taciturn** /'tæsɪˌtɜ:n/ *adj* неразгово́рчивый.

tack[1] /tæk/ *n* (*nail*) гво́здик; (*stitch*) намётка; (*naut*) галс; (*fig*) курс; *vt* (*fasten*) прикрепля́ть *impf*, прикрепи́ть *pf* гво́здиками; (*stitch*) смётывать *impf*, смета́ть *pf* на живу́ю ни́тку; (*fig*) добавля́ть *impf*, доба́вить *pf* (**(on)to** *+dat*); *vi* (*naut*; *fig*) лави́ровать *impf*.

tack[2] /tæk/ *n* (*riding*) сбру́я (*collect*).

tackle /'tæk(ə)l/ *n* (*requisites*) снасть (*collect*); (*sport*) блоки́ровка; *vt* (*problem*) бра́ться *impf*, взя́ться *pf* за+*acc*; (*sport*) блоки́ровать *impf & pf*.

tacky /'tækɪ/ *adj* ли́пкий.

tact /tækt/ *n* такт(и́чность). **tactful** /-fʊl/ *adj* такти́чный.

tactical /'tæktɪk(ə)l/ *adj* тактический. **tactics** /'tæktɪks/ *n pl* тактика.

tactless /'tæktlɪs/ *adj* бестактный.

tadpole /'tædpəʊl/ *n* головастик.

Tadzhikistan /ˌtædʒɪkɪ'stɑːn/ *n* Таджикистан.

tag /tæg/ *n* (*label*) ярлык; (*of lace*) наконечник; *vt* (*label*) прикреплять *impf*, прикрепить *pf* ярлык на+*acc*; *vi*: ~ **along** (*follow*) тащиться *impf* сзади; **may I ~ along?** можно с вами?

tail /teɪl/ *n* хвост; (*of shirt*) нижний конец; (*of coat*) фалда; (*of coin*) обратная сторона монеты; **heads or ~s?** орёл или решка?; *pl* (*coat*) фрак; *vt* (*shadow*) выслеживать *impf*; *vi*: ~ **away, off** постепенно уменьшаться *impf*; (*grow silent, abate*) затихать *impf*. **tailback** *n* хвост. **tailcoat** *n* фрак.

tailor /'teɪlə(r)/ *n* портной *sb*; **~-made** сшитый на заказ; (*fig*) сделанный индивидуально.

taint /teɪnt/ *vt* портить *impf*, ис~ *pf*.

Taiwan /taɪ'wɑːn/ *n* Тайвань *m*.

take /teɪk/ *vt* (*various senses*) брать *impf*, взять *pf*; (*also seize, capture*) захватывать *impf*, захватить *pf*; (*receive, accept*; ~ *breakfast*; ~ *medicine*; ~ *steps*) принимать *impf*, принять *pf*; (*convey, escort*) провожать *impf*, проводить *pf*; (*public transport*) ездить *indet*, ехать *det*, по~ *pf* +*instr*, на+*prep*; (*photograph*) снимать *impf*, снять *pf*; (*occupy*; ~ *time*) занимать *impf*, занять *pf*; (*impers*) **how long does it ~?** сколько времени нужно?; (*size in clothing*) носить *impf*; (*exam*) сдавать *impf*; *vi* (*be successful*) иметь *impf* успех (*of injection*) прививаться *impf*, привиться *pf*; ~ **after** походить *impf* на+*acc*; ~ **away** (*remove*) убирать *impf*, убрать *pf*; (*subtract*) вычитать *impf*, вычесть *pf*; **~-away** магазин, где продают на вынос; ~ **back** (*return*) возвращать *impf*, возвратить *pf*; (*retrieve, retract*) брать *impf*, взять *pf* назад; ~ **down** (*in writing*) записывать *impf*, записать *pf*; (*remove*) снимать *impf*, снять *pf*; ~ **s.o., sth for, to be** принимать *impf*, принять *pf* за+*acc*; ~ **from** отнимать *impf*, отнять *pf* у, от+*gen*; ~ **in** (*carry in*) вносить *impf*, внести *pf*; (*lodgers*; *work*) брать *impf*, взять *pf*; (*clothing*) ушивать *impf*, ушить *pf*; (*understand*) понимать *impf*, понять *pf*; (*deceive*) обманывать *impf*, обмануть *pf*; ~ **off** (*clothing*) снимать *impf*, снять *pf*; (*mimic*) передразнивать *impf*, передразнить *pf*; (*aeroplane*) взлетать *impf*, взлететь *pf*; **~-off** (*imitation*) подражание; (*aeron*) взлёт; ~ **on** (*undertake*; *hire*) брать *impf*, взять *pf* на себя; (*acquire*) приобретать *impf*, приобрести *pf*; (*at game*) сражаться *impf*, сразиться *pf* с+*instr* (**at** в+*acc*); ~ **out** вынимать *impf*, вынуть *pf*; (*dog*) выводить *impf*, вывести *pf* (**for a walk** на прогулку); (*to theatre, restaurant etc.*) приглашать *impf*, пригласить *pf* (**to** в+*acc*); **we took them out every night** мы приглашали их куда-нибудь каждый вечер; ~ **it out on** срывать *impf*, сорвать *pf* всё на +*prep*; ~ **over** принимать *impf*, принять *pf* руководство

+*instr*; ~ **to** (*thing*) пристрасти́ться *pf* к+*dat*; (*person*) привя́зываться *impf*, привяза́ться *pf* к+*dat*; (*begin*) стано́виться *impf*, стать *pf* +*inf*; ~ **up** (*interest oneself in*) занима́ться *impf*, заня́ться *pf*; (*with an official etc.*) обраща́ться *impf*, обрати́ться *pf* с+*instr*, к+*dat*; (*challenge*) принима́ть *impf*, приня́ть *pf*; (*time, space*) занима́ть *impf*, заня́ть *pf*; ~ **up with** (*person*) свя́зываться *impf*, связа́ться *pf* с+*instr*; *n* (*cin*) дубль *m*.

taking /'teɪkɪŋ/ *adj* привлека́тельный.

takings /'teɪkɪŋz/ *n pl* сбор.

talcum powder /'tælkəm 'paʊdə(r)/ *n* тальк.

tale /teɪl/ *n* расска́з.

talent /'tælənt/ *n* тала́нт. **talented** /-tɪd/ *adj* тала́нтливый.

talk /tɔːk/ *vi* разгова́ривать *impf* (**to, with** с+*instr*); (*gossip*) сплётничать *impf*, на~ *pf*; *vt & i* говори́ть *impf*, по~ *pf*; ~ **down to** говори́ть *impf* свысока́ с+*instr*; ~ **into** угова́ривать *impf*, уговори́ть *pf* +*inf*; ~ **out of** отгова́ривать *impf*, отговори́ть *pf* +*inf*, от+*gen*; ~ **over** (*discuss*) обсужда́ть *impf*, обсуди́ть *pf*; ~ **round** (*persuade*) переубежда́ть *impf*, переубеди́ть *pf*; *n* (*conversation*) разгово́р; (*lecture*) бесе́да; *pl* перегово́ры (-ров) *pl*. **talkative** /'tɔːkətɪv/ *adj* разгово́рчивый; (*derog*) болтли́вый. **talker** /'tɔːkə(r)/ *n* говоря́щий *sb*; (*chatterer*) болту́н (*coll*); (*orator*) ора́тор. **talking-to** *n* (*coll*) вы́говор.

tall /tɔːl/ *adj* высо́кий; (*in measurements*) ро́стом в+*acc*.

tally /'tælɪ/ *n* (*score*) счёт; *vi* соотве́тствовать (**with** +*dat*).

talon /'tælən/ *n* ко́готь *m*.

tambourine /ˌtæmbə'riːn/ *n* бу́бен.

tame /teɪm/ *adj* ручно́й; (*insipid*) пре́сный; *vt* прируча́ть *impf*, приручи́ть *pf*. **tamer** /'teɪmə(r)/ *n* укроти́тель *m*.

tamper /'tæmpə(r)/ *vi*: ~ **with** (*meddle*) тро́гать *impf*, тро́нуть *pf*; (*forge*) подде́лывать *impf*, подде́лать *pf*.

tampon /'tæmpɒn/ *n* тампо́н.

tan /tæn/ *n* (*sun*~) зага́р; *adj* желтова́то-кори́чневый; *vt* (*hide*) дуби́ть *impf*, вы́~ *pf*; (*beat*) (*coll*) дуба́сить *impf*, от~ *pf*; *vi* загора́ть *impf*, загоре́ть *pf*; (*of sun*): **tanned** загоре́лый.

tang /tæŋ/ *n* (*taste*) ре́зкий при́вкус; (*smell*) о́стрый за́пах.

tangent /'tændʒ(ə)nt/ *n* (*math*) каса́тельная *sb*; (*trigonometry*) та́нгенс; **go off at a** ~ отклоня́ться *impf*, отклони́ться *pf* от те́мы.

tangerine /ˌtændʒə'riːn/ *n* мандари́н.

tangible /'tændʒɪb(ə)l/ *adj* осяза́емый.

tangle /'tæŋg(ə)l/ *vt & i* запу́тывать(ся) *impf*, запу́таться *pf*; *n* пу́таница.

tango /'tæŋgəʊ/ *n* та́нго *neut indecl*.

tangy /'tæŋɪ/ *adj* о́стрый; ре́зкий.

tank /tæŋk/ *n* бак; (*mil*) танк.

tankard /'tæŋkəd/ *n* кру́жка.

tanker /'tæŋkə(r)/ *n* (*sea*) та́нкер; (*road*) автоцисте́рна.

tantalize /'tæntəˌlaɪz/ *vt* дразни́ть *impf*.

tantamount /'tæntəˌmaʊnt/ *predic* равноси́лен (-льна) (**to** +*dat*).

tantrum /'tæntrəm/ *n* присту́п

раздраже́ния.
tap[1] /tæp/ *n* кран; *vt* (*resources*) испо́льзовать *impf* & *pf*; (*telephone conversation*) подслу́шивать *impf*.
tap[2] /tæp/ *n* (*knock*) стук; *vt* стуча́ть *impf*, по~ *pf* в+*acc*, по+*dat*; **~-dance** (*vi*) отбива́ть *impf*, отби́ть *pf* чечётку; (*n*) чечётка; **~-dancer** чечёточник, -ица.
tape /teɪp/ *n* (*cotton strip*) тесьма́; (*adhesive, magnetic, measuring, etc.*) ле́нта; **~-measure** руле́тка; **~ recorder** магнитофо́н; **~ recording** за́пись; *vt* (*seal*) закле́ивать *impf*, закле́ить *pf*; (*record*) запи́сывать *impf*, записа́ть *pf* на ле́нту.
taper /ˈteɪpə(r)/ *vt* & *i* су́живать(ся) *impf*, су́зить(ся) *pf*.
tapestry /ˈtæpɪstrɪ/ *n* гобеле́н.
tar /tɑː(r)/ *n* дёготь *m*.
tardy /ˈtɑːdɪ/ *adj* (*slow*) медли́тельный; (*late*) запозда́лый.
target /ˈtɑːgɪt/ *n* мише́нь, цель.
tariff /ˈtærɪf/ *n* тари́ф.
tarmac /ˈtɑːmæk/ *n* (*material*) гудро́н; (*road*) гудрони́рованное шоссе́ *neut indecl*; (*runway*) бетони́рованная площа́дка; *vt* гудрони́ровать *impf* & *pf*.
tarnish /ˈtɑːnɪʃ/ *vt* де́лать *impf*, с~ *pf* ту́склым; (*fig*) пятна́ть *impf*, за~ *pf*; *vi* тускне́ть *impf*, по~ *pf*.
tarpaulin /tɑːˈpɔːlɪn/ *n* брезе́нт.
tarragon /ˈtærəgən/ *n* эстраго́н.
tart[1] /tɑːt/ *adj* (*taste*) ки́слый; (*fig*) ко́лкий.
tart[2] /tɑːt/ *n* (*pie*) сла́дкий пиро́г.
tart[3] /tɑːt/ *n* (*prostitute*) шлю́ха.
tartan /ˈtɑːt(ə)n/ *n* шотла́ндка.
tartar /ˈtɑːtə(r)/ *n* ви́нный ка́мень *m*.
task /tɑːsk/ *n* зада́ча; **take to ~** де́лать *impf*, с~ *pf* вы́говор+*dat*; **~ force** операти́вная гру́ппа.
Tass /tæs/ *abbr* ТАСС, Телегра́фное аге́нтство Сове́тского Сою́за.
tassel /ˈtæs(ə)l/ *n* ки́сточка.
taste /teɪst/ *n* (*also fig*) вкус; **take a ~ of** про́бовать *impf*, по~ *pf*; *vt* чу́вствовать *impf*, по~ *pf* вкус+*gen*; (*sample*) про́бовать *impf*, по~ *pf*; (*fig*) вкуша́ть *impf*, вкуси́ть *pf*; (*wine etc.*) дегусти́ровать *impf* & *pf*; *vi* име́ть *impf* вкус, при́вкус (**of** +*gen*). **tasteful** /-fʊl/ *adj* (сде́ланный) со вку́сом. **tasteless** /-lɪs/ *adj* безвку́сный. **tasting** /-tɪŋ/ *n* дегуста́ция. **tasty** /-tɪ/ *adj* вку́сный.
tatter /ˈtætə(r)/ *n pl* лохмо́тья (-ьев) *pl*. **tattered** /-d/ *adj* обо́рванный.
tattoo /təˈtuː/ *n* (*design*) татуиро́вка; *vt* татуи́ровать *impf* & *pf*.
taunt /tɔːnt/ *n* насме́шка; *vt* насмеха́ться *impf* над+*instr*.
Taurus /ˈtɔːrəs/ *n* Теле́ц.
taut /tɔːt/ *adj* ту́го натя́нутый; туго́й.
tavern /ˈtæv(ə)n/ *n* таве́рна.
tawdry /ˈtɔːdrɪ/ *adj* мишу́рный.
tawny /ˈtɔːnɪ/ *adj* рыжева́то-кори́чневый.
tax /tæks/ *n* нало́г; **~-free** освобождённый от нало́га; *vt* облага́ть *impf*, обложи́ть *pf* нало́гом; (*strain*) напряга́ть *impf*, напря́чь *pf*; (*patience*) испы́тывать *impf*, испыта́ть *pf*. **taxable** /ˈtæksəb(ə)l/ *adj* подлежа́щий обложе́нию нало́гом. **taxation** /tækˈseɪʃ(ə)n/ *n* обложе́ние нало́гом. **taxing** /ˈtæksɪŋ/ *adj* утоми́тельный. **taxpayer** *n* налогопла-

тéльщик.

taxi /ˈtæksɪ/ *n* такси́ *neut indecl*; **~-driver** води́тель *m* такси́; **~ rank** стоя́нка такси́; *vi* (*aeron*) рули́ть *impf*.

tea /tiː/ *n* чай; **~ bag** пакéтик с сухи́м ча́ем; **~ cloth, ~ towel** полотéнце для посу́ды; **~ cosy** чехóльщик (для ча́йника); **~cup** ча́йная ча́шка; **~-leaf** ча́йный лист; **~-pot** ча́йник; **~spoon** ча́йная лóжка; **~ strainer** ча́йное си́течко.

teach /tiːtʃ/ *vt* учи́ть *impf*, на~ *pf* (*person* +*acc*; *subject* +*dat*, *inf*); преподава́ть *impf* (*subject* +*acc*); (*coll*) проу́чивать *impf*, проучи́ть *pf*. **teacher** /ˈtiːtʃə(r)/ *n* учи́тель *m*, **~**ница; преподава́тель *m*, **~**ница; **~-training college** педогоги́ческий институ́т. **teaching** /ˈtiːtʃɪŋ/ *n* (*instruction*) обучéние; (*doctrine*) учéние.

teak /tiːk/ *n* тик; *attrib* ти́ковый.

team /tiːm/ *n* (*sport*) кома́нда; (*of people*) брига́да; (*of horses etc.*) упря́жка; **~-mate** член той же кома́нды; **~work** сотру́дничество; *vi* (**~** *up*) объединя́ться *impf*, объедини́ться *pf*.

tear[1] /teə(r)/ *n* (*rent*) прорéха; *vt* (*also* **~** *up*) рвать *impf*; (*also* **~** *up*) разрыва́ть *impf*, разорва́ть *pf*; *vi* рва́ться *impf*; (*rush*) мча́ться *impf*; **~ down, off** срыва́ть *impf*, сорва́ть *pf*; **~ out** вырыва́ть *impf*, вы́рвать *pf*.

tear[2] /tɪə(r)/ *n* (**~**-*drop*) слеза́; **~-gas** слезоточи́вый газ. **tearful** /-fʊl/ *adj* слезли́вый.

tease /tiːz/ *vt* дразни́ть *impf*.

teat /tiːt/ *n* сосóк.

technical /ˈteknɪk(ə)l/ *adj* техни́ческий; **~ college** техни́ческое учи́лище. **technicality** /ˌteknɪˈkælɪtɪ/ *n* формáльность. **technically** /ˈteknɪklɪ/ *adv* (*strictly*) формáльно. **technician** /tekˈnɪʃən/ *n* тéхник. **technique** /-ˈniːk/ *n* тéхника; (*method*) мéтод. **technology** /-ˈnɒlədʒɪ/ *n* технолóгия, тéхника. **technological** /ˌteknəˈlɒdʒɪkəl/ *adj* технологи́ческий. **technologist** /tekˈnɒlədʒɪst/ *n* технóлог.

teddy-bear /ˈtedɪˌbeə(r)/ *n* медвежóнок

tedious /ˈtiːdɪəs/ *adj* ску́чный. **tedium** /ˈtiːdɪəm/ *n* ску́ка.

teem[1] /tiːm/ *vi* (*swarm*) кишéть *impf* (**with** +*instr*).

teem[2] /tiːm/ *vi*: **it is ~ing (with rain)** дождь льёт как из ведра́.

teenage /ˈtiːneɪdʒ/ *adj* ю́ношеский. **teenager** /-dʒə(r)/ *n* подрóсток. **teens** /tiːnz/ *n pl* вóзраст от трина́дцати до девятна́дцати лет.

teeter /ˈtiːtə(r)/ *vi* кача́ться *impf*, качну́ться *pf*.

teethe /tiːð/ *vi*: **the child is teething** у ребёнка прорéзываются зу́бы; **teething troubles** (*fig*) нача́льные проблéмы *f pl*.

teetotal /tiːˈtəʊt(ə)l/ *adj* трéзвый. **teetotaller** /-lə(r)/ *n* трéзвенник.

telecommunication(s) /ˌtelɪkəˌmjuːnɪˈkeɪʃ(ə)nz/ *n* да́льняя связь. **telegram** /ˈtelɪˌgræm/ *n* телегра́мма. **telegraph** /ˈtelɪˌgrɑːf/ *n* телегра́ф; **~ pole** телегра́фный столб. **telepathic** /ˌtelɪˈpæθɪk/ *adj* телепати́ческий. **telepathy** /tɪˈlepəθɪ/ *n* телепа́тия. **telephone** /ˈtelɪˌfəʊn/ *n* телефóн; *vt* (*message*) телефони́ровать *impf* & *pf* +*acc*, о+*prep*; (*person*) звони́ть *impf*, по~ *pf* (по телефóну) +*dat*; **~ box** телефóнная бу́дка; **~ directory** телефóнная кни́га; **~**

exchange телефо́нная ста́нция; ~ **number** но́мер телефо́на. **telephonist** /tɪ'lefənɪst/ *n* телефони́ст, ~ка. **telephoto lens** /'telɪ ˌfəʊtəʊ lenz/ *n* телеобъекти́в. **telescope** /'telɪˌskəʊp/ *n* телеско́п. **telescopic** /ˌtelɪ'skɒpɪk/ *adj* телескопи́ческий. **televise** /'telɪˌvaɪz/ *vt* пока́зывать *impf*, показа́ть *pf* по телеви́дению. **television** /'telɪˌvɪʒ(ə)n/ *n* телеви́дение; (*set*) телеви́зор; *attrib* телевизио́нный. **telex** /'teleks/ *n* те́лекс.

tell /tel/ *vt* & *i* (*relate*) расска́зывать *impf*, рассказа́ть *pf* (*thing told* +*acc*, о+*prep*; *person told* +*dat*); *vt* (*utter, inform*) говори́ть *impf*, сказа́ть *pf* (*thing uttered* +*acc*; *thing informed about* о+*prep*; *person informed* +*dat*); (*order*) веле́ть *impf* & *pf* +*dat*; ~ **one thing from another** отлича́ть *impf*, отличи́ть *pf* +*acc* от+*gen*; *vi* (*have an effect*) ска́зываться *impf*, сказа́ться *pf* (**on** на+*prep*); ~ **off** отчи́тывать *impf*, отчита́ть *pf*; ~ **on,** ~ **tales about** ябе́дничать *impf*, на~ *pf* на+*acc*. **teller** /'telə(r)/ *n* (*of story*) расска́зчик; (*of votes*) счётчик; (*in bank*) касси́р. **telling** /'telɪŋ/ *adj* (*effective*) эффекти́вный; (*significant*) многозначи́тельный. **telltale** *n* спле́тник; *adj* преда́тельский.

temerity /tɪ'merɪtɪ/ *n* дёрзость.

temp /temp/ *n* рабо́тающий *sb* вре́менно; *vi* рабо́тать *impf* вре́менно.

temper /'tempə(r)/ *n* (*character*) нрав; (*mood*) настрое́ние; (*anger*) гнев; **lose one's** ~ выходи́ть *impf*, вы́йти *pf* из себя́; *vt* (*fig*) смягча́ть *impf*, смягчи́ть *pf*.

temperament /'temprəmənt/ *n* темпера́мент. **temperamental** /ˌtemprə'ment(ə)l/ *adj* темпера́ментный.

temperance /'tempərəns/ *n* (*moderation*) уме́ренность; (*sobriety*) тре́звенность.

temperate /'tempərət/ *adj* уме́ренный.

temperature /'temprɪtʃə(r)/ *n* температу́ра; (*high* ~) повы́шенная температу́ра; **take s.o.'s** ~ измеря́ть *impf*, изме́рить *pf* температу́ру +*dat*.

tempest /'tempɪst/ *n* бу́ря. **tempestuous** /tem'pestjʊəs/ *adj* бу́рный.

template /'templeɪt/ *n* шабло́н.

temple[1] /'temp(ə)l/ *n* (*religion*) храм.

temple[2] /'temp(ə)l/ *n* (*anat*) висо́к.

tempo /'tempəʊ/ *n* темп.

temporal /'tempər(ə)l/ *adj* (*of time*) временно́й; (*secular*) мирско́й.

temporary /'tempərərɪ/ *adj* вре́менный.

tempt /tempt/ *vt* соблазня́ть *impf*, соблазни́ть *pf*; ~ **fate** испы́тывать *impf*, испыта́ть *pf* судьбу́. **temptation** /temp'teɪʃ(ə)n/ *n* собла́зн. **tempting** /'temptɪŋ/ *adj* соблазни́тельный.

ten /ten/ *adj* & *n* де́сять; (*number 10*) деся́тка. **tenth** /tenθ/ *adj* & *n* деся́тый.

tenable /'tenəb(ə)l/ *adj* (*logical*) разу́мный.

tenacious /tɪ'neɪʃəs/ *adj* це́пкий. **tenacity** /-'næsɪtɪ/ *n* це́пкость.

tenancy /'tenənsɪ/ *n* (*renting*) наём помеще́ния; (*period*) срок аре́нды. **tenant** /'tenənt/ *n* аренда́тор.

tend[1] /tend/ *vi* (*be apt*) име́ть скло́нность (**to** к+*dat*, +*inf*).

tend² /tend/ *vt* (*look after*) ухáживать *impf* за+*instr.*

tendency /'tendənsı/ *n* тендéнция. **tendentious** /ten'denʃəs/ *adj* тенденциóзный.

tender¹ /'tendə(r)/ *vt* (*offer*) предлагáть *impf*, предложи́ть *pf*; *vi* (*make* ~ *for*) подавáть *impf*, подáть *pf* заявку (на торгáх); *n* предложéние; **legal** ~ закóнное платёжное срéдство.

tender² /'tendə(r)/ *adj* (*delicate, affectionate*) нéжный. **tenderness** /-nıs/ *n* нéжность.

tendon /'tend(ə)n/ *n* сухожи́лие.

tendril /'tendrıl/ *n* ýсик.

tenement /'tenımənt/ *n* (*dwelling-house*) жилóй дом; ~**-house** многоквarти́рный дом.

tenet /'tenıt/ *n* дóгмат, при́нцип.

tennis /'tenıs/ *n* тéннис.

tenor /'tenə(r)/ *n* (*direction*) направлéние; (*purport*) смысл; (*mus*) тéнор.

tense¹ /tens/ *n* врéмя *neut.*

tense² /tens/ *vt* напрягáть *impf*, напря́чь *pf*; *adj* напряжённый. **tension** /'tenʃ(ə)n/ *n* напряжéние.

tent /tent/ *n* палáтка.

tentacle /'tentək(ə)l/ *n* щýпальце.

tentative /'tentətıv/ *adj* (*experimental*) прóбный; (*preliminary*) предвари́тельный.

tenterhooks /'tentə,hʊks/ *n pl*: **be on** ~ сидéть *impf* как на игóлках.

tenth /tenθ/ *see* **ten**

tenuous /'tenjʊəs/ *adj* (*fig*) неубеди́тельный.

tenure /'tenjə(r)/ *n* (*of property*) владéние; (*of office*) пребывáние в дóлжности; (*period*) срок; (*guaranteed employment*) несменя́емость.

tepid /'tepıd/ *adj* тепловáтый.

term /tɜːm/ *n* (*period*) срок; (*univ*) семéстр; (*school*) чéтверть; (*technical word*) тéрмин; (*expression*) выражéние; *pl* (*conditions*) услóвия *neut pl*; (*relations*) отношéния *neut pl*; **on good** ~**s** в хорóших отношéниях; **come to** ~**s with** (*resign o.s. to*) покоря́ться *impf*, покори́ться *pf* к+*dat*; *vt* называ́ть *impf*, назвáть *pf.*

terminal /'tɜːmın(ə)l/ *adj* конéчный; (*med*) смертéльный; *n* (*electr*) зажи́м; (*computer, aeron*) терминáл; (*terminus*) конéчная остановка.

terminate /'tɜːmı,neıt/ *vt* & *i* кончáть(ся) *impf*, кóнчить(ся) *pf* (**in** +*instr*). **termination** /-'neıʃ(ə)n/ *n* прекращéние.

terminology /,tɜːmı'nɒlədʒı/ *n* терминолóгия.

terminus /'tɜːmınəs/ *n* конéчная остановка.

termite /'tɜːmaıt/ *n* терми́т.

terrace /'terəs/ *n* террáса; (*houses*) ряд домóв.

terracotta /,terə'kɒtə/ *n* терракóта.

terrain /te'reın/ *n* мéстность.

terrestrial /tə'restrıəl/ *adj* земнóй.

terrible /'terıb(ə)l/ *adj* ужáсный. **terribly** /-blı/ *adv* ужáсно.

terrier /'terıə(r)/ *n* терьéр.

terrific /tə'rıfık/ *adj* (*huge*) огрóмный; (*splendid*) потрясáющий. **terrify** /'terı,faı/ *vt* ужасáть *impf*, ужаснýть *pf.*

territorial /,terı'tɔːrıəl/ *adj* территориáльный. **territory** /'terıtərı/ *n* террито́рия.

terror /'terə(r)/ *n* ýжас; (*person; polit*) террóр. **terrorism** /'terə,rız(ə)m/ *n* террори́зм. **terrorist**

/'terərɪst/ *n* террори́ст, ~ка. **terrorize** /'terə,raɪz/ *vt* терроризи́ровать *impf* & *pf*.

terse /tɜ:s/ *adj* кра́ткий.

tertiary /'tɜ:ʃərɪ/ *adj* трети́чный; (*education*) вы́сший.

test /test/ *n* испыта́ние, про́ба; (*exam*) экза́мен; контро́льная рабо́та; (*analysis*) ана́лиз; **~-tube** проби́рка; *vt* (*try out*) испы́тывать *impf*, испыта́ть *pf*; (*check up on*) проверя́ть *impf*, прове́рить *pf*; (*give exam to*) экзаменова́ть *impf*, про~ *pf*.

testament /'testəmənt/ *n* завеща́ние; **Old, New T~** Ве́тхий, Но́вый заве́т.

testicle /'testɪk(ə)l/ *n* яи́чко.

testify /'testɪ,faɪ/ *vi* свиде́тельствовать *impf* (**to** в по́льзу +*gen*; **against** про́тив+*gen*); *vt* (*declare*) заявля́ть *impf*, заяви́ть *pf*; (*be evidence of*) свиде́тельствовать о+*prep*.

testimonial /,testɪ'məʊnɪəl/ *n* рекоменда́ция. **testimony** /'testɪmənɪ/ *n* свиде́тельство.

tetanus /'tetənəs/ *n* столбня́к.

tetchy /'tetʃɪ/ *adj* раздражи́тельный.

tête-à-tête /,teɪtɑ:'teɪt/ *n* & *adv* тет-а-те́т.

tether /'teðə(r)/ *n*: **be at, come to the end of one's ~** дойти́ *pf* до то́чки; *vt* привя́зывать *impf*, привяза́ть *pf*.

text /tekst/ *n* текст; **~ message SMS/CMC-**сообще́ние; *vt* посыла́ть *impf*, посла́ть *pf* **SMS** (+*dat*). **textbook** *n* уче́бник.

textile /'tekstaɪl/ *adj* тексти́льный; *n* ткань; *pl* тексти́ль *m* (*collect*).

textual /'tekstjʊəl/ *adj* текстово́й.

texture /'tekstʃə(r)/ *n* тексту́ра.

than /ðæn/ *conj* (*comparison*) чем; **other ~** (*except*) кро́ме+*gen*.

thank /θæŋk/ *vt* благодари́ть *impf*, по~ *pf* (**for** за+*acc*); **~ God** сла́ва Бо́гу; **~ you** спаси́бо; благодарю́ вас; *n pl* благода́рность; **~s to** (*good result*) благодаря́ +*dat*; (*bad result*) из-за+*gen*. **thankful** /-fʊl/ *adj* благода́рный. **thankless** /-lɪs/ *adj* неблагода́рный. **thanksgiving** /'θæŋks,gɪvɪŋ/ *n* благодаре́ние.

that /ðæt/ *demonstrative adj* & *pron* тот; **~ which** тот кото́рый; *rel pron* кото́рый; *conj* что; (*purpose*) что́бы; *adv* так, до тако́й сте́пени.

thatched /θætʃt/ *adj* соло́менный.

thaw /θɔ:/ *vt* раста́пливать *impf*, растопи́ть *pf*; *vi* та́ять *impf*, рас~ *pf*; *n* о́ттепель.

the /ðə, ði:/ *def article, not translated*; *adv* тем; **the ... the ...** чем ...тем; **~ more ~ better** чем бо́льше, тем лу́чше.

theatre /'θɪətə(r)/ *n* теа́тр; (*lecture ~*) аудито́рия; (*operating ~*) операцио́нная *sb*; **~-goer** театра́л. **theatrical** /θɪ'ætrɪk(ə)l/ *adj* театра́льный.

theft /θeft/ *n* кра́жа.

their, theirs /ðeə(r), ðeəz/ *poss pron* их; свой.

theme /θi:m/ *n* те́ма.

themselves /ðəm'selvz/ *pron* (*emph*) (они́) са́ми; (*refl*) себя́; -ся (*suffixed to vt*).

then /ðen/ *adv* (*at that time*) тогда́; (*after that*) пото́м; **now and ~** вре́мя от вре́мени; *conj* в тако́м слу́чае, тогда́; *adj* тогда́шний; **by ~** к тому́ вре́мени; **since ~** с тех пор.

thence /ðens/ *adv* отту́да. **thenceforth, -forward** /ðens 'fɔ:θ, -'fɔ:wəd/ *adv* с того́/э́того вре́мени.

theologian /ˌθɪəˈləʊdʒ(ə)n/ *n* теоло́г. **theological** /-ˈlɒdʒɪk(ə)l/ *adj* теологи́ческий. **theology** /θɪˈɒlədʒɪ/ *n* теоло́гия.

theorem /ˈθɪərəm/ *n* теоре́ма. **theoretical** /ˌθɪəˈretɪk(ə)l/ *adj* теорети́ческий. **theorize** /ˈθɪəraɪz/ *vi* теоретизи́ровать *impf*. **theory** /ˈθɪərɪ/ *n* тео́рия.

therapeutic /ˌθerəˈpjuːtɪk/ *adj* терапевти́ческий. **therapist** /ˈθerəpɪst/ *n* (*psychotherapist*) психотерапе́вт. **therapy** /ˈθerəpɪ/ *n* терапи́я.

there /ðeə(r)/ *adv* (*place*) там; (*direction*) туда́; *int* вот!; ну!; ~ **is, are** есть, име́ется (-е́ются); ~ **you are** (*on giving sth*) пожа́луйста. **thereabouts** /ˈðeərəˌbaʊts/ *adv* (*near*) побли́зости; (*approximately*) приблизи́тельно. **thereafter** *adv* по́сле э́того. **thereby** *adv* таки́м о́бразом. **therefore** *adv* поэ́тому. **therein** *adv* в э́том. **thereupon** *adv* зате́м.

thermal /ˈθɜːm(ə)l/ *adj* теплово́й, терми́ческий; (*underwear*) тёплый.

thermometer /θəˈmɒmɪtə(r)/ *n* термо́метр, гра́дусник. **thermos** /ˈθɜːm(ə)l/ *n* те́рмос. **thermostat** /ˈθɜːməˌstæt/ *n* термоста́т.

thesis /ˈθiːsɪs/ *n* (*proposition*) те́зис; (*dissertation*) диссерта́ция.

they /ðeɪ/ *pron* они́.

thick /θɪk/ *adj* то́лстый, (*in measurements*) толщино́й в+*acc*; (*dense*) густо́й; (*stupid*) тупо́й; ~**-skinned** толстоко́жий. **thicken** /ˈθɪkən/ *vt* & *i* утолща́ть(ся) *impf*, утолсти́ть(ся) *pf*; (*make, become denser*) сгуща́ть(ся) *impf*, сгусти́ть(ся) *pf*; *vi* (*become more intricate*) усложня́ться *impf*, усложни́ться *pf*. **thicket** /ˈθɪkɪt/ *n* ча́ща. **thickness** /ˈθɪknɪs/ *n* (*also dimension*) толщина́; (*density*) густота́; (*layer*) слой. **thickset** *adj* корена́стый.

thief /θiːf/ *n* вор. **thieve** /θiːv/ *vi* ворова́ть *impf*. **thievery** /ˈθiːvərɪ/ *n* воровство́.

thigh /θaɪ/ *n* бедро́.

thimble /ˈθɪmb(ə)l/ *n* напёрсток.

thin /θɪn/ *adj* (*slender; not thick*) то́нкий; (*lean*) худо́й; (*too liquid*) жи́дкий; (*sparse*) ре́дкий; *vt* & *i* де́лать(ся) *impf*, с~ *pf* то́нким, жи́дким; *vi*: (*also* ~ *out*) реде́ть *impf*, по~ *pf*; *vt*: ~ **out** проре́живать *impf*, прореди́ть *pf*.

thing /θɪŋ/ *n* вещь; (*object*) предме́т; (*matter*) де́ло.

think /θɪŋk/ *vt* & *i* ду́мать *impf*, по~ *pf* (**about, of** о+*prep*); (*consider*) счита́ть *impf*, счесть *pf* (**to be** +*instr*, за+*acc*; **that** что); *vi* (*reflect, reason*) мы́слить *impf*; (*intend*) намерева́ться *impf* (*of doing* +*inf*); ~ **out** проду́мывать *impf*, проду́мать *pf*; ~ **over** обду́мывать *impf*, обду́мать *pf*; ~ **up, of** приду́мывать *impf*, приду́мать *pf*. **thinker** /ˈθɪŋkə(r)/ *n* мысли́тель *m*. **thinking** /ˈθɪŋkɪŋ/ *adj* мы́слящий; *n* (*reflection*) размышле́ние; **to my way of** ~ по моему́ мне́нию.

third /θɜːd/ *adj* & *n* тре́тий; (*fraction*) треть; **T~ World** страны́ *f pl* тре́тьего ми́ра.

thirst /θɜːst/ *n* жа́жда (**for** +*gen* (*fig*)); *vi* (*fig*) жа́ждать *impf* (**for** +*gen*). **thirsty** /ˈθɜːstɪ/ *adj*: **be** ~ хоте́ть *impf* пить.

thirteen /θɜːˈtiːn/ *adj* & *n* трина́дцать. **thirteenth** /-ˈtiːnθ/

adj & *n* трина́дцатый.

thirtieth /ˈθɜːtɪɪθ/ *adj* & *n* тридца́тый. **thirty** /ˈθɜːtɪ/ *adj* & *n* три́дцать; *pl* (*decade*) тридца́тые го́ды (-до́в) *m pl*.

this /ðɪs/ *demonstrative adj* & *pron* э́тот; **like ~** вот так; **~ morning** сего́дня у́тром.

thistle /ˈθɪs(ə)l/ *n* чертополо́х.

thither /ˈðɪðə(r)/ *adv* туда́.

thorn /θɔːn/ *n* шип. **thorny** /ˈθɔːnɪ/ *adj* колю́чий; (*fig*) терни́стый.

thorough /ˈθʌrə/ *adj* основа́тельный; (*complete*) соверше́нный. **thoroughbred** /-ˌbred/ *adj* чистокро́вный. **thoroughfare** /-ˌfeə(r)/*n* прое́зд; (*walking*) прохо́д. **thoroughgoing** /-ˌgəʊɪŋ/ *adj* радика́льный. **thoroughly** /-lɪ/ *adv* (*completely*) соверше́нно. **thoroughness** /-nɪs/ *n* основа́тельность.

though /ðəʊ/ *conj* хотя́; несмотря́ на то, что; **as ~** как бу́дто; *adv* одна́ко.

thought /θɔːt/ *n* мысль; (*meditation*) размышле́ние; (*intention*) наме́рение; *pl* (*opinion*) мне́ние. **thoughtful** /-fʊl/ *adj* заду́мчивый; (*considerate*) внима́тельный. **thoughtless** /-lɪs/ *adj* необду́манный; (*inconsiderate*) невнима́тельный.

thousand /ˈθaʊz(ə)nd/ *adj* & *n* ты́сяча. **thousandth** /ˈθaʊz(ə)ntθ/ *adj* & *n* ты́сячный.

thrash /θræʃ/ *vt* бить *impf*, по~ *pf*; **~ out** (*discuss*) обстоя́тельно обсужда́ть *impf*, обсуди́ть *pf*; *vi*: **~ about** мета́ться *impf*. **thrashing** /-ʃɪŋ/ *n* (*beating*) взбу́чка (*coll*).

thread /θred/ *n* ни́тка, нить (*also fig*); (*of screw etc.*) резьба́; *vt* (*needle*) продева́ть *impf*, проде́ть *pf* ни́тку в+*acc*; (*beads*) нани́зывать *impf*, наниза́ть *pf*; **~ one's way** пробира́ться *impf*, пробра́ться *pf* (**through** че́рез+*acc*). **threadbare** *adj* потёртый.

threat /θret/ *n* угро́за. **threaten** /-t(ə)n/ *vt* угрожа́ть *impf*, грози́ть *impf*, при~ *pf* (*person* +*dat*; **with** +*instr*; *to do* +*inf*).

three /θriː/ *adj* & *n* три; (*number 3*) тро́йка; **~-dimensional** трёхме́рный; **~-quarters** три че́тверти. **threefold** *adj* тройно́й; *adv* втройне́. **threesome** *n* тро́йка.

thresh /θreʃ/ *vt* молоти́ть *impf*.

threshold /ˈθreʃəʊld/ *n* поро́г.

thrice /θraɪs/ *adv* три́жды.

thrift /θrɪft/ *n* бережли́вость. **thrifty** /-tɪ/ *adj* бережли́вый.

thrill /θrɪl/ *n* тре́пет; *vt* восхища́ть *impf*, восхити́ть *pf*; **be thrilled** быть в восто́рге. **thriller** /-lə(r)/ *n* приключе́нческий, детекти́вный (*novel*) рома́н, (*film*) фильм. **thrilling** /-lɪŋ/ *adj* захва́тывающий.

thrive /θraɪv/ *vi* процвета́ть *impf*.

throat /θrəʊt/ *n* го́рло.

throb /θrɒb/ *vi* (*heart*) си́льно би́ться *impf*; пульси́ровать *impf*; *n* бие́ние; пульса́ция.

throes /θrəʊz/ *n pl*: **in the ~** в мучи́тельных попы́тках.

thrombosis /θrɒmˈbəʊsɪs/ *n* тромбо́з.

throne /θrəʊn/ *n* трон, престо́л; **come to the ~** вступа́ть *impf*, вступи́ть *pf* на престо́л.

throng /θrɒŋ/ *n* толпа́; *vi* толпи́ться *impf*; *vt* заполня́ть *impf*, запо́лнить *pf*.

throttle /ˈθrɒt(ə)l/ *n* (*tech*) дро́ссель *m*; *vt* (*strangle*) души́ть *impf*, за~ *pf*; (*tech*) дроссели́ровать *impf* & *pf*; ~ **down** сбавля́ть *impf*, сба́вить *pf* газ.

through /θru:/ *prep* (*across, via,* ~ *opening*) че́рез+*acc*; (*esp* ~ *thick of*) сквозь+*acc*; (*air, streets etc.*) по+*dat*; (*agency*) посре́дством+*gen*; (*reason*) из--за+*gen*; *adv* насквозь; (*from beginning to end*) до конца́; **be** ~ **with** (*sth*) ока́нчивать *impf*, око́нчить *pf*; (*s.o.*) порыва́ть *impf*, порва́ть *pf* с+*instr*; **put** ~ (*on telephone*) соединя́ть *impf*, соедини́ть *pf*; ~ **and** ~ соверше́нно; *adj* (*train*) прямо́й; (*traffic*) сквозно́й. **throughout** *adv* повсю́ду, во всех отноше́ниях; *prep* по всему́ (всей, всему́; *pl* всем)+*dat*; (*from beginning to end*) с нача́ла до конца́+*gen*.

throw /θrəʊ/ *n* бросо́к; *vt* броса́ть *impf*, бро́сить *pf*; (*confuse*) смуща́ть *impf*, смути́ть *pf*; (*rider*) сбра́сывать *impf*, сбро́сить *pf*; (*party*) устра́ивать *impf*, устро́ить *pf*; ~ **o.s. into** броса́ться *impf*, бро́ситься *pf* в+*acc*; ~ **away, out** выбра́сывать *impf*, вы́бросить *pf*; ~ **down** сбра́сывать *impf*, сбро́сить *pf*; ~ **in** (*add*) добавля́ть *impf*, доба́вить *pf*; (*sport*) вбра́сывать *impf*, вбро́сить *pf*; ~**-in** вбра́сывание мяча́; ~ **off** сбра́сывать *impf*, сбро́сить *pf*; ~ **open** распа́хивать *impf*, распахну́ть *pf*; ~ **out** (*see also* ~ *away*) (*expel*) выгоня́ть *impf*, вы́гнать *pf*; (*reject*) отверга́ть *impf*, отве́ргнуть *pf*; ~ **over,** ~ **up** (*abandon*) броса́ть *impf*, бро́сить *pf*; ~ **up** подбра́сывать *impf*, подбро́сить *pf*; (*vomit*) рвать *impf*, вы́~ *pf impers*; **he threw up** его́ вы́рвало.

thrush /θrʌʃ/ *n* (*bird*) дрозд.

thrust /θrʌst/ *n* (*shove*) толчо́к; (*tech*) тя́га; *vt* (*shove*) толка́ть *impf*, толкну́ть *pf*; (~ *into, out of; give quickly, carelessly*) сова́ть *impf*, су́нуть *pf*.

thud /θʌd/ *n* глухо́й звук; *vi* па́дать *impf*, *pf* с глухи́м сту́ком.

thug /θʌg/ *n* головоре́з (*coll*).

thumb /θʌm/ *n* большо́й па́лец; **under the** ~ **of** под башмако́м у+*gen*; *vt*: ~ **through** перели́стывать *impf*, перелиста́ть *pf*; ~ **a lift** голосова́ть *impf*, про~ *pf*.

thump /θʌmp/ *n* (*blow*) тяжёлый уда́р; (*thud*) глухо́й звук, стук; *vt* колоти́ть *impf*, по~ *pf* в+*acc*, по+*dat*; *vi* колоти́ться *impf*.

thunder /'θʌndə(r)/ *n* гром; *vi* греме́ть *impf*; **it thunders** гром греми́т. **thunderbolt** *n* уда́р мо́лнии. **thunderous** /-rəs/ *adj* громово́й. **thunderstorm** *n* гроза́. **thundery** /-rɪ/ *adj* грозово́й.

Thursday /'θɜ:zdeɪ/ *n* четве́рг.

thus /ðʌs/ *adv* так, таки́м о́бразом.

thwart /θwɔ:t/ *vt* меша́ть *impf*, по~ *pf* +*dat*; (*plans*) расстра́ивать *impf*, расстро́ить *pf*.

thyme /taɪm/ *n* тимья́н.

thyroid /'θaɪrɔɪd/ *n* (~ *gland*) щитови́дная железа́.

tiara /tɪ'ɑ:rə/ *n* тиа́ра.

tick /tɪk/ *n* (*noise*) ти́канье; (*mark*) пти́чка; *vi* ти́кать *impf*, ти́кнуть *pf*; *vt* отмеча́ть *impf*, отме́тить *pf* пти́чкой; ~ **off** (*scold*) отде́лывать *impf*, отде́лать *pf*.

ticket /'tɪkɪt/ *n* биле́т; (*label*) ярлы́к; (*season* ~) ка́рточка; (*cloakroom* ~) номеро́к; (*receipt*) квита́нция; ~ **collector**

контролёр; ~ **office** (билéтная) кácca.

tickle /'tɪk(ə)l/ *n* щекóтка; *vt* щекотáть *impf*, по~ *pf*; (*amuse*) веселить *impf*, по~, раз~ *pf*; *vi* щекотáть *impf*, по~ *pf impers*; **my throat ~s** у меня щекóчет в гóрле. **ticklish** /'tɪklɪʃ/ *adj* (*fig*) щекотлúвый; **to be ~** боя́ться *impf* щекóтки.

tidal /'taɪd(ə)l/ *adj* прилúво-отлúвный; ~ **wave** прилúвная волнá.

tide /taɪd/ *n* прилúв и отлúв; **high ~** прилúв; **low ~** отлúв; (*current, tendency*) течéние; **the ~ turns** (*fig*) собы́тия принимáют другóй оборóт; *vt*: ~ **over** помогáть *impf*, помóчь *pf* +*dat of person* спрáвиться (*difficulty* с+*instr*); **will this money ~ you over?** вы протя́нете с э́тими деньгáми?

tidiness /'taɪdɪnɪs/ *n* аккурáтность. **tidy** /-dɪ/ *adj* аккурáтный; (*considerable*) порядочный; *vt* убирáть *impf*, убрáть *pf*; приводúть *impf*, привестú *pf* в поря́док.

tie /taɪ/ *n* (*garment*) гáлстук; (*cord*) завя́зка; (*link*; *tech*) связь; (*equal points etc.*) рáвный счёт; **end in a ~** закáнчиваться *impf*, закóнчиться *pf* вничью́; (*burden*) обýза; *pl* (*bonds*) ýзы (уз) *pl*; *vt* свя́зывать *impf*, связáть *pf* (*also fig*); (~ *up*) завя́зывать *impf*, завязáть *pf*; (*restrict*) ограничивать *impf*, ограничить *pf*; ~ **down** (*fasten*) привя́зывать *impf*, привязáть *pf*; ~ **up** (*tether*) привя́зывать *impf*, привязáть *pf*; (*parcel*) перевя́зывать *impf*, перевязáть *pf*; *vi* (*be ~d*) завя́зываться *impf*, завязáться *pf*; (*sport*) сыгрáть *pf* вничью́; ~ **in, up, with** совпадáть *impf*, совпáсть *pf* с+*instr*.

tier /tɪə(r)/ *n* ряд, я́рус.

tiff /tɪf/ *n* размóлвка.

tiger /'taɪgə(r)/ *n* тигр.

tight /taɪt/ *adj* (*cramped*) тéсный; ýзкий; (*strict*) стрóгий; (*taut*) тугóй; ~ **corner** (*fig*) трýдное положéние. **tighten** /-t(ə)n/ *vt* & *i* натя́гиваться *impf*, натянýться *pf*; (*clench, contract*) сжимáть(ся) *impf*, сжáться *pf*; ~ **one's belt** потýже затя́гивать *impf*, затянýть *pf* пóяс (*also fig*); ~ **up** (*discipline etc.*) подтя́гивать *impf*, подтянýть *pf* (*coll*). **tightly** /-lɪ/ *adv* (*strongly*) прóчно; (*closely, cramped*) тéсно. **tightrope** *n* натя́нутый канáт. **tights** /taɪts/ *n pl* колгóтки (-ток) *pl*.

tile /taɪl/ *n* (*roof*) черепúца (*also collect*); (*decorative*) кáфель *m* (*also collect*); *vt* крыть *impf*, по~ *pf* черепúцей, кáфелем. **tiled** /-d/ *adj* (*roof*) черепúчный; (*floor*) кáфельный.

till[1] /tɪl/ *prep* до+*gen*; **not ~** тóлько (**Friday** в пя́тницу; **the next day** на слéдующий день); *conj* покá не; **not ~** тóлько когдá.

till[2] /tɪl/ *n* кácca.

till[3] /tɪl/ *vt* возделывать *impf*, воздéлать *pf*.

tiller /'tɪlə(r)/ *n* (*naut*) рýмпель *m*.

tilt /tɪlt/ *n* наклóн; **at full ~** пóлным хóдом; *vt* & *i* наклоня́ть(ся) *impf*, наклонúть(ся) *pf*; (*heel* (*over*)) кренúть(ся) *impf*, на~ *pf*.

timber /'tɪmbə(r)/ *n* лесоматериáл.

time /taɪm/ *n* врéмя *neut*; (*occasion*) раз; (*mus*) такт; (*sport*) тайм; *pl* (*period*) временá *pl*;

(*in comparison*) раз; **five ∼s as big** в пять раз бо́льше; (*multiplication*) **four ∼s four** четы́режды четы́ре; **∼ and ∼ again, ∼ after ∼** не раз, ты́сячу раз; **at a ∼** ра́зом, одновре́ме́нно; **at the ∼** в э́то вре́мя; **at ∼s** времена́ми; **at the same ∼** в то же вре́мя; **before my ∼** до меня́; **for a long ∼** до́лго; (*up to now*) давно́; **for the ∼ being** пока́; **from ∼ to ∼** вре́мя от вре́мени; **in ∼** (*early enough*) во́-время; (*with ∼*) со вре́менем; **in good ∼** заблаговре́менно; **in ∼ with** в такт +*dat*; **in no ∼** момента́льно; **on ∼** во́-время; **one at a ∼** по одному́; **be in ∼** успева́ть *impf*, успе́ть *pf* (**for** к+*dat*, на+*acc*); **have ∼ to** (*manage*) успева́ть *impf*, успе́ть *pf* +*inf*; **have a good ∼** хорошо́ проводи́ть *impf*, провести́ *pf* вре́мя; **it is ∼** пора́ (**to** +*inf*); **what is the ∼?** кото́рый час?; **∼ bomb** бо́мба заме́дленного де́йствия; **∼-consuming** отнима́ющий мно́го вре́мени; **∼ difference** ра́зница во вре́мени; **∼-lag** отстава́ние во вре́мени; **∼ zone** часово́й по́яс; *vt* (*choose ∼*) выбира́ть *impf*, вы́брать *pf* вре́мя +*gen*; (*ascertain ∼ of*) измеря́ть *impf*, изме́рить *pf* вре́мя +*gen*. **timeless** /-lıs/ *adj* ве́чный. **timely** /-lı/ *adj* своевре́менный. **timetable** *n* расписа́ние; гра́фик.

timid /'tımıd/ *adj* ро́бкий.

tin /tın/ *n* (*metal*) о́лово; (*container*) ба́нка; (*cake-∼*) фо́рма; (*baking ∼*) про́тивень *m*; **∼ foil** оловя́нная фольга́; **∼-opener** консе́рвный нож; **∼ned food** консе́рвы (-вов) *pl*.

tinge /tındʒ/ *n* отте́нок; *vt* (*also fig*) слегка́ окра́шивать *impf*, окра́сить *pf*.

tingle /'tıŋglıŋ/ *vi* (*sting*) коло́ть *impf impers*; **my fingers ∼** у меня́ ко́лет па́льцы; **his nose ∼d with the cold** моро́з пощи́пывал ему́ нос; (*burn*) горе́ть *impf*.

tinker /'tıŋkə(r)/ *vi*: **∼ with** вози́ться *impf* с+*instr*.

tinkle /'tıŋk(ə)l/ *n* звон, звя́канье; *vi* (& *t*) звене́ть *impf* (+*instr*).

tinsel /'tıns(ə)l/ *n* мишура́.

tint /tınt/ *n* отте́нок; *vt* подкра́шивать *impf*, подкра́сить *pf*.

tiny /'taını/ *adj* кро́шечный.

tip[1] /tıp/ *n* (*end*) ко́нчик

tip[2] /tıp/ *n* (*money*) чаевы́е (-ы́х) *pl*; (*advice*) сове́т; (*dump*) сва́лка; *vt* & *i* (*tilt*) наклоня́ть(ся) *impf*, наклони́ть(ся) *pf*; (*give ∼*) дава́ть *impf*, дать *pf* (*person* +*dat*; *money* де́ньги на чай, *information* ча́стную информа́цию); **∼ out** выва́ливать *impf*, вы́валить *pf*; **∼ over, up** (*vt* & *i*) опроки́дывать(ся) *impf*, опроки́нуть(ся) *pf*.

Tippex /'tıpeks/ *n* (*propr*) бели́ла.

tipple /'tıp(ə)l/ *n* напи́ток.

tipsy /'tıpsı/ *adj* подвы́пивший.

tiptoe /'tıptəʊ/ *n*: **on ∼** на цы́почках.

tip-top /'tıptɒp/ *adj* превосхо́дный.

tirade /taı'reıd/ *n* тира́да.

tire /'taıə(r)/ *vt* (*weary*) утомля́ть *impf*, утоми́ть *pf*; *vi* утомля́ться *impf*, утоми́ться *pf*. **tired** /'taıəd/ *adj* уста́лый; **be ∼ of: I am ∼ of him** он мне надое́л; **I am ∼ of playing** мне надое́ло игра́ть; **∼ out** изму́ченный. **tiredness** /'taıədnıs/ *n* уста́лость. **tireless** /'taıəlıs/ *adj* неутоми́мый. **tiresome** /'taıəsəm/

adj надое́дливый. **tiring** /ˈtaɪərɪŋ/ *adj* утоми́тельный.

tissue /ˈtɪʃuː/ *n* ткань; (*handkerchief*) бума́жная салфе́тка. **tissue-paper** *n* папиро́сная бума́га.

tit[1] /tɪt/ *n* (*bird*) сини́ца.

tit[2] /tɪt/ *n*: **~ for tat** зуб за́ зуб.

titbit /ˈtɪtbɪt/ *n* ла́комый кусо́к; (*news*) пика́нтная но́вость.

titillate /ˈtɪtɪˌleɪt/ *vt* щекота́ть *impf*, по~ *pf*.

title /ˈtaɪt(ə)l/ *n* (*of book etc.*) загла́вие; (*rank*) зва́ние; (*sport*) зва́ние чемпио́на; **~-holder** чемпио́н; **~-page** ти́тульный лист; **~ role** загла́вная роль. **titled** /ˈtaɪt(ə)ld/ *adj* титуло́ванный.

titter /ˈtɪtə(r)/ *n* хихи́канье; *vi* хихи́кать *impf*, хихи́кнуть *pf*.

to /tuː/ *prep* (*town, a country, theatre, school, etc.*) в+*acc*; (*the sea, the moon, the ground, post-office, meeting, concert, north, etc.*) на+*acc*; (*the doctor; towards, up ~; ~ one's surprise etc.*) к+*dat*; (*with accompaniment of*) под+*acc*; (*in toast*) за+*acc*; (*time*): **ten minutes ~ three** без десяти́ три; (*compared with*) в сравне́нии с+*instr*; **it is ten ~ one that** де́вять из десяти́ за то, что; **~ the left (right)** нале́во (напра́во); (*in order to*) что́бы +*inf*; *adv*: **shut the door ~** закро́йте дверь; **come ~** приходи́ть *impf*, прийти́ *pf* в созна́ние; **~ and fro** взад и вперёд.

toad /təʊd/ *n* жа́ба. **toadstool** *n* пога́нка.

toast /təʊst/ *n* (*bread*) поджа́ренный хлеб; (*drink*) тост; *vt* (*bread*) поджа́ривать *impf*, поджа́рить *pf*; (*drink*) пить *impf*, вы́~ *pf* за здоро́вье +*gen*.

toaster /ˈtəʊstə(r)/ *n* то́стер.

tobacco /təˈbækəʊ/ *n* таба́к. **tobacconist's** /-kənɪsts/ *n* (*shop*) таба́чный магази́н.

toboggan /təˈbɒgən/ *n* са́ни (-не́й) *pl*; *vi* ката́ться *impf* на саня́х.

today /təˈdeɪ/ *adv* сего́дня; (*nowadays*) в на́ши дни; *n* сего́дняшний день *m*; **~'s newspaper** сего́дняшняя газе́та.

toddler /ˈtɒdlə(r)/ *n* малы́ш.

toe /təʊ/ *n* па́лец ноги́; (*of sock etc.*) носо́к; *vt*: **~ the line** (*fig*) ходи́ть *indet* по стру́нке.

toffee /ˈtɒfɪ/ *n* (*substance*) ири́с; (*a single ~*) ири́ска.

together /təˈgeðə(r)/ *adv* вме́сте; (*simultaneously*) одновре́ме́нно.

toil /tɔɪl/ *n* тяжёлый труд; *vi* труди́ться *impf*.

toilet /ˈtɔɪlɪt/ *n* туале́т; **~ paper** туале́тная бума́га. **toiletries** /-trɪz/ *n pl* туале́тные принадле́жности *f pl*.

token /ˈtəʊkən/ *n* (*sign*) знак; (*coin substitute*) жето́н; **as a ~ of** в знак +*gen*; *attrib* символи́ческий.

tolerable /ˈtɒlərəb(ə)l/ *adj* терпи́мый; (*satisfactory*) удовлетвори́тельный. **tolerance** /ˈtɒlərəns/ *n* терпи́мость. **tolerant** /-rənt/ *adj* терпи́мый. **tolerate** /-ˌreɪt/ *vt* терпе́ть *impf*, по~ *pf*; (*allow*) допуска́ть *impf*, допусти́ть *pf*. **toleration** /ˌtɒləˈreɪʃ(ə)n/ *n* терпи́мость.

toll[1] /təʊl/ *n* (*duty*) по́шлина; **take its ~** ска́зываться *impf*, сказа́ться *pf* (**on** на+*prep*).

toll[2] /təʊl/ *vi* звони́ть *impf*, по~ *pf*.

tom(-cat) /ˈtɒm(kæt)/ *n* кот.

tomato /təˈmɑːtəʊ/ *n* помидо́р; *attrib* тома́тный.

tomb /tuːm/ *n* моги́ла. **tombstone** *n* надгро́бный ка́мень *m*.
tomboy /ˈtɒmbɔɪ/ *n* сорване́ц.
tome /təʊm/ *n* том.
tomorrow /təˈmɒrəʊ/ *adv* за́втра; *n* за́втрашний день *m*; ~ **morning** за́втра у́тром; **the day after** ~ послеза́втра; **see you** ~ до за́втра.
ton /tʌn/ *n* то́нна; (*pl, lots*) ма́сса.
tone /təʊn/ *n* тон; *vt*: ~ **down** смягча́ть *impf*, смягчи́ть *pf*; ~ **up** тонизи́ровать *impf* & *pf*.
tongs /tɒŋz/ *n* щипцы́ (-цо́в) *pl*.
tongue /tʌŋ/ *n* язы́к; **~-in-cheek** с насме́шкой, ирони́чески; **~-tied** косноязы́чный; **~-twister** скорогово́рка.
tonic /ˈtɒnɪk/ *n* (*med*) тонизи́рующее сре́дство; (*mus*) то́ника; (*drink*) напи́ток «то́ник».
tonight /təˈnaɪt/ *adv* сего́дня ве́чером.
tonnage /ˈtʌnɪdʒ/ *n* тонна́ж.
tonsil /ˈtɒns(ə)l/ *n* минда́лина. **tonsillitis** /ˌtɒnsɪˈlaɪtɪs/ *n* тонзилли́т.
too /tuː/ *adv* сли́шком; (*also*) та́кже, то́же; (*very*) о́чень; (*moreover*) к тому́ же; **none** ~ не сли́шком.
tool /tuːl/ *n* инструме́нт; (*fig*) ору́дие.
toot /tuːt/ *n* гудо́к; *vi* гуде́ть *impf*.
tooth /tuːθ/ *n* зуб; (*tech*) зубе́ц; *attrib* зубно́й; **~-brush** зубна́я щётка. **toothache** *n* зубна́я боль. **toothless** /-lɪs/ *adj* беззу́бый. **toothpaste** *n* зубна́я па́ста. **toothpick** *n* зубочи́стка. **toothy** /-θɪ/ *adj* зуба́стый (*coll*).
top[1] /tɒp/ *n* (*toy*) волчо́к.
top[2] /tɒp/ *n* (*of object*; *fig*) верх; (*of hill etc.*) верши́на; (*of tree*) верху́шка; (*of head*) маку́шка; (*lid*) кры́шка; (*upper part*) ве́рхняя часть; ~ **hat** цили́ндр; **~-heavy** переве́шивающий в свое́й ве́рхней ча́сти; **~-secret** соверше́нно секре́тный; **on** ~ **of** (*position*) на+*prep*, сверх +*gen*; (*on to*) на+*acc*; **on** ~ **of everything** сверх всего́; **from** ~ **to bottom** све́рху до́низу; **at the** ~ **of one's voice** во весь го́лос; **at** ~ **speed** во весь опо́р; *adj* ве́рхний, вы́сший, са́мый высо́кий; (*foremost*) пе́рвый; *vt* (*cover*) покрыва́ть *impf*, покры́ть *pf*; (*exceed*) превосходи́ть *impf*, превзойти́ *pf*; (*cut* ~ *off*) обреза́ть *impf*, обре́зать *pf* верху́шку +*gen*; ~ **up** (*with liquid*) долива́ть *impf*, доли́ть *pf*.
topic /ˈtɒpɪk/ *n* те́ма, предме́т. **topical** /ˈtɒpɪk(ə)l/ *adj* актуа́льный.
topless /ˈtɒplɪs/ *adj* с обнажённой гру́дью.
topmost /ˈtɒpməʊst/ *adj* са́мый ве́рхний; са́мый ва́жный.
topographical /ˌtɒpəˈgræfɪk(ə)l/ *adj* топографи́ческий. **topography** /təˈpɒgrəfɪ/ *n* топогра́фия.
topple /ˈtɒp(ə)l/ *vt* & *i* опроки́дывать(ся) *impf*, опроки́нуть(ся) *pf*.
topsy-turvy /ˌtɒpsɪˈtɜːvɪ/ *adj* пове́рнутый вверх дном; (*disorderly*) беспоря́дочный; *adv* вверх дном.
torch /tɔːtʃ/ *n* электри́ческий фона́рь *m*; (*flaming*) фа́кел.
torment /ˈtɔːment/ *n* муче́ние, му́ка; *vt* му́чить *impf*, за~, из~ *pf*.
tornado /tɔːˈneɪdəʊ/ *n* торна́до *neut indecl*.

torpedo /tɔ:ˈpi:dəʊ/ *n* торпе́да; *vt* торпеди́ровать *impf* & *pf*. **torrent** /ˈtɒrənt/ *n* пото́к **torrential** /təˈrenʃ(ə)l/ *adj* (*rain*) проливно́й.

torso /ˈtɔ:səʊ/ *n* ту́ловище; (*art*) торс.

tortoise /ˈtɔ:təs/ *n* черепа́ха. **tortoise-shell** *n* черепа́ха.

tortuous /ˈtɔ:tjʊəs/ *adj* изви́листый.

torture /ˈtɔ:tʃə(r)/ *n* пы́тка; (*fig*) му́ка; *vt* пыта́ть *impf*; (*torment*) му́чить *impf*, за~, из~ *pf*.

toss /tɒs/ *n* бросо́к; **win (lose) the ~** (не) выпада́ть *impf*, вы́пасть *pf* жре́бий *impers* (**I won the ~** мне вы́пал жре́бий); *vt* броса́ть *impf*, бро́сить *pf*; (*coin*) подбра́сывать *impf*, подбро́сить *pf*; (*head*) вски́дывать *impf*, вски́нуть *pf*; (*salad*) переме́шивать *impf*, перемеша́ть *pf*; *vi* (*in bed*) мета́ться *impf*; **~ aside, away** отбра́сывать *impf*, отбро́сить *pf*; **~ up** броса́ть *impf*, бро́сить *pf* жре́бий.

tot[1] /tɒt/ *n* (*child*) малы́ш; (*of liquor*) глото́к.

tot[2] /tɒt/ *vt* & *i* : **~ up** (*vt*) скла́дывать *impf*, сложи́ть *pf*; (*vi*) равня́ться *impf* (**to** +*dat*).

total /ˈtəʊt(ə)l/ *n* ито́г, су́мма; *adj* о́бщий; (*complete*) по́лный; **in ~** в це́лом, вме́сте; *vt* подсчи́тывать *impf*, подсчита́ть *pf*; *vi* равня́ться *impf* +*dat*. **totalitarian** /təʊˌtælɪˈteərɪən/ *adj* тоталита́рный. **totality** /təʊˈtælɪtɪ/ *n* вся су́мма целико́м; **the ~ of** весь. **totally** /ˈtəʊtəlɪ/ *adv* соверше́нно.

totter /ˈtɒtə(r)/ *vi* шата́ться *impf*.

touch /tʌtʃ/ *n* прикоснове́ние; (*sense*) осяза́ние; (*shade*) отте́нок; (*taste*) при́вкус; (*small amount*) чу́точка; (*of illness*) лёгкий при́ступ; **get in ~ with** свя́зываться *impf*, связа́ться *pf* с+*instr*; **keep in (lose) ~ with** подде́рживать *impf*, поддержа́ть *pf* (теря́ть *impf*, по~ *pf*) связь, конта́кт с+*instr*; **put the finishing ~es to** отде́лывать *impf*, отде́лать *pf*; *vt* (*lightly*) прикаса́ться *impf*, прикосну́ться *pf* к+*dat*; каса́ться *impf*, косну́ться *pf* +*gen*; (*also disturb*; *affect*) тро́гать *impf*, тро́нуть *pf*; (*be comparable with*) идти́ *impf* в сравне́нии с+*instr*; *vi* (*be contiguous*; *come into contact*) соприкаса́ться *impf*, соприкосну́ться *pf*; **~ down** приземля́ться *impf*, приземли́ться *pf*; **~down** поса́дка; **~ (up)on** (*fig*) каса́ться *impf*, косну́ться *pf* +*gen*; **~ up** поправля́ть *impf*, попра́вить *pf*. **touched** /tʌtʃt/ *adj* тро́нутый. **touchiness** /ˈtʌtʃɪnɪs/ *n* оби́дчивость. **touching** /ˈtʌtʃɪŋ/ *adj* тро́гательный. **touchstone** *n* про́бный ка́мень *m*. **touchy** /ˈtʌtʃɪ/ *adj* оби́дчивый.

tough /tʌf/ *adj* жёсткий; (*durable*) про́чный; (*difficult*) тру́дный; (*hardy*) выно́сливый. **toughen** /ˈtʌf(ə)n/ *vt* & *i* де́лать(ся) *impf*, с~ *pf* жёстким.

tour /tʊə(r)/ *n* (*journey*) путеше́ствие, пое́здка; (*excursion*) экску́рсия; (*of artistes*) гастро́ли *f pl*; (*of duty*) объе́зд; *vi* (& *t*) путеше́ствовать *impf* (по +*dat*); (*theat*) гастроли́ровать *impf*. **tourism** /ˈtʊərɪz(ə)m/ *n* тури́зм. **tourist** /ˈtʊərɪst/ *n* тури́ст, ~ка.

tournament /ˈtʊənəmənt/ *n* турни́р.

tousle /ˈtaʊz(ə)l/ *vt* взъеро́шивать *impf*, взъеро́шить *pf* (*coll*).

tout /taʊt/ *n* зазыва́ла *m*; (*ticket* ~) жучо́к

tow /təʊ/ *vt* букси́ровать *impf*; *n*: **on ~** на букси́ре.

towards /tə'wɔːdz/ *prep* к+*dat*.

towel /'taʊəl/ *n* полоте́нце.

tower /'taʊə(r)/ *n* ба́шня; *vi* вы́ситься *impf*, возвыша́ться *impf* (**above** над+*instr*).

town /taʊn/ *n* го́род; *attrib* городско́й; **~ hall** ра́туша. **townsman** *n* горожа́нин.

toxic /'tɒksɪk/ *adj* токси́ческий.

toy /tɔɪ/ *n* игру́шка; *vi*: **~ with** (*sth in hands*) верте́ть *impf* в рука́х; (*trifle with*) игра́ть *impf* (с)+*instr*.

trace /treɪs/ *n* след; *vt* (*track* (*down*)) высле́живать *impf*, вы́следить *pf*; (*copy*) кальки́ровать *impf*, с~ *pf*; **~ out** (*plan*) набра́сывать *impf*, наброса́ть *pf*; (*map, diagram*) черти́ть *impf*, на~ *pf*.

tracing-paper /'treɪsɪŋ,peɪpə(r)/ *n* ка́лька.

track /træk/ *n* (*path*) доро́жка; (*mark*) след; (*rly*) путь *m*, (*sport, on tape*) доро́жка; (*on record*) за́пись; **~ suit** трениро́вочный костю́м; **off the beaten ~** в глуши́; **go off the ~** (*fig*) отклоня́ться *impf*, отклони́ться *pf* от те́мы; **keep ~ of** следи́ть *impf* за+*instr*; **lose ~ of** теря́ть *impf*, по~ *pf* след+*gen*; *vt* просле́живать *impf*, проследи́ть *pf*; **~ down** высле́живать *impf*, вы́следить *pf*.

tract[1] /trækt/ *n* (*land*) простра́нство.

tract[2] /trækt/ *n* (*pamphlet*) брошю́ра.

tractor /'træktə(r)/ *n* тра́ктор.

trade /treɪd/ *n* торго́вля; (*occupation*) профе́ссия, ремесло́; **~ mark** фабри́чная ма́рка; **~ union** профсою́з; **~-unionist** член профсою́за; *vi* торгова́ть *impf* (**in** +*instr*); *vt* (*swap like things*) обме́ниваться *impf*, обменя́ться *pf* +*instr*; (**~ *for sth different***) обме́нивать *impf*, обменя́ть *pf* (**for** на+*acc*); **~ in** сдава́ть *impf*, сдать *pf* в счёт поку́пки но́вого. **trader, tradesman** /-də(r), -dzmən/ *n* торго́вец. **trading** /-dɪŋ/ *n* торго́вля.

tradition /trə'dɪʃ(ə)n/ *n* тради́ция. **traditional** /-n(ə)l/ *adj* традицио́нный. **traditionally** /-nəlɪ/ *adv* по тради́ции.

traffic /'træfɪk/ *n* движе́ние; (*trade*) торго́вля; **~ jam** про́бка; *vi* торгова́ть *impf* (**in** +*instr*). **trafficker** /-kə(r)/ *n* торго́вец (**in** +*instr*). **traffic-lights** *n pl* светофо́р.

tragedy /'trædʒɪdɪ/ *n* траге́дия. **tragic** /'trædʒɪk/ *adj* траги́ческий.

trail /treɪl/ *n* (*trace, track*) след; (*path*) тропи́нка; *vt* (*track*) высле́живать *impf*, вы́следить *pf*; *vt* & *i* (*drag*) таска́ть(ся) *indet*, тащи́ть(ся) *det*. **trailer** /-lə(r)/ *n* (*on vehicle*) прице́п; (*cin*) (кино)ро́лик.

train /treɪn/ *n* по́езд; (*of dress*) шлейф; *vt* (*instruct*) обуча́ть *impf*, обучи́ть *pf* (**in** +*dat*); (*prepare*) гото́вить *impf* (**for** к+*dat*); (*sport*) тренирова́ть *impf*, на~ *pf*; (*animals*) дрессирова́ть *impf*, вы́~ *pf*; (*aim*) наводи́ть *impf*, навести́ *pf*; (*plant*) направля́ть *impf*, напра́вить *pf* рост+*gen*; *vi* пригота́вливаться *impf*, пригото́виться *pf* (**for** к+*dat*); (*sport*) тренирова́ться *impf*, на~ *pf*. **trainee** /-'niː/ *n* стажёр, практика́нт. **trainer** /-nə(r)/ *n* (*sport*) тре́нер; (*of animals*) дрессиро́вщик; (*shoe*) кроссо́вка. **training** /-nɪŋ/ *n* обуче́ние; (*sport*) трениро́вка; (*of animals*) дрессиро́вка; **~-college** (*teachers'*) педагоги́ческий институ́т.

traipse /treɪps/ *vi* таска́ться *indet*, тащи́ться *det*.

trait /treɪ/ *n* черта́.

traitor /'treɪtə(r)/ *n* преда́тель *m*, ~ница.

trajectory /trə'dʒektərɪ/ *n* траекто́рия.

tram /træm/ *n* трамва́й.

tramp /træmp/ *n* (*vagrant*) бродя́га *m*; *vi* (*walk heavily*) то́пать *impf*. **trample** /-p(ə)l/ *vt* топта́ть *impf*, по~, ис~ *pf*; ~ **down** выта́птывать *impf*, вы́топтать *pf*; ~ **on** (*fig*) попира́ть *impf*, попра́ть *pf*.

trampoline /ˌtræmpə'li:n/ *n* бату́т.

trance /trɑ:ns/ *n* транс.

tranquil /'træŋkwɪl/ *adj* споко́йный. **tranquillity** /-'kwɪlɪtɪ/ *n* споко́йствие. **tranquillize** /'trænkwɪˌlaɪz/ *vt* успока́ивать *impf*, успоко́ить *pf*. **tranquillizer** /-ˌlaɪzə(r)/ *n* транквилиза́тор.

transact /træn'zækt/ *vt* (*business*) вести́ *impf*; (*a deal*) заключа́ть *impf*, заключи́ть *pf*. **transaction** /-'zækʃ(ə)n/ *n* де́ло, сде́лка; *pl* (*publications*) труды́ *m pl*.

transatlantic /ˌtrænzət'læntɪk/ *adj* трансатланти́ческий.

transcend /træn'send/ *vt* превосходи́ть *impf*, превзойти́ *pf*. **transcendental** /ˌtrænsen'dent(ə)l/ *adj* (*philos.*) трансцендента́льный.

transcribe /træn'skraɪb/ *vt* (*copy out*) перепи́сывать *impf*, переписа́ть *pf*. **transcript** /'trænskrɪpt/ *n* ко́пия. **transcription** /træn'skrɪpʃ(ə)n/ *n* (*copy*) ко́пия.

transfer *n* /'trænsfɜ:(r)/ (*of objects*) перено́с, перемеще́ние; (*of money*; *of people*) перево́д; (*of property*) переда́ча; (*design*) переводна́я карти́нка; *vt* /træns'fɜ:(r)/ (*objects*) переноси́ть *impf*, перенести́ *pf*; перемеща́ть *impf*, перемести́ть *pf*; (*money*; *people*; *design*) переводи́ть *impf*, перевести́ *pf*; (*property*) передава́ть *impf*, переда́ть *pf*; *vi* (*to different job*) переходи́ть *impf*, перейти́ *pf*; (*change trains etc.*) пересаживаться *impf*, пересе́сть *pf*. **transferable** /træns'fɜ:rəb(ə)l/ *adj* допуска́ющий переда́чу.

transfix /træns'fɪks/ *vt* (*fig*) прико́вывать *impf*, прикова́ть *pf* к ме́сту.

transform /træns'fɔ:m/ *vt* & *i* преобразо́вывать(ся) *impf*, преобразова́ть(ся) *pf*; ~ **into** *vt* (*i*) превраща́ть(ся) *impf*, преврати́ть(ся) *pf* в+*acc*. **transformation** /ˌtrænsfə'meɪʃ(ə)n/ *n* преобразова́ние; превраще́ние. **transformer** /træns'fɔ:mə(r)/ *n* трансформа́тор.

transfusion /træns'fju:ʒ(ə)n/ *n* перелива́ние (кро́ви).

transgress /trænz'gres/ *vt* наруша́ть *impf*, нару́шить *pf*; *vi* (*sin*) греши́ть *impf*, за~ *pf*. **transgression** /-'greʃ(ə)n/ *n* наруше́ние; (*sin*) грех.

transience /'trænzɪəns/ *n* мимолётность. **transient** /'trænzɪənt/ *adj* мимолётный.

transistor /træn'zɪstə(r)/ *n* транзи́стор; ~ **radio** транзи́сторный приёмник.

transit /'trænzɪt/ *n* транзи́т; **in** ~

(*goods*) при перево́зке; (*person*) по пути́; ~ **camp** транзи́тный ла́герь *m*. **transition** /-'zɪʃ(ə)n/ *n* перехо́д. **transitional** /-'zɪʃənəl/ *adj* перехо́дный. **transitive** /'trænsɪtɪv/ *adj* перехо́дный. **transitory** /'trænsɪtərɪ/ *adj* мимолётный.

translate /træn'sleɪt/ *vt* переводи́ть *impf*, перевести́ *pf*. **translation** /-'leɪʃən/ *n* перево́д. **translator** /-'leɪtə(r)/ *n* перево́дчик.

translucent /trænz'lu:s(ə)nt/ *adj* полупрозра́чный.

transmission /trænz'mɪʃ(ə)n/ *n* переда́ча. **transmit** /-'mɪt/ *vt* передава́ть *impf*, переда́ть *pf*. **transmitter** /-'mɪtə(r)/ *n* (радио)переда́тчик.

transparency /træns'pærənsɪ/ *n* (*phot*) диапозити́в. **transparent** /-rənt/ *adj* прозра́чный.

transpire /træn'spaɪə(r)/ *vi* (*become known*) обнару́живаться *impf*, обнару́житься *pf*; (*occur*) случа́ться *impf*, случи́ться *pf*.

transplant *vt* /træns'plɑ:nt/ переса́живать *impf*, пересади́ть *pf*; (*med*) де́лать *impf*, с~ *pf* переса́дку+*gen*; *n* /'trænsplɑ:nt/ (*med*) переса́дка.

transport *n* /'trænspɔ:t/ (*various senses*) тра́нспорт; (*conveyance*) перево́зка; *attrib* тра́нспортный; *vt* /træns'pɔ:t/ перевози́ть *impf*, перевезти́ *pf*. **transportation** /ˌtrænspɔ:'teɪʃ(ə)n/ *n* тра́нспорт, перево́зка.

transpose /træns'pəʊz/ *vt* переставля́ть *impf*, переста́вить *pf*; (*mus*) транспони́ровать *impf* & *pf*. **transposition** /ˌtrænspə'zɪʃ(ə)n/ *n* перестано́вка; (*mus*) транспониро́вка.

transverse /'trænzvɜ:s/ *adj* попере́чный.

transvestite /trænz'vestaɪt/ *n* трансвести́т.

trap /træp/ *n* лову́шка (*also fig*), западня́; *vt* (*catch*) лови́ть *impf*, пойма́ть *pf* (в лову́шку); (*jam*) защемля́ть *impf*, защеми́ть *pf*. **trapdoor** *n* люк.

trapeze /trə'pi:z/ *n* трапе́ция.

trapper /'træpə(r)/ *n* зверoло́в.

trappings /'træpɪŋz/ *n pl* (*fig*) (*exterior attributes*) вне́шние атрибу́ты *m pl*; (*adornments*) украше́ния *neut pl*.

trash /træʃ/ *n* дрянь (*coll*). **trashy** /-ʃɪ/ *adj* дрянно́й.

trauma /'trɔ:mə/ *n* тра́вма. **traumatic** /-'mætɪk/ *adj* травмати́ческий.

travel /'træv(ə)l/ *n* путеше́ствие; ~ **agency** бюро́ *neut indecl* путеше́ствий; ~ **sick: be ~-sick** ука́чивать *impf*; укача́ть *pf impers* +*acc*; **I am ~-sick in cars** меня́ в маши́не ука́чивает; *vi* путеше́ствовать *impf*; *vt* объезжа́ть *impf*, объе́хать *pf*. **traveller** /-lə(r)/ *n* путеше́ственник; (*salesman*) коммивояжёр; **~'s cheque** тури́стский чек.

traverse /'trævəs/ *vt* пересека́ть *impf*, пересе́чь *pf*.

travesty /'trævɪstɪ/ *n* паро́дия.

trawler /'trɔ:lə(r)/ *n* тра́улер.

tray /treɪ/ *n* подно́с; **in- (out-)~** корзи́нка для входя́щих (исходя́щих) бума́г.

treacherous /'tretʃərəs/ *adj* преда́тельский; (*unsafe*) ненадёжный. **treachery** /'tretʃərɪ/ *n* преда́тельство.

treacle /'tri:k(ə)l/ *n* па́тока.

tread /tred/ *n* похо́дка; (*stair*) ступе́нька; (*of tyre*) проте́ктор; *vi* ступа́ть *impf*, ступи́ть *pf*; ~ **on** наступа́ть *impf*, наступи́ть *pf* на+*acc*; *vt* топта́ть *impf*.

treason /'tri:z(ə)n/ *n* измéна. **treasure** /'treʒə(r)/ *n* сокрóвище; *vt* высокó ценúть *impf*. **treasurer** /'treʒərə(r)/ *n* казначéй. **treasury** /'treʒərı/ *n* (*also fig*) сокрóвищница; **the T~** госудáрственное казначéйство.

treat /tri:t/ *n* (*pleasure*) удовóльствие; (*entertainment*) угощéние; *vt* (*have as guest*) угощáть *impf*, угостúть *pf* (**to** +*instr*); (*med*) лечúть *impf* (**for** от+*gen*; **with** +*instr*); (*behave towards*) обращáться *impf* с+*instr*; (*process*) обрабáтывать *impf*, обрабóтать *pf* (**with** +*instr*); (*discuss*) трактовáть *impf* о+*prep*; (*regard*) относúться *impf*, отнестúсь *pf* к+*dat* (**as** как к+*dat*). **treatise** /-tıs/ *n* трактáт. **treatment** /-mənt/ *n* (*behaviour*) обращéние; (*med*) лечéние; (*processing*) обрабóтка; (*discussion*) трактóвка. **treaty** /-tı/ *n* договóр.

treble /'treb(ə)l/ *adj* тройнóй; (*trebled*) утрóенный; *adv* втрóе; *n* (*mus*) дúскант; *vt* & *i* утрáивать(ся) *impf*, утрóить(ся) *pf*.

tree /tri:/ *n* дéрево.

trek /trek/ *n* (*migration*) переселéние; (*journey*) путешéствие; *vi* (*migrate*) переселя́ться *impf*, переселúться *pf*; (*journey*) путешéствовать *impf*.

trellis /'trelıs/ *n* шпалéра; (*for creepers*) решётка.

tremble /'tremb(ə)l/ *vi* дрожáть *impf* (**with** от+*gen*). **trembling** /-blıŋ/ *n* дрожь; **in fear and ~** трепещá.

tremendous /trı'mendəs/ *adj* (*huge*) огрóмный; (*excellent*) потрясáющий.

tremor /'tremə(r)/ *n* дрожь; (*earthquake*) толчóк. **tremulous** /-mjʊləs/ *adj* дрожáщий.

trench /trentʃ/ *n* канáва, ров; (*mil*) окóп.

trend /trend/ *n* направлéние, тендéнция. **trendy** /-dı/ *adj* мóдный.

trepidation /,trepı'deıʃ(ə)n/ *n* трéпет.

trespass /'trespəs/ *n* (*on property*) нарушéние грани́ц; *vi* нарушáть *impf*, нарýшить *pf* грани́цу (**on** +*gen*); (*fig*) вторгáться *impf*, вторгнуться *pf* (**on** в+*acc*). **trespasser** /-sə(r)/ *n* нарушúтель *m*.

trestle /'tres(ə)l/ *n* кóзлы (-зел, -злам) *pl*; **~ table** стол на кóзлах.

trial /'traıəl/ *n* (*test*) испытáние (*also ordeal*), прóба; (*law*) процéсс, суд; (*sport*) попы́тка; **on ~** (*probation*) на испытáнии; (*of objects*) взя́тый на прóбу; (*law*) под судóм; **~ and error** мéтод проб и оши́бок.

triangle /'traı,æŋg(ə)l/ *n* треугóльник. **triangular** /-'æŋgjʊlə(r)/ *adj* треугóльный.

tribal /'traıb(ə)l/ *adj* племеннóй. **tribe** /traıb/ *n* плéмя *neut*.

tribulation /,trıbjʊ'leıʃ(ə)n/ *n* гóре, несчáстье.

tribunal /traı'bju:n(ə)l/ *n* трибунáл.

tributary /'trıbjʊtərı/ *n* притóк. **tribute** /'trıbju:t/ *n* дань; **pay ~** (*fig*) отдавáть *impf*, отдáть *pf* дань (уважéния) (**to** +*dat*).

trice /traıs/ *n*: **in a ~** мгновéнно.

trick /trık/ *n* (*ruse*) хúтрость; (*deception*) обмáн; (*conjuring ~*) фóкус; (*stunt*) трюк; (*joke*) шýтка; (*habit*) привы́чка; (*cards*) взя́тка; **play a ~ on** игрáть *impf*, сыгрáть *pf* шýтку с+*instr*; *vt* обмáнывать *impf*,

обману́ть *pf.* **trickery** /-kəri/ *n* обма́н.
trickle /'trɪk(ə)l/ *vi* сочи́ться *impf.*
trickster /'trɪkstə(r)/ *n* обма́нщик. **tricky** /-kɪ/ *adj* сло́жный.
tricycle /'traɪsɪk(ə)l/ *n* трёхколёсный велосипе́д.
trifle /'traɪf(ə)l/ *n* пустя́к; **a ~** (*adv*) немно́го +*gen*; *vi* шути́ть *impf*, по~ *pf* (**with** с+*instr*). **trifling** /-flɪŋ/ *adj* пустяко́вый.
trigger /'trɪgə(r)/ *n* (*of gun*) куро́к; *vt*: **~ off** вызыва́ть *impf*, вы́звать *pf.*
trill /trɪl/ *n* трель.
trilogy /'trɪlədʒɪ/ *n* трило́гия.
trim /trɪm/ *n* поря́док, гото́вность; **in fighting ~** в боево́й гото́вности; **in good ~** (*sport*) в хоро́шей фо́рме; (*haircut*) подстри́жка; *adj* опря́тный; *vt* (*cut, clip, cut off*) подреза́ть *impf*, подре́зать *pf*; (*hair*) подстрига́ть *impf*, подстри́чь *pf*; (*a dress etc.*) отде́лывать *impf*, отде́лать *pf.* **trimming** /-mɪŋ/ *n* (*on dress*) отде́лка; (*to food*) гарни́р.
Trinity /'trɪnɪtɪ/ *n* Тро́ица.
trinket /'trɪŋkɪt/ *n* безделу́шка.
trio /'tri:əʊ/ *n* три́о *neut indecl*; (*of people*) тро́йка.
trip /trɪp/ *n* пое́здка, путеше́ствие, экску́рсия; (*business ~*) командиро́вка; *vi* (*stumble*) спотыка́ться *impf*, споткну́ться *pf* (**over** о+*acc*); *vt* (*also ~ up*) подставля́ть *impf*, подста́вить *pf* но́жку +*dat* (*also fig*); (*confuse*) запу́тывать *impf*, запу́тать *pf.*
triple /'trɪp(ə)l/ *adj* тройно́й; (*tripled*) утро́енный; *vt & i* утра́ивать(ся) *impf*, утро́ить(ся) *pf.* **triplet** /'trɪplɪt/ *n* (*mus*) трио́ль; (*one of ~s*) близне́ц (из тро́йни); *pl* тро́йня.
tripod /'traɪpɒd/ *n* трено́жник.
trite /traɪt/ *adj* бана́льный.
triumph /'traɪəmf/ *n* торжество́, побе́да; *vi* торжествова́ть *impf*, вос~ *pf* (**over** над+*instr*). **triumphal** /traɪ'ʌmf(ə)l/ *adj* триумфа́льный. **triumphant** /traɪ'ʌmf(ə)nt/ *adj* (*exultant*) торжеству́ющий; (*victorious*) победоно́сный.
trivia /'trɪvɪə/ *n pl* ме́лочи (-че́й) *pl.* **trivial** /-vɪəl/ *adj* незначи́тельный. **triviality** /ˌtrɪvɪ'ælɪtɪ/ *n* тривиа́льность. **trivialize** /'trɪvɪəˌlaɪz/ *vt* опошля́ть *impf*, опо́шлить *pf.*
trolley /'trɒlɪ/ *n* теле́жка; (*table on wheels*) сто́лик на колёсиках. **trolley-bus** *n* тролле́йбус.
trombone /trɒm'bəʊn/ *n* тромбо́н.
troop /tru:p/ *n* гру́ппа, отря́д; *pl* (*mil*) войска́ *neut pl*; *vi* идти́ *impf*, по~ *pf* стро́ем.
trophy /'trəʊfɪ/ *n* трофе́й; (*prize*) приз.
tropic /'trɒpɪk/ *n* тро́пик. **tropical** /-k(ə)l/ *adj* тропи́ческий.
trot /trɒt/ *n* рысь; *vi* рыси́ть *impf*; (*rider*) е́здить *indet*, е́хать *det*, по~ *pf* ры́сью; (*horse*) ходи́ть *indet*, идти́ *det*, пойти́ *pf* ры́сью.
trouble /'trʌb(ə)l/ *n* (*worry*) беспоко́йство, трево́га; (*misfortune*) беда́; (*unpleasantness*) неприя́тности *f pl*; (*effort, pains*) труд; (*care*) забо́та; (*disrepair*) неиспра́вность (**with** в+*prep*); (*illness*) боле́знь; **heart ~** больно́е се́рдце; **~-maker** наруши́тель *m*, **~**ница споко́йствия; **ask for ~** напра́шиваться *impf*, напроси́ться *pf* на неприя́тности; **be**

in ~ имéть *impf* неприя́тности; **get into ~** попáсть *pf* в бедý; **take ~** старáться *impf*, по~ *pf*; **take the ~** труди́ться *impf*, по~ *pf* (**to** +*inf*); **the ~ is (that)** бедá в том, что; *vt* (*make anxious, disturb, give pain*) беспокóить *impf*; **may I ~ you for ...?** мóжно попроси́ть у вас +*acc*?; *vi* (*take the ~*) труди́ться *impf*. **troubled** /'trʌb(ə)ld/ *adj* беспокóйный. **troublesome** *adj* (*restless, fidgety*) беспокóйный; (*capricious*) капри́зный; (*difficult*) трýдный.

trough /trɒf/ *n* (*for food*) кормýшка.

trounce /traʊns/ *vt* (*beat*) порóть *impf*, вы́~ *pf*; (*defeat*) разбивáть *impf*, разби́ть *pf*.

troupe /tru:p/ *n* трýппа.

trouser-leg /'traʊzə,leg/ *n* штани́на (*coll*). **trousers** /'traʊzəz/ *n pl* брю́ки (-к) *pl*, штаны́ (-нóв) *pl*.

trout /traʊt/ *n* форéль.

trowel /'traʊəl/ *n* (*for building*) мастерóк; (*garden ~*) садóвый совóк.

truancy /'tru:ənsɪ/ *n* прогýл. **truant** /'tru:ənt/ *n* прогýльщик; **play ~** прогýливать *impf*, прогуля́ть *pf*.

truce /tru:s/ *n* переми́рие.

truck[1] /trʌk/ *n*: **have no ~ with** не имéть никаки́х дел с+*instr*.

truck[2] /trʌk/ *n* (*lorry*) грузови́к; (*rly*) вагóн-платфóрма.

truculent /'trʌkjʊlənt/ *adj* свирéпый.

trudge /trʌdʒ/ *vi* устáло тащи́ться *impf*.

true /tru:/ *adj* (*faithful, correct*) вéрный; (*correct*) прáвильный; (*story*) правди́вый; (*real*) настоя́щий; **come ~** сбывáться *impf*, сбы́ться *pf*.

truism /'tru:ɪz(ə)m/ *n* трюи́зм.

truly /'tru:lɪ/ *adv* (*sincerely*) и́скренне; (*really, indeed*) действи́тельно; **yours ~** прéданный Вам.

trump /trʌmp/ *n* кóзырь *m*; *vt* бить *impf*, по~ *pf* кóзырем; **~ up** фабриковáть *impf*, с~ *pf*.

trumpet /'trʌmpɪt/ *n* трубá; *vt* (*proclaim*) труби́ть *impf* о+*prep*. **trumpeter** /-tə(r)/ *n* трубáч.

truncate /trʌŋ'keɪt/ *vt* усекáть *impf*, усéчь *pf*.

truncheon /'trʌntʃ(ə)n/ *n* дуби́нка.

trundle /'trʌnd(ə)l/ *vt & i* катáть(ся) *indet*, кати́ть(ся) *det*, по~ *pf*.

trunk /trʌŋk/ *n* (*stem*) ствол; (*anat*) тýловище; (*elephant's*) хóбот; (*box*) сундýк; *pl* (*swimming*) плáвки (-вок) *pl*; (*boxing etc.*) трусы́ (-сóв) *pl*; **~ call** вы́зов по междугорóдному телефóну; **~ road** магистрáльная дорóга.

truss /trʌs/ *n* (*girder*) фéрма; (*med*) гры́жевóй бандáж; *vt* (*tie (up), bird*) свя́зывать *impf*, связáть *pf*; (*reinforce*) укрепля́ть *impf*, укрепи́ть *pf*.

trust /trʌst/ *n* довéрие; (*body of trustees*) опéка; (*property held in ~*) довери́тельная сóбственность; (*econ*) трест; **take on ~** принимáть *impf*, приня́ть *pf* на вéру; *vt* доверя́ть *impf*, довéрить *pf* +*dat* (**with** +*acc*; **to** +*inf*); *vi* (*hope*) надéяться *impf*, по~ *pf*. **trustee** /trʌs'ti:/ *n* опекýн. **trustful, trusting** /-fʊl, tɪŋ/ *adj* довéрчивый. **trustworthy, trusty** /-,wɜ:ðɪ, -tɪ/ *adj* надёжный, вéрный.

truth /tru:θ/ *n* прáвда; **tell the ~**

говори́ть *impf*, сказа́ть *pf* пра́вду; **to tell you the ~** по пра́вде говоря́. **truthful** /-fʊl/ *adj* правди́вый.

try /traɪ/ *n* (*attempt*) попы́тка; (*test*, *trial*) испыта́ние, про́ба; *vt* (*taste*; *sample*) про́бовать *impf*, по~ *pf*; (*patience*) испы́тывать *impf*, испыта́ть *pf*; (*law*) суди́ть *impf* (**for** за+*acc*); *vi* (*endeavour*) стара́ться *impf*, по~ *pf*; **~ on** (*clothes*) примеря́ть *impf*, приме́рить *pf*. **trying** /ˈtraɪɪŋ/ *adj* тру́дный.

tsar /zɑː(r)/ *n* царь *m*. **tsarina** /zɑːˈriːnə/ *n* цари́ца.

T-shirt /ˈtiːʃɜːt/ *n* футбо́лка.

tub /tʌb/ *n* ка́дка; (*bath*) ва́нна; (*of margarine etc.*) упако́вка.

tubby /ˈtʌbɪ/ *adj* то́лстенький.

tube /tjuːb/ *n* тру́бка, труба́; (*toothpaste etc.*) тю́бик; (*underground*) метро́ *neut indecl*.

tuber /ˈtjuːbə(r)/ *n* клу́бень *m*. **tuberculosis** /tjʊˌbɜːkjʊˈləʊsɪs/ *n* туберкулёз.

tubing /ˈtjuːbɪŋ/ *n* тру́бы *m pl*. **tubular** /ˈtjuːbjʊlə(r)/ *adj* тру́бчатый.

tuck /tʌk/ *n* (*in garment*) скла́дка; *vt* (*thrust into*, *~ away*) засо́вывать *impf*, засу́нуть *pf*; (*hide away*) пря́тать *impf*, с~ *pf*; **~ in** (*shirt etc.*) заправля́ть *impf*, запра́вить *pf*; **~ in, up** (*blanket*, *skirt*) подтыка́ть *impf*, подоткну́ть *pf*; **~ up** (*sleeves*) засу́чивать *impf*, засучи́ть *pf*; (*in bed*) укрыва́ть *impf*, укры́ть *pf*.

Tuesday /ˈtjuːzdeɪ/ *n* вто́рник.

tuft /tʌft/ *n* пучо́к.

tug /tʌg/ *vt* тяну́ть *impf*, по~ *pf*; *vi* (*sharply*) дёргать *impf*, дёрнуть *pf* (**at** за+*acc*); *n* рыво́к; (*tugboat*) букси́р.

tuition /tjuːˈɪʃ(ə)n/ *n* обуче́ние (**in** +*dat*).

tulip /ˈtjuːlɪp/ *n* тюльпа́н.

tumble /ˈtʌmb(ə)l/ *vi* (*fall*) па́дать *impf*, (у)па́сть *pf*; *n* паде́ние. **tumbledown** *adj* полуразру́шенный. **tumbler** /-blə(r)/ *n* стака́н.

tumour /ˈtjuːmə(r)/ *n* о́пухоль.

tumult /ˈtjuːmʌlt/ *n* (*uproar*) сумато́ха; (*agitation*) волне́ние. **tumultuous** /tjʊˈmʌltjʊəs/ *adj* шу́мный.

tuna /ˈtjuːnə/ *n* туне́ц.

tundra /ˈtʌndrə/ *n* ту́ндра.

tune /tjuːn/ *n* мело́дия; **in ~** в тон, (*of instrument*) настро́енный; **out of ~** не в тон, фальши́вый, (*of instrument*) расстро́енный; **change one's ~** (пере)меня́ть *impf*, перемени́ть *pf* тон; *vt* (*instrument*; *radio*) настра́ивать *impf*, настро́ить *pf*; (*engine etc.*) регули́ровать *impf*, от~ *pf*; **~ in** настра́ивать *impf*, настро́ить (*radio*) ра́дио (**to** на+*acc*); *vi*: **~ up** настра́ивать *impf*, настро́ить *pf* инструме́нт(ы). **tuneful** /-fʊl/ *adj* мелоди́чный. **tuner** /ˈtjuːnə(r)/ *n* (*mus*) настро́йщик; (*receiver*) приёмник.

tunic /ˈtjuːnɪk/ *n* туни́ка; (*of uniform*) ки́тель *m*.

tuning /ˈtjuːnɪŋ/ *n* настро́йка; (*of engine*) регулиро́вка; **~-fork** камерто́н.

tunnel /ˈtʌn(ə)l/ *n* тунне́ль *m*; *vi* прокла́дывать *impf*, проложи́ть *pf* тунне́ль *m*.

turban /ˈtɜːbən/ *n* тюрба́н.

turbine /ˈtɜːbaɪn/ *n* турби́на.

turbulence /ˈtɜːbjʊləns/ *n* бу́рность; (*aeron*) турбуле́нтность. **turbulent** /-lənt/ *adj* бу́рный.

tureen /tjʊˈriːn/ *n* су́пник.

turf /tɜ:f/ *n* дёрн.

turgid /ˈtɜ:dʒɪd/ *adj* (*pompous*) напы́щенный.

Turk /tɜ:k/ *n* ту́рок, турча́нка. **Turkey** /ˈtɜ:kɪ/ *n* Ту́рция.

turkey /ˈtɜ:kɪ/ *n* индю́к, *f* инде́йка; (*dish*) индю́шка.

Turkish /ˈtɜ:kɪʃ/ *adj* туре́цкий. **Turkmenistan** /tɜ:kˌmenɪˈstɑ:n/ *n* Туркмениста́н.

turmoil /ˈtɜ:mɔɪl/ *n* (*disorder*) беспоря́док; (*uproar*) сумато́ха.

turn /tɜ:n/ *n* (*change of direction*) поворо́т; (*revolution*) оборо́т; (*service*) услу́га; (*change*) измене́ние; (*one's ~ to do sth*) о́чередь; (*theat*) но́мер; **~ of phrase** оборо́т ре́чи; **at every ~** на ка́ждом шагу́; **by, in turn(s)** по о́череди; *vt* (*handle, key, car around, etc.*) повора́чивать *impf*, поверну́ть *pf*; (*revolve, rotate*) враща́ть *impf*; (*page; on its face*) перевёртывать *impf*, переверну́ть *pf*; (*direct*) направля́ть *impf*, напра́вить *pf*; (*cause to become*) де́лать *impf*, с~ *pf* +*instr*; (*on lathe*) точи́ть *impf*; *vi* (*change direction*) повора́чивать *impf*, поверну́ть *pf*; (*rotate*) враща́ться *impf*; (*~ round*) повора́чиваться *impf*, поверну́ться *pf*; (*become*) станови́ться *impf*, стать *pf* +*instr*; **~ against** ополча́ться *impf*, ополчи́ться *pf* на+*acc*, про́тив+*gen*; **~ around** *see* **~ round; ~ away** (*vt & i*) отвора́чивать(ся) *impf*, отверну́ть(ся) *pf*; (*refuse admittance*) прогоня́ть *impf*, прогна́ть *pf*; **~ back** (*vi*) повора́чивать *impf*, поверну́ть *pf* наза́д; (*vt*) (*bend back*) отгиба́ть *impf*, отогну́ть *pf*; **~ down** (*refuse*) отклоня́ть *impf*, отклони́ть *pf*; (*collar*) отгиба́ть *impf*, отогну́ть *pf*; (*make quieter*) де́лать *impf*, с~ *pf* ти́ше; **~ grey** (*vi*) седе́ть *impf*, по~ *pf*; **~ in** (*so as to face inwards*) повора́чивать *impf*, поверну́ть *pf* вовну́трь; **~ inside out** вывора́чивать *impf*, вы́вернуть *pf* наизна́нку; **~ into** (*change into*) (*vt & i*) превраща́ть(ся) *impf*, преврати́ть(ся) *pf* в+*acc*; (*street*) свора́чивать *impf*, сверну́ть *pf* на+*acc*; **~ off** (*light, radio etc.*) выключа́ть *impf*, вы́ключить *pf*; (*tap*) закрыва́ть *impf*, закры́ть *pf*; (*vi*) (*branch off*) свора́чивать *impf*, сверну́ть *pf*; **~ on** (*light, radio etc.*) включа́ть *impf*, включи́ть *pf*; (*tap*) открыва́ть *impf*, откры́ть *pf*; (*attack*) напада́ть *impf*, напа́сть *pf* на+*acc*; **~ out** (*light etc.*): *see* **~ off**; (*prove to be*) ока́зываться *impf*, оказа́ться *pf* (**to be** +*instr*); (*drive out*) выгоня́ть *impf*, вы́гнать *pf*; (*pockets*) вывёртывать *impf*, вы́вернуть *pf*; (*be present*) приходи́ть *impf*, прийти́ *pf*; (*product*) выпуска́ть *impf*, вы́пустить *pf*; **~ over** (*page, on its face, roll over*) (*vt & i*) перевёртывать(ся) *impf*, переверну́ть(ся) *pf*; (*hand over*) передава́ть *impf*, переда́ть *pf*; (*think about*) обду́мывать *impf*, обду́мать *pf*; (*overturn*) (*vt & i*) опроки́дывать(ся) *impf*, опроки́нуть(ся) *pf*; **~ pale** бледне́ть *impf*, по~ *pf*; **~ red** красне́ть *impf*, по~ *pf*; **~ round** (*vi*) (*rotate; ~ one's back; ~ to face sth*) повёртываться *impf*, поверну́ться *pf*; (*~ to face*) обора́чиваться *impf*, оберну́ться *pf*; (*vt*) повёртывать *impf*, поверну́ть *pf*; **~ sour** скиса́ть *impf*, ски́снуть *pf*; **~ to** обраща́ться *impf*, обрати́ться *pf* к+*dat* (**for** за +*instr*); ~ **up** (*appear*) появля́ться *impf*, появи́ться *pf*; (*be found*) находи́ться *impf*, найти́сь *pf*; (*shorten garment*) подшива́ть *impf*, подши́ть *pf*; (*crop up*) подвёртываться *impf*, подверну́ться *pf*; (*bend up*; *stick up*) (*vt* & *i*) загиба́ть(ся) *impf*, загну́ть(ся) *pf*; (*make louder*) де́лать *impf*, с~ *pf* гро́мче; ~ **up one's nose** вороти́ть *impf* нос (**at** от+*gen*) (*coll*); ~ **upside down** перевора́чивать *impf*, переверну́ть *pf* вверх дном. **turn-out** *n* коли́чество приходя́щих. **turn-up** *n* (*on trousers*) обшла́г.

turner /ˈtɜːnə(r)/ *n* то́карь *m*.

turning /ˈtɜːnɪŋ/ *n* (*road*) поворо́т. **turning-point** *n* поворо́тный пункт.

turnip /ˈtɜːnɪp/ *n* ре́па.

turnover /ˈtɜːnəʊvə(r)/ *n* (*econ*) оборо́т; (*of staff*) теку́честь рабо́чей си́лы.

turnpike /ˈtɜːnpaɪk/ *n* доро́жная заста́ва.

turnstile /ˈtɜːnstaɪl/ *n* турнике́т.

turntable /ˈtɜːnteɪb(ə)l/ *n* (*rly*) поворо́тный круг; (*gramophone*) диск.

turpentine /ˈtɜːpən͵taɪn/ *n* скипида́р.

turquoise /ˈtɜːkwɔɪz/ *n* (*material*, *stone*) бирюза́; *adj* бирюзо́вый.

turret /ˈtʌrɪt/ *n* ба́шенка.

turtle /ˈtɜːt(ə)l/ *n* черепа́ха.

turtle-dove /ˈtɜt(ə)l͵dʌv/ *n* го́рлица.

tusk /tʌsk/ *n* би́вень *m*, клык.

tussle /ˈtʌs(ə)l/ *n* дра́ка; *vi* дра́ться *impf* (**for** за+*acc*).

tutor /ˈtjuːtə(r)/ *n* (*private teacher*) ча́стный дома́шний учи́тель *m*, ~ница; (*univ*) преподава́тель *m*, ~ница; (*primer*) уче́бник; *vt* (*instruct*) обуча́ть *impf*, обучи́ть *pf* (**in** +*dat*); (*give lessons to*) дава́ть *impf*, дать *pf* уро́ки+*dat*; (*guide*) руководи́ть *impf* +*instr*. **tutorial** /tjuːˈtɔːrɪəl/ *n* консульта́ция.

tutu /ˈtuːtuː/ *n* (*ballet*) па́чка.

TV *abbr* (*of* **television**) ТВ, телеви́дение; (*set*) телеви́зор.

twang /twæŋ/ *n* (*of string*) ре́зкий звук (натя́нутой струны́); (*voice*) гнуса́вый го́лос.

tweak /twiːk/ *n* щипо́к; *vt* щипа́ть *impf*, (у)щипну́ть *pf*.

tweed /twiːd/ *n* твид.

tweezers /ˈtwiːzəz/ *n pl* пинце́т.

twelfth /twelfθ/ *adj* & *n* двена́дцатый. **twelve** /twelv/ *adj* & *n* двена́дцать.

twentieth /ˈtwentɪɪθ/ *adj* & *n* двадца́тый. **twenty** /ˈtwentɪ/ *adj* & *n* два́дцать; *pl* (*decade*) двадца́тые го́ды (-до́в) *m pl*.

twice /twaɪs/ *adv* два́жды; ~ **as** вдво́е, в два ра́за +*comp*.

twiddle /ˈtwɪd(ə)l/ *vt* (*turn*) верте́ть *impf* +*acc*, *instr*; (*toy with*) игра́ть *impf* +*instr*; ~ **one's thumbs** (*fig*) безде́льничать *impf*.

twig /twɪg/ *n* ве́точка, прут.

twilight /ˈtwaɪlaɪt/ *n* су́мерки (-рек) *pl*.

twin /twɪn/ *n* близне́ц; *pl* (*Gemini*) Близнецы́ *m pl*; ~ **beds** па́ра односпа́льных крова́тей; ~ **brother** брат-близне́ц; ~ **town** го́род-побрати́м.

twine /twaɪn/ *n* бечёвка, шпага́т; *vt* (*twist*, *weave*) вить *impf*, с~ *pf*; *vt* & *i* (~ *round*) обвива́ть(ся) *impf*, обви́ть(ся) *pf*.

twinge /twɪndʒ/ *n* присту́п (бо́ли); (*of conscience*) угрызе́ние.

twinkle /'twɪŋk(ə)l/ *n* мерца́ние; (*of eyes*) огонёк; *vi* мерца́ть *impf*, сверка́ть *impf*. **twinkling** /-klɪŋ/ *n* мерца́ние; **in the ~ of an eye** в мгнове́ние о́ка.

twirl /twɜːl/ *vt* & *i* (*twist, turn*) верте́ть(ся) *impf*; (*whirl, spin*) кружи́ть(ся) *impf*.

twist /twɪst/ *n* (*bend*) изги́б, поворо́т; (*~ing*) круче́ние; (*in story*) поворо́т фа́булы; *vt* скру́чивать *impf*, крути́ть *impf*, с~ *pf*; (*distort*) искажа́ть *impf*, искази́ть *pf*; (*sprain*) подвёртывать *impf*, подверну́ть *pf*; *vi* (*climb, meander, twine*) ви́ться *impf*. **twisted** /-tɪd/ *adj* искривлённый (*also fig*).

twit /twɪt/ *n* дура́к.

twitch /twɪtʃ/ *n* подёргивание; *vt* & *i* дёргать(ся) *impf*, дёрнуть(ся) *pf* (**at** за+*acc*).

twitter /'twɪtə(r)/ *n* щёбет; *vi* щебета́ть *impf*, чири́кать *impf*.

two /tuː/ *adj* & *n* два, две (*f*); (*collect; 2 pairs*) дво́е; (*number 2*) дво́йка; **in ~** (*in half*) на́двое, попола́м; **~-seater** двухме́стный (автомоби́ль); **~-way** двусторо́нний. **twofold** *adj* двойно́й; *adv* вдвойне́. **twosome** *n* па́ра.

tycoon /taɪ'kuːn/ *n* магна́т.

type /taɪp/ *n* тип, род; (*printing*) шрифт; *vt* писа́ть *impf*, на~ *pf* на маши́нке. **typescript** *n* маши́нопись. **typewriter** *n* пи́шущая маши́нка. **typewritten** /'taɪp,rɪt(ə)n/ *adj* машинопи́сный.

typhoid /'taɪfɔɪd/ *n* брюшно́й тиф.

typical /'tɪpɪk(ə)l/ *adj* типи́чный. **typify** /'tɪpɪ,faɪ/ *vt* служи́ть *impf*, по~ *pf* типи́чным приме́ром +*gen*.

typist /'taɪpɪst/ *n* машини́стка.

typography /taɪ'pɒgrəfɪ/ *n* книгопеча́тание; (*style*) оформле́ние.

tyrannical /tɪ'rænɪk(ə)l/ *adj* тирани́ческий. **tyrant** /'taɪrənt/ *n* тира́н.

tyre /'taɪə(r)/ *n* ши́на.

U

ubiquitous /juː'bɪkwɪtəs/ *adj* вездесу́щий.

udder /'ʌdə(r)/ *n* вы́мя *neut*.

UFO *abbr* (*of* **unidentified flying object**) НЛО, неопо́знанный лета́ющий объе́кт.

ugh /əx/ *int* тьфу!

ugliness /'ʌglɪnɪs/ *n* уро́дство. **ugly** /-lɪ/ *adj* некраси́вый, уро́дливый; (*unpleasant*) неприя́тный.

UK *abbr* (*of* **United Kingdom**) Соединённое Короле́вство.

Ukraine /juː'kreɪn/ *n* Украи́на. **Ukrainian** /-nɪən/ *n* украи́нец, -нка; *adj* украи́нский.

ulcer /'ʌlsə(r)/ *n* я́зва.

ulterior /ʌl'tɪərɪə(r)/ *adj* скры́тый.

ultimate /'ʌltɪmət/ *adj* (*final*) после́дний, оконча́тельный; (*purpose*) коне́чный. **ultimately** /-lɪ/ *adv* в коне́чном счёте, в конце́ концо́в. **ultimatum** /,ʌltɪ'meɪtəm/ *n* ультима́тум.

ultrasound /'ʌltrə,saʊnd/ *n* ультразву́к. **ultra-violet** /,ʌltrə'vaɪələt/ *adj* ультрафиоле́товый.

umbilical /ʌm'bɪlɪk(ə)l/ *adj*: **~ cord** пуповина.

umbrella /ʌm'brelə/ *n* зо́нтик, зонт.

umpire /'ʌmpaɪə(r)/ *n* судья́ *m*; *vt* & *i* суди́ть *impf*.

umpteenth /ʌmp'ti:nθ/ *adj*: **for the ~ time** в который раз. **unabashed** /ˌʌnə'bæʃt/ *adj* без всякого смущения. **unabated** /ˌʌnə'beɪtɪd/ *adj* неослабленный. **unable** /ʌn'eɪb(ə)l/ *adj*: **be ~ to** не мочь *impf*, с~ *pf*; быть не в состоянии; (*not know how to*) не уметь *impf*, с~ *pf*. **unabridged** /ˌʌnə'brɪdʒd/ *adj* несокращённый. **unaccompanied** /ˌʌnə'kʌmpənɪd/ *adj* без сопровождения; (*mus*) без аккомпанемента. **unaccountable** /ˌʌnə'kaʊntəb(ə)l/ *adj* необъяснимый. **unaccustomed** /ˌʌnə'kʌstəmd/ *adj* (*not accustomed*) непривыкший (**to** к+*dat*); (*unusual*) непривычный. **unadulterated** /ˌʌnə'dʌltəreɪtɪd/ *adj* настоящий; (*utter*) чистейший. **unaffected** /ˌʌnə'fektɪd/ *adj* непринуждённый. **unaided** /ʌn'eɪdɪd/ *adj* без помощи, самостоятельный. **unambiguous** /ˌʌnæm'bɪgjʊəs/ *adj* недвусмысленный. **unanimity** /ˌju:nə'nɪmɪtɪ/ *n* единодушие. **unanimous** /ju:'nænɪməs/ *adj* единодушный. **unanswerable** /ʌn'ɑ:nsərəb(ə)l/ *adj* (*irrefutable*) неопровержимый. **unarmed** /ʌn'ɑ:md/ *adj* невооружённый. **unashamed** /ˌʌnə'ʃeɪmd/ *adj* бессовестный. **unassailable** /ˌʌnə'seɪləb(ə)l/ *adj* неприступный; (*irrefutable*) неопровержимый. **unassuming** /ˌʌnə'sju:mɪŋ/ *adj* скромный. **unattainable** /ˌʌnə'teɪnəb(ə)l/ *adj* недосягаемый. **unattended** /ˌʌnə'tendɪd/ *adj* без присмотра. **unattractive** /ˌʌnə'træktɪv/ *adj* непривлекательный. **unauthorized** /ʌn'ɔ:θəˌraɪzd/ *adj* неразрешённый. **unavailable** /ˌʌnə'veɪləb(ə)l/ *adj* не имеющийся в наличии, недоступный. **unavoidable** /ˌʌnə'vɔɪdəb(ə)l/ *adj* неизбежный. **unaware** /ˌʌnə'weə(r)/ *predic*: **be ~ of** не сознавать *impf* +*acc*; не знать *impf* о+*prep*. **unawares** /ˌʌnə'weəz/ *adv* врасплох.

unbalanced /ʌn'bælənst/ *adj* (*psych*) неуравновешенный. **unbearable** /ʌn'beərəb(ə)l/ *adj* невыносимый. **unbeatable** /ʌn'bi:təb(ə)l/ *adj* (*unsurpassable*) не могущий быть превзойдённым; (*invincible*) непобедимый. **unbeaten** /ʌn'bi:tən/ *adj* (*undefeated*) непокорённый; (*unsurpassed*) непревзойдённый. **unbelief** /ˌʌnbɪ'li:f/ *n* неверие. **unbelievable** /ˌʌnbɪ'li:vəb(ə)l/ *adj* невероятный. **unbeliever** /ˌʌnbɪ'li:və(r)/ *n* неверующий *sb*. **unbiased** /ʌn'baɪəst/ *adj* беспристрастный. **unblemished** /ʌn'blemɪʃt/ *adj* незапятнанный. **unblock** /ʌn'blɒk/ *vt* прочищать *impf*, прочистить *pf*. **unbolt** /ʌn'bəʊlt/ *vt* отпирать *impf*, отпереть *pf*. **unborn** /ʌn'bɔ:n/ *adj* ещё не рождённый. **unbounded** /ʌn'baʊndɪd/ *adj* неограниченный. **unbreakable** /ʌn'breɪkəb(ə)l/ *adj* небьющийся. **unbridled** /ʌn'braɪd(ə)ld/ *adj* разнузданный. **unbroken** /ʌn'brəʊkən/ *adj* (*intact*) неразбитый, целый; (*continuous*) непрерывный; (*unsurpassed*) непобитый; (*horse*) необъезженный. **unbuckle** /ʌn'bʌk(ə)l/ *vt* расстёгивать *impf*, расстегнуть *pf*. **unburden** /ʌn'bɜ:d(ə)n/ *vt*: **~ o.s.** отводить *impf*, отвести *pf* душу. **unbutton** /ʌn'bʌt(ə)n/ *vt* расстёгивать *impf*, расстегну́ть *pf.* **uncalled-for** /ʌn'kɔ:ldfɔ:(r)/ *adj* неуме́стный. **uncanny** /ʌn 'kænɪ/ *adj* жу́ткий, сверхъесте́ственный. **unceasing** /ʌn'si:sɪŋ/ *adj* непреры́вный. **unceremonious** /ˌʌnserɪ'məʊnɪəs/ *adj* бесцеремо́нный. **uncertain** /ʌn 'sɜ:t(ə)n/ *adj* (*not sure, hesitating*) неуве́ренный; (*indeterminate*) неопределённый, нея́сный; **be** ~ (*not know for certain*) то́чно не знать *impf*; **in no** ~ **terms** недвусмы́сленно. **uncertainty** /ʌn'sɜ:t(ə)ntɪ/ *n* неизве́стность; неопределённость. **unchallenged** /ʌn'tʃælɪndʒd/ *adj* не вызыва́ющий возраже́ний. **unchanged** /ʌn'tʃeɪndʒd/ *adj* неизмени́вшийся. **unchanging** /ʌn'tʃeɪndʒɪŋ/ *adj* неизменя́ющийся. **uncharacteristic** /ˌʌnkærəktə'rɪstɪk/ *adj* нетипи́чный. **uncharitable** /ʌn 'tʃærɪtəb(ə)l/ *adj* немилосе́рдный, жесто́кий. **uncharted** /ʌn 'tʃɑ:tɪd/ *adj* неиссле́дованный. **unchecked** /ʌn'tʃekt/ *adj* (*unrestrained*) необу́зданный. **uncivilized** /ʌn'sɪvɪˌlaɪzd/ *adj* нецивилизо́ванный. **unclaimed** /ʌn'kleɪmd/ *adj* невостре́бованный.

uncle /'ʌŋk(ə)l/ *n* дя́дя *m.*

unclean /ʌn'kli:n/ *adj* нечи́стый. **unclear** /ʌn'klɪə(r)/ *adj* нея́сный. **uncomfortable** /ʌn'kʌmftəb(ə)l/ *adj* неудо́бный. **uncommon** /ʌn 'kɒmən/ *adj* необыкнове́нный; (*rare*) ре́дкий. **uncommunicative** /ˌʌnkə'mju:nɪkətɪv/ *adj* неразгово́рчивый, сде́ржанный. **uncomplaining** /ˌʌnkəm'pleɪnɪŋ/ *adj* безро́потный. **uncomplicated** /ʌn'kɒmplɪˌkeɪtɪd/ *adj* несло́жный. **uncompromising** /ʌn'kɒmprəˌmaɪzɪŋ/ *adj* бескомпроми́ссный. **unconcealed** /ˌʌnkən'si:ld/ *adj* нескрыва́емый. **unconcerned** /ˌʌnkən 'sɜ:nd/ *adj* (*unworried*) беззабо́тный; (*indifferent*) равноду́шный. **unconditional** /ˌʌnkən 'dɪʃən(ə)l/ *adj* безогово́рочный, безусло́вный. **unconfirmed** /ˌʌnkən'fɜ:md/ *adj* неподтверждённый. **unconnected** /ˌʌnkə'nektɪd/ *adj* ~ **with** не свя́занный с+*instr.* **unconscious** /ʌn'kɒnʃəs/ *adj* (*also unintentional*) бессозна́тельный; (*predic*) без созна́ния; **be** ~ **of** не сознава́ть *impf* +*gen*; *n* подсозна́тельное *sb.* **unconsciousness** /ʌn'kɒnʃəsnɪs/ *n* бессозна́тельное состоя́ние. **unconstitutional** /ˌʌnkɒnstɪ 'tju:ʃən(ə)l/ *adj* неконституцио́нный. **uncontrollable** /ˌʌnkən'trəʊləb(ə)l/ *adj* неудержи́мый. **uncontrolled** /ˌʌnkən 'trəʊld/ *adj* бесконтро́льный. **unconventional** /ˌʌnkən 'venʃən(ə)l/ *adj* необы́чный; оригина́льный. **unconvincing** /ˌʌnkən'vɪnsɪŋ/ *adj* неубеди́тельный. **uncooked** /ʌn'kʊkt/ *adj* сыро́й. **uncooperative** /ˌʌnkəʊ 'ɒpərətɪv/ *adj* неотзы́вчивый. **uncouth** /ʌn'ku:θ/ *adj* гру́бый. **uncover** /ʌn'kʌvə(r)/ *vt* раскрыва́ть *impf*, раскры́ть *pf.* **uncritical** /ʌn'krɪtɪk(ə)l/ *adj* некрити́чный.

unctuous /'ʌŋktjʊəs/ *adj* еле́йный.

uncut /ʌn'kʌt/ *adj* неразре́занный; (*unabridged*) несокращённый.

undamaged /ʌn'dæmɪdʒd/ *adj* неповреждённый. **undaunted** /ʌn'dɔ:ntɪd/ *adj* бесстра́шный. **undecided** /ˌʌndɪ'saɪdɪd/ *adj* (*not settled*) нерешённый; (*irreso-*

lute) нереши́тельный. **undefeated** /ˌʌndɪ'fiːtɪd/ *adj* непокорённый. **undemanding** /ˌʌndɪ'mɑːndɪŋ/ *adj* нетре́бовательный. **undemocratic** /ˌʌndemə'krætɪk/ *adj* недемократи́ческий. **undeniable** /ˌʌndɪ'naɪəb(ə)l/ *adj* неоспори́мый.

under /'ʌndə(r)/ *prep* (*position*) под+*instr*; (*direction*) под+*acc*; (*fig*) под +*instr*; (*less than*) ме́ньше+*gen*; (*in view of, in the reign, time of*) при+*prep*; **~-age** несовершенноле́тний; **~ way** на ходу́; *adv* (*position*) внизу́; (*direction*) вниз; (*less*) ме́ньше.

undercarriage /'ʌndəˌkærɪdʒ/ *n* шасси́ *neut indecl.* **underclothes** /'ʌndəˌkləʊðz/ *n pl* ни́жнее бельё. **undercoat** /'ʌndəˌkəʊt/ *n* (*of paint*) грунто́вка. **undercover** /ˌʌndə'kʌvə(r)/ *adj* та́йный. **undercurrent** /'ʌndəˌkʌrənt/ *n* подво́дное тече́ние; (*fig*) скры́тая тенде́нция. **undercut** /ˌʌndə'kʌt/ *vt* (*price*) назнача́ть *impf*, назна́чить *pf* бо́лее ни́зкую це́ну чем+*nom.* **underdeveloped** /ˌʌndədɪ'veləpt/ *adj* слабора́звитый. **underdog** /'ʌndəˌdɒg/ *n* неуда́чник.

underdone /ˌʌndə'dʌn/ *adj* недожа́ренный. **underemployment** /ˌʌndərɪm'plɔɪmənt/ *n* непо́лная за́нятость. **underestimate** *vt* /ˌʌndər'estɪˌmeɪt/ недооце́нивать *impf*, недооцени́ть *pf*; *n* /ˌʌndər'estɪmət/недооце́нка.

underfoot /ˌʌndə'fʊt/ *adv* под нога́ми.

undergo /ˌʌndə'gəʊ/ *vt* подверга́ться *impf*, подве́ргнуться *pf* +*dat*; (*endure*) переноси́ть *impf*, перенести́ *pf.* **undergraduate** /ˌʌndə'grædjʊət/ *n* студе́нт, **~**ка. **underground** /'ʌndəˌgraʊnd/ *n* (*rly*) метро́ *neut indecl*; (*fig*) подпо́лье; *adj* подзе́мный; (*fig*) подпо́льный; *adv* под землёй; (*fig*) подпо́льно. **undergrowth** /'ʌndəˌgrəʊθ/ *n* подле́сок. **underhand** /'ʌndəˌhænd/ *adj* закули́сный. **underlie** /ˌʌndə'laɪ/ *vt* (*fig*) лежа́ть *impf* в осно́ве +*gen.* **underline** /ˌʌndə'laɪn/ *vt* подчёркивать *impf*, подчеркну́ть *pf.* **underlying** /'ʌndəˌlaɪɪŋ/ *adj* лежа́щий в осно́ве. **underling** /'ʌndəlɪŋ/ *n* подчинённый *sb.*

undermine /ˌʌndə'maɪn/ *vt* (*authority*) подрыва́ть *impf*, подорва́ть *pf*; (*health*) разруша́ть *impf*, разру́шить *pf.*

underneath /ˌʌndə'niːθ/ *adv* (*position*) внизу́; (*direction*) вниз; *prep* (*position*) под+*instr*; (*direction*) под+*acc*; *n* ни́жняя часть; *adj* ни́жний.

undernourished /ˌʌndə'nʌrɪʃt/ *adj* исхуда́лый; **be ~** недоеда́ть *impf.*

underpaid /ˌʌndə'peɪd/ *adj* низкоопла́чиваемый. **underpants** /'ʌndəˌpænts/ *n pl* трусы́ (-со́в) *pl.* **underpass** /'ʌndəˌpɑːs/ *n* прое́зд под полотно́м доро́ги; тонне́ль *m.* **underpin** /ˌʌndə'pɪn/ *vt* подводи́ть *impf*, подвести́ *pf* фунда́мент под+*acc*; (*fig*) подде́рживать *impf*, поддержа́ть *pf.* **underprivileged** /ˌʌndə'prɪvɪlɪdʒd/ *adj* обделённый; (*poor*) бе́дный. **underrate** /ˌʌndə'reɪt/ *vt* недооце́нивать *impf*, недооцени́ть *pf.*

underscore /ˌʌndə'skɔː(r)/ *vt* подчёркивать *impf*, подчеркну́ть *pf.* **under-secretary** /ˌʌndə'sekrətərɪ/ *n* замести́тель *m* мини́стра. **underside** /'ʌndəˌsaɪd/ *n* ни́жняя сторона́, низ. **undersized** /'ʌndəˌsaɪzd/ *adj* малорóслый. **understaffed** /ˌʌndəˈstɑːft/ *adj* неукомплектóванный.

understand /ˌʌndəˈstænd/ *vt* понимáть *impf*, поня́ть *pf*; (*have heard say*) слы́шать *impf*. **understandable** /ˌʌndəˈstændəb(ə)l/ *adj* поня́тный. **understanding** /ˌʌndəˈstændɪŋ/ *n* понимáние; (*agreement*) соглашéние; *adj* (*sympathetic*) отзы́вчивый.

understate /ˌʌndəˈsteɪt/ *vt* преуменьшáть *impf*, преумéньшить *pf*. **understatement** /ˈʌndəˌsteɪtmənt/ *n* преуменьшéние.

understudy /ˈʌndəˌstʌdɪ/ *n* дублёр.

undertake /ˌʌndəˈteɪk/ *vt* (*enter upon*) предпринимáть *impf*, предприня́ть *pf*; (*responsibility*) брать *impf*, взять *pf* на себя́; (*+inf*) обя́зываться *impf*, обязáться *pf*. **undertaker** /ˈʌndəˌteɪkə(r)/ *n* гробовщи́к. **undertaking** /ˌʌndəˈteɪkɪŋ/ *n* предприя́тие; (*pledge*) гарáнтия.

undertone /ˈʌndəˌtəʊn/ *n* (*fig*) подтéкст; **in an ~** вполгóлоса. **underwater** /ˌʌndəˈwɔːtə(r)/ *adj* подвóдный. **underwear** /ˈʌndəˌweə(r)/ *n* ни́жнее бельё. **underweight** /ˌʌndəˈweɪt/ *adj* исхудáлый. **underworld** /ˈʌndəˌwɜːld/ *n* (*mythology*) преиспóдняя *sb*; (*criminals*) престу́пный мир. **underwrite** /ˌʌndəˈraɪt/ *vt* (*guarantee*) гаранти́ровать *impf* & *pf*. **underwriter** /ˈʌndəˌraɪtə(r)/ *n* страхóвщик.

undeserved /ˌʌndɪˈzɜːvd/ *adj* незаслу́женный. **undesirable** /ˌʌndɪˈzaɪərəb(ə)l/ *adj* нежелáтельный; *n* нежелáтельное лицó. **undeveloped** /ˌʌndɪˈveləpt/ *adj* нерáзвитый; (*land*) незастрóенный. **undignified** /ʌnˈdɪgnɪˌfaɪd/ *adj* недостóйный. **undiluted** /ˌʌndaɪˈljuːtɪd/ *adj* неразбáвленный. **undisciplined** /ʌnˈdɪsɪplɪnd/ *adj* недисциплини́рованный.

undiscovered /ˌʌndɪˈskʌvəd/ *adj* неоткры́тый. **undisguised** /ˌʌndɪsˈgaɪzd/ *adj* я́вный. **undisputed** /ˌʌndɪˈspjuːtɪd/ *adj* бесспóрный. **undistinguished** /ˌʌndɪˈstɪŋgwɪʃt/ *adj* зауря́дный. **undisturbed** /ˌʌndɪˈstɜːbd/ *adj* (*untouched*) нетрóнутый; (*peaceful*) спокóйный. **undivided** /ˌʌndɪˈvaɪdɪd/ *adj*: **~ attention** пóлное внимáние **undo** /ʌnˈduː/ *vt* (*open*) открывáть *impf*, откры́ть *pf*; (*untie*) развя́зывать *impf*, развязáть *pf*; (*unbutton, unhook, unbuckle*) расстёгивать *impf*, расстегну́ть *pf*; (*destroy, cancel*) уничтожáть *impf*, уничтóжить *pf*. **undoubted** /ʌnˈdaʊtɪd/ *adj* несомнéнный. **undoubtedly** /ʌnˈdaʊtɪdlɪ/ *adv* несомнéнно. **undress** /ʌnˈdres/ *vt* & *i* раздевáть(ся) *impf*, раздéть(ся) *pf*. **undue** /ʌnˈdjuː/ *adj* чрезмéрный. **unduly** /ʌnˈdjuːlɪ/ *adv* чрезмéрно.

undulating /ˈʌndjʊˌleɪtɪŋ/ *adj* волни́стый; (*landscape*) холми́стый.

undying /ʌnˈdaɪɪŋ/ *adj* (*eternal*) вéчный.

unearth /ʌnˈɜːθ/ *vt* (*dig up*) выкáпывать *impf*, вы́копать *pf* из земли́; (*fig*) раскáпывать *impf*, раскопáть *pf*. **uneasiness** /ʌnˈiːzɪnɪs/ *n* (*anxiety*) беспокóйство; (*awkwardness*) нелóвкость. **uneasy** /ʌnˈiːzɪ/ *adj* беспокóйный; нелóвкий. **uneconomic** /ˌʌniːkəˈnɒmɪk/ *adj* нерентáбельный. **uneconomical** /ˌʌniːkəˈnɒmɪk(ə)l/ *adj* (*car* *etc.*) неэкономи́чный; (*person*) неэконо́мный. **uneducated** /ʌn'edjʊˌkeɪtɪd/ *adj* необразо́ванный. **unemployed** /ˌʌnɪm'plɔɪd/ *adj* безрабо́тный. **unemployment** /ˌʌnɪm'plɔɪmənt/ *n* безрабо́тица; ~ **benefit** посо́бие по безрабо́тице. **unending** /ʌn'endɪŋ/ *adj* бесконе́чный. **unenviable** /ʌn'envɪəb(ə)l/ *adj* незави́дный. **unequal** /ʌn'iːkw(ə)l/ *adj* нера́вный. **unequalled** /ʌn'iːkw(ə)ld/ *adj* непревзойдённый. **unequivocal** /ˌʌnɪ'kwɪvək(ə)l/ *adj* недвусмы́сленный. **unerring** /ʌn'ɜːrɪŋ/ *adj* безоши́бочный.

uneven /ʌn'iːv(ə)n/ *adj* неро́вный. **uneventful** /ˌʌnɪ'ventfʊl/ *adj* непримеча́тельный. **unexceptional** /ˌʌnɪk'sepʃən(ə)l/ *adj* обы́чный. **unexpected** /ˌʌnɪk'spektɪd/ *adj* неожи́данный. **unexplored** /ˌʌnɪk'splɔːd/ *adj* неиссле́дованный.

unfailing /ʌn'feɪlɪŋ/ *adj* неизме́нный; (*inexhaustible*) неисчерпа́емый. **unfair** /ʌn'feə(r)/ *adj* несправедли́вый. **unfaithful** /ʌn'feɪθfʊl/ *adj* неве́рный. **unfamiliar** /ˌʌnfə'mɪljə(r)/ *adj* незнако́мый; (*unknown*) неве́домый. **unfashionable** /ʌn'fæʃənəb(ə)l/ *adj* немо́дный. **unfasten** /ʌn'fɑːs(ə)n/ *vt* (*detach, untie*) открепля́ть *impf*, открепи́ть *pf*; (*undo, unbutton, unhook*) расстёгивать *impf*, расстегну́ть *pf*; (*open*) открыва́ть *impf*, откры́ть *pf*. **unfavourable** /ʌn'feɪvərəb(ə)l/ *adj* неблагоприя́тный. **unfeeling** /ʌn'fiːlɪŋ/ *adj* бесчу́вственный. **unfinished** /ʌn'fɪnɪʃt/ *adj* незако́нченный. **unfit** /ʌn'fɪt/ *adj* него́дный; (*unhealthy*) нездоро́вый. **unflagging** /ʌn'flægɪŋ/ *adj* неослабева́ющий. **unflattering** /ʌn'flætərɪŋ/ *adj* нele...

unfold /ʌn'fəʊld/ *vt & i* развёртывать(ся) *impf*, разверну́ть(ся) *pf*; *vi* (*fig*) раскрыва́ться *impf*, раскры́ться *pf*. **unforeseen** /ˌʌnfɔː'siːn/ *adj* непредви́денный. **unforgettable** /ˌʌnfə'getəb(ə)l/ *adj* незабыва́емый. **unforgivable** /ˌʌnfə'gɪvəb(ə)l/ *adj* непрости́тельный. **unforgiving** /ˌʌnfə'gɪvɪŋ/ *adj* непроща́ющий. **unfortunate** /ʌn'fɔːtjʊnət/ *adj* несча́стный; (*regrettable*) неуда́чный; *n* неуда́чник. **unfortunately** /ʌn'fɔːtjʊnətlɪ/ *adv* к сожале́нию. **unfounded** /ʌn'faʊndɪd/ *adj* необосно́ванный. **unfriendly** /ʌn'frendlɪ/ *adj* недружелю́бный. **unfulfilled** /ˌʌnfʊl'fɪld/ *adj* (*hopes etc.*) неосуществлённый; (*person*) неудовлетворённый. **unfurl** /ʌn'fɜːl/ *vt & i* развёртывать(ся) *impf*, разверну́ть(ся) *pf*. **unfurnished** /ʌn'fɜːnɪʃt/ *adj* немеблиро́ванный.

ungainly /ʌn'geɪnlɪ/ *adj* неуклю́жий. **ungovernable** /ʌn'gʌvənəb(ə)l/ *adj* неуправля́емый. **ungracious** /ʌn'greɪʃəs/ *adj* нелюбе́зный. **ungrateful** /ʌn'greɪtfʊl/ *adj* неблагода́рный. **unguarded** /ʌn'gɑːdɪd/ *adj* (*incautious*) неосторо́жный.

unhappiness /ʌn'hæpɪnɪs/ *n* несча́стье. **unhappy** /ʌn'hæpɪ/ *adj* несчастли́вый. **unharmed** /ʌn'hɑːmd/ *adj* невреди́мый. **unhealthy** /ʌn'helθɪ/ *adj* нездоро́вый; (*harmful*) вре́дный. **unheard-of** /ʌn'hɜːdɒv/ *adj* неслы́ханный. **unheeded** /ʌn'hiːdɪd/ *adj* незаме́ченный. **un-**

heeding /ʌn'hiːdɪŋ/ *adj* невнима́тельный. **unhelpful** /ʌn'helpfʊl/ *adj* бесполе́зный; (*person*) неотзы́вчивый. **unhesitating** /ʌn'hezɪˌteɪtɪŋ/ *adj* реши́тельный. **unhesitatingly** /ʌn'hezɪˌteɪtɪŋlɪ/ *adv* без колеба́ния. **unhindered** /ʌn'hɪndəd/ *adj* беспрепя́тственный. **unhinge** /ʌn'hɪndʒ/ *vt* (*fig*) расстра́ивать *impf*, расстро́ить *pf*. **unholy** /ʌn'həʊlɪ/ *adj* (*impious*) нечести́вый; (*awful*) ужа́сный. **unhook** /ʌn'hʊk/ *vt* (*undo hooks of*) расстёгивать *impf*, расстегну́ть *pf*; (*uncouple*) расцепля́ть *impf*, расцепи́ть *pf*. **unhurt** /ʌn'hɜːt/ *adj* невреди́мый.

unicorn /'juːnɪˌkɔːn/ *n* единоро́г.

unification /ˌjuːnɪfɪ'keɪʃ(ə)n/ *n* объедине́ние.

uniform /'juːnɪˌfɔːm/ *n* фо́рма; *adj* единообра́зный; (*unchanging*) постоя́нный. **uniformity** /ˌjuːnɪ'fɔːmɪtɪ/ *n* единообра́зие.

unify /'juːnɪˌfaɪ/ *vt* объединя́ть *impf*, объедини́ть *pf*.

unilateral /ˌjuːnɪ'lætər(ə)l/ *adj* односторо́нний.

unimaginable /ˌʌnɪ'mædʒɪnəb(ə)l/ *adj* невообрази́мый. **unimaginative** /ˌʌnɪ'mædʒɪnətɪv/ *adj* лишённый воображе́ния, прозаи́чный. **unimportant** /ˌʌnɪm'pɔːt(ə)nt/ *adj* нева́жный. **uninformed** /ˌʌnɪn'fɔːmd/ *adj* (*ignorant*) несве́дущий (**about** в+*prep*); (*ill-informed*) неосведомлённый. **uninhabited** /ˌʌnɪn'hæbɪtɪd/ *adj* необита́емый. **uninhibited** /ˌʌnɪn'hɪbɪtɪd/ *adj* нестеснённый. **uninspired** /ˌʌnɪn'spaɪəd/ *adj* бана́льный. **unintelligible** /ˌʌnɪn'telɪdʒɪb(ə)l/ *adj* непоня́тный. **unintentional** /ˌʌnɪn'tenʃən(ə)l/ *adj* нечая́нный. **unintentionally** /ˌʌnɪn'tenʃənəlɪ/ *adv* нечая́нно. **uninterested** /ʌn'ɪntrəstɪd/ *adj* незаинтересо́ванный. **uninteresting** /ʌn'ɪntrəstɪŋ/ *adj* неинтере́сный. **uninterrupted** /ˌʌnɪntə'rʌptɪd/ *adj* непреры́вный.

union /'juːnjən/ *n* (*alliance*) сою́з; (*joining together, alliance*) объедине́ние; (*trade* ~) профсою́з. **unionist** /'juːnjənɪst/ *n* член профсою́за; (*polit*) унионі́ст.

unique /jʊ'niːk/ *adj* уника́льный.

unison /'juːnɪs(ə)n/ *n*: **in** ~ (*mus*) в унисо́н; (*fig*) в согла́сии.

unit /'juːnɪt/ *n* едини́ца; (*mil*) часть.

unite /jʊ'naɪt/ *vt* & *i* соединя́ть(ся) *impf*, соедини́ть(ся) *pf*; объединя́ть(ся) *impf*, объедини́ть(ся) *pf*. **united** /jʊ'naɪtɪd/ *adj* соединённый, объединённый; **U~ Kingdom** Соединённое Короле́вство; **U~ Nations** Организа́ция Объединённых На́ций; **U~ States** Соединённые Шта́ты *m pl* Аме́рики. **unity** /'juːnɪtɪ/ *n* еди́нство.

universal /ˌjuːnɪ'vɜːs(ə)l/ *adj* всео́бщий; (*many-sided*) универса́льный. **universe** /'juːnɪˌvɜːs/ *n* вселе́нная *sb*; (*world*) мир.

university /ˌjuːnɪ'vɜːsɪtɪ/ *n* университе́т; *attrib* университе́тский.

unjust /ʌn'dʒʌst/ *adj* несправедли́вый. **unjustifiable** /ʌnˌdʒʌstɪ'faɪəb(ə)l/ *adj* непрости́тельный. **unjustified** /ʌn'dʒʌstɪˌfaɪd/ *adj* неопра́вданный.

unkempt /ʌn'kempt/ *adj* нечёсаный. **unkind** /ʌn'kaɪnd/ *adj* недо́брый, злой. **unknown** /ʌn'nəʊn/ *adj* неизве́стный.

unlawful /ʌn'lɔːfʊl/ *adj* незако́нный. **unleaded** /ʌn'ledɪd/ *adj* неэтили́рованный. **unleash** /ʌn'liːʃ/ *vt* (*also fig*) развя́зывать *impf*, развяза́ть *pf*.

unless /ən'les/ *conj* если... не.

unlike /ʌn'laɪk/ *adj* непохо́жий (на+*acc*); (*in contradistinction to*) в отли́чие от+*gen*. **unlikely** /ʌn'laɪklɪ/ *adj* маловероя́тный; **it is ~ that** вряд ли. **unlimited** /ʌn'lɪmɪtɪd/ *adj* неограни́ченный. **unlit** /ʌn'lɪt/ *adj* неосвещённый. **unload** /ʌn'ləʊd/ *vt* (*vehicle etc.*) разгружа́ть *impf*, разгрузи́ть *pf*; (*goods etc.*) выгружа́ть *impf*, вы́грузить *pf*. **unlock** /ʌn'lɒk/ *vt* отпира́ть *impf*, отпере́ть *pf*; открыва́ть *impf*, откры́ть *pf*. **unlucky** /ʌn'lʌkɪ/ *adj* (*number etc.*) несчастли́вый; (*unsuccessful*) неуда́чный.

unmanageable /ʌn'mænɪdʒəb(ə)l/ *adj* тру́дный, непоко́рный. **unmanned** /ʌn'mænd/ *adj* автомати́ческий. **unmarried** /ʌn'mærɪd/ *adj* холосто́й; (*of man*) нежена́тый; (*of woman*) незаму́жняя. **unmask** /ʌn'mɑːsk/ *vt* (*fig*) разоблача́ть *impf*, разоблачи́ть *pf*. **unmentionable** /ʌn'menʃənəb(ə)l/ *adj* неупомина́емый. **unmistakable** /ˌʌnmɪ'steɪkəb(ə)l/ *adj* несомне́нный, я́сный. **unmitigated** /ʌn'mɪtɪgeɪtɪd/ *adj* (*thorough*) отъя́вленный. **unmoved** /ʌn'muːvd/ *adj*: **be ~** остава́ться *impf*, оста́ться *pf* равноду́шен, -шна.

unnatural /ʌn'nætʃər(ə)l/ *adj* несте́ственный. **unnecessary** /ʌn'nesəsərɪ/ *adj* нену́жный. **unnerve** /ʌn'nɜːv/ *vt* лиша́ть *impf*, лиши́ть *pf* му́жества; (*upset*) расстра́ивать *impf*, расстро́ить *pf*. **unnoticed** /ʌn'nəʊtɪst/ *adj* незаме́ченный.

unobserved /ˌʌnəb'zɜːvd/ *adj* незаме́ченный. **unobtainable** /ˌʌnəb'teɪnəb(ə)l/ *adj* недосту́пный. **unobtrusive** /ˌʌnəb'truːsɪv/ *adj* скро́мный, ненавя́зчивый. **unoccupied** /ʌn'ɒkjʊˌpaɪd/ *adj* неза́нятый, свобо́дный; (*house*) пусто́й. **unofficial** /ˌʌnə'fɪʃ(ə)l/ *adj* неофициа́льный. **unopposed** /ˌʌnə'pəʊzd/ *adj* не встре́тивший сопротивле́ния. **unorthodox** /ʌn'ɔːθəˌdɒks/ *adj* неортодокса́льный.

unpack /ʌn'pæk/ *vt* распако́вывать *impf*, распакова́ть *pf*. **unpaid** /ʌn'peɪd/ *adj* (*bill*) неупла́ченный; (*person*) не получа́ющий пла́ты; (*work*) беспла́тный. **unpalatable** /ʌn'pælətəb(ə)l/ *adj* невку́сный; (*unpleasant*) неприя́тный. **unparalleled** /ʌn'pærəˌleld/ *adj* несравни́мый. **unpleasant** /ʌn'plez(ə)nt/ *adj* неприя́тный. **unpleasantness** /ʌn'plez(ə)ntnɪs/ *n* неприя́тность. **unpopular** /ʌn'pɒpjʊlə(r)/ *adj* непопуля́рный. **unprecedented** /ʌn'presɪˌdentɪd/ *adj* беспрецеде́нтный. **unpredictable** /ˌʌnprɪ'dɪktəb(ə)l/ *adj* непредсказу́емый. **unprejudiced** /ʌn'predʒʊdɪst/ *adj* беспристра́стный. **unprepared** /ˌʌnprɪ'peəd/ *adj* неподгото́вленный, негото́вый. **unprepossessing** /ˌʌnpriːpə'zesɪŋ/ *adj* непривлека́тельный. **unpretentious** /ˌʌnprɪ'tenʃəs/ *adj* просто́й, без прете́нзий. **unprincipled** /ʌn'prɪnsɪp(ə)ld/ *adj* беспринци́пный. **unproductive** /ˌʌnprə'dʌktɪv/ *adj* непродукти́вный. **unprofitable** /ʌn'prɒfɪtəb(ə)l/ *adj* невы́годный. **unpromising** /ʌn'prɒmɪsɪŋ/ *adj* малообеща́ющий. **unprotected** /ˌʌnprəˈtektɪd/ *adj* незащищённый. **unproven** /ʌnˈpruːvən/ *adj* недока́занный. **unprovoked** /ˌʌnprəˈvəʊkt/ *adj* непровоци́рованный. **unpublished** /ʌnˈpʌblɪʃt/ *adj* неопублико́ванный, неи́зданный. **unpunished** /ʌnˈpʌnɪʃt/ *adj* безнака́занный.

unqualified /ʌnˈkwɒlɪˌfaɪd/ *adj* неквалифици́рованный; (*unconditional*) безоговоро́чный. **unquestionable** /ʌnˈkwestʃənəb(ə)l/ *adj* несомне́нный, неоспори́мый. **unquestionably** /ʌnˈkwestʃənəblɪ/ *adv* несомне́нно, бесспо́рно.

unravel /ʌnˈræv(ə)l/ *vt & i* распу́тывать(ся) *impf*, распу́тать(ся) *pf*; *vt* (*solve*) разга́дывать *impf*, разгада́ть *pf*. **unread** /ʌnˈred/ *adj* (*book etc.*) непрочи́танный. **unreadable** /ʌnˈriːdəb(ə)l/ *adj* (*illegible*) неразбо́рчивый; (*boring*) неудобочита́емый. **unreal** /ʌnˈrɪəl/ *adj* нереа́льный. **unrealistic** /ˌʌnrɪəˈlɪstɪk/ *adj* нереа́льный. **unreasonable** /ʌnˈriːzənəb(ə)l/ *adj* (*person*) неразу́мный; (*behaviour, demand, price*) необосно́ванный. **unrecognizable** /ʌnˈrekəgˌnaɪzəb(ə)l/ *adj* неузнава́емый. **unrecognized** /ʌnˈrekəgˌnaɪzd/ *adj* непри́знанный. **unrefined** /ˌʌnrɪˈfaɪnd/ *adj* неочи́щенный; (*manners etc.*) гру́бый. **unrelated** /ˌʌnrɪˈleɪtɪd/ *adj* не име́ющий отноше́ния (**to** к+*dat*), несвя́занный (**to** с+*instr*); **we are ~** мы не ро́дственники. **unrelenting** /ˌʌnrɪˈlentɪŋ/ *adj* (*ruthless*) безжа́лостный; (*unremitting*) неосла́бный. **unreliable** /ˌʌnrɪˈlaɪəb(ə)l/ *adj* ненадёжный. **unremarkable** /ˌʌnrɪˈmɑːkəb(ə)l/ *adj* невыдаю́щийся. **unremitting** /ˌʌnrɪˈmɪtɪŋ/ *adj* неосла́бный; (*incessant*) беспреста́нный. **unrepentant** /ˌʌnrɪˈpent(ə)nt/ *adj* нераска́явшийся. **unrepresentative** /ˌʌnreprɪˈzentətɪv/ *adj* нетипи́чный. **unrequited** /ˌʌnrəˈkwaɪtɪd/ *adj*: **~ love** неразделённая любо́вь. **unreserved** /ˌʌnrɪˈzɜːvd/ *adj* (*full*) по́лный; (*open*) открове́нный; (*unconditional*) безоговоро́чный; (*seat*) незаброни́рованный. **unresolved** /ˌʌnrɪˈzɒlvd/ *adj* нерешённый. **unrest** /ʌnˈrest/ *n* беспоко́йство; (*polit*) волне́ния *neut pl*. **unrestrained** /ˌʌnrɪˈstreɪnd/ *adj* несде́ржанный. **unrestricted** /ˌʌnrɪˈstrɪktɪd/ *adj* неограни́ченный. **unripe** /ʌnˈraɪp/ *adj* незре́лый. **unrivalled** /ʌnˈraɪv(ə)ld/ *adj* бесподо́бный. **unroll** /ʌnˈrəʊl/ *vt & i* развёртывать(ся) *impf*, разверну́ть(ся) *pf*. **unruffled** /ʌnˈrʌf(ə)ld/ *adj* (*smooth*) гла́дкий; (*calm*) споко́йный. **unruly** /ʌnˈruːlɪ/ *adj* непоко́рный.

unsafe /ʌnˈseɪf/ *adj* опа́сный; (*insecure*) ненадёжный. **unsaid** /ʌnˈsed/ *adj*: **leave ~** молча́ть *impf* о+*prep*. **unsaleable** /ʌnˈseɪləb(ə)l/ *adj* нехо́дкий. **unsalted** /ʌnˈsɔːltɪd/ *adj* несолёный. **unsatisfactory** /ˌʌnsætɪsˈfæktərɪ/ *adj* неудовлетвори́тельный. **unsatisfied** /ʌnˈsætɪsfaɪd/ *adj* неудовлетворённый. **unsavoury** /ʌnˈseɪvərɪ/ *adj* (*unpleasant*) неприя́тный; (*disreputable*) сомни́тельный. **unscathed** /ʌnˈskeɪðd/ *adj* невреди́мый; (*predic*) цел и невреди́м. **unscheduled** /ʌnˈʃedjuːld/ *adj* (*transport*) внеочередно́й;

(*event*) незаплани́рованный. **unscientific** /ˌʌnsaɪən'tɪfɪk/ *adj* ненау́чный. **unscrew** /ʌn'skru:/ *vt* & *i* отви́нчивать(ся) *impf*, отвинти́ть(ся) *pf*. **unscrupulous** /ʌn'skru:pjʊləs/ *adj* беспринци́пный. **unseat** /ʌn'si:t/ *vt* (*of horse*) сбра́сывать *impf*, сбро́сить *pf* с седла́; (*parl*) лиша́ть *impf*, лиши́ть *pf* парла́ментского манда́та.

unseemly /ʌn'si:mlɪ/ *adj* неподоба́ющий. **unseen** /ʌn'si:n/ *adj* неви́данный. **unselfconscious** /ˌʌnself'kɒnʃəs/ *adj* непосре́дственный. **unselfish** /ʌn'selfɪʃ/ *adj* бескоры́стный. **unsettle** /ʌn'set(ə)l/ *vt* выбива́ть *impf*, вы́бить *pf* из колеи́; (*upset*) расстра́ивать *impf*, расстро́ить *pf*. **unsettled** /ʌn'set(ə)ld/ *adj* (*weather*) неусто́йчивый; (*unresolved*) нерешённый. **unsettling** /-'setlɪŋ/ *adj* волну́ющий. **unshakeable** /ʌn'ʃeɪkəb(ə)l/ *adj* непоколеби́мый. **unshaven** /ʌn'ʃeɪv(ə)n/ *adj* небри́тый. **unsightly** /ʌn'saɪtlɪ/ *adj* непригля́дный, уро́дливый. **unsigned** /ʌn'saɪnd/ *adj* неподпи́санный. **unskilful** /ʌn'skɪlfʊl/ *adj* неуме́лый. **unskilled** /ʌn'skɪld/ *adj* неквалифици́рованный. **unsociable** /ʌn'səʊʃəb(ə)l/ *adj* необщи́тельный. **unsold** /ʌn'səʊld/ *adj* непро́данный. **unsolicited** /ˌʌnsə'lɪsɪtɪd/ *adj* непро́шеный. **unsolved** /ʌn'sɒlvd/ *adj* нерешённый. **unsophisticated** /ˌʌnsə'fɪstɪˌkeɪtɪd/ *adj* просто́й. **unsound** /ʌn'saʊnd/ *adj* (*unhealthy, unwholesome*) нездоро́вый; (*not solid*) непро́чный; (*unfounded*) необосно́ванный; **of ~ mind** душевнобольно́й. **unspeakable** /ʌn'spi:kəb(ə)l/ *adj* (*inexpressible*) невырази́мый; (*very bad*) отврати́тельный. **unspecified** /ʌn'spesɪˌfaɪd/ *adj* то́чно не ука́занный, неопределённый. **unspoilt** /ʌn'spɔɪlt/ *adj* неиспо́рченный. **unspoken** /ʌn'spəʊkən/ *adj* невы́сказанный. **unstable** /ʌn'steɪb(ə)l/ *adj* неусто́йчивый; (*mentally*) неуравнове́шенный. **unsteady** /ʌn'stedɪ/ *adj* неусто́йчивый. **unstuck** /ʌn'stʌk/ *adj*: **come ~** откле́иваться *impf*, откле́иться *pf*; (*fig*) прова́ливаться *impf*, провали́ться *pf*. **unsuccessful** /ˌʌnsək'sesfʊl/ *adj* неуда́чный, безуспе́шный. **unsuitable** /ʌn'su:təb(ə)l/ *adj* неподходя́щий. **unsuited** /ʌn'su:tɪd/ *adj* неприго́дный. **unsung** /ʌn'sʌŋ/ *adj* невоспе́тый. **unsupported** /ˌʌnsə'pɔ:tɪd/ *adj* неподде́ржанный. **unsure** /ʌn'ʃʊə(r)/ *adj* неуве́ренный (**of o.s.** в себе́). **unsurpassed** /ˌʌnsə'pɑ:st/ *adj* непревзойдённый. **unsurprising** /ˌʌnsə'praɪzɪŋ/ *adj* неудиви́тельный. **unsuspected** /ˌʌnsə'spektɪd/ *adj* (*unforeseen*) непредви́денный. **unsuspecting** /ˌʌnsə'spektɪŋ/ *adj* неподозрева́ющий. **unsweetened** /ʌn'swi:t(ə)nd/ *adj* неподсла́щенный. **unswerving** /ʌn'swɜ:vɪŋ/ *adj* непоколеби́мый. **unsympathetic** /ˌʌnsɪmpə'θetɪk/ *adj* несочу́вствующий. **unsystematic** /ˌʌnsɪstə'mætɪk/ *adj* несистемати́чный.

untainted /ʌn'teɪntɪd/ *adj* неиспо́рченный. **untangle** /ʌn'tæŋg(ə)l/ *vt* распу́тывать *impf*, распу́тать *pf*. **untapped** /ʌn'tæpt/ *adj*: **~ resources** неиспо́льзованные ресу́рсы *m pl*. **untenable** /ʌn'tenəb(ə)l/ *adj* несостоя́тельный. **untested** /ʌn 'testɪd/ *adj* неиспы́танный. **unthinkable** /ʌn'θɪŋkəb(ə)l/ *adj* невообрази́мый. **unthinking** /ʌn 'θɪŋkɪŋ/ *adj* безду́мный. **untidiness** /ʌn'taɪdɪnɪs/ *n* неопря́тность; (*disorder*) беспоря́док. **untidy** /ʌn'taɪdɪ/ *adj* неопря́тный; (*in disorder*) в беспоря́дке. **untie** /ʌn'taɪ/ *vt* развя́зывать *impf*, развяза́ть *pf*; (*set free*) освобожда́ть *impf*, освободи́ть *pf*.

until /ən'tɪl/ *prep* до+*gen*; **not ~** не ра́ньше+*gen*; **~ then** до тех пор; *conj* пока́, пока́... не; **not ~** то́лько когда́.

untimely /ʌn'taɪmlɪ/ *adj* (*premature*) безвре́менный; (*inappropriate*) неуме́стный. **untiring** /ʌn'taɪərɪŋ/ *adj* неутоми́мый. **untold** /ʌn'təʊld/ *adj* (*incalculable*) бессчётный, несме́тный; (*inexpressible*) невырази́мый. **untouched** /ʌn'tʌtʃt/ *adj* нетро́нутый; (*indifferent*) равноду́шный. **untoward** /ˌʌntə'wɔːd/ *adj* неблагоприя́тный. **untrained** /ʌn'treɪnd/ *adj* необу́ченный. **untried** /ʌn'traɪd/ *adj* неиспы́танный. **untroubled** /ʌn 'trʌb(ə)ld/ *adj* споко́йный. **untrue** /ʌn'truː/ *adj* неве́рный. **untrustworthy** /ʌn'trʌstˌwɜːðɪ/ *adj* ненадёжный. **untruth** /ʌn'truːθ/ *n* непра́вда, ложь. **untruthful** /ʌn'truːθfʊl/ *adj* лжи́вый.

unusable /ʌn'juːzəb(ə)l/ *adj* неприго́дный. **unused** /ʌn'juːzd/ *adj* неиспо́льзованный; (*unaccustomed*) /ʌn'juːst/ непривы́кший (**to** к+*dat*); **I am ~ to this** я к э́тому не привы́к. **unusual** /ʌn'juːʒʊəl/ *adj* необыкнове́нный, необы́чный. **unusually** /ʌn'juːʒʊəlɪ/ *adv* необыкнове́нно. **unutterable** /ʌn 'ʌtərəb(ə)l/ *adj* невырази́мый.

unveil /ʌn'veɪl/ *vt* (*statue*) торже́ственно открыва́ть *impf*, откры́ть *pf*; (*disclose*) обнаро́довать *impf* & *pf*.

unwanted /ʌn'wɒntɪd/ *adj* нежела́нный. **unwarranted** /ʌn 'wɒrəntɪd/ *adj* неопра́вданный. **unwary** /ʌn'weərɪ/ *adj* неосторо́жный. **unwavering** /ʌn 'weɪvərɪŋ/ *adj* непоколеби́мый. **unwelcome** /ʌn'welkəm/ *adj* нежела́тельный; (*unpleasant*) неприя́тный. **unwell** /ʌn'wel/ *adj* нездоро́вый. **unwieldy** /ʌn 'wiːldɪ/ *adj* громо́здкий. **unwilling** /ʌn'wɪlɪŋ/ *adj* несклóнный; **be ~** не хоте́ть *impf*, за~ *pf* (**to** +*inf*). **unwillingly** /ʌn'wɪlɪŋlɪ/ *adv* неохо́тно. **unwillingness** /ʌn'wɪlɪŋnɪs/ *n* неохо́та. **unwind** /ʌn'waɪnd/ *vt* & *i* разма́тывать(ся) *impf*, размота́ть(ся) *pf*; (*rest*) отдыха́ть *impf*, отдохну́ть *pf*. **unwise** /ʌn'waɪz/ *adj* не(благо)разу́мный. **unwitting** /ʌn'wɪtɪŋ/ *adj* нево́льный. **unwittingly** /ʌn'wɪtɪŋlɪ/ *adv* нево́льно. **unworkable** /ʌn 'wɜːkəb(ə)l/ *adj* неримени́мый. **unworldly** /ʌn'wɜːldlɪ/ *adj* не от ми́ра сего́. **unworthy** /ʌn'wɜːðɪ/ *adj* недосто́йный. **unwrap** /ʌn 'ræp/ *vt* развёртывать *impf*, разверну́ть *pf*. **unwritten** /ʌn 'rɪt(ə)n/ *adj*: **~ law** непи́саный зако́н.

unyielding /ʌn'jiːldɪŋ/ *adj* упо́рный, неподáтливый.

unzip /ʌn'zɪp/ *vt* расстёгивать *impf*, расстегну́ть *pf* (мо́лнию+*gen*).

up /ʌp/ *adv* (*motion*) наве́рх, вверх; (*position*) наверху́, вверху́; **~ and down** вверх и вниз; (*back and forth*) взад и вперёд; **~ to** (*towards*) к+*dat*; (*as far as, until*) до+*gen*; **~ to**

now до сих пор; **be ~ against** иметь *impf* дело с+*instr*; **it is ~ to you**+*inf*, это вам+*inf*, вы должны+*inf*; **what's ~?** что случилось?; в чём дело?; **your time is ~** ваше время истекло; **~ and about** на ногах; **he isn't ~ yet** он ещё не встал; **he isn't ~ to this job** он не годится для этой работы; *prep* вверх по+*dat*; (*along*) (вдоль) по+*dat*; *vt* повышать *impf*, повысить; *vi* (*leap up*) взять *pf*; *adj*: **~-to-date** современный; (*fashionable*) модный; **~-and-coming** многообещающий; *n*: **~s and downs** (*fig*) превратности *f pl* судьбы.

upbringing /'ʌp,brɪŋɪŋ/ *n* воспитание.

update /ʌp'deɪt/ *vt* модернизировать *impf* & *pf*; (*a book etc.*) дополнять *impf*, дополнить *pf*.

upgrade /ʌp'greɪd/ *vt* повышать *impf*, повысить *pf* (по службе).

upheaval /ʌp'hi:v(ə)l/ *n* потрясение.

uphill /'ʌphɪl/ *adj* (*fig*) тяжёлый; *adv* в гору.

uphold /ʌp'həʊld/ *vt* поддерживать *impf*, поддержать *pf*.

upholster /ʌp'həʊlstə(r)/ *vt* обивать *impf*, обить *pf*. **upholsterer** /-rə(r)/ *n* обойщик. **upholstery** /-rɪ/ *n* обивка.

upkeep /'ʌpki:p/ *n* содержание.

upland /'ʌplənd/ *n* гористая часть страны; *adj* нагорный.

uplift /ʌp'lɪft/ *vt* поднимать *impf*, поднять *pf*.

up-market /ʌp'mɑ:kɪt/ *adj* дорогой.

upon /ə'pɒn/ *prep* (*position*) на +*prep*, (*motion*) на+*acc*; *see* **on**

upper /'ʌpə(r)/ *adj* верхний; (*socially, in rank*) высший; **gain the ~ hand** одерживать *impf*, одержать *pf* верх (**over** над+*instr*); *n* передок. **uppermost** *adj* самый верхний, высший; **be ~ in person's mind** больше всего занимать *impf*, занять *pf* мысли кого-л.

upright /'ʌpraɪt/ *n* стойка; *adj* вертикальный; (*honest*) честный; **~ piano** пианино *neut indecl*.

uprising /'ʌp,raɪzɪŋ/ *n* восстание.

uproar /'ʌprɔ:(r)/ *n* шум, гам.

uproot /ʌp'ru:t/ *vt* вырывать *impf*, вырвать *pf* с корнем; (*people*) выселять *impf*, выселить *pf*.

upset *n* /'ʌpset/ расстройство; *vt* /ʌp'set/ расстраивать *impf*, расстроить *pf*; (*overturn*) опрокидывать *impf*, опрокинуть *pf*; *adj* (*miserable*) расстроенный; **~ stomach** расстройство желудка.

upshot /'ʌpʃɒt/ *n* развязка, результат.

upside-down /,ʌpsaɪd'daʊn/ *adj* перевёрнутый вверх дном; *adv* вверх дном; (*in disorder*) в беспорядке.

upstairs /ʌp'steəz/ *adv* (*position*) наверху; (*motion*) наверх; *n* верхний этаж; *adj* находящийся в верхнем этаже.

upstart /'ʌpstɑ:t/ *n* выскочка *m* & *f*.

upstream /'ʌpstri:m/ *adv* против течения; (*situation*) вверх по течению.

upsurge /'ʌpsɜ:dʒ/ *n* подъём, волна.

uptake /'ʌpteɪk/ *n*: **be quick on the ~** быстро соображать *impf*, сообразить *pf*.

upturn /'ʌptɜ:n/ *n* (*fig*) улучшение. **upturned** /-tɜ:nd/ *adj* (*face etc.*) по́днятый кве́рху; (*inverted*) перевёрнутый.

upward /ˈʌpwəd/ *adj* напра́вленный вверх. **upwards** /-wədz/ *adv* вверх; ~ **of** свы́ше+*gen*.

uranium /jʊˈreɪnɪəm/ *n* ура́н.

urban /ˈɜ:bən/ *adj* городско́й.

urbane /ɜ:ˈbeɪn/ *adj* ве́жливый.

urchin /ˈɜ:tʃɪn/ *n* мальчи́шка *m*.

urge /ɜ:dʒ/ *n* (*incitement*) побужде́ние; (*desire*) жела́ние; *vt* (*impel*, ~ *on*) подгоня́ть *impf*, подогна́ть *pf*; (*warn*) предупрежда́ть *impf*, предупреди́ть *pf*; (*try to persuade*) убежда́ть *impf*. **urgency** /ˈɜ:dʒ(ə)nsɪ/ *n* сро́чность, ва́жность; **a matter of great** ~ сро́чное де́ло. **urgent** /ˈɜ:dʒ(ə)nt/ *adj* сро́чный; (*insistent*) настоя́тельный. **urgently** /ˈɜ:dʒ(ə)ntlɪ/ *adv* сро́чно.

urinate /ˈjʊərɪˌneɪt/ *vi* мочи́ться *impf*, по~ *pf*. **urine** /ˈjʊərɪn/ *n* моча́.

urn /ɜ:n/ *n* у́рна.

US(A) *abbr* (*of* **United States of America**) США, Соединённые Шта́ты Аме́рики.

usable /ˈju:zəb(ə)l/ *adj* го́дный к употребле́нию. **usage** /ˈju:sɪdʒ/ *n* употребле́ние; (*treatment*) обраще́ние. **use** *n* /ju:s/ (*utilization*) употребле́ние, по́льзование; (*benefit*) по́льза; (*application*) примене́ние; **it is no ~ (-ing)** бесполе́зно (+*inf*); **make ~ of** испо́льзовать *impf* & *pf*; по́льзоваться *impf* +*instr*; *vt* /ju:z/ употребля́ть *impf*, употреби́ть *pf*; по́льзоваться *impf* +*instr*; (*apply*) применя́ть *impf*, примени́ть *pf*; (*treat*) обраща́ться *impf* с+*instr*; **I ~d to see him often** я ча́сто его́ встреча́л; **be, get ~d to** привыка́ть *impf*, привы́кнуть *pf* (**to** к+*dat*); **~ up** расхо́довать *impf*, из~ *pf*. **used** /ju:zd/ *adj* (*second-hand*) ста́рый. **useful** /ˈju:sfʊl/ *adj* поле́зный; **come in ~, prove ~** пригоди́ться *pf* (**to** +*dat*). **useless** /ˈju:slɪs/ *adj* бесполе́зный. **user** /ˈju:zə(r)/ *n* потреби́тель *m*.

usher /ˈʌʃə(r)/ *n* (*theat*) билетёр; *vt* (*lead in*) вводи́ть *impf*, ввести́ *pf*; (*proclaim*, ~ *in*) возвеща́ть *impf*, возвести́ть *pf*. **usherette** /ˌʌʃəˈret/ *n* билетёрша.

USSR *abbr* (*of* **Union of Soviet Socialist Republics**) СССР, Сою́з Сове́тских Социалисти́ческих Респу́блик.

usual /ˈju:ʒʊəl/ *adj* обыкнове́нный, обы́чный; **as ~** как обы́чно. **usually** /-lɪ/ *adv* обыкнове́нно, обы́чно.

usurp /jʊˈzɜ:p/ *vt* узурпи́ровать *impf* & *pf*. **usurper** /-ˈzɜ:pə(r)/ *n* узурпа́тор.

usury /ˈju:ʒərɪ/ *n* ростовщи́чество.

utensil /ju:ˈtens(ə)l/ *n* инструме́нт; *pl* у́тварь, посу́да.

uterus /ˈju:tərəs/ *n* ма́тка.

utilitarian /ˌjʊtɪlɪˈteərɪən/ *adj* утилита́рный. **utilitarianism** /-ˌnɪz(ə)m/ *n* утилитари́зм. **utility** /ju:ˈtɪlɪtɪ/ *n* поле́зность; *pl*: **public utilities** коммуна́льные услу́ги *f pl*. **utilize** /ˈju:tɪˌlaɪz/ *vt* испо́льзовать *impf* & *pf*.

utmost /ˈʌtməʊst/ *adj* (*extreme*) кра́йний; **this is of the ~ importance to me** э́то для меня́ кра́йне ва́жно; *n*: **do one's ~** де́лать *impf*, с~ *pf* всё возмо́жное.

Utopia /ju:ˈtəʊpɪə/ *n* уто́пия. **utopian** /-pɪən/ *adj* утопи́ческий.

utter /ˈʌtə(r)/ *attrib* по́лный, абсолю́тный; (*out-and-out*) отъя́вленный (*coll*); *vt* произноси́ть *impf*, произнести́ *pf*; (*let out*) издава́ть *impf*, изда́ть *pf*. **utterance** /ˈʌtərəns/ *n* (*uttering*) произнесе́ние; (*pronouncement*) выска́зывание. **utterly** /ˈʌtəlɪ/ *adv* соверше́нно.

Uzbek /ˈʌzbek/ *n* узбе́к, -е́чка. **Uzbekistan** /ˌʌzbekɪˈstɑːn/ *n* Узбекиста́н.

V

vacancy /ˈveɪkənsɪ/ *n* (*for job*) вака́нсия, свобо́дное ме́сто; (*at hotel*) свобо́дный но́мер. **vacant** /-kənt/ *adj* (*post*) вака́нтный; (*post*; *not engaged*, *free*) свобо́дный; (*empty*) пусто́й; (*look*) отсу́тствующий. **vacate** /vəˈkeɪt/ *vt* освобожда́ть *impf*, освободи́ть *pf*. **vacation** /vəˈkeɪʃ(ə)n/ *n* кани́кулы (-л) *pl*; (*leave*) о́тпуск.

vaccinate /ˈvæksɪˌneɪt/ *vt* вакцини́ровать *impf* & *pf*. **vaccination** /-ˈneɪʃ(ə)n/ *n* приви́вка (**against** от, про́тив +*gen*). **vaccine** /ˈvæksiːn/ *n* вакци́на.

vacillate /ˈvæsɪˌleɪt/ *vi* колеба́ться *impf*. **vacillation** /-ˈleɪʃ(ə)n/ *n* колеба́ние.

vacuous /ˈvækjʊəs/ *adj* пусто́й. **vacuum** /ˈvækjʊəm/ *n* ва́куум; (*fig*) пустота́; *vt* пылесо́сить *impf*, про~ *pf*; ~ **cleaner** пылесо́с; ~ **flask** те́рмос.

vagabond /ˈvægəˌbɒnd/ *n* бродя́га *m*.

vagary /ˈveɪgərɪ/ *n* капри́з.

vagina /vəˈdʒaɪnə/ *n* влага́лище.

vagrant /ˈveɪgrənt/ *n* бродя́га *m*.

vague /veɪg/ *adj* (*indeterminate*, *uncertain*) неопределённый; (*unclear*) нея́сный; (*dim*) сму́тный; (*absent-minded*) рассе́янный. **vagueness** /-nɪs/ *n* неопределённость, нея́сность; (*absent-mindedness*) рассе́янность.

vain /veɪn/ *adj* (*futile*) тще́тный, напра́сный; (*empty*) пусто́й; (*conceited*) тщесла́вный; **in** ~ напра́сно.

vale /veɪl/ *n* дол, доли́на.

valentine /ˈvælənˌtaɪn/ *n* (*card*) поздрави́тельная ка́рточка с днём свято́го Валенти́на.

valet /ˈvæleɪ/ *n* камерди́нер.

valiant /ˈvæljənt/ *adj* хра́брый.

valid /ˈvælɪd/ *adj* действи́тельный; (*weighty*) ве́ский. **validate** /-ˌdeɪt/ *vt* (*ratify*) утвержда́ть *impf*, утверди́ть *pf*. **validity** /vəˈlɪdɪtɪ/ *n* действи́тельность; (*weightiness*) ве́скость.

valley /ˈvælɪ/ *n* доли́на.

valour /ˈvælə(r)/ *n* до́блесть.

valuable /ˈvæljʊəb(ə)l/ *adj* це́нный; *n pl* це́нности *f pl*. **valuation** /ˌvæljʊˈeɪʃ(ə)n/ *n* оце́нка. **value** /ˈvæljuː/ *n* це́нность; (*math*) величина́; *pl* це́нности *f pl*; ~**-added tax** нало́г на доба́вленную сто́имость; ~ **judgement** субъекти́вная оце́нка; *vt* (*estimate*) оце́нивать *impf*, оцени́ть *pf*; (*hold dear*) цени́ть *impf*.

valve /vælv/ *n* (*tech*, *med*, *mus*) кла́пан; (*tech*) ве́нтиль *m*; (*radio*) электро́нная ла́мпа.

vampire /ˈvæmpaɪə(r)/ *n* вампи́р.

van /væn/ *n* фурго́н.

vandal /ˈvænd(ə)l/ *n*ванда́л. **vandalism** /-dəˌlɪz(ə)m/ *n* вандали́зм. **vandalize** /-dəˌlaɪz/ *vt* разруша́ть *impf*, разру́шить *pf*.

vanguard /ˈvængɑːd/ *n* авангáрд.
vanilla /vəˈnɪlə/ *n* ванúль.
vanish /ˈvænɪʃ/ *vi* исчезáть *impf*, исчéзнуть *pf*.
vanity /ˈvænɪtɪ/ *n* (*futility*) тщетá; (*conceit*) тщеслáвие.
vanquish /ˈvæŋkwɪʃ/ *vt* побеждáть *impf*, победúть *pf*.
vantage-point /ˈvɑːntɪdʒˌpɔɪnt/ *n* (*mil*) наблюдáтельный пункт; (*fig*) вы́годная позúция.
vapour /ˈveɪpə(r)/ *n* пар.
variable /ˈveərɪəb(ə)l/ *adj* изменчивый; (*weather*) неустóйчивый, перемéнный; *n* (*math*) перемéнная (величинá). **variance** /ˈveərɪəns/ *n*: **be at ~ with** (*contradict*) противорéчить *impf* +*dat*; (*disagree*) расходúться *impf*, разойтúсь *pf* во мнéниях с+*instr*. **variant** /-rɪənt/ *n* вариáнт. **variation** /-rɪˈeɪʃ(ə)n/ *n* (*varying*) изменéние; (*variant*) вариáнт; (*variety*) разновúдность; (*mus*) вариáция.
varicose /ˈværɪˌkəʊs/ *adj*: **~ veins** расширéние вен.
varied /ˈveərɪd/ *adj* разнообрáзный. **variegated** /ˈveərɪˌgeɪtɪd/ *adj* разноцвéтный. **variety** /vəˈraɪətɪ/ *n* разнообрáзие; (*sort*) разновúдность; (*a number*) ряд; **~ show** варьетé *neut indecl*. **various** /ˈveərɪəs/ *adj* рáзный.
varnish /ˈvɑːnɪʃ/ *n* лак; *vt* лакировáть *impf*, от~ *pf*.
vary /ˈveərɪ/ *vt* разнообрáзить *impf*, менять *impf*; *vi* (*change*) менятьcя *impf*; (*differ*) рáзниться *impf*.
vase /vɑːz/ *n* вáза.
Vaseline /ˈvæsɪˌliːn/ *n* (*propr*) вазелúн.
vast /vɑːst/ *adj* громáдный. **vastly** /-lɪ/ *adv* значúтельно.
VAT *abbr* (*of* **value-added tax**) налóг на добáвленную стóимость.
vat /væt/ *n* чан, бак.
vaudeville /ˈvɔːdəvɪl/ *n* водевúль *m*.
vault[1] /vɔːlt/ *n* (*leap*) прыжóк; *vt* перепры́гивать *impf*, перепры́гнуть *pf*; *vi* пры́гать *impf*, пры́гнуть *pf*.
vault[2] /vɔːlt/ *n* (*arch, covering*) свод; (*cellar*) пóгреб; (*tomb*) склеп. **vaulted** /-tɪd/ *adj* сводчáтый.
VDU *abbr* (*of* **visual display unit**) монитóр.
veal /viːl/ *n* телятина.
vector /ˈvektə(r)/ *n* (*math*) вéктор.
veer /vɪə(r)/ *vi* (*change direction*) изменять *impf*, изменúть *pf* направлéние; (*turn*) поворáчивать *impf*, поворотúть *pf*.
vegetable /ˈvedʒɪtəb(ə)l/ *n* óвощ; *adj* овощнóй. **vegetarian** /ˌvedʒɪˈteərɪən/ *n* вегетариáнец, -нка; *attrib* вегетариáнский. **vegetate** /ˈvedʒɪˌteɪt/ *vi* (*fig*) прозябáть *impf*. **vegetation** /ˌvedʒɪˈteɪʃ(ə)n/ *n* растúтельность.
vehemence /ˈviːəməns/ *n* (*force*) сúла; (*passion*) стрáстность. **vehement** /-mənt/ *adj* (*forceful*) сúльный; (*passionate*) стрáстный.
vehicle /ˈviːɪk(ə)l/ *n* трáнспортное срéдство; (*motor ~*) автомобúль *m*; (*medium*) срéдство.
veil /veɪl/ *n* вуáль; (*fig*) завéса. **veiled** /veɪld/ *adj* скры́тый.
vein /veɪn/ *n* вéна; (*of leaf; streak*) жúлка; **in the same ~** в том же дýхе.
velocity /vɪˈlɒsɪtɪ/ *n* скóрость.
velvet /ˈvelvɪt/ *n* бáрхат; *adj* бáрхатный. **velvety** /-tɪ/ *adj* бархатúстый.

vending-machine /'vendıŋ/ *n* торго́вый автома́т. **vendor** /-də(r)/ *n* продаве́ц, -вщи́ца.

vendetta /ven'detə/ *n* венде́тта.

veneer /vı'nıə(r)/ *n* фане́ра; (*fig*) лоск.

venerable /'venərəb(ə)l/ *adj* почте́нный. **venerate** /-ˌreıt/ *vt* благогове́ть *impf* пе́ред+*instr*. **veneration** /ˌvenə'reıʃ(ə)n/ *n* благогове́ние.

venereal /vı'nıərıəl/ *adj* венери́ческий.

venetian blind /vı'ni:ʃ(ə)n blaınd/ *n* жалюзи́ *neut indecl*.

vengeance /'vendʒ(ə)ns/ *n* месть; **take ~** мстить *impf*, ото~ *pf* (**on** +*dat*; **for** за+*acc*); **with a ~** вовсю́. **vengeful** /'vendʒfʊl/ *adj* мсти́тельный.

venison /'venıs(ə)n/ *n* олени́на.

venom /'venəm/ *n* яд. **venomous** /-məs/ *adj* ядови́тый.

vent[1] /vent/ *n* (*opening*) вы́ход (*also fig*), отве́рстие; *vt* (*feelings*) дава́ть *impf*, дать *pf* вы́ход+*dat*; излива́ть *impf*, изли́ть *pf* (**on** на+*acc*).

vent[2] /vent/ *n* (*slit*) разре́з.

ventilate /'ventıˌleıt/ *vt* прове́тривать *impf*, прове́трить *pf*. **ventilation** /-'leıʃ(ə)n/ *n* вентиля́ция. **ventilator** /'ventıˌleıtə(r)/ *n* вентиля́тор.

ventriloquist /ven'trıləˌkwıst/ *n* чревовеща́тель *m*.

venture /'ventʃə(r)/ *n* предприя́тие; *vi* (*dare*) осме́ливаться *impf*, осме́литься *pf*; *vt* (*risk*) рискова́ть *impf* +*instr*.

venue /'venju:/ *n* ме́сто.

veranda /və'rændə/ *n* вера́нда.

verb /vɜ:b/ *n* глаго́л. **verbal** /'vɜ:b(ə)l/ *adj* (*oral*) у́стный; (*relating to words*) слове́сный; (*gram*) отглаго́льный. **verbatim** /vɜ:'beıtım/ *adj* досло́вный; *adv* досло́вно. **verbose** /vɜ:'bəʊs/ *adj* многосло́вный.

verdict /'vɜ:dıkt/ *n* пригово́р.

verge /vɜ:dʒ/ *n* (*also fig*) край; (*of road*) обо́чина; (*fig*) грань; **on the ~ of** на гра́ни+*gen*; **he was on the ~ of telling all** он чуть не рассказа́л всё; *vi*: **~ on** грани́чить *impf* с+*instr*.

verification /ˌverıfı'keıʃ(ə)n/ *n* прове́рка; (*confirmation*) подтвержде́ние. **verify** /'verıˌfaı/ *vt* проверя́ть *impf*, прове́рить *pf*; (*confirm*) подтвержда́ть *impf*, подтверди́ть *pf*.

vermin /'vɜ:mın/ *n* вреди́тели *m pl*.

vernacular /və'nækjʊlə(r)/ *n* родно́й язы́к; ме́стный диале́кт; (*homely language*) разгово́рный язы́к.

versatile /'vɜ:səˌtaıl/ *adj* многосторо́нний.

verse /vɜ:s/ *n* (*also bibl*) стих; (*stanza*) строфа́; (*poetry*) стихи́ *m pl*. **versed** /vɜ:st/ *adj* о́пытный, све́дущий (**in** в+*prep*).

version /'vɜ:ʃ(ə)n/ *n* (*variant*) вариа́нт; (*interpretation*) ве́рсия; (*text*) текст.

versus /'vɜ:səs/ *prep* про́тив+*gen*.

vertebra /'vɜ:tıbrə/ *n* позвоно́к; *pl* позвоно́чник. **vertebrate** /-brət/ *n* позвоно́чное живо́тное *sb*.

vertical /'vɜ:tık(ə)l/ *adj* вертика́льный; *n* вертика́ль.

vertigo /'vɜ:tıˌgəʊ/ *n* головокруже́ние.

verve /vɜ:v/ *n* жи́вость, энтузиа́зм.

very /'verı/ *adj* (*that ~ same*) тот са́мый; (*this ~ same*) э́тот са́мый; **at that ~ moment** в тот са́мый моме́нт; (*precisely*) как раз; **you are the ~ person I was**

looking for как раз вас я искáл; **the ~** (*even the*) дáже, оди́н; **the ~ thought frightens me** однá, дáже, мысль об э́том меня́ пугáет; (*the extreme*) сáмый; **at the ~ end** в сáмом концé; *adv* óчень; **~ much** óчень; **~ much** +*comp* горáздо +*comp*; **~**+*superl*, *superl*; **~ first** сáмый пéрвый; **~ well** (*agreement*) хорошó, лáдно; **not ~** не óчень, довóльно +*neg*.

vessel /'ves(ə)l/ *n* сосýд; (*ship*) сýдно.

vest¹ /vest/ *n* мáйка; (*waistcoat*) жилéт.

vest² /vest/ *vt* (*with power*) облекáть *impf*, облéчь *pf* (**with** +*instr*). **vested** /-tɪd/ *adj*: **~ interest** ли́чная заинтересóванность; **~ interests** (*entrepreneurs*) крýпные предпринимáтели *m pl*.

vestibule /'vestɪ,bju:l/ *n* вестибю́ль *m*.

vestige /'vestɪdʒ/ *n* (*trace*) след; (*sign*) при́знак.

vestments /'vestmənts/ *n pl* (*eccl*) облачéние. **vestry** /'vestrɪ/ *n* ри́зница.

vet /vet/ *n* ветеринáр; *vt* (*fig*) проверя́ть *impf*, провéрить *pf*.

veteran /'vetərən/ *n* ветерáн; *adj* стáрый.

veterinary /'vetə,rɪnərɪ/ *adj* ветеринáрный; *n* ветеринáр.

veto /'vi:təʊ/ *n* вéто *neut indecl*; *vt* налагáть *impf*, наложи́ть *pf* вéто на+*acc*.

vex /veks/ *vt* досаждáть *impf*, досади́ть *pf* +*dat*. **vexation** /vek'seɪʃ(ə)n/ *n* досáда. **vexed** /vekst/ *adj* (*annoyed*) серди́тый; (*question*) спóрный. **vexatious, vexing** /vek'seɪʃəs, 'veksɪŋ/ *adj* досáдный.

via /'vaɪə/ *prep* чéрез+*acc*.

viable /'vaɪəb(ə)l/ *adj* (*able to survive*) жизнеспосóбный; (*feasible*) осуществи́мый.

viaduct /'vaɪə,dʌkt/ *n* виадýк.

vibrant /'vaɪbrənt/ *adj* (*lively*) живóй. **vibrate** /vaɪ'breɪt/ *vi* вибри́ровать *impf*; *vt* (*make ~*) заставля́ть *impf*, застáвить *pf* вибри́ровать. **vibration** /vaɪ'breɪʃ(ə)n/ *n* вибрáция. **vibrato** /vɪ'brɑ:təʊ/ *n* вибрáто *neut indecl*.

vicar /'vɪkə(r)/ *n* прихóдский свящéнник. **vicarage** /-rɪdʒ/ *n* дом свящéнника.

vicarious /vɪ'keərɪəs/ *adj* чужóй.

vice¹ /vaɪs/ *n* (*evil*) порóк.

vice² /vaɪs/ *n* (*tech*) тиски́ (-кóв) *pl*.

vice- *in comb* вице-, замести́тель *m*; **~-chairman** замести́тель *m* председáтеля; **~-chancellor** (*univ*) прорéктор; **~-president** вице-президéнт. **viceroy** /'vaɪsrɔɪ/ *n* вице-корóль *m*.

vice versa /,vaɪsɪ 'vɜ:sə/ *adv* наоборóт.

vicinity /vɪ'sɪnɪtɪ/ *n* окрéстность; **in the ~** поблúзости (**of** от+*gen*).

vicious /'vɪʃəs/ *adj* злóбный; **~ circle** порóчный круг.

vicissitude /vɪ'sɪsɪ,tju:d/ *n* превpáтность.

victim /'vɪktɪm/ *n* жéртва; (*of accident*) пострадáвший *sb*. **victimization** /,vɪktɪmaɪ'zeɪʃ(ə)n/ *n* преслéдование. **victimize** /'vɪktɪ,maɪz/ *vt* преслéдовать *impf*.

victor /'vɪktə(r)/ *n* победи́тель *m*, **~**ница.

Victorian /vɪk'tɔ:rɪən/ *adj* викториáнский.

victorious /vɪk'tɔ:rɪəs/ *adj* победонóсный. **victory** /'vɪktərɪ/ *n* побе́да.

video /ˈvɪdɪəʊ/ *n* (~ *recorder*, ~ *cassette*, ~ *film*) ви́део *neut indecl*; **~ camera** видеока́мера; **~ cassette** видеокассе́та; **~ (cassette) recorder** видеомагнитофо́н; **~ game** видеоигра́; *vt* запи́сывать *impf*, записа́ть *pf* на ви́део.

vie /vaɪ/ *vi* сопе́рничать *impf* (**with** с+*instr*; **for** в+*prep*).

Vietnam /ˌvɪetˈnæm/ *n* Вьетна́м. **Vietnamese** /ˌvɪetnəˈmiːz/ *n* вьетна́мец, -мка; *adj* вьетна́мский.

view /vjuː/ *n* (*prospect*, *picture*) вид; (*opinion*) взгляд; (*viewing*) просмо́тр; (*inspection*) осмо́тр; **in ~ of** ввиду́+*gen*; **on ~** вы́ставленный для обозре́ния; **with a ~ to** с це́лью+*gen*, +*inf*; *vt* (*pictures etc.*) рассма́тривать *impf*; (*inspect*) осма́тривать *impf*, осмотре́ть *pf*; (*mentally*) смотре́ть *impf* на+*acc*. **viewer** /ˈvjuːə(r)/ *n* зри́тель *m*, ~ница. **viewfinder** /ˈvjuːˌfaɪndə(r)/ *n* видоиска́тель *m*. **viewpoint** *n* то́чка зре́ния.

vigil /ˈvɪdʒɪl/ *n* бде́ние; **keep ~** дежу́рить *impf*. **vigilance** /-ləns/ *n* бди́тельность. **vigilant** /-lənt/ *adj* бди́тельный. **vigilante** /ˌvɪdʒɪˈlæntɪ/ *n* дружи́нник.

vigorous /ˈvɪgərəs/ *adj* си́льный, энерги́чный. **vigour** /ˈvɪgə(r)/ *n* си́ла, эне́ргия.

vile /vaɪl/ *adj* гну́сный. **vilify** /ˈvɪlɪˌfaɪ/ *vt* черни́ть *impf*, о~ *pf*.

villa /ˈvɪlə/ *n* ви́лла.

village /ˈvɪlɪdʒ/ *n* дере́вня; *attrib* дереве́нский. **villager** /-dʒə(r)/ *n* жи́тель *m* дере́вни.

villain /ˈvɪlən/ *n* злоде́й.

vinaigrette /ˌvɪnɪˈgret/ *n* припра́ва из у́ксуса и оли́вкового ма́сла.

vindicate /ˈvɪndɪˌkeɪt/ *vt* опра́вдывать *impf*, оправда́ть *pf*. **vindication** /-ˈkeɪʃ(ə)n/ *n* оправда́ние.

vindictive /vɪnˈdɪktɪv/ *adj* мсти́тельный.

vine /vaɪn/ *n* виногра́дная лоза́.

vinegar /ˈvɪnɪgə(r)/ *n* у́ксус.

vineyard /ˈvɪnjəd/ *n* виногра́дник.

vintage /ˈvɪntɪdʒ/ *n* (*year*) год; (*fig*) вы́пуск; *attrib* (*wine*) ма́рочный; (*car*) архаи́ческий.

viola /vɪˈəʊlə/ *n* (*mus*) альт.

violate /ˈvaɪəˌleɪt/ *vt* (*treaty*, *privacy*) наруша́ть *impf*, нару́шить *pf*; (*grave*) оскверня́ть *impf*, оскверни́ть *pf*. **violation** /-ˈleɪʃ(ə)n/ *n* наруше́ние; оскверне́ние.

violence /ˈvaɪələns/ *n* (*physical coercion*, *force*) наси́лие; (*strength*, *force*) си́ла. **violent** /-lənt/ *adj* (*person*, *storm*, *argument*) свире́пый; (*pain*) си́льный; (*death*) наси́льственный. **violently** /-ləntlɪ/ *adv* си́льно, о́чень.

violet /ˈvaɪələt/ *n* (*bot*) фиа́лка; (*colour*) фиоле́товый цвет; *adj* фиоле́товый.

violin /ˌvaɪəˈlɪn/ *n* скри́пка. **violinist** /-nɪst/ *n* скрипа́ч, ~ка.

VIP *abbr* (*of* **very important person**) о́чень ва́жное лицо́.

viper /ˈvaɪpə(r)/ *n* гадю́ка.

virgin /ˈvɜːdʒɪn/ *n* де́вственница, (*male*) де́вственник; **V~ Mary** де́ва Мари́я. **virginal** /-n(ə)l/ *adj* де́вственный. **virginity** /vəˈdʒɪnɪtɪ/ *n* де́вственность. **Virgo** /ˈvɜːgəʊ/ *n* Де́ва.

virile /ˈvɪraɪl/ *adj* му́жественный. **virility** /-ˈrɪlɪtɪ/ *n* му́жество.

virtual /ˈvɜːtjʊəl/ *adj* факти́ческий; (*comput*) виртуа́льный. **virtually** /-lɪ/ *adv* факти́чески. **virtue** /ˈvɜːtjuː/ *n* (*excellence*) доброде́тель; (*merit*) досто́инство; **by ~ of** на основа́нии+*gen*. **virtuosity** /ˌvɜːtjʊˈɒsɪtɪ/ *n* виртуо́зность. **virtuoso** /ˌvɜːtjʊˈəʊsəʊ/ *n* виртуо́з. **virtuous** /ˈvɜːtjʊəs/ *adj* доброде́тельный.

virulent /ˈvɪrʊlənt/ *adj* (*med*) виру́лентный; (*fig*) зло́бный.

virus /ˈvaɪərəs/ *n* ви́рус.

visa /ˈviːzə/ *n* ви́за.

vis-à-vis /ˌviːzɑːˈviː/ *prep* (*with regard to*) по отноше́нию к+*dat*.

viscount /ˈvaɪkaʊnt/ *n* вико́нт. **viscountess** /-tɪs/ *n* вико́нте́сса.

viscous /ˈvɪskəs/ *adj* вя́зкий.

visibility /ˌvɪzɪˈbɪlɪtɪ/ *n* ви́димость. **visible** /ˈvɪzɪb(ə)l/ *adj* ви́димый. **visibly** /ˈvɪzɪblɪ/ *adv* я́вно, заме́тно.

vision /ˈvɪʒ(ə)n/ *n* (*sense*) зре́ние; (*apparition*) виде́ние; (*dream*) мечта́; (*insight*) проница́тельность. **visionary** /ˈvɪʒənərɪ/ *adj* (*unreal*) при́зрачный; (*impracticable*) неосуществи́мый; (*insightful*) проница́тельный; *n* (*dreamer*) мечта́тель *m*.

visit /ˈvɪzɪt/ *n* посеще́ние, визи́т; *vt* посеща́ть *impf*, посети́ть *pf*; (*call on*) заходи́ть *impf*, зайти́ *pf* к+*dat*. **visitation** /ˌvɪzɪˈteɪʃ(ə)n/ *n* официа́льное посеще́ние. **visitor** /ˈvɪzɪtə(r)/ *n* гость *m*, посети́тель *m*.

visor /ˈvaɪzə(r)/ *n* (*of cap*) козырёк; (*in car*) солнцезащи́тный щито́к; (*of helmet*) забра́ло.

vista /ˈvɪstə/ *n* перспекти́ва, вид.

visual /ˈvɪzjʊəl/ *adj* (*of vision*) зри́тельный; (*graphic*) нагля́дный; **~ aids** нагля́дные посо́бия *neut pl*. **visualize** /-ˌlaɪz/ *vt* представля́ть *impf*, предста́вить *pf* себе́.

vital /ˈvaɪt(ə)l/ *adj* абсолю́тно необходи́мый (**to, for** для+*gen*); (*essential to life*) жи́зненный; **of ~ importance** первостепе́нной ва́жности. **vitality** /vaɪˈtælɪtɪ/ *n* (*liveliness*) эне́ргия. **vitally** /ˈvaɪtəlɪ/ *adv* жи́зненно.

vitamin /ˈvɪtəmɪn/ *n* витами́н.

vitreous /ˈvɪtrɪəs/ *adj* стекля́нный.

vitriolic /ˌvɪtrɪˈɒlɪk/ *adj* (*fig*) е́дкий.

vivacious /vɪˈveɪʃəs/ *adj* живо́й. **vivacity** /vɪˈvæsɪtɪ/ *n* жи́вость.

viva (voce) /ˈvaɪvə (ˈvəʊtʃɪ)/ *n* у́стный экза́мен.

vivid /ˈvɪvɪd/ *adj* (*bright*) я́ркий; (*lively*) живо́й. **vividness** /-nɪs/ *n* я́ркость; жи́вость.

vivisection /ˌvɪvɪˈsekʃ(ə)n/ *n* вивисе́кция.

vixen /ˈvɪks(ə)n/ *n* лиси́ца-са́мка.

viz. /vɪz/ *adv* то есть, а и́менно.

vocabulary /vəˈkæbjʊlərɪ/ *n* (*range, list, of words*) слова́рь *m*; (*range of words*) запа́с слов; (*of a language*) слова́рный соста́в.

vocal /ˈvəʊk(ə)l/ *adj* голосово́й; (*mus*) вока́льный; (*noisy*) шу́мный; **~ chord** голосова́я свя́зка. **vocalist** /-lɪst/ *n* певе́ц, -ви́ца.

vocation /vəˈkeɪʃ(ə)n/ *n* призва́ние. **vocational** /-n(ə)l/ *adj* профессиона́льный.

vociferous /vəˈsɪfərəs/ *adj* шу́мный.

vodka /ˈvɒdkə/ *n* во́дка.

vogue /vəʊg/ *n* мо́да; **in ~** в

мо́де.

voice /vɔɪs/ *n* го́лос; **~ mail** голосова́я по́чта; *vt* выража́ть *impf*, вы́разить *pf*.

void /vɔɪd/ *n* пустота́; *adj* пусто́й; (*invalid*) недействи́тельный; **~ of** лишённый +*gen*.

volatile /ˈvɒlə,taɪl/ *adj* (*chem*) летýчий; (*person*) непостоя́нный, неусто́йчивый.

volcanic /vɒlˈkænɪk/ *adj* вулкани́ческий. **volcano** /-ˈkeɪnəʊ/ *n* вулка́н.

vole /vəʊl/ *n* (*zool*) полёвка.

volition /vəˈlɪʃ(ə)n/ *n* во́ля; **by one's own ~** по свое́й во́ле.

volley /ˈvɒlɪ/ *n* (*missiles*) залп; (*fig*) град; (*sport*) уда́р с лёта; *vt* (*sport*) ударя́ть *impf*, уда́рить *pf* с лёта. **volleyball** *n* волейбо́л.

volt /vəʊlt/ *n* вольт. **voltage** /ˈvəʊltɪdʒ/ *n* напряже́ние.

voluble /ˈvɒljʊb(ə)l/ *adj* говорли́вый.

volume /ˈvɒljuːm/ *n* (*book*) том; (*capacity, size*) объём; (*loudness*) гро́мкость. **voluminous** /vəˈljuːmɪnəs/ *adj* обши́рный.

voluntary /ˈvɒləntərɪ/ *adj* доброво́льный. **volunteer** /,vɒlənˈtɪə(r)/ *n* доброво́лец; *vt* предлага́ть *impf*, предложи́ть *pf*; *vi* (*offer*) вызыва́ться *impf*, вы́зваться *pf* (*inf*, +*inf*; **for** в+*acc*); (*mil*) идти́ *impf*, пойти́ *pf* доброво́льцем.

voluptuous /vəˈlʌptjʊəs/ *adj* сластолюби́вый.

vomit /ˈvɒmɪt/ *n* рво́та; *vt* (& *i*) рвать *impf*, вы́рвать *pf impers* (+*instr*); **he was ~ing blood** его́ рва́ло кро́вью.

voracious /vəˈreɪʃəs/ *adj* прожо́рливый; (*fig*) ненасы́тный.

vortex /ˈvɔːteks/ *n* (*also fig*) водоворо́т, вихрь *m*.

vote /vəʊt/ *n* (*poll*) голосова́ние; (*individual* ~) го́лос; **the ~** (*suffrage*) пра́во го́лоса; (*resolution*) во́тум *no pl*; **~ of no confidence** во́тум недове́рия (**in** +*dat*); **~ of thanks** выраже́ние благода́рности; *vi* голосова́ть *impf*, про~ *pf* (**for** за+*acc*; **against** про́тив+*gen*); *vt* (*allocate by* ~) ассигнова́ть *impf* & *pf*; (*deem*) признава́ть *impf*, призна́ть *pf*; **the film was ~d a failure** фильм был при́знан неуда́чным; **~ in** избира́ть *impf*, избра́ть *pf* голосова́нием. **voter** /-tə(r)/ *n* избира́тель *m*.

vouch /vaʊtʃ/ *vi*: **~ for** руча́ться *impf*, поручи́ться *pf* за+*acc*. **voucher** /-tʃə(r)/ *n* тало́н.

vow /vaʊ/ *n* обе́т; *vt* кля́сться *impf*, по~ *pf* в+*prep*.

vowel /ˈvaʊəl/ *n* гла́сный *sb*.

voyage /ˈvɔɪɪdʒ/ *n* путеше́ствие.

vulgar /ˈvʌlgə(r)/ *adj* вульга́рный, гру́бый, по́шлый. **vulgarity** /-ˈgærɪtɪ/ *n* вульга́рность, по́шлость.

vulnerable /ˈvʌlnərəb(ə)l/ *adj* уязви́мый.

vulture /ˈvʌltʃə(r)/ *n* гриф; (*fig*) хи́щник.

W

wad /wɒd/ *n* комо́к; (*bundle*) па́чка. **wadding** /-dɪŋ/ ва́та; (*padding*) наби́вка.

waddle /ˈwɒd(ə)l/ *vi* ходи́ть *indet*, идти́ *det*, пойти́ *pf* вперева́лку (*coll*).

wade /weɪd/ *vt* & *i* (*river*) переходи́ть *impf*, перейти́ *pf* вброд; *vi*: **~ through** (*mud etc.*) пробира́ться *impf*, пробра́ться *pf* по+*dat*; (*sth boring etc.*) одолева́ть *impf*, одоле́ть *pf*.

wafer /'weɪfə(r)/ *n* ва́фля.

waffle[1] /'wɒf(ə)l/ *n* (*dish*) ва́фля.

waffle[2] /'wɒf(ə)l/ *vi* трепа́ться *impf*.

waft /wɒft/ *vt* & *i* нести́(сь) *impf*, по~ *pf*.

wag /wæg/ *vt* & *i* (*tail*) виля́ть *impf*, вильну́ть *pf* (+*instr*); *vt* (*finger*) грози́ть *impf*, по~ *pf* +*instr*.

wage[1] /weɪdʒ/ *n* (*pay*) *see* **wages**

wage[2] /weɪdʒ/ *vt*: ~ **war** вести́ *impf*, про~ *pf* войну́.

wager /'weɪdʒə(r)/ *n* пари́ *neut indecl*; *vi* держа́ть *impf* пари́ (**that** что); *vt* ста́вить *impf* по~ *pf*.

wages /'weɪdʒɪz/ *n pl* за́работная пла́та.

waggle /'wæg(ə)l/ *vt* & *i* пома́хивать *impf*, помаха́ть *pf* (+*instr*).

wag(g)on /'wægən/ *n* (*carriage*) пово́зка; (*cart*) теле́га; (*rly*) ваго́н-платфо́рма.

wail /weɪl/ *n* вопль *m*; *vi* вопи́ть *impf*.

waist /weɪst/ *n* та́лия; (*level of* ~) по́яс; **~-deep, high** (*adv*) по по́яс. **waistband** *n* по́яс. **waistcoat** *n* жиле́т.**waistline** *n* та́лия.

wait /weɪt/ *n* ожида́ние; **lie in ~ (for)** подстерега́ть *impf*; подстере́чь *pf*; *vi* (& *t*) (*also* ~ *for*) ждать *impf* (+*gen*); *vi* (*be a waiter, waitress*) быть официа́нтом, -ткой; ~ **on** обслу́живать *impf*, обслужи́ть *pf*. **waiter** /-tə(r)/ *n* официа́нт. **waiting** /-tɪŋ/ *n*: **~-list** спи́сок; **~-room** приёмная *sb*; (*rly*) зал ожида́ния. **waitress** /-trɪs/ *n* официа́нтка.

waive /weɪv/ *vt* отка́зываться *impf*, отказа́ться *pf* от+*gen*.

wake[1] /weɪk/ *n* (*at funeral*) поми́нки (-нок) *pl*.

wake[2] /weɪk/ *n* (*naut*) кильва́тер; **in the ~ of** по сле́ду +*gen*, за +*instr*.

wake[3] /weɪk/ *vt* (*also* ~ *up*) буди́ть *impf*, раз~ *pf*; *vi* (*also* ~ *up*) просыпа́ться *impf*, просну́ться *pf*.

Wales /weɪlz/ *n* Уэ́льс.

walk /wɔːk/ *n* (*walking*) ходьба́; (*gait*) похо́дка; (*stroll*) прогу́лка; (*path*) тропа́; **~-out** (*strike*) забасто́вка; (*as protest*) демонстрати́вный ухо́д; **~-over** лёгкая побе́да; **ten minutes' ~ from here** де́сять мину́т ходьбы́ отсю́да; **go for a ~** идти́ *impf*, пойти́ *pf* гуля́ть; **from all ~s of life** всех слоёв о́бщества; *vi* ходи́ть *indet*, идти́ *det*, пойти́ *pf*; гуля́ть *impf*, по~ *pf*; ~ **away, off** уходи́ть *impf*, уйти́ *pf*; ~ **in** входи́ть *impf*, войти́ *pf*; ~ **out** выходи́ть *impf*, вы́йти *pf*; ~ **out on** броса́ть *impf*, бро́сить *pf*; *vt* (*traverse*) обходи́ть *impf*, обойти́ *pf*; (*take for* ~) выводи́ть *impf*, вы́вести *pf* гуля́ть. **walker** /'wɔːkə(r)/ *n* ходо́к. **walkie-talkie** /ˌwɔːkɪ'tɔːkɪ/ *n* ра́ция. **walking** /'wɔːkɪŋ/ *n* ходьба́; **~-stick** трость.

Walkman /'wɔːkmən/ *n* (*propr*) во́кмен.

wall /wɔːl/ *n* стена́; *vt* обноси́ть *impf*, обнести́ *pf* стено́й; ~ **up** (*door, window*) заде́лывать *impf*, заде́лать *pf*; (*brick up*) замуро́вывать *impf*, замурова́ть *pf*.

wallet /'wɒlɪt/ *n* бума́жник.

wallflower /'wɔːlˌflaʊə(r)/ *n* желтофио́ль.

wallop /'wɒləp/ *n* си́льный уда́р; *vt* си́льно ударя́ть *impf*, ударить *pf*.

wallow /'wɒləʊ/ *vi* валя́ться *impf*; **~ in** (*give o.s. up to*) погружа́ться *impf*, погрузи́ться *pf* в+*acc*.

wallpaper /'wɔːl,peɪpə(r)/ *n* обо́и (обо́ев) *pl*.

walnut /'wɔːlnʌt/ *n* гре́цкий оре́х; (*wood*, *tree*) оре́ховое де́рево, оре́х.

walrus /'wɔːlrəs/ *n* морж.

waltz /wɔːls/ *n* вальс; *vi* вальси́ровать *impf*.

wan /wɒn/ *adj* бле́дный.

wand /wɒnd/ *n* па́лочка.

wander /'wɒndə(r)/ *vi* броди́ть *impf*; (*also of thoughts etc.*) блужда́ть *impf*; **~ from the point** отклоня́ться *impf*, отклони́ться *pf* от те́мы. **wanderer** /-rə(r)/ *n* стра́нник.

wane /weɪn/ *n*: **be on the ~** убыва́ть *impf*; *vi* убыва́ть *impf*, убы́ть *pf*; (*weaken*) ослабева́ть *impf*, ослабе́ть *pf*.

wangle /'wæŋg(ə)l/ *vt* заполуча́ть *impf*, заполучи́ть *pf*.

want /wɒnt/ *n* (*lack*) недоста́ток; (*requirement*) потре́бность; (*desire*) жела́ние; **for ~ of** за недоста́тком +*gen*; *vt* хоте́ть *impf*, за~ *pf* +*gen*, *acc*; (*need*) нужда́ться *impf* в+*prep*; **I ~ you to come at six** я хочу́, что́бы ты пришёл в шесть. **wanting** /-tɪŋ/ *adj*: **be ~** недостава́ть *impf* (*impers+gen*); **experience is ~** недостаёт о́пыта.

wanton /'wɒnt(ə)n/ *adj* (*licentious*) распу́тный; (*senseless*) бессмы́сленный.

war /wɔː(r)/ *n* война́; (*attrib*) вое́нный; **at ~** в состоя́нии войны́; **~ memorial** па́мятник па́вшим в войне́.

ward /wɔːd/ *n* (*hospital*) пала́та; (*child etc.*) подопе́чный *sb*; (*district*) райо́н; *vt*: **~ off** отража́ть *impf*, отрази́ть *pf*.

warden /'wɔːd(ə)n/ *n* (*prison*) нача́льник; (*college*) ре́ктор; (*hostel*) коменда́нт.

warder /'wɔːdə(r)/ *n* тюре́мщик.

wardrobe /'wɔːdrəʊb/ *n* платяно́й шкаф.

warehouse /'weəhaʊs/ *n* склад.

wares /weəz/ *n pl* изде́лия *neut pl*, това́ры *m pl*.

warfare /'wɔːfeə(r)/ *n* война́.

warhead /'wɔːhed/ *n* боева́я голо́вка.

warily /'weərɪlɪ/ *adv* осторо́жно.

warlike /'wɔːlaɪk/ *adj* вои́нственный.

warm /wɔːm/ *n* тепло́; *adj* (*also fig*) тёплый; **~-hearted** серде́чный; *vt* & *i* гре́ть(ся) *impf*; согрева́ть(ся) *impf*, согре́ть(ся) *pf*; **~ up** (*food etc.*) подогрева́ть *impf*, подогре́ть *pf*; (*liven up*) оживля́ть(ся) *impf*, оживи́ть(ся) *pf*; (*sport*) размина́ться *impf*, размя́ться *pf*; (*mus*) разы́грываться *impf*, разыгра́ться *pf*. **warmth** /wɔːmθ/ *n* тепло́; (*cordiality*) серде́чность.

warn /wɔːn/ *vt* предупрежда́ть *impf*, предупреди́ть *pf* (**about** о+*prep*). **warning** /-nɪŋ/ *n* предупрежде́ние.

warp /wɔːp/ *vt* & *i* (*wood*) коро́бить(ся) *impf*, по~, с~ *pf*; *vt* (*pervert*) извраща́ть *impf*, изврати́ть *pf*.

warrant /'wɒrənt/ *n* (*for arrest etc.*) о́рдер; *vt* (*justify*) опра́вдывать *impf*, оправда́ть *pf*; (*guarantee*) гаранти́ровать *impf* & *pf*. **warranty** /-tɪ/ *n* гара́нтия.

warrior /'wɒrɪə(r)/ *n* во́ин.

warship /'wɔːʃɪp/ *n* вое́нный ко-

ра́бль *m.*
wart /wɔːt/ *n* борода́вка.
wartime /'wɔːtaɪm/ *n*: **in ~** во вре́мя войны́.
wary /'weərɪ/ *adj* осторо́жный.
wash /wɒʃ/ *n* мытьё; (*thin layer*) то́нкий слой; (*lotion*) примо́чка; (*surf*) прибо́й; (*backwash*) попу́тная волна́; **at the ~** в сти́рке; **have a ~** мы́ться *impf*, по~ *pf*; **~-basin** умыва́льник; **~-out** (*fiasco*) прова́л; **~-room** умыва́льная *sb*; *vt* & *i* мы́ть(ся) *impf*, вы́~, по~ *pf*; *vt* (*clothes*) стира́ть *impf*, вы́~ *pf*; (*of sea*) омыва́ть *impf*; **~ away, off, out** смыва́ть(ся) *impf*, смы́ть(ся) *pf*; (*carry away*) сноси́ть *impf*, снести́ *pf*; **~ out** (*rinse*) спола́скивать *impf*, сполосну́ть *pf*; **~ up** (*dishes*) мыть *impf*, вы́~, по~ *pf* (посу́ду); **~ one's hands (of it)** умыва́ть *impf*, умы́ть *pf* ру́ки. **washed-out** /wɒʃt'aʊt/ *adj* (*exhausted*) утомлённый. **washer** /'wɒʃə(r)/ *n* (*tech*) ша́йба. **washing** /'wɒʃɪŋ/ *n* (*of clothes*) сти́рка; (*clothes*) бельё; **~-machine** стира́льная маши́на; **~-powder** стира́льный порошо́к; **~-up** (*action*) мытьё посу́ды; (*dishes*) гря́зная посу́да; **~-up liquid** жи́дкое мы́ло для мытья́ посу́ды.
wasp /wɒsp/ *n* оса́.
wastage /'weɪstɪdʒ/ *n* у́те́чка.
waste /weɪst/ *n* (*desert*) пусты́ня; (*refuse*) отбро́сы *m pl*; (*of time, money, etc.*) тра́та; **go to ~** пропада́ть *impf*, пропа́сть *pf* да́ром; *adj* (*desert*) пусты́нный; (*superfluous*) нену́жный; (*uncultivated*) невозде́ланный; **lay ~** опустоша́ть *impf*, опустоши́ть *pf*; **~land** пусты́рь *m*; **~ paper** нену́жные бума́ги *f pl*; (*for recycling*) макулату́ра; **~ products** отхо́ды (-дов) *pl*; **~-paper basket** корзи́на для бума́ги; *vt* тра́тить *impf*, по~, ис~ *pf*; (*time*) теря́ть *impf*, по~ *pf*; *vi*: **~ away** ча́хнуть *impf*, за~ *pf*. **wasteful** /-fʊl/ *adj* расточи́тельный.
watch /wɒtʃ/ *n* (*timepiece*) часы́ (-со́в) *pl*; (*duty*) дежу́рство; (*naut*) ва́хта; **keep ~ over** наблюда́ть *impf* за+*instr*; **~-dog** сторожево́й пёс; **~-tower** сторожева́я ба́шня; *vt* (*observe*) наблюда́ть *impf*; (*keep an eye on*) следи́ть *impf* за+*instr*; (*look after*) смотре́ть *impf*, по~ *pf* за+*instr*; **~ television, a film** смотре́ть *impf*, по~ *pf* телеви́зор, фильм; *vi* смотре́ть *impf*; **~ out** (*be careful*) бере́чься *impf* (**for** +*gen*); **~ out for** ждать *impf* +*gen*; **~ out!** осторо́жно! **watchful** /-fʊl/ *adj* бди́тельный. **watchman** *n* (ночно́й) сто́рож. **watchword** *n* ло́зунг.
water /'wɔːtə(r)/ *n* вода́; **~-colour** акваре́ль; **~-heater** кипяти́льник; **~-main** водопрово́дная магистра́ль; **~ melon** арбу́з; **~-pipe** водопрово́дная труба́; **~-ski** (*n*) во́дная лы́жа; **~-skiing** водолы́жный спорт; **~-supply** водоснабже́ние; **~-way** во́дный путь *m*; *vt* (*flowers etc.*) полива́ть *impf*, поли́ть *pf*; (*animals*) пои́ть *impf*, на~ *pf*; (*irrigate*) ороша́ть *impf*, ороси́ть *pf*; *vi* (*eyes*) слези́ться *impf*; (*mouth*): **my mouth ~s** у меня́ слю́нки теку́т; **~ down** разбавля́ть *impf*, разба́вить *pf*. **watercourse** *n* ру́сло. **watercress** /-kres/ *n* кресс водяно́й. **waterfall** *n* водопа́д. **waterfront** *n* часть го́рода примыка́ющая

к бе́регу. **watering-can** /ˈwɔːtərɪŋ͵kæn/ *n* ле́йка. **waterlogged** /ˈwɔːtə͵lɒgd/ *adj* заболо́ченный. **watermark** *n* водяно́й знак. **waterproof** *adj* непромока́емый; *n* непромока́емый плащ. **watershed** *n* водоразде́л. **waterside** *n* бе́рег. **watertight** *adj* водонепроница́емый; (*fig*) неопровержи́мый. **waterworks** *n pl* водопрово́дные сооруже́ния *neut pl.* **watery** /ˈwɔːtərɪ/ *adj* водяни́стый.

watt /wɒt/ *n* ватт.

wave /weɪv/ *vt* (*hand etc.*) маха́ть *impf*, махну́ть *pf* +*instr*; (*flag*) разма́хивать *impf* +*instr*; *vi* (~ *hand*) маха́ть *impf*, по~ *pf* (**at** +*dat*); (*flutter*) развева́ться *impf*; ~ **aside** отма́хиваться *impf*, отмахну́ться *pf* от+*gen*; ~ **down** остана́вливать *impf*, останови́ть *pf*; *n* (*in various senses*) волна́; (*of hand*) взмах; (*in hair*) зави́вка. **wavelength** *n* длина́ волны́. **waver** /-və(r)/ *vi* колеба́ться *impf*. **wavy** /-vɪ/ *adj* волни́стый.

wax /wæks/ *n* воск; (*in ear*) се́ра; *vt* вощи́ть *impf*, на~ *pf*. **waxwork** *n* воскова́я фигу́ра; *pl* музе́й восковы́х фигу́р.

way /weɪ/ *n* (*road, path, route*; *fig*) доро́га, путь *m*; (*direction*) сторона́; (*manner*) о́браз; (*method*) спо́соб; (*respect*) отноше́ние; (*habit*) привы́чка; **by the** ~ (*fig*) кста́ти, ме́жду про́чим; **on the** ~ по доро́ге, по пути́; **this** ~ (*direction*) сюда́; (*in this* ~) таки́м о́бразом; **the other** ~ **round** наоборо́т; **under** ~ на ходу́; **be in the** ~ меша́ть *impf*; **get out of the** ~ уходи́ть *impf*, уйти́ *pf* с доро́ги; **give** ~ (*yield*) поддава́ться *impf*, подда́ться *pf* (**to** +*dat*); (*collapse*) обру́шиваться *impf*, обру́шиться *pf*; **go out of one's** ~ **to** стара́ться *impf*, по~ *pf* изо всех сил +*inf*; **get, have, one's own** ~ добива́ться *impf*, доби́ться *pf* своего́; **make** ~ уступа́ть *impf*, уступи́ть *pf* доро́гу (**for** +*dat*). **waylay** *vt* (*lie in wait for*) подстерега́ть *impf*, подстере́чь *pf*; (*stop*) перехва́тывать *impf*, перехвати́ть *pf* по пути́. **wayside** *adj* придоро́жный; *n*: **fall by the** ~ выбыва́ть *impf*, вы́быть *pf* из стро́я.

wayward /ˈweɪwəd/ *adj* своенра́вный.

WC *abbr* (*of* **water-closet**) убо́рная *sb*.

we /wiː/ *pron* мы.

weak /wiːk/ *adj* сла́бый. **weaken** /-kən/ *vt* ослабля́ть *impf*, ослабить *pf*; *vi* слабе́ть *impf*, о~ *pf*. **weakling** /-lɪŋ/ *n* (*person*) сла́бый челове́к; (*plant*) сла́бое расте́ние. **weakness** /-nɪs/ *n* сла́бость.

weal /wiːl/ *n* (*mark*) рубе́ц.

wealth /welθ/ *n* бога́тство; (*abundance*) изоби́лие. **wealthy** /-θɪ/ *adj* бога́тый.

wean /wiːn/ *vt* отнима́ть *impf*, отня́ть *pf* от груди́; (*fig*) отуча́ть *impf*, отучи́ть *pf* (**of, from** от+*gen*).

weapon /ˈwepən/ *n* ору́жие. **weaponry** /-rɪ/ *n* вооруже́ние.

wear /weə(r)/ *n* (*wearing*) но́ска; (*clothing*) оде́жда; (~ *and tear*) изно́с; *vt* носи́ть *impf*; быть в+*prep*; **what shall I** ~? что мне наде́ть?; *vi* носи́ться *impf*; ~ **off** (*pain, novelty*) проходи́ть *impf*, пройти́ *pf*; (*cease to have effect*) перестава́ть *impf*, переста́ть *pf* де́йствовать; ~ **out** (*clothes*) изна́шивать(ся) *impf*, износи́ть(ся) *pf*; (*exhaust*) из-

му́чивать *impf*, изму́чить *pf*.
weariness /ˈwɪərɪnɪs/ *n* уста́лость. **wearing, wearisome** /ˈweərɪŋ, ˈwɪərɪsəm/ *adj* утоми́тельный. **weary** /ˈwɪərɪ/ *adj* уста́лый; *vt* & *i* утомля́ть(ся) *impf*, утоми́ть(ся) *pf*.
weasel /ˈwiːz(ə)l/ *n* ла́ска.
weather /ˈweðə(r)/ *n* пого́да; **be under the ~** нева́жно себя́ чу́вствовать *impf*; **~-beaten** обве́тренный; **~ forecast** прогно́з пого́ды; *vt* (*storm etc.*) выде́рживать *impf*, вы́держать *pf*; (*wood*) подверга́ть *impf*, подве́ргнуть *pf* атмосфе́рным влия́ниям. **weather-cock, weathervane** /ˈweðəˌkɒk, ˈweðəˌveɪn/ *n* флю́гер. **weatherman** *n* метеоро́лог.
weave[1] /wiːv/ *vt* & *i* (*fabric*) ткать *impf*, со~ *pf*; *vt* (*fig*; *also wreath etc.*) плести́ *impf*, с~ *pf*. **weaver** /-və(r)/ *n* ткач, ~и́ха.
weave[2] /wiːv/ *vi* (*wind*) ви́ться *impf*.
web /web/ *n* (*cobweb*; *fig*) паути́на; (*fig*) сплете́ние; (*the Web*) (*comput*) Всеми́рная паути́на; **~ page** веб-страни́ца, страни́ца в Интерне́те. **webbed** /webd/ *adj* перепо́нчатый. **weblog** *n* сетево́й журна́л, блог. **weblogger** *n* бло́ггер. **website** *n* сайт, веб-са́йт.
wedded /-dɪd/ *adj* супру́жеский; **~ to** (*fig*) пре́данный +*dat*. **wedding** /-dɪŋ/ *n* сва́дьба, бракосочета́ние; **~-cake** сва́дебный торт; **~-day** день *m* сва́дьбы; **~-dress** подвене́чное пла́тье; **~-ring** обруча́льное кольцо́.
wedge /wedʒ/ *n* клин; *vt* (**~ open**) закли́нивать *impf*, закли́нить *pf*; *vt* & *i*: **~ in(to)** вкли́нивать(ся) *impf*, вкли́нить(ся) *pf* (в+*acc*).
wedlock /ˈwedlɒk/ *n* брак; **born out of ~** рождённый вне бра́ка, внебра́чный.
Wednesday /ˈwenzdeɪ/ *n* среда́.
weed /wiːd/ *n* сорня́к; **~-killer** гербици́д; *vt* поло́ть *impf*, вы́~ *pf*; **~ out** удаля́ть *impf*, удали́ть *pf*. **weedy** /ˈwiːdɪ/ *adj* (*person*) то́щий.
week /wiːk/ *n* неде́ля; **~-end** суббо́та и воскресе́нье, выходны́е *sb pl*. **weekday** *n* бу́дний день *m*. **weekly** /ˈwiːklɪ/ *adj* еженеде́льный; (*wage*) неде́льный; *adv* еженеде́льно; *n* еженеде́льник.
weep /wiːp/ *vi* пла́кать *impf*. **weeping willow** /ˈwiːpɪŋ ˈwɪləʊ/ *n* плаку́чая и́ва.
weigh /weɪ/ *vt* (*also fig*) взве́шивать *impf*, взве́сить *pf*; (*consider*) обду́мывать *impf*, обду́мать *pf*; *vt* & *i* (*so much*) ве́сить *impf*; **~ down** отягоща́ть *impf*, отяготи́ть *pf*; **~ on** тяготи́ть *impf*; **~ out** отве́шивать *impf*, отве́сить *pf*; **~ up** (*appraise*) оце́нивать *impf*, оцени́ть *pf*. **weight** /weɪt/ *n* (*also authority*) вес; (*load*, *also fig*) тя́жесть; (*sport*) шта́нга; (*influence*) влия́ние; **lose ~** худе́ть *impf*, по~ *pf*; **put on ~** толсте́ть *impf*, по~ *pf*; **~-lifter** штанги́ст; **~-lifting** подня́тие тя́жестей; *vt* (*make heavier*) утяжеля́ть *impf*, утяжели́ть *pf*. **weightless** /ˈweɪtlɪs/ *adj* невесо́мый. **weighty** /ˈweɪtɪ/ *adj* ве́ский.
weir /wɪə(r)/ *n* плоти́на.
weird /wɪəd/ *adj* (*strange*) стра́нный.
welcome /ˈwelkəm/ *n* приём; *adj* жела́нный; (*pleasant*) прия́тный; **you are ~** (*don't mention it*)

пожа́луйста; **you are ~ to use my bicycle** мой велосипе́д к ва́шим услу́гам; **you are ~ to stay the night** вы мо́жете переночева́ть у меня́/нас; *vt* приве́тствовать *impf* (& *pf in past tense*); *int* добро́ пожа́ловать!

weld /weld/ *vt* сва́ривать *impf*, свари́ть *pf*. **welder** /-də(r)/ *n* сва́рщик.

welfare /'welfeə(r)/ *n* благосостоя́ние; **W~ State** госуда́рство всео́бщего благосостоя́ния.

well[1] /wel/ *n* коло́дец; (*for stairs*) ле́стничная кле́тка.

well[2] /wel/ *vi*: **~ up** (*anger etc.*) вскипа́ть *impf*, вскипе́ть *pf*; **tears ~ed up** глаза́ напо́лнились слеза́ми.

well[3] /wel/ *adj* (*healthy*) здоро́вый; **feel ~** чу́вствовать *impf*, по~ *pf* себя́ хорошо́, здоро́вым; **get ~** поправля́ться *impf*, попра́виться *pf*; **look ~** хорошо́ вы́глядеть *impf*; **all is ~** всё в поря́дке; *int* ну(!); *adv* хорошо́; (*very much*) о́чень; **as ~** то́же; **as ~ as** (*in addition to*) кро́ме+*gen*; **it may ~ be true** вполне́ возмо́жно, что э́то так; **very ~!** хорошо́!; **~ done!** молоде́ц!; **~-balanced** уравнове́шенный; **~-behaved** (благо)воспи́танный; **~-being** благополу́чие; **~-bred** благовоспи́танный; **~-built** кре́пкий; **~-defined** чёткий; **~-disposed** благосклóнный; **~ done** (*cooked*) (хорошо́) прожа́ренный; **~-fed** отко́рмленный; **~-founded** обосно́ванный; **~-groomed** (*person*) хо́леный; **~-heeled** состоя́тельный; **~-informed** (хорошо́) осведомлённый (**about** в+*prep*); **~-known** изве́стный; **~-meaning** де́йствующий из лу́чших побужде́ний; **~-nigh** почти́; **~-off** состоя́тельный; **~-paid** хорошо́ опла́чиваемый; **~-preserved** хорошо́ сохрани́вшийся; **~-to-do** состоя́тельный; **~-wisher** доброжела́тель *m*.

wellington (boot) /'welɪŋt(ə)n (bu:t)/ *n* рези́новый сапо́г.

Welsh /welʃ/ *adj* уэ́льский. **Welshman** *n* валли́ец. **Welshwoman** *n* валли́йка.

welter /'weltə(r)/ *n* пу́таница.

wend /wend/ *vt*: **~ one's way** держа́ть *impf* путь.

west /west/ *n* за́пад; (*naut*) вест; *adj* за́падный; *adv* на за́пад, к за́паду. **westerly** /'westəlɪ/ *adj* за́падный. **western** /'west(ə)n/ *adj* за́падный; *n* (*film*) ве́стерн. **westward(s)** /'westwəd(z)/ *adv* на за́пад, к за́паду.

wet /wet/ *adj* мо́крый; (*paint*) непросо́хший; (*rainy*) дождли́вый; **~ through** промо́кший до ни́тки; *n* (*dampness*) вла́жность; (*rain*) дождь *m*; *vt* мочи́ть *impf*, на~ *pf*.

whack /wæk/ *n* (*blow*) уда́р; *vt* колоти́ть *impf*, по~ *pf*. **whacked** /wækt/ *adj* разби́тый.

whale /weɪl/ *n* кит.

wharf /wɔ:f/ *n* при́стань.

what /wɒt/ *pron* (*interrog*, *int*) что; (*how much*) ско́лько; (*rel*) (то,) что; **~ (...) for** заче́м; **~ if** а что е́сли; **~ is your name** как вас зову́т?; *adj* (*interrog*, *int*) како́й; **~ kind of** како́й. **whatever, whatsoever** /wɒt'evə(r), ˌwɒtsəʊ'evə(r)/ *pron* что бы ни+*past* (**~ you think** что бы вы ни ду́мали); всё, что (**take ~ you want** возьми́те всё, что хоти́те); *adj* како́й бы ни+*past* (**~ books he read(s)** каки́е бы

книги он ни прочитáл); (*at all*): **there is no chance ~** нет никакóй возмóжности; **is there any chance ~?** есть ли хоть какáя-нибýдь возмóжность?
wheat /wi:t/ *n* пшенúца.
wheedle /'wi:d(ə)l/ *vt* (*coax into doing*) уговáривать *impf*, уговорúть *pf* с пóмощью лéсти; **~ out of** вымáнивать *impf*, вы́манить *pf* у+*gen*.
wheel /wi:l/ *n* колесó; (*steering ~, helm*) руль *m*; (*potter's*) гончáрный круг; *vt* (*push*) катáть *indet*, катúть *det*, по~ *pf*; *vt* & *i* (*turn*) повёртывать(ся) *impf*, повернýть(ся) *pf*; *vi* (*circle*) кружúться *impf*. **wheelbarrow** *n* тáчка. **wheelchair** *n* инвалúдное крéсло.
wheeze /wi:z/ *vi* сопéть *impf*.
when /wen/ *adv* когдá; *conj* когдá, в то врéмя как; (*whereas*) тогдá как; (*if*) éсли; (*although*) хотя́. **whence** /wens/ *adv* откýда. **whenever** /wen'evə(r)/ *adv* когдá же; *conj* (*every time*) вся́кий раз когдá; (*at any time*) когдá; (*no matter when*) когдá бы ни+*past*; **we shall have dinner ~ you arrive** во скóлько бы вы ни приéхали, мы пообéдаем.
where /weə(r)/ *adv* & *conj* (*place*) где; (*whither*) кудá; **from ~** откýда. **whereabouts** /'weərə,baʊts/ *adv* где; *n* местонахождéние. **whereas** /weər'æz/ *conj* тогдá как; хотя́. **whereby** /weə'baɪ/ *adv* & *conj* посрéдством чегó. **wherein** /weər'ɪn/ *adv* & *conj* в чём. **wherever** /weər'evə(r)/ *adv* & *conj* (*place*) где бы ни+*past*; (*whither*) кудá бы ни+*past*; **~ he goes** кудá бы он ни пошёл; **~ you like** где/кудá хотúте. **wherewithal** /'weəwɪ,ðɔ:l/ *n* срéдства *neut pl*.
whet /wet/ *vt* точúть *impf*, на~ *pf*; (*fig*) возбуждáть *impf*, возбудúть *pf*.
whether /'weðə(r)/ *conj* ли; **I don't know ~ he will come** я не знáю, придёт ли он; **~ he comes or not** придёт (ли) он úли нет.
which /wɪtʃ/ *adj* (*interrog, rel*) какóй; *pron* (*interrog*) какóй; (*person*) кто; (*rel*) котóрый; (*rel to whole statement*) что; **~ is ~?** (*persons*) кто из них кто?; (*things*) что-что? **whichever** /wɪtʃ'evə(r)/ *adj* & *pron* какóй бы ни+*past* (**~ book you choose** какýю бы кнúгу ты ни вы́брал); любóй (**take ~ book you want** возьмúте любýю кнúгу).
whiff /wɪf/ *n* зáпах.
while /waɪl/ *n* врéмя *neut*; **a little ~** недóлго; **a long ~** дóлго; **for a long ~** (*up to now*) давнó; **for a ~** на врéмя; **in a little ~** скóро; **it is worth ~** стóит э́то сдéлать; *vt*: **~ away** проводúть *impf*, провестú *pf*; *conj* покá; в то врéмя как; (*although*) хотя́; (*contrast*) а; **we went to the cinema ~ they went to the theatre** мы ходúли в кинó, а онú в теáтр. **whilst** /waɪlst/ *see* **while**
whim /wɪm/ *n* прúхоть, каприз.
whimper /'wɪmpə(r)/ *vi* хны́кать *impf*; (*dog*) скулúть *impf*.
whimsical /'wɪmzɪk(ə)l/ *adj* капрúзный; (*odd*) причýдливый.
whine /waɪn/ *n* (*wail*) вой; (*whimper*) хны́канье; *vi* (*dog*) скулúть *impf*; (*wail*) выть; (*whimper*) хны́кать *impf*.
whinny /'wɪnɪ/ *vi* тúхо ржать *impf*.
whip /wɪp/ *n* кнут, хлыст; *vt* (*lash*) хлестáть *impf*, хлестнýть *pf*; (*cream*) сбивáть *impf*,

сбить *pf*; ~ **off** скидывать *impf*, скинуть *pf*; ~ **out** выхватывать *impf*, выхватить *pf*; ~ **round** быстро повёртываться *impf*, повернуться *pf*; **~-round** сбор денег; ~ **up** (*stir up*) разжигать *impf*, разжечь *pf*.

whirl /wɜːl/ *n* кружение; (*of dust*, *fig*) вихрь *m*; (*turmoil*) суматоха; *vt* & *i* кружить(ся) *impf*, за~ *pf*. **whirlpool** *n* водоворот. **whirlwind** *n* вихрь *m*.

whirr /wɜː(r)/ *vi* жужжать *impf*.

whisk /wɪsk/ *n* (*of twigs etc.*) веничек; (*utensil*) мутовка; (*movement*) помахивание; *vt* (*cream etc.*) сбивать *impf*, сбить *pf*; ~ **away, off** (*brush off*) смахивать *impf*, смахнуть *pf*; (*take away*) быстро уносить *impf*, унести *pf*.

whisker /ˈwɪskə(r)/ *n* (*human*) волос на лице; (*animal*) ус; *pl* (*human*) бакенбарды *f pl*.

whisky /ˈwɪskɪ/ *n* виски *neut indecl*.

whisper /ˈwɪspə(r)/ *n* шёпот; *vt* & *i* шептать *impf*, шепнуть *pf*.

whistle /ˈwɪs(ə)l/ *n* (*sound*) свист; (*instrument*) свисток; *vi* свистеть *impf*, свистнуть *pf*; *vt* насвистывать *impf*.

white /waɪt/ *adj* белый; (*hair*) седой; (*pale*) бледный; (*with milk*) с молоком; **paint** ~ красить *impf*, по~ *pf* в белый свет; **~-collar worker** служащий *sb*; ~ **lie** невинная ложь; *n* (*colour*) белый цвет; (*egg*, *eye*) белок; (~ *person*) белый *sb*. **whiten** /-t(ə)n/ *vt* белить *impf*, на~, по~, вы~ *pf*; *vi* белеть *impf*, по~ *pf*. **whiteness** /-nɪs/ *n* белизна. **whitewash** *n* побелка; *vt* белить *impf*, по~ *pf*; (*fig*) обелять *impf*, обелить *pf*.

whither /ˈwɪðə(r)/ *adv* & *conj* куда.

Whitsun /ˈwɪts(ə)n/ *n* Троица.

whittle /ˈwɪt(ə)l/ *vt*: ~ **down** уменьшать *impf*, уменьшить *pf*.

whiz(z) /wɪz/ *vi*: ~ **past** просвистеть *pf*.

who /huː/ *pron* (*interrog*) кто; (*rel*) который.

whoever /huːˈevə(r)/ *pron* кто бы ни+*past*; (*he who*) тот, кто.

whole /həʊl/ *adj* (*entire*) весь, целый; (*intact*, *of number*) целый; *n* (*thing complete*) целое *sb*; (*all there is*) весь *sb*; (*sum*) сумма; **on the** ~ в общем. **wholehearted** /-ˈhɑːtɪd/ *adj* беззаветный. **whole-heartedly** /-ˈhɑːtɪdlɪ/ *adv* от всего сердца. **wholemeal** *adj* из непросеянной муки. **wholesale** *adj* оптовый; (*fig*) массовый; *adv* оптом. **wholesaler** *n* оптовый торговец. **wholesome** *adj* здоровый. **wholly** /ˈhəʊllɪ/ *adv* полностью.

whom /huːm/ *pron* (*interrog*) кого *etc.*; (*rel*) которого *etc.*

whoop /huːp/ *n* крик; *vi* кричать *impf*, крикнуть *pf*; ~ **it up** бурно веселиться *impf*; **~ing cough** коклюш.

whore /hɔː(r)/ *n* проститутка.

whose /huːz/ *pron* (*interrog*, *rel*) чей; (*rel*) которого.

why /waɪ/ *adv* почему; *int* да ведь!

wick /wɪk/ *n* фитиль *m*.

wicked /ˈwɪkɪd/ *adj* дикий. **wickedness** /-nɪs/ *n* дикость.

wicker /ˈwɪkə(r)/ *attrib* плетёный.

wicket /ˈwɪkɪt/ *n* (*cricket*) воротца.

wide /waɪd/ *adj* широкий; (*extensive*) обширный; (*in measurements*) в+*acc* шириной; ~

awake по́лный внима́ния; ~ **open** широко́ откры́тый; *adv* (*off target*) ми́мо це́ли. **widely** /ˈwaɪdlɪ/ *adv* широко́. **widen** /-d(ə)n/ *vt & i* расширя́ть(ся) *impf*, расши́рить(ся) *pf*. **widespread** *adj* распространённый.

widow /ˈwɪdəʊ/ *n* вдова́. **widowed** /ˈwɪdəʊd/ *adj* овдове́вший. **widower** /ˈwɪdəʊwə(r)/ *n* вдове́ц.

width /wɪtθ/ *n* ширина́; (*fig*) широта́; (*of cloth*) поло́тнище.

wield /wiːld/ *vt* (*brandish*) разма́хивать *impf* +*instr*; (*power*) по́льзоваться *impf* +*instr*.

wife /waɪf/ *n* жена́.

wig /wɪg/ *n* пари́к.

wiggle /ˈwɪg(ə)l/ *vt & i* (*move*) шевели́ть(ся) *impf*, по~, шевельну́ть(ся) *pf* (+*instr*).

wigwam /ˈwɪgwæm/ *n* вигва́м.

wild /waɪld/ *adj* ди́кий; (*flower*) полево́й; (*uncultivated*) невозде́ланный; (*tempestuous*) бу́йный; (*furious*) неи́стовый; (*ill-considered*) необду́манный; **be ~ about** быть без ума́ от+*gen*; **~-goose chase** сумасбро́дная зате́я; *n*: *pl* де́бри (-рей) *pl*. **wildcat** *adj* (*unofficial*) неофициа́льный. **wilderness** /ˈwɪldənɪs/ *n* пусты́ня. **wildfire** *n*: **spread like ~** распространя́ться *impf*, распространи́ться *pf* с молниено́сной быстрото́й. **wildlife** *n* жива́я приро́да. **wildness** /ˈwaɪldnɪs/ *n* ди́кость.

wile /waɪl/ *n* хи́трость.

wilful /ˈwɪlfʊl/ *adj* (*obstinate*) упря́мый; (*deliberate*) преднаме́ренный.

will /wɪl/ *n* во́ля; (*~-power*) си́ла во́ли; (*at death*) завеща́ние; **against one's ~** про́тив во́ли; **of one's own free ~** доброво́льно; **with a ~** с энтузиа́змом; **good ~** до́брая во́ля; **make one's ~** писа́ть *impf*, на~ *pf* завеща́ние; *vt* (*want*) хоте́ть *impf*, за~ *pf* +*gen*, *acc*; *v aux*: **he ~ be president** он бу́дет президе́нтом; **he ~ return tomorrow** он вернётся за́втра; **~ you open the window?** откро́йте окно́, пожа́луйста. **willing** /ˈwɪlɪŋ/ *adj* гото́вый; (*eager*) стара́тельный. **willingly** /ˈwɪlɪŋlɪ/ *adv* охо́тно. **willingness** /ˈwɪlɪŋnɪs/ *n* гото́вность.

willow /ˈwɪləʊ/ *n* и́ва.

willy-nilly /ˌwɪlɪˈnɪlɪ/ *adv* во́лей-нево́лей.

wilt /wɪlt/ *vi* поника́ть *impf*, пони́кнуть *pf*.

wily /ˈwaɪlɪ/ *adj* хи́трый.

win /wɪn/ *n* побе́да; *vt & i* выи́грывать *impf*, вы́играть *pf*; *vt* (*obtain*) добива́ться *impf*, доби́ться *pf* +*gen*; **~ over** угова́ривать *impf*, уговори́ть *pf*; (*charm*) располага́ть *impf*, расположи́ть *pf* к себе́.

wince /wɪns/ *vi* вздра́гивать *impf*, вздро́гнуть *pf*.

winch /wɪntʃ/ *n* лебёдка; поднима́ть *impf*, подня́ть *pf* с по́мощью лебёдки.

wind¹ /wɪnd/ *n* (*air*) ве́тер; (*breath*) дыха́ние; (*flatulence*) ве́тры *m pl*; **~ instrument** духово́й инструме́нт; **~-swept** откры́тый ветра́м; **get ~ of** проню́хивать *impf*, проню́хать *pf*; *vt* (*make gasp*) заставля́ть *impf*, заста́вить *pf* задохну́ться.

wind² /waɪnd/ *vi* (*meander*) ви́ться *impf*; извива́ться *impf*; *vt* (*coil*) нама́тывать *impf*, намота́ть *pf*; (*watch*) заводи́ть *impf*, завести́ *pf*; (*wrap*) уку́тывать *impf*, укýтать *pf*; ~ **up** (*vt*) (*reel*) смáтывать *impf*, смотáть *pf*; (*watch*) *see* **wind**²; (*vt* & *i*) (*end*) кончáть(ся) *impf*, кóнчить(ся) *pf*. **winding** /ˈwaɪndɪŋ/ *adj* (*meandering*) извíлистый; (*staircase*) винтовóй.

windfall /ˈwɪndfɔːl/ *n* пáдалица; (*fig*) золотóй дождь.

windmill /ˈwɪndmɪl/ *n* ветрянáя мéльница.

window /ˈwɪndəʊ/ *n* oкнó; (*of shop*) витрíна; **~-box** нарýжный ящик для цветóв; **~-cleaner** мóйщик óкон; **~-dressing** оформлéние витрíн; (*fig*) показýха; **~-frame** окóнная рáма; **~-ledge** подокóнник; **~-pane** окóнное стеклó; **~-shopping** рассмáтривание витрíн; **~-sill** подокóнник.

windpipe /ˈwɪndpaɪp/ *n* дыхáтельное гóрло. **windscreen** *n* ветровóе стеклó; ~ **wiper** двóрник **windsurfer** /ˈwɪnd ˌsɜːfə(r)/ *n* виндсёрфингíст. **windsurfing** /ˈwɪnd,sɜːfɪŋ/ *n* виндсёрфинг. **windward** /ˈwɪndwəd/ *adj* навéтренный. **windy** /ˈwɪndɪ/ *adj* вéтреный.

wine /waɪn/ *n* винó; ~ **bar** вíнный погребóк; ~ **bottle** вíнная бутылка; ~ **list** кáрта вин; **~-tasting** дегустáция вин. **wineglass** *n* рюмка. **winery** /ˈwaɪnərɪ/ *n* вíнный завóд. **winy** /ˈwaɪnɪ/ *adj* вíнный.

wing /wɪŋ/ *n* (*also polit*) крылó; (*archit*) флíгель *m*; (*sport*) фланг; *pl* (*theat*) кулíсы *f pl*. **winged** /wɪŋd/ *adj* крылáтый.

wink /wɪŋk/ *n* (*blink*) моргáние; (*as sign*) подмигивание; *vi* мигáть *impf*, мигнýть *pf*; ~ **at** подмигивать *impf*, подмигнýть *pf* +*dat*; (*fig*) смотрéть *impf*, по~ *pf* сквозь пáльцы на+*acc*.

winkle /ˈwɪŋk(ə)l/ *vt*: ~ **out** выковыривать *impf*, выковырять *pf*.

winner /ˈwɪnə(r)/ *n* победíтель *m*, ~ница. **winning** /ˈwɪnɪŋ/ *adj* (*victorious*) выигравший; (*shot etc.*) решáющий; (*charming*) обаятельный; *n*: *pl* выигрыш; **~-post** фíнишный столб.

winter /ˈwɪntə(r)/ *n* зимá; *attrib* зíмний. **wintry** /ˈwɪntrɪ/ *adj* зíмний; (*cold*) холóдный.

wipe /waɪp/ *vt* (*also* ~ *out inside of*) вытирáть *impf*, вытереть *pf*; ~ **away, off** стирáть *impf*, стерéть *pf*; ~ **out** (*exterminate*) уничтожáть *impf*, уничтóжить *pf*; (*cancel*) смывáть *impf*, смыть *pf*.

wire /ˈwaɪə(r)/ *n* прóволока; (*carrying current*) прóвод; ~ **netting** прóволочная сéтка. **wireless** /-lɪs/ *n* рáдио *neut indecl*. **wiring** /-rɪŋ/ *n* электропровóдка. **wiry** /-rɪ/ *adj* жíлистый.

wisdom /ˈwɪzdəm/ *n* мýдрость; ~ **tooth** зуб мýдрости. **wise** /waɪz/ *adj* мýдрый; (*prudent*) благоразýмный.

wish /wɪʃ/ *n* желáние; **with best ~es** всегó хорóшего, с наилýчшими пожелáниями; *vt* хотéть *impf*, за~ *pf* (**I ~ I could see him** мне хотéлось бы егó вíдеть; **I ~ to go** я хочý пойтí; **I ~ you to come early** я хочý, чтóбы вы рáно пришлí; **I ~ the day were over** хорошó бы день ужé кóнчился); желáть *impf* +*gen* (**I ~ you luck** желáю вам удáчи); (*congratulate on*) поздравлять *impf*, поздрáвить *pf* (**I ~ you a happy birthday** поздравляю тебя с днём рождения); *vi*: ~ **for** желáть *impf* +*gen*; мечтáть *impf* о+*prep*. **wishful** /-fʊl/ *adj*: ~ **thinking** самообольщéние; принятие желáемого за действи́тельное.

wisp /wɪsp/ *n* (*of straw*) пучóк; (*hair*) клочóк; (*smoke*) стрýйка.

wisteria /wɪ'stɪərɪə/ *n* глици́ния.

wistful /'wɪstfʊl/ *adj* тоскли́вый.

wit /wɪt/ *n* (*mind*) ум; (*wittiness*) остроýмие; (*person*) остря́к; **be at one's ~'s end** не знать *impf* что дéлать.

witch /wɪtʃ/ *n* вéдьма; **~-hunt** охóта за вéдьмами. **witchcraft** *n* колдовствó.

with /wɪð/ *prep* (*in company of, together ~*) (вмéсте) с+*instr*; (*as a result of*) от+*gen*; (*at house of, in keeping of*) у+*gen*; (*by means of*) +*instr*; (*in spite of*) несмотря́ на+*acc*; (*including*) включáя+*acc*; ~ **each/one another** друг с дрýгом.

withdraw /wɪð'drɔː/ *vt* (*retract*) брать *impf*, взять *pf* назáд; (*hand*) отдёргивать *impf*, отдёрнуть *pf*; (*cancel*) снимáть *impf*, снять *pf*; (*mil*) выводи́ть *impf*, вы́вести *pf*; (*money from circulation*) изымáть *impf*, изъя́ть из обращéния; (*diplomat etc.*) отзывáть *impf*, отозвáть *pf*; (*from bank*) брать *impf*, взять *pf*; *vi* удаля́ться *impf*, удали́ться *pf*; (*drop out*) выбывáть *impf*, вы́быть *pf*; (*mil*) отходи́ть *impf*, отойти́ *pf*. **withdrawal** /-'drɔːəl/ *n* (*retraction*) взя́тие назáд; (*cancellation*) сня́тие; (*mil*) отхóд; (*money from circulation*) изъя́тие; (*departure*) ухóд. **withdrawn** /-'drɔːn/ *adj* зáмкнутый.

wither /'wɪðə(r)/ *vi* вя́нуть *impf*, за~ *pf*. **withering** /-rɪŋ/ *adj* (*fig*) уничтожáющий.

withhold /wɪð'həʊld/ *vt* (*refuse to grant*) не давáть *impf*, дать *pf* +*gen*; (*payment*) удéрживать *impf*, удержáть *pf*; (*information*) утáивать *impf*, утаи́ть *pf*.

within /wɪ'ðɪn/ *prep* (*inside*) внутри́+*gen*, в+*prep*; (~ *the limits of*) в предéлах +*gen*; (*time*) в течéние +*gen*; *adv* внутри́; **from ~** изнутри́.

without /wɪ'ðaʊt/ *prep* без+*gen*; ~ **saying good-bye** не прощáясь; **do ~** обходи́ться *impf*, обойти́сь *pf* без+*gen*.

withstand /wɪð'stænd/ *vt* выдéрживать *impf*, вы́держать *pf*.

witness /'wɪtnɪs/ *n* (*person*) свидéтель *m*; (*eye-~*) очеви́дец; (*to signature etc.*) завери́тель *m*; **bear ~ to** свидéтельствовать *impf*, за~ *pf*; **~-box** мéсто для свидéтельских показáний; *vt* быть свидéтелем+*gen*; (*document etc.*) заверя́ть *impf*, завéрить *pf*.

witticism /'wɪtɪˌsɪz(ə)m/ *n* острóта. **witty** /'wɪtɪ/ *adj* остроýмный.

wizard /'wɪzəd/ *n* волшéбник, колдýн.

wizened /'wɪz(ə)nd/ *adj* морщи́нистый.

wobble /'wɒb(ə)l/ *vt & i* шатáть(ся) *impf*, шатнýть(ся) *pf*; *vi* (*voice*) дрожáть *impf*. **wobbly** /'wɒblɪ/ *adj* шáткий.

woe /wəʊ/ *n* гóре; **~ is me!** гóре мне! **woeful** /-fʊl/ *adj* жáлкий.

wolf /wʊlf/ *n* волк; *vt* пожирáть *impf*, пожрáть *pf*.

woman /'wʊmən/ *n* жéнщина. **womanizer** /-ˌnaɪzə(r)/ *n* волоки́та. **womanly** /'wʊmənlɪ/ *adj* жéнственный.

womb /wuːm/ *n* мáтка.

wonder /ˈwʌndə(r)/ *n* чу́до; (*amazement*) изумле́ние; **(it's) no ~** неудиви́тельно; *vt* интересова́ться *impf* (**I ~ who will come** интере́сно, кто придёт); *vi*: **I shouldn't ~ if** неудиви́тельно бу́дет, е́сли; **I ~ if you could help me** не могли́ бы вы мне помо́чь?; **~ at** удивля́ться *impf*, удиви́ться *pf* +*dat*. **wonderful, wondrous** /ˈwʌndəˌfʊl, ˈwʌndrəs/ *adj* замеча́тельный.

wont /wəʊnt/ *n*: **as is his ~** по своему́ обыкнове́нию; *predic*: **be ~ to** име́ть привы́чку+*inf*.

woo /wu:/ *vt* уха́живать *impf* за +*instr*.

wood /wʊd/ *n* (*forest*) лес; (*material*) де́рево; (*firewood*) дрова́ *pl*. **woodcut** *n* гравю́ра на де́реве. **wooded** /ˈwʊdɪd/ *adj* леси́стый. **wooden** /ˈwʊd(ə)n/ *adj* (*also fig*) деревя́нный. **woodland** *n* леси́стая ме́стность; *attrib* лесно́й. **woodpecker** /ˈwʊdˌpekə(r)/ *n* дя́тел. **woodwind** *n* деревя́нные духовы́е инструме́нты *m pl*. **woodwork** *n* столя́рная рабо́та; (*wooden parts*) деревя́нные ча́сти (-те́й) *pl*. **woodworm** *n* жучо́к. **woody** /ˈwʊdɪ/ *adj* (*plant etc.*) деревяни́стый; (*wooded*) леси́стый.

wool /wʊl/ *n* шерсть. **woollen** /ˈwʊlən/ *adj* шерстяно́й. **woolly** /ˈwʊlɪ/ *adj* шерсти́стый; (*indistinct*) нея́сный.

word /wɜ:d/ *n* сло́во; (*news*) изве́стие; **by ~ of mouth** у́стно; **have a ~ with** поговори́ть *pf* с+*instr*; **in a ~** одни́м сло́вом; **in other ~s** други́ми слова́ми; **~ for ~** сло́во в сло́во; **~ processor** компью́тер(-изда́тель) *m*; *vt* выража́ть *impf*, вы́разить *pf*; формули́ровать *impf*, с~ *pf*. **wording** /ˈwɜ:dɪŋ/ *n* формулиро́вка.

work /wɜ:k/ *n* рабо́та; (*labour; toil; scholarly ~*) труд; (*occupation*) заня́тие; (*studies*) заня́тия *neut pl*; (*of art*) произведе́ние; (*book*) сочине́ние; *pl* (*factory*) заво́д; (*mechanism*) механи́зм; **at ~** (*doing~*) за рабо́той; (*at place of ~*) на рабо́те; **out of ~** безрабо́тный; **~-force** рабо́чая си́ла; **~-load** нагру́зка; *vi* (*also function*) рабо́тать *impf* (**at, on** над+*instr*); (*study*) занима́ться *impf*, заня́ться *pf*; (*also toil, labour*) труди́ться *impf*; (*have effect, function*) де́йствовать *impf*; (*succeed*) удава́ться *impf*, уда́ться *pf*; *vt* (*operate*) управля́ть *impf* +*instr*; обраща́ться *impf* с+*instr*; (*wonders*) твори́ть *impf*, со~ *pf*; (*soil*) обраба́тывать *impf*, обрабо́тать *pf*; (*compel to ~*) заставля́ть *impf*, заста́вить *pf* рабо́тать; **~ in** вставля́ть *impf*, вста́вить *pf*; **~ off** (*debt*) отраба́тывать *impf*, отрабо́тать *pf*; (*weight*) сгоня́ть *impf*, согна́ть *pf*; (*energy*) дава́ть *impf*, дать *pf* вы́ход +*dat*; **~ out** (*solve*) находи́ть *impf*, найти́ *pf* реше́ние +*gen*; (*plans etc.*) разраба́тывать *impf*, разрабо́тать *pf*; (*sport*) тренирова́ться *impf*; **everything ~ed out well** всё ко́нчилось хорошо́; **~ out at** (*amount to*) составля́ть *impf*, соста́вить *pf*; **~ up** (*perfect*) выраба́тывать *impf*, вы́работать *pf*; (*excite*) возбужда́ть *impf*, возбуди́ть *pf*; (*appetite*) нагу́ливать *impf*, нагуля́ть *pf*. **workable** /ˈwɜ:kəb(ə)l/ *adj* осуществи́мый, реа́льный. **workaday** /ˈwɜ:kəˌdeɪ/ *adj* бу́дничный. **workaholic** /ˌwɜ:kəˈhɒlɪk/ *n* труженик. **worker** /ˈwɜːkə(r)/ *n* работник; (*manual*) рабо́чий *sb*. **working** /ˈwɜːkɪŋ/ *adj*: ~ **class** рабо́чий класс; ~ **hours** рабо́чее вре́мя *neut*; ~ **party** коми́ссия. **workman** *n* рабо́тник. **workmanlike** /ˈwɜːkmən,laɪk/ *adj* иску́сный. **workmanship** *n* иску́сство, мастерство́. **workshop** *n* мастерска́я *sb*.

world /wɜːld/ *n* мир, свет; *attrib* мирово́й; ~**-famous** всеми́рно изве́стный; ~ **war** мирова́я война́; ~**-wide** всеми́рный. **worldly** /ˈwɜːldlɪ/ *adj* мирско́й; (*person*) о́пытный.

worm /wɜːm/ *n* червь *m*; (*intestinal*) глист; *vt*: ~ **o.s. into** вкра́дываться *impf*, вкра́сться *pf* в+*acc*; ~ **out** выве́дывать *impf*, вы́ведать *pf* (**of** у+*gen*); ~ **one's way** пробира́ться *impf*, пробра́ться *pf*.

worry /ˈwʌrɪ/ *n* (*anxiety*) беспоко́йство; (*care*) забо́та; *vt* беспоко́ить *impf*, о~ *pf*; *vi* беспоко́иться *impf*, о~ *pf* (**about** о+*prep*).

worse /wɜːs/ *adj* ху́дший; *adv* ху́же; *n*: **from bad to** ~ всё ху́же и ху́же. **worsen** /ˈwɜːs(ə)n/ *vt* & *i* ухудша́ть(ся) *impf*, уху́дшить(ся) *pf*.

worship /ˈwɜːʃɪp/ *n* поклоне́ние (**of** +*dat*); (*service*) богослуже́ние; *vt* поклоня́ться *impf* +*dat*; (*adore*) обожа́ть *impf*. **worshipper** /-pə(r)/ *n* покло́нник, -ица.

worst /wɜːst/ *adj* наиху́дший, са́мый плохо́й; *adv* ху́же всего́; *n* са́мое плохо́е.

worth /wɜːθ/ *n* (*value*) цена́, це́нность; (*merit*) досто́инство; **give me a pound's** ~ **of petrol** да́йте мне бензи́на на фунт; *adj*: **be** ~ (*of equal value to*) сто́ить *impf* (**what is it** ~? ско́лько э́то сто́ит?); (*deserve*) сто́ить *impf* +*gen* (**is this film** ~ **seeing?** сто́ит посмотре́ть э́тот фильм?). **worthless** /ˈwɜːθlɪs/ *adj* ничего́ не сто́ящий; (*useless*) бесполе́зный. **worthwhile** *adj* сто́ящий. **worthy** /ˈwɜːðɪ/ *adj* досто́йный.

would /wʊd/ *v aux* (*conditional*): **he** ~ **be angry if he found out** он бы рассерди́лся, е́сли бы узна́л; (*expressing wish*) **she** ~ **like to know** она́ бы хоте́ла знать; **I** ~ **rather** я бы предпочёл; (*expressing indirect speech*): **he said he** ~ **be late** он сказа́л, что придёт по́здно.

would-be /ˈwʊdbiː/ *adj*: ~ **actor** челове́к мечта́ющий стать актёром.

wound /wuːnd/ *n* ра́на; *vt* ра́нить *impf* & *pf*. **wounded** /-dɪd/ *adj* ра́неный.

wrangle /ˈræŋg(ə)l/ *n* препира́ние; *vi* препира́ться *impf*.

wrap /ræp/ *n* (*shawl*) шаль; *vt* (*also* ~ *up*) завёртывать *impf*, заверну́ть *pf*; ~ **up** (*in wraps*) заку́тывать(ся) *impf*, заку́тать(ся) *pf*; ~**ped up in** (*fig*) поглощённый +*instr*. **wrapper** /-pə(r)/ *n* обёртка. **wrapping** /-pɪŋ/ *n* обёртка; ~ **paper** обёрточная бума́га.

wrath /rɒθ/ *n* гнев.

wreak /riːk/ *vt*: ~ **havoc on** разоря́ть *impf*, разори́ть *pf*.

wreath /riːθ/ *n* вено́к

wreck /rek/ *n* (*ship*) оста́нки (-ов) корабля́; (*vehicle, person, building, etc.*) разва́лина; *vt* (*destroy, also fig*) разруша́ть *impf*, разру́шить *pf*; **be** ~**ed** терпе́ть *impf*, по~ *pf* круше́ние; (*of plans etc.*) ру́хнуть *pf*. **wreckage** /ˈrekɪdʒ/ *n* обло́мки *m pl* круше́ния.

wren /ren/ *n* крапи́вник.

wrench /rentʃ/ *n* (*jerk*) дёрганье; (*tech*) га́ечный ключ; (*fig*) боль; *vt* (*snatch, pull out*) вырыва́ть *impf*, вы́рвать *pf* (**from** у+*gen*); **~ open** взла́мывать *impf*, взлома́ть *pf*.

wrest /rest/ *vt* (*wrench*) вырыва́ть *impf*, вы́рвать *pf* (**from** у+*gen*).

wrestle /'res(ə)l/ *vi* боро́ться *impf*. **wrestler** /'reslə(r)/ *n* боре́ц. **wrestling** /'reslɪŋ/ *n* борьба́.

wretch /retʃ/ *n* несча́стный *sb*; (*scoundrel*) негодя́й. **wretched** /'retʃɪd/ *adj* жа́лкий; (*unpleasant*) скве́рный.

wriggle /'rɪg(ə)l/ *vi* извива́ться *impf*, изви́ться *pf*; (*fidget*) ёрзать *impf*; **~ out of** увили-ва́ть *impf*, увильну́ть от+*gen*.

wring /rɪŋ/ *vt* (*also* **~** *out*) выжима́ть *impf*, вы́жать *pf*; (*extort*) исторга́ть *impf*, исто́ргнуть *pf* (**from** у+*gen*); (*neck*) свёртывать *impf*, сверну́ть *pf* (**of** +*dat*); **~ one's hands** лома́ть *impf*, с~ *pf* ру́ки.

wrinkle /'rɪŋk(ə)l/ *n* морщи́на; *vt* & *i* мо́рщить(ся) *impf*, с~ *pf*.

wrist /rɪst/ *n* запя́стье; **~-watch** нару́чные часы́ (-со́в) *pl*.

writ /rɪt/ *n* пове́стка.

write /raɪt/ *vt* & *i* писа́ть *impf*, на~ *pf*; **~ down** запи́сывать *impf*, записа́ть *pf*; **~ off** (*cancel*) спи́сывать *impf*, списа́ть *pf*; **the car was a ~-off** маши́на была́ соверше́нно испо́рчена; **~ out** выпи́сывать *impf*, вы́писать *pf* (**in full** по́лностью); **~ up** (*account of*) подро́бно опи́сывать *impf*, описа́ть *pf*; (*notes*) перепи́сывать *impf*, переписа́ть *pf*; **~-up** (*report*) отчёт. **writer** /'raɪtə(r)/ *n* писа́тель *m*, ~ница.

writhe /raɪð/ *vi* ко́рчиться *impf*, с~ *pf*.

writing /'raɪtɪŋ/ *n* (*handwriting*) по́черк; (*work*) произведе́ние; **in ~** в пи́сьменной фо́рме; **~-paper** почто́вая бума́га.

wrong /rɒŋ/ *adj* (*incorrect*) непра́вильный, неве́рный; (*the wrong …*) не тот (**I have bought the ~ book** я купи́л не ту кни́гу; **you've got the ~ number** (*tel*) вы не туда́ попа́ли); (*mistaken*) непра́вый (**you are ~** ты непра́в); (*unjust*) несправедли́вый; (*sinful*) дурно́й; (*out of order*) нела́дный; (*side of cloth*) ле́вый; **~ side out** наизна́нку; **~ way round** наоборо́т; *n* зло; (*injustice*) несправедли́вость; **be in the ~** быть непра́вым; **do ~** греши́ть *impf*, со~ *pf*; *adv* непра́вильно, неве́рно; **go ~** не получа́ться *impf*, получи́ться *pf*; *vt* обижа́ть *impf*, оби́деть *pf*; (*be unjust to*) быть несправедли́вым к+*dat*. **wrongdoer** /'rɒŋˌduːə(r)/ *n* престу́пник, гре́шник, -ица. **wrongful** /-fʊl/ *adj* несправедли́вый. **wrongly** /-lɪ/ *adv* непра́вильно; (*unjustly*) несправедли́во.

wrought /rɔːt/ *adj*: **~ iron** сва́рочное желе́зо.

wry /raɪ/ *adj* (*smile*) криво́й; (*humour*) сухо́й, ирони́ческий.

xenophobia /ˌzenə'fəʊbɪə/ *n* ксенофо́бия.

X-ray /'eksreɪ/ *n* (*picture*) рентге́н(овский сни́мок); *pl* (*radiation*) рентге́новы лучи́ *m pl*; *vt* (*photograph*) де́лать *impf*, с~

pf рентге́н +*gen*.

Y

yacht /jɒt/ *n* я́хта. **yachting** /ˈjɒtɪŋ/ *n* па́русный спорт. **yachtsman** *n* яхтсме́н.

yank /ˈjæŋk/ *vt* рвану́ть *pf*.

yap /jæp/ *vi* тя́вкать *impf*, тя́вкнуть *pf*.

yard[1] /jɑːd/ *n* (*piece of ground*) двор.

yard[2] /jɑːd/ *n* (*measure*) ярд. **yardstick** *n* (*fig*) мери́ло.

yarn /jɑːn/ *n* пря́жа; (*story*) расска́з.

yawn /jɔːn/ *n* зево́к; *vi* зева́ть *impf*, зевну́ть *pf*; (*chasm etc.*) зия́ть *impf*.

year /jɪə(r)/ *n* год; **~ in, ~ out** из го́да в год. **yearbook** *n* ежего́дник. **yearly** /ˈjɪəlɪ/ *adj* ежего́дный, годово́й; *adv* ежего́дно.

yearn /jɜːn/ *vi* тоскова́ть *impf* (**for** по+*dat*). **yearning** /-nɪŋ/ *n* тоска́ (**for** по+*dat*).

yeast /jiːst/ *n* дро́жжи (-же́й) *pl*.

yell /jel/ *n* крик; *vi* крича́ть *impf*, кри́кнуть *pf*.

yellow /ˈjeləʊ/ *adj* жёлтый; *n* жёлтый цвет. **yellowish** /-ɪʃ/ *adj* желтова́тый.

yelp /jelp/ *n* визг; *vi* визжа́ть *impf*, ви́згнуть *pf*.

yes /jes/ *adv* да; *n* утвержде́ние, согла́сие; (*in vote*) го́лос «за».

yesterday /ˈjestəˌdeɪ/ *adv* вчера́; *n* вчера́шний день *m*; **~ morning** вчера́ у́тром; **the day before ~** позавчера́; **~'s newspaper** вчера́шняя газе́та.

yet /jet/ *adv* (*still*) ещё; (*so far*) до сих пор; (*in questions*) уже́; (*nevertheless*) тем не ме́нее; **as ~** пока́, до сих пор; **not ~** ещё не; *conj* одна́ко, но.

yew /juː/ *n* тис.

Yiddish /ˈjɪdɪʃ/ *n* и́диш.

yield /jiːld/ *n* (*harvest*) урожа́й; (*econ*) дохо́д; *vt* (*fruit, revenue, etc.*) приноси́ть *impf*, принести́ *pf*; дава́ть *impf*, дать *pf*; (*give up*) сдава́ть *impf*, сдать *pf*; *vi* (*give in*) (*to enemy etc.*) уступа́ть *impf*, уступи́ть *pf* (**to** +*dat*); (*give way*) поддава́ться *impf*, подда́ться *pf* (**to** +*dat*).

yoga /ˈjəʊgə/ *n* йо́га.

yoghurt /ˈjɒgət/ *n* кефи́р.

yoke /jəʊk/ *n* (*also fig*) ярмо́; (*fig*) и́го; (*of dress*) коке́тка; *vt* впряга́ть *impf*, впрячь *pf* в ярмо́.

yolk /jəʊk/ *n* желто́к.

yonder /ˈjɒndə(r)/ *adv* вон там; *adj* вон тот.

you /juː/ *pron* (*familiar sg*) ты; (*familiar pl, polite sg & pl*) вы; (*one*) *not usu translated*; *v translated in 2nd pers sg or by impers construction*: **~ never know** никогда́ не зна́ешь.

young /jʌŋ/ *adj* молодо́й; **the ~** молодёжь; *n* (*collect*) детёныши *m pl*. **youngster** /ˈjʌŋstə(r)/ *n* ма́льчик, де́вочка.

your(s) /jɔː(z)/ *poss pron* (*familiar sg; also in letter*) твой; (*familiar pl, polite sg & pl; also in letter*) ваш; свой. **yourself** /jɔːˈself/ *pron* (*emph*) (*familiar sg*) (ты) сам (*m*), сама́ (*f*); (*familiar pl, polite sg & pl*) (вы) са́ми; (*refl*) себя́; -ся (*suffixed to vt*); **by ~** (*independently*) самостоя́тельно, сам; (*alone*) оди́н.

youth /juːθ/ *n* (*age*) мо́лодость; (*young man*) ю́ноша *m*; (*collect, as pl*) молодёжь; **~ club** молодёжный клуб; **~ hostel** молодёжная турба́за. **youthful** /-fʊl/ *adj* ю́ношеский.

Yugoslavia /ju:gə'slɑ:vɪə/ *n* Югосла́вия.

Z

zany /'zeɪnɪ/ *adj* смешно́й.

zeal /zi:l/ *n* рве́ние, усе́рдие. **zealot** /'zelət/ *n* фана́тик. **zealous** /'zeləs/ *adj* ре́вностный, усе́рдный.

zebra /'zebrə/ *n* зе́бра.

zenith /'zenɪθ/ *n* зени́т.

zero /'zɪərəʊ/ *n* нуль *m*, ноль *m*.

zest /zest/ *n* (*piquancy*) пика́нтность; (*ardour*) энтузиа́зм; ~ **for life** жизнера́достность.

zigzag /'zɪgzæg/ *n* зигза́г; *adj* зигзагообра́зный; *vi* де́лать *impf*, с~ *pf* зигза́ги; идти́ *det* зигза́гами.

zinc /zɪŋk/ *n* цинк.

Zionism /'zaɪə,nɪz(ə)m/ *n* сиони́зм. **Zionist** /'zaɪənɪst/ *n* сиони́ст.

zip /zɪp/ *n* (~ *fastener*) (застёжка-) мо́лния; *vt* & *i*: ~ **up** застёгивать(ся) *impf*, застегну́ть(ся) *pf* на мо́лнию.

zodiac /'zəʊdɪ,æk/ *n* зодиа́к; **sign of the** ~ знак зодиа́ка.

zombie /'zɒmbɪ/ *n* челове́к спя́щий на ходу́.

zone /zəʊn/ *n* зо́на; (*geog*) по́яс.

zoo /zu:/ *n* зоопа́рк. **zoological** /,zəʊə'lɒdʒɪk(ə)l/ *adj* зоологи́ческий; ~ **garden(s)** зоологи́ческий сад. **zoologist** /zəʊ'ɒlədʒɪst/ *n* зоо́лог. **zoology** /zəʊ'ɒlədʒɪ/ *n* зооло́гия.

zoom /zu:m/ *vi* (*rush*) мча́ться *impf*; ~ **in** (*phot*) де́лать *impf*, с~ *pf* наплы́в; ~ **lens** объекти́в с переме́нным фо́кусным расстоя́нием.

Zulu /'zu:lu:/ *adj* зулу́сский; *n* зулу́с, ~ка.

Appendix I **Spelling Rules**

It is assumed that the user is acquainted with the following spelling rules which affect Russian declension and conjugation.

1. **ы**, **ю**, and **я** do not follow **г**, **к**, **х**, **ж**, **ч**, **ш**, and **щ**; instead, **и**, **у**, and **а** are used, e.g. **ма́льчик*и***, **кричу́**; **лежа́т**, **ноча́ми**, similarly, **ю** and **я** do not follow **ц**; instead, **у** or **а** are used.

2. Unstressed **о** does not follow **ж**, **ц**, **ч**, **ш**, or **щ**; instead, **е** is used, e.g. **му́жем**, **ме́сяцев**, **хоро́шее**.

Appendix II **Declension of Russian Adjectives**

The following patterns are regarded as regular and are not shown in the dictionary entries.

Singular	nom	acc	gen	dat	instr	prep
Masculine	**тёпл|ый**	~ый	~ого	~ому	~ым	~ом
Feminine	**тёпл|ая**	~ую	~ой	~ой	~ой	~ой
Neuter	**тёпл|ое**	~ое	~ого	~ому	~ым	~ом

Plural	nom	acc	gen	dat	instr	prep
Masculine	**тёпл|ые**	~ые	~ых	~ым	~ыми	~ых
Feminine	**тёпл|ые**	~ые	~ых	~ым	~ыми	~ых
Neuter	**тёпл|ые**	~ые	~ых	~ым	~ыми	~ых

Appendix III **Declension of Russian Nouns**

The following patterns are regarded as regular and are not shown in the dictionary entries. Forms marked * should be particularly noted.

1 *Masculine*

Singular nom	acc	gen	dat	instr	prep
обе́д	~	~а	~у	~ом	~е
слу́ча|й	~й	~я	~ю	~ем	~е
марш	~	~а	~у	~ем	~е
каранда́ш	~	~а́	~у́	~о́м*	~е́
сцена́ри|й	~й	~я	~ю	~ем	~и*
портфе́л|ь	~ь	~я	~ю	~ем	~е

Singular nom	acc	gen	dat	instr	prep
обе́д|ы	~ы	~ов	~ам	~ами	~ах
слу́ча|и	~и	~ев	~ям	~ями	~ях
ма́рш|и	~и	~ей*	~ам	~ами	~ах
карандаш|и́	~и́	~е́й*	~а́м	~а́ми	~а́х
сцена́ри|и	~и	~ев*	~ям	~ями	~ях
портфе́л|и	~и	~ей*	~ям	~ями	~ях

2 *Feminine*

Singular nom	acc	gen	dat	instr	prep
газе́т|а	~у	~ы	~е	~ой	~е
ба́н|я	~ю	~и	~е	~ей	~е
ли́ни|я	~ю	~и	~и*	~ей	~и*
ста́ту|я	~ю	~и	~е*	~ей	~е*
бол|ь	~ь	~и	~и*	~ью*	~и*

Plural	nom	acc	gen	dat	instr	prep
	газе́т|ы	~ы	~	~ам	~ами	~ах
	ба́н|и	~и	~ь*	~ям	~ями	~ях
	ли́ни|и	~и	~й*	~ям	~ями	~ях
	ста́ту|и	~и	~й*	~ям	~ями	~ях
	бо́л|и	~и	~ей*	~ям	~ями	~ях

3 *Neuter*

Singular	nom	acc	gen	dat	instr	prep
	чу́вств|о	~о	~а	~у	~ом	~е
	учи́лищ|е	~е	~а	~у	~ем	~е
	зда́ни|е	~е	~я	~ю	~ем	~и*
	уще́л|ье	~ье	~ья	~ью	~ьем	~ье

Plural	nom	acc	gen	dat	instr	prep
	чу́вств|а	~а	~	~ам	~ами	~ах
	учи́лищ|а	~а	~	~ам	~ами	~ах
	зда́ни|я	~я	~й*	~ям	~ями	~ях
	уще́л|ья	~ья	~ий*	~ьям	~ьями	~ьях

Appendix IV **Conjugation of Russian Verbs**

The following patterns are regarded as regular and are not shown in the dictionary entries.

1. **-е-** conjugation

(a) **чита́|ть**	~ю	~ешь	~ет	~ем	~ете	~ют
(b) **сия́|ть**	~ю	~ешь	~ет	~ем	~ете	~ют
(c) **про́б|овать**	~ую	~уешь	~ует	~уем	~уете	~уют
(d) **рис|ова́ть**	~у́ю	~у́ешь	~у́ет	~у́ем	~у́ете	~у́ют

2. **-и-** conjugation

(a) **говор|и́ть**	~ю́	~и́шь	~и́т	~и́м	~и́те	~я́т
(b) **стро́|ить**	~ю	~ишь	~ит	~им	~ите	~ят

Notes

1. Also belonging to the **-е-** conjugation are:

i) most other verbs in **-ать** (but see Note 2(v) below), e.g. **жа́ждать**; (жа́жду, -ждешь); **пря́тать** (пря́чу, -чешь), **колеба́ть** (коле́блю, -блешь).

ii) verbs in **-еть** for which the 1st pers sing **-ею** is given, e.g. **жале́ть**.

iii) verbs in **-нуть** for which the 1st pers sing **-ну** is given (e.g. **вя́нуть**), **ю** becoming **у** in the 1st pers sing and 3rd pers pl.

iv) verbs in **-ять** which drop the **я** in conjugation, e.g. **ла́ять** (ла́ю, ла́ешь); **се́ять** (се́ю, се́ешь).

2. Also belonging to the **-и-** conjugation are:

i) verbs in consonant + **-ить** which change the consonant in the first person singular, e.g. **досади́ть** (-ажу́, -ади́шь), or insert an **-л-**, e.g. **доба́вить** (доба́влю, -вишь).

ii) other verbs in vowel + **-ить**, e.g. **затаи́ть**, **кле́ить** (as 2b above).

iii) verbs in **-еть** for which the 1st pers sing is given as consonant + **ю** or **у**, e.g. **звене́ть** (-ню́, -ни́шь), **ви́деть** (ви́жу, ви́дишь).

iv) two verbs in **-ять (стоя́ть, боя́ться)**.

v) verbs in **-ать** whose stem ends in **ч**, **ж**, **щ**, or **ш**, not changing between the infinitive and conjugation, e.g. **крича́ть** (-чу́, -чи́шь). Cf. Note 1(i).

Английские неправильные глаголы

Инфинитив	Простое прошедшее	Причастие прошедшего времени	Инфинитив	Простое прошедшее	Причастие прошедшего времени
be	was	been	**drink**	drank	drunk
bear	bore	borne	**drive**	drove	driven
beat	beat	beaten	**eat**	ate	eaten
become	became	become	**fall**	fell	fallen
begin	began	begun	**feed**	fed	fed
bend	bent	bent	**feel**	felt	felt
bet	bet,	bet,	**fight**	fought	fought
	betted	betted	**find**	found	found
bid	bade, bid	bidden, bid	**flee**	fled	fled
bind	bound	bound	**fly**	flew	flown
bite	bit	bitten	**freeze**	froze	frozen
bleed	bled	bled	**get**	got	got
blow	blew	blown			gotten *US*
break	broke	broken	**give**	gave	given
breed	bred	bred	**go**	went	gone
bring	brought	brought	**grow**	grew	grown
build	built	built	**hang**	hung,	hung,
burn	burnt,	burnt,		hanged (*vt*)	hanged
	burned	burned	**have**	had	had
burst	burst	burst	**hear**	heard	heard
buy	bought	bought	**hide**	hid	hidden
catch	caught	caught	**hit**	hit	hit
choose	chose	chosen	**hold**	held	held
cling	clung	clung	**hurt**	hurt	hurt
come	came	come	**keep**	kept	kept
cost	cost,	cost,	**kneel**	knelt	knelt
	costed (*vt*)	costed	**know**	knew	known
cut	cut	cut	**lay**	laid	laid
deal	dealt	dealt	**lead**	led	led
dig	dug	dug	**lean**	leaned,	leaned,
do	did	done		leant	leant
draw	drew	drawn	**learn**	learnt,	learnt,
dream	dreamt,	dreamt,		learned	learned
	dreamed	dreamed	**leave**	left	left

Инфинитив	Простое прошедшее	Причастие прошедшего времени	Инфинитив	Простое прошедшее	Причастие прошедшего времени
lend	lent	lent	**speak**	spoke	spoken
let	let	let	**spell**	spelled, spelt	spelled, spelt
lie	lay	lain	**spend**	spent	spent
lose	lost	lost	**spit**	spat	spat
make	made	made	**spoilt**	spoilt, spoiled	spoilt, spoiled
mean	meant	meant	**spread**	spread	spread
meet	met	met	**spring**	sprang	sprung
pay	paid	paid	**stand**	stood	stood
put	put	put	**steal**	stole	stolen
read	read	read	**stick**	stuck	stuck
ride	rode	ridden	**sting**	stung	stung
ring	rang	rung	**stride**	strode	stridden
rise	rose	risen	**strike**	struck	struck
run	ran	run	**swear**	swore	sworn
say	said	said	**sweep**	swept	swept
see	saw	seen	**swell**	swelled	swollen, swelled
seek	sought	sought	**swim**	swam	swum
sell	sold	sold	**swing**	swung	swung
send	sent	sent	**take**	took	taken
set	set	set	**teach**	taught	taught
sew	sewed	sewn, sewed	**tear**	tore	torn
shake	shook	shaken	**tell**	told	told
shine	shone	shone	**think**	thought	thought
shoe	shod	shod	**throw**	threw	thrown
shoot	shot	shot	**thrust**	thrust	thrust
show	showed	shown	**tread**	trod	trodden
shut	shut	shut	**understand**	understood	understood
sing	sang	sung	**wake**	woke	woken
sink	sank	sunk	**wear**	wore	worn
sit	sat	sat	**win**	won	won
sleep	slept	slept	**write**	wrote	written
sling	slung	slung			
smell	smelt, smelled	smelt, smelled			

The Russian Alphabet

Capital Letters	Lower-case Letters	Letter names	Capital Letters	Lower-case Letters	Letter names
А	а	а	С	с	эс
Б	б	бэ	Т	т	тэ
В	в	вэ	У	у	у
Г	г	гэ	Ф	ф	эф
Д	д	дэ	Х	х	ха
Е	е	е	Ц	ц	цэ
Ё	ё	ё	Ч	ч	че
Ж	ж	жэ	Ш	ш	ша
З	з	зэ	Щ	щ	ща
И	и	и	Ъ	ъ	твёрдый
Й	й	и кра́ткое			знак
К	к	ка	Ы	ы	ы
Л	л	эль	Ь	ь	мя́гкий
М	м	эм			знак
Н	н	эн	Э	э	э
О	о	о	Ю	ю	ю
П	п	пэ	Я	я	я
Р	р	эр			

Английский алфавит

Заглавные буквы	Строчные буквы	Названия букв
A	**a**	/eɪ/
B	**b**	/biː/
C	**c**	/siː/
D	**d**	/diː/
E	**e**	/iː/
F	**f**	/ef/
G	**g**	/dʒiː/
H	**h**	/eɪtʃ/
I	**i**	/aɪ/
J	**j**	/dʒeɪ/
K	**k**	/keɪ/
L	**l**	/el/
M	**m**	/em/

Заглавные буквы	Строчные буквы	Названия букв
N	**n**	/en/
O	**o**	/əʊ/
P	**p**	/piː/
Q	**q**	/kjuː/
R	**r**	/ɑː(r)/
S	**s**	/es/
T	**t**	/tiː/
U	**u**	/juː/
V	**v**	/viː/
W	**w**	/ˈdʌb(ə)ljuː/
X	**x**	/eks/
Y	**y**	/waɪ/
Z	**z**	/zed/

Other titles in the Oxford Russian range

Oxford Russian Dictionary
ISBN 9780198614203
500,000 words, phrases, and translations – the most comprehensive Russian and English dictionary available

Concise Oxford Russian Dictionary
ISBN 9780198601524
310,000 words, phrases, and translations

Pocket Oxford Russian Dictionary
ISBN 9780198610069
210,000 words, phrases, and translations

Oxford Beginner's Russian Dictionary
ISBN 9780199298549
Designed for English speakers just starting to learn Russian

Oxford Russian Grammar and Verbs
ISBN 9780198603801
Comprehensive coverage of all the key points of Russian grammar

Abbreviations/Условные сокращения

abbr	abbreviation	сокращение
abs	absolute	абсолютный
acc	accusative (case)	винительный падеж
adj, adjs	adjective(s)	имя прилагательное, имена прилагательные
adv, adv	adverb(s)	наречие, наречия
aeron	aeronautics	авиация
agric	agriculture	сельское хозяйство
anat	anatomy	анатомия
approx	approximate(ly)	приблизительн|ый, -о
archaeol	archaeology	археология
archit	architecture	архитектура
astron	astronomy	астрономия
attrib	attributive	определительное, атрибутивное
aux	auxiliary	вспомогательный глагол
bibl	biblical	библейский термин
biol	biology	биология
bot	botany	ботаника
chem	chemistry	химия
cin	cinema(tography)	кинематография
coll	colloquial	разговорное
collect	collective	собирательное (существительное)
comb	combination	сочетание
comm	commerce	коммерческий термин
comp	comparative	сравнительная степень
comput	computing	вычислительная техника
conj, conjs	conjunction(s)	союз, -ы
cul	culinary	кулинария
dat	dative (case)	дательный падеж
def	definite	определённый
derog	derogatory	пренебрежительное
det	determinate	определённый
dim	diminutive	уменьшительное
eccl	ecclesiastical	церковный термин
econ	economics	экономика
electr	electricity	электротехника
electron	electronics	электроника
emph	emphatic	усилительное
esp	especially	особенно
etc.	etcetera	и так далее
f	feminine	женский род
fig	figurative	в переносном смысле
fut	future (tense)	будущее время
g	genitive (case)	родительный падеж
geog	geography	география
geol	geology	геология
geom	geometry	геометрия
gram	grammar	грамматика
hist	historical	история
imper	imperative	повелительное наклонение
impers	impersonal	безличное
impf	imperfective	несовершенный вид
indecl	indeclinable	несклоняемое
indef	indefinite	неопределённый
indet	indeterminate	неопределённый
inf	infinitive	инфинитив
instr	instrumental (case)	творительный падеж
int	interjection	междометие
interrog	interrogative	вопросительный
ling	linguistics	лингвистика